MOTION PICTURE
EXHIBITION IN
BALTIMORE

ALSO BY
ROBERT K. HEADLEY

*Motion Picture Exhibition in Washington, D.C.:
An Illustrated History of Parlors, Palaces and
Multiplexes in the Metropolitan Area, 1894–1997*
(McFarland, 1999; paperback 2006)

Motion Picture Exhibition in Baltimore

An Illustrated History and Directory of Theaters, 1895–2004

Robert K. Headley

McFarland & Company, Inc., Publishers
Jefferson, North Carolina, and London

The present work is a reprint of the illustrated case bound edition of Motion Picture Exhibition in Baltimore: An Illustrated History and Directory of Theaters, 1895–2004, *first published in 2006 by McFarland.*

LIBRARY OF CONGRESS CATALOGUING-IN-PUBLICATION DATA

Headley, Robert K. (Robert Kirk), 1938–
Motion picture exhibition in Baltimore : an illustrated history and directory of theaters, 1895–2004 / Robert K. Headley.
p. cm.
Includes bibliographical references and indexes.

ISBN 978-0-7864-7527-8
softcover : acid free paper ∞

1. Motion pictures—Maryland—Baltimore—History.
2. Motion picture theaters—Maryland—Baltimore—History.
3. Motion picture theaters—Maryland—Baltimore—Directories.   I. Title.
PN1993.5.U75H43   2013
791.43097526—dc22   2005031101

BRITISH LIBRARY CATALOGUING DATA ARE AVAILABLE

© 2006 Robert K. Headley. All rights reserved

No part of this book may be reproduced or transmitted in any form or by any means, electronic or mechanical, including photocopying or recording, or by any information storage and retrieval system, without permission in writing from the publisher.

Front cover: Baltimore's landmark Senator Theatre (photograph courtesy of Tom Kiefaber/Dave Pugh Design); back cover image © 2013 Comstock

Manufactured in the United States of America

McFarland & Company, Inc., Publishers
Box 611, Jefferson, North Carolina 28640
www.mcfarlandpub.com

To

My aunt, Mary Virginia (Smoot) Kromm,
who took me downtown to the movies. "Thank you, Diddy."

My trusty and well-beloved friends
my wife Anne
Robert Barnes
Martin Wasserman
Warren Edelstein
Roger Russell
with whom I have enjoyed countless movies for more than 50 years

The exhibitors, architects, managers, projectionists, ushers,
cashiers, janitors, and exchange men and women who have given us
so many hours of enjoyment at the movies

The battered, underrated, wonderful old city of Baltimore

Contents

ACKNOWLEDGMENTS — viii
PREFACE — 1

I. A History of Motion Picture Exhibition in Baltimore — 5

Chapter 1	The Wonder of the Century (1894–1906)	7
Chapter 2	The Triumph of Cheap Entertainment (1907–1913)	23
Chapter 3	Bigger and Better Theaters (1914–1920)	54
Chapter 4	Movie Palaces (1921–1927)	77
Chapter 5	A Theater Near You (1928–1939)	104
Chapter 6	The Movies in War and Peace (1940–1947)	127
Chapter 7	Shopping Centers and Drive-Ins (1948–1960)	141
Chapter 8	The Return of the Palaces? (1961–1967)	158
Chapter 9	Multiplexes to Megaplexes (1968–1990)	166
Chapter 10	Megaplexes (1990–2004)	182

II. Baltimore Area Theaters by Name — 187

APPENDICES
    1. Baltimore Area Theaters by Street Address — 447
    2. Architects of Baltimore Area Theaters — 450
    3. Theater Architecture — 452
    4. Theater Personnel — 456

NOTES — 461
BIBLIOGRAPHY — 493
INDEX — 497

Acknowledgments

It is a great pleasure to acknowledge the support of the many people and institutions who have helped make this book possible. The staffs at several libraries and archives have been very helpful, and I would especially like to acknowledge those at the Maryland Room, Hornbake Library, University of Maryland at College Park; the Maryland Room and Microfilm Reading Rooms, Enoch Pratt Free Library; the Maryland State Archives; the Special Collections Dept., Albin O. Kuhn Library, University of Maryland, Baltimore County; the Maryland Historical Society; the Anne Arundel County Historical Society; the Dundalk-Patapsco Neck Historical Society; the Laurel Historical Society; and the Theatre Historical Society of America. The Baltimore *Sun*, the Hearst Corporation, the Bel Air *Aegis*, *Boxoffice* magazine, the *Capital-Gazette* newspapers and *Baltimore Magazine* graciously gave permission to use material from their various publications. These people and the ones listed below have made my research a delight. I hope I have not omitted anyone, but, if I have, I apologize.

Floyd Adams
Max Alvarez (National Museum of Women in the Arts)
Ray Amtmann
Mrs. Arthur Armstrong
Leon B. Back (Rome Theaters)
Robert W. Barnes
Ben Beck
Harry Belsinger, Jr. (Belsinger Signs)
Marian & Nathan† Bernstein
Christ Bouloubassis
Steve Brenner†
W. M. Brizendine (Schwaber Theaters)
Lauren Brown (Hornbake Library, UMCP)
Mr. & Mrs. Clarence Bryant
Mark G. Cahill (Shapiro Petrauskas Gelber)
Oscar Coblentz, Jr.
Irwin & Scott Cohen (R/C Theaters)
David Colburn
Rodney Collier†
Robert Cramblitt†
Veazy Craycroft†
Peter Curtis
William Curtis†
Philomen DeRoché (Patuxent Publishing Co.)
Louis S. Diggs
Sanford H. Disney†
George H. Douglass†
Frank H. Durkee, Jr.
Frank H. Durkee, III
Thurman L. Durst†
Mike Dyer (Atkinson Dyer Watson)
Dr. Warren Edelstein
E. Bernard Evander†
William E. Eyring, Sr.†

John Freeland
Linda Geeson (Baltimore *Sun*)
Sam Goldman
Dr. Douglas Gomery
Rebecca Gundy (Baltimore City Archives)
Don & Diane Gunther
Sol Goodman
David H. Harrison†
The Hasslinger Family
Marjorie† and Robert K. Headley, Sr.†
Mary Henderson (Historical Society of Harford County)
Mr. & Mrs. Louis Hesson
Bill Hewitt
J. Russell Hildebrand, Sr.†
Harry R. Hitchcock
Eric Holcomb (CHAP)
William Hollifield
Thomas Hollowak
Vincent Holter
Henry Hornstein†
Roy Insley
Sam Isaacson†
Tom Kiefaber
John Kilduff†
Edward A. Kimpel
Martin Kircher
A. Briscoe Koger
Jeffrey Korman (Enoch Pratt Free Library)
Bob Kramer
Dean Krimmel
Adam Kromm†
Mary V. Kromm
Marvin Kushnick
William Lange
Meyer "Mike" Leventhal†
Joseph A. Liberto, Jr.
Charles A. Lipsey
Grace Lopresti
Randy & Debrean Loy
Eleanor Lukanich
Doug McElrath (Hornbake Library, UMCP)
John McGrain
Marian McKew†

Harry Macer
Robert T. Marhenke†
Mary Markey (Maryland Historical Society)
Sidney Marks†
Etta Cluster Mercur
David Millhauser†
Jack Nethen (Claude Neon Signs)
Barbara Nevens
Jackie Nickel
Elmer Nolte†
August Nolte†
Roland Nuttrell†
Helen Ohrenschall
Richard Parsons (Baltimore County Public Library)
Thomas Paul
Emily H. Penke
Paul Potter
Earl Pruce
M. Robert Rappaport
Philip Redman
Charles Reisinger†
H. Charles Robertson
John Robinson
John Rockstroh
Dan Rodricks
Alisha Rogers (Westfield)
Fabius Rollins†
Hon. Lawrence H. Rushworth
Maurice Rushworth†
Roger Russell
Mark N. Schatz (Anne Arundel County Historical Society)
George R. Scherman†
Fred Schmuff†
Mrs. John Seamon
Aaron Seidler
Martin Shargel, M.D.
Patrick J. Sheehan (Library of Congress)
Gene Shillman, Sr. (Jaeger, Inc.)
Samuel Shoubin
John A. Sipes
Tom Steuhler
Carroll Streeks
Emma Sweeting
Mr. & Mrs. Andrew Szpara
Mr. & Mrs. Roland Tankersley†

"Turkey Joe" Trabert
D. Edward Vogel
Allan Vought (Bel Air *Aegis*)
Roy Wagner
Brooks Walker[†]
Martin Wasserman
Robert Weinholt

Roger White
Irving Whitehill[†]
James L. Whittle[†]
James T. Wollon, Jr.
Ben Womer[†]
Dr. Leon Zeller[†]
Albert C. Zink

    I regret that many of those listed above ([†]) did not live to see this book completed. I would also like to acknowledge the considerable help of the delightful members of my classes at Glen Meadows, Charlestown, and Oakcrest retirement communities, Catonsville Community College, Dundalk Community College, the Friendly Seniors class at Essex Community College, and the Memories of Mars Website. I learned much from all these people, and I had the opportunity to try out many ideas that I have used in this book.

    Despite my best efforts, there are certainly errors of omission and commission in this book. I take full responsibility for them. I will be grateful for any corrections or additions, sent care of the publisher. Likewise, every effort has been made to locate the owners of copyrighted material and obtain permission to use it.

PREFACE

If you could move back in time, experience the events of some other year, which year would you choose? It would be difficult for me to choose a single year. I would like to go back to 1700 and talk to my earliest Headley ancestor on this continent and ask him where he was born, who his parents were, and why he came here. But, as I was writing a part of this book that dealt with the post–World War II years, I experienced a mighty wave of nostalgia, and I shamelessly wallowed in memories of the late 1940s. I was around 10 then, living in the greatest city in the greatest country on earth. We had just whipped the Axis, and the air was filled with optimism. Howard and Lexington was the center of Baltimore, and the blocks east on Lexington to Charles and north on Howard to Centre were filled with wonders. There were five 10-cents stores within two blocks on Lexington: Woolworth's, McCrory's, Schulte United, Grant's, and Kresge's. There were four grand department stores dominating the intersection. Read's Drug Store was on one corner; you could get great chow mein on the balcony there. There were several nut stores on Lexington Street; each one had a person out in front handing out samples of nuts. There was also a man who sold lavender from a small, glass-walled cart, and, I believe, an organ grinder with a little monkey up near O'Neil's. And there were the movies.

We almost never called them movie theaters. To us they were simply "movies." "What movie are you going to?" was usually answered by the name of a theater, the Stanley or the Ambassador, less commonly by the name of a film, *Shane* or *Fire Maidens of Outer Space*. Lexington Street was the center of Baltimore's downtown movie theater district with the New, Keith's, the Century, Valencia, and the delightful Laffmovie. Howard Street had the Howard, the Mayfair, the Little, and the Stanley. Further afield were the Town and the Hippodrome. What a choice!

A perfect Saturday was taking my allowance, catching the bus from Westport and riding downtown. First of all, making the rounds of the 10-cents stores—I collected toy dogs and plastic horses then. Schulte United had plastic horses for 5 cents or 10 cents, and I could afford enough to stage huge cavalry engagements on my living room floor. Then on to Nedick's for a hot dog and orange juice and finally a couple of wonderful hours at the movies. I guess that 1950 or 1951 would be one of the years I'd like to return to.[1] I have never lost the excitement of sitting in a theater, seeing the house lights dim and the curtain part. I loved it then, and I love it now. I hope this book will trigger pleasant memories of happy times at some of the lost "movies" of Baltimore. And, for those readers who did not grow up in Baltimore, I hope you will gain some understanding of how movie exhibition developed in one of the nation's great cities.

Baltimore had quite a reputation because of its attitude toward movies and theaters. It was considered a difficult town for live theater, and Baltimore audiences were thought to be generally unresponsive to happy endings in movies. We had no problem shedding tears at sad movies, but we drew the line at clapping or cheering when the hero finally got the girl or the fort was saved. As early as 1910, Baltimore was described as being "very critical" in its appraisal of motion pictures. In 1922, Guy Wonders, the manager of the Rivoli, put it this way: "Sometimes an enthusiastic person will start applause, but on the whole Baltimore audiences are rather cold and unresponsive."[2] A 1928 article[3] also commented on the impassive nature of Baltimoreans, claiming that they could take unhappy endings bravely, calmly, and stoically. Marie Presstman, of the State Censor Board, believed this showed that Baltimoreans were intelligent. The article compared this with the situation in Washington where, it was claimed, "they must have their happy endings." Some films shown around this time actually had two endings, one happy, the other sad.[4] The happy one was for distribution in Washington.

Baltimore was also tough on legitimate shows. In 1930 a drama critic commented that Baltimore's well-known peculiarities as a legitimate show-town were being reflected in movies. He said there was no predicting what any given picture would do here.[5] We were pleased in February 1937 when Cleveland ousted us as the worst theatrical town in the country. The popular comedienne Clara Bloodgood committed suicide in Baltimore's Stafford Hotel just before she was to appear at the Academy of Music; no motive was ever discovered.[6] Could she have been dreading the Baltimore audience that much?

On the other hand Baltimore received high marks for its toleration. A writer for the *New York World* said that Baltimore

> in many ways ... greatly resembles Boston ... but religious fanatics are numerous there too, much more numerous than is commonly supposed. And if these were left to their own devices the city would soon sink in the same morass that has swallowed up Boston, as indeed it almost did a few years ago. But are they left to their own devices? They are not. The moment one of them starts something nonsensical the civilized minority lays down a barrage that is deadly in the execution that it works.

H. L. Mencken was cited as one of the leaders of the "civilized minority."[7]

Baltimore and Maryland have produced a number of entertainers. We can claim, at least circuitously, Charlie Chase,[8] Ben Lyon, Geraldine O'Brien, Jeff Donnell, Howard Rollins, Clarence Muse, Edward Everett Horton, Dorothy Phillips,[9] Maxine Kavanaugh,[10] Margaret Hayes, Billie Holliday, Mildred Natwick, Mildred Dunnock, John Astin, Gary Moore, Eddie Mayehoff, Bess Armstrong, Glen Milstead (better known as Divine), Montel Williams, Charles S. Dutton, Toni Braxton, John W. Albaugh, Larry Adler, and vaudeville star Pat Rooney, Jr.[11] Cab Calloway attended high school in Baltimore.[12] Monte Blue worked here, shipping oysters and performing imitations of Charlie Chaplin outside local theaters. Baltimore-born directors include Barry Levinson and John Waters. The Warner brothers lived here with their parents between 1887 and 1897, although they confined their activities to selling newspapers and shining shoes around Baltimore and Gay streets. Perhaps they saw their first movies here. According to several sources, it was in Baltimore that Charlie Chaplin signed the contract for his first movie for Mack Sennett in 1913.[13] Fred Waring gave his first professional performance at the Rivoli.[14]

Over the years many motion pictures have been filmed in and around Baltimore. Baltimore even had its own film studios. In 1911 the Knickerbocker Motion Picture Company opened a studio on Virginia Avenue just west of Park Heights. Sadly, the studio did not last very long. The Knickerbocker Studio had closed by 1915 when another studio, the Triangle Corporation, opened nearby. That studio, too, closed quickly. The story of movies made in the Baltimore area, while interesting, is beyond the scope of this book.

Why *Motion Picture Exhibition in Baltimore*? There are several reasons. It is a complete revision of my *Exit: A History of Movies in Maryland*, privately printed in 1974. I have corrected many of the errors in that book. I have done more research, talked with many other people in the movie business, from whom I have learned a lot, and acquired new photographs of Baltimore theaters; I want to make this material available. A lot has happened in the movie business; old circuits have disappeared and new ones have appeared, and, sadly, many more old theaters have closed; I want to record this. I have also delved more deeply into the histories of Baltimore's legitimate theaters and summer parks, both of which played major roles in the early development of movie exhibition.

In 1974, when I finished the first edition of *Exit*, there were 67 four-wall theaters (with 80 screens) in the Baltimore metropolitan area; only five of those theaters (with 11 screens) remain.[15] Sixty-three theaters that were showing films in 1974 have closed during the past 27 years. Of the 10 drive-ins operating in 1974, only two remain. During the same 27 years, 24 new theaters opened with 181 screens. Since 1960, the Baltimore area has lost just about all of its old theaters. The Century, Stanley, Parkway, Town, New, Howard, Metropolitan, Apollo, Broadway, Strand, Ambassador, Walbrook, Patapsco, Hiway, Grand, Northwood, Arcade, Perring Plaza, Irvington, Alpha, and Westview have all closed; many of them have been demolished. But there is a bright side. A few have been preserved. Some of the new movie theaters are more like the glitzy palaces of the 1920s than the shoeboxes of the 1970s. They are more comfortable and have wonderful sound and projection systems. And now the climate appears favorable for saving at least a few of the older theaters. Maybe we can have the best of both worlds.

ROBERT K. HEADLEY, JR.
University Park, Maryland
February 2006

I
A History of Motion Picture Exhibition in Baltimore

1
THE WONDER OF THE CENTURY
(1894–1906)

Movies arrived quietly in Baltimore in October 1894, but nearly two more years passed before Baltimoreans had their first chance to see them projected on a screen. The movies of 1894 were viewed through a peephole in a wooden cabinet called a Kinetoscope. Two years later, projected movies were shown at Electric Park in suburban Arlington. Regular movie exhibitions began in the fall of 1904 when James Kernan brought Keith's vaudeville into his new Maryland Theater. In 1906 the first movie theaters were opened, and, by November 1908, there were 36 licensed moving picture theaters in the city.

In the 1890s, theater or stage-based entertainment in Baltimore was centered around the intersection of Baltimore and Gay Streets with major outlying theaters on West Fayette Street, North Howard Street, and North Charles Street. The most important theaters were:

> **Academy of Music,** N. Howard Street, opened in 1875, musicals, opera
> **Howard Auditorium,** N. Howard Street, opened in 1890, vaudeville, melodrama
> **Ford's,** West Fayette Street, opened in 1871, drama, vaudeville
> **Holliday Street Theater,** Holliday Street, opened in 1795, melodrama
> **Monumental,** East Baltimore Street, opened in 1837, variety, vaudeville
> **Music Hall,**[1] Mt. Royal Avenue, opened in 1894, concerts
> **Lyceum,** N. Charles Street, opened in 1892, drama, opera
> **Odeon,** S. Frederick Street, opened circa 1870, melodrama, burlesque
> **Front Street Theater,** Front Street, opened in 1829, melodrama
> **Lehmann's Hall,** N. Howard Street, opened in 1870, concerts, recitals

Ticket prices ranged from 25 cents to $1.50. There were also the Grand Musee and Theatre (or Dime Museum) at 418 E. Baltimore Street, the Museum of Anatomy at 708 E. Baltimore Street, the North Avenue Ice Skating Rink and 148 halls[2] scattered around the city. The Academy of Music, Monumental, and Ford's were the largest theaters, followed closely by the Holliday Street Theater, Lyceum, and Auditorium. The huge Front Street Theater burned in December 1895 and was never rebuilt.

The theatrical center of Baltimore extended to Center Street on the north and Baltimore Street on the south. The Lyceum, in the 1200 block of North Charles Street, was considered so far out of downtown that John W. Albaugh, the manager, used to get a lot of ribbing about it being out in the country. One performer, Rosina Vokes, autographed a photograph, "Rosina Vokes, playing the Lyceum near Baltimore."

The city was also ringed by open-air amusement parks, most of which had some kind of theater. These parks were exceptionally popular and very important in familiarizing large numbers of people with motion pictures. A five-cent fare from Pratt Street took you to Point Breeze where you could enjoy bathing, dancing, music, and fireworks and pick up a fish, crab or chicken supper for 50 cents at River View Park. A 1900 newspaper article estimated that "on a warm evening" 4,000 people visited River View Park and 2,500 visited Electric Park.[3]

There was a clear polarization of white audiences evident in these theatrical venues. The upper classes tended to patronize the Academy of Music, Ford's, the Music Hall, and Lyceum. The rapidly growing middle class frequented the Auditorium and the Holliday Street Theater, while the working class sought out less expensive theaters such as the Monumental, Odeon, and Front Street. At that time, theater entertainments for African American audiences seem to have been limited to performances at halls of churches and fraternal organizations.

The first commercial movie machine was Thomas Edison's Kinetoscope. That machine, which allowed a viewer to watch a short film through a slot, had its first public exhibition in New York in April 1894. Baltimoreans had learned about the new machine a month earlier, when articles about the Kinetoscope appeared in the Baltimore *Sun*. The Columbia Phonograph Company made arrangements for its showrooms in Washington and Baltimore to exhibit these new machines. Kinetoscopes were sent to Baltimore on October 3, 1894, from the Washington office.[4] They presumably were set up at the company's offices at 110 East Baltimore Street. Three months later another Kinetoscope parlor was opened in Baltimore. Neither of these places was well advertised, and they seemed to make little impression on the popular entertainment scene in Baltimore.

No advertisements have been located for movies in Baltimore until the spring of 1896. This period of time between 1894 and 1896 was marked by feverish attempts by inventors throughout the United States and Europe to develop a workable machine to project moving pictures onto a screen. Nearly simultaneously, in 1895, successful machines were invented in France, England, and the United States. In the United States, the first successful projector, later named the Vitascope, was developed by Thomas Armat and C. Francis Jenkins. The firm of Raff & Gammon acquired the rights to market the machine and gave its first public performance at Koster & Bial's Music Hall in New York on April 23, 1896. Two months later it came to Baltimore. Middlemen who had purchased the exhibition right from Raff & Gammon distributed Vitascope machines and films on a states' rights basis. Charles E. Ford thought the new machine might be just the thing to open the new Electric Park and began negotiations with one of these middlemen.

Electric Park was a summer park, not too far from Pimlico Race Track, built by August Fenneman. Fenneman fenced in the park and added a large casino. The park opened on Monday, June 8, 1896, under the management of Charles E. Ford; the price of admission was 25 cents. The park covered an area of about 24 acres with frontage on Belvidere Avenue and on Reisterstown Road. It became a popular summer entertainment center. The Vitascope shows were presented in the Casino, a large, comfortable oval building with a peaked roof in the center of the park. It seated about 5,000. The opening program at Electric Park advertised Prof. Fisher's String and Brass Band,

Edison's Vitascope, Princess Eulalie, Adele Purvis Onri, the Three Sisters Don, and the Three Bouffons.

Unspecified problems with the Vitascope forced a postponement of movies during the opening week. Available evidence indicates that the first showing of the Vitascope was actually on Tuesday, June 16. It was supposed to be exhibited on Monday, June 15, but according to the *Sun*,[5] "...when it was exhibited for the first time, it did not operate smoothly...." The problems were corrected, and the exhibition on Tuesday went well.[6] That show featured films of Broadway and 33rd Street in New York, an act from the play *A Milk White Flag*, some dance scenes and scenes of Niagara Falls, and the beach at Atlantic City. The review of the show in the *American* of June 16, 1896, mentioned the Vitascope first: "The Vitascope was the main feature of the evening, and the reproduction by it of scenes from life made one realize the greatness of the Wizard Edison, who invented it."[7] The Vitascope was featured at Electric Park for the next two weeks. During the week of June 21, there were movies of the famous May Irwin kiss, surf bathing, a blacksmith shop, and various dances. Several of these scenes, including the kiss, were repeated during the week of June 28. The Vitascope moved to top billing in the second week ads: "This Week's Wonders. THE VITASCOPE. Edison's latest and most marvelous discovery heads the list."[8]

Baltimore's indoor theater season[9] opened in mid–August 1896, and in a little more than a month, a second moving picture exhibition appeared in Baltimore. Charles Ford had a hand in this exhibition too, but he had experienced so much trouble with the Vitascope at Electric Park that he brought in a different machine. The vaudeville show at Ford's Theater the week of September 28 featured the Animatograph, an English projector, and movies of "a lone fisherman, sitting on the edge of a bridge, who was tipped overboard by an enraged farmer and floundered about in the water." This was called "one of the best scenes."[10] The following month, there was a movie exhibition at Kernan's Auditorium. As part of the Irwin Brothers Company of American and European artists there was an exhibition of the Centograph billed as "the latest French invention — the triumph of photography."[11] Films shown in this exhibition included scenes from the Russian War, 14th Street in New York, the Griffin-Dixon fight, a fire scene, and a bucking bronco. At Ford's, in a special election show during the week of November 2, 1896, among the minstrel acts there was an exhibition by the Biograph. The movies included McKinley receiving the Baltimore delegation at Canton, Ohio; the Royal Blue Express traveling at 60 miles per hour; Niagara Falls; and a stable on fire.

James Kernan was the major theatrical force in turn-of-the-century Baltimore; with his Auditorium, Monumental and Maryland theaters, Kernan tapped theatergoers of all classes of society. Kernan's friend, Frederick C. Schanberger, remembered that Kernan, at one time, did not think very much of movies, but was induced to pay $400 a week for a trial. As soon as word of the movies got around, the theater was packed for every performance.[12] Kernan might not have had a high opinion of movies at first, but he was a good enough judge of shows to quickly revise his opinion. Within two weeks, Kernan brought the Kinematographe to his Auditorium Theater as part of the Hopkins' Trans-Oceanic Star Specialty Company.

The movies were still novelties and the clear hits of this show, as suggested by the review in the *Baltimore American*. "The Kinematographe is a world-astounding marvel. The life motion of photography which it reproduces in life size is more than astonishing, and it is safe to predict that its effect in our city will be a repetition of its prior suc-

10   I. A History

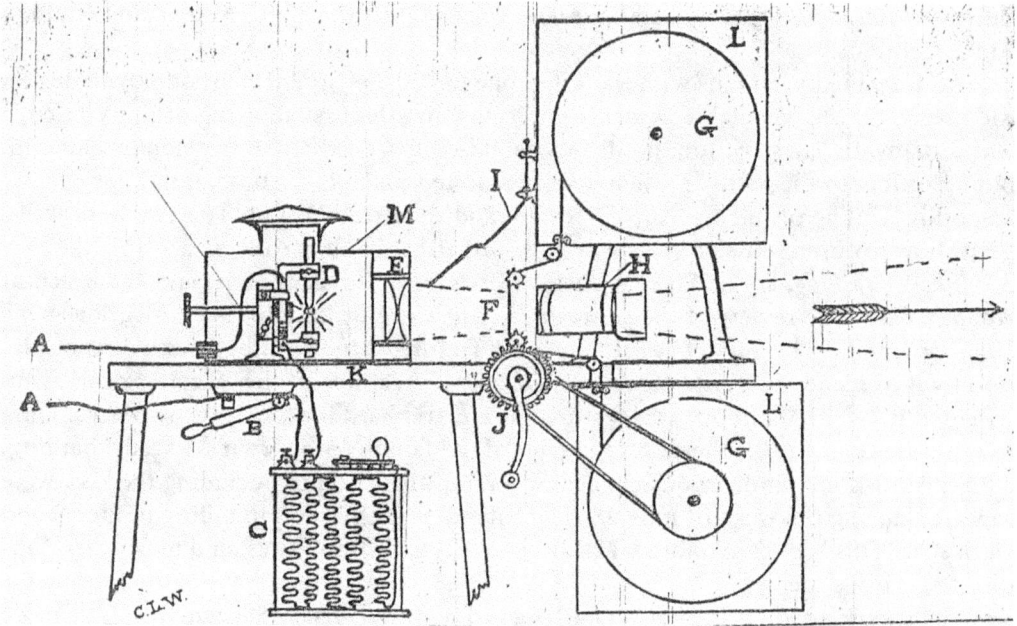

Diagram of an early projector showing (A) the power source, (C) the rheostat which controls the amount of current, (D) the carbon arc, (E) lens, (F) the film gate, (G) the supply and take-up reels, (H) lens, (I) the shield that drops down when the machine stops to protect the film from the concentrated heat of the arc lamp, (J) the hand crank, and (L) the metal cases that protect the film.

cess."[13] Despite this popularity, the Kinematographe exhibition was the last movie exhibition in Baltimore in 1896.

One of the best-known early movie exhibitions in Baltimore took place in January 1897. The Methodist Trades Bazaar, to benefit the City Missionary and Church Extension Society of the Methodist Episcopal Church, was held at Hamilton Easter's store at 23–27 East Baltimore Street between January 20 and 30. Governor Lowndes and Mayor Hooper were among the notables who attended the opening on the evening of January 20.

There were displays and booths on both floors of the Easter Building. The first floor featured a butter exhibit, a house furnishings department, a fine laundry and toilet soap display that included a three-and-a-half-foot column made of Castile soap, and a men's furnishings department. There was also a dining room and an automatic electric photograph machine. The second floor featured electric, nautical, and bicycle exhibits, furniture, and a typewriter exhibit. And at the far end, beyond the open well that looked down onto the first floor, was a large room containing a Cinematograph exhibit.

The writer for the *Baltimore American* made a valiant, but incomprehensible, attempt to explain motion pictures: "Another interesting thing is the photographing of motion, or, as it is termed, Lumiere's Cinematograph. Photographs taken at the rate of fifteen per second are placed upon a curtain with the assistance of electricity and magic lantern effects, with like rapidity. One does not see a break between the pictures, of which there are 900 a minute required to make the life-size pictures complete."[14] The reporter for the *Morning Herald* could not decide whether the exhibit that showed how a fire alarm works or the Cinematograph was the more interesting, although the latter was described in some detail:

> A very much visited apartment last night was that at the rear of this [second] floor in which the Cinematograph was stationed. There was a rush to see the moving photographic figures which this instrument showed. The more interesting of the subjects treated were "The Lion," "Niagara Falls," "Prairie Afire," "The Czar on the Place de la Concorde at Paris," ... "Cavalry Crossing La Saône at Lyons," "Children's Quarrel" and the arrival at a French railroad station. Music was furnished along with the pictures.[15]

This exhibition also marked the first instance of the use of music with a moving picture exhibition in the area. It was still vivid in the mind of Mrs. William T. Childs 40 years later. She reminisced in Carroll Dulaney's column:

> Mrs. Childs says she saw the first movies shown in Baltimore ... at the old dry goods store of Hamilton Easter ... a bazaar was held for the benefit of the Methodist Home for the Aged. Mrs. Easter offered the store for the purpose. The bazaar included a "cinematograph" exhibition of motion pictures made in France ... shown on the second floor of the store. The pictures included views of French Army maneuvers, ships sailing at sea, some comic scenes and animated reproductions of famous paintings, such as "The Angelus." The performance ... lasted 30 minutes and the charge was 15 cents. Her most vivid recollection of this ... was the attendance at one performance after another of Dr. John T. King, Sr., Dr. G. Lane Taneyhill and F. H. Davidson, who seemed so fascinated by the pictures that they could not tear themselves away.[16]

The next movie exhibition was at the Auditorium, where Joseph Menchen appeared with his Kineoptikon in January and April 1897. He showed movies of Mlle. Winnefred doing her famous "Butterfly Dance" during the January exhibition. Other moving picture exhibitions in the first half of 1897 included the Zinematographe, which showed films of the Maher-Choynski fight at Kernan's Monumental Theater during the week of March 15,[17] the Cinematascope, also at the Monumental, during the week of April 18, and the Cinematograph, which ended the 1897 theatrical season at Ford's with five consecutive weeks of motion pictures. Each week at Ford's, 12 new pictures were shown between acts of an operetta. The movies at the Monumental and Auditorium were just one act in a vaudeville show.

The summer season of 1897 opened at Electric Park with Cineograph movies as part of the vaudeville show. The films were changed every week. At about the same time, manufacturers of movie equipment, eager for new markets, began advertising in local newspapers. In July 1897, the Edison Manufacturing Company of Orange, New Jersey, advertised "Projecting Kinetoscopes" in the *Baltimore American*. The 1897 Model "complete with all accessories for projecting animated pictures, life size" was available for $100. For two weeks in August, Ford's presented Veriscope films of the Corbett-Fitzsimmons' fight. There were two performances daily, at 2:30 and 8:30; ticket prices ran from 25 cents to $1.00. New York exhibitor William A. Brady appeared onstage to announce the fight and "called attention to all points and people of interest which appeared in the pictures."

The first attempt to operate a place devoted to motion pictures in Baltimore was made in the fall of 1897. An enterprise called Lumiere's Wonderland opened on October 4, at 36 W. Baltimore Street. The second floor of the Wonderland contained an exhibition of Astley D. M. Cooper's painting, "The Morning of the Crucifixion," a life-sized painting of the arrival on Calvary. The first floor had been converted into a "cozy auditorium" where Cinematograph shows were offered. The exhibitions ran from 1:00 to 5:30 and from 7:00 to 10:30. Admission was 10 cents. The Wonderland lasted only about a week. The Baltimore public was not yet ready for a movie theater. A Cineograph exhibition, part of an election special during the week of November 1 at Ford's, was the last movie exhibition in the city in 1897. At 10:30, following Joseph Jefferson's performance of "Rip Van Winkle," patrons who wished to see the movies and hear Fisher's Big Band paid an additional 25 cents for admission.

In January 1898, the Biograph came to Baltimore after a successful six-week run at Willard's Hall in Washington. Beginning on Monday, January 17, there was a weeklong Biograph exhibition at the Academy of Music Concert Hall. Admission was 50 cents for adults and 25 cents for children. The first week's films included scenes of Queen Victoria's Jubilee parade, the Atlantic City volunteer fire department, a pillow fight, and a royal lawn party at Aldershot. Two weeks later, the Biograph was part of Hallen and Fuller's vaudeville show at the Auditorium Theater. The following month, for one week beginning on February 7, motion pictures of the Horitz Passion Play were shown at the Music Hall. Tickets cost 25 cents with reserved seats available at 35 and 50 cents. Shows were given every evening at 8:15 with matinees at 3:00 on Wednesday, Thursday, Friday and Saturday. This show came to Baltimore after a two-week exhibition in Philadelphia.[18] Movies of the Passion Play had the qualified support of the church. According to the *Baltimore American* of January 30, 1898, motion pictures of the Passion Play met with such strong endorsement from the clergy in Boston that the theater management decided the theater was not the proper place for it. The clergymen of Boston requested that they not produce it in theaters, but in halls or churches. The following week the *Baltimore American* provided a detailed description of this exhibition:

> A special presentation of the "Passion Play" was given in honor of Cardinal Gibbons yesterday ... at five o'clock at the Music Hall ... where a reproduction of the sacred drama as given by the peasants of Horitz, in Bohemia, will be seen each afternoon and evening this week. Cards of invitation were issued to all the clergy ... of the city ... and the presentation of the play by means of the cinematograph was highly commended on all sides. Cardinal Gibbons said: "It is most realistic and impressive, and I will recommend it." ... The presentation opens with a description of the village of Horitz ... with an instructive history of the "Passion Play." Then follow the tableaux, thirty-five in number. All the scenes are interesting and realistic, and some almost awe-inspiring. The moving pictures before your eyes, with all the apparent elements of life, except that of speech, lend to these scenes an altogether spiritual atmosphere which cannot but leave more than a passing impression.... During the presentation of these scenes selections are rendered on an organ and several solos are sung.[19]

Professor Ernest Lacy gave the introductory lecture. The Passion Play was so popular that it returned to the Music Hall in October 1898 and January 1899.

Movies of the Spanish-American War proved very popular in 1898 and attracted many new customers to see them. James Kernan brought the Biograph back to the Auditorium as part of a vaudeville program in late March 1898. Among the scenes shown were movies of the battleship *Maine* that had been blown up in Havana Harbor on February 15. Kernan replaced the Biograph with Schneider's American Cinematograph a month later as part of a gala spring opening of the Auditorium. Schneider also showed war movies featuring the *Maine* tragedy. The only advertised motion picture exhibitions during the summer of 1898 were a Veriscope showing at the Holliday Street Theater of the 1897 Corbett-Fitzsimmons fight in June and a "Wargraph" exhibition of Spanish-American War movies as part of the burlesque bill at Kernan's Monumental, also in June. Neither Electric Park nor River View Park advertised any movies during the summer season.

In September 1898 there were two motion picture showings. Kernan brought the Biograph, with the latest war films, including the great naval parade passing Grant's Tomb, back to the Auditorium. The first movies shown on "The Block"[20] were shown at the Bijou Theater which was the remodeled Grand Musee at 418 E. Baltimore Street. Egan and Michael opened the Bijou on September 12 after a three-month remodeling. It consisted of a Curio Hall where the D'Aljaris Collection of Spanish Torturing Instruments was exhibited and a theater where vaudeville was provided. Among the vaudeville acts was the Lumiere Cinematograph. The Bijou was open from 1:00 P.M. until 11:00 P.M. and charged 10, 15, and 20 cents, slightly less than the larger uptown theaters. The Bijou reduced its tickets to a flat 10 cents and gave the cinematograph top billing in its ads of September 18 and 25. A reviewer for the *Sunday Herald* of September 25 reported that the Bijou was doing a good business; nevertheless, its ads ceased after October 2.

The year 1899 began with three different motion picture exhibitions at the Music Hall. The first, during the first two weeks of January, was a return of the Passion Play, featuring lectures by James J. Skelly and vocal music by contralto Blanche Yewell and baritone F. DuShane Cloward. By all accounts this was a highly successful exhibition. According to the reviewer for the *American*, "Although this is the third time that the Passion Play has been at the Music Hall, yesterday was the largest attendance on the opening night."[21]

During the last week of January, there was a Biograph exhibition at the Music Hall which featured 37 pictures at each show. One of these films was the well-known movie of Pope Leo XIII obtained by W. K. L. Dickson. Other movies were of the coronation of Queen Wilhelmina, the Empire State Express traveling 60 mph, and a hotel fire in Paris. Reserved seats cost 50 cents with regular prices of 25 cents for adults and 15 cents for children. The Biograph continued for a second week. Beginning on the evening of January 24 and continuing for the next three Tuesdays, the popular travel lecturer, Burton Holmes, lectured at the Music Hall. This was Holmes' first engagement in Baltimore. Holmes, who was widely publicized as the successor to retired lecturer John L. Stoddard, gave lectures on exotic places illustrated with slides and motion pictures. The four lectures were: "The Hawaiian Islands," "Fez, the Metropolis of the Moors," "Grecian Journeys," and "The Grand Canon of Arizona." Tickets to all four cost $2.00, $2.50, or $3.00 while single tickets cost 25 cents, 50 cents, or $1.75.[22] Holmes would return to Baltimore many more times in the future.

Around the beginning of February 1899, a Mutoscope hall opened in the Sun Building at 305 East Baltimore Street. It operated, with little newspaper publicity, until as late as June. There was an exhibition of movies at Kernan's Monumental Theater during the week of March 27. An extra added attraction to the top-billed Clark Bros. Royal Burlesquers was "The Wonderful Moving Picture Machine, showing the Windsor Hotel Fire."[23] In early June, River View Park[24] began showing Biograph movies, changing the pictures every week. These exhibitions continued through the park's season until the week of September 11. During the weeks of August 7 and 21 the film *Man in the Moon* was shown. This film, by French filmmaker George Méliès, was one of the earliest special effect or "trick" films.[25]

The Biograph films were replaced at River View by American Vitagraph films in mid–August. There do not seem to have been any motion picture exhibitions at Electric Park in the summer of 1899. During the week of November 5, Kernan's Monumental advertised movies of Admiral Dewey's triumphal reception in New York and the Columbia-Shamrock yacht race as part of a burlesque review. On November 11, an ad by William Brady appeared in the *Sun*, warning the public that the films of the Jeffries-Sharkey fight made by the American Mutoscope Company were the only authorized genuine ones. Brady had purchased the rights to show the official fight film in Maryland, but other shorter, pirated, versions were also available. In the same issue of the *Sun*, the Monumental advertised that "The First Animated Moving Pictures to Be Completed of the Jeffries-Sharkey Fight Have arrived and will be introduced as a Special Feature in conjunction with The Gay Masqueraders." On November 25, Kernan's Auditorium advertised "First Time Here Jeffries-Sharkey Contest in the Edison Pictures taken at the Ring-Side."

Both of these films were so-called "stolen" pictures of the fight. The saga of this fight ended a month later at Ford's Theater when movies of the complete "genuine" 25-round bout were shown on December 16. Ford's advertised a week of movies of the Jeffries-Sharkey fight. There were two shows a day, at 2:15 and 8:15. Tickets cost 25 cents, 50 cents, 75 cents, and $1.00. The great popularity of movies of prizefights probably had a lot to do with introducing a large segment of the population to movies.

In January 1900 there were additional motion picture exhibitions at the Kernan theaters. During the week of January 22, there was a Cinematograph exhibition at the Auditorium as part of Weber & Fields vaudeville company, and during the following week, films of the McGovern-Dixon fight and the South African War were shown at the Monumental. On February 10, the Auditorium advertised the enormously popular film *Cinderella* in five scenes as part of its vaudeville bill for the following week. However, movies of the war between the English and Boers in South Africa got the most audience response. According to the *Sun's* reviewer:

> An indication of Boer sympathies was shown in the exhibition of pictures by the Vitagraph. Scenes were shown of Boer rough riders on a South African farm, portraits of Oom Paul and other Boer leaders, which were greeted with vociferous applause. Portraits of Generals Kitchener and Methuen and scenes of a regiment of British Lancers charging and of marines boarding a transport at Southampton were received with much fainter applause, with which was mingled a good supply of hisses.[26]

The same day, the Monumental advertised something called the "Tobascoscope," which showed films of Boer cavalry and a reproduction of the Maher-McCoy fight. These were the only film exhibitions advertised in Baltimore during the first half of 1900. For the second year in a row, River View Park showed Vitagraph films during the summer season. Again, movies of the Boer War seemed to be among the most popular. Only a single ad for movies at Electric Park has been located.[27]

Burton Holmes was back at the Music Hall for four Thursday evenings in November and December for his annual appearance in Baltimore. Series tickets were somewhat more reasonable this time, ranging from $1.50 to $2.50. Single ticket prices remained the same as in 1899. There was also a movie exhibition featuring the Cineograph at the Monumental during the week of December 22.

In early 1901, the Lyceum Theater was leased by the Chase organization and began to give vaudeville performances. Between February and April, there was usually a motion picture exhibition as part of the show. In February, the Comiograph was part of the Orpheum Show at the Lyceum. For the remainder of the spring theater season, a Biograph exhibition, with 12 new films each week, was part of every show there. The films shown during the week of March 11 included scenes of Maryland's Fifth Regiment marching. The Monumental continued its sporadic motion pictures; during the week of March 4, Lubin's Cineograph presented movies, including films of Carrie Nation's hatchet brigade on its crusade against the saloons.

During the summer season that year, movies were shown fairly regularly at Electric Park and, at least occasionally, at the River View Park Casino. Movies were also advertised "every evening this season" at Graubner's West End Park near the intersection of West Baltimore Street and Franklintown Road. The only movies during the fall and winter of 1901 were shown during Thanksgiving week at the Junior Order of United American Mechanics (O.U.A.M.). Bazaar held at the Fourth Regiment Armory on Fayette Street near Paca and during the week of December 30 at the Monumental. The latter were films of the Jeffries-Ruhlin fight.

In 1902 movies were shown as an extra feature with Sam A. Scribner's "Morning Glories" burlesque show at the Monumental during the week of January 20, 1902. These films featured scenes of President McKinley making his last speech and reviewing troops at Buffalo. Burton Holmes was at the Music Hall for another illustrated lecture series in January and February. The next movies in 1902 were Vitagraph films with Sandow and his company at the Auditorium during the week of April 21. A Biograph exhibition was one of the Midway features at the Maryland Industrial Exposition, which was held at Pennsylvania and North Avenues between May 27 and April 14. The exposition was divided into sections of the Midway, which also featured a Wild Animal Arena, Japanese and German Villages, a Crystal Maze, a Moorish Palace, and the Industrial Hall. The Hall contained booths from various local businesses such as Bernheimer Bros., the Maryland Telephone Company, the Lipton Tea Company, the American Tobacco Company, and five brewing companies.

When Electric Park opened for the 1902 season on June 2, the American Vitagraph was featured prominently in its opening ad and in most of its ads throughout that season. There was only a single ad for motion pictures at River View Park, on June 8, when Lubin's cinematograph [sic] showing scenes of St. Pierre before and after the eruption of Mt. Pelee was exhibited. Among the films shown at Electric Park were the "thrilling fire scene 'Midnight Rescue,'" "Red Riding Hood," and "the coronation of Edward VII." A special feature of the vaudeville show beginning on June 9 was the young comic juggler W. C. Fields. The last films of 1902 were the Vitagraph films shown at Electric Park during the week of September 8. There were no more motion pictures advertised in Baltimore until February 1903.

Three new theaters opened in Baltimore in 1903, and film exhibitions almost reached their 1899 high. The former United Railways powerhouse on the 1100 block of East Baltimore Street was converted into a 10–20–30-cent theater, the Convention Hall, in early 1903. It opened on January 19 with the Erwood Stock Company in a five-act production called "A Mortgaged Slave." The management of the theater introduced a new feature by having vaudeville performances during intermissions and between the acts. Among these vaudeville performances during the week of February 2 were motion pictures. During the week of March 16, the Oberammergau Passion Play by the American Vitagraph Company, with explanatory dialog by an announcer, was given there. The year's second new theater, the Empire,[28] opened in the former St. Mark's Lutheran Church at 315–319 North Eutaw Street on February 23. In April 1903, the Empire had Vitagraph motion pictures on the vaudeville bill for three weeks. Included in these films were scenes of the launching of Sir Thomas Lipton's racing yacht *Shamrock III* and "A Journey to Luna."[29] Burton Holmes appeared in Baltimore twice during 1903, both times at the Lyric. The Monumental continued to present occasional exhibitions of action films with a showing in April of the Corbett-McGovern fight film. As usual, the film was part of a larger show, in this case, Robie and Mack's World Beaters burlesque company. For three weeks in June, motion pictures could be seen at the Eagles' Industrial Exposition held at Industrial Park at North and Pennsylvania avenues. There were 200 industrial booths in the hall and Gaskill-Mundy-Levitt High Class vaudeville attractions, "30 mammoth shows and free acts ... dazzling electrical displays," and a "fine zoological aggregation." Among the advertised amusements were the German Village, House Upside Down, Jim Key, the Educated Horse, a Ferris Wheel, and Edison's Kinedrome. Admission was 10 cents.

More than 100,000 people visited the exposition during the first week.[30] The *Sun*'s reviewer failed to mention the Kinedrome in his review on June 7; a high diver, lion cubs, the crew of a French warship, and a women's brass band were singled out for special mention. In the summer of 1903, films moved back to Electric Park; this year, the Cineograph was featured with new views advertised nearly every week.[31] The Convention Hall changed its name to Bijou when it reopened on August 24; admission was still 10–20–30 cents. During the week of September 14, the Bijou advertised "Special first motion pictures of the Reliance-Shamrock yacht race."

The biggest theatrical event of 1903 was the opening of the Maryland Theater on Franklin Street. James Kernan opened the Maryland, one-third of his Triple Million Dollar Enterprise, on October 19 with the play *Mary Magdala*, starring Minnie Maddern Fiske. Tickets cost 25–50–75 cents at matinees and 25–50–75 cents to $1.00 in the evenings. The following month, Kernan made the Kinetoscope part of the vaudeville show at the Maryland, and during the last week of December the Vitagraph showed films as part of another vaudeville show. Over the next several years, the Maryland became one of the theaters in Baltimore that most consistently showed motion pictures.

Because of his willingness, albeit hesitant at first, to show early movies on a regular basis, James Kernan deserves much credit for launching the new medium in Baltimore. He was one of the major theatrical promoters in Baltimore and is credited with introducing refined vaudeville to the city. When he died in 1912, he was mourned by the entire city.

> James Lawrence Kernan — better known to his associates ... as "Addie" Kernan — theatrical manager, hotel proprietor, Confederate veteran and liberal giver to the orphans and the needy, died ... yesterday afternoon in his apartment in the Hotel Kernan.... He was 74 years old.
>
> Mr. Kernan was proprietor of the hotel, of the Maryland Theatre, adjoining; was interested in the amusement enterprises and was one of the most widely known citizens of Baltimore, as well as having a host of friends in the theatrical profession in all parts of the world.... Mr. Kernan was fond of admitting that he started his successful career in life "with a shoestring." He attributed all of his triumphs in business to hard work.... He was born in Baltimore at the southeast corner of Pratt and High streets on 26 July 1838.... His father was James Kernan, a leading feed dealer, whose place of business was on the site now occupied by the Maryland Theater....

He attended Loyola College on Holliday Street, and around that time boarded with the family of Junius Brutus Booth on Gay Street. Kernan completed his education at Mount St. Mary's College in Emmitsburg. After graduation from college, he was employed in a dry goods store, but became ill. To recover his health he signed on a ship, the brig *Romance*, on which his brother was a mate. A voyage to South America and the West Indies restored his health. Upon his return to Baltimore, he worked as a clerk for the B & O Railroad. When the Civil War broke out, Kernan enlisted in the Confederate Army, where he became friends with Colonel John Mosby. He served with the Baltimore Light Artillery and was captured in 1864. He spent the rest of the war at the Point Lookout Military Prison. In 1866, he and his brother, Eugene, took over Washington Hall Theater in the 700 block of East Baltimore Street.

Despite a destructive fire in 1874, the Kernans made a success of the theater and a new form of entertainment called burlesque. The Kernans gave the first performance of *Uncle Tom's Cabin* in Baltimore at the old Maryland Institute building. In 1890, Kernan took over the Holliday Street Theater and converted it into a popular-priced theater. That same year, he bought the Howard Auditorium Theater on Howard Street, where he booked vaudeville shows.

Kernan's greatest theatrical triumph was his "Million Dollar Triple Enterprise"[32] consisting of the Maryland Theater, the Hotel Kernan, and the Auditorium Theater, all clustered near the intersection of North Howard and Franklin streets. The enterprise was built in stages. The Maryland Theater was completed in 1903. The rebuilt Auditorium Theater and the Hotel Kernan opened in 1905. The grand opening of the Million Dollar Triple Enterprise took place on Monday, September 4, 1905, and it was billed, with typical theatrical modesty, as "the greatest combination of buildings in the world." The enterprise occupied 51,500 square feet of ground — 2,000 tons of steel; 100,000 tons of concrete, crushed stone and cement; and several million bricks went into the construction of the two theaters and hotel. Heat and electrical power for the enterprise were supplied by four sets of generators in Machinery Hall, a subterranean power plant with uniformed engineers, white tile and marble walls. A total of 350 employees was required to run the theaters and hotel. In 1903, when Kernan laid the cornerstone of the Maryland Theater, he controlled the Auditorium, Holliday Street, and Monumental theaters, the Convention Hall, and Hollywood Park in Baltimore; the Lyceum, Empire, and Lafayette Square theaters in Washington; and the Lafayette Square Theater in Buffalo, New York. Kernan also, at one time, operated the Bijou Theater and River View Park in Baltimore.

Short, white-haired, with a huge white mustache and immaculately tailored clothes, James Kernan was a real showman; he knew how to attract customers to his theaters. Kernan rushed to book exotic dancer "Little Egypt" following her sensational dance at the 1893 Chicago World's Fair. He pioneered burlesque and vaudeville in Baltimore, and he introduced a generation of Baltimoreans to motion pictures with exhibitions in all of his theaters from the late 1890s until well into the 20th century. Despite his affiliation with "Little Egypt" and burlesque, Kernan would not allow certain types of performances on his stages. He was not happy with Virginia Earle's act, "When Salome Meets the Devil," at the Maryland and ordered her to cut some of the lines. She refused, and he cut the whole act, replacing it with a movie.[33] He was one of the first showmen who could offer traveling performers more than one-week dates; for this reason he was able to book top acts.

But even Kernan made mistakes. One story tells of the time he contracted to pay magician Harry Houdini $20 for a vaudeville skit at the Lyceum Theater. He watched the act once, then went backstage and ordered Houdini to pack his handcuffs and get out. Kernan was also, apparently, reluctant at first to put motion pictures in his theaters. According to his long-time friend Frederick Schanberger,[34] Kernan could see no good in the early Biograph, but Schanberger and others persuaded him to give it a trial run.

While James L. Kernan is not remembered for his theaters, except by a dwindling number of senior citizens and a few historians, he is remembered for his charity, compassion and the establishment of a hospital for crippled children. In 1905, Ada Mosby, the daughter of Kernan's Civil War friend Colonel John Mosby, started work at the Hospital for Crippled Children on West 20th Street. One version of how she met Kernan is that she advertised for a piano for the hospital, and he paid them a visit. He is supposed to have told her, "You don't need a piano, Miss Mosby, you need a hospital!" Five years later, he purchased the 60-acre Radnor Park estate near Dickeyville in West Baltimore and deeded it to the hospital. The new institution built there became known as the Kernan Hospital for Crippled Children. He provided generously for the hospital while he lived and left it stock worth more than $300,000 after his death. It was Kernan's custom to pay weekly visits every Sunday to the hospital. For many years he organized Christmas parties for the poor children, African American and white, of Baltimore. He arranged matinees at the Maryland theater for every sick or poor child he could identify. "Give them the treat of their lives and send the bill to me" were his instructions every year.[35]

In February 1906, Kernan and others associated with the Empire burlesque circuit planned a huge new theater on Baltimore Street near Calvert. This was to combat the "invasion" of Baltimore by the rival Columbia circuit which had just opened the Gayety. When asked if Kernan would abandon his Monumental Theater after the new theater opened, he said, "Abandon the old Monumental! Well, I guess not! No matter what might happen, as long as I have a cent and one brick stuck to another of the house, I would continue it in operation, if only out of sentiment."[36] Four months later, the old veteran had had enough of the burlesque war. He sold his beloved Monumental, his Lyceum Theater in Washington and the Lafayette Square Theater in Buffalo. He still planned to continue as general manager of the Kernan Company which operated the Million Dollar Triple Enterprise. James Lawrence Kernan died in December 1912; his coffin was placed on public view in the art gallery of his hotel where it was visited by thousands of mourners.[37] An editorial in the *Baltimore American* called Kernan "broad-minded and liberal, far-seeing and a firm believer in Baltimore" and said that the city had no man of "larger heart, no man who put his charity to better use."[38] He left an estate worth about $1,500,000. His hospital became one of the most famous orthopedic centers in the United States.

Much of downtown Baltimore was destroyed by a terrible fire which began on February 7, 1904. The only theater destroyed was the ancient Odeon on North Gay Street which, strangely, never seemed to exhibit films. A month later, Kernan's Maryland Theater had Vitagraph films of the fire. These were shown during the week of March 7 as an addition to Vesta Tilley's vaudeville company. The *Sun*'s reviewer on March 6 was impressed by these films: "This moving picture sensation will be produced by means of the American Biograph [sic] and will show the great fire from its start to its finish. The scenes will be from photographs taken Sunday and Monday while the flames were raging. They make a remarkable photographic record of the greatest fire in modern history and are projected in such a real manner that it is hard to believe when looking at them that one is not gazing at the actual occurrence."[39]

The following week, the performances of George H. Primrose's vaudeville company concluded, "with the Kinetograph moving-picture machine portraying with startling realism a great train robbery and a number of other exciting and amusing scenes from real life." The former film was no doubt Edwin S. Porter's landmark film, *The Great Train Robbery*. This film, which made its debut in New York in December 1903, marked the beginning of "story" films and, according to film historian Charles Musser, "...is a remarkable film not simply because it was commercially successful or incorporated American myths into the repertoire of screen entertainment, but because it presents so many trends, genres, and strategies fundamental to cinematic practice at that time."[40] It has been called, "the first important western" and "the first dramatically creative American film."

All of this success and praise notwithstanding, neither Kernan nor any other local manager found any reason to exhibit movies in Baltimore for the remainder of the spring season. In a summer of only sporadic film exhibition, Electric Park showed *The Great Train Robbery* during the week of July 25. During the week of September 12, Electric Park advertised "Pearce and Scheck's moving pictures." This is one of the earliest appearances together of the two names which would soon become synonymous with motion picture exhibition in Baltimore.

Beginning in the fall of 1904, Baltimoreans could see weekly movies at the Maryland. Kernan had contracted with the B. F. Keith organization to supply Keith's high-class vaudeville to the Maryland, and Biograph films were part of each show. A typical show consisted of seven or eight acts plus movies. The bill for the week of October 24, 1904, consisted of seven acts and Biograph movies of *The Great Train Robbery*. One of these acts was "The Three Keatons" with a young Buster, "youngest comedian on the American stage." Movies were a regular feature at the Maryland for the remainder of 1904 and well into the nickelodeon era, although the Biograph was replaced by the Kinetograph in the fall of 1905.

The Biograph continued at the Maryland through the end of the 1905 spring theater season in late April. There was one Biograph showing at the Auditorium the second week of May and then no more movies until mid–June, when they appeared at Electric Park. Movies were shown at the park most of that summer; Pearce and Scheck provided the exhibitions for at least three weeks and possibly for the entire summer season. There were no movie ads for the weeks of May 15, 22, 29, June 3, 17, July 31, or August 7, 14, 28. It is possible that films were shown at the park, but not included in the advertisements on these dates.[41] Weekly films returned to the Maryland in September; this season they were exhibited using the Edison Kinetograph.[42] The only other exhibition of motion pictures advertised in 1905 was the Jimmy Britt–Battling Nelson fight at the Lyric Theater on October 3, 4, and 5. There were two shows a day, at 2:15 P.M. and 8:15 P.M.; admission was 25 cents with reserved seats at 50 cents and $1.00.

Most of the film exhibitions up to this time had been put on by exhibitors from out of state, but there were a few local exhibitors. They could not afford their own theaters so they moved from venue to venue. Some showed films almost exclusively in rented halls. Walter Hitchcock was one of these men. Hitchcock was born in 1874; he started out as a carpenter, but was also a singer. In 1899, he lost his sight. Around 1900, he got an Edison projector, and Hitchcock and his family began offering moving picture exhibitions around Baltimore. Among the venues for his exhibitions were the West Branch YMCA, the halls at Northeast and Broadway markets, the Germania Mannerchor Hall, Frohsinn Hall (on South Payson Street), Johnny Klein's Beer Park and Shadyside Beer Park (both near Westport), and St. Mary's Industrial School, where one of the brothers was always on hand to turn on the lights in case a movie got too suggestive. Hitchcock also formed his own lady minstrel show, recruiting stage-struck young women from the Vindex Shirt factory. Hitchcock served as the interlocutor, but he hired two professional end men, Harry Kettlebahn and Joe Sweeton.

Walter Hitchcock was also well known in Baltimore for his illustrated song slides. After an unsuccessful attempt to run a small movie theater north of Belair Market on Gay Street, Hitchcock opened an illustrated song slide business on the second floor of the Loeb Building at 15 S. Gay Street. Theater managers paid about 25 cents a night for a set of 16–18 song slides. On several occasions, Hitchcock got permission to close off Baltimore Street between Gay and Holliday and give an open-air movie show along with election returns. He would show advertising slides and slides with election returns along with interspersed short films. He had someone stationed in front of the Sun Building to write down the returns as they were posted; then boy runners would carry the returns to Hitchcock's wife, who would prepare slides with the returns on them.

The number of newspaper advertisements for motion picture exhibitions in Baltimore averaged around 20 per year, until 1905 when it suddenly doubled. Then, in 1906 it skyrocketed to 70 ads. Obviously something was happening. The people of Baltimore seemed ready to devour every movie they could find. Several conditions necessary for a successful movie theater had been met. There were potential customers from all classes of Baltimore society. Films, especially films with stories, were readily available. And cheaper movie projection equipment could be readily obtained. The time was ripe for a theater devoted entirely to movies.

The first successful movie theater in Baltimore opened in early 1906 at 406 East Baltimore Street.[43] It was called simply "The Moving Picture Theater."

> AUTHENTIC
> *EARTHQUAKE*
> AND
> *Fire Pictures*
> ALL
> THIS WEEK AT
> **The Moving Picture Theatre**
> **406 E. Baltimore St.**
> OPEN FROM 10 A.M. TO 11 P.M.
> ADMISSION 5¢

Ads for this theater continued into the late spring. In May it was advertising movies of the San Francisco earthquake. This was the first permanent movie theater operated by Marion Pearce and Philip Scheck, who both went on to become major players in the development of motion picture exhibition in Baltimore. In late 1905, William B. Brown set up a small movie house in one half of the penny arcade at 402–404 E. Baltimore Street on the western end of Baltimore's famous "Block."

On the opening day, before any of the show had begun, the film caught fire, and Brown's theater was wrecked.[44] Brown had nearly gone bankrupt when Pearce and Scheck

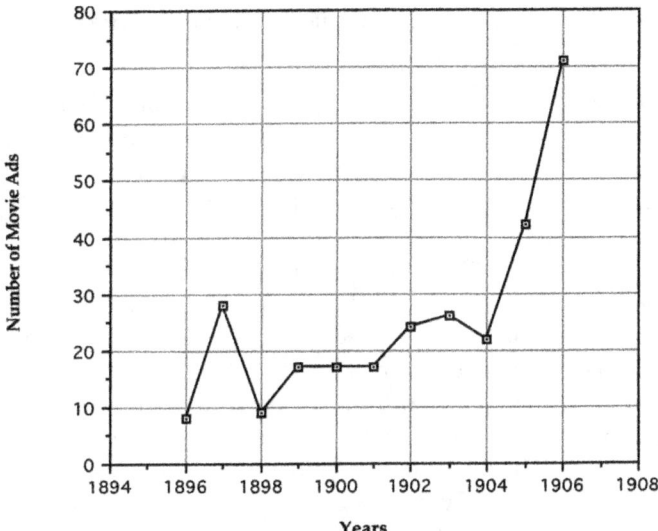

Chart 1. Number of Movie Ads in Newspapers, 1896–1906

stepped in. They bought him out, and rebuilt the theater. They installed about 75 seats, a projector, and a muslin sheet screen. They probably opened the theater in January 1906, charging five cents admission.[45] They rented films from P. L. Waters of New York for $25 a week; total expenses, including rent, were $125 a week. The shows—15-minute one-reel movies—were presented between 11 A.M. and 11 P.M. Films were changed on Mondays and Wednesdays. They had five employees—a doorman, two projectionists, one usher, and a ticket seller. In July 1906, Samuel Stuart, the owner of the building in which Pearce and Scheck were offering their shows, decided to remodel the building and combine the second and third floors into a vaudeville theater. In August 1906, Pearce and Scheck moved their movie exhibitions up to 227 North Eutaw Street, where they opened the Ideal Theater.[46] The new theater, in Stuart's building, was named the Colonnade; it was operated by W. Arthur Humbert of Pittsburgh. The Colonnade opened on September 10, 1906 with vaudeville and movies twice a day. The reviewer for the *Baltimore American* described the Colonnade as "a cozy little house." When it opened, the seats had not been installed so wooden chairs were used. The Colonnade was not very successful. It closed in early October, but reopened in the middle of the month under the management of local vaudeville booker John T. McCaslin. McCaslin lasted a little more than a month, and advertisements for the Colonnade disappeared around the beginning of December 1906.[47]

Four other nickelodeons opened in 1906. By late 1906, as reported by *Billboard* magazine, there were at least five movie theaters operating in Baltimore, seating a total of 437 people[48]:

>Moving Picture Parlor, 903 E. Baltimore Street; Jn. Donohue, mgr.; Seating Capacity (S.C.) 60
>Moving Picture Palace [Ideal], 227 N. Ontario Street [sic]; Wm. Wheeler, mgr.; S.C. 108
>Happyland, 611 E. Baltimore Street; H. L. Reichenback, mgr.; S.C. 84
>Moving Picture Parlor [Pickwick], 312 W. Lexington Street; Wm. B. Brown, mgr.; S.C. 110

> Moving Picture Parlor [Amusea], 406 E. Baltimore Street; Pearce & Schenk [sic], mgrs.; S.C. 75

The Maryland continued to have Kinetograph movies on its vaudeville bill throughout the spring, fall, and winter of 1906. The traveling exhibitor Lyman H. Howe gave his first motion picture exhibition in Baltimore at Ford's Theater in May 1906.[49] At that engagement he showed movies of the recent San Francisco earthquake and the siege and surrender of Port Arthur. Howe opened for two shows a day, matinees at 2:15 and evenings at 8:15. Matinee admission was 25 cents; evening prices were 50 cents on the first floor, 35 cents in the balcony, and 25 cents in the gallery. In addition to Pearce and Scheck's theater and Ford's, the Maryland and the Monumental also showed films of the San Francisco earthquake. Howe returned to Ford's at the end of the summer with his Lifeorama show that featured 30 international subjects. In the summer, Keith's vaudeville moved from the Maryland to Electric Park, where the Kinetograph was still advertised, at the end of each performance. The fall of 1906 saw Albaugh's Theater — the former Lyceum — and the Maryland in competition with vaudeville and movies. The Kinetograph remained at the Maryland while the rival Vitagraph was at Albaugh's. This competition lasted until late November when Albaugh's gave up.

1906 was a pivotal year. Theaters built especially for motion pictures began to replace vaudeville, burlesque, and legitimate theaters as the major venue for films. The popular amusement situation in Baltimore would never be the same.

2

The Triumph of Cheap Entertainment (1907–1913)

Movies were firmly entrenched in Baltimore by 1907. Within a year, there were 36 licensed moving picture theaters in Baltimore, one for every 14,805 inhabitants.[1] The average moving picture theater had an attendance of about 5,000 persons each week. Although no figures are available, the Baltimore movie-going public seemed to come from all social classes. Movies had been introduced to the upper classes through Burton Holmes and Lyman Howe exhibitions at the Music Hall/Lyric and Ford's. They had been introduced to middle-class audiences at the Maryland and to the working classes at the Monumental and at various halls throughout the city and at summer parks on all sides of the city. Movies continued to be exhibited at vaudeville theaters; the Maryland showed movies regularly during the September-through-May theater season for the next several years. Movies also appeared sporadically at the Lyric, Ford's, Academy of Music, Holliday Street Theater, and Auditorium and at smaller venues such as Ehmling's Music Hall.[2] Between May and September, when most indoor theaters closed, motion pictures moved outdoors to the amusement parks. "A month or so more, and the theatres will begin to close their doors for the summer season. The Academy will probably close the second week in May. Ford's will again have the Lyman Howe Pictures, and if they prove as successful as previously, they will probably be run through the entire summer, until the opening of the next theatrical season. The length of time the Auditorium will remain open is problematic, and depends upon the success of the stock company which opened there this week. The popular price houses will run well into May, and the cheaper vaudeville and picture houses will not close at all during the warm months. While the theatres are beginning to put on their 'dark' clothes, things about the parks are booming, and carpenters and painters are working overtime. Electric Park, Gwynn Oak, Bay Shore and a score or more of the smaller parks will be open about the middle of May...."[3]

In addition to Electric Park and River View Park, movies were shown at Bay Shore, Gwynn Oak, Luna Park, and Suburban Gardens.[4] Projectionist Sam Isaacson showed movies at one park, probably Joe Goeller's Hollywood Park on Back River, where the projection booth was a small roofless wooden structure. During the movies, drunken patrons occasionally tossed empty beer bottles into the booth.

Nickelodeons, as the small storefront movie theaters were often called, proved to

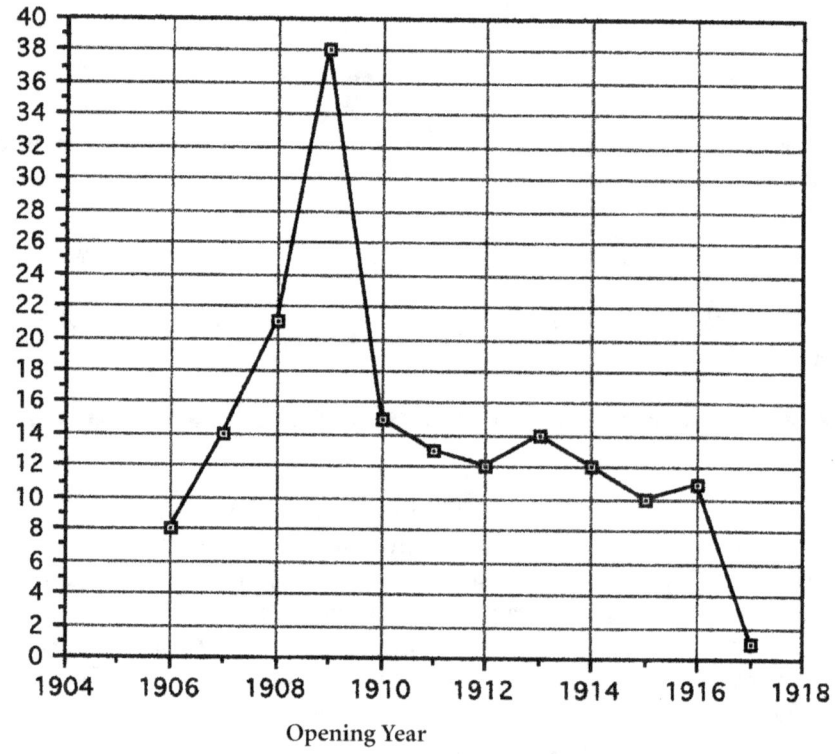

Chart 2. Nickelodeons Opened in the Baltimore Area, 1906–1918

be exceedingly popular. They were cheap to build and attend, and their shows were short; a patron could be in and out in less than an hour. Eclecticism, with liberal doses of pragmatism, was a major component of nickelodeon architectural styles. Exhibitors could hardly open them fast enough. Fourteen movie theaters opened in Baltimore in 1907. Six of these were in the downtown area and, significantly, eight were in outlying shopping districts: three on South Broadway, one on Gay Street, two on Pennsylvania Avenue, one in West Baltimore, and one in South Baltimore. The following year, 21 nickelodeons opened, and in 1909 — the greatest year ever for building movie theaters — 38 opened. Chart 2 shows the enormous spurt in the opening of movie theaters in 1908 and 1909 and the dramatic drop around the First World War.

A building could be converted into a basic nickelodeon for less than $1,000. The average cost of a nickelodeon in Baltimore was around $4,000. An article from a 1907 exhibitors' magazine describes how easy it was to open a movie theater:

> A 5-cent theater can be started for $500.... Between [$500 and $50,000] are 5-cent theaters of varying costs. The first thing to be considered ... is rent. Usually it is necessary to sign a lease for at least one year, and, as the business is considered objectionable by landlords, the rent is higher than for other enterprises. After the rent is paid it is necessary in many cases to make alterations in the building, and these have to be paid for by the owner of the theater. Seats have to be bought and a small amount of lumber is required for the stage.
>
> The largest item of expense is that of the front. If the theater is to catch crowds ... there must be an attractive front. In some of the more pretentious

2. The Triumph of Cheap Entertainment (1907–1913) 25

> downtown establishments ... the front is of the finest mosaic, with pictures painted by a recognized artist ... there must be extensive arrangements for light, and a sign, fairly scintellant [sic] with electric bulbs, must extend out over the sidewalk, where it can be seen for blocks. Lighting fixtures, including a sign, cannot be had for much less than $200.
>
> Every 5-cent theater has a [projector] with which to show its moving pictures. The lantern costs $100 ... and the films, which are rented, come at $50 a week for each....[5] For the illustrated songs there must be ... singers and these are not easily found for less than $10 a week each. Also there must be a piano and a man to play it. Two ticket sellers and one "barker" are necessary to look after the business of the front end, and one man is required to operate the lantern. Even in the cheapest of these theaters it is hard to get along without a salary roll of five or six men and women. To offset this expense there must be a large patronage, and that this patronage is available has been proved by the theater on State street, near Monroe. Sig Faller, its manager, says the average attendance there is 4,000, with perhaps 6,000 on Saturday. In this establishment there are three floors, with a shooting gallery in the basement, a penny arcade on the first floor, and the theater proper on the second floor. As a means of getting the people to visit the second floor Mr. Faller built a flight of steps with water running underneath them. The steps are of glass, and the water dashing below makes it appear to the visitor of the place that they are walking up over a waterfall. Thousands who would not ... climb an ordinary flight of stairs willingly go up this novel waterfall stairway. "There's tricks in all trades," said Mr. Faller, as he dumped 50,000 pennies into a sack.[6]

The first movie theaters were simply rooms with the bare necessities for showing films. They were often built in remodeled stores. They were usually long and narrow and decorated with flags, bunting, and posters. There might have been a separate box office. Inside, was a small lobby that opened directly into the auditorium. Radiators or a wood stove provided heat, and small fans on the walls provided ventilation. The floors were flat and the screen was a sheet or square of wall painted flat white. There was a piano down front. The projection booth, a 5' × 5' metal or asbestos box, might have been set up in the rear of the auditorium on the same level as the seats or hung from the top of the back wall. In 1907 it was usual to have continuous shows, as many as four an hour. The average number of seats in a Baltimore nickelodeon was 200; the largest seated about 400 while the smallest, only 79. The first ads for movie theaters appeared sporadically in Baltimore newspapers in 1906, but did not really become common until 1908.

The catalyst of an outsider opening a fancy nickelodeon in town in 1907 really started the burst of theater building in Baltimore. Sigmund Lubin, pioneer Philadelphia moviemaker, leased the failed Colonnade Theater at 406 E. Baltimore Street and brought in his architect, Franz Koenig, to remodel it. Koenig designed an elaborate new facade lighted by incandescent lamps and crowned with a large female statue. Lubin's theater opened on Easter Monday, April 1, 1907.[7] Lubin's was the first twin theater in Baltimore and one of the first in the world. The first-floor theater featured motion pictures and illustrated songs and the larger theater on the second and third floors specialized in vaudeville with motion pictures. The total seating for both theaters was around 800. Lubin had his cameraman take movies of scenes around the harbor and Lexington Market to attract local interest. Admission to the lower theater was 5 cents. Admission to the upper theater was 5 cents for balcony seats and 10 cents for seats in the orchestra. The *Baltimore American* was impressed.

J. G. Hoffmeister's nickelodeon, the Paradise, on Fleet Street; it didn't take much to convert a store into a movie theater around 1906.

With the advent of Lubin's a novel form of entertainment is to be introduced to Baltimore. Appreciating the popularity of life-motion pictures, Mr. Lubin, with an average stock on hand of over $100,000 in subjects to select from, has transformed the lower hall into a model auditorium for the exhibition of original life-motion pictures, exceeding in quality as in quantity any display of the kind ever attempted in any city. Briefly, the performance will be one that could not be duplicated by any other exhibitor in the country. Illustrated singing by vocalists of the highest class will be a feature of the performance. The performance will be of unusually long duration, much longer than that offered by the average entertainment.[8]

2. The Triumph of Cheap Entertainment (1907–1913) 27

Hot on Lubin's heels came the Miles brothers, from New York. They had organized one of the first film exchanges in the country several years earlier and seemed ready to build a national circuit of movie theaters. They purchased property on South Broadway and opened the Family Theater there in 1907. But local entrepreneurs were not standing idly by.

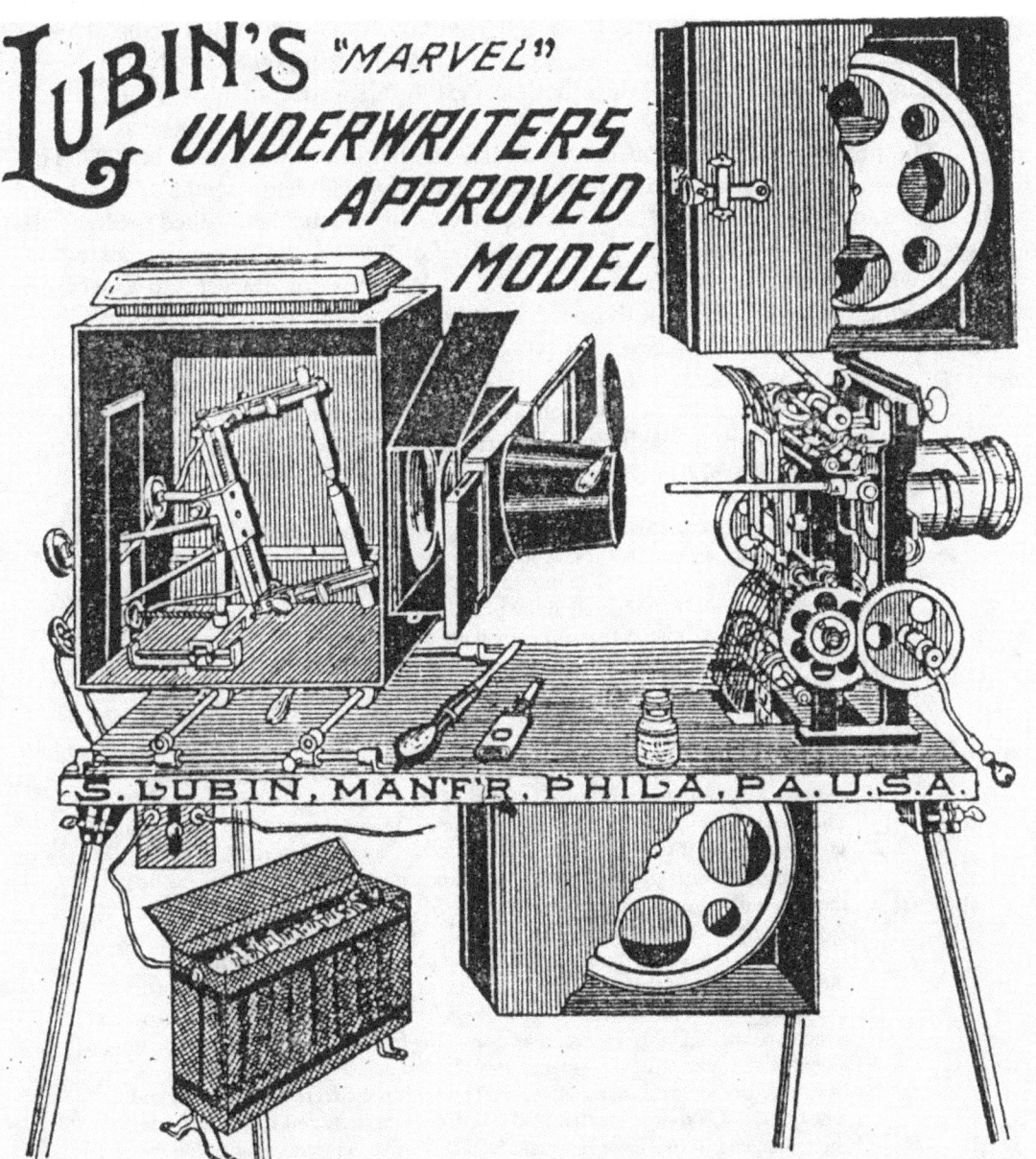

Lubin's Marvel was a popular projector in early nickelodeons.

Pearce and Scheck, operating as the newly incorporated National Amusement Company, had lost the lease on the theater at 406 East Baltimore Street in mid–1906 and opened a theater on North Eutaw Street. In January 1907, they moved back to Baltimore Street, where the action was, and opened the Amusea Theater. Three months later, they leased a building on West Lexington Street and made plans to erect a movie theater in its place. They also opened a nickelodeon on 36th Street in Hampden. Others active in the exhibition business were Harry Lewy and Tom Bohannon who built a string of Wizard theaters in town. By 1908 they had Wizards on West Lexington Street, North Eutaw Street, and Light Street. Most of the other local exhibitors were content with one or two small theaters.

The first African-American movie theaters in Baltimore were built in 1907. The Palace Theater (later called the Lincoln) at 936 Pennsylvania Avenue seems to have been the earliest. It was advertising as early as March 1907. The Avenue (later called the Renard) on Pennsylvania Avenue, which opened in the fall of 1907; Easter's on West Lexington Street, which opened in 1908; and the Eureka on West Saratoga Street and Queen on West Lexington Street, which both opened in 1909, were other early African-American theaters. There were at least two unsuccessful attempts in 1907 to build theaters for African-American audiences in the 600 or 700 blocks of West Lexington Street.[9]

By 1908, nickelodeons, or electric theaters, were permanent fixtures in the amusement landscape. *Billboard* magazine's local correspondent wrote that movies were thriving. He provided a snapshot of motion picture exhibition in Baltimore that spring.

> The moving picture has been before the public many years.... It has only been in the last four years that it has been recognized as an independent feature for public amusement.... The moving picture theatres have sprung up like mushrooms but if conducted along proper lines their permanency may be realized.... The subjects that are shown are varied in interest and include scenes of foreign travel as well as comic features. The moving picture has great possibilities. It is a boon to the common people and for the person whose worldly means for travel are hopelessly limited.... Important events and happenings have been presented with as much interest as they are chronicled in the daily newspapers. The doings of royalty and the peasant are received with much attention. The field of interesting topics is unlimited. The moving picture is a great factor in the commercial world as a person can see the making of steel products—locomotives, steamships, etc.... The latest development is the presentation of well-known plays and comic operas on the film with phonographic reproductions.
>
> The first moving picture theatre made its appearance here in 1904 [*sic*]. It was a small one and it gradually became popular. The presentation of the moving pictures in this manner soon became recognized, and its popularity increased to such an extent that the city is honeycombed with these theatres, which are springing up in every section. This field has developed to such an extent that a new building as large as a regular theatre is in course of erection, exclusively for moving pictures. The building covers half a block, and it will cost $100,000. It is located in the business district, and it will be under the management of Pierce [*sic*] and Scheck. These gentlemen have done much to build up the moving picture business in this city. They have in operation six of the finest places in the city ... all doing excellent business. Their success is due to their foresight and getting established before outsiders began to invade the field. They have adopted the name Amusea for all of their theatres.
>
> Bohannon and Lewey [*sic*] began by giving exhibitions for clubs, soci-

2. The Triumph of Cheap Entertainment (1907–1913)   29

eties, and other purposes and later they opened their handsome theatres which are known as the Wizard. They have shown much enterprise ... and they are very successful....

Lubin's Theatre on East Baltimore Street is the biggest hit in town. It has only been open one year and ... has reaped a vast fortune. The building is a handsome structure equipped with all modern devices for the comfort and convenience of the patrons and for their amusement as well ... High class vaudeville has been a great feature in addition to the moving pictures. When ... improvements are completed the building will have double its present capacity. Much of the success is due to the excellent management of Edward C. Earle....

The Cupid at Light and West Streets is one of the latest and most successful places in town.... The Crescent, at 1110 S. Charles Street, is the latest one to open which was May 20. It has a capacity of 180 persons.... Miles Brothers have two splendid places in operation ... They have established their Southern agency here. The Lincoln on Pennsylvania Avenue was recently opened by Charles L. P. Osbon, formerly of Cincinnati.... The Renard on Pennsylvania Avenue was recently opened by Fred H. Carley.... The Cluster, operated by Benjamin Cluster at 669 W. Baltimore Street is a new one in the field and business is good. The Family Theatre, The Majestic and Nicoland on Broadway are rivals and the business they are doing is awe-inspiring.... The Pickwick is doing well on West Lexington Street. The Arcadia on North Howard Street is under the management of James J. Ross.... Since the regular seasons at the Maryland and Holliday Street Theatres have close[d] moving pictures have been presented on an elaborate scale. The performances have pleased emmensely [sic] and the attendance has been large.[10]

Baltimore Street became a "Great White Way" in reality in the fall of 1908 when new street lighting was installed between Eutaw Street and Jones Falls. The street became a popular evening promenade and was host to as many as 10,000 pedestrians, especially young men and women, on a single evening. A romantic article described Baltimore Street this way, "On fine evenings it is thronged with shoppers and pleasure seekers, and on Saturdays and Sundays the crowd between Eutaw street and the bridge often exceeds 10,000. Gay young gallants and giggling maidens make up 50 percent of the throng. The girls sail along in groups ... arm in arm, and the gay young gallants follow after, or stand on the corners and admire. The heartless cops forbid flirting ... but there are many ways to get around the prohibition. So assiduously, indeed, is the game of love played beneath the white lights that the new promenade threatens to become a real lover's lane."[11] For at least six days a week—movies were forbidden in Maryland on Sunday—crowds like these were exactly what nickelodeon owners needed.

One of the first attempts to show Sunday movies in Baltimore was in 1911. Several writers opposed this attempt in letters to the editor of the *Sun* in June 1911. One writer claimed that Sunday movies would hurt "our youth and weak adults."[12] Another believed that, "The very suggestion of opening the motion-picture shows on the Sabbath Day is an offense to a great mass of our community, who hold the observance of the Sabbath and the welfare of the rising generation a most sacred trust of the American and Christian citizen."[13] As a matter of fact, there were Sunday movies and shows at this time, but they were supposed to be religious or charitable. The Victoria Theater got into trouble in December 1911 when what was supposed to be a religious Sunday show actually consisted of a ragtime music concert. The ever-vigilant Lord's Day Alliance pounced, and the theater manager had to do some fancy talking to exonerate himself. The Sunday closing laws were more lax in Baltimore County, but in December 1911, when Marshal Gorsuch found that moving picture theaters in Arlington had been open on Sundays, he ordered them closed.[14] Marshal Mahle of the county police force made a personal observation of methods of Sunday observance in Highlandtown and Canton in early 1912 and again ordered the movie theaters to close on Sundays. In the mid-teens, there was more agitation in the city for Sunday movies, but it would take many more years to be able to go to a movie on Sunday.

The northeast corner of Baltimore and Holliday streets was the beginning of theater row on the Block. The elaborate facades of the Grand and Lubin's and the Wilson are visible on the north side of the block. (Photograph courtesy of the Maryland Historical Society, Baltimore, Maryland)

The period between 1907 and 1913 was a simpler, less dangerous time; the above description of Baltimore Street seems to describe a street on a different planet. With those strolling crowds, it was an ideal location for a movie theater. Large numbers of pedestrians were crucial to the success of the early nickelodeons. Since most nickelodeons did not advertise in the newspapers, they were dependent on customers who were attracted by the advertising in front of the theater. Some theaters were literally covered with posters which, together with the brightly lit facades and the music from graphophones set up at theater entrances, acted as magnets to passersby. A correspondent for the *Moving Picture World* described "The Block" in December 1909, "I was fairly amazed at what should be called 'Moving Picture Row,' the section of Baltimore street between Holiday [sic] and Gay streets. Nine moving picture palaces, six of them one after the other, and all fine looking houses." This correspondent went on to describe the movie theater situation in the city, "They are tired of names like 'Bijou Dream,' 'Nickolet,' 'Palace,' etc., but they adopt originality in naming their places 'Blue Mouse,' 'Black Cat,' 'Red Moon,' Red Feathers' [sic], 'Rainbow,' etc. They do not seem to care for white or cream-colored fronts; they have a mixture of white or colored marble and the rich ornaments are either imitations of dark woods, old gold, old silver, bronze, etc. Most of the houses have very rich and artistic fronts."[15]

The movie novelty seemed to be wearing off by 1909, and exhibitors were trying new ways to attract customers. One of these was to make the silent movies talk.

> The Amusea, Messrs. Pearce and Scheck's Lexington Street house, present[s] a bill of talking motion pictures that can't help but make the best sort of impression this week. They are clear and sharp in detail and the lines accompanying them are rendered by professionals and this branch of the work, as well as the imitations are not entrusted to the hands of amateurs.[16]

Attempts to give sound to movies, with sound effects and live actors and actresses behind the screen, date back at least to 1907.[17] Lubin's was one of first movie houses in the city to use behind-the-screen talkers; it advertised talking motion pictures as early as May 1908. A year later, Pearce and Scheck and others began using talkers. In December 1909, Bohannon, Lewy and Fuld[18] began to use them at their new Wizard Theater on Lexington Street. According to the *Baltimore American*, "At the Great Wizard Theater ... a new feature was inaugurated yesterday, that of talking pictures. They made a distinct hit with the large audiences. This week the talking pictures are *The Engineer's Daughter* and *The Keeper of the Light*."[19]

By early 1911 many movie theaters had stock companies of four or five talkers. The Columbia and Leader were said to be among the leaders in this field. In the spring of 1911, a club called The Photo Players of Baltimore was organized; one of its purposes was the promotion of talking pictures and to teach men and women how to talk "behind the sheet."[20] The new organization, one of the first of its kind in the country, had 25 members including George Skillman (the manager of the Lyceum Song Slide Service), William O'Brien, Frank Schwartz, Lewis Fields, Joseph Fields, and Robert North.[21] Durkee's Colonial Theater advertised "picture-talkers" in February 1913. As late as 1915, Sigmund Lubin was still extolling behind-the-screen talkers. According to Lubin, the earlier talkers' "half-hearted speaking" was not very convincing, but he believed that well-equipped talkers would produce most satisfying results.[22] An article in 1928 credited singer and theater manager Joe Fields with inventing the idea of having actors and actresses behind the screen in 1910, but this is certainly too late.[23] Fields may have had some part in developing this kind of talkie in Baltimore, and his story is worth telling. According to the 1928 article, Fields was singing illustrated songs at Pearce and Scheck's Amusea on North Eutaw Street in 1910 when he came up with the idea, but Pearce and Scheck refused to put on regular talking shows. Fields then took his idea to Charles Whitehurst at the Red Moon Theater, where it became an instant success. Soon Fields was training five or six companies of talkers for other theaters in the city.

Behind-the-screen talkers worked this way. The entire company of talkers would review a film a couple of times before the first show to get an idea of what it was about. They would consider possible dialogue at this time. For comedies, they would plan humorous local references and, if they could have one of the characters say something like, "Let's go down on Baltimore Street," the audiences would respond with laughter and applause. Much of the dialogue was spontaneous. When the movie was shown, the company of talkers set up behind the transparent screen and supplied dialogue and sound effects. At times the talkers interacted with the audience. A talker at the Blue Mouse in 1911 admonished a group of noisy girls, "The young ladies out in front will please keep quiet." The talkers also supplied other sound effects. Around 1913 there was a sound effects machine available to exhibitors called the Dramagraph. This was a machine that could be operated by one person to produce many sound effects, such as the barking of dogs, train whistles, thunder, gunshots, bells, and chimes, for silent movies.

Not everyone was singing the praises of these talkers. Claude Woolley, writing in 1909, did not appreciate amateur talkers: "In the production of the so-called 'talking pictures,' where the talking does not proceed from a phonograph, it is produced by the cooperation of persons placed behind the screen, who endeavor to talk for the characters as they appear and to reproduce with mechanical contrivances the galloping of horses, the roaring of the wind, the rushing of water, etc. When well drilled these talking effects sometimes add much to the pleasing effects of the performance, but it only too often happens that the 'talkers,' unskilled and imperfectly drilled to the subject of the film, and with ludicrous squeaking voices or unduly bass ones, turn what the film-maker conceived as a tragedy into a comedy of a very ridiculous sort. This abuse has been carried to such a point that it is likely that, in the near future, the manager, who will announce that 'our pictures *do not* talk,' will receive the mead of praise and patronage."[24] Reminiscing about the behind-the-screen talkers at the beginning of the sound movie era, *Evening Sun* movie critic Q.E.D., who did not like talkies any more than he liked color movies, was not very complimentary.[25]

> There were those who heaved a great sigh of relief when they gave up trying to make the movies "sound" a number of years ago. You surely haven't forgotten those gruesome days, have you? Well, we haven't. Many an afternoon at the Pickwick, on Howard Street, do we remember.
>
> There would be a close-up of a hand touching a front doorbell and ... darned if a baby whistle didn't sound ... back of the sheet. A character, under great stress, would very obviously cry out "NO!" whereupon the audience would be treated to a long harangue by this same character's voice back stage, the sum and substance of the speech amounting to nothing more than "NO!" Sometimes the two or three merrymakers back of the curtain who were giving voice to the action would attempt getting over what in these days would be dubbed a nifty, but which, in those days and these, would be termed just plain terrible.
>
> When all this sort of thing was finally stopped, everybody felt that a great load was taken off his chest.

Another early sound movie device was the Cameraphone. This system, along with the Chronophone, the Synchroscope and the Theatrephone, depended on the synchronization of phonograph records with films. They were never very successful, mainly because of the inability to amplify the sound and the difficulty in synchronizing the phonograph with the projector. The Cameraphone opened in Baltimore at the Holliday Street Theater in April 1908. The program included the "Teddy Bear Song" sung in a "distinct French accent" and a number by George M. Cohan. It was popular enough to continue there well into the summer, but was gone within the year. In 1913 another invention, by Baltimorean George R. Webb, made a bid to give movies decent sound. This will be discussed later.

Music, instrumental and vocal, provided sound in most theaters. It is difficult for those of us living in an age of spectacular soundtracks, digital music, and painfully powerful amplification systems to appreciate the power of a theater orchestra or a large organ. A local movie critic once wrote that "Music is to the films what fragrance is to the flowers."[26] Music has been an important adjunct to movies from the beginning. Shortly after the first movie theaters were built, exhibitors realized that some kind of musical accompaniment was needed. Many tried pianos, and the theater piano player pounding out the "William Tell Overture" or "Every Morn I Bring Thee Violets" at the keys became an icon of the era.[27] The piano players did yeoman service for many years, but they were not universally appreciated. In 1910, there was a spate of letters to the *Sun* complaining about the excesses of poor piano playing. Typical of these letters was the one from "Distressed," which said, in part, "I have been in about a dozen of these places [movie theaters] the past week ... and the incessant piano playing has driven me well-nigh distracted. The pictures as a rule are not bad, though I must confess to being surfeited with murders and shootings ... but the piano playing is something awful, enough to drive one crazy.... The pianos in these places are always lusty instruments, sharp and strident in tone, with no soft pedals in their mechanism apparently. The performers are always young girls of quite astonishing vigor and endurance ... The playing in some of these places is worse than in others possibly, but it is all fearful, horrible, torturous, devilish."[28] One writer went so far as to suggest that piano players in theaters be licensed. In the early days of movie piano playing, the piano players decided what songs to play, but, by the late teens, elaborate cue sheets were made available with the film. A sample cue sheet for the Plaza Film Company's *Angel Child* in 1918 is given below.

1. At Screening—*Dew Drops*	Armstrong	3 min. 30 sec.	Allegretto
2. After the Shower—*Springtime*	Drum	2 min. 30 sec.	Waltz Intermezzo
3. After Years of Waiting—*Sunbeams*	Helliar	3 min. 15 sec.	Moderato
4. Gloria Leaves Office—*School Days*	Edwards	2 min. 45 sec.	Popular Song
5. Richard Grant, Att.—*Romance*	Mericanto	1 min. 30 sec.	Moderato
6. Girls Saying Prayers—*Ghost Dance*	Salisbury	3 min. 30 sec.	Moderato

The cue sheet also provided the piano player (or organist) with additional information. For the film *Angel Child* the following description was supplied: Character—comedy Drama; Atmosphere—neutral; Mechanical Effects—autos, slamming doors; Special Effects—none; Direct cues—none; Remarks—light opera selections throughout will fit this picture.

Another way to add sound to a movie was by hiring live singers. These singers were very popular attractions at many of the smaller theaters. A popular singer could have been shared among several theaters. Among the best-known in Baltimore were Hilt and Chick,[29] who sang at the Picture Garden; Archie Lloyd, tenor Herman Dick and Billy Frisch, at the New Pickwick; Alfred Armond, Pete Murray and Joe Combs at the Blue Mouse; Dick Queen at the Lexington; and soprano Edna Roseman and Harry Moorehead at the Grand. In 1912, the Wizard hired an opera singer, the Great Duero, to sing operatic selections every afternoon and evening.

Orchestras had been entertaining patrons and providing accompaniment in vaudeville and burlesque theaters for many years before they were used in movie theaters. The orchestra at the Monumental Theater used to assemble on the sidewalk in front of the theater and play for ten or fifteen minutes before going into the theater. Small orchestras were common in early Baltimore movie theaters. Prof. Farson's Gwynn Oak Orchestra was a popular attraction here. It played at the Colonnade in 1906 and opened the New in 1910 and the ill-fated Amusea on Lexington Street in 1911. Daly's airdome on Pennsylvania Avenue had the Goldfield Orchestra playing from a small balcony at the rear of the theater in 1912. The Flaming Arrow had a five-piece ladies' orchestra, and the Lord Baltimore had a four-piece orchestra around 1913.

The first specialized employees of movie theaters were the projectionists, and they were the first to get organized. By the time of the first convention of the International Alliance of Theatrical Stage Employees (IATSE) attended by delegates representing projectionists' organizations held in Minneapolis in July 1908, there were eleven branch projectionists' local unions.[30] Local 181 was organized in Baltimore in 1909 and chartered a year later. The founding meeting of the union was held by 13 members on April 13, 1909, in a room on the second floor of the Palace Theater building at 228 South Broadway. The first president was William F. Evans. G. Kingston Howard succeeded Evans in 1911. In 1913, the union was meeting on the first and third Monday of each month at 11:30 P.M. Its headquarters were in the Loeb Building, on South Gay Street.

A year after the projectionists' union local was chartered, the founding meeting of the State Board of Examiners of Moving Picture Operators[31] of Baltimore City[32] was held and the first licenses were issued. The first three members of the board were exhibitor Marion S. Pearce, fire underwriter Crofton S. Whitter, and projectionist George T. "Bunny" Gregory. The first nine licenses were issued on June 20, 1910, to George T. Kreis—Number 1[33], George S. Greener—Number 2, Thomas Finn—Number 3, F. Clarence Grote—Number 4, H. C. Schaum—Number 5, Edgar Gamble—Number 6, Clifford Hyde—Number 7, J. R. Goodman—Number 8 and A. H. G. Thompson—Number 9. In order to get a state license, a projectionist had to be 21 years old with at least a year's experience under a licensed operator and had to pass a practical and written examination. The initial cost of a one-year license was $10; annual renewals cost $5. During the first few years the board issued licenses and heard complaints about fires in theater booths, projectionists operating while intoxicated, and unlicensed projectionists. Anyone found guilty of using an unlicensed operator could be fined. The exhibitors were not happy with the provision of the new law that required all projectionists to be at least 21 years of age and have a year's experience. In one of the first arrests in a campaign against unlicensed operators, Isaac Cluster, who operated a small theater on West Baltimore Street, was fined $10 in 1914 for allowing his son, Benjamin, to operate the projector there. By the end of the 1914–1915 fiscal year, 189 projectionists had been licensed. The state's licensing law lasted 70 years, finally abolished by the 1980 session of the legislature.

The exhibitors competed against one another, but they joined together to take on their traditional opponents, the projectionists and the state legislature. The local exhibitors organized themselves soon after the projectionists did. In December 1910, about 150 local exhibitors met at the Rennert Hotel for the first annual banquet of the newly formed Moving Picture Exhibitors' Association of Baltimore.[34] The officers of this group were J. C. Weidman, president; A. G. Steen, vice-president; William Fait, secretary and treasurer, and Watson E. Sherwood,[35] counsel. In an address to the group, Sherwood said that the motion picture theaters in the city were bringing in more than $4 million a year. With this kind of money coming in, the exhibitors had to get organized. Three years later they formed a local branch and joined the Motion-Picture Exhibitors' League of America becoming the 36th state branch to join that organization. They held a convention in Baltimore in June 1913. On June 3 and 4, under the chairmanship of Harry Moorehead, and with the participation of Marion A. Neff, the national president of the League, the exhibitors of Baltimore and Maryland met at the Emerson Hotel to organize the state branch of the League. Marion Pearce was elected president with J. Howard Bennett as national vice-president, Oliver J. Allenbaugh as first vice-president, James J. Hartlove as second vice-president, Frank Durkee as secretary, Harry Moorehead as treasurer and S. I. Rosen of Annapolis as sergeant-at-arms.

At the convention there were exhibitions of various projectors and motion picture equipment; three newspapers, the *Sun*, *American* and *News*, had booths,[36] and the projectionists' union had a booth. There was a sound effects machine called the Lapin Dramagraph[37] and the martial sounding Tank piano which, to quote an enigmatic contemporary account, "proved once more that motion pictures need more sentimental playing than noise." The General Electric booth featured an "Ozonator" that purified a theater's air by blowing ozone through it. The Louis A. Dieter Company exhibited plaster relief and statuary work for theaters.

At the end of the convention a group photo of the attendees was taken on the steps of the courthouse. Nearly every one of the film pioneers in the state is in this photo. The object of the new organization was to protect the exhibitors and give them a powerful body to oppose what they considered unjust legislation. According to J. Howard Bennett, the first goals of the League would be to examine the question of national censorship and oppose unjust taxation. Bennett also came out against sensational posters.

The nickelodeon bubble was still expanding in 1910, and Baltimore was acquiring a national reputation, at least among the film exhibitors. This is how a correspondent for *The Moving Picture World* described the movie situation in Baltimore in early 1910.

> Shortly described, therefore, Baltimore is just a simple little semi–Southern, easy going, scattered village of half a million.... But it has one supreme recommendation in our eyes.... It loves the picture, respects the picture, encourages the picture.... It denied admission to the Jeffries-Johnson photographs,

Baltimore exhibitors convention in June 1913. Sadly few can now be identified; they include: #4 Isidore Weniz, #20 possibly Harry Lewy, #24 Abraham or Louis Benesch, #31 Sam Benjamin, #41 Harry Moorehead, #48 Marion Pearce, #50 John Heinz, #52 Joe Brodie, #55 Nat Keen, #58 Charles Hicks, #67 Eugene McCurdy, #70 Frank Durkee, #75 Guy Wonders, #78 Arthur Price, #84 Walter Pacy, #92 Frank Hornig, #99 Lou DeHoff, #104 Moses Millhauser, #113 Charles Pearce.

> for Baltimore is towards the South, where persons of color are not permitted to take undue liberties with white people.
>
> We were interested to learn ... that Baltimore is ... particular in the quality and class of subject which it tolerates in its picture houses. The latter are patronized by the very best local society. On our visit to the city ... we made it a point in the ... time at our disposal to study many audiences in and out of the theaters, and of meeting individual members of those audiences. These people were quite classy enough for the Metropolitan or Manhattan Opera House, New York City. We were impressed by the circumstance that in the character of the people who visited the picture houses in Baltimore, the picture is dignified as a valuable factor in the entertainment of the best classes of the public.
>
> Some of the Baltimore picture houses are amongst the finest and most comfortable in the county. They are administered with tact and ability. Just imagine now one charming little place that we visited, called "The Blue Mouse," an Independent theater ... giving for five cents the privilege of a waiting room for ladies, with telephone, writing facilities, and the like. It is this sort of thing which uplifts the picture and attracts the better classes of people....
>
> "Moving Picture Row," Baltimore (it is called ... East Baltimore Street), has all the aspects of Fourteenth Street, New York City. It is crowded with theaters, possibly overcrowded. Competition and the survival of the fittest will no doubt remedy a state of things which is possibly not profitable all round.... The foreign element in picture making is not liked there, or perhaps we ought to say, not understood.... Baltimore likes the Imp and the Bison pictures.... Baltimore is very critical, and properly so, for culture is rife there.[38]

The southern nature of the city was emphasized in July 1910 when Mayor Mahool decided that motion pictures of the Jeffries-Johnson prizefight should not be exhibited in Baltimore. The unthinkable had just occurred in Reno, Nevada, on July 4, 1910, when African-American boxer Jack Johnson knocked out James J. Jeffries. Jeffries, billed as the "Great White Hope," had retired undefeated in 1905, but was coaxed out of retirement to fight Johnson, who had won the championship in 1908 by defeating Tommy Burns.[39] In many places, as soon as word of Johnson's victory became known, there were riots; at least nine people were killed. There was no serious trouble in Baltimore. The governments of some cities, when they saw the disturbances that could result, were wary of films of the fight.[40] In Baltimore, Mayor Mahool made his opposition to boxing and to the exhibition of the fight movies very clear on several occasions—once, at least a week before the fight. Mahool had the support of the Police Board. The board's counsel believed that the police had the necessary authority to stop any exhibitions that might cause civil unrest. Police Marshal Farnan made a direct appeal to the mayor not to allow the movies to be shown in Baltimore. There was opposition to the fight pictures from important local exhibitors as well. Marion Pearce, of Pearce & Scheck, who controlled "90 percent of the moving pictures in this city and vicinity," William Ballauf, manager of the Gayety, and George Rife, of the Holliday Street Theater, made clear their personal opposition to showing the pictures. Pearce was quoted as saying, "I am opposed to the exhibition of them on moral grounds, but I think it would be unwise both from a moral and a financial standpoint to show them in this section of the country. Prejudice would be aroused and bitterness between the races ensues. I do not think that my patrons want them. I am personally against prize fighting and would not degrade my theatre for such exhibitions."[41] James Kernan "wouldn't think of allowing such pictures to be shown in the Maryland

Theater." The only showman who said he would show the films was John Weidman, who ran the Comedy Theater on Baltimore Street and the Family Theater on Broadway.

The major Baltimore newspapers opposed the exhibition of the fight films in Maryland. The *Baltimore News* demanded that the mayor prevent the films from being shown. The *Evening Sun* supported the opponents of the fight films, stating in a July 6 editorial that a failure to make money by the exhibition of these films would have a powerful negative effect on the boxing promoters. The *Baltimore American* not only opposed the Johnson-Jeffries films, but also wanted to see the end of prizefights throughout the country. Most of the local ministers took a firm stand against the showing of the fight films. While there were a few incidents in Baltimore, and about 70 African Americans were arrested, there were no serious injuries.

One of the few letters to the local newspapers in support of exhibiting the fight pictures said that poor men who could not afford to go to Reno to see the fight in person were being penalized.[42] One place in the area where the fight movies were shown was Ruppert's Park on Bladensburg Road, just outside the Washington, D.C., city limits in Prince George's County.[43] Ruppert's Park advertised "Johnson and Jeffries Contest Pictures. For White People Only." The movies were shown three times a day around the end of September 1910 despite the efforts of the clergy to have Governor Crothers suppress them.

As a direct result of the Johnson-Jeffries fight, a Federal law was passed in 1910 that prohibited interstate transportation of prizefight films.[44] But this would not be the last time that films of a prizefight caused problems in Baltimore. In 1927, films of the Dempsey-Tunney fight—featuring the infamous "long count"—were seized by Federal marshals as they were being shown at the Maryland, Clover, and Comedy Theaters. The films were in unmarked metal boxes so that no one associated with their transportation could be identified. Within days of the seizure, a Federal grand jury began an investigation into the alleged interstate transportation of the films. Attorneys for the owners of the three theaters said that the films had been manufactured in Baltimore and therefore were not in violation of the law. The grand jury, however, decided that it was correct to seize the films. A year later, films of the Dempsey-Tunney fight and the Dempsey-Sharkey fight were seized by police at the Flag Theater on Fort Avenue.

With all the vitriol being cast at the movie theaters, many people lost sight of the good that theaters could do. For most of the 20th century, movie theaters were running shows for charities and benefits as well as supporting the nation's several war efforts with bond and recruiting drives. Sadly, as the ownership of the theaters passed out of local hands, these activities largely ceased.

Early examples of charitable work by local exhibitors abound. In March 1911, 57 Baltimore theater managers donated a portion of their receipts to the Children's Hospital School. Following the devastating explosion of the Welsh freighter *Alum Chine* in Baltimore harbor in 1913, Nixon & Zimmerman donated the use of their Academy of Music for a benefit to aid the survivors and the families of those who were killed.[45] Actors and actresses from many legitimate theaters in Baltimore and Washington also donated their services.

Admission to the nickelodeons usually cost 5 cents, unless a very big show was playing and then tickets could cost 10 cents.[46] When the blockbuster *Quo Vadis* played at the Red Moon in 1913, patrons paid 10 cents, and the ads claimed that they were lucky; theaters in other cities were charging between 25 and 50 cents for the same movie. The

The interior of an unidentified Baltimore nickelodeon. Note the piano and small stage just below the screen and the very plain stenciled decoration on the walls. Some kind of heating device seems to be located along the right side of the auditorium.

Wizard raised its prices for a special program in October 1913. A vaudeville theater, like the Victoria, charged 10 cents admission with reserved seats at 20 cents and box seats at 30 cents. There was enormous resistance among exhibitors to raising the price of movie tickets to 10 cents. A 1914 article in *Moving Picture World* addressed this problem and the desirability of longer, better shows at 10 cents.[47] J. Hesser Walraven, manager of the New Theater, made a prediction about ticket prices in 1915; he said that Baltimoreans would soon see $5 admission prices. He thought they might come in a couple of years, but it would take more than 70 years to reach that level. Prices did go up in 1917; the price range at the Parkway was: Matinees— orchestra: 15 cents; balcony: 10 cents; box seats: 25 cents. In the evening, the prices went up to: orchestra: 25–35 cents, 15 cents, 50 cents, respectively. The West End was charging 10 cents for matinees and 15 cents in the evening. The Idle Hour charged 10 cents on Friday and Saturday nights.

As the second decade of the century moved forward, despite increasing ticket prices, the popularity of movies continued to increase, and the number of movie houses grew at a quickening pace. There were 106 licenses issued for moving picture theaters in Baltimore in 1910 and the Building Survey of the city in 1911 found 173 theaters and moving picture parlors in the city.[48] The *Baltimore News* exaggerated the ease of starting a movie theater: "The moving picture man ... rents him a little 'parlor,' buys an electric sign and a graphophone and he can't keep the people out. They all come, the shop girls, out for lunch, the office boy, out on an errand, the shopper, who wants a place to rest.

The roller-skating rink may be deserted, but there is always the S. R. O. sign up at the moving picture parlor."⁴⁹ Another 1911 article described the movie situation in Baltimore.

> "Let's go to the moving-pictures." This is the commonest expression in Baltimore these days. The moving pictures are at our door.... The moving pictures as a popular entertainment have been known in Baltimore more than a decade. One of the earliest films exhibited here showed scenes in Galveston immediately after the hurricane ... of 1900. It was a moving picture all right. It moved in every direction, wobbling so violently at times that the spectators had had moments very like incipient seasickness. There were no picture parlors in Baltimore then, and this film, with others equally as quavering, was shown by a department store.⁵⁰ They rigged up a place on the top floor and, in addition to the films illustrated songs were given. It was a nine-day wonder and all Baltimore flocked to see it. And to think this was only 10 years ago! If the Galveston film could be shown with one of today some idea of the wonderful strides in this art would be gained....
>
> The young women who attend the moving pictures are as entertaining as the films. Note their wide-eyed interest in tender scenes and the deep sigh of utter happiness and content when the lovers ... fall into each other's arms at last. Then go out and flatly contradict anyone who says sentiment is on the wane. Why, business girls, for all their boasted practicability are the deepest sighers of them all. It may be added that the pictures must be taken very seriously. There are those who think that a picture parlor is a place to jest and laugh, but a lively party who labored under this delusion were very sharply reprimanded at the Green Cheese Parlor.⁵¹ ... At the Green Cheese, they compose their own dialogue, and it is often quite novel. In one brilliant mediaeval picture in which king and queen and court wandered through a magnificent estate, the queen plucked a rose and, turning to the king, said, soulfully: "Ain't this rose swell?"
>
> The picture parlors have shown a tendency of late to give the people too much for their money. They throw in vaudeville between the films, the one-act sketch being a prime favorite for the purpose.... Illustrated songs have been a part of the moving-picture show from the beginning ... and after the second verse the words of the chorus are thrown on the screen and everybody is cordially invited to join in.... Sometimes a person in the audience stands up and insists upon singing alone. There is a hot dispute between him and the regular singer. Then the latter says he will leave it to the audience. Do they want to hear this curbstone tenor? Aw, give him a chance, the audience says good-naturedly.... The audience never knows from what direction to expect a voice in the illustrated songs. Sometimes a piercing tenor comes through the aperture in the rear whence flows the stream of light. Again, a bass rolls up from the music pit. Or a small boy in the midst of the spectators stands on a chair and pipes verse 2, while the singer on the stage feigns astonishment.
>
> The attitude of the public toward the picture show is to regard it as a part of the day's routine than an evening entertainment. Business folk hurry through luncheon that they may have a half hour for the films and house-mothers say that the working members of their flock come home an hour later than was their custom in other days. In one office there is a password sent around when the boss leaves early — "Four-thirty" — which means at this hour the staff will adjourn to the Green Cheese....⁵²

At the same time this article was written, the Baltimore City Council was making a decision that was to have a major effect on theater construction. This ordinance changed the building code so as to prohibit the erection of a motion picture theater without the approval of the Council. The ordinance was introduced because of the many protests against movie houses being built next to churches and in residential sections. Mayor Mahool signed it on May 6. This ordinance was to be the cause of numerous fights between supporters of opposing theaters. By 1915, so many ordinances requesting permits for movie theaters were being introduced into the Council that John F. O'Meara, president of the First Branch, said he would introduce a measure establishing a "movie belt" in the city where new theaters could be erected. The flood of requests for permits also occasioned a proposed ordinance that would void an ordinance issued for the erection of a motion picture theater if it were not used within six months of the date it was granted. It seems that real estate speculators were trying to secure permits on desirable locations and then selling them at inflated prices.

Rare color films added to the popularity of movies. Some of the first color movies in town were shown at the Auditorium Theater in August 1911. These were Kinemacolor films of English subjects including scenes from North Wales, troops passing in review, the Crystal Palace, and King George and Queen Mary. They lasted more than an hour and a half. A choir and an orchestra provided music; a lecturer provided commentary. The *Baltimore American* called them "the most wonderful in this line that have ever been exhibited."[53] The Kinemacolor films of the Panama Canal and the Balkan War, which were shown at the Auditorium in May 1913, also got wonderful reviews. Color movies were few and far between for many years. Kinemacolor films entitled *With the Fighting Forces of Europe*, which presented views of the various armies arrayed against one another in Europe, were shown at the Academy of Music in May 1916. The early color films had problems when the subjects moved suddenly and created a "fringe" or blurred outline of the subject. By 1922, this problem had been solved and better color movies appeared. The British costume drama, *The Glorious Adventure* and the American film *The Light in the Dark* were successful color films that year. The latter film, which only had certain scenes in color, was shown at the Rivoli in November 1922. It was called "one of the most interesting as well as significant film offerings of the fall season."[54] Color films were still regarded, at least by some,[55] as very special treats until well after World War II.

Baltimore Theaters 1910–1911

Academy of Music	N. Howard Street	Carrollton	1203 W. Balto. Street
Aladdin	930 W. Balto. Street	Celtic	839 Greenmount Avenue
Albaugh's	1213 N. Charles Street	Clifton	316 S. Broadway
Amusea	414 E. Balto. Street	Cluster	669 W. Balto. Street
Arcade	747 W. Balto. Street	Cluster	303 S. Broadway
Arcadia	121 N. Howard Street	Cluster	526 N. Gay Street
Auditorium	N. Howard Street	Colonial	1438 N. Gay Street
Aurora	7 E. North Avenue	Columbia	625 Columbia Avenue
Belnord	Philadelphia Road	Comedy	412 E. Balto. Street
Bijou	222 S. Broadway	Comic	3603 Eastern Avenue
Black Cat	1204 W. Balto. Street	Crescent	314 N. Broadway
Blue Bell	1717 Harford Avenue	Crescent	1110 S. Charles Street
Blue Mouse	28 W. Lexington Street	Crescent	1509 W. Lafayette Avenue
Bon Ton	563 N. Gay Street	Crown	756 Columbia Avenue
Brodie	1118 Light Street	Cupid	1130 Light Street

Daisy	1752 N. Gay Street	Lubin's	410 E. Balto. Street
Daly's	936 Pennsylvania Avenue	Lyric	Mt. Royal Avenue
Dixie	312 W. Balto. Street	Majestic	320 S. Broadway
Eagle	3610 Eastern Avenue	Maryland	Franklin Street
Eastern	3915 Eastern Avenue	Monumental	E. Balto. Street
Electra	1048 N. Gay Street	New Pickwick	115 N. Howard Street
Elektra	1039 N. Gay Street	Olympia	2938 O'Donnell Street
Elite	467 N. Gay Street	Palace	328 S. Broadway
Eureka	402 S. Fremont Avenue	Paradise	1727 Fleet Street
Eureka	1115 W. Saratoga Street	Paradise	1600 N. Washington Street
Excelsior	1358 W. North Avenue	Pastime	407 W. Lexington Street
Fairmount	101 N. Clinton Street	Patterson	1202 Laurens Street
Family	518 S. Broadway	Patterson	3136 Eastern Avenue
Federal	814 Light Street	Pickwick	312 W. Lexington Street
Flag	1318 E. Fort Avenue	Plaza	1107 N. Broadway
Ford's	W. Fayette Street	Pleasant Hour	2869 N. Fulton Avenue
Fremont	617 N. Fremont Avenue	Princess	1212 E. Balto. Street
Gayety	E. Balto. Street	Queen	666 W. Lexington Street
Gem	714 E. Balto. Street	Rainbow	426 E. Balto. Street
Gem	617 N. Duncan Street	Red Mill	1510 W. Lafayette Avenue
Gilmor	314 N. Gilmor Street	Red Moon	20 W. Balto. Street
Grand	400 E. Balto. Street	Regan	3327 Eastern Avenue
Great Wizard	30 W. Lexington Street	Renard's	1230 Pennsylvania Avenue
Highland	3511 Eastern Avenue	Royal	1727 N. Monroe Street
Holliday Street	Holliday Street	Savoy	315 N. Eutaw Street
Home	2211 Pennsylvania Avenue	Stockton	2 S. Stockton Street
Horn	2018 W. Pratt Street	Suburban	3155 W. North Avenue
Hull	1444 Hull Street	Teddy Bear	1741 E. Balto. Street
Ideal	903 W. 36th Street	Theatorium	11 E. North Avenue
Keystone	1105 N. Gay Street	Thirty-One	31 W. Lexington Street
Leader	248 N. Broadway	Traymore Casino	504 W. Franklin Street
Lexington	314 W. Lexington Street	Victoria	415 E. Balto. Street
Liberty	5 N. Liberty Street	Waverly	1105 York Road
Lubin's	404 E. Balto. Street	Wilson	418 E. Balto. Street

By 1912, movies were so popular that the saloon owners were complaining. There was the belief among many saloon owners that the heads of poorer families were taking their families to movies after dinner instead of stopping off at a local bar. Movies had been around for more than 15 years, and a long newspaper article in May 1912 summarized their history in Baltimore.

> Fifteen years ago when one wanted to marvel at the strides made in the amusement business he entered a converted store, put his eye to a peephole in a small wooden box, dropped a nickel in a slot, turned a handle and saw a moving picture. Now, for the same price, one may find a comfortable seat in a miniature theater and see three or four tabloid plays enacted in pictures almost as perfect as life itself thrown on a screen. Each ... reel has some story to tell ... an assortment of comedy, drama, melodrama, and education all

shown in pictures for one nickel. Between the pictures illustrated songs are given. That is the motion picture business of today. In Baltimore now there are 93 licensed motion picture theaters representing an investment of more than $500,000. They are found in every section of the city ... Highlandtown, Canton, Walbrook, Curtis Bay and all the suburbs have as many as their population will support.... In January 1906, the moving picture business ... today in Baltimore had its inception. A store ... at 402 and 404 East Baltimore Street near Holliday had been converted into a penny arcade. Half of it was used by the old Colonnade in which were displayed a number of miniature attractions. The other half was occupied by Pearce and Scheck who meant to test the public's taste for moving pictures. That establishment opened by Pearce and Scheck was the first motion picture parlor in the city.... The little parlor attracted attention, and its patronage was large from its opening day. During the evening the crowds were so great that the picture was rushed off in 10 minutes and until the place closed at night every seat was filled. Moving pictures struck the popular fancy and the nickels poured into the coffers.

Then came an awakening to the possibilities of the business akin to the rush to new gold territories and moving picture parlors sprouted up like mushrooms. Soon after Pearce and Scheck started the business, the Pickwick on Lexington Street near Howard was opened by Braun and Baum. Then Bohannon and Lewy built the Wizard on Eutaw and Lubin opened a theater on Baltimore Street near Holliday in the place where Pearce and Scheck had started their little place.... Pearce and Scheck left the Colonnade Building and built a place further down the street and Lubin acquired the Colonnade site. Then Baltimore got its first white way. In that block other motion picture houses were built and their presence heralded by glaring electric signs. The Gayety Theater ... added to the fiery display, and the Victoria ... in the same block later contributed its quota to the general glare.

All over town picture houses popped up. Stores were converted into theatres almost over night and the public craze for moving pictures supported them. It was an appeal to children that formed the foundation of success, for grown-ups displayed an enthusiasm for pictures that amounted almost to fanaticism.... Competition among the houses arose. At first one film a day, the pictures changed twice a week or in those parts of town where one house had things all its own way, once a week was sufficient. A 15-minute performance satisfied, and as the nickels rolled into the ticket booth in a steady stream big profits were assured. But downtown the competition got keener. Two films for each performance were shown and the film companies began to show an activity that assured that every demand would be met by an adequate supply. Between the shows illustrated songs were given. Then three pictures were offered, with two illustrated songs and finally the houses offered four pictures for a nickel with illustrated songs in the intermission....

Talking moving pictures came next. People were stationed behind the screen to give words to the pictured characters. The innovation was well received at first but finally people realized that the speaking of lines behind the screen was an anachronism, the managers realized it too, and the talking was dispensed with. Competition and growing critical attitude on the part of the public soon forced some of the houses out of business.... Comfort and safety were seen to be two elements that contributed to the success of a picture house ... proper exits were provided and ... each was marked by a red light. Operators of the machines were examined and licensed to prevent fires and accidents from inexperienced handling....[56]

One important event of that year not mentioned in the article was the prohibition of smoking in moving picture theaters. As early as 1909, smoking was prohibited in some theaters. A man was ejected from the Princess Theater on East Baltimore Street in March 1909 for smoking. In the fall of 1912, the Board of Public Safety adopted a measure prohibiting smoking in moving picture theaters. Building Inspector Stubbs said that he had received complaints that smoking was permitted in two of the largest moving picture theaters in the city. He said that the principal danger was of a panic caused by the striking of a match in a darkened theater, but he also noted that "there is always the danger of fire from the careless use of a match or the throwing of a lighted cigarette or the stump of a cigar on the floor. It was thought best to stop the practice before we had any serious accidents."[57] The terrible fire panic in the old Front Street Theater in 1895, the Rhoads Opera House fire in 1908, and the fire in the Flores Theater in Acapulco in February 1909 must have been still fresh in the inspector's mind.[58] Thanks to this ordinance, generations of Baltimoreans have been able to breathe freely in the city's theaters. It appears that smoking was still allowed in some of the larger vaudeville theaters in 1920 when a man wrote a letter to the newspaper protesting smoking in the Hippodrome. He had purchased a box seat and "did not enjoy my afternoon. Not only was I inhaling all brands of smokes but was in constant fear that any moment either a lighted match or a stub would be thrown carelessly on my feet or my wraps."

The quest for sound movies continued. Another attempt, this time a more sophisticated one by a Baltimorean, was made in 1913.

> The first public performance of Mr. George R. Webb's long-expected electric talking and singing pictures took place last evening [October 6, 1913] at Albaugh's Theatre before a very large and interested audience, which frequently indicated its approval by thoroughly spontaneous applause. The exhibition on the whole was a surprisingly successful one, the various kinds of pictures, showing vaudeville acts and monologues and grand opera, being presented with very few suggestions of misadventure. In fact, the only thing that served to crate [sic] an unfavorable impression was the breaking of a too wet film ... which had to be removed ... the Webb pictures so far exceed anything of a similar nature that has been shown here that they may be regarded rather in the light of an epoch-making offering. Probably the most striking thing about them is the perfection of the synchronism between the action and the voice of the performers. The picture is thrown on the screen and immediately the figure standing before the audience begins to sing or play or speak, as the case may be. The audience hears the words and actually sees them formed with the lips. All this is very interesting. In only one instance last evening — that of a humorous interpretation of the "Bill Simmons" song — did the synchronism seem imperfect.[59]

There had been private performances of Webb's talkies, one in New York in April 1913 and one in Baltimore a month later, but this was the first public performance. By all accounts Webb's talkies were very good.[60] George Register Webb was born in Baltimore in 1858, the son of William G. and Amanda Webb. His father operated a bell and brass foundry. George's brother, Henry, later built the Parkway and McHenry theaters. George Webb started out as a clerk with the Baltimore and Ohio Railroad and later helped to build the Pikesville to Emory Grove Railroad. Working with Alexander Brown he consolidated the street railways of Baltimore. In 1901, he became president of the United Railways and Electric Company. He also organized the Maryland Telephone Company, the Pittsburgh and Allegheny Telephone Company, the Delmarva Telephone Company, the Wilmington Light and Power Company, and the Duquesne Light Company of Pittsburgh. He collaborated with Pierre S. Dupont and Harry P. Scott to consolidate the street railways and the light and telephone system of Wilmington as the Wilmington and Philadelphia Traction Company. It was apparently Webb's involvement with the various telephone companies and his seemingly boundless energy that brought about his work on talking pictures. As he explained to a writer for *Technical World Magazine* in 1913:

> "We've been working on this thing [talking pictures], ten years," ... "I was president of some telephone lines down Wilmington way.... [O]ur plant wasn't paying as well as it should, so I began looking for ways to utilize the system. There was always a big lull in the evenings, ... and I wanted to see if we couldn't make use of our wires then. It occurred to me to send music by wire ... from a central station into the homes of our subscribers, to accomplish it in such a way that they wouldn't have to hold a receiver to their ears. In our Wilmington plant, we began experimenting. We rigged up a talking machine with some necessary mechanical changes and installed it in ... our private workshop. From this room we ran a wire to an office in another part of the building. Then we turned on the talking machine and hoped that the sounds would be reproduced in the other room." ... "And for two years the thing wouldn't even croak," [an associate] chuckled. "We thought Webb was cracked." But Webb kept on. He built different transmitters and different horns. One day a faint sound issued from the reproducer on the top floor.... Webb changed the reproducer a bit and tried again. In a few days he heard the song again, the whole song, but the tones were poor. In fact, they were scarcely audible. So he built still another kind of horn. In fact, he made a thousand different types before he obtained one that would reproduce full round tones, unspoiled by any metallic scraping. Then came a day when he added an inch and a half to the length of the horn and found he had the secret.... "I'll tell you what I did," said Webb, ... "I remembered the human throat as being the perfect mechanism for the utterance of articulate sounds; and I modeled the shape of my horn after it."[61]

Webb moved his experiments to Baltimore where he developed a system to send music over six different wires to six different rooms. Eventually he was able to send music by wire to 113 different Wilmington homes. The magnaphone, a loudspeaker system for announcing the arrival and departure of trains, developed out of Webb's music-by-wire system.[62] In 1910 Webb organized the Webb Talking and Singing Picture Company. He then turned his attention to talking moving pictures. He began working on an apparatus that would create a "'talkie' whose voices would seem to speak from everywhere."

> He began to direct a series of experiments. His first point of attack was the screen. He installed the vocal equipment in a different way. On the back of a moving picture frame, he placed eight of his musical reproducers, two on a side. This was to assure the voices coming from everywhere. Then he worked out a scheme for the synchronizing of these voices with the moving picture film to be shown.... He took a photoplay plot and had dialogue written into it. The company learned their parts. When they were perfect in them, they played the piece and a recording instrument took down every word. Then, they played the piece at the same tempo, speaking the lines so as to keep the time exactly the same and a camera caught their actions. There he had the two sides of it—for the eye, the ear. All he now had to do was to produce them together. He rigged up a talking machine beside the moving picture projector. Wires were run from the talking machine to the different reproducers behind the screen. Each wire took up mechanically its thread of the speaking. Then the projector and the talking machine were run in unison. The words of the characters came from that part of the screen where they happened to be.[63]

2. The Triumph of Cheap Entertainment (1907–1913) 45

Much of the credit for Webb's talking movies goes to his engineer, William P. Stunz. Stunz devised a system to synchronize film and music. One feature of this system was twin turntables on which records could be placed; as soon as one record was finished, the second one took its place. Stunz used a transmitter and loudspeaker that he had developed for sending music over the telephone lines. An African-American machinist whom Webb had met in Paris invented a governor to control the speed of his device.[64] Webb opened a studio near New York City and produced some sound movies. The Webb system, as installed in a theater, consisted of the projector and a phonograph, both operated by the same motor, in the projection booth. The phonograph was connected to a series of speakers behind the screen. On the first of April 1913, Webb unveiled his talking pictures at the New Amsterdam Theater roof.[65] According to an article in *Motography*, the pictures proved to be an extraordinary success.[66] The first Baltimore exhibition of Webb's talkies seems to have been a private screening at Albaugh's Theater on Charles Street on May 28, 1913.[67] Webb chose a good time for this exhibition. Two days earlier, pioneer exhibitor George Kleine, had told reporters that talking pictures would be the ultimate development of motion pictures, and Baltimore was set to host a motion picture exhibitors' convention the following month.

In the fall of 1913, Webb gave a public performance of his talking pictures at Albaugh's Theater. The exhibition, which ran for two weeks beginning on October 6, featured an hour of talking pictures. The performance consisted of an opera —*I Pagliacci, Rigoletto*, or *Faust* and a bill of ten vaudeville acts including De Wolf Hopper, Nat Wills, and Harry Lauder. The audience, with many society and musical people present on the first night, seemed to be impressed with the talkies and frequently burst into spontaneous applause. The reviewer for the *Sun* was equally impressed: "It may be said at once that the Webb pictures so far exceed anything of a similar nature that has been shown here that they may be regarded rather in the light of an epoch-making offering. Probably the most striking thing about them is the perfection of the synchronism between the action and the voice of the performers."[68] This reviewer, however, was not entirely satisfied with the quality of the sound, calling it "metallic" and describing the sound of the choruses as by no means so agreeable as the soloists. The Baltimore *Star* also praised the exhibition: "Mr. Webb's pictures 'talk' so naturally, in such harmony with the movements on the screen, that it is difficult for persons sitting before the darkened stage to realize that the performance is not that of people in the flesh."[69]

Theatrical producer William A. Brady came down from New York to attend the exhibition at Albaugh's. Brady was said to be delighted with the pictures. When he returned to New York, Webb traveled with him. Rumor had it that they were negotiating for control of Webb's talking pictures in the United States.

Even though they received generally favorable reviews, Webb's talking pictures never caught on, and they soon vanished from the movie news. Negotiations with Brady and with Adolph Zukor fell through, and Webb seems to have lost interest in talkies. There must have been at least a small market for them though, if we are to believe a 1914 article which claimed that, "...the Webb talking and singing picture machine, and hundreds of the high-tensioned instruments which make synchronization possible ... are turned out daily in the old Hoen Building at Guilford avenue, Lexington and Holliday streets."[70]

There were other local exhibitions of Webb's talkies in 1914 and 1917. The 1914 exhibition ran for two weeks in May at the Academy of Music. It consisted of selections by

De Wolfe Hopper and Nat Wills and several arias from *Rigoletto* and *Pagliacci*. The reviews, once again, were excellent. The reviewer for the *Baltimore American* wrote, "After seeing the truly marvelous singing and talking pictures that George R. Webb's genius has accomplished at the New Academy of Music, the question inevitably arises, Will future audiences be satisfied with pictures that do not speak as well as move?"[71] In 1928 an *Evening Sun* reviewer reminisced about them.

> Performances were given ... at 2.15 P.M. and 8.15 P.M., of "Webb's Electrical Talking and Singing Pictures." ... We got an awful thrill out of seeing them from about the fourth or fifth row in the center of the balcony. The program was divided into a number of parts and was devised to show the manifold possibilities of this new invention ... The first section was ... "Vaudeville" and offered banjo solos, xylophone solos, a recitation by De Wolf Hopper of his famous "Casey at the Bat" and, as an added attraction ... there was Nat M. Willis [sic], the famous tramp comedian.
> After an intermission of seven minutes, selections were given from the grand opera, "Pagliacci" ... An intermission of five minutes followed this ... and the program was turned over to an old-time minstrel show by Carroll Johnson and his company.[72]

Webb sailed for England in June 1914 on the *Aquitania*. He was planning to film several Gilbert & Sullivan operettas and show them in the fall. He returned to the United States at the end of August disappointed; the sudden outbreak of war in Europe had ended negotiations to sell his inventions there. The Webb sound movies were exhibited again in January 1917 at the Parkway Theater. While his earlier exhibitions had been of very short, four-minute films, the 1917 exhibition featured a 20-minute film of the entire second act of *Carmen*. Six speakers located above and behind the screen broadcast the singing of Signor Giuseppe Campanari, Leon Rothier, and Signora Maria Conesta. Again, the pictures got excellent reviews, and again they went nowhere.

The Webb movies were also shown at the McHenry Theater in October 1917. For the McHenry performances, speakers were set up throughout the auditorium in an effort to overcome the lack of electronic amplification. This exhibition did not bring in any support, and George Webb never did see his invention gain wide acceptance. He died of heart disease at his North Charles Street residence on July 5, 1920; he was 60 years old.[73] The following June, his talking pictures were exhibited at Westminster Cathedral Hall in London.[74] The London *Times* review pointed out the problems that would occur if a portion of film were damaged and suggested that one of the main arguments against talking pictures was that they would only be appreciated by people who understood the language of the movie.[75]

The equipment of The Webb Talking Pictures Company was auctioned off in 1923 at the company's factory in the Hoen Building. In the summer of 1927, when sound movies were back in the news, George Webb's brother, Henry, arranged an exhibition of an improved version of the Webb talking pictures at the Rivoli Theater. According to one newspaper account, "The synchronization of tone and action was convincing, the volume of sound ample, and it was shown that if the sound and action do not synchronize the defect can be corrected at once." Fred Schmuff, who was managing the State Theater at the time, said of the Webb sound system, "We put it down in the State Theater. We didn't use it, but he [Frank Durkee] wanted to try it out down there. For a big house like that the sound just wasn't big enough."

Pioneer movie exhibitors throughout the country gambled on the increasing popularity of the new medium. Many failed, but a few succeeded. In every major American city the story was the same with only minor variations. Businessmen of many different backgrounds, machinists, druggists, grocers, lawyers, jewelers, and electricians purchased movie outfits and began to show films.[76] Some became traveling exhibitors while others acquired more permanent places of exhibition. These entrepreneurs nurtured the film industry through its infancy, taking movies from minor roles on vaudeville bills to top billing in theaters constructed especially for them. Some of them moved into movie making and became the heads of Hollywood production companies, some remained in the exhibition business creating huge circuits or chains of theaters covering many states, and some gradually faded out of the picture. Others just stayed put, creating local circuits. Many, knowing little about the new business, failed after a few years and their companies went bankrupt.[77]

In Baltimore, Marion Pearce and Philip Scheck were important pioneers in the local movie exhibiting business. They reigned supreme in the city during the first 15 years of the 20th century, then gave way to newer exhibitors.[78] Of course, Pearce and Scheck were not the only ones who had the idea to create movie theater circuits. William Fait, Louis Schlichter, Tom Bohannon and Harry Lewy, James Hartlove and John Kahl, the Cluster family, William Daly, Louis Hornstein, Thomas Goldberg, Charles E. Whitehurst, J. Louis Rome, and Frank Durkee all started circuits. Fait had a circuit of eight small downtown theaters—Red Moon, Lexington, Little Pickwick, Dixie, Lubin's, Dream, Renard, and Comedy—in 1914. Local druggist, Dr. Frederick W. Schanze, built Schanze's Theater next door to his drug store at the corner of Pennsylvania and North avenues. He was successful there and built a bigger theater, the Metropolitan, across the street. That was enough of a circuit for him. Other early exhibitors were not interested in creating citywide circuits either. Frank Hornig was satisfied with his popular Horn Theater and his short-lived Royal down the street; Schlichter did not expand beyond his adjoining Edmondson and Bridge theaters. One of the earliest African-American exhibitors with several theaters was William H. Daly.[79] He took over the Lincoln in 1909. He also operated two open-air theaters on Pennsylvania Avenue and tried unsuccessfully to run the Princess Theater on East Baltimore Street.

The Hornstein family operated United Theaters, a circuit of African-American theaters that eventually included the Regent, Diane, and Lenox. The circuit was founded in 1914 by Louis Hornstein and enlarged by his sons, Isaac and Simon, and his grandson, Henry B. Hornstein. The Rome organization, founded in the mid-teens by William Hoffmeister, Samuel Back, Morris Klein, and J. Louis Rome, was one of the few local circuits to operate both white and African-American movie theaters. Frank Durkee went on to create the biggest local circuit in town.

Marion Pearce and Philip Scheck probably did more than any other early Baltimore exhibitors to foster the young movie business in town. They had a near monopoly on the exhibiting of movies in Baltimore before 1906, and they founded an organization that lasted more than 50 years. They started the first film exchange in town, and had a hand in the construction or operation of 22 theaters. Both men were Baltimoreans. Marion S. Pearce was born here in 1874, and Philip J. Scheck was born in 1877. Pearce had to leave the public school system before completing his formal education, but took correspondence courses in electrical engineering. He went to work for the United Railways of Baltimore, and, in 1898, he was made head of the electrical division.

The idea for exhibition of movies has been ascribed to Pearce.[80] Around 1899, he

Pearce and Scheck ran their fledgling movie business from their second floor office at 223 North Calvert Street.

got the idea to provide moving picture exhibitions for churches and other organizations. He apparently did some local exhibiting on his own at this time. A 1915 article said that Pearce and Scheck attended the Cinematograph exhibition at Hamilton Easter's in January 1897 and were so fascinated with motion pictures that they read up on them and bought a movie projector. They gave an exhibition at a church which proved so successful that they could not keep up with all the requests from other churches for movie exhibitions.

In 1901, Pearce took charge of the motor and generator work for the Southern Electric Company. He continued to give motion picture exhibitions at night. That same year, he formed a partnership with Scheck, a machinist, whom he had met at United Railways. Pearce supplied the projector and six sets of song slides and Scheck supplied the capital, about $200.

In 1902, Pearce and Scheck were operating their own electrical contracting and movie exhibiting organization at 16 S. Gay Street. They abandoned the electrical business in late 1903 in favor of the more lucrative and exciting film business. They provided 11 movie shows in 1903 including at least one at Electric Park. The devastating Baltimore fire of February 1904 almost ruined them. It destroyed their office on Gay Street, but they

The offices of Pearce and Scheck, on North Calvert Street; left to right: Arthur Meyer, Philip J. Scheck, Charles Pearce, Marion S. Pearce.

were able to salvage enough equipment to conduct one movie show at a time. According to Marion Pearce's son Wilbur, Marion and his sister Ida took a wagon driven by a hired man to pick up whatever they could salvage from the office. Among the items saved was a penny picture machine, which was repaired in Pearce's basement on Chester Street.[81] With the equipment they saved, they were able to offer 100 movie shows throughout Maryland in 1904. They had invested $400 and made a profit that year of $150. By 1905, movies had become so popular that Pearce and Scheck were able to book as many as 36 shows in a single week. During the summers of 1904 and 1905, they apparently took over the movie concession at Electric Park. This may have been where they earned the money to begin opening their movie theaters.

Many of the movie exhibitions given by Pearce and Scheck were traveling shows. These shows, which continued until the mid–1920s, were common around this time.[82] They were basically one-man operations. However, sometimes two or three men were involved. In the early days, Pearce and Scheck provided the shows themselves — Pearce cranked the projector while Scheck sang baritone solos between reels. They carried their own equipment — a projector, a bed sheet screen, film, and cylinders of oxygen and hydrogen gas — packed in trunks.[83] The gasses were used to produce the limelight to project the movies, as electricity was generally not available outside the major cities. Charles Pearce, Marion Pearce's brother, occasionally operated the projector, and Meyer Leventhal, Stephen Brenner, and George Matthews gave one-man shows for Pearce and Scheck. Robert J. Griffin sang illustrated songs for their exhibitions as early as 1902. The shows usually consisted of two or three reels of movies and a couple of illustrated songs. One, probably typical, show was given at the Harford Avenue Methodist Episcopal Church on May 5, 1902, for the benefit of the Sunday School carpet fund. A handbill advertised the show as an "Artoscope Entertainment."

Among the moving pictures shown that day were eight views of the Galveston, Texas, cyclone and scenes of the funeral of President McKinley. Philip Scheck sang the "latest beautifully illustrated songs" including "Hello, Central, Give Me Heaven," and "Stay in Your Own Back Yard." Miss Alphonsia R. Wilson, reader, offered several "humorous and pathetic selections." Marion S. Pearce was listed as manager of the entertainment.

Among their competitors at this date was George W. E. Brooks, who presented the "wonderful Edison Kinestoscope [sic]" at Philanthropy Hall, 1017 E. Baltimore Street, on May 19, 1902. While Pearce and Scheck concentrated their movie exhibitions in the Baltimore area, they did send traveling shows to Frederick, Cumberland, Ellicott City, Towson, and other Maryland cities. They also occasionally sent shows, by boat, as far away as the Northern Neck of Virginia. Churches, lodge halls, clubs, and camp meetings were the usual venues for the traveling shows; they were paid about $25 per show. Regular shows were also given at hospitals, jails, and other local institutions.

According to a family story, when Pearce and Scheck brought a show to St. Mary's Industrial School, a young George Herman Ruth — he had not become "Babe" yet — helped to carry their equipment.[84] As late as 1909, they were providing motion picture entertainments at Amusement Hall at Spring Grove State Hospital in Catonsville.

The projectors in the very early days did not have take-up reels and the film was allowed to run off the projector into a bag to be rewound later. This caused them some major problems, as recounted by J. M. Shellman, the local correspondent for *Moving Picture World*: "The projection machine was run entirely by gas, and they used a bag to catch the film, instead of a magazine. One evening they were just about to commence the performance at a lodge when the building inspector of Baltimore, who was present, asked them where their magazine was. They answered that they had none. The inspector said they could not go on with the show, and so, even though they had been running for some years without a magazine, they were forced to give up the entertainment for that night."[85]

In 1904, Pearce and Scheck opened an office at 214 N. Calvert Street. The following year they moved across the street to 223 N. Calvert Street, where they carried a complete line of films and moving picture supplies. They opened their first movie theater at 406 E. Baltimore Street in early 1906. This was the first successful movie theater in Baltimore and has been described above. In March 1906, Pearce and Scheck joined with William Brown, Watson E. Sherwood, and James Wallace Bryan to incorporate the National Amusement Company, "for the purpose of owning, operating, and conducting moving picture theaters and parlors and for the purpose of owning, operating, and conducting public exhibitions of amusement generally." In July 1906, the owner of the building on Baltimore Street in which Pearce and Scheck were giving their shows decided to remodel the building into a vaudeville theater.[86] The following month Pearce and Scheck transferred their movie exhibitions up to 227 North Eutaw Street where they opened the Ideal Theater.

In January 1907, Pearce and Scheck leased the first floor of the building at 414–416 East Baltimore Street and opened the Amusea Theater.[87] Three months later, they leased the property at 35 West Lexington Street for five years. They had the building on that site demolished and erected a one-story movie theater also called the Amusea. In November 1907, they began showing movies at the Opera House in Frederick, Maryland. In March 1908, there were 20 movie theaters in Baltimore; Pearce and Scheck ran four of them. They were ready for a bigger theater and began negotiating with Aaron Cohen, Michael Hartz, and Joel Gebhardt to operate a large vaudeville theater at 415 East Baltimore Street. The following month, they announced that they would build a small movie theater at 903 3rd Avenue in Hampden.[88] In May 1908, Cohen, Hartz, and Gebhardt announced that architect A. Lowther Forrest was preparing plans for the theater at 415 East Baltimore Street, and on June 6, Pearce and Scheck were awarded the contract to operate the theater. The new theater was the 1,500-seat Victoria; it opened at the end of December 1908.

By 1909, Pearce and Scheck were operating a circuit of 13 theaters. They had the Victoria, Grand, Leader, two Amuseas, two Ideals, the Hull, and the Y.M.C.A. in Baltimore; the Bijou Dream in Winchester, Virginia; the Ideal in Martinsburg, West Virginia; the City Opera House in Frederick, Maryland; and the Alhambra in Washington, D.C. After the Victoria was built, Pearce and Scheck moved their offices and film exchange from Calvert Street into that building. In March 1909, they acquired the Leader Theater on South Broadway. During 1909, Pearce and Scheck were interested in three corporations: Pearce and Scheck, Inc. (which sold motion picture supplies),[89] the National Amusement Company[90] and the Victoria Company. Through the Victoria Company, they controlled the Leader, Ideal (in Hampden), Grand, Victoria, and Amusea (on Baltimore Street); and through the National Amusement Company they controlled the Bijou Dream in Winchester, the City Opera House in Frederick, the Ideal in Martinsburg (West Virginia), the Y.M.C.A. in Baltimore, the Alhambra in Washington, and the theaters on North Eutaw Street.

In the summer of 1912, they bought the old Medical College on West Baltimore Street and announced that they would erect a large vaudeville and motion picture theater there. They were granted a building permit for this theater, the Lord Baltimore,[91] in November 1912. The Lord Baltimore opened in 1913. At that time, it was the largest theater in the city outside the downtown theater district.[92] Pearce and Scheck moved vaudeville into the Lord Baltimore from the Victoria, which was charging them too much rent, and kept it there for several months until their Hippodrome opened.

On April 5, 1913, Pearce, Scheck, and W. Stuart Symington applied for a charter for the Hippodrome Company with a capital stock of $400,000. On April 18, they announced that they would build a new theater on the site of the Eutaw House Hotel on Eutaw Street. The hotel had been extensively damaged by fire in May 1912 and was too expensive to rebuild. Pearce and Scheck were vying with Nixon & Zimmerman and Marcus Loew to buy the Eutaw Street property on which to build a theater. The owners were asking $350,000. Pearce and Scheck won out and purchased the ground and remains of the old hotel on July 1. Workmen began clearing the site in October 1913. By January 1914, Pearce and Scheck had selected an architect for the new theater. He was Thomas W. Lamb,[93] the dean of American theater architects. The cost of the theater was estimated at $225,000, and it was claimed that it would be the largest structure of its kind south of Philadelphia. The new theater would be called the Hippodrome. It opened in November 1914.

Prior to about 1910, Pearce and Scheck's film exchange handled films made by several producers. In February 1910, they attended the Fifth Semi-annual Convention of the Film Service Association in New York. There, they had the opportunity to associate with other pioneer exhibitors such as Tom Moore from Washington, Joseph and Herbert Miles from New York and San Francisco, J. R. Freuler from Milwaukee, William T. "Pop" Rock of Vitagraph, one of the Warner brothers from Pittsburgh, and H. Schwalbe from Philadelphia. Later in 1910, the Motion Picture Patents Company formed the General Film Company to distribute its products. Pearce and Scheck sold their film distribution business to the General Film Company for about $25,000[94] and got the Baltimore area franchise for General Film Company films. Competition was fierce and, like many other aggressive distributors,[95] Pearce and Scheck were not above using pressure to increase their business. In a July 1910 letter to the Motion Picture Patents Company, Hood and Schultz, the operators of the Carrollton Theater on West Baltimore Street, complained bitterly about the tactics of their rivals across the street, the Black Cat, and about Pearce and Scheck's shows at the nearby West Branch YMCA.

> The Black Cat open[ed] directly opposite to us, and put on licensed films and took service from Pearce & Scheck, Tom Moore, and Miles Bros. While taking service from Pearce & Scheck they boasted to us that they were not paying a license fee, although they were receiving each week from your office the postal card receipt ... they want to put on first run pictures to get ahead of us and the Aladdin, which in the first place they cannot afford to do, as their place has a bad name, and few first class people go there ... just a word about Pearce and Scheck. Their West Branch is one block from us, and they know ... what pictures we get, so they always put them on a night or two before we get them, and then tell our operator about it, and say they are going to keep on doing it until we take service from them. They are doing the same thing on Broadway to a party that gets our pictures after we have had them. While they are doing this their customers are suffering, and asking for better service and pictures.... When Miles Bros. licenses were canceled, we went to Pearce and Scheck..., but they wanted such a high price for their service, and then too they could not give us what we wanted, they offered us something like thirty day pictures, and of course after they had used them themselves at their place just one block from us.[96]

There were other complaints about the way Pearce and Scheck operated their film exchange. Charles Demme, who ran the Crescent on West Lafayette Avenue, said that he had dropped the General Film Company's service because of bad service from Pearce and Scheck.[97] The opening of a new theater on West Lafayette Avenue caused Demme additional problems in 1911. The first theaters on West Lafayette were Emmerich and Demme's Crescent at 1509 and the Red Mill across the street; both opened in 1909. The Lafayette opened in the spring of 1911 a block to the east. Soon after the opening of the Lafayette, the owners of the Red Mill wrote to the Motion Picture Patents Company complaining about service from Pearce and Scheck. They reported that they could only get films that had already been shown at the Lafayette and that when they complained to Charles Pearce, who was in charge of the film department, he told them that the Lafayette had been beating them out on pictures right along and would keep on doing so, that it was only a question of a short time before they beat the Red Mill out altogether.[98] One of the problems might have been that in 1911 and 1912, new films were not available as quickly as the 93

Baltimore movie houses could show them. Trying to meet this need, some local exhibitors, began to make their own films. According to one of Marion Pearce's sons, Pearce and Scheck made only newsreels. In 1913, Pearce and Scheck had the only licensed film exchange in Baltimore.[99] About a year later, they lost the General Film franchise. At the same time they left the Victoria and moved their offices across the street into the Grand Theater building. They remained there until the late 1930s when they moved to the Lord Baltimore.

The names Pearce and Scheck have been linked together for nearly a century, and it is often difficult to think of them as two separate and quite different people. Pearce generally handled the business side of the partnership while Scheck handled the mechanical side.

Marion Pearce, on the one hand was very innovative, but at the same time conservative in his views on the future of motion pictures. According to one of his sons, Pearce was against Sunday movies and spoke out against them in the state legislature. He also did not think that sound movies would succeed.[100] He was outgoing and very active in the fledgling Motion Picture Exhibitors' League of America. In 1913, he was elected the first president of the Maryland state branch of that organization, and two years later he was elected president of the national body. Pearce was also a projectionist, and in June 1910 he was elected the first president of the Maryland State Board of Examiners of Moving Picture Operators.[101] Pearce was one of the organizers of many of the early galas that featured top screen stars, put on by the local exhibitors at the Lyric Theater.

Philip Scheck seemed to be the exact opposite of Pearce. He was not an entrepreneurial type and was more introverted. He did not seem to take an active part in the exhibitor's organizations, although he was treasurer of the State Board of Examiners of Moving Picture Operators in 1920. He was content to remain in the background and exert a steady moderating influence on the partnership. Rarely did Philip Scheck appear in the group photographs of local exhibitors while the dignified Pearce and his brother Charles, with his prominent handlebar mustache, were always in these photos.

In a rare public statement in December 1910, Philip Scheck spoke out for a graduated theater license fee in Baltimore, "The small exhibitor should not be made to pay $50 for a license fee the same as a large exhibitor. The scale should be graduated according to the size of the theater. I would suggest that we band ourselves closely together and appear at the next meeting of the City Council and endeavor to have a graduated scale from $10 to $50 established."[102]

Pearce and Scheck not only worked together, but they also had adjacent homes. They purchased three lots on the north side of Egerton Road in Forest Park. The Schecks lived at 3708 and the Pearces lived at 3710 Egerton. Pearce's house had a 1 kilowatt radio transmitter on the top floor and a darkroom in the basement. The two men even shared the same car for a while.[103]

3

BIGGER AND BETTER THEATERS (1914–1920)

During this seven-year period, the size of individual movie theaters increased greatly, first-run theaters began to develop in the downtown area, methods for providing musical accompaniment for films became more elaborate, most of the film exchanges moved from Baltimore to Washington,[1] film censorship was taken over by the state, and a terrible flu epidemic devastated the country. The average weekly attendance at Baltimore theaters was about 322,500. The breakdown was given in a November 1914 article[2]:

100 Movie Theaters	150,000	Colonial	10,000
Hippodrome	30,000	Academy of Music	9,500
Victoria	30,000	Ford's	9,500
New	30,000	Palace	8,500
Maryland	15,000	Holliday Street Theater	5,000
Auditorium	10,000	Albaugh's	3,000
Gayety	10,000	Lyric	2,000

Based on these figures, movies and vaudeville were by far the most popular theatrical entertainments in Baltimore in the mid-teens. In a Woman's Page contest sponsored by the *Baltimore News* in the spring of 1915, going to the movies beat out romping with kiddies and an evening with books as the most popular form of amusement. Movies were changing the amusement habits of the city. Families could attend a movie show in their own neighborhood; they no longer had to go downtown. There were one or more neighborhood theaters in many of the commercial districts around the city such as North Avenue and Charles Street, Pennsylvania Avenue and North, Light Street, Greenmount and 33rd, Park Heights and Belvidere, Eastern Avenue, South Broadway, West Baltimore Street, and West Pratt Street. And people were staying up later, having after-theater suppers in a Chinese restaurant or going to a cabaret. There were many people lingering downtown on Howard and Eutaw streets after the theater as late as midnight. Movies even moved onto the Bay.

In September 1914, movies were shown on a ship for the first time in the Baltimore area; the ship was the steamer *Louise* returning from a trip to Tolchester. A projector was set up on the hurricane deck of the ship and four reels of movies were shown. The war in Europe and the U.S. involvement in it in 1917 had several effects on the local movie business. In 1916, Mayor Preston signed an ordinance that regulated the playing of "The Star Spangled Banner" in any public place or at any public entertainment or in any theater or moving picture hall, restaurant or cafe "except as an entire and separate composition or number, without embellishment of national or other melodies, nor shall 'The Star Spangled Banner' be played at or in any of the places mentioned for dancing or as an exit march."

Films of the war with lectures by military leaders were popular. Theaters proved excellent places to solicit for war bonds and aid for the boys at the front. A fuel crisis in early 1918 forced theaters and other places of amusement to close down on certain days. The amount of money spent on buildings began declining in 1915 and continued declining until 1918. Only a single movie theater, the McHenry, opened between the end of 1916 and 1919. Things changed in 1919 with a quadruple increase in building investments, and 1920 promised to be even better.[3]

What was it like to watch a movie in those days? J. M. Shellman, film writer for the *Sun*, writing in late 1919 describes it this way:

> The atmosphere in the moving-picture theatre is entirely different from that of a theatre playing road shows. When the public visits the latter they expect to spend three hours there. The ladies like to take their bon-bons, sit comfortably and exchange confidences during the intermission and the men like to have that ... between-the-acts smoke and (if it were before July 1 last) we might say that little quaff of inspiration. The air is filled with the low drone of many voices. The orchestra plays its lively airs from beginning to end.
>
> Then there is that little flicker of the lights over the music stands of the musicians, the director lowers his baton and the music faintly fades away. Then the footlights flash up and the play begins. But the atmosphere in the moving-picture theatre is entirely different. One goes into the playhouse. He or she passes many people coming out. In the main auditorium the lights are very dim. There is no low drone of voices. No orchestra is playing music that conforms and interprets the picture. It changes as the picture changes. Thus you are unconscious that there is music, except that it makes the play being shown more effective. You find a very comfortable chair just at the part of the theatre that suits your eyes best. You sit down and relax. And that relaxation is helped by the surroundings in which you find yourself. There are no harsh lights. The screen setting is one of soft, dusky colors. Or perhaps it is an elaborate set of plush curtains, either very dark green or very dark purple or very dark crimson. You immediately fall in with the play. You do not wait for the end or the beginning, you just get the play as it unfolds and if you haven't seen the first part you enjoy it just as much when it comes around again.[4]

Shellman goes on to criticize managers who added intermissions, saying that such a practice irritated the audience. You could enter a theater at any time to see a movie. Remember that? That practice lasted up until the late 1960s. It didn't seem to matter whether you went in at the beginning, middle or end of the movie; you stayed there until the picture reached the part you had already seen, then you asked a companion, "Isn't this where we came in?" People born after 1950 probably don't know what this phrase means.[5]

We talk of silent movies, but the interiors of movie theaters were anything but silent before talkies. Many writers have commented on the noise in early theaters. There was usually music of some kind, but there were also other sounds. John A. Grant, writing about attending the Maryland Theater in Oakland, Garrett County, describes the talking in the theater. "...[A]fter a few minutes of struggling [to read the dialogue], I found that I really didn't have to read; all I had to do was listen. People in the audience were reading the dialogue out loud.... All over the country, in addition to the music, there must have been a constant murmur of voices as the audience read the dialogue out loud."[6]

A 1909 article commented on early pests in movie theaters, mentioning men who laugh at every joke, people who know what's going to happen in the film before it happens and tell the whole audience, and the "chewing gum club" whose members crack gum five or six inches from a person's ear.[7] Talkers seem to have been annoying audiences for as long as there have been audiences. The talking was sometimes necessary; as one lady remembered, she had to read the subtitles for her grandmother who could not see well enough to read them. Children firing toy pistols were shooting up some of the movie theaters in Highlandtown in 1912. The Baltimore *Star* reported that once the sun went down, "From every court and alley the youngsters come out with the cap pistols on their hips and proceed to terrorize the 'movies.'"[8] Four boys tried to force a young woman cashier to give them free tickets. When she told them to run along, they opened fire and scared her so badly that she had to take a dose of aromatic spirits of ammonia.

Jacques Shellman devoted three of his 1919 Sunday columns to talking in the movies. In his August 3 column, Shellman listed the following annoyances in movie theaters: a young man holding an animated whispered conversation with his companion and snapping the rubber band against his straw hat; the smell of peanuts and the rustle of the paper bag in which they are carried; women eating bonbons and holding a running conversation; a woman singing along with the orchestra; a man keeping time with the music by tapping on the back of your seat. To Shellman's list, theater managers added pests like the little boys who hung around theater lobbies asking patrons for pennies and gangs of rowdy boys who created disturbances in their theaters. By November 1920, Shellman had formulated a new list of 11 things not to do in a movie theater. It included: Carry on an undertone conversation, read the sub-titles out loud and make witty remarks about them, whistle or warble the tune the orchestra is playing, keep time with the orchestra by tapping one's feet on the floor, eat peanuts or any other form of lunch, smoke in a theater whether it is allowed or not.

Sad to say, many of these annoyances are still with us today; plus you can also be robbed or shot in a theater.[9] Talking in the movie theaters was not tolerated in the 1920s. Magistrate Larkins of the Northwestern Police Court fined three men $6.45 each for "making noisy criticisms" in Schanze's Theater in March 1923. The music was often too loud. Patrons were complaining in the late 1920s about the volume excesses of theater orchestras. One woman wrote that she had seen a fellow patron "put her hands over her ears when the fairly bursting organ pipes made the theater shudder with its reverberation." She looked forward to leaving the theater for a "haven of peace," the street.[10]

The classic pest during the early days of the movies was the woman who kept her large feathered hat on during the show. Large hats had probably been annoying theater patrons who had to sit behind them since the first theaters. The managers of the Academy of Music asked ladies to remove their hats when attending performances in 1895, and Manager Schanberger at the Maryland was ready to get tough with women who did not remove their hats in the 1904 season. Letters to the editor of the *Evening Sun* in 1916 from "Pheebil Pheelicks" of Ellicott City and "Abel Ajacks" of Baltimore condemned such women. "Ajacks" pointed out that women entering New York City theaters were not allowed to take their seats until they had removed their hats. A writer to the *Evening Sun* in 1915 made the startling suggestion that men begin lighting cigars in the theater and applying them to the trimming of offending hats.[11]

The sale of concessions began to develop during the teens. It has become the salvation of exhibitors. These sales give them their profits, and increasingly more space is devoted to candy, popcorn, ice cream, nachos, hot dogs, and a host of other tasty tidbits. One of the earliest references to a concession stand in a Baltimore theater was in 1893. During a remodeling that summer, the Academy of Music moved its "confectionery stand" to a location just inside the entrance. In the days of the nickelodeons, people stopped by a local candy store, which was often located next door to or within a few doors of the theater, and stocked up on food to take into the theater. In a survey of 1910 movie theaters, 19 theaters (out of about 60) were in the same block as a confectioners—five were next door to one—10 theaters were in the same block as two confectioners, two theaters were in the same block as three confectioners, and one theater was in the same block as four confectioners. Peanuts, pickles, and fruit were some of the favorite items. Some early theaters, such as the Gayety, had penny candy machines attached to the backs of some seats. And there was the candy butcher who sold candy and other treats during intermissions at some burlesque and vaudeville theaters. At the Bijou on East Baltimore Street, the candy peddlers walked the aisles selling Meixner Brothers assorted chocolates for a nickel. Along with the chocolates the purchaser would get a song sheet containing the words to some of the current popular songs. Each day there was supposed to be one package of candy that contained an expensive gift, a wallet, pair of binoculars, or money.

At the Gayety, Charles Lipsey would make a pitch selling ice cream and candy during intermission. He had five boys working for him. As Lipsey made the pitch from the stage, his boys would fan out across the theater to sell ice cream, candy and prize packages. Small books with jokes and pictures of burlesque stars were also popular items.[12]

This practice of employing "pitch men" or barkers to sell candy and novelties during intermission caused problems at the Royal Theater in the fall of 1928. Numerous patrons complained of this "cheap ballyhoo" claiming that it did not belong in a first-class house like the Royal. Barkers were apparently still working at some theaters as late as 1949. An article on the newly opened Morgan Theater claimed that "The best of order, the absence of hawkers of soft drinks, peanuts and candies, and the services of courteous attendants" would be among the theater's new features.[13]

As late as 1919, patrons who wanted something to eat in the theater still depended on the nearby candy store, but the economic value of food sales inside the theater was becoming evident to exhibitors. A December 1919 article suggested that exhibitors should cash in on the public's fondness for snacks by installing automatic corn-popping machines in their lobbies. The Butter-Kist popcorn machine was touted as an excellent piece of equipment for this purpose. But it took a long time for popcorn to become universally available in theaters, and some parts of the country had popcorn machines well before others. Most theater owners resisted selling popcorn in their theaters. Andrew Smith, in his recent study of the social history of popcorn in the United States, writes that some exhibitors considered all concessions to be unnecessary nuisances or beneath their dignity while others believed that the profits were small compared with the trouble it took to sell popcorn and clean up afterwards.[14] Smith also notes that early popcorn machines "filled theaters with an unpleasant, penetrating smoky odor."[15]

Pearce and Scheck, who owned the exhibition business in Baltimore between 1900 and 1913, saw their empire crumble in the late teens. The building of the Hippodrome was the beginning of their end. In order to finance the project, they had to withdraw a large sum of money from their firm and from each partner's individual resources. By 1916 they were in default for non-payment of 1914 and 1915 taxes and had a considerable debt from other bills. Marion Pearce became seriously ill in 1916 and was unable to participate in the partnership. Watson Sherwood was appointed to handle Pearce's finances. Pearce recovered the following year, but he soon retired from the partnership. He had little to do with the theater business after 1916; he died in June 1953 at the age of 78. The Pearce and Scheck organization faded away during the 1920s. Philip Scheck and his brother John operated what remained of the theater business until 1932 when they both died. In that year, Philip Scheck's widow Mrs. C. Edna Scheck, his son Robert M. Scheck, and his friend Meyer Leventhal formed Philip J. Scheck Enterprises, Inc. They bought out the Pearce interests around this time and continued to operate a small circuit of theaters.[16] Robert Scheck died in his office in October 1964 and, in January 1966, the surviving partners sold their remaining movie house, the Lord Baltimore.

Meyer "Mike" Leventhal, who had started out as a 13-year-old usher at the Grand Theater in 1909, died in 1981 at the age of 85. Pearce and Scheck supplied their car when the young Leventhal eloped. His long career as an usher, projectionist, manager and theater owner spanned more than six decades.[17] He retired from the theater business in 1974. In addition to his duties with Pearce and Scheck, he was president of the State Board of Examining Motion Picture Machine Operators and president of the Allied Motion Picture Theater Owners of Maryland. "Mike" Leventhal was our last link to the old Pearce & Scheck organization and to the first years of the nickelodeons in Baltimore.[18]

As Pearce and Scheck was fading, other local exhibitors were getting organized. The Durkee circuit was formed in 1916 by Frank Durkee, Sr., Charles E. Nolte, Sr., and C. William Pacy.[19] All three men had started in the movie business around the same time. Durkee was born in Baltimore in 1888. He graduated from City College in 1906 and got a job as a clerk in the Commercial and Farmers Bank. While working in the bank during the day, he opened a small storefront theater on North Washington Street in 1909. He had a good voice and sang illustrated — often unkindly called "ulcerated"— songs at various theaters. By 1913, Durkee was running the Palace and Colonial, both on Gay Street. He began operating a film express between Baltimore and Washington in the spring of 1915. Charles Nolte and Gus Stenger had opened the Palace on South Broadway in 1909 and the Linwood in 1912. C. W. Pacy built the Garden on South Charles Street in 1910.

After the union of Durkee, Nolte, and Pacy, the three families controlled a group of theaters that stretched over one quarter of the city, from South to East Baltimore. Durkee Enterprises remained a neighborhood circuit. The closest it got to a downtown theater was the 2,000-seat State Theater in East Baltimore that it opened in 1927. The State was comparable in every way to a first-run downtown theater except it was not a first-run theater.

In March 1917, another group of local exhibitors united to incorporate their organization as the Exhibitors' League of Maryland, Inc. The new corporation was formed "...for the purpose of elevating the business of the motion picture exhibitors, creating a good feeling and friendship among persons engaged therein, advancing the interests and welfare of its members in all matters pertaining to the business and in general protecting and advancing to the mutual interest of members of the league...."[20] The office of the League was in the New Theater Building. The first board of directors consisted of Frank A. Hornig, J. Louis Rome, Thomas D. Goldberg, Louis A. DeHoff, and Frederick C. Weber.

By the early 1920s, the organization had become the Motion Picture Theater Owners of Maryland. In 1921, the Motion Picture Theatre Owners of Maryland, Virginia and the District of Columbia voted to join the national league. Over the years the name was changed to the Allied Motion Picture Theater Owners of Maryland and finally to the National Association of Theater Owners of Maryland. Members paid yearly dues based on the number of seats (for four-wall theaters) or number of cars (for drive-in theaters). The exhibitors' organizations appear to have been reluctant to become involved in politics or to take a stand on controversial issues. They were neutral or barely supportive in the long fight for Sunday movies, and they rarely endorsed candidates for local offices. In 1928, they did back a move in the United States Senate to make "block-booking" illegal. Annual meetings were held to discuss local and national problems and decide on future strategies, but there was also time for fun.

The social highlight of the exhibitors' year was the Annual Ball. Once a year, the local film community entertained itself and the public. The exhibitors organized annual movie balls beginning in 1914. The first one was a great success, with 4,000 people, who paid $1.00 a couple, jamming the Lyric Theater to dance to the music of Fritz Gaul's orchestra and hob-nob with popular film personalities, including Clara Kimball Young, Earle Williams, Norma Talmadge, Ormi Hawley, Henry Meyers, and Rosemary Theby. Forty-six actors and actresses came to Baltimore in April 1915 to attend the second annual Movie Ball at the Lyric Theater. Many of the most popular stars attended, including Francis X. Bushman, Clara Kimball Young, Viola Dana, Gertrude McCoy, Maurice Costello, and Norma Talmadge. Sigmund Lubin came down from Philadelphia with a detachment of his stars. One contingent of stars and their entourages paraded down from the Lyric to the Emerson Hotel. The ball was a great success and cheer after cheer rang out as master of ceremonies Marion Pearce, president of the local and national exhibitor's organizations, introduced the stars and other dignitaries. After the ball, members of the Vitagraph troupe stayed around to film some scenes for a new movie in Baltimore and at Bowie Race Track.

The movie balls were annual affairs for several years. The ball in 1917 was attended by 5,000 movie fans and stars Anita Stewart, Viola Dana, Edward Earle, Violet Mersereau, Thomas Meighan and Antonio Moreno. The fourth ball took place in April 1919. The balls were not held again until 1932. Another important social event of the exhibitors' year was the annual outing and picnic. This event was held first at the Hotel Bayou in Havre de Grace and later at Bay Ridge near Annapolis. The exhibitors and exchange men had a chance to unwind by playing baseball, competing in bag races and dancing.

In October 1914, the magazine *Motion Picture News* conducted a survey among exhibitors in major United States cities. The results suggested that movies were not doing so well in Baltimore. Three new theaters had opened since May 1. Two theaters had closed because of "summer dullness." Serials continued to be popular in residential sections. Conditions were depressed but were expected to improve.[21]

Summer dullness would continue into the late 1920s until theaters began to install air conditioning. Baltimore was entering a period of slow growth in movie theaters, and it would not end until after World War I. Among the 16 movie houses that opened in 1915 — eight of which would not last more than a few seasons — was the Gertrude McCoy, later known as the Fulton.[22] Sixty-one movie theaters opened between 1913 and 1920; 58 closed their doors during the same period.

The Gertrude McCoy, designed by Baltimore architect Francis E. Tormey, who also designed the Aurora and second Horn theaters, was fairly typical of the large neighborhood movie theaters built between 1914 and 1925 although it was smaller than many. It cost about $20,000 and seated fewer than 500. The Gertrude McCoy was one of the most up-to-date theaters in Baltimore for its day. Other theaters that opened that year were Berman's at Baltimore and High Street, the Bridge Theater on Edmondson Avenue, the Mount Royal on North Avenue, the Goldfield on Warner Street, and the best known of them all, the Parkway on North Avenue. Only a single theater, the McHenry, opened in 1917, and none opened in 1918.

Although not many new theaters were opened at this time, movies were more popular than ever. Attesting to this popularity were the expanded motion picture advertisements that filled several pages in the Sunday newspapers. Before 1912, few movie theaters advertised in the newspapers. Lubins, Pearce and Scheck's Amusea, the Wilson, Victoria, Great Wizard, Blue Mouse, New, Pickwick and Picture Garden advertised on an irregular basis in the *Sun*, *American*, and *News*. By late 1912, the *News* had a whole page of movie news with ads for the week's movies at 13 theaters as well as a page for vaudeville and legitimate theaters. The *Sun* also had a page of theater news with ads for 10 movie theaters. There were sporadic ads for movie theaters in the *Afro-American* between 1908 and 1915. The *American* had a special movie section in its Sunday issue by March 1914.[23]

By the end of 1915, the *Sun*, *News* and *American* each had a weekly page of movie news; the *News* had reviews for 22 theaters, the *American* had reviews for 18, and the *Sun* had reviews for 17. Curiously, the movie theaters listed in the *Sun*'s 1915 weekly Sunday listing were all west of Charles Street.[24] In 1916 the *News* had three pages of ads for 38 theaters. The *Sun* had a little more than a page on movies and a page and a half on live theaters. The *Afro-American* had one page with ads for seven theaters. In 1918 a writer for the *Moving Picture World* could report that "Baltimore's five dailies stand without exception as friends of the screen and the exhibitor."[25] The *Post* had a movie directory by 1922, and the *News* worked out an arrangement in late 1923 with the Exhibitors' League of Maryland to run daily ads for their theaters.[26] By the end of the 1920s, daily film schedules were appearing in all the major newspapers.

Movies were advertised in Sunday newspapers, but you still could not see a movie on a Sunday. A letter to the editor of the *Sun* in February 1914, signed by "A Six-Day-a-Week Worker," asked if "some of 'God's agents'" would "kindly give us their views as to why [theaters and moving-picture parlors] should be kept closed on Sundays?"[27] Despite the fact that movies were shown in some churches on Sundays and collections were taken up at these showings,[28] the Lord's Day Alliance protested the charity benefit film showing at a local theater on a Sunday organized by the Lloyd Street Synagogue and the Hebrew Ladies' Consumptive Association. The police said they would take no action unless the Police Board rescinded the Sunday permit.

The theaters tried, in vain, to court the favor of the churches by giving strong support to "Go-to-Church Day," Sunday February 7, 1915. But the exhibitors did not seem to be wholeheartedly in favor of Sunday movies at this time and indeed were lukewarm during much of the long fight. Perhaps they were scared off by news from other cities with Sunday movies. Frederick J. Herrington, president of the Motion Picture Exhibitors League of America, reported that competition had increased markedly in Philadelphia as soon as Sunday movies were okayed. And, he noted that wherever there were Sunday openings, the receipts from Saturday and Monday were invariably small.[29]

In 1919, the Baltimore City Council went on record as opposing the blue laws and urged the General Assembly to repeal them. An attempt to legalize Sunday movies was made in 1920 when Delegate George D. Iverson of Baltimore introduced a bill in the Maryland General Assembly that would have partly repealed the state's blue laws and legalized the opening of places of amusement in Baltimore on Sunday afternoons after 2 P.M. In a February 1920 editorial, the *Evening Sun* blasted those opposed to changing the Sunday laws. The editor wrote that their case rested on four assumptions that were obviously false: (1) "That the moral precepts and the religious doctrines of the Bible should be the law of the land," (2) "that communities that have the strictest Sunday laws are made better and kept better by those laws than communities that are more liberal," (3) "that religious denominations which believe in strict observance are more truly Christian and moral than churches that do not regard Sunday as the old Jewish Sabbath," and (4) "that a minority should dictate to a majority and force them to conform to the views of the minority."[30] The editorial concluded, "There should be one day of rest in every seven for every man. And the law should make that obligatory, not as a matter of religion, but as a matter of justice and efficiency. And churches and religious assemblies and the homes of the city should be protected from noise and disturbance. Changes in the Sunday law should not allow invasion of other people's rights. They simply propose ... to allow the majority of the community to exercise rights of which they are deprived by the minority."

The Exhibitors' League of Maryland decided it was still not the right time to take a stand and adopted the position expressed in Frank Durkee's motion that "the Exhibitors' League of Maryland take no active part neither for or against the bill...." At a hearing before the Judiciary Committee in late February, the manager of the Hippodrome, a representative of the Strand Theater, and members of the Whitehurst organization, which operated four large downtown theaters, were among the speakers in support of the bill. It was predicted that the Iverson bill would be reported favorably by members of the committee. Sensing that perhaps they had taken too weak a stand, the exhibitors reversed themselves and in March, with only Durkee and Julius Goodman, of the Ideal Theater, opposed, they voted in favor of supporting the Sunday opening bill. Ironically, at the same time the churches were benefiting by giving untaxed moving picture exhibitions that did not require licenses. This practice was the object of constant complaints of unfair competition by the exhibitors.[31]

Rival organizations arrayed themselves on different sides of the bill. The Lord's Day Alliance was opposed to it while the Liberty Defense League of Maryland was in favor of the bill. The Alliance charged that the opening of moving-picture theaters on Sunday would destroy the Christian religion. Nevertheless, the bill was passed and signed by Governor Ritchie in April 1920. Plans were made to put the question on the Baltimore City ballot in the fall. In the summer of 1920, the Lord's Day Alliance petitioned the Superior Court for a writ of mandamus forbidding the Supervisors of Elections from printing, on the official ballot, the question whether moving picture theaters should be open on Sunday.

An opinion by Superior Court Judge Morris A. Soper to allow the referendum was reversed by the Maryland Court of Appeals in October. The Court of Appeals declared the referendum unconstitutional; the people of Baltimore were denied the right to vote on Sunday movies. In an editorial in its October 18, 1920 issue, the *Sun* opined that there was not much popular "lamentation over the [court's] decision" and that it was not a great loss to the community in the matter of recreation. Nevertheless, the editor believed that the referendum would have been difficult to defeat because it had the support of "thousands of respectable voters" and regretted that the court had denied Marylanders the right to decide on the Sunday movie matter.

Shocked theater managers refused to make any comments. In a letter to the *Sun*, George Iverson, who had authored the bill, said that he believed the Court's decision showed that either the court was lax in its duty or it was being subjected to political pressure to delay the decision to keep the question off the ballot. Many Baltimoreans felt that the city was a "cheerless and dead town" on Sundays.

The rest of the week, Baltimore was a more exciting city. Vaudeville and films were offered at the Hippodrome, Garden, Victoria, and Maryland, while movies were playing at 112 theaters all over the city. The Gayety and the Palace were presenting burlesque, and dancing on the Garden roof was very popular. General admission to the ballroom was 15 cents, but it cost men 25 cents for admission to the dancing floor. Ladies were admitted free. Vaudeville at the Garden cost 10, 20, or 30 cents. A typical show there was the Black and White Review, which played during the week of October 3, 1915. It consisted of Cardo & Noll (comic opera stars), the 5 Musical Lundts (a high-class instrumental act), Col. Jack George (the William Jennings Bryan of Ethiopian oratory), Capt. Kidder & Company (in a short play), Earl & Bartlett (songs, chatter, and nonsense), and a film, *The Lingerie Shop*. Many of the movie theaters were still charging 5 cents for admission, but prices were on their way up. Some had already raised their prices to 10 cents.

By early 1915, the local projectionists' union had more than 100 members and had moved its headquarters into larger quarters on the second floor of the Gayety Theater building. Among prominent members were Sam Isaacson, Nelson Baldwin, Otto Niquet, John Bedford, Arthur Stewart and George "Bunny" Gregory. When a new contract was not being negotiated, the major event of the year for the projectionists was their annual ball. The first one was held in 1910. More than 3,000 people attended the ball at the Lyric Theater in November 1916. There was no ball in 1917, but one was held at Hazazer's Hall, on Franklin Street, in November 1919. A 40th Anniversary Ball was held at the Southern Hotel in May 1949.

There was a close relationship between the Baltimore local and Local 224 in Washington. Both had been organized around the same time and for many years they got together for baseball games[32] and attended each other's dances. Based on the correspondence exchanged between the presidents of the two unions, these affairs could sometimes become unruly. Sam Isaacson, the business agent for the Baltimore local, wrote to B. A. Spellbring of the Washington local in January 1914: "Just a few lines to remind you of our Fourth Annual Ball next Monday night. We want to see that bunch of twenty-five *gentlemen* that I hear you're going to bring over. We don't care if you bring a hundred as we don't fear your bunch and we *know* we can take care of them drunk or sober.... I am sending you twenty-five tickets ... as the law here won't allow anyone to enter the hall without a ticket and we want your bunch inside. Trusting to see you and your champions? next Monday...."

In the fall of 1915 the projectionists asked for a raise of $2.00 for a six-day week. The Baltimore exhibitors agreed and were praised as being liberal and progressive. The new contract also called for $1.50 per week for carrying reels one way or $2.50 per week for carrying them both ways. Overtime was 50 cents per hour. The new contract ran until November 3, 1918. The 1918 contract, which called for a raise in the daily salary to 70 cents an hour, was also signed with little argument. Appearances of peace were deceiving; the exhibitors were running schools where they quietly trained managers to operate projectors.[33] When the projectionists found out about this they were not very happy, and they no longer thought the exhibitors were so liberal and progressive. Five graduates from the exhibitors' school had received licenses by the time the matter was taken up by the state licensing board in the spring of 1919.

The licensing of managers continued to be a perennial thorn for the board throughout the 1920s. The dreaded word "strike" was whispered in the fall of 1920 when the projectionists asked for another raise, of 20 cents an hour, which would increase the average projectionist's wages from $45 a week to $55. The exhibitors formed a committee, under the chairmanship of Frank Durkee, to investigate the matter and advertised for all men who could operate projectors to attend a meeting on October 25. The following day the exhibitors' spokesman, Thomas Goldberg, said that there was a deadlock in negotiations—the projectionists wanted 90 cents an hour and the exhibitors were only willing to pay 80 cents. Goldberg said that the managers would run the theaters without union projectionists unless an agreement were reached within a week. In less than 24 hours a compromise was reached which gave the projectionists 85 cents an hour, and a strike was averted.

One of the most controversial movies of all time, *Birth of a Nation*, arrived in town in 1916. D. W. Griffith's film had nationwide repercussions that have lasted more than 80 years. It opened at the Liberty Theater in New York in March 1915, the first movie to cost $2 a seat. It reached Baltimore's Ford's Theater a year later, on March 6, 1916.[34]

> Before an audience which packed the house ... and which rocked with applause and hisses throughout the ... performance, the long-waited-for-film drama ..."Birth of a Nation," was presented for the first time in Baltimore at Ford's Opera House ... and opened the eyes of the beholders to what powerful wonders rest within the grasp of the "movies."
> To call "The Birth of a Nation" a drama is to belittle it, for the film production is a folio of dramas which unfolds in quick succession the most dramatic and most fearful periods of the country's history — the Civil War and the following crucifixion of the South in the era of the carpetbaggers. The story is taken from Thomas Dixon's novel, "The Clansman," with a number of changes in the original story to suit the purposes of the dramatist. In the latter half of the production the tensest situations in the problem of the South during reconstruction period are played up in a manner that kept the audience ... in a state of excitement that found outlet in bursts of applause that drowned frequently the beautiful musical setting that is given under the direction of Frederick Arundel.... Throughout the production an orchestra of 40 pieces supplies a remarkably beautiful and powerful accompaniment, the music of which is written by Joseph Carl Briel.[35]

The ad in the *Sun* for *The Birth of a Nation* took up nearly half a page; the film was called "D. W. Griffith's Eighth Wonder of the World." There were two shows a day, at 2:15 and 8:15. The ad warned that *The Birth of a Nation* would only be shown in the highest-class theaters at prices charged for the best theatrical attractions "and will positively not be shown in any other place in this vicinity this season." Matinee tickets cost 25 cents, 50 cents, 75 cents, and $1.00; for the evening show $1.50 and $2.00 seats were added.

Sound effects and music contributed a great deal to the impact of this film; the *Sun* of March 12, 1916 speaks of "the emotional appeal of the music and the cunning art of the mechanical effects." Among the mechanical effects were the use of coconut halves beaten on bricks to simulate horses' hoofs, wagon wheels mounted on axles to create the sound of wagons rolling along a road, sheets of deer skin stretched tightly over large frames that were struck with mallets to produce the sounds of distant artillery, and sticks that were snapped when characters in the film walked through the woods. This movie has brought controversy with it from the time it opened to 1998 when it was included in the American Film Institute's list of the 100 greatest American movies.[36]

According to film historian Garth Jowett, "[*The Birth of a Nation*] ... was a benchmark, not only in the development of American cinematic art, but also in the public acknowledgment of the motion picture as an important influence on American society and culture."[37] Wherever it was shown there was controversy. When it opened in Boston, in April 1915, hundreds of African Americans tried to break up the performance, and more than 200 police were needed to restore order. Much of the opposition to the movie was due to Griffith's stereotyping of African Americans. There was fear among many groups that the strong emotional impact of Griffith's images would undo years of civil rights work. The National Association for the Advancement of Colored people declared that it would mount a campaign to have the film either censored or stopped.

The reviewer in the *Evening Sun* was struck by the emotional impact of the film and confirmed the still strong Southern sympathies of Baltimore audiences. "While the pictures in the second half of the drama, in which the injustice which the Northern carpetbaggers did to the Southern whites will grip some who see the film with the greater dramatic power, the first scenes moved the audience mightily last night.... As the files of soldiers rode down the crowded streets with banners flying, the orchestra played *Dixie* and the crowd present showed that it was Southern by applauding wildly. There followed such scenes of battle as have seldom, if ever, been equaled in Baltimore."[38]

The *Afro-American* gave the film grudging praise for artistic merits but condemned the story, "Nearly everyone who sees the photo-play Birth of a Nation ... comes away with the conviction of Francis Hackett 'As a spectacle it is stupendous.' It lasts three hours, represents an immense investment of pains and money in the setting of whole battle scenes upon the canvas and compels an admiration by its very bigness. While on the one hand the play receives universal commendation as a production, on the other hand it receives universal condemnation as a 'vicious play with vicious methods.'"[39]

The same editorial criticized Ford's Theater for showing the film. "Ford's Theatre for many years has been looked upon as ... about the fairest theatre in Baltimore in its treatment of colored people, and at times they have been given privileges there which have not obtained in other quarters. In consequence of which it enjoyed perhaps the largest patronage of any theatre in Baltimore. Just for what reason ... it has allowed the most despicable play in the country to be staged on its boards is probably best known to itself." The editorial went on to suggest that every self-respecting African American in Baltimore should stay away from Ford's in the future.

Despite the criticism, *The Birth of a Nation* played to record audiences. The first four days, Ford's grossed $10,102.75 in seven shows. Due to contractual restrictions, the film could not be shown in any other Baltimore theater, but it returned to Ford's in early 1917 and grossed $8,947 over two weeks.[40] Beginning in 1923, it was revived several times. The Lyceum revived it at popular prices— 25 cents, 50 cents and 75 cents— on a reserved seat basis in May 1923; it played two weeks to large crowds. The 1958 showing at the Cameo Theater did not seem to arouse much interest, although the executive secretary of the Maryland Commission on Interracial Problems and Relations condemned it and asked that the exhibition be canceled.[41]

"It shall be unlawful to sell, lease, lend, exhibit, or use any motion picture film, reel or view, in the State of Maryland, unless the said film, reel or view has been submitted by the exchange, owner or lessee of the film, reel or view and duly approved by the Maryland State Board of Censors...."[42] This was the key section of the Maryland censorship law that went into effect on June 1, 1916. Prior to the establishment of a state censor board, the censoring of movies was a police matter.[43] It was the duty of the Police Department, at least as early as 1908, to report whether any improper movies were being shown. But this duty seems to have been imperfectly done, at best. Police began censoring live performances as well as movies at Baltimore theaters around the end of 1908. A police sergeant watched each initial performance, and if he disapproved, he would report it to headquarters. A theater manager had the right to object and present his opinion. When questioned about the qualifications of the police to act as theatrical censors, the president of the Police Board said, 'I consider the men of the Baltimore police force an especially intelligent body."[44]

When the Baltimore Marshal of Police, Thomas F. Farnan, ordered his men back into the theaters in September 1909, he told them that "he wanted to uphold the good morals of the community by keeping out all plays that were unfit for the wife or daughter or sweetheart."[45] Marshal Farnan asserted in June 1911 that he had frequently ordered the patrolmen working in areas where there were movie houses to act as censors and order the proprietors of the theaters showing suggestive pictures to stop showing them. The guideline given to a patrolman was to decide if he would let his own children see the movie.

Detectives, functioning as censors, were assigned theaters in their district to check every night.

A *Sun* editorial on June 8, 1911, called for a different censoring authority, saying that the policemen were generally too busy with other duties to attend to the censoring of movies and that they were "not chosen with respect to their discriminating taste and judgment in matters of art and morals."[46] To answer this, Marshal Farnan appointed the entire city to act as censors. Anyone could report an offensive movie by letter or telephone. He added an extra operator at police headquarters to take the calls. According to *Moving Picture World* there was no rush to phone, and not a single complaint was registered. The magazine went on to suggest that because of the lack of interest, local reporters had to write their own letters to the editor.[47] Exhibitor J. Howard Bennett, speaking just before the exhibitors' convention in 1913, said that policewomen were doing a good job as film censors. However, sometimes the movies were so bad that even presumably tough-skinned policewomen shrank from testifying with men present. Two of the three policewomen who witnessed a showing of *The Theft of the Secret Service Code* at Lubin's Theater were unable to testify and "shrank before the gaze of the many men" in Central Police Court. The third witness, Policewoman Eagleston, was made of sterner stuff. She "took the stand and defied the grinning males to 'rattle' her. She told a clear story, going into all the details, telling of the dancing and high kicking, etc. of the characters depicted on the film."[48]

The call for censoring films followed the rapid expansion of nickelodeons after 1908.

No one felt it necessary to censor newsreels and films showing the workings of factories, but as soon as movies that told stories appeared, there were people who objected to the stories and the way they were told. Partisans felt very strongly about censorship, and the pages of Baltimore newspapers of that time are filled with letters, pro and con, about it. Two major proponents of censorship were the church and women's clubs. Their main concern was the effect of movies on children.

One of the earliest attempts to establish a censor board in Baltimore was made in 1910 by J. Spencer Clarke, Collector of Water Rents and Licenses. Clarke proposed a six-member board composed of the mayor, the collector of water rents and licenses, the president of the Maryland Society for the Protection of Children and three other "upright and capable citizens." The board would be responsible for approving all films before they were exhibited to the public, and would have general supervision over all "performances, theatrical, dramatic, operatic or otherwise, plays, farces, exhibitions and other public amusement."[49] Clarke's ordinance was not adopted.

A 1910 editorial in the *Sun* reporting on the recent appointment in Frederick, Maryland, of a committee of ladies to formulate plans for the censorship of moving picture shows stated the editor's belief that "women are well qualified for this work, and it is a work that ought to be done. There is a craze among children to see the moving pictures and they resort to them in great numbers. It is therefore of the utmost importance that the exhibitions be kept clean and decent."[50] A collection of various groups[51] met in November 1910 to plan a campaign to elevate the moral tone of all the picture shows. They hoped to see one day a week set aside, preferably a Saturday, when only films approved by a committee of censors would be shown. At least one local exhibitor endorsed the idea.

There was a flurry of activity for censorship in Baltimore in 1911, reaching its peak that June. The Maryland Society to Protect Children from Cruelty and Immorality, at its annual meeting in 1911, urged the creation of a City censor board. The Photo Players of Baltimore pledged full cooperation with the plan, but several local exhibitors were opposed. William Fait, who managed five movie theaters, opposed a censor board; he believed managers were the best censors and thought it would be "pretty hard ... for any man or woman, or body of men and women to censor pictures for 600,000 Baltimoreans."[52] On the other hand, Charles Whitehurst said he would support a censor board.

Two months later, an editorial in the *Sun*, while stopping short of calling for censorship, said that "if those who manage [movie theaters] refuse to conduct them along decent lines they should be summarily suppressed."[53] Within three days of this editorial, the *Sun* printed a much stronger editorial advocating the passage of an ordinance for proper censorship. The paper again cited the danger movies posed for children, but also added their danger to the minds of "the untutored." It is hard to read all of these calls for censorship and not see them, at least partially, as an elitist or social class action.

Among the scenes that aroused the need for censorship in one writer at this time were the following: the attempted assault by a Russian landowner on a peasant's wife, a French ballet scene of "a most pronounced type," a trysting scene between a so-called lover and two sweethearts, and an employer slyly exhibiting to his employee's wife "a piece of nude statuary of a most vulgar character."[54] Sensational exploitation was also frowned on. In April 1912, Marshal Farnan considered banning movies "purporting to be of the Titanic disaster."

The *Sun*, in a long 1911 editorial, admitted many benefits of the movies, that they were easily affordable for even the poorest citizens and that they could be powerful educational tools for young people, but it warned that movies should be wholesome.[55] In a second editorial in June 1911, the *Sun* wrote that "The motion pictures are for the most part innocent and enjoyable and in many instances are educational as well, and it should be the endeavor of the governing bodies of communities to keep them so by refusing to allow the display of those that are false, suggestive and degrading."[56]

The Baltimore Association of Jewish Women adopted a resolution advocating censorship of movies in March 1912; the following month, a number of organizations and state political figures endorsed plans for film censorship. The *Sun* believed that public sentiment for film censoring was "growing more determined every day" and that it was only a matter of time before we had censorship. Following a meeting in early May, there was nearly unanimous agreement among the exhibitors that all films should be censored before being exhibited in the city. Tom Bohannon, of the Wizard theaters, said that he did not believe a single picture man in Baltimore would object to censorship if the manufacturers would send them the films earlier to be inspected.[57] Councilman Harry C. Kilmer, of the 15th Ward, introduced an ordinance in May 1912 which provided for the appointment of a five-member censor board, but that measure failed.

By 1915, the *Sun* was still calling for some form of film censorship. In an editorial this newspaper wrote, "...there can be no doubt that many of the moving-picture theatres could be subjected to censorship with advantage to the public."[58] At last, in February 1916, Delegate Howard Bryant of Baltimore County introduced a bill calling for the establishment of a State board of censors for moving pictures. The possibility of a state censor board had been buoyed by a Supreme Court decision in February 1915.[59] Bryant's Committee on Ways and Means held a session on February 17 that was attended by a large delegation of motion picture men. Guy Wonders, the president of the Exhibitors' League of Maryland; J. W. Binder, of the Motion Picture Board of Trade; Fulton Brylawski, a Washington lawyer[60]; Paul Cromelin, of the Cosmofoto Film Company; and W. Stephen Bush, of the *Moving Picture World*, spoke against the bill. Despite the spirited and often eloquent testimony of the movie men and others who opposed censorship and several attempts to weaken it, the Bryant Bill passed.[61]

There was also activity in Congress to establish Federal censorship of motion pictures in 1916.[62] Before the Maryland law was passed there had been dark rumors of a $15,000 fund set up by opponents to defeat it. If true, $15,000 was not enough. The *Sun* expressed the hope that the governor would appoint "intelligent and well-qualified" censors and not "prudes, fools or knaves." At least "one, if not two, educated women ... women who have children of their own" should be on the board according to the paper.[63] The *News* was against the bill, opining that the establishment of a state censor board seemed to be "a scheme to give someone a job" rather than "because there is some general feeling that such a measure is necessary." The *News* felt that the Police Board was qualified to carry out ordinary censorship of films and plays.[64]

Maryland established the Maryland State Board of Censors in the spring of 1916. It consisted of three members appointed to three-year terms by the governor. Governor Harrington appointed the first members of the Board of Censors at the end of May 1916. They were: William F. Stone, a Republican from Baltimore; Mrs. Thomas B. Harrison, a Democrat; and Charles E. Harper, the former mayor of Salisbury, also a Democrat. Each member received a yearly salary of $2,400. The job of the board was to examine all films to be exhibited in the state and approve those which were "moral and proper" and disapprove the ones that were "sacrilegious, obscene, indecent, or immoral."

Every film approved by the board received a certificate that it had been "Approved by the Maryland State Board of Censors." If the board ordered an elimination of any part of a film or disapproved any film, the exhibitor could appeal to the Baltimore City Court. In July 1916, the board set up its offices at 204 East Lexington Street and went to work.[65] During its first year, the board took in $23,316 in fees and other income and spent $22,722. Fines totaling $50 were levied for violations during that year. Among those fined were the Clover Theater ($25) for showing the film *Race Suicide* without making the board-ordered eliminations; the Strand Theater was fined ($5) for showing the film *Love Dope* without submitting it to the board first.

Initially, the board worked from 9 A.M. to 3 P.M. and only one member reviewed a film. That member could either approve or reject the film. If it was rejected, the exhibitor could request a second screening in the presence of two members of the board whose decision was final. The board also had supervision over posters displayed outside movie houses, and an inspector was detailed to check on all the advertising material used for the films. If an elimination was made in the movie, any posters showing the eliminated material had to be scrapped also. When sound movies first appeared, the censor board was momentarily stymied because they did not have the proper kind of projector to reproduce sound, but in August 1929, a new $7,000 projection system that could handle both types of sound films was installed. The censor board then assumed the power to censor the dialog in talking movies. Film companies believed that the dialog could not be censored and in some states, notably Pennsylvania, they filed suits to prevent the sound portions of movies from being censored.[66] In Maryland, there was no protest from the exhibitors, and the censor board reviewed the dialog, too.

For years after the censor board was created, it had to test the limits of its jurisdiction. It took many years and numerous court cases to establish the board's powers. Sometimes that power was exercised with a heavy hand. One early case, described as a test case by an assistant state's attorney, took place at the Little Pickwick Theater on Lexington Street in 1917.

> Irvine and Jack Levine, managers of the Little Pickwick theater, 312 West Lexington street, booked "Purity" ... for a two day run. The film was screened peacefully on Wednesday, Jan. 17, but on Friday Mrs. T. B. Harrison of the Censor Board, went into the theater in the afternoon, viewed the picture and then walked out perfectly "mum." At 6 p.m. she returned accompanied by a police sergeant and asked to see the manager. Jack Levine presented himself and Mrs. Harrison, it is reported, stated that certain parts were in the picture that had previously been eliminated, and requested that they be cut. "All right," said Mr. Levine, "I will very gladly cut out anything that is in the film that you order eliminated; but as this picture bears the seal of the Maryland Censor Board, I understood that it was all right to be shown." The required eliminations were made and Mrs. Harrison took possession of the film, about 200 feet, then without any warning, but it is thought a nod from Mrs. Harrison was the signal, the police officer presented Mr. Levine with a warrant.[67]

The Levines were fined $2.50 each. In 1917, the Maryland Attorney General ruled that exhibitors who violated the censor law were not entitled to jury trials and only had the right to appeal if their fines exceeded $50.

Perhaps no subject, not even Sunday movies, has so inflamed critics of movies as much as the showing of films that they believe are offensive or obscene. There have been more articles, letters, and editorials to the Baltimore newspapers on censorship than on any other aspect of motion pictures.[68] Some people thought that the censors were ineffective; they wanted a lot more censoring. Before the censor board had completed its first year, a coalition of women's groups—including the DAR, the Mothers' Congress, and the Child Welfare League—complained that immoral films were still being shown in Baltimore. When one of the women was asked to tell the board about the dozen "immoral" pictures she had seen, she said that she did not remember any except one, "and she had never seen anything so horrible as that."[69]

In 1917 the Rev. Clifford Twombley blasted movies, saying that "Thirty to fifty percent of the films of today deal with marital infidelity, illicit love, immorality and lust. Fifteen to twenty percent have realistic murders and suicides, and twenty to thirty percent show robberies, thieving, kidnapping, blackmailing, poisoning, gambling, etc." He believed that the country had to be aroused to the dangers of moving pictures, "a great menace to the morals of the young people of the nation and to the purity of the American home."[70]

Faced with this criticism, the censor board declared that it would not run under fire. Since most of the objections were about movies that the critics believed were unfit for children, the censors suggested that it was the responsibility of parents to control their children's movie going. Governor Harrington supported the censors.

Women's clubs and church groups opposed the censor board because they thought it was not doing enough; movie men opposed it because it was there. The Maryland Exhibitors' League launched an attack in 1918 to have the film censor law repealed. The campaign was led by Frank Hornig, Lou DeHoff and Jack S. Connolly. The exhibitors believed that the law was unpopular and that it had not become a major source of revenue for the state. They said that the censor law gave a small group of individuals the opportunity to pass on the views and tastes of the community without any public comment. They pointed out that Rudolph Valentino's hit movie *The Sheik*— eagerly anticipated as a "particularly 'peppy' picture"— was heavily censored when it came to Maryland; as soon as the public learned this, business trailed off at the Century Theater where it was being shown.

The exhibitors tried hard to have the censorship law repealed, but to no avail. In 1922, in response to the censor board's request for more power, the *Evening Sun*, which had opposed censorship for several years, editorialized that given the power it was asking for—the right to limit approval to films which were "moral and proper"—it would be impossible to show film versions of many Biblical stories in Maryland.[71] A writer to the *Evening Sun* in 1929 would have liked a lot more censoring: "I was shocked when I visited a local movie house last week. The picture was one of the modern type, which showed degraded youth at its worst. In this picture ... was shown a young woman smoking and also imbibing alcoholic liquors. A more degrading spectacle could never be shown.... To my way of thinking, both the producer of this picture and the Maryland State Board of Censors should be thrown in jail."[72]

Movies were not the only form of entertainment to be censored. The newspapers are filled with articles about chorus girls, exotic dancers, and burlesque stars being arrested for showing too much bare skin or doing dances that were deemed just a bit too suggestive. In 1922, Acting Marshal of Police Henry issued an order that prohibited "the appearance before the footlights or on the boards of the theatres of Baltimore of a single dimpled knee or a solitary shiny shin."[73] The Clover Theater on the Block seemed to have more than its share of run-ins with the law over its live shows. In June 1926, a vaudeville act, called "The Rescue of the Princess," described in theatrical parlance of the day as a "wow," was stopped by police, who entered the theater and tersely announced, "The company's pinched." The manager and the performers were fined $11.45 each. In addition to performing what the police magistrate called a "vulgar show," policemen testified that the actors used bad grammar. In 1934 the police arrested 22 men and four women for participating in and attending a show called "The Dance of the Ancient Nile."[74] A lawyer representing the theater told the judge, "On East Baltimore Street they call this dance the hoochie-coochie, but everywhere else they call it art." The judge disagreed and fined the offenders.

In the beginning, the First World War seemed to affect movies in Maryland only slightly. We were slow to take sides. Many local families had relatives in Europe, on both sides. One night in the spring of 1915, as janitor Fritz Nowak sat in the Academy of Music watching movies of the fighting, he was startled to recognize his brother, Adolph, among a group of German soldiers in a recently captured French village. Nowak told the manager, who cut out the frames of film with Nowak's brother in them and got them enlarged for him. In August 1916, Capt. Koenig and the crew of the German submarine *Deutschland* were royally entertained at the Garden Theater on Lexington Street as guests of the manager, George Schneider. After "The Star Spangled Banner" was played, the orchestra struck up "Die Wacht Am Rhein." Movies of the war in Europe were very popular; one called *War as It Really Is*, made under the direction of General Joffre, was shown at the Lyric in June 1917.

Once we entered the war, many theaters held benefits for local military units, and the movie industry helped to sell bonds. In October 1917, the Parkway held benefits for the Welfare Association of the 117th Mortar Battery that provided comforts such as tobacco, candy, sweaters and mufflers to the soldiers in the battery. Manager Guy Wonders of the Wilson placed a large fish bowl in the lobby of his theater; male patrons were encouraged to "drop in a cigarette for our boys at the front" or to drop in a penny if they did not have a cigarette. In November 1917, the New, Walbrook, Broadway, Horn, and Royal theaters held patriotic entertainments. Albaugh's Theater held a benefit for First Company, Maryland Coast Artillery Corps. Numerous rallies were held at theaters to benefit local military units returning from Europe.

Free rallies were held in May 1919 at 11 theaters all over town plus theaters in Catonsville and Ellicott City, to benefit the men of the 313th Regiment. A benefit for the 115th Infantry Regiment occurred that same month at the Auditorium. Dozens of other theaters, including the Rialto, Linwood, Brodie, and Gertrude McCoy, produced benefits for American soldiers. In 1921 Charles Whitehurst hosted a benefit at his New Theater to raise funds to maintain the home for disabled soldiers at Bentley Springs.

In January 1918, a man applauded a picture of the Kaiser in Ben Cluster's Family Theater on South Broadway. The disturbance he created resulted in his being locked up for disorderly conduct. We had finally figured out which side we were on. A fuel crisis in early 1918 forced theaters and other places of amusement to close down one day a week between January 22 and February 17.[75] Even the Maryland Theater, which was heated using "surplus" heat from the private power plant that heated the Hotel Kernan, had to close on those days. This arrangement caused many problems for the exhibitors, including the loss of a whole day's receipts each week and the need to rearrange their bookings.

In April 1918, a series of patriotic meetings in support of the Third Liberty Loan was held at the Bridge, Blue Bell, Crown, Fairyland, Pacy's Garden, Hampden, and West End. In the intensive drive to reach Maryland's War Savings quota of $28 million, the managers of the major downtown theaters and dozens of actors, actresses and vaudeville acts volunteered their services in June 1918. Lou DeHoff, manager of the Garden, in August 1918 hired Tobias Yarnith to impersonate the Kaiser in an advertising stunt. Yarnith, dressed in an imperial costume with a "haughtily curled mustache," was driven through the streets imprisoned in a cage guarded by Uncle Sam to advertise the movie *Four Years in Germany*. Unfortunately for Yarnith, the director of the Maryland Compulsory Work Bureau learned of his job and had him taken to court, where he was ordered to get a regular job. He was still wearing his Kaiser costume when he appeared in Central Police Court. The magistrate gave him a month to find work.

In the campaign for the Fourth Liberty Loan, just before the end of the war, Baltimore theaters sold $65,000 worth of Liberty bonds in one evening. The breakdown for the various theaters showed that the Maryland, with popular Keith's vaudeville, sold the most.

Maryland	$21,550	Folly	$2,100
Auditorium	$13,800	New	$1,500
Hippodrome	$8,700	Ford's	$1,200
Palace (Fayette Street)	$7,400	Victoria	$950
Academy of Music	$3,700	Garden (Lexington Street)	$750
Gayety	$2,700	Colonial (Eutaw Street)	$200

It was not only to help U.S. soldiers in the trenches that movie theaters raised money. A number of local theaters — including the Parkway, New Pickwick, Goldberg, Wilson, Eureka, Bridge, Idle Hour, and Brodie — donated all the money they took in between 5 and 7 P.M. on June 30, 1916, to the Fresh Air Society. In February 1917, Myer Fox, president of the Linden Company, entertained several hundred orphans at the Rialto Theater. Twice during March 1917, the Victoria Theater held a "Vegetable Matinee." Several thousand customers brought a vegetable which admitted them to the theater; the vegetables collected were donated to the Federated Charities of Baltimore. The New Theater offered rooms to military recruiters in April 1917. At the same time, Thomas Goldberg entertained crippled children from the Kernan Hospital at his North Avenue theater. In January 1918, a benefit held at the Victoria Theater by the Amalgamated Clothing Workers of America, to aid Jewish families displaced by the war, raised $15,000. The Hippodrome, Grand (Highlandtown), and the Lincoln Highway theaters raised money in the summer of 1919 for the St. Mary's Industrial School rebuilding fund.

Several times, during the late teens, theaters had to close because of epidemics of whooping cough and scarlet fever. An infantile paralysis epidemic broke out on the East Coast in the summer of 1916. That August, the Baltimore Health Commissioner issued an order prohibiting children under age 13 (later modified to children under age 9) from attending all indoor exhibition places in the city, including moving picture theaters. Originally the ban was to exclude children under age 16 only from movie theaters, but the exhibitors protested, and the ban was modified to include legitimate theaters. The ban lasted until the end of October. Two years later, a much worse epidemic hit.

It was romantically called "The Spanish Lady," but there was nothing romantic about it. It killed an estimated 21 million people worldwide.[76] It was the great influenza pandemic of 1918-1919. In the fall of 1918, just as the First World War was grinding to a close, it struck. One of the earliest local notices of the epidemic was in mid–September. An *Evening Sun* article offered the opinion that "Spanish sneeze disease isn't one to be trifled with."[77] There were only 25 reported cases in the United States at that time, and the government was trying to identify sick soldiers returning from Europe and quarantine them on board ships and in military hospitals. The disease was said to be a more dangerous form of the grippe that often led to pneumonia. A newspaper article said, "It is short-lived, and though it causes great discomfort for a while, leaves no ill effects to those who recover."[78] But great numbers of people did not recover.

By the 19th of September, concern was growing. Passengers from ships coming in to East Coast and Great Lakes ports were being examined by physicians. One high-ranking doctor suggested that the Germans could have started the disease by landing agents in submarines and turning the germs loose in a theater. By September 23, 4,500 sailors at the Great Lakes Training Station had influenza. In Maryland, the flu appeared at Camp Meade, Camp Holabird, and the Curtis Bay Ordnance Depot; 100 sick soldiers were sent to the hospital at Fort McHenry. Dr. John D. Blake, the Baltimore City Health Commissioner said there was nothing to be alarmed about, that a person suffering from the disease very seldom died.[79] Blake thought a quarantine was unnecessary. "I have no intention of adopting any quarantine measures in Baltimore, other than to ask the street car company, the moving-picture theatres and such people to be especially careful about their ventilation."[80]

Twelve suggestions to avoid the flu were published in the *Evening Sun*. Among them were: avoid needless crowding, smother coughs and sneezes, don't breathe through your mouth, keep cool when you walk and warm when you sleep, open windows, wash hands before eating, avoid tight clothing, and breathe all the pure air you can get. On September 24, 1,800 soldiers at Camp Dix, New Jersey, were reported flu victims.

The flu was raging in New England. In Boston, 100 people had died of the flu, and the public schools were closed. In spite of the rapid spread and high death rates in other areas, medical authorities in Baltimore were still unwilling to take measures that could have saved many lives. The population was urged to be "sensible" and not panic, to just go to bed at the first sign of the flu and call a doctor.[81] Between September 24 and 25, the number of cases of flu at Camp Meade tripled; more than 1,000 soldiers were ill. Some slight efforts at quarantining the military camps were made, and nurses and doctors were wearing masks to protect themselves from contagion. Elsewhere in Maryland, there were 2,921 cases of the influenza by the beginning of October; theaters at Camp Meade and Sparrows Point had been closed, and Baltimore theaters were set to close.

> ...the theatres of Baltimore may be closed if the number of cases of influenza ... in that city spread to a more alarming degree and warrant that action being taken by the Health Department due to it becoming an epidemic. The Liberty Theatre, at Camp Meade ... was ordered closed ... on ... September 25. No entertainments or festivities are being allowed. Two theatres at Sparrows Point, Md. ... were ordered closed on ... October 2. The public school at Sparrows Point was also ordered closed by the Baltimore County Health Commissioners. At the present writing forty-eight deaths have occurred in twenty-four hours, 900 new cases have been reported, the total in the city and state being 2,921. Camp Meade's total has been brought up to 6,300. A general conference was scheduled ... on ... October 4, and definite action by the Health Department officials and medical men will be determined upon.[82]

In Baltimore, during the week of October 7, there were 533 deaths from influenza. Many other cities were hit as hard as Baltimore. Louisville closed everything but the saloons; every theater in Atlanta was closed. Many theater owners used the time when their theaters were closed to carry out repairs and renovation. The epidemic peaked in October; things got so bad that even the churches in Baltimore were ordered closed on Sunday, October 13. The death tolls were nearly as bad as the war; 3,500 dead in Washington and 3,414 dead in Baltimore. Among the dead in Baltimore were four projectionists, John Reid of the Red Moon and the Patterson, Elmer Clark of the Peabody, Frank Lewis of the Victoria and David Seaman of the Walbrook. The local film exchanges offered to begin new bookings at the point they left off so that there would be less loss to exhibitors.

Beginning on October 28, Baltimore allowed limited opening of theaters between 7:30 P.M. and 11:30 P.M. The following day, the hours of opening were changed to between 6:30 and 10:30. Restrictions on theaters were also lifted in Elkton, Federalsburg, Cambridge, Easton, Cumberland, and Annapolis. The health commissioner banned smoking and spitting on the floors in theaters, one of the few positive results of the plague. By the beginning of November, the worst was over. All restrictions on Baltimore theaters were lifted on November 2. Washington theaters reopened on November 4.

On November 11, 1918, thousands of Baltimoreans took to the streets, delirious over the ending of the war. Governor Harrington declared a state holiday beginning at noon. Before daylight, church bells began to ring and factory whistles shrieked to announce the armistice. Schools and department stores closed; the courts and the Stock Exchange closed. There were impromptu parades everywhere.

One of the major problems faced by legitimate theaters as well as movie theaters was attracting audiences during the summer months. Despite banks of fans mounted on the walls, the temperatures in theaters could become unpleasant during the summer. In 1895, Charles E. Ford, who was running Ford's Theater, said that "the public will not sit in a close, warm theater on a hot night to see any theatrical show ... Almost everybody preferred to ride about and keep cool on open trolley cars...." Most legitimate theaters closed down between May and September. The bigger legitimate and vaudeville houses could afford to close, but the little movie theaters could not. Many attempts were made to cool and ventilate the theaters. By the late teens, a local film correspondent could glibly report that Baltimore movie theaters were...

PLEASANT ALL THE TIME

Just as soon as the first hot spell strikes us at the beginning of summer the moving-picture theatres suffer from decreased patronage. From all sections of the city the report is made that "business is rotten." And then let a cool night come along and the place is jammed with people.... Some ... say that it is caused by the people taking trips out into the country or to the shores. Some expect a falling off of business during the summer months. But what all do know and realize is that in the majority of moving-pictures [sic] theatres the atmosphere on hot summer days is from 20 to 30 degrees cooler than the outside temperature.

The reason that this condition of coolness can be guaranteed is that the moving-picture theatres are built upon lines that guarantee the best ventilation. No sooner hot weather begins than up go the 15-inch diameter oscillating fans, 8 or 12 of them; the huge rotary exhaust fans located in the roof of the theatres are set to work and a current of air is kept in circulation during the whole time that there are people in the theatre.

> Not only do the theatres have this method of keeping the interior of the theatre cool, but some of them are equipped with air-cooling systems so that before the current of air is forced into the theatre it is forced through an ice-cooling system and goes into the theatre a current of air that is cold.
>
> Of course, if the theatre that does not actually have a cool atmosphere ... advertises that it does, this ... tends to make people skeptical. But it was just the other day that we watched a ventilating system tried out and it was proved that the air was 20 degrees cooler inside than outside....
>
> When the public realizes that this condition exists it will attend the moving pictures just as much in the summer as in the winter. And when it is realized that the amusement offered will tend to take one's mind off the heat, as well as having artificial means of coolness, it will be found that the majority of the moving-pictures are pleasant all the time.[83]

"Pleasant" is certainly not the first word that comes to mind to describe an auditorium during a typical Baltimore summer before air-conditioning. Some theaters made valiant attempts to remain open during the sultry summer months, but many were forced to close. Other forms of amusement were more appealing and cooler. Norman Clark, writing in 1921, summed up the pre-air conditioning cooling methods, "Fans, whirling ventilators, ice water and so on are all right, but, boy, when a theatre seat gets warm, it's warm!"[84]

During a hot spell in 1916, 27 Baltimore theaters were forced to close. Theater owners tried everything, from giant Monsoon exhaust fans mounted on the roofs to rooms filled with ice to cool the air circulated through the theater. In the 19th century, before electric fans, theater patrons were sold hand fans—similar to those formerly found in many churches—along with a program. An article from 1909 suggested that the small fans along the walls were of more psychological than practical value. "Many of the theaters have in the past installed fans of the ordinary disc or 'buzz' fan type for use in hot weather, but such fans do not in any way improve the air in the room or make the place any cooler. They simply stir up the air, and the only cooling power they have is due to the direct draft and increasing the evaporation of the perspiration from the skin...."[85]

The same article goes on to say that what was needed was a method for removing the "foul air" entirely from the auditorium and replacing it with outside air. Large fans running at 450 to 700 rpm installed at the end of the auditorium away from the entrance were suggested as the best means for ventilation. The Victoria, in 1909, advertised an "iced-air" plant with "Fans Everywhere—The Victoria Has More Fans in Service Right Now Than Any Other Theatre in Baltimore Ever Had. It's Never Too Warm in the Victoria." Under the stage of the Hippodrome one could, until recently, still see the ice room that was part of that theater's early attempt at cooling the auditorium. The room was filled with a number of 300-pound blocks of ice that were sprayed with a fine mist of water to cool down the air. This created a cool fog that was then circulated throughout the theater. The Garden had the same kind of system that required at least two truckloads of 300-pound blocks of ice every day. Very early, theaters realized the appeal of ads for "pure" and "fresh" air. The New Pickwick in 1913 boasted that it was "ventilated by pure, fresh air not perfumed foul air." The reference to "perfume" was to the practice of spraying perfume throughout the theater to "freshen" the air.[86] The New Theater installed a "new refrigerating plant" in the summer of 1916 and, according to *Moving Picture World* (July 1, 1916), the patrons could "expect a polar region atmosphere when they enter the house." It would take another ten years before modern air conditioning came to town.

Theaters had always vied with each other to be the first to show a film in their area. This produced the "first-run theater." Now practically meaningless, first-run theaters were once important outlets for Hollywood product. A local film columnist explained the meaning of "first-run" in a 1920 article.

> What is a "first-run" picture? That is ... probably the most misunderstood term regarding the showing of moving pictures.... It was generally understood that seeing a picture ... advertised as "first-run" meant that you were seeing something better than usual. And it probably is understood that way by many today.
>
> When you see a "first-run" picture at a "first-run" moving-picture theatre you generally do see something a little better than usual, because then you see it before it is shown in any other theatre in that city, where it is advertised as "first-run," and generally the contract so reads that no other theatre will be allowed to run it until 30 days have elapsed after it is shown at the "first-run" theatre.
>
> When a picture is advertised as a "first-run" picture ... it does not mean that the picture is shown in that theatre before being shown any other place in the country. It simply means that it is being shown for the first time in the city where that theatre is located ... there are only about seven "first-run" theatres in Baltimore. When you take into consideration that there are about 100 producing companies always turning out pictures the fact is apparent that seven theatres cannot take care of the product of all the companies, because only seven new or "first-run" pictures can be shown during one week in Baltimore.[87]

The system of first-run downtown theaters began in the teens. The first-run theaters functioned like the legitimate theaters on Broadway in New York. They were the first places to show new films, and the reception of a new film at the first-run theaters had a great influence not only on exhibitors throughout the nation but also on the general public. Second-run theaters got movies 30 days after they played at a first-run theater. There were also third-run theaters, which got movies between 7 and 10 days after they finished playing at the second-run theaters.[88] According to a 1927 prospectus prepared by Halsey, Stuart & Company, "These first-run houses are regarded by the production end of the business as their 'show windows.'" Many of the Hollywood production companies, such as Paramount, Warner Bros., MGM, and RKO, controlled at least one downtown first-run theater in major United States cities. In Washington, Warner Bros. had the Earle (later the Warner) and the Metropolitan, MGM had the Capitol and Palace, and RKO had Keith's. To a great extent, Baltimore resisted the national circuits, and for many years the first-run theaters were controlled by local exhibitors. The national circuits were constantly looking for ways to acquire, through lease, purchase, or construction, a local first-run theater. As of January 1920, the following Baltimore theaters were first-run:

Blue Mouse	New
Parkway	Hippodrome
Strand (Howard Street)	New Wizard
New Pickwick	Garden
Victoria	Wilson

The Charles Whitehurst organization controlled the New and the Garden. It would soon add a third, the Century. After Whitehurst's death in 1924, Marcus Loew and

William Fox were quick to begin negotiating to buy the Whitehurst theaters. Loew won and gained the Century and Parkway for MGM films. The Maryland Theater offered first-string Keith-Albee vaudeville and the Hippodrome and Garden offered "small time" vaudeville. Warner Bros. was unable to obtain a downtown house and had to be satisfied with the Metropolitan as a showcase for their first-run films and for their new sound process that emerged in 1927.

In the first half of the 1920s, many of the smaller, older downtown theaters were forced out of the first-run category by bigger theaters. Each of the first-run houses seated more than 1,000 people.

4

Movie Palaces (1921–1927)

There was tremendous optimism in Baltimore among the exhibitors and the public alike on the eve of the third decade of the century. Almost half of Baltimore's 750,000 inhabitants attended moving pictures every day. Baltimore movie theaters took in $22 million between June 1920 and June 1921.[1] New theaters, larger and more opulent than their predecessors, were being planned and many older theaters were being remodeled.

The 1920s were a wonderful time for movie theaters. The size and grandeur of theaters continued to increase during this short period, and the largest movie theaters ever built in Maryland opened in Baltimore. Many large neighborhood theaters seating more than 1,000 were built; and two, the State and Regent, seated more than 2,000. The nine new theaters that opened in 1921 could seat more than 14,500 people. Many smaller theaters were forced to close, unable to compete with the new theaters. By 1925, Baltimore had 111 movie houses, three legitimate theaters and four vaudeville theaters.

A new local projectionists' union was formed during labor troubles in the late 1920s. Two scandals, one involving a slush fund to get a theater permit passed by the city council and the other involving the unexpected appearance of the unknown wife of a dead exhibitor, rocked the local theater world. Loew's and Warner Bros. gained footholds in Baltimore. The long trek out of the center of the city began during this era. Between 1920 and 1930, the balance of the city's population shifted to the residential wards; the population of downtown decreased by 56,098 persons, or 14.9 percent. After 1927, few new theaters would be built in old downtown. Modern air conditioning arrived in the late 1920s, and movies with sound appeared at the tail end of the period.

In 1922, despite all the big theaters being built, the average American movie theater still had fewer than 600 seats. A survey done by *Motion Picture News* found that the average theater had 507 seats, was open five days a week, employed seven people, charged 12–28 cents at matinees and 17–36 cents in the evenings, had an average daily patronage of 364 people, had seven changes of program every two weeks, and had three 8-reel shows a day.[2] The survey concluded that the small theater was still the "bread and butter" of the motion picture business. The best season for movie going seemed to be the fall; the worst was the summer. One of the best theater nights in the history of Baltimore was recorded on Thanksgiving in 1920 when virtually all of the theaters in town were packed to capacity. Thousands more people wanted to attend, but were unable to get tickets.

Ticket prices continued to climb in the 1920s. In response to grumbling about high ticket prices in 1921, Rome Theaters' Broadway, Capitol, and Apollo lowered their prices to 11 cents in the evening and 17 cents at night. A writer to the *Evening Sun*, outraged that one 10-cent theater had recently charged an astounding $1.50 for reserved seats, said that he had "personally forbidden any member of his family to attend any movie where the charge exceeds 25 cents."[3] Other writers in 1921 complained about paying 28 cents for an orchestra seat in the afternoon and 44 cents for one at night and that the better theaters were unwise to charge 55 cents, that 25 cents was plenty for the best movies. Almost as if they had been alarmed by these letters, the New and the Parkway reduced their prices in early 1922.

The subject of expensive tickets was brought up in an *Evening Sun* editorial in June 1922 in response to a waning in movie attendance. The paper said, "The big increase over pre-war prices ... has doubtless had its effect. We used to have five and ten cent movies. Now one rarely finds a place where tickets are less than twenty-five cents even in daytime and in some places the night rates almost reach those of the legitimate theatres."[4] Still, the movies cost less than live theater; a ticket to a big musical show could cost as much as $2.50 or $3.00, while a dramatic show could cost $2.00. A top-price ticket to Shubert vaudeville at the Maryland cost $1.00.

Two years later, even the movie critics were complaining. T.M.C. of the Sunday *Sun* asked "Will the nickel show ever return?"[5] By that time, first-run theaters were charging between 15 cents and $2.00, while neighborhood houses charged from 15 to 40 cents. Only a few movie houses "in more modest sections" charged 10 cents. The last five-cent theaters in town—an estimated 35 theaters—raised their prices to 10 cents in May 1924. Two months later, the Federal government abolished the war tax on tickets selling at 50 cents or less. Most admissions went down a few cents to 50, 40, 30, and 25 cents. However, three of the four 10-cent movie theaters on East Baltimore Street raised their prices to 15 cents. In 1927, the Royal Theater was charging 25 cents for all seats in the afternoons; evening prices beginning at 5 o'clock were 60 cents for box and loge seats, 40 cents for orchestra seats and 25 cents for balcony seats. T.M.C. believed high prices had something to do with the 15 million-person drop in daily movie attendance. The New Garden Theater lowered its rates to the level of the other first-run theaters in May 1928. The new rates were: 11 A.M. to 1 P.M.— 35 cents; 1 P.M. to 5:30 P.M.— orchestra 50 cents, balcony 25 and 35 cents; 5:30 P.M. to closing — orchestra 60 cents, balcony 35 and 50 cents.[6]

The shows of the 1920s, like the theaters, reached their elaborate zeniths, but by the end of the decade the number of vaudeville shows had declined markedly. The opening show at the Regent in January 1921 included vaudeville with Sidney Perrin's High Flyers featuring four acts: Iris Hall in Show Folks, "Once Again" with Allen and Stokes, "piano jazz boys" Brooks and Jackson in "Borrowed from the Big Time," and Margareto Rice in "Different," plus a movie. There were three shows daily with music by Ike Thompson's 10-piece orchestra.

In June 1923, the show at the Metropolitan consisted of (1) *Mirror Lake and Thereabouts*, Yosemite Park in Pathé Color; (2) *Flashes of Wild Life*; (3) *Speed Demons*, a Lyman Howe Novelty; (4) *The Mysterious Ocklawaha River in Florida*; (5) *Between Showers*, a one-act comedy; (6) Overture, *Maritana* with Julius Sokolove conducting the Metropolitan's orchestra; (7) *The Kingdom Within*, a thrilling tale of the California redwoods starring Pauline Starke and Gaston Glass; and (8) Sextet from *Lucia*, played by Kenneth G. Faulkner on the Robert Morton Organ. In November 1925, the Century presented a show that consisted of a first-run film, *Pretty Ladies*, with ZaSu Pitts, plus an Our Gang comedy, and onstage Ace Brigode and his Fourteen Virginians featuring Ethel Briant, the Charleston Queen.

The big movie theaters—such as the Apollo, Belnord, Boulevard, Capitol, Columbia, Royal, Horn, Met, and National—that opened in the early 1920s had house orchestras. During the 1920s, the conductors of the orchestras at the first-run theaters were as well known as many actors. The conductors and the members of the orchestras were first-rate musicians with large followings and strong fan loyalty. The film critic for the *Evening Sun* praised Baltimore's theater orchestras in a 1922 column, going so far as to state his belief that movie orchestras deserved a lot of the credit for the steady development of "the musical side of this country." He singled out the orchestras at the Rivoli (under Felice Iula) and the Century (under Frank Rehsen) for special praise.

Among the theater orchestra leaders in 1922 were Julius Sokolove at the Boulevard and Metropolitan, Hendrick Essers at the New and later the Parkway, E. V. Cupero at the Century and New, Edgar Hunt at the Hippodrome, Felice Iula at the Rivoli and later the Stanley, Robert Paul Iula at the Boulevard and later the Stanley, Mischa Guterson at the Valencia and later the Stanley, Emile S. Odend'hal at the Auditorium and later the Rivoli, George Wild at the Century, and V. Nessul at the Parkway and later the New.

All-women orchestras were popular in the teens and 1920s. The Flaming Arrow had a five-piece ladies' orchestra playing at each performance when it opened in 1913. In 1922, Frank Durkee's Palace and Belnord theaters engaged the 10-piece Ladies' Broadway Symphony Orchestra, conducted by Miss Julie Baker, to play at matinees and evening performances.

In 1923, the Century orchestra, under Frank Rehsen, was augmented to 28 pieces. The music column in the *Evening Sun* of October 5, 1926, praised the managers of the local theaters for "endeavoring to put the music of the several orchestras up to a higher plane than it had held for years." The writer of the column was especially impressed with the orchestra at the Auditorium, where a harp had replaced a drum, saying that the musical numbers were of a "more advanced order" and that "more or less subdued effects have taken the place of clamorous instrumentation." When the Stanley opened in 1927 it had a larger than usual orchestra, 35 members, under the joint direction of the Iula brothers, Felice and Robert. The Regent orchestra, conducted by Isaiah "Ike" N. Thompson, who later went on to the Royal, and Paul Harris, was one of the largest in an African-American theater. Thompson's orchestra had 12 musicians. They routinely played 30 to 40 numbers during each performance.

But not every moviegoer was pleased with theater orchestras. A writer to the *Evening Sun* in 1926 wrote that the only compliment he or she could pay the members of one local movie house orchestra was that they were industrious. The writer went on to describe this orchestra, "Their 'sad' selections, with a mournful cornet predominating, made me shiver, while their 'peppy' numbers, despite the frantic efforts of the drummer and the contortions of the violinist-leader, were ... hollow and arid attempts at gayety...." Robert Garland, in his "Day by Day" column in the *Daily Post* in 1927, was ambivalent about theater orchestras. "Attending the silent dramas frequently, I look forward to the sweet sounds that usually manage to emerge from one or two Baltimore orchestra pits. But, apart from one or two, I'd not object if most of our motion-picture orchestras didn't bother about playing at all. There're several I'd pay to stop...."[7] When the Century brought back its orchestra in the fall of 1930, the public was ecstatic. Paul R. Mooney described the audience as the orchestra began playing, "amid deafening applause, which was renewed every two to three minutes, whether the selection was completed or not. This ovation was ... extended to the stage show, ... which goes to prove that the Baltimore public will never be satisfied with any mechanical replacement of the actor in person."[8] The Rivoli's orchestra under Felice Iula was considered to be one of Baltimore's best. Movie critic T. M. Cushing wrote in 1924, "Thus far, it is believed that our Rivoli Theater has proved most successful in this respect, and one does not have to inquire extensively among the fans for hearty endorsement of the work of Felice Iula and his musicians."[9] Nathan Bernstein took his uncle, a musician from Austria, to a performance at the Rivoli where the orchestra was conducted by Felice Iula. When the orchestra had stopped, the uncle stood up, clapped his hands together and shouted, "Damn, now that's real music!" In 1926 Iula won a popularity contest for orchestra leaders conducted by the New York *Morning Telegraph*. He beat out such well-known bandleaders as Meyer Davis, Paul Whiteman, and Fred Waring.[10]

The Century's orchestra, under George Wild, was a close second to that at the Rivoli, and the orchestras at the Metropolitan, Boulevard and Parkway had their "inspired moments." The orchestras at the New, Garden and Hippodrome were less highly regarded.

Theater musicians received good salaries, but they had to fight for them; during World War I, they were getting $28 a week while common laborers were making $5–$6 a day. By 1921 the minimum wage paid to orchestra members at the Rivoli was $45 a week; in 1925 it had increased to $54. In 1932 a pit musician at the Hippodrome was paid $67.50 a week.[11] As sound movies became better and more popular, theater orchestras withered and died. Despite numerous complaints, most of the local theater orchestras disappeared during the 1930s.

By the early 1920s there were printed scores available for most of the movies released. The Synchronized Scenario Music Company offered complete scores for the national distributing organizations in early 1921.[12] Baltimore movie audiences, at least around 1922, seemed to prefer the old-time popular songs, such as "Last Rose of Summer," "Sweet Bessie," and "Slumber On, My Little Gypsy Sweetheart," and they could not get enough of "Dixie" or "Carry Me Back to Old Virginia." An organist or piano player could get a few laughs playing "The Prisoner's Song—If I had the wings of an angel..." during a wedding scene. Audiences had had enough jazz and opera melodies. Commenting on the state of downtown theaters in 1926, one moviegoer wrote that "a movie theater is certainly the wrong place to go in order to hear 'good music.'" This writer complained about the Rivoli orchestra—"about the best orchestra in Baltimore" with Mr. Iula, "a fine and popular conductor"—that played selections of the "race-horse" type like "Poet and Peasant" or "Orpheus."[13] Around 1914, composers, through the American Society of Composers, Authors and Publishers (ASCAP), established a tax on the proprietors of movie theaters that used their music in the programs accompanying motion pictures in their theaters. The tax was 10 cents per seat per year. The courts upheld the rights of composers in every case where they took a theater owner to court for refusing to pay the tax. The exhibitors fought fiercely, but the only recourse they had was to play music published by companies, such as G. Schirmer and the Boston Music Company, which were not members of the Society. In 1922, it was estimated that only about 10 percent of the music used in the country was taxed.

Piano players were gradually phased out. By the mid–1920s, they were found in only a few older neighborhood theaters. A movie critic writing in 1925 described attending a West North Avenue theater, probably the Walbrook, on a recent Saturday night.

"The house was crowded — all but capacity — with ... between 500 and 600 persons. It was warm and stuffy, but no one appeared visibly affected. And the solo music accompaniment was a steady piano bang-bang by someone who must have been playing all the day ... no one seemed to mind that, either. This theater, of course, belonged to the good old-fashioned variety of pre-war days...."[14]

The piano player sometimes received accidental attention. Mitzi Seamon who was a substitute piano player at the Lyceum Theater in Sparrows Point, believed that half the popcorn sold in the theater wound up in her hair during the exciting scenes. In a 1993 interview, she described piano playing at the Lyceum. "The piano was ... in the middle of the screen. I could look right up at the screen ... as I'm playing.... The music was stacked on the side ... if you were having a big movie, what they considered a big special which they tried to have once a week, they would send you advanced cue sheets with the movie and [there would be] maybe six or seven bars while Joe is coming out the door or seven or eight bars next to it where she came out and kissed Joe ... you would get those cue sheets a week or ten days ahead of time."

Mrs. Seamon learned from the regular piano player, Gladys, and filled in for her at a salary of $25 a week.

> I'd go up and sit on the bench with her and I'd learn how she would improvise. If it was a baby, [she'd play], 'Rock-a-bye Baby' ... the louder you got the louder the kids got ... for Saturdays, you had built up some noisy music because there was always the sequel next week and you could go to the same thing and you could go to this real loud, noisy type of music that you could meet any Saturday with any different picture ... they all were running after the Indians or the Indians were running after them.... Almost every Saturday you could use the same music ... when I would finish, I would be almost bent in two like a pretzel ... you played three hours steady like that, sitting straight up.[15]

The job of a piano player had its risks. The young woman playing at the Baltimore Theater on Fait Avenue liked oysters. She would send a boy out for a "small fry of oysters"—13 fried oysters. She would put the box of fried oysters next to her and eat them as she played. At one performance she suddenly started screaming and ran up the aisle. When the manager asked what the matter was, she said, "There's a rat eating my oysters."

The piano player — they were rarely called "pianists" in the theaters, which was considered too highbrow — or organist was a very important person in the early theaters. They were visible representatives of the theater. The manager remained a shadowy figure seen only occasionally and then usually to enforce decorum, and the projectionist was an invisible presence noticed only when something went wrong with the film. The piano players and organists were right there in front of the audience guiding them through the movie. A good piano player or organist could make a lot of difference in attendance at a theater.

A 1919 newspaper article told of a piano player who was lured away from one theater by a larger salary. After one week, the theater he left reported that the house receipts had dropped $600. When the management agreed to pay him more, he returned, and the receipts rose by $600. His playing was described in the same article: "He can play. He sits there all day long, and not only does he translate the pictures musically, but he is always inventing new turns to the various musical scores that he plays so that they will bring out more fully the hidden depths of emotion that the picture is endeavoring to convey. He is always suggesting new musical effects which will help him in his musical translations."[16]

On many occasions, these musicians saved lives by calming the audience and helping them evacuate the theater when fire threatened. In September 1925, a piano player helped to avert a panic when a reel of film exploded in the projection booth at the Flaming Arrow Theater. She began playing a popular song that calmed the crowd and they filed out of the theater without creating a stampede. Three years later a similar situation occurred at the Pimlico Theater. The organist stayed at her organ all the while playing until the audience had left the theater.

The organ was the natural successor to the piano; it could fill even a large theater with a greater variety of sounds and music. One of the first theaters in Baltimore to install a pipe organ was the Blue Mouse in the spring of 1910. J. Reginald Foard gave organ recitals there before every performance. Some early organs, such as the orchestral organ and the Fotoplayer, could replace a full orchestra.

The Fotoplayer, which was installed in the innovative New Pickwick Theater in 1917, was designed and built especially for movie theaters. The repertory of a Fotoplayer was heavy into percussion and could reproduce the sounds of chimes, xylophones, drums, bells, pistol shots, cymbals, thunder, wind, sirens, rain, fire gongs, whistles, and auto horns.

By the late 1920s, huge organs of incredible versatility were being installed in movie theaters. The most popular organs in Baltimore theaters were the ones made by the Moller Company of Hagerstown, Maryland. Twenty-eight Baltimore theaters had Moller organs. Over the years, the Hippodrome had three Moller organs. Other popular makes included Wurlitzer, Kimball, Robert-Morton, and Kilgen. Most of the theater organs had two manuals or keyboards, but there were big three-manual organs in the Boulevard, Metropolitan, Belnord, Rivoli, Century, Keith's, Hippodrome, and Stanley. In the late teens, a two-manual organ cost about $2,500; by the early 1920s they were running around $5,000. The 3/20 Skinner organ installed in the Boulevard in 1921 cost $16,000. The three-manual $50,000 Kimball installed in the Rivoli was a whole orchestra in itself.

> It contains trombones, bass horns, trumpets, bass viols, cellos, violins, violas at the various pitches, clarinet, oboes and a variety of flute colors, deep and pervading diaphonic diapason with a thunderous organ tone. Also the trap drummer's effects, snare drums, bass drums, cymbal, tympani, orchestral bells, xylophone, chimes, harp, it being possible to correctly interpret all the different types of music depicted on the screen, from the love scenes to the storm at sea, from the Oriental music, dances and Chinese effects of the Far East to a correct interpretation of Sousa's Band. The pipes in this instrument range from the large diaphone, 16 feet long, to the small piccolo pipes no larger than a lead pencil. All these instruments are at the command of one operator, being instantly changeable by the combination pistons set at the console.[17]

A picture of the new organ figured prominently in the Rivoli's ads. Concerts by well-known organists were touted in the advertising of many movie theaters. The Rivoli praised Walter Klotz, its "brilliant young organist, formerly of the Bijou and Colonial Theaters, Atlantic City," in its May 1920 advertising.

The elaborate shows at the big downtown theaters were still limited to six days of the week. No Sunday movies for Baltimore yet. Attempts to have a referendum on Sunday movies for Baltimore failed again in 1922. Those opposed to movies on Sunday cut the theaters no slack. In the fall of 1923, eight movie houses opened on Sunday night to help raise funds for the new West Baltimore General Hospital. They raised about $2,500. The Maryland Baptist Union Association immediately sent a petition to Police Commissioner Gaither asking him to stop future performances. To his credit, Gaither refused.[18]

In 1924 a bill supported by Councilman Howard Bryant which would have permitted Sunday movies was passed by the General Assembly after a tough fight only to be declared invalid by the courts. That bill was opposed by a coalition of women's and religious organizations and civic groups as well as by the projectionists who claimed that it would deprive them of a day of rest, but they withdrew their opposition when the exhibitors promised them a day off during the week. One group of opponents had an open letter published in the *Sun* in which they claimed that the Sunday movie legislation was class legislation in that it would permit one group of people to carry on business on Sundays while denying that right to other groups. They also used the arguments that this legislation would take away a day of rest for many workers, that the movies were already open six days a week and that was enough, and that if the proposed bill should become law, other businesses—such as billiard parlors, poolrooms, and bowling alleys—would ask for the same privilege.

The editor of the *Sun* said that there was no convincing proof that the public really wanted Sunday movies. One group that did not favor Sunday movies consisted of the wives of theater musicians. One wife wrote, in 1927, that she looked forward to Sunday as the only day that she could have "a little pleasure together" with her children and her husband.[19] A supporter of Sunday movies believed that they would give young people a place to go, thus reducing crime.[20]

It was late 1926 before the groups that wanted Sunday movies felt strong enough to challenge the blue laws again. That December, state senator Ambrose J. Kennedy, who supported Sunday movies, said he would introduce legislation to liberalize the blue laws. That same month the president of the Liberty Defense League, John G. Callan, who was also a member of the House of Delegates,[21] stated that the League would demand repeal of the blue laws. The League had the support of the Hotel Men's Association. Senators Bouse and Kennedy introduced legislation in 1927 to permit Sunday movies, but their bills died in committee.

By the following September, the Liberty Defense League and the Sunday Amusement League of Baltimore were able to announce a double-barreled attack on the blue laws. They were first going to have an actual test of the law, and secondly they were going to obtain 10,000 signatures on a petition for a referendum on repealing the blue laws. The members of the Sunday Amusement League were told that they would be arrested if they tried to test the law; but in October 1927, the League was negotiating with Baltimore exhibitors to show a movie on a Sunday night. According to Callan, the group wanted to test the laws to see why certain activities, such as the selling of gasoline, were permitted on Sundays yet they were clearly not charities or necessities and to find out whether those supporting the blue laws wanted them enforced strictly. The Police Commissioner warned theater owners that they would be arrested if they rented their theaters for Sunday movie shows. Callan and the League again had the support of the Hotel Men's League, but they were not ready to test the law until late January 1928.

The theaters continued to be active in charity fund-raising. Special Sunday shows raised funds to build West Baltimore General Hospital. Local movie theaters raised more than $1,000 for the city's relief fund in September 1926 to aid the victims of the terrible hurricane that had ravaged Florida that month; the Boulevard donated $275, and the New gave $450. On Sunday, May 8, 1927, under Red Cross auspices, 57 theaters throughout the state opened to raise money for flood victims in the Midwest. All of the theatrical employees—including musicians, projectionists, and stagehands—donated their services. All receipts were turned over to the Baltimore Red Cross Chapter for relief work for the victims of the Mississippi River floods.

Two big scandals involving movie theaters and local exhibitors occurred in the 1920s. In one, there were charges of money paid to influence the passage of a theater permit through the City Council, and in the other the unsuspected wife of a supposed bachelor exhibitor suddenly appeared to contest the exhibitor's estate. The first scandal began in the fall of 1920.

> Testimony that a slush fund of between $3,000 and $5,000 was used to put through the City Council the Boulevard Theatre Permit ordinance was brought forward. The testimony came during proceedings before the referee in bankruptcy in the United States District Court. Judge John C. Rose was forced to take a hand because of reluctance of witnesses to tell how the money was spent. Judge Rose sentenced to jail for contempt, until he tells what he knows of the disposition of the slush fund, Edward J. Wiley, stock promoter for the theatre.... Alfred G. Buck, president of the company, admitted drawing $3,000 from the theater's accounts, but refused to tell in court the disposition of it, on the ground that he would be incriminating himself. Buck ... declared he had given the money to Edwin T. Dickerson and Judge Harry W. Nice, of the Appeal Tax Court.... Despite his earlier refusal ... Buck declared last night that it had been paid to Dickerson & Nice for "legitimate legal expenses." False entries were made on the company's books to "cover up" the withdrawals of $4,500 of the company's funds, according to other witnesses, who also testified this $4,500 was "for lobbying purposes" and to "get the bill through."[22]

This explosive testimony added high-test fuel to one of the biggest scandals to rock the movie business in Baltimore. The resulting revelations and charges would bring down Alfred Buck, put an end to his planned deluxe theater on Park Circle, and dash hopes for the Washington Theater on Pennsylvania Avenue and the Irving Theater on Frederick Avenue.

The story began in October 1920 when partners Roy B. Palmore and Leo H. Homand had an ordinance introduced into the City Council to allow them to build a movie theater on the east side of Greenmount Avenue north of 33rd Street. The measure passed the Second Branch of the council easily, but it was held up in the First Branch largely through the efforts of Republicans and one faction of Democrats and especially Councilman Wilson J. Carroll, who represented the Twelfth Ward, where the new theaters would be.[23] Carroll had the measure transferred to the Committee on Building Regulations.

Meanwhile, the American Theaters Company was incorporated, with Edwin T. Dickerson of the law firm of Dickerson & Nice as president, Alfred G. Buck[24] of the Seaboard Film Corporation as vice-president and general manager, and Bernard H. Dundon of the Maryland Finance Corporation as secretary and treasurer. The American Theaters Company wanted to build a theater on the west side of Greenmount Avenue above 33rd Street. In January, while the Palmore & Homand measure was languishing in committee, Councilman Carroll introduced the measure to authorize a building permit for the American Theaters Company theater. Roy Palmore later testified that while the Palmore & Homand measure was blocked in the council, he was approached by two men who told him that if he put up $2,500, he could get the ordinance passed. Palmore also said that E. J. Wiley first proposed to promote the Palmore & Homand theater, but when they would not agree, he threatened to have another theater built across the street.

The matter came to a head on the evening of January 31, 1921, when there was a row, with name calling, in the City Council. Councilman Edward Gross, of the Eighteenth Ward, tried to have the Palmore & Homand measure recalled from the committee, but supporters of the American Theaters Company blocked his attempt. After a month of bickering, both ordinances were reported out of the Joint Committee on Building Regulations. The opponents of the Palmore and Homand ordinance had blocked it for nearly five months and allowed the American Theaters Company ordinance to catch up. In the Council meeting on March 7, 1921, Frank W. Jacoby, president of the First Branch, made the unusual move of installing another councilman as chair so that he could make a statement from the floor. He accused Carroll of making an offer to Palmore & Homand and said that if they would drop their plans for the theater, he would secure passage of an ordinance for them to build a theater anywhere else in the city. The two measures were a matter of rivalry between Democratic factions. The *Evening Sun* chided the Council for spending so much time wrangling over the ordinances.

By mid–March 1921, the coalition of Mahon Democrats and Republicans showed signs of breaking up. A vote on the Palmore & Homand theater was seen as a litmus test of its strength. The bill passed. The American Theaters Company bill also passed, and in April, Mayor Broening agreed to consider both at the same time, effectively wiping out the lead of the Palmore & Homand measure. Broening signed both ordinances on April 16.

Despite getting their permit, Palmore & Homand abandoned plans for their theater on Greenmount Avenue[25] and the American Theaters Company was able to begin construction of the Boulevard Theater unopposed. It opened on October 8, 1921. It was a beautiful structure that seated more than 1,000 people.

Within a month, troubles began. It was revealed that the building was undercapitalized by $250,000, and that the actual cost of land and building was $271,000. Shortly after a meeting between the stockholders and the contractors, the American Theaters Company was declared bankrupt. Many small stockholders were left penniless by the crash of the Boulevard.[26] The petition of bankruptcy alleged that the company was heavily in debt and that its officers had committed an act of bankruptcy by giving preference to certain creditors. Almost immediately, a New York group offered to buy the theater for $175,000. Councilman Carroll surfaced again, this time representing the creditors and supporting the New York offer. At that time he was accused by E. J. Wiley of saying, "to Hell with the stockholders; I am looking out for the creditors." Judge Morris A. Soper was appointed receiver to run the affairs of the theater.

The meeting of stockholders on November 15 was a stormy affair. Wiley and Carroll traded charges. Carroll accused Wiley of getting more than his legitimate promoter's share, and Wiley said that Carroll had been the company's guardian angel in the City Council. At the end of the meeting Wiley invited Carroll outside to settle the matter "in the alley."

The investors elected a new board of directors and supported a reorganization plan.

Veteran manager Bernard Depkin was appointed manager of the Boulevard. On November 16, Wiley charged that Carroll had been paid $750 and 1,000 shares of stock to secure passage of the Boulevard ordinance in the City Council. Carroll claimed that the money and stock were his attorney's fees. Wiley claimed that he was trying to arrange a settlement to protect the stockholders when Carroll said he was going to throw the company into the hands of receivers. Carroll demanded that the City Council carry out a full investigation of the charges against him. State's Attorney Robert F. Leach was watching the situation develop and seemed ready to take Wiley's charges to a grand jury. Things simmered until December 2, when Wiley testified before Judge John C. Rose during the bankruptcy proceedings.

At that hearing, Wiley testified that a $3,000–$5,000 slush fund was used to get the City Council to approve the permit for the Boulevard Theater. Wiley refused to tell what he knew about the disposition of this fund, and Judge Rose sent him to jail for contempt. Alfred Buck refused to provide information in court as to the disposition of the fund, but, when questioned at the Courthouse by detectives, he stated that he had given the money to Edwin T. Dickerson and Harry W. Nice of the law firm of Dickerson & Nice for "legitimate legal expenses."[27] Other witnesses told of false entries on the company's books to cover up withdrawals of $4,500 for "lobbying purposes" and to "get the bill through."[28]

State's Attorney Leach had heard enough and presented the case to the grand jury the same day; some members of the City Council began calling for a full investigation. Wiley was released from jail on December 3. The *Sun* pointed out some questions that had not been answered: Why were false entries made on the American Theaters Company's books to "cover up" payment of money for "legitimate counsel fees"? Why did Alfred Buck say he would incriminate himself by telling that he had paid the money only for "legitimate counsel fees"? Why were the checks for the "legitimate counsel fees" taken from the back of the book and no record kept on the stubs? Why was $1,500 drawn from cash receipts and used without any apparent entry in the books?

On December 5, the State's Attorney was said to have enough evidence for one indictment. That same day Dickerson & Nice refunded the $4,500 to Judge Soper as receiver for the theater. The City Council met that day but did not discuss the case and the *Sun* asked "Why did the City Council do nothing, not even discuss the charges which have thrown a cloud over every Councilman, when both branches met last night?"[29] The grand jury investigation began on the 6th, as did a meeting by the grievance committee of the Bar Association to consider Wiley's charges against Carroll.

By the end of the day, the grand jury had decided to ask for indictments of Buck, Dundon, Carroll, and Dickerson. Buck was indicted for embezzlement and larceny of $1,200 of the American Theatres Company's funds. Buck and Dundon were indicted for larceny of $1,500 of the company's funds on two different days in March 1921. Carroll was indicted on three charges of accepting bribes. All four men were indicted on charges of conspiracy to defraud the American Theatres Company. Nice was specifically excluded.

Dickerson denied that any of the $4,500 paid his firm by the Boulevard Company was paid out to any Councilman or city official. Testimony on December 9 indicated that Buck asked Wiley, in a letter, for $1,000 for Dickerson & Nice and $500 for Councilman Carroll to make certain the ordinance was signed. Wiley testified that Carroll received only $250 of the $500 and complained that "it was a mighty small cut."

On December 20, 1921, the grand jury returned criminal presentments against Harry

Nice, Edwin Dickerson, Wilson J. Carroll, Alfred G. Buck, and Bernard H. Dundon. Dickerson, Nice, Buck and Dundon were charged with conspiracy to acquire with intent to defraud certain moneys of the American Theaters Company. Buck, Dundon and Dickerson were charged with conspiracy to bribe Wilson J. Carroll and Buck and Dundon were also charged with larceny of $1,500 from the American Theaters Company. Meanwhile the grievance committee of the Baltimore Bar Association had recommended that Carroll be disbarred for his connection with the Boulevard Theater case. The grand jury indicted all of the above named men except Harry Nice on January 5, 1922. Carroll was indicted on three charges of accepting a bribe. Dickerson, Buck and Dundon were indicted on conspiracy to bribe Carroll. Buck was indicted on embezzlement and larceny, and Buck and Dundon were indicted on larceny.

The jury decided that there was not enough evidence to indict Nice, and State's Attorney Leach said that their refusal to indict him weakened the state's case against the others. Carroll's disbarment case went to the Supreme Bench in March. He was found innocent of accepting bribes, but was suspended from practicing law for a year. Wiley was the main witness against him. Finally, in July 1922, Leach decided that Wiley's testimony at Carroll's trial had been discredited and had tainted his testimony in the indictments of Buck, Dundon, Dickerson and Carroll. Leach said that he would enter a *nolle prosequi* since, with the State's main witness discredited, there was virtually no chance for a conviction. The *Baltimore American* was disappointed by the inability of the State's Attorney to try the case and editorialized that if everybody involved in this "grave public scandal" went free, it would be a failure of justice.[30]

In January 1922, after a bidding battle between stockholders and creditors, a group of stockholders purchased the Boulevard for $145,000. Operation of the theater was resumed at once. A new board of directors was elected; significantly none of the men who originally promoted and developed the theater were on the board. In the fall of 1922, another theater project in which Buck and Wiley had been involved, the Circle Theater on Park Circle, collapsed amidst complaints by a stockholder. Wiley's plans to build the 1,200-seat Irving Theater on Frederick Avenue in Irvington also fell through. Fallout from the Boulevard case had brought about the collapse of at least three major theater projects in Baltimore, ruined many investors, and destroyed the careers of several of the principals in the company.

Baltimore Theaters 1922

Academy of Music	N. Howard Street	Belvidere	819 Belvidere Avenue
Aladdin	930 W. Baltimore	Blue Bell	1713 Harford Avenue
Am	941 Pennsylvania Avenue	Blue Mouse	28 W. Lexington Street
Apollo	1506 Harford Avenue	Bridge	2104 Edmondson Avenue
Arcadia	320 S. Broadway	Broadway Garden	1105 N. Broadway
Argonne	926 S. Sharp Street	Broadway	509 S. Broadway
Artmore Casino	502 W. Franklin Street	Brodie	1118 Light Street
Auditorium	N. Howard Street	Bunny	1225 Columbia Avenue
Aurora	7–9 E. North Avenue	Capitol	Baltimore Street nr. Gilmor
Baltimore	3205 Fait Avenue	Carey	Carey nr. School
Belmar	Belair Road nr. Cherry Avenue	Century	18 W. Lexington Street
Belnord	2706 Philadelphia Avenue	Clover	414 E. Baltimore Street

Cluster	303 S. Broadway	Lubin's	404 E. Baltimore Street
Colonial	1438 N. Gay Street	Lyric	Mt. Royal Avenue
Comedy	412 E. Baltimore Street	McHenry	1032 Light Street
Community	3019 Hamilton Avenue	Maryland	Franklin Street
Crown	756 Washington Boulevard	Metro Photoplays	1–3 S. High Street
Crystal	530 N. Gay Street	Metropolitan	1524 North Avenue
Curtis	921 Curtis Avenue	Monument Open Air	Monument Street
Dixie	312 W. Baltimore Street	Mt. Washington Casino	South Avenue
Douglas	1329 Pennsylvania Avenue	New Gem	617 Duncan Street
Dunbar	621 N. Central Avenue	New Idle Hour	223 N. Howard Street
Eagle	3610 Eastern Avenue	New Lyceum	1209 N. Charles Street
Echo	124 E. Fort Avenue	New Patterson	3136 Eastern Avenue
Edmondson	2100 Edmondson Avenue	New Peabody	11 E. North Avenue
Elektra	1039 N. Gay Street	New Pickwick	115 N. Howard Street
Eureka	400 S. Fremont Avenue	New	210 W. Lexington Street
Excelsior	1358 W. North Avenue	New Wizard	30 W. Lexington Street
Fairmount	101 N. Clinton Street	Northwestern	1056 Pennsylvania Avenue
Fairyland	624 N. Chester Street	Nowosci	510 S. Broadway
Family	518 S. Broadway	Palace	311 W. Fayette Street
Fayette	2443 E. Fayette Street	Palace	1351 Gay Street
Flag	1318 E. Fort Avenue	Parkside	4707 Harford Road.
Flaming Arrow	1108 E. Preston Street	Parkway	3 W. North Avenue
Folly	E. Baltimore Street	Pastime	2028 Greenmount Avenue
Ford's	W. Fayette Street	Pennington	4911 Pennington Avenue
Forest Park	3306 Garrison Boulevard	Pictorial	3310 E. Baltimore Street
Frederick	3436 Frederick Avenue	Picture Garden	31 W. Lexington Street
Fremont	615 N. Fremont Avenue	Pimlico	5144 Park Heights Avenue
Garden	114 W. Lexington Street	Poplar	611 Poplar Grove Street
Garden	1102 N. Charles Street	Princess	1517 Eager Street
Gayety	E. Baltimore Street	Queen	666 W. Lexington Street
Gertrude McCoy	1563 N. Fulton Avenue	Rainbow	2117 Pennsylvania Avenue
Gilmor	314 N. Gilmor Street	Realart	719 W. Baltimore Street
Good Time	1405 N. Milton Avenue	Red Wing	2341 E. Monument Street
Grand	400 E. Baltimore Street	Regent	1627 Pennsylvania Avenue
Grand	515 S. 3rd Street, e.	Rialto	846 W. North Avenue
Hampden	911 W. 36th Street, n.	Rivoli	418 E. Baltimore Street
Harford	2618 Harford Avenue	Roosevelt	512 W. Biddle Street
Hippodrome	12 N. Eutaw Street	Schanze's	2426 Pennsylvania Avenue
Horn	2018 W. Pratt Street	Solax	1204 W. Baltimore Street
Ideal	903 W. 36th Street, n.	Star	1531 E. Monument Street
Lafayette	1433 W. Lafayette Avenue	Strand	404 N. Howard Street
Leader	248 S. Broadway	Sunset	1110 S. Charles Street
Lincoln	936 Pennsylvania Avenue	Superba	906 Columbia Avenue
Lincoln Highway	Washington Road	Victoria	415 E. Baltimore Street
Linwood	Linwood Avenue nr. Hudson	Walbrook	3100 W. North Avenue
Lord Baltimore	1114 W. Baltimore Street	Waverly	3211 Greenmount Avenue
Lord Calvert	1625 Harford Avenue	West End	1601 Baltimore Street

4. Movie Palaces (1921–1927)   89

Suddenly Baltimore found itself with a number of fairly large neighborhood theaters plus dozens of smaller ones, and many exhibitors believed that there were too many theaters. Charles Whitehurst gave his view of the situation in 1922.

> The consensus of opinion among the exhibitors of Baltimore seems to be that conditions are improving, but ... very slowly and it will be next fall probably before the improvements can be noticed. If the statements of the exhibitors ... can be held as a criterion this is undoubtedly a dull period, but all appear to hold the attitude that it will grow better and the one fact that stands out is that, so far as is known, no picture theatres have had to close because of the dull times.
>
> But the keynote of the exact condition of the picture business in Baltimore was struck when Charles E. Whitehurst ... operating the Century, Parkway, Garden, New and Peabody Theatres, said that the seating capacity of the picture theatres is becoming too large for the population of the city. "During the war," he said, "everyone was making huge wages. And those people who saved some of it are not feeling the depression as much as those who did not. People are going to shop for their picture entertainment. There are going where they can get the best for their money...."
>
> It will take time for conditions in the moving picture field ... to get back to normal.... The trouble in Baltimore with the moving picture business is that the seating capacity of the theaters is becoming greater than the population warrants and it's going to be a survival of the fittest. "But with regard to prices, it is a very hard thing to regulate them so that the exhibitors who show first run pictures can make enough to come out with a decent profit. The producers must come to the realization that prices for pictures must be more reasonable.... I made more money at the New Theatre four years ago when I used to charge 10 and 25 cents than I am making now at 25 and 75 cents. I could get a picture then for $500 a week. Now I have to pay about all I take in. And when I raise my prices in accordance, the public will not stand for it. It's the same way with other expenses ... ushers that received $8 now get $15 a week and musicians that received $30 now get $45 a week. "I am trying to meet these conditions, but the public will not stand the big prices unless I give them something extraordinary, and it is hard to keep the standard up for an 83-cent top price. And many people have written scathing letters to the forum columns of the newspapers denouncing these high prices. Conditions will right themselves eventually, but it will be very gradually."[31]

Of course Charles Whitehurst was the man who had just opened the 3,000-seat Century Theater. And the Century was about to crowd several smaller theaters off Lexington Street.

> Just what will be the ultimate effect of the gradual elimination of numerous small motion-picture theaters—more familiarly termed "neighborhood houses"—is ... causing considerable speculation among the people in the film industry. The fact that the smaller movie theaters are doomed to extinction has become apparent during the last six months or a year, and Baltimore seems merely to be following in the wake of the other larger cities, in which the more commodious picture palaces have succeeded in capturing practically all the patronage that was formerly distributed among the little exhibitors. Local conditions in this respect were brought forcibly to the public attention through the announcement in The Sun that more than 20 film theaters have been closed in Baltimore during the present year.
>
> The observed scarcely knows whether to deplore or approve the passing of the modest movie emporiums. Certainly the cheap, poorly ventilated

> houses did not make for ideal amusement conditions. The poor projection of films tended to add a severe strain to the eyes of the patron, while the crude tinkling of the player piano or wheezing of the ... organ did not contribute materially to the finer sensibilities of one's ears. On the other hand this type of theater has supplied a more economical and convenient center of amusement for a substantial proportion of the population and may ... have kept many persons out of mischief. In the early days of movie history these small exhibitors were able to skim a goodly amount of cream from the average filmplay at a comparatively low rental and had a low general upkeep expense. After a time, however, the film rentals began to go up ... until now the rentals have actually reached a prohibitive figure. This means that the owner of the large theatres, who formerly based their competition more directly upon the general attractiveness of their theater accommodations, now have become masters of the exhibiting business because they alone can afford to pay the high rentals for photoplays.
>
> And so, not only the neighborhood houses, but also the smaller first-run film theaters in the central part of the city have been forced to the wall. The last year has witnessed the closing of the Blue Mouse and the Picture Garden on Lexington street, and the Pickwick and the Strand on Howard street. Uptown the neighborhood houses have had to give way before various new theaters, of which there have sprung up one for each section (such, for example, are the Parkway, the Metropolitan, and the Boulevard). The tendency of the public has been more definitely established toward the larger, "first-run" houses. Many persons must see a picture during its first showing, or not at all. In the more remote sections of the city the patronage seems to have centered about one large neighborhood house to the exclusion of all the others....[32]

It had taken more than 10 years for the theater situation in town to reach a kind of equilibrium. The smaller, marginal theaters had to give way to the newer, larger ones. Theaters had to expand or die. The Wilson closed in 1920 only to be reborn the following year as the Rivoli. The Wizard, Horn, Regent, Belnord, and Cluster were all rebuilt as larger houses. The opening of a new movie palace in the neighborhood could doom nearby older theaters. The 3,000-seat Century was built in 1921 just east of the Wizard and Blue Mouse theaters. Neither of these nor the Picture Garden across the street could stand up to competition like that. All three closed within a few years of the Century's opening.

Among the other movie houses which closed in June 1923 were the West End, Lord Calvert, New Pickwick, Strand {1}, Victoria, and Superba. Some were just closed for the summer slump when many people deserted them for amusement parks, but the West End, Blue Mouse, and Strand would never reopen. Some reasons given for the closing of so many theaters were exorbitant film rentals, high overhead expenses, daylight saving time, and competition from larger theaters that offered vaudeville in addition to movies.

Neighborhood theaters were especially hard hit. According to Bernard Depkin, manager of the Metropolitan Theater, "The small exhibitor is doomed. His extinction is only a matter of months.... He can't afford the prices now demanded by the producers." Depkin cited the following example, "Several years ago I rented Harold Lloyd pictures at $700 a week. The last Lloyd picture we exhibited cost us $7,500 and the distributor first asked $12,000."[33] Films that had rented for $15 a week a few years earlier now rented for more than $15 a day. Theaters raised the prices of tickets.

A writer to the newspaper commented on the higher prices. "When the 'nuisance tax' was removed January 1 [1922] we sighed in relief. Where prices were 44 cents they would now be reduced to 40 cents. Were they? Not so one could notice it. They were boosted to 50 cents. Where the prices were 22 cents, including tax, now they are 25 cents. Only for the smaller and residential movie were people allowed to benefit by removal of the tax. It is very true that we are boobs—will stand for anything. But not forever. Even a worm will turn."[34]

Some downtown merchants were complaining to the Zoning Commission that there were too many theaters, and they were damaging their businesses. Management and labor finally found something they could agree on. In his report to the Baltimore Federation of Labor in July 1923, G. Kingston Howard, the delegate from the projectionists' union, said that Baltimore movie theaters were experiencing the worst summer season in their history. Howard noted the crowding out of small theaters by larger ones and reported that four small theaters in East Baltimore had recently closed due to a lack of patronage.

Size loomed more important as the 1920s moved on. The advent of the big neighborhood theaters began in the late teens with theaters like the Walbrook (1,400 seats, 1916), Rialto (500 seats, 1916), and McHenry (981 seats, 1917), but things did not really get going until after the war. In 1920, the new Horn (600 seats) opened and in 1921 the Capitol (800 seats), Columbia (1,300 seats), Apollo (1,300 seats), Douglass (1,349 seats), Regent (2,250 seats), Boulevard (1,625 seats), and the Belnord (1,269 seats) opened; the Ritz (1,175 seats) opened in 1926, and the State (2,044 seats) and Avalon (1,500 seats) opened in 1927. Downtown, the mighty 4,000-seat Stanley also opened in 1927.

T. M. Cushing, writing in 1926 discussed the plight of the older theaters. "One by one the small old-fashioned 'neighborhood' movie houses are giving up the ghost—those picturesque (and unsightly) little emporiums wherein one might see a feature 'fillum' for 5 or 10 cents. Gone is the old 'nickelodeon'—even the cheapest movie costs you 10 to 15 cents. In place of these modest establishments big and pretentious temples of cinema art are being erected. Among the first of the new type of neighborhood theater is the Boulevard.... Until now this theater has more or less set the pace for the second-run movies."[35]

At the beginning of the 1927 theater season, this was the first-run set-up in Baltimore:

Garden and **New** (Whitehurst)—Fox, Universal, Film Booking Office, Producers' Distributing Corporation
Hippodrome (Keith-Albee)—First National, Film Booking Office, Universal
Century, Valencia, Parkway (Loew's)—United Artists, Famous Players–Lasky, MGM
Rivoli—First National
Metropolitan (Warner Bros.)—Warner
Embassy—Famous Players–Lasky, Universal

Soon after the Stanley opened, the Stanley Company and Loew's made a deal whereby three of their Baltimore theaters—Stanley, Century, and Valencia—would be operated jointly under Loew's management. The theaters planned to use First National, Paramount, MGM, and United Artists product exclusively. Warner Bros. gained control of the Stanley Company in September 1928 and later moved their first-run operation from the Metropolitan to the Stanley. The cost of a ticket to a first-run theater in Baltimore was increasing, but it had not yet reached the New York top price of $2.00.

The second big theater scandal of the 1920s involved the story of a young New York dancer who suddenly appeared in Baltimore claiming to be the widow of local theater magnate Charles Whitehurst. Everyone believed that Whitehurst had been a bachelor when he died, but the dancer, Claire Ulrich, claimed that they had married in a private ceremony in a New York hotel room nine months before his death. During the next six years, the Whitehurst case became one of the most sensational court cases in Baltimore.

Charles E. Whitehurst was the son of Dr. Jesse Harrison Whitehurst, a photographer with studios in Baltimore and several other cities who also had founded the Juniper Tar drug firm. Charles was born in Baltimore around 1875. He was one of eight children, three girls and five boys.[36] Whitehurst was educated in the Baltimore public schools and then joined his brothers to work in his father's proprietary medicine business. Whitehurst entered the moving picture business in 1907 when he opened the Red Moon theater on Baltimore Street. Although he was successful there, he correctly foresaw that the center of downtown was moving north from Baltimore Street to Lexington Street.

In 1910, supported by the investments of his family and friends, he opened the New Theater on Lexington. Five years later he built the Garden in the next block, and in 1921 he opened the Century. The Century was the largest theater in Baltimore at the time. After the Wizard closed in late 1924, Whitehurst controlled all the Lexington Street theaters from the New to the Century. Each of the Whitehurst theaters installed huge illuminated signs; the street was dubbed the "Lane of Lights" and "Whitehurst's Baby Broadway."

Whitehurst showed his willingness to innovate and change with the times by booking vaudeville shows made up entirely of women during World War I. Women were filling many traditional male roles by the summer of 1918, and Whitehurst reasoned that, with so many male entertainers in the service, women would have to fill that role too. He decided to take a chance.[37] By the time of his death, in January 1924, Whitehurst controlled the New, Garden, Century and Parkway theaters, seating nearly 9,000 people and representing an investment of about $5 million.

Charles Whitehurst was characterized as a tireless worker in pursuing the interests of his theaters and a great booster of his hometown. In response to a question about moving his theater interests to other cities, he was quoted as saying, "I made my money in Baltimore, and here I will use it to promote the material growth of the city." He spent much of his time traveling among his theaters. "Early in the day and late in the evening his short, plump figure was encountered in all parts of the houses."[38] He opposed daylight saving time, but was in favor of Sunday movies.

Whitehurst was a member of the board and one of the founders of the Motion Picture Theatre Owners of America. In 1921, he was reportedly joining with New York interests to produce films. The first one was to star Lionel Barrymore, Virginia Lee, and Louise Glaum. His untimely death put an end to this enterprise. At least some of the credit for the success of the Whitehurst theaters must be given to Whitehurst's dynamic manager at the New, Louis A. DeHoff. DeHoff was a skilled manager and publicist who knew how to use the press effectively. His publicity stunts at the New during the late teens were legendary. DeHoff's efforts to furnish entertainment to inmates at the Maryland Penitentiary and to support American soldiers in the Liberty Loan drive and Red Cross drive earned him an award from the State Board of Parole in May 1918.

On Friday, January 25, 1924, while in perfect health, Charles Whitehurst was taken ill with influenza, apparently the same kind that had caused the terrible pandemic of 1918. Within a short time he developed pneumonia, and his condition deteriorated rapidly. He lapsed into a coma on the 30th, and 10 hours later, at 3 A.M. on January 31, he died. He was buried in Loudon Park Cemetery on February 1. At 2 P.M., as his funeral services were being conducted, more than 80 Baltimore movie theaters stopped their shows for 10 minutes in his honor. He has been the only local exhibitor so honored. The Whitehurst theaters closed for the entire day. Five days after the funeral, Dr. J. H. Whitehurst, Charles' brother, took over as president of the Whitehurst theater interests.[39] Charles left no will, but his estate was valued at $278,000.

Everyone assumed that Charles Whitehurst died a bachelor. But, in August 1924, a young dancer named Claire Ulrich shocked his family and the local theater community by filing suit against Whitehurst's mother for the widow's dower in Whitehurst's estate.[40] Even Whitehurst's close associates were unaware of his marriage. The resulting suit and appeals lasted until September 1929.[41] Miss Ulrich claimed that she and Whitehurst had been married in a private ceremony in April 1923. The ceremony, she said, had taken place in a New York apartment, where Whitehurst read the ceremony for the marriage of a Catholic to a non-Catholic out of a prayer book, in the presence of one witness.

Several months after she filed suit, Miss Ulrich stated that she was visited by a man who represented himself as an attorney. He showed her a letter that contained veiled threats of personal injury by the Ku Klux Klan if she persisted in her suit. Faced with these threats, she signed an agreement to accept $11,000 to waive all further claims. The agreement was acknowledged by M. Morris Whitehurst as one of the administrators. Ulrich paid the lawyer $1,500 but later learned that he had received $5,000 from the Whitehursts.

Miss Ulrich's lawyers filed a bill asking for a widow's share of half of the $278,000 estate of Charles Whitehurst. Whitehurst's mother immediately appealed, and the case went to the State Court of Appeals in October 1925. The Court upheld Judge George A. Solter's overruling of Whitehurst's demurrer to the petition filed by Ulrich and sent the case back to Solter. The trial got under way in Circuit Court in November 1925. In February 1926, Judge Solter handed down his opinion that Ulrich was indeed the legal wife of Charles Whitehurst and was entitled to press her claim to half the estate in court. Whitehurst's mother appealed, but in December the Maryland Court of Appeals again agreed with Judge Solter. In upholding Solter's ruling, the Court noted that the payment of $5,000 by members of the Whitehurst family to an attorney working for Ulrich carried with it "a strong implication of bribery."[42]

Charles Whitehurst's mother died soon after her appeal was denied, and Ulrich's suit against the estate did not begin for more than a year. On April 3, 1928, Claire Ulrich presented evidence before Judge Eugene O'Dunne in Baltimore Circuit Court. She charged that Whitehurst interests had organized a conspiracy, which included Ulrich's mother and her New York lawyer, in an attempt to get her to abandon her claim to a share of Charles Whitehurst's estate. During her testimony, Ulrich testified that she had met Whitehurst in 1922 when she came to Baltimore as a cabaret dancer.[43] Whitehurst "paid considerable attention to her" over the next year and finally, she said, they were married in a private ceremony in a New York hotel room. Whitehurst told her that he wanted the marriage kept secret because he had promised his mother that he would not marry while she was alive.

The defense lawyer argued that Ulrich was merely Whitehurst's mistress and that the alleged marriage contract had been forged. Both sides produced witnesses to support their case. The Whitehurst family's witnesses said that they all knew her as Claire Ulrich and that they had no reason to believe that Charles Whitehurst had married her. Miss

Ulrich's witnesses said that they had known her as Mrs. Whitehurst. One quoted Charles Whitehurst as saying of Ulrich in August 1923, "This is no longer Miss Ulrich. She is Mrs. Whitehurst." On April 4, a government handwriting expert identified penciled inscriptions in the Catholic prayer book reportedly used for the marriage ceremony between Whitehurst and Ulrich as being in the handwriting of Charles Whitehurst. Several days of testimony by various experts and witnesses, including Miss Ulrich, culminated in Ulrich's dramatic weeping flight from the witness stand on April 17. She had become upset as a defense lawyer read a letter from Whitehurst to her. One of the key pieces of evidence was the so-called "wifey" letter, quoted below[44]:

> Friday
>
> Dear Kiddo, Wifey and Decorator, and Movie Star, almost, not yet:
>
> Well, anyway, howsoever, you are right there with the mustard when it comes to certain performances and you will be awarded the golden medal in Class A or there will be trouble. Now, will you be good? Oh, yes, you are always a good little bad girl; no, you are my big girl, but will soon be my little girl.
>
> Just heard from Ditman and I hope to see him next week, but do not think he has a photo of you. Hurried, with love and kisses.
>
> CHAS.

A handwriting expert for the defense testified that the word "Wifey" had been inserted after the letter was written and was not in Charles Whitehurst's handwriting. Additional witnesses for the defense stated that they believed Ulrich was the "new girl" who succeeded a German girl as Whitehurst's girlfriend. Howard W. Bryant, president of the City Council, and a close friend of Whitehurst, said he believed that Whitehurst was "...keeping [his new girl] as he had kept other girls in New York."[45] The plaintiff's lawyer characterized Ulrich as a "credulous and foolish girl, gullible to an extreme degree" but of unblemished character and Charles Whitehurst as "a man of the world in the lowest sense of the word."[46] Louis Deal, an associate of Whitehurst, testified that he had served as advisor to Dr. J. Herbert Whitehurst in conversations with Miss Ulrich. Deal and another witness claimed that they could have made a settlement with her for $25,000 with "no widow strings attached." Declaring "I couldn't understand how Charlie could have been such a fool," Deal said that the estate finally made a payment of $11,000 to Ulrich "to keep it out of the newspapers in Baltimore."[47] A former employer of Miss Ulrich testified that Ulrich had forged the word "wifey" in the "Dear Wifey" letter.

The mass of often-contradictory evidence and hearsay was left for the judge to sort out on April 27. Four days later, in a 22-page opinion, Judge O'Dunne denied Ulrich's claim for a share in Whitehurst's estate, ruling that the alleged "prayer book" marriage between Whitehurst and Ulrich never took place and that the signatures "Charles" and "Claire" and the word "wifey" were forgeries. While expressing his sympathy for Miss Ulrich, Judge O'Dunne stated in his opinion that society had little respect for a man who "having substantial wealth at his command, takes a young and confiding girl, less than half his age, to his apartments for their mutual convenience and lives with her without the sanction of legal wedlock, and when suddenly taken off by an unexpected death leaves her wholly unprovided for." Ulrich filed an appeal in June.

The Maryland Court of Appeals heard her appeal in December 1928. In March 1929, by a split decision 5 to 3, the court reversed Judge O'Dunne's decision. The majority opinion was that the unorthodox ceremony did constitute a valid marriage under the law of New York. On July 10, 1929, Judge O'Dunne upheld the validity of the marriage. This would eventually give Miss Ulrich $150,000 from the estate. Lawyers for the Whitehurst estate said they would fight the award. On 22 July they unsuccessfully appealed for permission to review the proceedings claiming that new tests showed that the key words "Charles" and "Claire" written in the prayer book and the word "wifey" in the letter were forgeries. A hearing was held at the end of the month to determine the value of Charles Whitehurst's estate. The final decree was signed in late September. Everyone thought this was the end of the story, but three months later, Claire Ulrich's mother sued the Whitehurst brothers for $150,000, claiming that the family had agreed to set her up in business in Philadelphia and pay all her expenses to recompense her for helping them in the suit brought by her daughter. Her suit was dismissed in April 1931. The long battle over Charles Whitehurst's estate was at last over.

Whatever may have been the truth about the relationship between him and Ulrich, Charles Whitehurst was a visionary in the Baltimore theater world. He was one of the few local exhibitors who thought big and took the risks to build deluxe, downtown movie palaces.

Claire Ulrich Whitehurst returned to New York where she attended Columbia and Cornell. Later, she moved to Coral Gables, Florida where she was active in musical organizations. During World War II, she worked with the American Red Cross to coordinate housing for soldiers. President Truman awarded her a citation for this work. She died in Coral Gables in August 1994 at the age of 94.[48]

Baltimore exhibitors on the *Our Gang* set with Charlie Chase in Hollywood, 1926. [Standing, left to right]: unidentified, unidentified, Arthur Price, Walter Pacy, unidentified, Frank Durkee, Sr., Wilbur Whitehurst, unidentified, Jack Whittle.

Several national theater circuits saw Whitehurst's death as an opportunity to enter the lucrative Baltimore first-run market, which was virtually untapped by outside interests. The Whitehurst theaters—Century, Garden, New and Parkway—were valued at $4 million.[49] A struggle ensued between the Whitehurst family and a group of bankers for control of the Century Theater Company. By November 1925, the Whitehursts had purchased enough stock to gain control of the company. At the same time Marcus Loew was anxious to return to the city; the expanding Stanley Company was looking for another outlet, and Famous Players–Lasky and William Fox were lurking in the shadows.

Loew was determined to have a theater in Baltimore. During negotiations to buy the theaters, he said, "If this deal falls through I will build or buy a house [in Baltimore] for my productions…. I am certain on one point, however, and that is, regardless of the outcome of the present negotiations, I will have a theater in Baltimore."[50] As it turned out, Marcus Loew beat out Fox, his only serious competition. Loew wanted all four theaters, but he wound up with only the Century and the Parkway for which he might have paid approximately $1.9 million. The Garden was sold in 1927 to Schanberger interests. Morris Mechanic bought the New Theater in 1929.

The major national theater circuits had flirted with Baltimore for many years, but had failed to establish a major presence in the city. The Shubert organization had acquired control of the Lyceum in 1905, the Auditorium in 1909 and the Academy of Music in 1921; they tried unsuccessfully to purchase the New in 1921. Nixon and Zimmerman interests gained control of the Academy of Music in 1896, the Victoria in 1916, and the McHenry in 1920. They nearly acquired the Maryland in 1908 and wanted to build a theater on the site where the Hippodrome was eventually built.

Keith vaudeville played the Maryland, Garden, and Hippodrome, and Keith interests also planned a theater in Baltimore in 1926. Marcus Loew was very anxious to add a first-run Baltimore theater to his circuit. He had leased the Hippodrome from 1915 to 1924, and he shared the Stanley with Warner Bros. from 1928 to 1934. Loew had planned to build theaters on the Hippodrome site in 1913, at North and Charles in 1920, and on West Pratt Street in 1928. Warner Bros. had been trying to acquire a downtown house for a long time. They planned a large theater in the vicinity of Charles and Lexington Streets in 1931, but they abandoned that idea and took over sole control of the Stanley in 1934.

Loew's—with the Century, Valencia, and Parkway, and Warner Bros.—with the Stanley, were the only outside circuits to have theaters in Baltimore for any length of time until the 1960s when Boston-based General Cinema opened theaters in the suburbs. By the end of the 20th century nearly all of the theaters in the metropolitan area were owned by national chains. In 1998, national theater circuits controlled 65 percent of the theaters in the metropolitan area and 80 percent of the screens.[51] Of the 68 theaters (and 68 screens) operating in the same area in 1960, all were controlled by local interests.

The Censor Board worked throughout the 1920s to keep dangerous subjects out of Maryland's theaters. Dr. Howard A. Kelly, commenting in 1920 on the spread of vice in the city, declared that, "Of all the evil influences of the present day … exceeding by far the liquor traffic, I estimate the movies, as at present conducted, to be the worst, the most potent agents in producing crime and immorality."[52] There were constant calls for more censoring. The board seemed to be approving too many films. In 1921, only one out of every five movies submitted to the board was considered objectionable. In 1924, the board made cuts in 897 of the 5,512 pictures reviewed and completely rejected only one film.

In 1926, four films were rejected out of 6,482 reviewed; cuts were ordered in 684. A juvenile court judge in 1923 stated that moving pictures were the chief cause of juvenile crime as young boys attempted to imitate their screen heroes.[53]

What subjects did the board consider to be improper in movies? These varied with the composition of the board and the era. Films banned in one era were passed in a later era. In 1927, members of the board agreed that they were passing scenes that would have been cut a few years earlier. During the First World War, films which tended to discourage military recruiting were frowned on, but difficult to reject. Much of the material ordered to be eliminated from films seemed to be aimed at preserving the status quo.

When the board started out, these were some of the subjects it considered objectionable in a movie[54]:

- Improper exhibition of feminine underwear.
- Indelicate sexual situations.
- Nude figures.
- Overpassionate love scenes.
- Excessive use of firearms.
- Disrespect for the law, third degree scenes.
- Infidelity on part of husband justifying adultery on part of wife.
- White slave stories.
- Gruesome murders ... stabbing and shooting of persons.
- Deeds of violence ... throwing bombs, arson ... train wrecking.
- Birth control, malpractice.
- Venereal disease...
- Inflammatory scenes and titles calculated to stir up racial hatred or antagonistic relations between labor and capital.

Kissing scenes were a constant problem. In 1921, the Citizens' League for Better Motion Pictures told Governor Ritchie that a three-foot kiss was the longest kiss that motion picture spectators ought to be allowed to see.[55] They wanted on-screen kisses limited to three feet of film, or about two seconds, and requested that couples not be shown kissing while seated on a bench. A Baltimore exhibitor was arrested in March 1921 for exhibiting a movie which contained a kiss longer than three feet.

In 1926, there was an editorial on the kiss. It said, "It is possible that kisses might have remained what they were — a mere caress of butterfly wings— except for the movies. The motion pictures of passion, ... to make the patrons gasp and tremble with delight, invented a new kind of kiss—not new in method of application, but revolutionary in duration. It was not, in any scientific sense, a proper kiss, but rather a form of vulcanizing that stuck and stuck and stuck. It is still to be seen on the screen in some sections, but censors delete the greater part of the footage."[56] Local moviegoers in 1929 believed that Maryland censors cut more kissing scenes than other states' censors did, but censor board member Asa C. Sharp said they were mistaken. The board had just cut portions of two Greta Garbo kissing scenes "not ... because of the actual kissing, but for the manner in which the kissing was done."[57]

In the early 1930s, under chairman Dr. George Heller, the board ruled that films could only show someone kissing another on the neck if the person kissed was the kisser's mother-in-law, great-grandmother, grandmother, parent, sibling, child or wife. Prior to this ruling the censors had consistently eliminated kisses on the neck. Heller's successor,

Bernard B. Gough,[58] declared that "The length or location of a kiss or embrace will depend entirely upon the nature and purpose of the scene. Under certain circumstances a kiss might not be permitted at all. Under different circumstances, it might last for an indefinite period."[59] It is difficult to imagine a set of circumstances where a kiss might last indefinitely. One manager could not see what the fuss was all about. "Baltimore hardly ever gets over a three-foot kiss. The censor board is already about as strict as you can find and there's precious few six-foot or even four-foot kisses that get by."[60]

Audiences seem to have had seen enough kissing by 1933. John O'Ren reported seeing a Bette Davis movie at the Century "where much of the footage of what I consider a mediocre film" was taken up by the kisses of Miss Davis and a fair-haired youth. O'Ren said that there were no feminine gasps of astonishment and no breathless ahs. The spectators seemed to take the screen caresses rather disdainfully.[61]

The censors often seemed arbitrary. Gilbert Kanour, writing in the *Evening Sun* of July 16, 1936, reported that the line "Aw, he stinks" was allowed in the movie *America's Sweetheart*, but a similar line, "The princess says your music stinks," was cut from the film, *The Princess Came Across*.

During the interminable bickering over censorship, proponents of censoring often brought up the fact that motion picture theaters were the places of choice for children to play hooky. Ever since movie theaters first appeared in the city, kids skipping school had made beelines for them. Certain theaters developed reputations as friendly places that would wink at the young rascals. In 1921, the managers of Lubin's, the Clover, the Comedy, and the Rivoli were cited for "harboring" children in their theaters during school hours. In later years, the Howard was the place to go. Several generations of kids sought out the cool, dark interior of that theater instead of attending school. Shame on them.

As the turbulent 1920s were coming to an end, one final fight involving movie theaters remained. This one pitted the exhibitors against the projectionists. It ended up with the exhibitors forming their own union of projectionists that dominated the city theaters for the next generation. As regular as swallows returning to Capistrano, the projectionists and exhibitors faced off every September when the projectionists' contracts came up for renewal. The projectionists asked for raises and the exhibitors refused, saying they were hardly able to make ends meet. Contract negotiations would drag out well into the fall, and predictions of strikes were routinely made.

The troubles began in 1921; the Exhibitors' League of Maryland and the Theatre Managers' Association of Baltimore opposed the union projectionists, musicians, and stagehands. Technicalities over when certain letters were sent and when they were received blurred the usual argument over wages, and the two sides were deadlocked. The managers announced a 20 percent cut in the projectionists' wages. The operators of the Palace and Gayety declared "open shop" and prepared to open the season with non-union orchestras. In early September, the musicians and stagehands agreed not to strike for 60 days, and a temporary truce was arranged.

The theater owners pushed things a bit further in 1922 when the Cluster and Novelty theaters on South Broadway fired their union projectionists. The union distributed circulars asking people to attend other theaters in the area. A year later, with the Cluster family in the thick of things, union projectionists picketed Benjamin Cluster's Waverly Theater, which had also dispensed with the services of a union operator. In June 1923, after working nearly a year without a contract, there was a split in the exhibitors' ranks occasioned by a new wage scale that would cut some salaries. An impartial arbitration board agreed on a scale that would pay projectionists between 85 and 95 cents an hour depending on the size of the theater. The Exhibitors' League of Maryland said it was a decision for each exhibitor, whether or not to sign. Most of the large downtown houses, including all of the Whitehurst theaters, did sign with Local 181.

However, very quietly, in November 1923, a new union, the Independent Motion Picture Operators and Managers Union of Baltimore City, was incorporated. Nothing much was heard of this group until 1927. In 1925, the Baltimore projectionists asked for increases of 20 to 30 percent, which would put them on a par with projectionists in Washington and Philadelphia. On September 1, the projectionists' union issued an ultimatum demanding that the contracts be signed that night. Within 24 hours the owners, with the exception of a single neighborhood theater, had capitulated.

Events of 1927 brought to a head the long simmering hostility between the exhibitors and the projectionists, and before the year was over the two projectionists' unions in Baltimore were at each other's throats. The independent union was strongly supported by the major local exhibitors, Durkee, Rome, and Gaertner; Local 181 had the support of organized labor. Sam Isaacson, president of Local 181, saw a big fight coming.

> Baltimore's "biggest fight in moving picture labor disputes" looms between the Motion Picture Exhibitors' League and the Motion Picture Operators' Union, it was asserted last night at the meeting of the Baltimore Federation of labor.
>
> Samuel Isaacson ... reported that the union was making preparations for the presentation of a new wage schedule at the expiration of the present agreement with the managers, September 1. Some of the managers have learned of this proposed move, he said, and have canceled existing agreements. "This makes it look as if we are in for a fight," Mr. Isaacson said. "If that is the case, Baltimore will see the biggest fight in motion-picture labor disputes it has yet witnessed."[62]

Isaacson was right. The fight in 1927 split the projectionists completely, and split the exhibitors into two groups, depending on which union they used. The first salvos were fired in August 1927 as the two-year agreement, grudgingly accepted by the exhibitors in 1925, was nearing its end. The union was ready to ask for a new wage scale, and the owners did not like what they had heard about it. At the same time that the owners had nearly reached the breaking point, two members of the State Board of Examiners of Moving Picture Operators accused a former board member of operating a school for operators and providing his students with answers to the state examination.[63] Two years earlier, the *Afro-American* had predicted that the white local was headed for trouble and that there were enough non-union operators available to operate every theater in town.[64] The newspaper concluded that the African-American local had made a wise decision not to merge with the white local.

Board members John Bedford and William H. Miller charged, on August 27, that former member Harry Cluster, (1) while a member of the board and at the present time was conducting a school to prepare applicants to take the examination to be licensed as moving-picture machine operators before the board of which he was a member and for which he assisted in preparing the questions to be submitted in the examinations, (2) as a member of the board obtained the list of questions and approved answers and has taught his students the approved answers prior to their taking such examination, and (3) prepared and submitted certain questions that were not reasonable or proper and could only be answered by students specially instructed at his own school. William E. Stumpf, secretary of the owners' group, said that the school had been conducted for eight years and that Cluster was an instructor there. Governor Ritchie said he would investigate the charges.

The theater owners refused to agree to the new wage scale, and the projectionists threatened a strike on September 1 if they did not. The new scale seemed innocent enough; the wages of all projectionists, except those at first-run theaters, would remain the same. However, there were other changes from the previous agreement that were more difficult for the owners; an exhibitor could not fire a projectionist unless the projectionist agreed and if an exhibitor should sell or lease his theater, he had to guarantee that the same wage scale would be maintained by the new owner. The theater owners were adamant; their representative bluntly stated on the last day of August that "The motion-picture theatre owners will not agree to the demands made by the operators' union, and if the latter do not modify, then they will just have to strike."[65] It was clear that the owners had drawn a line in the sand and that they were prepared for a strike. The union seemed to be pushing its demands to the limit. Last-minute discussions on August 31 failed to resolve the issue.

On the first of September 1927, 44 neighborhood movie houses abandoned negotiations with IATSE Local 181, and signed two-year contracts with the independent Motion Picture Operators and Managers Union No. 1.[66] Eight downtown first-run theaters—Century, Valencia, Parkway, New, Garden, Hippodrome, Metropolitan, and Rivoli—signed with 181 and 26 theaters had not made up their minds. A spokesman for Local 181 made disparaging remarks about the independent union and said that his union had ordered a walkout in all the theaters that had signed with the other union as well as those theaters that had not signed with either union. The owners, headed by Frank Durkee, who hated Local 181,[67] locked that union's projectionists out of their 44 theaters. G. Kingston Howard, business agent, admitted that those theaters could probably put on shows because their managers had been trained to operate the projectors and could bring in apprentices from the exhibitors' school. One projectionist was arrested at the Avalon Theater, and some owners asked for police protection although business agent, Sam Isaacson, promised they would "fight clean." Three more theaters signed with the independent union on September 1, and all of the approximately 82 movie houses in Baltimore conducted their regular performances. The following day, police were instructed to canvass every theater in the city to make sure that all the projectionists were licensed.

On September 3, Local 181 began picketing nine theaters. On September 5, the Capitol, Avalon, Palace, and Idle Hour were picketed. Three days later, citing threats against one of its members, the independent union was granted an injunction forbidding Local 181 to picket neighborhood movie houses.[68] The situation settled down, but the two unions remained apart for the next 25 years.[69] Meanwhile, Governor Ritchie had conducted an investigation of the charges against Harry Cluster and completely exonerated him.[70] By 1929, Local 181 had gained back about 50 theaters, but local president G. Kingston Howard is reported to have said that they got "the hell beat out of them" in the strike.

The independent union, which was often derisively called the "Exhibitors' Union" or "Cluster's Union," was organized along the lines of 181, but it had no affiliation with any national labor organization. It seems clear that it was more or less controlled by the exhibitors. Harry Cluster, who had run the school for operators, was recognized as the man who organized the new union and who was in charge of the union's operation,[71] but it was widely believed that he took orders from the exhibitors. The independent union held its meetings at a number of locations over the years, among these were locations on North Howard Street, near Pulaski and Frederick Avenue, and on Foster Avenue. Frank Durkee reportedly told his operators that he would guarantee their jobs for life if they would leave 181. Some members did desert 181 and join the new union in order to keep their jobs. The two unions existed side-by-side until after World War II.

Not only were the projectionists pitted against the owners in yearly combat, but the projectionists themselves were divided along racial lines. For many years there were two unions, one for white operators and one for African-American operators. Prior to 1914, there were perhaps 20 African-American projectionists working in black theaters. "Doc" Clarence Lee, of the Pastime Theater on Lexington Street, seems to have been the first African-American projectionist who received a license. Five others, including Leonard Outen, George Douglass, William Causby, John Pitts, and Chester Seward had their licenses by 1916. Douglass, Causby, Pitts, Seward, and Lee applied for permission to affiliate with the white union, but were refused. In 1921, they formed their own union, the Colored Motion Picture Projectionists Association.[72] Three years later, the white union offered to let the black operators become an auxiliary of their union; the offer was refused primarily because of a set of highly restrictive conditions that they would have had to agree to.[73] Another offer, apparently with similar conditions, was made by the white union in 1926, but that too was refused.

At the end of 1924, seven African-American theaters — the Dunbar, Star, National, Roosevelt, Regent, Goldfield, and Douglass — employed operators who were members of the association. Two more theaters were added in 1925, and, by 1928, the association had 14 members working at ten theaters and its own school to train operators. William Causby was the president; Moxley Willis, vice-president; Charles Vodery, secretary[74]; Nathan Miller, recording secretary; George Douglass, business agent; and Richard Johnson, sergeant-at-arms. In August 1948, climaxing a 15-year struggle, the auxiliary status of Local 181-A was abolished at the convention of the International Alliance of Theatrical State Employees and Moving Picture Operators. The elevation of the Baltimore local to full voting status followed a resolution to that effect at the 1946 Chicago convention.

The motion picture projector has endured a complicated evolution since the first ones appeared in the 1890s. A projector once consisted of a lamp house and a motion head. Light was provided either by lime light — produced by a gas flame heating a piece of lime to incandescence — or by electric arcs. The motion head contained the shutter, intermittent film feed, two film magazines, and a safety shutter. The motion head also served as a support for the lens. The earliest projectors did not have take-up reels; the film tumbled into a large bag or other container after it was projected. Take-up reels were soon developed.

In 1907, Edison Projecting Kinetoscopes were selling for $75, $115, and $135. Other popular machines were the Lubin Marvel, the Powers Cameragraph, and the Motiograph. The improved Edison Kinetoscope 1913 Model sold for $250. In 1917, a motor-driven Motiograph projector cost $305. Hand-cranked projectors were replaced by motor-driven ones by 1915, although hand-cranked models were still available. A new Baird projector cost $500 in 1921. A Loew's theater projection booth in 1927 cost about $13,189 to equip.[75] In 1936, a new Motiograph projector, less the lamphouse and sound reproducer, cost more than $1,000.

Baltimore and Washington projectionists of locals 181-A and 224-A. [*Seated on the floor, left to right*] • Harry Robinson (224-A), Tompkins (224-A), Wiley Davis (224-A), Ralph Dines (224-A), Edward Tolson (224-A); [*seated on chairs left to right*] Willie Johnson (181-A) • • Edward Johnson (181-A), Robert Ford (224-A), Robert Johnson (181-A) • George Douglass (181-A), Charles Turpin (224-A), Augie Johnson (181-A), Guy Hunt (224-A), William Curtis (181-A) [*remaining rows mainly 224-A members or unidentified*]

For many years each reel contained 1,000 feet of film and ran for about 12 minutes. Many of us remember when the changeover from one reel to another was indicated by a small black dot in the upper right-hand corner of the screen.[76] The 2,000-foot reel was adopted in 1936. Individual projectionists welcomed this although the national union opposed it.[77] In the 1970s, the xenon bulb began to replace the carbon arc as the light source for projectors. Xenon bulbs were much easier to use and provided a very compact and bright light. Exhibitors were beginning to talk about automation in the projection booth in the late 1960s, and the "platter" system was becoming available in the early 1970s.[78] The Christie Electric Corporation was advertising its Autowind film handling system, which could handle four and a half hours of continuous projection.

By 1971 the technology was available, though costly, to fully automate a booth. Instead of projectionists, theaters would have technicians who controlled several booths from a single control room. In 1983 a new projector system that could handle 35mm and 70mm film could cost between $6,900 and $12,900. For many years theater equipment in Baltimore was sold by Pearce and Scheck, the Moving Picture Supply Company, Palmore & Homand, Isidor Weniz, the Haefele Company, the National Theatre Supply Company and the J. F. Dusman Company. J. F. Dusman founded his supply company in 1912; it operated for more than 60 years.

Modern theater air conditioning began to appear in larger theaters in the late 1920s. Theater historian Douglas Gomery identifies Balaban & Katz's Central Park Theater, which opened in Chicago in 1917, as "the first mechanically air cooled theatre in the world."[79] Much of the technology for practical air conditioning was developed in Chicago because that city was the center of the meat packing industry which required efficient refrigeration methods. Other air-conditioned Balaban & Katz theaters followed the Central Park. By 1925, the head of Paramount's theater division could announce that "the summer slump which hitherto has devastated the box office returns of motion picture theatres has been banished by the introduction of efficient cooling plants."[80] The Rivoli in New York, Grauman's Metropolitan in Los Angeles, the Palace in Dallas, and the Texan in Houston had all installed air conditioning by the summer of 1925.

In Baltimore, the New, Century, and Garden were advertising air conditioning by August 1925. The New claimed it was "Cooler here than anywhere." The Century said it was "20° cooler than the street." Theaters without air conditioning did the best they could; manager Depkin at the Metropolitan served his patrons ice water when the weather was hot. The management of the Little Theater tried to stay open all summer in 1928 by installing a large exhaust fan and several wall fans. The Carey advertised the "Arctic Nu-Air" system, which ensured 40,000 cubic feet of fresh air every minute to keep the theater cool. Two years later, after Loew's had acquired the Century, the Century and Valencia installed a gigantic $500,000 air conditioning system. This seems to have been the first modern air-conditioning system in a Baltimore theater.

At the end of this period, the greatest movie theater in Baltimore and in the state of Maryland was built on North Howard Street. The magnificent 4,000-seat alabaster Stanley Theater opened with impressive ceremony on September 23, 1927, a fitting architectural coda to bring the movie palace era to a close in the city. The Stanley, named for Philadelphia exhibitor Stanley Mastbaum, was built by the Stanley-Crandall Company during its expansion out of Pennsylvania to provide it a first-run outlet in Baltimore. It was built on the ruins of the Academy of Music according to plans by the Philadelphia firm of Hoffman and Henon who designed, among many other theaters, the Stanley, Mastbaum Memorial, and Boyd theaters in Philadelphia. The Stanley lasted only 38 years; it was unforgivably destroyed in 1965.

5

A Theater Near You (1928–1939)

During this era, sound movies were finally perfected. By 1930, most of the city's theaters had been wired for sound. The Little Theater tried returning to silents in 1930, but moviegoers had gotten a taste of talkies and few wanted to return. Sound was here to stay. Many people wanted to see a newsreel theater in Baltimore similar to a popular one opened in New York in 1930, and someone suggested that the Valencia would make a good one. In 1930 Baltimore had 11 first-run theaters seating 21,330 and taking in as much as $92,500 a week. The Century was the highest grossing theater in town, taking in about $16,000 a week; the Stanley was second with about $15,000 a week, followed by the New at around $10,000, and the Hippodrome at about $8,500. Business was good.

According to Morris Mechanic, the Depression was hurting ordinary productions, but people would still pay to see the super-specials. People seemed to be shopping around for movies, and the automobile was beginning to make itself felt as a means of getting to them.[1] There were fewer movie theaters built during the early years of this decade, and they were generally much smaller than ones built in the previous decade. When theaters were built, they were built in the suburbs and towns adjacent to the city. This was the era of the neighborhood theater.[2]

Oil was replacing coal as the fuel of choice to heat theaters by 1930. Air conditioning was more widely available. The architectural styles, art deco and Moderne, were markedly different from the baroque and beaux-arts designs of earlier theaters. It cost more to build and equip a theater. In 1930, the cost of a 1,000-seat movie theater was about $151,000. A 2,000-seat air-conditioned theater cost about $340,750. By 1933 the Motion Picture Theater Association of Maryland had decided that there were enough movie theaters in Baltimore and sent a resolution to the Mayor and members of the City Council opposing the erection of more.[3] Voluntary daylight savings time was adopted in 1930, and Sunday movies were finally permitted in Baltimore.

The first drive-in theater in Maryland, the Governor Ritchie Drive-In, opened in Glen Burnie in 1939. Burlesque and vaudeville were dying in the 1930s. In 1932, there were only four Baltimore theaters that offered vaudeville and film, the Hippodrome, Keith's, Century, and State. The Embassy had eliminated its vaudeville and orchestra in 1927 and the New, Rivoli and Stanley had eliminated their stage shows around 1928. One writer to *Evening Sun* movie critic Q.E.D. said that this pleased her because the New and Rivoli "offered very mediocre talent."

Many reasons were suggested to explain the death of burlesque. George Rife, president of the Empire Theater Company, which operated the Palace Theater, said that burlesque theaters could not afford to charge the prices that the movie and vaudeville theaters did. Top prices for movie-vaudeville combinations were 60 cents while burlesque houses had to charge $1.00 or more. Rife told a reporter that in the old days, the hottest thing in burlesque was the can-can, which was always performed in long skirts.[4] One theater manager thought that burlesque had died because women were permitted to attend burlesque performances which had previously been like men's clubs. A real estate man believed that burlesque had just gone too far and that there was nothing left to show after full nudity was allowed. The movie business continued to improve in the mid–1930s. In 1936 attendance at Baltimore neighborhood theaters was up 15 percent. In 1937, Baltimore had a total seating capacity of 74,038 for 90 theaters. Despite the large number of theaters in the city, Maryland was underseated with 12.5 persons for each theater seat.[5] Cartoons were becoming popular. Over 3,000 people, mainly children, attended an all-cartoon show featuring Mickey Mouse and *The Three Little Pigs* at the Century in January 1934.

The first-run situation in Baltimore became set in the 1930s and remained nearly unchanged for the next 30 years. In 1930, the first-run theaters in Baltimore were:

Auditorium (Schanberger)	Metropolitan (Warner Bros.)
Century (Loew's)	New (Morris Mechanic)
Hippodrome (Rappaport)	Rivoli (Wilson Amusement Co.)
Keith's (Schanberger)	Stanley (Loew's-Stanley-Crandall)
Little (Moviographs)	Valencia-Parkway (Loew's–UA)

Film critic Donald Kirkley wrote about the downtown movie theater situation in a 1931 column.

> Once a year ... there is a general shifting of the business elements and a readjusting of programs. The shifting has been more marked this year than usual, and changes in the operating policies in some theaters are still being made. The bookings for the 1931-1932 season are complete ... but exhibitors are still experimenting with the movie-going habits of Baltimoreans.
>
> The most important events so far as booking is concerned have been the shifting of the Warner Brothers' films from the Metropolitan to Keith's and the Auditorium; the Met's change to a neighborhood policy, removing it from the category of first-run houses; the distribution of Radio Pictures between the New and Rivoli theaters, and the opening of the Hippodrome which being late, must take such films as it can shop for, as a combination vaudeville and film house ... this means ... that certain stars will shine in different settings this year. There are now nine first-run theaters in town, including the Valencia, often used to replay hits from the Century or Stanley, and the Europa, which as its ... name indicates, is Baltimore's one outlet for the best films from abroad.
>
> There has been a steady tendency toward opening new pictures later in the week instead of on Monday, in accordance with a tradition long in vogue among playhouses and cinemas. Baltimore, where not many seasons ago all the theaters opened new shows on Monday, now has only three film houses changing bills on that day. They are the New, the Stanley and the Europa. Only last week the Century and Valencia switched to Friday, sharing that day

with Keith's and the Auditorium. The Hippodrome and the Rivoli switch on Saturday.

Laymen are unable to understand the reasons behind the changes, and indeed they are not without opponents among the exhibitors. The chief reason seems to hinge on word-of-mouth criticism. This can hurt a bad picture so much that if it opens on Monday by Friday and Saturday it will be cold and dead. Normally crowds flock to the movies Friday night and Saturday, and are willing to take chances on new films. A good film which opens Friday or Saturday will obtain the benefits of the praise spread by the thousands who see it, and will build up rapidly the coming week. Exhibitors seem to think this more than offsets the unfavorable effects on a poor film.[6]

Warner Bros. Vitaphone was the first successful sound system for movies. It would revolutionize the industry. Vitaphone was introduced to Baltimore at the Metropolitan Theater in January 1927. The first sound show, on the evening of January 30, consisted of a main feature, John Barrymore in *Don Juan* which had only musical accompaniment, and several special films with music and talking to show how Vitaphone worked. Adult tickets cost 50 and 75 cents; children's tickets cost 25 and 35 cents.

Film critic T. M. Cushing[7] devoted an entire column to the premiere. He estimated that about 1,000 patrons attended the theater for the Baltimore premiere of Vitaphone. Three of the Warner brothers—Jack, Sam, and Harry—were in the audience. Among the short introductory pieces that preceded *Don Juan* were the famous announcement by Will Hays and several musical numbers. Cushing was lavish in his praise while stating his belief that sound still had a way to go before it was perfected. "The performance revealed excellent synchronization of movement and sound, although the actual performance seems uneven and the mechanical limitations of phonographic reproduction are quite obvious...." He called the performance of "Vesti la Giubba" by Giovanna Martinelli "the supreme achievement of the program." The film, *Don Juan*, was described as a "jolly good movie."

The *Baltimore Daily Post* said, "So realistic was the impression given by the Vitaphone's accompaniment ... that time after time, the audience broke out into enthusiastic applause, as if the actors themselves were on the stage."[8] During the rest of the year, musical and talking Vitaphone shorts were usually part of the show at the Metropolitan. A year later, in January 1928, the first all-sound movie, Al Jolson's *The Jazz Singer*, arrived at the Metropolitan Theater with five two-hour shows every day. Coincidentally Washington's first sound movies also played at a theater named Metropolitan. Both Metropolitan theaters charged regular prices for *The Jazz Singer*; matinees were 25 and 35 cents and evenings cost 35 and 50 cents. The *Jazz Singer* got good reviews. The *Sun*'s reviewer called it a "supreme moment" when Al Jolson stepped up on the platform at the Winter Garden Theater and sang "Mother o' Mine" "right out to the assembled multitude at the Metropolitan Theater."[9]

People flocked to the Metropolitan; the first week of *The Jazz Singer* exceeded the theater's weekly attendance record by more than 5,000.[10] Although it was originally booked for only two weeks, *The Jazz Singer* stayed at the Metropolitan for an unprecedented nine weeks, then in April 1928 it moved to the Cluster.

By no means was everyone enthralled with the new talkies. One New York writer had written in 1922 that movies were essentially a pantomime art, and talking pictures would leave nothing to the imagination.[11] Movie critic Q.E.D. in his column of March 26, 1928, came out not only against talkies but also against color movies. The editor of the

Sun was worried that talkies would destroy the regional accents and everyone would sound the same.[12]

Numerous contributors to the Letters to the Editor in the *Sun* during 1929 also did not like sound movies. One writer, who signed her letter "An Old Lady," asked, "Why must all the moving pictures now be talkies?" She believed that many people, especially those advanced in years, preferred silent movies. She felt that talkies sounded unnatural and pointed out that subtitles made it easier to follow the story.[13] Another woman wrote to Q.E.D. expressing the opinion, "I think the talking picture is an abomination that we must bear.... Sound pictures are fine for small theaters like the Boulevard and the Waverly, but why have those tinny sounds at places like the Century or the Stanley, where they have a perfectly good orchestra on hand?"[14] Another correspondent admitted to loathing talkies when they first appeared, but she thought they were greatly improved by 1929. One letter complained of the poor quality of early sound films; "Last night, in the search of a little diversion, I went to see a much-touted motion picture, but after a few minutes, during which I was tortured by the falsetto tones and monstrous distortions of the human voice, in a poorly made 'talkie,' I could not stand it any longer, and went to the Auditorium, where I found a small but intelligent audience enjoying ... a charming play...."[15]

Some complained that talkies made it very difficult for deaf people to follow what was going on, and, at least one writer said that he envied the deaf because the sound in the talkies was so bad. Suddenly the public found out that their idols had accents! William N. Jones, the film critic for the *Afro-American,* wrote in July 1929 that talkies had just not clicked. He liked the music, but said the voices sounded wrong. All men sounded alike and all women sounded alike, except in the Fox Movietone system that made women sound like men.[16] An editorial in the *Evening Sun* in November 1929 commented on how some stars sounded on the screen and asked, "...who would have believed that so divine a creature ... could harbor an accent redolent of those regions where the nasal twang is at its strongest, a twang whose quality is not enhanced by the fact that she appears to be talking through a megaphone."[17] Another writer believed that "A theater can be transformed into either a barn or cathedral merely by the music played within it." This person was "not willing to spend an evening in a place filled with ghastly voices and metallic sounds, masquerading as music" when there were still legitimate theaters and a few places loyal to the silent drama.[18]

A curious letter of April 1929 told of the writer's yearning for silent films because, "up until a year ago we all liked the movies. They were a balm for ragged nerves, insomnia, fatigue or what have you. What," this person asked, "was more soothing than the hushed theater, with its golden silence broken only by the thrilling music sifting through the hidden pipes of the organ? ... Won't someone please shed a tear for those of us who used, of a Saturday night, to be lulled to sleep by incomparable music?" The writer went on to damn the movies with faint praise, "Silent drama wasn't beyond the comprehension of the average person. It didn't take a master mind to follow the thread of the plot, if any."[19]

In 1930, the management of the Little Theater decided to bring back a silent film, *The Passion of Joan of Arc,* just to see if people really preferred talkies to silent films. Judging from the theater's failure to try this again, people preferred talkies.

Despite all this criticism, people who disliked talkies were in a minority; most people were thrilled with talkies and color movies. By late 1929, a writer who signed his or her name "Old-Timer" praised the movies, writing in part that, "Thanks to science the 'squawk' has been practically eliminated from talkies and the 'flicker' from the movies. The recent advent of Technicolor ... has attained the pinnacle of perfection." Sound was very, very good for the theaters. The Stanley had averaged about $12,000 a week before sound; after sound the weekly average more than doubled to around $27,000. The Rivoli reported its first three months with sound movies were 60 percent, 15 percent, and 40 percent better than the corresponding months the previous year before sound. While some of this increase can be attributed to the elimination of the orchestras and the consequent savings from not having to pay the musicians — overhead expenses decreased by about 30 percent — most of it was certainly because of movies with sound.

After some hesitation, Baltimore exhibitors began wiring their theaters for sound. The Cluster Theater on South Broadway was the second theater in the city to install a sound system. Benjamin Cluster took his young daughter to New York and bought a $15,000 Vitaphone system. The Cluster attracted capacity crowds after the theater was wired in April 1928. By May, the Cluster was advertising "Vitaphone Acts Are Presented at Every Performance Every Day." In July the Loew's theaters — Century, Valencia, and Parkway — were equipped for sound, followed, in less than a month, by the New.

Vitaphone was soon followed by another sound system, Movietone.[20] One of the first Movietone films was *Street Angel* which played at the New in August 1928. In the fall of 1928, many exhibitors, having seen how good the Movietone system was, were installing both sound systems in their houses.

Durkee was uncharacteristically slow in equipping all his theaters; Rome's Apollo, Broadway, and Capitol had Vitaphone and Movietone systems by 23 September. Durkee's Palace got both systems in September, as did the Rivoli. In the spring of 1928, the Regent was the first African-American theater in Baltimore to get sound. *The Jazz Singer* opened there on Sunday May 13 at midnight.[21] Throughout 1928, the Regent had talkies as part of its weekly program.[22] Durkee's Boulevard installed both systems in late November and the independent Ideal got them in early December. By the end of 1928, 21 Baltimore theaters (about 24 percent) had been wired for sound; a year later, virtually all the theaters in town had some kind of sound system.

At the end of 1929, the price of Western Electric sound systems for small theaters had gone down to $5,500 for a sound-on-disc or sound-on-film system and to $7,000 for a system that could handle both. But there were cheaper systems on the market; the Electone sold for between $975 and $1,285 and the popular Royal Amplitone, from $2,350 to $3,500.

Projectionists had many problems with the new sound technology. One of the biggest was with the sound-on-disc systems. They worked this way. A 16-inch, one-sided record containing the soundtrack was supplied for each reel of a film. The record was placed on a turntable that was attached to the projector and synchronized with it, usually by means of a direct drive from the projector's motor. The needle of the tone arm was placed on an indentation near the center of the record, and the film was put in the projector with a frame marked "start" in the film gate. Starting the projector also started the record and, if everything went well, they both ran together for the whole reel.

The changeover was a little more complex. The operator had to start the second projector while the record for the first projector was still running. The second reel actually used sound from the first reel's disk for about four seconds, then the operator switched sound over to the second machine's disk. Projectionists didn't like the disk systems very much. The records were soft and easy to break or scratch, and the needle was also liable to jump a groove at the slightest bump or vibration. A passing bus or truck on a nearby street could play havoc with a sound-on-disk system. It was terrible when a needle got stuck in the same groove and the same line was repeated over and over.

The sound-on-film system was much easier for the projectionist. In this system, the film had a soundtrack along one edge and after it had passed through the film gate, it passed through a sound head where a device converted the soundtrack into electrical energy and fed it into an amplifier that powered speakers behind the screen. Both systems had problems when the film broke or censors removed an objectionable scene. With the sound-on-disk system the projectionist had to insert a black segment of film that was the same length as the section that had been removed. With the sound-on-film system, all that had to be done was to splice the two ends together.

Other less common problems were warped disks and hat racks under the seats that vibrated with certain volumes and frequencies of sound. The first photoelectric cells, used with the sound-on-film systems, lasted between a few days and two to three months. If one of these cells was broken near a basin of water, an explosion could result. The Vitaphone system was quickly phased out; at the New Theater, the turntables were removed at the end of 1931.

There have been sizable minorities in Baltimore which spoke other languages, but until European films became popular in the 1950s, foreign language films were few and far between in local movie theaters. The first French talkies were shown at the Little in November 1930 under the auspices of the Alliance Française. A letter to the editor of the *Evening Sun* in 1931 complained that there had been talkies in German and French but none in Jewish, by which the writer probably meant Yiddish, spoken by a sizable group in Baltimore.

There was a Polish theater, the Nowosci, on South Broadway for a few years. In 1923, during one of the many struggles between the union projectionists and the exhibitors, the union distributed flyers in Polish and Yiddish. This suggests that some patrons of the South Broadway theaters were more comfortable in those languages. In a 1923 court case, Benjamin Cluster noted that these flyers were distributed "to pedestrians and patrons of [the Cluster Theater], a large majority of whom are persons of foreign birth."[23] As late as 1939, both the Broadway and the Leader were advertising in Polish in the *Jednosc-Polonia*.

German, French, Italian, Greek, Japanese, and Swedish movies have appeared from time to time on art theater screens and in college auditoriums. The one German theater in town, the Hindenburg, was suspected of being an outlet for Nazi propaganda and was closed by the FBI in 1940.[24] The ancient Cluster Theater showed Chinese films for a short time, but no theater in Baltimore has been able to make a success of solely ethnic films.

The coming of sound brought with it many changes, including the need to remodel many older theaters so that the sound could be heard clearly. Baltimore architect G. R. Callis was quoted in a 1928 magazine article about changes in theaters that sound might cause. He said, "With the perfection of synchronized pictures and the announcement by Eastman of the perfection in color, the picture theatre has completed the stages of evolution, and will develop beyond all expectations."[25]

Many of the predictions about changes did come true, but the stock market crash and the depression that followed put an effective damper on larger theaters. After 1929, there would be no more large movie palaces built in Baltimore. From then on, the emphasis would be on the construction of neighborhood theaters. The only new downtown theaters before 1967 would be the Lexway (1938), Times (1939), Mayfair (1941), Roslyn (1942), and Town (1947), all built in existing buildings, and the Centre (1939), built from the ground up. A writer for *Motion Picture News* in 1929 clearly understood that sound would bring drastic changes in movies.[26] He could not have imagined multiplex theaters with tens of auditoriums, but he was correct about theaters aging fast. This has been especially true in the second half of the 20th century. Typically, movie theaters last as long as their leases last. Very few theaters are now owned by the exhibitors. They are simply another bit of commercial real estate that can be converted into a supermarket, sporting goods store, or series of shoe shops. Even the Egyptian grandeur of the Muvico theater at Arundel Mills is plastic and can be dismantled quickly.

One final change brought about by movies with sound was the rather sudden departure of the big theater orchestras, piano players, and organists. Live music was no longer needed and, besides, it was too expensive. Many theatergoers bemoaned the loss of popular orchestras, and the musicians' union fought tooth and nail to get them back in the theaters.

At first, film music was poorly reproduced, sounding, according to one person, "very flat ... like a beehive in full blast." It took some years before the sound equipment could reproduce full-range music. In 1928 Joseph N. Weber, president of the American Federation of Musicians, hopefully predicted that the public would "demand personal appearances instead of mechanized music," but the music critic of the *Evening Sun*, Frederick W. Strehlau, feared that continued improvement in sound movie technology would give the public better music than all but the largest theaters could afford.[27]

In 1930, the American Federation of Musicians put a large ad in the local papers asking the public to send back a coupon to enroll in the Music Defense League. The ad said: "One admission fee used to buy real music and a movie—Now it buys a movie, with talk, and mechanical music, which is cheaper—an economy for the theatre, not for the patron." The ad went on to suggest that "mechanical music" failed to please patrons, threatened corruption of musical taste, and discouraged development of musical talent. At least one musician suggested that since the public was not getting the live music it formerly paid for, the price of tickets should be cut in half. The exhibitors ignored this suggestion.

Judging from letters to newspapers, many moviegoers supported the musicians. Several writers in 1928 and 1929 complained that sound movies were putting "millions [sic] out of work," eliminating "from the movie field many good musicians with families," and depriving "many most deserving men and women of a means of earning a living." One writer called for the theaters to "Give us back the orchestra and banish this 'canned music,'" and another vowed not to patronize any movie theater using Vitaphone or any other machine.[28]

Oddly enough, it was not sound movies directly that nearly eliminated theater orchestras; rather, it was Sunday movies. By May 1932, when Sunday movies became legal in Baltimore, the few theater orchestras that remained were living on borrowed time. The Hippodrome and Keith's gave their orchestras notices of dismissal unless they would drop their demand for double pay—$22 for musicians and $33 for conductors—on Sundays. Some managers grudgingly agreed to pay, but they could only stand this a few weeks, and faced with their objection, the musicians' union offered to compromise at time and a half. The theater men objected to this also and threatened to dispense with vaudeville, throwing the musicians out of work. Fortunately for the musicians, the exhibitors found that there was strong public demand for live entertainment and the Century and Hippodrome agreed to continue vaudeville, paying their musicians time and a half on Sundays.

For much of its early history, air conditioning was too expensive for all but the largest downtown theaters. A Carrier Engineering Corporation ad from 1928 entitled "Can the Neighborhood House Afford Manufactured Weather?" addressed this expense. The ad pointed out that Carrier engineers had devised air conditioning equipment that was within the reach of smaller theaters of 900 or more seats. With air conditioning, movie theaters became places of refuge from the sultry Baltimore summers, but some theaters went too far. Air conditioning systems could be too powerful. An article in the *Evening Sun* of July 13, 1928 confirms this: "...the owners of movie theaters discovered a few years ago that by means of huge refrigeration plants, it was possible to lower the temperature of the interior of their houses to the point where a polar bear would regret having left off his heavy undies.... The exhibitors ... were not satisfied with [lowering the temperature] a degree or two; An Ice House or Nothing, was their motto." Another writer to the same paper echoed this sentiment: "Concerning those theaters which are using that horrible cooling system, I would like to say that going from the street into one of them is one of the quickest and surest ways of going to the cemetery I know of."[29]

John O'Ren, in his "Down the Spillway" column, also felt that theaters were getting too cold. He liked hot weather and asked us to consider his feelings, "...when I walked from a nice, melting pavement into one of the 'refrigerated' theaters ... the cold reddened my nose and chilled my body.... It was unearthly cold, and when I thought of the pleasantly steaming streets outside I had to hold on to my chair to keep from walking out during the denouement. I am told that hundreds just love this refrigeration and seek it as relief on hot days. For myself, I mean to find some ancient place wholly unequipped for using ice furnaces, and then I shall try to persuade the management to turn off the electric fans."[30]

Most people, however, appreciated air conditioning. Loew's claimed that its Century, Stanley, Valencia and Parkway were "Baltimore's Only Refrigerated Theatres." Temperatures reached 104 degrees in August 1930, and the air-conditioned theaters did a terrific business. *Sins of the Children* played to capacity crowds at the Valencia. In the summer of 1931, the Loew organization in Baltimore allowed patrons to remain in the Stanley or the Century after the last show and doze in their seats until the next morning. Police were present to see that there were no "pants burglars." The Century opened its doors again to the city in July 1936. Anyone who arrived after the last show was allowed to come into the air-conditioned theater and sleep until morning; performers appearing on-stage were allowed to sleep backstage. Loew's also came to the rescue of sweltering Baltimoreans when the city was hit with three consecutive days of 100-degree temperatures in August 1948. William K. Saxton, Loew's city manager, announced that he would keep the Century Theater open all night with the air conditioning turned on for anyone who wanted to spend the night there.

It took many years before all of the movie theaters were air-conditioned. As late as 1930, the Auditorium, Little, Rivoli, Palace, and Hippodrome were still closing during the hottest summer months, and other theaters were experiencing very low attendance. The neighborhood theaters lagged well behind the downtown theaters, but the mid–1930s found many of them installing air-conditioning systems. In 1935 and 1936, cooling systems were installed in the Harford, Patterson, Gwynn, Broadway, Lord Baltimore, Rialto, Apollo, and Astor. A letter to the *Afro-American* in 1939 pointed out the desirability of modern air conditioning in the theaters of northwest Baltimore and graphically described attending an un-air-conditioned theater in the summer: "One hesitates to enter these 'hot boxes' ... wearing ... good clothes. The audience sits uncomfortably through ... the best picture waiting anxiously until it has ended, so they can make a ... rush to the exits for a breath of ... clean air, or for an aspirin to get rid of an annoying headache."[31]

Three years later things had not changed. A writer to the same paper complained, "How much longer must the colored-theatregoers in Baltimore wait for air conditioning? ... This condition is terrible now, and on hot days many people are forced to leave before the show is over." Even some of the large downtown theaters were slow to install air-conditioning systems. At the beginning of the fall 1941 season, Donald Kirkley reported that the management of Ford's and the Maryland were trying to cope with the September heat by placing large fans offstage and opening all the doors during intermissions.[32] The Maryland still did not have air conditioning in the summer of 1946, and in 1949, Norman Clark could write, "One of these days, when the big city legitimate theaters have installed air-cooling systems, we shall be having plays, musicals, operettas the year round."[33]

As late as 1950, only about 20 percent of the motion picture theaters in the United States were air-conditioned. The ones that were boasted the fact with cardboard icicles dripping from their marquees and the motto, "It's cool inside."

The Durkee organization began a major expansion around 1930 and within two years controlled 15 theaters: Circle (Annapolis); Arcade, Belnord, Boulevard, Edgewood, Forest, Grand, Red Wing, State, Fulton, Linwood, McHenry, Garden, and Patterson (Baltimore); and the State (Havre de Grace). When Frank Durkee died in 1955 at the age of 68, F. H. Durkee Enterprises operated 23 theaters. Operation of the Durkee organization fell to Durkee's son, the Noltes, and Fred Schmuff. Charles Nolte, Sr., another senior official of Durkee Enterprises, died in 1967 at the age of 83.

The Durkee theater circuit was the powerhouse of Baltimore circuits. For nearly 40 years what Durkee said was gospel in the local movie business. Some idea of the power wielded by the Durkee organization was evident during a 1939 suit brought by a rival theater in West Baltimore. During the suit, brought by the Westway Theater, which claimed that Durkee's Edgewood Theater got films before the Westway, an agent for one of the film companies was quoted as saying, "Mr. Durkee has too many theaters. We can't go against him. When Mr. Durkee asks for protection, Mr. Durkee gets protection."[34] According to one source, Durkee had enough power to keep ticket prices in Baltimore lower than those in other areas even when the other exhibitors wanted to raise them.[35]

Neighborhood theaters were doing well in 1932, but the first-run theaters were suffering. It could cost 65 cents to see a show that consisted of a movie, newsreel, and comedy at a downtown theater.[36] Loew's Century and Stanley lowered their prices in 1932. The prices on Mondays through Fridays were 40 cents for all seats except loge seats (60 cents) after 6:00 P.M. Weekday matinee prices at the Century were 35 cents; Stanley tickets cost 25 cents for the orchestra and 35 cents for the loges. Tickets at the Valencia and Parkway were 15 cents at all times. Children's tickets ranged from 15 cents to 25 cents. The average admission price in 1938 was 22 cents; ten years later it was 44 cents.

During the Depression, sales of popcorn, at five to ten cents a bag, increased. Independent vendors leased lobby space in theaters to sell popcorn, or they leased space outside the theater, on the street or in a nearby store. In Baltimore, there were popcorn stores near the Hippodrome, State, and Grand theaters. The center for the introduction of popcorn into theaters seems to have been the Midwest, especially Texas, Kansas, Missouri, and Iowa. By the end of 1930, about 100 Chicago theaters were realizing between $40 and $100 a month from vending machines installed in their lobbies or lounges.

In 1937, the sale of nickel candy was bringing the nation's theaters a profit of about $4 million a year. Most of the candy was sold in vending machines; only about 10 percent of the theaters had concession stands.[37] When the Monroe Theater opened in 1939, it had two candy machines in the small standee area. A 1940 survey found that some cities had many theaters with concessions while other cities had very few.[38] Baltimore theaters lagged far behind those in other cities in sale of popcorn and installation of confectionery counters.

	Theaters	Popcorn Machines	Candy Machines	Confectionery Counters
Dallas	39	800[39]	few	500
Detroit	182	200	250	250
Boston	38	125	500	400
Cleveland	120	25	75	5
New Haven	24	5	12	20
Richmond	23	1	23	none
Baltimore	103	none	150	6

Robert Rappaport had the job of filling the candy machines at his father's Hippodrome Theater around 1941. He would fill the two machines downstairs and then go upstairs to fill the two machines there. By the time he had filled them, it was time to go back and fill the ones on the first floor.

Film censorship was still under attack in the 1930s. The Citizens' League of Maryland for Better Motion Pictures, a constant boil on the neck of both the exhibitors and the censors, launched attacks in 1921 and 1932. In each case, the League accused the censors of being too lax. Movie critic Q. E. D. criticized current movies of 1932 as getting "smuttier and smuttier," and Donald Kirkley criticized films such as *Kept Husbands*, *A Devil with Women*, *Madonna of the Streets*, and *Naughty Flirt* which had not been cut by the censors.[40] An editorial in the *Evening Sun* in 1933 suggested that the censor board should be scrapped. "So far as we know, the only people who want a Board of Motion-Picture Censors in this State are a few fanatics and the politicians who are afraid of them. No one else, certainly no intelligent person, believes that the board has any effect on the movies save to impair the good ones by bad cutting." The State Senate Finance Committee had called censorship wholly ineffectual and the editorial asked, "Since most people never wanted the board and since its friends are now admitting its uselessness, why is it necessary to continue to pay out the $32,158.81 that it costs the taxpayers to operate it every year?"[41] There was an unsuccessful attempt in the House of Delegates in 1933 to abolish the censor board.

Many movies became famous as targets of the censor board, and, in a number of cases, the courts had to step in. Judge Joseph Ulman reversed the board's decision to require deletions from the movie *Birth* in 1931. He said in part that "Many of the changes ordered by the board are in the form of substitution of inexact euphemisms for scientific terms. Such changes cannot be said seriously to rest upon a 'moral' basis. The court has no hesitation in concluding that no part of the film is obscene, sacrilegious or lewd."[42]

In 1933, Judge Samuel Dennis overruled the board in its censoring of the Marlene Dietrich film *The Song of Songs*. The judge said he did not see how the Board could insist on the deletions they had ordered without exposing themselves to the criticism of being arbitrary in view of other types of pictures they had permitted.[43]

Then, in 1936, along came Hedy Kiesler, better know in this country as Hedy Lamarr, in a Czechoslovakian film called *Ecstasy*. This film was condemned by nearly everyone in Europe — including the Pope and the Nazis — and in the United States. The film was first imported into the United States in 1935, but it was impounded by customs officials. A year later, a slightly revised version was allowed into the country by Judge Learned Hand who said he could see nothing harmful or immoral in the film. The Maryland censors banned the film twice, but, at a third hearing, Judge Ulman ruled that *Ecstasy* could be shown if certain parts were eliminated. The movie was shown at the Palace Theater which, then in its final years, specialized in controversial films. The Palace ads touted the controversy: "Now it can be shown! The film that was originally banned by the United States Customs — the film that the whole world is whispering about!"

Film critic Donald Kirkley did not think the film was worth all the fuss. In his review[44] he wrote, "...it is often difficult for the adult spectator to discover what is happening on the screen, and why. Except for occasional outbursts of one-syllable words in American, the film is silent, and the characters sometimes give the impression that they are fugitives from a Czechoslovakian psychopathic ward." Commenting on the censored scenes, he concluded, "As a result of [certain somewhat suggestive scenes] the spectator is apt to leave the theater slightly depressed, half asleep and mildly curious as to the nature of the missing scenes."

A revival at the Europa Theater, the former Dixie on West Baltimore Street, in November 1936 sparked renewed bickering, this time over advertising posters.[45] One poster showed the scene of the heroine floating nude on a pond; this was one of the scenes that Judge Ulman had ordered cut the previous spring. Problems arose when the judge ordered that poster be removed; it was not taken down in every place, and Judge Ulman threw the book at the owners and distributor of the film. Ulman also authorized the censor board to revoke any permission to show the film.[46]

Permission to show *Ecstasy* was requested again in 1940, and Judge Rowland Adams vacated the 1936 injunction issued by Judge Ulman. The movie was shown, minus 18 "obnoxious" scenes at the Lexway in April. In September 1940 it was shown at the Governor Ritchie Drive-In; it moved to the Three Arts the following month.

After high points in the early and mid–1920s, the opening of new movie theaters took a nosedive between 1928 and 1937, rebounding somewhat in the late 1930s before another steep decline in the war years. During the 1930s the number of new theaters being opened and the number of older theaters being closed was very low, and the two figures seem to parallel one another. This parallel trend is evident from the early 1920s until the end of the 1940s, as the chart on page 115 will show.

Note that the number of openings surpasses the number of closings around 1928. The cause of some closings was no doubt the Federal amusement tax in 1932 which was almost enough to break some of the smaller, marginal theaters. Then, beginning in 1933 the state tried to add a 10 percent admission tax on all amusements; united efforts by the exhibitors got the new tax reduced to one percent on gross admissions. The theater own-

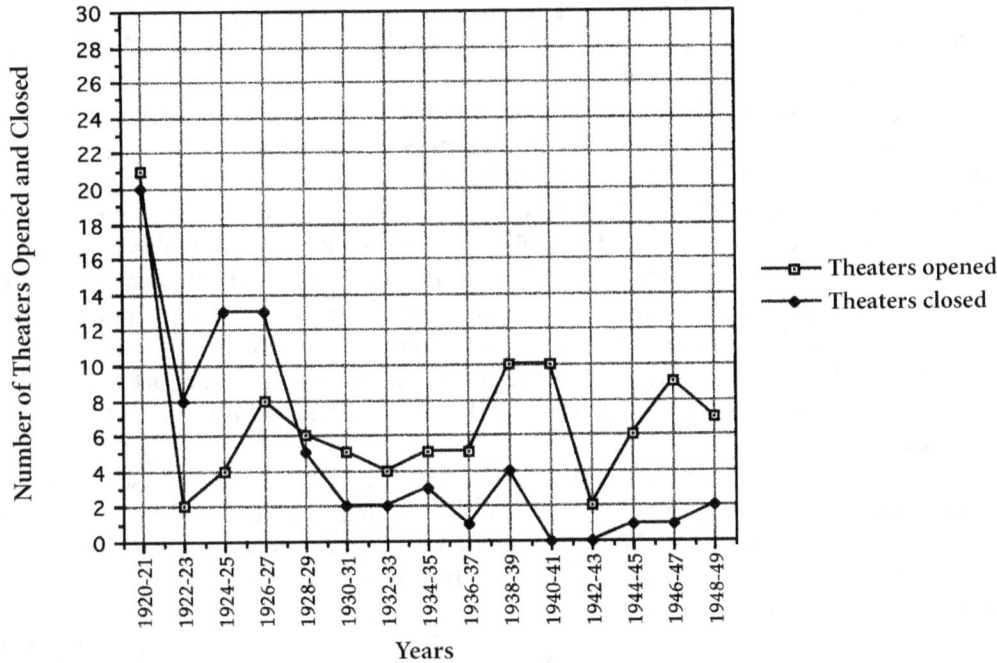

Theaters Opened and Closed 1921–1949

ers said that a lot of theaters could not afford all these increases and would have to close. In November 1941, this tax was reduced further to one-half of one percent.

The 1930s was a decade for tying up loose ends in the movie business. The first was daylight saving time. Although many workers in local stores, factories, and offices were in favor of adopting daylight saving time, exhibitors had opposed it vehemently from the beginning. In March 1918, Baltimore got daylight saving time as a war emergency measure. Howard Bryant introduced a daylight saving ordinance into the City Council in 1919, but it was not adopted until 1922.

That summer was terrible for the movies. The first evening performances were hit especially hard, and many films played to nearly empty houses. All the managers agreed that people just would not go to a movie while it was still light. Lou DeHoff, manager of the Century Theater said, "No one wants to go to a theater when it's still daylight at 9 o'clock, consequently we have a very small attendance at the earlier performances and at the later ones. We expected things to be bad, but they're even worse than we expected."[47]

Receipts at the Rivoli were running $2,000 to $3,000 behind those of the previous year. Things got so bad by the middle of June that the Exhibitors' League of Maryland proposed that all member theaters in the city close during July and August. The exhibitors unanimously rejected that idea, but some of the smaller ones eliminated matinees, and many reduced the number of their employees or cut the number of hours their staffs worked. As soon as daylight saving time ended, at the end of August, movie attendance rebounded. The manager of the Parkway said, "We have been fortunate in having one full house every evening this summer, but last night we filled the house twice, the first time to absolute capacity."[48]

Opponents of daylight saving time won the day in the summer of 1923, and Baltimore was one of the few Mid-Atlantic cities that did not move clocks ahead. There was partial daylight saving time in 1924, 1925, and 1926. Dr. Zechia Judd, who had formerly supported it, wrote in 1926: "Of all insane ideas which get lodgment in moron brains, the daylight-saving bug takes the medal for stupidity."[49] Plans to bring back daylight saving time, with the strong support of the Chamber of Commerce, were announced in March 1928; supporters expected continued opposition from the theaters. A spokesman for the musicians' union opposed daylight saving time because he said, that daylight was not so good for music as darkness. In April the City Council, by unanimous vote, adopted an unfavorable report on changing the time. In 1930, an estimated 740 local businesses, out of 859 surveyed, favored the adoption of daylight saving time.[50] In April of that year, 220 companies informed the Baltimore Association of Commerce that they would voluntarily adopt daylight saving time at the end of the month, and support for the time change seemed to be growing. Between April and September 1930 there was voluntary daylight saving time.

During this confusing period, adjacent businesses could be only inches apart in distance but an hour apart in time. Most downtown department stores, all banks, the Federal courts, railroad offices, and the post offices were on daylight saving time. Public and parochial schools, municipal offices, state courts, the Pratt library, and railroad train schedules were on standard time.

Theaters generally continued to oppose daylight saving time, but in mid–May 1930, the Rivoli and Metropolitan theaters announced that they would break ranks with the other theaters and adopt daylight saving time. They were soon joined by the Hippodrome. The New said that it would use daylight saving time only on Sunday evenings and the Metropolitan changed its mind again and opted to remain on standard time. The battle continued into 1931.

In a letter to the *Evening Sun*, an anonymous young woman said that she thought any mother would rather have her children "out of doors in the precious air and light than being in a closed-up moving-picture theater 'improving' their childish minds by viewing 'Seed — Woman Against Woman — Fighting for Love' or the elevating plays where gangsters are glorified and odd bits of humanity are 'taken for a ride' or 'put on the spot.'"[51]

Daylight saving time remained voluntary until February 1942. During the Second World War the country was on War Time. The city council shelved daylight saving time for the summer of 1946 and agreed to place it on the November ballot. The measure passed and daylight saving time began in April 1947.[52]

The final act of the Sunday movie saga began in a snowstorm. The heaviest snowfall in six years dumped 15 inches of snow on Baltimore on Saturday, January 28, 1928. Despite the blizzard, John Callan decided to test the blue law the following day, Sunday the 29th. Saying that he did not see where it was a crime for the poor man to be allowed Sunday amusement when the rich man could have his golf, Callan leased the Broadway Garden Theater and prepared to show a feature film — appropriately entitled *The Mockery*— and a comedy. Patrons would be asked to buy programs instead of tickets; this same system had been used successfully at Oriole Park for Sunday baseball games. Police Commissioner Gaither warned Callan that if he tried to show a movie on Sunday he would be arrested. Everything was very civilized.

A crowd estimated at about 2,000 gathered in front of the theater on Sunday evening. Then, as if it had been choreographed, the test took place. Shortly after 7 P.M. two police sergeants took up positions near the theater's entrance where they were soon joined by a police captain. The projectionist, Irving Schlossberg, began showing the comedy at about 8:30. As soon as the first two customers had paid their 50 cents for a program, Captain Mooney stated, "That's enough. We have enough to make a case. Lock the doors. John [Callan], we'll walk you to the station house; it's only a short distance." Arrested along with Callan were Charles F. Mules, vice-president of the Liberty Defense League, and Mr. Schlossberg. They were charged with working on Sunday. Magistrate Thomas O'Neill at the Northeastern Police Station released the men on their own recognizance.

Callan's case went to the grand jury, whose members refused to indict him and his co-defendants. Callan asserted that the dismissal of the charges showed that the exhibition of movies and the selling of programs on Sunday were legal, and he immediately made plans to test the law again. On Sunday night, February 5, 1928, Callan showed the movie *The Dumb-Bells*— perhaps another dig at the opposition — at the Harford Theater. An estimated 3,000 supporters appeared at the theater. As before, Callan and his colleagues were arrested. They were charged with not obtaining the necessary licenses to conduct a motion picture theater.[53]

Ironically, two other movie theaters were also open on that Sunday night. The Young Men's Ritchie League hosted a benefit at the Rialto Theater, and a Catholic church held another at the Capitol Theater. Neither organization had to get permits even though the projectionists were paid for their work.

This time Callan wasn't so lucky; a criminal court jury found him, Charles Mules, and projectionist Walter Stierhoff guilty. Callan appealed, but the supreme bench of Baltimore City sustained the convictions. Callan appealed to the State Court of Appeals, but, in January 1929, that court too upheld the conviction. Callan was fined $100. During all this time, the exhibitors kept silent.

Within a week of his loss in the Court of Appeals, Callan was ready to introduce a bill in the state legislature to permit the showing of movies on Sundays in Baltimore City. Callan's bill would have given the Mayor and City Council the authority to allow Sunday movies. The City Council overwhelmingly passed a resolution supporting the idea of a referendum on Sunday movies. The *Sun* and *Evening Sun* supported Sunday movies, recanting the position made in a 1924 editorial that "the Sunday movie drive does not at present appeal convincingly to the spirit of intelligent liberalism," admitting that they were probably wrong.

The *Evening Sun*, in an editorial on January 23, 1929, called Baltimore a "four-day town." This meant that very little business was transacted from Saturday to Tuesday. Few traveling men stayed in town if they could possibly get out. The editorial supported Callan's bill declaring that "moving pictures are among the most innocent forms of entertainment and cannot be said to be more demoralizing than Sunday radio programs."[54]

At the end of March 1929, after a bitter debate, the Maryland House passed an amendment giving the City Council a 30-day window to adopt or reject a Sunday movie ordinance. Supporters of the Lord's Day Alliance tried unsuccessfully to exempt Baltimore, Montgomery and Queen Anne's counties in a vain attempt to embarrass delegates from those counties who had voted solidly for the amendment. The passage of the amendment seemed to take some of the fight out of the opponents, and the so-called "Sunday amusements and sports bill for Baltimore City" was passed by the House by a 65-to-51 vote. Opponents in the Maryland Senate delayed consideration of the bill by having it referred to a committee, and efforts to bring it out of committee failed. The Committee on Judiciary failed to report it out and it died there.

The city tried again at the end of 1930, when the City Council passed a resolution calling on the State Legislature to permit Baltimore City to authorize amusements on Sunday.[55] Two bills were introduced in the General Assembly in January 1931. Baltimore delegate D'Alesandro introduced one which would grant Baltimore home rule on the Sunday entertainment question. Another bill would give the counties, towns and cities in Maryland the right to decide for themselves what amusements would be legal. These bills were denounced by the Lord's Day Alliance and the Citizens' League for Better Motion Pictures. The debate got ugly when Episcopal priest Robert Browning hinted that the major supporters of blue law reform were Jews.[56]

The home rule bill was finally passed and went into effect on June 1, 1931; the battleground shifted to Baltimore. The new bill said that "...the Mayor and City Council of Baltimore, in furtherance of the principle of Home Rule and for the purpose of promoting a reasonable and proper observance of Sunday, shall have full power and authority to prohibit, permit or regulate ... amusements, entertainments or games to be held, shown or played for recreation or profit ... within Baltimore City on the Lord's Day, commonly called Sunday...."[57] The Lord's Day Alliance called the home rule bill unconstitutional.

The City Council quickly drew up three separate ordinances so drafted that, in a referendum, the voters would be voting separately on the questions of sales, athletic games, and motion pictures. Eventually these were united in a single ordinance. For motion picture theaters, the key section was 6: "It shall not be lawful to keep open or use any dancing saloon, opera house, ten-pin alley, barber shop or ball alley within the City of Baltimore on the Sabbath Day, commonly called Sunday; provided, however that it shall be lawful to exhibit motion pictures, to give theatrical performances, or musical concerts, and to open or use bowling alleys after 2 o'clock P.M. on Sunday in said City, with or without a charge or admission fee."[58]

The opponents of blue law reform, led by The Rev. Davis and Cornelia Gibbs,[59] got more and more vicious in their attacks. Unswayed, the City Council enacted the ordinance, and Mayor Howard W. Jackson signed it. This paved the way for a citywide referendum in May 1932. Opponents went to court, but, thanks largely to Maryland Attorney General Preston Lane of Frederick County, were unsuccessful in their efforts to block the referendum. H. L. Mencken took the supporters of the blue laws to task in his *Evening Sun* column of April 25, 1932. An article in the *Afro-American* supported Sunday movies and cited Washington, D.C. as a city where Sunday movies were permitted and "had a stupendous effect in curbing the tendency to seek illegitimate amusements in houses of ill repute as is the custom in Baltimore on Sunday."[60]

The vote on the referendum was scheduled for May 2, 1932. Both sides predicted victory, but when an estimated 140,000 Baltimoreans packed the movie theaters for free shows on May 1, the outcome seemed certain.[61] When the votes were counted, the liberal Sunday ordinance was passed by the huge majority of 83,990 votes.[62] The people of Baltimore had spoken decisively, and Sunday movies were ensured. The *Philadelphia Record* contrasted the situation in Philadelphia, where many Sunday amusements were still illegal, with Baltimore's new-found freedom, "Next Sunday Baltimoreans will go to church in the morning and do as they please in the afternoon. They may go to baseball games, to the theater, to moving-picture shows, lawfully, openly as American citizens should do things, lawfully and openly."[63] On the other hand, Philadelphians would go to church and then return home "to irritation at forced idleness" or they would go to other cities for amusement.

With the headline, "Miss Baltimore Has Discarded Her Puritanical Garb of 200 Years Ago," the *Afro-American* announced the end of the ban on Sunday movies. According to this article, many theater managers were surprised that the ordinance had passed and had not made plans to be open on Sunday. Benjamin Flax, manager of the Royal Theater, said that his theater would open at 2 P.M. with a stage and screen show. The Carey and Lafayette were also planning to open, while the managers of the Regent and Dunbar were not sure.[64] The long battle for Sunday movies in Baltimore had at last been won.

The first Sunday with movies was May 8, 1932; all the first-run theaters were open. At first it seemed as if that Sunday would be the same sleepy kind of day as previous Sundays. Perhaps the thunderous sermons denouncing the new liberal Sunday laws as pagan had frightened the city. But when evening came, people began going downtown. Restaurants, hotels, and movie theaters saw the change. Taxis reported a thriving business. Visitors from out of town came to see what was going on. Crowds of window shoppers strolled past the department stores.

Business at the movie theaters started out slowly, but grew to standing room only by the end of the evening. There was a heavy demand for bags of candy that often found their way into theaters. Both J. Louis Rome of the Associated Motion Picture Theater Owners and Herman Blum of the Motion-Picture Theater Owners and Managers of Maryland reported that their member theaters had done a good business. The following Sunday was somewhat less boisterous, but nonetheless saw a slightly increased attendance at some theaters. There were crowds on downtown streets until after 11 P.M. African-American movie theaters did not seem to fare as well as the white theaters, and many managers of these theaters reported that they had not made enough money on Sundays to cover their operating expenses.

As soon as Baltimore City got Sunday movies, Baltimore County exhibitors wanted them. Representatives from Gaertner theaters, as well as Porter Siewell, who ran the Towson Theater, and Julius Requardt, who ran the Overlea Theater, asked the County Commissioners for permission to open their theaters on Sunday. The exhibitors argued that the proximity of their theaters to the city line put them in competition with the Baltimore theaters, and if they could not open on Sundays, it gave the Baltimore theaters an unfair advantage over them. The Commissioners said they were sorry, but they had no authority to grant this permission.

Harry Gaertner did not wait for the Commissioners' permission; he opened his Strand Theater in Dundalk on May 8, 1932.[65] Gaertner was taken to court, but his case was dismissed after he promised not to open on future Sundays. He decided not to make a test case of the charges against him. Fearing that other theaters would follow Gaertner, the county police marshal ordered policemen stationed at all the movie theaters in Baltimore County on May 15. Rather than risk arrest, the exhibitors decided to seek legislation to allow Sunday movies.

In the 1933 session of the Legislature, three counties—Baltimore, Prince George's, and Allegany—were working to get rid of their blue laws.[66] The Rev. Davis was right there to challenge them. The *Evening Sun* took Davis to task in an April 1933 editorial,[67] calling his arguments "as unvarying as they are fallacious." The editorial said that Davis and his colleagues claimed that movies were immoral on weekdays and consequently twice as immoral on Sundays, that the legislation was a "dastardly attack" on the Church since it tempted people to engage in other than religious acts on Sundays, that the legislation endangered the American Home, and that its only result would be to corrupt and undermine the moral stamina of the people in the three counties. The *Sun*, tongue in cheek, pointed out that, after nearly a year of Sunday movies in Baltimore: church attendance had increased, the number of divorces had dropped considerably, drunkenness had decreased, fewer foundlings had been reported, and the number of cases of certain diseases—chickenpox, dysentery, erysipelas, and malaria, to name a few—had decreased. The Baltimore Police Commissioner reported a 6- to 7-percent decrease in various crimes in the city during 1932. The legislature enacted a law legalizing Sunday movies in Baltimore County which went into effect on the first Sunday in June 1933.[68]

During the 20th century, Baltimore has had a large and growing African-American population. A minority until late in the century, African Americans had a disproportionately smaller number of theaters than whites in the city. A 1934 study by the Baltimore Urban League provides some information on African-American theaters at that time.[69] This study found that there were 12 movie theaters for African-American audiences in Baltimore, and three of these seated more than 1,000. It also found that Baltimore was "neither Southern nor Northern in its treatment of the Negro movie fan."[70] Contrasting treatment in the South where a balcony or a section of the movie house was set aside for African Americans with that in the North, where African Americans could be admitted to any section of the theatre, the study concluded that, "In Baltimore Negroes are not admitted to any motion picture except those catering exclusively to colored people. Three theatres permit Negroes to occupy the back rows of the balcony when legitimate productions are given."

Baltimore movie theaters had been segregated from the very beginning. Theaters for white patrons were built in white neighborhoods, and downtown was considered a white neighborhood in terms of the theaters. Theaters for black patrons were located in African-American neighborhoods. The black downtown was located along Pennsylvania Avenue, and the largest, most prestigious black theaters were built there. Other black neighborhoods were located in East Baltimore around Monument and Central Avenue and in South Baltimore around Hanover and Sharp streets. Each neighborhood had its theaters.

Pennsylvania Avenue Area: Lincoln, Daly's, Renard's, Royal, Carver, Regent, Lenox, Carey, Roosevelt, Queen, Fremont, Ruby, Harlem
Central Avenue Area: Dunbar, Radio (Star), National (Eden)
South Baltimore: Hill, Argonne (Goldfield), Goldfield (Dean)
Baltimore County: Anthony, Winter's
Annapolis: Star, Clay Street Theater

Occasionally, white theaters on the fringes of African-American neighborhoods had clauses in their leases that they could not be used as black theaters. At least once, in 1916, the court upheld such a covenant. Mrs. Nellie Larkin, who was operating the Artmore Casino in the 500 block of West Franklin Street, had claimed that it was "unconstitutional to prohibit in a lease the attendance of colored persons at a moving-picture theatre."[71] Circuit Court No. 2 decided that the lease was lawful.

Several of the larger cities in Maryland also had theaters for African Americans. In Annapolis, the Star on Calvert Street and the Clay Street Theater were black theaters. But

Baltimore was the main location of African-American theaters; in the mid–1930s, 80 percent of black theaters in Maryland were located in Baltimore. Some white exhibitors went to great lengths to maintain separation of the races, while others did their best to treat both races equally. The *Afro-American* praised James L. Kernan for his 1908 Christmas party at the Maryland. Kernan invited several thousand children, black and white, to attend the theater, see a show, and receive presents of candy, cake and toys. According to the *Afro-American*:

> Probably for the first time in the history of this city, the little unfortunates of this city were on an equal footing.... The treat was given at the Maryland Theatre, and ... several thousands, were not only invited to witness the performance at the expense of Manager Kernan, but were welcome[d] by him ... on the stage, and given each of them a handsome Christmas present of toys, candy, cake and other presents. Thursday was the winding up of the week, and no child that looked deserving was turned away ... over 5,200 bags containing toys and candy were given away.... Mr. Frederick Schanber[ger] was an able assistant to Manager Kernan, and deserves great credit for the admirable manner in which the affair ... was managed. The several hundred little Afro-Americans who were marshaled in the theater ... sat almost spell-bound during the entire performance.... It was a magnificent affair and the children are very grateful to their patron saint, Manager James L. Kernan."[72]

Some of the large legitimate theaters from time to time allowed black patrons in the balconies. Balconies were also reserved for black patrons in towns which only had a single theater. In October 1924, the manager of the Academy of Music was quoted in the *Afro-American*, "Tell the colored people if they will patronize this theatre they can have all of the balcony. If they have any trouble at any time, tell them to come to me and not to those who are under me."[73] At the time, the *Afro-American* was running ads for the De Wolfe Hopper Comic Opera Company in *The Chocolate Soldier* at the Academy of Music. Two months later, the new manager of the Academy of Music, Mr. Schanberger, told the same paper, "Colored people have been sitting in the first balcony all of this week. We will continue to sell them tickets for the first balcony."[74]

The policy of not allowing African Americans into the theater forced Loew's Century to cancel the engagement of a popular musical revue in 1928. The show was the *Merry Go Round*, which featured the all-black Pan American Quartet. Although the revue had just finished a week at Loew's Palace in Washington, the Century refused to allow it to open with the black quartet. Unwilling to be split up, the company returned to New York. The local manager, a Mr. Kingsmore, passed the buck saying that he had nothing to do with the cancellation; it was the responsibility of Loew's New York office. He also stated that, "The [Pan-American] quartet was probably the best part about the show."[75] The policy of racial segregation kept many first-rate films out of the big downtown theaters. In 1930 *Sun* film critic Donald Kirkley complained that the Baltimore first-run theaters were missing out on a good thing when they passed up the chance to show the film *Hallelujah*, which had a black cast. He declared it one of the best movies of 1929. *Hallelujah* did eventually play at the Little, where crowds had to be turned away, and at several neighborhood theaters.

Each of the local circuits in Baltimore seemed to have its own territory. Fred Schmuff, a Durkee executive for many years, said, "We'd never purposely run in opposition to anyone. Many a time we were offered property on York Road or Belair Road and

Gaertner was over there. [Frank] Durkee would say, 'Go over and see Lou Gaertner; he's on Belair Road; we're not interested.'"[76]

Competition did occur when several exhibitors wanted to open a theater at the same location. It did not take much for a savvy exhibitor to figure out good locations for a movie theater, and occasionally two exhibitors would clash. Sometimes they both built a theater. Harrison Stires and Thomas Goldberg clashed over who would build a movie theater in the 3100 block of West North Avenue in Walbrook. In 1913 they were denied permits, but the following year they both received permits, and they each built a theater. Goldberg's theater didn't last long, but he eventually acquired Stires' Walbrook Theater across the street.

In some cases both exhibitors built theaters and managed to work out a *modus vivendi*. The Hampden and Ideal operated within a few doors of each other in the 900 block of 36th Street in Hampden for 50 years. Sol Goodman, who ran the Ideal for many years, described the competition: "Well, we were friendly competitors. We split the product right down the middle. We had Metro and Warner Bros. and RKO; [they] were our basic majors. They had Paramount, Fox, and Columbia. And we had two minors, but they were very, very profitable; one was Republic Pictures who had Gene Autry and Roy Rogers and also John Wayne who made one or two pictures a year—I think *The Sands of Iwo Jima* was a Republic Picture, if I'm not mistaken—and Monogram Pictures with the Bowery Boys. So we would split the product."[77]

In 1921, Palmore & Homand clashed with Alfred Buck's American Theatres Company over who would build a theater in the attractive Greenmount and 33rd Street area. After much wrangling, the mayor decided that the ordinances should be considered together. Then, he signed both ordinances. Palmore & Homand could build their theater on the east side of Greenmount Avenue while Buck could build his theater on the west side. This was the beginning of the Boulevard Theater scandal, described earlier, that rocked Baltimore in 1921.

Powerful theater circuits clashed again in 1935 when the Durkee organization, then the largest theater circuit in the area, planned a theater on a wooded lot on the north side of Liberty Heights Avenue, across the street from the Gwynn Theater. The Rome circuit, the second largest theater circuit, had a half interest with Robert Kanter in the Gwynn Theater and vigorously opposed granting Durkee a permit.[78] The matter developed into a "nasty situation" in the city council when the committee considering the measure became divided. Things got so bad that the *Evening Sun* editorialized that perhaps the law giving the City Council permit authority over theaters should be looked upon with suspicion and distrust.[79] One person doubted the sanity of the Baltimore City Council in allowing Durkee to build across the street from the Gwynn and asked, "Must the residents of this vicinity tolerate another theater because a movie chain has 'pull' with the City Council members?" The Durkee supporters won and, after a year of bickering, a measure granting the permit for the new theater passed the City Council. Eventually Durkee and Rome got together and created one corporation out of the two theaters.

Exhibitors were often pitted against local property-owners, one side wanting to build a theater and the other fearing a theater would lower the value of their homes and businesses. There have been many cases where the local inhabitants of an area did not want a movie theater in their neighborhood. In 1910, a letter to the *Sun* protested the erecting of a movie theater on the corner of Mount Royal and Maryland avenues. The writer believed that these theaters "attract by day and by night undesirable crowds and detract from the taxable residential values."[80] The following year, there were protests by 100 people in the vicinity of Philadelphia Road and Linwood Avenue against the proposed Belnord Theater. One person complained that there was a library across the street from the proposed theater and asked if it was "proper to allow a moving-picture theatre, with its attendant features, to operate within the very shadow of an institution which seeks to elevate and educate the young and furnish recreation to the old?"[81] Former mayor Mahool and a judge came out against that theater. Louis Kolb and Charles Bender tried to placate the protesters by guaranteeing that the theater would be noise-proof, that they would not allow crowds to gather in front of the theater, and that they would not allow a hurdy-gurdy to come near. They must have convinced the opposition because the Belnord was built later that year. These protests were the cause of the May 1911 ordinance that gave the City Council the authority to grant building permits for new theaters.

A large protest by nearby churches stopped the erection of a movie theater on Madison near North Avenue in 1911, and, that same year, a protest by local residents kept the Home Theater from reopening. The North Avenue Baptist Church protested the building of a motion picture theater across the street around 1914. Several churches tried unsuccessfully to block the building of the Rialto Theater two years later.[82] In 1917 the Maryland Court of Appeals ruled that moving picture theaters conducted for the public were not nuisances per se and refused to block the building of the Community Theater in Hamilton. Four neighborhood churches were successful in blocking the Standard Amusement Company's attempt to build a theater at Park Heights and Oswego avenues in 1921, but the Avalon Theater was built a couple of blocks away six years later. In 1952, residents of the Owings Mills area successfully protested against the building of a drive-in theater on Reisterstown Road.

Movie theaters continued to aid charities and victims of disasters. Flood victims and the jobless were among the many recipients of aid raised by local theater owners. In 1929, the Stanley held a show to benefit the Palestine Red Cross. The theaters came to the aid of the jobless in 1930; a special Sunday benefit at Baltimore and Baltimore County theaters organized by the Maryland Motion Picture Theater Owners' Association took in more than $34,000 for the police department's unemployment relief program. The Independent Motion Picture Operators and Managers Union agreed to help and, even though many were themselves unemployed, members of the local musicians' union volunteered to play in orchestras for the benefit.

Two groups of mainly Baptist and Methodist ministers protested the Sunday movies, but Police Commissioner Gaither said that the fund was necessary, and he intended to see the benefit through. The Stanley held annual parties for orphans, and the Valencia gave Christmas parties for thousands of newsboys. In 1946, Maryland theaters set a goal of $200,000 for their contribution to the American Cancer Society; Baltimore's share was $143,000. Individual exhibitors also helped out their communities. Julius Goodman of the Ideal Theater in Hampden personally drove around and delivered Christmas dinner baskets to poor families. In 1945, Isador Rappaport gave all the profits from a Frank Sinatra short film to organizations helping underprivileged children.

The Variety Club was founded by a group of theater men in Pittsburgh in 1927. Local clubs called "tents" were later formed in other cities throughout the world. By 1955, there were 42 tents with a total membership of 9,488. Each tent sponsored one or more charities. Baltimore Tent, Number 19, was formed in 1938 by a group of local showmen that included J. Louis Rome, Frank Durkee, William Saxton, Isador Rappaport, Rodney Collier, J. Lawrence Schanberger, Morris Mechanic, and Samuel Diamond. Tent 19 sponsored Boys' Clubs and a children's clinic. The Baltimore club also gave $4,000 to West Baltimore General Hospital to remodel the accident room. The Variety Club sponsored Christmas shows at the Lord Baltimore and Broadway theaters for the Police Boys Clubs in 1945. The Variety Clubs also sponsored the Will Rogers Memorial Hospital. In addition to its charitable activities, the Variety Club was an important social club for people in the amusement industry.[83]

The movies fought a desultory war with radio in the late 1920s and early 1930s. Radio was becoming popular during the 1920s, and some exhibitors saw it as a powerful competitor. Others, like the Crandall theaters in Washington and the Whitehurst organization in Baltimore were not afraid of the radio. They enlisted radio to attract customers to the theaters.

The first Whitehurst radio broadcasts probably occurred in September 1925 from the Century Theater. The audience that packed the theater that evening was so enthralled that it remained until 12:45 a.m. In early 1926, the Whitehurst circuit set up radio broadcasting studios on the stages of the Century and New theaters. The broadcasts featured acts from various Whitehurst theaters.

Television was seen as an ally of radio against movies when it first appeared in 1928. The *Evening Sun*'s On the Air column admitted that the movies had the upper hand with the development of films with sound, but predicted that the real battle lay "in the future ... when television is promised as a public service."[84] And, in a 1928 editorial, the *Sun* opined that, "there is the suggestion that the movie houses themselves will be rendered obsolete by the perfecting of a television apparatus to carry film ... into every home."[85]

The struggle with radio competition reached its peak in the mid 1930s when radio ads appeared saying, "Stay home and get your entertainment free from the radio." Ad campaigns and the appearance of movie stars on the radio terrified some exhibitors, but by 1935, the New York *Times* was able to report that "There is no convincing proof that broadcasting has lowered box office receipts." One well-documented occasion when radio did affect movie attendance was on December 11, 1936, when King Edward VIII abdicated. His speech was carried by all the major networks at 5:00 P.M., and downtown theaters were practically empty. Managers at the Century and Stanley reported patrons hurrying out of their theaters as the time for the speech drew near. The management at Keith's also noted an unusually small audience.

Vaudeville was nearly dead in Baltimore by 1935, but a couple of theaters still had live shows. The Hippodrome and the State were the last holdouts. One show at the State just about put an end to vaudeville and became part of the theater lore of East Baltimore. On the evening of February 9, 1936, a young lioness named Ruthie, who was part of a vaudeville act, escaped from her cage backstage at the State Theater and raced into the auditorium, where she leapt into the laps of four boys in the fourth row. Then she passed in front of Mrs. Blanche Peart, who promptly fainted. Ruthie then headed up the aisle, with her two trainers in pursuit, while two comedians onstage tried to distract the audience. When she got to the lobby she encountered patrolman Alexander Jezierski, who had come in to warm up. Grover and Anita George, the lion's trainers, attempted to corner her by firing blank cartridges; Patrolman Jezierski covered them with his gun. As the snarling, cornered animal appeared ready to attack, the trainers told Jezierski to shoot her. He fired and hit her in the shoulder. A cage was quickly brought to the lobby, and the lion was taken to an animal hospital where she was declared "not badly hurt."

One of the boys, Edward Posluszny, was clawed on the knee as Ruthie climbed over him. Mrs. Peart was taken to Johns Hopkins Hospital, where she was treated for hysteria. Posluszny said he thought a large dog had jumped in his lap. "Something with fur on it streaked in front of us. It pounced onto my knees and made another spring across the section of seats opposite us to land in the center aisle. We could see ... that it was big and long and its tail was powerful strong. It struck all of us across the face good and hard." The lion was described as "only a baby, about 6 months old; gentle and well mannered," and "about two and a half feet long." Posluszny estimated it was six feet, while patrolman Jezierski said it was "about the size of a horse."[86]

The year 1936 could have been called the Year of the Lion. Ten months after the lion escaped at the State, a more serious incident involving a lion occurred at the Hippodrome. In December 1936, an act called "Beauty and the Beast" was part of the vaudeville bill. In it, a young woman came out and danced in mock terror in front of eight lions. A newspaper critic, reviewing an early performance, thought that the dance was artistic enough, but the lions looked old and tired and some were probably toothless. Upon learning of that review, the dancer, Gladys Cote, took the criticism personally and decided to spice up her act. On December 8, during the 4:00 P.M. stage show, as the act was ending, a lion named "George" suddenly turned on the young woman and attacked. The trainer leapt on the lion's back, firing his pistol in an attempt to rescue her. Finally he pulled the lion away and a stagehand was able to drag the girl to safety. She was rushed to University Hospital. Doctors found her in serious condition, but predicted that she would recover.

Miss Cote was well enough the following day to tell co-workers that she would resume her lion act as soon as she was able. It was not to be; on December 10, doctors noticed signs of infection and, despite injections of serum and blood transfusions, she died of gas gangrene in the early morning of the 11th. Doctors believed that matter under the lion's claws had caused the fatal infection. The coroner found that Miss Cote's death was an unavoidable accident caused by her "neglect and carelessness ... in not leaving the cage when she should have left it and as she was instructed and through her jealousy and her personal ambition and adverse criticism...."[87] The lion trainer noted that Miss Cote had received unfavorable publicity, apparently for leaving the cage immediately after the act ended, and had opted to remain inside even though it was considered more dangerous.

By 1938, there were 17,541 theaters in the United States. They grossed about $19 million a week and more than $1 billion a year. There were 117 theaters in the country that could seat more than 3,000 people; three of them were in Baltimore.

Capacities of United States Theatres (1938)[88]
(selections)

	Over 3,000 Seats	2,000 to 3,000	1,500 to 2,000	1,000 to 1,500	500 to 1,000	200 to 500	Less than 200	Total
California	5	38	60	146	401	261	40	951
Dist. of Col.	1	3	6	10	17	18	1	56
Maryland	3	1	9	21	69	95	14	212
New York	31	104	160	245	570	379	80	1,569
Pennsylvania	10	34	75	139	423	451	22	1,154
Virginia	1	1	5	20	93	113	39	272

Airdomes died out in Maryland in the 1920s, but, in 1939, a new kind of open-air theater appeared. These theaters tapped the popularity and availability of the automobile. They were called open-air theaters for a while, but later the name drive-in caught on. One of the earliest references to a local drive-in was at the end of a theater column in the *News-Post*. Norman Clark noted that "an open-air auto movie theatre is to be built on the Governor Ritchie Highway."[89] The first drive-in in the United States had been opened six years earlier in Camden, New Jersey, by Richard M. Hollingshead. Hollingshead had correctly surmised that the country was ready to watch movies in the more informal setting of the family car.

There were fewer than 100 drive-in theaters in the entire country by 1939. The nearest one to Baltimore, prior to the Governor Ritchie Drive-In in Glen Burnie in 1939, was the Mount Vernon Drive-In which had opened in Alexandria, Virginia, the previous year. World War II interrupted the development of the drive-ins, but after the war, some local exhibitors became interested in them. Durkee, somewhat grudgingly, built the North Point Drive-In in 1948[90] and Schwaber built the General Pulaski Drive-In in 1950. During the 1950s, drive-in theaters accounted for five out of the six movie theaters built in the Baltimore area. The last local drive-in was the Super 170 Drive-In built by Rome Theaters in Odenton in 1963. By that time, drive-ins were past their prime. The demise of the drive-ins was almost as quick as their rise.

In the 1970s and 1980s, as the suburbs spread farther and farther out from the cities, the once cheap land where the drive-ins had been built became a prime target for developers. The owners of drive-ins could make more money by selling the land than they could by showing movies. Against seemingly hopeless odds, a few drive-ins have held on, due in large part to enthusiastic owners and devoted fans, many of whom nostalgically associate drive-ins with the semi-mystical 1950s. The last remaining drive-in in the Baltimore area is the Bengies in Middle River.

6

THE MOVIES IN WAR AND PEACE (1940–1947)

A small spurt in theater openings occurred in the early 1940s, just before World War II put an end to new construction. As soon as the United States entered the war, exhibitors joined in the war effort, selling war bonds, collecting scrap metal and rubber, and providing much-needed entertainment to servicemen and women and civilians alike. Baltimoreans had to contend with wartime shortages and blackouts, but they went to movies in larger-than-ever numbers. On Sundays, pleasure-seekers forsook their old haunts in the city's many parks and packed the movie theaters from the first to the last show. Lines were long, and exhibitors were making money hand over fist.[1] There was a minor crisis when many of the younger men in the film industry joined the armed forces. Women and older men had to replace them. By 1944 exhibitors could see that we were winning and that the war would be over soon; they began to think about building new theaters. The movement to suburban residential developments that had begun in the 1930s continued with increased vigor in the late 1940s.

There were many film exchanges located in Baltimore during the early years of the movies. The early exchanges, like Pearce and Scheck, the Great Eastern Film Exchange, the Philadelphia Film Exchange, the Baltimore Film Exchange, Palmore and Homand, and the Mutual Film Corporation were concentrated near the intersection of East Baltimore Street and Gay Street. In the early teens, the exchanges began moving to Washington, which was more centrally located. At first, local exhibitors had to go down to the Washington, Baltimore and Annapolis Railway depot and pick up the films shipped from Washington. If a film had to be held over for another Baltimore theater, it was taken to Augie Pahl, who had a place behind Haefele's film supply store on Baltimore Street.[2] Pahl would keep the holdovers for 10 or 25 cents a night.

Frank Durkee and a man named Henderson formed a company called the Baltimore and Washington Film Express in 1915 to transport film between the film exchanges in Washington and the theaters in Baltimore. Trucks departed the company's headquarters in Baltimore at 1:00 A.M. and returned with new film at 8:00 A.M. Initially Durkee's company handled films of the General Film Company, Universal Film Company, and Mutual Film Corporation. Exhibitors paid between $10 and $12 a week for this service. This arrangement worked well and relieved the theaters as well as the distributors of the need

The members and wives of the Motion Picture Theatre Owners of Maryland pose for a panoramic shot at their first annual outing in September 1951. Those identified include: #1 Aaron Seidler, #4 Elmer Nolte, #5 Jack Whittle, #9 Frank Hornig, Jr., #10 Meyer Leventhal, #12 Lauritz Garman, #18 Morton Rosen, #23 Sol Klein, #26 Jack Levine, #27 Vernon Nolte, #28 William Meyers, #31 Harry Silver, #35 Ben Beck, #52 Henry Dusman, #53 Stanley Baker, #54 Rodney Collier, #60 Ed Kimpel, #61 Bob Marhenke, #64 Joe Walderman, #69 Leon Back, #73 Morris Oletsky, #77 Curtis Hildebrand, #78 Frank Durkee, Jr., #81 Oscar Coblentz.

to make daily trips to pick up or return films. Of course, putting all the films in one truck could cause a disaster if something happened to the truck.

By the mid–1930s all of the major exchanges had moved to Washington to better serve what came to be known as the Washington Territory. This territory covered Washington, D.C., Delaware, Maryland, Virginia and part of West Virginia. The distribution center was Film Row in Washington. At first, it was located around the old entertainment neighborhood at 9th and Pennsylvania Avenue, N.W. Later, it moved to New Jersey Avenue. Baltimore exhibitors traveled to the exchanges, by train or private car, to book films. These trips gave them a chance to socialize. Irwin Cohen, of R/C Theaters, remembered that he would take a whole carload of exhibitors to Washington. "It got to the point that, when I drove over, I used to have a whole ... crowd that I would take with me ... the Cohen boys from Essex ... lived a couple of doors down the street and directly behind us was Harry Silver who owned a theater in Overlea. All of a sudden they found out that I was going to Washington and first thing I knew I had a full car every Monday morning to drive to Washington."[3]

Sol Goodman, who ran the Ideal Theater in Hampden, went by train. "It was very common to take the B & O and you would have breakfast on the train, then you'd get to Washington and you would go to book pictures. It was usually done on Mondays. So you would see all your [Baltimore theater] people there, and they were all booking pictures ... just talking and kidding with the bookers."[4] The exchange employees remember these visits fondly because of the gifts and lunches the visiting exhibitors often provided. Long-time exchange employee, Gertrude Epstein, who worked for several Washington film exchanges, remembered the Baltimore exhibitors.

> All the exhibitors would come in ... from Baltimore, a lot of them, every week ... every Monday and it was a madhouse because there was a constant turnover.... It was nice because everybody knew everybody. We were one big

happy family.... Of course they [the Baltimore exhibitors] would go over to the major distributors first and get their licks in there and then they would come over to the smaller ones and you'd have three or four of them there at the same time, always arguing, always [saying things like] "This picture was so awful! This picture was terrible! This one you'll make money with and this one you won't." Most of them were lovely, [but] some of them were awful.... The Rome Circuit was lovely ... and Durkee.... The male bookers were very friendly ... with the Baltimore exhibitors. Sometimes they'd go out to lunch.... At Christmas time ... they gave beautiful presents, especially Rome. Rome was always very nice with their gifts.[5]

By 1940 the Auditorium, Metropolitan, and Rivoli had been deleted from the list of first-run theaters. The remaining first-run theaters were: Century, Stanley, Hippodrome, Parkway, Keith's, Centre, Little, Times, New. African Americans were unable to attend the first-run white theaters downtown until 1959. Their first-run films usually opened at the Regent, Royal, or Harlem and later at the Metropolitan. A first-run film usually played at a single first-run theater, but in August 1940 the movie *The Boys from Syracuse*, starring Allan Jones and Martha Raye, opened simultaneously at the Hippodrome and Keith's. This was the first time such a thing had happened in Baltimore. Ten years later, the Mayfair, Roslyn, and Town were added to the first-run theaters.

Baltimore Theaters 1941

Academy of Music	N. Howard Street	Diane	1429 Pennsylvania Avenue
Aladdin	930 W. Baltimore	Dunbar	621 N. Central Avenue
Aldine	3310 E. Baltimore Street	Earle	4839 Belair Road
Alpha	725 Frederick Avenue	Echo	124 E. Fort Avenue
Ambassador	4604 Liberty Heights	Edgewood	3500 Edmondson Avenue
Apollo	1506 Harford Avenue	Embassy	415 E. Baltimore Street
Arcade	5434 Harford Road	Eureka	400 S. Fremont Avenue
Astor	611 Poplar Grove Street	Ford's	W. Fayette Street
Aurora	7–9 E. North Avenue	Forest	3306 Garrison Boulevard
Avalon	4338 Park Heights	Fremont	504 N. Fremont Avenue
Avenue	1405 N. Milton Avenue	Fulton	1563 N. Fulton Avenue
Belnord	2706 Philadelphia Avenue	Garden	1102 N. Charles Street
Boulevard	3302 Greenmount Avenue	Gayety	E. Baltimore Street
Bridge	2104 Edmondson Avenue	Grand	515 Conkling Street
Broadway	509 S. Broadway	Gwynn	4609 Liberty Heights
Cameo	4707 Harford Road	Hampden	911 W. 36th Street
Capitol	Baltimore Street nr. Gilmor	Harford	2618 Harford Avenue
Carey	Carey nr. School	Harlem	616 N. Gilmor Street
Casino	1118 Light Street	Highland	3829 Eastern Avenue
Centre	10 E. North Avenue	Hippodrome	12 N. Eutaw Street
Century	18 W. Lexington Street	Horn	2018 W. Pratt Street
Clover	414 E. Baltimore Street	Howard	115 N. Howard Street
Cluster	303 S. Broadway	Ideal	903 W. 36th Street
Columbia	709 Washington Boulevard	Irvington	4113 Frederick Avenue
Comedy	412 E. Baltimore Street	Keiths	114 W. Lexington Street
De Luxe	1318 E. Fort Avenue	Lafayette	1433 W. Lafayette Avenue

Lane	60 Dundalk Avenue	Pimlico	5144 Park Heights Avenue
Leader	248 S. Broadway	Plaza	404 E. Baltimore Street
Lenox	2115 Pennsylvania Avenue	Preston	1108 E. Preston Street
Lexway	31 W. Lexington Street	Radio	627 N. Eden Street
Lincoln	936 Pennsylvania Avenue	Realart	719 W. Baltimore Street
Linden	910 W. North Avenue	Red Wing	2341 E. Monument Street
Linwood	Linwood Avenue nr. Hudson	Regent	1627 Pennsylvania Avenue
Little	523 N. Howard Street	Rex	4615 York Road
Lord Baltimore	1114 W. Baltimore Street	Rialto	846 W. North Avenue
Lord Calvert	2444 Washington Boulevard	Rio	1531 E. Monument Street
		Ritz	1607 N. Washington Street
Lyceum	Sparrows Point	Rivoli	418 E. Baltimore Street
Lyric	Mt. Royal Avenue	Roosevelt	512 W. Biddle Street
McHenry	1032 Light Street	Roxy	2443 E. Fayette Street
Maryland	Franklin Street	Royal	1329 Pennsylvania Avenue
Met	1538 W. North Avenue	Schanze's	2426 Pennsylvania Avenue
Monroe	1924 W. Pratt Street	Senator	5904 York Road
Northway	6701 Harford Road	Stanley	516 N. Howard Street
Nemo	4815 Eastern Avenue	State	2045 E. Monument
New	210 W. Lexington Street	Strand	1 Shipping Place
New Essex	416 Eastern Boulevard	Superba	906 Columbia Avenue
Overlea	6805 Belair Road	Times	1711 N. Charles Street
Palace	1351 N. Gay Street	Towson	512 York Road
Park	1105 N. Broadway	Vilma	3703 Belair Road
Parkway	3 W. North Avenue	Walbrook	3100 W. North Avenue
Pastime	2028 Greenmount Avenue	Waverly	3211 Greenmount Avenue
Patterson	3136 Eastern Avenue	Westport	2305 Russell Street
Pennington	4911 Pennington Avenue	Westway	5300 Edmondson Avenue
Pic	756 Washington Boulevard	York	2026 Greenmount Avenue
Pikes	1001 Reisterstown Road		

There was a considerable amount of litigation involving theaters and distributors during the 1940s and 1950s. It usually involved independent exhibitors against larger circuits or the distributors or new theaters against established theaters. The independents wanted to be treated as the equals of the big circuits, and they wanted better films. The courts tended to side with the distributors and the larger circuits.

In a major 1939 case, the independent Westway Theater sued seven major film distributors and Durkee's Lyndhurst Corporation, which operated the Edgewood Theater. The owners of the Westway claimed that there was a conspiracy between Durkee and the film distributors and a violation of the Sherman Anti-Trust Act. A Federal judge found for the defendants, concluding that there was no conspiracy, that the provisions of the license agreements between the distributors and the operators of the Edgewood granting runs and clearances were valid and not in violation of the Sherman Anti-Trust Act, and that each of the defendants had the right to select its own customers and to determine for itself whether or not it would deal with the Westway and upon what terms.[6]

In the same year, the Linden Theater sued the Durkee and Rome organizations for conspiring to violate the anti-trust laws. The owners of the Linden complained that they did not have the right to bid for films in open competition and that films were made available to the Linden only after they were out of date. In 1946 the Linden Theater brought a second anti-trust case against Durkee and Rome; the Harford Theater followed suit. Both of these suits came soon after the Jackson Park Case in Chicago where the Supreme Court upheld a lower court decision awarding damages to the Jackson Park Theater in its suit against Balaban & Katz and the major distributors. This case was seen as encouragement to other independent theater owners to institute damage suits. An out-of-court settlement was reached two years later that gave the Harford Theater a better break on playing time.

In 1948 the Windsor Theater filed an anti-trust suit against the nearby Walbrook and Hilton theaters and the six major distributors charging a conspiracy to deprive it of neighborhood-run features. An out-of-court settlement was reached with one of the distributors; Twentieth Century–Fox agreed to split its product between the Walbrook and Windsor on a first-neighborhood-run basis. Three years later the Windsor's suit against the Walbrook and Hilton was dismissed.

In 1954, the Supreme Court denied the request by the Crest Theater for anti-trust damages from eight major distributors. "The Supreme Court ... upheld the right of motion picture distributors to deny first-run films to neighborhood theaters with limited drawing power. The decision rejected contentions of the Crest Theater in Baltimore which had sought anti-trust damages from eight major distributors. The Crest charged conspiratorial action by the eight in refusing to license first-run pictures to it. The distributors denied any conspiracy and said their refusal was the result of independent judgment in solving a common business problem."[7] The Court noted the disparity between neighborhood and first-run theaters.

Justice Clark delivered the 7–1 decision, stating that, "An exclusive license would be economically unsound because the Crest is a suburban theater, located in a small shopping center, and served by limited public transportation facilities; and, with a drawing area of less than one tenth of that of a downtown theater it cannot compare with those easily accessible theaters in the power to draw patrons."

In 1941, anti-trust concerns took a back seat to World War II. On December 7, Baltimoreans were watching Abbott and Costello in *Keep 'Em Flying* at Keith's as the Japanese air force was blasting Pearl Harbor. The Stanley was showing Bogart's *Maltese Falcon*. Neighborhood theaters were showing *International Lady* and *Bowery Blitzkrieg*. Robert Marhenke, who was managing the Capitol Theater that Sunday, remembered that the theater was packed. When he heard the news, Marhenke had to make a decision. He could have made an announcement but, instead, decided to let people find out as they left the theatre. That way they could at least enjoy the show, and there "wasn't a darn thing they could do about it," anyway.

Throughout the war, the reality of the conflict would be brought home vividly by newsreels. Baltimoreans listened to Edward R. Murrow, Gabriel Heatter, and Lowell Thomas on the radio, and we saw with our own eyes, in the newsreels, jack-booted Huns marching through Belgium and our devastated navy at Pearl Harbor. The day after Pearl Harbor, the Hippodrome advertised that the "Latest War News Flashes" would be announced directly from the stage. An enterprising, if not very tactful, insurance agency advertised war and bombardment coverage. The call went out for 150,000 civilian volunteers. The city and the country were getting ready for war, and movies were in the thick of it.

An article in late December 1941 alerted exhibitors about what to expect.

> Baltimore will shortly experience its first total blackout alarm. Some local managers ... have drawn up their own rules and are instructing their staffs in the procedure to follow. Trailers are being made to acquaint the audiences with their part in an alarm. The opinion has been expressed by Governor O'Conor that Baltimore is most vulnerable to air raids due to the large scale defense activities in and around the city and for this reason an increasing number of practice blackout alarms will ensue as the war becomes intensified.
>
> Harry Cluster, business agent of The Motion Picture Projectionists Union, Inc., has been appointed an air raid warden, and Robert T. Marhenke, Capitol manager, was appointed some time ago to act in this capacity.
>
> Questionnaires are being mailed ... to owners of public buildings, including theatres, to submit data on available raid shelter space, amount of plate glass, etc. The slight business slump here is attributed to preholiday activities and radio war broadcasts. C. W. Hicks is having blue bulbs of small wattage installed in the box offices of his houses, to remain lit during blackouts as a precautionary measure.
>
> Five Japs comprising the Eno Troupe, appearing at F. H. Durkee's State Theatre, surrendered themselves to the federal authorities following Japan's declaration of war.
>
> By request of the Baltimore Civilian Defense Committee, a special trailer touching upon that subject is being shown in all theatres this week.[8]

The girls at the Gayety Theater did their part too. Organized in March 1941 by comedienne Dorothy Sevier, they donated clothing to the British War Relief Society. Presumably they didn't need much clothing and could spare it for England. Several films, described as "good-natured" spoofs of the navy, that were in production were quietly shelved. Hollywood thought it would be in bad taste to make fun of the navy after Pearl Harbor.

In Baltimore, preparations were being made to guard against air raids. In early 1943, there was a law enacted against pleasure driving, and movie theaters feared the worst. After a slight drop in patronage during the first few days of the law, attendance picked up, and soon several downtown theaters were reporting that they had sold out on Sunday evenings. Across the nation, movie theaters were doing spectacular business. During the war years, the estimated weekly attendance in the United States averaged about 85 million.

Even before Pearl Harbor, the war in Europe was affecting the local movie scene. The German Consul in Baltimore vigorously protested the State censors' January 1938 decision to allow the Hippodrome Theater to show the *March of Time* newsreel entitled *Inside Nazi Germany*. Consul Frederick F. Schneider had not actually seen the film, but he was afraid it was "likely to influence adversely the good understanding now existing between the Government of the United States of America and the Government of Germany." With narration like, "children are taught that they are born to die for Germany — they must act as they are told by the state" and "newspapers in Germany may print only what the state says they can print — and all letters are subject to censorship," it did not paint a flattering picture.

In 1940, the FBI began looking for propaganda and investigating the exhibition of German-language films. It turned out that many of the German-language films shown in Baltimore since October 1939 had been exhibited at the Hindenburg Theater on North

Howard Street. Projectionist Charles Reisinger was working at the Hindenburg during its last days. He described it in several interviews: "The Hindenburg Theater was up on the roof [of Lehmann Hall] and they had cut a hole in the roof and you used to shine it down into the theater ... [the projection booth was] just a little shed on the roof with two holes cut in the ceiling and they went down that way and they had to put glass over there in case something fell down on people's heads. I remember that I worked there; they came up and told me to shut it off. The next day they closed the Hindenburg up."[9] The Little Theater, under the management of Herman Blum, banned propaganda-laden Russian films, concentrating instead on British and French films.

Movie theaters proved to be excellent places to distribute information to the population.[10] Trailers detailing civilian defense measures were shown in theaters all over the city. Frank Hornig, president of the Motion Picture Theatre Owners of Maryland, was appointed acting chairman of the Theatre Committee for Civilian Defense; he coordinated the work of the Baltimore Committee on Civilian Defense with the member theaters. During late December 1941, local theaters showed trailers, such as *Fighting the Fire Bomb*, in an effort to recruit volunteers for home defense.

Beginning in April 1942, the weekly programs of the city's theaters began carrying excerpts from official publications of the Baltimore Committee on Civilian Defense. Topics covered in these excerpts included, "Blackouts," "Helpful Hints on Air Raids," "War Gases," and "Air Raid Shelters." In September 1942, the Baltimore Police Department published General Order No. 4248 which detailed procedures to be followed during an air raid and blackout. Generally speaking, during a blackout, between sunset and sunrise, no light was to be visible from any building. Offenders were subject to hefty fines of up to $500 or to imprisonment for not more than one year, or both. Smoking or the lighting of matches on the street during a blackout was prohibited; offenders could be arrested for disorderly conduct.

During blackouts, theater box offices could be illuminated by a single 25-watt bulb with an opaque coating and a one-inch circular aperture on the bulb, provided the bulb had a shade which shielded it from outside observation above the horizontal. Each theater was supposed to appoint a theater warden to be responsible for preparing the theater in blackouts, during an air raid, and in case it was hit by a bomb.

Theaters helped to provide financing for the war effort by selling war bonds. They held bond drives throughout the war. During a meeting sponsored by the Motion Picture Theater Owners' Association of Maryland in May 1942, exhibitors pledged $115,000 worth of war bonds. May 30 was proclaimed War Bond Day for the theaters. Touring Hollywood starlets[11] selling war bonds reached Baltimore in May 1942. They hoped to help Maryland reach its June quota of war bonds and stamps which had been set at $12,002,100.[12]

During June, July, August, and September 1942, the Ambassador Theater sold war bonds and stamps worth $52,171. Each day the theater honored a different local serviceman; 15 September was Staff Sergeant Mendes E. Morstein Day, and 24 September was Lieutenant Erwin A. Young Day. In September, local exhibitors took part in a one-month effort by the motion picture industry to sell $1 billion in war bonds and stamps. They planned rallies with bands and entertainers at all of the Baltimore movie theaters on September 1. Movie theaters throughout the state donated their total day's receipts on September 24, 1942 to the purchase of war bonds.

A series of Fourth War Loan motion picture premieres in Baltimore began in January 1944. The first film was *Life Boat*, starring Tallulah Bankhead, at the New Theater. Admission was by the purchase of a Series E bond. Subsequent bond premieres were scheduled for the Stanley, Century, and Hippodrome. Frank Durkee, state chairman of motion-picture participation in the war-loan drive, announced in November 1944 that all neighborhood theaters in Baltimore would admit purchasers of $25 bonds to performances free. Bond purchasers were admitted free to downtown theaters on Pearl Harbor Day. The Mayfair, New, Hippodrome, Stanley, Century and Keith's theaters aided the Seventh War Loan with special pre-release premieres in May 1945. The Hippodrome sold more than $91,000 worth of war bonds during the evening shows on June 4, 1945.

In the fall of 1945, downtown Baltimore theaters devoted one night each to special bond premiers known as Victory Shows. Theaters also collected scrap metal and rubber during the war. By November 1942, theaters across the country had collected about 167,000 tons of scrap metal. Some theaters would admit a person free for bringing in a certain amount of scrap. November 13 and 14, 1942, were designated as collection days in Baltimore. Anyone who brought 10 pounds of scrap metal or two pounds of scrap rubber to a collection center was entitled to one ticket for a matinee during the following week at a local movie theater. The movie theaters also reduced the cost of tickets for servicemen.[13]

Shortages of nearly everything affected the whole nation, but some were especially hard on theaters. Fuel oil was in short supply during much of the war, and theaters everywhere were rushing to convert from oil heat to coal. Government officials said that theaters and dance halls would come last on the fuel oil list, if they made the list at all. Many were operating on reduced schedules. Most theaters in the Baltimore area used coal and were unaffected by the shortage. A shortage of film made it impossible for film distributors to supply prints to all of their customers at the same time.

There was also a shortage of colored bulbs. Exhibitors tried dyeing clear bulbs, but the color wore off after a few days. The supply of strategic materials was so limited that, in May 1942, the War Production Board ordered that all construction of public amusement projects, which included movie theaters, be stopped by June 6. The Apex Theater was already under construction with building materials slated for a theater in Annapolis and just made it under the wire.

The role of women in the entertainment industry has always been viewed ambivalently. It was perfectly all right for them to show off their talents, charms, and beauty on the stage or screen, but they rarely got the opportunity to have anything to do with the operation of a theater. Female managers do appear occasionally in the history of the stage, and there were a few in early, usually small, movie theaters.[14] Piano players were generally women, as were cashiers. By about 1910, there were some female ushers at Baltimore theaters. Two years later, the Academy of Music, the Auditorium, and the New had hired, as the *Sun* reporter put it, "a dainty young lady to do the piloting down the aisle."[15] Aided by outside events, women moved slowly into the work force. The World Wars were major catalysts.

During World War I, one of the few local plants to employ women was the Bartlett-Hayward Company, but there were also conductorettes, elevator girls, and female messengers. During a dispute with musicians at the Maryland Theater in 1918, manager Frederick C. Schanberger filled their places in his orchestra with women. That same year, manager Bernard Depkin of the Parkway, Strand, Wizard, McHenry, and Peabody theaters actually stated that he would hire women projectionists if he could find any women he thought capable of doing the work, and he could get them trained.

Depkin was in the process of replacing male employees with young women at his theaters, but he never got as far as projectionists. Charles Whitehurst booked a six-act, all-female vaudeville show. He believed that, "if it actually becomes necessary to send all men over to lick the Kaiser, women can and will prove themselves as efficient as actor folk as they have in industrial activity...."[16]

When the members of the Motion Picture Theater Owners Association of Maryland drew up a code for the National Recovery Administration in 1933, they called for the payment of a minimum of $15 for a 48-hour week for men and $12 for a 40-hour week for women. Within days of the declaration of war in 1941, thousands of Maryland women flocked to the offices of the women's division of the Maryland Council of Defense; they all wanted to volunteer for the defense effort. Women broke out of their narrow world during the war; they would never turn back.

Theater owners were only too happy to move women into managerial jobs. In 1942, there were scores of managers and assistant managers, and there were reports that the newly-organized Women's Army Auxiliary Corps was going to train projectionists. Hundreds of thousands of women worked in war plants. Many industries began to get worried about males being drained out of the work force, but not the IATSE. Richard F. Walsh, president of that male bastion, would not even consider replacing men in the booth with women; he believed women were too "panicky."[17]

By the end of 1942, 2,500 of the 42,000 members of IATSE had been drafted. By the end of the Second World War, women proved they could do just about any job a man could do. But it would still be many years before there were any female projectionists in Baltimore.

During World War II, times were hard for factory workers of both sexes, but they were also difficult for women who stayed home to take care of children and keep house. One Baltimore woman had worked herself ragged, so on an evening in July 1943, her husband took her out to a movie, where she could relax. The film and the cool, dark theater worked their magic, and soon she was so relaxed that she fell asleep. She awoke later, suddenly, and, for some reason, began to clap. Unfortunately, at that moment there was a picture of Adolph Hitler on the screen. Her husband quieted her, but not before she was hissed from all parts of the theater. They left soon after that, and the woman said that, since then, she continually expected a visit from the FBI.

America's huge war industry was in motion day and night. As soon as one shift of workers finished, another began. Movie theaters responded to shift workers' needs by adding late shows. Staying open late was one of the ways that the Baltimore business community found to make its goods and services available to the large number of shift workers employed by local industries.

In 1943 at least 8,000 night-shift war workers at the Bethlehem-Fairfield shipyard wanted movie theaters and other places of business to remain open at night. Their first specific request was for a downtown movie theater to be open between 12:30 and 3:30 A.M. two nights a week.[18] A proposal for after-midnight movies was made during a meeting of representatives of the Civilian Mobilization Committee, the Association of Commerce, various labor organizations, and the moving-picture industry on March 24, 1943. Their first idea was to ask the neighborhood theaters to have late shows. Frank Hornig was appointed by the exhibitors to work with representatives of the AFL and CIO to explore the practicality of the proposal. One member of the committee studying the issue of keeping theaters open longer at night saw the lack of adequate mass transportation as a serious obstacle. He favored keeping the neighborhood theaters, rather than the downtown houses, open; then, the patrons could walk home. Everyone was within walking distance of a movie theater. On April 9, 1943, the Century and Stanley announced that they would have late shows; the Century planned a show at 12:30 A.M. Keith's responded with a midnight showing of *Frankenstein Meets the Wolfman* on April 11. The Hippodrome offered a midnight stage and screen show on April 20. The Stanley advertised a continuous show from midnight, Friday, April 23, to midnight, April 24, that featured a premier of the movie *Air Force*. The first after-midnight show at the Century brought more than 2,000 customers to the theater. The show was so successful that manager William K. Saxton scheduled another late show for the following Wednesday. In order to give workers time to go home and clean up, the feature film began at 1:30 A.M.

After a trial of several weeks at a number of downtown theaters—the Century, Keith's, Hippodrome, and Stanley—the late shows were declared a success. Managers were surprised by the large attendance and how well behaved the audiences were. The Times Theater inaugurated a policy of all-night movies in May 1943; it was the only downtown theater that continued late-night movies throughout the war. The Century and Keith's had occasional midnight and late shows in 1944.

Movies about the Frankenstein-Wolfman meeting and the air force were good choices for war workers. The men and women who built ships and planes preferred action movies, especially westerns. A 1942 newspaper article said that while people who wore coats and ties to work might have enjoyed *Mrs. Miniver* or a Judge Hardy film, most of the factory workers wanted to see a rip-roaring western.[19] Managers said that they could identify war workers because they were in their shirtsleeves at morning or afternoon shows and in sport shirts open at the neck at the evening shows. In earlier times people used to get really dressed up when they went to movies. It was not unusual for people to dress in evening clothes to attend movie theaters.

On a hot June day in 1925, the movie critic for the *Sun* found out the hard way that he was not welcome in the Century Theater, at least not in the orchestra or loges, if he took his coat off. The management said that the coat rules had been adopted because of the protests of lady patrons. An usher, who was interviewed in 1926 said that the audiences did not dress as much as they used to, but added that when a big musical movie played, large parties of society people came, and they were really dressed up. The Second World War seems to have put an end to dressing up for a movie. When after-midnight shows were not available, night shift workers usually patronized the afternoon shows, and day workers went to the first evening shows. By 1943, the public had apparently tired of war movies and the studios responded by producing fewer films of this type. The new movies were termed "super-escapist."[20]

Traditionally the war years have been regarded as good ones for the movie business. Attendance was high and theaters made huge profits. Motion picture attendance in Baltimore reached an all-time high in 1942 but then seemed to drop approximately 10 percent between October 1942 and September 1943.[21] The manager of one of the African-American movie theaters reported in 1942 that although evening patronage at his theater was better, attendance at matinees was worse because more people had jobs. Attendance was also down for the last evening shows because so many people had to get up early in the morning. Some of the theaters considered eliminating afternoon shows.

Weekend business was still excellent, but because so many people had gone into higher-paying war work, there was a problem staffing the theaters. Theaters also substituted for babysitters. Mothers had been using them since the days of the nickelodeons. An article in the *News-Post* in December 1943 reported that neighborhood theaters were being used as nurseries on Saturdays. Mothers brought their children to the theaters early in the day; they usually brought a bag of potato chips, some candy, and a pack of chewing gum. Sometimes they brought their lunches in bags. The mother would tell the child to stay at the theater until she came to pick him or her up or "not to come home until 7." A typical Saturday show was a Western, an action picture, a chapter of a serial, a comedy, a cartoon, previews of coming attractions, and maybe a newsreel.

When the new Federal amusement tax kicked in on April 1, 1944, the managers of the first-run theaters agreed not to raise their prices more than five cents per ticket. When questioned about an OPA request for Congress to put a price ceiling on movie admissions, Lauritz Garman, an official of the Motion Picture Theater Operators of Maryland, said that there was no reason for local complaints. Garman said that prices were much higher in New York and Philadelphia than in Baltimore. He said that the Baltimore theaters had decided long before 1944, when the Federal amusement tax was doubled, not to increase their prices.

By 1946, some distributors were specifying the minimum admission price a theater could charge. The following table shows some of these prices for Baltimore neighborhood theaters.

	Loew's	Warner	RKO	Fox	Columbia	U.A.	Universal
Ritz	25¢	28¢	none	25¢	X[22]	none	25¢
Vilma	25¢	28¢	none	25¢	X	none	X
Centre	30¢	33¢	X	30¢	X	X	30¢
Hampden	X	X	X	27¢	X	27¢	25¢
Columbia	25¢	28¢	none	25¢	X	X	25¢
Broadway	27¢	X	X	27¢	X	27¢	25¢
Apollo	25¢	X	X	27¢	X	25¢	25¢
Irvington	X	28¢	25¢	25¢	X	X	25¢

Presumably the Centre was considered more like a downtown theater than a neighborhood one and could charge higher prices. A survey by the *Afro-American* in May 1947 showed that the average top ticket price on Pennsylvania Avenue was 50 cents for adults and 25 cents for children. At the same time, the Hippodrome had top prices of 70 cents and 35 cents; the New charged 65 cents and 35 cents and the Town charged $1.50 and 74 cents. Baltimore neighborhood exhibitors had the lowest admission prices of any city in the country in 1949 according to exhibitors Milton Schwaber and Frank Durkee. Schwaber said that 95 percent of Baltimore's neighborhood theaters had not changed their prices since 1929. The prices at neighborhood movie houses then were 20 to 25 cents for matinee performances and 30 to 36 cents for evening performances. Children were 14 to 18 cents at all times.[23]

In the fall of 1944, members of the Motion Picture Theatre Owners of Maryland made plans to close their theaters on V-day. Managers were advised to prevent those in the theater from learning the news of the end of the war in order to prevent a panic. By 1945, everyone was dreaming of the end of the war. Germany capitulated first, in the spring, but the war in the Pacific dragged on into the summer. When President Truman authorized the use of the atomic bomb, the end was near. Acting Mayor C. Markland Kelly, who had lost a son in the war, announced that any parades would be saved until the fighting men were back to take part in them. He suggested that the city mark the day quietly at home or at prayer in churches. Stores were ready to close within 15 minutes of news of peace. The police department was braced for huge crowds downtown.

Suddenly, at 9:34 on the evening of August 12, a broadcast over WBAL announced that the war was over. Bedlam erupted downtown; then, just as suddenly, the crowds learned that it was a false report. The Translux — an electric bulletin sign — on the old Sunpaper building spelled out the message, "Report of Japanese surrender is false." On the 14th, the morning newspaper headlines read, "Japs to Quit: Tokyo," and, finally on August 15, the *Sun* announced, "The War Is Over."

At 7:00 P.M. on August 14, President Truman announced the Japanese unconditional surrender. Within an hour, a huge crowd of singing, dancing, and cheering people flooded the downtown streets. The crowd reached its peak at about 10 P.M. with more than 100,000 packed on Baltimore Street between Eutaw and the Fallsway. On Howard Street there were another 75,000 and Lexington Street had 25,000. At the same time, the African-American community was holding another celebration on Pennsylvania Avenue. The streets were still jammed at midnight and at 1:00 A.M. the sidewalks were impassable. Church bells throughout the city rang; nearly everyone had some kind of noisemaker. Servicemen in town kissed every girl they saw.

As soon as they heard the news, people in theaters poured out onto the streets. The manager of a theater on East Baltimore Street stopped the film to make the announcement and immediately the audience rose and left the theater cheering as they went. In another theater, a woman was leaving by a side door when she heard the celebration outside. She turned back into the theater shouting, "The war is over!" At least half the audience left. Performances at theaters on military bases were halted to spread the news. In the harbor, any ship with steam up was blowing its whistle. Just about every business in the city was closed on the 15th; it was very difficult for people to find places to eat. Taverns, nightclubs, and stores closed. Things got so desperate that some people bought tickets to movie theaters so they could buy candy in the lobby vending machines.[24]

Even before the war was over, exhibitors were planning post-war theaters. Because of the scarcity of building materials, very few theaters had been built during the war. A few that had been started in the early 1940s were completed in 1944 and 1945, but the real post-war building boom for theaters had to wait until 1946. A 1944 survey in the *Wall Street Journal* suggested that postwar theaters would be smaller and more comfortable than their pre-war predecessors. The survey predicted that the average number of seats in the new theaters would be about 800. Visions of the post-war movie theater seem to have been accurate, but these theaters would not be built by the big nation-wide circuits. The post-war years would belong to the independent local exhibitors.

Much of the new theater construction involved remodeling and renovation. As a result of the huge increase in movie-going during the war, theaters and their accoutrements were wearing out. William Saxton, manager of the Loew Theaters in Baltimore, said that even his cash registers were wearing out, and he planned to buy colored light bulbs to replace some of the white ones he had to use during the war.[25] Remodeling ranged from trivial redecorating — new carpeting or a new paint job — to completely rebuilding a theater. Isador Rappaport planned a new neon marquee for his Hippodrome. Morris Mechanic gutted his New Theater and completely rebuilt the inside. He also added a new cooling system and an escalator to carry patrons from the lobby to the mezzanine level. The Stanley was ready to be redecorated, and the Mayfair was to be enlarged.

But the end of the war did not mean the end of controls on strategic materials. Building material was hard to obtain unless it was for veterans' housing. Despite an order by the Civilian Production Authority banning nearly all construction except homes for veterans and authorizing "completion only of those jobs on which materials had been incorporated 'on the site,'" there was an enormous increase in applications for building permits. On the 26th and 27th of March, 1946, for example, 312 applications were filed with the Bureau of Buildings. That same month there were three permit applications for theaters worth a total of $125,000. Architect Kenneth C. Miller, the architect of Edmondson Village Shopping Center and Theater, said that construction would continue there. Builder Edward Eyring was more cautious and was waiting for clarification before beginning construction of "a $30,000 theater for the Ritz Enterprises at 1201–1203 Dundalk Avenue, and a $50,000 theater for the same sponsor on Belair Road at Erdman Avenue."[26]

The Victory and the Patapsco, only a few blocks apart in Brooklyn, got a jump on the end of the war, opening in the fall of 1944. The Patapsco had been planned in 1941, but problems obtaining building materials held it up for three years. The Midway, in Middle River, opened in 1945. Then, in 1946, despite the Civilian Production Administration's directive, the tap for construction material was turned on and nine movie houses opened around the city: Anthony, Dean, Edgemere, Hill, Hiway, Homewood, Madison, New, and Paramount. Of the 12 theaters opened in 1944, 1945, and 1946, all except one— the rebuilt New—were outside downtown. Six were in areas that had concentrations of defense industries, Brooklyn–Curtis Bay, Middle River, and Dundalk–Turner's Station. Again, with the exception of the New, these theaters were medium-sized, had fewer than 1,000 seats, and were unpretentious neighborhood theaters. They did not break any new architectural ground, opting instead to use pre-war plans and styles. Schwaber Theaters liked architect Hal Miller's design so much that they built four of their theaters—Apex, Homewood, Paramount, and Colgate—according to identical or nearly identical plans.

During World War II, exhibitors could make an 8-cent profit on a 10-cent bag of popcorn. This kind of money was too good to miss, and even exhibitors who disliked the mess associated with food in the theater began installing popcorn machines and more candy machines. The Rivoli, Embassy, and Cluster Theaters installed popcorn machines in 1946, and the Westport got a candy machine around the same time.[27] By 1947, popcorn and other snack foods were being sold in 85 percent of the theaters in the United States,[28] and the following year 98 percent of theaters in the country were offering some kind of refreshment service to their patrons. According to *Business Week*, candy and popcorn sales in a deluxe first-run house made up between 3 percent to 5 percent of the theater's weekly gross; in neighborhood houses between 12 percent and 25 percent of the box office gross.[29]

A somewhat different picture is suggested by the 1948 Business Census. According to that source, there were 236 movie theaters in Maryland with a revenue from admissions and fees for the year of $17,356,000. Ninety of these theaters sold merchandise which brought in $445,000 and 76 theaters made $304,000 from rented concessions. So, it seems that slightly more than 70 percent of the theaters in the state were selling some kind of snack food, candy, popcorn, ice cream, sandwiches, coffee, nuts or cookies. *Life* magazine in July 1949 reported that more than two billion bags of popcorn a year were sold in the United States, mainly to children. Between the mid–1940s and 1966, theater refreshment sales grew nearly 100 percent reaching sales of $400 million. Some of this increase was due to the greatly diversified line of foodstuffs sold in drive-ins. Everyone ate at a drive-in, and some drive-ins had snack bars that resembled large cafeterias.[30] In the 1950s, concession stands began appearing in downtown theaters and, by the end of the decade, nearly all theaters in Baltimore had them.

The year 1947 was a big one for censorship. David Selznick's movie, *Duel in the Sun*, was seen by many as so terrible that it was denounced in the United States Congress. The Maryland Board of Censors approved the film, but ordered the elimination of eight or ten scenes deemed "too hot" as well as scenes in which Jennifer Jones was "too scantily clothed." Howard Hughes's western, *The Outlaw*, starring a sultry Jane Russell, was unanimously condemned by the censors as being obscene, indecent, inhuman, immoral, and tending to debase morals and incite to crime.[31] The board objected to the scene in which a cowboy offers to trade Miss Russell for a horse, a scene showing the buildup to a kiss, and scenes where Miss Russell displayed her famous curves. Judge E. Paul Mason affirmed the board's ban in September 1947.

A short time later, the censors, led by board chairman Sydney R. Traub, denounced foreign-made movies and their "deteriorating" effect on Marylanders. Traub reported that the board found 42 percent of these films objectionable in 1948 and 52 percent objectionable in 1949. In 1949, the censors tried to expand their power by banning the Polish documentary, *On Polish Lands*, claiming that the film was subject to censorship as to its truth and sincerity. Despite a ruling from the State's attorney general that they had exceeded their legal authority and a protest from the Maryland Civil Rights Congress, the board members stuck by the ban.[32] Three years later the Roberto Rosselini-Ingrid Bergman movie, *Stromboli*, was the center of controversy. Strangely enough, even though many censor boards banned the film and many exhibitors refused to show it, the Maryland censors passed it.[33]

7

SHOPPING CENTERS AND DRIVE-INS (1948–1960)

In 1948 there were 18,631 movie theaters in the country, including 820 drive-ins. Maryland had 241 movie theaters; five of these were drive-ins. In the Baltimore metropolitan area, including Baltimore and Anne Arundel counties, there were 137 movie theaters (two were drive-ins), more than half the movie houses in the state. In 1948, after 11 years of litigation, the government finally won its anti-trust case against the major national movie producers. The first-run movie situation in most cities changed dramatically as a result of this case. The big circuits separated their production activities from their exhibition activities, in many cases selling off their theaters to local circuits. Loew's and Warner Bros., the only national circuits to gain footholds in Baltimore, sold out to Morris Mechanic. While indoor theaters continued to be built until the very early 1950s, there came a disastrous period when it seemed that no one wanted to go to the movies. Hollywood tried everything—wide-screen movies, 3-D movies, even vibrators under theater seats—but nothing seemed to work. Older theaters closed by the hundreds.

Only the drive-ins made money. The 1950s were the drive-in era.[1] In the Baltimore area, six drive-ins were opened during that decade. Only three drive-ins were opened after 1960. The painful racial integration of movie theaters began in the late 1940s and gained speed during the next decade. One bright spot in movie exhibition was the appearance of "art houses," smaller theaters that specialized in foreign films. In Baltimore, the Schwaber organization pioneered the development of art houses, converting the Homewood into the Playhouse (1951), the Linden into the Cinema (1956), and the Parkway into the 5 West (1956). In 1958 JF Theaters converted the Times Theater into the Charles. The others have closed, but the Charles is still going strong at the beginning of the new century. First-run films began to move out of downtown in the 1950s with the opening of these art theaters.[2] The Playhouse, 5-West, Cinema, and Charles all played first-run foreign movies and independent films. Other neighborhood theaters turned to art films in the 1960s as a last desperate attempt to remain open. This did not work for the Aurora, Edgewood, Rex, or Avalon.

By the end of the 1940s, a new kind of commercial construction began appearing in the suburbs of larger cities. It was called a shopping center. Shopping centers, later malls, would become the focus of most of the shopping and entertainment activity in the country over the next 60 years. In the fall of 1948, the writer of an article in *Boxoffice* believed that shopping centers might develop into "a boom comparable to the drive-in expansion of the past two years."[3] This article suggested that two factors were stimulating theaters in shopping centers: large-scale housing developments outside large cities and, especially for women shoppers, the availability of convenient free parking. The Hiway and Hill theaters, both opened in 1946, were the second and third Baltimore area theaters to be built in suburban shopping centers.[4] In the following year, the Watersedge opened in a small Dundalk shopping center. The larger Edmondson Village and Crest theaters opened in malls in 1949.

These theaters set the tone for the next 50 years of theater building. Nearly all of the movie theaters built after 1949 would be in shopping centers.[5] In contrast, prior to the late 1940s, nearly all the theaters built in the Baltimore area were in settled, commercial areas of the cities.

The development of motion picture exhibition in Maryland outside of Baltimore mirrored its development in the city, but on a smaller scale. The earliest movies were shown by traveling shows in legitimate theaters, opera houses, or halls. The first movie theaters outside Baltimore were built in Cumberland, Hagerstown, Frederick, and Annapolis around 1909. It took several more years for movies to reach the smaller towns. The first movie theater in Ellicott City was opened by Edward A. Rodey, by at least 1912, on the fifth floor of an ancient building on Main Street that had formerly been a tavern and town hall.[6] In Bel Air, movies were shown at the annual Chautauqua, and a movie theater had opened there by the mid-teens.

In the early twenties, in many suburban population centers, movies were still being shown in school auditoriums, halls and churches. There was a need for real movie theaters. The Community Church in St. Helena became the first movie theater in the Dundalk area in 1924. In Towson, movies were shown in an open-air theater in the summer of 1915. The first movie theater there, the Recreation Theater, opened in January 1916. Caltrider's Hall in Reisterstown had movies around 1925. In Catonsville, movies were shown at the old high school on Frederick Avenue and at the Odd Fellows' Hall on Ingleside Avenue around 1917. Within a few years, the populations of several suburban centers had increased to the point where they could support a movie theater. The Strand was built in Dundalk in 1927. The Alpha opened in Catonsville; the Argonne opened in Bel Air, and the Towson opened in Towson in 1928. A year later the Art opened in Glen Burnie. Later, the New opened in Reisterstown (1934) and the Hollywood opened in Arbutus (1936).

Annapolis was the only other city in the Baltimore area that could support several movie theaters. It appears that the population of a city had to be more than 5,000 before it could support more than one movie theater. Annapolis had a 1910 population of 8,609; Bel Air and Ellicott City were much smaller.

The earliest movie exhibition in Annapolis identified so far was given by Thomas Armat at the Opera House on December 18, 1901 for the benefit of the local Boys' Club. Tickets for the two-hour show cost 50 cents for reserved seats, 35 cents for general admission, and 25 cents for gallery seats. Music between the movies was provided by a "professional violinist and pianist from Washington."[7] Despite the audience, which was described as "small but appreciative," the exhibition was called a great success. The movies consisted of short scenes that included the funeral of President McKinley and the race between the yachts Columbia and Shamrock.

In 1906 there was an exhibition of Biograph movies at the Colonial Theater. The Maryland Avenue Methodist Episcopal Church hosted several early movie exhibitions. In February 1907 the American Entertainment Company presented the "Lifephonetic Combination" of moving pictures, and in December 1907 Prof. J. A. Loose showed movies there. The first movie theaters in Annapolis were clustered around the City Market (the Lyric and Burtis) or on Church Street (the Magnet and later the Republic). The large African-American population in Annapolis supported two theaters, an early converted hall on Clay Street and later the Star Theater. Annapolis was the only urban center in the Baltimore area to have early separate theaters for African Americans.

Integration of Baltimore movie theaters began in the late 1940s, but proceeded slowly. Before the 1960s, most Baltimore neighborhoods were either white or black, and consequently the theaters that served those areas were the same. Neighborhood theaters remained de facto segregated. Early targets for anti-segregation efforts were the Maryland and Ford's theaters. The management of the Maryland could not decide on one policy. In February 1947, after threats of a picket line, the Maryland Theater made seats in all parts of the theater available to African Americans.[8]

In May 1949, the Maryland announced that it had abandoned its policy of racial segregation and would be open to anyone, regardless of race or color. This announcement was made following a successful run of the play, *Anna Lucasta*, with an all-black cast.[9] For the first three nights, African-American patrons had been allowed only in the balcony and the theater had been picketed. On the fourth night, following discussions between the theater's management, the NAACP, and the editorial staff of the *Afro-American*, they were allowed to sit anywhere. The play ran an extra two weeks to full houses and was brought back for three additional days after a short engagement out of town.

Desegregation at the Maryland lasted less than a month. In June 1949 African-American patrons, who had received invitations to attend showings of *Maid in the Ozarks* at the Maryland, were refused admittance because "the second balcony 'reserved' for colored patrons had recently been condemned by the fire marshal."[10] In September 1949 the management officially reinstated its former policy of racial segregation. Picketing resumed at once. Other early protests took place outside Ford's Theater which had a long-standing policy of allowing African Americans to be seated only in the rear of the balcony.

One of the earliest cases of picketing a theater to protest the barring of African Americans was in 1947 in front of Ford's. A year later, on a bitter January day, members of the Progressive Citizens of America, the NAACP, the Baltimore Interracial Fellowship, and the Interfraternal Council of Baltimore added a picket line in front of the Town Theater. They were protesting what they called "the wishy-washy policy of the theatre on the matter of admitting colored persons to the show to see the film 'The Roosevelt Story.'"[11] Previously, a racially mixed audience had been admitted to see a preview of the movie and at another showing, in connection with the March of Dimes Campaign, there were no restrictions on admittance. Isador Rappaport, the owner of the Town, claimed that his hands were tied and that the matter was in the hands of the joint committee of theater owners, which set policies for all the local movie houses.

The *Afro-American* reported that the picket lines at the Town and across the street at Ford's had been very effective in reducing the patronage at both theaters.[12] Ford's was still being picketed in 1949, and its management declared that the theater would remain segregated "until the community 'pattern' of segregation is changed."[13] Finally, in 1952, there was a settlement after an appeal from Governor Theodore McKeldin in a letter to the chairman of the Commission on Interracial Problems and Relations which said, in part:

> Negro citizens of Baltimore have been needlessly affronted by a policy which excluded them from attending performances in Ford's Theatre, except in the rear of the balcony. The resulting humiliation and resentment has brought a picket line to the doors of the Theatre. The picketing has persisted for several years, and so has the policy.... Discrimination between the races in theatres and other cultural institutions is both offensive and illogical. The absurdity of the practice is illustrated by the grossly inconsistent and arbitrary manner of its application both in this State and elsewhere.... Negro artists are banished from the stage at the Lyric, but members of their race may and do sit through performances without challenge or complaint from white patrons. Ford's Theatre, on the other hand, follows the converse rule. It accepts Negro actors, but restricts Negro theatregoers.... Curiously, there was an interval from 1944 to 1946 when Negroes were not segregated while attending performances at Ford's.

The governor asked the newly formed Commission on Interracial Problems and Relations (CIPR) to find a solution. The committee met with a representative of Ford's in January 1952, and, after discussions, the management of the theater agreed to cooperate with the Commission. The Commission released a statement on February 1, 1952, that asked "all legitimate theatres in the communities of Maryland to lift such discriminatory practices as now exist in legitimate theatres." The management of Ford's accepted the recommendation.[14] In October 1953, the Lyric Theater refused to grant permission for singer Marian Anderson to appear at the theater in January 1954, but a month later, in response to meetings with the CIPR and numerous letters to local newspapers, the theater relented.

In 1956, a few downtown movie theaters quietly desegregated, and, by the beginning of 1959, for the first time in the history of Baltimore, all of the downtown movie theaters and a few neighborhood ones were desegregated. Many of the early desegregated theaters belonged to the JF, Rappaport and Schwaber organizations and included the Cameo, Century, Charles, Cinema, Ford's, Hilltop, Little, Lyric, Mayfair, New, Pulaski Drive-In, Stanley, Five-West, Hippodrome, Playhouse, Town, and Timonium Drive-In. Carlin's Drive-In adopted an anti-discrimination policy in 1959. The following year, the CIPR noted that most neighborhood theaters still refused to admit African Americans. It was not until 1964 that the Baltimore *Sun* began carrying advertisements for African-American theaters in its movie guide.

One theater in the unique position of being a white theater located close to a concentration of African Americans was the Northwood; serious, long-term problems developed there. The Northwood, operated by the Grant organization, was located in a strip mall near the intersection of Alameda and Havenwood Road, in the heart of heavily white northeast Baltimore, but it was only a few blocks from predominately black Morgan State University. The Northwood refused to admit black patrons, and protests began in April 1955.

The manager of the theater set up ticket-selling facilities in the inner lobby and screened customers at the entrance. He also posted a sign which read, "Until the Motion Picture Theater Owners of Maryland, of which this theater is a member, and the courts of Maryland advise otherwise, this theater reserves the exclusive right to restrict its patronage," at the entrance. The picketing began at the Northwood and extended to two black theaters—the Dunbar and Eden—which were also operated by the Grant organization. Students from Morgan State and Johns Hopkins picketed the Northwood during April and May 1955 and more sporadically for the next eight years, but little was accomplished until early 1963.

In late 1955, the CIPR tried to arrange a meeting between the opposing parties, but haggling over who would attend resulted in the collapse of this effort. Finally, a meeting attended by Irving Grant, Joseph Grant, Commissioner Otto Kraushaar, and two representatives of the picketers was held in March 1956. At this meeting it became clear (1) that the Grant brothers feared a loss of business if they admitted African-American patrons; (2) that the residents of the neighborhood around the theater were opposed to integration; and (3) "that if other theaters in the area would agree to operate on an integrated basis, no one particular theater owner would suffer a loss of business."

The CIPR tried to arrange a meeting with the owners of the area theaters,[15] but only Fred Perry of the Cameo was willing to attend. Three owners were willing to integrate if a majority of the other owners agreed to do likewise. No consensus could be obtained, and the Commission recommended that "a public accommodations act either on a statewide or municipal level be enacted making discrimination of this kind unlawful."[16]

By 1963, 60 percent of Baltimore movie theaters had been integrated. Encouraged by civil rights legislation introduced in the state legislature, protesters at the Northwood tried again. In February 1963, students from Morgan State, after trying unsuccessfully again to gain admission to the theater, renewed their demonstrations. They were joined by students from Goucher College and Johns Hopkins University. By February 20, 12 percent of Morgan State's student body of 2,628 had been arrested for trespassing. The following day, Mayor Goodman announced that the owners of the Northwood had agreed to desegregate the theater. According to the announcement, "The Northwood Theater Corp. has arrived at a peaceful, orderly solution by way of integration if the acts of trespass and mass protest demonstrations immediately cease. As soon as this good faith is proven by the demonstrators, (the theater) will admit all law abiding persons the following day."

The students stopped demonstrating, and on February 22, 1963, the first African Americans, Mrs. Ruth Lighston and her four children, were admitted to the Northwood Theater. The publicity which the theater got as a result of its stand resulted in a 30 percent drop in admissions. The remaining segregated theaters in town soon dropped their segregation policies, and Baltimore experienced no further problems with segregation at movie theaters. Maryland passed civil rights legislation in 1963 and amended it the following year to cover, among other businesses, motion picture theaters, legitimate theaters, concert halls, sports arenas, and other places of exhibition and entertainment. The struggle to integrate the Northwood Theater was important because it showed that demonstrations, which disrupted civil authority and overloaded the local police, judicial, and penal facilities, could be effective instruments in racial desegregation.[17]

In addition to the changing demographics of the city and suburbs and the popularity of television after World War II, there was another change that had far-reaching effects on the movie business. This was the well-known Paramount Consent Decree. In the late 1930s the five major movie studios—often called "The Big Five" (Paramount, MGM, RKO, 20th Century–Fox, and Warner Bros.)—controlled the film industry in the United States. They produced, distributed, and exhibited films in their own theaters. As a result, the government took them to court, contending that their ownership of theaters, especially first-run theaters, was in violation of antitrust laws. In November 1940 a consent decree between these studios and the government was signed. The studios agreed to cease the practice of blind bidding, where exhibitors bid on a block of films before they had been made.

Another result of the 1940 consent decree was the establishment of arbitration tribunals in 31 cities for settling disputes in the industry. The first complaint filed before one of these tribunals was by Baltimore exhibitor, Thomas Goldberg, in February 1941. Goldberg complained about the seven-day clearance granted three Durkee theaters— the Ambassador, Forest, and Gwynn — over his Walbrook Theater. On a split decision, the Ambassador retained the existing clearance, but the Walbrook got 20th Century–Fox and Warner product immediately after the Forest and Gwynn.[18] Soon after Goldberg filed his complaint, Leo H. Homand filed a complaint against Durkee's Edgewood Theater and the independent Alpha and Irvington theaters. Homand said his Westway Theater had not made a profit since it opened in 1939 because of the clearance granted to the other three theaters. Homand lost when the tribunal ruled that the 14-day clearance of the Edgewood was reasonable.

The government still was not satisfied, and after several more years of legal wrangling, it filed suit again against Paramount. In 1948 the Supreme Court ordered the studios to divest themselves of their theaters. It took 12 more years before all the studios gave up fighting the decree. Baltimore was not as strongly affected as many other cities—Washington, for example — because the Big Five producers had only four downtown theaters here. The history of this litigation was summarized in a 1949 article.

> Monday's opinion by the federal statutory court in New York is the latest development in 11 years of litigation during which the Justice Department battled to compel a divorce of exhibition from production and distribution. On July 27, 1938, the Department first entered the arena with a suit against the Big 5 — Paramount, 20th Century–Fox, Warner Bros., RKO, Loew's (MGM) — and the Little 3 — Universal, United Artists, Columbia. The charge was monopoly; the main relief, for the Big 5, was divorcement.
>
> A consent decree signed by the Big 5 Nov. 21, 1940, by which they agreed not to book pictures in more than blocks of five, established arbitration trade screenings, not to sell pictures blind or to expand their theatre holdings, suspended the action. Action was also suspended against the Little 3 which rejected a consent decree.
>
> On Oct. 8, 1945, the Department reopened the suit, again seeking divorce and reform of trade practices ... the court handed down an opinion on June 11, 1946 that was the father of the decree which they issued on Dec. 31, 1946. This decree established competitive bidding, prohibited admission fixing, roadshowing, formula deals, franchising, etc., but denied the Department divorce.
>
> All parties appealed, the Department primarily on divorce; the Big 5 principally on the court's findings as to their monopolistic practices; the Little 3 wanted franchises, clearance retention, admission prices, etc.
>
> On May 3, 1948 the Supreme Court affirmed the statutory court's monopoly findings and upheld it on trade practices, but rejected competitive bidding and sent the case back for further study. November 1, RKO got out through a consent decree providing for apparent divorce. November 8, the lower court started rehearing against what were now the Big 4 and were to be the Big 3 when Paramount dropped out Feb. 23 with a "divorce" consent

decree. The Big 5 continued to fight; so did the Little 3. July 25, the statutory court again ruled, this time in favor of divorce.[19]

The decree prohibited systems of clearances, block booking and theater pooling. Each movie had to be sold individually, and no film's sale could be conditioned on the purchase of another. Admission prices were to be fixed only by the exhibitor. The 1946 decree denied the government's request that the five major distributors be forced to divorce their theater operations; but on appeal, the Supreme Court ordered divorcement. This decree forced Loew's, Paramount, R.K.O., 20th Century–Fox and Warner Bros. to divorce their theater circuits. The Warner organization had to dispose of some theaters in Pittsburgh and York, Pennsylvania; Staunton, Virginia; Wilmington, Delaware; Washington, D.C., and other cities.

Baltimore was not affected by this since Warner Bros. had only the Stanley. Loew's, which did have theaters in Baltimore, was ordered to divest itself of the Parkway or have it subjected to product limitation if competing independent theaters could not get films with the same availability for five years. Loew's had to sell off 24 of its theaters in other cities. In 1954 Loew's separated its production and distribution business from its domestic theater operations by forming a new theater-holding company called Loew's Theaters, Inc. One year later, it sold the Century and Valencia to Morris Mechanic.

Movie attendance was high during and just after the war, but it took a nose-dive in the early 1950s. The chart below shows average national weekly attendance figures and grosses[20] between 1935 and 1953:

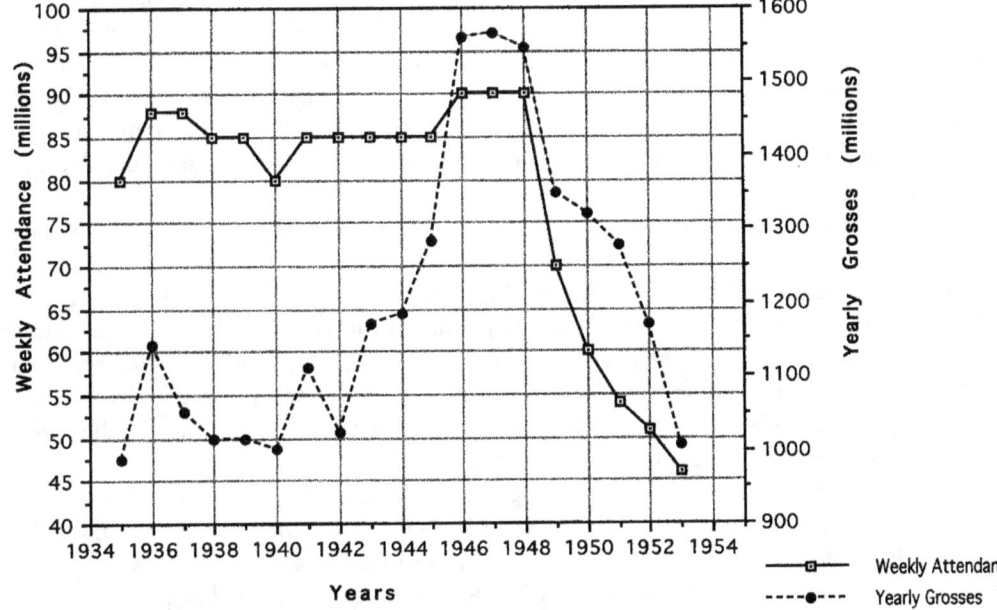

Average weekly attendance at movie theaters and yearly grosses between 1935 and 1953. The dramatic rise in both from a low in 1942 to a high plateau between 1946 and 1948 and the even more dramatic fall after 1948 can be seen clearly.

Chart 7. Weekly Attendance and Yearly Grosses for U.S. Movie Theaters 1935–1953

Movie grosses did not rebound to their 1946 and 1947 levels until 1972. In 1949, Baltimore was reported to have the lowest admission prices for neighborhood theaters of any city in the country; they ranged from 14 cents for children to 36 cents for adults at evening shows.[21] Despite these prices, local exhibitors saw a decline in theater attendance. In July 1949, concluding that the box office was being hurt by general indifference on the part of the movie-going public, the Motion Picture Theatre Owners of Maryland launched a campaign, financed by a 10-cent-a-seat assessment on each participating exhibitor, to bring audiences back to the movies. The campaign was aimed at children, dating couples, married stay-at-homes, workingmen, and housewives. It was apparently not very effective. The number of permits for motion picture theaters in Baltimore dropped from 113 in FY 1949 to 104 in FY 1950. New theater construction was curtailed in 1951 and 1952 by a lack of available building supplies. As of April 1953, 25.3 percent (70 theaters) of the theaters that were operating in Maryland in 1948 had closed. By late 1959, approximately 3,000 four-wall movie theaters in the United States had closed; the number of drive-ins had increased to 4,700. Things did not look good for hardtop theaters.

A 1950 survey listed nearly 100 brands of candy sold at the nation's theater concession stands. Among these were: Almond Joy, Baby Ruth, Black Crows, Chuckles, Dots, Goobers, Jujyfruits, M & Ms, Oh Henry, Raisinets, Sugar Daddy, Three Musketeers, and Tootsie Rolls. A few of these are still available. At the same time, drive-ins were beginning to offer fast food — hamburgers, hot dogs, and French fries. In 1953, *Motion Picture Herald* selected the Theatre Sales Champions from among all the concessions available in theaters. The winners included Almond Joy, Baby Ruth, Dots, Hershey Bar, Jujyfruits, M & Ms, Milk Duds, Mounds, Necco Wafers, and Tootsie Rolls.[22] Raisinets, one of the most popular candies today, did not even make the top 16. The most popular beverages were Canada Dry, Coca-Cola, Dad's and Hire's Root Beer, Mission Dry Orange, and Orange Crush. Art theaters served a different, "classier" array of refreshments, such as coffee and tea along with pastries and imported chocolates. Some even served cider and herbal teas.

The two projectionist unions co-existed in kind of an armed truce until the late 1940s. Around that time, Local 181 began actively trying to get the other projectionists to join them. There were semi-clandestine meetings at the Southern Hotel, where the leadership of 181 met with members of the independent union to coax them to join. Harry Cluster, the business agent of the independent union, and John Codd, who had replaced Harry Bauer as president, would reportedly go and watch the hotel to see which projectionists were going to the meetings. Local 181 went so far as to have a spy in the independent union who reported on the independent union's activities.

Two of the officers of Local 181 would go to the Horn and Horn Restaurant on Baltimore Street after their theaters closed on the nights that the independent union had its meeting. They would sit at a table with a telephone, and shortly after midnight, the phone would ring and their man in Cluster's union would report what had happened at the meeting. Many members of the independent union did join Local 181. Eventually Harry Cluster was forced out as leader of the independent union, and Charles Reisinger took over as business agent.

As a result of unfair labor practice charges, alleging that the union was a company-dominated union, filed against the theater owners' association in October 1951, Independent Union 1 was broken up the following April, and the money in the union's relief fund

A show of strength by the Independent Projectionists union at their ninth anniversary banquet in the New Howard Hotel, September 23, 1936. Among the members present were: #3 Philip Redmond, #7 Henry Nolte, #8 Steve Brenner, #28 Herman Cluster, #40 Charles Reisinger, #52 Harry Bauer, #53 Harry Cluster, #31 John Codd, #47 Fabius Rollins, and #48 Roland Tankersley.

was divided among the members. The union had 92 members at that time; 25 of them joined Local 181. Even though the owners agreed not to recognize any successor union, a new one was formed in 1952 called the Motion Picture and Television Operators of Maryland. Charles Reisinger was business agent of the new group.

Durkee theaters continued steadfastly to refuse to recognize Local 181 and, in 1954, several members of that union were fired from Durkee theaters. Local 181 set up picket lines around the Ambassador and the Belnord and publicized the names of several other theaters that did not employ members of its union.[23] The two unions continued to exist into the 1970s with some projectionists maintaining membership in both. They held a joint meeting at Reisinger's house in September 1971 to discuss the impending elimination of the state licensing board and, in March 1972, they met to discuss the possibility of uniting the two groups. The two groups had merged by 1974, when the president of IATSE Local 181 announced that the membership had reached more than 100 projectionists with the addition of 12 General Cinema Corporation projectionists.

Censorship received an unexpected setback in 1952. That May the United States Supreme Court unanimously ruled that New York State had no right to ban the movie *The Miracle* strictly on the charge that it was sacrilegious. This ruling extended the protection of the 1st and 14th amendments to motion pictures, reversing the court's 1915 ruling that the exhibition of movies was strictly for business and entertainment. The court did make it clear that this ruling was not a green light for any kind of movie and that it

Projectionists Irving Whitehill and Leroy Goldbloom look happy as they walk the picket line in front of the Ambassador during the 1954 strike by Local 181.

was not saying that censorship should be abolished. The statement of the court notwithstanding, it does appear that this decision opened a wide door for the foes of censorship. The Maryland Attorney General advised the board that it could "restrict the showing of a film only if it is obscene or indecent in the sense generally 'heretofore known to the law.' ... The Maryland statute, as presently drawn, was not intended to meet the test of constitutionality now required by the Supreme Court decisions. It is in no sense a tightly drawn or limited statute."[24]

In 1953, Judge Herman Moser reversed the censor board's ban on the film *The Moon Is Blue*. He criticized the board for not having any fixed standards by which to interpret what was indecent, immoral and obscene. He believed that it was time for the state courts to decide whether the state should even have a censor board.[25] In January 1954, the Maryland Attorney General recommended that the board only censor pictures found to be "obscene" or "indecent." Board member Traub disagreed, but in March a bill was introduced in the legislature to limit censorship to obscene films. The following year, Washington area exhibitor Sidney Lust asked for an amendment to the movie censorship bill which would exempt newsreels from censorship. By a very close vote, 59 to 57, the amendment passed.

In 1959, a battle raged in the state legislature over several bills to strengthen censorship, but the United States Supreme Court's ruling on *Lady Chatterley's Lover* seemed to invalidate the portion of the law about debasing or corrupting morals or inciting to crime.[26] The state attorney general told the board that all provisions of the law should be enforced except that portion which stated that the portrayal of sexual immorality as a desirable, acceptable or proper pattern of behavior in a film makes it of such a character that its exhibition would tend to debase or corrupt morals.

Historians have debated the impact of television on movie-going in post-war America. While it may not have been the only cause of dwindling movie attendance in the 1950s, it was certainly an important and obvious one. Ed Lachman, a New Jersey exhibitor, hoped the effect of television would be temporary and expressed the feelings of many small exhibitors. He noticed a significant decrease in the number of his regular customers, especially on Tuesday nights when the Milton Berle show aired. He said that his children stopped asking to be taken to the movies on Saturdays since the family had bought a television set. He also blamed bingo games.[27]

Television was only one of the competitors for the American entertainment dollar. In 1948, Gilbert Kanour wrote about Hollywood's jitters. He told of reports from the nation's exhibitors that business was off an average of 25 percent, as much as 50 percent in some areas. He mentioned the high cost of living as one cause. Another cause was "the ability of the housewife to buy almost anything her family requires in the way of household accessories." This cut into the amount of money available to spend on entertainment. Significantly, television was not even mentioned in this article.[28]

Richmond exhibitor Morton G. Thalhimer, in a 1952 article,[29] listed the following competitors that were taking people away from the movies: (1) television; (2) midget automobile races, night baseball, professional football games, better dance halls and traveling name-bands, skating rinks and bowling alleys; (3) continued expansion and overdevelopment of many college and professional sports; (4) increased popularity of traveling symphony orchestras and concert artists; (5) effects of installment sales; (6) young children keeping families tied down at home; (7) popularity of vacation cottages; (8) rising cost of living and higher taxes; (9) unsettled world conditions.[30]

The controversy over television echoed the controversy about radio in the 1920s and 1930s. Faced with its growing popularity, exhibitors tried offering television in theaters. Among the most successful theater television shows were the prizefights shown during the early 1950s. The first significant test of theater television was the broadcast of the Joe Louis–Lee Savold fight in June, 1951. The fight was shown in nine theaters in six cities, including Baltimore. It played at Loew's Century, which charged 65 cents admission and had to turn away several hundred patrons, and at the Harlem. In June 1952, the Sugar Ray Robinson–Joey Maxim light heavyweight fight was shown over a network of 38 theaters in 25 cities. Among those theaters were the Stanley and State in Baltimore. In September 1952, the Rocky Marciano–Jersey Joe Walcott bout was televised in 50 theaters including the Stanley and State. Tickets cost $3.00 at the Stanley and $2.50 at the State.

Another successful strategy used during the 1950s to attract customers was to have a theater specialize in the foreign movies that were becoming available. Many older theaters were converted into these art theaters. One of the first and most successful of these in Baltimore was the Playhouse, which Schwaber Theaters opened in November 1951. They had remodeled their Homewood Theater on West 25th Street into a comfortable art house for about $60,000. The remodeled neighborhood theater had a lounge with a tea and coffee bar, comfortable rocking-chair seats, and exhibits of the works of local artists. Patrons could sit in comfort, sip exotic beverages, munch imported chocolates and read high-class European magazines and newspapers. The new manager, Ted Routson, said in a newspaper interview that Schwaber Theaters was confident that, "good movies are going to go on being made, at one place or another in the Western World, and we are even more confident that there will prove to be enough persons of taste in Baltimore to warrant bringing such films here."[31]

They guessed correctly. The Playhouse was an immediate success, and Schwaber followed it up with the Cinema (the converted Linden Theater, 1954), the 5 West (the converted Parkway, 1956), and the 7 East (the converted Aurora, 1964). The "art" theater was not a new phenomenon. There had been earlier movie houses in the city, albeit usually short-lived ones, that specialized in European films. Probably the first of these was the Little (also known as the Europa from 1931 to 1933), which was Baltimore's haven for foreign films from the time it opened in 1927 until the 1970s. The Three Arts (or Film Art) on North Howard showed foreign films between 1935 and 1940. Another Europa, converted from the old Dixie Theater in 1936, lasted only until 1938. The World (later the Fine Arts) on West Lexington Street showed classic and foreign films between 1949 and 1952. The African-American community had two art houses—the Morgan, which opened as an art house in the fall of 1949, and the Carver which opened in 1953. Neither one of these theaters was successful.

Hollywood tried other strategies to bring patrons back to the movies in the 1950s. Many of these were technical, and the decade saw a number of new screen processes. One of these, in 1953, was the 3-D movie. These were cumbersome to watch, requiring special cardboard glasses, but they offered some spectacular special effects.

> The March of the Deepies is still going merrily on and it is coming into Baltimore.... Don't you know what "deepies" are? That's what they're calling the third dimension picture in Hollywood.... The first 3D picture made at Warner Brothers studio is "House of Wax" and that begins here at the Stanley.... Now on view at Keiths is also one of the first of the "deepies"—"Man in the Dark," recorded at the Columbia Studios. The Stanley will stage a special premiere of "House of Wax," Thursday, at 8 P.M.... Hollywood is in ... the throes of third dimension ... the public is in a state of mystification. Important changes are happening in Cinemaland.... As the Associated Press stated in a recent dispatch from Hollywood: Cinerama ... CinemaScope ... natural vision ... metrovision ... paravision ... Todd-AO ... Warnerphonic sound ... polarization ... stereophonic.... These words have entered film language in recent months.... Studios are not agreed on which system to use according to AP. 20th Century–Fox has thrown its entire future into its own wide-screen process, CinemaScope. MGM is using it also. Warners and RKO base their hopes on 3D gimmicks that require glasses. Paramount and Universal-International are experimenting with both 3D and wide-screen. In addition, MGM and Paramount are working on trick lenses which can project present films on wide screen....[32]

The term "deepies"—thank goodness—never caught on and neither did 3-D movies.[33] Until the mid–1960s, 3-D films were photographed using two cameras (which photographed the same scene from two angles comparable to the distance between the human eyes, roughly 2.5 inches) and shown using two projectors. In the anaglyphic 3-D process, the film in one camera was dyed red and that in the other camera was dyed green. The viewer watched the film through a pair of glasses with one red and one green lens, and each eye saw the scene from slightly different angles which were merged by the brain into one, thus causing the 3-D illusion. Later films used polarizing filters instead of colored glasses.

The first 3-D movies were short subjects in the 1920s.[34] Possibly the earliest one shown in Baltimore was *Ouch!*, a 3-D short filmed in Stereoscopik; it was shown at the New during the week of August 2, 1926. Apparently it was not even considered worth being reviewed; T.M.C. of the *Sun* ignored it, concentrating instead on the main feature, *Up in Mabel's Room*, and the accompanying stage show. A few more shorts were made during the 1930s and 1940s, and MGM's Pete Smith produced a short film in 3-D called *Third Dimensional Murder*; it played at the Century in March 1941.[35]

The first 3-D feature film using the polarizing 3-D process was Arch Oboler's *Bwana Devil*, which opened in Baltimore at the Stanley on January 29, 1953.[36] It got terrible reviews: "...a badly botched, amateurish affair ... the color is extremely poor, the picture is sometimes a bit fuzzy ... the story is so ineptly contrived and edited that one's feeling of horror ... is blunted. Mr. Stack, the other humans, and the sluggish lions are all too obviously puppets in a demonstration of 3-D film."[37] Nevertheless, *Bwana Devil* grossed $2.4 million in 10 weeks at about 1,200 theaters. At least some of the scenes had a good 3-D effect; the scene where a native warrior thrusts a spear at the audience provoked a lively reaction. *Bwana Devil* was followed quickly by Warner Bros.' *House of Wax*, Columbia's *Man in the Dark*, RKO's *It Came from Outer Space*, and Columbia's *Fort Ti*. The film *Fort Ti*, which played at Keith's, was described as "the throwingest picture yet," and Donald Kirkley noted in his review that "many times moviegoers were observed to duck as things seemed to come their way, breaking through the screen barrier."[38]

The glasses that viewers had to wear were uncomfortable for some, especially those who wore regular glasses, but the projectionists faced worse problems. The 3-D system used in the 1950s required two projectors running in perfect synchronization, and, despite Selsyn motors' attempt to interlock the projector motors, 3-D films gave projectionists ulcers.[39]

The most successful movie released in 1953 was *The Robe*, the first CinemaScope movie; it broke box office records all over the country. It did so well at the New that Morris Mechanic held it over for a tenth week rather than bring in a new Christmas movie. At this time, Hollywood was struggling to adopt a standard system from the bewildering number of wide-screen and 3-D processes. The cost to the exhibitor to convert a theater for one of the six new wide-screen systems could be as high as $150,000. Despite the lack of an industry-wide standard, showmen believed that these new processes were the "shot-in-the-arm" that movies needed, and they began their conversions. Exhibitors who could afford the high installation price remodeled their theaters. A lot of theaters lost their prosceniums and a few rows of seats when wide screens were installed. The widest of the wide screens—51 feet wide by 26 feet high—came to Baltimore in 1957.[40]

This Is Cinerama opened at the Town on August 28.[41] The Baltimore *Sun* movie critic gave the movie a good review.[42] He especially liked Lowell Thomas' introduction when the movie suddenly jumped from a small screen to the huge Cinerama screen and the audience found itself hurtling down a roller coaster, calling it "one of the most effective pieces of showmanship" he had ever seen. The searchlights set up in front of the theater for Cinerama's premiere had an unforeseen effect. The reflections of the bright lights darting around in the clouds made many people around the city think of flying saucers, and frightened residents telephoned their local police to see what was going on. The film was shown once a night with matinees on Wednesdays, Saturdays, and Sundays.

Other, less successful, attempts to give additional dimension to the movies were also made. "Smell-o-Vision" and other systems to provide the dimension of smell to the movies were dismal failures.[43] Curiously, with all the gimmicks introduced in 1953, the local box office champion was a "quiet little film, short on conventional glitter but loaded with charm, compassion and Leslie Caron."[44] The film was *Lili*, and it played for 12 weeks at the Playhouse.

The Rivoli curse? One of the strangest mysteries in the history of Baltimore movie theaters was resolved, albeit unsatisfactorily, in 1955. It involved the disappearance of the manager of the Rivoli Theater and would have made a good subject for a Hitchcock movie. The strange story of the disappearance of Henry Matcher began in 1917. In May of that year, when he was 16, Matcher started to work as an usher at the Wilson Theater. Matcher's boss was Guy L. Wonders. After the Wilson closed and the larger Rivoli had opened in its place, Matcher moved up the ladder from doorman to general manager of the Rivoli and Embassy theaters. He became a close friend of composer Victor Herbert. Herbert gave Matcher a baby carriage when his first daughter was born. His longevity as manager for six different theater owners attests to the quality of his work. Newspaper articles chronicled his anniversaries at the Rivoli, the 25th in 1942, the 28th in 1945, and the 30th in 1947. It seemed that he would go on forever.

On the morning of April 28, 1948, less than a month before he would have celebrated his 31st anniversary at the theater, Matcher left home at 8:00 A.M. for the Rivoli. That afternoon, at around 2:30, he spoke with his wife by telephone and told her, "I'll see you later." That was the last time she heard from him. That evening, Henry Matcher boarded the Old Bay Line steamer, *City of Richmond*, for its overnight trip to Norfolk. He registered as "Harry Cohen of Baltimore." At 11:00 P.M. he was seen in the ship's dining room by a bellman to whom he gave a letter to mail when the ship docked in Norfolk. When police later opened the envelope it was found to contain two blank sheets of paper and $31. It was addressed to "Henry D. Welcher" at 3501 Lucille Avenue, Baltimore; the address was Henry D. Matcher's.

The man who registered as Cohen asked to be awakened at 6:00 A.M., but when the bellman came to call him, there was no response. After the ship docked, the purser was informed that the door to Cohen's cabin was locked. An investigation revealed that it was locked from the inside. The purser opened the door with a duplicate key and found the room empty. The window which opened onto the deck was open, and it appeared that the bed had not been slept in.[45] The purser found $5 in bills on the chair, 15 cents on the floor, and 31 cents on the wash basin. There was no sign of "Harry Cohen."

A waiter on the *City of Richmond* later identified Matcher as the man who had registered as Cohen. He had eaten a chicken dinner the evening before he disappeared, and, according to the waiter, had not appeared nervous or worried. The Baltimore police asked the Coast Guard to have ships look for his body in the Chesapeake Bay between Baltimore and Norfolk. Matcher left a wife and three daughters.

Matcher's wife told police that he had been in good health and had no known business or personal worries. Neither Matcher nor Cohen was ever seen again. Seven years after he disappeared, Henry Matcher was declared legally dead.[46] There has been much speculation about the disappearance. Some have suggested that he fled to escape debts, and it is interesting to speculate on the name, Henry D. Welcher, he used on the envelope he gave to the bellman. The first part is identical to his real name; a welcher is a person who does not pay a debt or wager.[47]

Another tragedy connected with the Rivoli occurred in Washington, D.C., six years earlier. Matcher's old boss, Guy Wonders, died in August 1942 as the result of a fall from the fire escape on the seventh story of the Earle Theater Building. His wife had died a month earlier, and he had been worried about his own health. Co-workers speculated that he committed suicide. Wonders had been in the movie business for more than 30 years, the same number of years that Matcher had been at the Rivoli.

A new movie theater circuit, JF Theaters, was born in Baltimore in the late 1950s. JF stood for Jack Fruchtman, who came up to Baltimore from Greenbelt, Maryland in 1954 to run the New and Keith's theaters for his friend, Morris Mechanic.[48] According to one source, Fruchtman "knew all about film. He knew what people wanted and he just simply stepped in and he started managing them.... He took the theaters over on a share-the-expenses business."[49] In 1957, he acquired control of the Mayfair, and JF Theaters was born. JF expanded in 1958 when it got the Stanley, the Garmen-Beck theaters (Uptown, Pikes, and Avalon), and the Times and took over the management of the Rappaport Theaters. Fruchtman said that the only change would be fewer art films at the Little. By the end of the year Fruchtman controlled 14 theaters in the Baltimore area, including all of the first-run downtown movie theaters. The Stanley, Uptown, Pikes, and Avalon are long gone, but the Times lives on as the popular Charles Theater. JF took a month to remodel the Times; it reopened as the Charles on October 2, 1958.

> All revamped in modern style, the Charles Theater, in the 1700 block North Charles St.— it was formerly the Times— will reopen today at 2 P.M. As its first attraction the new management will present Jules Verne's famed comedy "Around the World in 80 Days," which in its prosperous movie career has won 52 international awards.[50]

This was a very small notice for a movie theater that would go on to become one of the most popular theaters in town. JF Theaters was one of the newest local circuits, but it eventually operated most of the downtown theaters and was the largest circuit in the state for a short time. JF may be remembered for one spectacular failure—the Tower Theater, which never lived up to its potential—and one spectacular success—the Charles, which has been far more successful than anyone ever dreamed.

At the end of the decade, the motion picture industry took stock of the situation. One survey, reported in the trade magazine *Boxoffice* in 1960, said things were going to slowly improve. Among its optimistic predictions were: an increase in the average weekly movie attendance to 51 million in 1965, and 68 million in 1980, with a 72 percent increase in the important under-30 age group. The survey also found that comfortable seats were of greater importance than in the past, probably because patrons compared them with comfortable seating watching television in their own homes. Lack of convenient parking was the most frequent complaint.[51]

Things did not quite work out as the survey suggested. Ten years later admissions were lower than they had been in 50 years. Since the peak of 80 million in 1946, weekly movie admissions dropped to 20.8 million in 1962 and to 15.8 million in 1971. Gross revenues were down by 25 percent by the early 1970s.[52]

The early 1950s provided a coda to the career of one of the great movie theater architects. In Maryland and adjoining states, during the great age of movie theater construction, Baltimorean John Zink was a theater architect *par excellence*. Working out of Baltimore and Washington, he designed nearly 100 movie houses in Maryland, the District of Columbia, Virginia, and Delaware.

John J. Zink was born in Baltimore, Maryland, on June 1, 1886. He spent most of his life in Baltimore where he raised a family and designed 12 movie houses. He began his training at the Maryland Institute, and worked for a while with the Baltimore architects Wyatt and Nolting.[53] By 1910 he was advertising in the Baltimore Business Directory and had an office in the Builders' Exchange Building. He went to New York for a few years prior to World War I. There he worked with the well-known theater architect Thomas W. Lamb[54] and became interested in this type of architecture. He attended evening classes at the Columbia School of Architecture.

Zink returned to Baltimore around 1916 and worked with Ewald G. Blanke for several years.[55] In 1922, Zink became associated with W. O. Sparklin.[56] Zink maintained an office in Washington, D.C., between 1917 and 1920. He designed his home at 2826 Overland Avenue in the Hamilton section of Baltimore and included an architectural office in its design. His son described him as "pretty much of a loner in the architectural business,"[57] and most of the theaters he designed during these 25 years were his own creations. During the last years of his career, Zink worked with two other architects, Raymond Snow on the Village Theater (1940) in Washington, and F. L. W. Moehle on the Smyrna (1948) in Smyrna, Delaware; the New (1949) in Elkton, Maryland; and Ontario (1951) in Washington, D.C.

According to his son, John Zink's "architectural M.O." was as follows. After determining what the client wanted, he would spend hours thinking about the site, the shape and color of the building, the materials, and the arrangement of the areas within the building. He would do this while staring off into space or gazing at a piece of blank paper, and create the whole building in his mind's eye. When he had the total concept defined, he would lay out a sheet of tracing paper, glue it down around the edges, moisten it with a damp cloth, and let it dry until it was stretched as tight as a drum head. The first sheet was the foundation layout plan showing the dimensions of the building. Next came the basement floor layout, the first floor layout, mezzanine or balcony layout, and roof layout, each stretched over the preceding sheet. Sometimes he would have 10 or 12 sheets of paper glued to the drafting table. When they were all finished, he would cut out the finished layouts with a razor blade and run blueprints on them.[58]

In old architects' parlance, Zink was a "plans man" as opposed to an "elevation man." That is, he was more concerned with the layout of the building than in its appearance. This was made clear in a list of criteria he used as a judge on a 1941 panel of architects selecting the "Perfect 36" theaters for Jay Emmanuel's *Theatre Catalog*. His criteria were sufficiency of exits; arrangement of entrances, exits, and rest rooms; and design of interiors and exteriors. The comfort and safety of the patron came first.

At a time when many theater architects were going wild over atmospheric designs and flights of exotic fancy in their theater designs, Zink kept his work very plain. Most of his theaters were in restrained Classic, Colonial, or Moderne design. He was more interested in the patrons and in the excellence of the sight lines and acoustics than in fancy frills. He felt that most people attended the movies at night, and would not even notice the gewgaws on a theater's exterior. He may have been one of the first theater architects to use the reverse curve design for the auditorium floor of a theater.[59] The reverse curve design places the lowest point in the auditorium floor about one third of the distance from the stage to the rear of the theater.

John Zink was characterized by one co-worker as having a good sense of humor, being very intelligent, good to work with, and very straight-laced. Zink was also a very private person. One reporter said that it was difficult to get Zink to talk about himself. "To find out something about himself was most difficult, although he very considerately gave all details about the theatre. He declined to tell anything about himself, and to get [a] photograph ... it was necessary to get the assistance of Mrs. Zink."[60]

Zink was well known for his honesty. One Baltimore theater owner, who had a reputation for suing everyone who ever worked for him, tried several times unsuccessfully to have Zink design a theater for him. Exasperated at being constantly dogged by the man, Zink finally chased him out of his office.

In Baltimore, he worked mainly with the builders E. Eyring and Sons. He knew his builders and suppliers well, and exercised tight control over them during the construction of a building. He supervised the construction of each theater personally; the final stages seemed to be as exciting for him as they were for spectators. As the Tivoli Theater in Frederick was nearing completion and the finishing touches were being put on the interior, "Mr. Zink was as much interested as a boy ... on Christmas morning. It is a wonder you are not tired of this place," said a reporter to Mr. Zink as they walked through the foyer, over which the architect had gone back and forth many times. 'Oh, no,' said he. 'This is just the interesting time, to see just how everything comes out.'"[61]

John Zink was a quiet man, well liked by the exhibitors he chose to work for. He was described by one exhibitor as "a perfectionist and a fine man." He was a member of the American Institute of Architects, and, at one time, the president of the Baltimore Chapter. In addition to architecture, he was very interested in music. At various times, he was a church organist, choir director, musical play director, and violinist. Once, he conducted the Baltimore Symphony Orchestra in a selection from Beethoven's 9th Symphony.

After battling cancer for several years, John Zink died in Baltimore in August 1952 at the age of 66. With his passing, an era of movie theaters passed also. Zink's theater legacy remains with us in such theaters as the Senator Theater in Baltimore, the Uptown and Takoma theaters in Washington, and the exteriors of Baltimore's Ambassador, Edgewood, Patterson, and Colony and Washington's MacArthur and Senator, beautiful monuments to a master.

8

THE RETURN OF THE PALACES? (1961–1967)

The movie industry began feeling its way through the 1960s, looking for the magic combination that would bring people back to the theaters. The year 1961 was pivotal; 142 new theaters (84 indoor theaters and 58 drive-ins) opened. By the following spring, despite the lowest grosses in 10 years, the nation was in the midst of a modest boom in theater building; 1961 was the first year in more than a decade when construction of indoor theaters exceeded that of drive-ins.

The beginning of the decade saw large single-screen theaters opening, but the end of the decade found them replaced by twin theaters. Nationwide, approximately 70 percent of the new theaters were in shopping centers; locally, the figure was closer to 100 percent. This was the wave of the future; exhibitors were building in the new centers of population. Homes and businesses along the York Road, Liberty Road, Route 40, Reisterstown Road and Ritchie Highway corridors were growing rapidly. Large new theaters, such as the Hillendale, Harundale Mall, Perring Plaza, Westview, and North Point Plaza were built.[1]

With the opening of the Hillendale Theater on Taylor Avenue in 1960, the swan song of the single-screen theater in Baltimore began. Between 1960 and 1967 the last single-screen theaters in the area were built. Schwaber Theaters, inspired by Howard Wagonheim, was again the most innovative exhibitor in the Baltimore area in the 1960s. Wagonheim pioneered the conversion of aging neighborhood theaters into art theaters in the 1950s and would pioneer the first twin theater in the state—the Cinema 1-2 in Lutherville—in 1964. The population base grew larger in the late 1950s and early 1960s, providing more potential movie customers. In 1959, the movie industry picked up an average of 2,333,000 patrons a week.[2] By 1964, even though the average weekly movie attendance was still around 19 million, grosses were starting to increase. First-run movies moved into the neighborhoods during the 1960s.

Still, the closing and destruction of theaters continued, and Baltimore lost some of its largest and most beautiful movie houses during that time. The Century closed after 40 years in 1961. In 1963, Baltimore lost the State (36 years), Ritz (37 years), Jewell (49 years), Harford (47 years), Columbia (42 years) and Avalon (36 years). Ironically, the State and Avalon had both opened on the same day in 1927. The Stanley closed in 1965. Most of these were demolished, lost forever.

On a brighter note, local theaters were finally desegregated in 1963. National theater circuits began returning to Baltimore during this period. The first of these appeared in town in 1962 when Trans-Lux leased the four Rappaport theaters. The New York–based chain obtained long leases on the Hippodrome, Town, Aurora, and Little, refurbished them and used them for some spectacular premiers during the next 10 years.[3] General Cinema opened the Harundale Mall Theater in 1964, the Perring Plaza Cinema in 1966, and the York Road Cinema in 1967. Increasing costs of films made concession sales more important. In some theaters, films became almost loss leaders, serving merely to bring customers in to the concession stands.

Baltimore Theaters 1962

Name	Address	Name	Address
Aero	1417 Fuselage Avenue	Howard	115 N. Howard Street
Alpha	725 Frederick Avenue	Ideal	903 W. 36th Street
Ambassador	4604 Liberty Heights	Irvington	4113 Frederick Avenue
Apex	110 S. Broadway	Lenox	2115 Pennsylvania Avenue
Apollo	1506 Harford Avenue	Lincoln	936 Pennsylvania Avenue
Arcade	5434 Harford Road	Linwood	Linwood Avenue nr. Hudson
Aurora	7–9 E. North Avenue	Little	523 N. Howard Street
Avalon Art	4338 Park Heights	Lord Baltimore	1114 W. Baltimore Street
Belnord	2706 Philadelphia Avenue	McHenry	1032 Light Street
Bengies Drive-In	Middle River	Mayfair	508 N. Howard Street
Boulevard	3302 Greenmount Avenue	Met	1538 W. North Avenue
Bridge	2104 Edmondson Avenue	New	210 W. Lexington Street
Broadway	509 S. Broadway	New Essex	416 Eastern Boulevard
Carlin's Drive-In	Druid Hill Drive	New Horn	2108 W. Pratt Street
Carlton	1201 Dundalk Avenue	North Point Drive-In	North Point Boulevard
Carver	1429 Pennsylvania Avenue		
Charles	1711 N. Charles Street	Northway	6701 Harford Road
Cinema	910 W. North Avenue	Northwood	1572 Havenwood
Clover	414 E. Baltimore Street	Paramount	6650 Belair Road
Cluster	303 S. Broadway	Park	1105 N. Broadway
Colony	8123 Harford Road	Patapsco	601 Patapsco Avenue
Crest	5425 Reisterstown Road	Patterson	3136 Eastern Avenue
Earle	4839 Belair Road	Pennington	4911 Pennington Avenue
Edmondson Drive-In	Route 40	Pikes	1001 Reisterstown Road
Edmondson Village	4428 Edmondson Avenue	Playhouse	9 W. 25th Street
		Plaza	404 E. Baltimore Street
5 West	3 W. North Avenue	Pulaski Drive-In	Pulaski Highway
Gayety	405 E. Baltimore Street	Regent	1627 Pennsylvania Avenue
Grand	515 S. Conkling	Rex	4615 York Road
Hampden	911 W. 36th Street	Rialto	846 W. North Avenue
Harlem	616 N. Gilmor Street	Roosevelt	512 W. Biddle Street
Hillendale	1045 Taylor Avenue	Royal	1329 Pennsylvania Avenue
Hippodrome	12 N. Eutaw Street	Senator	5904 York Road
Hiway	1812 Earhart Road	Stanton	516 N. Howard Street
Hollywood	5509 Oregon Avenue	State	2045 E. Monument

Strand	1 Shipping Place	Victory	1017 Patapsco Avenue
Timonium Drive-In	Timonium Road	Vilma	3703 Belair Road
Town	311 W. Fayette Street	Walbrook	3100 W. North Avenue
Towson	512 York Road	Waverly	3211 Greenmount Avenue
Uptown	5010 Park Heights	Westway	5300 Edmondson Avenue
Valley Drive-In	Reisterstown Road		

The first-run hegemony of the downtown theaters began breaking down in the 1960s. A neighborhood theater, the Crest, began showing first-run films in 1962. The following year the Ambassador, Boulevard, Hillendale, Senator, Strand {2}, and Uptown were added to the ranks of the first-run theaters. In 1963 United Artists instituted a new method of film distribution for neighborhood theaters. This experimental plan involved opening a film at a group of up to 11 neighborhood theaters, seven days after completion of its first-run showing. The first film selected for this plan was *Taras Bulba*, which was scheduled to open a week's engagement at the Broadway, Carlin's Drive-In, Governor Ritchie Drive-In, Hiway, Irvington, Northwood, Paramount, Patapsco, Towson, and Uptown. At the end of the week the film was to be released to another group of theaters. The distributors believed that this method would give the public more opportunities to see a particular movie. It also showed that the first-run downtown theaters were not really necessary.

At the end of 1964, the James Bond movie, *Goldfinger*, opened on a double first-run basis at the Northwood and Uptown where it played to 60,000 customers during its first 12 days, breaking attendance records at both theaters. The new Cinema 1–2 (1964), Westview Cinema (1965), Reisterstown Road Plaza (1965), North Point Plaza (1966), Perring Plaza Cinema (1966), Tower (1967), and York Road Cinema (1967) all began to show first-run films as soon as they opened. By 1968, first-runs had been effectively wrested from the few remaining downtown theaters, and the disturbances of April 1968 simply supplied an unneeded exclamation point to the demise of downtown first-runs. The year 1970 was the last to see the *Sun* separating first-run theaters from the others in its movie listings; from then on, nearly every theater was a potential first-run venue.

Sound technology continued to advance. Stereophonic sound had been used, experimentally, in Disney's *Fantasia* (1940). With the coming of the new processes of the 1950s, notably CinemaScope, stereophonic sound became an integral part of films. There were 2,000 theaters equipped to reproduce stereophonic sound by 1954.[4] In 1975 the first feature film with a stereo optical soundtrack was released.[5] By the 1990s we had Dolby, SDDS and DTS; there were digital stereo sound systems that could literally knock your socks off. The previews have become especially loud, reaching painful levels. Allegedly, the producers realized that they were alienating many viewers with such high decibel levels and they decided, in 2001, to lower them to a less toxic level.[6]

Just as some really nice large, single-screen theaters were opening up around the city, an upstart oddity appeared that would completely change the nature of movie exhibition and put an end to single-screen theaters within the decade. This oddity was the twin theater. There had been a few earlier twin theaters, but they were usually accidents. Baltimore had the two Lubin's theaters on East Baltimore Street and the Century and Valencia. Both of these were vertical twin theaters and were not planned as twins. The first planned twin auditoriums in Maryland opened in 1964.

> The Baltimore area's newest film theaters—Cinema One and Cinema Two—make their genteel bow today. Combined, the two houses have 1,300 seats—500 at Cinema One and 800 at Cinema Two. Most modern in every way, they are located in the Yorkridge Shopping Center.... They are part of the Schwaber chain of theaters. There will be a common ... lobby and one box office for both theaters. The first program for Cinema One will be "Seduced and Abandoned," which also will be shown simultaneously at the 5 West ... also a Schwaber.[7]

Schwaber's Cinema 1 and 2 in a small strip mall just west of York Road in Lutherville was the first twin theater in Maryland.[8] Within three years the only theaters built would be multi-screen.

Boston-based General Cinema Corporation was one of the first major players from outside the state to enter the local theater building market. General Cinema came on strong in 1964 when they opened the 1,100-seat Harundale Cinema in Glen Burnie. They opened the Perring Plaza Theater two years later and the York Road Cinema in 1967. John Broumas, who was building large, attractive theaters around Washington at a dizzying pace, tried to encircle Baltimore too, opening the Glen Burnie Mall in 1964, the Randallstown Plaza in 1965, and the North Point Plaza in 1966.

Local exhibitors were not inactive. Durkee opened the Liberty in 1964 and the Plaza in Annapolis in 1966; Schwaber opened the Valley Drive-In in 1961 and the Cinema 1 and 2 in 1964. In 1966, Jack Fruchtman opened his first new theater, the Village, and in 1967, he opened the Tower and leased the Edmondson Village; neither theater did JF much good.

Most of the theater-building activity was in the suburbs, but there was hope for downtown. The new Charles Center, near the site of the old Century Theater, was suggested as a good site for a downtown luxury movie theater. The Tower, the last theater built in downtown Baltimore until 1985, opened there in 1967. It was a valiant attempt, but a different scenario was playing in the city, and downtown movies were just bit players in it. The Tower had a big opening with a 60-piece band, a searchlight, a host of VIPs, and three "nightclub bunnies," but it went downhill after that. Eugene Feinblatt, director of the city's renewal agency, praised the theater for its contribution to making "Charles Center a showplace of the nation and a Mecca for city planners and architects all over the world." Peter Glenville, the director of the opening feature, *The Comedians*, was pleased with the proportion and size of the new movie house. Dr. Saul Perdue, of the city's renewal commission, believed that the theater was, "one more indication of 'the faith of the business community in the rebirth of the downtown area.'"[9]

Charles Center may have been "a Mecca for planners and architects" but it certainly did not attract many shoppers and moviegoers. In less than 20 years the Tower Theater had closed twice and then been replaced by a smaller auditorium for Johns Hopkins University. Except for a multiplex at the Inner Harbor which lasted only 15 years, no more theaters would be built downtown in the 20th century.

The grim specter of urban renewal came to Baltimore in the 1950s and 1960s, and it lingered into the final years of the century like some monster hiding under a child's bed. The city has suffered greatly from the wholesale destruction of much of its architectural and cultural heritage. Movie theaters suffered disproportionately, with more than 100 downtown and neighborhood theaters lost. Urban renewal came too early, before the climate was favorable for theater preservation. Or perhaps it was the fault of greedy developers and entrepreneurs who saw these structures merely as piles of bricks to be redistributed.

What have we lost? As it happens, almost everything. The 1950s, 1960s, and 1970s witnessed the closing of 114 Baltimore area movie theaters. By 1980 there were few old theaters left. Not only were neighborhood houses closing, Baltimore lost many of its irreplaceable downtown movie palaces during this period. The Valencia and Lexway closed in 1952; the Rivoli hung on until 1953. Keith's fell in 1955. The Century was lost in 1961, and four years later the Stanley was gone. The Gayety closed in 1969. Meekly bowing to "progress" we watched these great buildings fall. A sampling of theater obituaries suggests that, in the 1960s when most of the damage was done, few realized what was happening.

> Each Thursday Mary K. Gilliece, our secretary, leaves on this reporter's desk the names of the attractions that are coming to the first-run film theaters.... We picked up the list, preparatory to writing this column and the first entry shook our usual equanimity. It read: "Century—Closed forever." Of course, we knew that the Century was closing ... tonight ... to make way for the builders of Charles Center. However, Mrs. Gilliece's statement of such forceful finality gave us pause. Then we began to think of the many pleasant hours we had put in at the West Lexington St. house since it opened in May, 1921.... Now, all this grandeur of yesteryear must fall before the bulldozers of today. But that's the way of progress. We recall the singing organist—the first in the city, we believe—the big orchestra, the stage shows, the Hollywood stars who appeared in person ... the roof-garden atop the Century which later became the Valencia theater, in 1926, with its blue sky and twinkling stars.... After tonight's final performance—the Century becomes history.[10]

The Stanley was lost four years later. *Sun* critic R. H. Gardner wrote about the closing. He reported that Morris Mechanic, the owner of the Stanley and Ford's theaters, who was building a new legitimate theater in the Charles Center, was getting rid of both theaters because he "does not wish to add to the list of his competitors."[11] The Stanley was only 33 years old. Gardner noted that the Stanley was, "a longtime favorite of those Baltimoreans who enjoy viewing their movies in an atmosphere of awesome opulence." Thank goodness someone realized that. A condescending editorial several weeks later in the *Evening Sun* commented on the Stanley as it was being smashed down. The editor seems to be saying that what the Stanley had was not really splendor; we just stupidly thought it was. He didn't even think that it had any recognizable style. It is worth quoting this piece of nonsense in full because it expressed so well the attitude that lost so much for the city.

> ### REGRETFUL FAREWELL
>
> Now that the demolition crews are attacking the walls of the Stanton Theater—or the Stanley as it was longer and better known to those who will feel a pang or two at its passing—it will not be long before blankness replaces what another generation took, in its innocence, for splendor. The interior which once represented the most lavish form of cinema elegance, has already been pulled to pieces and hauled away to memory's rubble bin. Only the shell of all that bizarre and extravagant grandeur remains to be brought down.
>
> The lament for its disappearance is a sentimental one. The Stanley (or Stanton) was never an architectural monument in the true sense of course. Its style, if such it may be called, was that of an opulent, confused dream of

what a flourishing movie industry and its patrons took to be the magnificence of Ninevah, or perhaps Byzantium, crossed with some vague remembrance of Bavarian baroque. But, in its way it was enchantingly spectacular, and in all its ornament and elaboration somehow warmhearted as the bleak prosaic geometry of modern design so rarely is. It belonged to a period that is gone, an exuberant mood that has vanished, a brief age of popular taste for the emphatically palatial that is unlikely to be revived. Yet it remained a fascinating anachronism that many will be sorry to lose. In these colder, more severe times it was a reminder of a robust and rich vulgarity expressing a confidence which, in retrospect, seems touching and wonderful.

One is bound to wonder whether whatever in time replaces it will, when its time for destruction comes round, be remembered half as fondly.[12]

What this editorial seems to be saying is that anyone who appreciated the Stanley or would want to save it was naive or feeble-minded. Imagine actually being so innocent as to be awed by the grandeur of the Stanley. "Never an architectural monument in the true sense...." what does that mean? For anyone, except an oaf, the Stanley was one of the city's great architectural monuments, in *any* sense. But the editor hit the nail squarely on the head in the last paragraph; how many of us fondly remember the vacant, brick-strewn lot that replaced the Stanley? One writer was so besotted by the prospects of the new Mechanic Theater that he could see no reason for saving the Stanley even though "the Stanton's seedy grandeur has a certain eye appeal."[13] A decade later, things had changed. According to an article by Don Walls in the *Daily Record*, if the Stanley had been standing in 1979, "there would be little doubt that funds could be raised to restore it within the AFI program."[14] The Stanley, Mayfair, and Little formed a mighty outpost that anchored North Howard Street in the downtown hinterlands. Their loss helped to turn Howard Street into the wasteland it is today.

In 1963 death came to Baltimore's largest neighborhood theater, Durkee's 2,000-seat State Theater on East Monument Street. Reporter Andrew Sharp, writing about that closing, was one of the first to call attention to the rapid disappearance of local theaters.[15] Durkee Enterprises executive Fred Schmuff, who managed the State when it opened in 1927, provided some reasons for the 1969 closing of another Durkee theater, the Belnord. Schmuff said that the Belnord did a good business until two years before it closed and laid the blame on changing neighborhoods; fear of going out at night; the attraction of small, intimate auditoriums; and the high cost of heating and cooling the large theaters. But the coup de grace came from the movie producers who raised film rentals so high that many theaters simply could not survive.

Additional insight as to why all these theaters were closing can be gained from 1972 testimony by Durkee Enterprises executive William Pacy to the Maryland General Assembly on behalf of the National Association of Theatre Owners of Maryland. Speaking in support of continuing the exemption of the local theater industry from state minimum wage regulations, Pacy noted that the increase in the state admission tax put a lot of theaters out of business. He went on to say that neighborhood theaters were operating on a shoestring and could not afford further increases in expenses. Pacy pointed out that many theater employees were part-time workers who, because of Social Security limitations, lack of experience, age competition or scheduling problems, could not get other jobs. He believed that these employees were paid a fair wage that the theaters could afford and that they would lose their jobs if the state included them under minimum-wage standards.

Pacy noted that the theater industry employed many people who would otherwise be unemployable. Schoolboys and retired men could work as doormen and ushers, and schoolgirls and older women could work as cashiers or candy attendants to supplement their family incomes. He said that many older people, who could not compete with younger workers or who did not want to stay at home and be bored or be a bother to their families, found companionship and a paycheck at theaters. If the theaters were forced to pay their employees higher wages, Pacy foresaw the replacement of candy attendants with vending machines, the replacement of doormen with turnstiles, the replacement of cashiers by automatic ticket machines and the elimination of ushers. He also foresaw more theater closings. Pacy listed the Baltimore City theaters which had closed between 1950 and 1972. He found that 62 theaters out of the 97 open in 1950 had closed by 1972, leaving only 35 theaters still open in the city. Between 1967 and 1971, Durkee closed five of its 18 theaters and added only two new ones.[16]

There were price increases at many neighborhood theaters in the summer of 1950; the newly opened Northwood charged 44 cents. Other houses raised their prices from 32 to 36 cents and from 36 to 40 cents. The average adult admission price in 1954 was 49 cents; children paid 16 cents. Throughout the late 1950s and 1960s movie prices ranged between 75 cents and $1.65; road shows, like *Camelot* at the New in 1968, charged $2.00 for loge seats. A record high cost-of-living index in the spring of 1960 prompted JF Theaters to reduce ticket prices at all of its first-run downtown houses. The top price Monday through Thursday from 5:00 P.M. until closing was reduced from $1.49 to $1.00; Friday and Saturday from 5:00 P.M. until closing and all day on Sunday, tickets cost $1.25. The Shoppers Special—50 cents until 5:00 P.M. on Mondays—was also reinstituted. These reductions did not bring more people to the theaters, but JF opted to keep them in place throughout the summer.

When the Federal 10 percent admissions tax ended in December 1965, local exhibitors felt that they should maintain ticket prices at the same level and not pass the savings on to the customers.[17] But there were still other taxes. In 1970, the Baltimore City Council approved a bill that would eliminate the city tax of .5 percent on movie theaters. That left the 4.5 percent state tax on gross receipts. The city of Annapolis and Anne Arundel County must have seen movie theaters as vast untapped sources of revenue in 1971. The city imposed a tax of 3.5 percent and the county imposed one of 4.5 percent on admissions. David Colburn, the resident manager for the Durkee theaters in Annapolis said he would have to raise admission prices. Not to be out-done, Baltimore County got into the act and imposed a 5 percent admission and amusement tax.

Efforts to weaken the Maryland Censor Board intensified in the 1960s when the board was battered by several lawsuits. Local exhibitors Ronald Freedman and William Hewitt, Jr., waged war against the state censors throughout the 1960s. Several times between 1962 and 1968 they challenged the constitutionality of the state's censorship law. In October 1962, Freedman, who was operating the Rex Theater on York Road, deliberately exhibited the film *Revenge at Daybreak* without first submitting it to the censor board. He specifically wanted to test the constitutionality of the state's censorship law and bring about the overthrow of the law.

The following spring he was fined $25 plus costs by Judge Anselm Sodaro. Freedman immediately appealed to the Maryland Court of Appeals, which upheld Judge Sodaro's decision and the constitutionality of Maryland's motion picture censorship law. Freedman then appealed to the Supreme Court. In 1965, the Supreme Court found the

Maryland law unconstitutional and unanimously reversed Freedman's conviction. The high court did not rule on the constitutionality of censorship but rather that the Maryland law failed to provide adequate safeguards against undue inhibition of protected expression.

One day after the Supreme Court rendered its opinion, the Maryland Attorney General prepared an amendment to the statute governing the censorship of films. The General Assembly approved the revision which provided that "'the burden of proving that the film should not be approved and licensed shall rest on the board' and that legal proceedings should be cleared through-and-including an opinion from the Circuit Court of Baltimore City within fifteen (15) days after submission of the film to the Board."[18] If the censors objected to a movie, they now had to convince a court that their decision was proper and do it promptly.[19] Within a few months, Freedman, this time with Hewitt, was back in court, charged with 14 violations of the state's censorship statute. A grand jury charged both men in May 1965 for exhibiting uncensored, unlicensed films, and showing films that bore the seal of the State Censor Board but which the Board had never reviewed. By 1966, Maryland's State Censorship Board was the only one left in the nation. In 1968, Freedman and Hewitt were again charged with exhibiting unlicensed films. The two exhibitors immediately filed suit challenging the constitutionality of Maryland's film censorship law.

9

MULTIPLEXES TO MEGAPLEXES (1968–1990)

The year 1968 began on a somber note when Dr. Martin Luther King was assassinated in Memphis. The rioting that followed this tragic event was devastating for the remaining downtown movie theaters. Baltimore's once vibrant downtown became a ghost town of discount stores, boarded-up buildings, and vacant lots. People were afraid to go downtown. More old theaters were closed. Baltimore lost the Bridge and the Ambassador in 1968; the next year the Roosevelt, Waverly, Gayety, and Belnord closed. Over the next 26 years, 76 movie theaters closed in the Baltimore area.

Twenty-eight new movie theaters opened during the same time period. The year 1970 proved to be a watershed for multi-screen theaters. Between 1960 and 1970 only two had been opened; after 1970 only one new theater was a single-screen theater. Statistics for 1971 reveal that there were 540 new theaters planned in the United States, only 43 of which were drive-ins. Drive-ins were clearly on their way out. Mini-theaters (theaters seating 350 or less) accounted for 210, and 276 were multi-auditorium units.[1] A particularly good year for the opening of movie theaters, 1973 brought seven new theaters to the Baltimore area with 15 screens. On the other hand, 1973 was a bad year for several beautiful theaters, like the Perring Plaza, that were crudely twinned in the rush for more screens.

As food sales provided more and more of a theater's profit, it became important to prevent patrons from bringing in outside food. When legislation was introduced in the Maryland House in 1985 to allow theater patrons to bring their own food and drinks into movie theaters, it was defeated largely because of vigorous opposition by the theater owners.

Film ratings and distribution also changed in the early 1970s. The Motion Picture Association of America adopted a system of film ratings which, after several modifications, is still with us.[2] The film *Billy Jack* proved that it was profitable to open a film at many screens in a city rather than at a single screen. This was another factor in the demise of the downtown first-run theaters.

During the last decades of the 20th century, it became common practice for movie theaters to begin their shows with a series of commercials or advertisements interspersed with tidbits of information and questions to test the audience's cinematic knowledge.

This annoying trend has continued into this century with unbearably loud MTV–style commercials touting soft drinks and cars. The ultimate ancestor of these ads was, no doubt, the fire curtain of many early theaters on which were painted the names of local businesses. Locally produced commercials for bread, milk, dry cleaning services and furnaces appeared on theater screens in the 1920s. Each ad ran a week, usually in groups of six that lasted five minutes.[3]

The Maryland Theater showed such ads in December 1926. This "procession of advertisements" outraged one patron, and he wrote, "I don't believe that any city except Baltimore would tolerate such a Cheap John commonplace stunt — especially in a first-class theater. People buy tickets to see a theatrical performance and they do not pay their money to look at motion pictures of department and furniture stores."[4] In 1948, theaters in the United States were said to be making more than $5 million a year from the showing of advertising films. For many years neighborhood theaters continued to show short commercials for local merchants in the weeks before the Christmas holidays.

Theodore Wells Pietsch (c. 1870–1930) designed some of the most elaborate early movie theaters in Baltimore. (Photograph courtesy of Dr. Theodore Wells Pietsch, III)

America suffered a cruel blow in April 1968 when Dr. Martin Luther King, Jr., fell victim to a cowardly assassin. To this day, we feel the repercussions of this tragic event. Downtown entertainment was hit hard. Rioting, between April 6 and 9, was so serious that a 4:00 P.M. curfew was imposed. By the 10th, almost 11,000 Federal troops were in the city. One of the immediate effects of the assassination was to hasten the exodus from downtown.

There was little physical damage to local movie theaters, but the damage done to downtown theaters' business was irreparable, and the psychic damage to the theater-going public was terrible.[5] The fear of lawlessness, engendered in part by the rioting, drove people away.

Ten years later, discussing the dismal failure of his Tower Theater, Jack Fruchtman said, "It is simply very difficult to get people mentally in favor of coming downtown...." There was less reason to go downtown to the movies. The Century and Stanley were gone, and first-run movies were available in the suburbs. The riots of April 1968 gave Baltimoreans one more reason to stay away from downtown, especially in the evenings.

Later in 1968, the business manager for the independent projectionists' union announced that union business meetings would be held during the day; the midnight meetings, which had been traditional since the union was founded, were considered to be unsafe. But even as downtown was dying, new commercial centers were developing in the suburbs.

By 1973 much of the population of Baltimore, especially the white population, was in full flight to the suburbs. Exhibitors were right behind them. *Evening Sun* writer Jeff Valentine provided an interesting snapshot of the current movie situation. He saw a comeback of sorts in the area with the opening of 19 new theaters over the previous six months.[6] Valentine quoted Leon Back, the president of the National Association of Theater Owners of Maryland, from his summary of the exhibitors' strategy, "The trend of the theaters is the same as the shopping centers. We go where the people are." Valentine noted that the theaters being built then were small multi-theaters, "look-alike modernistic buildings with shopping center names." The new theaters were being built along important commercial corridors such as York Road and Reisterstown Road and in Harford County. Finally, Valentine commented on the sad state of the downtown theaters which he claimed were reduced to "R- and X-rated violence and sex flicks."[7]

In 1978 *News American* columnist Jacques Kelly, in his first Neighborhood Watch column, commented on the death of downtown movies, writing that "Downtown movie theaters, which once outnumbered legitimate theatrical playhouses tenfold, are in a coma. Our inventory of once well-patronized movie houses is in a sorry state." He noted that the Charles had just closed "for repairs" and so had the 5 West, the Tower, and the Mayfair II (former Little). Kelly felt that downtown Baltimore would have to have more movie houses if it was going to have a viable night life, and he believed that untapped potential there would need help from the city government to develop. He noted that the Hippodrome, New, Howard, and Mayfair were probably viable but that they tended to show violent films.[8]

The Gayety was not demolished, but it never functioned as a theater after 1969. The editor of the *Evening Sun* said goodbye to the Gayety in a December 1969 editorial. In it he noted that seamen, farm boys, urban derelicts, men, young and old, found "good-natured jollity" or flickers of feminine tenderness at the Gayety. The passing of the old theater was blamed on the era of permissiveness when "once prim movie houses ... everywhere elbow aside the competition to display the last gritty dregs of what once passed as romance."[9]

Even while people were shunning downtown theaters, in the mid–1970s they were headed to suburban theaters in large numbers. Was it X-rated movies, multi-screen theaters, better pictures or just a larger population that turned things around from the dreary situation in the first half of the 1970s?[10] Perhaps it was a combination of all these, or maybe people just wanted escape from high unemployment and inflation.

The fact remains that movie attendance picked up in 1975 even if the building of new theaters slowed almost to zero. Marylanders spent 22.5 percent more on amusements than in 1974. More people were going out. "'There's no question about it,' said Ronnee Greenberg, speaking for the JF Theatres circuit ... 'Admissions are way up this year. And the kind of films people are going to see are disconnected with reality. They're not the heavier, thought-provoking films. People clearly don't want to see their problems magnified on the screen.' Ms. Greenberg cited 'Jaws,' 'Mandingo' and 'The Return of the Pink Panther' as popular escapist shows."[11] Business was also improving at other entertainment venues, such as the Merriweather Post Pavilion in Columbia, particularly for pop and rock music concerts. Business at restaurants was booming, and attendance at Oriole games was up over that of 1974. What theaters were left downtown managed to keep going with black exploitation films. JF Theaters emphasized movies with appeal to African-American audiences in its downtown theaters, and Baltimore became one of the leading cities for showcasing films of this kind. But the public is fickle, and moviegoing plummeted again in the late 1970s.

Despite a modest victory in 1971, the State Censor Board was working on borrowed time. The controversial Swedish movie *I Am Curious (Yellow)* was banned by the censors in July 1969. Their decision was upheld by the circuit court in Baltimore and by the state's Court of Appeals. The Court was split 4 to 3 in supporting the censors; Judge Thomas B. Finan, speaking for the majority, found that the film was designed primarily "to purvey shocking and titillating sexual sequences" and was "utterly without redeeming social value." The case was taken to the Supreme Court where the distributor's lawyer argued that it was not pornographic and challenged the Maryland court rulings on the grounds that the censor board was unconstitutional and that the film was protected by the First Amendment. Maryland Attorney General, Francis Burch, described the movie as "hardcore pornography." The Supreme Court had a difficult time, and, in a March 1971 4-to-4 deadlocked decision in which Justice William O. Douglas did not participate, the High Court upheld Maryland's ban on the film. A year later, the censor board agreed to reconsider the film after cuts were made by the distributor. The cuts were deemed adequate, and the film was finally approved. Faced with an avalanche of X-rated films, the courts tended to support the censors on the most blatantly pornographic films.

In February 1971, another unsuccessful attempt was made to abolish the censor board. Perhaps the impassioned plea against the bill by censor board member Mary Avara saved the board.[12] Just before the 1971 session of the General Assembly ended, a bill to replace the censor board with a movie classification board was defeated in the House by two votes. In a 1972 opinion upholding the ban of two films, Circuit Court Judge James A. Perrott accused the censor board of being inconsistent in its rulings. He said that the board seemed to be more likely to grant approval to a smut film if it were more expensively made or if it were 'introduced or interlaced with some pseudo-scientific or pseudo-educational facade.'[13]

Drive-in theaters presented another problem; passing motorists could be presented with huge pictures of naked people or couples engaging in sexual acts on the drive-in screen. Legislators tried to pass laws to prohibit films with this kind of scenery from being shown in drive-ins with screens that were visible from the road. In 1974, state senator J. Lipin from Anne Arundel County introduced legislation—patterned after a similar Virginia law—to this effect. At the same time, the Baltimore County Council was considering a similar ordinance specifically aimed at the Pulaski Drive-In. The Baltimore County bill was passed in February and the drive-in stopped showing X-rated films. Everyone seemed happy, but the following year, in a case involving the Valley Drive-In, a district court judge struck down the law, saying that people driving by an open-air theater could avert their eyes.

The Supreme Court's decision, in June 1973, which abolished a national standard for offensiveness and left it up to local communities, gave more power to the states to fight pornography and reversed a 15-year trend toward more permissiveness. It gave the Maryland censors renewed hope. The court also ruled that instead of a work having to be "utterly without redeeming social value" to be declared obscene, a work would win this declaration only if it, "taken as a whole, does not have serious literary, artistic, political or scientific value."[14] The next, and one of the biggest hurdles for the censor board, occurred in 1974 with the film *Deep Throat*.

Deep Throat had been banned in four other states before Baltimore City Circuit Court Judge James W. Murphy enjoined its showing at the North Cinema in May 1974. Each time the police seized a copy of the film, the theater manager obtained another print. In July, Judge Murphy upheld the board's ban on the film, describing it as an "unartistic, unattractive, base performance by amateur thespians whose only talent was their ability to overcome any feelings of decency or morality to engage in a public display of the most sordid nature." The theater's lawyer appealed to the Maryland Court of Appeals declaring that the movie had "serious literary, artistic and scientific value." Its purported value to science notwithstanding, in November 1974, the appeals court upheld the lower court's ban declaring that the film would probably be deemed obscene "under any meaningful definition of that term."[15] The Maryland Court of Appeals overturned the state's 1967 obscenity law in December 1977, and the North Cinema asked the circuit court to lift the ban on *Deep Throat*.[16] The general assembly increased the censor board's budget in 1974. This increase enabled it to hire more inspectors; hundreds of people applied for the $25-a-day jobs. Nine new inspectors began their jobs in December.

The nearly unrestrained freedom that filmmakers enjoyed in the 1970s reached its ugly nadir in 1976 with a film called *Snuff* which many believed showed, at its climax, a real murder. In their first attempt to edit scenes solely because of violence, the Maryland censors banned it. The members of the board would have approved the film if the bloody scene at the end of the film had been eliminated, but the publicity director for the film's distributor claimed that that scene was where the picture got its "novelty." A local film critic who testified for the board said that the theme of this film was torture and murder "done in a way to favor sadistic interests," and he feared that it would make money. He doubted that the killing and disemboweling in the final scene was real, but he suggested that it was only a matter of time before somebody did film a real killing for a movie.[17] In March 1976, the censor board survived another of the increasingly frequent attempts to abolish it. The vote in the Senate was extremely close; 21 senators supported a bill to abolish the board while 22 opposed it. The next year, with censor board member Mary Avara riding to the defense again, another bill to abolish the board failed.

The censor board came close to abolition again in 1978. The Senate Proceedings Committee gave a favorable report on a bill to abolish the board, but the acting governor said that he opposed eliminating the board. He was worried about what he saw as "a constant movement further and further in the direction of pornography." Then something strange happened; perhaps in their rush to abolish the board, the senators acted too hastily. The Judicial Proceedings Committee sent their bill to the Senate floor saying that prosecutors could curb pornographic movies more efficiently than a censor board just by enforcing anti-obscenity laws. The senators forgot one thing; the Maryland Court of Appeals had struck down the state's anti-obscenity law a month earlier and refused to reconsider its ruling in that matter.

The Senate decided this was not the time to do away with the censors. It did, however, pass a measure to curb the board's powers. The board would no longer have the power of prior censorship. In a seemingly contradictory act, the 1979 session of the Maryland Senate was ready to consider a bill that would increase the maximum fine for showing unapproved films to a maximum of $250. At the same time, the board's existence was threatened by sunset legislation that could abolish it by the end of 1980.

The State Secretary of Licensing and Regulation, who was responsible for overseeing the censor board, declared that it should be allowed to die. He felt that the board's $100,000 a year budget could be better spent elsewhere. The reaction of the chairman of the board, Jerusa C. Wilson, was lukewarm, saying that the board's official position was not to lobby for its retention or removal. Only steadfast Mary Avara came to the board's defense. But the clock was ticking and the board had only a few months to live.

The end came quickly. The House of Delegates passed a measure in February 1980 that would have allowed the censor board to operate for another six years. The Senate took up the matter next, and the committee considering the abolition of the board deadlocked 4–4. The issue was turned over to the full Senate where preliminary approval was given to legislation that would have made submitting a film to the board voluntary. The House and Senate could not agree, and the General Assembly session ended with a Senate vote not to extend the life of the censor board. House and Senate conferees argued back and forth but could not agree.

Barring any strong last-ditch action, the board's fate was sealed; it would cease to exist on the last day of June 1981. In March 1981, the House of Delegates, the last bastion of censorship support, voted 85–42 to extend the board's life another six years, but Governor Hughes said that he would veto the bill if the Senate did not kill it first. Oddly enough, most of the local exhibitors were uneasy about the board's demise. Most of them favored continuing the board because they believed it offered them protection, acting as a kind of buffer between citizen groups and the exhibitors. Mary Avara predicted that the city would be flooded with porno movies, but theater bookers said they were going to move slowly, test the waters. The last meeting of the Maryland Board of Film Censors was held on June 25, 1981; for better or worse, movies shown in Maryland were going to be uncensored for the first time in 65 years.

Despite the fact that predictions about the movie industry had been notoriously unreliable, people continued to make them. Local film critic Lou Cedrone made some at the end of 1976. It had been a terrible year for exhibitors, but Cedrone liked the upcoming films *Islands in the Stream*, *The Amazing Dobermans*, *Demon Seed*, *Damnation Alley*, and *The Cassandra Crossing*. He thought that *Rocky* looked like a winner. He picked Nick Nolte, Cliff Potts, and Richard Jordan as new faces to watch and opined that there should be less violence in future movies because, "the open-wound, broken-bone movie is no longer the attraction it was.... The American people have demonstrated ... that they have had about all they want." About new theaters, he wrote, "The new houses will be a little bigger than those that were built in the last decade. Distributors still will be looking for small theatres, but they also will want the 700-to-900-seaters for movies that play to audiences that large." Cedrone saw fewer daytime screenings and the videocassette as the movie industry's biggest worry.[18]

How have these predictions turned out? *Rocky* was indeed a winner. The other movies were mainly forgettable. Violence has not abated; we have not, alas, had our fill of it. Nick Nolte has lasted, but what happened to Cliff Potts and Richard Jordan? New theaters, with very few exceptions, were not bigger, and there were certainly no 700- to 900-seaters built. Perhaps this is a lesson; it is very difficult to attempt to predict the future of the movie industry.

On the other hand, it is always fun to rate things. Many magazines have ratings of the best and worst once a year. Here is an excellent 1979 rating of local movie theaters.

The Top Ten — And Why

1. **Campus Hills**— Modern movie theater with 350 seats— large for a twin. Sense of space, cleanliness rather than sterility, and comfort. Large concession selection. First run.

2. **Arcade**— Built in 1928 and recently reopened. Frequent film changes. '30s decor. Second and third run.

3. **Harundale**— Very large auditoriums seating up to 560 each. Big lobby with seating and smoking areas. First run.

4. **Mini-Flicks**— Extremely well-planned. Small. Outstanding seats. Small screen. Inexpensive candy. Lobby walls covered with a collage of old movie posters. Very clean. Second run.

5. **Charles**— Baltimore's newest art house. Beautiful interior. Bonus ticket book. First and second run.

6. **Eastport Cinema**— Red and black decor with lobby seating in alcoves. Vending machines only. Clean. Pleasant. First run.

7. **Senator**— The ultimate art deco movie theater in Baltimore. May seem at bit ragged around the edges, but thank heavens it's still around. First run.

8. **Glen Burnie Mall**— Large screen, though theater is a little narrow. Great slant. Subdued, comfortable and quiet. First run.

9. **Village**— Immense theater with great slant. Very clean and attractive. Second and third run.

10. **The Playhouse**— One of the original Baltimore art houses. Fresh coffee. Student discount. Vending machines only. Revolving art exhibition on walls of lobby — one of the most comfortable in town. First run.

The Losers

1. **New**— Just about everything is done in this theater except watching the movie. Audience commentary is frequently and freely given.

2. **Howard**— Watching a movie in this small theater is like sitting in a very dark can of sardines. Kung fu and bloody flicks are the common fare. Since the doors open at 8:00 A.M., the theater has become home for many regulars.

3. **Ritchie**— They've installed Dolby sound (the newest thing in sound systems), but you'd never know it from the unintelligible noise emitted from the speakers. Also, the screen is so small and the theater so narrow, it's like watching a TV through a tunnel.

4. **Town**— Depressingly run down, but at one time a beautiful art deco movie theater.

5. **Movies I-V**— No floor slant, poor visibility and sound, small screen hung high on the wall, and uncomfortable seats.[19]

A year later, *News American* writer Mike Giuliano rated the Senator, Charles, Playhouse, Grand, and Boulevard as the five best and the Howard, Town, Hillendale, Ritchie, and Golden Ring as the five worst theaters in the area.[20] It's too bad these raters did not have much choice in what they were rating since so many good theaters had disappeared by the time they made their lists. One might quibble with a couple of their choices, but no two raters would agree on everything. The best theaters blend beauty of external and internal form with comfort and good service. The worst show little attempt at beauty only the desire to squeeze the most seats into the smallest space and attempt to take the viewer's mind off the theater's shortcomings with sound that is so loud as to cause pain.

The 10 best and 10 worst local theaters are rated by the author as follows. The theaters with asterisks after their names are gone, either demolished or completely remodeled.

The Top Ten
(in alphabetical order)[21]

Ambassador*—beautiful impressive exterior; comfortable interior with good sight lines; excellent ice cream sandwiches

Bridge*—wide art deco auditorium was one of the most beautiful in town; good sight lines

Crest*—luxurious lobby and mezzanine; beautiful auditorium; good sight lines

Eastpoint 10 (Auditorium 4)—spectacular auditorium, wonderful place to see big movies

Edmondson Village*—beautiful exterior blending in with rest of shopping center; large attractive lobby with wide comfortable auditorium

North Point Plaza* **(before conversion to 4 screens)**—drab exterior did not do justice to excellent auditorium; ruined by chopping auditorium up into smaller theaters

Perring Plaza* **(before twinning)**—odd, cube-like exterior contrasted with the large auditorium with excellent amenities; likewise ruined by terrible twinning

Senator—just about the best there is today; attractive, clean, well-run and lovingly cared for

Stanley*—spectacular facade; beautiful, palatial interior; best marble lobby in town; comfortable seats and good sight lines

Town*—beautiful exterior and interior; good sight lines (especially from balcony); ruined by twinning and neglect[22]

The Bottom Ten
(in alphabetical order)

Alpha*—hard wooden seats; sounds from bowling alley in basement made every movie seem to include a thunderstorm; tiny men's room in basement

Glen Burnie Town Center 7*—one of the most unattractive exteriors of any present-day theater in metropolitan area

Howard*—small, unpleasant auditorium; danger of stepping on someone sleeping on the floor

Loew's White Marsh 16—nice exterior with lots of neon; lobby too crowded and noisy; long trip to centrally located rest rooms; horribly loud sound in all auditoriums follows you even to the rest rooms

Movies 1-2-3 Etc. at Golden Ring*—small, flat-floored, cramped auditoriums with tiny screens; as with most present-day theaters, sound was far too loud

New* — odd feeling that inside was too small and angles were all wrong; bland funeral parlor interior

Perry Hall* — same criticisms as Golden Ring; only advantage was that Perry Hall was cheaper

Timonium Cinemas* — long, narrow "shooting gallery" auditoriums; too many seagulls in parking lot; don't see Hitchcock's *The Birds* here

Watersedge* — cinder block decor

World* — odd "L-shaped" dark auditorium; small screen; weirdly attractive; the wonderful movies shown here made it bearable

Some theaters were not only small and unattractive, but they charged too much. Since the 1950s, first-run movie theater prices have been rising like first-class postage stamps. We have always complained about the cost of theater tickets. Early movie theaters used to put their prices up in lights to attract customers; they have not done this in many years. Admission prices jumped to around $3.00 in the 1970s. But some theaters kept lower prices; in May 1971, the Village and Joppatown theaters were charging $1.00 at all times. In 1980, people were complaining about $4 tickets. A writer for the *Sun*, aghast at $4 tickets, suggested that theaters could attract more patrons by lowering the price to $2.[23] What a great idea! Someone must have been listening, because the following year discount movie theaters arrived. In an effort to turn marginal theaters into moneymakers, some exhibitors lowered their prices. The dark side of discount theaters was that they did not get first-run movies, but a little patience on the part of a moviegoer could save him or her a lot of money.

> A number of area theaters are now offering ticket prices of $2 or less for new and recent films. Some ... offer these prices all day for all seats, while others restrict the savings to daytime showings or matinees.... You can still afford to go to the movies. How did this phenomenon come about? "It was the economy," says Irwin Cohen, president of R. C. Theatres, the firm that manages the Hollywood Theater ... and the Village Theater...." We felt that there was a large number of people who were looking for entertainment, and ... for a lower ticket price." Those theaters currently offer $1.50 admission for all seats, with three shows per day at 2:00, 7:15, and 9:00 P.M. The films are generally new.... Walt Burgess of the Smart Brothers, who have introduced a 99-cent admission policy to the Apollo, the Crest, the Edmondson Village, and the Northwood theaters, says that comedy films, like the Richard Pryor triple-feature currently playing those houses, are among his chain's biggest draws.... Burgess says that he and his brother Pat came up with the idea for the 99-cent theaters when they asked themselves "what could you do as a kid for a quarter?"...
>
> The other side of current cinema savings comes with matinee showings. General Cinema ... which manages the Columbia, Harundale, Perring Plaza, Security Mall and York Road cinemas, expanded its matinee policy in early December. According to a spokesman..., "Our company is really the originator in the bargain matinee throughout the country. It's really the best thing we have." While the format is somewhat limited in time availability, covering only three out of the five showings on weekdays, it is more generous in the film fare it offers.... [T]he General Cinemas spokesman said, "We just want people to come to the movies."
>
> The latest entry into the matinee sweepstakes are four downtown theaters managed by JF Theaters. The Hippodrome, Mayfair, New, and Town theaters have instituted a "Shoppers' Special," which reduces admission to $2 every day until 5 P.M....[24]

Bel Air–based Greater Baltimore Cinema, founded by Bob Wienholt in 1979, specialized in discount theaters. Wienholt's chain of small multiplexes flourished during the 1980s. Wienholt concentrated on northeast Baltimore and adjacent Baltimore County, building theaters in a variety of commercial spaces. By 1992, Greater Baltimore Cinema was operating six multiplexes with 29 screens in Maryland and Pennsylvania.[25] Wienholt was preparing to expand, but the bottom seemed to fall out of the discount theater business in the mid–1990s, and, faced with poor summer ticket sales and serious competition from several new megaplexes, he filed for Chapter 11 bankruptcy in August 1997.

Reduced prices had been around for a long time, but they were usually available only at special times or for special occasions. In January 1981, the United Artists theaters at Golden Ring announced a "Special Inflation Fighting Price Policy;" all seats would be $2.00 between 10:00 A.M. and 6:00 P.M., Monday through Friday. Most Baltimore theaters were charging between $3.50 and $4.00. Faced with a huge 500-percent increase in the City amusement tax in 1989, some theaters passed the increase along to their customers. Tom Kiefaber said he would try to maintain adult ticket prices at the current $5.00 while the Charles raised its prices from $4.00 to $4.25. United Artists kept ticket prices at its Harbor Park theaters at $3.50 for matinees and $5.50 in the evening. The average ticket price in 1990 was $4.23. The list of discount theaters in December 1991 included the Hillendale ($1.50), the Hollywood Twin ($1.00 Monday–Thursday; $2.50 weekends), the Liberty Cinemas ($2.00), Jumpers Mall ($1.75), North Point Plaza 4 ($1.75), the Patterson 1 & 2 ($1.50), and the Village 3 ($2.50, $1.00 Tuesday and Wednesday).

First-run films at Towson Commons cost $7.00 in 1994. Golden Ring was charging $6.50 for evening movies while Timonium charged $4.25 for matinees in 1995. In 1996 and 1997 prices ranged between $4.00 at matinees and $6.50 in the evening. By 1998 matinees at some theaters had risen to $4.75 and evening shows cost $7.25. As the new century began, it was not unusual to find some theaters charging more than $8.00 or $8.50 for an evening ticket. One of the few benefits of growing older was the prospect of senior discount tickets.

One of the symbols of movie-going that has changed almost as much as theater architecture is the movie ticket. Long, accordion pleated books of colorful tickets were used for more than 50 years.[26] These tickets typically had the name of the theater, the price, and a preprinted serial number on one side with a disclaimer notice on the other. Color variations in the tickets indicated different prices. A device called the "automatic ticket-shooter" appeared in several Baltimore movie theaters in 1913.[27] The coming of multiplex theaters in the 1960s made the use of these tickets cumbersome since several mechanical ticket dispensers had to be installed to provide the wide assortment of colored tickets for each price and feature combination.

By the early 1980s, most new theaters were using computerized ticketing systems. A single computerized ticket dispenser could issue a ticket for any combination of film and price. At some theaters now, the patron receives a ticket on which is printed the name of the theater, a serial number, the date and time of the show, the date and time you bought the ticket, the cost of the ticket, the name of the movie, which auditorium the movie is playing in and the name of the cashier.[28]

Local exhibitors were disappearing along with downtown movie theaters. Many circuits that had been around since the early days went out of business as their older theaters were out-screened by richer national circuits. They sold off their real estate or went into other businesses. Pearce and Scheck, Whitehurst, Durkee, Rome, Schwaber, and JF were replaced by General Cinema, Loew's, Hoyt's, and United Artists. And some of these newcomers did not last much longer. At the beginning of the 21st century several of these circuits were in financial trouble. General Cinema, Loew's, United Artists, and Regal closed a number of their older theaters and applied for Chapter 11 bankruptcy protection. General Cinemas, which had given us so many big beautiful theaters in the 1960s, was acquired by American Multi-Cinemas in 2002. Regal emerged from bankruptcy stronger than ever and, by 2003, it was able to buy a number of theaters in the northeast, including the Hunt Valley and Bowie theaters from Hoyt's.

The Whitehurst Circuit, formed by Charles Whitehurst around 1909, was important because of its early emphasis on downtown first-run theaters. Whitehurst, discussed in Chapter 4, was the only local exhibitor who concentrated on large, downtown theaters and could round up the necessary financing to act on his visions. Only Pearce and Scheck were able to build theaters on a par with Whitehurst's New, Garden, and Century, but they seem to have peaked too early and built in the wrong areas.

Morris Mechanic was, in some ways, the successor to the Whitehurst group. Mechanic was born in Poland in 1904 and moved with his parents to Baltimore when he was very young. He owned a downtown chocolate company when he got his start in the theater business, buying the New Theater from Whitehurst interests, in 1929. He only built a single theater, the Centre, in 1939. In 1942 he bought Ford's Theater, and he later acquired the Century, Valencia, and Stanley. Mechanic went through Baltimore's first-run theaters like one of the Four Horsemen of the Apocalypse. He disposed of the Stanley and Ford's apparently because he did not want to add to the list of his new theater's competitors. He died in July 1966, just a few months before the Morris Mechanic Theater opened.

The Rappaport circuit never controlled many theaters; at its peak it had only the Hippodrome, Town, Little, Aurora, and Film Centre, but it did a lot with these five theaters. Isador Rappaport was a real showman, who pumped extraordinary life into every theater he touched.[29] He turned the Hippodrome into one of the most popular theaters in town and rejuvenated the Palace from a parking garage into the Town, which became a major first-run venue for 20 years. In 1958, all of the Rappaport theaters, except the Film Center, were put under the management of Jack Fruchtman, and for the first time in the history of Baltimore, all of the downtown first-run theaters fell under the same management. This move was made to eliminate the cutthroat competition that had existed between Rappaport and Fruchtman.

This situation lasted for four years; then, in 1962, Rappaport got out of the theater business entirely and leased his theaters to the Trans-Lux Corporation of New York. He died in 1973 at the age of 71. Two years later, his son, M. Robert Rappaport, returned to the local exhibition scene with two multi-screen theaters, one in Timonium and one in Glen Burnie.[30] He leased the Hillendale and Jumper's Mall theaters. He added a new screen to the Jumpers Mall Theater and was building a triplex at the Greenspring Shopping center when he sold all his theaters to Durkee Enterprises in 1985.

Schwaber Theaters was a major innovator among the Baltimore circuits. Schwaber was quick to sense the art house boom of the 1950s and converted several of their theaters into successful art houses. Schwaber also saw the potential of theaters with multiple auditoriums and built the area's first one in 1964. Milton Schwaber was a dealer in real estate before he got into the movie business in the early 1940s. He built a couple of small neighborhood theaters, the Apex and Homewood. Then, in 1947 he acquired a son-in-law, Howard Wagonheim, who transformed the circuit. Wagonheim began to chauffeur his father-in-law around town; while doing this, he became interested in the theaters, which, like many other neighborhood theaters, were not doing too well.

Wagonheim, who loved foreign films and did not believe they were being packaged correctly, began to think about how to do this. Everything clicked when he saw an ad for the new Heywood-Wakefield Airflo Rocking Chair theater seats. He talked Mr. Schwaber into replacing the original seats in the Homewood Theater on 25th Street with 359 of the new seats, widely spaced so that people had enough room to not have to stand when someone wanted to get past them. Wagonheim remodeled the lobby into a cozy carpeted lounge, with comfortable seating and original paintings on the walls. He served free coffee and tea and had the candy machines removed. He also designed new ads for the newspapers and renamed the theater the Playhouse. The first film at the new theater grossed $3,012 its first week. The Homewood had previously been averaging $800. Schwaber Theaters converted several other theaters into art houses, but the Playhouse was the most successful.[31]

In 1964, as downtown movie-going was beginning to fall off, Wagonheim correctly saw that multi-screen theaters were the wave of the future. He opened the Cinema I and II, the first twin theaters in Maryland, in Schwaber's newly built Yorkridge Shopping Center. Schwaber Theaters, renamed World Fare Cinemas, opened several other theaters, including the Valley Drive-In in Owings Mills, the Mini-Flick in Pikesville, and the Tollgate Movies in Bel Air. Schwaber died in 1981, and Wagonheim died six years later after leasing out most of his theaters. Their circuit had lasted only about 40 years, but it had been a major force in shaping the Baltimore movie scene.

Between 1970 and 1988, JF Theaters was the major local circuit. During the 1970s, JF opened the Joppatown Theater, the Rotunda twin theaters, the Jumpers Mall 3, and the Campus Hills twin. By 1975, JF operated 44 screens in Maryland, West Virginia, and Virginia.[32] JF seemed to be playing Monopoly, acquiring every theater it landed on. But JF leased most of its theaters, and leasing cost a lot of money. The reckoning came in 1978 when a shortage of cash, in part due to some bad leases, forced JF Theaters to file for Chapter 11 bankruptcy protection. The company worked its way out of bankruptcy under the leadership of Jack Fruchtman, Jr. The court allowed JF to terminate leases on the Tower, Charles, Little, Strand, Earle, Carlton, and Shore Drive-In and to sell the Rex and Lord Baltimore. In 1981, Continental Realty Corp., headed by Jack Luetkemeyer, Jr., and J. Mark Schapiro and primarily interested in real estate, infused new life into the circuit and eventually bought out the Fruchtman family.

By the mid–1980s, JF had gotten back some of its lost steam and had acquired two of John Broumas' theaters—the Randallstown Plaza and the North Point Plaza—and had leased World Fare Cinemas' Yorkridge Cinema 1 and 2 and Mini-Flick. In 1984, JF was the largest theater chain in Maryland with 22 screens in the Baltimore area; plus they were quadraplexing the North Point, adding five screens at Reisterstown Road Plaza, building a seven-screen theater in Glen Burnie, and a six-plex in Lexington Park and planning a theater in Annapolis (which was never built). JF added the nine-screen Columbia Palace Theater in 1986. Their goal was 100 screens by 1988, but they never made it.[33] They came close, after acquiring 15 screens from Durkee in 1988, bringing them to a total of 67 screens. But JF lasted only a few more months; Continental Realty sold its movie theater business to Loew's Theatre Management Corporation in September 1988 for nearly $30 million.

In 1984, in addition to the extensive expansion by JF, there was activity by Rappaport Management, Inc., George Brehm, and United Artists. On Route 40 in Catonsville, Brehm added three new auditoriums to his Westview Complex, giving him a total of eight. United Artists was planning a nine-screen complex of theaters, restaurants, and a parking garage in the Inner Harbor.[34] The end came for Durkee theaters in the 1980s. Durkee twinned and triplexed some of its larger theaters and purchased four theaters from M. Robert Rappaport in 1985. Then, in 1988, JF Theaters bought most of the Durkee theaters. The Patterson Theater was the last operating Durkee house when it closed in 1995. For the first time in 86 years, Baltimore was without a Durkee theater.

Movies may be escapist entertainment par excellence, but there is a sinister side to the dark auditoriums, and monsters are not only on the screens. There have always been people who will take advantage of the anonymity the darkness provides to harm or annoy others. Ushers were warned about "deviants" and "mashers" and how to handle them. Young women were favorite targets for these pests. One curious activity in theaters was cutting locks of hair from girls' heads. A 14-year-old girl lost five long curls to a phantom barber in a downtown movie house in February 1921. A slasher cut a nine-inch lock of hair from a woman's head as she and her husband watched a movie in a North Howard Street theater in February 1926. More heinous was the reported kidnapping of attractive women from theaters by injecting them with drug-laden syringes.[35] Fights over girlfriends, manners, and clothing have taken place in theaters, and, horribly, there have been shootings, murders, and suicides.

One of the earliest shootings in a Baltimore movie theater took place in the spring of 1912. Arthur Millard, enraged because the piano player at the Pickwick Theater would not marry him, walked into the theater on the evening of April 11, 1912, and fired two shots at her. He then turned the gun on himself. Millard died on the spot. His victim, Mrs. Hazel E. Pierce, was not seriously injured.

In October 1920, Wasil Sereclicz shot himself on the stairway to the balcony in the Palace Theater on Fayette Street. A burlesque comic on-stage at the time, upon hearing the gunshot, quipped, "That sounds like another Wall Street explosion." Sereclicz died before he got to the operating room.[36]

The year 1925 seems to have been a particularly bad one to go to the movies. A man shot himself in the head in Schanze's Theater in January 1925.[37] Frank M. Scholl, a drummer in the Hippodrome orchestra, died — according to the newspapers — from a sudden attack of indigestion while performing in July; his wife and daughter were in the audience at the time. At the Goldfield Theater, in August, there was a stage act that featured Susie Maturio and her sharpshooter husband, Pedro. Mrs. Maturio would hold a penny between her teeth and her husband would shoot it out with a .22 caliber rifle. He missed on August 8 and shot his wife in the lip.[38] A shoot-out in the Town Theater in 1953 resulted in two deaths.

People used to go to the movies to get away from this kind of thing. It has become harder and harder to do. Two theater patrons were beaten unconscious by a gang of ten noisy punks while attending a showing of *The Untouchables* at a theater in Columbia in June 1987. Oblivious, the rest of the 40-odd people in the audience kept watching the movie, ignoring pleas for help.

Several more unpleasant incidents occurred in local movie theaters during the 1990s. Guns, the weapon of choice of the late 20th century, have become easy to obtain and some patrons, for whom the line between reality and a fantasy on the screen has ceased to exist, think nothing about using a gun even in a crowded theater. Movies are not the safe wombs they once were. Recent accounts of people being beaten up, stabbed, and murdered in movie theaters suggest that the real world is no longer kept at bay by a box office. A gang of racist thugs assaulted some Hopkins students driving them out of the Harbor Park Theater in 1998. The management was forced to call the police and close the theater.

All of the movie pioneers have passed on. So have many second and third generation exhibitors, musicians, and projectionists. James Kernan passed away many years ago. Pearce and Scheck are gone, as are Joe Fields, the Gaertners, the Noltes, Frank Durkee, Isador Rappaport, John McCaslin, Maurice Cohen, Henry Hornstein, Frank Hornig, Ben Beck, Leon Zeller, and Lauritz Garman.[39] Sam Isaacson, John Bedford, Carroll Bayne, Maurice Rushworth, Russell Hildebrand, Bill Lange, Sr., and George Douglass are gone. Jack Whittle[40] died in 1977 and Mike Leventhal died in 1981. Steve Brenner "Bozo the Clown" died in 1982.[41] Jack Fruchtman died in 2001. Most of the theater architects are gone, John Zink, John Eyring, Theodore Wells Pietsch, A. Lowther Forrest, John Eberson, and Thomas Lamb. Piano players, organists and conductors have also passed away. Gone are the Iulas, George Wild, Harvey Hammond and Roland Nuttrell as well as Mary Barber, Audrey Hane, Eddie Mitnick, Marie Jackson, and Mrs. Westergaard. Some of our losses are highlighted below.

John T. McCaslin, a man who had been associated with Baltimore theaters and entertainments for nearly 50 years, died at the home of his daughter in New Jersey in 1944. He had done just about everything in the entertainment field. He sold patent medicine and worked as a high-wire walker in the circus. He was a magician, a theatrical booking agent, and an impresario. He arranged entertainments for wealthy Baltimoreans. Especially noteworthy was his $20,000 conversion of Lehmann's Hall into a replica of the Imperial Palace Hotel in Cairo for Van Lear Black.

McCaslin was born in Monkton, Maryland, June 19, 1876. His obituary says, "A large, jovial man, he began his own theatrical career at 12 as a 'boy baritone,' singing 'He Never Cared to Travel from His Own Fireside' and 'The Baggage Car Ahead.'"[42] He operated the Colonnade Theater, where early movies were exhibited in 1906. McCaslin billed himself as a vaudeville contractor, character comedian, and magician in his ad in the 1907-08 *Baltimore Business Directory*. His office then was at Gay and Lexington streets. The ad stated, "Amusements and attractions furnished from Balloon Ascensions to Punch and Judy.... Special rates to Clubs, Lodges, Smokers, Socials, Bands, Fairs and Churches— from 20 minutes to 10 hours of solid fun and amusement by the best and highest class of Vaudeville Performers, male and female — Strictly Moral, Chaste and Refined Singers ... Acrobats ... Magicians, Musical Teams ... Ventriloquists, Jugglers, Moving Pictures, Illustrated Songs, Comedians of all Characters, Mandolin Clubs, etc." McCaslin discovered Johnny Eck, known as the "half-boy," and was his agent for 10 years. A man who knew him in his later years described him as "the Barnum of Baltimore, a great big heavy-set man. He wore a 10-gallon hat all the time ... he had a big stomach and wore an elk's tooth on a gold watch chain." He was known as "John T., the Fixer." According to Fred Schmuff, "[McCaslin's] name has been synonymous with entertainment as long as I can remember. He was in everything. He booked ... if you had a lodge or something, you wanted entertainment, you went to John McCaslin."[43]

The projectionists' union lost one of its oldest members in 1953. G. Kingston Howard had received the very first projectionists' license when the state began issuing them in

June 1910. He became the second president of the union in 1911 and was its business agent for many years.

> G. Kingston Howard, first president [sic] of Operators Local 181, Baltimore, Md., and one of the outstanding leaders of the 1913 campaign for direct charters for operators' locals, died last July 20 at the age of 75. He was business Agent of the Baltimore union for a long period and Financial Secretary of the Baltimore Federation of Labor for 15 years, as well as Vice-President of the Maryland–District of Columbia Federation of Labor.
>
> Brother Howard's theatrical career dated back to 1896 when he and his brother-in-law (Howard and Johnson) toured with their own tent-show vaudeville act. This act used one of the first Edison Kinescope [sic] projectors, with a box or bag for the take-up on the film, and it used calcium instead of electricity for light. Brother Howard's career as a projectionist in Baltimore ended with about 15 years at Loew's Parkway Theatre.[44]

Movie veteran Fred Schmuff died in February 1991.[45] He started out in knickers at the old Community Theater on Hamilton Avenue in 1918 and went on to become an executive in the Durkee circuit. He retired in May 1983. In a 1986 interview, he spoke about his early days:

SCHMUFF: I retired May the 31st 1983....
HEADLEY: Where did you start out?
SCHMUFF: ...on Hamilton Avenue right near Harford Road, up the street from the Arcade.... It used to be St. John's Church, and Durkee turned it into a theater. It was a wooden building ... and they remodeled it.... That's what they called the Community.
HEADLEY: How did you get interested in the movie business?
SCHMUFF: I was always interested in theaters from when I was a kid up.
HEADLEY: What was your job there?
SCHMUFF: I was there Friday nights and Saturday nights, [I] was an usher. [They] didn't have any uniforms then. They cost money. [I got paid] a dollar a night. I'd just walk up and down the aisle and see that everything was peaceful and quiet and whatnot. If you had a crowd then you hunted for seats and showed people where vacant seats were.... They didn't teach you anything; they turned you loose in those days.... [Later] I became manager of the old Community during the nighttime and worked in the office over on Gay Street between 10 and 2.... I stayed to work that way until [I became] manager of the State. I opened the State.[46]

While managing the State Theater, Schmuff booked vaudeville shows for the big theater. He believed that he was instrumental in the success of Abbott and Costello. They were doing so well at the State that he suggested their agent book them in Atlantic City instead of Canton, Ohio. The agent agreed and they were a big success there too. Fred Schmuff remembered that he and his assistant manager at the State had to wear a tuxedo every night. He left the State in 1935 and worked as Durkee's division manager, supervising all their theaters in East Baltimore. He later became the circuit's film buyer.

Baltimore has lost many of its theater musicians too. Organist Roland Nuttrell died in April 1980 at the age of 66. He started his career as a theater organist when he graduated from Forest Park High School in 1932. He attended the University of Maryland, Johns Hopkins, and the Peabody Institute. He played the organ at the Century, Valen-

cia, Stanley and Parkway theaters. Roland Nuttrell is probably best known for his midnight radio program, "Nocturne." Nocturne included Nuttrell's organ music and poetry readings by Charles Purcell. It was broadcast on WCAO between 1937 and 1957.[47]

Baltimore Theaters 1985

Apex	110 S. Broadway	North Point Plaza 4	2399 North Point Blvd.
Beltway Plaza Twins	7636 Belair Road	Patterson 1 & 2	3136 Eastern Avenue
Bengies Drive-In	**Middle River**	Perring Plaza 1 & 2	8730 Satyr Hill Road
Boulevard 1 & 2	3302 Greenmount Avenue	Playhouse	9 W. 25th Street
Carlton	1201 Dundalk Avenue	Randallstown Plaza 2	8730 Liberty Road
Charles	**1711 N. Charles Street**	Reisterstown Road Plaza 2	6512 Reisterstown Road
Church Lane Cinema	Cockeysville	**Rotunda Cinemas 1 & 2**	**711 W. 40th Street**
Earle	**4839 Belair Road**		
Edmondson Drive-In	Route 40	Security Mall Cinemas 4	6901 Security Blvd.
Grand	515 S. Conkling		
Hillendale Twins	**1045 Taylor Avenue**	**Senator**	**5904 York Road**
Hippodrome	12 N. Eutaw Street	Strand	1 Shipping Place
Hollywood 1 & 2	5509 Oregon Avenue	Timonium 3 Cinemas	2131 York Road
Liberty 1 & 2	8632 Liberty Road	Town	311 W. Fayette Street
Little X	523 N. Howard Street	Towson	512 York Road
Mayfair	508 N. Howard Street	Village	11900 Reisterstown Road
Mini-Flick	Pikesville	Westview 8	6023 Baltimore National Pike
Movies at Golden Ring 5	6400 Rossville Blvd.		
New	210 W. Lexington Street	York Road Cinema 2	6376 York Road
New Carver	1429 Pennsylvania Avenue	Yorkridge 4	58 W. Ridgely Road

If a theater were lucky, it was tastefully remodeled for some other use and some shreds of its theatrical past were preserved. Many became churches—not just for the salvation of souls but of buildings as well—while others were turned into malls or offices. Still others were bulldozed into oblivion. Jacques Kelly, who has been one of the most faithful chroniclers of Baltimore's movie theaters and their slow extinction, lamented the loss of the Boulevard in 1989. "The loss of any neighborhood landmark is a sad day. But the demise of a classic movie theater, the place you first encountered Clark Gable or Doris Day, has a unique way of evoking distant times past."[48]

The owners tried to get rid of the Mayfair Theater in 1986, but no one wanted it. It was offered at auction as a "Valuable Historic Development Property," but no one offered more than $200,000, and the auction was canceled. A paltry offer for a beautiful building so rich in theater history. The Mayfair has been slowly disintegrating since then; its later acquisition by the City did not stay the process. The New Theater closed without any fanfare after a 76-year run in 1986. Also without a blip on the preservationists' radar, the Little closed in 1988 to be razed for a parking lot. Two years later the Hippodrome and Town were shuttered. Loew's gave no reason for the closing of the last of the old downtown first-run movie theaters.[49] Theater closings continued into the next decade, but the glimmers of hope seen by Jacques Kelly sparkled on the horizon.

10

MEGAPLEXES (1990–2004)

The last decade of the 20th century was that of the megaplex, a huge expensive structure of 12 or more screens. It was also a time of financial difficulties for the big national circuits, difficulties brought on in large part by the frantic building of megaplexes. Finally there was some hope that a few theaters might be preserved.

The Baltimore area entered the age of the megaplex tentatively, but, by the late 1990s, the multiplex of six or eight screens was as passé as the single-screen theater. In 2000 the earlier megaplexes with 14 and 16 screens were dwarfed by Muvico's 24-screen complex near BWI Airport. The wide open spaces on York Road, now as far out as Cockeysville, along the I-95 corridor, at White Marsh — near the once tranquil stream of the same name where black snakes used to slither through the grass— along the Reisterstown Road corridor in Owings Mills, and into Anne Arundel County along the still beautiful Baltimore-Washington Parkway — all beckoned to developers of the megaplex. Not all of the planned theaters were built, however.

In 1995 it was predicted that Towson would have 34 screens by 1997. That proved only partially true. As of 2002, there were only eight screens there. Neighborhood opposition doomed the American Multi-Cinemas theater at Towson Marketplace, and the proposed Regal megaplex has not materialized.[1] At the beginning of the 21st century there may be places in the Baltimore suburbs that cry out for new theaters, but the huge cost of megaplex theaters will make building them more and more difficult.[2] It will be surprising if any new theaters are opened in Towson in the foreseeable future.[3]

As bigger and fancier theaters with stadium seating opened, many of the remaining older ones closed. One exhibitor predicted that it would not be long before slant-floor theaters were completely obsolete. Between 1992 and 2001 the Perring Plaza, Patterson, Village 3, Westview, North Point Plaza, Greenspring 3, Reisterstown Plaza Five Star, Movies at Harbor Park, Yorkridge 4, Columbia Cinema, Rotunda, Glen Burnie Town Center, and Columbia Palace 9 closed. The Columbia Palace 9 and the Movies at Harbor Park were only 15 years old; the Patterson was 65.

Prior to the mid–1980s, most of the Baltimore movie theaters had been owned by independent, local exhibitors.[4] But, beginning in 1985, there were rapid changes in who controlled the theaters. First of all, Durkee theaters purchased Rappaport's Associated Cinemas, which operated the Timonium, Hillendale, Ritchie and Jumpers Cinemas, giving them 41 screens. Then, in July 1988, JF Theaters bought 15 of Durkee's screens, giving them a total of 67 screens, and essentially ending Durkee's movie business. Two months later Loew's theaters acquired JF. Loew's was the fifth largest theater chain in the country and in the midst of a major nationwide expansion in 1988, but it did not have any theaters in the lucrative Baltimore-Washington area until August of that year when it acquired the 48-screen (13 theater) Roth circuit in the Washington suburbs. The acquisition of the Roth and JF theaters gave them a major piece of the local movie market. After an absence of more than 30 years, the name Loew's was back in Maryland.

By 1990, the Loew's organization controlled most of the theaters in the Baltimore area, and Hoyt's was moving up quickly. The following table shows the relative strengths of the major theater owners in the Baltimore area between 1990 and 2000.

Circuit	1990 Theaters	1990 Screens	1998 Theaters	1998 Screens	2000 Theaters	2000 Screens
Loew's	16	64	0	67	6	47
Independents	11	36	8	18	4	13
UA	3	26	5	48	4	43
General Cinema	4	15	3	19	4	36
Hoyt's	1	12	2	26	2	26
R/C Theaters	2	5	2	14	2	14
K/B Theaters	1	6	—	—	—	—
Premier Theaters	—	—	2	11	3	19
Regal Theaters	—	—	1	14	1	14
Total	38	164	33	217	26	212

Out of 26 theaters in 2000, only three were single screens.

Movie exhibitors finally realized, by the 1990s, that patrons wanted something more than a darkened room with a screen at one end. AMC's Grand 24 opened in Dallas, Texas, in 1995 bringing a dramatic end to the 30-year multiplex theater era and ushering in the age of the megaplex.[5] AMC's stunning success attracted the attention of exhibitors all over the nation. R/C Theaters decided to try stadium seating when they added a bigger-than-usual auditorium to their Eastpoint theater in 1995. Auditorium 4, with modified stadium seating, is a wonderful place to see spectaculars like *Twister* and *Independence Day*.[6] Auditorium 4 is the only new theater that has the feel of the spacious theaters of half a century ago. Regal Theaters' Bel Air 14, which opened in July 1997, started the next wave of intensive theater building and brought the first megaplex to Maryland. The Bel Air 14 features stadium seating and digital sound with two large concession stands, a cafe, and a video game room.[7]

As the movie companies were building bigger and more expensive theaters, they were sowing the seeds of their own downfalls. In 1997 and 1998 two mergers created huge theater chains. Cineplex Odeon Corp. merged with the Loew's Theaters unit of the Sony Corp. to form Loew's Cineplex Entertainment, a chain of 460 theaters with 2,600 screens. Soon after this merger was announced, another, even larger, merger was announced. This merger combined the theaters owned by Hicks, Muse, Tate & Furst of Dallas and Kohlberg

Kravis Roberts & Company of New York with Regal Cinemas of Knoxville to form the largest theater chain in the world, with more than 5,000 screens.

By 1999, it was apparent that construction costs for the new megaplexes were eating up the theater companies' profits. The stocks of General Cinema, Loew's Cineplex and AMC fell. The following year, the big circuits began to slow down. They pulled out of deals to build new theaters in several areas. General Cinema and Loew's Cineplex backed out of plans to build multiscreen theaters in Columbia. In early 2001, AMC and Loew's Cineplex announced that they were going to close a large number of their older, under-performing theaters. AMC said that it would close about 80 of its 186 theaters over the next three years. A spokesperson for Loew's Cineplex stated that most of the theaters it planned to close were 15 to 20 years old. Loew's filed for Chapter 11 bankruptcy in February. United Artists was reorganizing under Chapter 11 at the same time, and Regal Cinemas filed for bankruptcy that October. General Cinemas was bought out by AMC in 2002.

Notice that the city of Baltimore, with its nearly 700,000 people, did not figure in any new theater building. In 1975 there were 32 movie theaters in Baltimore and 15 years later there were seven. Seriously underscreened now, the city became the scene of active speculation about new theaters. Speculation, but no actual theaters. Regal was looking around for the right spot. Magic Johnson was also looking at several sites, including Mondawmin Mall. A developer promised an 18-screen theater east of the Inner Harbor. As of 2003 there were only five operating movie theaters (with 10 screens) in the city— the Senator, Rotunda (two screens), Charles (five screens), Apex, and Earle. The latter two show X-rated movies.

Concession sales continued to increase in importance as sources of movie theater revenue. In 1972, concession sales accounted for about 8.8 percent of total theater income; by 1991, that percentage had risen to 27.3 percent. As the 20th century drew to a close, most movie theaters featured the same generic candy and snack foods. There was very little variation between a General Cinema, Loew's, Hoyt's or R/C theater. Raisinets, thank goodness, are still sold along with Snickers, Twizzlers, Goobers, Junior Mints, Gummi Bears, Sno-Caps, Mike & Ike, Milk Duds and Sweetarts.[8] Trays of Nachos with cheese dip are popular items. Some theaters sell bulk candy from large bins, and a few have coffee bars.

There was a scare about theater food in 1994 when a study released by the Center for Science in the Public Interest revealed that much of the popcorn in theaters was popped in unhealthy coconut oil. Fortunately, most theaters in Baltimore popped their corn in the healthier vegetable oil. Tom Kiefaber, of the Senator Theater, said that his theater had been using canola oil since 1989. A spokesperson for General Cinemas said that they had used canola oil since 1990, but United Artists believed that people preferred the taste of corn popped in coconut oil so most of their theaters were still using it.[9]

The loss of Baltimore's theaters continued into the 21st century. Despite successful theater restorations throughout the country, the City appeared not to care very much. Baltimore has had a terrible record on theater preservation. We have stood by, seemingly uncaring, as the Stanley, Century, Keith's, Little, Ford's, Rivoli, Grand, and a host of neighborhood theaters were demolished or otherwise ruined. Other cities have fought to save their theaters; they have lost many battles, but they have also won some. Sadly, in many cases, the city government has lacked the backbone to risk the ire of a building's owner by putting it on the historic landmarks list. Events in the City Council in 1987 showed what could happen.

Second District Democratic Councilman Nathaniel J. McFadden took a bill out of the Urban Affairs Committee that would have added 15 buildings, including the Senator and Gayety theaters, to the list of Baltimore's historic landmarks. The owners of ten of the buildings, fearing that placement on the list would prevent them from developing the property or altering the structure, asked to have their properties kept out of the legislation. In the end, the Council sided with the owners and, in most cases, only gave landmark status to buildings whose owners wished it. The Euchtman-Macht House, the only building in the city designed by Frank Lloyd Wright, was excluded, as were the two theaters.[10]

"It's all politics," sums up Baltimore's disgraceful record in theater preservation. The safeguarding of our architectural heritage has been left up to the very persons we were trying to protect it from. We thought that the City's indifference to theater preservation had evaporated at the end of the century, but it's still there. As of 2004, there are only a few hopes for salvaging pieces of our movie legacy. We still have the Senator, thank goodness. The Patterson Theater on Eastern Avenue has been saved and turned into an arts center with a copy of its beautiful vertical sign still lighting up the corner. The Parkway is still hanging on. It may be saved, but has suffered such dreadful interior vandalizing that much of its beauty is gone. The beautiful old Auditorium-Mayfair building sits forlornly, roofless, amidst the ruins of North Howard Street. It will probably become an apartment building. It looked for a while as if the Grand Theater on Conkling Street might have been saved, but City and Enoch Pratt Library officials turned deaf ears on the pleas of preservationists, and the Grand was needlessly destroyed. Finally, there is the delightful prospect that the Ambassador Theater may be restored.

The super-nova in local theater restoration is the Hippodrome. Things looked bleak when the Hippodrome and the nearby Town closed in the summer of 1990, but an editorial in the *Sun* on these closings seemed to signal a changed attitude toward theater preservation. Noting that both theaters had been reduced to "mere shadows" of their past, the editorial suggested that "a way should be found to return at least the Hippodrome to life as an artistic venue." It concluded that the Hippodrome had too much to offer to disappear from the scene.[11]

The University of Maryland had been investigating the feasibility of acquiring the Hippodrome as an auditorium for shows and graduations in the early 1980s. Nothing came of this. In 1993, Don Hicken, a teacher at the Baltimore High School for the Performing Arts, developed an ambitious plan to restore the Hippodrome as a vaudeville museum. Hicken's plan was enthusiastically supported by many, but the financing never developed. The Hippodrome was offered for sale at prices ranging between $600,000 and $1.5 million, but there were no buyers.

Then, remarkably, in 1997, the Hippodrome and Town were donated to the University of Maryland. The buildings' owners, J. Mark Schapiro and John A. Luetkemeyer, Jr., both Baltimoreans, said they wanted to see something positive happen in the area. It looks like they have gotten their wish; good for them. In early 1998 the Greater Baltimore Committee, Inc. and the Downtown Partnership, with the endorsement of the Baltimore Center for the Performing Arts, suggested that the Hippodrome be restored into a "site for large-scale Broadway productions." They put a price tag of $25 million on the project. The 1998 Maryland General Assembly granted authority to the Maryland Stadium Authority to prepare studies, including site studies, architectural programs, and budget estimates, and design and construct facilities for State agencies or local governments. The

Baltimore Hippodrome Performing Arts Center was one of the projects approved for study, and it received a $1.7 million grant in Fiscal 1999 for design development. Hardy Holzman Pfeiffer Associates of New York was chosen as architects for the project.[12] By the fall of 1998, the estimated cost of restoration had risen to nearly $50 million, and in early 1999 it had increased to $53 million. Amid much ballyhoo, the Hippodrome reopened with Mel Brooks' *The Producers* on February 10, 2004, a red-letter day for Baltimore.

The only somber note was the wanton destruction of Highlandtown's Grand Theater a week earlier. The Hippodrome's neighbor, the Town Theater, may also be preserved as a theater. Nothing better could happen to transform the blighted west side of the city into a thriving theater district.

Signs of an encouraging trend for theater preservation have appeared around the state. Although most of the old downtown theaters have been lost, there is at least one active, restored theater in nearly every Maryland county. Cumberland, Hagerstown, Frederick, Westminster, Church Hill, Chestertown, Easton, Berlin, and Pocomoke City all have saved historic theaters. Other cities have not fared as well. Annapolis, Ellicott City, and Bel Air have lost all of their downtown theaters.

For the 21st century we can hope that some representative movie theaters from all of the different eras will be saved and restored to show the future what 20th Century movie theaters were like. And while we're trying to save movie palaces from the 1910s and 1920s, and neighborhood theaters from the 1930s and 1940s, let us not forget the theaters of the last half of the century. It may be too late for the 1960s theaters. There is not a single one of the beautiful, big 1960s theaters left intact in the Baltimore area.[13] We can still save a representative theater of the 1970s, 1980s and 1990s. Are any worth saving? Certainly one or two of the multiplexes or megaplexes are worth saving, if only to compare them as quaint ancestors to whatever the 21st century may bring. Perhaps the Campus Hills for the 1970s, the Security Square 8 for the 1980s, and Hoyt's West Nursery 14 for the 1990s.[14]

I hope we have learned from past mistakes and blindness. As the new century unfolds, we must make our voices heard above the clamor of those irresponsible people who would ravage our movie heritage. The movie theater is an important part of the social and cultural history of America. Theaters deserve equal protection.

II
Baltimore Area Theaters by Name

Entrance to Electric Park

This is a listing of movie theaters and other theaters where moving pictures have been shown. No attempt is made to list every venue where movies have been shown. Each theater is described under its earliest name even if it were better known under a later name. Each write-up contains the name of the venue, the address, dates of operation, architect, and seating capacity as well as, in most cases, a description and an historical narrative. Dates given in parentheses are estimates. Numbers in brackets { } are used to distinguish among theaters with the same name. Numbers not in brackets are part of the theater's name, e.g. Rotunda 1-2. An asterisk preceding the name of a theater indicates that that theater was never completed.

Abbey Lane (see Lane)

Academy of Music, 516 North Howard Street, 1875–1927, J. Crawford Neilson, Baldwin & Pennington (of 1893 remodeling), J. D. Allen (of Philadelphia, of 1896 remodeling); c. 1,800 (main auditorium), 1,200–1,400 (concert hall). The first theater at 516 North Howard Street was the Academy of Music, which opened in January 1875. Designed "to compare favorably with any grand music hall in the world," the Academy of Music was a large Romanesque multi-purpose theater filling a lot 120 by 250 feet. It cost an estimated $460,000. The facade rose 100 feet above the grand entrance on Howard Street. Arched doorways led into a marble-lined hall. Adjacent to this hall was a café. Two grand stairways led up to a combination concert hall and lecture room on the second floor. The hall had a folding floor that could be laid down to convert it into a ballroom. Further on, the entrance hall led to the center and rear of the building occupied by the main auditorium or Grand Opera House with a stage that measured 80 by 75 feet with a depth of 36 feet. The fire curtain featured an idyllic scene of pleasure boats on Lake Como painted by Philadelphia artist Russell Smith for $2,800. The box-circle was arranged into two rows of boxes with four seats and rows of single seats. In the center of the opera house was a crystal dome from which hung a huge chandelier containing 240 candle-shaped lights and 994 crystal chains. The opera house walls were traced in gilt. It seated about 1,800; 750 in the orchestra, 464 in the balcony, and 600 in the gallery. The building was heated by steam. The original lighting system used gas lamps, but by 1895 the interior was illuminated by 2,000 16-candle-power electric lights.

The opening of the Academy of Music was celebrated with a grand ball and concert on the evening of January 5, 1875. The front of the theater was brilliantly lit by 25 globe lights; inside more than 1,500 gaslights provided illumination. The doors opened at 7:30, and the crowd of about 1,200 guests strolled in to music provided by the U.S. Marine Band. H. M. Jungnickel's 40-piece orchestra played dance music in the main auditorium. Supper rooms opened at 10:00 P.M. The best champagnes were available at $2.50 a bottle. Tickets were expensive, $10 per couple.

President Grant had been invited to the opening, but he was unable to attend. Distin-

Multiple boxes, elaborate wall decorations, and the famous painting of Lake Como made the Academy of Music one of Baltimore's most impressive theaters. (Photograph courtesy of the Maryland Historical Society, Baltimore, Maryland)

guished invitees from Baltimore, Philadelphia, New York, Richmond, New Orleans, and Washington did attend the "successful and brilliant inauguration."

The opening was notable for the beautiful women and their outfits. As one newspaper wrote, "The private boxes, stalls, loges and chairs bloomed with beautiful ladies in full evening dress. Toilettes were conspicuous everywhere. Belles were numerous—there were a hundred belles of the evening. The style of dressing showed due appreciation among the ladies of the inauguration event, and gave it éclat. There were many décolleté toilettes; there were some powdered coiffures; all dresses were *en train* with colors generally of delicate, tasteful shades and modes, of the prevailing clear-cut Grecian style."[1] The first public attraction at the theater was the opera *Lucia Di Lammermore* on the night of January 7. The reviewer for the *Baltimore American* was impressed by the crowd and by the theater's excellent acoustics.

During its 52-year lifetime, the Academy of Music was one of Baltimore's premier theaters, hosting such diverse attractions as the weightlifter Sandow, health lecturer Bernarr McFadden, noted actors Sir Henry Irving and Otis Skinner, Sarah Bernhardt, Julia Marlowe, and Maude Adams, lecturer Thomas Huxley, the D'Oyley Carte Gilbert and Sullivan operetta company, early Biograph movies, stage productions of Klaw & Erlanger and Charles Frohman, the Ziegfeld Follies, and the Imperial Russian Court Balalaika Orchestra. Irving declared that the Academy of Music was the most spacious and attractive playhouse in which he had acted during his American experience. For approximately the last 20 years of its existence, the Academy of Music alternated its productions between vaudeville and legitimate shows.

The theater changed hands several times. It was organized in March 1870 by a group of local men that included Dr. J. Hanson Thomas, Israel Cohen, William T. Walters, W. F. Frick, and J. Hall Pleasants. In 1887 it was leased to Patrick Harris. Harris joined with his brother-in-law, R. L. Britton, and Tunis F. Dean in 1890 to run the theater. In 1893, the building was extensively remodeled. Electric lights replaced gas in the lobby chandelier and the entire front portico was illuminated around the border by strings of incandescent lights. The offices to the right of the entrance were replaced by a ladies' reception room and a confectionery stand. Inside, the auditorium and the boxes were hung with pale blue tinsel armure of colonial design. The new asbestos drop curtain featured a picture of Baltimore Harbor painted in New York by Milton C. Slemmer.[2] Harris, Britton & Dean operated the Academy of Music until they lost their lease in 1895. In 1896, the powerful Nixon and Zimmerman[3] theatrical syndicate gained control of the theater for $12,000 a year, and remodeled it during that summer. The new owners had the theater gutted, leaving only the four walls and roof. The *Baltimore American* reported on the remodeling:

> The entire building has been frescoed, from the most obscure dressing-room to the very topmost part of the dome—fresco work of the most exquisite character and such a blending of bright tints as to produce a scene of fairyland, The dome is a work of art.... The Italian artist devoted six weeks to this part of the fresco-work, and the result is a picture worthy of a place in Walters' Art Gallery.
>
> The coloring all through the house is delicate, yet of sufficient warmth to make the general effect cozy. The proscenium arch has received some of the most artistic touches to be seen anywhere in the building. One of the most conspicuous changes is the elimination of the great chandelier, and ... of the glass dome which formerly covered so much space ... in its present shape the entire ceiling is unobstructed, and one beautiful picture after another fills the space and charms the eye. Figure painting, which is the most difficult of all work of this character, is seen here in life-size poses and with striking naturalness. Garlands of flowers and wreaths are intermingled here and there between the figures and the whole effect is beautiful.... In the rear of the lower floor, popularly known as the orchestra circle, five rows of chairs have been removed and the space ruled off as a promenade or for standing room.... The aisles have been widened ... and will admit of four people walking abreast.... Persons can now pass to their seats without disturbing those already seated, and the chairs in themselves, made as they were expressly for the firm are perfect cradles of rest.[4]

The number of box seats was increased from six to 12 and the number of seats on the lower floor was reduced from 1,057 to 700. The *Sun* waxed lyrical describing the new theater.

> Richly blended tints of white, ivory and pink salmon prevail in the decorations, which, with the remodeled interior, are after the French Renaissance. Six roomy and attractive boxes are on each side of the proscenium arch. A rainbow effect is worked out on the balconies, which, under the glow of electric lights shedding their rays through globes cut with the French fleur de lis is quite unique. The dome is artistic. Literature, Tragedy, Comedy and Music are represented by figures of young women, while garlands and cupids enhance the ornamentation. The curtain represents the "Court of Love." Frank Simra of Philadelphia was the artist.[5] Roomy aisles and an inner foyer, adding much to the comfort of the audience, were secured by sacrificing many seats. The new seats are large and are finished in maroon-colored corduroy velvet.[6]

The remodeled theater opened with John Philip Sousa's comic opera *El Capitan*, starring popular De Wolf Hopper, on September 28, 1896. Many well-known theatrical people attended this performance, including Nixon and Zimmerman, Daniel Frohman, Marc Klaw, and Abraham Erlanger. Among the improvements introduced in the theater in the summer of 1901 was an innovative stage feature. This was a 32 × 34-foot area of floor in the middle of the stage to replace the traps which formerly had to be cut for each show. Custom traps could be prepared for each show by simply rearranging the movable joists under this area of floor.

In 1902, a new lobby entrance to the main auditorium was constructed. In the summer of 1904, the Academy of Music was completely rewired. The building required 3,000 incandescent lights distributed over 244 circuits and 41 fused panel boards. There were about 1,300 lights on the stage. The border and footlights were composed of red, white, and blue lamps, each color on a separate dimmer. There were five sets of border lights, each containing 120 lamps. Klaw & Erlanger began producing shows for the theater in 1907, but Nixon and Zimmerman continued to hold the lease. The original drop curtain featuring the painting of Lake Como by Russell Smith was restored by local artist Milton

C. Slemmer during alterations to the theater in the summer of 1907. The theater was completely refurnished in 1911. The *Sun* reported on the improvements:

> The improvements inside the theater are complete. The lobby windows are draped in old rose silk, while the balcony and lower floor have been supplied with large new chairs like those in the Metropolitan Opera House.... Red velvet carpets cover the floors, foyers, and stairways, and a new electric plant has been installed.
>
> One improvement is a new smoking room on the lower floor.... This is a comfortable lounging room and will afford a delightful change from the former smoking room in the basement. There is also a handsome ladies' room on the main foyer. All the doors have been supplied with the latest modern exit appliance making it one of the safest theatres in the country. The employees will be uniformed and there will be girl ushers.
>
> The color scheme on the boxes is white and gold, while the walls are paneled in old rose damask silk. The chairs in the boxes are after the style of those used in the palm room at the Plaza Hotel, New York. Instead of the steps in the orchestra circle leading to the orchestra chairs, they have been supplanted by an incline or runway after the style of the Nixon Theatre, Pittsburgh.... Beautiful new chandeliers adorn the lobbies and the foyers.[7]

The remodeled theater reopened with *The Pink Lady* on September 30, under the management of Tunis F. Dean. In 1921 Sam S. & Lee Shubert, Inc. acquired the property, and when the lease expired two years later, they paid Nixon and Zimmerman approximately $500,000. In the spring of 1925, arrangements were made between Fred C. Schanberger and the Shuberts to pool the interests of the Academy of Music and the Auditorium. The former theater would be used for grand opera and symphony concerts while the latter theater would continue regular Shubert bookings. The theater columnist for the *Daily Post* called the Academy of Music an "emergency house," a theater that got shows that had to play a week in Baltimore, if all the other theaters were booked.[8] The Shubert organization sold the Academy of Music to the Stanley-Crandall Company in March 1926. The end came that same year. Most of the theater was demolished, and the Stanley opened on the site the following year. During the demolition, nearly $100 in change was found among the old seats.

Many of the most important theatrical stars in the country and world played the Academy of Music. Sarah Bernhardt appeared there in 1882. Henry Irving made his only visit to Baltimore there in 1883. Lily Langtry, Edwin Booth, Joseph Jefferson, Nat Goodwin, and Madam Modjeska also appeared at the Academy of Music. Opera singers who sang there included Patti, Christine Nillson, Melba, and Emma Abbott. One source claims that John Charles Thomas made his professional debut in the show *Her Soldier Boy* at the Academy in 1916.[9] Several early movie exhibitions were held at the Academy of Music. There was a Centograph exhibition in October 1896, a Biograph exhibition in January 1898, and in October 1905 an exhibition of the Britt–Nelson prizefight.

When word of the demolition was announced, the *Sun* received a letter signed "Old-Timer" who suggested one last memorial performance with some of the performers who had appeared at the Academy of Music. The writer said, "We would all like to see the Lake Como curtain rise and fall once more." *Daily Post* critic T. O. Head praised the Academy of Music and regretted its passing in his column of March 22, 1926:

> The seats were designed for men whose legs did not stop at the knee, and they were comfortable. The shape of the house was excellent for acoustics, and there was a spaciousness that is not often found in theaters. The stage was large enough for almost anything that was desired and — oh, it was just plain nice and comfortable and satisfactory.... It was a great old theater in its time.... I liked it.

Aero, 1417 Fuselage Avenue, Middle River, 1942–1977, Skidmore, Owings & Merrill, c. 660. The Aero was located in the Aero Shopping Center built by the Glenn L. Martin Company.[10] It was a large, barn-like theater with a small lobby and an unusual auditorium where the side walls leaned inward. The lights on the sidewalls were in the shape of the Glenn L. Martin Company logo. It opened, under the management of Edward F. Perotka, on May 30, 1942, with *The Gold Rush* starring Charlie Chaplin and a special feature entitled *Cavalcade of Aviation*. The first ad in the *Evening Sun* on June 26, 1942, was for the *Corsican Brothers* with Douglas Fairbanks, Jr. Perotka's Victory Theater Company purchased the theater and shopping center in 1948. Later it was operated by the Vogel Circuit, which closed it on July 1, 1977. Soon after it closed, it was reopened for an unsuccessful stint as a live venue for country music. The theater and strip shopping center have been replaced by a supermarket.

Airdome, Irvington, c. 1912. A series of letters to the *Sun* in the spring of 1912 indicates that an open-air theater was operating in a back yard in Irvington around that time and arousing some local opposition.[11]

Airdome, corner of Mullikin Street and Mullet Court. The Red Fox Amusement Company was granted a permit for an open-air moving picture theater in March 1915 at this location, which had been a large vacant lot in 1914. It is not known whether the theater actually opened.

Airdome, Division and Presstman Streets, c. 1915. There was an African-American open-air theater at this location in the summer of 1915.

Airdrome, 300 block York Road, south of Pennsylvania Avenue, Towson, 1915. This open-air theater opened on July 3, 1915 and lasted until the middle of August. According to the *Jeffersonian* of August 28, 1915, the proprietor packed up and left leaving unpaid bills behind him. The theater was reportedly doing good business the month before it closed.

Aladdin, 930–932 West Baltimore Street, 1908–(1938), Otto G. Simonson (of 1915 remodeling), J. F. Dusman (of 1933 remodeling), c. 250, increased to 499 in 1915. The Aladdin was begun around October 1908 when James W. Bowers, Jr. planned an $8,000 moving picture theater at 930–932 West Baltimore Street. In March 1909 a man named Friedman was planning a $12,000 moving picture theater at 926–928 West Baltimore Street. Bowers won out. He was granted a permit to convert the building at 930–932 West Baltimore Street into a movie house in August 1909. The Aladdin opened in late 1909. William Bamberger acquired it in 1915 and planned to improve the theater with a one-story 49 × 40-foot addition for $6,000. The remodeled theater opened on December 20, 1915. The seating capacity was nearly doubled and a new stage installed. Bamberger's wife managed the theater and, according to *Motion Picture News*, "through her able management of it the business has been built up from a losing proposition to a very profitable investment."[12]

In 1916, the Investment Company of Maryland purchased the theater for about $10,000, considered a higher than usual price for a small neighborhood house. The theater changed hands again in April 1916. J. Louis Rome reopened it on January 13, 1917. Apparently it was open for only about a month. Newton R. Henderson took it over, made $2,000 worth of improvements, and reopened it on June 23, 1917. Graul's orchestra played for the reopening. The Aladdin was acquired by C. E. Nolte's Greater Baltimore Theater Company in April 1918. It closed for renovations during the summer of 1922. A new owner, Harry Morstein, who also operated the Queen Theater, acquired it in early 1927. He reopened it as an African-American theater that March. The New Aladdin advertised motion pictures and vaudeville. It was called the New Queen in 1930, and apparently closed for several years around that time. It reopened as the Booker T on October 19, 1933, and continued under that name until about 1938 when its doors closed for good. The building, drastically remodeled, was standing as of the early 1990s.

Albaugh's (see Lyceum {1})

Alcazar (see Arcadia)

Aldine (see Pictorial)

Alert (see Elektra {2})

Alhambra (see Crystal)

Alpha, 725 Frederick Avenue, Catonsville, 1928–1961, Joseph Henry Steinacker, possibly John J. Zink (of 1938–39 remodeling), 625 (later 547). Elmer Cashmeyer and Robert E. Kanode opened the Alpha. A local architect designed the Alpha and local builders, Ammenhauser Brothers & Raab, built it. The original Alpha had a front with three sets of double doors and a decorative arch above them. There were two retail spaces on either side of the entrance. The name was spelled out at the top of the arch. It opened on Thursday, March 1, 1928. Music was provided by Stanley Bowsil on the "Kilgen Wonder Organ."[13] Soon after it opened, it was taken over by Oscar Coblenz and his son. It was remodeled in 1938 and 1939 for nearly $20,000. The remodeled front kept the two retail spaces — the one on the east side of the entrance was an Arundel Ice Cream Store — but the rest of the facade was completely redone. A triangular marquee with neon lighting and the name Alpha spelled out in large letters on the top of either side was added, and the simple arch was replaced by an art deco tower topped with the name Alpha and illuminated by neon. Mr. Coblenz Jr. operated the the-

Drawing of the original front of the Alpha Theater (725 Frederick Avenue, Catonsville) designed by Joseph Henry Steinacker.

ater in association with the Hicks organization from 1939 until 1960; it closed down the following year. Coblenz and Hicks at one time leased the Westway at North Bend and ran it in tandem with the Alpha. They split product between the two theaters.

For many years, the Alpha was the only theater in the greater Catonsville area. The seats in the Alpha were the hard, wooden-backed kind. Downstairs there was a small bowling alley with 11 lanes that predated the Alpha; the thunder of the balls could be heard during the movies. The tiny rest rooms were located adjacent to the bowling alley. The theater building has been extensively remodeled. It was used by a sporting goods store, and an archery range was set up in the auditorium.

Am (see American)

*Ambassador {1}, 1803–1809 North Charles Street. The Ambassador Theatre Company, incorporated in 1921 by Harry E. Karr, Jacob W. Hook, Bernard Depkin Jr., Carl Fenhagen, and Theophilus White, planned this 1,600-seat theater. The cost was estimated at $150,000–$200,000. Revised plans by Thomas W. Lamb in early 1922 called for a $500,000 theater with a roof garden and ballroom. The company applied for a building permit in March 1922, but the project was canceled.

*Ambassador {2}, west side of Fulton Avenue, south of Pennsylvania Avenue. Charles Raith was granted a permit to construct a 2,500-seat Italian Romanesque theater for movies and vaudeville in March 1926. The architects were Clyde N. and Nelson Friz. It would cost $1,250,000. New plans were announced in 1928, but the project was soon abandoned for lack of funds. In May 1921, August Malthan had Otto G. Simonson prepare plans for a $150,000 theater near this same location.

Ambassador {3}, 4604 Liberty Heights Avenue, 1935–1968, John J. Zink, 925. Durkee Enterprises and the Rome organization battled in the City Council for a year over the permit to build the Ambassador. Finally, in January 1935, the council passed the bill, and Durkee's supporters won. The Rome organization had opposed the new theater because they had a half interest in the Gwynn Theater across the street from the proposed site. There was also some opposition from local homeowners. The Ambassador opened on September 18, 1935, with *Page Miss Glory* starring Marion Davies and Dick Powell. The opening ceremonies featured addresses by Governor Harry Nice and Mayor Howard Jackson. Frank Durkee was lavish in his praise of his new theater:

> It gives me great pleasure to witness the completion of the Ambassador Theatre and its dedication to the amusement of the people of Baltimore. I say, advisedly, "dedicated to amusement," for laughter and enjoyment are undeniably part of our birthright. It was this thought that first inspired the design of the Ambassador. The Ambassador Theatre is the realization of an ideal, a crowning achievement, for no city in the world has a more modern,

The 1938 front of the Alpha Theater, designed by John Zink, featured lots of neon and a waterfall effect.

more luxurious, or more perfectly conceived theatre. The Ambassador offers a standard of comfort unknown even 10 short years ago—a magnificence of interior that is equal to that of any theatre in the world. If the people of Baltimore derive enjoyment and pleasure from the Ambassador to the extent we believe they will, then our ambitions will have been fully realized.

The Ambassador, the twentieth Durkee house, was indeed a beautiful theater. It was built by E. Eyring and Sons. The facade, of beige glazed bricks, featured a tall vertical tower. Originally, the Ambassador had a canopy that led from the street to the marquee overhang; there were small shrubs on either side of the canopy. Inside, there were a lounge, cosmetic and rest room for the ladies and smoking room for the men. A soundproof nursery was located on the second floor. Architect John Zink prepared a description of the theater for *Motion Picture Herald*.[14]

Entrance Area

The ticket office is of the attached type and its facing is of black Vitrolite on which designs have been sand-blasted. This black Vitrolite is set in highly polished aluminum sash bars. In the center is an octagonal panel of clear plate glass through which the speaking and dispensing holes have been cut. The cornice of the office is made of three lines of neon tubes of blue set in metal channels. The base is of verde antique marble.

On either side of the ticket office are sets of double entrance doors with plate glass panels

John Zink's most perfect theater, the beautiful Ambassador (4604 Liberty Heights Avenue, 1935–1968) in a 1949 photograph showing the protective canopy in place.

ornamented with sandblasted designs.... On each of the one-story wings adjoining the entrance section the poster frames have been installed.... Under and in front of these display frames have been placed provisions for plants.... In front of these evergreen beds are circles ... for plants.

The round-ended protrusions over the one-story wings conceal the stairs to the nursery and, on the other side, to the projection department....

The attraction board section of the marquee is made of removable raised glass letters illuminated from behind in the usual manner, Over the center of the front attraction board is the name of the theatre made of reversed channel letters with neon tubes of red behind them illuminating a recessed background. Other parts of the marquee signs are of blue neon tubes, and the monogram is of green tubes. The vertical sign consists of three line red neon tube letters on a black background.... The cap and marginal lines are of blue neon tubes, as are also the tubes running up the front on the right. At the top of the tower supporting the vertical sign are light beacons in amber color.

Behind the four recesses over the center portion of the front are colored lights, throwing blue, red, green, and amber reflections against the walls. All display lighting on the front is continuous, no flashers having been used.

Foyer Area

Approximately 5 feet behind the front doors is another set of doors forming a small vestibule. The foyer runs through full two stories in height. The floor is laid with a perforated rubber mat in sections, thus forming a protection to the carpeted floors of the auditorium. The base, to the top of the doors, is of Marsh Marble, the joints of which are of polished aluminum. The marble is of black and gold. Above the doors the walls are of plaster, and the relief ornamentation is of plain Celotex boards, cut and grooved. At either end of the foyer is a large sandblasted plated glass panel, protected on the outside with wire glass. The standee posts are finished with cast aluminum trimmings. At the right of the foyer, on entering, is a reception room with a fireplace equipped with electric logs.... The floor of this room is of marble tile. Easy chairs, tables and

Despite the seeming flatness of the floor, the Ambassador had excellent sightlines and was a perfect place to see movies.

lamps compose the furniture and are in the modernistic style.

The projection room ... is 40 feet long and 12 feet deep.... The nursery is 24 feet long and 14 feet deep....

Auditorium

The auditorium floor gives the appearance of being level, since both the floor of the rear area and that in front of the proscenium are on the same elevation. However, the floor slopes to the center from both, providing safe access to the seats. For greater comfort and accessibility the rows have been set 34 inches from back-to-back. The seats are air-cushioned as are also the backs.... Each of the our emergency exits are provided with a separate vestibule by which the afternoon light, seeping through cracks between the double doors is entirely eliminated.... Over the two exits near the stage there has been arranged a balcony effect. Between the back wall of each recess and the front is a perforated ornamental plaster grille. Behind these and through the openings a variable lighting effect has been installed, while on the front a contrasting effect is provided. The stage itself is formed in steps. Footlights are provided between the pedestals, and the pedestals conceal colored floor lights.... The curtains, valences, legs, etc. are of high-nap plush and are lined. The sidewalls of the auditorium have been lined with Acousti-Celotex in decorative combination with plain and ornamental Celotex.... Lighting effects on the sidewalls have been produced by chromium brackets, each of which contains three colors in addition to the emergency light. The ceiling effects are obtained through louvres set at certain angles for diffusing the various colors.

When the plans were filed in April 1934, the cost of the theater was estimated at $45,000. Durkee added new reclining seats in the spring of 1956. In February 1963, the Ambassador became a

The AMC megaplex, adjacent to the Mall in Columbia, Maryland, opened in late 2003.

first-run theater, one of the first outside downtown, with its showing of *Two for the Seesaw*. The Ambassador remained in the Durkee circuit until they sold it in October 1968. The last movie at the Ambassador was *The Fox* on October 8, 1968. The building is still standing; it has been used as a dance hall and school. The Ambassador was one of the best theaters in which to watch a movie in Baltimore; the seats were comfortable and the sight lines were excellent. In 2004, an organization was formed to restore the Ambassador as a movie theater.

AMC Columbia 14, The Mall in Columbia, 2003–present. AMC opened this 14-screen megaplex adjacent to Columbia Mall on December 17, 2003. Among the opening features was the blockbuster *Lord of the Rings: The Return of the King*.

American, 941 Pennsylvania Avenue, (1921)–(1929), 250–300. This theater was built for Kalem Flaks around 1921 in a remodeled store. The permit, issued in early December, called for converting the building into a theater 20 feet wide at one end, 33 feet wide at the other, and 140 feet long. A year later, Louis Ulman got a contract for $5,000 alterations to the theater for the Rosen Candy Company next door. It was occasionally referred to by its abbreviated name, Am. In the spring of 1924, Abraham Rosen was granted a permit to conduct an open-air theater surrounded by 15-foot-high brick walls behind the American. The entrance was through 941 Pennsylvania Avenue. Lights were hung from the walls. The theater could seat 1,000 patrons on new benches. There was also a stage with dressing rooms underneath.[15] Among the opening attractions at the theater was a former heavyweight prizefighter named Sandow, who planned to lift a seven-passenger touring car, filled with people, with his teeth. The *Afro-American* claimed that Rosen's theater was the only airdome for African Americans in the city.

The hardtop theater was extended back to Pear Street, taking in the former open-air theater in the fall of 1924. It reopened on October 17, 1924. A four-piece orchestra accompanied the movie. The American advertised double seating capacity and complete lighting, heating and ventilating systems all under cover. Around 1925, the theater was taken over by the Flaks organization, which changed the theater's name to Lincoln Number Two, to distinguish it from the other Lincoln. It closed around 1929, but the building lasted until it was demolished before 1969.

Amusea {1}, 414–416 East Baltimore Street, 1907–c. 1965, Louis Levi (of 1906 building), A. Lowther Forrest (of 1914 remodeling), 75 (later 275, 375) The Amusea {1}, one of the earliest movie houses in Baltimore, was the converted first floor of a store on the north side of East Baltimore Street. It was leased by Pearce and Scheck for $3,250 a year in January 1907 after they vacated their movie house at 404–406 East Baltimore Street. At first, they presented only movies and illustrated songs, but refined vaudeville was added in August 1908. The shows ran from 11:00 A.M. to 11:00 P.M. The projection booth, like most booths in early movie houses, was very small and had a low ceiling. For many years the booth had no air conditioning, and the temperature in it could reach 100°. The popular strongman, Cameroni, hanging by his teeth, slid down a wire from the Munsey Building 1,000 feet to the roof of the Amusea in 1911.

In 1913, the shows consisted of one reel and were changed daily. In December 1914, architect A. Lowther Forrest prepared plans for remodeling the Amusea with a new front and lobby, new seats, and a new heating and ventilating system. The name was changed to Clover in January 1915 when the theater reopened. In 1920 the seating capacity was increased by 100 seats by removing the emergency hallway exit and building new exits at the rear. A new screen, indirect lighting system, and pipe organ were added and a sloping floor replaced the former level one. The Clover operated well into the 1970s. Between the mid-1920s and the late 1940s, the Clover was operated by the Livingston family.

It was a place where the unexpected often happened. Striptease shows held there were routinely raided. The proprietor and three performers were fined for putting on a show that was too "peppy" in November 1928. Police raided the Clover in September 1935, arresting the chorus girls, actors, and ticket seller for providing an indecent show and also rounding up about 25 boys between ages 14 and 19 who were in the audience. The theater was packed for the next performance, but "the gags were wholesome, the girls stuck strictly to a song-and-dance routine that was even more wholesome, and the audience soon sensed that burlesque wasn't what it used to be."[16]

In the early 1950s, a show at the Clover (and at the nearby Globe) consisted of two old movies and five or six "semi-amateur" strippers. A piano and drums provided music. According to Bernard Livingston, who grew up around the Clover and helped his father and mother run it, "Most of the strippers and chorus girls, who had come ... from ... West Virginia and Tennessee, ... had a strong sense of personal morality ... they stuck to one guy, sent money to their family and eventually got married." Livingston said that, "many girls envisioned it as a starting point for the theater."[17]

Amusea {2}, 225 North Eutaw Street, 1907–(1910), unknown, 125. This was another of the many Amusea theaters opened by Pearce and Scheck. The original building was converted into a movie house in the early summer of 1907. Some of the earliest uses of behind-the-screen-talkers in Baltimore were at this theater.

Amusea {3}, 35 West Lexington Street, 1907–(1914), Louis Levi, 114. Pearce and Scheck built this early theater in the spring of 1907. It was a one-story brick and stone building, 16'6" × 80' with an ornamental front covered with mirrors and a large, arched entrance finished in stucco and studded with electric lights. The cost was estimated at between $3,000 and $6,000. Pearce and Scheck ran it until the spring of 1909 when they sold it to the Flag Amusement Company. The new owners changed the name to Red Feather. Walter C. Hooper operated it, as the Alhambra, for a short while around 1910. It did a terrible business, and Hooper was forced to leave the city for his health. Hooper's sister, Mrs. Laura Talbot, remembered the mirrors on the front of the theater and the purple-liveried doorman. Hooper later operated a movie theater in York, Pennsylvania. The Spurrier Amusement Company took over the Alhambra in early 1911 and changed the name to the Lemon, apparently because of the awful business it did.

It was renamed again in May 1911 when it opened with another curious name, the White Dog. Despite an impressive opening that featured singers Charles Jefferson, Prof. J. Albert Loose,[18] Nick Weems, and child contralto Zella Jewell supported by Farson's Gwynn Oak orchestra, the White Dog did not last out the year. In the summer of 1911, there were plans to erect a four-and-a-half-story building on the site. In March 1912 there was a hosiery shop at 35 West Lexington Street, yet there appeared to be a theater there two years later. A 1914 advertisement reads, "The Lemon, 35 West Lexington Street, Superior Amusement Company operating theaters from coast to coast. R. J. Dawes, resident manager."[19] This was the last heard of this movie house.

Amusea {4}, 8030–8034 Main Street, Ellicott City, c. 1912–c. 1928. This theater was located on the fifth floor of a large building that is believed to date from the 1780s.[20] This building was variously used as a tavern, town hall, opera house and Yates' grocery store. The theater was used for minstrel shows and other types of entertainment. Opened by Edward A. Rodey, this theater was known as Rodey's Amusea and was operating as early as 1912. In 1921 it seemed to be used as much for dances as for movies. In 1922, W. S. Hoffman was running the theater. According to a description in a Historic American Building Survey, the "fifth floor is entirely taken up by a large stage, orchestra and balcony." By 1928, Charles Yates was the proprietor, M. L. Meade was the manager, and it was known simply as the Amusea Theatre.

Anderson's Picture Parlor (see Majestic {1})

Anthony, 103 South Main Street, Turner's Station, 1946–(1963), David Harrison, c. 600. Dr. Joseph H. Thomas, a prominent local physician and Realtor, built this theater in the African-American steelworker community of Turner's Station near Dundalk. The Anthony was named after Dr. Thomas' father. The one-story concrete and cinder-block building with brick facing cost an estimated $80,000. It had an asymmetric facade with the right third half a story higher than the left two-thirds. It opened on March 22, 1946. The first feature was *Dakota* starring John Wayne. The first manager was Robert R. Lee, who had been showing movies in churches and halls in Turner's Station before the war.

Apex, 110 South Broadway, 1942–present, Hal A. Miller, 640 (580 by 2003). The Apex was built by the Schwaber organization. It was constructed of material slated for a theater that Milton Schwaber had planned to build in Annapolis. There was some local resistance to the theater and, in March 1942, an injunction was sought by neighborhood residents and the operators of two existing theaters on South Broadway to block it. It opened on July 1, 1942, with *Remember Pearl Harbor*. Typical of other Schwaber-built theaters, also designed by Miller, the Apex was a rather plain, functional theater with a beige-face brick facade. Much of the original marquee and neon survive. The Apex has been operating as an X-rated film house for many years.

Apollo, 1500 Harford Rd., 1921–1981, Herbert C. Aiken, 1,300 (850 in orchestra, 450 in balcony; later 764). The Apollo Theater was opened on January 8, 1921 by the Apollo Theater Company (C. Constantine, president, and Leo H. Homand,

Apollo Theater (1500 Harford Road, 1921–1981, Herbert C. Aiken); the little store on the left sold ice cream and other items for patrons to carry into the theater in the days before concession stands.

The entrance to the Arcade (5436 Harford Road, 1928–1983, Oliver B. Wright) led back through an arcade to the theater's box office. The headquarters of the Durkee circuit was on the second floor.

secretary-treasurer). It cost about $175,000. The building measured 63 by 125 feet. The tall distinctive exterior of red and white terra cotta brick featured a facade dominated by six windows, three on each story, above the marquee with two smaller windows flanking each set, and ornamental limestone trim. The original interior colors were ivory and old rose with old rose draperies. The ceiling of the lobby was beautifully decorated with relief work of mythological scenes. There was also a balcony. The interior walls and ceilings have been covered with acoustic tiles and cloth. The original seating capacity was announced as 1,000, but while it was under construction in November 1920, this figure was increased to 1,300. William E. Stumpf, who was also operating the Good Time Theater, was the first manager. A two-manual Robert-Morton organ and a house orchestra provided music.[21] Miss Eva Rhinehart was the organist in 1924.

According to the Apollo's opening announcement, the theater had a Gold Fibre Screen and Powers Projection that guaranteed "soft, smooth, non-flickering pictures." For a number of years there was a small ice cream shop at the south end of the theater building. The interior of the Apollo was redecorated in November 1927 in pale blue and gold with large techstone panels. In June 1933, a new ventilation system was added, and the interior was repainted in cooler greens and blues. The Apollo was acquired by Morris Klein's State Theatre Corporation (later Rome Theaters) in May 1921, just a few months after it opened, for about $200,000; they operated it until 1981. One of the most successful movies ever shown there was *My Wild Irish Rose*. The Apollo was being used as a church in 2004.

Arcade {1}, 741–747 West Baltimore Street, (1909)–1913, Milton C. Davis (of 1909 remodeling). This building, originally known as China Hall, was said to have been built in 1840 and was the scene of many political and social gatherings. It was so named after the China store, which early in its history occupied the ground floor. For many years, China Hall was famous for its dancing school directed by, among others, Professors Spies, Farson, and Tuttle. Morris Lasky and C. E. Barry remodeled it into a movie house. The remodeled hall opened on February 5, 1910. A moving picture theater and stores were on the first floor. The second floor contained a large dance hall and six different lodges, and the third floor contained a banquet hall. Barry said that he had one of the finest dance halls south of New York. An Arcade Theater was operating at this address between 1910 and 1913. As of July 1923, the building was called Forresters' Hall; it was a four-story building containing three stores, a large ballroom and a number of lodge and meeting rooms on the upper floors. New buildings of the University of Maryland Medical School now occupy the site.

Arcade {2}, 5436 Harford Rd., 1928–1983, Oliver B. Wight, John F. Eyring (of 1949 remodeling), c. 1,000 (545 reported in 1972). The Durkee Organization opened the Arcade on May 18, 1928.[22] Its birth certificate was an October 1927 ordinance permitting the Community Company to erect a brick and steel building 160' long by 51' wide at 7 West Hamilton Avenue, with entrances on Harford Avenue and Hamilton Avenue, for the exhibition of motion pictures, vaudeville, and theatrical performances. The auditorium was located in a separate building at the end of a long corridor behind the Arcade Building, which has housed the headquarters of Durkee Enterprises since October 1928. The theater itself was fairly plain, but large; it seated nearly 1,000 on a single floor. The inaugural program contains a short, rather fanciful description of the Arcade: "In the rear of the Arcade one steps into a fairyland. The beauty and delicacy of the lobby treatments can hardly be described in mere words. The elaborate ceiling is most unusual and is a masterpiece of decorative art. From the lounging chairs to the unusual graceful doors, the entire effect is a veritable cymposium [sic] of art and beauty. In the rear of the theatre is a smoking room for gentlemen.... A luxurious lounge has been provided for the ... ladies. The auditorium holds a thousand comfortable chairs, and as an unusual feature, there has [sic] been placed lounge chairs (in the center of the auditorium) for the convenience of those that come early."

The Arcade had a Kilgen organ (Opus 4126). The Arcade {2} served the Hamilton area until 1972 when falling attendance prompted the Durkee organization to begin showing X-rated films. Faced with opposition from local business and church leaders, the Durkee leadership dropped the X-rated movies and began showing historical and educational films. Business jumped by 100 percent and the theater almost lasted out the decade.

The Arcade {2} closed in March 1979 after the final performance of *The Bermuda Triangle*. Local community organizations petitioned Durkee to reopen the theater. Durkee agreed and reopened the theater in December 1981 as a repertory house. That was a failure, and the theater closed again the following year. Bill Hewitt leased the Arcade in 1982 and 1983, but he had to close it in mid-1983. In May 1998, a group of students from Goucher College proposed several plans for recycling the Arcade. The marquee was removed in 2002.

Arcade Moving Picture Parlor (see Nowosci)

Arcadia {1} (see Majestic {1})

Arcadia {2}, 121 North Howard Street, 1908–(1916), unknown, 144. Sam Benjamin converted the penny arcade at 121 North Howard Street into the Arcadia in early 1908. It was renamed the Alcazar in January 1911 and lasted until 1916.

Argonne, 924–928 South Sharp Street, 1922–(1960), Edward J. Storck, 750. Wallace High acquired the property in the fall of 1921 and opened this African-American movie house on January 18, 1922. It was built for High by the Guilford Building Company and cost about $15,000; it was a one-story, 30 by 155 ft., brick theater. The facade was of ornamental, white-glazed brick. It had a small stage with a narrow, rectangular addition to the roof, apparently where scenery could be flown. The *Afro-American* gave this description of the new theater and its opening:

> Last Wednesday another, new theatre was added to the rapidly growing number of houses in the city that cater exclusively to colored patronage, when the Argonne on Sharp Street ... threw open its doors to the public.
> This latest house is a very worthy addition ... equaling ... the best that are now in opera-

tion. It is built substantially, with a high ceiling and is roomy in its seating arrangement which accommodate some 750 persons.

All the latest conveniences for the benefit of patrons have been installed and the latest operating devices for giving the best and most satisfactory exhibition of pictures. The house is owned by Mr. Wallace High (white) but with the exception of the camera operator, all the other employees are colored, namely, Moses Johnson, manager; Miss Lillian Mason, cashier; and an orchestra composed of Anthony Farrell, violinist; Edgar Gibson, piano; Wallace Jones, cornetist, and Frank Butler, traps.[23]

According to one source, the screen could be flown to allow access to the stage. There was a large room above the theater that was used as a pool hall, party room, and storage area. There were problems about the roof of the Argonne when it opened, and a temporary building permit had to be issued to allow a non-fireproof roof.[24]

In March 1922, the Argonne was advertising a beauty contest on Tuesday nights, country store on Wednesday nights, an amateur contest on Friday nights, and a pie-eating contest on Saturday nights. It became the Goldfield {2} or New Goldfield in 1926. Later, George Jacobs, who had worked for Rome Theaters, bought their interest in the Goldfield {1} and Goldfield {2} theaters. These two theaters served the African American community in South Baltimore, and it was common for patrons to come from as far away as Annapolis and Glen Burnie. Jacobs would start the evening shows late to give patrons a chance to get to the theater from distant locations in Anne Arundel County. The Goldfield {2} had stage shows from time to time, but they ceased in the 1940s. In the spring of 1925, a Charleston contest with $100 in prizes was held at the Goldfield. Chuck Richards appeared there a few times. The Goldfield {2} closed in the early 1960s. After being used as a church for several years, it was abandoned and later torn down.

Arlington {1}, 5202 Park Heights Avenue, 1914–1921, Fred E. Beall, unknown. In early 1914, Jacob Cohen had this one-story motion picture theater built. It was 23' × 100' and cost an estimated $5,000. The Cluster Amusement Company took over the Arlington in the spring of 1917. After it closed, around 1921, it was converted to a garage and later an auto supply company.

Arlington {2} (see Star {1})

Arrow, 808–810 South Conkling Street, 1913–1918, unknown, c. 350. The Arrow was operated by the Canton Amusement Company and built by E. Eyring and Sons; it opened with movies and vaudeville in the early spring of 1913. In March 1913, the management of the Arrow gave away a box of chocolates each night to the per-

The Glen Theater (43 Annapois Boulevard, Glen Burnie, 1929–1961) opened as the Art Theater in 1929. It was Glen Burnie's first real movie theater. (Photograph courtesy of the Archives of the Anne Arundel County Historical Society, Inc.)

son who held the lucky number on the stub of their admission ticket. The Arrow was for sale in February 1916. At that time the equipment in the theater included two Powers No. 6 projectors, 350 chairs, a piano, screen, box office, and electric fans. William E. Eyring, Sr., remembered that his father and uncle, Richard, took turns operating the projector at the Arrow. The building was still standing as of the mid-1970s when it housed the Eastern Industrial Clinic.

Art {1}, 43 Annapolis Boulevard at Crain Highway, Glen Burnie; 1929–1961, unknown, c. 500. Maurice Glick's Arundel Amusement Corporation opened the Art on August 31, 1929. Unspecified problems, probably related to the design of the building, caused the theater to be closed after only a few months. It was remodeled and reopened, as the Glen, under the management of J. Henry Gruver. New sound equipment was installed. New exits were created, and a new projection room was built within a fireproof concrete vault. The Glen opened on May 24, 1930. It was remodeled again in 1937. The Glen was a long, narrow theater; the auditorium connected to the lobby at a 45-degree angle. A fire damaged the theater in 1948, but it reopened that June completely remodeled and fireproofed. After it closed, the theater was extensively remodeled, but traces of the tiny box office still remain near the spot where the entrance was on Annapolis Boulevard.

Art {2} (see Three Arts)

Artmore Casino, 502–504 West Franklin Street, (1906)–(1922), unknown, unknown. This hall showed movies occasionally between about 1906 and 1922. It was also called the Traymore Casino or Traymore Amusement Garden. It was called the Traymore Casino in April 1909 when Charles R. Rosenbrock bought it. It was a saloon, cafe, and music hall at that time. In May 1914, M. V. P. Montgomery was granted a permit to convert the premises to exhibit movies, vaudeville, and theatrical performances. It was showing movies in 1916 when the operator was involved in a court case trying to break a lease that stipulated that the theater should not be used for African-American patrons. The court ruled against her.

Astor (see Poplar)

*****Astoria**, 2418–2428 Saint Paul Street. This three-story, $350,000, Italian renaissance theater was planned in mid-1924. The plans were being prepared by Lucius R. White, Jr., but the City Council denied the ordinance.

Auditorium {1} (see Walbrook)

Auditorium {2}, 508 North Howard Street, 1880–1986, possibly William Bruce Gray (Washington, of 1891 remodeling), J. B. McElfatrick & Sons (New York, of 1895 remodeling), Paul E. McClelland (of 1896 Palm Garden), J. D. Allen & Company (Philadelphia, of 1903 theater), E. Bernard Evander (of 1941 remodeling into Mayfair), Austin X. Dopman (of 1963 redecorating); 1,760 (as Auditorium), 850, later 783 (as Mayfair). Around 1880, an association called "The Natatorium and Physical Culture Association of Baltimore City" was formed by Dr. James A. Steuart and others. They selected a spot on North Howard Street, somewhat north of the main business district and built the Natatorium, a 60 by 244-foot bathing house and swimming school. The Natatorium opened on June 17, 1880. A contemporary ad described it as "...a hygienic agency, supplying with the most approved means, a source of healthful acquatic [sic] exercises, and furnishing instruction in the delightful and most necessary art of swimming."

After a promising opening, the Natatorium foundered, and in 1885 the building was acquired by the Oratorio Society. Five years later, James Lawrence Kernan, Confederate veteran, wealthy philanthropist, and theater man, acquired the building and, in January 1891, he announced his intention to convert it into a legitimate theater. Kernan first remodeled the building's interior.[25] He changed the name to the Howard Auditorium and reopened it on April 6, 1891. Quickly the name was shortened to "Auditorium"; it was called that for the next 49 years.

The lobby of the new theater was filled with wax statuary with De Munkacsy's famous "Christ Before Pilate" tableau in the center. On the left side of the hall was a Spa where mineral waters and soda were available. The opening attraction was Jules Levy's Great American Band with several solo singers.

Kernan was planning a new theater on the site of the Auditorium in the summer of 1893, but it took several more years before he was able to build it. The following spring, he converted the Auditorium into an "Ice Palace" for year-round skating. The skating floor was 50 by 150 feet, surrounded by seating on the main floor and gallery. An ice cave with dangling icicles replaced the stage. There were only six other ice palaces in the world in 1894.[26] The Auditorium

The present front of what's left of the Auditorium (508 N. Howard Street, 1880–1986) dates from 1903, when it was rebuilt from plans by J. D. Allen & Co. of Philadelphia.

ice palace was plagued with problems, notably the failure of the ice-making equipment to freeze the skating floor for opening day. At the same time that he opened the Ice Palace, Kernan opened a roof garden on top of the theater with an Oriental pagoda at one end and a promenade around the roof.

By the spring of 1895, Kernan believed that the Baltimore public wanted a first class family vaudeville theater, so he took steps to give them one. He hired New York theater architect J. B. McElfatrick to completely remodel the theater. The front was painted in Pompeii red-lined brick effects, and a portico was erected over the entrance. The facade was illuminated by powerful electric arc lights and a new sign, visible for several blocks, spelled out the name "Auditorium" with 600 alternating double-flash lights. The lobby was lined with white marble tiling. A contemporary newspaper account described it this way:

> The lobby ceiling is ... beautifully ornamented in gold, green and bronze designs, elaborated with ... cathedral glass, each design being surrounded by hundreds of tiny vari-colored electric lights in clusters, vines and trigonals. The lobby is divided into two ... sections. The first, extending from the main doorway, about twenty feet and separated from the main lobby by an ornamental automatic gate, will be an open vestibule. The front entrance and arch lobby transoms are finished in richly

designed beveled-plate cathedral glass, specially imported for the Auditorium.... To the right of the lobby is located the Crystal Reception Room, 25 × 45 feet ... it is called the Crystal Reception Room because its walls and ceilings are adorned with electrically lighted crystal chandeliers and fixtures.... To the left of the lobby are located the ladies' reception and retiring rooms, the manager's private office and the box office.... On entering the theater proper the real splendor of Manager Kernan's enterprise will be fully appreciated and enthusiastically admired. Not even a vestige remains to recall the interior of the old structure.... The transformation is ... complete.... The former ... hall-shaped appearance of the Auditorium no longer exists. It is now in every sense a handsome theater, with thoroughly theatrical aspect. About the first important improvement that catches the eye ... is the circular balustrade opening in the ceiling, which gives one an upward glance at the balcony promenade and conversazione on the second floor. This balustrade circle is finished in handsomely-ornamented stucco work and is encircled by one hundred electric lights.... A sterio-relief wainscoting, finished in majolica effects, extends around the lower wall of the theater, and also follows the course of the stairway leading to the balcony.... The theater ceiling and walls are beautifully frescoed, the prevailing tints are in cream, gold and green in Byzantine and Renaissance decorations elaborated by unique bronzings. There are twelve cardinal-throned proscenium boxes (three lower and three upper) each seating six persons. The boxes are embellished in soft green shadings and bronze ... lighted by three hundred tiny electric lights.

The elaborately-frescoed ceiling ... is studded by three hundred and ninety-six lights, which can be lessened to any number desired ... to produce dark effects in the house. The sloping ceiling of the orchestra circle is embellished with hundreds of small incandescent lamps designed in running vine and prong-shaped formations. The dimensions of the stage are 63 feet wide and 69 feet deep, with opening proscenium arch 32 feet wide and 30 feet high. The rear of the proscenium arch is circled with electric lights, by which shadow and light effects can be ... produced on the stage. A double row of white and green foot lights is also provided. There are six rows of border lights, comprising in all 300 incandescent lamps, the first and third rows being double. The entire electric system of the house, comprising 2,600 white-frosted and colored lights, is instantly regulated by two switchboards. The stage lights are controlled on the stage and the house lights in the box office. There are twelve dressing rooms....[27]

Kernan planned to adopt a New York innovation and employ uniformed women ushers in the theater. The remodeled Auditorium opened with The New York Vaudeville Club on September 30, 1895.

In less than a year, Kernan announced that he would remodel the theater again. Again, his first thought was to build a completely new theater on the site, and he turned to J. B. McElfatrick & Sons a second time for the plans. It was estimated that the new building would cost $150,000.

By July 1896, Kernan had scaled back his plans. He converted the Auditorium into a concert hall and added a second floor with a roof garden and a palm garden, connected to the dress circle, where spectators could watch the performance and have refreshments at the same time. At the entrance to the palm garden were four large, soft green, scagliola columns. The front wall of the theater was raised thirty feet and the dress circle was extended to make room for the garden. In one corner of the garden, a Hungarian orchestra played during intermission and before and after the performance. Broad oak stairways led from the Palm Garden to the roof garden. Improvements in the main auditorium included a new $1,500 drop curtain featuring a copy of Maignan's "The Parting of Hector and Andromache," painted by the Lee Lash Company of Philadelphia.

The remodeled Auditorium opened on October 5, 1896. During the summer of 1897, Kernan gave double performances at the Auditorium. One performance was given inside the theater until 10:30; this was followed by one in the roof garden that lasted until midnight.

In December 1902 Kernan announced plans for the greatest entertainment complex ever built in Baltimore, the Million Dollar Triple Enterprise. He selected the Auditorium and the area adjacent to it for this complex of two theaters and a luxury hotel. The cornerstone of the Maryland Theater around the corner at Franklin and Eutaw Streets was laid on March 19, 1903, and seven months later that theater opened.

Plans called for a new theater on the site of the old Auditorium. The facade of the new building would be granite and white terra cotta with a mansard roof. The corridors and lobbies would be wainscoted eight feet high with Italian marble; the stairways would be of marble with bronze balustrades. Finishings around the boxes would be of polished brass with nickel rails and posts. The old Auditorium closed on April 4, 1903, and workmen began demolition within the week. The new Auditorium opened on September 12, 1904 with the William A. Brady production of *Foxy Grandpa*. Kernan called it "without question the coziest and prettiest theater of its size in America." A description of the $250,000 theater appeared in a local newspaper.

> The removal of the scaffolding of the Auditorium ... has revealed one of the handsomest theatre fronts in America. On a foundation of substantial granite rises a beautiful white terra-cotta structure, with wide arched doorway and windows, with graceful female figures on each side of the main entrance. The magnificent relief work and dainty ornamentation presents the acme of sculptural art and artistic designing.... The interior, with a seating capacity for 2,000 persons, will be truly a revelation in artistic beauty.... The prevailing shade will be green, ranging from dark at the bottom to lighter shades at the top, with dainty floral wreaths and festoons in pleasing profusion. Green marble columns will support the cantilever balcony and gallery, which will do away with uprights in positions where they would ... obstruct the view of the stage, which can be seen from every seat in the house. The hangings, tapestries, upholstery, furnishings and carpets will all be in ... shades of green, while opera chairs ... will give the extreme of comfort.... The floors of the lobby and foyer will be of the most expensive tiling and mosaic, laid in colored designs. The

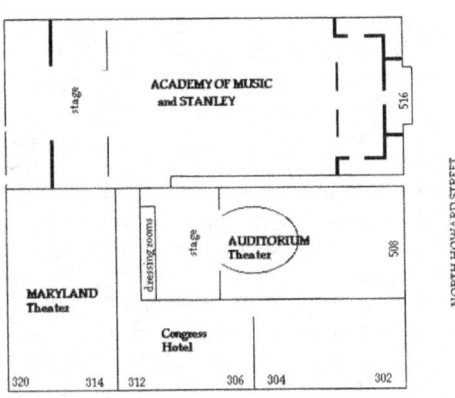

> exits number 30 ... making it possible to empty the house in less than five minutes ... 5,000 incandescent lights will illuminate [the theater] within and light up with resplendent brilliancy its white front.... On the stage the electrical effects will be dazzling, with a number of new features in illumination from the sides and top that have never before been used in a Baltimore theatre.... [The stage] is, from curtain line to back wall, 40 feet; width, 70 feet, and height to flies, 60 feet....[28]

On Christmas Eve 1904, Kernan opened the Turkish baths in the basement of the Auditorium.[29]

The grand opening of the Million Dollar Triple Enterprise took place on Monday, September 4, 1905. It was billed as "the greatest combination of buildings in the world." It was certainly the greatest combination of theatrical buildings in Maryland. Within the three buildings—the Auditorium Theater, the Maryland Theater, and the Kernan Hotel—there were 120 hotel rooms, a barbershop, a $50,000 Turkish bath, a rathskeller, an art gallery, an oriental banquet room, a billiard parlor, 3,600 theater seats, and a huge underground electrical generating plant called Machinery Hall. The two-story Machinery Hall, which was lined with glazed bricks, was located beneath the rathskeller and provided electricity for all three buildings. Four electric generators powered the 6,000 incandescent lights that illuminated the enterprise. Patrons could tour the hall and admire the white-uniformed mechanics and attendants operating the generators.

The opening show at the Maryland featured Keith's vaudeville—including the latest Kinetograph moving pictures—and the Auditorium presented Mason and Mason in the musical comedy *Fritz and Snitz*. Seats at both theaters sold for 15, 25, 50, and 75 cents. Vaudeville had been the regular fare at the Auditorium, but with the opening of the Maryland, vaudeville moved to the newer theater. The Auditorium became a house for "strictly high-class & refined" musicals and legitimate shows. It had a stage that was 20 feet deep with a proscenium opening 32 feet wide by 28 feet high. Ed Rollman conducted the nine-piece orchestra in 1907. The fire curtain reportedly featured a rustic scene with a young woman making eyes at a young man. It was taken down around 1915. According to longtime manager Leonard McLoughlin it was dreadful.

The management of the Auditorium was shared between Kernan and veteran theater manager, George W. Rife. An inspection by building inspectors in the spring of 1909 revealed that one of the theater's main wooden trusses that supported the gallery had rotted away from the wall causing the gallery to sag. Building Inspector Preston ordered the Auditorium closed until repairs could be made. At around the same time, the Auditorium was leased to the Shubert organization. The Shuberts had been trying to get a Baltimore theater for several seasons and

The dome and gallery of the Auditorium remained above the false ceiling of the Mayfair until the theater's roof collapsed in 1998.

had booked their shows intermittently at the Lyric and Lyceum. After Kernan died, in 1912, his close friend Frederick C. Schanberger became president of the Kernan theatrical interests. A bitter fight occurred in September 1913 when the newly merged Klaw-Erlanger organization and Shubert booking office signed an agreement by which their attractions would no longer be presented at the Auditorium, but would be moved to either Ford's Theater or the Academy of Music. According to the terms of the agreement, Ford and Samuel F. Nixon, owner of the Academy of Music, would assume the Shubert lease of the Auditorium, pay the $15,000 yearly rental to the Kernan Company, make repairs to the Auditorium, and rent it out. Schanberger disputed the whole arrangement, and declared the lease void. He leased the Auditorium to New England theater magnate Sylvester Z. Poli for his stock company at the end of September, and the Shuberts filed suit five months later.

The Poli Players lasted until June 1915. By 1918, everybody was back on friendly terms, and Schanberger arranged a five-year booking arrangement with the Shuberts. The Auditorium was to play all of the shows in Baltimore produced by the Shuberts, Al Woods, Elliott, Comstock, and Gest, and Selwyn and Company. The theater remained under the personal direction of Schanberger with Leonard B. McLaughlin as business manager. Facilities for showing movies—presumably a permanent projection booth—were added to the Auditorium in the fall of 1915. One evening in November, 1926, during the opening performance of the play *One of the Family*, as the players were complaining about a storm and shaking their raincoats, a 15-foot square section of the ceiling fell on the gallery. No one was injured, but, after the act had finished, Grant Mitchell, a member of the cast remarked that something had apparently brought the house down.

During most of the 1920s and 1930s, the Auditorium presented stock shows, with such greats as Marie Dressler, Marjorie Rambeau, Henry Hull, Spencer Tracy, and Pat O'Brien, as well as occasional movies. In January 1929, Spencer Tracy was paid $300 a week for his role in *Excess Baggage*; Pat O'Brien received $175. In the summer of 1929, the Auditorium was redecorated and wired for sound. It reopened on September 14, 1929, with two-a-day movies and a large orchestra—conducted by Mischa Guterson—accompanying them.

After a few shows the theater went dark. An attempt was made at this time to lease the Auditorium as a supplementary house to the New, but that fell through.[30] The Auditorium did not reopen until early November. It was on thin ice again by early 1932. Some said it was brought on by the kind of pictures it played or that the owners did not give movies enough chance to catch on there. Mortgage foreclosure and receivership proceedings were instituted against the Kernan interests, including the Auditorium and Maryland Theaters and the Kernan Hotel in March 1932. The court appointed receivers and a trustee to sell the properties. In July, the Penn Mutual Life Insurance Company of Philadelphia bought all three properties at auction for $225,000. By the late 1930s, a hodge-podge of legitimate shows, movies, political conventions, and lectures on cooking was not enough to keep the Auditorium open.

C. W. Hicks, who operated a chain of neighborhood theaters, acquired the Auditorium in the summer of 1940 for about $63,000. He commissioned local architect E. Bernard Evander to draw up plans for an extensive remodeling job which would result in a new theater for films within the shell of the older theater. Credit is due to Evander for the preservation of much of the original building, including the beautiful Beaux Arts facade. To create a new theater within, the old auditorium was gutted between the dressing rooms and the front entrance and between the first floor and the bottom of the second balcony. A new, false ceiling was installed just below the second balcony and a new proscenium for the screen was erected. A new floor was laid, and the lobby area was completely remodeled. Incredibly, the original ceiling, projection booth, second balcony, dressing room area, and basement were left virtually intact. On the exterior of the theater, the major changes were the addition of a massive modern marquee and the modernization of the entrance beneath it. The remodeling lasted from June 1940 to January 1941.

The new theater, called the Mayfair, opened on January 31, 1941 with *A Night at Earl Carroll's* starring Ken Murray. At that time, the Mayfair was the first theater in the country equipped with facilities to accommodate TV and the new third dimensional sound. It also featured "black light," an ultraviolet lighting system that illuminated designs on the carpet. The "airplane seats" were coral and green. The seat rows in the Mayfair were fairly close together, and the front row of a crossover aisle on the left side of the auditorium near the exit was one of the few places where people with long legs could sit comfortably. In December 1941, the Mayfair became a first-run theater with the Australian film *Forty Thousand Horsemen*.

Jack Fruchtman acquired the Mayfair in early September 1957. By 1960, it was equipped with 70mm equipment, and the seating had been reduced to 783. The theater was completely remodeled in 1963 for the Baltimore premier of *Lawrence of Arabia* that June. The front of the building, as well as the marquee and lobbies, were all redone. The inner lobby was paneled with polished walnut. A new curtain of tangerine red was installed, and the auditorium walls were covered with green and blue cloth. New, deep red carpeting was laid, and new glass box offices flanked the black-tiled front. The main entrance was formed of three large, circular doorways framed in gold-colored metal. Above the entrance was a marquee of back-lighted Plexiglas with a curved soffit of translucent panels.

The Mayfair operated as a movie theater until April 1986. It was offered for sale at an auction in May 1986, but the sale was canceled when bidders offered no more than $200,000 for the property. It has been boarded up since then, slowly disintegrating. The city acquired the building in 1987 and hired an architect to investigate renovating the theater, but that did not stop its decline. The Mayfair has become a victim of benign neglect and a dismaying lack of imagination. In 1993 there was a brief period of hope when the mayor announced a campaign to make Howard Street an "Avenue of the Arts" with a renovated Mayfair Theater as its northern anchor. This plan died quickly too. A roof collapse in 1998 has raised serious questions about the theater's preservation. We should say our good-byes to this historic old building soon; it cannot last much longer.

The Auditorium was important in Baltimore movie exhibition history because it provided an early inexpensive venue for movies. Beginning with a Kinematograph exhibition in November 1896, the Auditorium showed movies every year until 1900. Many of the early projectors—the Kineoptikon, Biograph, Cinematograph and Vitagraph—had exhibitions there with short-story films such as *Cinderella,* prize fights such as the Jeffries-Sharkey fight, and news films such as those of the Boer War in 1900.

Aurora, 7 East North Avenue, 1910–1984, Francis E. Tormey, 485 (303 after 1964 remodeling). Plans to build a motion picture theater were announced by Eugene Cook's Paradise Amusement Company in early 1910, and the Aurora opened on October 15, 1910. It cost between $15,000 and $25,000. A description of the Aurora appeared in the *Sun*.

> The building will have a frontage of 40 feet on North Avenue and will extend back 95 feet 6 inches to the rear ... it will be 35 feet high on the North avenue front, divided into two stories. The center of the first story front will be used as an entrance and lobby to the main auditorium. The interior will take up the entire height of the building having a seating capacity of about 500.... On the west side of the lobby will be a storeroom.... On the east side ... will be the entrance to the bowling alleys ... in the basement and also to a stairway leading to the billiard room on the second floor.... The North avenue front will be of a unique treatment, eliminating the general type of amusement building fronts. This will be constructed of tapestry brick, with a bronze effect harmonizing with the bronze finish of the copper bay windows, cornice, etc. A special feature of the front will be the heavy overhanging cornice, covered with a warm, rich red slate.[31]

There was also a very small balcony. A 2/8 Moller organ (Opus 2832) was installed in 1919. A new marquee was added to the theater in late 1920. In 1921, the Aurora was extensively remodeled. The auditorium and lobby were redecorated and repainted gray, old ivory, and gold. New maroon draperies were hung, and a new concrete floor was laid. A deep rose carpet was also installed. Blue and bronze poster cases and a box office were placed in the lobby, and a leaded art glass window was installed over the lobby entrance. This remodeling cost about $6,000. A new ventilation system installed in the summer of 1921 provided a cooler theater with a complete change of air every three minutes. A new electric sign and interchangeable electric board were installed in the fall of 1925.

The Aurora was redecorated again in November 1927. At that time, the interior was textoned throughout in old rose and old ivory with antique gold trim and matching new velvet carpets and draperies. New crystal lighting fixtures were also installed. A new marquee was installed in the spring of 1948. Rappaport Theaters acquired the Aurora in 1949 for $150,000. It passed into the JF organization in 1958 and became a first-run theater. It was remodeled in 1960 and reopened with *Psycho* on 20 July. In 1962, the Aurora, along with the other former Rappaport theaters, was leased to the Trans-Lux Corp. for 25 years. This arrangement lasted only two years. In the fall of 1964, the Schwaber organization bought the theater at auction and reopened it as the 7 East. They widened the aisles, reduced the seating capacity from 369 to 303 and added a new sound system.

Ten years later, Schwaber sold the theater, and in May 1974, it became a soft-core porn theater, the Cinema North or North Cinema. The grand opening of the North Cinema, on May 24, was interrupted when the vice squad arrived and arrested the manager for showing the film *Deep Throat* without the censor board's approval. The theater battled the censors throughout the late 1970s, and, in 1979, it was for sale again for $60,000. It was purchased by film buff Robert L. Brown, completely renovated, and reopened in November 1981 as a repertory house. Despite Brown changing the name back to Aurora, the theater lasted less than a year. Competition from the well-established Charles a few blocks away doomed it. In October 1982, the Aurora went back to showing X-rated films. It closed in 1984.

By 2003, the theater was being used as a church. About the only traces of the original theater are some lions' heads above the windows on the second floor.

Avalon, 4338 Park Heights Avenue, 1927–1963, Frederick A. Fletcher, c. 1,500. The Avalon opened on April 16, 1927. It was built by S. Hoffberger's Real Estate Holding Company and leased for five years by Arthur Price's Avalon Theaters Corporation. At the time it opened, the Avalon was one of the largest theaters in northwest Baltimore; it was nicknamed "The Downtown Theater Uptown." It cost about $200,000. The exterior was done in a Moorish style, although it was described as Gothic in a contemporary newspaper article. Five arches supported by six twisted columns above the marquee dominated the facade. This was balanced by smaller triple-arches on either side. The columns and arches appeared to be of cast concrete. The second-story facade was a diaper of diamonds in dark brick on a beige brick background. The large marquee contained 4,000 incandescent light bulbs. There were also three small stores located in the building. The interior was designed in a restrained Spanish style. A contemporary account described the interior:

> The auditorium has walls of techstone with travertine bases. A semi-indirect lighting

The staff of the Aurora (7 E. North Avenue, 1910–1984, Francis E. Tormey) poses in front of the theater in this early photograph, c. 1910; the man with the goatee, fourth from the left, is probably the owner, Eugene Cook. (Photograph courtesy of Mrs. Audrey Winter)

system has been used and in the auditorium have been placed eight large soft-colored domes. Various colors and shades can be thrown upon the walls and ceiling at will. The plush carpets and velour hangings are of burnt orange with dull gold trimmings and this color scheme for decorations is carried out through the house.[32]

The Avalon's organ was a two-manual Kimball which was played by several organists including Roy Seiler, John Varney, and John

The beautiful Moorish facade of the Avalon (4338 Park Heights Avenue, 1927–1963, Frederick A. Fletcher) with a new marquee in 1947.

Decker. Loritz Garman took over the theater from Price in October 1928. The Garman-Beck organization leased the Avalon in November 1930 and purchased it in 1956. A new marquee was installed in early 1942.

Following a citywide trend in the early 1960s, it became an art-film house. Robert Hyatt took the theater over, redecorated it and reopened it on December 26, 1961. R. Freedman made a last-ditch effort to save the Avalon when he took it over in the summer of 1962, but he had no more success than Hyatt, and the Avalon closed for good in early November 1963. Within a few years of its closing as a theater, it was acquired by the United Broadcasting Company and converted into a radio-TV studio. The first TV programs were broadcast from the theater in March 1967. It was abandoned a few years later, and was vacant for many years until it was demolished.

Avenue {1}, 1230 Pennsylvania Ave, 1907–1915, 1943–1960; David Harrison (of New Albert); 148 (as Renard), 624 (as New Albert). This movie house opened in the fall of 1907 as the Avenue, under the management of H. H. Lee. It was one of the first movie theaters for African Americans in Baltimore. Fred H. Carley changed the name to the Renard Moving Picture Parlor in 1908. It was usually called Renard until around 1915, but in one 1909 listing, it was called the No Name Theater. Apparently it was a storefront theater. Clinton J. Johnson operated it for several years. The Renard was advertised as the "only picture parlor conducted exclusively by colored people, every person [connected] therewith, from manager to operator being a member of the race."

After the Renard closed, a large auditorium, the New Albert Hall, was built in the rear of the original structure. There was a 40-car garage on the first floor of the new building and a dance hall on the second. In the late 1920s the New Albert Hall became a major Baltimore venue for jazz performances. Louis Armstrong and "Jelly Roll" Morton played there, and there were "battles" between local jazz bands. Prizefights were also held there. In 1943, David Harrison designed a theater to be built in the garage portion for Joseph Garfink. The New Albert Theater opened on September 10, 1943. Isidore K. Makover was the manager. In 1947 he renovated it and converted it into a first-run black theater.

Aaron Seidler, who started at the New Albert in 1947, described the theater in a 1991 interview:

> The New Albert in its day was a very popular place. It was the largest and only ballroom

in the city of Baltimore [for blacks ?]. It was called the New Albert Ballroom and all the big name bands, Duke Ellington, Jimmy Lunsford ... Count Basie, the biggest bands in the days when dancing was very popular.... The New Albert, before it was the New Albert, was a big garage.... The theater was actually built where the garage was, on the level ground. Right above it, which would be the second floor of the garage, but the equivalent of a third floor as far as distance was concerned, was the New Albert Hotel, a black hotel. Above that, covering the whole expanse of the property was this gigantic, open ballroom, called the New Albert Ballroom. And ... while I operated the New Albert Theater, I also leased out the hotel and ... on a couple of occasions, was able to book some big bands in the ballroom. Bands will come out of Norfolk, Richmond, and North Carolina and have a "dead night" in traveling and they would call around, and we had the only really available ballroom and it might be on a Tuesday or Wednesday night where you could buy Count Basie very cheap. He'd be willing to work just to make ends meet. We would book on quick notice with maybe ten days notice to get the advertising together and book Count Basie in the ballroom. I did not do too much of that; maybe over the years about 10 or 12 good band bookings.... Inside of the theater was a big, open spaced place. When I first went to work there, there were just seats down the center section because there were steel columns holding up the whole area. So the sides were wide open; we could stand more people than we could sit and on a popular show we often did that ... more people would stand for an hour and a half or two than were seated. Business was pretty good, so the owners decided to do the construction to eliminate these columns, there were two on each side supporting the upper area, so we could put seats down. We did that [and it] limited me because I could now seat less than I could before, sitting and standing, but it was a much better arrangement. We also air-conditioned the theater finally at that time. It ran successfully; everything was double feature. One of the biggest things that we had, that made me come into my own, was a picture called "Pinky."³³

The theater closed in the summer of 1950 for a complete remodeling; it reopened in October with additional seats, a new air-conditioning system, and first-run films. One of the main results of this remodeling was the removal of the posts which had obscured the view in the auditorium. The New Albert closed again around 1960, and, along with much of lower Pennsylvania Avenue, it was demolished in 1971.

Avenue {2} (see Good Time)

Avon (see Community {1})

Baby Wizard (see Wizard {3})

Baltimore, 3205–3209 Fait Avenue, 1914–1930, poss. A. Lowther Forrest, c. 300. The Baltimore opened in 1914 and lasted until 1930. It may have been the $5,000 brick theater designed by A. L. Forrest in late 1913. The Broadway Theater Company purchased it in the summer of 1916 and completely renovated it. Charles Nolte's Linwood Amusement Company bought it in the fall of 1921 for about $10,000. According to a local resident, several seats at the rear of the theater were modified into a single seat to accommodate the extremely large wife of a local butcher. The building is still standing, but has been extensively remodeled.

Baltimore Theater (see Princess {1})

Baltimore Hebrew Theater (see Princess {1})

Baltimore Moving Picture Company, 2329 East Chase Street, 1908. This company gave traveling movie shows at African-American churches and halls around the end of 1908.

Battlefront Airdome (see Daly's)

Bay Shore Park, North Point, Baltimore County; Otto Simonson & Theodore Wells Pietsch, 1906–1947. The United Railways Company built this park on a portion of the Franklin Roberts tract near Fort Howard. The total cost was half a million dollars, $200,000 for the 30-acre park and $300,000 for the streetcar line. After several delays, Bay Shore finally opened, under the management of M. J. Fitzsimmons, on August 11, 1906, with Giuseppe Aiala and his Royal Artillery Band, borrowed for the occasion from River View Park, as the main attraction. The original buildings included a three-story restaurant, a two-story dancing pavilion with bowling alley, a bathhouse, a 2,000-seat music pavilion, carousels, pagodas, a railway station, and a 1,000-foot pier that extended into the bay. The buildings, interspersed among oaks and elms, were all painted white. One criticism in the early years of the park was the long time it took to get there by streetcar. Streetcars departed Howard and Franklin streets for Bay Shore every 10 minutes beginning at 7 A.M., but they took one hour and 15 minutes to get to the park. The one-way fare was fifteen cents.

In March 1907, architects Simonson and Pietsch drew plans for new construction at the park, including an amusement building, a moving picture hall, and a soda water and candy pavilion. The style was called "highly ornate, "angular," and "very pretty ... especially appropriate to a bayside amusement resort, giving an impression of lightness and animation."[34] According to Mueller, the movie theater was located in an enclosed portion of the Pavilion.[35] Local politician George P. Mahoney leased Bay Shore from the transit company in 1939. The resort closed at the end of the 1947 season when it was acquired by Bethlehem Steel. Later it was given to the state park system, and the site is now part of North Point State Park. A fountain and streetcar shelter there have been restored.

Beacon (see Brodie)

Bell, Grundy Street. The Bell was one of the very short-lived nickelodeons in Highlandtown. It was operated by Scotty Pugh.

Belmar, 6313 (now 6309) Belair Road, c. 1920–1927, R. C. Brockmeyer, c. 200. The Belmar was a small brick and concrete block movie house, about 26 feet wide by 60 feet deep, that operated for about seven years. It was built by Henry Gyr for about $12,000. It was usually open only two days a week. A fire damaged the theater in the fall of 1926. The owner, Alexander Baliko, planned a $50,000 addition with 300 to 400 extra seats according to plans by R. E. Tyr in 1928, but it probably was not built. The building is still standing. It has been extensively remodeled and is currently used by the Olympic Upholstery Company.

Belnord, 2700–2706 (2716) Pulaski Highway, 1911–1969; John Freund, Jr. (1911 theater), William O. Sparklin (1921 theater); unknown (1911 theater), 1,269 (790 1st floor, 479 balcony — 1921 theater). Louis Kolb and Charles Bender received a permit in May 1911 to build a theater on the site of Riley's Stables and Miller's Oyster Bar. It was a one-story, brick and stone theater with a tile roof and floors of Virginia pine and terrazzo. It cost about $8,000. There was an open-air theater, surrounded by a corrugated iron fence, located just west of the theater. During the summer, movies were shown at the open-air theater. Occasionally local performers appeared in live acts on the stage.

In the spring of 1919, the Greater Baltimore Theater Company announced plans to build a large new movie theater on the site of the 1911 Belnord. They purchased the original theater and an adjoining lot in 1919. This new theater was one of the largest in town, seating nearly 1,300. It was designed by William O. Sparklin[36] and built at a cost of $130,000. It opened on May 14, 1921. The second Belnord was built of brick, concrete and steel and measured 75 × 150 feet. The front of the new theater was of terra cotta brick, trimmed in limestone, with a marquee over the entrance.

Inside, the walls were cream and ivory. There was a huge dome in the auditorium ceiling which was finished in gold leaf and lighted by indirect multi-colored lights. The seats were upholstered in morocco leather. Music was provided by an orchestra conducted by Harry M. Nolan and a $10,000 three-manual Kimball organ. Charles Nolte was the first manager. A permit was granted in October 1921 to allow the owners to install a gallery approximately 38 feet deep by 70 feet wide which would contain about 400 seats. By 1930, the Belnord had been equipped with a Western Electric synchronized sound system. In 1954 it was remodeled for Cinema-Scope.

Declining attendance and unruly audiences finally closed the Belnord in the fall of 1969. It is still standing, with most of the facade intact, and is being used by a food market. Above the false ceiling, the auditorium ceiling and balcony are still intact.

Beltway Movies 6, 7660 Belair Road, Fullerton, 1997–present, Kelly Clayton & Mojzisek, c. 825 (1 — 210, 2 — 85, 3 — 85, 4 — 147, 5 — 148, 6 — 150). Local independent exhibitor Robert Wienholt opened this attractive theater on March 7, 1997, and closed it the following December. It reopened in June 1998 and is currently (2004) operating as a subsequent-run theater. Behind a very plain brick front, the theater is arranged in a T-shaped floor plan. A fairly large lobby — with concession stand and rest rooms on the left and video games and several booths on the right — leads back to the middle of a corridor on which the six auditoriums are located. Although there is little or no slope to the auditorium floors, the screens are placed at a comfortable angle. The theater also has a birthday party room.

Beltway Plaza 2, 7636 Belair Road, 1980–1986, Kelly Clayton & Mojzisek, 375. This small twin theater opened in the Bel Air Beltway Plaza Shopping Center in July 1980. Auditorium 1 opened on July 11 and auditorium 2 opened on

This Belnord (2700–2706 Pulaski Highway, 1921–1969, William O. Sparklin) was built in 1921 on the site of a 1911 theater and airdome. (Photograph courtesy of the Maryland Historical Society, Baltimore, Maryland)

July 18. It lasted only six years. It was located at the rear end of the east-west section of the shopping center and has been replaced by three stores.

Belvedere (see Star {1})

Bengies Drive-In, 3417 Eastern Boulevard, Middle River, 1956–present, Jack K. Vogel, 585 cars. The Frog Mortar Corp.[37] opened the Bengies Drive-In on June 6, 1956. There was a spacious concession building with a completely unobstructed view across the front of the large screen. On either side of this building were twin, heated auditoriums which each seated 60 walk-in patrons. The projection booth was above the concession area. The entrance to the Bengies was enhanced by the installation of a theater marquee–type channeled chaser and California redwood and jalousie windows. The original marquee, similar to the 1940s theater marquees, was replaced by a larger, more elaborate one in 1973. By the summer of 1996, Bengies was one of only two operating drive-in theaters in Maryland. Under the dedicated management of D. Edward Vogel, who has managed it since 1988, it has had more staying power than most of the other drive-ins in the country and has lasted up to the present. For many years it has been the tradition to begin every show with the playing of the National Anthem.

When steelworkers at Bethlehem Steel and other local steel plants went on strike in July 1956, manager Hank Vogel announced that they would be admitted to the Bengies without charge Monday through Thursday. In the summer of 1998, the Bengies management announced with great fanfare that the drive-in was closing for good at the end of the season with a night of films on Halloween. However, when the 1999 season rolled around, the Bengies opened as usual, much to the delight of its many fans. The 52 × 120-foot screen at the Bengies is perfect for CinemaScope films.

Berman's, 913 East Baltimore Street and 1–3 South High Street, 1915–1922, John Freund, Jr., c. 400. Pawnshop owner Isaac Berman opened this theater on February 12, 1915. The original permit called for the entrance to be on High Street, but it was repealed in December 1914 and replaced by one that located the entrance on Baltimore Street. The building was described as fireproof throughout with an extremely decorative front. It was "L" shaped with the entrance on Baltimore and the exit on High Street. It measured 32 feet, seven inches by 102 feet. The cost was estimated at between $10,000 and $20,000.

Berman's was located in an old Jewish neighborhood and featured slides with captions in Yiddish. At one time, Berman hired a projectionist who had just come over from Russia and could speak no English. He was an asset because he knew Yiddish, and did not put the Yiddish slides in upside down.

The theater was sold for $25,000 in the summer of 1915. New owners remodeled and reopened the theater on October 17, 1916. According to *Moving Picture World* of November 4, 1916, the new theater was practically rebuilt. A new ventilation system and a gold fiber screen were installed and the entrance was moved from Baltimore Street around the corner to High Street.

Morris Flaks acquired it around 1919. He changed the name to Flaks Photoplay Theater. The name was changed again, in 1921, to Metro Photoplays. It closed in 1922, and Louis Fisher purchased the theater at auction in July 1923 for $11,000. The name may have been changed to Karp just before it closed. Permission was granted in July 1939 to convert the building into a public garage.

Bernheimer's (see Little Moving Picture Palace)

Biddle, 1235 East Biddle Street, 1948–1970, David Harrison, 457. The partnership of Samuel Schwartz, Anne Rosenberg, and Evelyn Kaminsky opened this plain-looking theater. The grand opening was held on June 4, 1948. Formerly a garage with a hall on the second floor, it may have, at one time, also been a stable. For many years, it was operated by [Robert] Lee, who also ran the Madison.

Bien's (see Lincoln Highway)

Bijou {1}, 222 South Broadway, 1907–1913, unknown, 100. The Bijou {1} opened around 1907. It was known as the Bijou-Dream in 1908 and as the Broadway {2} in 1910 and 1911. It probably closed in 1913.

Bijou {2} (see Convention Hall)

Bijou (see Palace Museum)

Black Cat, 1204 West Baltimore Street, 1908–1928, unknown, c. 300. Andrew G. Steen and Frank P. Durham leased the first floor of the building at 1204 West Baltimore Street and converted it into the Black Cat Theater. It probably opened in December 1908 since it celebrated its anniversary during the week of December 20, 1909. Improvements costing about $1,500 were announced in July 1909. This theater was very long and narrow; "perhaps the longest hall in existence" in 1909 according to one source.[38] The projector had to be set up behind the screen in order to get a good picture. Later, a booth was set up halfway between the screen and the rear of the auditorium.

In 1910, the Black Cat was offering vaudeville shows along with four or five reels of movies. Their rivals across the street, the Carrollton, wrote in 1910 that the Black Cat also gave away ice cream pies and had pie-eating contests and amateur nights but that few "first class people" attended.[39] The name was changed to Solax, after an early film company, in 1913 when the Black Cat Amusement Company was purchased by Chisolm & Tall. G. W. Hamilton, Harry Bentum, and George A. Baldwin purchased the Solax in January 1920; they reopened it on January 22.

Blaney's (see Empire {1})

Blue Bell {1}, 1713–1715 Harford Avenue, 1909–1925, William Emmerich, c. 300. This movie house, with its wide stucco front, was one of the more important early neighborhood theaters in the city. It was well advertised in the newspapers. Charles W. Demme and William Emmerich received a permit for the theater in September 1909 and opened it in late 1909 or early 1910. It measured 33 by 100 feet and cost about $5,000. Emmerich and Demme purchased the property at 1717 Harford Avenue in October 1911 with the intention of enlarging the Blue Bell to a capacity of 1,000 seats, but they were unable to do so. They did remodel the Blue Bell to in-

Much of the facade in this 1968 photograph of the Blue Bell (1713–1715 Harford Avenue, 1909–1925, William Emmerich) was original.

crease the seating capacity and improve the ventilation in late 1912. In 1915, Emmerich and his sister Henrietta bought Demme's share of the theater. It was purchased by John L. McDonald and Elmer Hutchins in 1920 and operated by them for several years. McDonald supervised the music. Myer Abramson and Abraham Oliver acquired the Blue Bell for about $25,000 in August 1924. They leased it to Arthur Price and Jack Whittle in September 1924 for $2,400 a year.

The Theater closed in 1925. The building was sold in March 1926 and converted into a furniture store. The State Theater Company, which operated the nearby Apollo Theater, purchased the building in April 1926. It was remodeled in the early 1940s according to plans by David Harrison for the Rome organization, but it apparently never reopened as a movie theater. At one time, the Blue Bell {1} had a three-piece orchestra; Mickey McDonald and Charlie Gorsuch played the piano.

A ladder against the rear wall of the auditorium led to the projection booth. When all of the seats were filled, kids would climb up and hang on to it to watch the movie. One person remembered that, in the summer, the door into the auditorium would be open with only some curtains across the doorway. Children would saunter back and forth past the doorway hoping to catch a peek at the movie when a breeze opened the curtains. It was used as a church in the 1970s, but was demolished about ten years later.

Blue Bell {2} (see Eureka Amusement Company)

Blue Bird (see Rialto)

Blue Mouse, 28 West Lexington Street, 1909–1921, A. Lowther Forrest, c. 300. The Consoli-

The Blue Mouse (28 W. Lexington Street, 1909–1921, A. Lowther Forrest) was one of the most popular of the early downtown movie theaters.

dated Amusement Company, one of the pioneer exhibitors in Baltimore, opened the Blue Mouse and operated it for many years. H. A. Fitzjarrell, president of the company, leased the Dime Savings Bank building in early 1909 for five years at $8,500 a year and had the first floor converted into the Blue Mouse for about $7,000.

In January 1910, the Blue Mouse advertised vaudeville and moving pictures, and it claimed to be the only moving picture theater in the country equipped with a mirror screen and a $3,000 pipe organ.[40] Jack Whittle, during a 1973 interview, remembered the mirror screen as being made of frosted glass two inches thick. Among the early live entertainers at the Blue Mouse was J. Reginald Foard, who played the organ and offered illustrated recitations of classic poems.

Leonard Chick, Alfred Armond, and Joe Combs all sang there around 1912. The Blue Mouse was sold to a syndicate in June 1913. Joseph Blechman, who was also operating the Picture Garden across the street, bought the theater in April 1914. It was redecorated and practically rebuilt in 1918 for about $10,000. *Moving Picture World* described the remodeling.

The lobby of the Blue Mouse has been entirely remodeled. The box office, which was formerly located to the right as you enter, has been set in the framework of the outer doors. A floor of small tiles has been laid, with an ornamental border. A paneled ceiling, from which hang three inverted lights with ivory finished globes, gives a clear, soft effect. The color scheme is old ivory and brown. The operating room has been widened by about three feet, with two large windows opening on the lobby. The interior of the house has been redecorated and painted and the color scheme of old ivory and brown is here carried out. Brown damask curtains hang at the double entrances.[41]

The proscenium arch was redecorated and new Simplex projectors were installed. First-run films were to be the exclusive fare. The Blue Mouse reopened under the management of Arthur Price on August 26, 1918. Additional remodeling, to include the installation of a new organ, was planned in the spring of 1919. The pipes of the new organ were behind the screen with the console in the orchestra pit.

The theater was redecorated again in the summer of 1921. At that time, the front was painted white and the lobby was painted a light blue, lined with white, to resemble large tiles. A new box office was also installed. The seats were replaced, two new exhaust fans were installed, and new dark blue draperies were hung.

It closed in May 1923. The theater was leased to a New York company that sold women's clothing and converted into retail space.

Bon Ton (see Gay Street Museum)

Booker T (see Aladdin)

Boulevard, 3302 Greenmount Avenue, 1921–1989, Ewald G. Blanke, 1,625 (later 1,484 c. 1935; 1,088; 762 reported in 1972). The opening of the Boulevard was announced in 1920; the newspapers that November carried sketches of the exterior and interior. It was built for Alfred Buck's American Theaters Company for an estimated $225,000. Ground was broken for the theater on April 11, 1921. It opened on Saturday October 8, 1921, to a specially invited audience. It opened to the public two days later.

Architect Ewald Blanke designed the exterior of the Boulevard in a Classical style with an Adamesque interior. It was built around the corner lot occupied by the Burriss and Kemp drugstore. Interior decorations featured mulberry silk tapestry panels and a color scheme of shades

Ewald Blanke's Boulevard Theater (3302 Greenmount Avenue, 1921–1989, Ewald G. Blanke) shown in 1940.

of pearl gray, azure blue, gold, and violet. The floors were covered with Axminster carpet. The 38-foot central dome in the auditorium ceiling was decorated with four classic figures representing Music, Song, Dance, and Myth. Two paintings by New York artist Leo Sielke flanked the ladies' lounging room; one was entitled "A Nymphal Sunset Dance" and the other, "Fountain of Inspiration." There were two small balconies, seating about 125 people.

The classical motif was carried out on the exterior of the theater in a bas-relief of dancing maidens. As Blanke described it, "Both facades are decorated in classic architecture with colonnade and relief panels in Greek architecture. Pompeian pressed brick, granite, and limestone will be used for the decorative features of the two fronts. Handsome marquises will extend over the entrance for the protection of the public."[42] Music was provided by an orchestra under the direction of Robert P. Iula with Roy C. Frazee at the $16,000 3/20 Skinner organ (opus 338)

The new Boulevard marquee in 1948.

and Victor C. Hargrave at the piano. There were children's shows, which featured vaudeville acts, on Saturday mornings in the early days of the Boulevard. The American Theaters Company did not own the Boulevard for very long. In January 1922, in the middle of a long court case alleging illegal activities by various members of the theater company, the theater was sold at auction for $145,000 to the Boulevard Theater Company. Bernard Depkin became the new manager, and Margaret McManus took over at the organ. A. Sokolove conducted the orchestra during the 1922 and 1923 seasons.

It was not a commercial success when Harry Schwalbe, of the Novelty Amusement Company of Philadelphia, purchased the Boulevard in March 1926.[43] Schwalbe was believed to be representing Stanley interests. Schwalbe renovated the building placing large electric signs around the marquees at both entrances to advertise coming attractions, installing a $3,000 chandelier in the auditorium, and laying new carpets.

The Durkee organization acquired it later in 1926 for more than $100,000.[44] They reopened the theater on August 1, 1927, and operated it until it closed in 1989. Durkee typically switched movies between the Boulevard and the Senator. If a movie opened at the Senator on a Sunday it would play three days and then go to the Boulevard on Wednesday. A huge new curved marquee was added in the spring of 1948. In late 1960 the Boulevard was renovated; a wide screen and a new automatic projection system were installed at this time. The theater was twinned in 1984. After it closed, the auditorium was converted into retail space.

Bridge {1}, 2100 Edmondson Avenue, 1915–1929, W. O. Sparklin and G. S. Childs, c. 700. This theater was part of a double-theater enterprise of the Edmondson Amusement Company. It was built next to the Edmondson Theater and opened on May 19, 1915. Built by the Consolidated Engineering Company at a cost of about $14,000, the two-story, art brick and stucco building measured 42 × 100 feet. It featured a modern ventilation system and had a balcony.

A unique feature of the Bridge {1}, foreshadowing designs of 60 years later, was a projection booth connected to the booth of the adjacent Edmondson Theater. Architects Sparklin and Childs were preparing plans for alterations to the Bridge and Edmondson in December 1916. As early as 1917, Louis Schlichter, president of the Edmondson Amusement Company, was considering consolidating the Bridge and the Edmondson into a single 1,400-seat theater. It took more than 10 years for a single theater to be erected on the site. A new cooling system was installed for the summer of 1918 and a new $4,000 2/10 Moller organ (Opus 2903) was installed the following summer. Both theaters were razed in 1929–1930 to build the new Bridge {2}.

Bridge {2}, 2100 Edmondson Avenue, 1930–1968, John J. Zink, 912. This handsome building occupies the site of the earlier Bridge {1} and Edmondson Theaters. Apparently the original plan, in 1927, was to build a third theater west of the Edmondson and Bridge {1}, and then rent out the Edmondson as a garage. This plan was abandoned, and a new plan to tear down the two older theaters and replace them with a single new one was announced in the fall of 1929.

The Bridge {2} was built for the Edmondson Amusement Company for about $270,000. The building, described as in the Colonial style, was built of brick, concrete, and steel. A large new marquee replaced the original one in the late 1930s. The facade was of beige brick with cream and blue glass tile. The art deco interior, one of the nicest in Baltimore, was done in ivory, old gold, and tan with a wall design of modernistic trees on either side of the screen. The Bridge {2} opened on March 15, 1930.

Someone must have been angry about the new theater because they tried to blow it up soon after it opened. On the night of May 7, 1930, ten minutes after the last person had left the theater, a mysterious explosion ripped a one-foot hole in the theater's portico. The building inspector stated that a dynamite bomb had caused the explosion. Earlier reports attributed the damage to a firecracker thrown by "mischievous boys." The police department investigated the incident, but apparently was never able to identify the bomber or the reason for the bombing.

The Hicks Circuit purchased the Bridge {2} for $36,000 in 1936 and operated it until it closed. The Bridge closed in mid–December 1949 and reopened—as an African-American theater with a second-run, double-feature policy—on December 29. A newspaper article praised the theater for being located in a non-restricted parking area and easily reached by the No. 4, 9, and 14 streetcars and Monroe Street bus. Despite these conveniences, it closed in 1968 and was sold to a church in November 1970. The marquee was torn off in late 1970, and the building has been used as a church for many years. The huge projection booth was remodeled into a dining room.

Broadway {1}, 509–513 South Broadway, 1914–1915, A. Lowther Forrest (of conversion), c. 500; 1916–1977, Benjamin Frank, 848 (700 reported in 1972). The original Broadway {1} opened on February 23, 1914, in a six-story warehouse that had been occupied by Rosenstein Bros. department store. The ordinance granting permission for the Broadway Theater Company to convert the first floor of the building was granted in October

Within six years of its opening, the Bridge (2100 Edmondson Avenue, 1930–1968, John J. Zink) had replaced a rather plain, narrow rectangular marquee with this unique one shown in 1940.

The beautiful art deco interior of the Bridge was a pleasant surprise, given the plain Colonial exterior.

A c. 1969 photograph of the Broadway Theater (509–513 S. Broadway, 1916–1977, Benjamin Frank); this is the 1916 theater that replaced the earlier one destroyed by fire.

1913. The remodeling cost about $7,000. The project was under the personal supervision of Harry Lewy. The lobby was an arcade with glass-fronted stores on either side and marble wainscoting. The front was decorated with thousands of incandescent lights and "life-sized figures suggestive of dramatic mythology."

The Broadway was gutted by fire on December 16, 1915, causing damages estimated at $30,000. The original building was demolished and a second theater built on the site. The new theater opened on May 20, 1916. The *Sun* described the new theater:

> The illumination is all of the indirect type. The interior is finished in hardwood, the color scheme in shades of French gray, giving a very soft and pleasing effect to the eye. By increasing the depth of the house it has been possible to keep the nearest seat about 20 feet from the screen, saving from eye fatigue those in the front seats.[45]

In March 1919, the Broadway hired a four-piece orchestra to provide music for their films. A Robert-Morton 2/4 organ was installed in 1920. The Broadway {1} was extensively remodeled in 1925 and 1927. A balcony was added and a half-ton crystal chandelier with 200 lights was hung from the auditorium ceiling. The new color scheme was ivory, gold, and old rose. The new marquee was 50 feet long with a 50-foot, 5,000-light sign above it. The stage was enlarged, the seating capacity was increased to around 900, and the lobby was remodeled. The marquee was replaced in the spring of 1948, and the entire theater was renovated and redecorated in December 1949.

During a 1950 showing at the Broadway {1} of *The Black Hand*, starring Gene Kelly, there was a large contingent from nearby Little Italy. When the scene in which Kelly pulls a knife to show how he will avenge his father's murder came on the screen, the entire audience stood up and cheered. The theater played mainly MGM, RKO, United Artists, Columbia, and Universal movies.

The Broadway {1} closed on April 4, 1977. Edward D. Idzi purchased it and spent almost $600,000 to remodel it into a club called the Polish Castle. The Polish Castle lasted only a few months. By October 1982 it had become the Yueh

The Brooklyn Theater (3730 S. Hanover Street, 1928–1959) lasted 30 years as a theater, but 50 years after it closed it still stands as a ladder and scaffolding store.

Yang Lou Chinese Restaurant. In September 1985, the building was reopened as the Fells Point Dinner Theater. It is now a restaurant, the Latin Palace.

Broadway {2} (see Bijou {1})

Broadway Garden (see Plaza {1})

Brodie (see Wizard)

Brooklyn, 3730 South Hanover Street, 1928–(1959), unknown, J. E. Moxley (of 1941 alterations), c. 400 (later c. 700). Louis Tunick opened the Brooklyn on Saturday, April 7, 1928. It was the first movie theater in Brooklyn, although there is some evidence that an earlier theater was planned on South Hanover Street in 1914. The Brooklyn is probably the theater "on the west side of Annapolis Boulevard 200 feet west of Potomac Street, Brooklyn" that the National Engineering Corporation received permission to erect in August 1927.[46] The Brooklyn opened with a Kimball orchestral organ; by 1929, it was equipped with an RCA sound system.

The building, which has changed little on the exterior, is still standing; the present front is plain brick with alternating light and dark horizontal stripes at the top. Tunick spent an estimated $30,000 to put on a 40-foot addition to the theater and install new booth equipment and seats in the summer of 1937.

Tunick made plans for additions and alterations to the Brooklyn in 1941. After the Brooklyn closed, the canvas murals of monumental people and horses were removed, restored, and installed on one wall of the Club Charles on North Charles Street. For many years now, it has been used by a ladder company.

Bunny, 1225 Washington Boulevard, 1912–1924, Frederick E. Beall (of conversion), 298. The Bunny was probably named for silent film comedian John Bunny. It was built, in a two-story building, for George P. Klein in late 1912 for about $1,200. It has had a long history of openings and closings. F. H. Rothrock reopened it in the fall of 1916 after it had been closed for a while. It was repainted and redecorated in the summer of 1919. R. L. Rubenstein, who operated the Pastime Theater on Greenmount Avenue, acquired the Bunny in April 1922 and planned a thorough renovation. The name was changed to the Ruby in August 1922 when it was renovated again. In 1923, it was sold at auction for $8,000. Harry Morstein operated this theater at one time.

Caltrider's Hall, 20 Main Street, Reisterstown, c. 1925–(1932). Movies were shown at this hall (also called Goodwin's Hall) on a regular basis during 1925 and 1926 and possibly later. This was probably the hall and garage that was leased by Philip Freedman and Jack B. Fagan for motion picture exhibition in October 1932.

Cameo (see Parkside)

Capitol {1}, 1518 West Baltimore Street, 1921–1970, Wyatt & Nolting, 1,200 (later 800). The Capitol was built in 1920–1921 by the J. Henry Miller Company for Morris Klein's Capitol Theatre Company. The Capitol was announced in March 1920. A month later, an ordinance granting the building permit was passed. The theater cost about $300,000. The Capitol advertised one of the first nurseries, "where young children can be kept while the mothers see the pictures," in a Baltimore theater. The building also contained several small stores and a second floor hall that had a small stage; billiard and pool parlors were planned for the basement. The original seating capacity was announced as 1,200.

The Capitol opened on February 5, 1921; music was provided by an organ and the Capitol Orchestra conducted by Herman Federoff. The opening of the Capitol was probably a major factor in the closing of the West End just up the street. The Capitol held Charleston dance contests in the mid–1920s. These popular contests lasted five weeks and the three best couples appeared in the finals. The original plain marquee was replaced, by the late 1930s, with a spectacular neon outlined marquee and vertical sign that featured large images of the Capitol dome. The theater was remodeled in 1946–1947 and reopened on February 22, 1947. Around that time, murals depicting the story of St. George and the dragon were painted on the ceiling and walls of the lobby.

The theater closed in 1964, and the ominous "Closed Temporarily" sign appeared on the marquee in 1970. An organization called the United Western Front was working on a plan to purchase the closed theater in 1968 and 1969 and convert it into a community hall, but those efforts failed. Later the marquee was removed, and, in 1973, the Capitol {1} was sold and converted into a plastics factory.

Capri (see Linden)

Carey, 1440 North Carey Street, 1915–1953, Stanislaus Russell, 480. The Carey was built for James C. Cremen at a cost of about $15,000. Cremen opened the Carey in September 1915. The building had a red brick facade. In 1920, it was advertised as "the best ventilated colored theater in the city." Cremen distributed handbills advertising the Carey as a high-class theater:

> The Carey Theatre is one of the most commodious and well-appointed amusement houses for colored people in the city. Every possible courtesy is extended by the management to patrons. An entire corps of colored attendants is employed at this theatre. Modern ventilating apparatus has been recently installed for the special purpose of having a cool place in summer. Only the very highest grade of pictures is used. The very best of order is maintained. With gratitude to those who are now our patrons and with earnest solicitent of the patronage of those who have not yet visited us, I am,
>
> Very truly yours,
> James C. Cremen.

The Capitol Theater (1518 W. Baltimore Street, 1921–1970, Wyatt & Nolting) with the 1938 marquee and impressive vertical sign.

The Carey Theater (1440 N. Carey Street, 1915–1953, Stanislaus Russell), shown here in 1925, was one of the major African-American movie houses in the Pennsylvania Avenue area. (Photograph courtesy of the Photography Collections, Albin O. Kuhn Library, University of Maryland, Baltimore County)

In the summer of 1926, the Carey installed an "Arctic Nu-Air" cooling system, which could supply 40,000 cubic feet of fresh air per minute. Patrons at the Carey in 1930 preferred "melodramas with action and mystery, Western pictures and serials ... especially with ... Tom Mix, Ken Meynard and Hoot Gibson."[47]

The Carey was completely redecorated in early 1941; reporter Lillian Johnson of the *Afro-American* was so impressed that she wrote an article on it. Johnson attended the Carey on a Thursday afternoon to see a double feature. The interior of the theater had been painted and redecorated. The walls and ceilings were white with radiators and ornamental wood in a deep orange. The walls were decorated with panels of tapestry framed in white. The lights along the sides of the auditorium were tubular and contained colored bulbs that varied from daylight green to pink.[48] After it closed as a movie house in the fall of 1953, the Carey was used as a church. It was abandoned by late 1970. In 1971–1972, it was razed to build a school.

Carlin's Park (see Liberty Heights Park)

Carlin's Drive-In, 2920 Druid Park Drive, 1958–1977, Stephen Hazzard (of Philadelphia) with Stanislaus Russell, 1,700 cars. Carlin's Park had been considered the prime site for the new Baltimore civic center, but, in the spring of 1957, the owners of the park requested a permit to erect a drive-in theater on part of the 49-acre tract. Carlin's Drive-In was operated by the Northeast Drive-In Theatre Corporation. It was located near the western end of Carlin's Park, where the roller coaster had been. It opened on the evening of June 20, 1958 with dancing on the terrace, with disc jockeys, and free souvenirs. When it opened, Carlin's Drive-In was believed to be the largest drive-in in the heart of any city in the United States. Special features of the drive-in included: a concrete terrace for dancing; a six-lane cafeteria-style concession stand; a playground for children with slides, swings, a carousel and Ferris wheel; electric car heaters for chilly weather; and a new ultra-bright pro-

Carlin's Drive-In (2920 Druid Park Drive, 1958–1977, Stephen Hazzard with Stanislaus Russell) was the only drive-in within the city limits of Baltimore.

jection system. The huge curved screen measured 64 by 142 feet; the screen tower was 90 feet high.

The Redstone theater circuit acquired the drive-in in 1961. The remains of the drive-in were razed in the spring of 1978 for construction of the Baltimore subway system. As the only drive-in within the city limits of Baltimore, Carlin's often ran afoul of a seldom-enforced blue law that prohibited the showing of movies after 1:00 A.M. on Sunday mornings.

Carlton, 1201 Dundalk Avenue, 1949–1978, John F. Eyring, 810. The Carlton was built for the Gaertner organization. The entrance, with a triangular neon-illuminated marquee, was located to the left to the auditorium. A neon sign, which spelled out the name Carlton in script, topped the marquee. There was also a flat sign on the rear wall of the auditorium to the right of the entrance. The lower half of the auditorium walls was covered with a quilted fabric in a diamond-shaped pattern while the upper half was decorated with modernistic murals.

The Carlton opened on February 22, 1949. It was leased by the JF organization in the spring of 1970. Shortly before it closed, the Carlton showed the X-rated film *Alice in Wonderland*, starring Playmate Christine DeBell. Miss DeBell appeared in person along with a lingerie fashion show. The show played to a standing-room-only audience with lines stretching far down Dundalk Avenue.

The Carlton closed on December 3, 1978, with a showing of *Grease*. Plans were made in 1989 to convert the building into a medical office building, but, after being closed for several years, the Carlton was finally converted into an attractive funeral parlor in 1992.

The interior of the Carlton (1201 Dundalk Avenue, 1948–1978, John F. Eyring) was typical of the movie theaters built in the late 1940s and early 1950s.

Carrollton, 1203–1205 West Baltimore Street, (1907)–1915, John F. Kunkel, c. 186. William E. Coulbourne, a wholesale fruit dealer, may have operated a movie house on this site as early as 1907. In late 1908, the Mercantile Bank erected a one-story brick and cement moving-picture theater there at a reported cost of $2,000. Hood and Schultz operated the Carrollton between about 1908 and 1913. In early 1913, this theater put on two-reel shows which were changed three times a week. The Carrollton closed in 1915. An unsuccessful attempt to reopen it was made by Lord Calvert Theaters in September 1915. The building has been torn down and replaced by a bank.

Carrollwood Twin, Carroll Island Rd., Middle River, 1974–1984, Jack K. Vogel, 400 (200 for each auditorium). The Carrollwood Twin was opened by Vogel Theaters in the small Carroll Island Shopping Center on November 27, 1974.

Carver (see Diane)

Casino {1} (see Wizard {3})

Casino {2}, Sparrows Point, c. 1909–1910. This was probably the public hall with a second floor theater that opened in March 1909 at Fifth and D streets.

Caton Moving Picture Parlor, 8–10 Ingleside Avenue, Catonsville, c. 1917–1928. Heine C. Andrae and Peter G. Olson showed movies in the Odd Fellows' Hall on Ingleside Avenue, just north of Frederick Avenue, in Catonsville.[49] In April 1919, Andrae applied for a license to operate a movie theater at the Odd Fellows' Hall "to be known as the Caton Theatre." This may have been the "Catonsville moving-picture theater" referred to in a May 1919 article.[50] In February 1922, Andrae had plans by architect Walter M.

Gieske for $30,000 alterations to a one-story brick theater in Catonsville. This was probably the Caton, but it is doubtful that the alterations were ever completed.

Catonsville High School, Frederick Avenue, Catonsville, c. 1919–1920. A group of local businessmen, including several members of the Catonsville Presbyterian Church, promoted the showing of movies at the high school in Catonsville in order to make money to support the school. J. R. Y. Savage was in charge of the exhibitions, which were held in the school's assembly hall every Friday.

Celtic Moving Picture Company, 839 Greenmount Avenue, 1909–1915, John K. Stack, c. 300. The Celtic Amusement Company opened this theater, usually called simply The Celtic, in mid–March 1909. It cost an estimated $3,500 to convert the original building, located opposite the long-gone hay scales, where farmers on their way to market used to weigh in. Jack Whittle rented it after the original owners could not make a go of it. He booked local talent such as Jim Barton, comedian and roller skate champion; Johnny Barry, also a roller skate champion; and Dick Wellby, a local singer, to appear onstage and augment the screen shows. The Celtic closed around 1915. The building was razed in the early 1970s.

Center Stage (see Theatorium)

Central, H Street, Sparrows Point. There is evidence of this very short-lived African-American movie house on the north side of Sparrows Point. It lasted about a year and was operated by Ed Snavely. Later, it became a pool hall, lunchroom, bowling alley, and barbershop. It was torn down long ago. The local African-American community could also see movies at the Union Baptist Church or the Methodist Church.

Centre, 10 East North Avenue, 1939–1958, Armand Carroll, 975. Armand Carroll, of Philadelphia, designed the Centre for Morris Mechanic. Interior decorations were by Armando T. Ricci. The estimated cost of the Radio Center — which included the theater, a radio studio, a branch of the Equitable Trust Company, a store, and a garage — was $400,000. It was one of the most modern theaters of its day when it opened in 1939. A writer for *Gardens, Houses and People* said that the Centre "gave Baltimore its first impressive manifestation of 'functional architecture' as applied to a place of public entertainment."[51] The Centre was built despite the objections of the owners of the Aurora Theater across the street. The facade was constructed of black Virginia marble and light marble from Italy. At the center of the facade was a dark blue column, still standing, which rose above the top of the facade and was surmounted by a powerful searchlight. The rounded ticket booth was of blue and gold mosaic. In the inside lobby, above the entrance to the auditorium, was a mural by Baltimore artist R. McGill Mackall. This mural, of two heroic nudes in blue-green, cream, silver, and gold, was symbolic of the motion picture industry, and bore the inscription "Man works by day; night is for romance." The color scheme of the interior was dark green, terra cotta, and gold. The ceiling was painted a neutral tint so that it could reflect any color through an elaborate indirect lighting system. Seating was on one floor.

The small, but fully-equipped stage was set off by a gold leafed, circular proscenium arch, and was equipped with microphones so that news items, such as election returns, could be relayed to the audience as they were broadcast from the studios of WFBR, located above the theater. The upper side walls of the auditorium were of asbestos transite and flowed on either side into the proscenium arch, while the lower walls were covered with aqua and gold damask with a walnut plywood wainscot. The Centre claimed to have the first circular proscenium arch in the United States and was also the first Baltimore movie theater to be completely equipped for radio broadcasting. In 1940, a quiz program "Drama-Grams" was broadcast live from the Centre's stage.

The opening of the Centre on February 1, 1939 was a glamorous occasion. One thousand guests, including film executives, Governor and Mrs. Herbert R. O'Conor and Senators Tydings and Radcliffe attended. The theater opened to the public on February 2 with *Kentucky* starring Loretta Young. The prices before 6:00 P.M. were 20 cents for adults and 10 cents for children. During the time that Morris Mechanic operated the Centre, it was a second-run house that ran films after they had played at his New or another downtown theater.

In March 1954, Isador Rappaport leased the Centre for five years. Rappaport closed the theater for a month in July, renovated it, and reopened it as the Film Centre[52] with Disney's *Vanishing Prairie* on August 1, 1954. The new theater featured a lounge where coffee and tea

The art deco front of the Centre Theater (10 E. North Avenue, 1939–1958, Armand Carroll) in 1939.

were served. It had deeply-piled sofas, beige carpeting, and a background of large drapery on which there was a Toulouse Lautrec print. There were magazines from all over the world, and beverages were served in china cups and saucers with copper spoons. The management planned arts and crafts exhibits in the lobby.

The Todd-AO movie *Oklahoma* played at the Film Centre in early 1956. Baltimore was the fourth city in the country to show a film in that wide-screen process. The Film Centre closed after a run of *Gigi* in the fall of 1958. The building, still (2004) standing, was used by a bank and the WFBR radio studios.

Century, 18 West Lexington Street, 1921–1961, John J. Zink, John Eberson (of 1926 remodeling), c. 3,076–3,450. This grand old theater was built in 1921 by the Whitehurst organization. The land for the entrance on Lexington Street was purchased for about $75,000 in the summer of 1919, and plans for the theater were prepared by John J. Zink. The huge structure, with a 24-foot wide entrance, occupied a lot 178 by 200 feet and housed two auditoriums. The lower one, which originally seated 3,450, was designed especially for motion pictures; the upper one, which could hold 3,000, contained a high-class cabaret for vaudeville and dancing. Three 30-

Architect Carroll carried the art deco theme into the auditorium of the Centre. The Centre claimed the only circular proscenium in Baltimore.

passenger elevators carried patrons up to the cabaret. It featured two bands, one for dancing and one for concert music. A three-part, telescoping stage could be rolled out for vaudeville. Later this upper auditorium was remodeled into the Valencia Theater.

According to Charles E. Whitehurst, the Century contained 1,560,000 cubic feet of interior space. It cost about $1,500,000 and was the largest movie house in town when it opened. The carpeting alone cost about $20,000, and the Monsoon ventilation system was installed at a cost of $36,000. The *Baltimore News* described the Century.

> The entrance ... opens into a long lobby leading to the theatre proper, which covers a lot running from the rear of the stores on the north side of Lexington street through to Clay street. The Lexington street front is of limestone. The vestibule is done in Verde antique marble with a mahogany ticket office standing in the center. The ceiling is in mauve blended to a light purple with gold decorations and the lighting is by invisible lights around the sidewalls up near the ceiling.
>
> The doorways from the vestibule to the lobby are of black and gold marble as are the walls of the lobby. The lobby is of striking design. High arches of hundreds of small mirrors stand out in the black and gold marble setting and run from the baseboard to the ceiling, reflecting like diamonds the lights of the three large chandeliers that hang suspended from the ceiling, the color scheme and decoration of which are similar to the vestibule.
>
> Around the topmost part of the side walls runs the row of invisible lights which send forth a mellow glow enhancing the richness of the ceiling and giving a soft touch to the first of Mr. Mackall's paintings which hangs in the lobby just above the entrance. To the right of the lobby is the ramp leading to the lower lobby where will be found the ticket offices for the roof theatre and the elevators leading thereto. On the left is the runway leading to the foyer.
>
> From the center of the foyer a marble

The entrance to Loew's Century Theater (18 W. Lexington Street, 1921–1961, John J. Zink) harkens back to the days of the nickelodeons with its entrance nearly obliterated by advertising in this 1953 photograph. (Photograph courtesy of Thomas Paul)

The ornate mirrored ramp led up to the Century or down to the Valencia's box office. (Photograph courtesy of Thomas Paul)

stairs leads upward and on each side of it is a marble arch leading to the first floor of the main auditorium. The walls of the foyer are finished in Circassian walnut above a baseboard of which hang a row of art needle tapestry panels. These encircle the foyer, except on the extreme left where will be found the three large elevators each with a capacity of 35 persons, to convey patrons to the balcony. Above the tapestry panels is another row of panels in which hang the series of Mr. Mackall's mythological paintings.

The foyer lighting is similar to that of the lobby, except that instead of three chandeliers there is only one, but that one is as large as the three of the lobby combined. The walls above the paintings are in mauve which also blends to a light purple and has gold decorations. At the top of the foyer the stairway divides the two parts turning and running to the balcony, while in the center a decorative art marble arch leads into the mezzanine floor. There are a number of alcoves around the floor, and they are furnished as cozy corners. The furniture is antique. There are restrooms, smoking rooms, and writing-rooms on the floor.

The decorations inside the main auditorium are similar to those of the mezzanine floor. The dome of the auditorium with a bright colored mural painting standing out in the glow in invisible light lends an attractive touch to the decorations.

There are but two boxes in the entire auditorium but they are spacious and furnished with large armchairs upholstered in the same tapestry to be found on the walls. Similar chairs are to be found in the loges, which run five rows deep across the front of the balcony.[53]

The seven oil murals of Greek mythological motifs were painted by R. McGill Mackall of the Charcoal Club.[54]

The Century opened to the public on May 7, 1921, with the Mae Murray film *The Gilded Lily*. Admission was 27 cents for orchestra seats and 20 cents for balcony seats at matinees; in the evening, orchestra seats cost 50 cents while balcony seats were 30 cents. The first show, however, was on May 6, for invited guests and featured Warren M. Willpaine and Helen MacNier Marshall of the Metropolitan Grand Opera Company in a duet from *Aida*. The feature film was Ernest Lubitsch's *Deception*. The audience, which included Governor Ritchie and Mayor Broening, sang American folk songs. A 30-piece orchestra, conducted by E. V. Cupero, provided the music. The members of the corps of usherettes, all under five feet tall, were dressed in Peter Pan costumes of black silk, with knee pantaloons and black silk hose. George Wild replaced Cupero in 1924 and brought with him a larger orchestra.

On Saturday, October 29, 1921, the Century Roof Garden opened. The opening attraction there was Ernie Young's Passing Parade and Fashion Show which included torch singer Ruth Etting. A jazz band provided music for dancing. Dinner was served between 6:30 and 8:00, and light refreshments were available until 1:00 A.M. A combination ticket to the Century Theater and the balcony of the roof garden with dancing privileges cost a modest 75 cents. For $1.75, a patron was entitled to dinner (catered by E. B. Taylor), dancing, and a show on the roof garden. The Century Roof was a large rectangular hall with a dance floor in the center and tables for patrons on a slightly elevated platform at both sides and one end. The open end of the hall had a stage with steps leading down to the dance floor. There was also a U-shaped balcony which seated 1,000 people.

A scare about the safety of the theater in 1925 brought a team of architects in to investigate. Theater patrons had become nervous when vibrations occurred during dances at the Roof Garden, but the architects found only "a slight and insignificant vibration" and declared that the structure was "absolutely safe." Nevertheless, the garden was closed and corrective measures were taken to stop the vibrations.

The Shubert organization tried to buy the Century soon after it opened, but Charles Whitehurst refused to sell. In October 1925, more than a year after Whitehurst died, Marcus Loew made an offer of $1,850,000 for the Century and Parkway Theaters, but interests headed by Dr. J. H. Whitehurst, president of the Century Theatre Company, wanted to keep the four Whitehurst theaters together. Finally, in May 1926, after control of the theater had passed into the hands of a faction that wanted the sale, the Century and Parkway were sold to Loew's for an estimated $1.8 million.

As soon as Loew's took over, they brought in the well-known theater architect John Eberson to remodel the Century and convert the ballroom upstairs into an atmospheric movie theater. In the Century, Eberson covered up some of the murals of naked nymphs and cavorting fauns with damask. The new auditorium color scheme was in green and silver with gold and dark blue used in the foyer and subfoyer. Eberson added plaster busts of great literary figures, such as Milton and Shakespeare, and a copy of the Laocoön statue in the middle of the grand staircase. A walnut screen was placed between the last row of seats and the auditorium entrance and a sunburst electric chandelier was hung from the auditorium ceiling. A new feature was the organ console elevator which lifted the organist into the auditorium as he was playing.

The remodeled Century opened on October 4, 1926 with a special show featuring live movie, stage, and radio stars, tours of the theater, and a parade through downtown. George Wild conducted the symphony orchestra[55] and John Elterman played the organ. The huge vertical sign erected in the summer of 1927 contained 4,365 lamps and was the largest electrical theater sign in the city. In the spring of 1927, the Century and Valencia installed a $500,000 air-conditioning system; it was operational by the end of May. On several occasions in the 1930s and 1940s, the Century allowed patrons to spend the night in the air-conditioned theater to escape mid-summer hot spells. In mid-1927, as a result of a partnership formed between Loew's, Inc. and United Artists, the Century, Valencia, and Parkway began exhibiting movies under the joint management of both organizations.

In September 1938, the Century began a new policy called "Streamlined Divertissements," that featured vocalists, choral groups, ballet ensembles, and instrumentalists. The new show was produced by Gene Ford, and the hand-picked 50-piece orchestra was under the direction of Don Albert. The first program included singer Helen Forrest, Broadway dancer Joan Engel, and the B & O Woman's Music Club. Joint management of the Century and other theaters by Loew's and United Artists ended in 1954 and, for a very short time, Loew's became full owners of the theater.

The Century was one of the most popular theaters in Baltimore. Many Baltimoreans remember the theater's imposing entrance and marquee that dominated the narrow block of West Lexington Street between Charles and Liberty. Just inside the doorway, on the left, was a long carpeted ramp that led up to the lobby of the Century. To the right was another ramp that led down to the Valencia's ticket booth and to the adjacent elevators that carried patrons up eight stories to that Moorish garden. For many years, a pretty girl in the lobby, dressed in a blue outfit and spotlighted by a blue light, directed patrons to the Century or Valencia. In the ladies' lounge of the Century there was once a mechanical bird of paradise (or canary according to less romantic sources) which had to be wound up daily.

The inner lobby of the Century was an impressive two-story space lined with mirrors and lighted by a huge chandelier. The later installation of a candy stand diminished the elegance. The balcony and mezzanine lobbies were straight out of a medieval castle with gargoyles and semi-nude carvings on the walls and pillars. If the inner lobby was sparkling and bright, these latter places were dim and eerie. After seeing a horror film at the Century, you wandered through the upper levels at your peril.

The first organ at the Century was a three-manual Moller (Opus 2955), but, by mid–1926, it had been replaced by a 3/11, Style 235 Wurlitzer (Opus 1422).[56] Harvey Hammond and Roland Nuttrell entertained audiences on the Century's organ for years. *Gone with the Wind* opened at the Century on a reserved-seat basis on January 26, 1940. Reserved seats cost $1.10. Baltimore had its first blackout of the war on June 3, 1942. The Century was showing *I Married an Angel*, starring Jeanette McDonald and Nelson Eddy, and it advertised "continuous performances throughout tonight's blackout."

The first major sporting event to be televised in a Baltimore theater was at the Century in June 1951, when the bout between Joe Louis and Lee Savold was shown there. Three months later more than 3,000 fans watched a second televised bout, this one between Robinson and Turpin at the Century. The line for tickets stretched around the block twice and management had to turn away an estimated 7,000 patrons. In 1953 the Century installed a new screen that was three times the size of the old one. To coincide with the showing of the movie *Battle Circus* in April 1953, an Army Signal Corps unit set up transmitters at the Century and anyone could send a free 20-word greeting to a serviceman or woman anywhere in the world.

Morris Mechanic bought the Century and Valencia from Loew's in 1955. The Valencia closed almost immediately, and the Century, a victim of what some called progress, closed on January 8, 1961. The city paid $1.45 million for the theater and the land it stood on. By April the theater had been stripped of most of its fixtures, including the statue of Laocoon.[57] Demolition of the Century began in the summer of 1962 and, by the end of the year, there was no trace of the old theater. It was replaced by part of the new Charles Center.

Charles (see Times)

Church Lane Cinema, 9950 York Road, Cockeysville, 1973–1986, unknown, 314. Charles Hagwood and Steve Finnerty opened this theater in the Church Lane Shopping Center on April 25, 1973. The minimalist entrance consisted of a flat marquee over a doorway in the shopping center. A small sign with the name of the theater and the current attractions appeared on top of the marquee. There was a single poster case to one side of the doorway. All traces of this theater have vanished.

Cinema {1} (see Linden)

Cinema {2} (see Schanze's)

Cinema I–Cinema II, 58 West Ridgley Road, Lutherville, 1964–2000, Morris Zimlin, 1,192 (408-Cinema I and 784-Cinema II). Schwaber Enterprises opened the Cinema I and II on August 19, 1964, in the Yorkridge Shopping Center north of Towson. These theaters were the first of the new wave of multiplex theaters to be built in Maryland. Ground was broken in December 1963. The following description is from *Boxoffice* of February 15, 1965.

> The building covers 14,000 square feet. Cinema I, the smaller of the two auditoriums, is 96 × 54 feet. It seats 500 in 27 rows, divided into three sections by two aisles. The Airflo Rocking Chairs are 24 inches wide and spaced four feet back-to-back. The screen is 16'6" × 34'6".
>
> Cinema I's seats are beige, blending smoothly with the soft green patterned sidewalls of wall fabric and gold draperies curving across the front to the sidewalls. Aisle runners are a rich green-blue diamond pattern.
>
> Cinema II seats 800 in its 117 × 59 feet area. The chairs, 28 rows in three sections, are a new design similar to that used in the recently completed auditorium of near-by Goucher College.
>
> The 18'6" × 40'6" screen in Cinema II ... is anchored to the rear wall with braces not visible to the audience. To enhance the unique floating effect, a cove of blue neon lighting is installed

Architect's drawing of the Cinema I and II (58 W. Ridgley Road, Lutherville, 1964, Morris Zimlin), the area's first twin theater.

around the back of the screen's perimeter. This halo of subtle light remains illuminated throughout the program. Here a pumpkin hue is used for chairs and draperies. The walls are turquoise fabric, and aisle runners are the same green-blue pattern.

The theaters operate with only one cashier, one ticket taker, and one manager.

For Cinema I, the spacious, high-ceilinged lounge area serves as a holding area, but in Cinema II there is a standee area eight feet deep and 50 feet wide ... with the standee rail 31 inches high to give wheel-chair patrons an unobstructed view of the screen. Each theatre has its own booth, equipped with water-cooled projectors. Both theatres can handle CinemaScope. Two to three ushers work the two auditoriums as demand requires.

The lobby is divided into two areas by an aluminum-framed glass partition with two pairs of glass double doors.

The lively green-blue rug pattern continues wall-to-wall through the dual lobby area. in Cinema I's lobby, the carpeting is carried right up several column-like panels to bring a degree of warmth where ceiling height is 26 feet. Floor-to-ceiling drapes in Cinema I's lobby are solid turquoise; in Cinema II's, the drapes are gold.

In the lobby of Cinema II, the entrance lobby, is the cashier's box-office equipped with two units — one for overload — the refreshment bar and the ticket taker's post. The candy counter is operated by Berlo Vending and is augmented by several coin-operated candy and soft drink machines in the Cinema I lobby and in both auditoriums.... Restrooms and powder rooms are located in the lounge in Cinema I and in the rear of the auditorium in Cinema II. Mosaic tile was used in all restrooms.

"For this theatre, we decided against a conventional marquee," [Howard] Wagonheim [president of the corporation which owns the theater] said. "Historically, the marquee is an impulse reactor as is the outside cash box. Today we depend on entertainment habit patterns. People make up their minds before leaving the house." Accordingly, the marquee has become an abbreviated overhang for patron convenience, and it bears no lettering at all. Instead, the two concurrent features are quietly advertised on an attraction board to the right of the ten-door entrance and in two small poster cases to the left. The result is one of dignity in this residential area shopping center. Changing the legends is a simple ground-level operation.

The $400,000 cinder block masonry building is faced with red brick on the exterior sidewalls and unpainted beige brick, in two tones, on the facade. It was completed in six months by the Yorkridge Realty Co. The architect was Morris Zimlin, Baltimore; interior decoration by Paramount Associates, Philadelphia....

Local residents did not mind the first opening film, *The Carpetbaggers*, but they were not sure they wanted *Seduced and Abandoned* shown in their neighborhood. The Cinema was renamed the Yorkridge 2 in 1979. JF Theaters leased the Yorkridge 2 in 1982 and converted it into a four-plex in the summer of 1983. In January 2000, Loew's Cineplex Entertainment, which had acquired the theater along with other JF theaters in 1988, closed the Yorkridge. According to a spokesman for the owners. "Yorkridge was not performing up to our standard. It was an old location. Four-screen theaters don't fit into the model of new theaters today. Its time had come."[58] The historic, first twin theater in the state, was just 35 years old. The Cinema was demolished in mid-2004.

Cinema Center (see Centre)

*Cinema Eastpoint, General Cinema Corporation of Boston announced plans for a 1,200-seat theater adjacent to Eastpoint Shopping Center in January 1965. Robert Kahn, of New York, was the architect.

Cinema North (see Aurora)

*Circle, Park Circle. The Circle Theater Corporation was incorporated in January 1921 with a capitalization of $650,000 to build and operate a 2,500-seat luxury theater on Park Circle. Ewald G. Blanke drew up the plans for the new theater. Alfred G. Buck, president of the corporation, acquired property on Park Circle and began excavations for the theater in August 1921. By October, work on the foundations and retaining walls was under way. The plans called for a classic theater with a concourse that would take in a vestibule, lobby, and foyer on the sidewalk level. Terraced walks were planned to connect the theater with nearby Carlin's Park. The project was abandoned in 1922 in the wake of the Boulevard Theater scandal that involved Buck. The foundations remained until at least 1927.

Circus, 1720 East Fayette Street, c. 1915–1916, unknown, c. 2,500. The Circus was an open-air theater, on Fayette Street opposite Jackson Place, that lasted only a year or two. It was built around a circus theme in the spring of 1915 by James J. Hartlove. According to a contemporary account, "The ground leading to the Circus will be covered with sawdust and large circus pictures will be displayed about the front entrance. The fencing around the lot will be topped by canvas, giving the appearance of a massive circus tent. Tickets are to be sold from a window the surroundings of which will resemble a circus wagon, and the general surroundings will be of the 'greatest-show-on-earth' order."[59]

Clifton, 314–316 South Broadway, 1909–1927, E. A. Moller, 234. Work to build the Clifton Theater began in late April 1909. Costing about $6,000, it was opened and operated by Samuel B. Ward and a Mr. Viola until around 1914.[60] Ward continued to operate it alone, and, in the spring of 1920, renovated the building. Ward sold the theater in early 1921.

Clover (see Amusea {1})

Clown, 112 North Howard Street, c. 1909, Jacob F. Gerwig (of conversion), c. 150. The Clown lasted about a year. Robert B. Bull announced plans to convert the business property at 112 North Howard Street into a $2,000 moving-picture theater in December 1908. The Clown was one of the earliest nickelodeons in Baltimore to advertise in the newspaper. On March 14, 1909, it advertised an exhibition of "about twenty reels" of independent moving pictures by the International Projecting and Producing Company of Chicago.

Cluster {1}, 303 South Broadway, 1909–1921. This was the original Cluster that was built and operated by pioneer exhibitor Benjamin Cluster. The rear wall of the auditorium painted white was used for the screen. Cluster closed this theater in June 1921; he razed it along with an adjacent building to build the present Cluster {2} Theater.

Cluster {2}, 303 South Broadway, 1921–1982, unknown, c. 900 (later 589, 450 reported in 1972 and, in 1980, 280). This Cluster replaced the earlier Cluster on the same site. It opened on September 24, 1921. It had a high balcony and a pressed metal ceiling. The front was of ornamental red brick with limestone trim. The unusual marquee was divided into two wings by a flat, indented section across the front of the theater. Later the name "Cluster" was spelled out in script neon letters in the middle portion. The ancient vertical sign above the marquee was one of the last signs of this kind in the state.[61] In the summer of 1929, Ben Cluster installed an Arctic Nu-Air Cooling and Ventilating system in the theater. This was one of the earliest air-conditioning systems in the city; large blowers were installed in a garage next door and these blew fresh air into the theater. A $12,000 orchestral organ was installed in the Cluster in early 1923 for organist Jesse Kremer. In 1926 the Cluster {2} acquired a new organ, a Wurlitzer (opus 602).[62] In March 1928, it was the second movie theater

The historic Cluster Theater (303 South Broadway, 1921, architect unknown) with its vertical sign still intact, c. 1976).

in Baltimore to show *The Jazz Singer*. Mrs. Etta Cluster Mercur, Ben Cluster's daughter, remembered going with her father in the late 1920s to buy a Vitaphone sound system in New York so that the Cluster {2} could show talkies. The sound system cost a fantastic $15,000. It was a success, and the theater drew capacity crowds for weeks. The management installed a popcorn machine in the Cluster in the summer of 1946.

Rome Theaters operated the Cluster {2} for many years after the Cluster family gave up the day-to-day operation, but the theater remained in the family. It closed in February 1977, reopened on October 21 and closed again in December 1977. It was used as a church in 1979, but reopened as a movie theater for Chinese films a year later. The Cluster lasted less than a year as a venue for Chinese movies; in July 1981, it reopened as Cinema-X. Cinema-X had an even shorter life span than the Chinese theater.

The theater was opened and closed several times between the end of July and December 8, when it closed for good. There were plans in 1982 to convert it into a community center. By 1999, when it was again used as a church, the vertical sign had been removed and the front had been repainted.

Cluster {3}, 667–669 West Baltimore Street, 1908–1916, Oliver B. Wight (of 1912 and 1914 alterations), 105. Benjamin Cluster and his brother Isaac began exhibiting movies at 669 West Baltimore Street in early 1908. It appears that a new theater was erected in the summer of 1912, when Isaac Cluster was granted permission to convert the building into a motion picture theater. It was a two-story building measuring 15 [sic] by 106 feet. The theater was remodeled in the summer of 1914. According to the 1914 insurance map, this theater consisted of two adjacent buildings, 667 and 669 West Baltimore Street. Both were labeled "moving picture theater," so it is possible that there were two separate Cluster theaters, although the one at 669 carried the additional notation, "This side not in operation." The Cluster's ad in the *Baltimore News* of October 20, 1912, suggests that a single theater was located at 667–669 West Baltimore Street.

Colgate, 1718 Dundalk Avenue, Dundalk, 1948–1953, Hal A. Miller, c. 700. Schwaber Enterprises opened the Colgate on December 18, 1948, with a gala community Christmas party. The Gaertner circuit bought it in January 1951. It lasted as a theater until the fall of 1953. Since then it has been used as a hall for many years. Boxing matches were held here on many occasions. The Colgate is nearly identical to the Apex, Paramount and Playhouse theaters, which were designed by the same architect.

Colonial {1}, 1436–1438 North Gay Street, c. 1910–1925, poss. George S. Greener (John Freund of 1920 addition), 275 (later 499). The Colonial {1} was one of the string of early movie houses along North Gay Street. It was opened in late 1909 or early 1910 probably by Frank Durkee's Colonial Theater Company. In 1913, the Colonial {1} ran shows of three reels which were changed three times a week. The theater closed for several years until J. McLaughlin reopened it in May 1920. McLaughlin made ambitious plans that summer to build a new ornamental brick front, a 29 by 91-foot addition to the theater, and install 200 new seats, a new ventilating system, and a new lighting system. The new theater measured 160 by 30 feet. The interior color scheme was old rose and gold. This remodeling cost about $20,000. The Colonial reopened on October 23, 1920, with a small orchestra to provide music for the films. Durkee's Northeastern Amusement Company purchased the Colonial in December 1924 for more than $50,000. Plans were under consideration at that time to convert the theater for other commercial uses.

Colonial {2} (see Blaney's)

Colonnade, 404–406 East Baltimore Street, 1906–present, Freund & Crawford (of 1906 remodeling), Franz C. Koenig (of 1907 remodeling), Fred. E. Beall (of 1916 remodeling); 75 (Pearce and Scheck movie theater on 1st floor), 270 (Colonnade). This plain four-story brick building, dating from late 1904, is surely one of the most interesting structures associated with motion pictures in Baltimore. It was not only the site of the first movie theater in town, but it was also the site of one of the first twin theaters in the country. There was a movie theater on the first floor and a vaudeville theater on the second and third floors. The theater history of this building began in late 1905, when William Brown took over part of the first floor and converted it into a small movie theater. About half an hour after the start of the first show, the film caught fire, and his theater was wrecked.

Pearce and Scheck bought Brown out and opened their own theater in January 1906. It had 75 seats. The earliest ad for this theater is in the *Baltimore American*, February 11, 1906, "Moving Picture Theater, 406 East Baltimore Street, Ladies-Children-Gentlemen, 5¢ Admission 5¢." During the week of May 13, 1906, "authentic earthquake and fire pictures" were being shown at "the moving picture theater, 406 East Baltimore Street." It was open from 10:00 A.M. until 11:00 P.M.

In July 1906, Samuel Stuart, the owner of the building remodeled the second and third floors into a vaudeville theater. The improvements were described in the *Sun* of July 17, 1906. "The building is four stories high, and the second and third floors are to be made into one.

Sigmund Lubin was so impressed with Baltimore's Block that he built side-by-side movie theaters there in 1908. The theater in the foreground is the site of the Colonnade and Pearce and Scheck's 1906 theater. Lubin's Family Theater is under construction adjacent to it. (News American photograph courtesy of Special Collections, University of Maryland Libraries)

The structure is 32 feet wide and 100 feet deep. A stage, 25 by 32 feet with a proscenium arch projecting, will be erected and the floors will be sloped. A gallery will be built at the Baltimore street front and iron stairways will lead up from the entrance." The remodeling cost an estimated $50,000.

The new theater was called the Colonnade. It was operated by W. Arthur Humbert of Pittsburgh. It opened on September 10, 1906 with two vaudeville performances a day, at 7:30 and 9:30. The vaudeville was booked by the William Morris organization out of New York. Prof. Farson's Gwynn Oak orchestra provided the music. Movies formed part of each vaudeville show. The reviewer for the *Baltimore American* described it as "a cozy little house" with an interior color scheme of cream, gold, and red. When it opened, the Colonnade had not been completely finished. The seats were not installed so wooden chairs were used. There was also a problem with the building permit; the building had been declared vacant, but it turned out that a tailor shop employing 125 people occupied the fourth floor. The shop was forced to relocate before further matinee performances could be given.

The Colonnade was not very successful. It closed in early October, but reopened in the middle of the month under the new management of local vaudeville booker John T. McCaslin. McCaslin lasted a little more than a month, and advertisements for the Colonnade disappear around the beginning of December 1906. Sigmund Lubin, a pioneer Philadelphia producer and exhibitor, leased the building in 1907, and spent several thousand dollars renovating it. His architect, Franz Koenig, designed a new facade lighted by incandescent lamps and crowned with a large female statue. Lubin's {1} opened on Easter Monday, April 1, 1907.[63] The *Sun* described the new theater:

> This new place of amusement is one of the handsomest of its kind in the country. The ... facade is cream white ... beautified by four female figures as crown. The lobby is of white cement and marble and contains two more figures. The color scheme on the first floor is dark green and yellow. At the back the wall is white and is adorned with mythological figures. The first floor will be devoted exclusively to moving-picture exhibitions.
>
> The floor above is given over to vaudeville, and there will be performances afternoons and evenings. There is a theatre with balcony and proper exits. The seats are cushioned.... Mr. Lubin has spent several thousand dollars on his new place and says he is going to make it one of the most up-to-the-minute enterprises of its kind in the East.[64]

The lower hall advertised "Life Motion Pictures, including Baltimore subjects, and illustrated singing by high class vocalists." Admission was 5 cents. The upper hall advertised "perfect vaudeville" and life motion pictures. According to the *Baltimore American*:

> With the advent of Lubin's a novel form of entertainment is to be introduced to Baltimore. Appreciating the popularity of life-motion pictures, Mr. Lubin ... has transformed the lower hall into a model auditorium for the exhibition of original life-motion pictures, exceeding in quality as in quantity any display of the kind ever attempted in any city. Briefly, the performance will be one that could not be duplicated by any other exhibitor in the country. Illustrated singing by vocalists of the highest class will be a feature of the performance. The performance will be of unusually long duration, much longer than that offered by the average entertainment.[65]

Admission to the upper theater was 5 cents for balcony seats and 10 cents for seats in the orchestra. This theater was one of first movie houses in the city to use behind-the-screen talkers; it advertised talking motion pictures as early as May 1908. Lubin operated the theaters at 404–406 West Baltimore Street and a theater next door at 408–410 West Baltimore Street until early 1910. In July 1910, both buildings were purchased by the Knickerbocker Amusement Company which planned a new, 2,000-seat theater on the site.[66] These plans fell through. Local exhibitor William Fait leased the theater in October 1910 when it was described as having been vacant for several months. A major remodeling of the theater was announced in July 1916. It reopened that fall.

> The color scheme is old rose and ivory. Large panels of old rose bordered by festive designs decorate the walls, around which runs a broad old ivory molded flowered cornice. The ceiling is paneled in ivory white. Four hundred mahogany, modern, ventilated chairs have been installed, and the gold fibre screen was shipped back to the factory and entirely resurfaced. New curtains of dark green ornament the doorways and granite finished linoleum now covers the floor. A Kimball orchestral organ has been installed. The indirect lighting system is used. A thirty-six-inch exhaust fan has been placed in the rear, and four sixteen-inch oscillating fans ... have been installed on each side of the auditorium.[67]

The ornamental stucco facade of the theater was removed in the spring of 1917 to avoid paying the new minor privilege tax on it. In May 1921, the Baltimore Theatre Company, which had leased the theater for a number of years, purchased it from Samuel Stuart for $100,000. They immediately deeded it to the newly formed People's Theatre Company for $155,000. In 1927, the theater was renovated and its name changed to Plaza. *Sun* columnist Lee McCardell describes an amateur show in what was probably the Plaza, in a 1929 article,[68] and nicely captures the seedy character of the place.

> The theater is one of these places where the cashier calls "Go on in" when you have shoved your 15 cents through his wicket. You part the greasy curtains that hang across the main entrance and step into a deep, narrow auditorium where a moving picture is being projected through a thick haze of cigarette smoke that hangs despondently between the audience and the low ceiling. The floor is strewn with candy wrappers and empty paper cups.... Down in the corner, to one side of the cramped stage, a pianist and a drummer ... grind out improvised sound to suit the romance shining over their shoulders.
>
> When ... the musicians pause to slip outside for a breath of fresh air, a high-powered, out-spoken, peanut-chewing-gum-and-popcorn salesman takes their place. This gentleman's wares include prize packages containing such premiums as genuine ladies' silk hose, genuine solid gold fountain pens and genuine gold-filled wrist watches.... [After selling his prize packages] the salesman retires back-stage to return with a basket of "those big milk choclit bars—fi' cents...." Then he doubles in ice-cold soda water, both bottled and paper-cupped, and "those good ice-cream cones with ice-cream right down to the bottom...."

Following the movie, the screen rolled up to reveal a shallow stage where the resident vaudeville company—"four scantily clad ladies, a Jewish comedian, a burlesque Irishman and a straight man"—performed. When they finished, the amateur show began. That consisted of a girl who sang—off-key—and danced, a second girl who also sang and danced, a man named "Chinch" who sang about a racehorse named Tennessee, two young men who played banjo and guitar, a kid who played a musical washboard, a duo who played a mandolin and jazz whistle, a tap dancer, a male singer, and finally a man who sang "Casey Jones." After the Second World War, the Plaza began specializing in "girlie" movies.

When the Gayety, across the street, burned in December 1969, its name and shows were moved into the Plaza. The theater was still operating as of 2001. The only external sign of its past history is the faded word "LUBIN'S..." high on the facade.

Colony, 8123 Harford Rd., 1949–1974, John J. Zink and Frederick L. W. Moehle, 630. Durkee Enterprises operated this neighborhood house. It opened on October 13, 1949. The opening ceremonies featured a parade led by the St. Dominic's Drum and Bugle Corps. Baltimore County Commissioner Christian Kahl and Frank H. Durkee gave speeches. Durkee said that his ambition was to give residents of the community a theater of which they could justly be proud. The Colony cost about $75,000; it had a concrete foundation and brick walls. The walls of the auditorium were covered with coral wall fabrics. Sensitive to the growing availability of cars, the Durkee organization provided the Colony with a large parking lot at the side and rear of the theater. The Colony lasted only 25 years. It closed on Monday, September 2, 1974, and became a VFW Hall.

Columbia {1}, 625–627 Washington Boulevard, c. 1908–c. 1916, Callis & Callis (of 1910 theater), unknown. A movie theater at this location may have opened as early as 1908; it probably lasted until about 1916. John Chesno obtained a permit in mid–1910 to erect a one-story $1,500 movie and vaudeville theater at this address. It was also called, sometimes simultaneously with Columbia, the Rex in 1911, 1912, and 1913. In the summer of 1915, Frank Ephraim's Twilight Amusement Company purchased the theater from Annie Chesno. In October 1915 Ephraim sold the property to William Nagosanosky, who apparently operated it as the Twilight Theater, at least into the fall of 1916. The 1914 insurance map shows 627 Columbia Avenue (= Washington Boulevard) as an empty lot with a house set back some distance from the street, suggesting that this theater was an open-air theater.[69]

Columbia {2}, 709–715 Washington Boulevard, 1921–1963, J. E. Moxley, 1,300. The Eureka Amusement Company, owned by Eugene McCurdy and William Kolb, took title to the property at 709–715 Washington Boulevard, then known as Columbia Avenue, in January 1921. There they built the Columbia for an estimated $150,000. The *Sun* described the theater:

> J. E. Moxley ... designed the building ... in the Adams [sic] style. It is beautifully planned and decorated, the colors used being French

gray, Kings blue and old ivory. Draperies of mulberry and Alice blue will harmonize with the general decorative scheme. There are 1,300 seats, including the balcony, and the measurements of the entire building are 60 by 125 feet.

In the center of the ceiling over the auditorium is a beautiful dome ... around which ... are a number of concealed lights, giving double the radiance of the usual dome effect. This is something new in lighting construction, according to Mr. Moxley, and gives a very fine effect.

Terra cotta and gray tapestry finished

Top: The Columbia theater (709–715 Washington Boulevard, 1921, J. E. Moxley), shown here in 1922, was demolished to build Martin Luther King Boulevard. ***Bottom:*** The tiny screen seems dwarfed by the cavernous interior of the Columbia.

brick were ... used for the facade. A large marquee rises over the entrance doors. Productions will be projected by two of the latest make projection machines with high intensity arcs.... Two large, six-foot fans have been placed behind the grill over the proscenium for ventilation and these are augmented by a natural flow of air through the ceiling ventilators. The theater will be heated by steam-heated indirect radiators. Music will be furnished by an orchestra, and a $10,000 organ....[70]

Four large urns adorned the top of the facade. Inside there was a small lobby lined with white marble. The exit signs were made of cream and wine-red stained glass. The original screen was set against the rear wall, and was surrounded by a square, molded plaster proscenium arch. There was a small stage in front of this screen. Later a new screen was installed in front of the stage. The Columbia {2} opened on November 19, 1921. Eugene McCurdy, who also managed the Lafayette and the nearby Eureka, operated the theater for many years. During the late 1920s, the Columbia's small stage was used for the popular bank nights and country store nights. The Columbia Orchestra with William T. Owens at the $10,000 Moller 2/10 organ (Opus 3181) provided music for the silent films.

In the spring of 1929, the Columbia was wired for sound with a Cinephone sound system. Patrons of the Columbia often visited the Arundel Ice Cream store at 683 Washington Boulevard to get ice cream before a show. The stage was enlarged in the summer of 1950 and live acts, such as Harry Kahn's "Fun Quiz" were presented. In September 1959, just after it was integrated, the Columbia {2} received a bomb threat, which fortunately was a hoax. The theater lasted into the early 1960s, when it closed. For a time, it was used as the Christian Temple Faith Church, and then it was completely abandoned. It was demolished during the summer of 1972 to make way for Martin Luther King Boulevard. The bits and pieces of the theater were dumped at a landfill on Potee Street to help make land for a park.

Columbia {3} (see Recreation Theater)

Columbia Cinema III, 10205 Wincopin Circle, Columbia, Md., 1973–2000, William Riseman (with Marks and Cooke of Towson), 1,000 (600 and 400) for theaters I and II (later 891 for three auditoriums; 1— 247, 2 — 384, 3 — 260). The developer of Columbia tried for two years to find an exhibitor to open a movie theater. Finally, General Cinema agreed and opened this theater with a Hollywood-style premier that featured searchlights and champagne on May 23, 1973. The first film was *Hitler: The Last Ten Days*. The reviewer for the *Columbia Flier* complained that it was too bad a "remarkably tasteless" movie was selected for the opening. A third auditorium was added in October 1982.

The Columbia Cinema has been noteworthy for the famous people who have attended shows there. Among these were John Denver, members of the Osmond family, and other entertainers performing at the nearby Merriwether-Post Pavilion. The opening of the megaplex at Snowden Square in December 1997 hurt the business of the Columbia Cinema. By March 2000, the name had been changed to Columbia City 3 Cinema, and it was showing art films and second-run movies. It lasted only another seven months, closing on October 19, 2000.

The Columbia Theater was one of 36 older theaters closed by General Cinema in September and October 2000 after it filed for bankruptcy protection. The theater was demolished in the fall of 2001; as of this date, luxury high-rise apartments are planned for the site.

Columbia Moving Picture Parlor, Mt. Winans. This theater was listed in Polk's *Maryland State Gazetteer* for 1909–1910–1911. It might have been identical to the Columbia Hall in Mt. Winans listed in Baltimore city directories between 1906 and 1925. There were several Columbia Halls, and it is difficult to determine if the one at 2125 Washington Boulevard in 1923, 1924 and 1925 is the same one as the one listed in 1922 at Washington Road and Annapolis Avenue and if either is the Mount Winans theater.

Columbia Palace 9, 8805 Centre Park Dr., Columbia, Md., 1986–2001, Kelly Clayton & Mojzisek, 1,714 (total seats; auditorium 1—153, 2—156, 3 and 4—203 each, 5—383, 6, 7, 8, and 9—154 each). This theater was JF Theaters' answer to the under-screening of Columbia. An earlier survey revealed that 80 percent of the first-run films that were available in Baltimore did not play in Columbia.[71] Despite protests by some local homeowners who believed that it would draw too much traffic and lead to noise, Baltimore-based JF Theaters opened the Columbia Palace 9 on October 3, 1986. This state-of-the-art, freestanding complex was built for $4.3 million. It featured a marble box office, a pink and purple lobby lined with marble, and rocking-chair style seats in three of the audito-

Elegant furnishings did not save the beautiful Columbia Palace 9 (8805 Centre Park Drive, Columbia, Maryland, 1986, Kelly Clayton & Mojzisek). It lasted only 15 years.

riums. Mirror-covered columns set off the centrally located concessions stand. Two of the auditoriums had 70mm projection capability. Six of the auditoriums were small, seating fewer than 200 persons. The largest had a 41-foot screen and seated 383; the smallest seated about 153. They were arranged in a U-shape around the centrally located concession stand immediately behind the entrance. The problem of crossover sound, at least in the large auditorium, was solved by constructing the walls of 12-inch concrete blocks filled with sand and placing a ¾-inch layer of insulation over them.

The Columbia Palace 9 became a Loew's theater when they acquired JF Theaters in 1988. The Columbia Palace 9 and the Columbia City Cinema 3 were both hurt by the opening of United Artists Snowden Square 14 in December 1997. Neither would last much longer. The Columbia Palace 9 closed on September 27, 2001, and a new strip mall has obliterated all traces of this attractive theater.

Comedy, 412 East Baltimore Street, 1907–c. 1952, unknown, 225 (later c. 400). This building has had a long and important history in the Baltimore movie business. Frank A. Fisher, a motion picture promoter from Philadelphia, leased the first floor of the three-story building at 412 East Baltimore Street in late January 1907 and began showing films there. The Miles Brothers seem to have been operating it around 1909.[72]

William Fait added the Comedy to his small circuit of theaters in October 1913. New owners took over in August 1916 and renovated it, installing a new screen and cooling system. A $4,500 pipe organ was installed in the summer of 1920, and it became the Globe around 1927–1928. Peter Oletsky operated the theater for many years. In its last years the Globe showed old double features and offered raunchy burlesque shows. In addition to the movie theater, the building at 412 East Baltimore Street housed several film exchanges and, for a few years after its formation, Local 181 of IATSE.

Comet, 1130 Light Street, c. 1907–c. 1919, unknown, 60 (later 175). The Comet, also known as the Cupid, was owned by Karl G. Harig and Sylvester C. Staylor who together operated as the

Cupid Amusement Company. The theater was located on the first floor of an attractive three-story brick building on the corner of Light and West streets that is still standing. It may have been in existence as early as 1906 and was certainly one of the earliest movie theaters in South Baltimore. On March 20, 1909, it re-opened as the "Greater Cupid," and it advertised vaudeville and movies for 5 cents with "fans galore." In 1913, it was running three reels of pictures changed three times a week.

The theater was purchased by the C. D. Rudolph Hardware Store in April 1920 at which time it was still referred to as a moving picture theater. There was a poolroom on the second floor, and gangs of local toughs used to hang out in front of the building and harass pedestrians. In 1999, the building housed a computer store.

Comic, 3603 Eastern Avenue, c. 1909–1913. The Comic was one of the earliest movie houses in East Baltimore. John A. Ertel and Walter Albers, who operated the Eagle across the street, purchased the Comic in September 1912, shortly after it had been enlarged. They planned to rename the theater "The Picture Garden." In October 1912, the Comic inaugurated "talking pictures," which were apparently silent movies using talkers behind the screen. The building has been completely remodeled.

Community {1}, 3019 Hamilton Avenue, 1916–1927, 1933-[1950], unknown, Oliver B. Wight (of Avon); 250 (as Community), 399-450 (as Avon). This movie house, the first in Hamilton, had a long career. Work on converting the original building into a movie theater was scheduled to begin in the fall of 1916. It was opened on December 25, 1916, by Capt. Warren A. Blake and Henry P. Mann, as the Community in what had been the Hamilton Presbyterian Church.

Blake and Mann's Hamilton Corporation was also planning to build a bowling alley on the same lot as the theater, and a local property owner brought suit against them claiming that the theater and bowling alley would be nuisances and "impair the reasonable enjoyment of the plaintiff's property as a residence and a boarding house." The case went to the State Court of Appeals in 1917 where the lower court's ruling for the plaintiff was sustained. It would seem that the theater had already opened by this time, so the effect of the decision probably resulted in the decision not to open a bowling alley.

Frank Durkee booked the films for the Community. His brother, Harry, bought the Community from Charles B. Eyer in the summer of 1919. It was a movie house until 1927, when it was converted into a bowling alley. In late 1927, plans were announced for a new brick theater to replace the original frame structure, and was expected to cost about $35,000. The new building, designed by Oliver B. Wight, was a one-story brick theater, 50 × 149 feet, with a mezzanine. It opened as the Avon on September 30, 1933. The Durkee organization operated the Avon from then up to the time it closed.

It was a popular local theater. One woman remembered that on Friday nights there used to be a singer and piano player at the Community; during intermissions they had sing-alongs. The ushers sold sheet music to the audience for 10 or 15 cents a sheet. There was a bowling alley at the rear of the theater, but despite the combination of movies and bowing, the Avon was torn down around 1950.

Community {2}, Turner's Station, 1945-unknown. According to *Boxoffice* of August 11, 1945, the United Project Company opened this theater on August 10.

Community Hall {1}, Glen Burnie (see Glen Burnie Theater)

Community Hall {2}, St. Helena Avenue at Willow Spring Rd., St. Helena, 1921–c. 1926. C. Robert Moore showed movies in the St. Helena Community Church or Hall during the 1920s. They were among the earliest exhibitions of movies in the Dundalk-St. Helena area. According to one source, when the movies were shown in the church, a screen was erected in front of the altar. There was a projection booth installed at the rear of the church.

Community Theater, Towson. This theater was located in the Independent Order of Odd Fellows (I.O.O.F.) Building in Towson. Movies were shown here in 1927 and 1928.

Convention Hall, 1100 East Baltimore Street, 1903–1909, Jackson Gott (of 1892 power plant), Edward H. Glidden (of 1903 remodeling), c. 2,000. Plans in November 1902 called for improvements to the two-story brick Romanesque Revival building that had originally been a cable car powerhouse built in 1892 for the City Passenger Railway Company. The improvements included remodeling the entrance for use as a theater with the box office and manager's office on the right side of a 15 × 18-foot tiled lobby. The auditorium was 45 × 90 feet with a 24 × 30-foot stage and six boxes.

A contemporary account described the theater: "A pleasing and commodious family theater.... Its furnishings are neat, and a warm color scheme makes the stage effects attractive. Boxes are at each side of the orchestra, and a good view of the stage can be had from all parts of the house."[73]

In January 1903 this theater opened as the Convention Hall. A new feature was the vaudeville performances given between acts. It was managed by Kernan, Schanberger, and Irvin as the American Amusement Company. In February 1903 one of the intermission acts was a series of short Vitagraph movies. During the week of March 16, 1903, Vitagraph films of the Oberammergau Passion Play were exhibited.

The theater was acquired by the Lafayette Amusement Company and reopened as the Bijou, a melodrama house, on August 24, 1903. It closed down after a short time and was not reopened again until 1906, when James Kernan installed new scenery and stage settings as well as new heating and electric lighting systems. It reopened under his management on February 5. Plans were developed, in the spring of 1907 by the Hebrew Free School Society, to purchase the building and convert it into a school, but these were abandoned.[74] For a short time, in mid–1907, it was called the Baltimore Theater and was apparently run as a Jewish theater.

Another attempt to use the building as a theater was made in the fall of 1907, when New York manager Leopold Spachner acquired the lease and reopened it as the Princess. The first attraction at the Princess was the Van Den Berg English Grand Opera Company's production of *Il Trovatore*, which opened to excellent reviews on November 22. The *Sun* reviewer noted that the opening night audience contained many residents who seldom visited the section of the city east of Jones' Falls.[75]

The Bijou {2} was listed as a movie house in 1908 and 1909. In its later years, the Bijou {2} was again used for Yiddish theater. Hendler's Creamery purchased the building in 1913. It was still standing in 2003.

*Cosmopolitan Architect D. E. Kubitz was preparing plans for the Cosmopolitan Theater Company for a theater on Baltimore Street near Greene in late 1910.

Crescent {1}, 314 North Broadway, c. 1909–c. 1915. The Crescent {1} was located next to the Hotel Hopkins and was operated by a Mr. Kiernan, who also operated a horse-drawn sightseeing bus that made trips to places like River View Park.

Crescent {2}, 1509 West Lafayette Street, 1908–c. 1920, H. R. McComas (of 1913 theater), c. 50 (300 by 1917). The Crescent {2} was opened around 1908, probably by John Kahl and James Hartlove who also operated the Crescent {4} on South Charles Street. In 1911, Charles W. Demme, Sr., and William Emmerich bought the theater. To distinguish it from the other Crescent Theaters, it was sometimes called the North Crescent.

In the fall of 1913, Demme had a new theater built on the site. It was a 20 × 69-foot one-story brick movie theater and cost about $2,200. The Crescent {2} was located immediately adjacent to #10 Firehouse, and the firemen could sit in the firehouse windows and watch the movies. The Crescent {2} had one piano player and charged 5 cents admission. In 1916, the name was changed, probably by the new owner Harry E. Volkmer, to the New Crescent, and the theater was completely renovated. The New Crescent opened on May 20, 1916. It featured a special Saturday matinee from 2:00 to 5:00 P.M., and regular performances every evening from 7:00 to 11:00. The theater was offered for sale at a public auction on November 22, 1917. It closed in 1920 and was razed to build a new firehouse.

Crescent {3} (see Eureka {1})

Crescent {4}, 1110 South Charles Street, 1908–c. 1925, F. E. Beall (of 1913 theater), 180–250 (later, as Sunset, c. 400). The original movie house was opened on May 20, 1908, by John Kahl and James J. Hartlove. Hartlove erected a new one-story theater on the site in 1913. It measured 30 by 123 feet and cost about $10,000. In 1913 the Crescent {4} was showing two reels of pictures, changed daily, as its exclusive entertainment. In an unusual publicity stunt in February 1915, manager Hartlove arranged for a wedding to take place in the theater. Local merchants donated $500 worth of gifts to the newlyweds.[76]

Between 1915 and 1919 it was called the New Crescent. In 1919, the theater was renovated; the interior was repainted, the floors were recovered with battleship cork linoleum, and two new Simplex projectors and a new piano were installed. At the same time, a contest to choose a new name for the theater was held; out of 975 names submitted, Sunset, submitted by Stanley Degges, was selected.

The theater changed hands several times before it closed around September 1925. The following month it was sold to the Provident Savings Bank for $25,000.

Crest, 5425 Reisterstown Road, 1949–1981, Julius Myerberg, 1,538. Located across the street from the Hilltop Diner, made famous by Barry Levinson in his movie *Diner*, the Crest was one of the most attractive and luxurious neighborhood theaters in the city. It opened on February 26, 1949, with *Adventures of Don Juan*, starring Errol Flynn. It was built by the Myerberg organization in the Hilltop Shopping Center despite last-minute opposition from a member of the City Council.[77] In its Modern Theatre Section, *Boxoffice* magazine of November 5, 1949 provided a detailed description of the new theater:

> Striking a happy combination of modern simplicity and gracious decor is the new Crest Theatre ... designed by architect Julius Myerberg. One of several outstanding characteristics of this ... house is the effective treatment accorded the back of the theatre auditorium. With decorative emphasis in the auditorium usually localized on the screen area and stage, Myerberg has employed a semi-circular canopy over the standee area to create a unique center of interest. Containing cove lighting for a colorful mural depicting Show Business, the canopy is set off by vertical waves of mauve-colored fabric dropping to the floor.
>
> Unusual treatment of this part of the theatre extends to the arrangement of the projection booth which opens into the auditorium through a rectangular window over the standee canopy. By locating it a full 21 feet from the seating floor, both the noise nuisance and the unsightly porthole effect are eliminated. Rectangular windows at either side of the back enclose comfortably equipped loges.
>
> The theatre exterior combines planes and sweeping curves in a treatment that softens the accustomed angularity of modern architecture....
>
> Small recessed spotlights are combined with indirect lighting to illumine the theatre front and lobby which are divided by a glass front and glass doors.
>
> Lobby walls are paneled in pickled finish oak and the area is highlighted by two curving staircases leading to the lounge above.
>
> Semicircular in shape, the television lounge has wall paneling of the same design as the lobby, topped with a three-foot frieze painted in an overall floral design.
>
> The front section, which overlooks the theatre entrance, consists of five glass panels with an etched mural in the center panel.[78] Over the staircase wall is a six by eight-foot television screen which may be enjoyed by patrons sitting in the modern sectional groupings with which the lounge is furnished.
>
> On the main floor the standee area is decorated with a figured ceiling of unusual pattern. Within the auditorium a unique stage effect has been obtained by the use of a curved curtain wall flaring to each side of the house. Set out four feet from the proscenium wall, these wings conceal vertical lighting for the fuchsia-colored plush curtain. Main walls and ceiling are divided into four sections with verti-

The elegant Crest Theater (5425 Reisterstown Road, 1949–1981, Julius Myerberg) was the focal point of the early strip shopping center on Reisterstown Road at Rogers Avenue.

cal lighting coves on either side joined across the ceiling by a trough. Cold cathode light is used. The walls are covered in a forest green fabric. An irregular dado top is trimmed with specially designed rococo plaster ornamentation. The same figure is continued in a painted design on the fabric walls. the acoustical plaster ceiling is painted mauve gray.

The rear wall of the auditorium was composed of mauve fabric in vertical waves surrounding "a central mural accented by a huge semi-circular ceiling cap and side pilasters."[79] The television lounge could accommodate up to 200 people. Additional features included soda and candy counters, water fountains, glass-enclosed smoking rooms and the latest in air-conditioning equipment. The facade was constructed of pattern-set face brick and granite. The theater cost an estimated $495,000 including equipment.

The Crest was awarded the Exhibitor Merit Award Plaque for outstanding design. When it opened, admission prices were 25 cents for adults at matinees Monday through Friday, and 40 cents in the evenings and on Saturdays, Sundays, and holidays. Children paid 18 cents at all times. The GFS Theatre Corporation, headed by Joseph Grant, Jack Fruchtman, and Aaron Seidler signed a long-term lease to operate the Crest in the spring of 1963, and in the early 1970s it was leased to JF Theaters. Rome theaters acquired the Crest and reopened it on December 25, 1975. The entire staff from Rome's recently closed Harlem Theater moved up to the Crest. It closed again in early 1976 and then reopened as the Crest 99 in 1980. By 1998, the auditorium of the theater had been converted into a church and the entrance and lobby had become a pawnshop. No one seems to remember anyone ever watching television in the television lounge. The Hilltop Shopping Center also included Holtzman's Bakery and Mandell-Ballow's Jewish deli.[80]

Crown, 756 Washington Boulevard, c. 1908–1950, unknown, 250–280 (375 in 1916). J. George Hoffmeister opened the Crown around 1908. A succession of many operators followed him; Jones and Heimiller, Morris Lasky, Charles Habighurst, Nat Keen and J. J. Hartlove (in 1917), Max Cluster, E. B. McCurdy (who kept it closed), Leon Zeller and Roger Hurlock, Samuel Shoubin, and finally, a Mr. Brown. The name was changed to Imperial between 1932 and 1934. Zeller changed the name to Roy in 1934. It was called the Pic from 1938 until it closed in 1950. According to *Motion Picture Herald* of June 10, 1950, the Pic was closed and would probably become a store.

The Crown building was still standing as of early 2004 when it was a variety store. In the middle of the lobby floor there was originally a large red tile design of the figure "5¢" and the name "ROY" was set in the front sidewalk.[81]

***Crown Imperial**. Crown Theaters announced a 4,500-seat 18-screen megaplex for the seventh floor of a retail and parking tower just east of the Inner Harbor in September 1998. It has not opened, as of 2004.

Crystal Maze, 612–614 East Baltimore Street, 1908–1909. J. E. Cahill, who later operated the Opera House in Centreville, Md. and the Music Hall in Easton, opened this theater. The name was changed to the Edisonia in 1909. It became the Elite in early April 1909 under the management of J. W. Jefferson, who promised "New Vaudeville Features That Have Never Appeared in Baltimore" and "New Moving Pictures Every Day."

Crystal Moving Picture Parlor, 526–530 North Gay Street, 1913–1927, unknown, c. 500 (750 after 1920 remodeling). Benjamin Meyer was granted a permit to build a one-story motion picture theater, 32 by 100 feet, at 526–528 North Gay Street in July 1911, but the Crystal Theater was not actually built until 1913. In June 1913, Meyer requested a permit to alter the building at 526–528 North Gay Street for use as a moving picture parlor.

The Crystal opened in August 1913. It was advertised as "Baltimore's Largest and Best Equipped Motion Picture Theater." The Crystal was extensively renovated in the fall of 1916. The exterior was repainted in dark colors and the lobby was redone in a mahogany finish with a border of paneled paintings edging the wall around the ceiling. Plans were made in the spring of 1920 to take out the stage and enlarge the theater to 750 seats. The back wall of the box office had a small window that looked into the theater so that the cashier could watch the movie. Around 1924, the Crystal staff consisted of two cashiers, a doorman, an organ player, an usher, a projectionist, a manager, and a boy who changed the posters. After managing the theater for several years, Harry Cluster leased it in January 1925.

In April 1923, a new $10,000 orchestral organ was installed in the Crystal. Title to the Crystal was conveyed by the Crystal Amusement

The Crystal Theater (526–530 North Gay Street, 1913–1927). (Drawing by Robert W. Kramer)

Company to the Real Estate Holding Company for about $30,000 in December 1924. It was called the Alhambra in its last year of operation. The large building that housed the Crystal was still standing as of late 2000, but most of the interior seemed to be missing.

Cupid (see Comet)

Curtis, 921, later 4704, Curtis Avenue, c. 1920–1926, unknown, c. 100. The Curtis was a frame building with a fairly plain, pressed metal front. According to one source, the Curtis opened in 1905, but this is almost certainly too early.[82] It was operated by a Lithuanian man named Rafael Shimanauskas. A pot-bellied stove provided heat for the theater.

Dainty (see Jewell)

Daisy (see Hasslinger's Daisy)

Daly's (see Palace {2})

Daly's Why, 1115–1117 Pennsylvania Avenue, 1912–(1917), possibly A. Lowther Forrest. The Modern Amusement Company of Baltimore City was granted a permit to build an airdome at this location in December 1911. The following June, the curiously named Daly's Why opened, offering motion pictures, singing, ice cream, sodas and sundaes, and a brass band. It was a one-story brick summer garden, 20 × 38 feet. It cost about $1,100 to build. The music was provided by the Goldfield Orchestra from a balcony at the rear of the airdome. Eubie Blake performed at Daly's during the week of May 20, 1912. The theater was advertised simply as Daly's Airdrome in the summer of 1916.

Dean (see Goldfield {1})

Deluxe (see Flag)

Deluxe Roosevelt (see Roosevelt)

Diane, 1429–1431 Pennsylvania Avenue, 1934–1986, David Harrison, 440. The announcement of the remodeling of the two-story buildings at 1429–1431 Pennsylvania Avenue into a movie theater was made in December 1933, but the Diane did not open until April 18, 1934. A huge crowd gathered in front of the theater before it opened and stormed the doors; special police had to be called before the theater could open. The Diane was operated by the Hornstein family.

Barry Goldman reopened it as the Carver Playhouse, an African-American art theater, on July 4, 1953. The most elaborate decorations were the sandblasted and figured glass panels in the front doors and transom. A life-size mural of Dr. George Washington Carver was featured in the foyer. There was also a lounge furnished with sofas, lounge chairs and coffee tables where attractive hostesses served refreshments. The rows of extra-wide seats were spaced 37 inches apart to provide more legroom. The management of the Carver stated that no child under 12 would be admitted. The opening feature was *Man on the Tight Rope*, with Frederick March. The marquee was removed around 1971 and the front was painted chrome yellow.

Dixie, 312 West Baltimore Street, 1909–1938, unknown, 175–200. The Dixie was built by the Dixie Amusement Company in the five-story building they leased in March 1909. It cost a reported $3,000, and opened on April 24, 1909.[83] It was a long, narrow theater with only three or four seats on either side of a single central aisle. A brief description of the theater in April 1909 adds, "The exterior will be of ornamental metal, while the interior will be of fancy carvings, with vari-colored electric lights."[84] The Dixie advertised in the May 2, 1909, issue of the *Sun* that a box of Guth's Gold Medal Candies would be given free to every lady and child purchasing a ticket beginning Monday, May 3. In October 1909, the Dixie Amusement Company bought the theater and planned extensive improvements. In 1913, the Dixie was offering a show made up of four reels of pictures for 5 cents. Nat Keen purchased the Dixie in August 1916.

Tragedy struck the theater in February 1926 when a statue fell from the facade and killed a four-year-old child, Elizabeth Baugher, who was walking past the theater. The owner of the theater and the manager were found guilty of criminal negligence in connection with the girl's death.

Philip Scheck Enterprises leased the theater for five years in the spring of 1928 and remodeled it. During the $10,000 remodeling, craftex walls, woodwork in old ivory, and draperies of dark blue with old gold figures were installed. On October 1, 1936, it reopened, under the joint management of Gibbons O'Hare and Moses Cohen, as the Europa {2} with *Cloistered*. It was a venue for foreign films until it closed about a year later. The building was scheduled for demolition in 1939.

Douglass, 1329 Pennsylvania Avenue, 1922–1970, Lachman & Murphy (of Philadelphia), 1,349 (later 1,190, 721— orchestra and 469 — balcony). This theater, as the Royal, was the best known of the several Royals in Baltimore. For many years it was one of the most popular theaters in town, attracting African American and white patrons alike to enjoy the live music there. The idea to build the Douglass was said to have been inspired by the opening of the 1,400-seat Dunbar Theater in Philadelphia in 1919. Unidentified Philadelphia buyers, believed to be E. C. Brown and Andrew P. Stevens, who were looking for a place to build a new theater, purchased a site on the east side of Pennsylvania Avenue between Lanvale and Lafayette in April 1920. The Douglass Amusement Company filed plans for a new theater in October 1920. Stock in the amusement company was offered at $10 a share. F. H. Keiser of Pottstown, Pennsylvania, built the theater for a reported $400,000.

It had a massive facade that dominated the entire 1300 block of Pennsylvania Avenue; the building measured about 90 × 172 feet. Inside the cavernous auditorium there was a large balcony, several boxes and false boxes, a wide, deep stage, and a tiny projection booth that had to be entered by climbing up an iron ladder at the rear of the balcony. The Douglass opened with a live show, *Within the Law*, presented by the Lafayette Players, on February 15, 1922.

The first few years were troubled. A suit was instituted to force the Douglass Amusement Company to sell the theater in March 1922. It closed for a while and reopened in October 1923. The Douglass Amusement Corporation promised Keith and Loew vaudeville acts with first-run movies that would appeal to everyone including people coming home from work, but crowds of patrons failed to materialize. Perhaps the Douglass was too pricey. For the production of *Follow Me* starring Billy Higgins and Clifford Ross that reopened the theater on October 8, 1923, the prices ranged from 39 to 55 cents for matinees and between 39 and 85 cents in the evening; boxes were 85 cents to $1.10.[85]

The Douglass closed in late December 1923 after the Sandy Burns Company refused to appear without a guarantee. The following year it reopened. Prices were reduced: matinees were 25 cents, and evening tickets cost 25 and 50 cents. In early 1924, the Lafayette Players and other acting groups appeared at the Douglass. The main attraction for the week of January 21, 1924, was supposed to be Oscar Micheaux's controversial film *Birthright*, but "owing to some defect in the reels" manager Cress Simmons was unable to show it.⁸⁶

In 1925, the newly formed Royal Theatre Company, acquired the theater. Title to the Douglass Theater was conveyed to J. Elmer Porter and Samuel H. Porter for about $125,000 in March 1925. They remodeled it and changed the name to Royal. The Royal opened on November 30, 1925, with two-a-day vaudeville and films. The first show was *Hello Dixie*, a musical starring Gus Smith. The *Afro-American* of January 23, 1926, was able to report that, "The Royal Theatre has entered the amusement field in Baltimore with an energy that is attracting a most substantial patronage. Within the last month the attendance has increased ... until standing room seems to be the order at all performances.... The former Douglass seems to have struck its stride, and bids fair to be among the city's most popular institutions for amusement lovers." The new management did seem to have hit upon a strategy that would finally make the huge theater pay. They had a top admission of 30 cents. They brought back the popular Sunday midnight shows. They brought in Paul Harris' six-piece orchestra and popular African American entertainers such as Gonzella White and the Smoky City Quartet.

The new policy appeared to work, and the corporation running the Royal decided to dissolve in the spring of 1926 to admit additional capital. Occasionally contests were added to the midnight shows. In April 1926, local girl "Little Bits" Randolph won the Charleston contest, the Taskiana quartet of Philadelphia won the quartet contest, and Johnny Jones' Valley Inn Orchestra won the jazz band contest.

Dr. J. Elmer Porter, of Pottstown, Pennsylvania, became the sole owner of the Royal in September 1926 for $140,000. But problems continued to plague the theater, and it went through several other operators, including Abe Lichtman of Washington who took over the operation of the theater in 1927. He immediately angered local musicians by replacing the Royal's orchestra with non-union musicians. Soon after that, Lichtman decided that stage shows had not done well at the Royal, so he decided to try a movies-only policy.

Lichtman gave up his lease on the Royal and closed it in June 1928 following a year of losses. Dr. Porter, the owner of the theater, announced that he would not allow the theater to be opened until he had sold it; the sale price was set at $175,000. Peter Oletsky took over operation of the Royal in September 1928 and brought back a union orchestra, the Royal Symphonic Orchestra, under the direction of Irvin Hughes. He reopened the Royal on October 15, 1928, under the management of Cincinnatus Major.

The first show was the movie *Four Walls*, starring John Gilbert, and *Sugar Cane*, a musical revue. This was to be the pattern in the Royal for several years, a weeklong engagement by a musical comedy or vaudeville show along with movies changed three times a week. In December 1928, Broadway promoter Sam Grisman was coaxed to see the show *Deep Harlem* at the Royal. Grisman was at first bored, but by the time the show was over, he called it the most astonishing performance of his whole theatrical career. He took the show over and moved it to Washington for a try-out, where it grossed more than $11,000 and then moved to New York.⁸⁷ The management of the Royal got in trouble with theatergoers later in the fall of 1928 when numerous patrons wrote to the *Afro-American* complaining about the practice of having barkers selling cheap candy and novelties in the theater during intermissions.

Oletsky had sound equipment installed in 1929. The first talkie, *The Scar of Shame*, was advertised for the week of April 15. In June, Oletsky announced that the Royal would be closed for two weeks in order to install "one of the most complete talking picture outfits of any theatre in Baltimore." Oletsky was ultimately unable to come to terms with the Royal's owner, and the Flaks organization took over operation of the theater in the fall of 1929. By the early 1930s Pennsylvania Avenue was one of the centers of African-American music; and the Royal, under the management of Morris Flaks, was one of the main venues. Flaks continued Oletsky's pattern of shows, a movie plus a stage show. The Sunday Midnight shows were especially popular. According to Count Basie, as reported by M. Sigmund Shapiro in a letter to the editor of *The Evening Sun* on February 11, 1971, Baltimore "was, during the early "30's, the eastern terminus of the so-called 'stride' piano school. James P. Johnson, 'Jelly Roll' Morton, Willie 'The Lion' Smith, Fats Waller and others would indulge in 'cutting' contests at the Strand Ballroom, the New Albert Hall and sundry other spots along the Avenue."

Nathan Stiefel was operating the Royal in October 1936 when he had the theater completely remodeled for $50,000. The Royal became famous throughout the country, and all major African-American entertainers played there at one time or another. Well-known stars who appeared at the Royal included Pegleg Bates, Mamie Smith, Butterbeans & Susie, Jackie "Moms" Mabley,[88] Earl Hines, Louis Armstrong, Count Basie, Cab Calloway, and Duke Ellington. Heavyweight champion Jack Johnson once gave an exhibition on the Royal's stage and Pearl Bailey appeared there as a chorus girl.

The Royal {4} ranked with the Apollo in Harlem, the Howard in Washington, and the Regal in Chicago as one of the premier African-American theaters in the country. Attendance by white patrons helped the Royal bring in additional revenue, but this attendance caused a minor problem for the management in 1932. A letter to the *Afro-American* complained of discrimination at the Royal. Manager Benjamin Flaks denied discrimination, pointing out that whites could more often afford the higher prices for box seats and that this gave the appearance of segregation. For many years, Tracy McCleary led the house orchestra, which once had included Charlie Parker.

In the summer of 1948, Washington-based District Theaters — ironically a direct descendant of Lichtman Theaters, which had unsuccessfully operated the Royal in 1927 and 1928 — acquired the Royal; the theater's policy was to have first-run double features every other week and a single feature plus a stage show the other weeks. The Royal became part of the JF Circuit in February 1965. The last stage show at the Royal was performed on November 12, 1968; it was the *Jewel Box Review*. The Royal closed on July 21, 1970, with the double feature *I Spit on Your Grave* and *Alley Cats*. A week later the theater fixtures and equipment were auctioned off, and in 1971 the building was demolished. The community has been lamenting the loss of the Royal since then. An historical marker in memory of the Royal Theater was dedicated on August 15, 1986. It's a small memento for such an important building. As one woman remembered, "You knew you were something if [your date] took you to the Royal and you put on your best outfit."[89] In the summer of 1999, the Pennsylvania Avenue Committee announced that it had raised $240,000 to erect a two-story brick monument to the Royal on the southeast corner of Pennsylvania and Lafayette avenues. Groundbreaking for the monument was set for June 2000.

Dream, 582 North Gay Street, 1913–1917, A. Lowther Forrest. In July 1913, Isidore W. Hirshberg was granted a permit to alter the buildings at 582–584 North Gay Street into a single building for use as a moving picture theater. The Dream opened around November 1913. William Fait purchased it in January 1914. On September 5, 1915, the Dream advertised, "Starting 6 September we will begin to show all new and up-to-date star feature shows. Something new for Northeast Baltimore."

The theater was renovated in the summer of 1916. Dr. Leonard K. Hirshberg, a local physician and newspaper writer, took over the Dream in May 1917 and immediately brought in a team of interior decorators to remodel the theater. Martin Berger, who also managed the Star and Poplar theaters, became manager in May 1917. It must have closed shortly thereafter. The Dream was a dress shop in 1973; in late 2000 it was a laundromat.

Dreamland, Virginia Avenue, Belvedere. Between 1912 and 1914, this mysterious movie house was reportedly operating somewhere near the intersection of Reisterstown Road and Virginia Avenue. C. T. Wilkinson was named as the manager in September 1912.

Dunbar, 619–621 Central Avenue, 1916–1958, Callis & Callis (Oliver B. Wight & E. A. Lockhart of 1921 remodeling plans; J. F. Dusman of 1929 remodeling), 200–350 (after 1923 remodeling, 500; after 1929 remodeling, 944).[90] The Dunbar was built in 1916 for Josiah Diggs and Henry S. Trimble's Crown Amusement Company It claimed to be the first African-American owned moving picture theater in Baltimore.[91] Diggs and Trimble bought two buildings in the 600 block of Central Avenue for the new theater. The plans, filed in August 1916, called for a one-story brick and stucco building 31 × 100 feet which would cost about $25,000. It opened on November 22, 1916. The Dunbar Amusement Company took title to the adjacent property at 623–625 North Central Avenue in August 1921 and planned to enlarge the Dunbar. In November 1923, they enlarged the theater to 75 × 100 feet. In 1923 the Dunbar advertised Paramount, Fox, Metro Goldwyn, Warner Bros., and First National films and featured the orchestra of Carlos Daugherty.

The theater was remodeled and enlarged again in 1924, reopening that April. Charles Vodery, one of the first African Americans to be licensed as a projectionist in Maryland, was the projectionist, among many of the early African-American projectionists who received training at the Dunbar. Charles Harris' orchestra provided the music. The Dunbar also had a piano player and, sometimes, a drummer, Chick Webb.

A 1941 night photograph of the Dunbar Theater (619–621 Central Avenue, 1916–1958, Callis & Callis, Oliver B. Wight & E. A. Lockhart of the 1921 remodeling; J. F. Dusman of the 1929 remodeling).

In the summer of 1929, the Dunbar was remodeled again. The seating capacity was nearly doubled, and it became the first African-American theater in Baltimore to install both Vitaphone and Movietone sound systems. At the same time, an Arctic Nu-Air cooling system, which offered a complete change of air every three minutes, was installed. The temperature was 10° cooler than outside.

The Dunbar offered first-class movies so that members of the African-American community in East Baltimore did not have to go "up town" to the movies. A writer in 1930 noted that patrons at the Dunbar preferred "thrilling and exciting melodramas" to "sob-pictures."[92] The Dunbar had a small stage, and occasionally would put on a live show. In 1933, the management turned the theater over to local youngsters on Friday nights; they put on their own show and received 20 percent of the evening's gross. The children's show was directed by Miss Odessa Bacote with Robert Carr as master of ceremonies. A serious fire nearly destroyed the theater in June 1945.

Joseph Grant's Calvert Theater Company acquired the remains of the Dunbar and rebuilt it in the summer of 1946. It reopened on July 5 with a western double feature. The City purchased the site in 1957, and the theater was razed to build a housing project.

Eagle, 3608–3610 Eastern Avenue, 1908–1929, unknown, 218. Walter Albers, John A. Ertel, and Steve Brenner operated this small theater for many years. It opened in 1908 and was one of the few movie theaters advertising in the newspaper in 1910. Just before it closed in 1929, the name was changed to New Eagle. For many years it was regarded as a favorite theater of the elderly; it was said that a view from the rear of the Eagle showed more bald heads than that of any other movie house in town.

The Eagle Theater introduced Sunday religious movies with organ accompaniment in early 1911. These shows proved extremely popular and, according to one observer, kept young men from street corners and fathers from looking for secret entrances to saloons.

In April 1912, the well-known strongman Cameroni appeared onstage at the Eagle, where he performed feats of strength. Outside the theater, he held back two horses each pulling in opposite directions. The Eagle building was still standing in 2000, with the date "1908" clearly visible at the top of the facade.

Earle {1}, 8059 Main Street, Ellicott City, c. 1925–1946, unknown, c. 180. The Earle seems to have been the second movie theater in Ellicott City. It was opened around the end of September 1925, apparently by Edward A. Rodey, who operated it until 1934. Jackson D. Wheat took it over in 1935 and ran it until it was destroyed by fire in December 1941. Wheat rebuilt the Earle in eight months. He reopened it on September 11, 1942. It was a very small, plain movie theater with wooden seats and a tiny balcony next to the projection booth. After it was rebuilt in 1942, the Earle was described as having "the latest in sound equipment and 'Day-lite' screen" with an interior that was "modernistic with checkerboard ceiling and deep tinted side walls."[93] Helen Hogan was the piano player for a number of years at the Earle. Patrons could buy candy to take into the theater at nearby Valmis Brothers or Frizzle's confectionery. Children used to sit in the balcony armed with peashooters and a 5-cent pound of dried peas shooting people in the audience until the manager threw them out.

The Earle Theater Company was incorporated in October 1943 by Isaac and Rose Taylor and Max and Ethyl Goodman. It closed around November 28, 1946.

Earle {2}, 4847 Belair Rd., 1937–present, John Eyring, 796 (425 by 2003). The Gaertner organization opened the Earle on November 17, 1937. It cost about $30,000 and measured 81 × 141 feet. In flowery language, the opening program of the Earle described the new theater:

> Designed along strictly modern lines and constructed of brick and ornamental stone, it is indeed "supreme in beauty and all the arts," with a battery of many colored floodlights playing upon its facade and a brilliantly lighted marquee, its entrance is both imposing and inviting, a lobby beautifully decorated in a modern motif, with handsome gun metal mirrors and made more attractive with modern semi-indirect lighting effects. A luxurious lounge adjoining the lobby will be found convenient and enjoyable…. The decoration of the auditorium is almost awe-inspiring in its beauty and interest…. The walls are decorated with alternating blocks of fawn and ivory Celotex…. Circulating ice water supplied by a specially installed cooling system will be found at convenient locations…. The arrangement of the seats are [sic] unique in theatre construction. They are scientifically set in a concave semicircle in such a way that the occupant … may enjoy a full, clear view of the screen. These seats are oversized, with ample space between rows for your comfort and freedom of entry and exit.

The first show at the Earle began with a Mickey Mouse cartoon; it was followed by a Three Stooges comedy and then the feature presentation, *Back in Circulation*, with Pat O'Brien and Joan Blondell. The building next door to the theater was originally an Atlantic Confectionery; later it became the headquarters for Ritz Enterprises. In 1970, the Earle became a JF theater. As an independently operated theater, it has been showing X-rated movies for many years.[94]

East (see Takoma)

Eastern, 3915–3917 Eastern Avenue, 1909–1914, unknown, 627. The Eastern, built by the Baltimore Amusement Company, was one of the largest movie houses in the city — measuring about 40 by 140 feet — when it opened in the spring of 1909. It had an 18-foot stage and cost an estimated $15,000. Movies and vaudeville were featured.

The opening show cost 10 cents and con-

The sparkling art deco Vitrolite front of the Earle Theater (4847 Belair Road, 1937–present, John Eyring) matched that of the next-door Atlantic Confectionery.

sisted of three vaudeville acts, illustrated songs—by Dorothy Phillips—and moving pictures. Sam Phillips of the Maryland Theatrical Agency was the manager, and vaudeville was booked by H. W. Taylor of Philadelphia. John B. Cook, who ran the Aurora at North Avenue and Charles, bought the Eastern from the Great Eastern Amusement Company in May 1913. He reopened it in June with three acts of vaudeville and seven reels of movies.

The theater closed in 1914, probably as a result of competition from the newly opened Grand {2} on Conkling Street. Cook had architects Callis and Callis prepare plans to convert the theater into a sub-post office in March 1914. The plans called for an entirely new front and some interior alterations. This handsome building is still standing. It was used as a post office for many years.

*Easterner, 7930 Eastern Avenue. The Easterner was the first of three theaters planned for this site. The Durkee organization planned to begin construction on this 1,200-seat theater opposite Eastpoint Shopping Center in the fall of 1964. Durkee broke ground for the new theater in January 1965, but it was never completed.

Easter's, 407 West Lexington Street, 1908–1916, Robert C. Ulrich. This theater was named after its owner, George Easter. It was a one-story, 20 × 64-foot brick moving picture hall. It cost an estimated $2,300. It was operated in turn by Easter, Horace Lutwyche, Russell and Causby, and Lee and Causby, and lasted until about 1916. The name was changed to Pastime soon after it opened.

*Eastpoint 4, Eastern Avenue. Rappaport Theatres announced that they would build a 1,500-seat fourplex opposite Eastpoint Shopping Center. The plans were being developed by architect Donald B. Ratcliffe and the opening was set for early 1976.

Eastpoint 10, 7938 Eastern Avenue, 1995–present, John Carroll Dunn, c. 2,798 (for 10 auditoriums). R/C Theatres of Reisterstown opened this multiplex in a small strip mall opposite Eastpoint Mall. Irwin and Scott Cohen reasoned that

One of several theaters designed by the late John Carroll Dunn, the Eastpoint 10 (7938 Eastern Avenue, 1995–present), has a very plain exterior, but Auditorium Number 4 is nearly as big as many single screen theaters.

the Eastpoint area would be a good location for a theater since there were no other theaters serving the southeastern quarter of the city. After waiting for more than 30 years, there was a theater at Eastpoint. The Eastpoint 10 opened, in stages, in 1995. It began on May 17 with a showing of *Crimson Tide*; two days later *Die Hard with a Vengeance* and *Little Princess* opened.

Nine of its auditoriums are typical of theater auditoriums of the early 1990s, opening off of a long corridor. But the ninth auditorium, Auditorium Number 4, which opened six months after the others, is a real gem — a large, 626-seat, stadium-style theater with a 50-foot-wide screen and a blue waterfall curtain. With state-of-the-art projection and sound, this auditorium has been a perfect venue for such blockbuster films as *Twister* and *Independence Day*. Auditorium 4 has excellent acoustics, probably because the walls do not have 90-degree angles, which would cause sound waves to bounce back.

Much of the theater complex was constructed within two vacant store lots. The entrance runs between two ticket booths and up several stairs into a huge lobby, with video games and a large concession counter. One set of restrooms is located off this lobby. On the right side of the lobby is a wide corridor running back from the street; the entrances to the auditoriums open into this corridor. At the far end of the corridor is Auditorium Number 4, where a small concession stand and second set of rest rooms are located near the entrance. The smallest auditorium seats 108. Television actor Richard Belzer, who starred in the series *Homicide*, was reportedly a regular at this theater. The Eastpoint 10 annually heads the *Dundalk Eagle*'s list of the Best Places for a Date. R/C Theatres is to be congratulated for this outstanding theater.

Eastway (see New Essex)

Echo, 124–126 East Fort Avenue, 1914–1953, Albert H. Friese (?), 340. Paul Klein and Dr. Herman O. Weinholt received a permit to erect this movie theater in July 1913. Some problem must have come up because, in December 1913, Albert H. Friese, John C. Vollbracht, and Bruno Rosenbauer were also granted a permit to build a theater at the same location. The Riverside Amusement Company finally opened the Echo in mid–1914. It measured 29 × 109 feet and cost about $5,000. Maurice Zimmerman's Maryland Theatres Corporation purchased the Echo in the spring of 1921. Herbert Zimmerman operated it from 1926 to 1936, and William G. Myers ran it from 1936 until it closed in 1953.

In the early 1930s the front of the Echo was

As late as this 1931 photograph, the Echo Theater (124–126 East Fort Avenue, 1914–1953, possibly Albert H. Friese) still retained much of its original front, illuminated by dozens of incandescent lights. (Photograph courtesy of the Maryland Historical Society, Baltimore, Maryland)

decorated with hundreds of incandescent lights. The name was spelled out in these lights above the old arched entrance and on the front of the marquee. Large, elaborate bronze poster cases flanked the entrance, and there was a large sunburst at the top center of the facade. The building was later sold to a nearby undertaker.

Eden (see National)

Edgemere, North Point Road at Sparrow's Point Road, 1944–1958, unknown, c. 400. The history of this theater may go back to April 1941, when *Boxoffice* reported that a new theater was under construction in Edgemere. The Fradkin family purchased the building in which this theater was located prior to 1944. The portion of the building that was later converted into a theater had housed a car dealer. The first ad for the Edgemere was in the newspapers on September 15, 1944; *King of the Cowboys*, with Roy Rogers, was playing that day. The Fradkins leased the Edgemere to Joe Walderman in the fall of 1948. After it closed as a movie house in 1958, a church leased it. In 1972 it was used as a hall. It was still standing as of 2000, when it was used by a computer company.

Edgewood, 3500 Edmondson Avenue, 1930–1961, John J. Zink, 1,250 (later reduced to 675). This beautiful theater was built by the Durkee-controlled Lyndhurst Corp. In the spring of 1928, the Durkee organization announced that it was planning a $200,000 movie theater building with four stores, eight apartments and a library at the corner of Edmondson Avenue and Edgewood Street. Scaled-down plans were filed in July 1930. The Consolidated Engineering Company had to dynamite portions of a hill to build the theater. Herman Feldman protested the Durkee theater because he claimed that he had been denied a permit to build on the same site after he had purchased the property for $18,000. Thomas Goldberg, who operated the Walbrook Theater, also protested the building of the Edgewood because it would compete with his Walbrook Theater.

The Edgewood measured 83' × 150' and cost about $150,000. It was a beautiful red-brick neoclassical structure. The facade was dominated by a central vertical sign, similar to the one at the Patterson, illuminated by incandescent lights, suspended above a rectangular marquee. Inside, the auditorium had a wide square proscenium flanked by four niches containing art deco floral designs. It opened on October 3, 1930.

In April 1954, the Edgewood installed CinemaScope. In a desperate attempt to remain in business, on September 13, 1960, after extensive remodeling and the installation of new rocker seats, the Edgewood reopened as an art theater. Every other row of seats was removed so that the remaining rows were 54 inches apart. In addition, two rows of seats were removed at the rear of the auditorium to make room for two new lounges; a new screen was also installed. The first film, as an art house, was *The Red Inn*, starring Fernandel. The newly organized Baltimore Film Society held Monday night showings there in 1960 and 1961.

The Edgewood finally closed on May 18, 1961. It was tastefully remodeled as a church in the 1970s. The facade, minus the marquee, which was removed in the summer of 1971, is well preserved.

Edisonia (see Crystal Maze)

Edmondson, 2100 Edmondson Avenue, 1914–1930, Otto G. Simonson (or F. E. Beall), c. 400. The Edmondson Amusement Company opened the Edmondson Theater on September 5, 1914. It had been planned since about 1912, when the building permit was granted. The original cost was about $10,000. It was a one-story, fireproof, brick building with an extremely elaborate galvanized iron front. The theater measured 26 by 85 feet. The architect at that time was listed as

John Zink's beautiful Edgewood Theater (3500 Edmondson Avenue, 1930–1961, John J. Zink) around 1930. The vertical sign was very similar to that of the Patterson, which opened the same year.

The Edmondson Theater (2100 Edmondson Avenue, 1914–1930, Otto G. Simonson). (Drawing by Robert W. Kramer)

F. E. Beall. However, according to a notice in *American Builder* (May 23, 1914), the theater was built from plans by Otto G. Simonson. The management planned to show Vitagraph, Lubin, Selig, Biograph, Kalem, Essanay, Edison, and Kleine films.

The Bridge {1} was later built next to the Edmondson. In May 1919, plans were announced that the Edmondson and Bridge {1} would be converted into a single theater, but this was not accomplished until 1930, when they were both demolished to build the Bridge {2}.

Edmondson Village, 4428 Edmondson Avenue, 1949–1974, Kenneth Cameron Miller, 1,205. The Edmondson Village was one of the first shopping center theaters in the Baltimore area. It opened on June 3, 1949, during the shopping center's second-anniversary celebrations. It was designed in a neo-colonial style of red brick to harmonize with the rest of the shopping center.

The seating was on one floor. Advertisements touted the comfort and beauty of the theater.

> See an entirely new design in theatres—a theatre worthy of being part of the shopping center that has been called America's most beautiful. Kenneth Cameron Miller, Edmondson Village architect, has done a superb piece of work in proportion, color and design. See the ticket counter (no booth) in the interior lobby (no outside waiting), the beautiful lounge, and many other interesting and unusual features.

A bowling alley opened in the basement of the theater later in the summer. In 1954, the operators of the Edmondson Village brought a $150,000 anti-trust suit against Durkee Enterprises, Twentieth Century–Fox, and Loew's Inc., alleging that Durkee's Edgewood Theater, located about three-quarters of a mile to the east, was getting an unfair advantage over the Edmondson Village. A year later the management

The Edmondson Village Theater (4428 Edmondson Avenue, 1949–1974, Kenneth Cameron Miller) blended in with the Colonial style of the adjacent shopping center.

of the Edmondson Village sued to prevent a new drive-in, further west on the Baltimore National Pike, from using the word Edmondson in its name; they lost and the Edmondson Drive-In opened. Sam Weinberg of Honolulu purchased the theater and shopping center in 1967, and JF Theaters took over the operation of the Edmondson Village in December 1967. It closed in 1974 and has been converted to other uses.

Edmondson Drive-In, 6026 Baltimore National Pike, 1954–1991, Jack K. Vogel, 950 cars. George Brehm and Joseph Einbinder opened the Edmondson Drive-In on May 30, 1954. It did such good business from the day it opened that Brehm and Einbinder were able to acquire the funds to begin work on the adjacent Westview Cinema. From the early 1970s until it closed, a flea market was held on the grounds of the Edmondson Drive-In every Sunday.

The drive-in closed in 1991 and was demolished the following year; a Home Depot was built on the 19-acre site. The sign at the intersection of Route 40 and Winters Lane was retained and used by Home Depot. With the closing of the Edmondson Drive-In, there were only two drive-ins left in Maryland.

Electric Park, Belvedere Avenue, 1896–1916, Henry L. Copeland (New York, of 1908 additions), 5,000 (for casino). Electric Park was built by August Fenneman's Electric Park and Exhibition Company. The site was the John L. Kreis (or Crise) estate, also known as the Arlington Racecourse, which Fenneman had purchased in 1893. Fenneman put a fence around the park, built a large casino, and converted the poolroom into a dance hall.[95] In late 1895 Fenneman asked Charles E. Ford, who was managing Ford's Opera House, to give a season of comic opera at the theater he was building on the grounds of the race track. Ford was convinced that people would not sit in a close, warm theater on a hot night to see any theatrical show, but would enjoy the ride to a suburban park to attend the theater. Fenneman agreed, and Electric Park opened on Monday June 8, 1896, under his management. It was a summer park covering an area of about 24 acres, with a 1,350-foot frontage on Belvidere Avenue and a 500-foot frontage on Reisterstown Road. The park included a large theater or casino, a roof garden, lake, a swimming pool with a bottom covered with sand brought from Ocean City, and a racetrack. Water for the pool and lake was supplied by two artesian wells. The theater was described in a newspaper article.[96]

> The theatre is ... on the south side of Arlington racetrack, inside of the course. It is to be entirely of iron, of oval shape, three hundred feet long and one hundred and fifty feet wide. The stage will be at one end of the building, and, in size, will be about the dimensions of the stage at Ford's Opera House.... The dressing-rooms ... are to be on the stage floor, ranged in a semicircle around on the outer edge of the building. The orchestra, or main floor, will be sunk half a dozen feet below the level of the stage, while the first balcony will be a narrow semicircle surrounding it on the same level as the stage.
>
> The two upper balconies of the theatre will be of novel construction. Mr. Fenneman proposes to continue this summer the races ... so popular at the track last summer, and for this reason the upper balconies have been designed to serve both as places to watch the theatrical show inside and the races on the track outside. This is done by planning them both as outside porticoes, with extra large glass windows looking into the interior and everywhere around the building, commanding a good view of the stage.

The drop curtain was 33 feet wide and featured a Persian motif.

Electric Park was important as the site of the first projected motion pictures in the Baltimore area in June 1896, and, according to one "old-timer," the first ice cream cones in Baltimore were sold there. The *Baltimore American* reviewed the park's inaugural performance and described the summer casino where the show was given.

> The casino is a large and comfortable structure in the shape of an elongated circle, with a peaked roof. The auditorium is encircled by a broad platform, the floors of both being on a level, and separated by a railing. Tables and chairs are arranged ... for the convenience of those who desire to smoke or to sip some cooling beverage during the performance.... Curtains are provided along the outer edge of the platform, so that those sitting near the edge may be protected from sunshine or shower. The auditorium is cool and inviting, the sides being open. The ceiling is high and open, showing the steel rafters and beams, which are painted red. The first nine rows of seats nearest the stage, which is at the north end of the casino, constitute the orchestra circle, and they are separated from those in the rear by a broad space. At night the building is illuminated by arc lights.[97]

The opening program featured Prof. Fisher's String and Brass Band, Edison's Vitascope, Princess Eulalie, Adele Purvis Onri, the Three Sisters Don, and the Three Bouffons. Four thousand people attended despite threatening weather.

Electric Park became a very popular entertainment center. It featured motion pictures from its opening season until as late as 1909. Electric Park lived up to its name and the light generated there must have been visible for miles. "The electrical illuminations will be the most brilliant and extensive yet seen anywhere and will include thousands of incandescent and arc lights.... Electric lights of all colors are strung across the deck, shedding a soft and pleasing light.... The entire area of the main entrance, clubhouse and lawns will be covered by a huge canopy of lights which is of dazzling gorgeousness and beauty.... Sixty big arc lights encircle the track, and everywhere will there be an abundance of illumination."[98]

The park experienced financial difficulties in 1904. Fenneman leased it to Schanberger and Irvin in May 1906. They planned many improvements, including a "cuisine service" featuring traditional Maryland specialties under the personal supervision of Mr. Irvin. The Casino was converted into a vaudeville theater for the 1906 season.

When it reopened in May 1907, the park advertised an Electric Theater that showed "Sensational Moving Pictures" between 3:30 P.M. and midnight. Many improvements had been added prior to this opening; these included a new promenade deck on top of the clubhouse, a new vaudeville theater, new pool and billiard parlors, new dining-room and kitchen, and an Electric Theater, "where the latest and most sensational moving pictures will be presented by the scientific marvel, the Kinetograph."[99] Music was supplied by Italian bandmaster Vincent Del Manto's military band.

The United Amusement Company leased the park for 15 years in 1908 and planned a major upgrading. New attractions, including a large building called "The Johnstown Flood," and numerous shade trees were added to the park for the 1908 season. The Johnstown Flood building contained a scale model of the Pennsylvania city that could be flooded as a lecturer described the tragedy.[100]

In 1909, the park announced the opening of a special building devoted to moving pictures. August Fenneman re-acquired Electric Park for an estimated $200,000 in September 1910[101] and enlarged it, remodeling the deck into an open-air theater that could seat 5,000 people. It had a 40 × 30-foot stage. Above this deck was a new "hurricane deck" seating 1,000 where parties could be held. But the park's days were numbered; it was sold to the Electric Park Improvement Company in February 1916 for a figure between $75,000 and $100,000, and work began at once to raze the park structures in order to erect semi-detached "sunlight" and cottage dwellings.

Elektra {1}, 1039–1041 North Gay Street, 1910–1924, Theodore Wells Pietsch, 240–275. Moses Millhauser opened this small movie and vaudeville house in the spring of 1910. Architect Pietsch suggested the name. The site originally contained two small stores, but they were gutted, and an addition was added in the rear to build the Elektra {1}. Milhauser leased this property for $7,500 a year. The building measured 90' × 26'. It was brick trimmed with stone, with an incredible ornamental plaster facade dominated by a figure of Pan playing his pipes. The front was decorated in two tones of ivory and gold. The interior was done in tan and cream, illuminated by clusters of electric lamps, with Georgia pine and tile floors. One man remembered that there were two small gas-lit exit signs down near the piano. The floor was steeply pitched, utilizing a natural incline.

The Elektra {1} had a small stage, most of which was behind a muslin screen that could be rolled up and down. Music was provided by a piano with a violin or other instruments brought in as needed. The theater employed behind-the-screen talkers—Robert North and Margaret Matthews. In 1913, it featured shows of three reels changed three times a week. The United Theater Company purchased the theater in January 1917 and renamed it the New Elektra. Frank Durkee acquired the theater the following month and made plans to renovate it. It closed for several months in the summer of 1922 and reopened in September, only to be sold at auction in November. It closed in 1924, and the building was razed in late 1972.

Elektra {2}, 524–526 Eastern Avenue, Essex, 1930–1949, unknown, 285–320. This may have been the $40,000 brick theater and stores planned by the Essex Amusement Company in early 1930. Steve Brenner operated it from about 1930 until 1932. He used the sign from the Elektra {1} on Gay Street. The Elektra {2} was located on the second floor of a commercial building. According to one source, the building was built by a man named Gutermuth, who operated a grocery store on the first floor.

There were outside stairs on either side of the building that led up to the theater. The auditorium was equipped with hard, wooden pull-down seats. A piano player provided music. Brenner went bankrupt, and donated the theater's organ to St. Mary's Industrial School. It may have closed around 1939–1940 since the owners of the New Essex Theater were planning to reopen it around October 10, 1940.

The name was suddenly changed to Alert on July 9, 1943. The Alert and the Midway were the "Action Houses" of the Essex–Middle River area. The Alert closed

Architect Theodore Wells Pietsch designed some of the most elaborate theater fronts in Baltimore as this photograph of the Elektra (1039–1041 North Gay Street, 1910–1924) attests.

for remodeling in June 1947, and reopened in November. By the fall of 1948, it was open only on weekends. It closed for good on May 11, 1949. It had become a church by 1959 and was being used for religious services when it was extensively damaged by a five-alarm fire in August 1963.

Elite (see Paradise {3} and Crystal Maze)

Elkridge Drive-In, 6200 Washington Boulevard, Elkridge, 1948–c. 1982, unknown, 740 cars. The Elkridge Drive-In opened on or about August 1, 1948, with two shows nightly. It was completely remodeled for the 1950 season. The Elkridge closed around 1982. The site was overgrown as of the late 1990s with bits and pieces of the drive-in, including the attraction board, scattered about it.

Ellicott, 8217 Main Street, Ellicott City, 1941–1997, Stanislaus Russell, 386 (reduced to 125 by 1996). This theater has been opened and closed numerous times in its 56-odd year history. It was built by the Ellicott Theater Company, which was incorporated by Isaac and Rose Taylor and Max Goodman in February 1941. It first opened on July 18, 1941. The original theater had a modern facade with a triangular marquee. The facade was divided—by dark, fluted vertical bands—into five bays with a single window in all but the middle bay. The floor plan had to accommodate the oddly shaped lot, so the auditorium is at an angle to the entrance and lobby.

Bill Hewitt took over the lease in the fall of 1960, and Lawrence Perry leased the theater in the spring of 1968 after it had been closed for eight years. Perry planned to renovate and reopen it in April. The theater was reopened in 1970, but closed in the summer of 1971, when plans were made to convert it into a young adult entertainment center. In 1973 and 1974, the theater was used as a discotheque. After that it was used as a store for several years. Again in 1980, plans were made to revive it as a movie theater. It was also used as a children's theater, a laundromat, a grocery store, and a comic book store.

Jill Porter reopened the Ellicott as a theater in December 1994. It lasted less than a year, and by December 1995, when Tony McGuffin took it over, it had become a performing arts center for plays, puppet theater, and live music. The theater's second season in March 1997 began with a critically acclaimed production of Milan Stitt's play, *The Runner Stumbles*. McGuffin's theater could not make it for a third year; it closed in 1997 and was bought by the Precious Gifts store. Despite this drastic change, we should not assume that the Ellicott is finished as a theater.

Embassy (see Victoria)

Empire {1}, 315–319 North Eutaw Street, 1903–1922 (demolished 1986), Charles M. Anderson, c. 1,000 (1,900 after 1904 remodeling). The Empire Theater opened on February 23, 1903, in what had been a church built originally in 1851.[102] The *Sun* gave a short description of the new theater:

> The old St. Mark's Church building has been transformed into a cozy and handsome little playhouse with a seating capacity of about 1,000. The color scheme of the interior is red and gold making a rich and effective decoration. Red velvet curtains are draped about the windows and the chairs are of veneer polish and very comfortable. Artistically arranged groups of electric lights illuminate the theatre. It will be conducted as a family house, without bar or café, and is managed by Mr. Louis H. Baker.[103]

Movies came early to the Empire. During the week of April 13, 1903, as part of the vaudeville show, there were 30 Vitagraph films, including *A Journey to Luna*. George Fawcett leased the theater for a stock company in October 1903 and changed the name to the Oriole.[104] Fawcett took over for Leonard Scarlett, who had been arrested for setting fire to the theater on October 13.[105] Repairs to the fire damage were under the direction of Patrick J. Cushen and included an addition to the stage. In 1904, the theater was acquired by Charles E. Blaney of New York who changed the theater's name to Blaney's. Blaney announced that he would remodel the theater for the 1904–1905 season.

> Only the sidewalls of the church ... remained, and the building has been extended back over the alley in the rear about 40 feet. Handsome decorations and a plenitude of lights make the latest amusement venture in the city a most handsome house home for popular-price attractions.... A rose-color scheme is carried in varying tints in the interior effect, and the walls and ceilings are arranged with the main ceiling effect in the Louis XV style as the center. The lights are effectively grouped about the boxes and through the entire auditorium, so that it can be brilliantly illuminated. The chairs are comfortably placed, and 10 boxes ... occupy the space immediately next the stage. Two large galleries increase the capacity to about 2,200. The stage is Mr. Blaney's pride, and is 88 feet

wide, 58 feet deep, and the "gridiron" is 72 feet high.... Work on the theatre was completed only in time to ring up the curtain.... Milton C. Davis was the builder, and it is said that only local union labor was employed.[106]

In early 1909, Blaney's abandoned melodrama and turned to vaudeville and moving pictures. Charles E. Wright was the conductor of Blaney's orchestra from 1906 to 1911. It consisted of Herman Rolfs (clarinet), William Wankoff (cornet), Bill Novek (flute), George Smith (string bass), Charles Brunker (drums), John Guardaboscia (trombone), and Charles Schmidt (piano). The orchestra played Sousa marches from an outdoor balcony before every show.

Blaney sold the theater to David M. Newbold, Jr., for around $100,000 in 1909. George W. Rife, manager of the Holliday Street Theater, took over management. The name was changed to the Savoy when it was renovated in August 1910. As the Savoy it was mainly a vaudeville theater. During the fall of 1910, movies by the "Savoygraph" were part of nearly every show.

Theatrical producers and managers Stair & Havlin took over the theater in 1913. They reopened it on September 15 with popular plays. It was called the Colonial until 1921. The Stair & Havlin operation was dissolved in 1916, and the Quality Amusement Company, an African-American organization, leased the theater. They were not very successful, and the theater was sold at auction to New York producer Lee Shubert in 1918. Movies were shown there during the summer of 1919 and, late in 1920, it was auctioned again. A contest was held in January 1921 to rename the theater; the first prize was $50. The theater reopened as the Playhouse, a popular price musical comedy house, on February 7, 1921.

The Callahan Film Company, which was leasing the theater in the fall of 1921, sub-leased it to Miss Roma Reade and her stock company for a year. The Colonial reopened on August 23, 1920, with the social hygiene picture, *Some Wild Oats*. The Maryland Censor Board ordered it to be shown to audiences of the same sex, and the young women ushers were ordered to remain outside the doors while men were watching the film. Men were admitted between 4:00 and 6:00 and 9:00 and 11:00 P.M.; women were admitted between 2:00 and 4:00 and 7:15 and 9:00 P.M. The theater finally closed after going into receivership in 1922. It was sold at auction for $63,500 and converted to other uses.

In 1934, Hutzler's Department Store purchased the building and, after extensive remodeling, opened it as the Hutzler Annex. For many years the Annex was the site of Hutzler's Toytown and record department. The City acquired the building in the 1980s and had it demolished; no one — except Jacques Kelly — seemed to notice. Kelly wrote an obituary for Blaney's and rightly asked, "Why it wouldn't have made a good candidate for preservation through conversion into offices or apartments has never been explained."[107]

Blaney's was used for just about every kind of theatrical entertainment and many well-known performers played there, among them George M. Cohan, Mary Miles Minter, Charlotte Walker, and the magicians Thurston and Blackstone. As the Colonial it was the only theater in Baltimore daring enough to put on the controversial play *Sappho*.

Empire {2}, 311–315 West Fayette Street, 1911–1937, 1947–1990, Otto Simonson (William H. McElfatrick of Philadelphia, consulting architect, of Empire), John J. Zink and Lucius R. White, Jr. (of Town), 2,200 (as Empire-Palace; 835 — lower floor, 507 — balcony, 800 — gallery, 220 — boxes), 1,550 (as Town). The Empire began life as a vaudeville and burlesque theater on the Empire Circuit. It was built on the site of the old Mechanics Hall. It was supposed to replace the aged Monumental, but never did. Two lots on West Fayette Street were purchased for the theater for $50,000 in the spring of 1910. The Empire opened there on December 25, 1911, with Barney Gerard's "Follies of the Day" which got great reviews: "It begins lively, moves along interestingly and closes with energy."[108]

The management hoped to attract large numbers of women to the theater, and, indeed, one article reported that there were hundreds of women in the matinee and evening audiences on opening day. Matinee ticket prices were 10 cents for gallery seats, 15 cents for balcony seats, 25 and 50 cents for orchestra seats and $1 for box seats. At night the prices of balcony seats increased to 25 cents and orchestra seats went up to 50 and 75 cents.

Local architect Otto Simonson teamed with Philadelphia architect William H. McElfatrick to design the Empire in the French Renaissance style. It cost about $400,000 and was the first theater constructed in Baltimore under a new building code. The Empire was three stories high with a partially Grecian facade of brick and concrete with ornamental stone and white enameled terra cotta trim. It measured 100 feet wide by 150 feet deep. The entrance was constructed

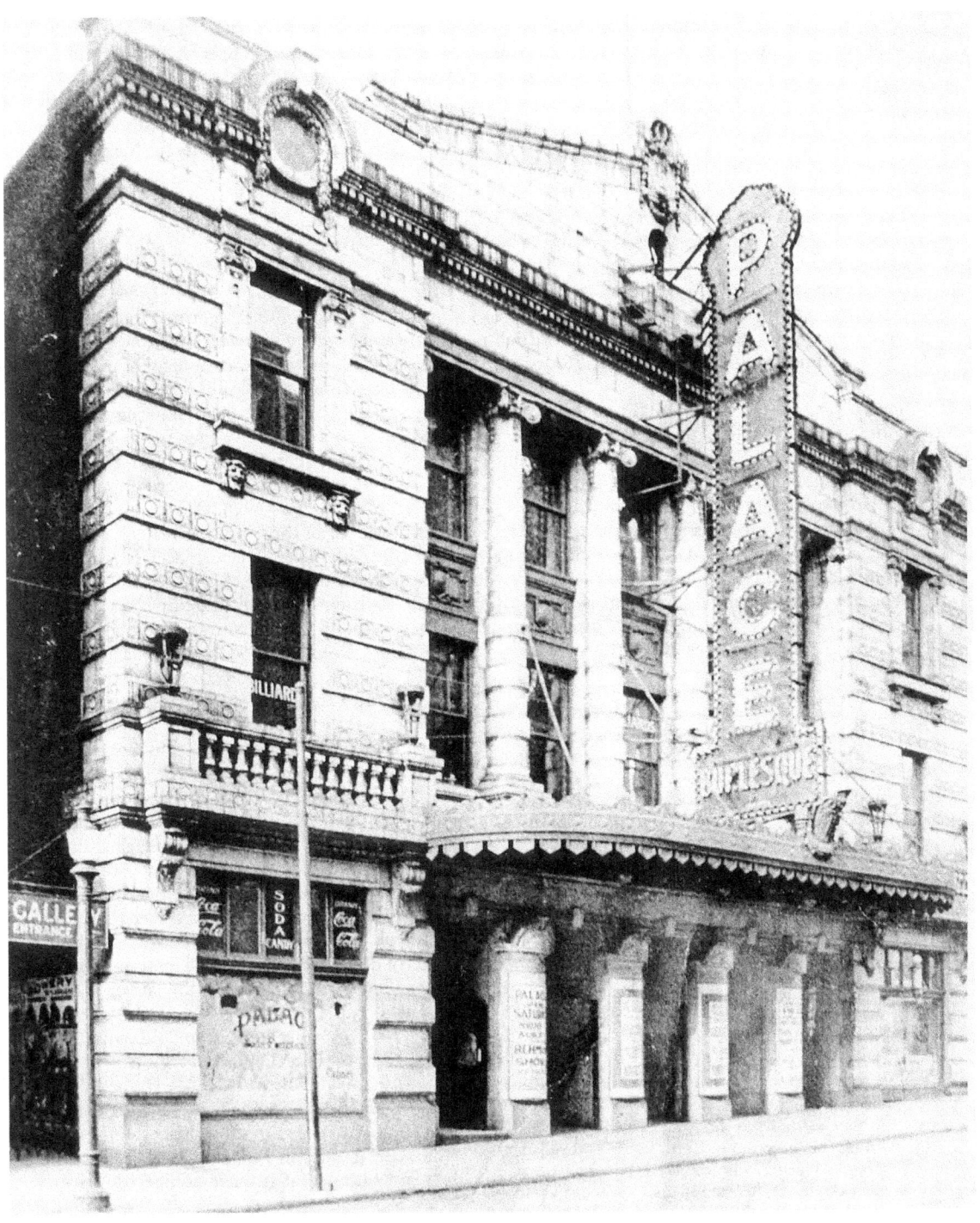

This theater building had a long second life as the Town (311–315 West Fayette Street, 1911–1937, 1947–1990, Otto Simonson of Empire, John J. Zink and Lucius R. White, Jr., of Town), one of the classiest theaters in Baltimore.

of onyx, white marble, colored granite and ivory with terrazzo flooring; the color scheme was gray, blue and gold.[109] The stage measured 70 feet wide by 70 feet high and 32 feet deep. Above the arch was a large painting depicting a scene from Greek mythology, and there were four boxes on either side of the stage. The original interior colors were a mellow green and gold. The draperies were soft rose; the carpets, deep red. The lighting fixtures were gleaming brass with globes by Tiffany.

There were 12 dressing rooms arranged in three tiers. On either side of the main foyer were large rooms used as stores. The two-story high foyer was completely lined in marble. Added attractions included pool parlors on the second floor, a magnificent soda fountain on the ground floor, and a rathskeller.

The Empire, Holliday Street Theater, and the Monumental passed into the control of the United Booking Office in May 1913. Soon afterward the name of the theater was changed to the Palace. The Palace opened on May 26, 1913, with three-a-day vaudeville and movies. The first program included Ismed "The Turkish Musical Marvel," Countess Leontine, and "Edison's masterpiece Talking Pictures" with three "Palacescope photo-plays." The *Sun* described the reopening in glowing terms.

> A new vaudeville theatre opened yesterday when the Palace gave its first bill to a representative and crowded house. There was a matinee performance at 2:30 o'clock and two performances at night. Occupying a box were Frederick C. Schanberger and George W. Rife, directing manager of the playhouse, and Eugene Kernan, booking representative in New York. Nearly every seat on the first floor was occupied and the balcony and gallery held a large number of spectators.
>
> Fresh in new paint and the lobby filled with palms, beneath which have been placed a number of comfortable lounges for the accommodation of visitors, the theatre presented a delightful appearance. The cooling system worked so perfectly that it was chilly within the walls of the theatre. The staff of young women ushers, formerly at the Auditorium, worked under the direction of Capt. Louis Cadwallader. Charles Warner, who directed the orchestra at the Maryland Theatre for many years, is wielding the baton at the Palace.[110]

There were daily shows at 2:30, 7:00, and 9:00 P.M. for prices ranging from 10 to 50 cents. The advertising emphasis for the new theater was on its clean and wholesome entertainment. It was touted as "a strictly first-class family theater," without a bar or smoking, that would be "for the ladies and children first, last and always."[111]

In March 1914, the Palace was reportedly the first vaudeville theater in the country to offer first-class vaudeville at 15 cents for the best seat in the house. On the first day, the management invited 100 old soldiers from the Confederate Home in Pikesville to be their guests.[112]

The Palace flourished during the late 1910s and early 1920s with such entertainers as Joe E. Brown, Mae West, Gus Hill, and Dave Marion; but, in the late twenties, bad times loomed over the theater, and it was used for all kinds of other shows. The policy was changed again in March 1922. This time, vaudeville and movies were added to the burlesque show. Between 1:00 and 2:15 and 4:30 and 8:15, vaudeville; and movies were shown between 2:15 and 4:30; and between 8:15 and 10:30, burlesque acts were presented.

In early January 1928, George W. Rife, the vice-president of the Empire Theater Company that controlled the Palace, declared that the Palace was in danger of closing. The Columbia Circuit, which had been booking shows at the Palace, discontinued business. Rife blamed the problems at the Palace on movie theaters that could offer the public a good, continuous run of movies and vaudeville at lower prices than the burlesque theaters could afford. In an attempt to increase patronage, controversial movies such as *Birth* and *Ecstasy* were shown. Even the old warhorse *Some Wild Oats* was dusted off and shown. It opened at the Palace on November 5, 1928. The advertising campaign was again aimed at women. According to one ad, "men and women will not be admitted together to this picture." Other ads carried the message, "'It's your fault, you never told me' is the daily cry of thousands of daughters and sons!" "Ignorance or innocence may mean misery—the law of eugenics—who is the man your daughter is going to marry?—The most sensational, daring, and spectacular motion picture ever shown."[113]

Some Wild Oats was the last straw; by December 23, 1928, the Palace was up for rent by the day, week, or season. It reopened for a short time with movies in February 1929. The Palace lost out because of intense competition from other burlesque theaters. According to the Sunday *Sun*, a rivalry arose between the Palace, the Gayety, and the Embassy, and the Palace lost.

> That was one of the weirdest situations ... in Baltimore. The regular Mutual wheel shows were coming to the Gayety. Down the street at the Embassy a group of entertainers, many of

them Baltimoreans, did their best to outbid their neighbors. At the Palace was a queer organization of passé show girls and visiting stars who gave a combination of singing, dancing, and joking that was neither musical comedy, nor revue, nor vaudeville, nor burlesque, nor Coney Island tent show, although it partook of some of the qualities of each. The prima donna was large and blonde, and, oh so weary ... there was, in contrast, a henna-haired "mamma," ... who fascinated the boys with her knowing ways and slightly daring stories about traveling salesmen. There was a wild scramble for girls and material.... By Friday, often, one could go into any one of the three burlesque houses and see pretty much the same skits and novelties.

When the three-cornered rivalry began, "the fancy" and the curious flocked to the Palace, but in a few weeks even the henna-haired mamma lost her appeal and the audience fell away to nothing. As a desperate expedient the management tried a strange combination. They offered continuous burlesque and motion-picture entertainment. It was simply awful; and the Palace closed.[114]

Amateur shows, Yiddish dramas, boxing, and bingo parties were held there for the next couple of years. New York producer John G. Jermon leased the theater for five years in the summer of 1930. It was then sold in 1931 for $14,000, subject to two unpaid mortgages representing an unpaid balance of $200,000. Howard Burkhardt and William Proctor tried to run the Palace as a vaudeville theater in December 1931, but that was also a failure, lasting less than a month. In January 1932, the financial situation got so bad that an entire vaudeville bill walked out before the evening show.

In May 1932, the theater was sold again, at auction, for $50,000. It struggled along until December 1933, when it was renovated and reopened on Christmas Eve. Although equipped with the latest RCA sound system to show movies, nothing seemed to work. Finally, Minsky's wide-open strip tease shows in 1934 and 1935 brought in the police. Four female performers were charged with indecent exposure. One more partial season of burlesque in the fall of 1936 finished the Palace. It closed and was converted into a three-floor parking garage in 1937. Neither Ford's Theater nor the Hippodrome had any objections to the conversion of the Palace to a garage.[115] It lay fallow until 1945, when Isador Rappaport acquired it and made plans to reopen it as a movie theater. The preliminary name for the new theater was Esquire,* but, when it opened it was called the Town. Rappaport said that he wanted a theater that would be "different ... beautiful, but not gaudy ... magnificent, but intimate ... lusciously luxurious, but simple and chaste."[116] In another interview, he said, "The theater will include every new device and innovation of modern film projection. It is my intention to provide this city with a theater comparable to the best in the country. Baltimore will be proud of its newest theater and the policy planned for its operation."[117]

We were indeed proud; the Town was a magnificent theater that served the city well for more than 30 years. Rappaport hired local architects John J. Zink and Lucius R. White, Jr., and spent about $500,000 remodeling the building into a 1,550-seat movie house. The garage was gutted, leaving only the walls of the original Empire Theater.

Zink and White's treatment of the new theater included indirect lighting, serpentine walls, panels of back-lighted corrugated glass, and modernistic metal sculpture by Oscar Bruno Bach.[118] The exterior of the first floor was completely remodeled, mainly by the addition of a huge curved marquee with the name Town spelled out on each side in hundreds of incandescent bulbs. A centrally located stainless steel and chrome box office was surrounded on both sides by two sets of plate-glass entrance doors. The interior decorations were by S. Brian Baylinson, a relative of the Rappaports. The lobby was separated from the outer foyer by three pairs of solid glass, all-mirror doors. On either side of these doors was a metallic "garden" by Bach. Irregularly shaped display frames were located on the right and left walls. The standee area featured blues and greens on the walls with pink and mulberry tones on the ceiling. The mezzanine lounge contained several more of Bach's metallic gardens.[119]

In the auditorium, the architects used inward curving sidewalls of Caribbean blue and a central path of light on the rose-colored ceiling running from the screen to the rear of the auditorium to bring the screen close to the audience. Two Bach metal compositions, one on each side of the screen, represented light, motion and music and were symbolic of the movie industry. The screen curtain was a shade of mulberry. The seats and carpets were shades of soft blues and greens. The seats were slightly wider than typical theater seats and the rows were spaced a few inches further apart. There were also two lounges finished in gray marble and beige tile, one on each floor, for men and women.

The Town opened on January 22, 1947, with

The Town Theater retained the massive facade of the Palace, but added an impressive art-deco marquee.

James Stewart and Donna Reed in Frank Capra's *It's a Wonderful Life*. Mr. Stewart attended the opening. Local film critics were lavish in their praise of the film and theater. Prices at the Town were deliberately set at 70 cents, five cents higher than those at the Hippodrome, in order to make the Town seem classy and important. For a short time after it opened, the Town had valet parking for patrons on Saturday nights.

There were many changes in the Town after 1947. The standee area was closed off from the auditorium with soundproof glass partitions. A concessions stand was built there. When the *Big Sky* opened at the Town in October 1952, it was shown on a special "full-vision" RCA synchroscreen, which was said to make movies more life-like. A stereophonic sound system was installed for the opening of the 3-D film *It Came from Outer Space* in 1953. In 1957, the Town was remodeled to show Cinerama.[120] Three projection booths were installed on the orchestra level at the rear of the auditorium and a large, curved screen replaced the older one. *This Is Cinerama* opened there on August 28. In September 1958, the Town was one of the Rappaport theaters acquired by the JF organization. In 1960, the Town was selected for the premiere engagement of the MGM blockbuster *Ben-Hur*. In 1962, the Town, Hippodrome, Little, and Aurora were leased to Trans-Lux for 25 years for a reported $3.5 million.

The most exciting event in the long history of this theater occurred on September 25, 1953, when the mezzanine of the Town was the scene of a bloody gun battle between FBI agents and a west coast outlaw. The outlaw, John Elgin Johnson, had made a call to a Los Angeles newsman on the morning of the 25th, and the newsman alerted the FBI. Johnson called again around 7:30 P.M., and the call was traced to a phone booth on the mezzanine of the Town. An FBI team, including agents J. Brady Murphy and Raymond J. Fox, raced to the theater, and the gunfight began. Johnson fired first, hitting Murphy in the stomach and Fox in the hip. Other agents emptied their guns, riddling the phone booth with bullets. Johnson was killed on the spot and Agent Murphy died later. The audience was almost oblivious to the drama upstairs as they watched the celluloid gunplay of Mickey Spillane's *I, the Jury* on the screen.

The Town closed in 1990. Its fine facade has remained virtually intact for more than 80 years, but the interior has nearly disintegrated. In 1997, along with the nearby Hippodrome, it was given to the University of Maryland. By mid–2003, it stood surrounded by redevelopment. We can only hope that imaginative developers find a good use for this historic building.

Essex Theatre, Essex. There was an Essex Theater operating at an unknown location in Essex in September 1927. It may have been another name for Essex Hall, where movies were also shown.

Eureka, 400–404 South Fremont Avenue, 1908–1952, unknown, c. 300 (later c. 450). This longtime movie house was the first one built by William Kolb and Eugene McCurdy's Eureka Amusement Company. According to one story, McCurdy and another man were laying carpet in the Cupid Theater on Light Street. The other man — probably McCurdy's partner, William Kolb — said, "Say, why don't we open one of these shows." A few months later McCurdy and Kolb opened the Eureka. The original structure was altered and enlarged in 1913. That same year the Eureka was advertising a five-cent show that consisted of two reels of pictures changed three times a week.

The Eureka was a one-story brick theater. The facade centered on an arched entrance into a shallow, open lobby where a ticket booth flanked by double doors was located. On either side of the entrance there were two brick pilasters topped with "T-shaped" capitals. The projection booth was hung from the rear wall and ceiling of the auditorium and was still intact when the theater was torn down.

In 1919 the Eureka purchased a 2/8 Moller organ (Opus 2753) for $2,600. By the 1950s a modern triangular marquee had been installed. The Eureka presented some vaudeville on its small stage and had behind-the-screen sound effects. On Saturday afternoons in the late 1930s, live acts, using local talent, appeared onstage. During the 1940s western movie stars sometimes appeared at the Eureka.

The Eureka closed as a white theater in mid–1951 and reopened as an African-American theater on December 23, 1951. It lasted about another year and then closed for good. After several years as a church, it was torn down in early 1973 to clear land for Martin Luther King Boulevard.

Eureka Amusement Company {1}, 1115–1117 West Saratoga Street, 1909–c. 1924, Walter T. Michael, c. 400. This interesting and many-named little movie house was built for about $1,500 in the fall of 1909 by Alfred H. Pitts and

Top: The lobby of the Town Theater featured modernistic metal sculptures by Oscar Bruno Bach.
Bottom: Similar to the auditorium of the New, yet more appealing, the Town's auditorium had more Bach sculptures on either side of the screen.

The front of the Eureka Theater (400–404 South Fremont Avenue, 1908–1952) was outlined in incandescent lights like many other early movie theaters.

Charles J. Jones' People's Amusement Company of Baltimore City. When it opened, it was advertised as "the only moving picture parlor in the city that is absolutely owned, operated, and controlled by colored people, and opened to all the people." In 1912, it was called the Crescent; in 1914, the Ruby; and in 1915, the Blue Bell. Usually, however, it was called the Eureka.

An early advertisement claimed that it was the prettiest, most convenient, and best-equipped house for African Americans in the city. It had a "lovely slope and situation of the chairs" which provided everyone in the audience with a comfortable seat and a good view. A four-foot hallway on either side, between two fireproof walls, served as the exit. The "lovely slope" turned out to be a mixed blessing; it usually flooded halfway up the theater when there were heavy rains. In the early years, this Eureka featured illustrated songs and light vaudeville in addition to movies.

By the summer of 1925, the theater had been converted to a church. It was still standing as late as 1973; a new formstone front had been added and it was still being used as a church.

Eureka Amusement Company {2} (see Eureka)

Europa (see Little; also see Dixie)

Excelsior, 1358–1360 West North Avenue, 1911–c. 1926, Theodore Wells Pietsch, 380. This theater, also know as Benesch's or Benesch's Excelsior, was opened by Abraham and Louis Benesch on July 22, 1911. It was a one-story brick structure built for about $10,000. The ivory, gold, and green facade was described as one of the gaudiest in town. Inside, the Excelsior featured a steeply pitched floor, a large balcony that could seat about 100 persons, and complete backstage dressing room facilities.

When it opened, the Excelsior presented continuous performances of licensed films and vaudeville from 3:00 to 11:00 P.M. Louis Benesch sold it to David Kaufman's Excelsior Theater Company in 1920, and Louis Schlichter took over the duty of booking the films. Just before it closed, the Excelsior was shut down by the building inspector because of the potential danger of plaster ornaments falling from the facade.

Fairmount, 101 North Clinton Street, 1912–1927, unknown, c. 400. The Fairmount was opened on May 4, 1912, by Edward Schuck. It was a wide two-story brick structure. The original heating system of the Fairmount consisted of two eggshell coal stoves, one near the entrance and one near the screen. The coal bin was located behind the piano. The presence of stoves gave the theater a country store-like atmosphere. While the women and children took their seats, the men would stand around the stoves and talk. According to Wallace High, the manager, "They would light their pipes even though it was not supposed to be allowed, and then stand around the stove with one foot on the railing ... and gossip with each other. When the show started they would all go down and sit with their families and everything would go along nicely until the fires would get low and the theatre became cool. Then someone would call out, 'Gettin' cold in here, put some coal on the fire.' When this reminder was given the usher would go down and fill both stoves with coal...."[121]

This idyllic system ended in 1920 when the theater was remodeled and a new heating system was installed. Among other improvements at the same time were new seats and a new screen. Wallace High purchased the theater for $20,000 in January 1921, and four months later sold it for about $23,000. Harry Gaertner leased the theater for five years in January 1922, but had given it up by September 1923 when several hundred people signed a petition asking Wallace High to come back and reopen the theater. As of 1974 the space belonged to an auto radio and TV service. Traces of what may have been the original screen remained on the back wall. That screen appeared to have been painted on the rear wall with a silver paint and outlined in black. By the 1990s, the theater was abandoned.

Fairyland, 624–626 North Chester Street, 1908–c. 1927, Clarence E. Anderson (of 1909 theater), 225–275. Nicholas Vito, who operated a fruit stall in Northeast Market, opened the Fairyland in 1908. In October 1908, he was planning a $3,000 one-story buff brick and tin addition with steam heat to be used as a moving picture theater. In January 1909, he was planning a $500 renovation to the theater. He commissioned plans for the addition, but in June 1909, the plans were changed to construct a new $2,500 theater. There is also some evidence that an addition to the theater was built in late 1911.

In 1913, the Fairyland was charging five cents admission for a two-reel show that changed daily. Occasionally called the New Market, probably because of confusion with another theater on Duncan Street, the theater was operated by Wallace High for a while before he sold it in November 1919. In 1994, the building was used as a church.

Family Theater, 518 South Broadway, 1907–1921, Henry J. Tinley (of conversion), 250. Plans to remodel the store at 518 South Broadway into a "moving picture hall" were made in August and September 1907. The cost was estimated at $2,500. The Miles Brothers, pioneers in movie exhibition and exchanges, purchased the land for $10,500, but sold the building in December 1908.

In the spring of 1914 the Family was enlarged and redecorated. A new screen and ventilating system were installed at that time. The shows then consisted of five reels of movies changed daily. Benjamin Cluster, who had operated the theater for several years, purchased the building in 1920. The building is still standing.

Fayette, 2239–2243 East Fayette Street, 1916–1957, John Freund, 385. Joseph A. Gallagher received a permit to build a theater on this site in May 1916, although it was probably built for Louis Helldorfer who filed plans in the fall of 1916. The plans called for a one-story motion picture theater to cost between $10,000 and $17,000.

Ground was broken in November 1916, and the theater probably opened in early 1917. Philip Blum and A. Kremen bought it in January 1921 for a reported $40,000. It was advertised for sale again in November 1923. In February 1924, the title was conveyed to the Patterson Realty Corp. for $25,000. Jack Levine was operating the theater in early 1924 when he installed a new Kimball organ and brought in Miss Lilly King, a concert soloist, to sing three nights a week.[122]

The Fayette closed in 1925 and was used as a bowling alley for seven years. Leon Zeller remodeled it back into a movie theater, which he called the Roxy, and reopened it in October 1932. Zeller used to broadcast over WCBM from the Roxy stage; he held kiddie shows there every morning.

In its later years, the Roxy was reportedly a wild theater where a patron was more than likely to get hit on the head with a jawbreaker. Still, at

Saturday matinees, you could see two movies and about 10 cartoons for a dime. Zeller sold out to the local radio personality Happy Johnny a short time before the theater closed in 1957.

The Roxy was also remembered fondly for its Amateur Night shows. One person remembered that the children tried to get as close to the front of the theater as they could on those nights. She said that "they stopped the movie and then they had the amateur [night] onstage and then they went back to the movie. They had some really nice singers there."[123] The Roxy was later converted into a church.

Federal, 814 Light Street, 1908–c. 1915/16, unknown, c. 300. The Federal was definitely open by January 1909, but had probably opened some weeks earlier. The Jones Brothers, who ran a coffee business near Cross Street, obtained the two-story brick dwelling at 814 Light Street and converted it into a moving picture theater in late 1908. They remodeled the theater for about $3,000 in 1910. Joe Brodie purchased the Federal in the fall of 1914, but was forced to close it around 1915 or 1916 due to poor business.

Local movie pioneer Meyer Leventhal remembered that he used to stand outside the Federal in the summertime and watch the projectionist through a big front window cranking a Power's 5 projector. The rheostat for the projector was kept on a ledge outside the booth window so that the room would not get too hot; it had to be moved inside quickly if it began to rain.

From the 1950s to the 1970s, the building was used by Hobelman Motors; in 1998, the Salvation Army opened its new divisional headquarters in the building.

Fields Photo Play Theatre (see Royal {3})

Filmart (see Three Arts)

Film Center (see Center)

Fine Arts (see Thirty-One)

Five West (see Parkway)

Flag, 1318–1320 East Fort Avenue, 1913–1958, J. C. Spedden (of 1916 remodeling), 250 (later c. 400). John T. Langville was granted a permit to build a moving picture theater at this location in December 1913. The original Flag Theater was an open-air theater. In November 1916, Langville probably remodeled it into a hardtop theater. In June 1917 and July 1919 he was granted permits for new construction at this location. James J. Hartlove took over the Flag in the summer of 1925 and modernized it. It became the Deluxe around 1929. William G. Myers operated the Deluxe from 1936 to 1958, when it closed.

The building was badly damaged by a six-alarm fire in December 1959. By 1968, as the result of a completely new brick front, it was difficult to determine that the building had ever been a movie house. Only the faded words, "Deluxe Theater — Modern Air Conditioning" on the side bore witness to that former life.

Flaming Arrow, 1108 East Preston Street, 1913–1944, F. E. Beall, c. 300. James Hartlove and Edward J. Rossiter's Crescent Novelty Company opened the Flaming Arrow in July 1913. For a while after the theater opened, a five-piece ladies' orchestra played at each performance. The building is a one-story structure of ornamental brick measuring 26 by 135 feet. It cost an estimated $3,000. Rossiter sold the Flaming Arrow to Alexander Kremen in 1922. The theater closed for several months for "extensive improvements" in early 1922. In July 1922, the Flaming Arrow purchased the old organ from the Rivoli Theater.

The name of the theater was changed to New Preston in the summer of 1925 after Arthur B. Price acquired it. Price spent about $10,000 renovating the theater. Improvements included new seats, lighting fixtures, draperies, projectors, heating and lighting systems, and floor coverings. On September 15, 1925, the piano player and projectionist were credited with saving many lives during a film fire. A newspaper account described the fire:

> A panic was averted last night at the New Preston ... when Mrs. Clyde Westergaard, the pianist, turned from the thrilling musical score of "The Birth of a Nation" and played "My Best Girl," a favorite of the kids and a song that usually starts a gay response from the youngsters. The youngsters, however, were far from gay, and many of them yelled "fire" in a way that threatened to spread terror in the crowd of 300 persons. With louder bangs on the keyboard than ever, Mrs. Westergaard ... stuck to her post near the screen as the people in the front filed past her ... she could see that the film had exploded, and that the operator, C. Robert Moore, was standing by bravely in his asbestos lined box ... doing all he could to prevent flames from spreading to the theatre. The operator stuck his head out of the projection box opening and called to the people to take their

The Flaming Arrow (1108 East Preston Street, 1913–1944), F. E. Beall) was a neat little nickelodeon with a pretentious name. It became the Preston in 1925.

seats. Later he told them to file out front and rear, but to avoid rushing. After that display of coolness, he fell back into the box and was overcome by the fumes.... William R. Marchstein ... after seeing most of the people leave, realized that the operator was the only person in real danger. Marchstein ran ... and dragged the operator out, carrying him to the open front door, where he was revived. The operator's eyelids were inflamed by the smoke and for a few moments he suffered from fumes in his lungs.[124]

DeForest sound equipment was installed in July 1929. Rome theaters acquired the theater and completely remodeled it in 1936. The entire building was remodeled along modernistic lines. The exterior was done in black glass with chrome trim. The auditorium was lined with ivory and brown Celotex connected by strips of black and silver, and the ceiling was painted ivory. New chairs and a new lighting system were installed. It reopened on October 25, 1936.

This fine building has been used as a furniture warehouse for many years, but the exterior is in beautiful condition.

Flax Photoplay Theater (see Berman's)

Ford's Theater, 320 West Fayette Street, 1871–1964; James J. Gifford (of 1871 theater), J. B. McElfatrick & Son (of New York, of 1893 and 1903 remodelings); 2,250 (800–first floor, 600–balcony, 850–gallery and private boxes). This grand old theater of the legitimate stage deigned, on numerous occasions, to show movies. Many of its theatrical seasons were sprinkled with movies, including some major blockbusters. Two of the earliest movie exhibitions in Baltimore—the Animatograph and Biograph exhibitions—were given at Ford's in 1896. In May 1897 there was a Cinematograph exhibition, and in August of that year, the famous Corbett-Fitzsimmons fight films were shown there. Movies of the Jeffries-Sharkey fight were shown in December 1899.

Ford's was built by and named after John T. Ford, who also operated the more famous Ford's Theater in Washington. The architect patterned Ford's after Booth's Theater in New York. The *Sun* gave a detailed description.[125]

The Fayette-street front ... is of pressed brick, painted white, three stories high, with Mansard roof and five wide doors.... The stage entrance is from Marion street ... the building having 86 feet front by 156 feet depth.... Iron steps and a hand rail of the same material with posts to correspond with massive lamps, lead to the vestibule of the new temple of the drama.... Immediately upon passing the portal, the visitor finds a spacious vestibule, elegantly frescoed, lighted by three exquisite chandeliers. To the right is the ticket office, to the left the broad stairway leading to the ladies' reception-room above.... All the floors ... are stained, from the vestibule to the gallery, and carpeted with drugget. The grand stairway is nearly eight feet in width, the steps of durable ash, and landings of walnut and ash in strips. The balustrade and hand-rail are also of heavy walnut, the whole oiled and polished so as to give, under the brilliant gaslight, an air of superb elegance new to the places of amusement of Baltimore.... A light exquisite balustrade of iron-fretted work extends around the balcony, surmounted with a rail covered with green plush, in very elegant contrast with the gilding below it, and the back ground of crimson cloth.... The main walls are of buff, or... "French drab;" the lofty ceiling, studded with stars, is frescoed to represent clouds; the pillars are of white ground, touched with light blue and gilding, with gilded capitals; the private box hangings are of the richest lace and yellow silk damask. A green cloth curtain, richly bordered, keeps the stage from view when the play is not going on.... The proscenium is pierced for three tiers of boxes, and the stage is of immense size, occupying fully one-third of the area of the whole house.

The theater also had several lounges, including "Conversation and Smoking Rooms" for gentlemen in the basement and on the third floor and a "Withdrawing Room" for the ladies on the second floor. Gas lights, ignited by electricity, provided illumination. The proscenium opening measured 38 feet wide by 35 feet high. The stage had a depth of 45 feet from the footlights to the back wall. Ford's was supposed to open on October 3, 1871, with a performance of *As You Like It*, but problems completing the stage prevented this, and a free impromptu entertainment was given instead.

The interior of Ford's Theater was entirely rebuilt in 1893. The interior was gutted; nothing remained except "the strong walls and massive roof." The *Sun* of July 6, 1893 described the new interior, said to be similar to that of the Empire Theater[126] in New York.

> The entire first floor is so graded that no step of any kind is required at any point.... The seating capacity of this floor will be somewhat increased. The space on the front of the stage, before the curtain, technically known as the apron, has been cut off and the lines of sight much improved by the elevation of the floor.
>
> The new dress circle in the first gallery has a balcony attachment, giving room for two rows of seats and so arranged that they can be converted into stalls when desired. This improvement gives about 150 additional seats. The circle will also have stairways on each side at the boxes, descending to the first floor, in addition to the main stairways in front.

The Ford family, including Charles E. Ford and John T. Ford, Jr., sons of John T. Ford, operated Ford's Theater until it was acquired in 1897 by New York interests. For the 1899 season, two statues—idealized representations of "Comedy" and "Tragedy" by E. Berge—were placed on either side of the proscenium arch.

In 1903, Ford's was remodeled again. The *Sunday Herald* gave a description of the new theater.

> The dimensions of the new interior, including the stage and lobby, are 86 by 156 feet, and altogether there is a seating capacity for 2,532 persons ... the galleries ... are brought much farther forward than in the old structure.
>
> The main coloring of the interior is rose, melting from a deep crimson into a pale pink.... The walls are bordered with a festoon of bowknot design. On each side of the stage are the tiers of boxes, 18 in number, arranged three in a row. They are of a striking Moorish design, the lower tier being square, the second with a round portico and the third finished in an oval curve. The decorations are exquisite and of a new effect in relief of plaster, hemp and cement set off with ornamentations of burnished gold, silver and bronze in metal finish. The supporting columns have an onyx finish and are hung with terra cotta and pink brocades. In the rear of each box is a small anteroom fitted with divans and chairs....
>
> The large sounding-box over the stage is painted with a reproduction of Guido Reni's celebrated painting in Florence, the Aurora. It ... shows the chariot of the sun being driven through fleecy clouds, while surrounding it are graceful female figures bearing flowers.... The painting was the work of Austin Burrill. The new drop curtain ... shows a Turkish interior....
>
> ...The ticket office has been placed in the centre of the lobby. It is a pretty little structure, with illuminated glass roof. At the right of the lobby there is an antique mantel, with hooded chimney. It is finished in a new French tint of mallard gray, with silver finish. The ceiling of the lobby is ornamented with free-hand designs

in foliage. At the left an oaken staircase leads to the floor above. The theatre is illuminated with incandescent lights set in stalactite fixtures....[127]

Chicago artist, Albert Fleury, supervised the interior redecoration of Ford's in the summer of 1905. In 1911, the theater was remodeled again and provisions were made so that movies could be shown. Extensive renovations to the theater, costing between $45,000 and $60,000, were carried out during the summer of 1921. During this remodeling a new box office was installed and a new floor was laid. The balcony foyer was decorated like a French salon as a lounging room. The auditorium was entirely redone in ivory and blue with new seats in the same colors and draperies of gold and blue. The orchestra pit was raised and a new heating system, which eliminated the annoying cracking of the pipes, was installed.

Ford's stayed open during the summer of 1914 with a series of movies. During the week of June 14, 1915, F. T. Neely of the *Baltimore News* gave a talk accompanied by 6,000 feet of movies of the war in Europe. Ford's was also used for road show films for a number of years. Among the well-known movies that played at Ford's were *David Copperfield* in 1914, *Birth of a Nation* in 1916, *Intolerance* in 1917, Cecil B. DeMille's *Ten Commandments* in 1925, and *Ben Hur* in 1927. A. L. Erlanger, of New York, who had been leasing it since 1921, purchased the theater in June 1929.

Morris Mechanic bought Ford's from Erlanger's estate for $50,000 in 1942 and immediately announced plans for "extensive additions and improvements." He ran it until it closed in February 1964 after the final performance of *A Funny Thing Happened on the Way to the Forum*. Mechanic, who was planning a new theater in Charles Center, sold Ford's to the Hecht Company, which promptly demolished it to build a parking garage. One of the most historic theatrical sites in the state, sold because one man wanted no competition and others wanted parking spaces. It was a shameful loss. A New York theatrical producer told a local theater critic that "it would be a shame to lose Ford's. It's one of the oldest theaters in the country and with such a rich theatrical history, it should be refurbished, and you'll still get the Broadway shows."[128] Nearly every famous stage personality of the previous 93 years had played at Ford's. The list includes Edwin Booth, Charlotte Cushman, Julia Marlowe, Buffalo Bill, Lily Langtry, Lew Dockstader, George M. Cohan, and Houdini.

According to one story, Billy Rose proposed to Fanny Brice backstage at Ford's. Another favorite story tells about the time Edwin Booth appeared onstage drunk to do a Shakespeare play; he told the audience, "I'm drunk, but if you bear with me, I'll give you the greatest performance of King Lear you've ever seen."[129]

Ford's was the Baltimore home of numerous great opera companies, and the original American production of *H.M.S. Pinafore* played there. In the early 1900s, at the end of each theatrical season, it was the custom of Ford's management to hold a benefit performance and turn over the proceeds to the ushers. Ford's is probably the only Baltimore theater with a part in a play. Cole Porter set the opening of his musical *Kiss Me, Kate* in Ford's.

Forest, 3300 Garrison Boulevard, 1919–1961, Edward H. Glidden, 650. The Forest, or Forest Park as it was first called, was built by the Forest Park Motion Picture Company. It opened on Monday, December 22, 1919. The theater was financed by Herbert M. Hartman of the Zeit Motor Car Company. The first manager was the versatile Charles E. Ford. The exterior of the theater was done in Italian Romanesque style in brick with a green tile roof. The small foyer was red brick trimmed with statuary white Italian marble and a marble floor. The decorations in the auditorium were in delicate plaster relief colored in polychrome. The cost was estimated at nearly $100,000. The organ was not installed in time for the opening, but there was an orchestra under the direction of Lazarus Fisher. By 1922, the Forest had a 2/10 Moller (Opus 2780) organ that cost $3,100; Miss M. Louise Jones was the organist.

A grisly robbery took place at the Forest in March 1923. A robber took night receipts of $138.65; during his get-away, his little finger was severed when a window slammed on it. He left it on the steps at the rear of the theater. The police captured a man with a missing little finger shortly after the robbery. When confronted with the missing finger, the man confessed.

The Forest was acquired by the Durkee Circuit by 1928, and was remodeled in its final years. Its owner sought to attract customers by showing foreign and classic films. The last show at the Forest was a Marlon Brando double feature of *On the Waterfront* and *The Wild One* on Saturday, May 13, 1961, the day that actor Gary Cooper died. The management announced that it would be open from then on only on Friday, Saturday, and Sunday, but, in fact, it never re-

The original Forest Theater (3300 Garrison Boulevard, 1919–1961, Edward H. Glidden) lacked a marquee; the one in this photograph must have been added before 1935.

opened. After it closed as a theater, the Forest was used for religious services. The marquee has been removed and a partially new facade has been added.

Frederick, 3436 Frederick Avenue, 1912–c. 1924. The Frederick was one of the first movie theaters in West Baltimore. It was a long, two-story building standing alone on a lot on the north side of Frederick Avenue just east of Irvington, and was operated for a while by Roy A. Collison. Years after it closed, it was converted into a popular seafood restaurant, Duffy's Tavern. The first-floor brick front is recent.

Fremont {1}, 615–617 North Fremont Avenue, 1909–c. 1922, Alfred Mason (Oliver B. Wight & E. A. Lockhart of 1921 remodeling), c. 250 (c. 700 after 1921 remodeling). The Fremont {1} may have been opened by a local druggist who tore down a couple of houses or a livery stable to build it. There is also evidence that two men named Greenbaum and Evatt had something to do with building it. The two-story theater had a white facade with twin pilasters on either side of a wide entrance, and its name was spelled out in incandescent lights above the entrance. Charles H. Imwold operated it until 1921, when Walter Windsor and Charles Nolte's Fremont Amusement Company acquired the theater. The Fremont closed that summer while it was being enlarged by the new owners.[130] Nolte advertised the theater for sale for $12,000 in February 1923.

Fremont {2}, 504–506 North Fremont Avenue, 1935–1951, J. F. Dusman, 170. A permit to erect this theater was granted to the Fremont Amusement Company in November 1934. This Fre-

The proud owner of the Fremont Theater (615–617 North Fremont Avenue, 1909–c. 1921, Alfred Mason) probably on opening day.

mont opened on April 9, 1935. Opening day patrons received free beer and ice cream. Joseph Walderman was the first manager. According to *Showman's Trade Review* of February 28, 1948, the Fremont had reopened the previous week after being remodeled. Despite being extensively remodeled by the Flaks Brothers in the spring of 1950 — a chromium and glass front was added along with a new neon-light marquee — it only lasted about another year.

Fulton (see Gertrude McCoy)

Garden {1} (see Picture Garden)

Garden {2}, 1100–1102 South Charles Street, 1910–1960, J. E. Laferty, c. 500 (c. 900 after 1916 remodeling). This theater was built by the C. W. Pacy Company for about $6,500. It was a one-story brick structure originally 35 × 75 feet. For a number of years, beginning in 1912, there was an open-air movie theater on the roof of the Garden.

The Garden was closed temporarily in the summer of 1916 and completely rebuilt, reopening on September 20, 1916. The new building measured 126 × 70 feet, with a 40-foot lobby. The facade was of ornamental brick. The walls of the 40-foot-wide lobby were painted a soft pink. During this remodeling, a plant to cool the air was installed and ads claimed that the Garden had more cubic feet of air per person than any other theater in the city. The projection booth was relocated to the roof of the theater.

The Garden was redecorated in the summer of 1919; the lobby floor was repainted red and the walls were repainted steel gray to give them a stone panel effect. The walls of the auditorium were repainted to give the appearance of tapestry with stenciled figures of red on a background of old rose.

The theater was owned and operated for many years by the C. W. Pacy organization and often called Pacy's Garden to distinguish it from other Garden theaters in town. The Garden Bowling and Billiard Academy, with four bowling alleys and ten pocket billiard tables, was located in the basement of the theater with an entrance at 1104 South Charles Street. According to one source, one of the first miniature golf courses in Baltimore was located in the basement of the Garden {2}.[131]

The Garden created some of the more innovative publicity stunts in town, especially in its early days. In July 1918, large crowds attended the theater to watch movies being made in the theater with some local talent. A real movie studio was set up on the stage as part of a live vaudeville act. July 15 was "Vampire Day" and the local Theda Baras were on hand at the theater to vamp their way into fame.

Garden {3}, 114 West Lexington Street, 1915–1955, Thomas W. Lamb, c. 2,700. An older generation of Baltimoreans knew this theater as the Garden; those of you younger than age 80 knew it as Keith's, and those of you younger than age 50 didn't know it at all. It was built on the site of Stewart Central Stables by the Charles E. Whitehurst organization. Whitehurst hired the well-known New York theater architect Thomas W. Lamb to design the Garden. It was built by the George A. Fuller Company, also of New York, at a cost of nearly $1,000,000. The Garden building's main entrance was on Lexington Street; the auditorium extended back to Clay Street. Above the theater was a ballroom, the famous Jardin de Danse, or Garden Roof, as it was usually called. The building, which could accommodate 6,000 people, was claimed to be the largest palace of amusement under one roof in the country.

Great precautions were taken to make it fireproof. The scenery, stage properties, and draperies were fireproofed, and the fire escapes were larger than required. A "down-and-out escape," which was a large tubular chute that ran from the roof to the pavement could evacuate people from the ballroom in less than a minute.[132] The balcony was constructed on a cantilever plan, eliminating sight-obstructing pillars and posts. The mezzanine floor featured what one newspaper described as "a great well-hole," which allowed an unobstructed view of the lower hall.[133]

The interior of the theater was originally done in melrose and gold with rich, red silk damask. The seats were upholstered in red plush and trimmed in old rose velour. Boxes on either side of the auditorium were arranged in tiers following a French Renaissance style. The opening advertisement described the treatment of the boxes: "For the side boxes of the theater a flat valance of plain velour in combination with a draped valance of brocade velour, with side hangings to conform, have been employed. The entrances to the boxes are treated from the overhead with cut out valances. The rails of the boxes and gallery have also been covered with a rose-colored velour and are surmounted with brass rails. A draped apron of velour containing the imprimitur of the Baltimore coat of arms is attached to each box."

C. W. Pacy's first theater was the Garden (1100–1102 South Charles Street, 1910–1960, J. E. Laferty) in South Baltimore; this photograph must date before the 1916 remodeling.

The proscenium was also described: "A beautiful effect is produced by the proscenium arch over the stage, which has been draped with a cut out valance of rose tinted velour trimmed with appliqué of illumined gold cloth and embroidery. This valance affords a background for two medallions, which contain a replica of Washington's Monument on Mount Vernon Place. Adding to the richness of the combination is the heavy gold bullion fringe of the valance."

The draperies, proscenium furnishings and other interior decorations were designed, made up and placed in position by Hutzler Brothers Company. The walls were white marble. The entrance to the building was likewise of white marble with a long entrance lobby. Next to the lobby there were two large elevators that held 28 people each to carry patrons up to the rooftop ballroom. The ventilation system could cool the air in the theater to 20° below the outside air temperature. The Baltimore Star, in describing the interior of the new theater, said: "Artistically the house surpasses anything seen in this section of the country, the highest salaried interior decorators in the country having been given carte blanche with regard to expense."[134]

The Jardin de Danse was decorated by the J. G. Valiant Company of Baltimore in Japanese style with "pretty blue-eyed girls gowned in rich Japanese garments."[135] Seating was available in 600 reed chairs. Patrons could sit and dine or go out on the dance floor and learn the latest dances. The large staff of the theater included female ushers dressed in steel color gowns of the Elizabethan period and male employees wearing black uniforms with braid and gold trimming.

In 1918, the popular roof garden was renovated. The walls were done in red, gold, and blue and a new lighting system was installed. The ceiling was covered with foliage that concealed shaded lamps; there was also trelliswork and foliage on the walls. The Garden Roof was redecorated again during the summer of 1925. This time a new dais, shaped like a seashell, was built for the orchestra. The Garden Roof was operated by Thomas J. Tobin; Fred Robbins and Oscar Apfel led the band on the Garden Roof. The Jardin de Danse was a very popular spot. A three-night endurance dance in 1923 yielded receipts of $7,000 and a profit of $2,000.

The Garden Theater opened to a select audience of about 500 people with an additional 2,000 people who had been waiting outside since the afternoon on January 30, 1915, with a vaudeville bill that featured Adele Ritchie, "the Dresden China prima donna" and comedienne, singing "Has Anybody Here Seen Rover?" There were continuous performances from 1:30 to 11:00 P.M. at prices from 10 cents to 30 cents.

For the first two decades of its life, the Garden was primarily a vaudeville theater with films as part of the show. Four-a-day or five-a-day vaudeville acts packed the house day after day. A typical bill consisted of six acts, three of which were unpaid "fillers." If these "fillers" were successful, they could stay on for pay; if not, off they went. A new 60-foot high animated sign was in-

Garden 283

Keith's Theater (Thomas W. Lamb, 1915) and the Garden Roof above it were popular attractions in the 1920s and 1930s. The theater was surrounded by candy stores, which supplied theater patrons with sweets. Note the banner across Lexington Street in this 1931 photograph. (Photograph courtesy of Thomas Paul)

stalled on the Lexington Street facade of the Garden in January 1925. An additional 200 seats were added at the same time.

The Garden closed in July 1927—for the first time since it opened—for about two weeks of extensive remodeling that cost about $250,000 and left little more than the original walls standing. New lighting effects were placed onstage; a new organ was installed; new carpets were laid; new dark blue drapes were hung; new lighting fixtures were installed. The color scheme of the auditorium was gray, ivory, gold and brown while the lobby was done in Caenstone and colors of green, ivory, gray, and gold. Brown techstone panels were put on the walls of the auditorium and green techstone panels were used in the lobby. The seating capacity was increased by 500 seats.

Charles Whitehurst's theater circuit began to disintegrate within a few years of his death in 1924. The directors and major stockholders of the Garden Theatre Company began discussing plans in early 1927 to sell the theater, apparently because of the need for a larger venue for vaudeville,[136] the rapid growth of competition and the breaking up of the Whitehurst theaters. In November 1927, the Garden was sold to Frederick C. Schanberger's James L. Kernan Company for about $1,000,000. When Shubert attractions were booked into the Maryland, plans were made to move Keith-Albee vaudeville to the Garden.

The theater was remodeled and reopened as the New Garden on December 26, 1927. It was open from 11:00 A.M. to 11:00 P.M. From 1927 until 1952, the Garden was managed by J. Lawrence Schanberger. In June 1928 he introduced a new summer service at the Garden; ushers carried trays filled with glasses of ice water up and down the aisles for thirsty patrons. The name of the theater was changed to Keith-Albee in 1928 in honor of those two powerful vaudeville rulers. The name was shortened to Keith's in 1930. Most of the major vaudeville stars and the big bands played at Keith's. Among the popular vaudeville acts booked there in the 1930s and 1940s were Morton Downey, John Steele, Arthur Tracey—better known as "The Street Singer"—the Avon Comedy Four, and Fanny Ward. Keith's showed its first talkie in March 1929. Three years later, vaudeville ended there, but the big bands, such as those conducted by Paul Whiteman, Tommy Dorsey, and Artie Shaw continued to play at Keith's.

The entire theater was reserved for African-American patrons on June 1 and 2, 1932, for a midnight presentation of *Old Kentucky*, with George Dewey Washington and Hamtree Harrington. The show was a disaster; only about 20 people attended the Wednesday night show and seven showed up for the Thursday performance. The second night's show was canceled. Members of the cast complained that they couldn't get anything to eat downtown without being insulted.

Keith's prospered during the war years, except for a financial crisis and subsequent reorganization in 1941 and 1942. Morris Mechanic, who controlled the nearby New Theater, in an apparent bid to stifle competition, purchased the mortgages on Keith's and immediately filed foreclosure proceedings against Keith's.

After lengthy litigation, Judge William C. Coleman granted the owners of Keith's the right to attempt reorganization of the corporation, and he specifically restrained the institution or continuance of any suit against the debtor during the period of the reorganization. Finally, in August 1942, the court approved a plan for the financial reorganization of the theater. A key element of the plan was a 10-year lease at $50,000 a year granted to the Schanbergers. Morris Mechanic was at least temporarily thwarted in his effort to control all of the downtown theaters.

Dancing continued on the roof garden for several years after World War II. In the late 1940s and early 1950s, when TV and other factors were making times difficult for movie theaters, Hollywood tried several new gimmicks to lure viewers back to the movie houses. Three of these were tested at Keith's. A large-screen TV was installed in the spring of 1948. In 1953, it was the first theater in Baltimore to install an extra-wide screen for its showing of *Shane*, and, around the same time, it showed some of the early 3-D films such as *Fort Ti*.[137]

None of these gimmicks could save Keith's. Its last films were forgettable ones with unknown stars. Finally, on December 3, 1955, to the sounds of a rock-and-roll stage show featuring Bill Haley and his "Comets," this grand old theater's 40-year life came to an end. The auditorium was demolished to build an uninspired parking garage which has since also disappeared. Many of us will miss Keith's and the scratchy recording of "Artist's Life" played there during intermissions.

Gay Street Museum, 563 North Gay Street, 1907–1913, unknown, 100. The Gay Street Museum was listed at this address between 1907 and 1910. It may have been an arcade, although, in the 1909 telephone directory, it was listed as a moving picture parlor. It became the Bon Ton in 1911.

Gayety, 405 East Baltimore Street, 1906–1969, J. B. McElfatrick, 1,600 (730 — orchestra, 390 — balcony, 480 — gallery). Although the Gayety was certainly not noted for its movies, it did occasionally show films. It was the western theatrical anchor and doubtless one of the major attractions of the Block, and outlasted most of the other theaters there. James Kernan thought that rumors of another burlesque theater on Baltimore Street in competition with his Monumental were a bluff, but when the Columbia Amusement Company obtained a site in the 400 block of East Baltimore Street, he probably rethought the matter. The Columbia organization applied for a permit for the Gayety on the site of Raine's Hall in August 1905, and it opened on February 5, 1906. It was one of the last theaters designed by the well-known theatrical architect, J. B. McElfatrick. The theater's first manager was William L. Ballauf.[138]

In 1910 the theater experienced financial troubles, and it was sold to John "Hon" Nickel. Nickel was an excellent promoter and turned the Gayety into one of the best burlesque houses in the country.[139] The Baltimore correspondent, Sylvan Schenthal, described the Gayety for *Billboard* magazine of February 17, 1906:

> It has a frontage of 64 feet and extends back 172 feet. The interior embraces every feature of modern methods in theatre building. The orchestra floor is 81 feet 4 inches from the curtain line to the rear wall and is 60 feet wide. There are twenty-five rows of seats spaced thirty-one inches apart.... There are two wide stairways on each side of the foyer leading to the balcony, and four exits direct to the street. The balcony contains thirteen rows of seats.... The height of the auditorium is 43 feet 6 inches from the foyer level....
>
> The interior is handsomely decorated.... The general style of architecture is French with stucco relief and the old gold and ivory effect. The sidewalls are tinted with a shade of rose DuBarry blended into olive green. The main ceiling and the ceiling under the balcony are tinted with a light shade of cream with festoons and wreaths. A large 60-foot chandelier hangs from the main ceiling. Sufficient gaslights have been provided in case of injury to the electric system.
>
> The stage is 30 feet from the back wall to the curtain line. It is 62 feet between sidewalls. The proscenium opening is 34 feet. A steel plate girder with iron curtain grooves and the latest approved asbestos curtain gives protection to the auditorium. The fly galleries on each side are 30 feet and the rigging loft is 65 feet above the stage. There are twenty dressing rooms all facing a small court in the rear of the building.

The theater's exterior facade was of buff-colored brick with pressed sheet metal decorations. The two-story-high central window is flanked by two marble columns. Architect Craig Morrison describes the facade, "Above, a male and female figure hold a plaque bearing the name of the theater. To either side is an arcade of two-story, arched windows, separated by metal heads which serve as impost blocks for the arches. Highlighting the decorative scheme are two large metal devices composed of human and satyr masques, the thyrsus and crescent mace, and a pair of inflated bladders, objects associated with Bacchanalian rites, and long-tailed birds frame large projecting breasts."[140] The interior featured two balconies, six boxes, and 1,600 seats on the main floor.

The first show at the Gayety featured Fred Irwin's "Majestics," who were young women described in a bewildering array of adjectives, such as "sweet, smooth, rich, musical, clinging, nervous, lively, big, musicular, cold, dreamy, and city [sic]." They appeared in the satire "Down the Line." Also on that first bill were Larry McCale, "The Man Behind the Comedy Gun," and the Accust Family in eccentricities followed by the travesty "For Girls Only."

As early as March 1907, there were movies on the program at the Gayety. It advertised a realistic film of the celebrated Thaw-White murder case. The Gayety introduced moving pictures as part of its regular programming in 1922. That same year the Baltimore Theatre Company, representing the Columbia Amusement Corporation, sold it. The property was assessed at $235,000 at that time.

The Gayety featured burlesque, or "burlesk" as the marquee proclaimed. Over the years all of the major stars of burlesque played there. Comedians Red Skelton, Joe Penner, and Phil Silvers and strippers Sally Rand, Gypsy Rose Lee, and Blaze Starr performed at the Gayety. Occasionally the shows exceeded what was considered proper, and the nearby police vice squad raided the theater. The 25-year manager, Gus Flaig, said that his girls were not stripping — that was vulgar — they were "beauty flashing," and that was an art. Flaig and his wife Dottie ran a tight ship backstage at the Gayety. They auditioned and hired the chorus girls; Dottie re-

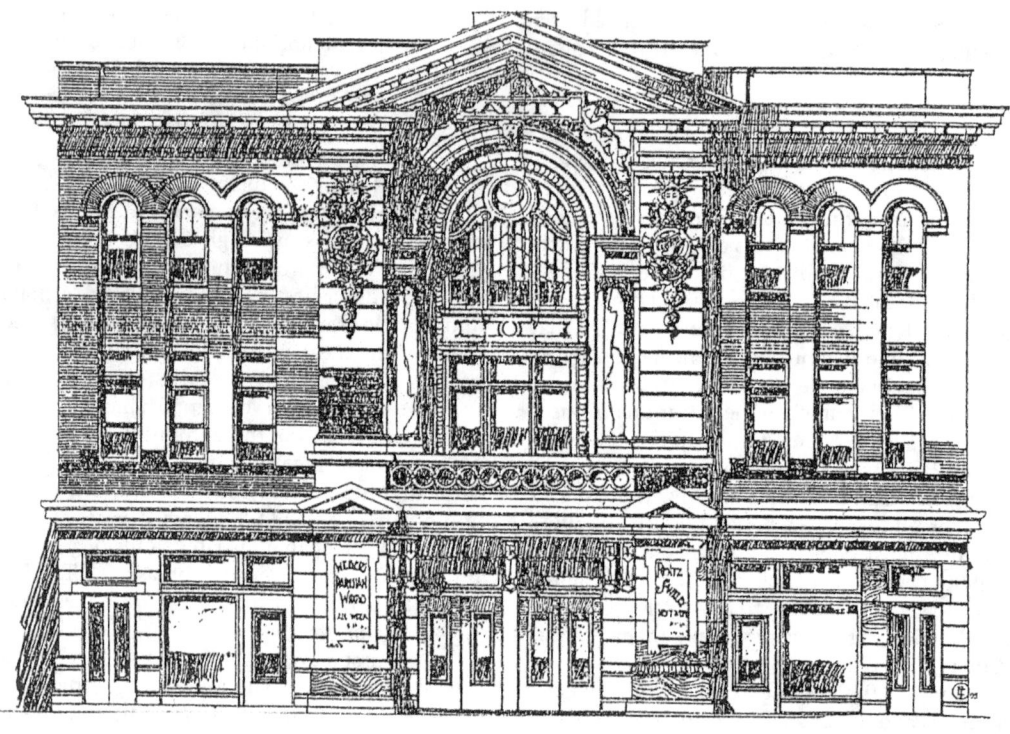

Drawing of the Gayety Theater, 1906.

hearsed them. A typical show at the Gayety ran about two and a half hours, and included a star stripper, a number two stripper, and often a number three stripper, plus three minor "take-it-off" performers. In addition to the strippers, there were several comedians and a singer who did a couple of songs while the chorus of showgirls danced.

The Gayety had been living on borrowed time, reduced to X-rated films and mediocre live shows, for several years when a five-alarm fire swept through it early on the morning of December 21, 1969. The age of explicitness and permissiveness had just about destroyed burlesque at the Gayety; the fire provided the coup de grace. The Gayety has been remodeled into commercial spaces and the front has been nicely cleaned.

Gem {1}, 714–716 East Baltimore Street, 1908–c. 1917, unknown, c. 100. This early movie house probably started out as a penny arcade since it was first called the Gem Museum. In June 1908, the owner of the building converted the structure into a moving picture theater. The second floor was removed, and an elaborate front was installed. The Gem was probably the only movie house in town with revolving seats. It had a flat, wooden floor with a canvas screen that could be rolled up when live acts performed. It became the first movie house on Baltimore Street to show independent films when John H. Heinz bought it from W. G. Spurrier in the spring of 1909. In January 1910, it advertised vaudeville and motion pictures, and in 1913, it was running shows of two reels changed daily.

In early 1916, extensive improvements, including a new ticket office, new exits, and a new floor were planned. The Gem closed around this time, so it is not clear whether or not the improvements were ever made.

Projectionist William Lange was John Heinz's brother-in-law and went to work as an usher and later projectionist at the Gem in 1909. He remembered many details about the theater.

> I used to get time off for lunch and ... supper and come back, help the operator, help practically anyone around the place, take tickets ... usher ... on Fridays and Saturdays we used to pack them in and the children.... The show would run about an hour. They would get the kids some lunch; they wanted them to stay there all day, so we let them see two shows and gave them timed tickets ... that was on busy

days and they wanted to make some money. Admission was only a nickel and they had to move some of them out after they saw the show two times. I had it in my mind that when the place was full we had five dollars.... I didn't make much, maybe about five bucks a week. The operator got about ten bucks a week.

[A show] was all short subjects. They didn't have features like they do today.... Instead of having 15-inch reels like today, they had 10-inch reels.... [The speed a projector was cranked] was up to the operator. You could turn them too slow and it wouldn't be natural. You got the swing of it, just how fast to turn it.... [There was] just one projector until I got there, [then we] put two projectors up. After every reel, they put a sign on the screen, "One Minute, Please." Then you'd re-thread.

We had a piano player and a drummer and he used to race time when the cowboys would come on. They used to play "William Tell"; that was a favorite one for the cowboys. And the kids would jump on the floor and keep time to the music. We had a good piano player.... Her name was Carrie McCorney.... They'd have music for matinees then they'd come back at 7:30 at night and they [also] had a drummer named Brown.

They had a cashier and when he first got the place, we used to clean up ourselves at night.[141]

Gem {2} (see New Gem)

General Pulaski Drive-In, Pulaski Highway, White Marsh, 1950–1985, unknown, 670 cars. Schwaber theaters opened the General Pulaski Drive-In on July 6, 1950. It advertised a free playground and train rides on the B&O Royal Blue Jr. for the children. It was generally just called the Pulaski Drive-In. It was twinned in 1983 and closed after the 1985 season. The two screens were still standing in 2001, forlorn remnants in the woods, which have grown a great deal since the theater closed.

Gertrude McCoy, 1563 North Fulton Avenue, 1915–1951, Francis E. Tormey, c. 495. The Lord Calvert Amusement Company, which operated the Lord Calvert on Harford Road, the Pastime Theater on Greenmount Avenue, and the Carrollton Theater, began planning this theater in the spring of 1915. The permit was granted in May, and the theater opened on October 30, 1915. Frederick C. Weber, the new president of the company, explained that the theater was named after Miss McCoy "because we think Miss McCoy is one of the greatest moving picture actresses in the world today."[142]

The opening program featured the four-reel Edison film, *Through Turbulent Waters*, starring Miss McCoy and Edward Earle. Music was provided by Prof. F. H. Nichols' orchestra, a violinist and a piano player. Miss McCoy, Mr. Earle, and Duncan McRae were present in person for the opening, and patrons were guided to their seats by young female ushers. Miss McCoy presented the theater with a life-sized oil painting of herself. In an interview, she told reporters, "I love Baltimore. Its people are so hospitable. Some day, when I grow old I expect to make this city my home."[143] She visited the theater regularly on its anniversary for the next several years.

The theater's architect had studied many large movie theaters in the east before he designed the Gertrude McCoy. It measured 37 by 145 feet and was described as a brick theater in the Italian Renaissance style, with a spacious 16-foot-deep vestibule and a light gray stucco exterior. The facade consisted of an arched entrance with a pilaster topped by an Ionic Capital on each side. The cornice above each pilaster was

The Gertrude McCoy (1563 North Fulton Avenue, 1915–1951, Francis E. Tormey) has not changed very much since it opened.

The Gertrude McCoy, renamed the Fulton in 1927, was acquired by Durkee Enterprises three years later.

decorated with a lion's head. At the top of the entrance arch was a female head. Flanking the arch on the second floor level were two roundels. The interior of the theater was finished in ivory and sky blue. The seats were set on a six-foot pitch to provide a clear view of the screen. The theater cost between $20,000 and $25,000 to build. The projection booth was a large, spotless, concrete room with a skylight and two projectors.[144] When it opened, the Gertrude McCoy claimed to be the largest theater in Baltimore devoted exclusively to movies. In August 1920, Weber announced that patrons would no longer stumble in soft spots on the floor caused by the rotting of the wooden floor under the rubber runners—a new floor of concrete had been laid.

The theater closed in June 1923 because of bad business. The following May it was sold at public auction for $16,000. In 1927, the name was changed to Fulton. Durkee Enterprises bought it in 1930 and operated it about 15 years before selling it to Henry Hornstein just after World War II. It closed in August 1945 and reopened on September 13 as an African-American theater. The management donated the first three days' receipts to the Police Boys Club. The opening day festivities included a drum and bugle corps that marched to the theater from Pennsylvania Avenue.

The Fulton closed on March 2, 1952. For many years, it was a food market, but it was converted to a church around 1973. The building was still standing as of 2000.

Gilmor, 314 North Gilmor Street, 1909–1922, John K. Stack, 250. The Gilmor was built by the Gilmor Amusement Company for about $4,000. The theater utilized a remodeled dwelling for the entrance; the auditorium was built in the rear. At first it was a white theater, but it had become an African-American theater by 1917, when it was operated by George Douglass and featured vaudeville and movies. Oscar M. Scherr, who formerly operated the Plaza Theater on North Broadway, purchased the Gilmor in 1920. Scherr remodeled the theater and reopened it as the New Gilmor on October 16, 1920. A jazz band provided music for the occasion. The Gilmor lasted another two years.

Glen (see Art {1})

Glen Burnie Mall, 6718 Ritchie Highway, Glen Burnie, 1964–1984, G. Limbert (?), 750. Broumas Theaters opened the Glen Burnie Mall theater on January 15, 1964. Local political leaders and film officials attended the opening. The Glen Burnie Mall Theater was located in the middle of the mall, where its auditorium towered above the adjacent stores. The word "THEATRE" illuminated in neon was affixed to the outside rear wall. Durkee Enterprises acquired the Glen Burnie Mall Theater in February 1968.

Glen Burnie Theater, Central Avenue & A Street, Glen Burnie, c. 1927–1929. Bill Diller ran movies at the Glen Burnie Theater in the Community Hall every Monday, Wednesday and Saturday night in 1927 and 1928. In November 1927, a four-piece orchestra played at every show. The first sound movie in Glen Burnie, *The Jazz Singer*, was shown at the Glen Burnie Theater in May 1928. By December 1929, movies at the Community Hall were under the management of V. Larkin Dicus.

Glen Burnie Towncenter 7, 7480 Baltimore Annapolis Boulevard, Glen Burnie, 1986–2002, unknown, 1,800 (including two 300-seat auditoriums). JF Theaters opened this seven-plex with a special preview benefit for the Johns Hopkins Kennedy Children's Center on July 17, 1986. It opened to the public the following day.

The Glen Burnie Town Center 7 is a triumph of minimalist design. The exterior of the building looks quite like a brick parking lot; this is not surprising since the theater is part of a 550-car garage. The main clue that a movie theater is inside is a rather plain, freestanding attraction board. The entire structure cost $3.8 million; the theater cost $1.3 million. JF leased the theater space in the county-owned building for 40 years at $1 per year. The wide sunken lobby was decorated with mirrors and dominated by a 50-foot concession stand.

The auditoriums, which ranged in size from 170 to 360 seats, were insulated from each other by walls of 12-inch concrete blocks filled with sand as well as by acoustical curtains on the walls. Each auditorium had a wide screen, four-track stereo sound, decorative aisle lighting, and offset seating. The two large auditoriums had 40-foot screens. This project was the first time that a public facility in the county had been combined with a private one.

Glen Burnie Town Center 7 became a Loew's theater in 1988 when that chain acquired the JF Theaters. It closed for a week in March 2001 in the wake of Loew's bankruptcy, and the county took it over. Wheaton-based Dunnagan Technical Services leased the theater and planned to reopen it as Glen Burnie Town Center Cinemas on the weekend of March 10, 2001. It lasted slightly over two months before closing again on May 13; an official said that ticket sales were too low.

By October 2002, there were plans to use the theater as an arts center. A town meeting in March 2003 produced additional ideas for the theater's re-use. Finally, in the summer of 2003, the Anne Arundel County Government announced that two of the theaters would house

A new marquee for an old theater. Thomas Goldberg reopened the long-closed Hilton (3117 West North Avenue, 1914–1917, 1941–1950) in response to the imminent opening of the adjoining Windsor Theater.

the county's public access television studios; three of the other theaters would be used by the Workforce Development Corporation.

Globe (see Comedy)

Globe Moving Picture Parlor (see Nowosci)

Goldberg's Gwynn Park Theater, 3117 West North Avenue, 1914–1917, 1941–1950, unknown, c. 400. Thomas D. Goldberg[145] received a permit for this theater in May 1914 and opened it around October 1, 1914. The plans called for a one-story $10,000 building measuring 37.9 by 98 feet. It was usually called Goldberg's Theater, and it lasted until about 1917. In April 1917,

Goldberg offered the theater equipment for sale; this included 500 chairs, two Simplex projectors, a Gold Fibre screen and a piano. The theater was converted into the West North Avenue Garage.

Plans to reopen it as a theater were announced in early 1937. In the spring of 1941 it was remodeled back into a movie house, the Hilton, which opened on April 25. The Hilton lasted about ten years. In later years a storm window company and a supermarket occupied the building. Much of the facade seems to be original.

Golden Arrow, 305 South Broadway, 1911–1912. This small movie house operated for about a year. It was located in a building next to the original Cluster {1} and was probably razed when the present Cluster was built.

Golden Ring (see Movies at Golden Ring Mall)

Goldfield {1}, 913–919 Warner Street, 1915–1927, 1946–1951, David Harrison (of 1946 remodeling), c. 200, later 400 (as the Dean/Jean). This theater opened as the Goldfield in 1915. The earliest reference to the Goldfield is in the Baltimore *Afro-American* of December 11, 1915,[146] where it was reported that the theater was in its sixth successful week. It is unclear just what this theater was, since a permit to build the Goldfield was not granted by the city until December 2, 1915. The Miller Mercantile Corporation purchased the theater from the Central Theatre Company for about $26,500 in September 1921. Live acts were presented occasionally. In August 1925, the theater achieved notoriety when a marksman wounded his wife, attempting to shoot a penny out of her mouth on the stage.

Ads for the Goldfield appeared in the *Daily Post* in the fall of 1925 suggesting that it was, at least for a short time, operated as a white theater. It closed in 1927 and was used as a church for several years. George W. Jacobs remodeled it back into a movie theater, and it reopened around August 16, 1946. The name was changed to Jean or Dean.[147] It was a plain rectangular brick structure with a square, shallow storm lobby. There is no trace of any marquee in 1943 photographs. The screen was mounted on the rear wall. It operated in the evenings with a double-feature policy. After being closed for a while, the theater was reopened on October 8, 1949. Jacobs died suddenly in January 1950, and the Dean closed a year later, after which it closed as a theater and was used as a chemical warehouse. The building was demolished for the construction of parking lots for Oriole Park at Camden Yards.

Goldfield {2} (see Argonne)

Good Time, 1401–1405 North Milton Avenue, 1914–1958, unknown, 300 (later 362). William Stumpf was granted a permit to build a one-story theater at this location in October 1913. He opened it as the Good Time in May 1914. It was a brick building, 30 by 113 feet, and cost about $7,000. The plans were reportedly prepared by the owner. The theater went into receivership in April 1921, and Solomon Hoffman bought it for $25,000. The Good Time was remodeled in the summer of 1922 and enlarged in 1928. In early 1930, it was acquired by the State Amusement Company and redecorated; the latest sound equipment was installed. Jack Whittle became manager at that time. The name of the theater was changed to Avenue in 1932. Whittle was granted a permit to build a one-story brick addition to the theater in April 1942. The Avenue is still standing, but it has been extensively remodeled. It was a church for many years after it closed as a theater in 1958.

Gordon, 2435 West Baltimore Street, 1916–1918, Herbert C. Aiken, 400 (650 for airdome). The Gordon was a neighborhood movie theater that lasted only a few years. Plans for the theater were announced in April 1915. It was a brick structure, measuring 117 × 87 feet, that contained four stores in addition to the theater; it was built for about $12,000 by the Gordon Realty Company. There was an airdome in the rear of the theater that seems to have opened in the spring of 1916 when it was advertised as, "Baltimore's prettiest and most modern open-air dome." The hardtop theater opened in October 1916 under the management of Henry E. Cook, who also operated the Waverly Theater Company. Joe Brodie and Thomas Goldberg leased the Gordon in late 1916 with an option to purchase it. It was sold in October 1917 for $10,600 and closed soon thereafter.

Govans, 5005 York Road, 1914–1921. The Govans was another small neighborhood movie house with a short life-span. It was probably opened in the fall of 1914 by William C. O'Brien. Frank R. Batchelor purchased it in October 1915. Miles E. Mitchell leased the theater in June 1916. It apparently closed in 1918 or early 1919. Harris and Rullman reopened it in the spring of 1919. R. L. Rubenstein, who also operated the Pastime Theater, purchased the Govans in 1921; he planned to remodel it and increase the seating capacity to 300. The Govans was a one-story frame structure with a two-story addition in the rear. The entrance was from a raised porch under an overhanging gable roof with a central box office. The name "Govans" was painted on the gable.

Governor Ritchie Open-Air, 1706 Ritchie Highway, Glen Burnie, 1939–1984, unknown, 450 cars (also given as 500, 750 or 786). E. M. Loew's of Boston opened this drive-in, the first one in the state, on the evening of May 14, 1939. Opening-night ceremonies featured speeches by Governor O'Conor and Baltimore Mayor Jackson. The St. Patrick's Boys' Band supplied the music and there was a fireworks display. The first film was *Gunga Din*.

A detailed description of the theater appeared in the *Sun*.

> The ceremonies over, the floodlights will be quenched, and the spectators ... in their own cars ... will see an image forty feet high and fifty feet long flashed against the screen. The nearest of the ten ramps or terraces, capable of parking 786 automobiles, is 150 feet from this gargantuan image, and the farthest point of vantage will be 575 feet away. Ten acres of Anne Arundel soil, enclosed ... by 3,600 plantings of California privet hedge, roses and assorted shrubs comprises this open-air auditorium.
>
> Six thousand square yards of gravel were dumped into the plot, in order to provide a smooth rise ... after the new earth has settled, it will be surfaced with an asphalt mixture. Dim lights, close to the ground, will mark the entrances to the ramps, and others, placed at intervals on posts set into the hedge, will give additional illumination.
>
> The projection room is ... in a brick dugout located unobtrusively at front center. Machines equipped with three-and-one-half-inch lenses will throw the super-picture on the screen, using a beam three times as bright as the ordinary indoor projector. The screen housing tower is a steel frame covered with composition board and rimmed with silvery, gleaming metal. The screen itself is masked in black, and five huge horns are in a rectangular space above it. They can be reached by means of a steel ladder inside the shell. Also enclosed in the shell are dressing rooms for the thirty ushers, the control room from which all lights are handled, and a freshly dug well. From ground to roof, the screen tower rises sixty-four feet.
>
> By day the place is striking enough and will be more striking when tables, shaded by colored umbrellas are placed in front of the rose garden. By night, the powerful floodlights throw the gray facade into sharp relief, and the red, blue and green name-piece and billboards glow bravely against the countryside.
>
> The two shows nightly will go on in rain, dark or moonshine. Ushers with flashlights will guide the automobiles to the desired location of the ramps. The entrance is on the right, and the exit is on the left side of the tower and between shows the field will be lighted in order to facilitate the flow of traffic.[148]

The war was a disaster for the drive-in. Because of gas and rubber rationing, few people were able to attend the theater. Bernard Farwell, the manager, reported that business was so bad by October 1942 that he was closing the drive-in for the duration. The Governor Ritchie Drive-In reopened in June 1944. In 1954 a radio program called "The Martin Manor," hosted by radio commentator Ray Martin, was broadcast from the drive-in over WASL. In 1974, the drive-in was leased out for rock concerts. It continued to draw good crowds, mainly young adults and teenagers, until the end, when it closed in January 1984. The site of the drive-in is now a strip mall.

Grand {1}, 400 East Baltimore Street, 1909–c. 1939, A. Lowther Forrest, 246 (later c. 400). The Grand {1} was one of the many early movie houses on the Block. Pearce and Scheck took a 10-year lease on the M. Weinberg clothing store on the corner of Baltimore and Holliday Streets in October 1908 for $7,000 a year. It cost them about $15,000 to remodel the first floor of the three-story building into a moving picture theater. They opened the theater in late January 1909. According to one source, the Grand {1} was a fine example of heavy plastic relief ornamentation which was painted in different hardwood colors. In January 1909, Joseph D. Keenan leased the second floor of the building to open a billiard parlor.

Around 1910, the Grand {1} changed shows daily. Each show lasted about 40 minutes and consisted of four reels. The feature was usually two reels with the other two reels devoted to comedies or other short subjects. Harry Moorehead was the manager for many years; billed as, "The Prince of Song Illustrated," he also sang illustrated songs. Miss Dorothy Decker played the piano in 1911, and a stock company "talked the pictures." In 1913, the Grand {1} was running two-reel shows that changed three times a week.

The offices of Pearce and Scheck were in the Grand {1} building from about 1915 until 1936 when their successor, Phillip J. Scheck Enterprises, moved to the Lord Baltimore. The Grand {1} lasted until about 1939 when it became a bar. The building is still standing, but all traces of the theater have vanished.

Much of Anne Arundel County was farmland when this aerial photograph of the Governor Ritchie Drive-In (1706 Ritchie Highway, Glen Burnie, 1939–1984) was taken. (Photograph courtesy of the Archives of the Anne Arundel County Historical Society, Inc.)

Grand {2}, 511–517 South Conkling Street, 1913–1985, Henry Bickel (Henry L. Maas and Son of 1929 remodeling), 1,600 (1,130–1,485 after 1929 rebuilding, 1,375 reported in 1972). Conkling Street was called 3rd Street in 1913 when the Grand opened. The Highland Amusement Company announced plans for the theater in April 1913.[149]

The building was 65 by 150 feet with an auditorium 95 feet deep and a stage measuring 30 by 65 feet. It included two pool parlors on the second floor and three store fronts. The lower front arches contained handsome stained glass windows. The auditorium had private boxes on either side with a huge semi-circular gallery. The owners of the theater held a contest to select a name for the new theater and "Grand," submitted by John Hoffman of North Linwood Avenue, was selected from several thousand entries. The Grand {2} opened on November 10, 1913, with six acts of vaudeville and movies. Opening day festivities included an afternoon parade led by William Schluderberg and Henry Schenning and featured the Fort Howard Band.

Shortly after 7 o'clock Monday evening the 1600 seats in the theatre were taken and 564 persons were standing in the rear of the seats. Crowds lined the lobby of the playhouse and the sidewalk in front and it was necessary for Mr. Charles S. Anderson, the manager, to inform them that there was no more room within the building for them. Attorney John Holt Richardson, counsel for the Highland Amusement Company, owners of the Grand Theatre, made the opening address. At the conclusion of his speech he was presented with a large bouquet of flowers by Mr. J. Wilson Brown, manager of the Highlandtown Branch, State Bank of Maryland, in behalf of the Highland Amusement Company.[150]

294 II. BALTIMORE AREA THEATERS BY NAME

The Grand (511–517 South Conkling Street, 1913–1985, Henry Bickel) in Highlandtown in 1940. The Grand had one of the largest stages in the city outside downtown. It was foolishly demolished for a regional library.

Vaudeville shows were changed on Mondays and Thursdays, and films were changed daily. According to several sources, the site of the theater had previously been a slaughterhouse, but an article in the *Baltimore County Sentinel* described the location as "on Third Street, adjoining the property of *The Sentinel*, to the south and will include the dwellings Nos. 511, 513 and 515, with the driveway adjoining, making four ordinary house lots."[151]

There were two slaughterhouses on the alley behind and to the south of the site of the Grand; Ludwig Sellmayer's pork packing plant was on the southeast corner of the block. Cattle were also driven up the alley to be slaughtered. Rumor has it that traces of the old pens are still there. The billiard parlor on the second floor of the theater was managed by "Al" Knight a crack billiardist. In 1922, a two-manual Robert-Morton organ (Wicks opus 432) was installed.[152]

Durkee Theaters acquired the Grand {2} in 1926 and spent an estimated $20,000 for an extensive remodeling. The lobby and foyer were rebuilt, a new entrance to the balcony was added, the exterior and interior were repainted and redecorated, and new equipment and lighting fixtures were installed. It reopened on September 11, 1926. It was around this time that vaudeville ended at the Grand. Durkee erected a large new electric sign at a cost of about $7,000 in November 1926.

A fire in the projection booth in January 1928 routed 900 persons; the projectionist, William Holthouse, was seriously burned on the hands and face, but refused to leave the theater until the show was completed. The Grand {2} was wired for sound by the fall of 1928.

The theater was completely rebuilt for an estimated $150,000 in the summer of 1929. The seating capacity was increased to nearly 2,000.

The interior was described as in the Egyptian style with a green and gold color scheme. It reopened on September 23, 1929.

The world premier of *Baltimore Bullet* was held at the Grand in March 1980. It adopted a discount policy in the fall of 1982, charging $2.00 all day. Durkee used the Grand for their action house in Highlandtown; the more serious movies were shown at the Patterson. It was in beautiful condition, typical of the care given theaters by Durkee Enterprises, at the end of its long career.

The Grand {2} closed after the final showing of *Invasion USA* in October 1985. Only about 15 people attended the last night. The Grand stood empty for a number of years after it closed. In 1997 the Eastern Avenue Partnership suggested that the Grand be reopened as a three-screen movie theater and film-editing studio. George Figgs, who operated the Orpheum Theater on Fells Point, would operate the theater. This plan fell through in 1999. Local director, John Waters, spruced up the front of the Grand in the fall of 1999 and used it in his new movie, *Cecil B. Demented.*

In 2000 plans were announced to demolish the Grand and put a new Enoch Pratt library building on the spot. In a shameful act by the city government, the demolition of the Grand began on January 19. This was done despite calls for its preservation by major national and local preservation organizations. Highlandtown has lost one of its great icons, and the city is the poorer for it. Sad to see the Enoch Pratt as the agent for destruction of this great old theater.

Graphic (see Paradise {3})

Gray's Theater, 4600 or 4700 block of Eastern Avenue. According to a source familiar with this area, a saloonkeeper named Gray opened a small movie house near his saloon around 1912.

Great Wizard (see Wizard {2})

Greenmount Gardens, 2600 block Greenmount Avenue near Lorraine Avenue, c. 1915. Greenmount Gardens was a short-lived airdome on the west side of Greenmount Avenue between Lorraine Avenue and 27th Street. It probably lasted only a single summer. The permit to build the theater was granted to the Greenmount Amusement Company in May 1915, and it opened around July 11, 1915. The theater was arranged to give the impression of an enclosed garden with floral decorations. The building permit allowed the owners to erect a roll canvas awning on a pipe frame for use in rainy weather.

Greenspring 3, 2835A Smith Avenue, 1985–1999, unknown, 880 (255, 400, and 225). The Rappaport organization began this triplex in 1984, but Durkee Enterprises acquired it before it opened on May 31 of the following year. It was located in the Atrium at Greenspring Shopping Center on the site of the Greenspring Bowling Alley, and cost around $750,000. The Greenspring 3 theaters were plain and utilitarian with a computerized box office and fully automated projection booth. The original decor consisted of blue and white walls with blue carpeting. The original idea of the Durkee management was to use two of the auditoriums for popular first-run features and the third for commercial or art films. In 1986, the Greenspring 3 was showing daily matinees aimed at the senior citizen market. It closed on March 4, 1999.

Guild, 12 West 22nd Street, 1925–1942, unknown, 150 (200 after 1929 remodeling). The Guild opened in November 1925 with *The Charles Street Follies*. The *Sun* described the Guild:

> Many new ... features ... have been incorporated in the plans of the new Guild Theater, which in size and completeness of detail, will be more elaborate than any of the little theaters in the city. There will be a two-story stage, with an area of 550 square feet; a cozy auditorium with upholstered opera chairs, seating 150 persons, and with a sloping floor to insure easy range of vision; special lighting ... a regular box-office, hat-wires under the chairs ... and sundry conveniences such as one might expect to find only in the most up-to-date Broadway playhouses....[153]

The Guild was enlarged in 1929, adding more seats and a larger stage. During the late 1920s and early 1930s, this tiny theater was called the Play-Arts Guild. It was listed among moving picture theaters. It was better known for puppet shows and plays. The famous Tatterman Marionettes made annual appearances at the Guild in the early 1930s. Gilbert and Sullivan operettas also played there. Edwin Smith, Jr., redecorated the Guild in 1942, creating a new lobby and adding a new curtain. This attractive little building is still standing, and is used as a church.

*Guilford, 3301–3311 Greenmount Avenue. Palmore and Homand had plans by Oliver B. Wight in November 1920 for a 1,400-seat at this loca-

The Gwynn (4607–4609 Liberty Heights Avenue, 1933–1951, A. Murray Myers) was across the street from the Ambassador and was used mainly for action films.

tion; it was across the street from where the competing Boulevard Theater was planned.

Gwynn, 4607–4609 Liberty Heights Avenue, 1933–1951, A. Murray Myers (Kubitz & Koenig, engineers),[154] c. 700. The Gwynn was built for Robert Kanter with the assistance of Rome Theaters in 1933. It opened on November 27, 1933. The original theater had a large rectangular marquee that stretched across the front of the building. There was a vertical sign with the theater's name in the center of the facade. The box office was also centrally located and was flanked by entrance doors. Above the first story, the front was divided into four sections by three square pilasters. For two years, until the plushier Ambassador was built by Durkee Theaters across the street, the Gwynn had no rivals. Durkee Theaters acquired the Gwynn in 1935 and used it primarily for action movies. The Gwynn closed in 1951. For several years, it was neglected and became a neighborhood eyesore. By 1969, it had been spruced up and in 1973, it was a 5 cents–10 cents store. It later became a drugstore and then a discount shoe store.

Halethorpe (see Strand 3)

Hampden, 909–911 West 36th Street, 1911–1974, 1976; J. E. Laferty (R. E. Chambers of 1912 remodeling,[155] George Schmidt of 1926 building, E. Bernard Evander of 1938 remodeling); 300 (later 784). Charles A. Hicks built the Hampden for about $1,500 in what had been a tin shop. The *Morning Sun* of March 14, 1911, reported that Hicks was planning to erect a motion picture theater and office building at a cost of about $5,000. It probably opened in the late spring or summer of 1911. By the summer of 1912, Hicks was planning to enlarge the theater with a 27 by 30 foot extension. The present building dates from 1926 when architect George Schmidt designed a new $70,000 theater.

The new Hampden opened in September

The Hampden (909–911 West 36th Street, 1911–1974, 1976, J. E. Laferty; R.E. Chambers of 1912 remodeling; George Schmidt of 1926 building; E. Bernard Evander of 1938 remodeling) was one of the 36th Street duo of movie theaters.

1926, near its neighbor, the Ideal, which reopened after remodeling in the same month. The exterior was described as in the Spanish style while the interior was in the Adam style. The Hampden was the only movie theater in Baltimore with a Gottfried organ. Extensive alterations, including a new front, were made in 1938. The Hampden was the first theater in what became the Hicks (later Hicks-Baker) Circuit.

The Hicks-Baker organization closed the Hampden in January 1974, and retired businessman Edward Makowski bought the building in 1976. He leased it to Fred Speckmann who reopened it in May 1976. Speckmann refurbished the 1930s decor, which included leaded glass exit signs, a "halo of red indirect lighting around the interior" of the auditorium, a marble countered ticket booth and a fountain in the lobby. He wanted to make the theater an alternative to X-rated theaters and show classic films and family-oriented movies. Speckmann's attempt failed, and the Hampden was soon closed again.

Local baker, Bernard Breighner, bought the closed theater around 1978 and converted it into a split-level mall. The $600,000 Avenue Mall opened in 1981. The interior of the theater was gutted and the floor leveled, but a few bits of the original theater, including the original plaster ceiling, were kept. The facade was completely remodeled, and the marquee and vertical sign were removed. The mall was not successful, and by 2002 the building had become a restaurant.

Happyland, 611 East Baltimore Street, 1906–1907 unknown, 84. H. L. Reichenback was managing this theater in late 1906. It lasted only about a year.

The front of the Harford Theater (2618–2620 Harford Road, 1916–1963, A. Lowther Forrest) in 2003 shows few changes from this 1940 photograph.

Harford, 2618–2620 Harford Road, 1916–1960, 1962–1963, A. Lowther Forrest (Ewald Blanke and John Zink of 1920 remodeling), c. 500 (700 after 1920 remodeling). Vincent A. Valentini opened the Harford in 1916. The original theater measured 32 by 90 feet. Thomas Goldberg, who managed the Walbrook Theater, purchased an interest in the Harford Theater in July 1920. It was remodeled for an estimated $15,000 in 1920. The new structure measured 54 by 108 feet; it reopened in October. The front was of spotted brick with Indiana limestone trimming. The lobby was lined with marble and tile. There was a very small balcony with only a couple of rows of seats. In 1921 the Harford purchased a two-manual Moller organ (Opus 2987). It closed in 1960, but reopened two years later as the Harford Art Theater. It closed for good in 1963, and since then has been remodeled into a church.

Mr. and Mrs. Louis Hesson remembered that manager Goldberg would often walk down the aisle during a crowded Saturday matinee and shout a kid's name, "Alan, your mother wants you." All the Alans in the audience would get up and leave. Many people who went to the Harford in the 1940s remember Wilbert Baxter, a longtime usher there who used to arrive at work on a little motor scooter. On Saturdays at some point during the show the children would start shouting, "We want Wilbert! We want Wilbert!" Manager Goldberg would stop the film, turn on all the lights and threaten to throw them all out.

Harlem, 614–618 North Gilmor Street, 1932–1975, Wilson Porter Smith (Frank E. and Henry R. Davis of 1903 church), 1,488–1,534. Plans for a movie theater on the site of the Harlem Park Methodist Episcopal Church, an imposing structure of gray Port Deposit granite with Indiana limestone trim on the west side of Harlem Park,[156] had been made as early as the summer of 1928 when the Fidelity Amusement Company announced it would raze the church and build a $200,000 theater.

Theodore Wells Pietsch prepared plans for this theater, but it was never built — one reason, perhaps, due to objections from local businesses. An official of the H. M. Rowe Company located two doors from the church wrote a letter to the acting mayor protesting the conversion of the building into a movie theater. In addition to complaining that he was out of town when the ordinance was being discussed in the City Council, he wrote, "we also have in our office nine or ten young white women who are employed as stenographers, bookkeepers, and clerical workers. I submit to you, Sir, that the situation created would undoubtedly result in annoyance of

The similarity between churches and movie theaters is clear in this 1946 photograph of the Harlem Theater (614–618 North Gilmor Street, 1932–1975, Wilson Porter Smith, Frank E. and Henry R. Davis of 1903 church) which was actually built in a former church.

one kind or another to these girls as they come to and go from their work at our office."[157]

The Rome organization built the Harlem within the original church structure. When it was being converted into a movie house, some people in the neighborhood said that it would probably be struck by lightning. The Harlem, which cost an estimated $150,000, opened on October 7, 1932, with *Chandu, the Magician*, starring Edmund Lowe. Opening day festivities included a huge parade that featured local organizations such as the Elks, Penrose Club, and the South Baltimore Republican Club, and many civic leaders. Five thousand people marched in the parade and 30,000 watched it. J. Finley Wilson, Grand Exalted Leader of the Elks, gave an address inside the theater.

The original marquee was rectangular, 65 feet long, contained 900 50-watt bulbs, and illuminated all of Harlem Square. There was also a 40-foot vertical neon-illuminated sign. The auditorium was restrained Spanish atmospheric with twinkling electric lights set in the ceiling to simulate a starry night sky. The interior colors were cream and blue. Before the opening of the Harlem, the management held a contest to select a slogan for the new theater. The winner of the $10 first prize was Oberlin Perry of North Mount Street. His slogan was "First with the best." In June 1933, the Harlem installed a Western Electric Wide Range sound system, reportedly the first such installation in Baltimore. In the 1950s, the first floor walls were draped, but tile roofs and other atmospheric touches were still visible in the balcony. During the riots of April 1968, all of the front glass was smashed.

Up until the early 1970s the Harlem put on live shows. Rome Theaters closed the Harlem in

General Cinema's Harundale Cinema (800 Aquahart Road, Glen Burnie, 1964–1989, William Riseman Associates), shown here about 1964, was one of the big 1960s movie houses that ringed Baltimore. (Photograph courtesy of the Archives of the Anne Arundel County Historical Society, Inc.)

1975 and sold it to the Rev. Raymond Kelly, Jr. His Harlem Park Community Baptist Church converted it back into a church. By the 1990s the interior had been remodeled; pews replaced the first floor seats and an altar replaced the stage. The Harlem was an African-American theater during its entire 40-odd year existence, and was regarded as one of the classier theaters for African Americans in Baltimore. One young patron remembered the delicious kosher hot dogs at the Harlem and cited them as one reason he went there.

Harundale Mall Cinema, 800 Aquahart Rd., Glen Burnie, 1964–1989, William Riseman Associates, 1,105. In the spring of 1963 James Rouse, the developer of Harundale Mall, announced plans for a new theater adjacent to the mall. General Drive-In Corporation signed the lease to operate the new theater, and ground was broken in December 1963. It was a large, freestanding, square building with a wrap-around porch in front. Patrons entered through two sets of glass doors, one on the corner and one in the middle of the front. The only decoration on the facade was a sign near the top that spelled out "Cinema" in large letters.

Inside, the theater had a 62 × 28-foot picture framed screen,[158] pushback chairs arranged in a staggered seating plan, and a lobby art gallery. The Harundale Cinema was similar to another General Cinema theater, the Perring Plaza Cinema. The Harundale Mall Cinema opened with searchlights and festivities broadcast live on WISZ on the evening of July 16, 1964. The first film shown was *Zulu*. Twinned in June 1973, the theater lasted until 1989.

Hasslinger's Daisy, 1752 North Gay Street, 1908–c. 1917, unknown, c. 125. Louis Hasslinger converted a two-story brick building, which had formerly housed a bowling alley on the first floor, into this small theater in late 1908 for an estimated $1,000. He named it after his youngest daughter, Daisy. The lobby was painted pale blue with the name "Daisy," formed in painted daisies, on the wall. The auditorium had a single aisle with three seats on either side. The projection booth was at the rear of the auditorium on a three-foot high platform. Movies were shown from 6:00 P.M. to 11:00 P.M. on weekdays and from 2:00 P.M. to 11:00 P.M. on Saturdays. The Saturday afternoon shows were mainly for children. Mr. Hasslinger gave them free candy, and, if they couldn't afford the nickel admission, he would often let them in free. He sat in a high wire chair in the lobby to collect tickets. On Saturday nights he made the children sit on the floor, but, as one man remembered, it was kept clean and they didn't mind as long as they could see the show six times.

The Daisy used at least one behind-the-screen talker, a Mr. Hall. Emma Mandler played the piano and John Bishop sang. The theater staff lived in the neighborhood, and if any member had an increase in the size of his or her family, Mr. Hasslinger would give him or her a raise. One woman remembered that a man used to spray some kind of perfume in the theater, and people in the neighborhood could tell when you had attended the Daisy because you smelled like that perfume. The building is still standing.

Hawkins Airdome, Preston Street between Druid Hill Avenue and McCulloh Street, 1921. John W. Hawkins opened this open-air theater in the rear of the Pythian Castle Hall (930–932 McCulloh Street) on June 1, 1921. Hawkins called the enterprise Hawkins Air Dome and Summer Garden, and he sold all kinds of soft drinks in the summer garden. The *Afro-American* of June 10, 1921, called it "The most pretentious open air picture garden so far constructed here for colored Baltimoreans...." Business was apparently not so good; after about four weeks, Hawkins closed it down and replaced it with an open-air cabaret. By the summer of 1925 it was a dance pavilion called Madison Square Garden.

Highland {1}, 3509–3511 Eastern Avenue, 1895–1919, Mottu & White (of 1913 alterations). This theater was on the second floor of the Highland Academy building. It operated from about 1909 until 1919. The Highland Academy, also known as Conkling Hall, was built for Philip Wagner. A popular place for dances and meetings of various fraternal organizations, it opened on March 20, 1895, with a large celebration that included fireworks. Webber's Band provided the music. Costing between $10,000 and $15,000, the Academy had a 50-foot frontage on Eastern Avenue and a depth of 68 feet. The front of the three-story building was constructed of pressed brick with brown stone trim. There was a banquet-reception hall on the first floor and two large lodge rooms on the third floor. The second floor was also used as a ballroom. The Academy was an early home for the Eichenkranz Society, a German social club and singing society founded by Philip Wagner. Early movies were also shown there, especially before the opening of the nearby Grand Theater.

Furniture dealer William J. Wieland bought the building in the summer of 1913 and converted it into a furniture store. By 1999, it had been converted into office space.

Highland {2}, 3829 Eastern Avenue, 1940–1951, J. O. Chertkof, 500. The Flax Brothers opened this Highland on June 25, 1940; it cost an estimated $12,000. It closed in the summer of 1949, but later reopened. In 1950, the theater was sued for $12,000 by the owner and two employees of an adjoining restaurant who claimed contamination by fumigation gas being used in the Highland. After the theater closed, it was converted into a supermarket and later a sportswear store.

Highland {3} (see Purity Moving Picture Parlor)

Highland Airdome, rear 3505 Eastern Avenue, c. 1913–1920, unknown, c. 1,800. This large, open-air theater was adjacent to the Highland Academy. It was open as early as June 1913, when it was mentioned in litigation to dissolve the partnership between Walter Albers and John A. Ertel who also operated the nearby Comic and Eagle theaters.[159] It reopened on May 18, 1914, with movies and vaudeville headed by the Musical Russells. The entrance and ticket booth were on Eastern Avenue, and there was a second entrance on Conkling Street near the Highlandtown Engine House. A stage was at the rear of the airdome. Thomas J. Kane operated it in 1915.

Highland Park (see Pitt's Park)

Hill, 610 Cherry Hill Rd., 1946–1971, Hal Miller,[160] 926. The Hill was built in a shopping center in Cherry Hill by District Theaters of Washington, D.C. It was a brick and concrete structure with a limestone front, and the front of the building featured a clock tower. The marquee was finished in glass and stainless steel with the latest type of fluorescent lighting. The walls and doors of the entrance lobby were finished in walnut. The Hill opened on Easter Sunday April 21, 1946, and closed in early 1971.

Hillendale, 1045 Taylor Avenue, 1960–1996, 2001–2004, Fenton and Lichtig, 910. Joseph Grant's investment company opened this beautiful, modern theater on November 23, 1960. The first show at the Hillendale was an exclusive engagement, along with the Boulevard, of *Can-Can*. The Hillendale was part of a large building project that included the theater, a bowling alley, and 10,000 square feet of office space. A special exception permit to build the $350,000 theater above the existing bowling alley was approved by the Baltimore County zoning commissioner in April 1960.

The Hillendale was the first hardtop theater built in the Baltimore area in ten years and claimed the first multi-channel transistorized sound system in the world.[161] The Century 70–35mm projectors were equipped with multiple-channel transistorized amplification and electronic sound changeovers. There were five Altec Lansing theater speakers behind the screen with 12 surround speakers permanently installed in ceiling coves.

The Hillendale had "Continental Seating" which eliminated center aisles and provided more choice seats with added space between rows. The front of the Hillendale was faced with brick and ceramic tile. There was a liberal use of glass and recessed lighting with a blue and gold color scheme in the lobby, and the same color scheme throughout the interior. The Mohawk carpeting was also blue. Haywood-Wakefield supplied the blue and orange seats. The theater and bowling alley were located on a four-and-one-half-acre tract that also had parking space for 500 cars. The bowling alley was on two levels with 28 lanes on the first and 14 on the upper level.

Aaron Seidler described the building of the theater:

> ...the Grants ... owned a piece of property that they were going to build bowling alleys ... and a little office building over top of the bowling alleys where they were going to move their offices.... They had just tried to do a joint operation with Durkee in a shopping area not too far from Hillendale ... right between where the Hillendale is and Towson. In any event, the joint venture didn't work out, and when it didn't work out, I said, "You guys are getting ready to build this bowling alley and this office structure, why not plan a theater in there?" So they got their architect and [he] said, yes the bowling lanes are really ... under ground, and they physically built a bridge structure over top the bowling lanes, just like you build a bridge with steel and figured out a way to pour lightweight concrete so it wouldn't be a heavy load on the bowling lane and it was there we created the Hillendale Theater. Over top of the bowling lanes and adjoining an office structure that was over top of the other end of the bowling lanes. We developed that and ran it very successfully.[162]

In 1979, the theater was rather crudely twinned into a 255-seat and a 461-seat theater. It was acquired by Durkee Theaters and closed by them in the spring of 1988. Tom Kiefaber remodeled the Hillendale and reopened it later that year. Kiefaber operated the theater as a sub-run house for several years, but it was never very successful. It was closed by the beginning of 1997 and negotiations were held to convert it into a community center.

Edward Copeland refurbished the Hillendale and reopened it as a first-run house on June 30, 2001, but it closed again in 2002. Michael Johnson leased it in 2003 as the latest venue for his Heritage Shadows of the Silver Screen. Johnson moved from the Parkway to the Hillendale in March and reopened the theater in May as a showplace for African-American films. He renamed the 255-seat auditorium the Howard Rollins Cinema I and the 461-seat auditorium the Grand Oscar Micheaux Cinema II. Again, lack of support proved fatal for Johnson, and he closed the theater in September 2004.

Hilton (see Goldberg's Theater)

Hindenburg (see Three Arts)

Hippodrome {1}, Light and McComas Streets,[163] c. 1911. This Hippodrome was a short-lived open-air theater at the Union League Baseball Park in South Baltimore. It opened in June 1911 with a vaudeville show that included "a fine motion-picture program."

Hippodrome {2}, 12 North Eutaw Street, 1914–1990, Thomas W. Lamb (John J. Zink of 1941 remodeling), c. 2.250 (originally 3,000 with 1,300 seats on the first floor). The Hippodrome is one of the best-remembered theaters in Baltimore. It is also among the longest-lived theaters in town, lasting more than 70 years, with more to come. Pearce and Scheck built the Hippodrome on the north portion of the site of the old Eutaw House — a luxury hotel that dated from 1835.[164] The hotel had been extensively damaged by fire on May 25, 1912, and was too expensive to rebuild. By early 1913, Pearce and Scheck were vying with Nixon and Zimmerman, and Marcus Loew to buy the $350,000 property on which to build a theater. Pearce and Scheck won out, but were unable to make a success of the theater, and Marcus Loew gained control of it for a few years.

Pearce and Scheck and W. Stuart Symington organized the Hippodrome Company and applied for a charter in April 1913. The new company had a capital stock of $400,000. They brought the well-known theater architect, Thomas W. Lamb, to Baltimore from New York

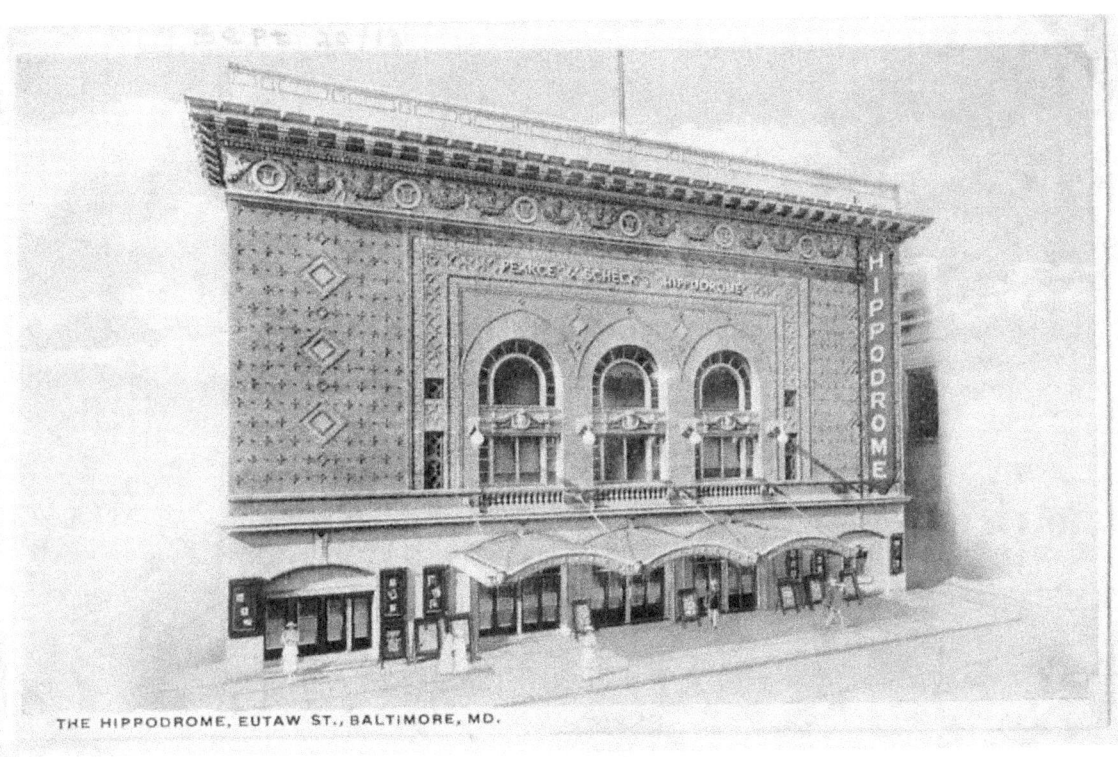

THE HIPPODROME, EUTAW ST., BALTIMORE, MD.

A postcard view of the Hippodrome (12 North Eutaw Street, 1914–present, Thomas Lamb) when it opened.

to design the Hippodrome.[165] The Singer-Pentz Construction Company was awarded the contract to build it. The theater measured 77 by 140 feet and cost an estimated $225,000. With steel, cement, brick, and stone construction, the building facade is a fine example of decorative brickwork with a frieze featuring classical motifs.

A contemporary description of the front is from the *Baltimore News*.

> The front is built with granite and terra cotta base, with tapestry brick laid in pattern work and surmounted with a handsome terra cotta cornice and balustrade. The marquise is an especial feature with a carriage-call signal display which will be visible two blocks away.[166]

The marble box office had provisions for two cashiers. The interior was even more elaborate and featured many new elements.

> The interior will be handsomely executed in decorative plaster and Green Alps marble. The wall treatment will be of silk and the fixtures for lighting are extremely new, having been especially designed for this house. The lobby will be treated in quiet, refined tones with marble wainscot, decorative arched ceiling and marble floor. The balcony has been made different from anything heretofore attempted in Baltimore, some of the features being the wide crossover, the two vomitories and inclined passageways leading to the stairs, eliminating the inconvenience of climbing the stairs to top of balcony and then having to walk down. This balcony is a monstrous affair supported on a hammock truss so that no columns obstruct the sight lines. There are five loggia boxes at the front of the balcony each accommodating about 24 people which can again be subdivided into two compartments each. The proscenium boxes are handsome, being designed on the order of a throne with large canopy over the top, which is studded with myriads of electric lights.[167]

The prevailing color was brown with the walls covered in brown silk panels. Above the stage was a huge allegorical mural featuring Greek goddesses and Muses painted by Vincent Maragliotti. The stage opening was 43 feet wide. Sixteen dressing rooms were available backstage. A large Moller pipe organ (2/17, Opus 1766) was built especially for the Hippodrome.[168] The ventilating system could change the air in every portion of the building every five minutes.

The magnificent marquee added by Isador Rappaport in 1931, as it was in 1953.

When it opened at 8:00 P.M. on Monday, November 23, 1914, the Hippodrome was called the largest playhouse south of Philadelphia. It presented vaudeville acts furnished by Marcus Loew's booking agency and also showed films. The opening program consisted of a two-reel movie, *The Iron Master*, and seven vaudeville acts. A reviewer for the *Sun* panned the vaudeville, and concluded that the only acts "that seemed to arouse enthusiasm" were Von Cello, Robinson's Elephants, and Lemaire & Dawson. On the other hand, the *Baltimore Star* liked the vaudeville, especially Roland West's Dairy Maids. The contractor was terrified when he heard that elephants were going to walk on the stage; he worried that the stage was not strong enough to support them.

The Hippodrome offered three vaudeville performances — one in the afternoon, followed by some movies during the supper hour, and two in the evening. The early ushers wore light gray uniforms, and the orchestra members dressed in semi-military attire. Frederick Weaver gave a 15-minute organ recital at 8:00 each evening during the opening week. The orchestra, which claimed to be the only theater orchestra in the United States that used "semi-military uniforms," was conducted by William J. Hopper. C. E. Lewis, who had managed the Victoria for Pearce and Scheck, became the first manager of the Hippodrome; the stage manager was S. Harry Kaufman. In the fall of 1915, the theater was leased by the Loew's organization, and Marcus Loew got his first foothold in Baltimore.

Beginning in October 1916, Loew's offered first-run feature films along with the vaudeville show. By 1917, the Hippodrome, which was not doing very well — some said that it was too far west of downtown — was charging 10 cents–15 cents (afternoons) and 15 cents–25 cents–30 cents (evenings) to see two movies and Marcus Loew's "Supreme Vaudeville."

A serious fire in the booth of the Hippodrome in July 1918 badly injured the operators, George F. Stenz and R. Patten. Loew's continued to lease the Hippodrome for six months at a time until January 1924. The theater then passed into the B. F. Keith organization, becoming the second Keith vaudeville house in town. It presented "Family Time," a second-class Keith attraction that consisted of vaudeville and movies.

Manager E. A. Lake installed a public address system in the theater in the summer of 1928 so that he could announce each vaudeville act from a microphone in his private office. The speaker was located under the proscenium arch.

During the summer of 1929, a sound system was installed in the Hippodrome. In May 1930, the Hippodrome adopted daylight saving time, and, probably coincidentally, closed early the following year during a run of the movie *Birth*.[169]

Things looked bad. In January 1931 a receiver was appointed for the theater, and it was ordered to be sold at auction; it could not pay its debts. L. Edward Goldman purchased it in February 1931 for $14,000 even though it was subject to more than $350,000 in debts. Goldman was the only bidder. Then, in mid–1931, Goldman leased the Hippodrome to Isador Rappaport. Rappaport had just come to Baltimore from Philadelphia and would show the city what a great theater the Hippodrome could be. He reopened it in grand style on August 28, 1931 with movies and vaudeville.

Governor Ritchie and George Jessel were among the notables present at the reopening. The movie shown was *Three Who Love*, with Conrad Nagel. The vaudeville, booked through Edward Sherman, included King, King, and King (three dancing brothers), the Misses LaMarr and Boyce (a singing team), and "Doc" Baker and his "Flashes of 1931." Rappaport provided four shows a day, at 12:30 P.M., 3:30 P.M., 6:45 P.M., and 9:00 P.M. Admission was 25 cents before 12:30, 35 cents between 12:30 and 6:00, and 50 cents after 6:00. A spectacular new marquee containing more than 8,000 lights was erected in 1931; and in May 1933, the Hippodrome was the fifth theater in the country to install the new wide-range speakers developed by Bell Telephone Laboratories.

Rappaport purchased the theater in early 1934 for about $300,000. He closed it for six weeks that summer, reopening it with a gala show on August 2. The theater had been spruced up with a thorough cleaning of its facade and the installation of new black Bakelite poster cases with chromium frames to match the box office and doors. Inside, there were new draperies and carpeting, and deluxe seats patterned after those in Radio City Music Hall.

Singer Sylvia Froos headed the stage show while Leslie Howard and Bette Davis starred in the film, *Of Human Bondage*. A special arrangement allowed Eddie Cantor to speak to the audience by long-distance telephone from the United Artists' Studios. For many years Rappaport organized special anniversary shows at the Hippodrome to celebrate his taking the theater over. The Hippodrome did its part for the war effort even before hostilities began, reducing prices for servicemen in July 1941. That same month, there was another of the grand reopenings, this time after a three-week remodeling. Dinah Shore appeared on stage.

News-Post critic Norman Clark described the changes in the theater:

> A facade entirely refurbished with chrome and walnut frame boards and heavy plate-glass doors of the most modern design. The lobby ... illuminated by indirect fluorescent lighting.
>
> The theatre's walls recovered with embossed leather fabric, highlighted with hand-carved moldings. The standee rail covered with padded natural leather, which will blend with the walls. Hidden lights casting their glow upon new carpets.... The decorative scheme of the stage and the proscenium will include rich festoons and drapes of silks, velours and plushes. There will be a new system of stage lighting. Also new screen and sound equipment, a larger screen and improved amplifiers. Furthermore, a newly built ladies' lounge on the lower floor, with an entrance from the main auditorium.[170]

In August 1949 the Hippodrome management informed the local musicians' union that its contract at the theater would not be renewed. It was believed at the time that vaudeville was ending at the Hippodrome, but it returned in October 1949 for two more years. Regular vaudeville ended at the Hippodrome on May 30, 1951, with Pee Wee King and his Golden West Cowboys onstage. The theater closed after a fire in April 1952, and, for a while, was put up for sale for $350,000 or to rent for $40,000 a year — but not as a theater. It reopened again and, in 1958 and 1959, the last stage shows were presented. One of the last of these occurred on June 3, 1958, when Diane Jergens and Jackie Coogan, starring in *High School Confidential*, appeared in a stage show with emcee Hugh Cherry of radio station WCAO. The Three Stooges appeared during a special show in June 1959.

Rappaport leased his theaters, including the Hippodrome, to Trans-Lux in 1962. The following summer, Trans-Lux spent about $250,000 to completely remodel the theater; they installed new seats, carpeting, and projection equipment, and put up a new marquee. It reopened on June 26 with *Cleopatra*. In the spring of 1964, the Trans-Lux organization was considering converting the Hippodrome into a legitimate theater,[171] but this never happened. The Baltimore premier of *My Fair Lady* did appear there in late 1964. After a gala premier of the film *Slaves* in May 1969, life was all downhill for the Hippodrome. The cornice on the Eutaw Street facade was removed in 1974 because there was fear that it might fall. The Hippodrome was acquired by JF Theaters and passed again into the Loew's organization when they bought out JF. It closed in August 1990 after showings of *Die Harder* and *Night Breed*.

Why is the Hippodrome, that started out so inauspiciously, the best-remembered theater in Baltimore? Perhaps because every important vaudeville performer and band between 1914 and 1951 played there. Or maybe because it was managed by one of Baltimore's best theater managers.[172] You may wonder who played there. To name them all would take more space than is available here, but some of the better-known performers are: Gene Autry, Milton Berle, Victor Borge, Cab Calloway, Bob Hope, Jerry Colonna, Benny Goodman, Betty Grable, the Three Stooges, Spike Jones, Molly Picon, Red Skelton, Al Jolson, Abbott and Costello, Danny Kaye, Jimmy and Tommy Dorsey, and Uncle Jack's Kiddie Club. A formidable lineup.[173]

While the Hippodrome lay in limbo during the early 1990s, some people were trying to think of ways to save it. One early call to save the Hippodrome was from local historian Jacques Kelly in his column on October 24, 1991. Kelly wrote about successful theater renovations in Toronto and suggested another look at the Hippodrome. Archivist Mary Markey echoed Kelly's sentiments in a letter to the *Sun* the following month.[174] The Hippodrome was put on Baltimore Heritage's list of endangered properties in 1992.

The first serious plan to save the theater was developed in 1993 by Donald Hicken, the head of the theater department at the Baltimore School for the Arts. Hicken organized the National Museum of Live Entertainment and secured an option to purchase the theater. His idea was to create a museum to honor live theater, but he could not get the financing. Then, in the spring of 1997, Continental Realty donated the theater to the University of Maryland at Baltimore. The stage was set for something really grand, which happened in 1998. Three groups, the Greater Baltimore Committee, Inc., the Downtown Partnership, and the Baltimore Center for the Performing Arts, proposed a $25 million renovation of the Hippodrome to turn it into a venue for big Broadway shows.[175] Plans called for enlargement of the Hippodrome's stage, demolition of the Eutaw Building on the south side of the theater, and renovation and reuse of the two late 19th century bank buildings to the north creating a massive entertainment complex. Governor Glendening pledged state support.

In mid–1998, New York architects Hardy

Holzman Pfeiffer Associates were selected to head the design team for the Hippodrome's restoration.[176] Despite the skepticism of some state legislators, rising cost estimates, and threatened loss of state funding in 1998 and the mean-spirited reneging by the Baltimore County Council on a promised $500,000 contribution, restoration work continued through 1998 and into 2000. The work of cleaning out and stabilizing the Hippodrome made progress in 2001; Clear Channel Entertainment was selected to run the theater. By the fall of 2001, the cost of the project had risen to $63 million.

The France-Merrick Foundation agreed to contribute $5 million, but there was a string attached. The Towson-based group wanted naming rights, and there was the outrageous possibility that the name Hippodrome would be replaced.[177] Thankfully, this did not happen; it's still the Hippodrome. Work had progressed far enough by the fall of 2003 to ensure a 2004 reopening. The restoration, supervised by local architects Schamu Machowski Greco, got rave reviews. The original marquee was rebuilt, and a new cornice with recreated lions' faces was installed. Inside, the long-gone boxes were rebuilt, the mural above the stage was restored, and the plasterwork was repaired and repainted. The spectacularly restored theater reopened on February 10, 2004 with *The Producers*. The show got great reviews.[178] Baltimore has another theater to be proud of.

Hiway, 1812–1814 Earhart Rd., Essex, 1946–1977, possibly Hal A. Miller, 720. Nicholas Schwartz seems to have opened the Hiway on October 22, 1946, with *Northwest Mounted Police*.[179] Just before the theater opened, the management had a free showing and let a gang of kids in to see the movie.

The Hiway had a narrow entrance and a long lobby lined with posters that led to the auditorium. The auditorium was large and plain with a round loudspeaker grill in the shape of the letter "H" below the bottom of the screen. Miss Edna's Hiway Kiddie Show appeared each Saturday morning on the Hiway's stage. In January 1949, the Hiway was the first movie theater in the area to show television movies. Manager Robert Marhenke obtained special equipment to show pictures of the Middle River Essex Community Children's Christmas party at the Hiway which were previously presented on WMAR-TV. On Monday nights in the summer of 1949, Happy Johnny's Talent Hunt Show was broadcast on WBMD from the Hiway's stage. On Saturdays, around 1950, the Hiway had live stage shows featuring singer Peggy Shoemaker and the Lazy H Ranch Boys. WSID broadcast the shows from the theater's stage. Elvis Presley and Walt Disney movies did well at the Hiway.

The front of the theater was severely remodeled and the auditorium was used for storage before it was demolished in 2004.

Holliday Street Theater, 100 block North Holliday Street, 1874–1917, James J. Gifford (of 1859 remodeling and 1874 rebuilding), c. 2,000 (1,000 — gallery, 418–426 — balcony, 489–601— orchestra). The first Holliday Street Theater was a frame building built in 1795 by Wignall and Reinagle on the site of City Hall Plaza. It was replaced by a brick building in 1813. A group that included John T. Ford acquired the theater in 1856 and ran it for the next 20 years.

After a serious fire in September 1873, a third theater was erected. The rebuilt theater opened on August 3, 1874. It was described in a contemporary account as, "built entirely of brick, painted outside a light drab color, the front resembling the old structure, though the present building is capable of comfortably seating about 1,750 persons."[180] The first floor lobby had flowered glass windows. One improvement noted in the description was the abolition of the stage boxes. The interior color scheme consisted of blue and light drab with crimson plush upholstery on the seats. The proscenium opening measured 38' × 35'.

John W. Albaugh leased the theater in 1878. In 1881 two of the new electric lights were installed in the front of the theater. In 1890 James Kernan, George W. Rife and George H. Houck acquired Albaugh's lease. The Holliday Street Theater was mainly a legitimate theater, but did occasionally show movies. The earliest films were shown there in June 1898 for a Veriscope exhibition. In April 1906, during a movie exhibition, Building Inspector Preston complained to the mayor that the projector was placed in the gallery among the spectators and was not in a fireproof room.

William Saunner directed the orchestra around 1907. In May 1908, the theater showed a new movie every day and changed illustrated songs on Monday and Thursday. During the summer of 1908, as a filler between seasons, the Cameraphone or "talking pictures" were exhibited. A popular feature at the Holliday Street Theater was the Paragon Baseball Scoreboard which was installed in May 1911.[181] This was the scoreboard's first appearance in Baltimore.

The city purchased the Holliday Street Theater for $86,500 in December 1914. This purchase and that of the adjacent Gordon property were the first steps in the development of the War Memorial Plaza. In early April 1915, the theater was leased to Oliver J. Allenbaugh who planned to begin showing high-class moving picture shows. This was the swan song of the old theater; it was torn down in 1917–1918. The Baltimore tradition of tearing down historic theaters had begun.

Certainly the most famous event in the history of the Holliday Street Theater was the first public performance of Francis Scott Key's "Star-Spangled Banner" a short time after the bombardment of Ft. McHenry. Well-known performers who appeared at the Holliday Street Theater include Junius Brutus Booth and his sons Edwin and John Wilkes, Edwin Forest, Laura Keene, John Howard Payne (the author of Home, Sweet Home), Lotta Crabtree, and Nat C. Goodwin. Charles Dickens lectured at the Holliday Street Theater during his trip to the United States.

One of the many stories about the Holliday Street Theater concerns Junius Brutus Booth, the great Shakespearean actor. During a performance of *Richard III* in the late 1850s, Booth was playing Richard. After a duel at the end of the play, Richmond slays Richard and, putting one foot on the king's body says, "The day is ours, the bloody dog is dead." During this performance, however, Booth was playing the title role with great energy, and "so far was Booth taken and driven by his dramatic personality that night, that he forgot to die. Time and again Richmond hissed 'That is your cue to die.'" But Richard refused to die and he drove the young actor playing Richmond all over the stage. At last the young man realized that he was in a real fight — to the death, and he fled the stage, jumping over the footlights and racing up the aisle with Booth in hot pursuit. They both disappeared into the street. Booth was next seen several hours later sitting on a fireplug on Howard Street, still dressed as Richard and holding his sword.[182]

Hollywood {1}, 5509–5511 Oregon Avenue, Arbutus, 1936–1995, Carl Ganter, John Carroll Dunn (of 1985 twinning), 475 (after the 1985 twinning — 204 and 271). The Hollywood was built in the Arbutus commercial district by the Tunick organization. It probably opened on September 5, 1936, with *Call of the Wild*, starring Clark Gable. It was an attractive art deco building with a facade of cream face brick. Inside the lobby, there was a tiny candy stand. There was also a glassed-in "crying room," where families with babies could watch a movie without disturbing others. The Hollywood was acquired by R/C Theaters and twinned in 1985; then, unfortunately, it was destroyed by fire on October 15, 1995.

The Hollywood was one of the most successful of Baltimore's suburban neighborhood theaters. It was closely identified with the Arbutus community for 60 years. Generations of young people had their first jobs and first dates at the Hollywood. There was so much outpouring of loss by local residents that R/C Theaters decided to build a new Hollywood Theater, with the help of a $350,000 loan from the county, on the same site.

Hollywood {2}, 5509–11 Oregon Avenue, Arbutus, 1998–present, Getz Taylor, 750 (for four auditoriums). The Hollywood {2} was built on the site of the Hollywood {1}. Immediately after the fire that destroyed the first Hollywood, R/C Theaters announced that it would build a new theater for Arbutus. With the aid of community and county support a new, four-screen, theater was built. As a sign of support, local community leaders sold engraved bricks at $25 each to help get the theater rebuilt. It cost about $1 million and took nearly three years to complete.

The new Hollywood opened on May 22, 1998. Ironically there was a fire alarm, caused by an overheated popcorn machine, on opening night. R/C planned to show first-run films at two auditoriums and bargain movies at the other two. The handsome facade of the new Hollywood is of white split-face brick with bands of red, blue and gray. The entrance is sheltered by a large rectangular marquee with the name of the theater spelled out in red letters on the street side. The auditoriums vary in seating capacity from 108 to 304.

Home, 2211 Pennsylvania Avenue, c. 1909–1911. The Home was advertising "the finest moving pictures" and vaudeville for 5 cents in 1909 and 1910. In the spring of 1911 nearly 100 residents near the theater signed a petition asking that the theater be closed because a rough element had taken to hanging out around the theater. There was so much opposition that by the fall of 1911 the owner agreed not to reopen the theater.

Homewood, 9 West 25th Street, 1946–1985, Hal A. Miller, 700 (after 1951 remodeling — 359, after 1967 remodeling — 450). The Schwaber or-

R/C Theaters built this new Hollywood (5509 Oregon Avenue, Arbutus, Getz Taylor, 1998–present) to replace the beloved Hollywood which burned in 1995.

ganization opened the Homewood on May 25, 1946. The opening advertisement featured this statement by the owners:

> We wish to present to the people of Homewood ... the theatre befitting their station in life, and worthy of their ideals and environment. We have spared no expense in installing the finest in sound and projector system obtainable. The lighting effects thruout the theatre are entirely indirect, with soft and blending tones enhancing the real beauty of the theatre. The modern air-cushioned seats were designed and built exclusively for this theatre. Also Acousticon Hearing Aids for the hard of hearing.

An amusing incident occurred when this theater was only a few months old. On November 25, 1946, a terrified nurse reported to the police that there was a dead body with a knife sticking in it in the lobby of the theater. Upon closer investigation, the body was found to be a dummy advertising the theater's latest attraction, *Who Done It?* starring Abbott and Costello.

The Homewood might have remained an unremarkable neighborhood theater if not for the vision of the owner's son-in-law. The idea to convert the Homewood into an art theater was the brainchild of Milton Schwaber's son-in-law, Howard "Boots" Wagonheim. Wagonheim described this conversion in a 1983 article[183]:

> Among the theaters owned by my father-in-law was the Homewood, at 25th and Charles streets. I talked him into letting me replace its tightly spaced rows of 800 seats with 359 of the new loges—the first theater in the country to be so equipped. I called the remodeled theater the Playhouse. I also thought that every theater should have a personality of its own. Going to the movies should be like visiting a friend's home. This gave me the idea of a lobby that was like a living room. With wall-to-wall carpeting, club chairs and sofas. On the walls should be paintings. Originals not reproductions. And, most important of all, no candy machines. Instead, there would be coffee and tea served free.

The Playhouse opened on November 7, 1951, with *The Emperor's Nightingale*. The new theater grossed $3,012 in the first week; the Homewood had been averaging about $800 a week. In November 1952, the editors of *Theater Catalog* awarded the Playhouse a bronze plaque for excellence in patron comfort, efficiency, and courtesy of management.

The *Sun* described the new theater:

> A new first-run motion picture theater, specializing in "the latest — and best — international films," will open here next month. To be called The Playhouse, it will be located... "well away from downtown congestion and convenient to the northern suburbs," in the words of H. Ted Routson, managing director. "New York and Washington have long had a monopoly on theaters where discriminating persons can see intelligent films in civilized surroundings," Mr. Routson said, "Now Baltimoreans will have a chance."
>
> The owner is Milton Schwaber ... who reports he is putting $60,000 in improvements into the building. When the refurbishing is finished ... the house will have only 400 seats instead of its present 700. These will be the new, foam-rubber, "rocking-chair" type, with broad base, 184 broad armrests and enough room between rows (45 inches from seatback to seatback) for patrons to enter and leave without forcing the seated to get to their feet.
>
> A tea and coffee bar ... will be located in a lounge walled off from the auditorium. With carpets and divans, it will offer, in addition to free beverages and crumpets, art and literature. New work by Baltimore painters and sculptors will be exhibited.... European newspapers and magazines will be provided for the leisure moments before the feature movie begins.
>
> A cycloramic screen will afford an equally good view from side and center seats. In front of the screen, a special auxiliary stage is being built. Here, Mr. Schwaber envisions occasions when small ensembles will offer chamber music or when dramatic readings or choral concerts may be presented. Admission rates will be the standard first-run house prices.[185]

Decorator Vincent Peranio did the art deco mural on the lobby walls. The walls of the auditorium were decorated with diagonal patterns of brown and green. Patrons who attended the opening show were impressed with the new seats. The world premier of *Uncle Vanya* was held at the Playhouse on January 23, 1959. As of January 1962, the longest run film at the Playhouse was the very popular *Never on Sunday*, which ran for 45 weeks.

The theater was remodeled and redecorated in 1967 at a reported cost of $75,000. During this remodeling the proscenium arch was removed and the screen was mounted against the rear wall. The ticket counter was moved inside and the lounge was completely refurbished. New airflow rocking chair seats were installed, and the seating capacity was increased to 450. The interior was re-done in red, black and white.

David Levy, who also leased the Charles and operated the Key Theater in Washington, leased the Playhouse between 1982 and 1984. Levy planned to operate the theater as a first-run art-film house, but had to give it up because of competition from suburban theaters.

The Playhouse closed in May 1985 and remained vacant for some time. Plans by the state to open a field office in the theater for the Division of Parole and Probation were scrapped in the face of strong objections by residents, businesses, and the city government. In 1987, plans to convert the theater into a huge retail liquor outlet also fizzled, thank goodness. Between 1989 and 1994, it was used as a church. In 1996, Michael Johnson's Group 7 Media partnership leased the theater, planning to showcase African-American films. They reopened it as the Heritage Playhouse Theater on January 31, 1997. The lobby was renamed in honor of the late Baltimore actor, Howard E. Rollins, Jr.

The new theater lasted less than a year, and by December 1997 it was closed and for sale. Korean businessman, Brian Bok Ok, purchased the theater to show Korean movies and, in 1999, he reopened it as the Kobko Theater. The Paragon Theater, which presented live shows, reopened in the Playhouse in February 2002 with the play *Lost in Yonkers*. It, too, was closed in 2004.

Hood and Schultz (see Carrollton)

Horn, 2016–2020 West Pratt Street, 1909–1920, 1920–1970, Francis E. Tormey (of 1920 theater), 192 (662 for 1920 theater). Frank and Paul Hornig chose a major West Baltimore shopping area as the site for their first theater. According to a family legend, Frank Hornig's mother-in-law had a dream about where to build the Horn. The contract for the theater was drawn up in May 1909, and ground was broken on June 3. Pearce and Scheck supplied the plans for $125. The theater cost $4,334. The following table gives a breakdown of this sum.

Plans	$125.00
Water Permit	2.00
Tickets	10.89
Chairs	269.97
Projector	139.70
Publicity and Printing	10.60
Four Fans	40.00
Muslin for Screen	2.75

Frank Hornig's original Horn on West Pratt Street proved so popular that he built a bigger one in 1920.

Curtains for Doors	1.50
Silkoline	1.44
Brackets, Portieres, Fixtures	6.05
Piano	252.50
Heating System	401.00
For Regrading Inclines	3.00
For Digging Well	10.00
Miscellaneous Expenses	257.00
Construction of Theater	2800.00

The first Horn Theater opened on September 4, 1909. The features were *Boys Will Be Boys*, *House of Terror*, and *Ben's Kid*. On opening day Frank Hornig started out with $14. He took in $62. After expenses of $4.25 for film rental and $2 to pay the projectionist were deducted, he had made a profit of $55.75. In 1913, the Horn was running two reels of ten-day-old pictures, which were changed daily. Hornig showed films made by several companies; Biograph and Selig films on Mondays and Thursdays, Edison and Vitagraph films on Tuesdays, Essanay and Pathé films on Wednesdays, Kalem and Pathé films on Fridays and Vitagraph and Essanay on Saturdays.

The Horn had a piano player on opening day; by May 1911 a drummer had been added. Occasionally live acts were brought in. Among these acts were the Baltimore City Quartet, the acrobats Somers and Spielman, and singers J. Warfield and P. Levy. Frank and Paul Hornig both managed the theater; Frank was the day manager, and Paul managed in the evenings.

The Horn was enlarged during the summer of 1910. Plans for building a new theater on the site were announced in the spring of 1920, and work began with the razing of an adjacent building in late July 1920. The old Horn closed in late July, and its films were shown down the street at Hornig's other theater, the Royal.

The new Horn was designed by Francis E. Tormey and lasted until 1970. (News American photograph courtesy of Special Collections, University of Maryland Libraries)

The new theater cost about $100,000 and measured 50 by 115 feet. The facade was red brick trimmed in stone, either granite or limestone. The interior was finished in panel effect with indirect lighting. The shallow lobby had attractive stained-glass transoms above the outer doors. The auditorium was vaguely Egyptian with squared pilasters on the sidewalls and a "scaled" proscenium arch. The proscenium was draped in dark blue velvet. A tiny balcony seated about 100. The original exit signs were apple-green stained glass with red lettering. The well-attended formal opening occurred on November 25, 1920. E. V. Cupero conducted the orchestra.

The Horn was extensively remodeled in the summer of 1926 and there were some alterations in 1959. It was called the New Horn between 1958 and 1970. Many of the customers of the Horn worked for the B & O Railroad; they would come for the 2:00 P.M. show and leave at 4:00.[186] After it closed, the Horn was used as a church.

Hornsby (see Teddy Bear Parlor)

Howard (see New Pickwick)

Howard and Johnson, 1430 Federal Street. G. Kingston Howard, one of the founders of the projectionists' union, and his brother-in-law were early exhibitors. They began as early as 1896 and lasted at least until 1908. It is not known if they exhibited films at the Federal Street address, but their offices were probably there. They toured with tent-show vaudeville and movies.

Hub Comedy Company (see Comedy)

Hull, 1444 Hull Street, 1909–1920, William C. Ritz (of 1916 addition), 75. There was a theater at this address since at least 1909. In a 1940 article, projectionist Frank Gibson told how he opened the Hull in an abandoned grocery store.[187] Gibson managed the theater for about a year. His wife was the cashier, and a neighborhood boy got $1 per week as doorman. Jack Whittle was the projectionist. When Gibson left to work at the Idle Hour, Whittle took over. During the summers he showed movies in an open-air theater in the back yard. The building was not strong enough to hold all of the customers, and Whittle had to brace the floor after a capacity crowd caused it to buckle.

Admission was 5 cents, and the 30- or 40-minute programs were changed daily. In late 1916, James Goeller, who must have acquired the theater after Whittle, contracted to erect a $3,000, 21.4 by 87-foot brick addition to the Hull. The Hull closed down around 1920.

Hunt Valley Cinema 12, 11511 McCormick Road,[188] Cockeysville, 1998–present, Arrowstreet Inc. (Somerville, MA), ca. 2,600 (auditoriums 8 — 298, 9 — 229, 10 and 11—193 each). This megaplex was one of three opened in the Baltimore-Washington area by Hoyt's Theaters in November 1998.[189] The others were in Alexandria, Virginia and Bowie, Maryland. They all had stadium seating with comfortable widely spaced, high-back chairs, large screens, and sound systems that were much too powerful for the small auditoriums. In addition to the usual concession stands, the $3 million Hunt Valley theaters had a Quickava Cafe where patrons could buy gourmet coffees and pastries.

The Hunt Valley Cinema 12 opened on November 20, 1998. Free popcorn was given away with the purchase of each ticket. The theater, located behind the Hunt Valley Mall, was added in an attempt to rejuvenate the mall, which some considered somewhat of a white elephant. The theater has a central two-story lobby with two ticket counters and a concession stand. There are two video game rooms. Auditoriums 1–7 are located off a corridor running from the left side of the lobby, and auditoriums 8–12 are located off a similar corridor on the right side. The auditoriums vary in size from 100 to 300 seats. There is a feeling of cut-rate quality about this megaplex. Crossover sound makes it difficult to concentrate on the films and, at least in one of the auditoriums, the screen is too high on the wall for comfortable viewing from the first six or eight rows. Regal Theaters bought the Hunt Valley megaplex in 2003.

Huntington, 221–225 West 25th Street, 1913–1920. The Huntington Theater Company planned a one-story moving picture and vaudeville theater at this location in the summer of 1913. It

The Hunt Valley Cinema 12 (11511 McCormick Road, Cockeysville, 1998–present, Arrowstreet Inc.) is one of many theaters acquired by Regal Cinemas in 2005.

The Ideal (903–905 West 36th Street, 1908–1963), shown here in 1932, was the other half of the 36th Street theater duo in Hampden. It retained Pearce and Scheck's second favorite name for a movie theater.

was to cost about $20,000. A City ordinance dated June 4, 1913 gave permission to construct a one-story building in the rear of 221 and 223 West Twenty-fifth Street, for exhibiting moving pictures and vaudeville, with an entrance from Twenty-fifth Street through an arcade building to be constructed along the west side of 223 West Twenty-fifth Street. Then, in September 1913, an application was filed by the Huntington Building Company to remodel the premises at 221 West 25th Street into a moving-picture theater. It lasted as a theater about six years and then became Huntington Hall, which had bowling alleys. Later it was converted into a rug store.

Hutchins and McDonald (see Pictorial)

Ideal {1}, 227 North Eutaw Street, 1906–1909, Jacob F. Gerwig (of conversion), 108. Pearce and Scheck converted the store at 227 North Eutaw Street into a small nickelodeon in mid–1906, but only lasted a few years. In December 1907, the Ideal celebrated its first anniversary with a week-long special show featuring instrumental music and illustrated songs. Every lady attending during the week received a handsome perfumed chrysanthemum.

Ideal {2}, 903–905 West 36th Street, 1908–1963, unknown, c. 300 (later c. 685, 580). Pearce and Scheck built a small $1,500 movie theater at this location in 1908. In September 1909, they added a large one-story addition. Julius Goodman leased the Ideal sometime before 1916, then purchased it for $18,000 in 1922. In its early days, the Ideal {2} was known as the "madhouse." It was remodeled many times. Information about these remodelings is contradictory. Sources in May 1923 name both Fred Beall and John Freund as the architect of a new theater for

The Ideal and Hampden theaters all lit up in 1938 create a miniature White Way on 36th Street in Hampden.

Julius Goodman.[190] The following spring, another source names Callis and Callis as architects of a new theater the same size as the previous ones planned by Beall and Freund.

The Ideal closed for a month and a half for remodeling in the summer of 1926, then reopened on September 20, 1926. In the fall of 1927, the Ideal was redecorated in blue with gold trimmings and large techstone panels on the walls. In 1930, plans were made to enlarge the theater by removing a partition, presumably between 903 and 905 West 36th Street. The newly rebuilt theater opened on September 1, 1930. Schwaber Theaters bought the Ideal {2} from the Goodman family in the spring of 1960.[191]

The last movie shown there was *PT 109*, starring Cliff Robertson, in September 1963. The building had been remodeled into a Salvation Army store by 1973. As late as 2000, portions of the auditorium decorations were visible.

The Goodman family and the Hicks family, who operated the nearby Hampden Theater, were friendly competitors. They split film product; the Ideal got MGM, Warner Bros. and RKO films while the Hampden got Paramount, Fox and Columbia. The Ideal also got Republic and Monogram pictures.

Ideal Airdome, 910 West 36th Street, 1911–c. 1922, unknown, c. 500. Pearce and Scheck purchased a portion of the lot occupied by the American Ice Company on the north side of 36th Street in Hampden in 1911 and erected an open-air theater on it. A year later they purchased the entire lot and planned to build a new theater, which was never built. Julius Goodman purchased the airdome in 1916 and operated it until at least the summer of 1922. A bank and later a department store were erected on the site.

Writing in 1957, Mrs. Ella Lott Goodman, the wife of Julius Goodman, described the airdome and its operation. It consisted of a lot surrounded by four wooden walls with seating on wooden benches. At the front of the lot was a stage with dressing rooms behind it for the vaudeville performers. Most of these performers were from the neighborhood. On Friday nights there were wrestling matches; admission was raised from 10 to 25 cents on those nights. "Spike Webb, former boxing coach at the Naval Academy was a great favorite in the neighborhood. The audience rioted one evening when he lost a match after a fine winning streak. The Airdome was closed for two days while repairs were made."[192] The arch enemy of the Airdome was rainy weather, which is why many films were run in tandem at a nearby hard-top theater. At the Ideal Open-Air, if a sudden storm came up, the staff and patrons raced across 36th Street to the hardtop Ideal, where the show continued.

Among the early members of the staff at the open-air theater were Miss Florence Mules, cashier; Miss Bell Kerney and Elmer F. Bernhardt, piano players; Adam and Earl Barnes (father and son), ushers; and Philip Smisel, projectionist. Another projectionist, Philip Redmond, remembered that the projection booth that housed the single, hand-cranked projector, looked like an outhouse on stilts. Goodman was planning a 750-seat theater with a removable roof on the site of his airdome, but he was never able to build it.

Idle Hour, 223 North Howard Street, 1913–1933, John Freund, Jr., c. 350. C. C. Waskey altered the three-story building at 223 North Howard Street into a moving-picture theater in July 1913. The alterations, which cost about $4,500, included remodeling the interior and putting a 24 × 25-foot addition on the rear.

The Idle Hour opened on October 15, 1913, and was very popular with downtown shoppers. A souvenir box of Lipps' Society Chocolates was presented to everyone who attended between 10:00 A.M. and 5:00 P.M. on opening day.

In 1915, the Triangle Film Corp. had a studio and general offices in the Idle Hour Building. In April 1920, Jacob Gomprecht, Jesse Benesch, and Reuben Ottenheimer purchased the building for $105,000. The Idle Hour was closed until mid–1921, when it was remodeled and the auditorium was repainted old ivory and brown. The name was changed to New Idle Hour when it reopened under the management of H. A. Blum on August 29, 1921. It had a Tonophone sound-on-disk system by 1928.

The building was sold in early 1934 and plans were made to remodel it as a modern retail establishment. The building is still standing.

Imperial (see Crown)

***Irving**, 4007–4011 Frederick Avenue, Ewald G. Blanke, 1,200. E. J. Wiley and Alfred Buck, both of whom were implicated in the Boulevard Theater scandal, planned a large theater in Irvington. Wiley's company purchased a lot on Frederick Avenue in Irvington in 1921 for the $250,000 movie theater. The new theater was described as "duplicating the Boulevard."

Irvington, 4113 Frederick Avenue, 1925–1971, Oliver B. Wight and E. Lockhart, 575. The Irvington was named for the West Baltimore community where it was located and which it served for nearly 50 years. The Irvington Theater Company acquired a lot on Frederick Avenue in the center of the Irvington shopping district in the fall of 1921 and received a permit to build the theater in December. According to one source, there might have been an earlier open-air theater on the site of the Irvington.

The Irvington was originally described as a one-story brick building measuring 50 by 100 feet, but a later description calls it a two-story limestone structure, 40 by 140 feet. Whichever, it cost a reported $50,000. The exterior of the Irvington did not change very much over the years. The interior had some of the hardest, wood-backed seats in town. The theater was under construction for some time and then sat idle for more than a year. It was acquired by Sigmund Kleiman who completed construction and opened the theater in mid–January 1925.

The first movie advertised at the Irvington was *A Self-Made Failure* on January 16. In February 1925, the Irvington advertised live music provided by an eight-piece orchestra under the direction of Lloyd H. Hemmick at all the evening shows. Jack and Irvin Levine acquired the theater in July 1925 and operated it for more than 40 years. The Irvington had a $7,000 2/10 Moller organ (Opus 3122), and was wired for sound in the spring of 1929.

Some interesting information about the finances of a neighborhood theater is available on the Irvington. In 1937, the theater was grossing an average of $3,771 a month giving it a total yearly gross of $42,256. The best months were January ($4,257), August ($4,182) and October ($4,176); the worst month was December ($3,036).[193]

The Baltimore Film Society obtained the Irvington from Jack Levine in the summer of 1967. Refurbished and remodeled in September 1967, and renamed the Irvington Cinema, it showed movie classics and foreign films, but failed to gain much public support. In 1969, the

Shown here in 1968, nearing the end of its movie life, the Irvington Theater (4113 Frederick Avenue, 1925–1971, Oliver B. Wight and E. Lockhart) presided over the south side of the Frederick Avenue shopping district in Irvington.

theater's proprietors took the next step toward movie-house oblivion and began to show "adult" films. After closing for a while, it reopened in April 1970 with adult film double features.

The Irvington was hit by pickets protesting the X-rated films in May 1971. As a result of these protests, the operators of the theater agreed to try family films for 90 days. But when the theater showed them, no one came. The Irvington closed for good in September 1971 and was converted into a church.

Ivanhoe, 3413–3415 Boston Street, 1913–1914, unknown, c. 100. Charles Kocourek opened this small movie and vaudeville theater in May 1913. There was a film fire at the theater a week after it opened; no one, except Joseph Helm, the projectionist, was injured. At that time the theater had not yet been named. Thomas Kane operated the theater for a short time around 1914. According to the 1914 Sanborn Insurance map, there was a saloon on the first floor of the building and a hall on the second floor. This suggests that the Ivanhoe may have been on the second floor.

Jean (see Goldfield {1})

Jewell, 719 West Baltimore Street, 1914–1963, Harry H. McClellan (Oliver B. Wight of 1920 rebuilding), 400 (of 1920 theater). The Jewell had almost as many names as the Picture Garden. It was opened on April 13, 1914, by Miss Theresa D. Marks. It was a two-story brick building, measured 23.6 by 127 feet, and cost between $4,500 and $10,000. The contract to build the theater was awarded to Harry H. McClellan, who also designed it, in December 1913. Miss Marks' father manufactured Tiffany lamps in a shop behind the theater.

The Jewell was offered for sale at a public auction on October 30, 1917, and reopened on February 9, 1918. It closed again and was sold in 1920 when plans were announced to convert it to other uses. It is unclear whether the old Jewell was rebuilt or whether it was razed and a new theater erected on the site.

Jack and Irvin Levine opened the new theater, called the Realart, on July 26, 1920. Miss Elizabeth Dell or Bell won a $25 prize for suggesting the new name. The theater was redecorated and had the latest sound system installed in early 1930. It was usually called the Realart between 1920 and 1957, although it was called the Dainty in 1934. In 1949, as the Realart, it was advertising in the *Afro-American*, suggesting that it might have been an African-American theater at that time. Between 1958 and 1963 it went through three rapid changes of name and film fare: Perry Center, 1958–1960; New Center Follies, 1961; New Paris Follies, 1961–1963. As the Perry Center, it showed classic films such as Sergei Eisenstein's *Alexander Nevsky* and *The Battleship Potemkin*. By mid–1972, the building was used as a church. It was razed in the fall of 1972.

Johnson and Foreman (see New Albert)

Jones and Heimiller (see Crown)

Jumpers Mall, 8186 Jumper's Mall, Ritchie Highway, Pasadena, 1974–present, Developers General Corp., 1,200 (400 for each auditorium). JF Theaters opened this unimpressive triplex on December 20, 1974. Robert Rappaport purchased it in late 1978 and added two additional 400-seat auditoriums in late 1979. In 1984 another two auditoriums were added, making a total of seven. The smallest theaters seated 180 persons. It was still operating, as a discount theater, as of 1998, but appeared rundown and badly in need of a good cleaning. Loew's closed the Jumpers Mall theaters on January 21, 1999. Baltimore-based Premier Cinemas took over the lease of the theater and renovated it, then reopened it as a discount theater in September 1999.

Kane (see Plaza {1})

Karp (see Berman's)

Keith's (see Garden {3})

Keystone, 1105 North Gay Street, 1910–1912, J. E. Laferty, unknown. David Newman operated this movie and vaudeville theater near the intersection of Gay Street and Broadway for several years.

Kidd's Amusement Theater, 1705 Westwood Avenue, c. 1915. Frank L. Kidd, who also ran the Traveler Theater on North Avenue, probably operated this small and very short-lived movie house. It was probably an airdome.

Kobko Theater (see Homewood)

Lafayette, 1433–1435 West Lafayette Avenue, 1911–1952, Niederhauser & McCluskey (Morris Zimlin, of 1936 alterations), 550 (468 in 1947), The Lafayette was built on the site of John N. Pickering's coal yard for Eugene McCurdy's Eureka Amusement Company at a cost of between $15,000 and $20,000. It opened in early March 1911. The building was two stories high, of brick and stone, with a wide, fancy metal facade and a narrow arched entrance of marble, granite and ornamental metal. It measured 40 by 125 feet.[194] The theater's name was spelled out in large letters across the front, above the box office. The auditorium was on the first floor; a pool parlor and hall were on the second.

Going to see a show at the Lafayette was a real treat for my mother's family during the years between 1910 and 1920. The Crescent and Red Mill up the street were all right, but the really good movies came to the classier Lafayette. On the way there, one could stop at a nearby Italian grocery and buy peanuts or pickles and pretzels, look in at Number 10 Engine House, then race down to the theater.

The theater was slightly damaged by a fire in March 1914; quick thinking by two Northwestern district patrolmen and theater employees prevented a panic. Later, the theater was enlarged, by extending the rear of the building back 20 feet, and renovated in the summer of 1919. The Lafayette closed in the mid–1920s and reopened on March 21, 1925, as an African-American theater. Peter Oletsky acquired it in the fall of 1925. J. C. Cremen, who also operated the Carey, was running the Lafayette by 1930. In 1930 he made several improvements to the theater, including providing "adequate rest room accommodations for lady patrons." He remodeled the marquee and ticket booth in 1936. The Lafayette was sold in January 1954 and demolished later to build a new school.

Laffmovie (see Thirty-One)

Lane, 60 Dundalk Avenue, 1940–1959, John Eyring, 400–495 (later 300 as Abbey Lane). Louis Gaertner's Ritz Enterprises built the Lane. They purchased a half-acre lot for the new theater on Dundalk Avenue near St. Helena Avenue in January 1940, and the Lane opened on November 22, 1940.

The facade consisted of buff face brick with an orange brick trim. The ventilation system of the new theater was touted in a newspaper article of November 22, 1940.[195] "In planning the new theatre, the directors kept in mind ... the patron's health, the assurance of an influx of fresh air at all times. The air in the new theatre is completely changed every minute to assure a

The Lafayette (1433–1435 West Lafayette Avenue, 1911–1952, Niederhauser & McCluskey) was the classiest of the three movie theaters on West Lafayette Avenue in the Harlem Park neighborhood.

supply of clean air ... a uniform temperature, regulated by thermostatic control, prevails in all parts of the theatre...." It closed as the Lane on May 6, 1951.

In 1954, the theater was completely renovated and reseated with luxury seats; it reopened as an art theater on June 4, 1954. The name was changed to Abbey Lane, and the opening feature was *The Moon Is Blue*. Described by one writer as "the cozy Art Theatre with coffee on the house,"[196] it was converted into a Goodwill Store in 1962 and, as of 2003, is still standing.

Latrobe, 1501 Fort Avenue, 1910–1914, Jacob F. Gerwig. The Latrobe was built for an estimated $4,000 by the George Brothers in the spring of 1909. By 1970, it was a funeral parlor. It is still standing.

Leader, 248 South Broadway, 1909–1959, John Freund, Jr., 363–382 (later 500). The Leader was one of the longest operating movie houses in town. Joseph Berman built it for about $5,000 in late 1908 and early 1909, then sold the theater to George E. McLaughlin in early 1909 for $22,000. Pearce and Scheck purchased it from McLaughlin in February 1909, and opened the Leader on February 8, 1909, with continuous vaudeville and motion pictures, and operated it for many years. It was a handsome theater with a large lobby and an auditorium decorated with oil paintings. In 1913, the Leader was running shows consisting of two reels of 30-day-old pictures and one act of vaudeville. The Link Brothers orchestra played there around 1915.

Pearce and Scheck planned to rebuild the Leader and increase the seating capacity to 1,200 seats, but this was never done. The Leader was closed and extensively remodeled in 1921, when improvements included a new marquee, floors, and ventilating system. The theater reopened on October 17, 1921.

Arthur Price's Alhambra Theatre Corporation leased the Leader in 1928 and remodeled it again. Joe Fields was the manager for many years. He often used behind-the-screen talkers at the Leader and, one time, he had a "human fly" climb the outside of the theater and walk across Broadway on a tightrope. Maurice Cohen took over the Leader in 1932. When the Carrier Company came around asking the Broadway theaters if they wanted air conditioning, only Cohen took the chance, and the Leader became the only air-conditioned theater in the neighborhood.[197]

Rome Theaters purchased the Leader in the 1940s, and it closed in May 1959. The building is still standing, but it has been extensively remodeled.

Lee and Causby (see Pastime {1})

Lehmann Hall, 844–856 North Howard Street, 1870–1956; Wyatt & Nolting (of 1910 remodeling), Walter M. Gieske (of 1913 remodeling); c. 1,000 (after 1913 remodeling), c. 900 (as Roslyn).

Lehmann Hall was built by Edward G. Lehmann, a local dancing teacher, in 1870. It was used for many functions over its 86 years. For many years, the Bachelor's Cotillions were held there.

Prof. James Bangert bought the hall in 1890, and in 1910 had architects Wyatt & Nolting prepare plans for a $15,000 remodeling. The plans called for four ornamental alcoves of brick, stone, and marble, replacing existing flooring with hardwood, and installing ornate metal ceilings. The hall was purchased by the Germania Maennerchor Society in 1912. At that time the building was extensively remodeled in a kind of 18th century Dutch style. The adjoining buildings at 848 and 850 North Howard Street were razed, and the new structure built there became headquarters for the Society. The lower walls were made of buff-colored rough brick, topped by stuccoed walls of a cream tint and a red-tiled roof.

The following description gives details of the planned remodeling.

> A great deal of the basement has never been excavated. There is room in the basement ... for four bowling alleys ... occupying ... the basements of the adjoining buildings, and running almost the entire depth. There will also be a dressing room ... and a big storeroom.
> The hall and stage of the present hall will practically be left intact, as its dimensions, 53 feet wide by 85 feet long, provide ample space, while the stage is commodious. There will also be a large dining room, a reception room and a woman's retiring room on the first floor.
> On the second floor, the room which will correspond to the dancing hall behind the gallery, which overlooks the main hall, will be used as a public barroom. On the same floor, but over the site where the new building will be erected, in place of the stores will be two card rooms, a music library, a room for the secretary of the association and in the far rear a kitchen. Much of the space of this floor is occupied by the upper part of the hall room. The third and top floor will be occupied by two large bedrooms, a reception hall, a large kitchen and a bathroom.[198]

The auditorium was enlarged to seat 1,000 people by extending it back 14 feet. The beautiful wood floor was still vivid in the memories of people living in 2002. The remodeled hall opened on November 17, 1913, with a concert under the direction of Prof. Theodore Hemberger, the musical director of the Germania Maennerchor. This auditorium was used for movies several times. It was also used for such diverse activities as a giant sale of women's and

The facade of Lehmann Hall (844–856 North Howard Street, 1870–1956, Walter M. Gieske of 1913 remodeling) rises behind the 1942 marquee of the Roslyn Theater in this 1954 photograph.

children's clothing in June 1920 and a meeting of the local Communist Party. The Baltimore Civic Opera also put on operas at the hall.

In October 1941, the Four-Star Corporation purchased the building for around $60,000 and converted the auditorium into a full-time movie theater. The Roslyn opened at 846 North Howard Street on January 16, 1942, with the first local showing at popular prices of *Sergeant York*, starring Gary Cooper. The Roslyn was advertised as "Baltimore's swankiest first-run theater."

The following description of the new theater is from the Baltimore *News-Post*:

> The Roslyn, Baltimore's newest downtown first-run theatre, will open the evening of January 16 ... at 850 North Howard Street, location of the former Lehmann's Hall. Everything from the marquee, ... one of the largest in the city, to the silver screen represents the last word in modern motion picture and theatre equipment. Wired for television, the RCA sound apparatus is equipped with both high and low frequency loud speakers, so that it will reproduce ... the entire frequency range of sound. It is also equipped with true cellular design that assures uniform distribution of every sound to every seat in the theatre.... The heating and cooling system will guarantee comfortable air-conditioning at all times. The floor has been designed according to the new "bowl-shape" principle to provide perfect vision from any seat in the house. Indirect wall lighting, deep carpets and the most up-to-the-minute decorative scheme will be other features. The seats feature the new "full floating cushions" for utmost comfort.[199]

One of the most impressive features about the Roslyn was the massive neon-lit marquee.

Dr. Leon Zeller operated the Roslyn for many years. A 1955 article suggested that union members on swing shifts could find entertain-

The ornate box office and facade of the Lexington Theater (314 West Lexington Street, 1909–c. 1918, Harry H. Brown); note the candy machines flanking the entrance.

ment there and described the Roslyn as a "first run double feature theatre" that was open until 4:00 A.M. and showed "the type of pictures that the He-Man likes, plenty of action."[200] The Roslyn closed in May 1956, and the building was demolished to widen Howard Street and erect additions to Maryland General Hospital.

Lehmann's Hall is probably best known for the first Monday germans where Baltimore's debutantes came out. These germans were usually held on the first Monday in December.

Lemon (see Amusea {3})

Lenox (see Rainbow {2})

Le-Roi (see Recreation Theater)

Lexington, 314 West Lexington Street, 1909–c. 1918, Harry H. Brown, c. 500. The Lexington was one of the earliest movie houses on Lexington Street. Thomas A. Keene and William S. Smith opened it in a converted store next to the Pickwick Theater in March 1909. In an early ad, on March 28, 1909, the Lexington claimed, "Our pictures have never been shown before in this city. Change Monday, Wednesday, Friday. Return engagement of Miss Lillian Yorley of New York, in all new songs. Hear this great artist sing. Get Wise. Visit the Lexington...."

The Lexington used behind-the-screen talkers. According to a 1910 ad, "the Lexington is devoted to the most select and artistic class of moving pictures, and maintains a large stock company to make real and humanize the action of the screens ... the seating capacity ... is large; the ventilation excellent; and every convenience is provided for the comfort of its patrons." In its early days, the Lexington had a front that resembled a florist shop. Potted palms grew in rank abundance in a niche above the ornate ticket booth, and floral swirls set with naked light bulbs outlined the sides and top of the outer lobby.

William Fait purchased the Lexington from Keene and Smith in the summer of 1913. In late 1913, Fait had architect John Freund, Jr., prepare plans for combining the Lexington and Pickwick into a single theater, but these plans never got beyond the drawing board stage.

Lexway (see Picture Garden)

Liberty {1}, 5 North Liberty Street, 1909–1916, unknown, 189. The Liberty Amusement Company leased a four-story warehouse on North Liberty Street in October 1908 and converted the first floor into a moving picture theater. In December 1910, the owners were granted permission to erect a sign at least 10 feet above the pavement with the words "The Liberty Moving Pictures, 5¢" spelled out in incandescent lights. Shows at the Liberty {1} in 1913 consisted entirely of movies, one 10-day-old reel, one 30-day-old reel, and two reels of commercials.

John English purchased it in June 1916 and redecorated it. At the time it was reported that the theater "was in very bad straits and ... located in an out-of-the-way location."[201] English could not turn business around, and a receiver was appointed by the Circuit Court in December 1916.

Liberty {2}, Fort George G. Meade, Odenton, 1918–?, Edward L. Tilton (New York), 2,661. There was a large theater called the Liberty operating at Fort Meade around the time of the First World War. It was one of a number of theaters built at military camps around the country by the Commission on Training Camp Activities. Designated as a Type A Theater, it cost an estimated $50,000.

The Liberty opened on February 13, 1918, with Gus Edwards' Song Review, which was also playing at the Maryland Theater in Baltimore. The huge theater was filled to capacity and before the show, the audience was led in singing by Kenneth Clark, the musical director of the camp, who originated "mob singing." Before the show started, Mr. McTuerny of the Knights of Columbus addressed the audience; "See here, fellows, this is a real theatre and a real show. We don't want any stamping of feet, yelling, whistling or personal remarks. If you want to applaud, clap, but cut out the rough stuff."[202]

An official opening was held five days later. Camp commander Major General Joseph E. Kuhn and the wife of the Secretary of War appeared onstage. There were three brigadier generals, a dozen colonels, and thousands of American doughboys, as well as French and British soldiers in the audience. The show was Victor Herbert's musical comedy, *Princess Pat*. Lou Fisher, of the 313th Regiment, directed the theater orchestra.

A theater critic attended a show at the Liberty in May 1918 and described the Liberty: "The theater is a large wooden structure and is equipped with everything that a first-class theater should have. The seats are all on one floor, which slopes up gradually from the orchestra pit, and the seating capacity, I understand, is 2700.... There are no soft sides to the seats, but when one has been in the army for six months or so, one does not need soft things to sit on."[203] Acoustics in the Liberty Theaters were said to be very good. There was little decoration, and the ventilation system was primitive. According to a contemporary writer, "The whole building is a purely utilitarian machine, efficient though hardly beautiful."[204]

Liberty {3}, 310 South Broadway, c. 1919–1921, unknown, 300. Benjamin Cluster operated this little movie house for a few years. He sold it to Nathan Goldberg for about $10,000 in the fall of 1921.

Liberty 1–2, 8632 Liberty Road, Randallstown, 1964–1987, 1989–1998, Mitchel Abramowitz (Liberty 2); 722 (Liberty 1), 378 (Liberty 2), c. 1,000 (1989 rebuilding). Durkee Enterprises opened the Liberty 1 in the Liberty Court Shopping Center on October 29, 1964. Built in spaces that had originally been a store, it had a 40 × 19-foot screen and a full-fidelity stereophonic sound system. The aisles and lobby were covered with miracle fibre rugs, and the floors in the auditorium were made of non-slip concrete. The Liberty 1 cost an estimated $350,000.

Within four years, plans for a second theater were being made. Although construction was scheduled to start on the adjoining Liberty 2 in December 1968, it did not open until August 25, 1971. The Liberty 1 and 2 shared a common lobby and box office.

In 1978, the Liberty 1 was completely remodeled. The theater was gutted leaving only the walls and roof after Durkee gave up the lease. In 1989, Tom Harmon, of Value Cinema Inc., rebuilt the theater and reopened it on August 3, 1989, as a $1 theater with four auditoriums. The three-story facade of the new theater was topped by the words "Liberty Cinemas" spelled out in bright red letters on a blue background. Below the name were four attraction boards, one for each theater. A thin marquee sheltered the ticket booth on the right. Three sets of central doors led into the theater. The Liberty closed in 1998.

Liberty Heights Park, Reisterstown Road and Park Heights Avenue, 1918–1955. John J. Carlin's huge amusement park had several movie theaters during its nearly 40-year existence.[205] The park opened on August 13, 1919, as Liberty Heights Park. It became Carlin's Park a few years later. The main attractions were the Carrousel, the Old Mill, Chute the Chutes, the Octopus, the Caterpillar, and a popular Mountain Speedway, which had an 800-foot tunnel of love built in the shape of a question mark.

When the park opened there were plans for a large coliseum for band concerts, a huge concrete swimming pool, sunken gardens, pagodas and Japanese tearooms, a casino, and a "pretentious moving-picture theatre." The theater was never built.[206] A fight arena opened in the park in the summer of 1924. In 1923 Rudolph Valentino danced the tango at Carlin's and was mobbed by hordes of admirers.

Over the years, fires claimed several buildings at Carlin's. In 1939 a sports arena with a seating capacity of 6,000 was opened at the park; it replaced the earlier one that had been destroyed by fire. An open-air theater was destroyed by fire in April 1944. At the time it was used for outdoor entertainments, plays and motion pictures and was described as a stage building with rows of wooden seats under the trees. In the spring of 1953, local exhibitor, Robert Marhenke, opened a nickelodeon at the park. The park closed two years later. Carlin's Drive-In was built where the roller coaster had been, but that too has disappeared.

Lincoln (see Palace {2})

Lincoln, 934–936 Pennsylvania Avenue, 1916–1971, unknown, c. 280 (later 400, 870). Kalman Flaks opened this theater as the New Lincoln Theater, "the only real colored vaudeville house in the city," on August 28, 1916. The opening vaudeville act was a play called *In Chinatown* by Brown Demont & Company; other acts were Professor Oliver, a musical ventriloquist, and Miss Clodius, a buck and wing dancer. Films were also shown at the Lincoln.

The theater was remodeled several times.

In 1938, two additional lots were acquired and the theater was enlarged to seat about 870. The Lincoln was one of the few integrated theaters in Baltimore when it opened; it was divided down the middle by an aisle. Whites sat on one side and African-Americans sat on the other.[207] It may have been the only African-American movie house to employ behind-the-screen talkers.

In 1917, the Lincoln was presenting vaudeville, which changed every Thursday, and movies that changed daily. Music was provided by Professor Charles Harris' orchestra, and a show cost 10 cents. The original Lincoln Theater had an open lobby with a central ticket booth. In its later years the facade of the Lincoln was remodeled in an art deco style which featured an unusual neon sign in the shape of President Lincoln's head. In the summer of 1927, the Lincoln was offering vaudeville twice a week, on Mondays and Saturdays, with movies only on the other days. The theater, razed in late 1971, was built on or very close to the site of William H. Daly's open-air theater. Among the well-known entertainers who played the Lincoln were Cab Calloway, Ethel Waters, Bessie Smith, and Stepin Fetchit. In its later years the Lincoln was known for being a rough house, where fights frequently broke out.

Lincoln Highway, 2536 Washington Boulevard, 1919–1935, unknown, c. 200. The Lincoln Highway overlooked the train tracks in the Morrell Park section of southwest Baltimore. A long frame building, in the beginning it was open only two or three days a week. By May 1927 the name had been changed to Morrell. John H. Bien operated it at one time, and after it closed as a movie house, it was converted into a club.

Lincoln Number Two (see American)

Linden, 910 West North Avenue, 1938–1965, John J. Zink, 884 (later 460 as the Cinema; 625 as the Sutton). The Linden opened as a neighborhood movie house on September 17, 1938. Located on the site of the McCormick Memorial Baptist Church, the Linden was the first theater in the Schwaber Circuit and cost an estimated $150,000. The facade was in buff brick.

The auditorium decoration consisted of contrasting panels with horizontal strips interrupted by broad vertical forms. The auditorium walls were finished in Celotex and the ceiling, in Kalite acoustic plaster. Cove lights on either side of a broad recessed ceiling panel, extending from

Charles Nolte's Linwood Theater (902–904 South Linwood Avenue, 1915–1952) in 1940.

the proscenium to the rear, illuminated the auditorium. With specially designed Heywood-Wakefield seats, set 34 inches apart, there was not a single step in the entire building. It also had the latest air-conditioning equipment — which cost about $9,000 — and an RCA sound system. The Linden was one of only four Baltimore theaters equipped with Acousticon hearing aids. The prices were 15 cents at matinees, 25 cents in the evenings, and 10 cents for children at all times. In February 1939 every lady attending the Linden on Wednesday and Thursday evenings received a piece of "fine 20 kt. gold dinnerware."

Following the successful conversion of the Homewood into the Playhouse, Schwaber closed the Linden in July 1953 and reopened it on July 29, 1954, after a $70,000 remodeling, as a second art film house renamed the Cinema. The predominant colors of the Cinema were brown, beige, and green. The carpeting was cocoa, and the stage and proscenium draperies were green. The old seats were replaced with 460 thickly upholstered rocking chair seats, with a back-to-back distance of 45 inches, that cost a total of $25,000. At the time the Cinema opened, there were reportedly only about a dozen theaters in the country completely seated with this type of seating. Coffee and tea were served in the lounge, and patrons could view the works of Baltimore's leading artists there while waiting for the movie to start.

The Cinema lasted until the spring of 1963 when the name was changed to Capri, which opened on May 15, 1963. The films shown were X-rated. Four months later, there was another name change, this time to the Sutton. The Sutton opened on Tuesday, September 17, 1963, as a first-run theater with the film, *Marilyn*. The Sutton lasted only two years, after which the building stood, almost isolated, in a sea of uninspired urban renewal that was described as "a complex of high-rise apartments, garden apartments, a shopping center, town houses, and office buildings." It was used as a bank in the early 1970s; by the 1990s, it was deserted and boarded up.

Linwood, 902–904 South Linwood Avenue, 1915–1952, unknown, 456. Charles E. Nolte and Walter Windsor opened the Linwood. A permit to use the lot on the west side of Linwood Avenue between Hudson and Dillon Streets for the exhibition of open-air moving pictures was granted to Windsor in May 1915. He operated the open-air theater on the lot in the summer of 1915 before building a hard-top theater.[208] The hard-top theater was built for about $2,500 in 1916. The permit granted to the Linwood Amusement Company called for a one-story building approximately 45 by 70 feet. It had a very small balcony.

While the original Linwood was being built, movies were shown on the lot under a tent. At the time, Nolte was also the projectionist. There were plans in August 1919 to enlarge the Linwood to seat 1,200 people, but these were not carried out. It was, however, enlarged in the fall of 1921. Elmer and Gus Nolte used to carry their father's supper to him at the theater. The day's receipts were taken home each night in a small bag, and once or twice a week the bank would send somebody to the house to pick them up.

The Linwood lasted until the early 1950s; the final show occurred on May 3, 1952. The building has been completely remodeled with little remaining of the theater except for the small section of tile spelling out the name "Linwood" at the old entrance.

Little, 523 North Howard Street, 1927–1989, Stanislaus Russell (John J. Zink, of alterations in 1933 and 1935), 238. This tiny theater was built for the Motion Picture Guild of Washington, which also operated the Little Theater in Washington.[209] It was built near the site of the old Diamond Bowling Alleys, where duckpin bowling was introduced around the turn of the century.[210] In 1955, on the fifty-fifth anniversary of the introduction, a commemorative plaque was displayed in the lobby of the Little.

The Guild leased the lot for the theater from Hochschild, Kohn, and Company and had it cleared by early August 1927. The theater cost about $25,000 and measured 30 by 110 feet. It opened with an informal preview on December 8, 1927. The first public performance was the following day, featuring the film *Tartuffe*, starring Emil Jannings. According to the *Evening Sun*, "Those who attended the inaugural ceremonies found broad and comfortable chairs, tasteful decorations, a cozy lounge and a friendly, intimate atmosphere."[211] There was a string orchestra on hand to play for the opening from a tiny rear balcony. The prevailing colors inside were brown and black.

The seats were arranged so that late arrivals could pass between the rows without disturbing patrons already seated. During the fifteen-minute intermissions between shows, cigarettes and coffee were served in the tiny lounge. Norman Clark liked the "sufficient room between the rows of seats to satisfy him who likes to wiggle his knees."[212] Clark also wrote that one of his highbrow friends remarked, "Thank God. I have at last found a picture theatre without a touch of Spanish," an apparent reference to the Valencia, which opened a year earlier. The theater's policy was to show only unusual and artistic films of intellectual appeal for intelligent persons. The Motion Picture Guild said that it was not concerned with education or uplift, but rather "solely in the beauty, artistry, color, and distinctiveness of the screen and in presenting pictures that exemplify those qualities to those who are interested."

In March 1928, an organization called The Cinema Club was incorporated by Louis Machat, James Bachelor, and Charles Shuman, "to act as censors of the photoplays proposed to be exhibited by the Motion Picture Guild." The Little was not an outstanding success, and it was placed in the hands of receivers in August 1929. Max Goldberg, of New York, the president of Moviographs, Inc.[213] leased the Little for an annual rent of $6,000 for three years in the fall of 1929. He redecorated it and reopened it on October 30, 1929. Goldberg sent Herman G. Weinberg from New York to manage the Little. Weinberg planned to stay just six weeks but remained for six years. He put an ad in the *Sun* that read: "Wanted: Four attractive girls as ushers. Apply Little Theatre...." One of the girls who applied so impressed Weinberg that he later married her. The ushers wore uniforms of deep blue velveteen blouses with scarlet velveteen pants.

In good weeks the Little grossed as much as $1,200 to $1,500 a week; in bad weeks, only $400. The Little was well attended by local movie critics and movie columnists, including H. L. Mencken. In 1931 a smoky fire broke out in the basement of the theater forcing patrons out of the theater and blocking North Howard Street. The coolness of manager Weinberg and his staff of girl ushers prevented a panic. Later in the year, the theater was redecorated again, and the name was changed to Europa; it reopened on September 7, 1931, again with Emil Jannings, this time in *Der Grosse Tenor*. A typical show at the Europa, beginning on January 19, 1933, consisted of Fox Movietone News, a Walt Disney Silly Symphony, a travelogue, a Laurel & Hardy comedy *Any Old Port*, previews of the next attraction *Men and Jobs*, a Soviet film comedy, and the main feature, *Cruiser Emden*.

Architect John J. Zink prepared plans for alterations to the theater in 1933 and for improvements to the interior in 1935. Among the planned improvements in 1935 was a balcony which was never installed. A. M. Tolkins and Louise Noonan Miller, who operated the Little Theater in Washington, were planning to take over the management of Baltimore's Little Theater in June 1940, but this probably did not occur. William Hicks bought the Little a year later just a few months after he had acquired the Mayfair across the street. Hicks played older American movies as well as recent English and Russian films. Occasionally, he had first-run American films.

In July 1946, the Rappaport organization acquired the Little from the Hicks Circuit and remodeled it. It reopened on July 19 with *Henry V*. Under Rappaport, the Little became the Baltimore home for British films. The name of the theater was supposed to change to the Franklin in May 1954, but the change never took place. The Trans-Lux organization leased the Little for 10 years in 1962. For many years, under Rappaport and Trans-Lux management, the Little was one of the few theaters in town where Baltimoreans could see foreign films. After Trans-Lux gave up the lease, the management of the Little reverted to JF Theaters.

In February 1971 the name was changed to the Little Cinema, and to Mayfair II in September 1973. By 1984 it was called the Little X Theater and occasionally featured live acts. An actress was arrested there in July 1984 for putting on an obscene sexual performance. It closed in January 1989. The last films were grainy triple-X-rated rubbish shown on projection TV.

This was a sad ending for a theater with a distinguished record of wonderful movies. The Little was demolished along with the rest of the block to build a large parking lot.

Little Moving Picture Palace, 302–306 West Fayette Street, 1908–1915, Charles E. Cassell (of Fayette Street building), c. 300. The six-story Bernheimer Brothers department store on Lexington Street opened with great ceremony on November 29, 1907. The following March a new store, this one facing Fayette Street, opened with another great ceremony. A theater for vaudeville and movies was located on the fourth floor of the Fayette Street building. According to an advertisement, this was a "full-fledged" theater "with actors, actresses, stage hands, and stage carpenters. The 300 seats were arranged in three sections. Admission was 5 cents or free with a receipt for merchandise purchased at the store. The first show, on March 9, 1908, featured Mac, the Crayon Man; a magician, the Great Lester; and "The Famous Ford," an escape artist. According to *Billboard* magazine, the vaudeville shows at Bernheimer's were highly successful. The opening show, which took in $300 at the box office, was described as "a good one ... evoking roars of laughter from the audience." The Bernheimer store was later incorporated into the May Company building.[214]

Little Pickwick (see Pickwick {1})

Little Washington Theater (see Paradise {2})

Lombard, 3903 East Lombard Street, c. 1909–1913, unknown, c. 35. This tiny movie house was in business only a short time, between 1909 and 1913. It was apparently located on one floor of a two-story dwelling.

Lord Baltimore, 1110–1116 West Baltimore Street, 1913–1970, J. C. Spedden,[215] c. 1,000 (later 850). Pearce and Scheck purchased the old Maryland Medical College Building[216] and lot on West Baltimore Street in the summer of 1912 and opened the Lord Baltimore for movies and vaudeville there on November 24, 1913. It cost between $35,000 and $60,000, and measured 119 by 150 feet. It originally had an ornamental brick facade, but the idea was to make it imposing rather than merely garish.

The Lord Baltimore had a large stage — 45 feet wide at the footlights — with at least four dressing rooms under the stage. The auditorium floor was steeply sloped. The original plans called for a balcony, but one was never built. The opening show featured Walter Milton — "The Hospital Surgeon," and The State Fair Girls. A four-piece orchestra provided the music. Opening week prices were 5 cents for general admission, 10 cents for reserved seats, and 25 cents for box seats.

When it opened, the Lord Baltimore was the largest theater in Baltimore outside the theater district.[217] Pearce and Scheck moved vaudeville into the Lord Baltimore from the Victoria, which was charging them too much rent, and kept it there for several months until the Hippodrome opened. In later years, amateur shows were given at the Lord Baltimore. Friday night stage shows at the Lord Baltimore featured "Professor" Cockey, who operated a North Avenue dance studio in the 1920s.

The projection booth was located on the roof of the lobby and had to be entered by going outside the theater and climbing up a narrow

The elaborate modern marquee of the Lord Baltimore (1110–1116 West Baltimore Street, 1913–1970, J. C. Spedden) in 1941.

stairway on the side of the building. According to one source, the builders of the Lord Baltimore forgot the projection booth and had to add it later.[218]

Pearce and Scheck had architect Stanislaus Russell prepare plans for improvements to the theater in June 1921. These improvements included storefronts on either side of the lobby. The offices of Philip J. Scheck Enterprises, the successor to Pearce and Scheck, were located in the Lord Baltimore building after about 1936. While the theater was being remodeled in 1941, the marquee fell and three persons narrowly escaped injury. JF Theaters purchased the theater in 1969 for about $50,000. It closed in mid–1970 and by 1973 had been converted into a church.

Lord Calvert {1} (see Northern)

Lord Calvert {2}, 2444 Washington Boulevard, 1936–c. 1953, Oliver B. Wight, 650. The permit for this $35,000 theater was granted in November 1935, and construction work began in May 1936. The original plans were designed by architect Fred Beall, but for some reason, possibly because they were too expensive, were canceled in March 1936, and new plans were prepared by Wight. The Lord Calvert opened under the management of Philip J. Scheck Enterprises on August 28, 1936. The Amusement Company, Inc. purchased the Lord Calvert in September 1940, and C. W. Hicks took it over from them in January 1942. After the theater closed, it was remodeled into a church with a formstone front.

Lubin's {1} (see Colonnade)

Lubin's {2}, 408–410 East Baltimore Street, 1908–1911, poss. Franz C. Koenig,[219] unknown. Sigmund Lubin signed a 10-year lease in February 1908 on the amusement arcade at this location. The yearly rental was $7,000 for the first five years of the lease, and $8,000 for the second five years. He converted it into a theater, which opened on August 24, 1908, with a "rattling vaudeville performance and interesting motion pictures and illustrated songs." It advertised Lubin's Cineograph with 45 minutes of the latest motion pictures. The *Sun* contained a full description of the new theater.

> When the woodwork [= scaffolding] in front of the new theatre is torn away a strik-

ingly pretty facade will be revealed. Over the box office stands an unusually graceful female figure, and other figures are worked out in plaster on the right and left walls. The panels are decorated with figures in bas-relief. The interior is in white and gold. Gold bands a foot wide running up from the columns and pilasters extend entirely across the ceiling at regular intervals. Each of these bands is studded with incandescent globes, more than 1,000 being used in all. The pitch of the orchestra floor is considerable — enough to give everybody in the audience an unobstructed view of the stage. The stage ... slopes ... and at back are arranged half a dozen white and gold female figures — a sort of permanent chorus.... At the front of the house, above the entrance, is a large concrete box for the moving picture machines. The house is fireproof throughout, with spacious aisles and wide exits. One of these exits leads into Lubin's present theatre, which adjoins the new place on the west.[220]

The theater measured 36 by 110 feet. Lubin told reporters that the new theater was "perhaps the very prettiest on his circuit and that he was pleased with every detail."[221] Sigmund Lubin and his wife attended the opening, which featured Benny Reinbold who did a comic monologue and Flosie Levan who wore a "sheathy sheath skirt" as "The Lively Lady." In February 1911, the Moving Picture Company of America leased the theater to Victor G. Pappas and C. Constantine for seven years at a yearly rental of $5,500. Despite reports that they were going to renovate for first-class moving pictures, they hired architect Theodore Wells Pietsch to prepare plans to remodel it into a restaurant and hotel.

Lumiere's Wonderland, 36 West Baltimore Street, 1897. This was a very short-lived exhibition of Astley D. M. Cooper's 11 by 13-foot painting entitled "The Morning of the Crucifixion" and movies projected by the Lumiere cinematographe. The theater opened on October 4, 1897. The painting was on one floor and the lecture room where movies were shown was on another floor. According to the advertisements, seats were free, but admission was 10 cents.

Luna Park Theater, Northwest corner of West Baltimore Street and Garrison Lane, 1910–c. 1914, Clarence E. Anderson, Jacob F. Gerwig (of new 1910 auditorium). Luna Park opened on May 30, 1910, on a five-and-a-half-acre tract, part of the old Shipley estate, at the western end of Baltimore Street next to West End Park.[222] It was built by the Luna Park Amusement Company. The opening featured the requisite Italian band, in this case, Signor E. Dell'Archiprete's Royal Roman Band, and an appearance by Mayor Mahool.

The new park was described in the Sunday *Sun*:

At the corner of Garrison Lane and Baltimore Street has been erected the Auditorium Building, which includes a cafe, over which are the administration quarters, retiring rooms, pantry, kitchen, storage room, dining hall, cloak room, and dance hall. At the end of this is a stage stretching the entire width of the building. The furnishings include a heating plant ... to keep this portion of the park in operation during the winter.

The building is skirted on the park side by a 10-foot piazza. There are gravel walks running the entire length, and to the centre of the park, along which have been erected amusement devices. This section is known as the Midway. A large carousel occupies a central position.... Toward the southwest has been erected a band shell.... The Fourth Regiment Military Orchestra will furnish dance music.

Approximately 5,000 incandescent lights will be used to illuminate the various buildings, and in the park proper have been erected 50 tall poles surmounted by Tungsten incandescent lamps. Visitors enter under an electric arch.[223]

The Luna Park Company planned to erect a $2,000, one-story, 30 × 90-foot moving-picture parlor in the park. A spectacular fire in July 1910 closed the park down for a short time. The main building—which contained the bar, hotel, dancing pavilion, dining room, offices, stage, and kitchen—was ruined, as were the shooting gallery, soda-water fountain, and popcorn booth. The moving-picture parlor was still under construction when the fire hit and was only slightly damaged.

Financial problems late in the summer placed the park in receivership, but it opened again the next season under new management. Among the new attractions in 1911 were a pool parlor, photograph gallery, Walking Charlie, and the Electric Ball Game. The Boston Orchestra under the direction of Signor Castellucci provided music.

At the beginning of August 1911, the park once again went into receivership. Finally, in the spring of 1913, the Paragon Amusement Company bought the park, and changed its name to Paragon Park by May of that year for a formal opening on May 30. It had a movie theater, the Paragon Picture Parlor, as early as May 1914. In 1915, the parlor advertised "high class moving pictures that were changed daily.[224] The park had closed by 1918 when it was sold to a developer who planned to build a number of dwellings on the site.

Lyceum {1}, 1209–1213 North Charles Street, 1879–1925; George A. Fredericks, William G. O'Brien (of 1887 remodeling), W. Bruce Gray (of 1890 remodeling; interior decoration by John Gibson); 750 (later 1,300: 629 — orchestra, 333 — balcony, 352 — gallery). Among the many famous people who appeared at this uptown theater were Edwin Booth, Sarah Bernhardt, Helena Modjeska, and Eddie Foy.

The basement bar room was a favorite hangout for artists, journalists, and musicians. Numerous motion picture exhibitions, starting in January 1900 with a series of Burton Holmes illustrated lectures, were given at the Lyceum, which had formery been known as the Wednesday Club Building.[225] The building was described as "semi-Gothic" with a front made of Baltimore County pressed brick and ornamental tiles. The proscenium was decorated in white papier-mâché. The figure above the stage represented the god Pan, instructing Cupid in music. The clubroom was on the second floor. The theater opened on December 29, 1879, with a musical program.

John W. Albaugh[226] purchased the Lyceum in February 1887 and reopened it with the same name on September 26 of that year.

The new theater was described in a contemporary newspaper account:

> The first floor contains an orchestra and a circle, the two being divided by handsome brass-mounted posts, connected with a rope of blue plush.... There is ... one gallery ... supported by eight iron columns, resting on brick and stone piers ten feet deep. The windows are finished in hard wood ... and contain heavy curtains of the same color as the drop curtain. The floors are covered with Brussels carpet.... A new proscenium arch has been placed in the auditorium at a height of thirty-five feet and with an opening of thirty feet. The arch is decorated with clusters of leaves and flowers, each leaf being raised and put on by hand and surmounted by red plush drapery. The sides are covered with a terra cotta colored paper which shows to good effect. The stage has been brought forward and ... measures forty-five feet deep. The stairs and floors of the inner lobby parlor and ladies' toilet-room are covered with Moquet carpet.... The walls of the lobby are finished in a bluish tint with a decorated border. The ticket office is in the front lobby.... The opera chairs, which are of the Demarest patent, are made of cherry wood and are finished in blue plush.... The entire house will be heated by steam and illuminated by gas, which will be lighted by electricity....[227]

The new proscenium was designed by stage carpenter and architect William O'Brien. The first show was Strauss' *The Gypsy Baron*, presented by the Conried Opera Company. The orchestra was conducted by Adam Itzel, Jr., who also composed an inaugural march for the occasion. Tickets cost from 50 cents to $1.25. The theater was remodeled again and reopened on November 3, 1890, with Edwin Booth in *The Merchant of Venice*. According to the *Herald*, the theater had been entirely rebuilt and "not a portion of the old theater" remained.[228]

The new three-story facade was of pressed brick and carved brown stone. The entrance was formed of three arched doors trimmed with brown stone. The 80-foot-deep auditorium contained two proscenium boxes on each side of the stage; there were two boxes in addition to the first dress circle on the second floor. The boxes were finished in ivory white, enriched and hatched with gold and silver with Louis XVI draperies in Nile green silver and yellow pink. The auditorium was painted orange pink with ivory, silver, and gold designs. The drapery of the proscenium arch was shrimp brown velvet plush.

The drop curtain, apparently quite impressive as all the newspaper accounts of the theater commented on it, was made of Nile green silver plush decorated with fleurs-de-lis with a fringe of colonial design in shrimp and old gold. The curtain was made in Philadelphia at a cost of $2,100. The stage dimensions were: proscenium opening — 33 × 40 feet, depth of stage — 55 feet, between side walls — 45 feet, to rigging loft — 65 feet, to fly gallery — 30 feet.

The seats were of cherry, upholstered in shrimp gray. The first four rows of the orchestra were officially known as the "fauteuils," but the public usually called them "love seats." They were large two-seater chairs, richly upholstered in silk plush, resting on Axminster carpets. The Lyceum had two star dressing rooms on the stage and ten ordinary dressing rooms downstairs.

The Nixon & Zimmerman circuit leased it in 1896. John W. Albaugh, Jr., took back the lease of the theater in the summer of 1897 and established a stock company there that fall.[229] For many years the Lyceum was one of the major local legitimate theaters, undergoing many name variations. It was known as Chase's Lyceum between 1901 and 1905 after it had been acquired by Washington theater owner Plimpton B. Chase. In the spring of 1905, it was leased by Robert E. Erwin and became part of the Shubert-Fiske-Belasco group of theaters.

There were extensive changes in the theater before its reopening on September 23, 1905. The *Sun* described some of the remodeling:

> The theatre has been overhauled ... and many improvements installed. The lobby has been redecorated, the green and red color scheme being carried out with green burlap panels with red borders....
>
> A novel convenience will be the lounging room, smoking parlor and art gallery combined and the cafe on the lower floor beneath the lobby. In this apartment will be newspapers, magazines, writing material, a telephone booth, lounges and chairs and other comforts. There is a large collection of old portraits ... these will be hung in the art gallery. Among them are large photographs of ... N. C. Goodwin, Beerbohm Tree, Sir Henry Irving, Richard Mansfield, ... and other famous artists and oil paintings of John W. Albaugh, Sr., Joseph Jefferson, and William H. Crane.
>
> All the seats in the balconies and the main auditorium have been refinished and the boxes have been beautified with rich Du Barry draperies.... The electrical apparatus has been enlarged and rearranged to meet the requirements of such plays as "The Darling of the Gods" and "Adrea" wherein the reproduction of sunshine, lightning and atmospheric conditions is really wonderful.[230]

It reopened as a Shubert house for the 1905-1906 season, and was called Albaugh's Theater until 1919. The following season it was operated by the Irwin-Luescher Company on the William Morris vaudeville circuit. There was more remodeling at this time; two illuminated eight-sheet billboards were set up on either side of the entrance, the lobby was repainted in cream and gold, and several new murals were added inside. The first balcony was converted into a mezzanine by removing several rows of seats around the horseshoe curve and dividing the space into a series of boxes. During the 1906-1907 season Albaugh's presented vaudeville. During the fall each show usually featured moving pictures.

Managers Irwin & Luescher permitted smoking on the mezzanine floor. They also began serving tea during performances, something new in Baltimore theaters. At the beginning of each intermission young ladies with tea trays circulated throughout the theater.

Irwin & Luescher did not last out the year, and George Fawcett leased the theater in December 1906. Fawcett reopened the theater on December 24 with a stock company that featured his wife, the famous Miss Percy Haswell. In October 1913, George R. Webb exhibited his talking movies to a large and enthusiastic audience at the Lyceum. It was called the Albaugh Lyceum Theater in 1920. Frederick C. Schanberger acquired the theater in May 1920 for an estimated $80,000 for the James L. Kernan Company. It was called the New Lyceum in 1921 when it showed the popular Griffith film, *Way Down East*, but reverted to Albaugh's in 1923.[231] A season of films was started at the Lyceum for the summer of 1923. Frank Wilcox and DeWitt Newing leased the theater in the fall of 1924 for their stock company.

The Lyceum fell on hard times in its last few years and showed some controversial movies and plays, including *White Cargo*, and *Getting Gertie's Garter*. One of the plays that the self-appointed moralists who harried the Lyceum decried was *Seduction*. It was the last play at the theater. Mr. H. Charles Robertson related the following incident that took place during one performance.

The play was widely publicized as a great love story, and, from the talk around town, it was pretty risqué. Such snatches of conversation as, "I heard you could actually see her bare breast" or "She was entirely nude on the stage in front of that Arab" were whispered all over town. The play was about an Arabian tribe fighting the British and the love affair between an Arab prince and his hostage, the lovely daughter of a British nobleman. During one performance, as British forces were closing in on his desert hideout, the prince and the girl — by now deeply in love — stood gazing into each other's eyes. Suddenly the prince could not endure the situation any longer. He tore off her clothing, and appeared ready to make passionate love to her. Then a pang of conscience hit him and he cried, "Oh God, I can't!" There was a moment of silence, then some wag in the balcony shouted, "Aw go ahead!" The audience roared with laughter, and the show had to be stopped momentarily. Apparently there had been a lot of improvisation on the part of the cast; nothing like that happened at later performances.

A group of prominent local women complained of the performance to Police Commissioned Gaither, and several members of the cast as well as the manager of the theater and the producer of the play were arraigned in Central Police Court. Mrs. Howard D. Bennett was so

For almost 40 years the Lyceum (5th and D streets, 1912–c. 1950, L. H. Fowler, Ewald G. Blanke of 1921 remodeling), shown here with an earlier marquee, probaby from the 1921 remodeling, was the main movie theater in Sparrow's Point. (Photograph courtesy of the Baltimore County Public Library Legacy Web)

shocked that she went back to the theater a second night to see if her first viewing had been correct. Her husband said that once was enough for him. Other women said the play was "grossly immoral, " "most indecent," and "an insult to the motherhood of Maryland." Magistrate Cadden dismissed all the charges.

On April 25, 1925, during a run of the comparatively tame *Romola*, starring Lillian Gish, the Lyceum Theater was destroyed by fire, apparently started by careless smoking in the theater's cabaret. Dr. Wyatt Brown, rector of St. Michael and All Angels, said that he was glad it had burned because of the character of its shows.

Undertaker William Cook waged an unsuccessful campaign to rebuild the Lyceum as a funeral parlor in the summer of 1925. There were many plans to build on the site, but none of them was successful. The site of the Lyceum has been a parking lot for more than half a century.

Lyceum {2}, 5th and D Streets, Sparrows Point, 1912–c. 1950, L. H. Fowler (Ewald G. Blanke of 1921 remodeling), 578. This is probably the theater mentioned in the May 18, 1912, *Exhibitor's World*, which said that the Home Amusement Company was planning a $20,000 motion picture theater in Sparrows Point. The plans were being prepared by architect L. H. Fowler, and called for a two-story structure, 112 by 50 feet of hollow tile construction[232] with a slate roof and steam heat. There were pool parlors and a bowling alley in the basement and a dance hall on the second floor.[233] The Home Amusement Company sold the theater to Erhard Eyring, G. R. Vincenti and E. G. Blanke in the summer of 1921 and plans were made to remodel it according to designs by Blanke. In 1928, the Lyceum purchased a Kimball organ. The Lyceum catered to the white population of Sparrows Point.

Heavy rains caused portions of the Lyceum's ceiling to collapse as a near-capacity audience was watching a movie in June 1947. No one was hurt, but there were reports of "burly adults" knocking down children in a rush to get out of the building. The J. S. J. Amusement

Company took over operation of the Lyceum in early 1948; it closed two years later. The building has been torn down along with most of the town of Sparrows Point.

Live shows were occasionally presented at the Lyceum. Meetings of Bethlehem Steel and high school graduations were also held there. During the silent film era, the Lyceum had a piano player named Gladys; her substitute was a young woman named Mitzi McDonough. Before World War II no food was sold in the Lyceum, and patrons often bought candy and treats at a newsstand near the theater.

Lyric {1} (see Music Hall)

Madison, 818–820 Madison Avenue, 1946–1951, David Harrison, 464. The Madison was built for James Kourkoules in what had been two stores. It opened on December 3, 1946. Despite a popular-priced program, air conditioning, luxury seating, and Naturaltone Sound, the Madison lasted only about five years. It closed first in July 1949, reopening with a new screen and refreshment stand in December 1949. It closed permanently on November 25, 1951, and the building was damaged by fire in 1952. The Madison did poorly because it was in a bad location, and the competition from the nearby Lincoln and Roosevelt was too much. In a 1947 article it was described as "off the beaten path."

Main (see Amusea {1})

Majestic {1}, 320 South Broadway, 1907–1926, George Clothier, Jr. (of conversion), 150–214. This storefront theater was opened in mid-1907. Business was so good, that a 20 by 61-foot addition, costing about $2,500, was added in the fall of 1907. The theater was operated by a Scot named Anderson in 1912; as a result, the name was changed to Anderson Picture Parlor on July 15, 1912. The theater was remodeled with paintings of Indian, Western, and battle scenes on the walls, a concealed electric lighting system, a new ventilation system, and 12 new electric fans. In the spring of 1919 it was acquired by J. Louis Rome, who renovated the theater and held a contest to give it a new name. Five people sent in the winning name, "Arcadia," and divided the $10 prize. The Arcadia opened on April 21, 1919, with more seats and a new ventilating system. Rome sold it in 1920, and it closed around 1926.

Majestic {2} (see Brodie)

Majestic {3} (see Superba)

*Majestic Motion Picture Parlor (see North Avenue Casino)

Maryland, 320–322 West Franklin Street, 1903–1951, John D. Allen (of Philadelphia); 1,356, 1,972, 1,750, 1,680 (after 1940 remodeling). The Maryland was one-third of James L. Kernan's "Triple Million Dollar Enterprise."[234] Kernan laid the cornerstone on March 19, 1903, to the tune of *Dixie*, and the theater opened on October 19, 1903.[235]

The *Baltimore American* described the new $500,000 theater on its opening day.

> The building ... is constructed upon the cantilever plan throughout, thereby securing a view unbroken by a post or pillar, the latter all being in the rear of the seats. These pillars are all hollow steel cylinders, encased in Vermont marble, hewn in semi-cylindrical form. By this cantilever system it is also possible for the seats to be elevated one above the other and the view of the stage even from the top gallery is unbroken.
>
> The galleries form with the boxes a semicircle. The boxes do not, therefore, interfere with the view at the side, a very unusual improvement ... there is a mezzanine floor composed of little boxes holding eight persons, in the rear of which is a handsomely decorated smoking room and manager's office.
>
> The lobby ... is wainscoted with Vermont marble and paved with tiles. On the left hand is the box office, faced with marble and on either hand in front rise the marble and steel fireproof steps.... On the first floor there is no center aisle ... but the aisles are removed to the sides to save the center space for seats. The first floor and the mezzanine floor are wainscoted with Vermont marble in harmony with the prevailing red of the walls.... The fire towers, into which both galleries and the mezzanine floor open, are made of steel, marble and concrete and provided with a winding stair from the top gallery to the ground.... The top gallery is very steep, but commands a fine view of the stage....
>
> The prevailing color of the boxes and the dome is old ivory, shading to tints of green, while the walls are red, shading from dark at the floor to a light color at the roof. The dome is decorated with four mural paintings costing $5,000 and a magnificent chandelier of incandescent lights, which cost $2,500....
>
> Adjacent to the lobby on the first floor is Mr. Kernan's art gallery.... Principal among the collection is the original of "And Every Soul Was Saved."[236]
>
> A handsome green asbestos curtain pro-

Kernan's Maryland Theater (320–322 West Franklin Street, 1903–1951, John D. Allen) on the left with a portion of the Hotel Kernan on the right. The Maryland was a major venue for movies between 1903 and the mid-teens.

tects the regular curtain depicting a Venetian scene. On the left-hand side of the stage behind the scenes is the fireproof building for the players' dressing-rooms rising in four tiers.... The building is of solid brick and cement, with metal-sheathed doors.[237]

The four mural paintings in the auditorium's dome, by Frank Sima of Philadelphia, represented music, art, literature, and drama. The stage measurements of the Maryland were: depth — 40 feet, width — 70 feet, height — 65 feet, proscenium opening — 33 by 35 feet. The Maryland opened as a legitimate theater with *Mary of Magdala*, starring Minnie Maddern Fiske. The opening, attended by Governor Smith, Mayor McLane, and architect John D. Allen, was a brilliant success. Everyone agreed that the Maryland was one of the prettiest theaters in town. A month after he opened the Maryland, James Kernan paid the astronomical sum of $12,500 to coloratura soprano Adelina Patti to sing there for one night. The Maryland's rathskeller, opened in December 1903, was located under the orchestra and was divided into three sections, American, Dutch, and Swiss with "heavy furnishings of the Flemish type." In September 1904, Kernan booked B. F. Keith vaudeville, and movies formed part of its vaudeville shows from the beginning. The Maryland was one of the principal early venues for movies in Baltimore. As early as March 1904, movies of the Baltimore Fire were shown. During the week of March 14, 1904, the vaudeville program included *The Great Train Robbery*.

In 1905, admission prices were 15 cents, 25 cents, 50 cents, 75 cents, and $1. In 1907, the Maryland had a nine-man orchestra. Patrons at the Maryland could visit the art gallery during intermissions. The establishment of vaudeville at the Maryland faced rough going in its first few years, and, at one point in 1908, Kernan had decided to sell his entire Triple Million Dollar Enterprise to the Nixon & Zimmerman organization. He was, however, persuaded to turn it over to Fred C. Schanberger, who made it a success. Kernan announced plans in 1909 to build a roof garden and theater with a seating capacity of 1,800 on top of the Maryland Theater and Hotel Kernan. Thomas W. Lamb was hired to prepare the plans, but the additions were never built. In the summer of 1911, the interior was completely repainted in deep old ivory and gold; the walls were hung with rose-colored silk damask, and a new enlarged stage was installed.

After what he considered unreasonable demands by the musicians' union, manager Frederick Schanberger, Sr., replaced his regular orchestra with a women's orchestra in August 1918.[238] Expensive stage draperies were installed in the summer of 1921. The grand drapery was gold and red with tormentor hangings of gray silk velour with gold and red trimmings. The theater was closed for four weeks in the summer of 1925 when a new switchboard was installed.

The vaudeville shows at the Maryland were booked by Fred Schanberger, Sr., who personally selected the acts each week in New York. The Maryland abandoned full-time vaudeville in 1927 after nearly 25 years. That September, the management announced that it would have two vaudeville shows a day, plus movies four times a day. It closed for a week in December 1927 and then began showing movies almost exclusively when it reopened. Shubert attractions moved to the Maryland that year, and Keith-Albee vaudeville moved to the Garden {2}. Vaudeville did not return to the Maryland until it was revived in 1939. Kurt Robitscheck presented his variety revue, *Laughter Over Broadway* for an eight-day run beginning on February 25. Louis Azrael thought it was a "pretty good show," but had not revived enough interest in vaudeville in town to keep it going.

In 1932 the Penn Mutual Life Insurance Company, which held the mortgage, foreclosed on several of the former Kernan properties, including the Maryland Theater. On July 20, 1932, Penn Mutual purchased the Maryland and Auditorium theaters and the Kernan Hotel at auction for $225,000. The Maryland was immediately put up for sale, but it continued to operate.

It had been for sale for nearly 10 years in April 1942 when C. William Hicks, who ran the Hicks Circuit, purchased it for an estimated $75,000. Hicks said that he would air condition the theater at once. He reopened the Maryland with vaudeville and first-run movies on January 15, 1943. Gloria Swanson opened summer stock season that year. During the war the Maryland presented stage shows and films. A typical show of 1943 featured Stan Kenton and his orchestra onstage, a couple of other live acts and a grade B movie. Hicks remodeled the theater in 1946. It reopened on September 12.

In November 1946, the New York–based group Consolidated Radio Artists, Inc. (CRA), took over the operation of the Maryland. CRA reopened it as a legitimate house with Lillian Hellman's *Another Part of the Forest*. In June 1948, the Maryland was sold at auction for $79,500, and was subject to a clause that stated it could not be used as a movie theater for 25 years. The Maryland Theater Corporation tried "glorified burlesque" with a chorus line called the "Hollywood Honeys" in October 1948. The management announced that the Maryland would abandon its policy of racial segregation in May 1949 after a successful experiment with desegregation during a run of *Anna Lucasta*. Joe Louis and Canada Lee praised the new policy when they attended the opening of the play *The Happy Journey* in November 1949. Burlesque alternated with other forms of theater in 1949 and 1950.

Miriam Hopkins, Kay Francis, and Eva La Galliene appeared at the Maryland during the 1949 season, but, despite good crowds, they simply could not put the theater in the black. The European Jewish Actors' Ensemble put on a series of excerpts from classic Yiddish plays in May 1950. Burlesque was back again in September 1950, but even the great Minsky could not save the Maryland.

By early 1951, the theater was for sale again, but no one wanted it as a theater. The Maryland was torn down in the spring of 1951 to make a parking lot. The scars left by the mezzanine and balcony are still visible on the wall where it adjoined the Congress Hotel. They are the only traces of the historic theater where the cream of America's live entertainers appeared. Among these performers were Al Jolson, Will Rogers, Eva Tanguay, Jack Benny, DeWolf Hopper, Houdini, George M. Cohan, W. C. Fields, Charlie Chaplin, and Fanny Brice. Sarah Bernhardt played Baltimore for the last time in 1918 at the Maryland. While they were members of the University Repertory Theater appearing at the Maryland, Margaret Sullavan and Henry Fonda were married in the dining room of the Hotel Kernan.

Leonard McLaughlin managed the Maryland from 1927 to 1942. Under his management, the Maryland established a local box office record when Katherine Cornell appeared in *The Barrets of Wimpole Street*. In one week, the theater took in $30,000.

One item that was salvaged from the Maryland was a huge crystal chandelier. It went to Trinity United Methodist Church on Capitol Hill in Washington until that structure too was demolished, then, in 1964, Congress purchased it and it was installed in the Small Rotunda of the Senate wing of the U.S. Capitol.[239] During the demolition of the Maryland, the copper box, which James Kernan had placed in the cornerstone nearly 50 years earlier, was located and opened. Kernan had left instructions that the box and its contents should be given to the most popular theater in the city or to the Maryland Historical Society. The box seems to have disappeared.

Mascot, 2421 Greenmount Avenue,[240] 1909–1915, Harry W. Fox. The Mascot opened in 1909. It was built for George R. Sumner at a cost of about $2,400. The building was a one-story brick structure measuring 20 by 90 feet.

Mayfair (see Auditorium)

McCoy (see Gertrude McCoy)

McHenry, 1032 Light Street, 1917–1971, Oliver B. Wight, 981–1,220. Henry Webb's Southern Amusement Company built the McHenry for a reported $75,000. The building permit was granted in October 1916. Often referred to as "The Southern Parkway," the McHenry was modeled after the Majestic in Detroit and the New Victoria in Buffalo and was described as having an Italian exterior with a Colonial interior. It was designed by Oliver Wight who had also designed the Parkway Theater.

The facade was of gray ornamental tapestry brick with stucco trim. In the center of the facade, directly over the galvanized iron marquee, was a tall French latticed window. The long lobby had walls of Caenstone with wainscoting and trim of Tennessee marble and a floor of white tile. The auditorium, at the end of a long lobby, measured 65 by 120 feet with all the seats on a single floor. An early press notice stressed the fact that there were no stairways in the McHenry, "thus minimizing accidents and providing great safety." The interior colors were old rose and gold or, according to another source, light gray and gold. The ceiling had six small domes and one large central one. The proscenium arch was gently rounded with an escutcheon at its apex. Two pilasters with Ionic capitals were on each side of the organ grills. Indirect lighting provided illumination. The screen was muslin covered with "liquid tungsten," and the organ was a $3,000 2/13 Moller (Opus 2256).

The McHenry was the first high-priced first-run movie house in South Baltimore. It opened on Saturday, May 26, 1917, with a program that included Olga Petrova in *The Undying Flame* and *The McHenry Topical Review* with "special scenes of South Baltimore" taken by the theater's cameramen. Prices ranged from 10 cents to 25 cents (for a reserved loge box seat). On Tuesdays, Fridays, and Saturdays, the McHenry offered Market Matinees at 10:30 A.M. On other days the first show began at 12:30 P.M. and the last show began at 9:15 P.M. In the fall of 1917, vaudeville, booked through Fred G. Nixon-Nirdlinger, was added to the show at the McHenry.

The Whitehurst organization acquired the McHenry in the fall of 1919 along with the Parkway. They turned around and sold it to Nixon-Nirdlinger in the spring of 1920. The Rex Amusement Company took over the lease on the McHenry the following summer for an annual rent of $6,000 with an option to buy the theater for $105,000 within six months. Ownership of the theater changed again in May 1923 when the title was conveyed to the McHenry Theater Company for $72,000.

In the summer of 1930, a $20,000 one-story brick addition, measuring 55.2 by 79.8 feet was planned. Architect Oliver B. Wight was planning alterations to the McHenry that included a new storefront, rest room and offices in March 1933.

The theater was operated by the Durkee organization for many years until it closed on August 22, 1971. It has been used as a thrift store, an indoor sports center, a Thai restaurant, and other things since then. There was some talk in 1980 about restoring it as a theater, but — except for some preliminary plans and a grant from the National Endowment for the Arts — nothing came of it. In December 1996 the theater was for sale for more than $600,000; some talked of tearing it down to build a parking lot. In 2001 developer Patrick Turner announced that he would convert the theater into office space and keep much of the original interior decoration. On the evening of August 28, 2001, Turner hosted a last performance at the McHenry. In a very classy move, Turner brought in food, live entertainers, and silent movies — supplied by Tom Kiefaber and personnel from the Senator Theater — to end the McHenry's movie career in style. Several hundred people attended this event.

Soon after it opened, the McHenry (1032 Light Street, 1917–1971, Oliver B. Wright) had a marquee installed. One of the two men on the left may be C. W. Pacy. (Photograph courtesy of the Maryland Historical Society, Baltimore, Maryland)

Metro Photoplays (see Berman's)

Metropolitan, 1524–1530 West North Avenue, 1922–1977, Otto G. Simonson, 1,450 (900 — main floor, 550 — balcony; later 1,200). The Metropolitan, or Met as it was usually known, was built for the Metropolitan Theater Company[241] It was the first white neighborhood theater to show first-run movies. The site for the theater was purchased for about $33,000 in the spring of 1921, and bids for its construction were taken at the end of the year. The Colonial Style building included six stores, a bowling alley, offices, and a large billiard room on the second floor. It cost about $325,000.[242] It had two entrances, one at the corner of North and Pennsylvania, through a two-story brick and limestone store and office building, and one further east on North Avenue. The corner entrance served as the main entrance until it was closed off in 1947. The North Avenue entrance was the main entrance for the next 30 years.

The *Sun* described the Metropolitan:

> Terra cotta, granite and red brick were ... used in constructing the facade. At each entrance there are spacious doorways over which metal marquees have been hung. Both the lobbies and the foyers are finished with a wainscoting of green Italian marble and have floors of terazza. Subdued illumination is furnished in all parts of the theater by the indirect lighting system and in the lobbies and foyers the illumination is furnished by artistic ceiling lights. ... Mulberry, ivory, gray and gold are the colors that have been used throughout the playhouse for decorations and draperies. The ... draperies will be mulberry colored tapestry. The chairs are of ebony with mulberry colored leather. A delightful place ... is the mezzanine promenade ... comfortably furnished with wicker furniture. The ... floor covering is heavy taupe velvet carpet.[243]

The Metropolitan immediately joined the ranks of Baltimore's first-run movie houses. After a private show for invited guests, including Mayor William F. Broening, on December 15, the Metropolitan opened to the public on December 16, 1922. Bernard Depkin, Jr., directed and staged the presentations of the shows. The Metropolitan Concert Orchestra, conducted at first by local violinist Walter Lee and later by Julius Sokolove, provided music. In September 1923, the Metropolitan Soloist Ensemble, under the direction of Sokolove, included Jules Simms—cello, Gerhard Helmers—violin, Angelo Figrani—clarinet, Harold Sokolove—piano, Paul Spitzbarth—bass, Winnet Dashiell—flute, Joseph Soistman—tympani and drums with Miss Dorothy Coats—harp. The three-manual Robert-Morton organ was played by Mrs. Josephine Schanze, Kenneth G. Faulkner, and George Finster, among others.[244] In 1925, the Warner brothers, looking for an outlet for their films in Baltimore, purchased the theater for $375,000.

The Metropolitan's chief claim to fame is that it was the first movie house in the area to show successful sound movies. *Don Juan* was shown there during the week of January 31, 1927, and the first real "talkie," *The Jazz Singer*, opened on January 8, 1928. People came from all over the city to see talkies at the Metropolitan.

In July 1928, the Metropolitan was closed for $25,000 renovations; plans called for redoing the theater in a "modernistic manner." An Italian garden was added in the foyer for the showing of another early talkie, *The Lights of New York*, in September 1928. The garden included several evergreens, a fountain, and a bench. The walls resembled the exterior of a Mediterranean garden wall.

In 1930 the Metropolitan was one of the first theaters in Baltimore to adopt daylight savings time. Warner Bros. shifted their first-run films from the Metropolitan to Keith's and the Auditorium in 1931 and the Metropolitan became a neighborhood house. The Metropolitan passed out of the Warner organization when it was leased by the Rome Circuit in 1937. Rome operated it until the fall of 1946 when it was leased to the Schwaber circuit, which maintained offices in the theater building and operated it until it closed. In early 1947 Schwaber extensively remodeled the Metropolitan.

They closed the original entrance at the corner of North and Pennsylvania and remodeled the one on North Avenue, adding a marquee and making it the main entrance. They also renovated the theater, putting in new seats and carpet and installing new lighting. A year later Schwaber converted it into a first-run African-American house, and it reopened on March 24, 1949. The Metropolitan closed on July 26, 1977. In August 1977 the theater's equipment and furnishings were auctioned off; fewer than 30 people attended the auction. The theater was demolished in 1978 to build the Penn-North subway station.

Mickey (see Teddy Bear Parlor)

Midway, 1909 Eastern Avenue, Middle River, 1945–1950, Frederick L. W. Moehle & Associates, c. 650. Harry and Al Vogelstein opened the Midway on September 20, 1945. It was built in a hall at the rear of Buedel's Tavern. A description of the new theater appeared in a local newspaper: "Deep upholstered seats for 700 patrons are placed on an inclined floor for clear vision. The building ... of fireproof construction is air conditioned and has seven exits. Rest rooms are just off the spacious lobby.... Hand painted murals adorn the walls.... The floor and aisles are covered with deep carpets."[245] A typical Saturday

This entrance to the Metropolitan Theater (1524–1530 West North Avenue, 1922–1977, Otto G. Simonson) was created in 1947 when the original entrance at the corner of Pennsylvania Avenue and North Avenue was closed off.

show at the Midway in 1945 consisted of Bill Boyd in *Undercover Man*, Ruth Terry in *Jamboree*, a chapter of *Jungle Queen* and two color cartoons. It only lasted about four years as a movie theater, closing in January 1950, but the building is still standing and has been used for many years as a hall. Much of the original theater, including the ceiling, proscenium, and ticket booth, remains.

Military Theaters. There were several movie theaters located on local military installations. Fort Howard and Fort Holabird had one theater each, built according to the same plans as many other theaters scattered about the country on army posts. The theater at Fort Howard has been closed for many years, but was still standing as of 2002. The Fort Holabird theater has been demolished. Both of these theaters were built according to the same plans and seated about 398. They were Colonial Style brick structures with a central ticket booth flanked by two sets of double doors.

Fort Meade had six theaters by 1943, Theaters Number 1 to Number 6. Theaters Number 2 through Number 5 were TH-3 Theaters, built during World War II; they seated about 1,000 people. Number 1 is the only one still functioning as a movie theater. The locations of the theaters at Fort Meade were as follows:

Theater Number 1— Llewelyn and Roberts Avenues (1933–present)

Theater Number 2 — Clark Road between 25th and 26th streets (c. 1941)

Theater Number 3 — Chamberlain Avenue and 7th Street (c. 1941–1978)

Theater Number 4 — A Street between 20th and 21st streets

Theater Number 5 — Zimborski and Rock avenues

Theater Number 6 — Zimborski Avenue and Simonds Street (an open air theater)

Another theater, the Liberty (q.v.), operated at Ft. Meade around the First World War. An open-air movie theater at Fort Meade was in operation in the early 1930s; it was apparently part of the Citizens Military Training Camp. A postcard shows this theater as a wooden structure with three sections of seats, a covered stage area and a projection booth above the entrance.[246] It probably seated between 750 and 950 people.

Mini-Flick, 1110 Reisterstown Road, Pikesville, 1973–1986, unknown, 300 (150 for each auditorium). Another creation of Schwaber innovator Howard Wagonheim, this tiny twin theater was opened by Schwaber World-Fare Theatres on June 21, 1973. Wagonheim designed most of the two theaters. The auditoriums were described as "compact," featuring a "modern decor." The seats were Heywood-Wakefield rocking-chair seats. The Mini-Flick was a popular theater where foreign films such as *La Cage aux Folles* had long runs. JF Theaters leased it in 1982. Just before it closed in 1986, the Mini-Flick became a discount theater, charging $1 at all shows. Two years after the theater closed, the building was acquired by a carpet company which gutted the building for a new showroom.

Monarch, 111 South 5th Street (= Eaton Street), c. 1909–1914. The Monarch was on Eaton Street just below Lombard; it lasted about five years. It last appeared in a 1914 listing. According to one source, it became a German saloon and later a food market. There was also a bowling alley in the southern half of the building.[247] The building on the site in 2002 appears to be more recent.

Monroe, 1924 West Pratt Street, 1939–1953, David H. Harrison, 500. Architect Alexander G. Porter prepared the original plans for the Monroe in 1938, but they were abandoned, and new plans were drawn by David Harrison. The Monroe was built for the Monroe Theater Company at a cost of about $30,000. The facade was of buff face brick with trim of dark face brick. The auditorium was long and narrow with a ceiling of Sabonite acoustical plaster, and the interior carpeting was gold and burgundy on a claret field. Yellow brocade and coral velour draperies and stage curtains completed the decor. The Monroe opened around July 6, 1939. One source said that Frank Hornig, who ran the competing Horn Theater a block to the west, bought a house next to the Monroe so that the theater could never be enlarged. The Monroe closed in early August 1953. The building was still standing as of 1999.

Monumental (see Washington Hall Theater)

Monumental Open Air Theater, 2241 East Monument Street, 1909–c. 1913, 2515 East Monument Street, c. 1914–1925. August "Augie" Pahl opened his first airdome around 1909 on the spot where the Red Wing Theater was later built, a 137 by 147-foot lot on the southwest corner of Patterson Park Avenue and Monument Street. In June 1913, Pahl upgraded this theater by erecting a roll canvas awning on pipe frame to be used in rainy weather. When the lot was sold to build the Red Wing, Pahl closed his airdome and moved three blocks east to the corner of Monument and Rose streets.[248] Both theaters had galvanized iron, double-decker billboards, and a 7–8-foot-high fence. They had rollback canvas roofs that could be opened when it got dark and could provide protection against rain. Inside there were long, wooden benches.

The theater at Monument and Rose had a small stage. Pahl's theaters were only open in the summer. He used behind-the-screen talkers and rear projection. Children were usually let in free; they could sit on the floor and watch the last show of the evening. The theater at Monument and Rose included a restaurant and bar and the one at Monument and Patterson Park had a soda fountain. After Pahl died, the theater closed; a food market was built on the site.

Morgan (see Schanze)

Morrell (see Lincoln Highway)

Morris Mechanic, 25 Hopkins Plaza, 1967–present, John M. Johansen, 1,854. For this unattractive block of concrete we lost the Stanley and Ford's; it was a bad trade. Although some people liked the unfinished concrete surfaces that carried the imperfections of the wooden molds, others felt that the $4 million theater was a graceless monstrosity. Brennen Jensen described it well when he wrote, "The 1967 building has all the hallmarks of unbridled Brutalism: the rawly exposed cement, the purposeful championing of function over form, the relentless drabness. It looks like an insecticide factory or an electric-power substation rather than a palace for the performing arts."[249]

The Mechanic Theater opened on January 16, 1967, with Betty Grable in *Hello, Dolly*. Sadly, Morris Mechanic had died a few months earlier. Despite a packed house, the opening was not a very happy occasion. Critics panned the show, and patrons complained of poor sightlines and terrible acoustics. In 1973, after two money-losing years, the Mechanic Theater was in trouble and was nearly turned into a movie theater. Motion picture equipment was actually installed there that summer, but no decision was made to convert it. It was rescued by Baltimore Theatre, Inc.—formed by fire commissioner Howard Owen, Jack Fruchtman, and Frank G. Roberts—which agreed to lease the theater for $65,000 a year. The theater lasted two years; then they gave up, and the theater went dark for a year and a half.

In 1976 the city spent $500,000 remodeling the Mechanic, improving the acoustics and enlarging the orchestra pit. The remodeled theater opened that November. Since its opening, the Mechanic Theater has been the major venue for Broadway shows in Baltimore.

Moses and Michael (see Pastime {2})

Mount Airdome An open-air theater, probably on Mount Street, was listed as seating 300 persons in 1926.

Mount Royal, 617–619 West North Avenue, 1915–c. 1920, William O. Sparklin and George S. Childs, c. 500. The Mount Royal Amusement Company built this movie theater in 1915 in a former garage building. It cost about $8,000, and opened on September 7, 1915. There was a store in the front of the building.

> The picture-house has an entrance fronting 22 feet on North Avenue, and the lobby will extend back 50 feet. The main auditorium, entered from this lobby, is 44 × 100 feet.... The front is decorated with a large marquis, and the general color scheme is a delicate cream tint. The interior decorations are very elaborate, the color scheme being in old ivory. The walls are decorated with large panels, having a background of blue satin damask.[250]

The ventilation system could change the air in the theater every three minutes. A new 2/9 Kimball organ was installed in 1916. In a primitive attempt at stereophonic sound, the organ pipes were placed in all sections of the auditorium. The house organist was a Mr. Benny, but

The Mount Royal (617–619 West North Avenue, 1915–c. 1920, William O Sparklin and George S. Childs) lasted only about five years, the fate of bad location. (Drawing by Robert W. Kramer)

Prof. Fred Wolff, the organist at Grace and St. Peter's Church, gave evening recitals.

In the fall of 1916, the lobby was redecorated. The moldings, wainscoting, borders, and doorframes were painted ivory white and the woodwork of the doors was done in mahogany. Tom Bohannon and Harry Lewy acquired the theater in December 1916. After the theater closed, around 1920, it was used by the Nichols Auto Company for a while, but it was razed many years ago.

Mount Washington Casino, South Avenue and First Street, Mount Washington. The Mount Washington Casino was a Queen Anne style building with a central tower. Movies were shown there between about 1914 and 1922. It was remodeled and redecorated in the spring of 1942 and reopened that June as a summer theater. Also used for dances and other community events, it was razed in 1958.

Movies at Golden Ring Mall, 6400 Rossville Road, 1976–2000, Woodbay Construction Company (of 1976 theaters), 900 (300 for each of the original three auditoriums; another source gave the total number of seats as 766).[251] The United Artists Theater Circuit opened this triplex on June 30, 1976. The original three auditoriums were located on the upper level of Golden Ring Mall at the east entrance. They were served by a single box office, refreshment center and projection booth. A new feature, between shows, was the "light curtain," a display of colors and changing patterns on the screen created by a separate projection unit.

Within a year, two new auditoriums, on the lower level and at the opposite end of the mall, had been added. Four auditoriums were added in 1985 above the 1977 auditoriums. In 1994, three more auditoriums were added. The original box office was moved to the lower level and served the original auditoriums as well as the new ones on the lower level. The original three auditoriums were barely adequate, but the later auditoriums were very poor excuses for movie theaters.

A 1979 survey of local movie theaters rated this theater near the bottom of the 47 theaters surveyed.[252] The reviewer's comments say it all: "No floor slant, poor visibility and sound, small screen hung high on the wall, and uncomfortable seats."

The mall was put up for sale in 1998, and plans were announced to raze it. The Movies at Golden Ring closed in April 2000. By mid-2001 Golden Ring Mall had been almost completely demolished.

Movies at Harbor Park, 55 Market Place, 1985–2000, Land Design/Research, Inc. (Columbia, Md.), 2,250 (for nine auditoriums). Plans to build a multi-screen theater complex in the Inner Harbor began as early as July 1980, when the Oxford Development Corporation announced that a 2,500-seat, eight-screen theater would be built within the Harbor West luxury condominium adjacent to McCormick & Company. In February 1983, the Cineplex Corporation announced that it was contemplating a multiplex theater in downtown Baltimore. One possibility was the northeast corner of Lombard Street and Market Place where plans for a multistory garage were being developed. Finally, on December 13, 1985, United Artists Communications beat out J-F Theaters and B. S. Moss Enterprises of New York, and opened a $3 million, nine-theater complex in the Harbor Park Garage.[253] A month before the theater opened, United Artists applied to transfer a liquor license from a closed White Coffee Pot restaurant on North Howard Street to the new theater. The city liquor board approved the request but limited the beverages to the lobby.

The theater was located on the lower levels of the 777-car garage. The nine auditoriums had staggered seating, wall-to-wall screens, and a computerized ticketing system. The interior design was contemporary. The Lombard Street entrance led into a large front hall with brick walls and terra cotta tiles on the floor. On one side of the lobby was a large refreshment stand and above that was the bar. On the lobby wall, a large mural by local artist Raoul Middleman depicted a fictitious historical Baltimore. The floor of the lobby was of patterned bricks while brown and green carpeting covered the floor of the promenade leading to the theater entrances. Each of the nine auditoriums, which opened off either side of a long hallway, seated between 200 and 240 people. The staff consisted of five managers and 35 employees.

Film critic, Corinne F. Hammett, described the individual auditoriums as "from the horrendous shoe-box school of design," but said that the screens were large and the projection was good.[254] Jacques Kelly did not like the design of the theater either, complaining that, "the place seems about as lackluster as such local architectural snorefests as the Science Center, the Walters Art Gallery and Lyric additions."[255]

United Artists closed the Movies at Harbor Park in March 2000. The theater had fallen into disrepair, and an official with United Artists said that it was not making enough money to keep it open. Ugly incidents like the harassment of several Hopkins students by a gang of punks in 1998, and several robberies did not help. In June 2001, Baltimore City Community College was making plans to take over the closed theater and convert it into classrooms and computer labs.

Movies at Marley Station, 7900 Governor Ritchie Highway, Glen Burnie, 1987–present, unknown, c. 1,990 (for eight auditoriums). United Artists opened this eight-screen multiplex in Marley Station Mall just south of Glen Burnie on June 5, 1987. The theaters are located in the middle of the lower level of the mall, where they take up 25,000 square feet. Entry to the theaters is on either side of a freestanding box office into a very small lobby with two sides devoted to a concession area. Decorations consist mainly of movie posters. The auditoriums open off a wide hallway that leads from the lobby. The largest auditorium seats about 330. Three auditoriums seat 270, two seat 250 and two seat 225.

Moving Picture Theater A movie house was located at 2634 Francis Street according to a 1914 listing of movie theaters.

Mozart Airdome, probably the northeast corner of North Avenue and Wolfe Street, c. 1921–c. 1923. The city council granted the Dudley Amusement Company a permit to build "an enclosure ... for the purpose of exhibiting moving picture shows" 50 by 100 feet at this location in October 1921. This theater lasted about three years.

Music Hall, 130 Mount Royal Avenue, 1895–present, Henry Randall, 2,244. The idea for building the Music Hall belongs to Frank Frick, who with Capt. Frederic M. Colston and several others formed the Auditorium Company and purchased a site on Mount Royal Avenue from the McKim estate in 1892.

When the Boston Symphony gave its first concerts in Baltimore, they were in the Concordia Opera House. After the Concordia was destroyed by fire in 1891, the concerts were held in the Academy of Music in the afternoons; the theater was not available in the evenings.[256] Frick and the others decided that Baltimore needed a concert hall.

The Music Hall has been used mainly for opera, ballet, and musical productions. The architect designed it using the proportions of the Leipzig Gewandhaus as a model. The money for building it ran out before the front had been completed and, for many years, the entrance remained very modest. The opening performance in 1895 featured Nellie Melba as soloist with the Boston Symphony. In October 1903 the name of the theater was changed to Lyric because the lessees believed that the name Music Hall conjured up images of lower class vaudeville and burlesque theaters. Despite excellent acoustics, the Lyric was not a financial success in its early years and, in 1906, it went into receivership. In 1907, the Lyric was sold at auction for $126,000 to the lessees, the Gottleib-Knabe Company.

Numerous movies have been shown at the Lyric. The first was a film of the Passion Play in February 1898, which was brought back the following January along with the first Burton Holmes illustrated lecture and Biograph films of Pope Leo XIII. Burton Holmes played the Lyric in 1900 and twice in 1903. Several other travel lecturers appeared at the Lyric with their movies over the next decade. These included Miss Emma R. Steiner, Woodworth Clum, and the Karmata Travelogues. As the century moved on, the Lyric was used less and less for movies and more and more for opera, ballet and concerts. In the spring of 1917, the film, *War as It Really Is*, made by Capt. Donald M. Thompson under the direction of General Joffre, was shown at the Lyric.[257]

Mutoscope [Parlor], 305 East Baltimore Street, c. 1899. A Mutoscope parlor opened at this address in early 1899.

Muvico Egyptian 24 Theater, 7000 Arundel Mills Circle, Arundel Mills Mall, Harmans, Anne Arundel County, 2000–present, Development Design Group (Ahsin Raheeb),[258] 5,400 (for 24 auditoriums; 1—141, 2—146, 3—106, 4—106, 5—141, 6—291, 7—291, 8—205, 9—101, 10—101, 11—485, 12—390, 13—390, 14—485, 15—101, 16—106, 17—205, 18—291, 19—291, 20—136, 21—101, 22—101, 23—?, 24—141). Florida-based Muvico Theaters announced in November 1999 that they would build a 5,000-seat "retro movie palace" with an Egyptian decor at the new Arundel Mills Mall in Harmans. The new theater opened, with full-page color newspaper ads for 17 films, on December 8, 2000. The Egyptian 24 was the first of the new "themed" movie theater complexes to open in the Baltimore-Washington area, and it appears likely that it represents the trend of the future. The facade resembles an Egyptian temple with rows of columns[259] covered with hieroglyphics leading from a mammoth porte cochere and supporting a canopy past a statue of Anubis, the Egyptian god of the underworld, to the mall entrance. Patrons buy tickets at twin box offices and pass, between sand-colored reproductions of Sphinxes, into the lobby.

The huge theater—117,000 square feet—is laid out like a short, wide "H," with a central lobby as the crosspiece. Passageways with walls resembling ancient temple walls run off to the right and left past rest rooms to 12 auditoriums opening off the sides of the "H." A huge concession counter stretches across the back wall of the lobby. Patrons can buy candy, sodas, and popcorn in addition to quesadillas, popcorn shrimp, chicken wings, and pizza.

On the floor of the lobby the Nile River is depicted as a sinuous line of blue tiles. The walls are lined with real marble imported from Egypt. The new megaplex has stadium seating, valet

The Egyptian god of the underworld welcomes patrons to Muvico's Egyptian 24 Theater (7000 Arundel Mills Circle, Arundel Mills Mall, 2000–present, Development Design Group).

parking, and a playroom for children. Some of the auditoriums have wide crossover aisles that offer extra legroom and an easy way to get from one side of the auditorium to the other. The walls of the auditoriums and the halls are decorated with scenes of ancient Egypt. All auditoriums have wall-to-wall curved screens, digital surround sound, and high-backed seats upholstered in red velour.

By the spring of 2001, this theater was among the top grossing movie theaters in the country. Muvico is to be congratulated for giving theatergoers a theater like this; it is glitzy, well run, and comfortable — an unbeatable combination. It will be interesting now to see what happens to Hoyt's nearby West Nursery 14. Muvico has the reputation for devastating any older theaters in its vicinity.

National, 1401–1407 East Monument Street, 1921–1952, E. A. Lockhart and Oliver B. Wight[260], 1,000 (as the Eden c. 450). The National opened as an African-American theater on October 1, 1921, on the site of the Charles A. Sefton wagon and truck factory. The National was built for H. C. Shipley's National Athletic and Amusement Company for a reported $100,000. It was built on a roughly triangular plan measuring about 90 × 125 feet with the entrance at one corner and the screen opposite it. The original 1,000 seats were arranged in a semi-circle. Mahogany-finished seats and cork carpet completed the decorations.

There was a dance hall on the second floor, described as the largest African-American dancing hall in the state.[261] The greater part of the Monument Street side of the building was occupied by a soda fountain. Samuel Crawford conducted the orchestra that consisted of violin, banjo, piano, and drums. The popular African-American vaudeville star, Sherman Dudley, took over the financially ailing National in the spring of 1923, but gave it up after only a month.

The National lasted until about 1925. It did not reopen as a theater until January 31, 1947, when it became the Eden.[262] The seating capacity of the Eden was between 400 and 500, much less than the National. The theater closed in 1952, and the building was demolished to construct a housing project.

Nemo (see Takoma Moving Picture Parlor)

New {1}, 210 West Lexington Street (202 Park Avenue after 1967 remodeling), 1910–1986; A. Lowther Forrest and Oliver B. Wight, Armand Carroll (of 1945 remodeling); 1,400 (1,700 after 1914 remodeling and 1,800 after 1945 remodeling). Charles E. Whitehurst's New Theatre Company[263] announced plans to build the New in the spring of 1910; it opened, as a vaudeville theater, on December 17, 1910. Whitehurst correctly saw that the shopping district in Baltimore was centered on three or four blocks of West Lexington Street between Charles and Eutaw. The New was his first effort to tap the enormous potential of this area. The architects used the New Amsterdam Theater in New York and the Majestic Theater in Boston as models. The plans called for a 1,400-seat theater that would cost about $100,000. The original stage measured 97 feet wide by 87 feet high. The entrance was built where Magary's store had been located. The original facade was in the French Renaissance style with buff-colored Roman brick and terra cotta trim. Above the marquee was a large copper and glass window, set in a recess of terra cotta.

A reporter described the theater just before it opened.

> The entrance at Lexington street is of Venetian marble, and this long, broad corridor leads to the theatre proper, the building being L-shaped. The walls of this corridor are of green veined marble, especially imported, and the ceiling is elaborately carved and decorated. Through this wide archway toward the rear of the corridor and we're in the auditorium. The color scheme of the interior is old rose and gold, and the opera chairs, carpets, and box draperies are in harmony. The ceiling shows a blue sky, with just the suggestion of floating clouds. This effect is brought out by hidden lights which cast a faint glow of dawn. Both of the galleries are of the cantilever pattern, and an unobstructed view of the stage can be obtained from every part of the house. The broad promenade immediately in the rear of the orchestra circle is one of the features. Opening onto this promenade are the writing, cloak, and retiring rooms. These will be in charge of maids. The painting "Beauty" over the proscenium arch was done by Oskar Gross,[264] the celebrated mural artist. Ten other paintings from his brush will grace the panels in the corridor. The air pumped in through the roof is water-washed in summer and heated to 68° Fahr. in winter. ... Twenty-seven safety exits have been provided and the auditorium can be entirely emptied in 84 seconds.[265]

Another source described the seats as maroon and mahogany and the curtain as dull gold and "a great relief from the usual blatantly hideous curtains in the Baltimore theatres."[266]

Much of the original 1910 facade of the New Theater (210 West Lexinton Street, 1910–1986, A. Lowther Forrest and Oliver B. Wight, Armand Carroll of 1945 remodeling) is visible in this 1944 photograph.

One source described the lobby decorations as in the style of Francis I with carved oak paneling and green Connemara marble, interspersed with lattice panels and huge mirrors.[267] The east wall of the lobby had two arched openings, decorated with marble pillars representing Satyr heads, leading into the auditorium.[268] The manager's office had a pivoting stained-glass window arranged so that the manager could look out into the lobby. The *Baltimore News* considered the decorations as being in the style of Louis 16th.[269]

Charles Whitehurst was quoted as saying, "We have decided to devote our theatre to continuous vaudeville, running from noon until 11:00 P.M. It will in no sense be a moving-picture house. Being in the heart of the shopping district, we will cater especially to women and children. It will be our policy to offer only the very best and cleanest acts in vaudeville at prices within the reach of everyone."[270]

The opening of the New was a lavish affair. Eugene O'Dunne, a former deputy state's attorney who would go on to become a judge and play a pivotal role in several movie cases, gave the inaugural address, comparing the theater to an ancient Greek theater. Farson's Orchestra provided music. The opening show featured eight acts of continuous vaudeville and Theaterscope movies. Admission was 10 cents, and the theater played to capacity audiences during its first week.

The New was renovated and remodeled many times during its lifetime. The theater was enlarged, and, despite Charles Whitehurst's earlier pronouncement, converted into a movie theater in the spring of 1914. This remodeling cost about $25,000 and increased the dimensions of the theater to 87 feet wide by 78 feet deep. At the same time, an elaborate ventilation and heating system was installed, and the entire lighting system in the auditorium was changed. A new refrigerating system was installed in the summer of 1916. Plans were announced in February 1917 to install a three-manual Moller organ.[271]

In the summer of 1921, it was remodeled again for $15,000. The *Sun* reported on this reopening.

> The playhouse presents an entirely new and comfortable appearance. New lighting fixtures have been installed and the softly glowing lamps are covered by Japanese silk shades in the auditorium and foyer, while in the sub-foyer large Japanese lanterns, which throw out a mellow radiance, furnish the light. Ceiling decorations blend ... with the French gray damask effect.... An effect of rich Caen stone is carried out on the walls of the foyer while a soft tone of gray is used on the paneled woodwork of the sub-foyer, contrasting with the mahogany-colored doors. Through the foyer and sub-foyer carpet of a dark tone of old rose has been laid, harmonizing with the furniture. New comfortable seats, furnished in blue velour, have been installed.... The principal curtain of the stage is wine-colored velour, while the curtains covering the screen when not in use are of orange colored silk.[272]

The theater reopened on September 5, 1921, with D. W. Griffith's *Way Down East*, starring Lillian Gish. Shubert interests were negotiating with Whitehurst in the fall of 1921 to acquire the New and convert it into a musical comedy house, but these negotiations fell through. In the spring of 1922, the management adopted a new policy of presenting live plays instead of movies, but this did not last very long.[273]

In August 1926, a new heavy plush carpet was laid, a new crystal chandelier was installed in the foyer, and a new electric marquee was erected over the exit. The foyer was redecorated in bronze, old gold, and brown. The New installed Movietone and Vitaphone sound systems in the summer of 1928. Then, on April 1, 1929, the last theater remaining in the former Whitehurst chain, the New was sold to Morris Mechanic. He remodeled it in 1929 and again in 1935. In 1938, the New began a policy of showing first-run 20th Century–Fox movies such as *Rebecca of Sunnybrook Farm*.

Between October 1945 and February 1946, by a miracle of the builder's art, the interior of the New was gutted and completely rebuilt.[274] Baltimore Contractors first spent two months stripping the interior of the theater down to the bare walls, ceiling, and floor. After that, construction work was completed in one month. The stage was rebuilt, and the original two balconies were replaced by a single one. Most of the 115 tons of new steel used in the reconstruction of the theater went into building the framework for the balcony.

Philadelphia architect Armand Carroll, who had designed the Centre for Mechanic, redesigned the New. *Boxoffice* described the remodeling:

> Major structural, architectural, and artistic changes are planned for the theatre proper, the mezzanine, the lobby, and the facade. The entire interior will be torn down and a greatly enlarged first floor orchestra area and enlarged mezzanine will be constructed eliminating the second balcony entirely....
>
> The Lexington St. facade and marquee will

The exuberant interior of the New before it was sterilized by Armand Carroll in 1945. (Photograph courtesy of the Maryland Historical Society, Baltimore, Maryland)

suggest but not be identical with those at the Centre Theatre on North Ave. Over a V-shaped marquee, a V-shaped tower will rise 60 feet. The base or rear of the tower's prism will be built against the facade of the theatre. The edge of the prism will point to the street, while the two slanted sides of the tower will carry the name of the theatre and the titles of the current pictures.

The lobby, with mural decorations, and the box-office will be redesigned. Luxurious lounges and rest rooms will be installed.[275]

One description of the remodeled interior described the "lines of utter simplicity ... mostly long, straight lines and gentle curves so composed that the spectator has an illusion of space greater than that which actually exists." Concentrating mainly on good sight lines, architect Carroll created an auditorium that was about as sterile as one could imagine. The New reopened to an audience of 1,800 on February 12, 1946 with *Leave Her to Heaven*, starring Cornell Wilde and Gene Tierney. Mechanic celebrated the remodeling of the theater with a cocktail party the evening before the reopening. John Payne and his wife Gloria DeHaven were there, along with Mayor McKeldin and representatives of most of the film companies.

On March 31, 1949, the world premier of *Mr. Belvedere Goes to College* was held at the New to celebrate the 20th anniversary of Morris Mechanic's ownership of the theater. In August 1953, a new 50-foot wide screen and a directional sound system were added. Jack Fruchtman became manager of the New in August 1954. On February 12, 1957, traffic on Lexington Street was snarled for two hours, and policemen were swamped by about 10,000 school children trying to get in to see *The Ten Commandments*. The premier of *The Road to Hong Kong* was held at the New in July 1962. In March 1966, *The Sound of Music* celebrated a one-year run at the New. In 48 weeks it had outgrossed the previous record holder, *Around the World in 80 Days*.

The New was completely remodeled again between October and December 1967 at a cost of about $130,000. The *News-American* described the changes.

> The remodeling includes the relocation of the entrance of the theater from Lexington St. to a new facade at 200 Park Ave.... Inside the theater, seating will be completely redesigned to give each patron an uninterrupted sight line of the screen — the 1,408-seat theater will be completely outfitted in new theater chairs. Other changes will be evidenced in a completely redecorated lobby and auditorium, the installation of all new fixtures and rest rooms. The screen and stage area is also being restyled to allow for the latest in screen viewing. A shadow box halo screen with no visible masking, which represents the newest development in fine motion picture presentation, will be instituted at the New Theatre. All new projection equipment ... plus a newly engineered balanced solid [sic] sound system ... are also a part of the "new" New Theatre.[276]

The New suffered the same decline in attendance in the late 1960s as the other downtown theaters. By 1971, it was showing triple features of questionable merit — three films for $1.25 before 5:00 P.M. — like the show on January 24: *No Blade of Grass* — "See A Baby Born Before Your Eyes! See Innocent Women Violated! See Brutal Bloodthirsty Cycle Bums Attack!" — *Scars of Dracula*, and *Horror of Frankenstein*. The New limped into the 1980s and finally closed in September 1986. In 1987, local actor and writer, Edward Heath, took over the New and renamed it The Tower Showcase Theater. He reopened the theater with his own musical, *We're Moving On*, in the fall of 1987.

In December 1987, the New was offered for sale at auction. According to the advertisement it had 879 seats on the first floor and 50 on the balcony and it was being rented for $4,000 a month. Heath purchased the building in 1988 and continued presenting live stage productions there. By 2001 it had become a clothing store.

New {2}, 49 Reisterstown Road, Reisterstown, 1934–1967(?), John F. Eyring, c. 500. Lauritz Garman and his Northern Amusement Company opened this theater on October 19, 1934. An enthusiastic crowd estimated at nearly 1,200 people attended the two evening shows. The New, which cost about $75,000, was a classic 1930s neighborhood theater. The front was divided into three vertical sections faced with raw sienna bricks. In the center of each section, above the first-floor level, were vertical inserts of corrugated concrete with windows at the second-floor level.

Irwin Cohen took over the New from the Durkee organization in the spring of 1965. Cohen changed the name to Squire, in keeping with the tradition of horsemanship in the area, and remodeled it accordingly. The Hitching Post Coffee and Tea Bar was added at this time; it had a bark wall and hitching posts. The Squire opened on June 17, 1965, with *Goldfinger*.

A theater was planned in Reisterstown in 1922, when J. Edward Christhilf had architect Joseph Henry Steinacker prepare plans for a $10,000 movie theater, but this theater was never built.

New Albert (see Avenue {1})

New Aurora (see Aurora)

New Brodie (see Brodie)

New Cameo (see Parkside)

New Carver (see Diane)

New Center Follies (see Jewell)

New Crescent (see Crescent {2} and Crescent {4})

New Dixie (see Dixie)

New Eagle (see Eagle)

New Essex, 416 Eastern Boulevard, Essex, 1934–1968, unknown, 625. Abraham and Louis Cohen built the New Essex in 1934.[277] Work began on the theater in early June 1934, and it opened on October 5. The name was changed to Eastway in December 1965. It reopened on December 25 with a double feature of *Cat Ballou* and *Tickle Me*. It closed on January 7, 1968, and the building was destroyed by fire five days later.

New Flaming Arrow (see Flaming Arrow)

New Garden (see Garden {3})

New Gem, 617–619 North Duncan Place, 1909–c. 1925, John Freund (of 1912 remodeling), 427 (in 1922). The New Gem, or simply the Gem as it

The staff of the New Gem (617–619 North Duncan Place, 1909–c. 1925, John Freund of 1912 remodeling) poses in front of the theater around 1913. The first four men, from left to right, are: Ray Levee, George Culp, Charles Bender, and Nick Burns.

was often called, was opened by Charles Bender around 1909. Prior to that time, the building was apparently used as a bowling alley. It was called the New Gem to distinguish it from the Gem on East Baltimore Street.

There is some confusion as to the later history of this theater. In the spring of 1912, Nicholas Ertel planned to erect a $4,000 moving picture theater at 617 North Duncan Place. Other records show that Nicholas Burns and Charles Bender bought the property at 619 North Duncan Place in mid-1912.

The exterior of the New Gem featured painted wreaths and flowers, and the walls of the auditorium were decorated with painted scenes, including one of the sinking of the Titanic. Burns, Bender, and Henry Kolb were part owners of the New Gem for many years, and Augie Pahl was associated with it in some way.

A piano player and a violinist furnished music. Among the piano players were Lou Shubert, Sam Shoebridge, and "Doc" Seitz. Ray Levee was one of the projectionists as well as the manager around 1919. In the summer of 1919, the theater was renovated, and the seating capacity was increased by 100. It closed for several weeks in the summer of 1921; a new cement floor was installed to replace the old wooden one, and a new screen and projection machines were installed. At the same time the auditorium was extended back, probably all the way to Collington Avenue, so that 100 new seats could be added.

The Baltimore Amusement Company acquired title to the New Gem in December 1921 for $15,000. Louis Greenberg bought the theater in November 1922 for $23,500; it was subject to a mortgage of $22,000 at the time. Among the equipment inside the theater at the time of the

Typical of many smaller theaters, the New Gem offered occasional live shows. This photograph, around 1913, shows a group apparently rehearsing. Note the fans mounted along each wall and the murals, including one of the *Titanic* sinking.

1922 auction were a piano, two Simplex projectors, a rewinding machine, and 14 electric fans. The theater closed for about six months in early 1924, but was renovated and reopened on November 3, 1924. It was advertised as "The Theatre With Two Entrances 617–19 Duncan Place And Log Cabin Entrance 604–6 Collington Avenue." The building, called "the former movie theater known as the Gem," was sold in August 1928. Just before it closed, it presented burlesque shows. It later became a hardware store.

New Glen, 130 Crain Highway, Glen Burnie, 1941–1978, John J. Zink, 600. Bob Gruver opened the New Glen on November 19 or 20, 1941. The front of the theater was asymmetrical with the entrance and marquee on one side and a store on the other. Above the marquee was a vertical sign. Inside were the latest Bodiform seats, a special calling system for patrons, a powder and ladies' room, a smoking lounge and men's room and a private soundproof room for parties. Gruver installed CinemaScope in August 1954. The theater was remodeled in the spring of 1960.

Competition from the new Glen Burnie and Harundale Mall theaters forced the New Glen to close in 1966. It reopened in November 1966 with a policy of showing adult foreign and domestic films with children's matinees on weekends. In 1968, it was leased out and converted into a teen dance club, the Hullabaloo. The club did not last long, and in the summer of 1970 the theater was sold at auction for $60,000. In November 1970, the building was reopened as the New Glen Art Theatre which specialized in X-rated films. It closed on December 23, 1978.

The county paid $128,000 for the theater as part of a 42-acre urban renewal district. It was demolished in 1978, and most people seemed to be glad to be rid of it.

New Goldfield (see Goldfield {2})

New Horn (see Horn)

New Idle Hour (see Idle Hour)

New Lincoln (see Lincoln)

New Market {1}, 613 North Duncan Street, 1912–1913. This storefront movie house lasted for about a year. It was opened by Nicholas Vito, who also ran the nearby Fairyland. It was a long, very narrow theater, measuring 17 feet-9 inches wide by 125 feet deep.

New Market {2} (see Fairyland)

New Nemo (see Nemo)

New Paris (**Follies Theater**) (see Jewell)

New Patterson (see Patterson {2})

New Peabody (see Peabody)

New Pickwick, 113–115 North Howard Street, 1908–1985, Franz Koenig (Oliver B. Wight of 1920 remodeling), 250–293. The New Pickwick, in its later reincarnation, the Howard, was the neighborhood movie house of downtown Baltimore. Robert H. Baum and J. Howard Bennett opened it in late September 1908. It cost about $5,000 to build and measured 28 by 90 feet. The facade was topped by a giant face in a sunburst and illuminated by 800 incandescent bulbs. Heroic figures flanked the wide entrance. A large picture window in the wall above the ticket booth allowed passersby to look into the projection booth. The interior was described as roomy and comfortable with excellent ventilation.

It opened with the entire operetta *The Mikado* on the Cameraphone; the first act was shown Thursday, Friday, and Saturday, and the second act was shown on Monday, Tuesday, and Wednesday. It was called the New Pickwick to distinguish it from the Little Pickwick on Lexington Street. Enlarged and improved for about $3,500 in the spring of 1911, it was open from 10:00 A.M. to 11:00 P.M., and, for 5 cents, you could see one reel of first-run pictures and one reel of two-week old material. The films were changed on Monday, Wednesday, and Friday.

Nick Weems and Billy Frisch were singers at the New Pickwick in 1912. Archie Lloyd was billed there in 1913 as "that pleasing lad in merry melody," and tenor Herman Dick sang there in 1913. In August 1913, manager Bernard Depkin installed, at a cost of $4,500, what he claimed was the first orchestral organ in Baltimore in the New Pickwick.[278]

J. Howard Bennett sold the theater to G. Horton Gaffney in the summer of 1916. In the fall of 1916, Gaffney, announced an all picture policy at the theater. He also hired female ushers and engaged a string orchestra to play during the performances. Gaffney reinstituted the policy of interspersing the movies with popular songs and hired three well-known local singers, H. Dick, J. Morrison, and B. Peterson. In August 1917, the Pickwick installed another new musical instrument, the $10,000 Fotoplayer. This instrument was said to be equal in sound-producing power to a 21-piece orchestra and was the first of its kind in Baltimore.

The New Pickwick was sold at auction on October 18, 1917. It was extensively remodeled in the summer of 1920, and a new front of terra cotta and brick was added. In March 1924, Samuel Soltz of Pittsburgh leased the theater for nine years. Soltz changed the name to Howard and redecorated the theater, repainting it brown, gray, and gold. He reopened it in April 1924. A new marquee was installed in the spring of 1948. As one of the less expensive downtown theaters, the Howard tended to attract unusual clientele. One had to watch one's step lest stepping on a drunk peacefully sleeping it off between the seats. The Howard was also a notorious place for school kids to play hooky. In December 1955, two employees were arrested for allowing six children under 16 to attend movies there during school hours.

The Howard lasted until early 1985. After it closed as a theater, it was converted into a Dunkin' Donuts branch. As of 2004, the building was still standing. Boarded up, its future did not look secure.

New Preston (see Flaming Arrow)

New Queen (see Aladdin)

New Wizard (see Great Wizard)

Newsreel (see Picture Garden)

Nicoland (see Palace {1})

North Avenue Casino, 6–8 East North Avenue, c. 1892–c. 1918. The North Avenue Casino was erected as a skating rink around 1892. It was a large building with a 40-foot frontage on North Avenue and a depth of about 206 feet. In addition to the skating rink, there were bowling alleys on the first floor. The skating rink was converted into the European Summer Garden, Museum and Vaudeville Theater in May 1898. It contained what was billed as "The Largest Curio Hall in the World," and admission was 10 cents.

The North Avenue Casino Company, incorporated in 1908, acquired the building. That summer, the North Avenue Casino was operating as a "moving picture palace." It featured a palm garden, music, and refreshments. It may have been an open-air theater since the first show did not start until 8:15, when it was getting dark enough to show a movie outdoors. The second show started at 9:15. Children paid a nickel, and adults paid a dime for admission.

The Casino was sold to the New Casino Company, headed by John D. Farson, the leader of the Gwynn Oak Band, in 1910 for $175,000. The main hall, which had previously been used as a skating rink, was to be remodeled into a ballroom. The building, called the "Arcadia" on the 1914 Sanborn Insurance Map, had bowling alleys on the first floor and a dance hall and poolroom on the second floor. Near the end of its career, there were several unsuccessful attempts to convert the Casino into a movie theater.

In July 1916 the North Avenue Casino Company had ambitious plans calling for a $150,000 remodeling from plans by A. Lowther Forrest. The ordinance for remodeling was held up in the city council for several months until October 24, 1916; by late November, Blanke and Zink were preparing plans for this remodeling. The theater, to be called the Majestic Motion Picture Parlor, would cost about $85,000. The size of the new structure was given as 75 feet on North Avenue with a depth of 303 feet back to 20th Street. In November 1917, the Homewood Amusement Company had Blanke and Zink prepare plans for a 2,000-seat, $150,000 theater on the site of the old Casino. Plans had changed again by February 1918; Blanke and Zink were drawing plans for a garage instead of a theater. The North Avenue Casino Company was dissolved in 1920.

North Point Drive-In, 4001 North Point Boulevard, 1948–1982, unknown, 888 cars. Durkee theaters opened this drive-in, the second one in the Baltimore area, with a special show on June 25, 1948. The opening feature was *Panhandle*, with Rod Cameron. The theater cost an estimated $300,000 and covered 27 acres. Like most drive-ins, it claimed to have the largest screen in the world, covering 15,100 square feet. Among the amenities of the new theater were a bottle-warming service, a snack bar, and a playground. It also had something called "moonbeam lighting" which consisted of blue and amber lights at the top of a 100-foot steel tower. When turned on, these lights cast a subdued glow over the entire drive-in.

All members of the Durkee organization were not enthusiastic about the drive-in. Soon after it opened, one of the officials reportedly said, "You guys are crazy; the mosquitoes were eating them up the first night."[279] Nevertheless, the North Point Drive-In did well enough to last 34 years. It closed after the 1982 season, and the site of the drive-in is now a large flea market.

North Point Plaza, 2399 North Point Boulevard, 1966–1998, Charles L. Culchia, 911. This freestanding theater was built by Broumas Theaters.[280] It opened on March 16, 1966, and sat rather forlornly, isolated, at the northwest end of North Point Plaza. The third Broumas theater in the Baltimore suburbs, it featured six-channel stereophonic sound and one of the widest screens in the state; it could show 70mm and Todd-AO films. By 1974 it was being operated by JF Theaters, and in 1984, it was divided into four small theaters. On the exterior, the North Point Plaza presented a very plain boxy appearance, but there was some attempt to make the front interesting. Local artist Quentin Moseley created a neon sculpture that was placed on the facade above the entrance. Before it was subdivided, the interior was attractive and the auditorium was well designed, providing excellent viewing. It had become a discount theater when it closed in the summer of 1998. After it closed it was quickly demolished, and a large store was erected on the site.

North Pole (see Palace Moving Picture Parlor)

Northeastern Amusement Company (see Palace {2})

Northern, 1625–1627 Harford Road, 1912–1922, Callis & Callis. The Northern was built by the Northern Amusement Company in 1912 for an estimated $7,000 to $10,000. The building was one story and measured 32 by 120 feet. The Lord Calvert Theaters Company acquired it in the spring of 1914 as the first in a planned circuit of theaters. The name was changed to Lord Calvert in 1914.

The Neo-Classical screen tower of Durkee's North Point Drive-In (4001 North Point Boulevard, 1948–1982). This was one of the earliest drive-ins in the Baltimore area.

In March 1920, the management arranged to have an amateur quartet sing several songs by local songwriters after the first show every evening. A committee of three newspapermen served as judges, and the best song was announced on Saturday night. Participation was high. The theater must have closed in 1922 since the building, with all of its theater equipment, was auctioned off in October 1922. A petition to alter the building, described as "a one-time mo-

The Northway's (6701 Harford Road, 1937–1979, John J. Zink) massive glass brick addition was probably added in 1941.

tion picture theater," was denied by the Board of Zoning Appeals in early 1924. It razed in 1973.

Northway, 6701 Harford Rd., 1937–1979, John J. Zink, 655 (later 421). The Northway was built for Durkee Enterprises. It cost about $35,000, and opened on September 16, 1937. The glass block tower was added later, probably in 1941 when a $5,000 contract for additions to the theater designed by Zink was awarded. In the 1960s, the original entrance on Harford Road was sealed

The entrance to the Northwood Theater (1572 Havenwood Road, 1950–1981, Fred Dixon) was not much to look at, but the attractive interior was very well designed.

off and a new entrance was constructed around the corner on Northern Parkway. For a while, the Northway was the only Durkee theater to show X-rated films, but in June 1978 it reverted to general films. Neither strategy worked, and the theater closed in 1979. It was acquired by an adjacent drugstore, but as of 2004 the marquee remains.

Northwestern, 1056 Pennsylvania Avenue, 1913–c. 1925, Callis and Callis, 150. The Northwestern, located on the first floor of a three-story building, was one of the smallest movie houses in Baltimore. It was built in early 1913 for Alexander J. Meyers. Kalem Flaks operated it at some point. The theater was completely remodeled in early 1922, reopening on February 14. It was converted into a confectionery in 1925 after a "price-cutting war" with the American and Lincoln Theaters.

Northwood, 1572 Havenwood Rd., 1950–1975, 1976, 1980–1981, Fred Dixon, 1,144–1,572. The Northwood was built by Joseph Grant's Northwood Theater Corporation in the ritzy Northwood Shopping Center. The Northwood could draw on a white-collar population of about 100,000, nearly all of whom were white. Work on expanding the shopping center and building the theater began in August 1949, and the theater opened on August 5, 1950. It was a very comfortable, attractive theater. The name of the theater and current attraction were presented on a large sign tower, more typical of drive-ins than four-wall theaters, located on a small raised walkway in front of the theater. The facade was of marble with three double, glass entrance doors to the left of the box office. A long lobby led back to the auditorium, which was located behind several stores. The interior color scheme was in shades of brown, green, and strawberry. The walls of the auditorium were decorated with modernistic figures. In 1951 Jay Emanuel Publications, publishers of *Theatre Catalog*, selected the Northwood as the "best-constructed theater built in 1950," and presented a bronze tablet to the managing director.

Between 1955 and 1963 the Northwood was

embroiled in a struggle with African-American organizations and students from several schools to desegregate the theater. After it closed temporarily in mid-1975, Fred Speckman leased it from the Northwood Partnership, which was owned by Schwaber World-Fare Cinemas, for a short time in the summer of 1976; he planned to concentrate on family films. The theater reopened again in the spring of 1980 as a discount theater, the Northwood 99, then closed in June 1981. The building was still standing as of 2002, when it was used as a lounge.

Novelty (see Nowosci)

Nowosci, 510 South Broadway, unknown, 1919–c. 1927. The Nowosci (Polish for "novelty") opened in the spring of 1919, but there may have been a movie theater in the building as early as 1916. In the summer of 1916, W. Urbanski, president of the National Polish Home Association, announced plans to alter the three-story building and moving picture theater at 510 South Broadway. Two years later the Polish National Home received permission to alter the building into a theater on the first floor. When it started out, the Nowosci presented vaudeville and live plays in Polish and showed Polish films. A newspaper article in 1919 described the vaudeville: "Their vaudeville stars appear in the barbaric colors that can be found among the happy peasants in Poland today, and their songs, most of them being patriotic or borrowed from folklore, have touches of Oriental music."[281]

The name was changed to Globe Moving Picture Parlor for about a year in 1926, and changed again, in 1927, to Arcade Moving Picture Parlor. It closed around 1927, but may have had a final name change to Sideman Moving Picture Parlor around that time. This may have been one of the theaters where the projectionist had to view the screen indirectly by means of a mirror. In 1921 or 1922, a local strongman, Antone Matysek, who had once lifted 2,900 pounds, held back two teams of horses in front of the Nowosci.[282] As of 2004, the large brick Polish Home building was still standing.

O'Donnell (see Olympia)

Oella Hall, Oella, c. 1920. During 1920, movies were shown at Oella Hall every Monday and Thursday night. The show cost 15 cents and featured "good music."

Olympia, 2938 O'Donnell Street, 1909–1915, Alfred Mason. This theater was built for an estimated $4,000. It was a one-story structure with an ornamental front of stamped metal. The screen was reportedly so high that patrons had to keep their heads up and bent back to watch a movie. The building was used as a laundromat as of 2000.

Oriole, 1202–1204 Laurens Street, 1908–1921, Clarence E. Anderson, 265–350. Herman S. Hackerman announced in September 1908 that he was planning to convert the dwelling at 1204 Patterson Avenue (now Laurens Street) into a motion picture theater. Carey Stockton announced his plans, in the spring of 1909, to remodel the building at the same address. Then, in December 1909, Hackerman announced that he was going to build a new, 265-seat, $1,200 picture theater at 1202–1204 Patterson Avenue. It is not clear exactly what was going on at this address, but someone built a movie theater there. The ads for the Patterson Theater during the week of December 9, 1912 announced special features every evening to celebrate the theater's fourth anniversary, suggesting that films had been exhibited there as early as December 1908. Hackerman's second announcement may have referred to an enlarged theater. It cost about $575 to equip the theater.

The theater's name was changed to Patterson around 1911. After having been closed for six years, the Patterson reopened in the late fall of 1917. Then it became the Pastime around 1918. In late 1918, when it was sold at auction for $2,000, the Pastime contained about 350 chairs, a piano, and a projector.

It was called the New Patterson in January 1919, and featured vaudeville and a jazz orchestra. It was sold to a company represented by Julius Goodman for $14,800 in August 1919. Goodman took over and was planning to renovate it, but it was sold again, this time for $11,600, in May 1920. The theater reopened as the Virginia on October 15, 1921, and closed within a year.

Oriole Park, Greenmount Avenue between 28th and 29th streets. This park, which had earlier been Federal League Park, was the home of the International League Orioles from 1902 to 1944. It burned to the ground on the 4th of July in 1944. Open-air movies were shown there during the summer between 1916 and 1920. The open-air theater opened on May 12, 1916, with movies under the management of S. B. Cook. During that summer, Oriole Park advertised moving pictures every night, from 7:45 to 11:00. Jack

Dunn, the manager of the Orioles, arranged for the showing of movies at the park every night in the summer of 1920. The screen was set up on the ball field behind home plate; the audience sat in the grandstand which had the advantage of being covered. Prominent in the advertisements was the phrase, "Smoking Permitted."

Orpheum {1} (see Washington Hall Theater)

Orpheum {2}, 2307–2309 Jefferson Street, 1911–1917, George S. Greener. The Orpheum cost about $3,000 to build in the spring of 1911. It was a one-story brick and stone building measuring 32 × 75 feet on the southwest corner of Jefferson and Bradford streets. It was built and operated by John M. Alexander. The theater was put up for sale at auction to close an estate in April 1918. It was then described as a complete and up-to-date moving picture parlor, with patent folding chairs with leather seats and backs, two motor-driven Powers moving-picture machines, and an upright Weber piano. The building was used as a laundry in the early 1970s, but by 1995 it was closed and boarded up.

Orpheum {3}, 1724 Thames Street, 1990–1999, George Figgs, 80. George Figgs opened the Orpheum on the second floor of the building at 1724 Thames Street in November 1990. The ancient building in which the Orpheum was located was a former horse car stable. Figgs wanted to recreate a typical neighborhood theater of the 1940s and 1950s, and the conversion cost about $70,000.

The entrance to the theater was through a door on the west side of the building. Above the entrance was a small, flat attraction board topped by the name "Orpheum" spelled out in white letters. The seats were from the old Clover Theater on Baltimore Street and had been in storage for many years. The opening attraction was a triple feature, Jean Cocteau's *Orpheus*, Billy Wilder's *Sunset Boulevard* and Fellini's *Roma*. The movies were shown using a 16 mm rear-screen projection system. Figgs booked classic films as well as foreign films, and while the Orpheum became a mecca for serious film buffs, it eventually closed in May 1999.

Overlea, 6805–07 Belair Rd., 1927–1953, unknown, c. 450. Louis Tunick opened the Overlea in late October 1927. It lasted until the early 1950s, spending its final years opening and closing. It was reopened in December 1949 by Morris Oletsky's newly formed Overlea Theater Company. It must have closed down again before November 1951 since it reopened in that month with a new double-feature policy. It closed again and was remodeled during the summer of 1952. It reopened a third time in September 1952 with the film *Little Egypt*. It closed for good soon thereafter.

In its 10th anniversary program, the Overlea manager, H. H. Silver, praised the friendliness of the theater: "The Overlea — a friendly theatre. No mile-long corridors filled with priceless Object D'Art [sic], no cathedral-like auditorium or vaulted lounge.... No staff of over-dressed, over-bearing, military trained attaches to order you about.... We cannot boast a mammoth stage or prancing, dancing ladies; not even a large orchestra ... we are proud of the airy cleanliness of our little theatre. We are happy too, to have so many friends who patronize the Overlea because of its intimate atmosphere, its comfortable seats, its perfect sound, its neighborly friendliness. It pleases us that our employees were born and raised among you people and know most of our patrons by name."

After it closed, in early 1953, the Overlea was purchased by a catering company. There was a bowling alley under the theater.

Overlea Hall, Belair Road near Overlea Avenue, Overlea, c. 1915. Exhibitor Arthur Gans applied for a county license to conduct a moving picture parlor in Overlea Hall in the spring of 1915.

Owings Mills Cinema 17, 10100 Mill Run Circle, Owings Mills Town Center, Shapiro Petrauskas Gelber (Philadelphia), 1998–present, 3,000 (120, 88, and 64 for the three Premium Cinemas). General Cinemas soared back into the Baltimore movie scene with this mammoth movie megaplex. Built to take advantage of the huge number of new residents expected to move into the area, the massive 64,000 square-foot Owings Mills Cinema 17 is located next to Owings Mills Town Center, not far from the Metro Station. The main entrance faces the shopping mall but is separated from it by a road and large parking areas. Within the megaplex are 14 regular auditoriums and three luxury auditoriums with a separate entrance.

The 14 regular screens opened on December 18, 1998. Among the first movies at the theater were *Pleasantville* and *Antz*. The small auditoriums, which vary from 122 to 297 seats, have stadium seating with rocking chair seats and a few special wide seats called "Love Seats." They feature THX and digital sound and 25 by

The massive entrance to Owings Mills Cinema 17 (10100 Mill Run Circle, Owings Mills, 1998–present, Shapiro Petrauskas Gelber); it was acquired by AMC in 2002.

40-foot screens. There is also a game room and a cafe — the Café Noir — with Starbucks coffee.

The three Premium Cinemas opened on February 5, 1999. These auditoriums are furnished with leather-upholstered seats and serve champagne, fine wines, and gourmet food. Admission to the Premium Cinemas cost $12 a ticket and was restricted to people 21 years old or older. After General Cinemas declared bankruptcy, the property was bought out by AMC in 2002. By that summer, the Premium Cinemas at Owings Mills were used as conventional auditoriums.

Pacy's Garden (see Garden {2})

Palace {1}, 228 South Broadway, c. 1906–c. 1914, unknown, 150[283] (later c. 250). Charles E. Nolte and Gus Stenger opened the Palace {1} around 1906 on the first floor of a three-story house. It cost $5,000, and at first it had about 150 chairs. Later, 100 more seats were added. The screen was a piece of white muslin, and the projection booth measured only six feet square.

When it first opened, the Palace {1} had a staff of four including a cashier and a doorman who each received $6.00 a week. Early shows there lasted between 15 and 20 minutes; as many as 20 shows were given during a single day. The electricity bill could have run as high as $100 a week. After a while, people were afraid to live in the two apartments above the theater because of frequent fires in early movie theaters. One fire in August 1909, luckily confined to the projection booth, did considerable damage, but no one was injured except the projectionist. The Palace {1} employed a singer and later hired talkers to speak behind the screen.

The theater's name was changed to Nicoland around 1908 when it was operated by the Zerker Brothers. It was again called the Palace in 1909, but became the Red Raven in 1910, when it closed because of competition from larger, newer theaters such as the Cluster and Leader. A Busy Moon theater was listed at this address in 1914. The founding meeting of the projectionists' union was held in April 1909, in a room on the second floor of the Palace Theater building.[284]

Palace {2}, 936 Pennsylvania Avenue, 1907–c. 1912 unknown, 280. In the earliest reference to this theater, it was advertised in the *Afro-American* of March 2, 1907, as "A new and commendable enterprise. The only colored theatre in Maryland." Henson and Lee operated this Palace as a legitimate theater and movie theater.

Cincinnati comedian Charles L. P. Osborn ran it in 1908 when it was called the Lincoln. By November 1909 the theater had been acquired by William H. Daly, who operated it until 1912. Evidence suggests that Daly had an open-air theater adjacent to a hard-top theater at this location. He later moved to 1115 Pennsylvania Avenue, where he operated another airdome called Daly's Why. A 1911 newspaper article said that this theater "boasts a bright yellow front and a big electric sign."[285] Daly's advertised electric fans and plenty of ice water with polite attendants in the summer of 1911. It was also advertised as "the only theater in Baltimore serenading pictures with orchestra bells."

An interesting feature of Daly's open-air theater was a bare electric wire running along the top of the wooden fence surrounding the theater. This wire could be energized to discourage kids from trying to climb over the fence and sneak inside. According to an article in the *Afro-American* of May 23, 1924, Miss Lottie Gee, who starred in Sissle and Blake's show *Bamville*, played at Daly's Theater the week of May 20, 1912. Eubie Blake was there the same week. The Lincoln Theater was built on this site in 1915.

Palace {3}, 1351 North Gay Street or 1901–1907 East Hoffman Street, 1913–1951, Otto G. Simonson (Theodore W. Pietsch of 1917–18 remodeling), 500 (1,000 after 1919 enlargement; 1,400 after 1921 remodeling). Frank Durkee's Northeastern Amusement Company opened the Palace {3} in early 1913. It was located on the southeast corner of the intersection of Gay, Hoffman and Wolfe Streets with the auditorium running parallel to Wolfe Street. The original theater was one story high, 30 × 31 feet, and seated about 500 persons; it cost an estimated $7,800. Durkee installed a $2,000 Wurlitzer Stringed Orchestra in October 1913. In July 1915, the Northeastern Amusement Company purchased two lots on Wolfe Street adjacent to the theater for the purpose of enlarging the auditorium. It was altered in 1917–1918. In 1919, plans for enlarging the theater were announced again. According to one article, many of the planned improvements in 1919 were modeled on the Rialto and Strand theaters in New York. At that time three sites, which measured a total of 50 by 60 feet, east of the theater on Hoffman Street were acquired and razed. The auditorium was enlarged to about 75 by 100 feet. The lobby was also enlarged and the stage was rebuilt. The seating capacity was increased to about 1,000 and a new Moller 2/10 organ (Opus 2664), a new ventilation system, and new seats were installed.

Two years later, a store and dwelling in front of the theater were razed for another addition to the theater. The number of seats was increased to 1,400 this time. In October 1922 Frank Durkee engaged the Ladies' Broadway Symphony Orchestra to play at the theater. An additional story for the Durkee offices was added to the building at Wolfe and Eager Streets adjoining the Palace in 1926.

Durkee Enterprises operated the Palace {3} until the fall of 1928, when they traded it to the Gaertner organization for the Red Wing Theater. The Palace was remodeled again in the summer of 1930; a new cement floor replaced the former wooden one, new seats were installed, new draperies were hung, and new carpets were laid. The interior was repainted green, cream, and gold. The Palace {3} barely lasted into the 1950s, closing in May 1951.

The handsome building was still standing in the 1970s. The inside had been gutted and the floor leveled, but the exterior was still attractive. The marquee was long gone, but the unique triptych-like windows remained. It was used as a warehouse for awhile, but much of it had been demolished by 2004.

Palace {4} (see Empire)

Palace Moving Picture Parlor {1}, 334–336 North Howard Street, c. 1908–1910, John K. Stack (of conversion), 240. This theater was built for Joseph Archer, the proprietor of Archer's Laundry, in late 1908. It had a frontage of 23.7 feet and a depth of 78 feet with an ornamental stamped metal front with papier-mâché covering. In the spring of 1909, the Palace was advertising "moving pictures and light vaudeville"; tickets cost 5 cents. The Consolidated Amusement Company, which operated the Blue Mouse on Lexington Street, leased the theater from Archer in late 1909 and changed the name to North Pole. It lasted about another year. In 1910, plans were made to convert the theater into stores.

Palace Moving Picture Parlor {2} (see Palace {3})

Palace Museum, 418 East Baltimore Street, before 1890–c. 1898. As early as 1890 there was a dime museum on this site. By 1894 it was called the Grand Musee and Theatre. It featured a curio hall, where oddities such as Jo-Jo the Dog-Faced Boy were exhibited, and an auditorium, where minstrel shows were presented. It was renamed the Palace Grand Museum in 1895. By 1896 it was called the Palace Musee.

In September 1898, new owners remodeled the building and changed the name to Bijou. They added "a full new set of scenery, frescoed ceilings and beautiful electric effects." The Bijou opened on September 12, 1898, with an eclectic show that included Lumiere's Cinematograph, Rawson and Baisley, the D'Aljaris collection of Spanish torturing instruments, and Mlle. Corinne's sacred goat and baboon. The management presented silver spoons to ladies who attended the opening.

The Bijou did not last very long, disappearing from the amusement pages of the newspapers by November 1898. In 1909 the site was used as an entrance to the Wilson Theater.

Paradise {1}, 1727 Fleet Street, 1905?–1912, unknown, 125–200. This movie house was one of the earliest in Baltimore. It may have opened as early as 1905, but accurate data is lacking. Pearce and Scheck reportedly opened it, but sold out to J. George Hoffmeister after less than a year. The Paradise was located on the first floor of a three-story building. It was a true storefront nickelodeon; about the only remodeling needed to change the original store into a theater was the widening of the entrance and the addition of a ticket booth. Programs consisted of two or three films an evening with slide programs or vaudeville acts during intermissions. Mr. Bredelmeyer was the piano player, and Frank Sousa was the projectionist. At one time, the Paradise had behind-the-screen talkers, Agnes Herckey and Francis LaCoda. Margaret Tolly sold tickets and Mr. Agner collected them. Inducements, such as free china and lollipops, were sometimes used to bring in customers. Children under four were admitted free. The building was still standing as of the early 1970s.[286]

Paradise {2}, 1600 North Washington Street, 1909–1912, poss. Paul Emmart, 75. This movie house operated between early 1909 and 1912. It was on the first floor of a two-story corner building that was still standing as of 1973. Built for the Ades Brothers, this was the first theater operated by Frank Durkee when he was working in a bank during the day, but E. A. Cook probably operated it before him. According to one source, Durkee rented a small store and converted it into the theater. He added a screen, a projector and some pine chairs and did most of the jobs there himself.[287] According to a notice in the Real Estate Section of the Baltimore *Sun* on September 29, 1909, Durkee was planning to build a $4,000 brick motion picture theater with plans by Paul Emmart in the northeastern section of the city. The dimensions were to be 28 by 75 feet. It is possible that this was the Paradise {2}, although it is also possible that Durkee was already operating the Paradise and these were his plans to build a new theater on the same site.[288] Sometimes called the Paradise Amusement Company, this theater was referred to as "The Little Washington Theatre" by Judge Eugene O'Dunne in his speech at Durkee's testimonial dinner in April 1938.

Paradise {3}, 467 North Gay Street, 1906?–1914, unknown, 76 (200 as Graphic). This Paradise may have opened as early as 1906. It was a penny arcade before E. A. Cook, a wholesale grocer and early exhibitor, converted it to a movie house. The theater was located on the first floor of a two-story building.

Jack Whittle, who went on to manage numerous local theaters and become the secretary of the Maryland branch of the National Association of Theater Owners, started out in the movie business as an usher at this theater. He arrived at work around 10:00 A.M. and performed duties that included cleaning up the inside and hosing down the outside, cleaning the graphophone machine which provided music for the slide shows between films, relieving the cashier and projectionist for lunch and supper, and selling candy up and down the aisles. He was paid $3.00 a week.

Whittle remembered that Mr. Cook used to play the harp every day when the show opened and that he also painted the advertising posters. As a result of his painting activities, his goatee was usually stained with various colors. The Paradise {3} became the Elite in 1909 and probably the Graphic in 1913. The tall, narrow building that housed the Paradise was still standing as of late 2000.

Paradise Amusement Company. (see Aurora, Paradise {2}, and Paradise {3})

Paragon Picture Parlor (see: Luna Park)

Paramount, 6650 Belair Rd., 1946–1978, Hal A. Miller, 840–937 (later 745). The Paramount was opened by the Schwaber Circuit to invited guests on October 3, 1946, and to the public the following day. The lobby was small, but the auditorium was fairly large. The auditorium had a stenciled ceiling, and the proscenium was outlined in chrome strips with cascading chrome bands on the sidewalls. It cost about $25,000 to build. It was similar to several of Miller's other theaters, including the Colgate, Homewood, and Apex.[289] It closed on September 13, 1978, and has been converted into an attractive office building.

Paramount Hall, Ware Avenue, Towson, 1916–1919. The Church of the Immaculate Conception showed movies in this parish hall for three years before its priest, Father Sheridan, moved them to a former theater at 506 York Road. Movies were shown at the hall on Tuesday and Friday evenings. The weekly movies were canceled and replaced by monthly shows in January 1918.

Parisienne (see Pennington)

Park {1} (see Pleasant Hour)

Park {2} (see Plaza {1})

Parkside, 4703–4709 Harford Road, 1921–(1959), Arthur Towne,[290] c. 498.[291] Plans to build the Parkside were announced in the summer of 1921, and it opened on December 30 that year. *The Sun* described the new theater:

> The Parkside Theatre ... is now open.... It has just been completed at a cost of $65,000 and is owned and operated by Michael C. Engelmeyer who designed and built it. There are 498 seats in this playhouse which measures 70 feet across the front, 45 feet across the back and has a depth of 154 feet. It is a fireproof structure. The interior is decorated in tan and green. Music is furnished by a four-piece orchestra, and the pictures are thrown on the screen by two ... projection machines. Performances are given every night from 7.15 to 11 and matinees are given on Mondays, Wednesdays, Fridays, and Saturdays from 2.15 to 5.[292]

The front of the theater, which contained two stores, was stucco. It must have closed a few months after it opened. J. Flax leased the theater in the summer of 1922 and reopened it in late August showing three or four films a week. Success eluded the Parkside, and it was sold at auction in December 1922. For sale again in April 1923, the Parkside was rebuilt for $30,000 in 1930 by Robert Kanter's newly-formed Hamilton Amusement Company. Kanter installed sound equipment, repainted the interior in old rose, gold, and green with matching draperies and carpets, and opened it as the Cameo on October 6, 1930. In 1937, the Rome organization operated the Cameo. It was renovated and reopened by two GIs fresh from military service, Henry Sauber and Bernard Manekin, in May 1946. Fred Perry took over the theater in the fall of 1951, and in December 1951 Hilltop Producer, Don Swann, Jr., announced that he would reopen the Cameo as a fine arts theater.

Under Swann, the Cameo had an art gallery featuring works of local artists. He also published a four-page newsletter in 1951 and 1952. For its final six or seven years, the Cameo showed foreign films and classic American films, and on Christmas day 1953, it began showing German films. For a few years the Cameo had some success with foreign language films. Artistic Films, which also operated the Stanton in Washington and the Ambassador in Philadelphia, took over the Cameo in 1958 and planned to operate it as an art house. It became the New Cameo Art Theatre on October 28, 1958, with *Birth of a Nation* and closed soon thereafter.

Parkway, 5 West North Avenue, 1915–1977, Oliver B. Wight[293]; 1,100 (800 orchestra, 300 balcony), 942–987 (after 1926 remodeling; 546 orchestra, 382 balcony, 14 boxes),[294] 435 (after 1956 remodeling). Henry W. Webb's Northern Amusement Company built the Parkway for about $120,000 in 1915. It was modeled after two theaters, the West End (later Rialto) Theater near Leicester Square in London and the Strand Theater in New York.[295] According to one account, a friend of Mr. Webb visited the West End Theater while in England in 1913. He was so impressed with it that he got photographs of the theater and copies of the plans and sent them to Webb. Webb was equally impressed and promptly organized a company to build the Parkway.

The original permit to build the theater was issued on December 9, 1914. The work of razing the four buildings that occupied the site began in February 1915. A lot 24.3 by 90 feet on North Charles street was purchased by the Forest Park Company in February 1915 in what was believed to be a move to get an entrance for the theater on Charles Street, but none was ever built. A new permit was granted in April 1915.

The front of the theater was described as simple and dignified. It was done in the Italian Renaissance style of light gray terra cotta with a mixture of light and dark texture brick. Originally, the marquee was a simple iron canopy, but it was remodeled several times. Access to the auditorium was through a small, marble-lined lobby with marble stairs leading from either side to a large lounge and tea room on the mezzanine. The chandelier in the lobby was a replica of one in the palace at Versailles, while the mezzanine lounge contained fixtures modeled after those at Fontain Bleu. The interior was furnished in the Louis XIV style.

Motion Picture News provided the following description of the Parkway as it was planned:

> The exterior of the structure is of buff colored brick, while a huge canopy of bronze extends over the entire sidewalk and front of the structure. The interior decorations are very elaborate. The general color scheme for the walls is gray and old gold, while the hangings and draperies are of old rose velour. The seats will be of the old rose color to harmonize with the general decoration.
>
> ...[T]he lighting fixtures and general scheme carried throughout is of the style of the Louis XIV period. The lighting is extremely novel. All lights in the gallery are put in the risers of the steps so that the patrons ... can move up and down the steps with perfect safety yet the lights do not interfere with the picture.... The ceiling lights are of the sunburst variety and when the auditorium is illuminated it has a particularly brilliant effect.
>
> The theatre will seat eleven hundred persons.... There will be a rest and retiring room for the ladies, while on the mezzanine floor there will be a tea and refreshments room. Both the rest room and the tearoom will be in charge of matrons. There will also be embossed writing paper provided in the rest room. A soda fountain with marble chairs will be located on the first floor.
>
> On the stage arrangements have been made for fresh flowers which will be grown in artistic receptacles and the general view of the stage will show an old French street scene. In the main auditorium there will be eight rows of seats, behind which will be the loge seats, while the boxes will be entered from the first and second floors.
>
> All of the employees will be in uniform, the men to wear Eton coats of gray, trimmed with gold and velour.[296]

In later remodelings, buff was the predominant color. On each side of the stage there was a "Royal Box" for special occasions. The ceiling of the auditorium contained a large ornamental dome with a suspended sunburst. The stage dimensions were: height 47 feet, width 45 feet, and depth 11 feet. Early writers praised the "chasteness" of the Parkway's design. An article in *Motography* put it this way, "A distinct feature of this picture playhouse, both from an interior and exterior point of view, is its chasteness of design. There is nothing garish; nothing to smite the senses with a feeling of the bizarre. Everything is in good taste, down to the smallest detail."[297] The Parkway had to be in good taste, it catered to the residents of some of Baltimore's most exclusive residential sections. Originally, it had a 2/15 Moller organ (opus 1962). Additional music was provided by an 11-piece orchestra conducted at first by Sidney Seidenman.

The Parkway opened to a packed house on October 23, 1915, with *Zaza*, starring Pauline Frederick. The management promised the exclusive showing of Paramount pictures. The Parkway had its own cameraman who filmed local news items that were shown on the screen within 24 hours. In the same month it opened, the Parkway Theater Company assumed control of the Parkway from the Northern Amusement Company. Henry Webb was president of the new company. There were plans by architect Thomas Lamb in 1916 to enlarge the Parkway, but they were never carried out.[298]

The Parkway's first anniversary was a gala affair. The local correspondent for *Moving Picture World*, gave a detailed description.

> ...It opened with the showing of the "Beauty Spots of Baltimore," together with the playing of the national songs, then came a Keystone comedy, an orchestral recital, the "The Parkway Topical Review," then a harp solo, then the big D. W. Griffith feature "A Sister of Six," and during the short intermission an organ recital. On this day 1,500 roses were ordered ... and one was presented to every lady patron.... In addition ... a handsome souvenir in the form of a four-page booklet was presented with a cut of the interior of the house on the cover, a word of appreciation to its clientele and with the program for the week on the inside. The lobby, auditorium, tea room and stage were beautifully decorated with autumn leaves, chrysanthemums and palms and besides these flowers the tea room was a bower of roses on Monday night, when a special reception was held after the performance for sixty invited guests.... Many of Baltimore's most noted men and women attended, and the appearance of the lobby ... seemed to resemble something that had been read about the first nights at the Parisian operas. At the curbing outside 26 limousines, touring cars and runabouts were banked and the thought came to us that how could any one use the word "movie" in connection with such dignity and such art as this.[299]

The restrained elegance of the Parkway Theater (5 West North Avenue, 1915–1977, Oliver B. Wight) can be easily seen in this 1916 photograph. (Photograph courtesy of the Photography Collections, Albin O. Kuhn Library, University of Maryland, Baltimore County)

On January 5, 1917, after changes that required a year to perfect, George R. Webb's "singing pictures" were exhibited at the Parkway. There was some discussion in 1917 of building an addition to the rear of the Parkway that would face Charles Street and of remodeling the auditorium to increase seating capacity. Thomas Lamb completed plans for this work, but they were never implemented.

Under the management of Bernard Depkin, the Parkway was one of the classiest movie theaters in Baltimore. Depkin set up a "beautiful and luxuriously furnished" library with the latest newspapers and magazines on the mezzanine floor. Fresh cut flowers, changed daily, were kept in the center of a large mahogany library table. On matinee days, tea and wafers were served.

The Whitehurst organization acquired the Parkway in early 1920, and Loew's bought it along with the Century in 1926. As soon as Loew's acquired the theater they brought in their architect, John Eberson, to make plans for extensive remodeling. During the remodeling, which began on August 7, 1926, the upper boxes were removed and replaced with ornamental panels; a 2/8 Wurlitzer style "F" organ (opus 1421) replaced the Moller; the lobby was enlarged; new carpets, draperies, and lighting fixtures were installed; and the entire building was repainted. The remodeled Parkway and Century both reopened on October 4, 1926. The feature that day at the Parkway was *Aloma of the South Seas*. Movietone and Vitaphone sound systems were installed in 1928.

As a Loew's theater, the Parkway had a staff of 18 including a manager, cashier, doorman, chief usher, two day ushers and four night ushers, two porters, four projectionists, a publicity

The original, elaborate Baroque interior of the Parkway around 1916. (Photograph courtesy of the Photography Collections, Albin O. Kuhn Library, University of Maryland, Baltimore County)

man and a maintenance man. In the 1930s the average weekly payroll was $538. The theater was remodeled again in 1939 at a cost of $30,000. At that time a new marquee was added, the mezzanine was remodeled, and the interior was redecorated.

Morris Mechanic bought the theater in June 1952 and promptly closed it. Don Swann, Jr., leased it for his Hilltop Players in October 1953 and reopened it on November 23, 1953 to a full house. The opening show—John Newland in *The Moon Is Blue*—got excellent reviews. Despite the encouraging opening, Swann gave up after two seasons.

Jack Fruchtman acquired the Parkway in April 1955. A year later, the vacant theater was sold to the Schwaber organization which remodeled it into an art theater, the Five West. The original seats were replaced by 435 Airflo rocking chairs spaced four feet from back to back on the first floor and five feet four inches from back to back on the balcony. There were two lounges. Imported coffees and teas were served in the downstairs lounge; patrons could view works by local artists there. There were no candy machines and no popcorn was sold. The main interior colors were brown, beige, and green. The stage and proscenium draperies were gold; the carpeting was hunter green.

The Five West opened with Alec Guinness in *The Ladykillers* on May 24, 1956. After closing in 1974, and being closed for more than a year, the Five West reopened for a few months in late 1976 and early 1977, but closed again by January 1978. In 1983, the Left Bank Jazz Society was planning to acquire the theater and restore it, but that plan fell through. In 1985, the owners commissioned an architect to study the possibility of remodeling the theater as a retail store. Jacques Kelly made a plea for the restoration of the theater in his column of August 30, 1985, but it fell on deaf ears.

In the fall of 1989, three local Korean businessmen paid $300,000 for the theater. They leveled the floor and converted the building to retail space, but they preserved the ceiling and upstairs walls. The theater remained closed for many years, suffering damage from neglect and being trashed by vandals.

It was used as office space for several years in the 1990s before it was leased by Michael Johnson's Heritage Shadows of the Silver Screen African American Film Museum and Cinema in the summer of 1998. Johnson had plans to convert the theater into a museum with an exhibition hall on the first floor and a 200-seat theater in the balcony. Much of the original interior decoration, including most of the paintings on the sidewalls of the balcony, had, by this time, been destroyed. Johnson hoped to open in November 1998, but was unable to, and, by mid-1999, the project was dead. The following year another attempt was made to save the Parkway as a performing arts venue combined with a restaurant. The necessary finances did not materialize, and this project was abandoned too.

At this writing, Charles Dodson has new plans to restore and reopen the Parkway, which could be restored as a beautiful, comfortable, useful theater, and help to restore the blighted area around North and Charles. It will take money, dedication, imagination, and the support of the City.

Pastime {1} (see Easter's)

Pastime {2}, 2026–2038 Greenmount Avenue, 1909–1953, S. Gordon Hopkins, c. 290 (c. 500 after 1915 remodeling). H. Barry George and Edward N. O'Malley opened the Pastime {2}. It was operating as early as the spring of 1909 when R. Griffin sang illustrated songs there. The original building was a one-story structure with a frontage of 28 feet and a depth of 100 feet. In the fall of 1912, the Pastime Company bought two lots at this location on which to erect a motion picture theater. It is not clear whether this was an addition to the already-existing theater or a completely new structure. George Schacker transferred management of the theater to the Lord Calvert Theaters Company in early 1915, and they remodeled it later that year. Harry Rubenstein bought the Pastime in March 1916. The theater was completely rebuilt and enlarged in 1922. It reopened as the York on October 14, 1922 under the supervision of Harry Cluster.

It was described in the *Sun*, as follows:

> A new front of ornamental brick has been built and the lobby is inclosed. The box office is now located in the right side wall of the lobby, which has a terezza cement floor. The indirect lighting system is used and soft tones of gray and brown have been used for decorating the theater. The new gold fiber screen, a new motor generator and two new moving-picture projection machines have been installed.[300]

The York was one of many theaters, in the days before concession stands, that had a candy store next door. It became an African-American theater in December 1951, and lasted until about 1953.

Pastime {3} (see Oriole)

Pastime {4}, Sparrows Point. Art Solz was the new manager of a Pastime Theater in Sparrows Point in October 1936. The location of this theater has not been determined.

Patapsco, 601–645 Patapsco Avenue, 1944–1977, David Harrison, 800. Planning for this art deco theater began just before the outbreak of World War II. The permit was granted in October 1941. The plans for the Patapsco were prepared by local architect David Harrison for Louis Tunick in April 1942, and work began on the building, but, due to wartime shortages of building materials, the theater did not open until September 9, 1944.

The Patapsco was unusual in several respects. It was built at a time when building materials were extremely difficult to obtain, and the week it opened, Baltimore experienced one of its very rare earthquakes. The curved facade of the Patapsco was of beige face brick with a rectangular central element containing five narrow vertical rows of glass blocks. Six horizontal "speed lines" run from the central element following the curve of the facade around each corner.

The last operating movie theater in Brooklyn, the Patapsco was remodeled into offices for the Baltimore Department of Social Services in 1977.

Patterson {1} (see Oriole)

Patterson {2}, 3136 Eastern Avenue, 1910–1929. This Patterson opened in 1910. Harry Reddish bought it in the fall of 1918. It was closed for complete renovation and redecoration in the summer of 1919. Between 1920 and 1929 it was called the New Patterson. There was a dance hall on the second floor. One source remembered it as being quite large and attractive with a wide stage. The organ was in the front center of the auditorium with pipes on either side. The organist had to climb back under the stage to turn the organ on. This Patterson closed in 1929; it was razed the following year, and the Patterson {3} was built on its site.

Patterson {3}, 3136 Eastern Avenue, 1930–1995, John J. Zink, 908–1,200 (two 500-seat auditoriums after 1975 twinning). This Patterson Theater was built for the Durkee organization on the site of the Patterson {2}. It measures 85 by 150 feet. The brick exterior of the theater is very plain, one of the plainest that John Zink did, but the beautiful vertical sign helps to offset the simplicity of the facade. The interior color scheme was red, orange, and gold with matching draperies. Lighting was indirect and by crystal chandeliers. The chairs were a special low-backed style with spring-cushioned seats.

The Patterson {3} was operated by the Grand Theater Company, an affiliate of Durkee Enterprises, which also operated the Grand Theater a few blocks away on Conkling Street. It opened on September 26, 1930. In November 1958 a fire started by one of the ushers did considerable damage to the interior. The theater was twinned in the spring of 1975. In 1986, a refrigeration company employee was asphyxiated in the basement air-conditioning unit of the Patterson as he was repairing it. The theater continued in operation until the end of 1995 when it was showing discount films. It was the last theater operated by the Durkee Circuit.

Plans were announced by the Eastern Avenue Partnership to convert the theater into art studios, exhibition galleries, and a small auditorium. By 2000, an arts group called the Creative Alliance was actively working on transforming the theater. The building was gutted and the inside rebuilt. The new building contains a 200-seat theater, several art galleries, and artists' studios. The spectacular vertical sign, probably the last one in the state, was removed in 2002. It had deteriorated to such an extent that restoration was impossible, and plans were made to have the makers of the original sign construct an identical replacement. On May 16, 2003, the completed arts center was opened with a dinner and gala ball featuring local senator Barbara Mikulski.

Peabody (see Theatorium)

Pell Mell, 221 North Eutaw Street, 1915–1916, Charles Montgomery Anderson, c. 300. Joseph Blechman leased the four-story building at 221 North Eutaw in November 1914. The theater, built on the first floor, measuring 22 by 93 feet, cost about $2,500. A permit to alter the building was issued on December 10, 1914, construction began the same month, and it opened on February 6, 1915. Blechman operated the Pell Mell during its short life. A description appeared in an exhibitors' magazine:

> The Pell-Mell is an extremely handsome house. In addition to the white marble and crystal entrance, the interior of the auditorium is extremely decorative. The screen as well as the operating machinery is of the latest patterns. General Film service is used. The Pell-Mell is the first picture house to open on Eutaw Street, one of the busiest shopping streets in Baltimore and the center of the department store district.[301]

The front was embellished with large columns and mythical figures. The Pell Mell closed because of poor business; it was advertised for rent in January 1916. It reopened, under new management, in late February 1916, but did not last out the year.

Pennington, 4911–4913 Pennington Avenue, 1920–1962, Smith & May, c. 400. The Pennington served the Curtis Bay area for almost 40 years. Owner G. H. Panitz hired architects Smith & May to design the Pennington in the fall 1919. The building consisted of a two-story theater and several stores and measured 85 by 106 feet. The Pennington opened on May 27, 1920. It was operated by Thomas Goldberg in the early 1920s and by Robert Marhenke between 1955 and 1962. The auditorium, which ran parallel to Pennington Avenue, had a small stage. There was a small bowling alley on the second floor of the building.

In 1962, the name was changed to Parisienne. As the Parisienne Fine Arts Theatre it advertised "the finest imported & domestic adult motion pictures." It closed in the spring of 1962. The building was still standing in the early 1970s when it was occupied by a plumbing supply company. A serious fire destroyed parts of the theater, including the entrance and lobby in the winter of 1978. By 1997, little was left of the Pennington and it was unrecognizable as a theater.

Penny Arcade, 606 East Baltimore Street. Movies were apparently shown at this penny arcade around 1908.

368   II. Baltimore Area Theaters by Name

The last great vertical sign at the Patterson Theater (3136 Eastern Avenue, 1930–1995, John J. Zink) could not be salvaged, but a replica replaced it.

The Perring Plaza Cinema (8730 Satyr Hill Road, 1966–1992, William Riseman) was one of William Riseman's many theaters for General Cinemas.

Penny Arcade, 238 South Broadway. A movie house by this name operated for a short time around 1919.

People's (see Lubin's {1})

Perring Plaza Cinema, 8730 Satyr Hill Road, 1966–1992, William Riseman (Boston), 1,184 (two 550-seat theaters after twinning). This attractive cube-shaped theater was built, off by itself, south of the Perring Plaza Shopping Center by the General Cinema Corp. It opened on February 16, 1966, with Sophia Loren in the first-run film *Judith*. A large, comfortable theater with pushback seats that had extra wide spaces between the rows to provide 25 percent more legroom than older theaters, it had a large screen — 62 feet wide by 28 feet high. There was an art gallery in the small lobby.

The Perring Plaza was a very popular neighborhood theater and was reportedly one of the top grossing theaters in the country for Disney movies. It was horribly twinned in June 1973.[302] The manager was robbed and kidnapped in November 1966. General Cinemas closed the Perring Plaza Cinemas in January 1992, and it was razed to build a Home Depot store.

Perry Center (see Jewell)

Perry Hall Movies 5, 8740 Belair Road, Perry Hall, 1990–1999, Kelly Clayton & Mojzisek, c. 500 for five auditoriums. Bob Wienholt opened this discontinuous complex of miniature movie auditoriums in Perry Hall Square, a strip mall at the intersection of Belair and Ebenezer Roads, in November 1990. The theaters were built in what had been commercial spaces. The auditoriums were small, poorly insulated against crossover sound, and had flat floors. They resembled the tiny auditoriums of the 1970s more than the more attractive, well designed multiple theaters we expected in the last decade of the 20th century.

The most attractive thing about these theaters was the price of a ticket, which was usually $1 or so cheaper than other first-run theaters. For a while they did well, offering a less expensive alternative to larger first-run theaters. The opening of the huge Loew's megaplex at White Marsh in 1997 doomed the Perry Hall theaters. Facing this competition, auditoriums 4 and 5 closed in 1997, and the other three closed in 1999.

Pic (see Crown)

Pickwick {1}, 312 West Lexington Street, 1906–c. 1920, possibly Jacob F. Gerwig, 110–125. In May 1906, William B. Brown planned to convert the building at 312 West Lexington Street into a penny arcade, but it became a movie theater instead. There was a theater on the site by December 1906. The plans called for metal ceilings and an ornamental front.

In September 1908 it was operated by the

Baltimore Amusement Company and was called the Pickwick. The management of the Pickwick formed a stock company to provide behind-the-screen dialog for the movies or, as the ad said, "to talk our pictures." After the New Pickwick was built on Howard Street, this theater was usually called the Little Pickwick. The Pickwick {1} was located adjacent to the Lexington Theater. William and John Fait operated it in 1913. At that time, the theater was open from 10:00 A.M. to 11:00 P.M. and a show consisted of four reels that were changed daily. Irvin and Jacob Levine purchased the Pickwick {1} in December 1914. The Levine brothers operated the theater until it closed.

Bernard Depkin, Jr., who went on to manage the Stanley and other large Baltimore theaters, started his movie career as assistant to manager J. Howard Bennett at the Little Pickwick soon after it opened. In a 1927 interview, Depkin remembered one of the popular illustrated songs, "The Little Lost Child," that was sung at the Pickwick and said music was supplied by a player piano.

Pickwick {2} (see New Pickwick)

Pictorial, 3310–3312 East Baltimore Street, 1913–1951, unknown, 285 (340 in 1917). The Pictorial Amusement Company opened the Pictorial in 1913 despite a spirited protest by nearby residents. The two houses on the site were razed in May 1913, and the theater was built for about $8,000. In early 1917, the owner, C. E. Meddinger, whose tea business was growing, sold the theater to Harry Blechman. In June 1918, it was put up for sale. Elmer Hutchins and John L. McDonald acquired the theater in the spring of 1919 and reopened it. It was acquired by Arthur Price's Alhambra Theater Corporation in 1927 and remodeled at a cost of about $5,000. Charles Castoro purchased the theater and an adjacent dwelling for $16,000 in the summer of 1928. The name of the theater was changed to Aldine that same year.

Four years later the Vestry of St. Paul's Parish bought the theater at auction for $6,000. As the Aldine it enjoyed some local popularity and was one of the first movie houses in town to show revivals of old films. The theater closed in December 1951, and was then used as an office and a church. The marquee had been removed by 1973. By 2002 a new formstone front had been added to the building.

The Aldine was remembered because the rest room was in the front of the auditorium and below the screen. Every time someone opened the door, light would flood out.

Picture Garden (see Thirty-One)

Pikes, 1001 Reisterstown Road, Pikesville, 1938–1984, John Eyring, 650. The Pikes is a handsome art deco structure on the eastern edge of Pikesville. The Garman-Beck organization opened the Pikes on March 25, 1938, and operated it for many years. The theater was acquired by the JF circuit and became a first-run theater in the 1960s.

Extensive renovations were completed on the Pikes in May 1965. These included a new lobby and screen and new air-conditioning, sound, and projection systems. The sidewalk was made coral-colored to match the new decor. On March 1, 1968, police evacuated 300 people from the theater when an oil-burner blew up during a showing of *The Graduate*. The explosion was so powerful that the outside furnace room doors were blown 15 feet out into the parking lot, and a section of the brick wall was moved out about one inch. The Pikes suffered from occasional flooding during heavy thunderstorms. It closed in 1984 and was put up for sale the following summer.

The real saga of the Pikes Theater began after it had closed and lasted 13 years. This terrible tale shows what can happen when there is no strong local preservation organization with a clear goal for a theater. Numerous well-intentioned attempts to save the Pikes as a theater failed. By the spring of 1997 there were two proposals for the site. One would have renovated the theater as a state-of-the-art classy movie theater; the other called for turning it into a gourmet Italian market. In August, a county review panel decided on the Italian market proposal. Ground for the market was broken the following year along with any chance for the rebirth of the Pikes Theater. The conversion of the Pikes into a restaurant resulted in a beautiful building where the architects retained much of the original theater's structure and decoration. Unfortunately, the market was not successful and it had closed by 2004.

Pimlico, 5132 Park Heights Avenue, 1914–1952, John R. Forsythe (John F. Eyring, of 1935 alterations), 600 (later c. 1,000). Copenhagen-born Lauritz Garman, the founder of the Pimlico, settled down in Baltimore around 1909. Several years later his friend George Flint, a patent attorney from Philadelphia, suggested he open a

Early nickelodeons, such as the New Pickwick (113–115 North Howard Street, 1908–1985), probably Franz Koenig) shown here around 1910, often used Classical motifs for their facades. J. Howard Bennett is the man in the derby hat next to the ticket booth. (News American photograph courtesy of Special Collections, University of Maryland Libraries)

The front of the Pimlico (5132 Park Heights Avenue, 1914–1952, John R. Forsythe, John F. Eyring, of 1935 alterations), shown here in a 1938 night photograph, was at least the third front for the theater.

movie theater in Pimlico and agreed to provide the money. They formed the Suburban Amusement and Development Company (George Flint, president; Lauritz Garman, vice-president and manager; Morris H. Wolf, treasurer; Benjamin Beck, secretary and counselor) and purchased a lot in a small commercial strip on the south side of Park Heights Avenue, just east of Belvedere, in November 1913. They opened the Pimlico there on March 28, 1914. The contract was let in January 1914, and the theater was to be completed in 60 days. It was a one-story brick and stucco building, 30 by 100 feet; the estimated cost was $15,000. The original theater had a metal front decorated with numerous electric lights.

In 1922, architect Forsythe prepared plans for alterations to the theater. These alterations included the extension and enlargement of the building, which increased its seating capacity from about 600 to over 1,000. The enlarged Pimlico opened on October 19, 1922. It boasted a $6,000 2/11 Moller organ (opus 3449). In July 1928 the organist, Mrs. Kate Wynants, averted panic during a fire that broke out in the theater during a showing of *Two Arabian Knights*. While she kept playing the organ, all the patrons marched calmly out. Extensive alterations were made to the lobby and front in 1935. It closed in September 1952, and was converted to a Read's Drugstore soon afterward.

Pitt's Park (later Highland Park). Highland Park opened in May 1912 and featured moving pictures under the direction of Charles Williams.

Playhouse (see Homewood)

Plaza {1}, 1105–1107 North Broadway, 1910–1971, J. Edward Laferty (David Harrison of 1940s remodeling), 210 (later 350–415). David Newman purchased the clubhouse of the Eighth Ward's Pioneer Republican Club in March 1909. He spent between $3,000 and $5,000, adding a 19 by 68-foot addition and a new front, to convert it into the Plaza {1}.

The theater opened in mid–1910. It had a very elaborate ornamental metal front decorated with vari-colored electric lights. It was strictly a five-cent theater. Frank Durkee acquired it in early 1914 and remodeled it. It was sold to Hyman Miller, of Washington, in early February 1919, and it reopened on February 22, 1919. In 1921, the theater was acquired by Maryland Theaters, Inc., and the name was changed to Broadway Garden. It was remodeled again in 1921; the heavy stucco ornamentation was stripped and the arches were filled in with brick. The lobby was enclosed and a marquise was added to the front.[303] The seating capacity was increased by moving the screen further back. It was sold at auction in November 1922.

In January 1928 the Broadway Garden was the site of an early test of the Sunday Blue Laws in Baltimore. John G. Callan, president of the Liberty Defense League, leased the theater for a Sunday evening show. Before the show could start, police arrested Callan and two others. The charges were later dismissed.

In 1929, it became the Park {2}. It was remodeled in the mid–1940s. In the riots of April 1968, the Park {2} was damaged by rioters. William Kane reopened it as the Kane or New Kane in the summer of 1969, but it lasted only another year. It was sold to a church in December 1970 and, as of 2004, the building was still being used as a church.

Plaza {2} (see Colonnade)

Plaza {3} (see Arcadia)

Pleasant Hour, 2869 (later 2269) North Fulton Avenue, 1909–c. 1920, E. Selckmann, c. 250. The Pleasant Hour was built next to the old Parkwood Hotel by Theodore Doukas and George Konstant in mid–or late 1909. It measured 28 by 50 feet with an ornamental metal front and a foundation of heavy stone. In 1913, the shows consisted of two reels of pictures changed daily; admission was 5 cents. The name was changed to Park in 1915. It was entirely remodeled in the summer of 1916 and reopened on August 28. It closed for a while in 1919, and J. L. Rome reopened it for a short time on May 3, 1919.

Poplar, 611–613 Poplar Grove Street, c. 1913–1955, F. E. Beall (J. F. Dusman of Astor), c. 200 (later 500). The Poplar, or "Popular" as it was sometimes called, was probably the theater which the Poplar Amusement Company received a permit to build in July 1913. It was a one-story building measuring 86 by 26 feet. In December 1921, the owner, Martin A. Berger, was granted a permit to enlarge the Poplar.[304] Louis Tunick leased the Poplar until Robert Kanter bought it in 1926 for $30,000.

Kanter's Amusement Corporation of America erected a new $85,000 Spanish style brick theater, named the Astor, on the site of the Poplar. The interior colors were rose and gold. There was a small balcony with box seats for private parties; these could accommodate about 15 people. An innovation at the Astor — the first of its kind in Baltimore — was a nursery room where children could be left in the care of an attendant.

The Astor opened on November 14, 1927. It had a Kimball organ, and Kanter installed Vitaphone and Movietone sound systems in July 1929. In 1930, he had plans to expand the Astor into a 2,000-seat theater. He acquired some adjoining land, but was unable to complete the project. The Astor was completely redecorated in the summer of 1939. Rome Theaters leased the Astor from the early 1940s until around 1951.

Kanter closed the theater and put it up for sale in the fall of 1953. Abel Caplan, who operated the Westway, took over in April 1954 and reopened it as an African-American theater, which lasted until 1955. Converted into a supermarket, the front has been extensively remodeled.

Popular (see Poplar)

Preston (see Flaming Arrow)

Princess {1}, 1212–1216 East Baltimore Street, 1906–1911, D. Millard Callis (of 1906 conversion), c. 1,200. This building was used for religious services until it was remodeled into a theater in the fall of 1906. The Metropolitan Hall and Amusement Company purchased St. Wenceslas Bohemian Catholic Church in the spring of 1904 and announced plans to convert it into a theater. The original plans, by Charles E. Cassell & Son, called for a two-story theater seating 1,800 people. The front of this theater was to be cream-colored brick with terra-cotta trim and statuary. The owners opted to convert the original church instead of completely rebuilding it in late 1906. The building consisted of a theater with stage, private boxes, and gallery on the second floor with ticket booth, cloakrooms, toilets, a cafe, and a large rathskeller on the first floor.

The Baltimore Hebrew Theater opened there on April 30, 1907, with a performance of *Ben Shomrin* by the Baltimore Theater Opera Company. An estimated 1,000 people attended the opening. Light opera, vaudeville, melodramas, and movies were presented there. The theater was put up for auction in May 1908 and purchased by Samuel Siegal, who planned some improvements. The building inspector ordered the theater closed in the spring of 1910, when an inspection revealed that a large number of burned-out fuses had been bypassed with wire.

Edward A. Relkin, of New York, leased the theater in the summer of 1910. Relkin made plans for $5,000 in improvements and to use it for Jewish plays. William H. Daly, who operated Daly's Theater on Pennsylvania Avenue, took over the Princess in the spring of 1911. He reopened it with vaudeville and movies on March 27, 1911, but some of the people living around the theater complained about the theater being operated by an African American. Also used for burlesque in its final year, it closed in 1911.

The building was sold to the Jewish Educational Alliance for about $30,000 in the spring of 1912. Workmen began tearing it down in July 1912 in order to build the M. S. Levy Memorial School. During the demolition, some bones and an old skull were discovered under the theater.

Princess {2}, 1517–1521 East Eager Street; 1916–1927, 1929–1930; William Freitag, Jr. (?), c. 400 (later 600). William Freitag and George Kirschenhofer, a wagon builder, were granted a permit to remodel the buildings at 1517–1521 East Eager Street into a movie theater in 1916. The theater, which measured 42.6 by 70.3 feet and cost a reported $3,500, opened on March 8, 1916. Robert L. Byrum purchased it in early 1917 and made extensive improvements. A balcony was added in the fall of 1919. Byrum operated it until 1929.

The Klein Amusement Company reopened it as an African-American theater in August 1929. The theater advertised a "grand opening … with Talkies" on February 12, 1930. The Lin-

The Princess (1517–1521 East Eager Street, 1916–1927, 1929–1930, possibly William Freitag, Jr.) had been a church longer than it had been a movie theater when this photograph was taken around 1975.

coln's Birthday opening was to feature free souvenirs for everybody. While it is not certain that it did open in 1930, it appears likely that it did, but did not remain a movie theater very long after that. It became a church and was still standing with very few exterior changes in the 1970s. Since then, it appears to have been demolished.

Progress Garden, St. Helena, c. 1920–1921. The name Progress Garden suggests an open-air theater. It was probably associated with the Progress Building in St. Helena, near Dundalk. The records of the Exhibitors' League of Maryland show that H. H. Hupfeldt was operating the Progress Garden in St. Helena in the spring and summer of 1921.

Purity Moving Picture Parlor, 227–229 South Highland Avenue, 1914–1920. The Purity was open by November 1914. Harry F. Griggs, who was in the butter and eggs business, operated the theater for a while in 1914 and may have opened it. In 1916, the name was changed to Highland. Wallace High, who also ran the Fairmount, may have operated it as the Highland. There are no obvious traces of the theater remaining.

Queen, 666 West Lexington Street, 1909–1933, C. H. Callis, c. 300. The Queen was one of the earliest African-American movie houses in Baltimore. It was built in 1909 for an estimated $3,500, by Edward T. Bates and Harry Morstein, and operated by the Queen Amusement Company (Clinton Johnson, president; Charles Forman, treasurer; Clay Burrell, secretary). The Queen seemed to be integrated in its early years. When it opened, the Queen advertised as "a refined place for refined people entertaining as many white as colored." Shows ran from 7:00 to 11:00 weekdays and from 4:00 to 11:00 on Saturdays. In the summer of 1914 new management consisting of Harry S. Boone, John R. Jones, and George Douglass took over the Queen. They promised, "Superb pictures, polite vaudeville, sane, sober, and courteous treatment to all" and "Positively no annoyance by unintelligent speechmaking and otherwise."[305] The Queen also offered vaudeville shows. Jack Whittle acquired it and operated it for a while, before selling it back to Morstein. The theater reopened under the management of Charles W. Mosely in March 1916; the name was changed to the New Queen.

The *Afro-American* described the reopening.

The New Queen Theater ... will open on or about March 11 ... presenting all of the latest and best serial pictures as well as some of the best acts in vaudeville. The house has been thoroughly repaired and renovated and two big new machines installed. The management has arranged ... for the best pictures and also with the Dudley Circuit of Washington, and the United Circuit of New York, for the best acts. This little theater, though small, will fill a long-felt want in ... Baltimore, as there is no house in the city where one can go and see special feature pictures and high class vaudeville acts combined for such a small price of admission.[306]

The New Queen also featured female ushers to look after the ladies and children. In August 1921, four little barefooted children sang several songs including "Mammy" and "Indiana" in front of the Queen. They did such a good job that onlookers took up a collection for them to pay for tickets to the theater. The site where the Queen stood is now occupied by a factory.

Radio, 627–629 North Eden Street, 1938–1957, David Harrison, 668. The Radio was built in a five-story building that had been used as an icehouse by the American Ice Company. It was often called the "Icehouse Theater." The permit to reconstruct the building was granted to the Radio Amusement Company in November 1937, and the Radio opened during the last week of March 1938. The front was Vitrolite, and the lobby had a terrazzo floor. It was air-conditioned and had leather upholstered seats with spring cushions. Joseph Schwaber leased the theater in the 1940s, and Schwaber theaters handled the management and booking for several years. The name was changed to Star in 1944. The theater, along with much of the surrounding area, was razed to construct a housing project.

Raffle's Theater, 816 Curtis Avenue. Raffle's or Raphle's movie theater may have been the name of an airdome at Marek's Outdoor Garden on Curtis Avenue. The name seems to have been based on the first name of Rafael Shimanauskas, who operated the Curtis Theater. The projection booth was enclosed, but the seats were out in the open.

Rainbow {1}, 426 East Baltimore Street, 1909–1913, unknown, possibly 300. This Rainbow lasted about four years. There is some evidence that Louis T. Deetjan converted a store into this theater. Professor Brown, a music teacher, operated it for a while.

The Lenox (2115–2117 Pennsylvania Avenue, 1919–1925, 1936–1964, probably Sparklin and Childs, David Harrison of the 1936 rebuilding) started life as the Rainbow Theater in 1919. It became a garage around 1926 and a theater again in 1936.

Rainbow {2}, 2115–2117 Pennsylvania Avenue; 1919–1925, 1936–1964; probably Sparklin and Childs[307] (David Harrison of 1936 rebuilding), c. 406. The Rainbow {2} was a one-story, 32' by 154,' brick and stucco theater that cost between $12,000 and $25,000. The Rainbow opened in December 1919. The first newspaper ad, on December 12, indicated that the Rainbow had a live orchestra and presented vaudeville and movies. The owner was Benjamin Sachs; George Woodlen was the first manager. Isador L. Blaustein acquired the Rainbow in January 1920.

According to the *Afro-American* of August 17, 1923, the theater was in deep trouble. An unidentified Washington man had tried to operate it for five weeks, but had run off. It closed around 1925 and was used as a church. Later, it became a garage for ten years. The Hornstein organization rebuilt it and reopened it on December 25, 1936, as the Lenox. The name Lenox was the prize-winning suggestion of Calvin Johnson. Adam Goelz leased the Lenox in March 1964; it closed later that year. The building was standing as of 1973, when it was used as a church.

Claude Neon Signs, shown here in 1948, at the Radio Theater (627–629 North Eden Street, 1938–1957, David Harrison) put up the marquees of many Baltimore theaters.

Randallstown Plaza, 8730 Liberty Road, Randallstown, 1965–1986, unknown, 928. Broumas theaters opened this large theater on July 14, 1965, in the Liberty Plaza Shopping Center. It had six-channel stereo sound; nearly 1,000 living-room-comfort chairs;, an all-weather, triple-filtered heating and cooling system; and a huge screen. The original name of the theater was Plaza-Randallstown Theater. JF Theaters took over the theater in November 1974. The Randallstown Plaza Theater was twinned in 1980. It closed in 1986 and was demolished to build a grocery store.

Recher Theater (see Towson Theater)

Recreation Theater, 506–508 York Road, Towson, c. 1919–1922, unknown, possibly 500. John Mariner, of Norfolk, purchased a building on York Road in the fall of 1915. He leased a large room in the rear to an unidentified Baltimore man, who turned it into a movie theater. The Recreation Theater opened there on January 11, 1916. Its opening was heralded by a band driving around Towson in an automobile. The owners must have underestimated the theater's heating system because they had to install another stove the week after it opened. Shows started at 6:30 with matinees on Wednesdays and Saturdays. Admission for adults was 10 cents on Mondays, Wednesdays, and Saturdays and 5 cents on Tuesdays, Thursdays, and Fridays.

A fire in August 1916 forced the theater to close for two weeks. New owners acquired the theater in late October 1916, and changed the name to Le-Roi. The Le-Roi lasted until early 1917. It seems to have remained closed until October 1919, when the Rev. Philip H. Sheridan of the Catholic Church of the Immaculate Conception purchased it for about $10,000. Father Sheridan planned to show movies "of a high moral order" two nights a week. A professional piano player was hired in June 1920. Father Sheridan operated it as the Columbia as late as March 1922. Notices posted around the theater indicated that smoking was prohibited.

After the movie theater closed, the building became the Mayflower Laundry. Since 1949 it has been used as the Kent Lounge. A 1922 article complained about the lack of a movie theater in Towson and had this to say about Father Sheridan's activities:

> Not so long ago the pastor of the Immaculate [sic] Catholic Church obtained a machine

Entrance to the Recreation Theater (506–508 York Road, c. 1919–1922, unknown) in Towson. (Photograph courtesy of the Baltimore County Public Library Legacy Web)

and exhibited motion pictures in the parish house a few nights each week. The attendance caused the moving of the shows from the church to a hall on the York road. Then a religious question arose and shows were discontinued and the town was once more "movieless."[308]

Towson continued "movieless" until the Towson Theater opened in 1928.

Red Mill, 1510 West Lafayette Avenue, 1908–c. 1916, Paul Emmart (of 1909 addition), 250. The Red Mill, its neighbors the Crescent across Lafayette Avenue and the Lafayette down the street, formed a mini theater district in West Baltimore. The Red Mill Amusement Company leased the building at 1510 West Lafayette in 1908 and opened a small theater there. The following September, the company purchased that building and the adjacent building at 1512 West Lafayette Avenue. The two buildings were converted into a larger theater.

The theater closed for a short time when the Red Mill Amusement Company dissolved in late 1913. In the fall of 1914, Eva J. Wasky and Margaret C. Cahill bought the Red Mill and planned a number of renovations. New owners took over in January 1916, promising "new and extremely attractive" films. It had apparently been closed and reopened again after being redecorated, under the management of Miss B. P. Smallwood, by the fall of 1916. It closed permanently soon afterwards, and the Red Mill was converted into a church, which lasted until the building was razed in 1971.

Red Moon, 20 West Baltimore Street, 1908–1918, Paul Emmart (of conversion), c. 400. Charles E. Whitehurst leased this three-story building next to the B & O Railroad Building in October 1908 and opened the Red Moon there later that year. The conversion cost about $10,000. The facade consisted of a recessed entrance with a decorative freestanding box office; above the entrance were several large classical statues and, in the middle, a small electric sign made up of the words "Red" and "Moon" sandwiching a half-moon. The entrance and lobby were finished in English veined marble. By 1913, it was running three-reel programs that were changed daily. William Fait bought the Red Moon from Whitehurst for about $12,000 in April 1913, and ran it

Durkee Enterprises traded their Palace Theater to Gaertner Theaters for the Red Wing (2239–2241 East Monument Street, 1916–1960, Wilson Raymond Russell, Blanke & Zink, of 1917 remodeling; John R. Forsythe, of 1920–21 remodeling) in 1928.

for about six years. The Red Moon was one of the earliest movie houses in town to use behind-the-screen talkers. It was demolished many years ago.

Red Raven (see Palace {1})

Red Star, Frederick Avenue, c. 1913. Nothing more is known about this theater.

Red Wing, 2239–2241 East Monument Street, 1916–1960; Wilson Raymond Russell, Blanke & Zink (of 1917 remodeling), John R. Forsythe (of 1920–21 remodeling), c. 500. Augie Pahl operated an open-air theater on this site for several years before the Red Wing was built (see Monumental Open Air Theater). Plans for the Red Wing were begun in the spring of 1914 by the Cortes Amusement Company of J. M. Carlos and George A. Paulus, but George Gaertner bought them out, plans and all. He opened the Red Wing in early 1916. It was a one story, ornamental brick and terra cotta building, 35 by 150 feet. The cost was variously estimated at $8,500, $9,150, and $20,000.

In the spring of 1917, extensive improvements, including the installation of a gold fibre screen and a typhoon fan for ventilation, were made to the theater. It was remodeled and enlarged in January 1921. Adjacent property on Monument Street was razed to increase the seating capacity and a new front of ornamental red brick trimmed with granite was erected. It reopened on January 22, 1921. Among the improvements in the 1921 remodeling was the replacement of the open lobby with a terra cotta front. The organ in 1921 was a 2/9 Moller (opus 3086). In 1927, a balcony was added and the stage was enlarged. It reopened on August 25, 1927.

In the spring of 1928, Durkee Enterprises traded their Palace Theater to the Gaertners for the Red Wing. This was no doubt to ensure their supremacy on Monument Street by eliminating the competition; the Red Wing was only three blocks from Durkee's State Theater. The Red Wing reopened as a Durkee theater on September 1, 1928. The Red Wing was a "100 percent action house"; it played last runs or films that did not play at either the State or the Belnord. After it closed in the fall of 1960, the Red Wing was converted into a department store.

A fire heavily damaged the building in January 1975. One day, while the Red Wing was being closed down, a woman came in and asked if she could have the seat in which she had sat for 40 years. The manager had it removed and gave it to her. Theater employees said that she attended the first show of the day and that she often ate her lunch in that seat and fell asleep there.

Regan's Casino, 3327 Eastern Avenue, 1910–1913. "Joe" Regan, a colorful local character who operated the nearby Grand Hotel and Cafe, ran this storefront movie theater for a few years.[309] It was acquired by William F. Gabriel and Richard Miller who reopened it on April 8, 1912, and gave away more than 400 chocolate eggs to patrons. The building was still standing as of the early 1970s when it was used as a Montgomery Ward catalogue store.

Regent, 1619–1629 Pennsylvania Avenue, 1916–1974, Sparklin and Childs (George S. Childs of 1921 theater), 500 (2,250 for 1921 theater including 400 in the balcony, later 1,474). Louis Hornstein and his sons Simon C. and Isaac L. received a permit for this theater in November 1915. It was a one-story brick building, 33.7 by 140 feet, located at 1627–1629 Pennsylvania Avenue, and cost about $10,000. Several exhibitors, including the Pitts Amusement Company in 1912 and Diggs and Trimble in 1914, had planned a theater at this same location. The Regent opened on June 19, 1916, with "high-class photo plays and vaudeville" and, as an extra-added attraction, John W. Cooper "world-famous colored ventriloquist." The Regent was billed as the largest, coolest, and best ventilated house in the city. In 1917, Charles Mosely was the manager and Ike Thompson's orchestra provided the music. By 1920, Paul Harris was conducting the Regent's own orchestra.

In 1920, the Hornstein organization bought several adjoining lots in order to enlarge the Regent. The new building incorporated the entrance to the old theater. It cost about $50,000 and measured 83 by 170 feet. The seating capacity was more than quadrupled to 2,250. Originally there were box seats. The new Regent opened on January 31, 1921, with vaudeville and movies. Ike Thompson's 10-piece orchestra again provided the music with the help of a new organ.[310]

The *Afro-American* reviewer gave the new theater a good review.

> On last Monday evening, colored theatergoers of Baltimore who wended their way to the newly enlarged Regent Theater, witnessed ... an age long dream, namely: a theater building which would meet the requirements of a legitimate playhouse on whose stage it would be possible to have ... some of the very best theatrical talent among the race and above all, a legitimate playhouse where colored patrons would not be humiliated by the odious presence of... "Mister James Crow." The realization of this dream has been brought to pass by the Hornstein Amusement Corporation, and ... they deserve great credit for their achievement, and should receive the support of the theatregoing public of Baltimore. When the doors were thrown open ... a mighty host of playgoers flooded the spacious aisles led by a corps of ushers in the person of some of the most charming damsels of our city. As the vast audience took its seat in the soft glow of hundreds of vari-colored electric lights, wave after wave of audible admiration swept through the ... auditorium culminating in an outburst of applause when the curtain arose disclosing the deep outlines of a real stage. ... A ten-piece orchestra under the leadership of Mr. Isaiah Thompson dispensed music as only professional musicians can. ... The occasion was ... an epoch-making one in the history of theatricals among colored folks of Baltimore, and the Hornstein Amusement Corporation, and ... Mr. T. E. Owsley, are to be congratulated for the success of the auspicious event.[311]

The management installed a new $18,000 two-manual Robert Morton pipe organ in June 1922. The organist was Jerome Carrington. The Regent presented three-a-day vaudeville in the 1920s until talking pictures arrived. In February 1925, Isaac Hornstein canceled plans to show a series of two-reel films featuring heavyweight champion Jack Dempsey because of Dempsey's disparaging remarks about African-American contenders. Hornstein was quoted as saying, "I am playing to colored patrons, and I would certainly be insulting them should I play a picture

The entrance to the Regent Theater (1619–1629 Pennsylvania Avenue, 1916–1974, Sparklin and Childs) about 1929. (Photograph courtesy of Don Gunther)

featuring a man having the sentiment as expressed by Dempsey in the press. I stand unalterably by my original refusal, and you may say for me that this picture or no other that may in any way offend our patrons will ever be flashed from this screen."[312]

The Regent was the first African-American theater in Baltimore to get sound and show *The Jazz Singer*. Hornstein installed a Vitaphone sound system in the Regent in the spring of 1928. Large crowds attended the showing of *The Jazz Singer* in May 1928; they were not exceeded until 1949, when the Regent showed *Lost Boundaries*. In March 1949, the manager canceled a showing of the film *Belle Starr* at the Regent after complaints from the local NAACP chapter. He had earlier refused to show *Song of the South* and *Forever Amber*.

In April 1953, the Regent installed equipment for 3-D movies, and in 1964, it was leased to JF Theaters. When Louis Hornstein ran the Regent, a person could not get into the theater if he or she were not properly dressed. Mr. Hornstein would send that person home to put on more suitable clothes. The Regent closed in December 1974 and was demolished, without any protests, in 1980. Among the many famous entertainers who had appeared on the Regent's stage were Cab Calloway, who made his first Baltimore appearance there, Sissle and Blake, Lena Horne, Ethel Waters, and heavyweight boxing champion Jack Johnson.

Reisterstown Plaza, 6512 Reisterstown Rd., 1965–1989, Drew Eberson, 850 (later 687). The Trans-Lux Corp. opened this theater in Reisterstown Road Plaza on June 30, 1965 as a first-run theater. Trans-Lux executives, two Maryland congressmen, and state senator Thomas D'Alesandro attended the opening ceremonies. It cost about $350,000 to build. The *News-American* provided a description of the theater:

> The theater has an 850-seat capacity, a parking area for 4,000 cars, and is equipped with the latest in scientifically engineered projection equipment, including 35 mm, CinemaScope and 70 mm, and a 6-channel stereo sound system. ... White marble has been used on the exterior walls and this effect has been carried over into the theater lobby, creating a continuous design. The interior blends red, gold, and white tones in walls, theater curtain, and carpeting. A coffee lounge is included.[313]

In 1980, the Reisterstown Road Plaza was remodeled into twin theaters which reopened on December 12. It closed in 1989.

Reisterstown Road Plaza 5 Star Cinema, 6764 Reisterstown Road, 1985–2000, John Carroll Dunn, c. 1,200 (for five auditoriums ranging in size from 225 to 275). JF Theaters built this five-plex for $1.5 million in the former Hochschild-Kohn store at Reisterstown Road Plaza in 1985.

A newspaper described the new theater:

> The projectors, the ticket office and even the concession stand are computerized. 5 Star manager Leon Sprouse pushes a button in his office to get the number of tickets sold for each show on a screen.... The computer system also prints the tickets, so moviegoers can buy in advance.
>
> Upstairs, five huge computerized film projectors ... light up 31-foot screens. They can hold entire movies, so only one projector is needed per screen. If a movie is in two of the complex's ... theaters, the film can be threaded through both projectors.... These sights are denied to ordinary moviegoers, who must be content with the art deco facade and interior. A gold-mirrored ceiling reflects the pink-orange walls and the red patterned carpet (designed by computer so the pattern never repeats).[314]

Another source gave a somewhat different description, "The house ... has been designed with a number of rococo flourishes meant to recall the old movie palaces of the Twenties and Thirties. In a predominant burnt orange color with such flashy amenities as twinkle-lights in the interior of the halls for illumination...."[315]

The entrance to the theaters was located at the rear of the plaza; it featured twin towers and a large marquee. The Reisterstown Road Plaza 5 Star Cinema opened on May 22, 1985. For four years the five-plex operated in the same plaza as the earlier Reisterstown Road Plaza 2. JF closed the twin in 1989. In the same year, two new auditoriums were added to the five-plex. For several years before it closed in June 2000, the Reisterstown Road Plaza 5 Star Cinema was operated by Premier Cinemas.

Renard Moving Picture Parlor (see Avenue {1})

Rex {1} (see Columbia {1})

Rex {2}, 4617–4625 York Road, 1933–1974, J. F. Dusman, 482 (later 780). Louis Schecter's Homeland Amusement Company was granted a permit to build a theater at this location in June 1933. It cost an estimated $13,000. The Rex {2} opened on October 20, 1933. When it opened, the manager, Charles Warren, received messages of congratulations from Jimmie Durante, Mae West, and Eddie Cantor.

The Rex had a very plain brick front, a small lobby, and a very wide auditorium. Next to the projection booth there was a narrow balcony with a single row of seats. Several artists contributed to the decorations in the Rex. J. J. Libertini did some decorative panels. Donald Vincent Coale did the lobby murals, and Louis Rosenthal did a relief "The Dawn of Maryland Freedom." In 1934, local artist M. Paul Roche, was commissioned to paint a series of murals for the Rex.

In late 1960, a Washington-based group took over the Rex for a weekend showing of Greek films. For a short time in the early 1960s, Ronald Freedman's Baltimore Film Society had its home in the Rex {2} and showed such film classics as Renoir's *Rules of the Game*. While Freedman was operating the Rex in 1962, he used the theater as a venue to try to overthrow Maryland's motion picture censorship law. By the mid-1960s, it had become an X-rated film house. A new stone-effect front was added in 1964. The Rex lasted until 1974, and has since been converted into a church.

Rialto, 846–848 West North Avenue, 1916–1964, Sparklin and Childs, 499 (650 after reseating and 785 c. 1935). Ambrose S. Brown planned a movie theater at 842–844 West North Avenue in June 1915, but he was denied a permit.[316] Three months later an announcement was made that the lot at 846–848 West North Avenue had been purchased to erect a moving picture theater. The permit for the theater was granted on December 4, 1915.

The first name for the theater was Blue Bird, suggested by Miss Louise Twele, but the management decided that Rialto would be a better name. Rialto was chosen because the New York Rialto had recently opened, and it was considered to be "the most handsome and best equipped theater in the country." Despite opposition from a nearby church and a few residents, the Rialto opened on June 24, 1916. It was built for Meyer Fox's Linden Amusement Company at an estimated total cost for the theater and ground of $75,000.[317] The theater measured 40 × 150 feet.

The *Moving Picture World* printed a detailed description of the Rialto, one of the most complete descriptions we have of an early Baltimore movie theater. Portions of this are given below.

> The exterior design of the Rialto is a typical Italian Renaissance and while the impression it gives is of sturdiness, strength and lasting qualities, still this is blended with what is beautiful in this style of architecture. The structure is built of tapestry brick and terra cotta ... in the center of the building is ... a huge archway of paneled glass and from the center of this, just above the three pairs of mahogany, plate glass doors, hangs a bronze and glass marquee on the inner side of which are located 50 incandescent lights. At night this theater presents the appearance of a spark of radium on an indigo velvet background, blazing out light from the three 1,000 watt nitrogen lights, two of which are located on the corners of the marquee and the other placed just over the center portion of the cornice.... As one enters the lobby, the impression is that you have gained admission to the palace of some wealthy oriental prince. ... The space taken up by the lobby measures 21 by 26 feet, the floor of which is tile and marble worked in a clean cut design. The substantial pilasters and walls are built of Italian Pavanaza and Tavanel marble ... the cornices of which are decorated in gold. The walls run up into a kind of half dome or archway effect, and kahnstone [= Caenstone] trimmed with a gold design forms the basis of its construction. Directly from the center of this ceiling hangs an indirect dome light of kahnstone [sic] trimmed with gold which, when the suffused glows of its rays shoot up into the ceiling and return to mingle with the natural colors of the marble, cause a gorgeous mingling of exquisite hues.
>
> To the left, directly as you enter, a small bronze, grilled window of unique design faces the lobby. Behind this is located the ticket office, which measures 4 by 8 feet, from which tickets are dispensed from an automatic ticket seller and an attractive cashier. The entrance to the main auditorium is gained through a double mahogany, plate glass door while on each side a double door of the same size and material is used for the exits. ... All three of the plate glass doors are hung with figured, old rose, silk curtains.
>
> Old rose and ivory is the keynote for the color scheme of the interior decorations, while gold is used extensively for the trimming effects. Large panels of old rose silk damask, with a unique border molding of ivory and gold decorate the walls, while at the top there is mounted a cornice of ivory designed in the style of the old Italian Renaissance.[318]

Music was provided by a Kimball organ.[319] Permission to increase the seating capacity from 499 to 650 was granted in December 1919. The newly formed Rialto Theatre Company purchased the Rialto from the Linden Company in the fall of 1920 for about $150,000. In December 1920, the Rialto Theatre Company took title to two properties adjoining the theater and was

Much of the grace of the Rialto's (846–848 West North Avenue, 1916–1964, Sparklin and Childs) original facade has been marred by the huge modern marquee.

planning to spend $21,000 to enlarge the theater to a seating capacity of 1,600. Plans were drawn by Oliver B. Wight.

J. Louis Rome booked first-run films into the Rialto in the spring of 1923. The theater was remodeled in the summer of 1927. At that time, the box office was placed in the middle of the lobby. When the theater reopened on August 26, 1927, a new gimmick, serving coffee during intermission, was tried. The theater was equipped with Vitaphone and Movietone sound systems in the spring of 1929. The Rome organization used the Rialto as its headquarters for many years. A first-run policy was inaugurated at the Rialto when it reopened after renovation on April 6, 1960. The Rialto, along with its neighboring buildings, has been razed.

Rio (see Winona)

Ritchie Cinemas 1–2–3, 6637 Governor Ritchie Highway, Glen Burnie, 1973–1988, Peter D. Paul,

The Ritz (1607 North Washington Street, 1926–1963), located near Frank Durkee's original theater, with nearly 1,200 seats, was Gaertner's largest theater.

1,100 (for three auditoriums). Robert Rappaport opened the Ritchie Cinemas on October 24, 1973, in Governor Plaza Shopping Center. It was the first three-screen movie theater in Anne Arundel County. There was a 25-foot refreshment counter in the lobby.

In a 1979 survey of local movie theaters,[320] the Ritchie 1-2-3 was rated one of the worst: "They've installed Dolby sound ... but you'd never know it from the unintelligible noise emitted from the speakers. Also, the screen is so small and the theater so narrow it's like watching a TV through a tunnel." Many of the problems with the Ritchie 1-2-3 were no doubt due to the newness of the technology involved in the theater. The owner flew the architect to Ohio to show him what kind of a theater he wanted. Durkee Theaters closed the Ritchie in the spring of 1988. It was replaced by a Chuck E. Cheese restaurant.

Ritz, 1607 North Washington Street, 1926–1963, J. H. Stehl, 1,175. The Gaertner organization opened the Ritz on November 23, 1926. It cost an estimated $75,000-$100,000. The Ritz was a one-story theater of red brick with cream brick and sandstone trim. The interior was gray with side walls paneled in maroon with gold stencil work that resembled silk damask. There were two small balconies, one on each side of the projection booth. The Ritz was wired for sound in 1929. The interior was remodeled in Spanish atmospheric style in 1933.

The theater closed temporarily in May 1956, then reopened as an African-American theater in June. After the Ritz closed permanently in 1963, it was converted into a food market. By the 1990s the building was closed and boarded up. Many people in this section of town viewed the Ritz as the high-class movie theater in the neighborhood, rating it more highly than the Apollo and Harford.

River View Park, Point Breeze, 1898–1929; Simonson & Pietsch (1906 additions), Clarence E. Anderson (1909 movie theater), Otto G. Simonson (1909 rebuilding). The predecessor to River View Park opened just after the Civil War; it did not become River View until 1898, when a stock company acquired the 25-acre site. John Lowery had a small beer garden, known as Lowery's Place on Colgate Creek, around 1868; it was located on Point Breeze where Colgate Creek joins the Patapsco River.[321] Harry McGowan and his son, George, bought Lowery's place in the 1870s. They sold out to William Folk who operated it for several years. Then a man named Joseph Smith set up the first amusement devices there.

River View, called by many "The Coney Island of the South," opened on May 30, 1898. It featured a 2,000-seat casino, on the waterfront, where vaudeville shows were given. There were also a scenic railway running through the park, a hotel and restaurant, a band stand, carousel, shooting gallery, facilities for boating and bathing, and "dazzling electrical displays." River View was served by Consolidated Railway streetcars from any part of the city for 5 cents after 1:00 P.M. Admission to the park was free, but it cost 25 cents for admission to the Casino.

One of the most popular attractions at the park in its early years was the Italian Royal Artillery Band, which always ended the evening with the "Anvil Chorus." One of the musicians hammered on a real anvil during that number. The Fourth of July fireworks display was another popular attraction.

The park was acquired in 1899 by local impresario James L. Kernan, who made it famous.[322] He planned a hotel, transformed the Casino into a "graphophone building," and erected a new and larger bandstand. Kernan also increased the capacity of the park's electric plant and lit the entire place with thousands of incandescent bulbs. River View Park had movie exhibitions as early as June 1899 when films of the Jeffries-Fitzsimmons prizefight were exhibited.

Long-time projectionist Sam Isaacson said that movies presented by the American Mutoscope and Biograph Company were shown at the River View Casino around the turn of the century. Vitagraph, Biograph, and Cinematograph exhibitions continued during the summers of 1900, 1901, and 1902. Isaacson also described the Metropolitan Railway, where George "Bunny" Gregory was the projectionist. This was a railroad coach rigged up to sway from side to side as if it were moving along a real track. As the coach rocked, movies of scenery taken from a moving train were projected outside the windows so that the audience inside felt that they were taking a real train ride.[323] An eyewitness described this ride in a 1911 article, "The spectators sit in a railway coach, with the picture screen arranged at the upper end. When the show is about to begin the trainmen slam the doors, whistles blow, the wheels turn rapidly, and you're off. A stiff breeze blows in the windows during the show and the car ... seems to swerve as on horseshoe curves. The audience leaves the car bruised and shaken and ill, but gasping to each other, 'Wasn't it grand!'"[324]

Improvements, including an elaborate portico at the artificial lake, were made to the park in 1906. For the 1909 season, Clarence E. Anderson prepared plans for a 500-seat Moorish style moving picture theater. The advertisements said, "Don't fail to visit the new park theater. Hear 'Storey' the great saxophone artist, and the latest moving pictures and illustrated songs."

The park was nearly destroyed by a spectacular fire in October 1909. Among the structures destroyed were the Casino and the Bandstand. Otto G. Simonson was commissioned to design buildings to replace those damaged or destroyed. The new oriental-style bandstand — illuminated with 2,000 incandescent light bulbs — was built over the water to give customers more room and make it cooler for the musicians. Repairs were made quickly, and the park reopened as usual in early May 1910. River View was one of the most popular summer parks in the Baltimore area. In 1882, Mr. McGowan boasted that more than a thousand people had come to his Point Breeze park. By 1924, River View had been visited by more than a million people. It still had a loyal following, but by that summer it was a little tattered around the edges.

A reporter wrote about the park in July, "River View, it will be remembered by those of us who used to answer the wild cry of 'Who wants the handsome waiter?' is the last of the old-time parks — and the best. It is the only amusement park within a Sabbath day's journey on the water and although there is some slight tinge of oil and scum it cannot kill enjoyment.... At night, when all the lights are lit and the ships outside are each picked off by pin pricks of light one can almost believe he is back in the old sweet days when a scuttle of suds and a cooling breeze made even the hottest summer night bearable — aye enjoyable."[325]

River View lasted until 1928, when the United Railways and Electric Company sold it to the Western Electric Company. Much of the original shoreline was filled in and a new plant was built on the site. One relic of River View that lasted long after the park's razing was a little steam engine that was parked in front of an electrical supply store on Pratt Street near Gay for many years. That locomotive had pulled a children's train at River View. In the summer of 1961, workmen doing excavations for an addition to the Western Electric plant discovered the remains of River View's Olympic pool. When it was filled in, the last relic of the old park disappeared.

Rivoli, 418–420 East Baltimore Street, 1921–1953, Ewald G. Blanke, c. 1,900.[326] Architect Blanke designed the Rivoli, incorporating the entrance and lobby of the Wilson Theater as a long lobby for the Rivoli. Wilson Theater interests purchased the Church of the Messiah[327] at Gay and Fayette streets in January 1920 for an estimated $195,000; the auditorium of the Rivoli was built on the site of the church. It appears that at least part of the church was used in the construction of the Rivoli's auditorium.

Before it opened, the Rivoli was often referred to as "The New Wilson," suggesting that the name Rivoli was selected fairly late in its construction. The Rivoli opened on January 3, 1921, with a special, by invitation only, performance of *Passion* starring Pola Negri. The public opening took place the following day with a show that included a film *Go and Get It*, a Harold Lloyd comedy, and a newsreel. The Rivoli had two entrances, one on Baltimore Street, which was the entrance to the former Wilson Theater, and one on Fayette Street facing City Hall Plaza.

White and gold were the predominant colors in the auditorium with draperies of old velour and gold at the boxes. The long lobby and foyer were done in mulberry with ivory and gold panels. The sub-foyer was painted white and gold to match the auditorium. The act curtain was of old velour and gold with a Grecian motif.

The ventilation system, by the Monsoon Company of New York, received great acclaim. It could supply 2,300,000 cubic feet of fresh air every hour. To air-condition the theater, large blocks of ice were delivered by the American Ice Company, and the air was directed over them before being pumped into the auditorium. The Baltimore Gas and Electric Company reported that the Rivoli was the largest theater in the country to be heated entirely by artificial gas.

The Rivoli had a state-of-the-art projection booth. It was supplied with the following equipment in October 1921[328]: Three Powers 6B projectors, Peerless arc controllers, speed and footage film indicators, a shadow box, automatic fire shutters, three liquid fire extinguishers, three powder fire extinguishers, a motorized rewinder, a spotlight, film cabinet, and an optical system condenser. Conrad F. Hagert was chief of the projection room staff; he was assisted by Carroll H. Bayne and Sidney Marks.

For many years, Felice Iula conducted the Rivoli's famous 25–30-piece orchestra.[329] Victor Herbert was the guest conductor for a few days in 1923. A typical show at the Rivoli in the spring of 1921 consisted of six parts: (1) Overture — *Poet and Peasant*, Rivoli Symphony Orchestra; (2) Rivoli News of the World; (3) Special — Marye Stuart Edwards, coloratura soprano; (4) *The Kiss* — L. Arditi; (5) Feature — *Nineteen and Phyllis*, Charles Ray; and (6) Comedy — *Now or Never*, Harold Lloyd. The Rivoli made arrangements to play First National pictures just before it opened, and, for several years, it had its pick of that company's output. Seventeen different streetcar lines ran within three blocks of the Rivoli, making it easy for patrons from other parts of the city to attend. A new $50,000 three-manual Kimball orchestral organ was installed in July 1922.

The Rivoli closed for nearly two months in the summer of 1923 while the interior was redecorated in a new color scheme of mulberry, gray, and gold.

The stage was extensively altered during the summer of 1925, and the theater was redecorated in July 1927 at a cost of about $50,000. New crystal lighting fixtures were installed and wall panels were refinished in green techstone with gray and gold trim. The box alcoves were redecorated in green and gold with cyclorama backgrounds and drapings to match. In the same month, Emile S. Odend'hal, formerly at the Auditorium, replaced Iula as conductor. Business fell off considerably during the 1927 season, and the Rivoli cut back on much of its newspaper advertising. This marked the beginning of the theater's 26-year decline.

The Rivoli installed Vitaphone and Movietone sound systems in the summer of 1928. Occasionally during the first few years of sound films, patrons could hear radio calls from Baltimore City police cars over the Rivoli's sound system. The Rivoli was the first theater in town, in February 1931, to install headphones on some of the seats for hearing-impaired patrons.

In the spring of 1932, William Martien & Company bought the Rivoli at auction for $90,000. It continued to show first-run films until 1934. Veteran exhibitor Joe Fields bought

Nothing of the earlier Wilson Theater remains in the entrance to the Rivoli (418–420 East Baltimore Street, 1921–1953, Ewald G. Blanke). Note the entrances to the ancient Amusea and Comedy theaters to the left of the Rivoli in this 1933 photograph.

it in 1936, temporarily restoring its popularity, but, probably as a result of the movement of the entertainment center of the city northwest to Lexington Street, the Rivoli continued to decline. It was offered to the city for $575,000 in the spring of 1944, but the city declined.

Harry C. Racoosin, Barney Krucoff and Harry S. Brown purchased the Rivoli from Fields in February 1946. By the spring of 1948, it had been reduced to playing films 21 days after first-run. It was sold in June 1952 for $243,000, and closed the following year. It was torn down to build a parking garage.

Guy Wonders was the first manager of the Rivoli; he was replaced by Henry Matcher who managed it until his strange disappearance in 1948. In the mid-1920s, the orchestra at the Rivoli was considered one of the best in Baltimore. From the time it opened until Loew's took over the Century in 1926 and Stanley-Crandall built the Stanley in 1927, the Rivoli was considered the premier movie house in town.

Rodey's Theater (see Amusea {4})

Roosevelt, 512–514 West Biddle Street, 1921–1969, Stanislaus Russell, 500 (given as 940 in 1966). The Roosevelt was built for an estimated $25,000 in a three-story building that had earlier been an I.O.O.F. Hall and a firehouse. It opened on June 18, 1921. Jacob Friedlander operated the Roosevelt with Mrs. Isaiah Thompson as organist and George Douglass as projectionist. The interior featured lighting by means of large, disk-like, vari-colored globes set in the ceiling. There was a poolroom on the second floor. The theater was sold in May 1924 because of declining patronage.

The interior of the Rivoli around 1921. Note the wicker chairs on the sides of the balcony.

Former owner Friedlander purchased the theater and took over operations again. In the spring of 1925, the *Afro-American* reported that it was "a pleasure to see the Roosevelt prospering," that "Mr. Friedlander, white, the proprietor and manager, has a city-wide reputation for square dealing," and that the Roosevelt was "a good place to visit." The theater was acquired by Morris Flaks, who also operated the Lincoln Theater, in 1925; he renovated it and reopened it in November 1925 with movies and vaudeville. It was also called the Deluxe Roosevelt. The Roosevelt was seriously damaged by a fire in November 1938, but Flax was able to reopen it. Acquired by the city in 1969, it was later demolished for a redevelopment project.

Roslyn (see Lehmann Hall)

Rotunda Cinemas 1, 2, 711 West 40th Street, 1974–2001, 2003–present, Jack Lawrence, 486 (250 and 236). JF Theaters opened this popular twin theater in Rotunda Mall in the Maryland Casualty Building on September 13, 1974. The theaters were located on the mall level with a single common box office. Inside was a small, plain concession counter illuminated by stage lighting from above. One wall of the lobby was decorated with movie posters. The Rotunda, according to Jack Fruchtman, was a natural in terms of location. It had plenty of free parking and could draw on different populations of moviegoers from University Parkway, Bolton Hill, Charles Village, Johns Hopkins, and Hampden.

The popularity of the Rotunda did not help it survive Loew's bankruptcy. Loew's closed the Rotunda at the end of March 2001. Tom Kiefaber, who operated the Senator Theater, leased the Rotunda in the summer of 2001. He completely renovated the theater, reseated it with wider aisles and about 150 seats per theater and replaced the projectors and screens. The Rotunda reopened quietly as the "Rotunda Cinematheque" in late December 2002.

Roxy (see Fayette)

Roy (see Crown)

Royal {1}, 1727 North Monroe Street, 1911–1915, unknown, c. 100. Aursler and Foss operated this little movie house. In 1913 it offered two reel shows, which changed daily. The building may have been converted into a funeral parlor.

Royal {2}, 1940–1942 West Pratt Street, 1911–1927, F. E. Beall, 250. The Royal was opened by Frank Hornig, who also ran the nearby Horn Theater. The brick and stone structure, which measured 30 by 80 feet and had fancy metal trimming, cost about $8,000. The Royal featured movies with some vaudeville. In October 1925, when a fire broke out in the theater, the piano player — Miss Ruth Davis — averted panic by staying at her piano and playing a lively march to which the patrons exited. Leonard Davidson, the operator, was severely burned and only escaped from the booth by climbing through a window onto the marquee and jumping to the sidewalk. An usher, Morris Jaffe, tried to put out the fire, but he was also burned badly. The building was standing in the early 1970s. It has been, in turn, a dry-goods store, a bottling company, a bar, and a church.

Royal {3}, 308 South Broadway, 1912–1917, Callis & Callis (of conversion). This theater was announced in July 1912, when it was described as a new moving picture theater for Realtor H. J. Skrentney. Plans called for a 28 × 109 foot building of pressed brick with a limestone front and stone trim. The cost was estimated at $7,000. In early 1917, Skrentney sold the theater to Joe B. Fields, who renamed it Fields Photo Play Theatre and reopened it on January 8. He planned to have talking pictures there. The singer at Field's theater was Carl Hazelhoff, billed as "the second Al Jolson." It was still called "motion picture theater property" when it was sold by Benjamin Cluster to Nathan Goldberg in November 1921.

Royal {4} (see Douglass)

*****Royal {5}** John Zink drew plans in 1928 for a $100,000, 1,100-seat movie theater in Catonsville for the Catonsville Theatre Corporation. Frank Paul Bland, of Catonsville, won the first prize of $75 for suggesting the name Royal for the theater. The Royal was pre-empted by the Alpha in March 1928.

Royal Amusement Company (see Lincoln)

Royal Moving Picture Parlor, 1543 Orleans Street, c. 1908–1909. This movie house, on the southwest corner of Orleans and Bond streets, lasted about a year. The name seems to have been changed to Victor in 1909.

Ruby {1} (see Eureka Amusement Company {1})

Ruby {2} (see Bunny)

Russell and Causby (see Pastime {1})

Schanze, 2426 Pennsylvania Avenue, 1912–1949, Paul Emmart, 495 (430 as the Morgan in 1947). The Schanze (pronounced shawn-see or shan-see) was built as a moving picture and vaudeville house by local pharmacist Dr. Frederick W. Schanze, who had a drugstore next to the theater. He purchased the livery stable that had been a terminus for the horsecar line that ran out to Pimlico and Pikesville in late 1911 and opened the $26,000 theater the following year. The building was constructed of reinforced concrete with granite and marble trim. It measured 33.8 × 140 feet. The interior was finished in hardwood and oak. There was a dance hall on the second floor.

The opening of Schanze's was described in the *Sun*.

> Schanze's Theater, Northwest Baltimore's newest amusement place ... was opened last night. A reception was held by the proprietor, F. W. Schanze, and a free concert was given by Emerick's Orchestra. A large crowd attended ... the playhouse and the large hall over it. The theater has a ... large stage adaptable to vaudeville productions. The daily performance will consist of two acts of vaudeville and three picture films.... In recognition of Mr. Schanze's spirit in erecting the building, the officers of the American Exchange and Savings Bank presented him with a silver loving cup.[330]

In 1913, Schanze's and the West End Theater were sharing the same vaudeville acts. Harry Reddish leased the Schanze in the spring of 1920. It was redecorated in March 1930 at a cost of $3,000. The new decor featured a color scheme of rose, cream, and gold with floral designs; new carpets and draperies were also installed. In

1938, the theater was leased by the Rome circuit; it was remodeled and renovated and reopened as the Morgan on November 5, 1938.

In March 1940 it reopened as the Uptown, under the management of the Irving Amusement Company. The Uptown announced that it would hire an African-American staff and cater to African-American patrons. In January 1941, S. Ashkenazi began to show Yiddish movies and foreign films there and changed the name to the Cinema Theatre. The first Yiddish film was *A Letter to Mother*, shown on January 12. The second-floor hall was known as Tel Aviv Hall around this time.

Barry Goldman remodeled the theater in the spring of 1942, adding a new facade of Vitrolite and an illuminated marquee. He reopened it on April 24 with a double feature. Goldman purchased the theater from Dr. Schanze's widow in 1944, then sold it to Samuel Shoubin in June 1946. Shoubin reopened it as an African-American theater, using the name Morgan again, on July 21, 1946. He advertised it as the "One and Only Scientifically Air-Conditioned Ultra-Modern Theatre in N. W. Baltimore."[331] It closed in the summer of 1949, but Shoubin reopened it again on September 1 as an African-American art house.[332] The new theater reopened to an enthusiastic audience with *Quartet*.

A serious fire in November 1949 ended its movie career. In the spring of 1950, Shoubin remodeled the building into an amusement arcade, "Porkie House Sportland," with pinball machines and a soda fountain on the first floor. The upstairs hall was called Morgan Hall and was rented out for parties. The owners of the adjacent Wilson's Restaurant purchased the building in 1955 and used it as expansion space for their popular restaurant.

In 1972, the Arch Social Club bought both

The beautiful damsels still adorned the facade of Schanze's Theater (2426 Pennsylvania Avenue, 1912–1949, Paul Emmart) many years after it closed.

buildings. After the restaurant was demolished, the club renovated the theater as a banquet hall and clubroom. The first floor facade has been remodeled drastically, but the two beautiful statues of muses still adorn the upper portion.[333]

Security Square Cinema, 1717 North Rolling Road, 1972–1987, 1987–present, unknown, unknown (between 176 and 428 each for the eight 1987 theaters). The first theater at Security Square Mall was a two-screen complex located inside the mall. The twin theaters opened on December 24, 1972. In 1979 two more auditoriums were added. The interior four-plex lasted until 1987, when General Cinema built a freestanding, eight-screen complex adjacent to the mall. The space where the original theaters had been became a food court.

The carpeted lobby of the 1987 theaters contained a large concession area. The aisles in the auditoriums were lined with Tivoli floor lighting. The pushback seats were upholstered in red and blue. The new theaters also had wall-to-wall screens, 70 mm projection, Dolby sound systems, and a computerized box office. They opened with great festivities on November 20, 1987. Miss Maryland was in attendance for the ribbon-cutting ceremonies, and door prizes were given to the first 500 patrons.

Senator, 5904–5906 York Road, 1939–present, John J. Zink, 1,024 (later 987, 934). The Art Deco Senator was built for Durkee Enterprises' Govans Corporation by E. Eyring & Sons. The building permit was granted in December 1938, and excavation began in May 1939. The theater cost an estimated $250,000. It was called "Govans" on the original plans. The theater consists of two main elements, a facade-lobby and an auditorium. The auditorium is at a slight angle to the facade-lobby portion. The facade is dominated by a limestone tower containing glass bricks and a huge curved marquee in its center topped by the name "Senator" in neon-traced letters. The facade of the theater below the marquee is faced with black structural glass with horizontal metal strips. At night, fluorescent lights behind the glass bricks provide a multi-colored effect.

On either side of the centrally located box office, glass doors lead into a large two-story, circular lobby. The lobby has a terrazzo floor with lower walls of antique walnut—the paneling was hand selected and steam-heated to fit the curvature of the lobby—and upper walls decorated with murals painted by Baltimore artist M. Paul Roche in shades of ivory on an aquamarine field. The murals depict the progress of visual entertainment.

Glass cases set in the walls of the lobby originally held aquariums containing tropical fish, but now they serve as display cases for movie memorabilia. The walls of the auditorium were originally covered with Dubonnet and tan damask with a maroon plaster dado trimmed in shades of tan. The stage curtains were gold with silver appliqué work. In the center of the ceiling at the front of the auditorium is a sunburst lighting fixture of light ivory hard-plaster; the sides and rear of the ceiling are richly decorated in a mural design in ivory and rose on a deep blue field. On one side of the projection booth there was a soundproof party room and on the other side there was a soundproof nursery.

When the Senator was built, the area where it was located was not considered to be capable of supporting a large movie theater. Frank Durkee was quoted as saying, "Sure, it is a beautiful place, but I'll never live to see it make any money."[334] The Senator opened on October 5, 1939, with *Stanley and Livingston*, starring Spencer Tracy. The Senator started out as a neighborhood theater, but in the early 1960s it became the first neighborhood house in town to show first-run films. In 1963, United Artists chose the Senator as its first-run theater in Baltimore. Its premier first-run film was *Irma la Douce*.

In 1984 readers of the *City Paper* selected the Senator as the best movie theater in town. In 1985, despite some neighborhood concern, the Durkee organization received zoning approval to build a 230-seat house, designed by Mitchell Abramowitz, next to the Senator. This theater was never built. In 1988, as the Durkee theater empire was selling off most of its theaters, Tom Kiefaber, a grandson of Frank Durkee, put together a company called Limelight, Inc., with several friends. They bought the Senator with a $2 million financing package from Equitable Bank.[335]

Early in 1989, the Senator held its first local premiere—*The Accidental Tourist*—hosted by its new owners. Kiefaber's enlightened and affectionate guidance has made the Senator one of the most important film venues in the state and the scene of countless premieres. The sidewalk in front of the theater bears the handprints and autographs of directors, actors and actresses who have attended these premieres. Kiefaber has continued to welcome audiences every evening and remind them to behave themselves.

In September 1989, the Senator celebrated

Top: Very little has changed at the Senator Theater (5904–5906 York Road, 1939–present, John J. Zink) since it opened in 1939. *Bottom:* The unique circular art-deco lobby of the Senator now houses movie memorabilia instead of previews of coming attractions.

its 50th anniversary with a showing of *The Wizard of Oz*. A readers' poll in *USA Today* in 1991 named the Senator one of the top four movie houses in the country. A survey rating U.S. movie theaters for presentation and sound quality by the THX Theater Alignment Program ranked the Senator number 1 along with a California theater.[336] Kiefaber has been planning to add extra screens to the theater for a number of years, a large auditorium seating about 450 named the Ambassador, and a smaller one seating about 175 named the Blue Mouse. Fortunately these screens will be built in spaces adjacent to the original auditorium. Despite plans for additional auditoriums, as of 2004 none have been built. The Senator had major financial problems in the summer of 2000, but was able to solve them. Against overwhelming odds the Senator is still operating, nearly in its original condition, as a first-run house, a bright jewel in Baltimore's movie theater crown.

Seven East (see Aurora)

Shore Drive-In, Mountain Road west of Tick Neck Road, Pasadena, 1954–1978, unknown, 750 cars. The Shore Drive-In was located on the southwest side of Mountain Road (Route 177) in the Armiger Neighborhood. The central building that housed the projection booth, rest rooms, and concession area was designed to resemble a ranch house. The Shore Drive-In was opened by Ritz Enterprises on August 12, 1954. The first film on what was advertised as "the largest screen in the world"— 115 feet wide and 70 feet high — was the Cinemascope feature *Three Coins in the Fountain*. The site of the drive-in is now a subdivision.

Sideman Moving Picture Parlor (see Nowosci)

Snowden Square 14, 9161 Commerce Center Drive, Columbia, 1997–present, Grieves Worrall Wright & O'Hatnick, 2,948. United Artists opened the Snowden Square 14 on December 19, 1997. This $5 million megaplex is located behind the Snowden Square Shopping Center on the eastern edge of Columbia. Its massive patterned brick and tile facade features a three-story-high, glass-fronted lobby and indoor ticket booths. Silver metal letters spell out "United Artists Theatres" on the facade. A narrow marquee extends the length of the facade. The rest of the exterior is composed of gray bricks with a horizontal red band at the second-floor level. Inside, there is a centrally located lobby, which contains the main concession area and rest rooms located to the right. The color scheme of the lobby is bright purple, yellow and green. Entrance to the auditoriums is also to the right of the concession area.

The auditoriums, all of which have stadium seating, are located along either side of the central corridor running the length of the theater. All of the auditoriums are small, seating fewer than 400; the largest seat 361 while the smallest seat 162. The seats are all thickly cushioned, high-backed rockers with cupholder armrests. The two largest auditoriums are located immediately behind the entrance. There are additional concession counters and rest rooms located along the central corridor. The opening of the Snowden Square 14 was one of the factors in the closing of the Columbia City 3 in 2000.

Solax (see Black Cat)

Solomon's, 525 North Fremont Avenue. C. H. Imwold managed this theater around 1920.

Southside Movies Four, 835 East Fort Avenue, 1992–1997, Kelly Clayton & Mojzisek, 550 (for four auditoriums). Greater Baltimore Cinema, Inc. opened this small quadraplex in SouthSide Marketplace in November 1992. It was a discount theater throughout its short life.

Squire (see New {2})

Stanley, 516 North Howard Street, 1927–1965, Hoffman & Henon, c. 4,000 (1,860 first floor, 1,800 balcony, 280 mezzanine, 60 boxes). When workers completed demolition of the Stanley Theater in Baltimore in 1966 they destroyed the largest most opulent movie theater the city ever knew or would ever know. With nearly 4,000 seats and a white marble facade that dominated North Howard Street for 40 years, the Stanley was the peak of movie-going elegance in Baltimore. The history of the Stanley goes back many years before that September night in 1927, when it opened to a select audience of 2,000.

The intersection of North Howard Street and Franklin Street lies a few blocks north of the traditional center of downtown Baltimore. During the last quarter of the 19th century and first half of the 20th century it was a center for entertainment. Within two blocks there were, at one time or another, three movie theaters, three legitimate theaters, and a major hotel. Theatrical entrepreneur James Kernan chose this intersection for his "triple million dollar enterprise."

Baltimore's biggest and best, the 1927 Stanley (516 North Howard Street, 1927–1965, Hoffman and Henon).

He built the Maryland Theater on Franklin Street in 1903, and next door to that he built a luxurious hotel. Around the corner, at 508 North Howard, he acquired the old Natatorium and turned it into the Auditorium Theater. Next door to the Auditorium was 516 North Howard, the site of two, very different, theaters, the Academy of Music and the Stanley.

By 1925, movies had become so popular that huge theaters were being built all over the country to accommodate the millions of viewers that attended movies every day. The newest movie palace in Baltimore, the Century, had opened in 1921. The seven other theaters that showed first-run films were older and smaller. The Academy of Music was more than 50 years old, out of date, and had limited seating. Clearly the city was ready for something special.

In July 1925, the *Baltimore News* announced that the Stanley Company of Philadelphia was planning to erect a movie theater in Baltimore. A month later, Stanley joined with the Crandall organization of Washington to form the Stanley-Crandall Company, and they were ready to expand. Eager for a presence in Baltimore, they began negotiations for the Academy of Music and the Boulevard Theater, and, in the spring of 1926, purchased the Academy for about $750,000.

In March 1926, Harry Crandall, the vice-president of the company, announced that they would begin razing the Academy of Music in six weeks and replace it with a 4,000-seat motion picture theater. They expected to use three shifts of workers night and day to erect the new theater. It was scheduled to open in December 1926. Construction was delayed when it was found that the foundations for the new theater had to be 12 feet deep rather than five feet that the Academy of Music had required. The side and rear walls of the Academy were so sturdy that they were retained in the Stanley.

The Stanley opened at 8:30 on Friday evening, September 23, 1927. Four thousand people, including 2,000 invited guests, attended the opening. Mayor Broening was there along with officials of the Stanley Company, including John J. McGuirk, the president, and Harry Crandall and E. F. Albee of the Keith-Albee organization. Before the premier, there was a formal dinner for the movie executives at the swanky Hotel Belvedere. Mayor Broening and his wife toured the new theater with its manager, Bernard Depkin. Guests strolled around and viewed the wonders of the Stanley while pianist Emanual Wad, of the Peabody Conservatory, played compositions by Chopin, Grieg, and Liszt on one of the six Steiff pianos in the mezzanine lounge. The ushers were dressed in "dapper uniforms and black patent leather belts." They carried kits that contained everything from smelling salts to pads and pencils.

During the seating of guests, organist Ernie Cooper played in the auditorium. Finally, the 35-piece orchestra, conducted by Felice Iula, who shared conductor duties with his brother Robert, played the national anthem, and the show began. First there was the Dedication, followed by the Stanley Symphony Orchestra playing Sigmund Romberg's "My Maryland" with a chorus of twenty under the direction of George Castelle. Dancers Carlos and Valeria did what was politely called "an interesting dance"; they were followed by the tremendously popular Fred Waring and his Pennsylvanians.

The movie program consisted of The Stanley News, a cartoon — *Ko-Ko the Cannibal* — and the main feature, *The Stolen Bride*, with Billie Dove. Interestingly, the villain in the movie was played by Armand Kaliz, who had played in musical comedy at the Academy of Music. Many members of the audience remembered Kaliz. Inaugural prices were 40 cents for a balcony seat, 60 cents for an orchestra seat, and 75 cents for a seat in the boxes and loges. The Stanley opened daily, except Sunday, at 10:30 A.M.; there was a 15-minute organ recital from 10:45 to 11:00, when the first regular performance began. Performances were continuous until closing time at 11:00 P.M.

Paul J. Henon, Jr., and D. T. Henon of the Philadelphia architectural firm of Hoffman-Henon designed the Stanley. Theater publicity quoted the cost as $2.5 million, but, according to notes by Paul Henon, the actual cost was $1,303,453. The Stanley was a huge theater; the front measured 120 feet, and its depth measured 350 feet. The facade was of white marble and white glazed terra cotta in a Romanesque style. The original marquee was rectangular with a cartouche in the middle containing the letters "ST" for "Stanley Theater." Above the marquee was a high second story consisting of three bays containing large arched windows, each flanked by columns. On either side of the middle bay was a massive urn on a pedestal. A cornice separated the second story from the top of the facade that featured a decorative floral relief and a cartouche. The facade could be illuminated by 50 multicolored floodlights installed on the top of the marquee. On the roof of the theater was a huge electric sign, "Stanley Theatre Photoplays," that was visible for many miles.

Beneath the marquee was a ticket booth with stations for four cashiers. The lower half of the booth was serpentine while the top was glass framed in bronze with a copper marquee. Across the top of the ticket booth was a "talking sign" announcing current and future attractions. Entrance doors on either side of the ticket booth led into a shallow entrance foyer. A stairway at either end led up to the balcony. Six sets of dou-

Top: The cavernous lobby of the Stanley was lined with several kinds of marble, had three crystal chandeliers and murals of Maryland history. *Bottom:* Proscenium arch and orchestra of the Stanley.

ble mahogany doors led from this area into the grand lobby. Above the series of double doors in the outer lobby and in the grand lobby were murals depicting events in the history of the state of Maryland.[337]

The grand lobby was paved with a decorative terrazzo marble floor inlaid with brass and on either side was a wide Italian marble[338] staircase. Several murals decorated the walls of the two-story grand lobby. Three chandeliers hanging from the 100-foot high ceiling and lights in wall sconces illuminated this lobby.

There were rooms to check coats and hats under each staircase. The staircases led up to the mezzanine lounge and balcony. The mezzanine lounge extended the width of the theater and was furnished with divans, easy chairs, decorative floor lamps, tables and other decorations.

From the grand lobby another six sets of double doors led into the Medieval Romanesque auditorium. The seats were arranged into sections divided by two long central aisles with a wide crossover aisle in the middle. The auditorium measured 120 by 250 feet and was divided into a front and a back section by an archway that flowed out from the proscenium. The front section was flanked by three bays, repeating the facade motif, each containing a chandelier. Above the front section was a huge medallion on the ceiling. The back section was covered by the balcony; a Tiffany cut-glass chandelier hung from the domed ceiling above it. The main colors of the auditorium were buff, gray, and pale blue set off with gold and terra cotta. The draperies, carpets, and silk wall panels were of deep rose or terra cotta and maroon. Twenty-four 1000-watt spotlights were located on the arch above the balcony. The Stanley's stage measured 50 feet wide, 30 feet deep and 38 feet high. The gridiron was 110 feet above the stage floor.

The Stanley had enough dressing rooms backstage to accommodate twelve complete acts. The switchboard that controlled the stage lighting was said to be one of the largest south of New York City. Under the stage were facilities for stagehands and musicians; these impressive stage facilities were not used very much. Cosmetic and rest rooms for ladies and smoking rooms and rest rooms for men were located in the basement and on the mezzanine. These rooms were furnished with antique furniture. On either side of the projection booth there were orchestral rehearsal rooms. There was also a screening room.

There were four Powers projection machines, three spotlights, and three effect machines in the projection booth. There was a joke among employees at the Stanley that the screen was so far away from the projection booth that the projectionist needed binoculars to focus the picture.

It took the services of many to build the Stanley. The David C. Butcher Company of Baltimore and Washington was the bricklaying contractor. The sheet metal work and marquee were done by the local W. A. Fingles Company. Marble was supplied by the Hilgartner Company, and granite was provided by Law & Burrell of Philadelphia. Gibelli and Company from Philadelphia did the mural and fresco painting, and another Philadelphia company, the Philadelphia Electric Sign Company, erected the signs for the theater. The uniforms were specially made by A. Jacobs & Sons of Baltimore.

When the Stanley opened, the staff consisted of Bernard Depkin, Jr.,[339] resident manager; W. A. Busch, house manager; Charles E. Ford, art director; William Dryden, stage manager; Lawrence O'Hare, chief projectionist; Harry E. Wallace, master electrician; Adrian Anthony, floor captain; Ernie Cooper, organist; and Dr. R. E. Keyser, house physician. There was also a 35-piece orchestra, a corps of ushers, and a large number of other employees including box office attendants, doormen, checkroom attendants, additional projectionists, and custodial personnel. New employees received special training. Employee benefits included sick leave and insurance. Each employee was required to have a bank account.

After a few years, Bernard Depkin was replaced by Washington manager, Harry Lohmeyer. Lohmeyer was there only a short time before he was replaced by another Washingtonian, Rodney Collier. Collier stayed at the Stanley for 23 years. In 1957, Lohmeyer returned, and Collier went to Washington to become a district manager for the Stanley-Warner Corp. Lohmeyer's time at the Stanley was short again; in 1958 the theater was sold to Morris Mechanic.

A cabaret called Sherry's, under the direction of E. A. Sherwood, opened on the roof of the Stanley on November 10, 1927. Opening night at the club featured music by Washington's Wardman Park Hotel orchestra under the baton of Moe Bear. Sherry's was decorated in a Spanish style.

Music was important throughout the history of the Stanley. The opening program for the theater set the tone, "Music will play an important part in the Stanley's appeal to the discriminating taste of Baltimore theatergoers and in establishing this incomparable Stanley-Crandall house as one dedicated to the utmost in superlative entertainment."

The first conductors of the Stanley's 35-piece symphony orchestra were the Iula brothers, both Baltimore natives. Felice S. Iula had been the conductor of the Rivoli Theater orchestra for some years and his brother, Robert Paul, had conducted the Park Symphony orchestra. Felice conducted the overtures and Robert did the stage shows and scored the pictures.

Between August 1928 and September 1929, Loew's conductor, Mischa Guterson, led the combined Parkway and Valencia orchestras at the Stanley. In the auditorium, there was a $50,000 triple-manual Kimball Concert Organ (Opus 6946).[340] It had 210 stops and 31 ranks of pipes in divided chambers on either side of the proscenium, behind ornate grills. The main chamber with 25 ranks of pipes, the electrical relays, glockenspiel, and chrysoglott were located on the left side. The solo chamber, on the right, contained the remaining six ranks plus assorted traps and percussions and a Kimball upright piano that was playable from the organ console. The Stanley organ featured a series of harmonic couplers which allowed the organist to play chords with one finger. The organ console was mounted on an electrically controlled mechanical screw lift.

Paul Tompkins was the chief organist from 1928 to 1930; Al Hornig was his relief. Roland Nuttrell took over for Hornig in 1930. The organ was used until the early 1950s; then it was not played again until members of the Potomac Valley Chapter of the American Association of Theatre Organ Enthusiasts restored it for the Maryland premier of *The Music Man* on July 31, 1962. The public reaction to this was so positive that JF Theaters, which was operating the theater at that time, decided to make organ interludes a regular feature of the weekend shows. The console of the Stanley's organ survives in the auditorium of Dickinson High School in Wilmington, Delaware.

Despite receipts of $30,000 the first week and more than $25,000 the next three weeks, business at the Stanley in its first year was not as good as expected. In July 1928, the Stanley-Crandall Company and Loew's agreed to pool their Baltimore theater interests. This included pooling expenses and profits and exchanging movies. First National films were made available to Loew's theaters and Metro-Goldwyn, United Artists, and Paramount films were made available to the Stanley. The following month, the Stanley was leased to Loew's. The Stanley was the site of the world premier of *Tarzan the Ape Man*, starring Johnny Weissmuller and Maureen O'Sullivan, on March 11, 1932.

In November 1933 Loew's decided to experiment with a combined vaudeville and movies policy at the Stanley, but it lasted only one season. The first vaudeville show starred popular singer Morton Downey along with a new orchestra under the direction of Robert Lansinger. Loew's relinquished operation of the Stanley in April 1934.

In 1938 it was among the first theaters in the country to install a new kind of sound reproduction equipment that reproduced sounds between 40 and 10,000 cycles; the older machines could only handle frequencies between 100 and 3,000. According to Frank Cahill, director of sound for Warner Bros. Studios, "The reproduction achieved by this machine is the nearest thing there is to natural sound. It covers the entire audible sound spectrum." The movie *Battle Cry*, by local author Leon Uris, had its premier at the Stanley in February 1955.

Going to the Stanley was always a grand occasion, one to which people assumed they should wear special clothes, maybe Sunday clothes. The anticipation of the show began even before one approached the theater; it could be seen from several blocks away, towering over North Howard Street.

You passed quickly by the adjoining Mayfair which was maybe showing a Republic film and hardly noticed the tiny Little Theater across the street. By some strange quirk of fate, the Little — one of the smallest theaters in Baltimore — had opened less than three months after the Stanley. As you bought your ticket, you could hardly wait to go inside. You gave your ticket to the uniformed doorman, walked into the grand lobby and suddenly you were transported into another world. You were walking on marble; you didn't realize it was Italian. You passed the marble stairs and could imagine kings and queens walking down them attended by ranks of courtiers.

By the time this writer came along, there was a concession stand in the lobby. It would have been blasphemy to anyone not so fond of ice cream sandwiches. After buying some treat, you entered the hushed auditorium. Movies were shown continuously, so you could go in at any time. You could almost feel the weight of the tons of bricks, marble, steel, and concrete that composed the theater as you entered that cavernous hall.

Where to sit? You had your choice of thousands of seats; the Stanley was almost never filled in the 1950s. The best seats were on the crossover aisles where you could put your legs straight out in front and really relax. Unless you were seated when the house lights were on, you didn't pay much attention to the wall hangings or the gold leaf highlights on the sculptured plaster. But, if you got there before a show started, that was best of all, because you could feel the unimaginable thrill of the house lights dimming and the huge curtain opening. Then came the movie, and you became a part of it, one of the unnamed extras. You were there when the beast from 20,000 fathoms attacked hapless citizens, and you marched through the Russian winter as Napoleon retreated from Moscow. When you left the Stanley, and you put it off as long as you could, it was like walking through a time tunnel into another world, a more drab, unexciting world. Seeing a movie at the Stanley was the peak movie-going experience in Baltimore. We will never see its like again.

The beginning of the end came for the Stanley in February 1958, when Morris Mechanic bought it from Stanley-Warner. One of the first things he did, the following fall, was to change the name to Stanton. He then leased the theater to JF Theaters. After that it was used for movies and just about anything else an auditorium could be used for. Legitimate shows, closed circuit TV shows, variety shows, and movies were all presented at the Stanley during its last eight years. Mechanic announced plans to convert the theater into a legitimate house in the spring of 1964. Just before it closed, Mechanic retrieved control of the theater and used it for live shows, as a replacement for Ford's, which he had closed and sold to a local department store.

The last movies at the Stanley were shown in March 1965. The following month, after the last show of the musical *Oliver* on April 17, the Stanley closed forever. There were some, half-hearted attempts to mobilize public support to save the Stanley, but it was the wrong time; theater preservation had not become popular and some, misguided at best, narrow-minded, stupid, or greedy at worst, people said, "Tear it down!" The drama critic for the Baltimore *News American*, who didn't even know when the theater had opened, felt that the Stanley did not deserve saving. He wrote, "My own view is that while the Stanton is representative of Hollywood baroque, circa 1929 [sic], it is unsatisfactory for any present-day theatrical use to which it could be put" but he grudgingly admitted that, "in comparison with the boxy plainness of so many of the new downtown structures, the Stanton's seedy grandeur has a certain eye appeal. And the city ought to have a large downtown movie theater for first-run films." He wanted to renovate the old barn-like Lyric. He praised Morris Mechanic's "splendid plans for a new theater in Charles Center."

Demolition began in July 1965, and by August the front of the theater had been ripped off and the auditorium gutted. Only the side and rear walls remained; perhaps they contained parts of the old Academy of Music. It is ironic that the oldest part of the building was the last to go. Local homeowners collected bricks from the rubble and used them to line their patios.

Baltimore's grandest movie palace was replaced by a parking lot.

Star {1}, 3910 Belvedere Avenue, 1910–1939?, unknown, 350. The Star {1}, one of the earliest movie houses in northwest Baltimore, opened around 1910. It was probably operated by the Arlington Amusement Company. which was incorporated in Baltimore County in July 1910. The name was changed to Belvedere, or Belvedere Picture Garden, around 1915. J. C. Cremen, who operated the Carey Theater, took over the Belvedere in May 1917, and Charles Nolte's Greater Baltimore Theaters leased it in 1919. Nolte remodeled it, installed a new flush front, and reopened it in October 1919. Sometime prior to 1939 it was evidently renamed the Arlington. It must have opened on a very limited basis, since the last record of it as a theater after 1928 was in a news item that said that the Arlington Theater that had been "unused for many months" was damaged by fire early on April 13, 1939.

Jack Whittle ran this theater for a while early in its career. During the summer, he used to take the equipment from the theater, carry it across the street to Electric Park, and set up an open-air movie on the deck of the dancing pavilion. The building was still standing as of the early 1970s.

Star {2} (see Winona)

Star {3} (see Radio)

State, 2045 East Monument Street, 1927–1963, George Schmidt and C. C. Fulton Leser, 2,044. The State was the largest neighborhood movie theater in town. It was built by the Durkee organization as a movie and vaudeville theater. Built in what was called an "Antique Spanish" style, itt cost a reported $450,000. The ordinance granting the building permit, dated July 8, 1926, specified that the exterior walls would be constructed of four-inch-thick brick, backed with eight-inch-thick terra cotta, wall tile, or cinder block, and that the walls would be bonded with brick at each second course of tile or block. The building measured 123 by 126 feet.

The *Baltimore American* described the interior of the new theater.

> From the large lobby at the side of the auditorium, a wide staircase leads to the balcony and mezzanine promenade. The walls are finished in ornamental plaster, colored in various tints, with burnt orange predominating.
>
> Green and orange drapings are hung in the arches between the lobby and auditorium, and also at intervals on the walls of the theatre. Soft carpets in rich colorings cover the floor of the foyer, while tapestry art squares add a richness to the walls of the mezzanine promenade. From the beautiful dome in the ceiling an immense crystal chandelier is hung, while smaller ones of similar design are placed in other parts of the interior.[341]

There was a full stage, but it was fairly shallow. Dressing rooms were located to the right of the stage. The 20 bowling alleys in the basement of the State were opened several months before the theater. The State opened, under the management of Fred Schmuff, on Saturday April 16, 1927. The Avalon Theater on Park Heights Avenue opened on the same day. George Schmidt, one of the architects who designed the State, died before the theater opened.

Stage shows, booked through the Edward Sherman vaudeville agency in Philadelphia, were a regular attraction at the State; they were changed on Sundays and Wednesdays. There were three stage shows a day, and each show contained three, sometimes four, acts. The State was probably the last movie house in town to play vaudeville. A typical show, from September 1935, included a movie *Every Night at 8*, with Alice Faye and George Raft, and, on stage, Foster & Batie in "Modernistic Harlem," Frank and Ethel Carmen in "Surprises," and "Melody Rhythm" a rhythmic revue.

The State had a Wurlitzer 2/7 style "E" (opus 1539) organ, which has been saved and is now in a private home. The first organist at the State was John Decker, formerly of the Paul Specht Orchestra. Sound came to the State in May 1929.

The theater was extensively remodeled in mid-1940. Among the many changes was a new, larger, but rather plain marquee. The foyer was modernized and a new chandelier and doors were installed. The auditorium was repainted and reseated. In a 1998 interview, Roy Insley recounted details about the State when he worked there as an usher and stage hand in the 1950s.[342]

> Now, when I was working there were at least four acts. I think they had eight or nine people in the orchestra ... and towards the end, just before vaudeville totally shut down.... I think they only had four ... the piano player, the drummer, bass, sax, and one other instrument ... trumpet.... The theater opened at 12:30; the movie started at 1 and then at 3 there would be a stage show and then there would be one at around five or six and then there would be another one.... I know there were three stage shows and ... it would always start off with a movie. I guess the movies were an hour and a half ... if the movie was a long ... one they cut the stage show ... they would maybe only book three acts or four acts.... If you're looking at the stage from the audience, the dressing rooms were to the right and as you go out the exit door alongside of the stage there was a slight ramp and the dressing rooms were off to that right side. I think they only had three dressing rooms. Some of the acts would share ... one of the dressing rooms was large and had several mirrors so they would share a dressing room.
>
> And also the State owned one or two of the row houses in the back on Castle Street, and they used to put the acts up in those houses. It was like a furnished ... apartment.... And then behind the theater was a garage, in that little alleyway, where we stored some of the big draperies and curtains and backdrops.
>
> There was one curtain I would have loved to have had and I think it was just destroyed and it was kind of sad ... it was such a beautiful red velvet curtain with a gold stripe. That curtain was actually red velvet with a gold stripe around the bottom. And it was really so pretty when the proscenium was closed off with that curtain. Then it was replaced with a gold, like a Damask, heavy Damask curtain....
>
> Well, you had the manager of the theater and, you had about eight or nine, originally, in the orchestra. There was a stage manager and an assistant stage manager and ... I think there were six or seven ushers. And, the woman who sold tickets. There probably were more than that. I think there were probably two and they alternated. And then you had two or three people working the snack bar. In those days they didn't have all the stuff they have in theaters now. They just mainly sold candy and popcorn. They had one ... two ladies that did cleaning in the theater. One was an elderly woman and she had a younger woman that helped her. So ... I

Top: Vaudeville lasted into the 1950s at the State. Note the adjoining popcorn store in this 1940 photograph. *Bottom:* East side of the State's auditorium. Note the annunciator just to the left of the curtain.

guess if you totaled it up, the total staff was probably maybe 25 or 30 ... and also you had the projection people. I think they probably had ... four projectionists, two working at a time....

During the 1950s, theater television came to the State. In December 1952, the complete production of Bizet's opera *Carmen* was telecast from the stage of the Metropolitan Opera House to the screen of the State Theater. And, in September 1955, the State was one of 100 theaters in the country to carry the Rocky Marciano-Archie Moore heavyweight title bout on closed-circuit TV. The State closed on December 1, 1963. The final show was *Phantom Planet* and *Terror from the Year 5000*. For several weeks in August and September 1967 a "Healing Revival," led by the Rev. Gene Ewing, packed the theater. Later, it was renovated and used by the Soul's Harbor Full Gospel Church. At the present time, the facade has been cleaned, and the interior has been converted into office space by Johns Hopkins Hospital.

Fred Schmuff felt that he had a hand in launching the careers of Abbott and Costello while managing the State. He related his experience in a 1988 interview.

> Abbott and Costello were playing the State. They were going over so big. I booked them for three days; so I called Eddie Sherman [their agent] and said, "I want to hold these guys for three more days, for the rest of the week." He said, "You can't do that. I've got them booked into Canton." I said, "I'll buy an act for Canton; I'll pay for the act." So, I did. They played Canton and went over big there. In talking to Eddie, I said, "You know. Eddie, I've got an idea. Why don't you put them in Atlantic City for the summer, say at the Steel Pier?" Eddie booked the Pier. This was in March. He said, "I don't think Frank [Gatti] would go for that." I said, "I'm playing them next week; why don't you have Frank come up and look at them and see what he thinks?" ... So Frank came up. He said, "I think you're right. I'm going to put them down there." And from then on in, they made it big.[343]

Stockton, 2–4 South Stockton Street, c. 1910, F. E. Beall, 200. There is some evidence that W. S. Riggins had this building altered into a movie house in early 1910. The building was still standing as of 1995. It has been a church for many years.

Strand {1}, 404–406 North Howard Street, 1916–1923, Sparklin and Childs, c. 500. The hard luck Strand {1} was built for the Howard Amusement Company and cost, exclusive of fixtures, about $10,000. The plans, announced in December 1915, called for a 37 × 121 foot, brick, steel, and timber building.

The *Baltimore News* described the new theater:

> The structure is ... well decorated; the exterior ... of cr[e]am stucco, is embellished with a large bronze marquis. The lobby of the theater is the first of its kind in the East. The lighting arrangement is entirely unique, the rays of light being absolutely diffused. The decorations of the main auditorium are in rose, gold and old ivory, the walls being paneled in old rose satin damask. The floor covering is of Wilton velvet, matching the satin wall panels. The lighting effect is totally indirect and invisible and is effected by rays from the coves. The Swartout automatic ventilating and cooling system has been installed. This enables the air in the house to be completely changed every 21 minutes. A concert organestra has ... been installed ... the first of its kind in the South. Warren Hackett Gailbraith, a Scotch musician of some note, presides at the console of this instrument in recitals and accompanying the pictures....[344]

The seats were 19-inch mahogany cabinet chairs. The Strand {1} opened on March 16, 1916, and seems to have been in trouble as soon as it opened. During its first year, there were several changes in management. It reopened under new management and with a newly installed cooling system in June 1916. In December 1916, T. T. Hildebrandt took over management. He lowered the admission price from 30 cents to 15 and planned to have fashion shows with live models. The Strand {1} featured Fisher's orchestra in late 1916. The first of several remodelings took place in the summer of 1917. The ticket booth which had been centrally located, was placed inside the lobby on the right wall. The lobby had a wainscoting of Maine marble with upper walls of Caenstone. The new interior color scheme was old ivory and soft gray with gold trim and wall panels of old rose silk.

The theater reopened under the management of the Parkway Theater Company on September 10, 1917. A month later a new policy of three-day runs replaced the earlier weekly runs. It was renovated in early 1919, and the lobby was lined with lattice-covered mirrors. It was remodeled again in August 1921 and repainted in soft grays and ivory; mahogany doors were also installed.

In August 1922, under the direction of

Original front of the Strand Theater (1 Shipping Place, Dundalk, 1927–1985, John F. Eyring) c. 1927 before the marquee was replaced. (Photograph courtesy of William E. Eyring, Sr.)

Thomas D. Goldberg, the Strand reopened with a new policy of showing three movies rather than one a week. Nothing worked for the Strand. It closed on January 13, 1923, and was sold to a men's clothing company that November. The building is still standing, with traces of the theater clearly visible in the front and rear.

Strand {2}, 1 Shipping Place, Dundalk, 1927–1985, John F. Eyring, 900. The Strand {2} was the premier movie house in Dundalk and the second oldest one in that area. Generations of Dundalkians watched their first movie at the Strand. It was built by the Gaertner circuit in the early strip shopping center on Shipping Place in the heart of downtown Dundalk. Construction was under way by the first of December 1926, and the estimated cost was $75,000.

The Strand {2} was nearly identical to the Vilma, another Eyring theater. The facade was of pink marble with maroon glazed tiles on the first floor and buff face brick on the second. Originally the entrance was protected by a small narrow marquee, but that was later replaced by a much wider one that ran across the entire front of the theater. It opened in February 1927 and closed on December 4, 1978, with *Blazing Saddles*.

JF Theaters had leased the Strand, but financial difficulties in 1978 forced them to terminate the lease. Robert Wienholt took the Strand over in 1979 and operated it until 1985. A moment of fame in the life of the Strand came in 1981 when director Barry Levinson selected it for one of the scenes in his film *Diner*.

It was twinned in the summer of 1982 when a small theater seating about 70 people was built in the balcony. The conversion of the North Point Plaza Theater into a four-plex in 1983 helped seal the doom of the Strand as it siphoned additional patrons away from the older theater. Wienholt closed it in November 1985.

In 1989, the theater was sold to a developer for around $198,000. Plans to convert it into an indoor sports center were announced in October 1992. Finally, in 2000, the theater was turned into a Family Dollar Store. Many patrons still remember the blue velvet curtain with figures of "lords and ladies" at the Strand.

Strand {3}, 1309 Francis Avenue, Halethorpe, before 1925–1935, unknown, 220. A local hardware merchant, Mr. Spindler, operated this movie theater on the second floor of his large cinder-block store. It was open only a few days a week. There were several other operators after Mr. Spindler. It was called the Halethorpe in 1925. Harry Kahn acquired it in the summer of 1927. The building seems to have disappeared by 2002.

Suburban, 3055–3057 West North Avenue, 1909–1918, Stanislaus Russell (of August 1909 addition), 250. The Suburban was the first movie theater in Walbrook. It was probably the "new moving picture theater or nickel theater" that was being planned by William Fernandis at North Avenue and 9th Street in Walbrook in March 1909. The theater was on the first floor of the three-story building that is still standing. It cost an estimated $2,000 to build. Fernandis had architect Russell draw up plans for a $1,000 brick addition in August 1909. Ranft and Krug operated it for a while.

Thomas Goldberg purchased the Suburban in September 1915 and planned a number of improvements. It did not last very long after Goldberg bought the much larger Walbrook, cater-cornered across North Avenue, in 1917. Later the building was used by S. Abrahams & Sons, a hardware and plumbing company. Portions of the theater's tiled vestibule were visible many years after the theater closed.

Suburban Hotel and Gardens, 4600 block of Park Heights Avenue, [1890]–[1923], unknown, 500. Around 1890, Egbert Halsted built the hotel and gardens on Park Heights Avenue, a few blocks above Cold Spring Lane; he ran it as a summer resort. In addition to a 42-room hotel, there was a music hall, summer garden, stables and carriage sheds. Edmund J. McGraw bought the hotel for $32,500 in May 1912.

The Suburban Gardens was remodeled for the 1914 season. It opened on June 6. After the remodeling it could seat 500 people and boasted two stages for vaudeville shows. A grotto at the rear of the main stage provided protection in case of inclement weather. A 1,600-square-foot dance floor was located in the middle of the garden, and the dining room featured special chicken and crab dinners. The hotel was torn down in the early 1920s and replaced by St. Ambrose's Catholic Church. Movies were shown at the Suburban Hotel and Gardens from time to time, beginning as early as July 1910.

Sunburst, 1705 Fleet Street, c. 1909. Two men named Robinson & Waldorf possibly operated this theater for a very short time around 1909.

Sunset (see Crescent 4)

Super 170 Drive-In, 8229 Telegraph Road, Odenton, 1963–1985, Bert-Core Associates, 700 cars. Leon Back and Edward Kimpel, Jr., of Rome Theaters built this drive-in for an estimated $350,000. Scheduled to open on June 29, 1963, it did not actually open until July 25. The drive-in was located on a 28-acre tract between Odenton and Friendship Airport on Maryland Route 170. It consisted of a 100 × 50 foot steel screen tower, a 90 × 60-foot concessions building, a fenced-in playground, and two box offices serving four lanes of traffic. The Super 170 Drive-In was twinned for the 1982 season. It was the last operating drive-in in Anne Arundel County, lasting through the 1985 season when it was operated by R/C Theaters. It was torn down to construct the interchange with Route 100.

Superba, 906–908 Washington Boulevard, 1910–1935, unknown, 300. The attractive Superba Moving Picture Parlor was opened and operated for many years by Daniel H. Braun. It cost about $3,000 to build. Robert Marhenke and Roger Hurlock—later with United Artists—operated it as the Majestic between 1932 and 1935. After it closed, it housed a laundry and washing machine repair shop for some years. The building is still standing with some of the original facade intact. Up until recently, the name "Superba" was clearly visible in the white brickwork above the entrance. In 1994 the IDS Group bought several buildings on Washington Boulevard, including the Superba building, and renovated them. The former theater became office spaces. The adjacent building was supposed to become a small live theater.

Sutton (see Linden)

Takoma Moving Picture Parlor, 4815–4817 Eastern Avenue, 1925–1966, J. Bisson (of 1930 remodeling), c. 297. This small movie house opened as the Takoma. A building permit was granted to John Wischhusen in November 1924 to alter and convert the building at 4815–4817 Eastern Avenue to exhibit moving picture shows. The theater must have opened the following year. Oscar Bocutti owned and operated the Nemo for many years. It was remodeled in 1930, became the Nemo in 1933, and operated under that name until 1946, when it became the New Nemo under the management of the Joseph Grant organization. It closed in 1955. The theater was advertised for sale in November 1964. After being closed for 10 years, it was completely refurbished by the new owner, Michael Spanos, who reopened it as the East on December 25, 1965.[345] The East specialized in foreign, especially Greek, films. It lasted only about two years. The theater was damaged extensively by fires in 1966 and 1967, and the building is now a church. In a lively 1975 article, Brian Constantini recalled attending the Nemo in the 1950s.

> But my clearest memory of growin'-up on The Hill [the area of Highlandtown between the Eastern Avenue underpass and City Hospital] was Saturday morning at the neighborhood movie. It was called "The Nemo" until they remodeled, then it was cleverly called "The New Nemo." However, the only apparent renovation was the substitution of popcorn and soda machines where the candy counter had once stood. Actually, this was a much needed renovation, because one man ran the entire movie house. He sold the tickets from a booth that faced out on Eastern Avenue then swiveled around as you walked in and took the ticket back from you. After everyone was in, but not necessarily seated, he ran upstairs and ran the projector....
>
> The Nemo would open, supposedly, at 11 A.M. on Saturday. I say supposedly because if the owner was late for work you just waited outside 'til he got there. Then he would have to fight his way thru the jeering line of kids to open up. Sometimes it was 11:15 or 11:30, or even noon before he arrived.... He was cantankerous and quick-tempered and appeared to openly dislike his young, Saturday morning patrons. But I still felt sorry for him. Can you imagine catering to dozens of smart-mouthed, little kids when you had a name like Oscar Bacooti?[346] I'm not sure of the spelling, but I am sure that he got weary of the kids who picked on the last two syllables of his last name and constantly hooted, "Cooty! Cooty! Cooty!"
>
> The theater ... had only one aisle, with no more than 10 to 12 seats on each side. Those rows tapered down toward the screen 'til there were only four or five seats across the front on either side of the aisle. In front of the screen was a pit with an organ in it left over from the silent screen days ... a reminder of a time 20 to 30 years past, while the small screen above it glowed with futuristic shows like "Destination Moon."
>
> Old Oscar had a strange habit of combining new shows like "Destination Moon" or the latest Lex Barker Tarzan flick with Roy Rogers or Gene Autry westerns that were showing on TV at the same time. ... The film invariably broke two or three times a showing, which was the signal for the young moviegoers to bombard the screen with candy and yell, "We want our money back! We want our money back!" If the crowd got too raucous or physical Oscar had no qualms about shutting off the projector and yelling down from the booth, "Shuddup or I'll throw all youse kids out!" Followed by a very audible deep breath and a stage-whispered, "I don't need this."
>
> ...[I]t was one helluva good bargain! An entire afternoon's worth of entertainment for a quarter: 14¢ to get in, 5¢ for popcorn from the new machine ... 5¢ for a box of stale "Black Crows," and a penny for two pretzel sticks from the Eastern Bakery on the way home.

The Nemo was described by one projectionist as a "gold mine." At one time a poster outside the entrance showed too much of Betty Grable's legs and they had to be covered. And, once, a bomb was discovered behind one of the radiators.

Teddy Bear Parlor, 1741 East Baltimore Street, 1909–1920, Jacob F. Gerwig, 268. Adam Leicht spent about $4,000 to convert the building on this site into the Teddy Bear. It was a one-story brick and stone theater with a plaster-of-Paris facade. There was a store adjacent to the Teddy Bear where patrons could purchase large sodas for two cents and take them into the theater. In the summer of 1910, Leicht put a $900 addition on the rear of his theater. Bill Leicht, remembered as a terrific piano player, was also associated with this theater.[347] The Teddy Bear used behind-the-screen talkers occasionally.

In September 1919, under a popular new manager, John Leo McDonald, the theater was reopened. McDonald held a contest to find a new name for the theater; the winning name was Mickey.[348] Mickey was apparently chosen because it was the nickname of manager McDonald who had also been a piano player at the Broadway Theater. In May 1921, J. Winer bought the Mickey for $7,400. Movies may have been at this theater as late as 1923–1924, when it was called the Hornsby on a card, printed in Polish, prepared by the projectionists' local 181 to advertise theaters that employed union operators. The building was standing, in the mid-1970s, when it was a bar and poolarama. It has since been demolished.

*Terrace, Essex. Work on this 750-seat theater designed for Abraham and Louis Cohen by David Harrison had begun by March 1942, but it was never completed

Terrapin Park Open Air Theater, Greenmount Avenue between 29th and 30th streets. This 13,000-seat park was the home of the Federal League Baltimore Terrapins baseball team from 1914 to 1916. The stands were designed by Otto G. Simonson. Movies were shown there during the summer of 1915 with two shows every evening at 10 cents a seat. After the afternoon ball game, a large screen was erected on the field and movies were shown after dark, rain or shine. The screen was located near first base so that patrons in the grandstand had a good view. The airdome was under the direction of Bernard Depkin.

Thalia Theater (see Washington Hall Theater)

Theater, 903 East Baltimore Street, 1906–1907, unknown, 60. John Donohue was operating a small, unnamed theater on East Baltimore Street in late 1906 and early 1907.

[*Many theaters were planned but never completed. The portion of the listing below provides information on some of them.*]

*Theater, Lexington Street near Fremont. There were plans for an $80,000 African-American theater at this location in February 1907. Washington architect John A. Lankford prepared the plans. In August 1907, another African-American theater was planned at 655–658 West Lexington Street. This one was to be a 650-seat theater in a $25,000, multi-story building designed by John Freund for the Grand United Order of Brothers and Sisters of Good Hope.

*Theater, 349 North Gay Street. Plans were made in October 1907 to remodel the lower floor of the building at this address into a moving picture parlor.

*Theater, 356–358 North Gay Street. Otis P. Thompson leased the two-story store at this address in October 1907 and planned to remodel the lower floor into a moving picture parlor.

*Theater, 612 East Baltimore Street. The large three-story building at this address was the site of at least two projected movie theaters. In September 1908 it was leased to the J. E. Cahill Amusement Company for five years. They were planning to spend $10,000 to convert it into a moving picture theater. The following April, the owner leased the building to John W. Jefferson, of Washington, who planned to spend a more modest $2,500 to convert it into a moving picture theater. Neither project succeeded.

*Theater, 1405 Ashland Avenue. Benjamin Schleisner planned to remodel this dwelling into a 300-seat moving picture theater in December 1908.

*Theater, 1637 Pennsylvania Avenue, unknown, c. 500. F. O. Singer planned $800 alterations to this large dwelling to convert it into a moving picture theater in January 1909.

*Theater, Gilmor and Mosher streets. The Baltimore Traction Company had converted the original Baker Church into a cable powerhouse for the Gilmor and Druid Hill Avenue car lines. Joseph Olevich purchased the powerhouse and planned to convert it into a vaudeville and movie theater and amusement hall.

*Theater, 2110 East Monument Street. E. Potts received a permit to erect a $4,000 moving picture theater at this address in March 1909.

*Theater, 404–410 East Baltimore Street. In March 1909 Sigmund Lubin was planning to raze his two theaters on Baltimore Street and build a new, $150,000 theater on the site. In July 1910, both buildings were purchased by the Knickerbocker Amusement Company, which had B. Eustace Simonson prepare plans for a new, 2,000-seat theater on the site. These plans fell through.

*Theater, east side of Milton Avenue south of Eastern Avenue. Thomas L. Jeter had architect Herbert C. Aiken prepare plans for a $1,200 moving picture theater at this location in 1909.

*Theater, northwest corner of Baltimore and Calvert Streets. Parr & Parr were organizing a stock company to build a $150,000 moving picture and vaudeville theater seating 1,800 on the site of the former B & O Railroad central building and, at an earlier date, the Baltimore Museum in the summer of 1909. Architect Paul Emmart was preparing the plans.

*Theater, 1034–1036 North Gay Street. In February 1910, at the same time he received a permit to build the Elektra Theater across the street, Moses Milhauser was granted a permit to convert the three-story building at this address into a movie theater.

*Theater, 417 North Paca Street. The Bernheimer Brothers planned a $1,200 motion picture theater at this address in the fall of 1910.

*Theater, southwest corner of Mount Royal and Maryland avenues. Local citizens successfully protested the erection of a moving picture theater at this location in the spring of 1910.

*Theater, 122 East Baltimore Street. William N. Yearly planned a moving picture theater at this address in early 1911.

*Theater, 1728–1734 Harford Avenue. Loritz Brothers planned a motion picture theater for this location in March 1911.

*Theater, North Avenue between Aisquith and Ensor streets. Rush and Deruff planned a $6,000 motion picture theater on the south side of this block in March 1911. By April, architect J. A. Katz had completed the plans.

*Theater, 1900 East Lanvale Street. J. M. Alexander planned a $9,000 movie theater here in April 1911.

*Theater, southwest side of Madison Avenue between Gold and Bloom streets. Francis E. Tormey prepared plans for a $10,000 motion picture theater for Schmidt and Cook on Madison Avenue near Gold Street in May 1911, but the theater was never built because of objections by local religious groups.

*Theater, Lexington Street between Liberty and Howard streets. Otto Simonson was preparing plans for a $175,000, 2,000-seat vaudeville theater on the north side of Lexington Street in October 1911.

*Theater, 523–527 North Howard Street. Architect A. Lowther Forrest prepared plans for a huge French Renaissance style theater with an 80-foot frontage and a depth of 170 feet, massive white marble columns, a lobby trimmed in onyx and colored marble at this location in February 1912. The seating capacity was to be greater than any other theater south of New York. It is ironic that this theater was never built, but 15 years later the tiny Little Theater opened at the same address.

*Theater, Brunt Street between Wilson and McMechen streets. The Pitts Amusement Company planned a $10,000 movie and vaudeville theater at this location in June 1912.

*Theater, 322 Forrest Street. H. P. Roth planned a vaudeville and movie theater at this address from plans by H. V. Gemmel in July 1912.

*Theater, 961–963 Frederick Road. The Carroll Amusement Company was granted a permit to build a theater at this address in May 1912.

*Theater, 1627 Pennsylvania Avenue. J. C. Spedden prepared plans for a $7,000 motion picture parlor at this address in September 1912. The Regent Theater was later built there.

*Theater, Harford Road near Chase Street. Pearce and Scheck were reported to have purchased a site for a movie theater on Harford Road in November 1912.

*Theater, Madison Avenue above North Avenue. Samuel E. Reinhard planned to convert the Shaw Stables on Madison Avenue into a movie theater in 1913.

*Theater, 3505–3507 Eastern Avenue. The Ertel and Albers Company had plans prepared in early 1913 for an 1,800-seat moving picture theater at this address. Building operations were scheduled to begin in March, but Walter Albers and John Ertel had a falling out, and the theater was never built.

*Theater, 2927–2929 Hudson Street. Charles Kocourek was granted a permit in April 1913 to convert the buildings at the corner of Hudson and Curley Streets into a theater.

*Theater, northwest corner of Lexington and Gay streets. Garnett Clark and Andrew Steen, who operated the Black Cat Theater, were negotiating to build a theater next to Zion Lutheran Church in May 1913.

*Theater, Madison Avenue near McMechen Street. The Metropolitan Amusement Company planned a 750-seat movie theater at this address in the spring of 1913.

*Theater, 1524–1526 Fleet Street. Mrs. Bridget Vaughn was granted a permit to convert the buildings at this address into a one-story theater in July 1913.

*Theater, 524–528 West Biddle Street. Erwin H. Schleunes, Jr., was granted a permit to erect a two-story movie and vaudeville theater here in July 1913.

*Theater, 38–44 South Broadway. Pearce and Scheck announced in September 1913 that they would build a large vaudeville and moving picture theater at this location.

*Theater, Druid Hill Avenue and Whitelock Street. A. Lowther Forrest prepared plans for a motion picture theater here in November 1913.

*Theater, 1362–1368 West North Avenue. There were plans to build a theater at this location as early as December 1913.

*Theater, Light and German streets. Baltimore investors headed by Robert W. McBride, manager of the Auditorium Theater, announced plans for a burlesque theater on the site of the old Carrollton Hotel in the spring of 1914. Thomas Lamb prepared the plans.

*Theater, 826–828 Hanover Street. George R. Callis, Jr., obtained a permit to build a moving picture theater at this address in June 1914.

*Theater, 1008 Pennsylvania Avenue. The Daly Amusement Company was planning to erect a $75,000 movie and vaudeville theater on this site in the summer 1914. The plans were drawn by A. Lowther Forest.

*Theater, 1118–1124 Pennsylvania Avenue. At the same time that W. H. Daly was planning a large new theater on Pennsylvania Avenue, the Mutual Amusement Company had architect Theodore Wells Pietsch prepare plans for a similar theater to be erected on the next block. Ground was apparently broken for this theater, but it was never completed.

*Theater, 18–30 Garrison Lane. Hyman Gereson purchased the Brunier Hair Plant at the intersection of Garrison Lane and West Baltimore Street in the fall of 1914; he planned to improve it with a large motion picture theater, bowling alleys, and a dancing academy.

*Theater, 1801 Presstman Street. Gottfried Helwig planned a large move theater on the southwest corner of Presstman Street and Kirby Lane in late 1914. Stanislaus Russell drew the plans.

*Theater, 801 East Baltimore Street. Plans were under consideration by Colman Klein to build a $15,000 theater at this location in April 1915.

*Theater, 619–621 Federal Street. The Baltimore Amusement Company was planning a theater at this location in May 1915.

*Theater, 2804 Pennsylvania Avenue. Susan Raith contemplated building a $5,000 moving picture theater at this location in December 1915. The permit was granted in March 1916. J. R. Forsythe was working on revised plans in October 1916.

*Theater, Liberty Heights and Garrison Boulevard. William Strom drew plans for a $10,000 movie theater at this intersection in January 1916.

*Theater, Calverton Rd. near West Franklin Street. James P. McClurg was granted a permit to build a one-story motion picture theater here in January 1916.

*Theater, 2523 Greenmount Avenue. The property at this location was leased to a Mrs. Halling for a moving picture theater in February 1916.

*Theater, 2205–2207 Madison Avenue. The Madison Amusement Company planned a theater at this location as early as October 1915. Plans were prepared by Callis and Callis in 1915. Sparklin and Childs prepared revised plans in February 1916.

*Theater, 400 block South Broadway. Pearce and Scheck planned a large theater at this location in June 1916.

*Theater, 607–613 North Fremont Avenue. In September 1916, Oliver B. Wight was preparing plans for a $25,000 moving picture theater at this location for Bohannon and Lewy.

*Theater, Gay and Federal streets. Henry W. Webb planned a 2,500-seat, $80,000 theater at this location in mid-1917. He had architect Thomas Lamb view the site in May, but nothing came of the project.

*Theater, Annapolis Junction. Henry Webb's Parkway Theatre Company was contemplating a large theater near the planned military installation east of Annapolis Junction in the summer of 1917. The theater was never built, but the installation was built and became Fort George G. Meade.

*Theater, Odenton. The Camp Meade Mercantile and Amusement Company, formed in 1917, planned a large theater at Odenton in the fall of 1917.

*Theater, Milton Avenue and Hoffman Street. An elaborate, 1,000-seat movie theater, said "to represent the last word in theater construction," was planned for this corner in July 1919.

*Theater, southeast corner of O'Donnell and Third streets, Canton. Rupert W. Wright was granted a building permit in December 1919 to erect a $25,000 movie house at this location, part of the old Bayview Brewery site.

*Theater, 602–610 North Howard Street. There were ambitious plans by S. Friedberg, president of the Grafanola Company of Norfolk, for a large amusement complex with stores, a motion picture theater, billiard room, bowling alleys and a dance hall at this location in late 1919. Plans were being prepared by Norfolk architects Neff & Thompson in the spring of 1920. The project got as far as demolition work in July 1922.

*Theater, 1600 block of Druid Hill Avenue. There was much controversy about this theater project. In early 1920, architect Oliver Wight prepared plans for a 2,000-seat luxury theater on Druid Hill Avenue for Robert Ennis. The project was abandoned because of local opposition.

*Theater, 238–244 South Broadway. Pearce and Scheck planned an 1,800-seat movie theater from plans by Zink & Sparklin at this location, in the same block as the Leader Theater, in 1919–1920.

*Theater, Southwest side of Calverton Road near Harlem Avenue. The Central Theater Company took title to two lots at this location in December 1920 for a moving picture theater.

*Theater, Park Heights and Oswego avenues. The local civic association received more than 400 complaints against a proposed theater in this location in February 1921. It was never built, but the Avalon was built six years later a few blocks away.

*Theater, 12–16 East 25th Street. Louis Schlichter, president of the Edmondson Amusement Company, had architects Smith and May prepare plans for a $250,000 Italian Renaissance style movie theater at this location in May 1921.

*Theater, Northwest corner of North and Harford avenues. A syndicate was reportedly interested in building a theater here in the spring of 1921.

*Theater, Madison Avenue near North. Joseph Castleberg had plans for a $200,000 theater at this location, the site of the old Cafe Kaluna, drawn by E. G. Blanke in March 1921, but the city denied him permission to build it in June 1921.

*Theater, north side of 36th Street east of Roland Avenue. An ordinance granting the Ideal Theatre Company permission to build a theater at this location was passed by the city council in September 1921, but the theater was never built.

*Theater, 615–621 East Fayette Street. The Central Theatre Company, incorporated in 1920 by members of the Rome family and others, was planning a theater at this location if the city did not acquire the property to widen Fayette Street.

*Theater, Catonsville. Heine C. Andrae had plans by Walter M. Gieske for a $30,000 theater in Catonsville in January 1922.

*Theater, between North Avenue, Maryland Avenue, Charles Street and Twentieth Street. A large movie theater was to be included in a $3,000,000 community building planned for this location in 1923.

*Theater, Park Avenue and Fayette streets. The Stanley organization, based in Philadelphia, was looking at a site, near the southwest corner of Park and Fayette, for a theater in September 1925. Stanley eventually selected the Academy of Music site for their new theater, the Stanley.

*Theater, Baltimore and Fremont streets. Plans were made for a motion picture theater at this location in November 1925.

*Theater, 4432–4442 Park Heights Avenue. The Real Estate Holding Company was granted a permit to erect a large movie theater at this address in June 1926. There is some confusion between a theater at this address and the Avalon, also planned in 1926, but located at 4338 Park Heights Avenue.

*Theater, 1909 West Pratt Street. G. I. Marks had plans in August 1926 by C. Callis for a two-story building at this location that would contain a movie theater, four stores, bowling alleys and a hall.

*Theater, Park Heights near Spaulding Avenue. The Associated Theatre Company was planning a 1,500-seat movie theater designed by Ewald G. Blanke at this location in February 1927. The Uptown Theater was built near this location in 1941.

*Theater, Sparrows Point. J. O. Blair prepared plans for a $25,000 theater in Sparrows Point in February 1927.

*Theater, 5200 York Road. Philip J. Scheck planned an 800-seat theater at this location from plans by S. Russell in June 1927. Bids were rejected in the spring of 1928, and the architect was going to take new bids on the general contract in the fall of 1929.

*Theater, 1941–1949 West Pratt Street. The Loew's organization was considering building a 2,000-seat theater at this location in January 1928.

*Theater, Gwynn Oak Avenue between Maine and Woodbine avenues. A movie theater was part of the original commercial plan for this block in the summer of 1928, but the theater was eliminated because of local opposition.

*Theater, 614–618 North Gilmor Street. The Fidelity Amusement Company was granted a permit for a theater at this location in August 1928. The Harlem Park Methodist Episcopal Church was located at this address; when it burned, the church was converted into the Harlem Theater.

*Theater, 7–13 Chesapeake Avenue, Towson. The 1929 Sanborn insurance map of Towson showed a large movie theater at this address, just east of the Towson Ice Company. The legend "to be movies" appeared in the middle of the proposed auditorium. This theater was never opened, but, according to a 1927 newspaper ad, a pipe organ, 700 seats, and projection equipment had been installed, and the theater was scheduled to open on September 5, 1927. If all these preparations had indeed been completed, it is difficult to see why it never opened as a theater.

*Theater, Parkville. David Harrison prepared plans for a movie theater in Parkville for I. L. Hornstein in the summer of 1932.

*Theater, 3122–3124 Greenmount Avenue. William and Helen Harris were granted a permit to convert the buildings at this address into a movie theater in May 1935. A. C. Radziszewski prepared the plans in July 1935.

*Theater, 1528–1534 Pennsylvania Avenue. The Radio Amusement Corp. planned a $25,000 movie theater at this location in April 1936. Jerome Kahn prepared the plans.

*Theater, Clifton Avenue. Leo Homand, vice-president of the Lord Calvert Theaters Company, was planning an 850-seat movie theater on Clifton Avenue in 1937. The architect was Oliver B. Wight.

*Theater, southwest corner Belair Road and Mary Avenue. T. B. Gatch & Sons was granted permission to build a theater at this location in July 1937.

*Theater, 419–423 North Caroline Street. The Radio Amusement Company received permission to erect a movie theater here in July 1937. The ordinance was repealed in January 1938.

*Theater, 8–34 West North Avenue. The North Avenue Market was granted a permit in July 1937 to alter a portion of its building to construct a motion picture and vaudeville theater.

*Theater, 5127–5131 Park Heights Avenue. Myer H. Stern had a permit for a movie theater at this location in February 1938.

*Theater, 3633–3637 Park Heights Avenue. Plans were made for a movie theater at this location in 1939.

*Theater, 663–665 West Saratoga Street. David Harrison prepared plans for Nathan Feldman's movie theater at this location in January 1939.

*Theater, Parkville. David Harrison had plans for a theater in Parkville in August 1939, but the project was canceled.

*Theater, 4925 Park Heights Avenue. A permit was granted to the Park Heights Amusement Company on June 10, 1940, to erect a $30,000 movie theater at this location. The permit for the Uptown, a block further out on Park Heights, was granted the same day. A judge reversed the Zoning Board's permission in September 1940. Apparently the planned theater would have covered the entire lot, and zoning law provisions limited construction coverage to only 75 percent of the site. The Park Heights Amusement Company filed plans again for a theater at the same location in 1941. Bernard F. Owens and Associates were the architects. The project was abandoned.

*Theater, 3202 West Belvedere Avenue. Joe Walderman and Morton H. Rosen were granted a permit to build a $15,000 movie theater at this location in June 1940. David Harrison was selected as the architect.

*Theater, 2801–2805 Greenmount Avenue. The Oriole Theatre Company was granted permission to build a movie theater on this site in June 1940.

*Theater, 3540–3544 South Hanover Street. David W. Chertkoff received permission to build a theater here, a block north of the Brooklyn Theater, in November 1940.

*Theater, 839 West Franklin Street. David Harrison prepared plans for a movie theater at this location in December 1940.

*Theater, Ellicott City. Baltimore exhibitor, C. W. Hicks, had Bernard Evander prepare plans for a movie theater in Ellicott City in 1940.

*Theater, Leeds Avenue and Colchester Road, Arbutus. J. E. Moxley was preparing plans for a theater and bowling alley at this location in March 1941.

*Theater, Reisterstown Road, Park Circle and Sequoia Avenue. The Park Circle Theatre Company planned a movie theater at this perennial favorite location in the summer of 1941.

*Theater, 6643–6645 Belair Road. The Overlea Shopping Center, Inc. was granted permission to build a one-story brick movie theater at this location in September 1941.

*Theater, 3539 South Hanover Street. The Hudson Realty Company received permission to convert this building into a movie theater in December 1943.

*Theater, 5701 Pulaski Highway. A $20,000 motion picture theater was planned for this site in October 1944.

*Theater, 621 South Fremont Avenue. A group of African-American clergymen and some white supporters blocked the construction of a movie theater at this location in November 1945.

*Theater, 1007–1013 Madison Avenue. After a year-long battle in the City Council, sponsors of this $70,000 theater gave up in June 1946; opposition from the NAACP and the Baltimore Housing Authority proved too much to overcome.[349]

*Theater, McCulloh Street at Cloverdale Road. Jerome and Joseph Grant planned a new theater on the site of a stable. Neighborhood residents strongly opposed the theater, and it was not built.

*Theater, 3309–3315 Belair Road at Erdman Avenue. John F. Eyring designed a $75,000 theater for Ritz Enterprises at this location in April 1949.

*Theater, 17 West Mount Royal Avenue. An ordinance to zone this address for a new movie theater was introduced in the City Council in December 1970.

*Theater, 500 block East Baltimore Street. An ordinance to zone this address for a new movie theater was introduced in the City Council in December 1970.

*Theater, Old Columbia Pike and Montgomery Road. George Brehm and Joseph Einbinder planned a 2,000-seat quadraplex at this location in 1973.

*Theater, Troy Hill Shopping Center, Elkridge. In 1997, the Manekin Corp. announced a 20-screen 5,000-seat megaplex for Loew's Theaters.

*Theater, Village at Waugh Chapel, Gambrills. In 2003, Flagship Cinemas of Everett, Mass. was planning a megaplex at the Village at Waugh Chapel.

*Theater, New York–based Madstone Theaters was planning to open an art theater in the rapidly developing area between Little Italy and the Inner Harbor in 2004.

*Theaters, North Avenue and Charles Street. Several large theaters were planned at or near this intersection in 1920. Among those interested in building there were Pearce and Scheck and Marcus Loew. Both were planning 3,000-seat theaters that would have cost about $1,000,000. Another large theater was planned for Charles Street between Lafayette Avenue and North Avenue. None of these projects got beyond the planning stage, although the Hippodrome Theater Company purchased the Shriner lot on the northeast corner of North and Charles in early 1920.

Theatorium, 11–13 East North Avenue, 1909–1923, Otto G. Simonson, c. 500 (350 seats as Center Stage). The Theatorium was opened by a Delaware-based corporation capitalized at $100,000, and headed by Samuel Buckman with Harry E. Jenkins. It was the first motion picture and continuous vaudeville house in the northern part of the city. It cost about $30,000—a high figure for 1909. The *Sun* contained a drawing of the theater along with this description:

> The design ... of modern Gothic architecture ... consists of one large arch entrance, banked on each side by smaller decorative openings, leading into one domed vestibule having a depth of 35 feet. In this vestibule is the ticket office and above is a shell for the musician's balcony. By means of double doors at each side of the vestibule entrance is had to the auditorium which will be about 28 feet wide and 100 feet long,[350] having a seating capacity of about 500 with two spacious aisles leading directly to the rear exits, one on each side of the stage. The stage will have the usual proscenium accessories, with fireproof curtain, dressing rooms, fly galleries, paint bridge, sliding skylights, and hose standpipe system.[351]

The interior color scheme was gold, green and white. The building permit was granted in April 1909, and the Theatorium opened on October 11, 1909, with a vaudeville and movie program. The vaudeville acts were interspersed with movies. The Theatorium presented two shows a day, from 2:00 until 5:30 and from 7:00 until 11:00. The Joe Wood Agency furnished the vaudeville acts. In 1913 only moving pictures were exhibited there. A show consisted of three reels of two-week-old pictures, which were changed daily; admission was 10 cents. The name was changed to Peabody in 1913 and to New Peabody in 1920. The Parkway Theater Company, which operated the Parkway Theater less than a block to the west, leased the Peabody in the fall of 1918.

The new owners remodeled the theater. A description of the remodeling is given in *Moving Picture World*.

> The interior has been made a delight to the eye, with soft gray, old ivory and old rose predominating. The pilasters are in old ivory, while the panels have been done in gray. Simple scroll works ornament the tops of the panels, and these, with the pilaster tops of Corinthian design are trimmed in old ivory and gold. The wainscoting has been finished in old rose, while the carpets and damask at the exits are of the deep old rose color. New seats have been installed. The lighting system has been entirely changed, and the inverted bowls, located one on each of the fourteen pilasters, throw a rich, soft glow over the entire auditorium. The ceiling is heavily beamed.[352]

In 1919 a $3,000 2/9 Moller organ (Opus 2867) was installed. A new front was added and the front of the lobby was enclosed in glass during improvements in August 1920.

During its last few years, it was operated by the Whitehurst chain. In September 1924, the Peabody was leased for 10 years to the Saunders Drive It Yourself Company of Kansas City which planned to convert the building into an automobile rental agency. It was later converted into an Oriole Cafeteria. In 1965 it was remodeled back into a theater, Center Stage. After some years of considerable success, the theater was destroyed in a fire set by arsonists on January 9, 1974.

Thirty-One, 31 West Lexington Street, 1906?–1923, 1938–1952; Alfred Lowther Forrest (of 1907 theater), Oliver B. Wight (of 1920 remodeling); c. 400 (as Picture Garden; 350 as the Lexway; later 297). Of all the movie houses in Baltimore, none has had more changes of name than this one. It started out, as early as June 1907, as the Thirty-One when Sperry and Hutchinson leased the four-story building in which it was located to Bohannon and Lewy.[353] Bohannon and Lewy called it the Wizard and operated it until March 1910 when they moved their business across the street, where they built the Great Wizard.

Bohannon and Lewy were great promoters. On July 13, 1908, the *Sun* carried this advertisement for the Wizard, "Special! On account of the numerous requests the sensational attraction 'The Directoire Gown on the Streets of Baltimore' will be shown Monday, Tuesday, and Wednesday of this week in addition to an excellent program of all new pictures."[354] The Wizard specialized in Biograph Films.

In the spring of 1911, it was remodeled for about $20,000 and the name was changed to Picture Garden. The new theater, decorated to resemble an Italian garden, was scheduled to open on May 20, but problems with the decorations caused several postponements. It finally opened with first-run pictures and singer Archie Lloyd on July 8, 1911, modestly advertising itself as "the most luxurious Photo-Play Theatre in America." Admission was 5 cents.

A contemporary account[355] called it "a handsome and rather unique moving picture theater," and described it in these words:

> It is provided with a waiting room and no one is permitted to enter the theater proper until there are available seats. The color scheme is green and gold. Along the walls are twelve handsome panels representing flower scenes. These were executed in Bordeaux, France. The dome is covered with lattice work through which are twined vines of green that twist in all directions. Up above the latticework is the blue dome. By an ingenious electrical device this dome can be lighted so as to represent the break of day, with its delicate shadings of gray, and can be changed to that of night with the deep blue of early evening showing the rising stars. The floor is covered with red velvet carpet. The house is well supplied with electric fans.

Another description added, "The electrical effects in the nature of great clusters of flowers and fernery suspended from the ceiling and illuminated by varicolored electric lights were the center of attraction in the decorative scheme. The Picture Garden is so arranged as to carry out, as nearly as possible, the appearance of a beautiful garden."[356] From these descriptions, it appears that the Picture Garden was an early attempt to create an atmospheric decor similar to the kind perfected in the 1920s by architect John Eberson.

Soon after it opened, the Picture Garden installed a pay-as-you-enter system. Instead of buying a ticket from a cashier, patrons put nickels into a register operated by a doorkeeper. The new system was said to have "aroused much interest."

J. Howard Bennett purchased the theater in late 1911; he hired violinist Sidney Seidenman to lead the orchestra and Paul Levy—described as "Atlantic City's idol"—to sing. In February 1912, the Picture Garden began using behind-the-screen talkers. Joseph Blechman leased it in late 1913. A new 2/12 Moller organ (Opus 2082), which cost nearly $3,000, was installed in the spring of 1916. In early 1918, the lobby was enclosed. Blechman purchased the theater for $155,000 in March 1920, and operated it until it closed in 1923. Four months later, he announced plans to remodel it. It reopened on September 20, 1920.

The Sun described the new theater:

> Since the remodeling ... has been completed the playhouse now has a very beautiful and comfortable appearance. After the plans of Architect Oliver B. Wight, the cost of reconstruction was about $25,000. The Adam style of design has been used. American-Italian marble forms the wainscoting of the lobby, the walls of which are of imitation Caenstone; there is a vaulted ceiling exquisitely decorated in the Adam style, and the floor is of marble tiles. On either side of the foyer are ... two handsome mirrors, and the floor is covered with green velvet carpet. In the auditorium the panels are stippled in an artistic design and the color system ... is tan and old ivory. The light is furnished by shaded bracket lamps ... near the screen the ceiling has been formed into an arbor effect with colored lights. A marquee has been put over the entrance.[357]

The remodeled theater lasted less than two years. Unable to compete with the Century, which opened across Lexington Street a year later, the Picture Garden closed. The building was leased to milliners in December 1922.

In May 1938, plans were made to remodel it back into a movie house. The permit to alter the building was granted in June 1938. When it reopened, in late July 1938, it was named the Lexway, and lasted until 1942. It was leased by a West Coast group, Newsreel Theaters of America, in that year and reopened as Baltimore's second newsreel theater on June 5, 1942—renamed the Newsreel. The first attraction included 62 news events and shorts with exclusive war analyses by H. V. Kaltenborn and Tex McCrary, and the latest issue of *The March of Time*.

Appropriately enough, one of the biggest news stories of 1942 was taking place at the same time that the Newsreel was opening—the U.S. fleet was blasting the Japanese navy near Midway Island. The newspaper headlines read, "Hard Hit, Jap Fleet Flees." The Newsreel had mechanical turnstiles instead of ticket takers. There was also a large map showing world battlefields and what time it was in each zone, and the management planned to display photomurals of Baltimore war heroes. The entire proceeds of the first two days' shows were donated to the Army and Navy relief funds.

In announcing the opening of the Newsreel,

Sun film critic Donald Kirkley commented on its chances of success: "Baltimore's needs for a cinema which offers an outlet for all the documentaries, undiluted by escapist fiction, has been argued pro and con for many years. Some say such a project will succeed here, in an ideal location, some say it will collide with the city's chronic antipathy toward novelties. We shall see."[358] Apparently Baltimore was not ready for an all-news theater. A year after it opened, the Newsreel added older feature films to its programs.

The name changed again; between June 11, 1944 and 1946, the theater was known as the Vogue. Manager Walter Gettinger began experimenting with all comedy shows, or "Laff Shows," as early as January 1946 and into the summer. Probably as a result of the success of these shows, the theater changed its film fare. After a brief attempt at showing first-run British films in October 1946, the theater switched completely to comedies.

On Thanksgiving Day in 1946, the Vogue became the Laffmovie.[359] Shows consisted of a humorous feature film with dozens of cartoons and comedy shorts. One early show, in November 1946, featured the Three Stooges, Donald Duck, Laurel & Hardy, Leon Errol, Billy Gilbert, Ben Blue and "other laff hits." A January 1948 show at the Laffmovie included 15 comedies— with 50 comedians— and six cartoons. It was a child's delight. One of the features of the Laffmovie was a series of distorting fun-house mirrors— the kind that made people look tall and skinny or short and fat— in the lobby. In the spring of 1948, radio station WBMD broadcast live from the Laffmovie's stage on weekdays between 2:00 and 2:30 P.M.

For unknown reasons, the Laffmovie folded in 1949. In March 1949, Martin J. Lewis of New York took over the theater; he remodeled and refurbished it and renamed it the World.[360] In the remodeling, a slight pitch was given to the floor, new seats were installed, and a small lounge was added. The World opened on March 23, 1949, with *Symphonie Pastorale*, starring Michele Morgan. A *Sun* movie critic was pleased that Baltimore would have another theater dedicated to the exhibition of foreign films. He also appreciated that the theater had been redecorated "in good taste" and provided with "a dignified lobby." He probably did not like the fun-house mirrors. The World ran many double features and revivals, including Marx Brothers' comedies and Flash Gordon space operas. It closed in the summer of 1951.

In November 1951, the theater reopened again — this time would be the last — as the Fine Arts. The Fine Arts opened with Yvonne De Carlo in *Hotel Sahara*. In December 1951, the theater rode out a violent attack by Sydney R. Traub, chairman of the Board of Motion Picture Censors, over the theater's showing of the film *Dante's Inferno* without having the censor board's seal. A magistrate found that manager Gettinger was guilty of only a technical violation and not a "willful intention to break the law."[361] However, the Fine Arts did not last out the year. It closed by July 1952.

The World and Fine Arts were among the few venues in town that showed older classic films. All traces of this theater and even the street on which it stood have vanished forever beneath broad pavements and sterile modern office buildings. This theater, in its last years, was a cozy, oddly shaped, seedy little house. It was roughly L-shaped and very narrow for more than half its length before opening up to the left a dozen or so rows back from the screen. According to Donald Mettee, the booth at the Laffmovie was very low and the operator had to lie on his stomach to focus the picture. The take-up reel was placed in a slot in the floor of the booth. Along with the Idle Hour and the Howard, this theater was one of the pleasant spots to relax downtown in the midst of a hard day of shopping.

Three Arts, 844 North Howard Street, 1935–c. 1942, unknown, 260–325. In 1935 a theater called the Three Arts (or Fine Arts) was opened in what had been the Hi-Hat Club.[362] The Three Arts was apparently located next to Lehmann Hall, but, with the conflicting evidence available, it is difficult to establish the exact location.[363] It opened on the evening of September 25, 1935, with a production by the Bekefi-Delaporte Institute of the Dance, Drama, and Music.

The *Evening Sun* described the interior of the theater as "decorated in silver and red with heavy multi-colored ceiling beams and a scarlet-draped entrance" with a flowered carpet that ran "the length of the interior to the foot of the deep stage, with its backdrop of blue and crimson."[364] Other articles added that the theater had a sloping floor, a commodious stage, a large storeroom for properties and scenery, and a number of dressing rooms. The decorations were designed by John McGrath, president of the Charcoal Club.

At some point before July 1937, it was renamed, this time as the Hindenburg. On September 8, 1937, Moe Kohn began showing movies in the theater with the film *Tales from the Vienna Woods*. Kohn changed the name to the Filmart or the Fine Arts. A. H. Young-O'Brien was the manager. The management planned to cater to students of foreign languages and had installed a new, up-to-date sound system. It was called the Three Arts again in 1938 and 1939 when it was leased by William R. Streett whose Ramsay Streett Players presented Broadway plays. During the 1938 season, plays were presented three days a week and foreign films were shown on a different three days.

The theater seemed to be closed off and on during 1940. In May 1940, it was again called the Hindenburg when it was showing pro–German movies and the Three Arts when it was presenting stage shows and other movies. The Hindenburg was investigated and closed by the FBI for showing German films.

According to projectionist Charles Reisinger, who was working at the Hindenburg when it closed, the theater was located in a hall on the second floor of Lehmann Hall. The projection booth had been built on the roof and had two ports, covered with glass, through which the film was projected into the theater. The exact location of the Hindenburg has proved extraordinarily difficult to pin down. For several weeks in the fall of 1940, the Three Arts showed the controversial film *Ecstasy* with Hedy Lamarr; six months earlier this film had played for several weeks at the Lexway. The theater seemed to be open sporadically after 1940, and was called the Art in the spring and summer of 1942.

Times, 1711–1715 North Charles Street, 1939–present; John W. Lawrence (of 1969 remodeling), Alex Castro (of 1999 additions); 725 (later 558, 485), c. 1,145 (after 1999 addition of four screens). The Times, Baltimore's first newsreel theater, opened on October 6, 1939, four months after the Charles Street Theatre Company had received a permit to convert the building at 1711–15 North Charles into a movie theater. The one-story brick and stone building in which the theater was built had originally been a powerhouse and car shed for the City Passenger Railway Company, dating from 1892. Part of the powerhouse became the Times and part was converted into a ballroom. The first attraction at the Times was Hendrik Van Loon's *The Fight for Peace*, which received excellent reviews.

The theater, built by William Gay, had an interior decorated with murals of news events done with a wide brush in black highlighted in yellow by Paul Roche, who had also done some of the murals in the auditorium of the main Enoch Pratt Library building. The Times was the first theater in Maryland to use the new Mirrorphonic Deluxe sound system. The floor was constructed in a bowl shape or reverse incline to provide good viewing from every seat.

The clean, modern lines of the new theater impressed a writer for the *Home News* of October 5, 1939: "Baltimore is presented with an impressively handsome movie theater ... a theater that would exemplify the highest standards in motion picture exhibition.... While the Times is not a sumptuous cathedral of the cinema, it is an excellent example of fine architecture and first rate artistic values. Here you will find stylism expressed in graceful and charming manner. Its beauty has not been defiled by unnecessary frills and furbelows."

A stainless steel time capsule called a "time rocket" was buried in front of the theater to be opened on the 50th anniversary of motion pictures. On November 8, 1939, a bronze tablet, sculptured by Mildred Caplan to celebrate the 25th anniversary of the first newsreels, was placed in the Times' lobby. The building was remodeled in June 1941, and a new marquee, twice the size of the former one, was added.

The Times Theater maintained a policy of all-night movies from May 1943 until the end of the war. For many years, the Times was part of the Zeller circuit which also included the Rex, Roslyn, and Roxy. By the late forties, it had ceased being a newsreel theater and was specializing in double features, often playing them at the same time as the Roslyn. In 1958, the Times was acquired by JF Theaters. They closed it in August 1958 for a complete remodeling and reopened it as the Charles on October 2, 1958, with a re-run of *Around the World in 80 Days*.

The 1958 remodeling consisted of a rebuilt front, renovated seating, new interior decorations, and a refurbished marquee. The Charles claimed a local record in 1961 by showing just four films during the whole year.[365]

In late 1969, the theater was completely renovated again. Based on the newspaper description, the renovation was extensive.[366] Much of the remodeling was done to enhance the acoustics of the theater. The auditorium was covered with acoustical panels, and, "Masonry walls on the sides of the screen have been used to create a proscenium frame and the stacked masonry units create a tile-like effect." The lobby was enlarged and a new lounge was built next to it. The front of the theater was refaced with brick. Inside, the predominant colors were various shades of blue. The renovated theater opened on Christmas Day 1969.

The Charles closed in the fall of 1978, and the following May it was leased for six years by Washington exhibitor David Levy.[367] Levy, who had wanted a theater in Baltimore for several years, began a very successful operation, featuring art and repertory films, that lasted until 1993. After redecorating the Charles in an art deco design, Levy reopened it with a screening of Claudia Weill's *Girl Friends* on May 31, 1979, to benefit the Baltimore Film Forum. The Charles did well — providing the city with many films that otherwise would probably never have played here — until the early 1990s.[368] The Charles had many hit movies over its 14 years under Levy's management, including *Cinema Paradiso*, *Kiss of the Spider Woman*, and *sex, lies and videotape*. The Charles was also the venue for controversial films; one of the most controversial — Jean-Luc Godard's *Hail Mary* in 1986.

Then, on December 12, 1993, after a 25 percent decline in attendance and reportedly several months in arrears with the rent, Levy closed the theater. He blamed the plight of the Charles on three trends: crime,[369] VCRs, and competition, especially from the Senator and the Rotunda. Everyone wondered where local moviegoers would turn for art films. Fortunately, they did not have to wonder long. Former manager, John Standiford and his uncle James "Buzz" Cusack stepped in and signed a five-year lease in February 1994 to run the Charles. George Mansour, a nationally known art film booking agent, booked the films. Cusack and Standiford added security guards and an espresso bar. The Charles reopened on March 10, 1994, with a sold-out event that benefited two local charities.

By 1996, the Charles was still open, but just barely. It was around this time that the operators announced that they would like to add a second screen in an adjoining space, where the Famous Ballroom was once located. A year later, they carried out a $1.6 million expansion that added four new screens in the ballroom space and increased the seating capacity to more than 1,000.[370]

The largest new auditorium seats 250 while the other three seat 155, 145, and 110; the new auditoriums have stadium seating with new high-backed seats. The lobby of the original Charles Theater was converted into the Cafe Metropole while a new entrance to all five auditoriums was constructed at the front of the ballroom space. The new box office is located at one end of the lobby. It was described by *Sun* columnist Edward Gunts as "made of dark metal and shaped like two rocket ships on a launching pad." The decor of the largest of the new auditoriums is similar to the original auditorium. Again, good acoustics was an important concern, and there are corridors separating the auditoriums from each other so that they have no common walls; crossover sound is virtually eliminated. Each of the new auditoriums differs from the others.

The concessions stand and the rest rooms are located beneath the rear seats of the new theaters. The projection booth serving the largest of the new auditoriums is located above the lobby. A window in the black-painted booth has been designed to resemble the diaphragm of a camera. The interior color scheme is in shades of yellow and blue.[371]

The grand reopening of the Charles multiplex took place on April 21, 1999. Lt. Gov. Kathleen Kennedy Townsend told the crowd that they were witnessing the "resurrection of a great Baltimore landmark," and Mayor Kurt L. Schmoke joined director John Waters in cutting a ribbon of film to open the new showplace. The theater, which started off as one of the locations for the Maryland Film Festival, has consistently been named as the best city theater by the readers of the *Baltimore City Paper*.

In its 110-year history the building at 1709–1711 North Charles Street has gone from a power plant, bowling alley, ballroom, newsreel theater, second-run theater ("where bums sleep"), first-run theater to the city's premier art theater. The exhibitors who cared for this theater — Leon Zeller, Jack Fruchtman (who converted it to the Charles), David Levy (who developed it as an art house), and John Standiford and James Cusack (who took it into the new century), and the Shecter family (the first owners of the theater and owners of the Famous Ballroom who have nurtured the theater and kept it in local hands) deserve a big round of applause.

Timonium I–II, 2131 York Road, Timonium, 1973–2000, Donald B. Ratcliffe, 500 (theater 1) and 425 (theater 2). M. Robert Rappaport opened this twin theater in the Timonium Shopping Center across the street from the State Fairgrounds on June 27, 1973. A third auditorium was added in the spring of 1976 by dividing the larger auditorium. The new twin auditoriums were too long and narrow to make them good for movie going, but the second auditorium was very comfortable and had good sight lines. Loew's closed the Timonium theaters in late 2000.

Timonium Drive-In, Timonium Road, Timonium, 1955–1982, unknown, 2,479 cars (1,400 reported in 1972). General Cinema Corp. of Boston opened this huge drive-in just west of York Road south of the fair grounds on August 3, 1955. Opening ads claimed that it was the "world's largest, most luxurious theatre" with a large, super CinemaScope screen and space for nearly 2,500 cars.

A full-page ad in the *Sun* of August 3, 1955 described the new drive-in:

> Bigness is only important to us for the pleasure it will give you and your family at Timonium Drive-in Theatre! The world's largest CinemaScope screen is important because it gives you the brightest, clearest, and most exciting picture possible, with easy vision for the passengers on each seat in your car.
>
> Same with our two giant RCA projectors, our marvelous new sound system with the latest in-car speakers.... Our ... delicately graded ramps, and our soft beams of artificial moonlight from high towers throughout the arena. *All* these things are the biggest, the newest, the best that money can buy.
>
> Then ... there's the fabulous refreshment building ... that lets you serve yourself delightful hot or cold snacks during intermission time without pushing or shoving or waiting in line. And ... for the small fry is the gay and colorful kiddieland where everything is free and all the rides are operated by two funny, entertaining clowns.

The drive-in also featured free diaper service, free bottle service for all babies, electronic ticket booths, and a six-lane toll plaza.

The Timonium Drive-In was torn down in 1982 to clear the way for a $30 million business park and Holiday Inn.

Tower, 222 North Charles Street (2 Charles Center), 1967–1977, 1981, unknown, 605. The Tower was the first new movie theater in downtown Baltimore in 20 years. It was also one of the most stunningly unsuccessful movie theaters in the city. It was built by the JF organization and so deeply buried in the new Charles Center that it was difficult to find. City renewal officials praised the theater for its contribution to Charles Center and considered it an indication of the business community's faith in the downtown area's rebirth.

The Tower was a great disappointment to the owners and the city. It never did well. Ground was broken for the $500,000 theater on November 16, 1964. It boasted a $25,000 automatic Norelco projection system. According to one source, the Tower was the first theater in the state to have an automated projection system.[372] The interior was decorated in avocado, green, and brown. The Tower opened on December 19, 1967, with a gala premier of *The Comedians*, starring Elizabeth Taylor and Richard Burton. The festivities were attended by JF head Jack Fruchtman, director Peter Glenville, three Playboy bunnies, and a select audience. A 60-piece band from Archbishop Curley High School provided music.

The Tower began losing money after its showing of *The Exorcist* in mid-1974 and, by its final years, it had been reduced to showing exploitation films. The Tower closed on November 15, 1977, with *Bucktown, USA* and *The Mack*. It took in just $400 in the picture's seven-day run. The next day, the theater's ad announced, "Closed for renovation. Reopen Xmas." Jack Fruchtman said that he was stymied. He could not seem to develop a mix that would attract customers to the theater. Nothing worked, from first-run films to sex films to black films and art films.

Charles Productions, a local company operating several of the former JF neighborhood theaters, reopened the Tower in March 1981. After extensive remodeling, the Tower quietly began showing movies again in late March. A grand reopening was held on April 17 with *Mon Oncle d'Amerique*. The new exhibitors did no better than Fruchtman, and the theater closed again. A group of developers had plans in 1985 to remodel and reopen the Tower, but that attempt was also a failure. The Tower remained closed for four years, then, in 1989, the family of Allan L. Berman, a local developer who had died in 1977, gave $1.3 million to the Johns Hopkins University to help fund the school's Downtown Center. The money was used to convert the space where the Tower Theater had been into a 222-seat lecture and performance hall called the Jean and Allan L. Berman Auditorium.

Town Theater (see Empire {2})

Towson, 512 York Road, Towson, 1928–1992, George Norbury MacKenzie III, 537. The Towson was opened by Porter G. Seiwell and W. A. Allen on March 1, 1928. It was built, for a reported $100,000, on the site of the Towson Hotel stables.

The *Jeffersonian* contained a full-page advertisement for the new theater and the following description:

The original front of the Towson Theater (512 York Road, Towson, 1928–1992, George Norbury MacKenzie, III) can still be seen, little changed from this 1938 photograph.

The building is constructed of brick with reinforced concrete floors and foundations. An elaborate and artistic entrance faces the York Road, and immediately inside a pretentious and beautifully furnished lobby with comfortable table seats, thick carpets, lighted by soft toned floor lamps make an ideal place for patrons to meet their friends or wait for the show to be completed before entering the main auditorium ... the theatre itself ... is, indeed, a work of art. Nothing is missing, from two projectors to make the pictures continuous, to the thick rich carpet on the floor. Seats that are so comfortable that we feel the management will have to provide entertainment of unusual interest to keep the patrons awake; lighting effects that are of every color of the rainbow; walls that are carefully decorated and hangings of unusual beauty and richness. The stage ... is provided with curtains of rose velour and also footlights. Two dressing rooms are provided..., with all the modern and latest conveniences.... The [manager's] office ... is provided with an elaborate system of telephones which permit the one in charge to keep in close touch with every section of the building at all times ... it is heated by vapor-controlled heat ... supplied by the latest and most efficient oil burner.... An insulated, reinforced gypsum roof carries the double advantage of being cool in the summer and warm in the winter. Two large electric fans erected on the roof assure the supply of ... clean air at all times.[373]

The theater had a Kilgen organ (Opus 4017).

Siewell operated the theater for many years, finally selling it to the Hicks-Baker organization in 1959. The theater was completely renovated in early 1967. Durkee Theaters operated the Towson for a few years before they were bought out by Loew's. In early 1984, the theater was twinned into two 250-seat auditoriums. In 1986, the Towson became the Towson Art Cinemas and, along with a different kind of film, came new treats at the concession stand — Perrier, frozen Cannoli pops, sunflower seeds, and Haagen-Dazs ice cream. Loew's operated the Towson as the successor to Durkee Theaters until early

1992. A new month-to-month lease was negotiated, and Loew's reopened the theater. Loew's gave up in July, two months after the eight-screen Towson Commons theaters opened a block away.

The Towson was converted into Rec Room Billiards in 1996, opting to keep the original arcade intact. Three years later, the Recher Brothers, co-owners of the theater, turned it back into a theater. The Recher Theater is a concert hall that can seat about 700 people. It has two full-service bars and a full-service kitchen.

Towson Commons 8, 435 York Road, Towson, 1992–present, Cambridge 7 (mall designed by RTKL Associates), 2,624 (for 8 auditoriums). The large enclosed mall and parking garage, on the southwest corner of York Road and Pennsylvania Avenue in downtown Towson, was planned by developer James J. Ward, III, in 1985. The next year General Cinema Corporation agreed to lease space in the new mall. Work on the ritzy mall began in the spring of 1989, and General Cinema Corporation opened its eight-screen complex there on May 22, 1992. The estimated cost of the theater was $2 million. The auditoriums ranged in size from 202 to 368 seats. The opening of Towson Commons forced the closing of the Towson Theater and the York Road Cinema.[374]

Traveler Theater, 2507 West North Avenue, 1913–1917. Frank L. Kidd operated this small movie theater. It may have been on the first floor of a row house or it may have been an airdome.

Traymore Casino (see Artmore Casino)

Twilight Amusement Company (see Columbia {1})

United Amusement Company (see Elektra {1})

Uptown {1}, 5010–5018 Park Heights Avenue, 1941–1975, John F. Eyring, 1,100. The Uptown {1} was built for the Uptown Amusement Company of Lauritz Garman, Benjamin Beck, George Flint, and Chauncey Wolf. Permits for three movie theaters within a few blocks of each other in Pimlico were granted on June 10, 1940, but only the Uptown {1} was built. The fireproof theater was built of brick and steel and measured 80 by 198 feet. It cost an estimated $200,000. It featured the recently perfected ultra violet lighting system called "invisible light," which brought out hidden luminous patterns in the fabric and plastic detail of the stage and proscenium. The arcaded side aisles were an unusual feature, as was the glass-enclosed box office located in the center of the lobby. The seating was in large, reclining seats, or, for 40 cents, you could sit in a glass-enclosed soundproof box or loge. The souvenir program of the Uptown's opening contained a flowery description of the theater:

> A large space ... adjacent to the theatre building is available for quick and convenient parking. The stately modernistic lines of the theatre exterior reflect substantial construction and quality standards. Three illuminated marquees list current and coming attractions and a specially devised clock ... over the front entrance ... gives the running time of the performance and exact time of arrival or departure.
>
> An entirely revolutionary system of enclosed ticket selling has placed the beautiful box office of the UPTOWN in the center of a large enclosed lobby permitting the purchase of tickets conveniently INSIDE the theatre and not in the outmoded and obsolete method of sidewalk buying in queues.
>
> Opening upon this first lobby is a spacious inner foyer. ... Large mirrors, subtle lighting and carefully selected musical programs are outstanding features immediately encountered by the patron. From this foyer ... are exquisitely appointed ladies' and gentlemen's lounges and retiring rooms.
>
> An ornamental staircase leads to ... glass enclosed loges and private boxes where private ... parties may be accommodated by appointment and previous reservation.
>
> The auditorium ... is graced by an extra large space for standing and two arcaded side aisles ... for quick and convenient seating or egress. Specially loomed, double thick carpeting of unique design and color gives warmth and comfort to the entire interior. The walls are covered in embossed fabric and walnut paneling. Indirect fluorescent lighting is restful and artistic.
>
> Oversized chairs ... specially designed by Heywood-Wakefield, are comfortably spaced permitting the utmost in accessibility and seating. The large stage is draped in gorgeous silks, velours and plushes and specially contrived proscenium panels are brilliantly illuminated by the recently discovered "black light." The amazing possibilities of this new light are further displayed in a specially painted feature curtain which takes on a third dimension when lit.
>
> Careful attention has been given to picture projection and sound amplification. An extra large 24-foot plastic screen reveals every interesting nuance of the projected image....

Top: A night shot of the beautiful front of the Uptown Theater (5010–5018 Park Heights Avenue, 1941–1975, John F. Eyring) just before it opened in 1941, showing its unique three marquees. This theater was John Eyring's most ambitious design. *Bottom:* The broad auditorium of the Uptown.

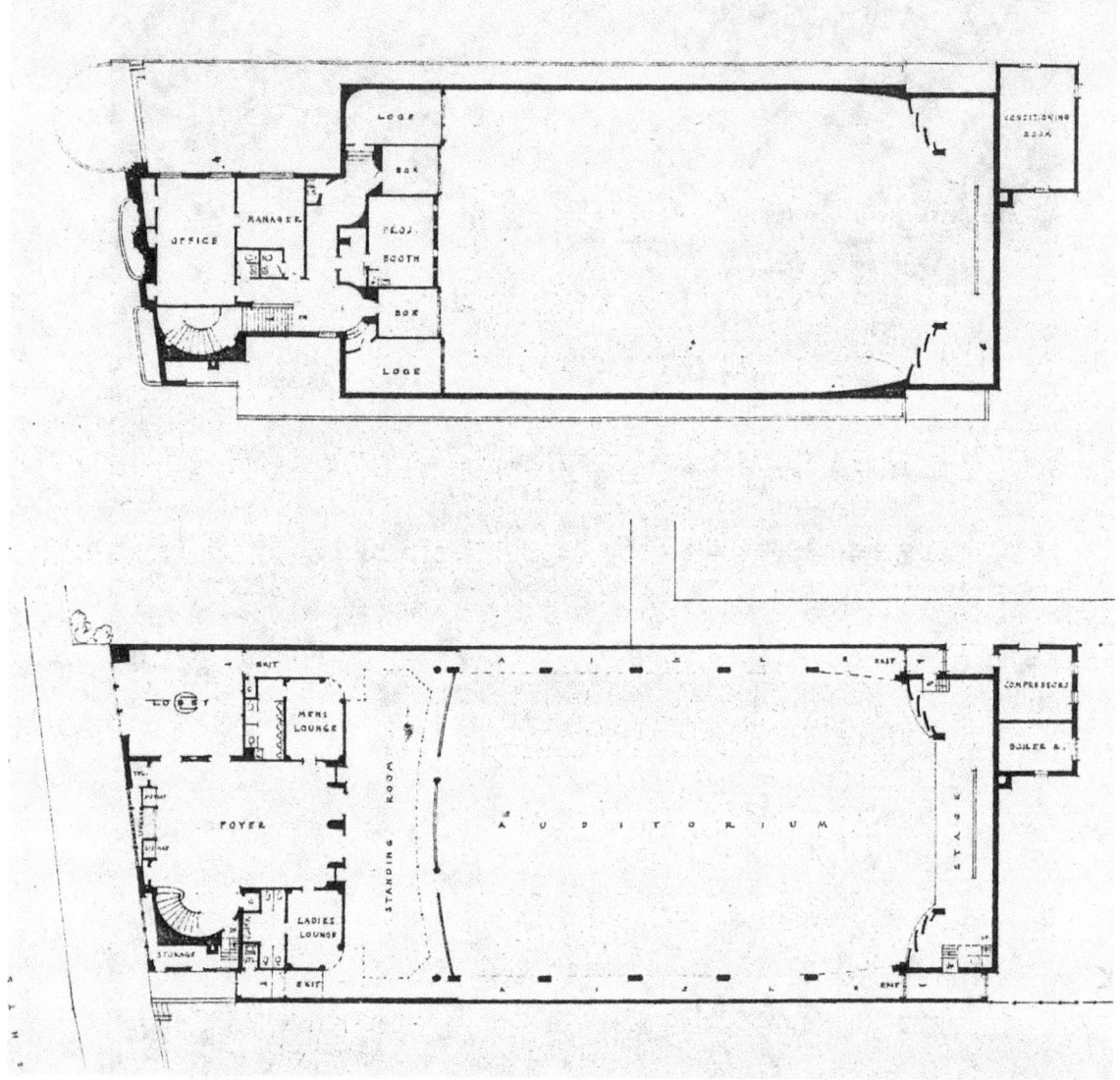

Plans for the main floor and mezzanine level of the Uptown Theater.

The Uptown {1} opened on June 27, 1941. Between 1955 and 1966, a new triangular marquee replaced the original curved marquee. The Uptown slowly ceased to function as a theater. Open on a part-time basis in the early 1970s before finally closing in 1975, it later became a church.

Uptown {2} (see Schanze)

Valencia, 18 West Lexington Street, 1926–1952, John Eberson, 1,466. When Loew's acquired the Century they brought in John Eberson, master of the atmospheric theater, to design a new theater above the Century where a rooftop ballroom known as the Century Roof had been. When the Valencia was built, local wits said it was the newest and oldest theater in town; it was "over a century!"

Eberson had the ballroom gutted, and in it created an auditorium that was "the grand inner courtyard of a Spanish grandee's Madrid palace." He added an atmospheric ceiling, where small lights with quartz lenses twinkled as stars. Cloud machines were installed in vases in niches on either side of the screen. A 2/8 Wurlitzer organ

John Eberson took the Spanish ballroom above the Century and converted it into a Mediterranean courtyard as the atmospheric Valencia Theater (18 West Lexington Street, 1926–1952, John Eberson). (Photograph courtesy of the Theatre Historical Society)

(Opus 1463) was added to provide music. The walls were rough stucco with carvings, small lamps, stained glass insets, and other decorations strewn about on them. An awning over the screen, installed just a few hours before opening, was the final touch.

Most of the 1,400 seats were on one floor, but there were two tiny balconies for VIPs on either side of the projection booth. Patrons entered the Valencia from the Lexington Street entrance by going down a long ramp to the right of the ramp that led up to the Century. At the end of the ramp was a ticket booth, and beyond that there were elevators to carry patrons eight floors up to the theater. The outside display sign, which consisted of 4,365 light bulbs, was, in 1927, the largest electrical theater sign in Baltimore.

The Valencia opened on December 23, 1926, with a private showing of *Valencia*, starring Mae Murray. The Grand Opening for the public was held the following day. The original staff at the Valencia, except for the projectionists, from the elevator operators to the usherettes, was made up entirely of women. The usherettes were "Baltimore girls, carefully selected for their beauty, courtesy and savoir faire," dressed in Spanish provincial uniforms with black sailor hats, gay blouses, and pleated skirts. Prices at the Valencia ranged from 25 cents to 65 cents.

Baltimore News movie critic Norman Clark thought the Valencia was, "Without fear of contradiction ... one of the loveliest theaters in these United States." He also said that George Wild's orchestra gave "promise of developing into an excellent organization." Clark also praised organist John Elterman, saying that he could do anything with the organ except make it sneeze. Apparently the movie was not as interesting as the theater, at least to one woman who wrote to the *Evening Sun*, "From my point of view, Mr. Loew displayed rare good judgment in giving us that silly Mae Murray as an opening attraction for his Valencia. There was so much to see and admire in that really, truly palace that what was going on on the screen wasn't noticed much. Imagine what we would have missed if the picture should have been worthwhile."[375]

The Century and Valencia installed their first air-conditioning system in the spring of 1927. It was touted as, "Baltimore's first and only theater refrigerating plant." According to the Gas and Electric Company, the Century and Valencia together were one of the eighty largest electrical power consumers in Baltimore. In June 1928, the Valencia installed Movietone and Vitaphone sound systems. In March 1930, Loew's City Manager was considering the possibility of converting the Valencia into a newsreel theater. It closed down for several years between 1936 and April 22, 1942.

The Valencia served as a "move-over house" for the Century; after a movie had played at the first-run Century, it was moved to the Valencia for an additional week. At one time, the Valencia was the home of a light opera company that specialized in the material of Gilbert and Sullivan.

The Valencia closed on May 18, 1952. Morris Mechanic bought the Century and Valencia from Loew's in October 1955, and announced that no more movies would be shown there and that it was to be converted into office space. But even that was not to be. The Valencia was demolished in 1962 along with the Century and other fine old buildings in that irreplaceable block. The Valencia was probably a terrible firetrap, which could be why many people were afraid to go up there. Joseph Eyring, a son of the builder Erhard Eyring, refused to attend movies at the Valencia. Still, the theater provided a touch of the exotic; it was an exciting place to see a movie.

Valley Centre 9, 9616 Reisterstown Road, Owings Mills, 1990–present, Kelly Clayton & Mojzisek, 2,200 (also reported to be 1,900; for nine auditoriums ranging from 120 to 375 seats). Negotiations between the owners of Valley Centre Mall and JF Theaters to build this theater began in 1988. JF had obtained the land for this theater complex behind the Valley Center shopping center and had planned the theater just before they sold out to Loew's. The theater opened on February 9, 1990.

The Valley Centre 9 resembles other theaters designed by Kelly Clayton & Mojzisek, such as the Center Park in Calverton and the Columbia Palace 9. A large conical cupola or rotunda, illuminated from the outside, covers the external box office. The huge concessions stand — 65 feet long, with six serving stations, and computerized soft-drink dispensers — was at that time one of the largest in the area. The auditoriums are located off the central lobby and off the wings, which extend from the lobby. Each auditorium is equipped with Dolby stereo sound. Infrared hearing aids for hearing-impaired patrons are also available in all the auditoriums. The Valley Centre 9 is located near the site of the Valley Drive-In.

Valley Drive-In, 910 Reisterstown Road, Owings Mills, 1961–1977, unknown, 600 cars. Schwaber Theaters opened this drive-in on July 6, 1961. It had a 45 × 105-foot metal screen and a combination snack bar and projection room. Children could play in the drive-in's "Candy Cane Land" playground. In 1975 the owner of the Valley Drive-In was charged, under a new county law, with showing an X-rated film on a screen that could be seen by the non-paying public. A district court judge struck down the law and dismissed the charges in November 1975. After the theater closed, a developer planned to build a sports resort on the site, but financing was not available.

Victor {1}, 1900 Frederick Avenue, c. 1911–c. 1918, unknown, 175. This movie house occupied a handsome brick building on the northwest corner of Frederick Avenue and Monroe Street. It was a movie house as early as 1911. Carl W. Seibel purchased it in 1915 and reopened it on September 4, 1915, as the New Victor with a special five-reel show that included a two-reel Charlie Chaplin comedy.

Victor {2}, 2038 Wilkens Avenue (or 500 South Fulton Avenue), 1913–1915. This Victor was an open-air theater owned by Edward J. Leitz. It was actually located on the south side of Cole Street, just east of the intersection with Wilkens Avenue, and was surrounded by a high board fence.

Victor {3} (see Royal Moving Picture Parlor)

Victoria {1}, 415 East Baltimore Street, 1908–1951; A. Lowther Forrest (with decorations by Henry Arntz), E. H. Glidden (of 1916 alterations), A. Lowther Forrest (of 1922 rebuilding), William H. Lee (of 1925 remodeling); 1,500

The Valley Centre 9 (9616 Reisterstown Road, Owings Mills, 1990–present, Kelly Chayton & Mojzisek) was one of the first of a new generation of luxurious multiplexes.

(later 1,250). The Victoria was built for Aaron Cohen, Michael Hartz, and Joel Gebhardt and operated by Pearce and Scheck as a vaudeville theater. Cohen, Hartz, and Gebhardt purchased two pieces of land on the south side of the 400 block of East Baltimore Street in the spring of 1908. Plans for a $100,000 theater there were completed by the end of May.

The original exterior was elaborately ornamented with plaster nymphs and trumpet-playing cherubim. A huge chandelier hung in the arched entrance. A long, narrow lobby, 15 × 94 feet, led to the auditorium, which was parallel to Baltimore Street, and measured 88 by 104 feet. Seating was on the main floor, the balcony, and in eight boxes. The color scheme was terra cotta and green. The stage was 80 feet wide, 50 feet high, and 28 feet deep. Downstairs there were 11 bowling alleys. With 10 exits, it was claimed that the theater could be emptied in two minutes.

The Victoria opened on December 28, 1908, with a program that featured the Four Musical Kings, who played 25 different musical instruments; Humes and Lewis, comedy acrobats; Shayne and King, who gave "Hebrew impersonations of a new sort"; the Divo Twins, vocalists and dancers; plus assorted motion pictures. The full house for the first show at 7:00 P.M. gave an enthusiastic reception to the new theater; many people had to be turned away.

A reviewer commented, "As a standard of excellence the opening bill augers well for future programs ... from every viewpoint the opening of the Victoria was a success. The audience was highly appreciative and the smoothness with which the first performance was presented gives ample proof of the care and forethought exercised by the management ... to provide ... a theater popular with the best class of patrons."[376] The orchestra was conducted by Mr. Steinwald.

During the summer of 1910, the Victoria split its vaudeville acts with the Casino Theater in Washington. It was the first theater in Baltimore built especially for vaudeville, and it claimed to have been the first 10–20–30-cent vaudeville theater in the country. Motion pictures formed a part of every show. Perhaps the most famous performer to play at the Victoria was Charlie Chaplin, who appeared there in May 1913 in "A Night in an English Music Hall."

In 1913, the Victoria was described as "an exceptionally good paying investment." Even so, Pearce and Scheck gave up their lease on the Victoria soon after they built the Hippodrome in 1914. The Fred G. Nixon–Nirdlinger booking agency of Philadelphia leased the Victoria in 1916 for $15,000 annually. Plans were made then to remodel the theater. New seats and draperies were installed, and the walls and ceilings were repainted and frescoed. The lobby was finished in white marble.

Disaster struck when the theater was partially destroyed by fire on March 25, 1922. The fire started soon after the last show had ended at 11:00 P.M. Within ten minutes, flames had burst through the roof. It was believed that the fire had resulted from a carelessly discarded cigarette. It took firemen two hours to get the blaze under control. The interior of the theater was wrecked, as much from the fire as from the water used to put it out. At one point, it was thought the balcony would collapse because of the tons of water directed on it.

The Victoria was rebuilt for an estimated $125,000. The present terra cotta facade which replaced the original plaster front and is still visible on Baltimore Street, dates from this rebuilding. A metal marquee was added over the entrance, and a huge sign containing hundreds of incandescent lights was erected above the marquee. The wainscoting in the lobby was of brown-tinted marble while that in the auditorium was of the gray-veined variety. The lines of the interior and the decorations retained their former Renaissance flavor, but the colors were changed to old rose and gold. It reopened with second-run films on November 25, 1922. Despite rebuilding, the Victoria did not do well and was closed until Hyman Blum took over operation of the theater in 1924. In August 1925, when the Victoria reopened for the fall season, music was provided by a six-piece string orchestra under the direction of Emanuel Schwartz. In November 1925, the Independent Film Company of Philadelphia, headed by Baltimorean Louis Berman, leased the theater. They changed the name to Embassy and brought Philadelphia architect William H. Lee down to completely remodel it in a 16th century Spanish style at a cost of more than $225,000. Walnut beams formed the motif of the ceiling decoration while the atmosphere of an old Spanish castle was carried out in the arch over the stage and in the decoration of the foyer and lobby. A huge 2/8 Wurlitzer-Hope-Jones orchestra organ, Style "F" (opus 1265) was installed to augment the 30-piece orchestra under the direction of Jules Corcozza.[377] Corcozza was later replaced by Mischa Guterson. The organists were Louis Jackobson and Earle Tobias. The golden pipes of the big organ were divided equally on either side of the stage; some of them reached the ceiling.

The theater reopened as the Embassy on February 28, 1926, with a private showing of *The Phantom of the Opera*. The organist that night did a bang-up job, and when a subtitle announced that the chandelier was falling, he pulled out all the stops. The resulting sound, that startled the audience out of its wits, resembled a real chandelier crashing to the floor.

American Theaters Corporation acquired the theater in August 1926, and reopened it with some improvements on September 6, 1926. The Embassy had a tough time after 1926. It was used for burlesque, vaudeville, movies, Yiddish theater, and occasional sporting events. The theater closed down in late 1927. M. Levine reopened it as a stock burlesque house in early 1928. John H. Nickel, who ran the nearby Gayety, purchased the theater in June 1929 in order to eliminate any possibility of competition. The J & L Theater Corporation acquired the Embassy in late 1934 and planned extensive alterations. The theater was sold in February 1946. It finally closed in 1951.

The auditorium was replaced by a parking garage in 1953. The lobby was used as a hamburger joint and later as a show bar.

Victory, 1017 Patapsco Avenue, Brooklyn, 1944–1973, David Harrison, circa 1,000. The Victory was a large barn-like theater, designed for Edward F. Perotka, which opened on November 30, 1944. It was a plain red brick structure and cost an estimated $25,000. The auditorium, which ran parallel to Patapsco Avenue, was located behind a row of stores. Louis Tunick acquired it in 1953 and operated it for many years. One regular patron of the Victory remembered that the management opened the theater free to children on the last day of school before the Christmas vacation. They provided soda, doughnuts and hard candy, and showed a movie with cartoons and a serial.

The Embassy (415 East Baltimore Street, 1908–1951, A. Lowther Forrest, E. H. Glidden of 1916 alterations, A. Lowther Forrest of 1922 rebuilding, William H. Lee of 1925 remodeling), which started life as the Victoria, had begun its downhill slide in this c. 1934 photograph. (Photograph courtesy of the Maryland Historical Society, Baltimore, Maryland)

Village, 11900 Reisterstown Road, 1966–1997, John Carroll Dunn (1991 alterations), 900 (after 1985 triplexing — 320, 250, and 200). The JF organization opened the Village in the Reisterstown Shopping Center on August 24, 1966. A typical suburban theater of the 1960s, a large rectangular structure at one end of the Reisterstown Shopping Center, it had all the requisite amenities, including a nursery service under the direction of a matron, a birthday room, and a room for private parties. R/C Theaters acquired the Village in 1979 and triplexed it in 1985. R/C

Ritz Enterprises' Vilma Theater (3403–3407 Belair Road, 1928–1973, John Eyring) had a front very similar to Eyring's Strand Theater in Dundalk.

operated it as a discount theater until 1997, when it was converted into a video store.

Vilma, 3403–3407 Belair Road, 1928–1973, John Eyring, 900. The Gaertner circuit purchased the land in the fall of 1927 and opened the Vilma on May 5, 1928. It cost about $125,000 and was designed in Spanish Mission style, very similar to the Strand in Dundalk, with interior colors of ivory, gray, and gold. There were two small balconies on either side of the projection booth. The auditorium ceiling was made of rather elaborate pressed metal. The Vilma had a two-manual Marr & Colton organ. It closed in the fall of 1973 and was converted into an attractive banquet hall, La Fontaine Rouge, by caterer Tom Stuehler. The new hall utilized much of the original front, but the inside was gutted.

Virginia (see Oriole)

Vogue (see Thirty-One)

Walbrook, 3100 West North Avenue, 1916–1966, J. Edward Laferty, c. 1,400. The Walbrook is a massive, fairly unattractive, dark brick structure on the northwest corner of West North Avenue and Roseland Street. It was built for the Walbrook Amusement Company (Harrison L. Stires, president, and Marion Pearce and Phillip Scheck directors) at an estimated cost of $20,000.[378] Stires became locked in a fight with Thomas Goldberg about which one of them would build a movie theater in the 3100 block of West North Avenue. After a long battle in the City Council, the permit was granted to Stires on June 3, 1914. The Council also approved Goldberg's plans for a theater across the street. Building began in December 1915.

Moving Picture World provided a detailed description of the new Walbrook.

> The building has been constructed so as to be absolutely fireproof throughout. The exterior is of Colonial brick with metal cornices ... a marquee has been placed over the triple

arched doorways of mahogany of the main entrance on North Avenue. The building measures 48 × 121 feet....

The lobby measures 10 × 45 feet. The walls are of old ivory, while the wainscoting is of Marvelo marble. The box office, which has a verdi-antique [sic] base and is paneled with heavy plate glass on three sides, is located in the center of the inner wall between two large mahogany doors paneled with glass which lead into the auditorium. Directly at each end of the lobby, large doors open upon spacious staircases of ornamental cast iron with slate treads which lead to the mezzanine floor, where private rest rooms for women and men ... are located; and thence to the balcony. The seating capacity of the balcony is 200 and the first row is arranged as boxes, which may be engaged for parties....

The operator's booth is located directly over the mezzanine floor and back of the balcony. It is equipped with ... two Simplex ... projection machines, a motor generator and a rewinder. The ventilation of this booth is done by a large rotary exhaust fan. ... The throw of the projection machine to the gold fibre screen, measuring 15 × 18½ feet, is 110 feet.

Situated in the ceiling, under the balcony ... is located a dome, finished in old ivory, which emits a beautiful diffused glow from the cove lighting system with which it is equipped. The floor is bowled so that the screen can be plainly observed from every seat. There are two four-foot aisles. There is a row of eleven seats in the center and on each side of this row is a four-foot aisle, and next to the walls on both sides is a row of six seats. These seats, which measure 19 × 20 inches, like the woodwork, are done is French grey. The ceiling is 30 feet high. The walls are done in old ivory, with large panels of Rose du Barry silk, topped by flower festoons. Below this is a wainscoting of old leather

The Walbrook Theater (3100 West North Avenue, 1916–1966, J. Edward Laferty) was built into the side of a hill at North Avenue and Rosedale. (Photograph courtesy of the Photography Collections, Albin O. Kuhn Library, University of Maryland, Baltimore County)

dado. A large chandelier ... is suspended from a heavy beamed and paneled ceiling with enriched cornices and moldings. The orchestra pit measures 9 × 14 feet and has room enough for a baby grand piano and six musicians. A heavy maroon colored carpet covers the floors. The seating capacity, including the balcony, is about 1,400.

A low-pressure steam heating system is used. Three large radiators have been placed in recess panels on each side of the main auditorium and one small radiator is located in each rear exit. Other radiators have been placed throughout the building, so that a uniform temperature is produced.

Both natural and artificial ventilating systems have been installed. There are ten ceiling ventilators. Large, rotary, ball-bearing fans have been placed in a vent house situated on the roof ... to force the air either in or out of the theater.[379]

The projection booth was quite small with barely enough room for the two projectors.

The Walbrook opened on May 29, 1916. It offered a program that changed every day, with performances running from 2:00 P.M. to 10:45 P.M., and there was an orchestra in attendance. Prices were a uniform 5 cents in the afternoon, but in the evening there were 250 seats for 5 cents, 700 seats for 10 cents, and 50 box seats for 25 cents. In the fall of 1916, the floor and seats on the sides of the auditorium were completely changed because the "bowl" in the floor was at too great an angle. This remodeling was probably from plans by Ewald G. Blanke and John J. Zink.

Thomas Goldberg, who operated Goldberg's Theater across the street, bought the Walbrook in March 1917. Arrangements were made in the summer of 1919 to install a new 2/8 Moller organ (opus 2726). The theater was renovated again in the summer of 1926. The exterior was repainted, new seats were installed in the boxes and on the first floor, new draperies were hung and the interior was redecorated. The troublesome rise on the sides of the lower floor was finally eliminated.

By the early 1960s, the Walbrook had a concession stand, a popcorn machine and a soft drink machine. It outlasted its neighbors, the Hilton and Windsor, by several years. The Walbrook began advertising as an African-American theater in 1956, and closed in 1966 to become a church. The Walbrook's marquee has been removed, but otherwise little else has changed.

Washington, 811–815 Pennsylvania Avenue. David Schwaber was granted a permit to build a theater at this location in December 1919. By June 1920, Ewald Blanke was drawing the plans. Schwaber, Blanke, and Alfred G. Buck incorporated the Washington Theater Company for $300,000 in 1921. Blanke was making revised plans that February. The theater was scheduled to open in September. Then the Boulevard Theater Scandal, which involved Buck, members of the City Council and the law firm of Dickerson and Nice, came along, and the Washington Theater project was scrapped.

Washington Hall Theater, 725–729 East Baltimore Street, 1837–1928, John D. Allen Company (Philadelphia, of 1906 remodeling), 2,000 (600—first floor, 400—balcony, 1,000—gallery). This ancient theater was built as the Washington Hall Theater in 1837 on the site of Hart's Tavern. It was later called the Baltimore Opera House, Olympic, Central, Monumental, and finally Folly. The Baltimore Opera House was located on the upper floors of a building that had the Calverton Carpet Manufacturing Company on the first floor. Destroyed by a fire in 1874, in 1875 it was rebuilt as the New Central Theater.[380]

The new theater opened to a packed house on August 16, 1875, under the management of the Kernan brothers, with "specialty acts, music, dancing, song and farce." Tickets cost 25 and 50 cents. Locals often referred to it as "The Bridge" because it was just east of the Baltimore Street Bridge over Jones Falls. It was a large theater. The proscenium opening measured 35 feet wide by 37 feet high; the stage was 40 feet deep and 62 feet wide. Behind the theater was a summer garden.

The entrance was to the west of the theater, and a long, covered walk led along the east side of Jones Falls to the garden. In the middle of the garden were tables and chairs, and around the garden was a sawdust track, about ten feet wide, where six-day walking matches were held.... Later the annex was converted into a roller skating rink and still later into a bicycle rink.... At one time there was a big glass tank in the garden, and Clara Beckwith, woman diver, would give exhibitions. Also there were boxing matches and battle-royals which always drew a big crowd. In the battle-royals four or five pugilists entered the ring, and the survivor was the winner.... Large glasses of beer were five cents, drinks of the best whiskey were ten cents and fancy drinks, like mint juleps, were 15 cents. A band gave nightly concerts and every Friday after school hours children were admitted free. Big revolving fans, made of framework covered with canvas were turned by a steam engine, which was in full view, and kept the place remarkably cool in hot weather.[381]

The Monumental was remodeled under the direction of George J. Roach & Sons in the summer of 1893. The exterior was painted a colonial buff and the interior was refrescoed in cream and gold. In December 1897, James Kernan opened the Thalia Theater in the rear of the Monumental; it could seat 1,000 and accommodate an additional 500 standees. The entrance to the Thalia was on Plowman Street. With an eye to attracting customers from the large nearby Eastern European Jewish population, Kernan made an arrangement with a New York theatrical syndicate to produce plays at the Thalia in Russian and Polish. The Thalia opened on December 24 with the comic opera *The Star of Prague*.

During the summer of 1898, the Monumental installed electric lighting. A new drop curtain done by the Lee Lash Company of Philadelphia was added; it was decorated with a picture of the stairway and hall of the Paris Opera House. Kernan often included movies—usually sensational ones—as part of the burlesque or vaudeville bill at the Monumental. In 1897 he exhibited movies of the Maher-Choynski fight, and the following year he played the Wargraph with events in the Spanish-American War. Films of the Windsor Hotel Fire, Admiral Dewey, and the Jeffries-Sharkey prizefight were shown there in 1899. The year 1901 brought an exhibition of movies of Carrie Nation's "hatchet brigade." In April 1903, Kernan played movies of the Corbett-McGovern fight.

The Empire Circuit acquired the theater in 1906 and remodeled it that summer. The remodeling, under the supervision of Edward D. Preston, included rearranging the galleries, rebuilding the boxes, and installing new chairs and interior decorations. In 1907, the Monumental had an eight-man orchestra conducted by Fred Heller. Between 1914 and 1916, it was called the Orpheum, which seems to have opened as a movie house on April 20, 1914. Louis Schaffer gave Yiddish theatrical performances there in 1917.

John H. "Hon" Nickel, who at the time operated the Nachmann Hotel, acquired the Monumental in October 1917. He reopened it with burlesque. The burlesque got him in trouble with the army in 1919. An officer at Camp Meade complained to the police that the "language of the actors and actresses playing at the Folly Theater was intolerable and a moral menace to soldiers and sailors."[382] Nickel had to post a $1000 bond to continue operation after his theater, hotel and cabaret were the target of attacks by the Maryland Hygiene Society in early 1923. The society complained that there was vice and a general disregard of prohibition at these places. Nickel denied that there was any vice and said that many of the best citizens of the city were among his patrons.

For the fall 1924 season, Nickel moved his burlesque from the Folly to the Gayety. A hodgepodge of shows played out the last years of the old theater. Tragedy struck in September 1924 when boxer Charlie Holman collapsed in the 12th round of his fight there with Lew Mayrs. Holman died a few hours later at Mercy Hospital. Yiddish films were shown at the Folly in 1926 and 1927. In May 1926, the famous Yiddish tragedian, Joseph Kessler, appeared in a Yiddish version of *Hamlet* at the Monumental, which was called Schorr's Yiddish Theater then.

Wrestlers and boxers would often tag along with the burlesque shows. Meyer Leventhal remembered a wrestler named Hassan "The Turk," who offered $50 to anyone who could stay in the ring with him for three minutes. A huge beer wagon driver named Shad Link jumped in with him and beat him. The Monumental was also the place where noted Baltimore wrestler Americus (Augustus "Gus" Schoenlein) got his professional wrestling start.[383]

Fire hit the old theater again in March 1928, and this time destruction was complete. Norman Clark remembered early days at the Monumental in a nostalgic article a few days after the fire:

> ...[O]n Monday afternoons one of my assignments was to drop in at the Monumental and cover the show.... There I'd sit in a box—Treasurer "Buck" Sadtler always put me in a box—in all my critical splendor. The air would be blue with tobacco smoke and it would make my eyes smart, but bigad, I was a critic! The shows were rough and ready, but they were freer of smut than many big revues I have seen in recent years. And there were no bare hides shown on the stage. The girls were a little fatter then than nowadays—men liked them plump.[384] If the players had dared to use the profanity down at the Monumental that has disgraced the uptown stages the last two or three seasons—the theatre would surely have been closed by the police. But men thought they were ... seeing hot stuff when they besat themselves in the Monumental.

I remember I trembled for fear that my Sunday-school teacher would find out I was the great Monumental critic.[385]

Many years later, Baltimore artist John McGrath also had vivid memories of the Monumental from the previous century. He remembered standing in line from 6:30 P.M. and paying 10 or 15 cents for the thrill of seeing Nellie, the Beautiful Cloak Model, from the front row of the gallery.[386] The remains of the old theater were razed in 1932 to build a parking lot.

The Monumental had featured many famous entertainers such as David Warfield, Maggie Cline, Weber and Fields, and May Irwin. "Little Egypt" created such an uproar that police had to be brought in to restore order. Another sensation was the appearance of "the Great Otillie" doing the Danse du Trilby in "stockingless feet" in January 1896.

Watersedge, 7910 Dundalk Avenue, 1947–1950, John Carroll Dunn, 600. The Watersedge Theater Company built this unimpressive cinderblock movie house behind the Watersedge Shopping Center in Dundalk. One cost estimate was $100,000; this is difficult to believe. The interior was carpeted with red-gold carpets and the color scheme was in matching pastels. The theater opened on October 9, 1947. Bob Marhenke operated it during its last years and closed it in April 1950. The building was later used as an auto repair shop.

Waverly, 3211 Greenmount Avenue, 1910–1969, Herbert C. Aiken (John Zink, of 1934 remodeling), 485 (750 after 1921 remodeling; figures of 1,250 and 1,325 were listed for the theater after the 1921 remodeling, but these are probably too high; 722 c. 1935). The Waverly Amusement Company purchased the land in October 1909 and opened the $6,000 Waverly the following year. The original theater measured 27 by 100 feet.

A brief description appeared in the *Star*: "It will be constructed of brick and will have the latest safety apparatus to guard against fire. The entire front will be of ornamental plaster staff, which will be brilliantly illuminated with a profusion of vari-colored lights."[387]

The Waverly featured movies and vaudeville. Shows ran from 3:30 P.M. to 10:30 P.M.; admission was 5 cents. Soon after it opened, the Waverly's popularity made an increase in seating capacity necessary. Therefore, several plans were made. In November 1913, a new theater was planned at 3205–3213 Greenmount Avenue, and in January 1914, the owners applied for a permit to build a $2,500, one-story, brick motion picture theater there. Apparently the plans for a new theater were dropped in May 1914 in favor of a 16 by 93-foot addition to the rear of the existing theater.

At some point, prior to 1914, the management of the Waverly ran an open-air theater in a vacant lot behind the four-wall theater. It was called the Waverly Summer Garden. Customers bought their tickets at the same box office but walked through the theater, out the rear door, and sat on wooden folding chairs under the stars.[388]

Ben Cluster and Peter Oletsky's Crystal Amusement Company, which ran the Crystal Theater on Gay Street, acquired the Waverly in December 1914. The Crystal Amusement Company acquired the lot adjoining the Waverly in 1919 in order to enlarge the theater at a cost of $100,000. The original theater closed on December 11, 1920; it was gutted and used as the entrance to a larger brick and concrete auditorium in the rear. The new Waverly opened on February 21, 1921. A five-piece band and a two-manual Robert-Morton organ provided music. The new theater had a front of colonial red brick with a large arch filled in with framed glass. The lobby walls were paneled with mirrors. The interior decorating, featuring old rose and gold on a base of green tiling, was completed in October 1921.

Durkee Enterprises acquired the Waverly and reopened it on December 21, 1929. It was extensively remodeled in the summer of 1934. For much of its later life, the Waverly showed "action" films. Just before it closed, in 1969, its patrons were terrorized by a gang one evening. The patrons fled and the employees sought refuge in the booth until the police arrived. Incidents such as this helped to close the theater. The building is still standing. It was used as a Goodwill Store for many years.

West End, 1601 West Baltimore Street, 1911–1923, Paul Emmart, 450. The West End was planned as a vaudeville and motion picture theater in late 1910. It was built by the West End Amusement Company for an estimated $30,000 on the site of an old factory at the apex of the triangle where Frederick Avenue meets Baltimore Street, just west of Gilmor. There is some evidence that an open-air theater was located near the spot where the West End was built.

The West End was described as a large "semi-fireproof" motion picture theater of fancy pressed brick, with stone trim. It faced 124 feet

The Waverly's (3211 Greenmount Avenue, 1910, Herbert C. Aiken, John J. Zink of 1934 remodeling) massive vertical sign was still attracting customers in 1935.

Hoyt's West Nursery 14 (1591 West Nursery Road, Linthicum, 1998–present, Arrowstreet Inc.) is typical of the megaplexes of the 1990s.

on Baltimore Street, 133.6 feet on Frederick Avenue and was 35 feet wide at the rear. The first floor had cement floorings and the second had hardwood floorings. A stage extended the whole width of the theater.

The facade was ornamental marble, onyx, terra cotta, and metal. There was a large dance hall above the theater. While the Emmart brothers operated it for many years, it was sold at public auction in 1918 for $25,000. A new Hinners organ with cymbal, chime and human voice sound effects was installed in the spring of 1921.

The West End never did very good business, and the opening of the luxurious new Capitol Theater, less than a block away in 1921, was the last straw. The Rome organization purchased the West End for $43,500 and reopened it for a short time in February 1923. It closed later that year and was acquired by the Salvation Army for about $13,500 in June 1924. The building, with its unusual domed entrance, is still standing.

West Nursery Cinemas 14, 1591 West Nursery Road,[389] Linthicum, Anne Arundel County, 1998–present, Arrowstreet Inc. (Somerville, Massachusetts), 2,736. Hoyt's theaters opened this megaplex on March 13, 1998. More than 11,000 people attended opening weekend shows at the 14-screen theater. The $8.5 million theater complex occupies a 57,300-square-foot sand-colored building in an office park near the intersection of the Baltimore-Washington Parkway and West Nursery Road. It features all stadium seating, a self-serve concession area, a gourmet coffee bar, and a game room. The entrance, which consists of four quadruple doors in a three-story glass wall, is flanked on the right by a dark blue panel with a large yellow number "14" mounted in the middle, and on the left by a pylon, which extends beyond the top of the roof and is topped by a blue globe ringed by the word "Hoyts." The auditoriums range in size from 123 to 373 seats. Each theater has digital sound, extra-wide aisles and wall-to-wall screens. AMC had proposed

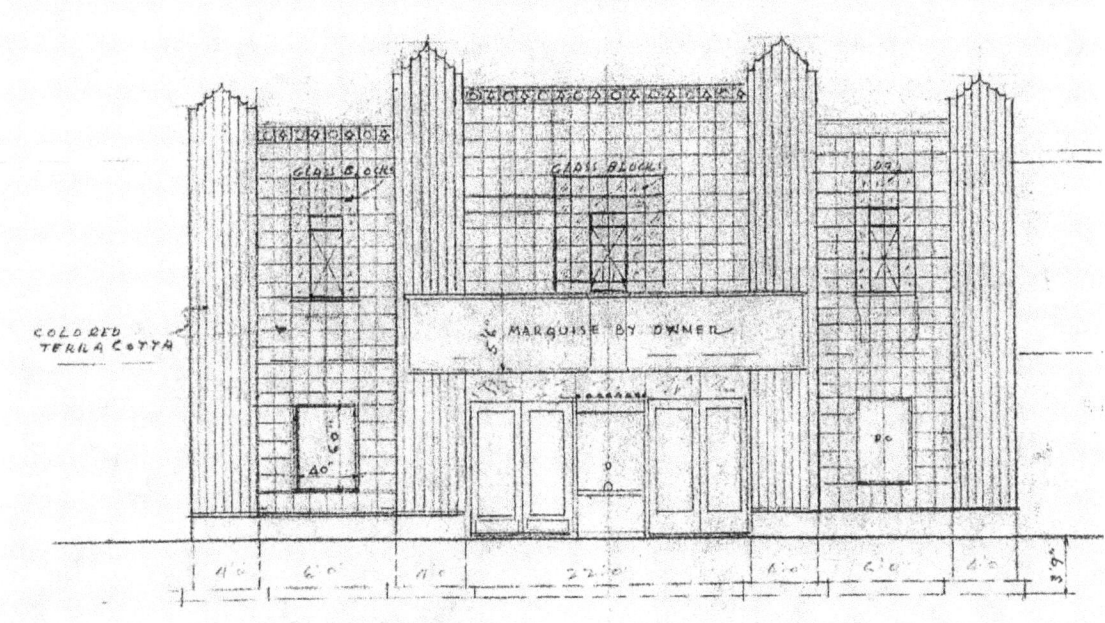

Architect's drawing for the front of the Westport Theater.

building a megaplex in the nearby Airport Square Industrial Park in 1995, but this theater never got beyond the planning stage.

Westport, 2305 Russell Street, 1940–1957, E. Bernard Evander, c. 500. The Westport was a quintessential neighborhood theater operated by the Hicks Circuit. It opened on June 20, 1940. It was a freestanding brick theater with the typical triangular 1940s marquee. The front was of colored terra cotta with three sections of glass blocks on the second-floor level. The Westport closed on October 26, 1957. It was torn down and replaced by a bank, which has been closed for many years. In the late 1940s, the Westport first had a single candy machine on the right side of the auditorium, where I bought Tootsie Rolls for 5 cents. Later a primitive popcorn machine was installed in the lobby; the popped corn was warmed by an electric bulb. A bag cost 12 cents.

Westview Cinemas, 6023–6026 Baltimore National Pike, 1965–1997, Fenton & Lichtig (of Westview I), 1,160 (Westview I), 895 (Westview II), 450 each (Westview III and IV). George Brehm and Joseph Einbinder opened the first five theaters within a five-year period on property adjoining the Edmondson Drive-In.

Westview I was a real showplace. The exterior was of stone, white split block, and multi-colored glass with a canopied entranceway and a freestanding marquee. The large foyer featured a pool with a life-sized statue, ceiling-high glass and multi-colored plastic windows, and a candy stand. The auditorium had gold drapes with split block coral walls. The carpeting was in various shades of green, blue, and gold. The seats were dark blue Heywood-Wakefield models with upholstered arms. The Technikote screen was 22 feet high by 51 feet wide. There was also a VIP party room with rocking chairs. Adjacent to the theater there were heated sidewalks to melt off the snow and ice and a parking lot with space for 450 cars. Westview I cost about $435,000. It opened on June 2, 1965; at the same time, demolition crews were attacking the Stanley Theater. From the very beginning, the theater made money, and within three years the owners added a second theater.

Westview II opened on November 19, 1968. It shared the stonewalled lobby containing a 10-foot waterfall with Westview I. Westview II featured rocking chair seats, an automated booth, and a closed-circuit TV connecting the booths of theaters I and II. General manager George Brehm described the second Westview Theater

The Westport Theater (2305 Russell Street, Westport, 1940–1957, E. Bernard Evander), a classy facade for a quintessential neighborhood theater; c. 1940.

as "really luxurious." He added, "We designed it with a discriminating, sophisticated audience in mind. We want to play pictures which will attract these people, reserving the Westview Cinema I for more general audiences."[390]

Four years later, two additional theaters opened in the complex. Westview III and IV cost $483,000 and opened in December 1972. The Westview IV, located on top of Westview III, opened on December 14. Westview III and IV were served by a single projection booth; the film was projected directly on the screen of one theater but required Periscope Optics to project on the other screen.

By the spring of 1984, there were six auditoriums in the Westview complex. At that time, the management decided to triplex the largest, Westview II, creating one 450-seat theater and two 250-seat houses from the original theater. One of the new theaters was scheduled to become an art house. In March 1989, Walter A. Robinson, the night manager of the Westview Cinemas, was stabbed to death in his office at the theater.

The management continued to subdivide the theaters. In mid-1990, the auditoriums of the complex's two largest remaining theaters, Westview VII and VIII, were twinned into four 200-seat auditoriums, and by November 1990, the Westview complex had been diced up into 10 smaller theaters.

The Westview Cinemas closed on May 29, 1997. A representative for the owner said that they hated to close. Apparently the deal with Circuit City was too good to turn down, and the competition from the United Artists Westview Mall 9 just down the street was too much. On the last day, the owners rolled back prices to $1, and many customers came by to say good-bye to the 32-year-old theaters. Some parts of the Westview were auctioned off in June and demolition began the next month. Within a few months there was no trace of the theaters.

Westview Mall 9, 5824 Baltimore National Pike, 1992–present, R·K Architects, c. 2,000. United Artists opened this nine-plex near the western

Westview Mall 437

Top: The original Westview Theater (6023–6026 Baltimore National Pike, 1965–1997, Fenton & Lichtig) was certainly one of the most interesting movie theater designs. *Bottom:* Pool and statue in the lobby of the Westview Theater.

end of Westview Mall on April 17, 1992. The entrance to the theaters is inside the enclosed mall and consists of little more than a ticket counter and two concession stands. The nine auditoriums range in size from 200 to 400 seats.

Westway, 5300 Edmondson Avenue, 1939–1978, J. E. Moxley, c. 700 (later 564). The Westway was located on the corner of Edmondson Avenue and Aldershot Road in the small commercial center known as North Bend.[391] It was a one and one-half story brick theater with a unique, nearly circular marquee over the corner entrance. The ticket booth was covered by the marquee but was separate from the main theater building. The Westway, which opened on April 22, 1939, seems to have been one of the last theaters in Baltimore to have Country Store Nights. In January 1941 the theater had Country Store and Gift Nights on weekday nights. Monday was Borden's Ice Cream Pie night, Tuesday and Wednesday were China Nights, Thursday was Field's Millinery Hat Night, and Friday was Forsythe Shoes Night. There were also occasional live shows with magicians and other entertainers. C. W. Hicks took over the Westway in January 1942.

In 1964, it was one of the first theaters in Baltimore to install xenon lamps for projection. After it closed, it was sold at auction in the spring of 1978 for $100,000 and converted into a church.

White Dog (see Amusea {3})

White Marsh 16, 8101 Honeygo Boulevard, White Marsh, 1997–present, David Rockwell, c. 3,525 (1—175, 2—175, 3—175, 4—370, 5—480, 6—370, 7—275, 8—275, 9—175, 10—80, 11—80, 12—85, 13—85, 14—175, 15—275, 16—275). The 16-screen, $7 million White Marsh megaplex was the largest movie theater complex in the state when it opened in 1997. It forms the centerpiece of The Avenue, a complex of shops and restaurants across Honeygo Boulevard from White Marsh Mall. The White Marsh 16 is a long, rectangular brick building, oriented on a northeast-southwest axis, with an enclosed three-story lobby that cuts through the middle. Above the marquees, which have the words "Loew's Theatres" spelled out in bright red letters, there is a two-story window above which the word "Loew's," in the same bright red, is repeated.

The first floor is constructed of beige and red split-face block. The upper stories are cream-colored brick. The two computerized ticket counters are located at the northwestern entrance of the lobby, and the concessions stands

The long eastern side of the White Marsh 16 (8101 Honeygo Boulevard, White Marsh, 1997–present, David Rockwell). The crowded lobby has entrances on the east and west sides of the complex.

are located in the center of the narrow lobby.[392] The auditoriums are located on either side of corridors which run to the northeast and southwest from the lobby. The restrooms are located inconveniently on one side of the central lobby. The stadium seating in high-back rocking chair seats with cupholder armrests is comfortable although the distance between rows is not quite enough. The sight lines are excellent. The auditoriums range in size from tiny rooms, seating 80, to a good-sized theater that can seat nearly 500 people. The White Marsh 16 is 100-percent THX certified, offering the Lucasfilm sound system as well as Sony's Dynamic Digital Sound in each auditorium.

As soon as it opened, the White Marsh 16 was doing a spectacular business, selling 57,000 tickets its first two weeks and averaging 25,000 to 30,000 tickets per week thereafter. Despite the often frenetic crowds milling about in the cramped lobby and the high-volume music that follows you into the restrooms, it has proved to be an extremely popular theater.

Wilson, 418 East Baltimore Street, 1909–1920, Theodore Wells Pietsch, 1,200.[393] George Wilson of Tyrone, Pennsylvania, purchased the building at 418 East Baltimore Street[394] and vacant lots around the corner on North Gay Street in early 1909. His Wilson Amusement Company was incorporated in April and erected the $50,000 Wilson theater on the site. Construction began in late July 1909, and it opened on November 22, 1909, with a vaudeville program that included Barnes and King (burlesque magicians), Kurnel-the-Great (a highly educated dog), and a series of movies. A large crowd attended the opening; among the guests were the architect, Theodore Wells Pietsch; the builder, Henry Maas; the muralist, Henry Arenz; the exhibitor, Herbert Miles, and numerous local officials.

A contemporary newspaper described the Wilson:

> The new theater is one of the most attractive ... in the city. It is built of steel and brick and is absolutely fireproof. The auditorium ... will accommodate 1,200 persons, while a spacious lobby forms the entrance on Baltimore street. The decorations in the interior of the theater are rich and handsome. Mural paintings decorate the walls, while suspended from the ceiling are two large clusters of lights. The murals, [by] Mr. Henry Arenz ... are exceedingly pretty and have attracted much attention.
>
> The seats are located on the ground floor, save a small balcony for private parties. The pronounced pitch to the floor, which is dished

The entrance to the Wilson Theater (418 East Baltimore Street, 1909–1920, Theodore Wells Pietsch) occupied the site of the earlier Palace Grand Museum. (Drawing by Robert W. Kramer)

and not a straight incline, gives an excellent sight line from any part of the house. The lighting fixtures are of solid bronze ... and the electric lighting effects, both on the exterior and the interior, are harmonized and in character with the work. The most complete heating and ventilating system has been installed, and powerful exhaust fans will keep the air of the auditorium in even circulation and constantly pure and fresh.[395]

A contemporary illustration shows a four-story facade with a wide, one-and-a-half-story arched entrance. The name "Wilson" appears to be spelled out, perhaps in tile, on the floor of the outer lobby; the name is repeated on a flat sign above the entrance arch. On the top of the building is a large star-shaped ornament, 18 feet in diameter, which seems to be composed of numerous pointed rays.

Business was very good during the Wilson's first year, but it closed temporarily in 1911. It reopened under new management with films and vaudeville in December of that year. Vaudeville was discontinued in January 1912 in favor of an all-film policy.

A 1914 article praised the stage decorations: "The [Wilson] has a most magnificent decoration of the stage, and has aroused much interest. It is known as a rose garden. Leading from the stage on either side of the screen is a trellis of beautiful roses and rose leaves which also continues across the top end of the picture screen. To the front of the stage is a very attractive electrical fountain. This fountain throws multiple streams and is so arranged as to reflect vari-colored illuminations."[396]

In the spring of 1917, in order to avoid paying the new minor privilege tax, manager Guy Wonders had the electric sign removed from the front of the theater and replaced the huge gilt ball on the roof with a flagpole. Wonders installed a new ventilation and cooling system in the summer of 1917 that consisted of a six-foot fan on the roof. The fan could deliver 94,000 cubic feet of fresh air into the auditorium.

The Wilson closed, with a final performance on July 31, 1920, to make way for a new theater, the Rivoli, which opened the following year. The old Wilson Theater auditorium on Gay Street was converted into several stores.

Windsor, 3113–3115 West North Avenue, 1941–1956, David Harrison, 650. Morris Oletsky and Morton Rosen's Baltimore Investment Corporation purchased a lot on West North Avenue for $15,500 in the spring of 1941 and opened the Windsor there in November. It was converted from the building that had been George Doebereiner's bakery. It was a very plain theater with a blue and maroon Vitrolite and stippled ivory terra cotta front and the traditional triangular marquee. The Windsor faced tough competition from the adjacent Hilton, which had opened a few months earlier, and the Walbrook across the street, both of which were operated by Thomas Goldberg.

In 1948, the owners of the Windsor unsuccessfully sued Goldberg, the Walbrook Amusement Company, and the Hilton Amusement Company for $600,000, charging restraint of trade. The Windsor became an African-American theater in late 1954 and closed two years later. The building is still standing but is being used for other purposes.

Winona, 1529–1531 East Monument Street, 1911–1957, F. E. Beall (of 1915 theater), 400. William Green opened the Winona on April 17, 1911, promising daily performances of high-grade dramatic and comic pictures with illustrated and spotlight songs. Because of numerous complaints from the theater's neighbors, Collector of Water Rents and Licenses Scully revoked Green's license the following month. Despite this, Green reopened his theater and was promptly arrested.

The Kay Bee Amusement Company announced plans for a new theater on the site in the summer of 1915. The name was changed to Star in December 1915. The permit "to erect a one-story brick or reinforced concrete building on the premises known as 1529–31 East Monument Street, for the exhibition of moving picture shows and for theatre purposes for colored people only...."[397] was granted in March 1916. The new theater measured 45 by 55 feet and cost about $6,000.

During its early years, movies and vaudeville were presented at the Star {2}. Among the well-known vaudeville acts were Billy Walker and "Babe" Brown and Ernest Watts and Muriel Ringgold, "the peer act of colored vaudeville." The name was changed to Rio around 1939.

It closed in March 1950. The Rio was reportedly opened once again, but no ads for it have been located.

Winters, Winters Lane, Catonsville, 1941–1945. There was a Winters Theater on Winters Lane in Catonsville in the 1940s. Robert R. Lee opened it in the fall of 1941 for African-American patrons.[398] According to the research of local historian Louis S. Diggs, movies were shown to

Bohannon and Lewy's Great Wizard (30–34 West Lexington Street, 1909–1924; Baldwin & Pennington) in 1909. The lobby was enclosed in the 1919 remodeling. (News American photograph courtesy of Special Collections, University of Maryland Libraries)

African-American audiences in two locations on Winters Lane. One was the Odd Fellows Hall, where movies, perhaps as early as 1910, were exhibited by a man from Baltimore. The other was the one-room schoolhouse on the corner of Winters Lane and Edmondson Avenue where movies were shown around 1940.[399] It is possible that the latter venue was the Winters Theater.

Projectionist Floyd Adams remembered that Lee rented a hall in Catonsville where he set up a 16 mm projector to show movies.

Wizard {1}, 219 North Eutaw Street, 1906–c. 1913, unknown, 66. The exact year that Harry Lewy and Tom Bohannon opened their first Wizard Theater on Eutaw Street, just below Clay, is not known. Harry Lewy claimed that it was opened in 1904, but that is almost certainly too early. It probably opened in the early summer of 1906[400] making it possibly the second movie theater in the city. The name Wizard came from Thomas Edison's nickname, "The Wizard of Menlo Park." The Wizard {1} was a storefront theater with a shallow lobby, a small arched entrance lit by incandescent bulbs, and a tiny ticket booth decorated with two globe lights. It had a large, plate-glass window above the entrance that allowed passersby to watch the operator cranking his projector. Early shows at the Wizard lasted about eight minutes and cost the customary nickel. A show consisted of a comedy followed by a more serious film. One early program consisted of a comedy, *The Poor Little Pig*, about boys trying to catch a greased pig, and a feature on the harvesting of coffee beans. The Wizard {1} lasted only a few years, but it was important as one of the earliest movie theaters in Baltimore.

Wizard {2}, 30–34 West Lexington Street, 1909–1924; Baldwin & Pennington (of 1909 theater), Oliver Wight (of 1919 remodeling); 250 (later c. 470). Tom Bohannon and Harry Lewy operated the original Lexington Street Wizard on the south side of Lexington Street, at 31 West Lexington, from 1907 to 1910.[401] In 1907 and 1908, Thomas O'Neill purchased the ancient buildings at 30–34 West Lexington Street. He razed them and, in early 1909, erected a new building containing a $35,000 theater on the site. He leased the theater to Bohannon, Lewy and Fuld's Greater Wizard Company.[402] The new structure measured about 42 × 110 feet.

The following description appeared in the *Sun*.

> The construction will be of brick walls and steel girders, with a finished front of wood, marble and ornamental stucco. The style will be Colonial with large columns and pilasters supporting the ornamental entablature, and will embrace a large lobby ... with mosaic floor and high marble wainscot. The interior, which will seat nearly 500 persons, will be arranged with a floor sloping toward the large stage at the rear. There will be three wide exits at the front and three at the rear.... A mezzanine floor will contain ... offices and [a] large fireproof room for the operator. In the front will be a private reception room for the ladies, and in the rear will be dressing rooms[403] in connection with the stage, smoking rooms, etc. The interior decorations will be of simple and subdued colors, to harmonize with the Colonial front. The building will be heated by steam, ventilated by large ventilators ... and in summer will be cooled by fresh air forced through the auditorium.[404]

The facade was painted red and gold and ornamented with a number of carved figures.

The new theater opened on October 14, 1909, with continuous vaudeville and movies from 11:30 A.M. to 11:00 P.M. Regular admission was 10 cents, with reserved seats available for an additional 10 cents. The deeply bowled floor, the cold air ventilating system, and the ladies' retiring rooms were judged to be especially attractive improvements in the new theater.

The Great Wizard was a very popular theater; according to the *Baltimore American*:

> Judging from the crowds that are in attendance continuously from morning till night, this model new theater has filled a long-felt want. Located, as it is, in the heart of Baltimore's busiest thoroughfare, it affords the most convenient place for those desiring rest and entertainment. Well conducted, roomy, spotlessly clean, comfortably seated, having retiring rooms especially for the ladies, and presenting the best of moving pictures and the highest class of vaudeville, this little theater is indeed a model of perfection.[405]

Bohannan, Lewy and Fuld continued to operate their other Wizard on the south side of Lexington Street until March 1910. The Consolidated Amusement Company leased that theater and advertised it as "The Original Wizard." Bohannan, Lewy and Fuld took them to court, claiming that they were not entitled to use the name "Wizard."[406] On June 9, 1912, the Great Wizard advertised that their "Wonderful new ICED AIR and OZONATING PLANT is a GREAT SUCCESS. During the hot and sultry days of last week the air in this theatre was ALWAYS COOL AND FRESH."

In 1913, the Great Wizard was open from 10:00 in the morning until 11:00 at night and ran shows consisting of two reels of pictures, which changed twice a week. Films were provided by the Swaab Film Exchange of Philadelphia. In early 1918, Henry W. Webb became a partner and acting head of the newly formed Wizard Theater Company. By 1919, the Wizard was being operated by Webb's Parkway Theater Company, which also controlled the Strand {1}, Parkway, and McHenry. In the spring of 1919, architect Oliver Wight prepared plans for major improvements. A new 2/6 Moller organ (Opus 1930), with a player piano console, was installed. The interior decorating was completed under the direction of Arthur Brunet of New York. The Wizard closed at the end of June for this remodeling. It reopened on September 15, 1919.

Moving Picture World described the new theater:

> The old structure was almost completely razed and the new structure was erected from the plans drawn up by ... Oliver B. Wight. The exterior is of old Colonial design, while the interior is of the Italian Pompeiian period, with a color scheme of tan and blue. The indirect lighting system has been employed and the thousand vari-colored bulbs are all controlled from a central switchboard located in the projection room. In the center of the [auditorium] ceiling there is ... a beautiful figured dome. Roomy and deeply upholstered chairs with tan backs and soft blue leather cushion seats, were built to order. The music is furnished by a large Moller organ which ... cost $10,000 and a concert orchestra of soloists which is under the direction of Prof. Herman Federoff.[407]

Among the organists were Kenneth G. Faulkner and Mary Soule. Federoff's Orchestra played at the Great Wizard in 1919 and 1920, and Bernard Depkin was the manager.

Faced with overwhelming competition from the newly opened Century Theater a few doors east, the Wizard closed in 1924. The Wizard ended its show business career in a blaze, if not a blaze of glory; at the final show on the evening of November 29, 1924, a smoky fire in the basement forced patrons to leave the auditorium.

Wizard {3}, 1118 Light Street, 1906–1957, J. C. Spedden (of 1911 remodeling and 1916 rebuilding), A. Lowther Forrest (of 1925 remodeling), 110 (later 450, 700). This theater was one of three Wizard Theaters operated by Bohannon and Lewy. The original theater was built in a converted three-story brick building in the winter of 1906.

At some point, before March 1910, it was acquired by Joseph Brodie, who ran a haberdashery next door. Brodie changed the name of the theater to the Brodie and made plans to build a larger theater on the site. In early 1912, Brodie gutted the original building and built his new theater. Information on this theater is plentiful, but contradictory. According to the Baltimore *Sun* of December 17, 1911, the new building, which was expected to cost $20,000, would measure 26 feet on Light Street with a back of 59 feet on Elizabeth Lane and a depth of 168 feet. A long lobby was to lead into the theater, which would have a spacious stage, ceilings of ornamental metal, and walls of pressed brick and concrete. It was to have an ornate facade illuminated with vari-colored electric lights and would seat about 800. According to another source,[408] the contract for the erection of the new theater called for an ornamental front of granite and copper; it was to seat 450 and cost $10,000.

In the spring of 1912 Brodie was planning to erect a $5,000 brick theater that would measure 32' × 78'. This may have been his airdome that opened in the summer. The open-air theater could seat 1,000 people and had a portable roof that could be spread over the entire auditorium in case of rain. The following summer, Brodie announced that the theater would be enlarged and remodeled into a semi-air dome theater. The auditorium was set up with a removable roof so that it could function as an open-air theater in warm weather, but in cold weather it could be enclosed and heated.[409]

An eyewitness said that Brodie retained the original building, but tore out the back wall and extended the theater toward Elizabeth Lane. While the builders were working on the extension, Brodie kept the theater open. At night, the screen of the original building would be removed and a second screen put up at the far end of the lot. Additional chairs were set up in the open area, and the projectionist would install a longer focus lens so that he could project movies on the more distant screen. Brodie used a novel scheme at this theater. He would hire a movie cameraman to take movies of people leaving certain local churches, such as St. Mary's Star of the Sea, on Sundays; then, he would advertise these movies during the week.

At one time, early in its history, the Brodie presented stage shows, and there is a story about one stage show that a booking agent mixed up. He apparently sent a first-class act, that had been originally scheduled to play in one of the big Chicago theaters, to the Brodie instead, much to the delight of the local patrons. Another story about the Brodie relates how Mr. Brodie got miffed with a film distributor, so he placed a sign on the marquee which read something like this, "I do not care to have your patronage. This film stinks." This sign attracted crowds of curious people.

Numerous reports in the summer of 1916 described a planned remodeling of the Brodie, but there is no evidence that it took place. Brodie made a one-week trip to New York and Philadelphia in September 1916 to collect information for the interior arrangements and furnishings of this remodeling. Plans called for an increase in the seating capacity to 2,000, but it is doubtful that this many seats were ever added.

Joe Brodie's Wizard Theater (1118 Light Street, 1906–1957, J. C. Spedden of 1911 remodeling and 1916 rebuilding, A. Lowther Forrest of 1925 remodeling) had seen a lot of remodeling by the time this 1938 photograph was taken.

Big cars and big theaters were characteristic of the 1960s. General Cinema's York Road Cinema (6376 York Road, 1967–1993, William Riseman Associates in association with Donald Ratcliffe) had an understated facade but a luxurious interior.

Joseph and Nathan Flax took over the Brodie in August 1920 and planned additional improvements. These included a $6,000 organ and 100 additional seats. Sigmund Kleiman acquired the theater in the winter of 1922. He added 100 seats by moving the front forward about 25 feet and also added a stage. During the summer of 1925, A. Lowther Forrest prepared plans for a major $25,000 remodeling consisting of a new front in Spanish Mission style. It reopened on October 23, 1925.

In 1927 and 1928 it was called the Majestic. Joe Brodie regained control of the theater in March 1928. He had an RCA Photophone sound system installed in September 1929. In 1935, the name was changed to Casino, and, around the same time, it was leased by the Durkee organization. Durkee reopened the theater as the Casino on December 25, 1936, and ran it until the summer of 1950. In 1950 it was completely remodeled and reopened with a new name, Beacon, on September 9, 1950. The Beacon closed around June 1, 1957. The building, still standing, has been completely remodeled into a store.

World (see Thirty-One)

YMCA, 1222–1232 West Baltimore Street, 1909–c. 1914 unknown, 415. The main hall on the first floor of this YMCA was used for entertainments since as early as 1896, when the stereopticians Kennard and Aler put on a show there called "Illuminated Wonders of Nature and Art." Pearce and Scheck rented the Hall for several years between 1909 and about 1913 to show movies. At that time they were showing five reels of pictures for 5 cents. Charles Pearce was the manager. Around 1912–1913 it was also called the West Baltimore Theater. The building was still standing as of 1999.

York (see Pastime {2})

York Ridge Cinema {2} (see Cinema I–Cinema II)

York Road Cinema, 6376 York Road, 1967–1993, William Riseman Associates in association with Donald Ratcliffe, 1,048. The General Cinema Corporation opened this attractive theater in the York Road Plaza Shopping Center on June 28, 1967. It was the fourth General Cinema theater in the Baltimore area; the others were the Perring Plaza Cinema, Harundale Cinema, and Timonium Drive-In. The York Road Cinema advertised "acres of free parking," "push-back seats," an art gallery in the lobby, a giant screen, and transistorized sound.

The *News American* described the new theater:

> Dark reds and light blue predominate in the decorating scheme, and one wall of the lobby has been paneled in natural wood. One of the theater's unusual features is its three separate ticket-selling areas, all of them inside the lobby ... designed to eliminate long box office lines, and to spare patrons the inconvenience of waiting outside in bad weather.
>
> Inside the theater ... there are pushback seats on an inclined floor. The seats combine both retraction and pushback movement, providing 25 percent more room than is normally found in conventional seating arrangements. Patrons will be able to pass between rows without causing anyone to rise, and the staggering seating plan will give an unobstructed view of the screen from any seat in the house.
>
> The screen is a large one, and not covered by a curtain. Instead, it is surrounded by a sort of picture frame, and colored lights play on it between shows.[410]

Paintings by Matthew Mack were on display in theater's art gallery during the opening. The original auditorium was twinned in the spring of 1977. The theater closed in 1993 and was demolished shortly thereafter.

APPENDICES

Appendix 1. Baltimore Area Theaters by Street Address

The information given is **Street**—*address* Theatre Name(s) opening date.

Numbers in brackets { } are used to distinguish among theaters with the same name. Numbers not in brackets are part of the theater's name, e.g. Rotunda 1-2.

5th St., Sparrows Point—*at D St.* Casino, Lyceum {2} (1909)

16th St., Highlandtown—*at Foster Ave.* Pitts Electric Park (1907)

22nd St.—*12 W.* Guild (1925)

25th St.—*9 W.* Homewood, Playhouse (1946), *221 W.* Huntington (1913)

36th St.—*903 W.* Ideal {2} (1908), *910 W.* Ideal Airdome (1911), *909 W.* Hampden (1911)

40th St.—*711 W.* Rotunda 1-2 (1974)

Aquahart Rd., Glen Burnie—*800* Harundale Mall Cinema (1964)

Arundel Mills Circle, Hanover—*7000* Muvico Egyptian 24 (2000)

Baltimore St., East—*305 E.* Mutoscope Parlor (c. 1899), *400 E.* Grand (1909), *404 E.* Colonnade, Lubin's (1906), *405 E.* Gayety (1906), *408 E.* Lubin's (1908), *412 E.* Comedy (1907), *414 E.* Amusea, Clover (1907-08), *415 E.* Victoria (1908), *418 E.* Wilson (1909), *418 E.* Rivoli (1921), *426 E.* Rainbow {1} (1909), *606 E.* Penny Arcade (1908), *611 E.* Happyland (1906), *612 E.* Crystal Maze, Edisonia, Elite (1908), *725 E.* Washington Hall Theater (1837), *714 E.* Gem (1908), *903 E.* Moving Picture Parlor (1906), *913 E.* Berman's (1914), *1100 E.* Bijou (1903), *1212 E.* Princess {1} (1906), *1736 E.* Cluster, Benj. (1912-13), *1741 E.* Teddy Bear (1909), *3310 E.* Pictorial, Aldine (1913)

Baltimore St., West—*at Butcher Lane* West End Park (1910-11), *at Garrison Lane* Luna Park (1910), *20 W.* Red Moon (1908), *36 W.* Lumiere's Wonderland (1897), *312 W.* Dixie, Europa (1909), *667 W.* Cluster (1908), *719 W.* Jewell, Realart (1914), *741 W.* Arcade, China Hall (1909), *930 W.* Aladdin (1908), *1110 W.* Lord Baltimore (1913), *1203 W.* Carrollton (1907), *1204 W.* Black Cat, Solax (1908), *1222 W.* Y.M.C.A. Hall (1909), *1518 W.* Capitol (1921), *1601 W.* West End (1910), *2435 W.* Gordon (1916)

Baltimore-Annapolis Rd., Glen Burnie—*43* Art, Glen (1929), *7480* Glen Burnie Town Center 7 (1986)

Baltimore National Pike—*5824* Westview Mall 9 (1992), *6023* Westview Cinemas I-II-III-IV (1965), *6026* Edmondson Drive-In (1954)

Bay Shore Park—Moving Picture Theater (1907)

Belair Rd.—*3703* Vilma (1928), *4839* Earle (1937), *6313* Balmar (c. 1920), *6650* Paramount (1946), *6805* Overlea (1927), *7636* Beltway Plaza 2 (1980), *7660* Beltway Movies (1997), *8740* Perry Hall Movies 5 (1990)

Belvedere Ave.—*at Reisterstown Rd.* Electric Park (1896), *3910* Star {1} (1910)

Biddle St.—*512 W.* Roosevelt (1921), *1235 E.* Biddle (1948)

Boston St.—*3413* Ivanhoe (1913)

Broadway, North—*314 N.* Crescent {1} (1909), *1105 N.* Plaza {1}, Broadway Garden, Kane (1910)

Broadway, South—*110 S.* Apex (1942), *222 S.* Bijou, Bijou-Dream, Broadway (1908), *228 S.* Palace, Nicoland, Red Raven, Busy Moon (1906), *238 S.* Penny Arcade (1919), *248 S.* Leader (1909), *303 S.* Cluster (1909, 1921), *305 S.* Golden Arrow (1911), *308 S.* Royal {3} (1912), *310 S.* Liberty {3} (c. 1919), *314 S.* Clifton (1909), *320 S.* Majestic, Anderson, Arcadia (1907), *509 S.* Broadway (1914, 1916), *510 S.* Nowosci (1919), *518 S.* Family (1907)

Carey St.—*1440 N.* Carey (1915)

Carroll Is. & Bowleys Qtr. Rd., Middle River—Carrollwood Twin (1974)

Central Ave.—*619 N.* Dunbar (1916)

Central Ave., Glen Burnie—*at A St.* Glen Burnie Theater (c. 1927)

Centre Park Dr., Columbia—*8805* Columbia Palace 9 (1986)
Charles St., North —*222 N.* Tower (1967), *1209 N.* Lyceum (1892), *1711 N.* Times, Charles (1939)
Charles St., South—*1100 S.* Garden {2} (1910), *1110 S.* Crescent {4} (1908)
Cherry Hill Rd.—*610* Hill (1946)
Chesapeake Ave., Towson—*at Delaware Ave.* Chesapeake Hall (c. 1920)
Chester St.—*624 N.* Fairyland (1908)
Clinton Ave.—*101 N.* Fairmount (1912)
Commerce Center Drive, Columbia— *9161* Snowden Square 14 (1997)
Conkling St.—*511 S.* Grand (1913), *808 S.* Arrow (1913)
Crain Highway, Glen Burnie—*128* New Glen (1941)
Curtis Ave., Curtis Bay—*816* Raffle's Theater (?), *921* Curtis (c. 1920)
Division St.—*at Presstman* Airdome (1915)
Druid Park Drive—*2920* Carlin's Drive-In (1958)
Duncan Pl.—*617 N.* New Gem (1909), *613 N.* New Market (1912)
Dundalk Ave.—*60* Lane, Abbey Lane (1940), *1201* Carlton (1949), *1718* Colgate (1948), *7910* Watersedge (1947)
Eager St.—*1517 E.* Princess {2} (1916)
Earhart Rd., Essex —*1812* Hiway (1946)
Eastern Ave.—*3136* Patterson {2}, Patterson {3} (1910, 1930), *3327* Regan's Casino (1910), *3505 rear* Highland Airdome (1913), *3509* Highland Academy (1909), *3603* Comic (c. 1909), *3608* Eagle (1908), *3829* Highland (1940), *3915* Eastern (1909), *4815* Takoma, Nemo, East (1925), *7938* Eastpoint 10 (1995)
Eastern Ave., Essex—*416* New Essex, Eastway (1934), *524* Elektra, Alert (1930), *1909* Midway (1945)
Eastern Ave., Middle River—*3417* Bengies Drive-In (1956)
Eaton St.—*111 S.* Monarch (c. 1909)
Eden St.—*627 N.* Radio, Star (1939)
Edmondson Ave.—*2100* Edmondson (1914), *2100* Bridge (1915, 1930), *3500* Edgewood (1930), *4428* Edmondson Village (1949), *5300* Westway (1939)
Eutaw St.—*12 N.* Hippodrome (1914), *219 N.* Wizard {1} (1907), *221 N.* Pell Mell (1915), *225 N.* Amusea (1907), *227 N.* Ideal {1} (1906), *315 N.* Empire, Blaney's (1903)
Fait Ave.—*3205* Baltimore (1914)
Fayette St.—*302 W.* Little Moving Picture Palace (1908), *320 W.* Ford's Grand Opera House (1871), *311 W.* Empire, Town (1910)
Fayette St.—*1720 E.* Circus (c. 1915), *2239 E.* Fayette, Roxy (1916)
Fleet St.—*1705* Sunburst (1909), *1727* Paradise (c. 1906)
Fort Ave.—*124 E.* Echo (1914), *835 E.* Southside Movies 4 (1992), *1318 E.* Flag, Deluxe (1913), *1501 E.* Latrobe (1910)
Francis Ave., Halethorpe—*1309* Strand 3 (c. 1925)
Francis St.—*2634* Moving Picture Theater (c. 1914)
Franklin St.—*320 W.* Maryland (1903), *502 W.* Traymore Casino (c. 1906)
Frederick Ave.—*1900* Victor {1} (c. 1911), *3436* Frederick (1912), *4113* Irvington (1925)
Frederick Ave., Catonsville—*725* Alpha (1928)
Fremont Ave., North—*504 N.* Fremont {2} (1935), *525 N.* Solomon's (c. 1920), *615 N.* Fremont {1} (1909)
Fremont Ave., South—*400 S.* Eureka (1908)
Fulton Ave.—*1563 N.* Gertrude McCoy, Fulton (1915), *2869 N.* Pleasant Hour (1909)
Fulton Ave.—*500 S.* Victor {2} (1913)
Fuselage Ave., Middle River—*1417* Aero (1942)
Garrison Blvd.—*3300* Forest (1919)
Gay St.—*115 N.* Gem, Odeon Music Hall (1904), *349 N.* moving picture parlor (1907), *356 N.* moving picture parlor (1907), *467 N.* Paradise {3}, Elite, Graphic (c. 1906), *526 N.* Crystal (1913), *563 N.* Gay Street Museum, Bon Ton (1907), *582 N.* Dream (1913), *1034 N.* moving picture theater (1910), *1039 N.* Elektra (1910), *1105 N.* Keystone (1910), *1351 N.* Palace {3} (1913), *1436 N.* Colonial (c. 1910), *1752 N.* Daisy (1908)
Gilmor St.—*314 N.* Gilmor (1909), *614 N.* Harlem (1932)
Governor Ritchie Hwy., Glen Burnie—*1706* Governor Ritchie Drive-In (1939), *6637* Ritchie Cinemas 1-2-3 (1973), *6718* Glen Burnie Mall (1964), *7900* Movies at Marley Station (1987)
Governor Ritchie Hwy., Pasadena—*8186* Jumpers Mall 1-2-3 (1974)
Greenmount Ave.—*839* Celtic (1909), *2026* Pastime {2}, York (1909), *2421* Mascot (1909), *nr. Lorraine* Greenmount Gardens (1915), *at 29th* Baltimore Baseball Park (1916), *between 29th & 30th streets* Terrapin Park Open Air (1915), *3201* Waverly Gardens (1912), *3211* Waverly (1910), *3302* Boulevard (1921)
Grundy St.— Bell ?
H St., Sparrow's Pt.— Central ?
Hamilton Ave.—*3019* Community, Avon (1916, 1933)
Hanover St.—*3730 S.* Brooklyn (1928)
Harford Rd.—*1500* Apollo (1921), *1625* Northern, Lord Calvert (1912), *1713* Blue Bell (1909), *2618* Harford (1916), *4703* Parkside, Cameo (1921), *5434* Arcade (1928), *6701* Northway (1937), *8123* Colony (1949)
Havenwood Rd.—*1572* Northwood (1950)
High St.—*1 S.* Berman's (1915)
Highland Ave.—*227 S.* Purity (1914)
Hoffman St.—*1901 E.* Palace {3} (1913)
Holliday St.— Holliday Street Theater (1874)
Honeygo Boulevard, White Marsh—*8101* White Marsh 16 (1997)
Hopkins Plaza—*25* Morris Mechanic (1967)
Howard St.—*112 N.* Clown (c. 1909), *113 N.* New Pickwick, Howard (1908), *121 N.* Penny Arcade, Arcadia, Alcazar (1906–07), *223 N.* Idle Hour (1913), *334 N.* Palace Moving Picture Parlor (c. 1908), *404 N.* Strand {1} (1916), *508 N.* Auditorium (1880), *516 N.* Academy of Music (1875),

516 N. Stanley (1927), *523 N.* Little (1927), *844 N.* Three Arts (1935), *844 N.* Lehmann Hall, Roslyn (1870, 1942)
Hull St.—*1444* Hull (1909)
Ingleside Ave., Catonsville—*8–10* I.O.O.F. Hall, Caton (c. 1917)
Jefferson St.—*2303* Orpheum {2} (1911)
Lafayette Ave.—*1433 W.* Lafayette (1911), *1509 W.* Crescent {2} (1908), *1510 W.* Red Mill (1908)
Laurens St.—*1202* Oriole, Patterson, Virginia (1908)
Lexington St.—*18 W.* Century (1921), *18 W.* Valencia (1926), *28 W.* Blue Mouse (1909), *30 W.* [Great] Wizard (1907), *31 W.* Wizard, Thirty One, Picture Garden (1906), *31 W.* Lexway, Vogue, Laff Movie, World (1939), *35 W.* Amusea, Red Feather, Lemon (1907), *114 W.* Garden {3}, Keith's (1915), *210 W.* New {1} (1910), *312 W.* Pickwick {1} (1906), *314 W.* Lexington (1909), *405 W.* Easter's, Pastime (1908), *666 W.* Queen (1909)
Liberty St.—*5 N.* Liberty {1} (1909)
Liberty Heights Ave.—*4604* Ambassador (1935), *4607* Gwynn (1933), *8632* Liberty 1–2 (1964), *8730* Randallstown Plaza (1965)
Light St.—*814* Federal (1908), *1032* McHenry (1917), *1118* Wizard {3}, Brodie, Casino, Beacon (1906), *1130* Comet, Cupid (c. 1907), *and McComas* Hippodrome (Union League Park) (1911)
Linwood Ave.—*902 S.* Linwood (1915)
Lombard St.—*3903 E.* Lombard (c. 1909)
Madison Ave.—*818* Madison (1946)
Main St., Ellicott City—*8030* Amusea (c. 1912), *8059* Earle (c. 1925), *8217* Ellicott (1941)
Main St., Turner's Station—*103 S.* Anthony (1946)
Market Place—*55* Movies at Harbor Park (1985)
McCormick Rd., Cockeysville—*11511* Hunt Valley 12 (1998)
Mill Run Circle, Owings Mills—*10100* Owings Mills 17 (1998)
Milton Ave.—*1401 N.* Good Time, Avenue (1914)
Monroe St.—*1727 N.* Royal {1} (1911)
Monument St.—*1401 E.* National, Eden (1921), *1529 E.* Winona, Star, Rio (1911), *2045 E.* State (1927), *2239 E.* Red Wing {2} (1916), *2241 E.* Monument Open Air (1909), *2515 E.* Monument Mov. Pict. Garden (1914)
Mount St.—Mount Airdome (c. 1926)
Mt. Royal Ave.—*130* Lyric (1895)
Mountain Rd., Pasadena—Shore Drive-In (1954)
Mullikin St. & Mullet Ct.—open-air moving picture theater (1915)
North Ave., East—*6 E.* North Avenue Casino (c. 1892), *7 E.* Aurora (1910), *10 E.* Centre (1939), *11 E.* Theatorium, Peabody (1909), *at Wolfe St.* Mozart Airdome (c. 1920)
North Ave., West—*5 W.* Parkway, 5 West (1915), *617 W.* Mount Royal (1915), *846 W.* Rialto (1916), *910 W.* Linden, Cinema (1938), *1358 W.* Excelsior (1911), *1524 W.* Metropolitan (1922), *2507 W.* Traveler (1913), *3055 W.* Suburban (1909), *3100 W.* Walbrook (1916), *3113 W.* Windsor (1941), *3117 W.* Goldberg's, Hilton (1914, 1941)

North Point Blvd.—*2399* North Point Plaza Th. (1966), *4001* North Point Drive-In (1948)
North Point Rd.—*at Sparrow's Point Rd.* Edgemere (1944)
O'Donnell St.—*2938* Olympia (1909)
Oregon Ave., Arbutus—*5509* Hollywood (1936, 1998)
Orleans St.—*1543* Royal Moving Picture Parlor, Victor (c. 1908)
Park Heights Ave.—*4338* Avalon (1927), *4600 block* Suburban Hotel & Gardens (c. 1890), *5010* Uptown (1941), *5132* Pimlico (1914), *5202* Arlington (1914)
Patapsco Ave.—*601* Patapsco (1944), *1017* Victory (1944)
Patterson Ave.—(see: Laurens St.)
Pennington Ave., Curtis Bay—*4911* Pennington (1920)
Pennsylvania Ave.—*936* Palace {2} (1907), *934* Lincoln (1916), *941* American, Lincoln {2} (c. 1921), *1056* Northwestern (1913), *1115* Daly's Why (1912), *1116* Lincoln (1914), *1230* Avenue, Renard's, New Albert (1907), *1329* Douglass, Royal (1921), *1429* Diane, Carver (1934), *1619* Regent (1916), *2115* Rainbow {2}, Lenox (1919), (1936), *2211* Home (c. 1909), *2426* Schanze, Morgan (1912)
Point Breeze—River View Park (1898)
Poplar Grove St.—*611* Poplar, Astor (c. 1913)
Pratt St.—*1924 W.* Monroe (1939), *1940 W.* Royal {2} (1911), *2018 W.* Horn (1909), *2016 W.* Horn (1920)
Preston St.—*bet. McCulloch & Druid Hill* Hawkins Airdome (1921)
Preston St.—*1108 E.* Flaming Arrow, Preston (1913)
Pulaski Highway—*2700* Belnord (1911, 1921)
Pulaski Highway, White Marsh—General Pulaski Drive-In (1950)
Reisterstown Rd.—*at Park Circle* Liberty Heights Park, Carlin's Park (1918), *5425* Crest (1949), *6512* Reisterstown Plaza (1965), *6764* Reisterstown Plaza 5-Star (1985)
Reisterstown Rd., Owings Mills—*910* Valley Drive-In (1961), *9616* Valley Centre 9 (1990)
Reisterstown Rd., Pikesville—*1001* Pikes (1938), *1110* Mini-Flick (1973)
Reisterstown Rd., Reisterstown—*11900* Village (1966), *49* New {2} (1934)
Ridgely Rd., Timonium—*58 W.* Cinema I–II (1964)
Rolling Rd.—*1717 N.* Security Square Cinema (1987)
Rossville Blvd.—*6400* Movies at Golden Ring (1976)
Russell St.—*2305* Westport (1940)
Saratoga St.—*1115 W.* Eureka, Crescent {3}, Ruby (1909)
Satyr Hill Rd.—*8730* Perring Plaza Cinema (1966)
Security Blvd.—*6901* Security Mall Cinema (1972)
Sharp St.—*924 S.* Argonne, Goldfield (1922)
Shipping Pl., Dundalk—*1* Strand {2} (1927)
Smith Ave.—*2835A* Greenspring 3 (1985)

South Ave. & 1st, Mt. Washington—Mt. Washington Casino (c. 1914)
St. Helena Ave.—at *Willow Spring* Community Hall (1921)
Stockton St.—*2-4 S.* Stockton (c. 1910)
Taylor Ave.—*1045* Hillendale (1960)
Telegraph Road, Odenton—*8229* Super 170 Drive-In (1963)
Timonium Road, Timonium—Timonium Drive-In (1955)
Thames St.—*1724* Orpheum {3} (1990)
Virginia Ave.—Dreamland (c. 1912)
Warner St.—*913* Goldfield, Dean (1915, 1946)
Washington Blvd.—*625* Columbia, Rex (c. 1908), *709* Columbia (1921), *756* Crown, Roy, Pic (c. 1908), *906* Superba (1910), *1225* Bunny (1912), *2444* Lord Calvert (1936), *2536* Lincoln Highway, Morrell (1919), *6200* Elkridge Drive-In (1948)
Washington St.—*1600 N.* Paradise {2} (1909), *1607 N.* Ritz (1926)
West Nursery Rd., Linthicum—*1591* West Nursery Cinemas 14 (1998)
Westwood Ave.—*1705* Kidd's Amuse. Th. (c. 1915)
Wilkens Ave.—*2038* Victor {2} (1913)
Wincopin Circle, Columbia—*10205* Columbia Cinema III (1973)
Winter's Lane, Catonsville—Winter's (c. 1941)
York Rd.—*4617* Rex (1933), *5005* Govans (1914), *5904* Senator (1939), *6376* York Road Cinema (1967)
York Rd., Cockeysville—*9950* Church Lane Cinema (1973)
York Rd., Timonium—*2131* Timonium Cinemas (1973)
York Rd., Towson—*435* Towson Commons (1992), *506* Columbia (c. 1919), *512* Towson (1928)

Appendix 2. Architects of Baltimore Area Theaters

The following abbreviations are used: addit.—addition; alt.—alterations; assoc.—associate; conv.—conversion; rebuild.—rebuilding; remodel.—remodeling.

Numbers in brackets { } are used to distinguish among theaters with the same name. Numbers not in brackets are part of the theater's name, e.g. Rotunda 1-2. An asterisk indicates that the theater was never completed.

Abramowitz, Mitchel Liberty {2} (1968)
Aiken, Herbert C. Waverly (1910); Gordon (1916); Apollo (1921)
Allen, J. D. & Co. (*Philadelphia*) Auditorium (1905 rebuild.), Monumental (1906 remodel.)
Anderson, Charles Montgomery Empire {1} (1903), Fairyland (1909 rebuild.); Pell Mell (1915 conv.)
Anderson, Clarence E. Oriole (1910); Moving Picture Theater at River View Park (1909)
Arrowstreet Inc. (*Somerville, MA*) Hoyt's West Nursery Cinemas 14 (1998); Hoyt's Hunt Valley Cinema 12 (1998)
Baldwin & Pennington Wizard {2} (1909)
Beall, Fred E. Stockton (1910); Royal {2} (1911); Bunny (1912 conv.); Edmondson (1913) (?), Crescent {4} (1913); Flaming Arrow (1913); Poplar (1913); Arlington {1} (1914); Renard (1916) (?); Star {2} (1916); Lord Calvert (canceled) (1936)
Bert-Core Assoc. Super 170 (1963)
Bickel, Henry Grand {2} (1913)
Bisson, J. Takoma (1930 remod.)
Blanke, Ewald G. Circle* (1921); Boulevard (1921); Rivoli (1921); Lyceum {2} (1921 remod.)
Blanke, Ewald G. & John J. Zink Red Wing (1917 remod.); Harford (1920 remod.)
Brockmeyer, R. C. (?) Belmar (1920)
Brown, E. H. C. (?) Gwynn (1933)
Brown, Harry H. Lexington (1909)
Callis, C. H. Queen (1909)
Callis & Callis Columbia 1 (1910); Northern (1912); Royal {3} (1912 conv.); Northwestern (1913); Dunbar (1916)
Callis, D. Millard Princess 1 (1906 conv.)
Cambridge 7 (*Boston, MA*) Towson Commons (1992)
Carroll, Armand Centre (1939); New (1945 remod.)
Cassell, Charles E. Princess* (1904), Little Moving Picture Palace (1908)
Chertkof, J. O. Highland {2} (1940)
Childs, George S. Regent (1921 rebuild.)
Clothier, George Jr. Majestic {1} (1907 conv.)
Copeland, Henry L. (*New York*) Electric Park (1908 addit.)
Culchia, Charles L. North Point Plaza (1964)
Davis, Milton C. Arcade {1} (1909 remod.)
Developers General Corp. Campus Hills 1 & 2 (1973); Jumpers Mall 3 (1974)
Development Design Group, Inc. Muvico Egyptian 24 (2000)
Dixon, Fred Northwood (1951)
Dunn, John Carroll Watersedge (1947), Hollywood (1985 remod.), Reisterstown Road Plaza 5 (1985), Village (1991 alt.), Eastpoint 10 (1995)
Dusman, J. F. Astor (1926); Dunbar (1929 remod.); Rex (1933); Fremont {2} (1935)
Eberson, Drew (*New York*) Reisterstown Road Plaza (1965)
Eberson, John (*New York*) Valencia (1926); Century (1926 remod.); Parkway (1926 remod.)
Emmart, Paul Red Moon (1908 conv.); Paradise {2} (1909) (?); Red Mill (1909 remod.); West End (1911); Schanze (1912);
Emmerich, William Blue Bell (1910) (?)
Evander, E. Bernard Grand (c. 1927-28, alt.); Hampden (1938 alt.); Westport (1940); Mayfair (1942)

Eyring, John F. Strand 2 (1927); Vilma (1928); New (Reisterstown) (1934); Pimlico (1935 alt.); Earle (1937); Pikes (1937); Lane (1940); Uptown (1941); Carlton (1949); Arcade {2} (1949 remod.)
Fenton & Lichtig Hillendale (1960); Westview I (1965)
Fletcher, Frederick A. Avalon (1927)
Forrest, A. Lowther Thirty-One (1907), Victoria (1908); Blue Mouse (1909); Grand {1} (1909); Daly's Why (1912); Dream (1913); Broadway (1913 conv.); Baltimore (1914) (?); Harford (1916); Victoria (1922 rebuild.)
Forrest, A. Lowther & Oliver B. Wight New (1910)
Forsythe, John R. Pimlico (1914); Red Wing (1920 remod.)
Fowler, Lawrence H. Lyceum {2} (1912)
Fox, Harry W. Mascot (1909)
Frank, Benjamin Broadway (1916 rebuild.)
Freund, John Jr. Colonnade (1906 remod.), Leader (1909); Belnord (1911); New Gem (1912 remod.); Idle Hour (1913); Berman's (1915); Fayette (1916); Colonial {1} (1920 addit.);
Frieberg, William Jr. Princess {2} (1916) (?)
Friese, Albert H. Echo (1914)
Friz, Clyde N. & Nelson Friz Ambassador* (1926)
Ganter, Carl Hollywood (1936)
Ganter, William Century (1934 alt.)
Gerwig, Jacob F. Pickwick (1906) (?); Ideal {1} (1906 conv.); Teddy Bear (1909); Clown (1909 conv.)
Getz Taylor Hollywood (1998)
Gieske, Walter M. Lehmann Hall (1912 remod.)
Gifford, James J. Ford's (1871)
Glidden, Edward H. Bijou {2} (1903 remod.); Victoria (1916 alt.); Forest (1919)
Gott, Jackson Bijou {2}, (of 1892 power plant)
Gray, William Bruce (*Washington*) Auditorium (1891 remod.)
Greener, George S. Orpheum (1911)
Grieves Worrell Wright & O'Hatnick Snowden Square 14 (1997)
Harrison, David Diane (1935); Rainbow (1936 remod.); Monroe (1939); Radio (1939); Plaza {1} (1940s remod.); Windsor (1941); New Albert (1943); Patapsco (1944); Anthony (1945); Victory (1945); Goldfield (1946 remod.); Biddle (1947)
Hazzard, Stephen & Stanislaus Russell Carlin's Drive-In (1958)
Hoffman & Henon Stanley (1927)
Hopkins, S. Gordon Pastime {2} (1909)
Kelly Clayton & Mojzisek Beltway Plaza 2 (1980); Columbia Palace 9 (1986); Valley Center 9 (1990); Perry Hall 5 (1990); Southside Movies 4 (1992); Beltway Movies 6 (1997)
Koenig, Franz C. (*Philadelphia*) Lubin's (1907 remod.); Lubin's {2} (1908) (?); New Pickwick (1908)
Kunkel, John F. Carrollton (1908)
Lachman & Murphy (*Philadelphia*) Douglass (1921)
Laferty, J. Edward Garden {2} (1910); Keystone (1910); Plaza {1} (1910 conv.); Hampden (1911); Walbrook (1916)
Lamb, Thomas White (*New York*) Hippodrome (1914); Garden {3} (1915); Ambassador* (1921)
Land Design/Research, Inc. Movies at Harbor Park (1985)
Lawrence, John W. Charles (1969 remod.); Rotunda (1974)
Lee, William H. (*Philadelphia*) Victoria (1925 remod.)
Leser, C. C. Fulton *see* Schmidt, George & C. C. Fulton Leser
Levi, Louis Amusea {3} (1907)
Limbert, G. (*Youngstown, Ohio*) Glen Burnie Mall (1964)
Lockhart, E. A. *see* Wight and Lockhart
Maclellan, H. H. Jewell (1913)
Mason, Alfred Fremont {1} (1909); Olympia (1909)
McComas, H. R. Crescent {2} (1913)
McElfatrick, John B. Gayety (1906)
McElfatrick, William H. Empire (1910, consulting architect)
McKenzie, George Norbury Towson (1928)
Michael, Walter T. (or Mitchell) Eureka Amusement Co. (1909)
Miller, Hal A. Apex (1942); Homewood (1946); Paramount (1946); Colgate (1948)
Miller, Ken Edmondson Village (1948)
Moehle, Frederick L. W. Dunbar (1945 rebuild.); Midway (1945)
Moller, E. A. Clifton (1909)
Mottu & White Highland {1} (1913, alt.)
Moxley, Jonathan E. Columbia {2} (1921); Westway (1939); Brooklyn (1941 alt.)
Myerberg, Julius Hill (1946), Crest (1949)
Myers, A. Murray Gwynn (1933)
Neilson, J. Crawford Academy of Music (1875)
Niederhauser & McCluskey (**Charles P. Niederhauser and Perry T. McCluskey**) Lafayette (1910)
Paul, Peter Ritchie Cinemas 1-2-3 (1973)
Pietsch, Theodore Wells Wilson (1909); Elektra {1} (1910); Excelsior (1911); Lincoln (?) (1915); Palace {3} (1917/18 remod. ?)
Ratcliffe, Donald Timonium 1-2 (1973)
Riseman, William (*Boston, MA*) Harundale Cinema (1964); Perring Plaza Cinema (1966); Columbia Cinema (1973)
Riseman, William Associates & Donald Ratcliffe York Road Cinema (1967)
Ritz, William C. Hull (1916 addit.)
Rockwell, David White Marsh 16 (1997)
Russell, Stanislaus Suburban (1909 addit.); Carey (1915); Roosevelt (1921); Little (1927); Ellicott (1940); Carlin's Drive-In (1958 assoc.)
Russell, Wilson Raymond Red Wing (1916)
Schmidt, George Hampden (1926 rebuild.)

Schmidt, George & C. C. Fulton Leser State (1927)
Selckmann, E. Pleasant Hour (1909)
Shapiro Petrauskas Gelber (*Philadelphia*) Owings Mills Cinema 17 (1998)
Simonson, Otto G. Theatorium (1909); River View Park (1909 rebuild.); Palace {3} (1912); Edmondson (1914); Aladdin (1915 remod.)
Simonson, Otto G. (& Lucius R. White, Jr.) Metropolitan (1922)
Simonson, Otto G. (& W. H. McElfatrick) Empire (1911)
Skidmore, Owings & Merrill Aero (1942)
Smith & May Pennington (1920) (?)
Smith, Wilson Porter Harlem (1932)
Sparklin, William O. Belnord (1921)
Sparklin, William O. & George S. Childs Bridge {1} (1915); Mount Royal (1915); Regent (1916); Rialto (1916); Strand {1} (1916); Rainbow (1919)
Spedden, J. C. Wizard {3} (1911 remod.); Lord Baltimore (1913); Wizard {3} (1916 rebuild.); Flag (1916 remod.)
Stack, John K. Palace Moving Picture Parlor (1908 conv.); Celtic (1909); Gilmor (1909)
Stehl, J. H. Ritz (1926)
Steinacker, Joseph Henry Alpha (1928)
Storck, Edward J. Argonne (1922)
Tilton, Edward L. (New York) Liberty (Ft. Meade, 1918)
Tinley, Henry J. Family (1907 conv.); Waverly (1913 addit.)
Tormey, Francis E. Aurora (1910); Gertrude McCoy (1915); Horn (1920 rebuild.)
Towne, Arthur Parkside (1921)
Ulrich, Robert C. Easter's (1908)
Vogel, Jack K. Edmondson Drive-In (1954); Bengies Drive-In (1956); Carrollwood 1–2 (1974); Edgewater Twin (1974)
White, Lucius R. Jr. *see* Simonson and White, Zink and White
Wight, Oliver B. Cluster {3} (1912); Cluster {3} (1914 conv.); Parkway (1915); McHenry (1917); Wizard {2} (1919 rebuild.); New Pickwick (1920 remod.); Picture Garden (1920 remod.); Arcade (1928); Avon (1930); Lord Calvert (1936)
Wight, Oliver B. & E. A. Lockhart National (1921); Dunbar (1921, remod. ?); Fremont 1 (1921, remod.); Irvington (1925)
Wyatt & Nolting Lehmann Hall (1910, remod.); Capitol (1921)
Zimlin, Morris Lafayette (1939, alt.); Cinema I–II (1964)
Zink, John J. Century (1921); Bridge {2} (1930); Edgewood (1930); Patterson {3} (1930); Ambassador (1935); Little (1935, alt.); Waverly (1935, alt.); Northway (1937); Linden (1938); Alpha (1938, remod.); Senator (1939); Hippodrome (1941, alt.)
Zink, John J. & Frederick L. W. Moehle Colony (1949)
Zink, John J. & Lucius R. White Jr. Town (1947)
Zink, John J. *see* Blanke & Zink

Appendix 3. Theater Architecture

For the first 30 years of movies, eclecticism, with liberal doses of pragmatism, was a major component of movie theater architectural styles. Storefront theaters and nickelodeons were built where space was available according to the whims of the owners and their architects within the limitations of the site and local building codes. During the late teens and 1920s, the huge profits that films were making allowed the exhibitors to give their architects nearly carte blanche, and modest nickelodeons turned into palaces.

The first movie theaters were little more than rooms with the bare necessities for showing films. They were often built in remodeled stores or even houses. They were usually long and narrow, the width of the original structure. The fronts were decorated with flags, bunting, and posters. There might have been a separate box office.

Inside, was a small lobby that opened directly into the auditorium. Heating was provided by a few radiators or even a wood stove, and ventilation by small fans on the walls. Some had windows that could be opened. The floors were flat and the screen was a bed sheet or square of rear wall painted flat white. In the space between the front seats and the screen was a piano. The projection booth, a metal or asbestos box 5' × 5', may have been set up in the rear of the auditorium on the same level as the seats or hung from the top of the back wall. Examples of these early theaters are the Paradise (Fleet Street), Wizard (Eutaw Street), Lubin's (Baltimore Street), Grand (Baltimore Street, 1910), and New Pickwick (Howard Street).

By 1909, movie theaters had become more sophisticated. They had arched entrances outlined with incandescent lights. One theater architect referred to this style as the "Coney Island front."[1] There might have been some statuary on the pressed metal facade to give it depth and make it stand out. Figures from classical architecture abounded. Fancy brass cases flanking the box booth held the posters. There was usually a separate box office, perhaps with an illuminated dome, set back under the entrance arch.

Inside, there was a larger lobby and standee area. The floor was sloped to provide better sight lines. Architect Franz Koenig, who did many of Sigmund Lubin's theaters, wrote in 1911[2] that the store front theaters were "rather repulsive" at first and that the owners tried "amateur decoration" with bunting and flags to improve the appearance of their buildings.

The equipment was similar in all these theaters.

An auction advertisement for the 1908 New Pickwick Theater provided a list of the furnishings of a typical small theater of this era.[3]

- two moving picture machines
- one spotlight; one grand piano
- cash register; typewriter and desks; iron safe; ticket chopper and machine; filterer and drinking cups; three fire extinguishers; vacuum cleaner
- two 36-inch exhaust fans in roof; three 8-inch desk fans; 13 16-inch wall fans
- framed pictures; six sheet brass frames; brass easels and banner frames
- ushers and doorman's uniforms
- telephones; ladders; stools; chairs; brass railing; screens; portieres
- 260 folding seat moving-picture parlor chairs

The major local architects between 1906 and 1913 were Fred Beall, A. Lowther Forrest, John Freund, J. Edward Laferty, Theodore Wells Pietsch, and Otto Simonson.

The first modest movie palaces were built in the late teens. Although some of these buildings were simply magnified nickelodeons, most owed little in style to their nickelodeon antecedents. They were the lineal descendants of the vaudeville and burlesque theaters modified for films. They were much larger than the nickelodeons. The facades were plain, often Classical in style, and made of brick or limestone with trim of marble or other ornamental stone and usually had a decorative marquise protecting the entrance.

The lobbies were heavily decorated with marble and hardwoods. They had sloping floors, multiple aisles, orchestra pits, and elaborate prosceniums. Many could seat more than 1,000 people. Orchestras and organs replaced pianos. Forced air heating systems provided heat, and huge fans in the roofs provided ventilation. Most had balconies and stages for live presentations. Examples of these first palaces were the Lord Baltimore (J. C. Spedden, 1913), Oliver Wight's Parkway (1915) and McHenry (1917), Ewald Blanke's Rivoli (1921) and Boulevard (1921), Columbia (J. E. Moxley, 1921), and Metropolitan (Otto Simonson, 1922).

One style of movie theater that reached its peak during the 1910s and then disappeared was the open-air theater or airdome. Not to be confused with drive-in theaters, the airdomes were walk-in theaters. In Baltimore, the first ones appeared around 1909, and the last one closed in the late 1920s. In its simplest form, an airdome was a vacant lot surrounded by a high wooden fence with a screen at one end, a ticket booth and projection room at the other and rows of wooden benches in between. More elaborate airdomes had roofs of canvas or metal that could be spread across the theater in case of rain.

Running an airdome was a chancy proposition. A rainy summer could spell the doom for one of these theaters. On the other hand, airdomes were cheap to build and easy to maintain. However, they were not long lived. Hawkins' Airdome on Pennsylvania Avenue lasted only a few weeks. Airdomes were sometimes operated in places, such as ballparks, that already existed for other purposes. In cases such as these, they provided excellent sources of income for parks that might otherwise be empty after dark. A couple of airdomes were operated in tandem with hardtop theaters. Patrons could start out in the cooler airdome, and, if a storm came up, they could hurry into the covered theater to finish the show.

Movie theaters reached their peak in size and grandeur in the late 1920s. Their facades towered several stories above the street. Patrons purchased tickets at box offices of marble and ornamental bronze. There were usually two sets of lobbies, an outer one and a grand multi-storied inner one; both were lined with ornamental stone and illuminated by great crystal chandeliers. Marble stairways led to mezzanines and wide balconies. The lobbies, promenades, and lounges were furnished with period furniture, often real antiques. The elaborate prosceniums incorporated organ grills. Ornamental plaster decorations and rich fabrics covered the auditorium walls. Box seats were attached to the sidewalls and a huge crystal chandelier hung from a distant domed ceiling. The stages were large and fully equipped; the orchestra pits held symphony orchestras. All had impressive organs. Air conditioning cooled these mammoth structures and forced-air heat warmed them.

During this era, marquees, with white letters on black backgrounds, became structures for advertising films and actors or actresses instead of simple projections to protect patrons. In many cities theaters were built in wildly exotic styles, Egyptian, Mayan, Oriental, and atmospheric; but Baltimore theaters, like those in neighboring Washington, followed more conservative lines. The best examples of this style in Baltimore were the Century (John Zink, 1921), Valencia (John Eberson, 1926), State (George Schmidt & C. C. Fulton Leser, 1927), and Stanley (Hoffman and Henon, 1927).

The depression put an end to the elaborate movie palaces of the late 1920s. Size and ornamentation changed markedly. The theaters of the 1930s and 1940s were very similar in style. Most were in outlying neighborhoods and suburbs, and there was little experimentation with exotic styles.

There was movement away from the elaborate decorations of the 1920s. Theater architect Ben Schlanger, writing in 1931,[4] wanted to do away with the "over-ornamented" theaters and replace them with plainer ones. He suggested simplifying the proscenium arch and decorating the sidewalls and ceilings of the auditorium with horizontal elements that would pull the patron's eyes toward the "main focal point," the screen.

Art deco and Streamlined or Moderne became the prevailing styles. Seating capacities decreased. The average theater seated about 850 people. The facades were cream face brick with bands of darker colors and trim of Vitrolite or ornamental stone. The use of glass bricks, one of the identifying characteristics of the art deco style, arrived in Baltimore during the mid–1930s. The rectangular marquees of the 1920s became triangular structures with black letters on a white background that could be read easily from cars driving by. Candy and popcorn machines appeared in lobbies, especially at the end of this period. The auditoriums had reverse curve slopes where the low point was several rows back from the screen instead of at the base of the screen. Highly decorated prosceniums and orchestra pits disappeared.

Ultraviolet lighting provided spectacular shows of color inside the auditorium. On the outside, neon lighting, introduced to Baltimore by Claude Neon Signs around 1924, began replacing incandescent lights on theater marquees. John Zink's Edgewood (1930), Bridge (1930), Ambassador (1935), and Senator (1939); John Eyring's Pikes (1938), and Uptown (1941); David Harrison's Patapsco (1944); and Bernard Evander's Westport (1940) are good examples of theaters of this era.

The movie theaters built in the first few years after the war did not differ markedly from those built immediately before the war. A 1944 article described likely characteristics of the new post-war movie theaters.[5] They would be smaller, with an average of 800 seats, but would be more comfortable than pre-war theaters. Seats would be larger, softer and arranged to give a better view of the screen. They would offer more legroom. More fireproof fabrics—spun glass, asbestos and new plastics—would be used. Small, low-cost air conditioning systems were expected.

Because of the government's anti-trust litigation, the large national theater circuits were not expected to be active players in the construction of new movie theaters. Most would be built by local, independent exhibitors. Amazingly, these predictions turned out to be true ... for a time. By 1948 theaters were indeed getting smaller. A theater cost about $200 per seat to build.

Then, in 1949 and 1950, three new theaters were built that represented a very different style. The Edmondson Village (1949), Crest (1949), and Northwood (1950) were all built in shopping centers by small, local organizations. They were large theaters, seating more than 1,200 people each. With the possible exception of the Crest, they blended in with the rest of the shopping center. They had large lobbies and big concession stands. The wide auditoriums were filled with heavily padded seats. Adequate parking was available close to the theater. With theaters such as these, things were looking up. Then, as if a tap had been turned off, the building of hardtop theaters suddenly ceased.

Most of the theaters built in the 1950s were drive-ins. A typical drive-in consisted of a 6- to 30-acre tract. Drive-ins were often located on major roads far enough outside the urban area for cheap land to be available. A drive-in could hold from 600 to 2,000 cars. Near the entrance was a roadside attraction board and sign. An entrance drive led to the ticket booth, similar to a tollbooth, and then continued along one side of the drive-in to the rear of the parking area. Rows of sloped parking spaces with post speakers were arranged in concentric curves radiating out from the screen tower. The larger-than-normal screen was mounted on a tower structure. In the middle of the parking area was a bunker-like building which housed the projection booth, the concession area, and the rest rooms.

An exit drive was located on the opposite side of the parking area from the entrance drive. Cars entered the holding drive from the highway; they stopped to get tickets at the box office that usually served two lanes of vehicles, one on each side. They then entered the theater along an entrance drive and drove into a parking spot. Many drive-ins had seating areas for "walk-ins" and playgrounds for children. Classic early drive-ins were the Governor Ritchie Drive-In (1939) in Glen Burnie and the Elkridge Drive-In (1948). Later drive-ins became larger and more elaborate. The Timonium Drive-In (1955), with a capacity of nearly 2,500 cars, was one of the largest in the country.

A writer for *Motion Picture Herald* in 1952 saw several trends in motion picture exhibition.[6] One was the move to increase the size of the picture that gave rise to CinemaScope, Cinerama and, more recently, IMAX. Along with this went the elimination of the screen border. The writer saw "a trend away from the long-established practice of regarding the auditorium as a room unrelated in architectural details and finishes to the physical character of the performance." In what was called the "random assembly," where seats were placed in the row wherever the position offered the least obstruction, the performance took precedence over the decor. Another trend was the gradual elimination of the marquee and its replacement with a vestibule that was integrated with both the front of the theater and the lobby.

Hard-top theaters returned in 1960 with a handsome theater in Hillendale. The Hillendale Theater was the first of a new breed of big luxury theaters. The typical theater built in the 1960s seated just fewer than 1,000 people and was located in a shopping center. The walls were made of pre-cast concrete frames, sometimes with brick curtain walls. The fronts of these theaters were often of large glass panels, and the box offices were no longer separate structures, but part of the lobby. The lobbies were large, brightly lit, and often two stories high. Concession stands were larger and sold a huge variety of refreshments.

The auditoriums were plain with large screens covering almost the entire front wall; prosceniums had nearly disappeared. Decorations consisted mainly of draperies. The Crest, Edmondson

Village, and Northwood were direct ancestors of these theaters of the mid–1960s. Typical of the later theaters were Fenton & Lichtig's Hillendale (1960) and Westview I (1965) and William Riseman's Harundale (1964) and Perring Plaza (1966).

Over the 30 years between 1968 and 1998 the architectural style of movie theaters went through a series of radical changes. The theaters built in the 1970s could not have been more different from the theaters of the mid–1960s. After 1969 the number of movie theater auditoriums per theater began to increase, but the individual auditoriums became smaller. *Boxoffice* magazine, in 1969, reported that small, intimate "mini-theaters" were attracting the attention of exhibitors.[7] Multi-auditorium pioneer Durwood Theaters of Kansas City, announced a six-auditorium theater in Omaha in 1968.

Washington exhibitor Paul Roth visited Stanley Durwood in Kansas City and realized the enormous potential of multiplexes. He described the advantages of the new theaters in a 1992 interview.

> I saw that all of the auxiliary spaces in the theater, the rest rooms, the lobby, the refreshment stand, all those things could be made to produce better because, if you staggered the show times, you could use them a multiple number of times during the evening rather than in a thousand seat single theater, you used the lobby fifteen minutes before each show started. The parking ... if you were full on Saturday night you had 900 people trying to get their cars out of the parking lot at 9:30 and 900 people trying to get their cars into the parking lot for the 9:45 show. The other way was just so great with the shows breaking about every 15 or 20 minutes.[8]

Between 1960 and 1973, the few theaters that were built were fairly luxurious structures with one or two screens. In 1973 things took a dramatic turn. The first local three-screen theater — the Ritchie Cinemas in Glen Burnie — appeared, and auditoriums began degenerating into narrow, ugly boxes with little attempt at decoration. Other triplexes followed, and it was not too long before theaters with four or more auditoriums appeared. A typical theater during the late 1960s and early 1970s, such as the Timonium Cinemas, Jumpers Mall or the Movies at Golden Ring Mall, was a plain, box-like structure adjacent to a shopping center or built into a mall. The two or three auditoriums and restrooms opened off a central lobby, which contained the concession stand. Most of these theaters had very plain auditoriums that tended to be long and narrow with a single central aisle. The average auditorium seated fewer than 200 people.

Although the average number of auditoriums per theater steadily increased from two in the early 1970s to six in 1975, the styles remained the same. Out of 285 new theaters reported in 1975 to *Boxoffice* magazine, only 16 were single screens. The remaining theaters included 115 twins, 41 triplexes, 37 quads, eight five-plexes, six six-plexes, two eight-plexes, and one nine-plex.

Speaking in 1976, Florida exhibitor Sidney Dreier believed that the striking changes — especially theater location and auditorium size — in theater design were for the better. He noted the importance of having theaters in shopping centers, "Nothing brings more people into a shopping center than does a theatre — thousands of visitors every week." Shopping center theaters called for new architectural designs. The new theaters were "intimate, luxurious and very comfortable." Dreier pointed out that new projection technology made it possible for each auditorium to show the same film at the same time using the same print.[9] Well, they were certainly intimate.

In the late 1980s, theater styles changed again, this time for the better. They stopped hiding inside malls and became more visible as large, freestanding buildings.[10] In 1986, the number of auditoriums jumped to an average of 10, and the designs changed markedly. There were fewer theaters built within shopping malls; they were more often built in separate buildings. Several of the auditoriums in a typical eight- or 10-plex, such as the Columbia Palace 9 or Valley Center 9, were large, seating between 400 and 500; the rest would seat between 300 and 170.

The basic layout was square or rectangular with a central box office, large lobby, and a huge central concession area. Some lobbies were lined with marble and were two stories high with windows providing natural light. Patron comfort was stressed in the design of theaters of the late 1980s. The auditoriums — nine seemed to be the magic number — were often arranged asymmetrically around three sides of the lobby. The floors were sloped with two aisles, lined with pinlights. Decorations, curtains, and murals returned. The Baltimore firm of Kelly, Clayton & Mojzisek designed some outstanding theaters in the late 1980s and early 1990s. But even nine auditoriums were not enough.

In the last half of the 1990s, megaplexes appeared. These were mammoth, usually freestanding complexes seating more than 3,000 people in 14 or 16 auditoriums. Most of the auditoriums built after 1995 had stadium seating where patrons enter at the lowest level, and the seats rise row-by-row back toward the projection booth. The megaplexes, much like the Wal-Mart, Costco, and Target stores, felt strong enough to stand on their own; they did not require adjacent shopping centers. Most of the megaplexes have comfortable seating and excellent sight lines in auditoriums that are remarkably similar; indeed, one would be hard put to distinguish between them in the dark. They all have huge multi-stationed concession areas.

In 2000, the Florida-based circuit Muvico took megaplexes to undreamed-of regions with its 24-

screen Egyptian-themed theater at Arundel Mills. Surely we have almost reached the maximum number of auditoriums. What will come next? Perhaps more theme megaplexes. Maybe a theater based on science fiction themes with exotic aliens manning the snack bar? Time will tell and the evolution of movie exhibition will continue to be interesting.[11]

Appendix 4. Theater Personnel

Many of the people who run the theaters are largely invisible. It is only when something goes wrong that they appear. The size of a theater's staff depends on the size of the theater. Nickelodeons needed only a few people — a projectionist, a cashier, a ticket-taker, and a manager, as a minimum. The more pretentious theaters added ushers, doormen, janitors, and musicians. In some smaller neighborhood theaters all the personnel might have been members of the owner's family. The son of the owner of the Paradise Theater on Fleet Street remembered his father bringing home bags of nickels and the family helping him count them on the kitchen table. In the early 1920s the staff of a large neighborhood theater could number as many as 11 people. The Gertrude McCoy listed the following staff members and their weekly salaries in a 1922 court case[1]:

> Projectionist (F. C. Grote) $50.00
> Cashiers (Nellie D. Fittro) $9.00, (Anna Haubert) $9.00
> Bookkeeper & Stenographer (F.J.W. Eisenhart) $20.00
> Charwoman (Bess Wolf) $9.00
> Doorman (George Norris) $20.00
> Usher & Errands (G. Burn) $5.00
> Manager (F. C. Weber) $30.00
> Piano (Emma Mandler) $17.50
> Violin & Piano (R. Uhlig & wife) $30.00
> Weekly Total Payroll $199.50

In 1937, the Irvington, in addition to a manager and possibly an assistant manager, had a staff of seven, which included a cashier ($14 a week), a janitor ($20), two ushers (one at $10 and one at $4.50), a boy who did odd jobs (at $1 to $2.50), and two projectionists (a chief projectionist at $43.50 and an assistant at $15.90). As theaters increased in size and complexity, their staffs grew. The Parkway had a staff of 18, including a manager, cashier, doorman, chief usher, two day ushers and four night ushers, two porters, four projectionists, a publicity man and a maintenance man. The Stanley had a huge staff with 28 ushers. If the theater had a stage and presented live acts, an additional staff of stagehands and backstage personnel was required. The stage personnel might have included a stage carpenter/manager, an assistant stage manager, an electrician, a property man, and a flyman.

The cashiers are the first members of a theater staff that the public meets. It is their job to sell the tickets and provide information about the show. In 1911, the Photo Players Club of Baltimore did not want to allow cashiers to become members. The cashiers, who were overwhelmingly female, said that they had just as much right to be called "artistes" as the musicians, singers, and talkers who performed in the nickelodeons. They believed that "the art of being able to attract public attention and get the nickels is one of the fine arts."[2] One of the club's directors quickly backed down and apologized; the club would reconsider its policy. The cashier at the Grand, Mamie Tegges, was voted "Highlandtown's most popular young lady" in a 1915 contest. According to writer Helen Paul White, a cashier had to have, "A brain built along the lines of an adding machine, a mind semi-detachable from the surging crowds, a capacity for working twenty-five hours in the day, a sense of humor ... and a sturdy pair of shoes."[3]

Cashiers are probably in the most dangerous position of any theater employee. They are the ones who are most often robbed, and many respond with extraordinary courage. When a would-be hold-up man tried to rob the box office of the Palace in December 1928, he got more than he bargained for. The cashier, Miss Olive Rooks, an attractive, six-foot tall blond from Virginia was not about to give him anything. After she noticed a small dark-haired man loitering near the box office too long, she told him, "Get away from here, you dirty bum!" At that, he reached through the window and grabbed for the money drawer. Miss Rooks was too fast for him and seized his hand. The robber told her to let go, but she held tight and said, "Let go of that money, runt." Then she began shouting for help. The robber, with one last desperate tug, broke free and fled.

On an evening in April 1940, a young man who had been standing in line for the second show at the Broadway Theater handed a note to Elizabeth Bloom, the cashier. The note said: "Give me what's in the register or I will kill you. Keep quiet for four minutes. I got a gun." A woman in line behind the robber ran into the theater and reported the holdup. Several theater employees rushed out, and when the would-be robber saw them, he stuck his hand through the window opening, grabbed a handful of money, and ran. The manager, Robert Marhenke, and others chased him into a blind alley. Marhenke, stuck his hand in his coat pocket to pretend he had a gun, and snarled, "I've got a gun on you. Come out now or I'll shoot." Marhenke's bluff worked; the man came out. When the robber got close enough to realize that it was a bluff, he tried to get away, but Marhenke was able to subdue him and turn him over to the local police.[4]

It was the cashier who had to face the gun of the

midget robber at the Royal in 1951. In February 1962, a bandit approached the box office at the State Theater, leveled his gun at Mrs. Olive White, the cashier, and growled, "This is it!" Unfazed, Mrs. White replied, "Get going!" and the thug beat a hasty retreat.

Hopefully the current trend of putting cashiers inside lobbies will remove them from the dangerous position outside.

Little has been written about the greeters who stand at the entrances of the auditoriums and collect tickets. They are the ones who welcome us to the theater and tell us where our movie is playing. They tear the tickets in two and give back half. They also tell us where the toilets are and let us back in the theater after a rest stop. The line between ushers and ticket-takers has blurred.

The big theaters used to also have doormen. Alas, these have disappeared. They gave a touch of class to the theater. Doormen like Albert C. Blackiston ensured that order would be maintained. Blackiston was the doorman at the Auditorium, Victoria, and Academy of Music during the first decade of the 20th century. He looked like a field marshal at the Victoria, magnificent in gold-banded cap and dark blue frock coat with a double row of polished brass buttons, sleeves decorated with broad gold bands and trefoils up to the elbows, and two heavy gold cords draped across his chest.[5] A friendly, enthusiastic, welcoming ticket-taker can start your movie visit on a high note; a sullen, silent one can make you want to turn around and get your money back.

The life of an usher can be summed up in the quote from a young female usher in 1926: "We don't get much money, but we have a lot of fun."[6] Ushers are important members of the theater staff. They are the personnel with whom the public most often come in contact. In the past, ushers often had to submit to a rigid, almost military-style of discipline while dealing with every kind of oddball and crank imaginable. They helped people find seats, looked for lost objects, listened to complaints, asked people to remove hats, watched out for mashers, and kept an eye on young couples. They had to be diplomatic and polite; not an easy task. They were the enforcers, the ones who told us to take our feet off the backs of seats and to pipe down. They were the ones who knew all the tricks and were ever vigilant to thwart kids trying to sneak in or toss them out if they were too boisterous.

In many theaters, ushers were forbidden to watch the movies or even to look at the screen. They wore fancy uniforms and, at the first-run downtown theaters, they were drilled like soldiers. Perhaps this was appropriate; they were the front-line troops.

At Loew's Century, Valencia and Parkway, ushers received monthly efficiency ratings. They were graded service (50 percent), personal (30 percent) and organization (20 percent). Service included courtesy, tolerance, speech, efficiency on duty and alertness. Personal consisted of neatness, personality, and appearance; and organization consisted of cooperation, loyalty, responsibility, and attendance. At Loew's Century they wore two-tone trousers, stiff shirtfronts, wing collars, ties and jackets. They were inspected daily.

One of the major duties of the ushers during the heyday of the downtown theaters was to find patrons seats. In those days you could walk into a theater at any time and, if a night scene was on the screen, it was too dark to negotiate the aisles without the help of an usher with a flashlight. At the State Theater, ushers progressed, up from aisle three to aisle one, before finally reaching the zenith, head usher. The balcony there was coveted by ushers because it was quiet and off the usual route of the manager.

Before about 1910, "when the profession of theatrical ushering was thrown open to women in Baltimore," ushers in theaters were all men.[7] Even after 1910, the overwhelming number of ushers, especially before World War II, were young men. There were a few female ushers in 1912, "dainty young ladies," at the Academy of Music, the Auditorium, and the New. Those at the Academy of Music wore gray skirts and gray bobtailed jackets with 17 brass buttons down the front and the name of the theater on the collar in gold letters. A lot of teenagers got their first jobs as ushers. Today, one of the main jobs of the usher is to clean the mountains of trash left in the auditorium after a show.

The manager is similar to a ship's captain. He or she was in charge of the theater, and much of the credit for a successful theater was due to an imaginative, innovative manager. With a few, very rare, exceptions, today's theater managers are not like the managers of old. Leon Back, president of the National Association of Theater Owners of Maryland, said that formerly a theater manager's main job was to "sell the picture, do promotional advertising, street stunts, distribute throwaways."[8] Managers used to have more responsibility. Many were able to select the films that played at their theaters and had control over the advertising. Today they may be little more than the owner's representatives, keeping order, hiring, firing, and turning over admission money.

It was different in the 1910s. Lou DeHoff and Bernard Depkin were two of the most popular and effective managers in Baltimore during the first several decades of the 20th century. DeHoff was particularly skilled at publicity. A 1918 article described DeHoff, who was managing the New Theater for Charles Whitehurst, as "one of the newer type of managerial personalities ... by instinct of the reportorial trend of mind. He knows news values, he knows 'angle'; every show he plays in Whitehurst's New Theatre fills him with dozens of ideas."[9]

Another article described Depkin, who was the

general manager for Henry Webb's Parkway Theater, as a shrewd and accurate buyer of films and a workaholic. Depkin paid attention not only to the films he bought, but also to the comfort of the patrons at his theaters. He was skilled at advertising and personally arranged the lobby displays.[10]

Robert Marhenke spoke for many managers when he said that there was as much action off screen as on in his reminiscence about his years as the manager of the Broadway Theater. A manager had to deal with hold-ups, women in labor, mashers, and rowdy kids. A manager had to be a jack-of-all-trades who could fix anything that went wrong.

The rowdy audience at Saturday matinees was one of the manager's greatest trials. With a leavening of cartoons, comedies, a serial chapter, and a shoot-'em-up cowboy film, the auditorium filled with energetic kids slowly fermented. Malted milk balls, jawbreakers and other missiles filled the air. The sound level rose to a dull roar. Many of the children had arrived at 10:00 A.M.—fully armed with peashooters, cap guns and slingshots, and their lunches—and stayed until 6:00 P.M. If things got too bad, the manager could stop the film and tell the unruly audience that there would be no more movie until they quieted down.[11] Sometimes this worked. A young man set off firecrackers in the Carlton in December 1958. He and five companions were ejected by the manager; and when he returned for a confrontation, the manager dealt with him using a "blunt instrument."

At the Crystal Theater, one night in December 1917, thieves set the theater on fire. It was discovered and put out before it could do much damage. Mr. Cluster, who lived above the theater, was able to get things ready for the next day's show by working through the night. He had to perform some minor repairs, get a new piano, and fix the screen.

"When you go to see motion pictures, whether in the first-class theatre or the nickel house, there is one man upon whom the whole picture show practically depends, one man who can either make or mar the entire entertainment for which you have paid your admission, and that man is ... a man you don't see at all, perhaps way up in a little 6 × 7 coop near the roof, the chap they call 'the operator.'"[12] The projectionists are the invisible men (rarely women) of the exhibition industry.

What was a projectionist's life like? In the early days it was hard and boring. The working conditions were terrible. The booths were small, cramped and hot, and the projectionists had to be constantly ready in case of fire. For many years, there were no toilets in the booths, and the projectionists had to use buckets. The booth at the Idle Hour was very small. "You had to lay down in the booth to look out the port windows to see the show, to see what was going on. You couldn't stand up. They took the legs off of the projectors and had them right down on the floor and you looked through a little hole down at the bottom that was on the floor. That's how you used to make the changeover."[13]

One early projectionist in New York described his day this way: "I reported at nine o'clock in the morning at whatever exchange supplied me with films for that day ... I received my 6 single reelers and went to some other place for my posters ... I generally reached the theatre about noon and then began at once to prepare for the show." He fixed the carbons, adjusted the lamps, and tightened all the loose chairs in the auditorium before he was ready for the show. "From then on until eleven o'clock I would alternately grind out a reel and then show slides while I was getting set for the next reel. I ate with one hand and ground with the other. I showed slides when I wanted a few minutes rest. After eleven o'clock I packed the reels and the posters and started back to the exchanges to give them back. Then a snack at a restaurant and home."[14]

Being a projectionist could be a hazardous job. The early booths were cramped, with inadequate ventilation. Breathing the vaporized carbon could cause lung disease. A letter to the editor of the *Sun* in 1921 commented on conditions in Baltimore projection booths: "Most of the projection rooms ... in this city are actually not fit for a 'human being' to work in. About 75 percent of the rooms have no ceiling ventilators, so as to let the carbon gas escape, which is so injurious to the health of the operator; more than 50 percent have no windows ... to let in pure, fresh air; only about 25 percent have ... running water and drainage washstands, and as for toilets they are a novelty."[15]

Film was highly flammable and many projectionists were seriously burned combating film fires. Fires were relatively common, but, fortunately there were no serious film fires in Baltimore.[16] The projectionist at the Royal Theater on West Pratt Street, Leon Davidson, was badly injured in 1925 when a fire in the booth forced him to jump out the window with his clothes in flames.[17] Three years later, projectionist William Holthouse was seriously burned on his hands and face while battling a fire in the booth at the Grand; he refused to leave the theater for treatment until after the show was completed.

Until the 1950s, the film used was highly inflammable, and film fires were common. Many of the booths were lined with asbestos and adding that to the vaporized carbon the projectors gave off, we can only guess at the toll on the projectionist's lungs. The heat in a booth could rise to more than 100 degrees, and some projectionists worked in their undershirts.

Still, it was a good job for many. The pay was better than that of many jobs, thanks to a strong union. Most projectionists loved the job. Despite all the dangers and bad working conditions, being a projectionist was considered a very good job. During the Depression, projectionists worked six days a week and made $54. In the 1930s, according to one projectionist, "It was like being a millionaire." Another said, "That was supposed to have been a top-notch job; yes sir, that was a good job in those days." One man making $25 a week as a bookkeeper in 1930 increased his salary to $45 a week when he became a projectionist. At one time the projectionists made more money than workers in the steel mills. The big first-run theaters had a staff of five projectionists, two working at a time with one relief man on call 24 hours a day.

Let us end on a sweet note, with the people who sell snacks. With theaters getting more and more of their profits from concessions, surely these people are among the most important employees. They are certainly among the youngest and lowest paid employees of a theater, but they provide us with a host of delicious treats to enjoy as we watch a movie.

Notes

Preface

1. And that's in spite of horrible memories of walking down the long, dark, bilious green corridor of the Medical Arts Building to my dentist, who didn't believe in Novocain, and plotting ways to avoid a bully who wanted to do something unnamed but awful to me.
2. "Throngs at Movies Found Unresponsive," Baltimore *Evening Sun*, (hereafter ES) June 2, 1922, p. 25.
3. "Local Movie Goers Immune to Unhappy Film Endings," *ES*, April 28, 1928, p. 3.
4. Baltimore *Evening Sun* columnist Christopher Billopp mirrored this in his May 2, 1930 column. He describes attending a movie that "portrayed a lovable old fellow thrown out of his job and starving" and "an equally lovable little boy ... crippled" who was beaten by a bully. Billopp hoped the movie turned out well, but he didn't wait to see the ending. He left "with tears streaming down my cheeks" when a doctor told the boy's parents that the child would always be a cripple. He must have been from Washington.
5. [Donald Kirkley], "Footnotes on the Films," [Baltimore Morning] *Sun*, (hereafter, MS) January 8, 1930, p. 7.
6. One motive suggested in a 1912 newspaper article was debt. At the time of her death in 1907, Miss Bloodgood was in debt for $35,225. "Reason for Suicide of Clara Bloodgood," Baltimore *Star*, September 10, 1912, p. 12.
7. "Baltimore Given High Praise for Tolerant Ideas," *ES*, September 23, 1929, p. 19. The reference to Baltimore nearly sinking into a morass a few years before may refer to the attack on motion pictures and on what they considered a lax censor board by the Citizens' League for Better Motion Pictures in 1921.
8. Chase, whose surname was Parrott, had a brother named James Parrott who was a director for Hal Roach comedies. Chase began his theatrical career singing illustrated songs in a Baltimore theater when he was 12 years old.
9. Miss Phillips was born in Baltimore in 1894. After she graduated from Eastern High School, she joined the Fawcett Stock Company to play ingénue roles. She went on to make movies for Essanay and Universal.
10. Miss Kavanaugh was also a successful playwright. She was born in Baltimore and attended the College of Notre Dame.
11. Rooney, the son of Irish comedian Pat Rooney, grew up in West Baltimore; he honed his talents hanging around on the corner of West Pratt and Stricker streets.
12. Francis X. Bushman was born in Norfolk, Va., but moved to Baltimore when he was a baby. He went to school at Mosher and Division Street.
13. Henry Bederski, "Chaplin Began His Career Here," *MS*, June 20, 1983, p. A8. Bederski says that Chaplin was appearing in the review "A Night in an English Music Hall" at the Victoria Theater when he was approached by Kassel and Bauman who were the financial backers of Sennett. Charles Chaplin was advertised as the featured player in the review when it opened at the Victoria in late May 1913. Curiously another story associates the beginning of Chaplin's movie career with Washington, D.C. During a run of Chaplin's show at the Cosmos Theater there, he asked Aaron and Julian Brylawski—who operated the theater—to have lunch with him. Over lunch he told the Brylawskis about a full-time movie-acting offer he had received, and he asked for their advice. They advised him to accept it. Chaplin became a good friend to the Brylawskis. (*The Brylawski Family in Washington's Motion Picture Business*, unpublished ms by Henry H. Brylawski, 1997.)
14. "Baltimore," *Boxoffice*, November 6, 1972, p. E-8.
15. There was a Hollywood Theater and a Security Square Twin, but they are both gone. The original Hollywood burned and the original Security Twin has been replaced by the Security Square 8.

Chapter 1

1. The Music Hall was renamed the Lyric in 1903.
2. Among the better-known halls were: the Canton Academy, China Hall, Eintracht Hall, Germania Maennerchor, Hampden Hall, the Labor Lyceum, Lehmann's Hall, Mozart Hall, Thalia Hall, and the Vernant Halls.
3. "Car Riding for Fun," Baltimore *Sunday Herald*, July 29, 1900, p. 25.
4. According to an invoice dated October 3, 1894 in the Raff & Gammon Collection (vol. 1, p. 11), Baker Library, Harvard Business School, one Kinetoscope (#183) was sent to the "Exhibition Department" in Baltimore. That machine cost $775.

5. "Wonders of the Vitascope," *MS*, June 17, 1896, p. 6.

6. Correspondence from Charles Ford to Raff & Gammon details the difficulties Ford had arranging the 16 June exhibition. On 11 May, Ford wrote that he had been in contact with [Peter W.] Kiefaber of Philadelphia, who had the Vitascope rights for New Jersey, Massachusetts, Illinois, and Maryland, and that he wanted a 50-day contract instead of the 100-day contract that Kiefaber had suggested. On 2 June, Ford told Raff & Gammon that he had invested more than $40,000 in Electric Park and he begged them to make every effort to deliver the Vitascope by Sunday [7 June]. Nine days later, Ford wrote that he had signed a contract with Kiefaber and that Kiefaber had sent J. H[unter] Armat to set up the machine. Armat, a brother of Thomas Armat who was one of the developers of the Vitascope, found that Electric Park had only alternating current and refused to set up the machine. Ford suggested that he could run a 500-volt direct current in from the streetcar system. In a letter of 16 June, Ford said that C[hristopher] Armat (a more experienced brother) had been working for two days with the chief electrician of the traction company to set up the Vitascope. On 20 June, Ford expressed his continuing dissatisfaction with Kiefaber and the Vitascope. Ford to Raff & Gammon, 11 May, 2 Jun, 11 June, 16 June, 20 June 1896, Raff & Gammon Collection, Baker Library, Harvard Business School; Musser (1990: 114, 129).

7. "Electric Park's Casino," *Baltimore American* (hereafter, *BA*), June 16, 1896, p. 2.

8. *Baltimore Herald*, June 14, 1896, p. 7.

9. Before air conditioning and efficient ventilation, theaters usually closed during the hottest summer months. They reopened between mid–August and mid–September. Traces of this cycle remained for many years even after air conditioning made possible comfortable year-round theater going. Contracts for projectionists and contracts between exhibitors and distributors ran from September to September. A new theater season still begins in the fall.

10. *MS*, September 29, 1896, p. 10.

11. *BA*, October 4, 1896. p. 14. Musser (1990:167) considers the centograph little more than a pirated Vitascope although this ad suggests that it may have been based on the Lumiere cinematographe.

12. "Arriving Actors Tell Ups and Downs of Stage," *MS*, March 3, 1913, p. 7.

13. *BA*, November 15, 1896, p. 22.

14. "The Methodist Bazaar," *ibid*, January 21, 1897, p. 9.

15. "Methodists' Big Bazaar," *Morning Herald*, January 21, 1897, p. 11.

16. "Day by Day by Carroll Dulaney," *BNP*, April 4, 1938, p. 17.

17. Boxing was extremely popular at this time. During the week of March 15, Ford's was advertising the Corbett–Fitzsimmons fight at Carson City, Nevada reproduced by means of Automatic Figures "about three feet in height representing the pugilists. These Automatons are so constructed that they can give EVERY ACTION of the ORIGINALS at the very second of its occurrence." Ford's Theater, the Monumental, and the Academy of Music had made arrangements to receive round-by-round news of the fight by means of special telegraph hook-ups. Meanwhile the fight was being filmed by Enoch Rector. These films debuted in New York on May 22, 1897; they reached Baltimore in August.

18. Baltimore was the fourth city in the country to get these movies. They had played in Philadelphia, Boston, and Washington.

19. "Passion Play at Music Hall," *Baltimore American* [hereafter *BA*], February 8, 1898, p. 4.

20. The Block is the local name for the well-known 400 block of East Baltimore Street between Holliday and Gay streets. It has been a center of entertainment since the turn of the century and has often been the subject of close police scrutiny. By the teens and 1920s, the Block had acquired a reputation for cheaper and more exotic amusements in its many nightclubs and theaters.

21. "Passion Play at Music Hall," *BA*, January 3, 1899, p. 9.

22. Compared with the prices of other items, tickets to the Holmes' lectures were expensive. Coffee cost 8 and a half cents a pound; sirloin steak was 12 cents a pound; a bottle of port, sherry, or claret cost 25 cents; women's skirts cost between 30 and 98 cents and men's suits were between $6.25 and $18.

23. The Windsor Hotel in New York was destroyed by fire on March 17 with the loss of 45 lives including a woman from Baltimore.

24. River View or Riverview Park was located on Point Breeze at the southeast corner of Baltimore where Colgate Creek empties into the Patapsco River. Opinion is divided on whether "Riverview" is one word or two. Early writers preferred two words which is what will be used herein.

25. The original title was "La Lune à un Mètre"; it was also called "A Trip to the Moon." It used dissolves and slow fades from one scene to another, between scenes.

26. "Theatres Last Night. Banda Rossa at Auditorium," *MS*, February 13, 1900, p. 7.

27. This ad was on July 7, 1900, for a vaudeville show with "Emmerson's Famous Moving Pictures."

28. This Empire was somewhat more expensive than the Convention Hall — admission cost 15 to 25 cents at matinees and 25 and 50 cents in the evenings — and should not be confused with the Empire at 315 West Fayette that later became the Palace and Town.

29. This was probably another title for Méliès' *La Lune à un Mètre*.

30. "Eagles Exposition Booming," *MS*, June 7, 1903, p. 8.

31. No movie ads were found for the weeks of August 10 and 17.

32. Also called the "Triple Million Dollar Enterprise."

33. "Kernan Orders Act Off," Baltimore *American Star*, September 29, 1908, p. 11.

34. Schanberger had been involved with theaters since he was 11 years old when he got a job clipping notices for the Academy of Music. He joined the Kernan organization in 1892. He soon became Kernan's business manager, and, upon Kernan's death in 1912, Schanberger became the president of Kernan enterprises. He even continued Kernan's habit of visiting the children at the Kernan Hospital for Crippled Children every Sunday. Schanberger was born in Baltimore, nearly at the back door of the Academy of Music, in 1872. He died there in 1947. His two sons, J. Lawrence and Frederick C. Jr., followed their father in the theater business.

35. Quoted in "Santa Claus Kernan Has His Own Empty Stocking Club," *MS*, December 20, 1908, p. 13.

36. "For Another Theatre," *MS*, February 17, 1906, p. 7.

37. I have borrowed freely here from the excellent unpublished biography of James Kernan written by Shirley Cammack of the James Lawrence Kernan Hospital. See also, "Mr. Kernan Dies in His Hotel," "Long Career as Theater Manager," and "Tributes from His Admirers," *BA*, December 15, 1912, p. A7.

38. "Mr. James L. Kernan," *BA*, December 15, 1912, p. A8.

39. "Theatres Next Week," *MS*, March 6, 1904, p. 8.

40. Charles Musser, *Before the Nickelodeon*, p. 254.

41. The ads did not always mention motion pictures, even when they were shown.

42. Biograph lost the movie contract for the Keith circuit to the Kinetograph Company in July 1905. (Musser, 1990:388) This may have been the reason for the switch at Electric Park from Biograph films to the "Casinograph" for the remainder of the summer.

43. There are several references to a movie theater opening in Baltimore in 1904, but these are almost certainly in error. One of these sources, an article in *The Film Index*, "Banquet for Baltimore Picture Men," December 31, 1910, claimed that J. Spencer Clark, collector of city water rent and taxes, issued the "first license to a motion picture theatre shortly after the big fire of 1904."

44. Much of this account of the theater at 404-406 E. Baltimore St. is based on J. M. Shellman, "Baltimore Has Long List of Motion Picture Pioneers," *Moving Picture World*, [hereafter *MPW*] July 15, 1916, p. 384. According to a slightly different account, the fire broke out about half an hour after the show had started. A still different account was provided by Harry R. Hitchcock, the son of early exhibitor Walter Hitchcock. According to Hitchcock, Brown came from Pittsburgh. He opened an arcade on the block that had movie machines—kinetoscopes or mutoscopes—in the front and a curtained-off area in the rear where he planned to exhibit projected movies. He hired Pearce and Scheck to do the electrical work and Walter Hitchcock to sing illustrated songs. A fire broke out in the theater before he could open it, and Brown couldn't pay Pearce and Scheck, so he gave them the theater instead.

45. The earliest newspaper ad is in the *BA* of February 11, 1906.

46. Pearce and Scheck had two small movie theaters side by side at 225 and 227 North Eutaw Street between 1906 and 1908. The one at 225 was called the Amusea and the one at 227 was called the Ideal.

47. The following year, Philadelphia-based Sigmund Lubin Enterprises leased the building and opened two theaters in it. The first floor was used mainly for motion picture shows, while the theater on the second and third floors was used for vaudeville. Both theaters showed movies.

48. The listing was published in December 1906 and again in March 1907 with the same errors. The theater on N. Ontario St. is Pearce and Scheck's Ideal on N. Eutaw St. Early theater listings are notoriously inaccurate. Information for the list had probably been gathered in mid-1906 which explains why Pearce and Scheck's Baltimore St. theater was still listed. Unlisted is the Wizard at 1118 Light St. which probably also opened in 1906.

49. Howe's shows were similar to those of Burton Holmes, but they were cheaper to attend.

Chapter 2

1. "Baltimore Has One Moving Picture Theatre to Every 14,805 Inhabitants," *MS*, November 29, 1908, p. 15. The population of the city was 573,000 in 1908.

2. Typical of shows at these smaller places was the show in January 1907 at Ehmling's which consisted of vaudeville, with Harry Moorehead singing illustrated songs and moving pictures.

3. "Baltimore, MD," *Billboard*, April 24, 1909, p. 10.

4. Although these were the major summer amusement parks in the Baltimore area there were many more; and most, if not all, presented vaudeville, usually booked by local promoter John T. McCaslin. A May 1909 listing in *Billboard* magazine named the following parks: Flood's, Herman's New Electric Park, Mitchell's Back River View Park, Weber's, Klein's Deer Park, North East Park, Hedden's Casino, Shadyside Park, Walnut Spring, Easter's Park, Pabst Park, Stoddard's Palm Garden, Electric Park, Suburban, Gwynn Oak Park, Bay Shore, River View, Hollywood, Hoffman House Casino, and Kline's Shore Line Park.

5. A 1908 article on conditions in Grand Rapids, Michigan, provided more detailed information on the cost of building, equipping, and running a nickelodeon. According to this article, rent cost between $100 and $400 depending on location and size; the cost of the equipment ran from $3,000 to $6,000. In one theater, the costs were: $1,750 for woodwork, $525 for the walls, $550 for staff work, $315 for the seats, $350 for painting, and $237 for tile. Seats cost between $1.50 and $3.50 apiece. The projector and accessories cost about $200. Film rental ran about $50 for first-class service. Typical salaries were: $9 to $21 a week for projectionists, $10 to $18 a week for singers, and $4 to $12 a week for piano players. "The Nickelodeon as a Business Proposition," *MPW*, (July 25, 1908), pp. 61–62.

6. "5-Cent Show Easily Started," *MPW*, August 17, 1907, p. 376.

7. The upper theater was scheduled to open during the week of 18 March with C. Nelson Camp & Company's electrical spectacular "Doomsday," but some problems developed and the opening was postponed until April.

8. "Lubin's," *BA*, March 31, 1907, Part 2, Section 2, p. 2.

9. Architect John A. Lankford was preparing plans for an $80,000 five-story theater on West Lexington near Fremont in February 1907, and The Grand United Order of Brothers & Sisters of Good Hope planned a 650-seat theater at 655–657 West Lexington.

10. Sylvan Schenthal, "Electric Theatre Conditions. Baltimore, Md.," *Billboard*, June 27, 1908, p. 14.

11. "The New White Lights Have Made a Lover's Lane of Baltimore Street," *MS*, November 8, 1908.

12. "Moving-Picture Shows Should Not Be Allowed to Open on Sunday," *MS*, June 11, 1911, p. 6.

13. "All Right-Thinking People Should Oppose Sunday Picture Shows," *MS*, June 13, 1911, p. 6.

14. In addition to movie houses being open on Sundays in Arlington, the poolrooms and bowling alleys had also been open; Gorsuch ordered them closed too. "Orders Arlington 'Lid' On," *ES*, December 22, 1911, p. 14.

15. John M. Bradlet, "Baltimore," *MPW*, December 25, 1909, p. 924.

16. "Talking Pictures at Amusea," *BA*, January 10, 1909, Part 2, p. 17.

17. In 1907, traveling exhibitor Lyman H. Howe employed a small company of people to provide sound effects for his movies. O. J. Tasker directed two assistants and a number of small boys behind the screen. They worked at a long table set up behind the screen. The apparatus they used when they appeared at Ford's Theater in August 1907 consisted of drums, boards, tin cans, sheets of sandpaper, and various musical instruments. Various assistants imitated the sounds of barking dogs; Tasker, himself, shouted in some gibberish to imitate the voices of Chinese coolies. For more details on Howe's sound effects, see "Art of the Noisemaker Adorns Moving Pictures," *MS*, August 18, 1907, p. 13.

18. This was Manes Fuld who died in 1956 at the age of 93. He founded the Voltamp Electric Manufacturing Company in 1904. Voltamp manufactured toy electric trains that have become collector's items. Fuld was also a Shakespearean actor and a pharmacist.

19. "The Great Wizard," *BA*, December 7, 1909, p. 13.

20. Frank Schwartz, a member of the club's board of directors, said, in April 1911, that the club had been formed several weeks earlier "for the benefit of piano and violin players, singers and talkers, and for the uplifting of moving-picture work in general." At one of the meetings, someone suggested that the club take in cashiers as honorary members, but another member objected and the suggestion was rejected. This rejection was not received favorably by the cashiers who felt that they were just as much a part of the movie business as the other members. The club beat a hasty retreat and invited the cashiers to join as honorary members. "Are Real 'Artistes,' Say Girl Cashiers," *BN*, April 8, 1911, p. 12.

21. *Motography*, March 18, 1911, p. 315.

22. "Actors to Speak the 'Lines' Behind Screen," *MS*, April 18, 1915, Sect. 3, Pt. 4, p. 3.

23. Sidney Daniels, "City 20 Years Ahead of Time in Talkies," *MS*, October 21, 1928, Magazine Section.

24. Claude L. Woolley, "Tricks of the Trade in the Making of Thrilling Moving Pictures," *MS*, May 16, 1909, p. 24.

25. "Movie Close-Ups," *ES*, March 26, 1928, p. 10. Q.E.D. was Gustav Klemm.

26. Filmland Gossip, *ES*, October 24, 1921, p. 5. Organist Gaylord Carter echoed this sentiment in a 1986 Smithsonian documentary on picture palaces when he told of a manager who asked him to "perfume the air with music."

27. Other stock pieces included Tobani's "Hearts and Flowers" for sad scenes, Waldteufel's "Skater's Waltz" for neutral scenes, and "A Hot Time in the Old Town Tonight" for a happy, boisterous scene. Sometimes, when the choice of musical accompaniment was left entirely up to the piano player or organist, terrible mistakes were made. One story relates how, during the scene in the film *The Crisis*, where President Lincoln lay dying surrounded by weeping family and friends, the piano player "broke into the rollicking, rhythmic chorus of 'Poor Butterfly!'"

28. "From the People. There Isn't Any Bar to Promiscuous Piano Playing in Picture Shows. Maybe a Censor of Music Would Help," *MS*, August 26, 1910, p. 6.

29. When Leonard Chick sang at the Blue Mouse in 1913, he was billed as "The Splendid Tenor."

30. These were in New Orleans; Indianapolis; St. Louis; Boston; Los Angeles; Lynn, Mass.; Denver; Chicago; Spokane; Vancouver; and Oakland.

31. Projectionists were usually referred to by the term "operator" but they will be called projectionists herein since that word is in more common use today. See, for example, *Laws of Maryland*, Chapter 195, April 18, 1918 for the amended law governing the board.

32. Only those projectionists operating machines in Baltimore City had to be licensed; those operating across the border in Baltimore County or in Frederick, Salisbury, or Oakland did not require any license. As it turned out, many operators at Baltimore County theaters did get licenses, presumably because they might be called to go into the city.

33. Kreis was better known by the name G. Kingston Howard that he began using shortly after he obtained his license.

34. A national exhibitors' organization, the Exhibitors' League, had also been formed in 1910 by exhibitors from Ohio, Illinois, Pennsylvania, Michigan, Indiana, West Virginia and Wisconsin. In 1911, the Washington, D.C. exhibitors joined. By 1920 there were four national exhibitors' groups, the Motion Picture Exhibitors of America, the Independent Motion Picture Exhibitors of America, the Motion Picture Theatre Owners of America, and the National Association of the Motion Picture Industry. A new organization, the Allied States Association was formed in 1923 by several independent exhibitors. By the 1930s, there were two major groups, the Motion Picture Theater Owners of America and Allied States Association of Motion Picture Exhibitors. Both organizations worked hard to obtain better deals from the distributors, but it was widely believed that the former was more closely tied to the producers and distributors than the latter.

35. Sherwood (1875–1950) was a relative of Marion Pearce.

36. The correspondent for *Exhibitors' Times* noted in his article on the convention that Baltimore was "perhaps the first city to have changed the policy [against motion pictures] of the big newspapers." He went on to say, "The Baltimore *Sun*, so well known and so powerful, was the leader on the attacks on motion pictures. At the eve of the convention, we are pleased to state that the Baltimore *Sun* has been the first paper to recognize the merits of motion pictures and for some time past, has been devoting much space to the movies. Today, the *Sun* is following the march and it is stated that the three largest papers of Baltimore, viz: the *Sun*, the *American* and the *News*, will devote full pages in their next Sunday editions, as a fitting opening of the convention. " "Notes on the Baltimore Convention," *Exhibitors' Times*, May 31, 1913, p. 6.

37. The salesman for the Dramagraph offered $100 to anyone who could name a noise that the machine could not imitate. It seemed to be able to produce a wide variety of sounds, from departing trains, thunder storms, squawking chickens, automobile horns, goats, to melodeons.

38. Thomas Bedding, Fellow of the Royal Photographic Society (F.R.P.S.), "Baltimore and the Picture," *MPW*, vol. 2 (1910), p. 399.

39. An unnamed film, probably about Johnson's fight with Burns, had been the subject of some protest in the spring of 1909. One letter to the editor of the *Sun* stated that prize fighting was illegal in Maryland, deplored the showing of the film at "one of our best theatres," and protested "in the name of decency against such a show in Maryland."

40. The fight had been filmed using three cameras by the Vitagraph Company. They had spent an estimated $250,000 to make the films.

41. "Stop It," Says Mayor," *MS,* July 6, 1910, p. 14.
42. "Every Man His Own Censor," *BA,* July 8, 1910, p. 15.
43. The films were shown in a building erected especially for the exhibition.
44. The Gayety advertised films of the Wolgast–Moran featherweight championship fight in July 1911 so presumably these films were made in Maryland to avoid Federal prosecution.
45. The *Alum Chine* blew up on the morning of March 7, 1913, while loading 500 tons of dynamite scheduled for use in building the Panama Canal. The ship was blown to bits. Windows were broken in Baltimore, and the explosion was felt in Atlantic City, New Jersey. Thirty-three men were killed, and 60 were injured in the disaster.
46. A 1913 nickel was equivalent to 90 cents in 2002; a 1913 dime was equivalent to $1.79.
47. W. Stephen Bush, "Is the 'Nickel Show' on the Wane?" *MPW,* February 28, 1914, p. 1065. The writer ended by claiming that even in the poorest European countries, such as Italy and Spain, it was rare to find a movie theater charging less than the equivalent of 10 cents.
48. A count of the theaters and moving picture parlors in published lists shows only 91 theaters in the same period. One reason for the discrepancy is that many motion picture shows were unnamed, short-lived affairs that lasted only a few months. These theaters never got listed in city directories and phone books and hardly ever advertised in newspapers.
49. "Local Film Shows Are Very Popular," *BN,* March 11, 1911, p. 13.
50. The author seems to be referring to the Cinematograph exhibition held at Hamilton Easter's store on East Baltimore Street in January 1897 which was widely believed to have been the first showing of projected movies in the city.
51. Could this be a thinly veiled reference to the Blue Mouse Theater on Lexington Street?
52. "A Thrill Per Minute at the Moving Pictures," *MS,* April 9, 1911, Part 4, p. 7.
53. "Auditorium," *BA,* August 29, 1911, p. 12.
54. "Success Follows Many Long Years of Experiment," *MS,* November 5, 1922, Pt. 6, p. 9.
55. Ida Smith complained in a letter to the editor that color films hurt her eyes and she dreaded the time when all movies would be in color. "But Many Movie Goers Find Color Pictures Less Tiring Than Black and White Ones," *ES,* May 21, 1938, p. 8.
56. "The Lure of the Moving Pictures," *MS,* May 5, 1912, pt. 4, p. 1.
57. "Maryland," *Motography,* October 12, 1912, p. 303.
58. The Front Street Theater, at Front and Low streets, opened in 1829. It burned during a performance in 1838. Within a year it had been rebuilt. It was a huge structure, four stories high, with seating for 4,000. Many of the leading actors and actresses of the 19th century performed there. In 1850, Swedish singer Jenny Lind appeared at the theater; seats for her performances sold for as much as $100 apiece. During a performance of a Yiddish play on December 27, 1895, someone shouted "Fire!" when a stage employee accidentally ignited a leaking gas fixture. In the ensuing panic to escape the theater 23 people were killed. The theater was demolished in 1904. The Rhoads Opera House Fire occurred in Boyertown, Pennsylvania, in January 1908. 171 people were killed. The theater fire in Acapulco, caused by a film fire, claimed between 250 and 300 lives.
59. "Webb Pictures Talk," *MS,* October 7, 1913, p. 7.
60. There were other systems being developed at the same time to provide sound for motion pictures. Among these were the Edison Kinetophone, the British Vivaphone, and a French system developed by Gaumont. None of these systems was able to evade "the hollow sound of the phonograph."
61. Edward Lyell Fox, "Bringing the 'Talkies' to Your Home," *Technology World Magazine,* Vol. 19 (August 1913), pp. 814–818.
62. A variation of these systems was used on the battleships *Utah* and *North Dakota* in order to send orders to various parts of the big ships.
63. Fox, *op. cit.,* p. 818.
64. Sidney Daniels, "City 20 Years Ahead of Time in Talkies," *MS,* October 21, 1928, Magazine Section, pp. 7–8. U.S. Patent Office records indicate that Webb used several inventions which were issued to Henry Theodore Crapo of New York. Might he have been the French machinist?
65. Daniels, *op. cit.,* says that Webb exhibited his talkies in London and Paris in 1911, but Daniels was not entirely accurate in all his facts in this article.
66. "Webb's Talking Pictures Shown," *Motography,* Vol. IX:8 (January–June 1913), p. 290.
67. Edison talking pictures, which seem to have used the same basic system as Webb's, were exhibited at the Maryland Theater in February 1913.
68. "Webb Pictures Talk, " *MS,* October 7, 1913, p.7.
69. "Mr. Webb's Talking Pictures," *[Baltimore] Star,* October 10, 1913, p. 8.
70. "Some of Geo. R. Webb's Wonderful Inventions," *MS,* May 10, 1914, Section 3, p. 4.
71. "Webb Pictures, Academy," *BA,* May 12, 1914, p. 10. Apparently the answer to the reviewer's question was "yes."
72. Q.E.D., "Movie Close-Ups," *ES,* October 8, 1928, p. 14.
73. A good account of Webb's career and talking pictures is given by Mark Miller, "Talking Pictures: A Baltimore Invention?" *Baltimore Magazine,* February 1982, p. 66–68, 108–109.
74. The only film named in the account in the London *Times* was *I Pagliacci,* suggesting that these may have been the 1913 films dusted off and shown again eight years later.
75. London *Times,* June 6, 1921, p. 8.
76. In 1906, a complete projecting outfit could have been purchased for as little as $68.50 at Sears. A year later, Wards was selling the same set, an Optigraph No. 4, for $75. Both companies published extensive catalogues of motion picture supplies.
77. The records of the Baltimore City circuit courts are filled with cases of early exhibition companies going into receivership because of lack of experience and poor management.
78. I am grateful to many people for their help in providing information on Pearce and Scheck. They include Wilbur Pearce, the Rev. E. Maurice Pearce, Mrs. Ruth Scheck, Mrs. Ruth Getchey, Mrs. Hilda Smith, Mrs. Gretchen L. Schlenger, Mrs. Louis Hesson, and Meyer Leventhal.
79. Daly was born in Virginia in 1859; he came to Baltimore around 1886 where he worked as a waiter and later a pork dealer. After his first business failed he went into the jewelry business and in 1909 loaned some money to the manager of the Lincoln Theater. Daly had to take over the theater to protect his loan.
80. *Baltimore Its History and Its People,* p. 855.

81. Wilbur Pearce, letter to the author, June 2, 1974.

82. One of the latest of these traveling shows was organized in 1919 by C. W. Simpson, who had managed the Latrobe and Huntington theaters. He took several reels and a projecting outfit and began showing movies at small towns in York County, Pennsylvania.

83. According to the Rev. E. Maurice Pearce, the motion picture equipment was carried in large, red, fiberboard trunks about the size of footlockers but deeper.

84. This is certainly possible. Ruth was taken to St. Mary's by his parents on June 13, 1902, and stayed there until he joined Jack Dunn's Baltimore Orioles in 1914.

85. J. M. Shellman, "Baltimore Has Long List of Motion Picture Pioneers," *MPW*, July 15, 1916, p. 384.

86. The unsuccessful vaudeville theater was called the Colonnade. The following year, Philadelphia-based Sigmund Lubin Enterprises leased the building and opened Lubin's Theater in it.

87. According to the *MS*, Real Estate Section, January 26, 1907, the rent was $3,250 a year.

88. This theater was called the Amusea in one early listing, but this was probably a mistake for Ideal — the other favorite name for a Pearce and Scheck theater — it cost an estimated $1,500.

89. Pearce and Scheck, Inc. was incorporated in June 1909.

90. Marion Pearce was president of the National Amusement Co. and the Victoria Co., while Philip Scheck was secretary of both companies.

91. The Lord Baltimore cost about $60,000; it could seat about 900.

92. The largest theater in the Baltimore metropolitan area outside downtown was the 1,600-seat Grand in Highlandtown, which was then in Baltimore County.

93. According to *Engineering News Record*, May 3, 1913, Michael McElfatrick had been engaged to prepare plans for the Hippodrome; however, Lamb was indicated as the architect by September 1913, and all of the plans were signed by Lamb.

94. Scheck later said that he and Pearce had discussed selling their exchange business and would have been satisfied with $15,000.

95. The motion picture industry consists of three different sectors: production, distribution and exhibition. The major interest here will be the exhibition, but an understanding of how the three sectors work may be useful. Simply stated, they may be equated to the manufacturer, wholesaler and retailer. The production sector makes the movies; the distribution sector delivers the movies to the exhibitors, and the exhibitors provide them to the public. A discussion of film production is beyond the scope of this book. The Washington *Herald*, in its Motion Picture News Column of August 17, 1913, described the film distribution system in Washington, but it could also have applied to Baltimore:

> At one time ... motion pictures were sold outright ... to exhibitors ... the cost of each film was about $100 ... the programs were limited to a few subjects of general interest. The next step was the establishing of "exchanges".... These exchanges assumed the purchase cost of films and undertook to rent them to the theaters. However, because each worked independently of the other without regard for price or schedule, conditions soon became chaotic. A theater manager would advertise a program he had arranged to get from one exchange, and wake up the morning before it was to be run to find that his competitor had secured the same pictures from another exchange a day ahead. One manager would run a certain number of films for 5 or 10 cents. His competitor would go him one better. Then the first would add one more ... and so on until they both found there was no money in the business.
>
> Another evil in those days was the frequent "repeating" of films. The supply was not as plentiful as now, and since there was no system of "booking," one never knew when he would pay admission to see films that he knew by heart. The public did not take kindly to the existing conditions, and exhibitors with large investments to protect them were heartily discouraged at the outlook for the future. It began to look as if the picture shows were merely a passing fancy.
>
> The first move toward rehabilitation was the formation of an organization known as the General Film Company (Inc.). In 1910 this company purchased a ... number of exchanges ... and established the first efficient system of "booking" films according to a definite schedule. This system, still in use in a modified form, undoubtedly did more than any other single thing to establish the permanency of the motion picture business. Briefly, the system operates like this: The manufacturers of films assign a release date to each picture the date upon which it may be rented by exchanges to the theaters. The film is handled thereafter according to its age, and automatically fits into what are known as "runs." When a theater advertises that it shows "first-run pictures," that means pictures that have not been run before. Every theater wants a well-balanced program, and most theater managers ... insist upon a program that has not been shown in the houses of any of their competitors.
>
> It is ... impossible to consider all theaters in a city ... as being in active competition with each other. Consequently, each city is divided by the exchanges into "situations." For example three theaters in the business section of a town within a radius of a few blocks are considered as conflicting, and the same is true of three houses in the residential section of a town within a radius of half a mile or so. But in "booking" films usually the two groups are treated as if they were in different cities.
>
> A theater manager goes to an exchange and explains that he wants a certain number of films per day of a certain age, and relies upon the booking system to divide his programs properly among comedies, dramas, etc. The "booker" opens an account with each theater and with every film released. By closely watching the route of each film and keeping in mind the theaters in the same situation, it is possible in most cases to arrange the programs of the different theaters so that they not only never run the same picture twice, but do not run a film after it has been run in a competing theater.
>
> In the larger cities automobiles collect the films from the theaters after 11 P.M., rush them to the various exchanges, where they are rewound, inspected, and redistributed into the boxes of the theaters to which they go on the following day....

The producing companies originally charged a flat rate for films, but they quickly saw that they could make more money by charging a percentage of the film's gross receipts. The Maryland exhibitors unsuccessfully fought this tooth and nail. At a meeting of the Exhibitors' League of Maryland in January 1920, Thomas Goldberg introduced a motion that would forbid members to book any picture on a percentage basis. Samuel Berman accurately predicted that, "It may come to the point where there will never be a flat rate again for booking pictures" ("Maryland Exhibitors Vote Against Percentage and Bond Themselves," MPW, February 7, 1920, p. 863).

Berman also believed that in a short time, percentage booking would not be a 50/50 proposition but would become 75/25 with 75 percent going to the producers. How right he was!

By the late 1930s, films were booked in groups of pictures or blocks; an exhibitor had to buy the entire block at the beginning of the season, usually in September. The individual pictures could be rented on different percentages. For example, out of 52 first-run features in one block, an exhibitor might get four pictures at 35 percent of gross receipts, six pictures at 30 percent of gross receipts, 12 pictures at 25 percent of gross receipts and the remaining 30 pictures at a flat rental. In Baltimore in 1939, after being shown at a first-run downtown theater, films were withdrawn from circulation for 21 days and then distributed to the neighborhood theaters. From the neighborhood theaters they went to third-run houses, which usually ran them as double features and charged less for tickets.

After World War II, things changed; block booking disappeared, and films were rented on an individual basis. The percentages of the gross receipts that went to the distributors gradually increased. When the original *Star Wars* opened at the Westview Cinemas in 1977, 84 cents of every dollar paid by customers went to the distributor. In 1981, a typical contract might have required an exhibitor to pay the distributor 90 percent during the opening week of a film after the theater's operating expenses had been deducted. In subsequent weeks the percentage might have gone down to 50 or 60 percent. It has now reached the point where exhibitors may receive only 10 percent of the gross receipts. The sale of food products has become crucial for exhibitors.

96. Letter, Hood and Schultz to Motion Picture Patents Co., July 23, 1910, Defendants' Exhibit No. 58, The United States Government v. The Motion Picture Patents Company. Equity No. 889. District Court. Eastern District of Pennsylvania, pp. 1366–1368 in six-volume transcript. There were three early movie theaters in the commercial area centering on the 1200 block of West Baltimore Street—the Carrollton, the Black Cat at 1200–1204, and Pearce and Scheck's YMCA at 1222–1230.

97. Letter, Charles W. Demme to Motion Picture Patents Company, August 3, 1910, ibid., p. 1414.

98. Letter, George C. Willis, Motion Picture Patents Company, March 28, 1911, ibid., p. 1415–1416.

99. Up until the mid-teens Baltimore had many film exchange branches, but by 1917 most of them had moved to Washington. Indeed, the only major exchange remaining in Baltimore in September 1917 was the Mutual Exchange on East Baltimore Street.

100. Interview, the Rev. E. Maurice Pearce, Fallston, Md., May 23, 1974.

101. The first meeting of the Board was held on June 10, 1910, in the Pearce and Scheck offices in the Victoria Theater Building.

102. Quoted in "Baltimore Exhibitors Have a Jollification," MPW, December 17, 1910, p. 1413.

103. According to Wilbur Pearce, the first car they bought together was a Stevens-Duryea around 1904.

Chapter 3

1. One of the first moves was in 1911 when the Baltimore branch of the General Film Company closed down. Film distribution was consolidated in the Washington branch. Most of the film exchanges felt that Washington was more centrally located than Baltimore to serve their territory, which included most of Maryland, Virginia, West Virginia, and Delaware. Stricter fire regulations in Washington nearly drove all the exchanges back to Baltimore in 1917, but that move was never implemented. For more on the local film distribution system, see Headley (1999).

2. William F. Braden, "Over 300,000 a Week in Theatres and 'Movie' Shows in Baltimore," MS, November 29, 1914, Section 3, p. 1. These figures do not quite agree with figures from 1913 claiming that between 75,000 and 100,000 people were attending moving-picture theaters in Baltimore every day. This would have meant that in one week the number of moviegoers in Baltimore was almost equal to the city's population. The 109 movie theaters in Baltimore took in about $30,000 a week.

3. The actual figures for investments in new buildings are: 1914—$13,572,283; 1915—$12,095,482; 1916—$11,096,998; 1917—$7,559,571; 1918—$6,464,225; 1919—$26,768,884; 1920—$23,030,380 (first six months). "1920 Building Program To Double That of 1919," MS, July 3, 1920, p. 13.

4. J. M. Shellman, "Regarding the Atmosphere," MS, December 7, 1919, Pt. 4, p. 11.

5. As I recall, the only movies that you would not ordinarily go in before they were over were Alfred Hitchcock movies because you wanted to get the full effect of the surprise ending, and you wanted to spot Hitchcock in his usual walk-on scene at the beginning of the film.

6. John A. Grant, "Let's Go to the Movies," *The Glades Star*, 6:5 (March 1987), p. 92.

7. "Sidelights on the Moving Pictures," BN, May 16, 1909, p. 6.

8. "Little Gunmen Are on Warpath Again," Baltimore Star, September 18, 1912, p. 14.

9. In the 1970s, managers were still citing problems with rowdy teenagers. Readers interested in movie horrors of this sort should see an article entitled "Mr. Coyle Pays a Visit to a Movie Theatre and Has a Hectic Experience," by Wilbur F. Coyle in the *Sun* of September 26, 1920. Problems of modern theater managers are nicely covered in Curtis Mees' "Motion Picture Theatre Management," *Motion Picture Herald* [hereafter MPH], March 7, 1953, pp. 12–15 and J. William Joynes' "Movie Managers Face Reel-Life Challenge," *News American* [hereafter NA], March 18, 1973, p. 1F.

10. "Movie Close-Ups," ES, August 26, 1927, p. 7. People have been complaining about sound that is too loud in the theaters for many years, but it doesn't seem to do any good. A contributor to Letters to the Editor in the *Sun* in November 1926 asked, "Why is it that theaters of Baltimore and other cities have such loud orchestra playing in time of acts?" We are still waiting for the answer.

11. "Ingenious Plan for Making Women Remove

Their Hats in the 'Movies,'" *ES*, December 31, 1915, p. 6. People were still complaining about "silly women who persist in gabbing at the cinema" and large hats that blotted out part of the screen in 1945.

12. Interview, Charles A. Lipsey, Baltimore County, Md., November 2, 1994. Marian McKew, the daughter of "Hon" Nickle, the owner of the Gayety, remembered that her father called the candy concession at the Gayety "the icing on the cake." A New York company paid Nickel several thousand dollars a year for that concession.

13. "New Deal at Morgan Bids for Cultural Film Bills," Baltimore *Afro-American* [hereafter *AA*], August 20, 1949, p. 22.

14. Andrew F. Smith, *Popped Culture. A Social History of Popcorn in America*, University of South Carolina Press, 1999, especially pp. 99–103.

15. This is curious since today the smell of popping popcorn is widely considered to be a pleasant appetizing aroma.

16. This circuit included the Carroll Theater in Westminster, Md. in which Robert Scheck and his wife had a controlling interest.

17. The author owes a particularly great debt to Mike Leventhal, the first person interviewed when research began on Baltimore movie theaters in the late 1960s. He was eager to help and shared his many memories of the early movie business generously.

18. "Meyer Leventhal, Theater Official, Dies," *MS*, August 21, 1981, p. C8.

19. William Pacy's three sons operated the Pacy theaters after their father's death. Charles William died in February 1950 and his brother Walter D. died that October. The third brother died in the early 1940s. Durkee was associated with the Pacy theaters for booking power only.

20. Baltimore City Incorporation Charters, SCL 64, p. 548.

21. *MPN*, October 31, 1914, pp. 20–21.

22. The Gertrude McCoy was named after a silent film actress who seemed to have been a favorite of the Lord Calvert Theatres Company executives or of Frederick Clement Weber, the company's president. The name of the theater was changed to Fulton in 1927. After it closed in 1952 it was remodeled into a food market and later into a church. It was still standing as of 2002 with much of the original facade still in place.

23. The issue of March 22 contained advertisements for the Blue Mouse, Majestic (South Broadway), Wizard, Lexington, Palace (Gay Street), Horn, Gem (East Baltimore Street), and Red Moon theaters.

24. Although the listing seemed to change from week to week, very few movie theaters east of Charles were included. On October 3, 1915, the list included: New, Wizard, Fremont, Edmondson, Pickwick, Bridge, Eureka, Schanze's, West End, and Aladdin.

25. "De Hoff of Baltimore Strong for Newspapers," *MPW*, June 15, 1918, p. 1551.

26. Three months earlier, the *News* had moved its stage and screen news from its Sunday edition to the Monday edition. There were ads for 38 theaters in the *News* at this time.

27. "Wants Moving Pictures on Sundays," *MS*, February 25, 1914, p. 6.

28. A letter to the editor of the *Evening Sun* complained about church halls showing movies "three nights a week, 52 weeks a year" without paying any taxes. "Moving Pictures in Church Halls," *ES*, October 20, 1915, p. 8.

29. "Maryland 'Get Together' Meeting," *MPW*, December 11, 1915, p. 1989.

30. "The Sunday Laws," *ES*, February 5, 1920, p. 18.

31. Donald Kirkley, in an April 17, 1930, article, pointed out that Sunday movies were regularly and legally shown at the Alcazar, the Maryland Yacht Club, the Y.M.C.A. and at several churches.

32. The Baltimore lineup for one baseball game played in Washington in June 1913 was Roy Collison—short stop, Sam Isaacson—second base, William George—first base, Howard Farcier—third base, William Reed—right field, Nelson Baldwin—center field, Edward Ryland—left field, Basil Morgan—catcher, Robert Hulse and George Ewell—pitchers and Harry Hess—substitute. B. A. Spellbring, president of the Washington projectionists and G. Kingston Howard, president of the Baltimore group, were the umpires.

33. One school was located in a "North Gay Street" theater, probably Harry Cluster's Crystal Theater. Cluster was also running a school for managers at the Exhibitors' League headquarters, 420 East Lexington Street, in 1921. An early reaction against this school occurred in 1923 when Basil Morgan, president of the projectionists' local preferred charges against the three members of the State Board of Motion Picture Operators. Morgan charged that the board was licensing inefficient operators and was working in sympathy with non-union movie houses in furnishing operators and in trying to undermine the union. The members of the board then were Harry Cluster, John H. C. Bedford and William H. Miller. Bedford was the representative of Local 181.

34. The film had been shown in Hagerstown and Cumberland prior to its coming to Baltimore. Ford's Theater was often used for road shows until as late as 1927.

35. "'Birth of a Nation' Here," *MS*, March 7, 1916, p 7.

36. It received 95 of a possible 205 votes; only *Citizen Kane* (1941), *Sunrise* (1927), *Greed* (1924), and *Intolerance* (1916) ranked higher. This film also ranked near the top of a list of "most important and misappreciated" American films through 1976. Richard Koszarski, *An Evening's Entertainment*, 1990, pp. 317, 319.

37. Garth Jowett, *Film. The Democratic Art*, 1976, p. 103.

38. "Notable Movie Seen at Ford's," *ES*, March 7, 1916, p. 3.

39. Editorial, "The Birth of a Nation." *AA*, March 4, 1916, p. [4] There had been an earlier protest in August 1915 when the NAACP asked the Police Board to ban any performance of the film in Baltimore.

40. Figures on the grosses are from the 1916–1917 Treasurer's Statements, Ford's Theater Collection at the Maryland Historical Society. The film's popularity is also attested to by the fact that the Ford's management was willing to break into a run of successful stage shows to play it in February 1917.

41. None of the classic films that played the Cameo seemed to generate any interest and the theater closed for good within a year.

42. Chapter 209, *Laws of Maryland, 1916*, pp. 411–416; Article 66A Moving Pictures, Annotated Code of Maryland 1924, pp. 2211–2216.

43. Some places in Maryland had censorship prior to 1916. In Frederick, Maryland, there was a moving picture committee. In 1910 the committee requested that managers of local movie theaters furnish it with a résumé of their films before exhibiting them so that "objectionable ones" could be censored.

44. Quoted in "Police Censor Had His Thumbs Down," Baltimore *Star*, February 23, 1909, p. 12. The anonymous writer did little to hide his or her skepticism for the qualifications of the average policeman to act as a censor.

45. "Police to Act as Theatrical Censors," Baltimore *Star*, September 1, 1909, p. 9.

46. "For Proper Picture Shows," *MS*, June 8, 1911, p. 6.

47. "Baltimore Censorship Flurry," *MPW*, July 22, 1911, p. 102.

48. "Women Cops Become Rattled," *MS*, January 29, 1913, p. 12. The police censors had been busy in January 1913. On the 27th three policewomen and two male officers had testified to help convict the manager of the Comedy Theater of showing the film *The Girl from Maxim's*. They said it "depicted a cafe scene with men and women drinking and numerous other objectionable features" and, in one scene, showed "women sitting on the knees of their men escorts and acting in an affectionate manner." The manager said it was a comedy, but the judge decided it violated the Baltimore City Code against indecent exhibitions on stage.

49. For the complete ordinance, see, "Clarke Defends Censor Ordinance," Baltimore *Star*, April 2, 1910, p. 14.

50. "Censorship of Moving Pictures," *MS*, August 4, 1910, p. 6.

51. Representatives of the Moral Education Board, Social Settlement School Board, Mothers' Club of Baltimore, Women's Christian Temperance Union, Sons of the American Revolution, Society of Social Hygiene, Oratorio Society, and the Young People's Association attended the meeting. "To War on 'Loose' Films," *MS*, November 10, 1910, p. 8.

52. "Object to Censor of Moving Pictures," *BN*,, April 15, 1911, p. 9.

53. "Censorship of the Picture Shows," *MS*, June 3, 1911, p. 6.

54. "Improper Motion Pictures Recently Exhibited In Baltimore—Where Are the Censors?" *MS*, June 6, 1911, p. 6.

55. "Value of Moving Pictures," *MS*, June 13, 1911, p. 6. The portrayal and exaltation of lawlessness and vice were common criticisms of the movies. A letter to the *Sun* on June 14, 1911, claimed that movies taught about extra-marital affairs and such things as "the exact spot in a man's back where a dagger may be used for greatest effect," and "that a woman is easily overcome by brute force."

56. "A Defense of Moving Pictures," *MS*, June 28, 1911, p. 6.

57. "Picture Managers Indorse Censorship," *BN*, May 5, 1912. Much of the increased interest in film censorship at this time was apparently caused by a robbery and murder committed by a South Baltimore boy who said that he got the idea from moving pictures. See also, "Urges Censorship," *ibid*.

58. "The Moving-Picture Show," *MS*, February 25, 1915, p. 6.

59. In the case of the Mutual Film Company against the states of Ohio and Kansas, the February 23, 1915, decision upheld the constitutionality of state censorship.

60. Fulton Brylawski was associated with his father Aaron, and his brother Julian, in the Washington exhibition business. He had spoken against a Federal censorship bill in 1914.

61. One of the bill's strongest opponents was Delegate Lloyd Wilkinson of Baltimore City. Wilkinson sponsored an unsuccessful last-ditch attempt to keep Governor Harrington from signing the bill. The vote was 52 to 41 against Wilkinson's bill. For additional information on this attempt, see: "Censorship Bill Wins in House," *BA*, March 14, 1916, p. 4.

62. One censorship bill offered by Georgia Representative Hughes, chairman of the House Committee on Education, received wide support, including support from the Maryland Congress of Mothers and the Society of Friends of Baltimore. The Hughes' Bill was not passed even though it was re-introduced in 1919. The Upshaw Movie Censorship bill was introduced in 1926, but it did not have enough support and again Federal censorship of films was defeated. In 1922, Congressman Appleby of New York introduced a bill (H. R. 10577) to establish a Federal Motion Picture Commission which would approve a film unless it was "obscene, indecent, immoral, inhuman, depicted a prize fight, or was of such a character that its exhibition would tend to impair the health, debase or corrupt the morals of children or adults or incite to crime, or produce depraved moral ideas or debase moral standards or cause moral laxity in adults or minors. For more on this bill, see "Bill for Federal Motion Picture Commission Before Congress," *MPW*, March 18, 1922, p. 1597 et seq.

63. "Moving Picture Censorship," *MS*, April 10, 1916, p. 6. The membership of the board has always been a serious problem. It seems clear, over the years, that many of the members were appointed to the board as pay-offs for party loyalty. Exhibitors were angered in 1917 when the trade magazine *Moving Picture World* reported that the stenographer working for the censor board had been doing a good deal of the censoring.

64. "A Censorship Bill That Should Be Killed," *BN*, March 25, 1916, p. 6.

65. In 1920, the board moved to 211 N. Calvert Street. These quarters proved adequate until 1929 when a plague of fleas invaded the censor board's offices and forced the board into a temporary retreat. Fleas continued to pester the censors as late as 1945.

66. The Vitaphone Company filed suit and lost in a lower court, but the Appellate Court reversed the lower court's decision declaring that the Pennsylvania Board of Censors had no jurisdiction over the talking movies.

67. "Maryland Censors Feel Oats," *MPW*, February 10, 1917, p. 883. The Levines were convicted on a technicality. The Censor Board contended that even though the film carried the state seal, the exhibitors should have obtained a list of the eliminations and seen that they were properly made before exhibiting the film. The same film had been shown in more than 20 other theaters in the city.

68. The author determined this by the rather unscientific method of measuring the height of clippings in his folder on censorship; it was more than 5 inches. The next thickest folder concerned Sunday movies, a mere ¾ inch.

69. "Women Attack Movies," *MS*, December 16, 1916, p. 14. Apparently one of the films was *War's Women*.

70. "Condemns Movie Standards," *MS*, November 27, 1917, p. 14.

71. "Moral and Proper," *ES*, January 27, 1922, p. 17.

72. "A Sad, Sad Story," *ES*, June 25, 1929, p. 19.

73. "Ban on Bare Legs Brings Sniffs from Chorus Girls," *ES*, January 4, 1922, p. 5.

74. Those arrested included the manager, the dancers, the barker, the piano player, the lecturer on crime and its consequences, the ticket chopper, and the audience.

75. At first the fuelless day was Monday, but that was soon changed to Tuesday. The formal notice said, "No fuel shall be burned (except to such extent as is essential to prevent injury to property from freezing) for the purpose of supplying heat for: ...(C) Theaters, moving picture houses, bowling alleys, billiard rooms, private or public dance halls, or any other place of public amusement."

76. For further information on the pandemic, see Richard Collier, *The Plague of the Spanish Lady*, New York: Atheneum, 1974.

77. "Keeping Out 'Flu,'" *ES*, September 13, 1918, p. 28.

78. *Ibid*. Of course, the key phrase here was "who recover."

79. "Hundred Soldiers Have the Influenza," *ES*, September 23, 1918, p. 16.

80. *Ibid*.

81. "'Flu' Nothing but Old-Fashioned Grip," *ES*, September 24, 1918, p. 20.

82. "Capital City Theatres Are Closed," *MPW*, October 19, 1918, p. 353.

83. J. M. Shellman, "Pleasant All the Time," *MS*, June 15, 1919, part 4, p. 4.

84. Norman Clark, "Nothing in Particular," *BN*, August 7, 1921, p. 17.

85. "Ventilation of Moving Picture Theaters," *The Nickelodeon*, May 1909, p. 143.

86. This practice was common during the nickelodeon era and lasted well into the 1920s. An usher or other employee would walk up and down the aisles with a large atomizer bottle spraying perfume throughout the theater. Patrons sometimes complained that they smelled "like they had been in a whorehouse" instead of a movie theater. A device that attached to a fan and perfumed the air as the fan was in operation was also available.

87. J. M. Shellman, "The First-Run Situation," *MS*, October 3, 1920, part 6, p. 9.

88. By the 1940s, films became available to second-run theaters 21 days after playing at a first-run theater, and third-run theaters could get films 28 days after playing at a first-run theater.

Chapter 4

1. "138 Baltimore Picture Houses Collect $2,196,071 in Year; Have 83,121 Seats," *MPW*, August 13, 1921, p. 694. The $2,196,071 was collected in war taxes from 138 movie theaters. According to this article the average yearly income of a Baltimore movie theater was $159,135. This was despite numerous complaints that Baltimore was not getting new films as quickly as some other cities.

2. L. C. Moen, "Statistics of the Motion Picture Industry," *MPN*, November 18, 1922, p. 2527, 2531; November 25, 1922, p. 2644–2645; December 2, 1922, p. 2772; December 16, 1922, p. 3024, and December 23, 1922, p. 3178.

3. "Cheap Movies or None for Him," *ES*, November 28, 1921, p. 12.

4. "What Ails the Movies?" *ES*, June 15, 1922, p. 23.

5. T. M. C. was the byline of *Sun* critic T. M. Cushing.

6. The previous prices that went into effect when the remodeled New Garden opened in December 1927 were: matinees—orchestra 50 cents, balcony 35 cents; evenings—orchestra 75 cents, balcony 50 cents; on Saturdays and holidays the evening prices were orchestra $1.00 and balcony 50 cents.

7. "Day by Day," *Baltimore Daily Post*, January 14, 1927, p. 3.

8. "For Orchestras and Stage Shows," *ES*, November 18, 1930, p. 25.

9. "Movie Music Is Improving Steadily," *MS*, August 10, 1924, p. 3.

10. He was presented with a silver loving cup and a diamond watch for winning this contest. Each band member received a gold medal. George Wild at the Century came in third and Fred Robbins at the Garden Roof came in sixth. Iula received 39,760 votes; Elmer Grosso, of the Greenwich Village Inn who came in second, received 38,281. Other major bandleaders who received votes were: Vincent Lopez—1,342, Paul Whiteman—354, Fred Waring—147, Paul Ash—33, Meyer Davis—16. "Felice S. Iula, Baltimore, First in Leaders' Contest," New York *Morning Telegraph*, March 4, 1926, p. 1. Felice and Robert Paul were sons of Frank and Teresa Iula, who had come to America from Italy as newly-weds. Robert Iula, known as "Bob," had been a charter member of the Baltimore Symphony since it was formed in 1916. He had his own band and played for most of the society parties in Baltimore. A third son, Ruffino, also became an orchestra leader. Ruffino led the orchestra at Ford's for many years. The Iula brothers' father, Frank, had been a harpist who organized his own orchestra in Baltimore. He sent his sons to study at the Peabody Institute and lived to see all three leading their own orchestras. Felice Iula later became the musical director of WBAL. He died in 1966 at age 74. His brother Robert died in 1952.

11. Musician Holly Mullinix described the typical day of a pit musician at the Hippodrome. He wrote that there were four stage shows a day with four or five acts apiece. Between the stage shows, there would be several hours of movies so the members of the orchestra could take long breaks. During the breaks the musicians would play pinochle, take naps, watch the movie—usually only once—read, or walk around downtown. Holly Mullinix, "I Remember ... Vaudeville's Golden Years," *MS*, September 29, 1974, The Sun Magazine, p. 52.

12. The scores were simplified so that any musician could play them. They were scored for twelve-piece orchestras—piano, organ, and ten other instruments—by Carl Edouarde, director of music at the Strand Theater in New York, composer James C. Bradford, and C. J. Breil who wrote the musical score for "The Birth of a Nation." "Synchronized Music Service To Be Available by April 1," *Exhibitors Herald*, February 26, 1921, p. 41.

13. "A Criticism of Movie Music and Other Things," *ES*, September 24, 1926, p. 29.

14. "Music at Movie Theaters Is Improving, says T.M.C.," *MS*, April 19, 1925, p. 3.

15. Interview, Mrs. John Seamon, Dundalk, Md., May 19, 1993.

16. J. M. Shellman, "Music for the Pictures," *MS*, June 1, 1919, part 4, p. 7. Within a short time this piano player's salary had risen from $20 a week to $150.

17. "Rivoli's New Organ," *BN*, July 23, 1922, p. 19.

18. Exhibitors' News and Views: Baltimore, *MPW*, November 10, 1923, p. 223.

19. "Sunday Movies from the Viewpoint of a Musician's Wife," *ES*, February 14, 1927, p. 17.

20. "Sunday Movies as a Crime Preventive," *ES*, January 2, 1928, p. 26.

21. Callan, a Democrat, represented Baltimore's Second District.

22. "$5,000 Slush Fund Charge Made in Theatre Scandal," *MS*, December 3, 1921, p. 1.

23. According to a letter to the editor of the Baltimore *Sun*, Carroll ignored the wishes of his constituents who did not want any theater built. "The Boulevard Theatre Affair," *MS*, November 27, 1921, p. 17.

24. Buck had been in the movie business since around 1906, when he worked for Thomas Edison as representative to the Keith vaudeville organization and as manager of 25 road companies in the U.S. He had been operating a film exchange in Baltimore since 1918. In 1921 he was also president of the Circle Theatre Corporation, which was planning a large theater on Park Circle and managing director of the Washington Theater Company which was planning a theater on Pennsylvania Avenue.

25. In less than a year, Palmore and Homand, Inc. went into receivership.

26. There were many pathetic stories about people who had invested their life's savings in the theater, seduced by promises that the preferred stock would pay 8 percent. A crippled boy invested $40 he had saved by selling newspapers. A woman invested $1,650 to provide for her son who was blinded in the war.

27. In testimony on December 12, E. D. Schwaber, who, with Buck and architect Ewald Blanke, was planning the Washington Theater on Pennsylvania Avenue, stated that Wiley told him to pay $500 to Dickerson & Nice to have the company incorporated. When he complained that $500 was too much, Wiley allegedly said that Dickerson & Nice could influence both the Republicans and Democrats in the Council.

28. "Money Alleged to Have Been Used to Obtain Final Passage of Ordinance by City Council," *MS*, December 3, 1921, p. 1.

29. "Dundon Says Lawyers Got Extra $1,000 as Fee; Nice Firm Issues Denial," *MS*, December 6, 1921, p. 22.

30. "A Grave Public Scandal," *BA*, July 15, 1922, p. 6.

31. "Baltimore Conditions Show Improvement; Too Many Theatres for the Population," *MPW*, January 7, 1922, pp. 35–36.

32. "Big Theaters Crowd Others Off the Map," *MS*, June 24, 1923, p. Section 3, Part 2, p. 3.

33. "Small Movie Houses on Road to Extinction, Exhibitors Say," *MS*, June 18, 1923, p. 5.

34. "But This Nuisance Tax Was Not Removed on the Prices Mentioned," *ES*, June 22, 1922, p. 21.

35. T. M. Cushing, "New Movie Season Here Opens Gayly," *MS*, October 24, 1926, section 3, p. 7.

36. Two of the brothers, Milton and J. Herbert became doctors. A sister, Camelia, became a well-known artist.

37. The show, which included the Petticoat Minstrels, played at the Garden during the week of August 12, 1918. The reviews were fair. The *Baltimore News* called it "mighty good," but the *Sun* merely noted the names of the acts.

38. "C. E. Whitehurst, Theater Owner, Dies at His Home," *ES*, January 30, 1924, p. 30.

39. Dr. Whitehurst had been an associate and confidential adviser to his brother for many years and had managed the first Whitehurst theater, the Red Moon.

40. Miss Ulrich was born in Philadelphia on July 1, 1900. She studied language and dance at the Merciacordia Academy in Marion, Pennsylvania, before moving to New York where she pursued a career as a dancer and met Charles Whitehurst.

41. The litigation connected to the Whitehurst case actually dragged on until 1931, when a suit by Claire Ulrich's mother against the Whitehurst brothers was dismissed.

42. "Hint of Bribery in Whitehurst Case Is Noted," *MS*, December 11, 1926, p. 22.

43. Ulrich said that she had met Whitehurst first in New York at a rehearsal hall and then later in Baltimore where she was to appear in a revue. In Baltimore, she had a disagreement over the costume she was to wear in the revue, claiming that it was indecent. Whitehurst interceded and ordered six yards of red satin to be worn as a skirt under the black lace costume. Just before she left Baltimore, Ulrich said that one of Whitehurst's nephews invited her and other girls in the company to attend a party at Milton Whitehurst's farm on Back River. She saw Charles Whitehurst often during the next five or six months. He proposed to her in the lobby of the Martha Washington Hotel in New York where she was living. The day before Whitehurst died, Miss Ulrich testified that she had received a message saying that he was very ill. She took a midnight train to Baltimore where she registered at the Hotel Rennert and tried to telephone Whitehurst. His brother, Herbert, told her that Whitehurst was getting on nicely but could have no visitors. She continued telephoning and finally went to his home where she was refused entrance. Three days later she learned that Charles Whitehurst had died. The most detailed accounts of Ulrich's testimony are found in newspaper articles of April 5, 17, and 19, 1928.

44. Newspaper versions of the letter differ in certain details including punctuation, the phrase "when it comes to certain performances," and the name in the last paragraph. One source has it Ditman while another has Ditmar.

45. "Expert Asserts 'Wifey' Forgery in Ulrich Case," *ES*, April 19, 1928, p. 46.

46. "Pact Bride Is Called Foolish," *BN*, April 24, 1928, p. 1.

47. "Call Forgery at 'Bride' Trial," *BN*, April 19, 1928, p. 1.

48. "Claire Ulrich Whitehurst, Helped Found Music Club," *Miami Herald*, August 11, 1994, p. 4B.

49. Of the four theaters, the Garden was said to be the best moneymaker. "Whitehurst Theater Sale Is Expected," *ES*, October 6, 1925, p. 44.

50. "Theater Negotiations Resumed in New York," *ES*, October 15, 1925, p. 49.

51. The numbers had changed only slightly by mid–2003. At that time national circuits controlled 54% of the 24 local theaters and 80% of the 199 local screens.

52. Quoted in "Dr. Kelly Attacks 'Movies' as Cause of Spread of Vice," *BN*, October 3, 1920, p. 30. Kelly was the president of the Howard Kelly Hospital on Eutaw Place.

53. "Says Movies Drive City Boys to Crime," *MS*, March 4, 1923, p. 17. The judge cited a case where three young boys caused a train wreck on the Pennsylvania Railroad in imitation of a wreck they had earlier seen in a movie.

54. A more complete list may be found in the *1924 Film Daily Yearbook*, p. 273, and in subsequent volumes of the yearbook.

55. The three-foot kiss was the invention of Canadian censor Samuel Clarke. He also did not approve of men kissing women on the beach. The head of the Chicago Law and Order League was opposed to all kissing. He recalled at least two deaths due to kissing on the mouth.

56. "The Kiss," *ES*, June 24, 1926, p. 25.

57. "Maryland Movie Fans Not Deprived of Kissing Scenes," *ES*, September 27, 1929, p. 52. In a 1925 interview, Marie Presstman, a member of the censor board, said that the board usually let the first 10 feet of a kiss go, but that many kissing scenes had to have 20 or 30 feet of film cut. "Says Man Is 'Maid' in New Movie Films," *MS*, May 5, 1925, p. 30.

58. The State Senate, much to the delight of Mrs. Rufus M. Gibbs and the Citizens' League of Maryland for Better Motion Pictures, refused to confirm Heller's reappointment in 1933. Apparently both the Senate and the League thought that under Heller's leadership the board was allowing too many "degrading, indecent or salacious" movies to be exhibited in Maryland. Gough, who was not a frequent moviegoer, was seen as a force for stricter censorship.

59. "Stricter Movie Censorship Seen," *MS*, May 3, 1933, p. 20.

60. "She Deplores Movie with Shortened Kiss," *ES*, March 11, 1921, p. 15.

61. John O'Ren, "Down the Spillway," *MS*, June 7, 1933, p. 10.

62. "Movie Labor Fight Looming, Union Head Says," *MS*, August 4, 1927, p. 24.

63. According to Maurice Rushworth, the first school was held in the New Theater after the regular projectionists had left for the night. Rushworth, who was the chief operator there, noticed that some of the switches in the booth were not as he had left them. After he complained to the management, the school moved to another theater.

64. "Colored Operators in New Theatres," *AA*, September 5, 1925, p. 4.

65. "Owners Defy Theatre Union," *BN*, August 31, 1927, p. 1.

66. The theaters that signed with the new union included all the Durkee theaters, the Rome theaters, the Gaertner theaters, the Garman-Beck theaters, and a number of independents such as the Hampden, Ideal, Irvington, Belmar, Eagle, Flag, Harford, Walbrook, and Morrell.

67. According to one projectionist, Durkee said that he would never hire a projectionist from 181 as long as there was a breath in his body. In May 1928 someone threw gas bombs into Durkee's home. During that month, several gas bombs, which released a sickening stench, were also thrown into the home of L. Wesley Cooper and into the Belnord Theater. During one of the strikes, Charles Nolte armed himself with eggs and threw them from the window in the Linwood Theater's projection booth at picketing projectionists on the street below.

68. A temporary injunction was granted in September 1927 with a final injunction in October 1930. For more details on this case, see: Independent Motion Picture Operators and Managers Union of Baltimore City, Incorporated v. Moving Picture Operators Protective Union No. 181 et al., Baltimore City Circuit Court No. 1, Equity Papers, September 5, 1927, Maryland State Archives, Series T53, Box 3685.

69. In February 1928, a union newspaper printed a list of "Fair Motion Picture Houses," those that had projectionists who belonged to Local 181. Thirty-three of Baltimore's approximately 85 movie houses were on that list. Ironically, the Cluster Theater operated by Ben Cluster was listed as one of the fair theaters. *The Baltimore Federationist*, February 10, 1928, p. 3.

70. Cluster said that the charges against him had resulted from a misunderstanding and he wanted to put the matter behind him. Cluster was apparently exhausted by the struggle to form the independent union and suffered a severe nervous and physical breakdown in November.

71. Many projectionists had run-ins with Cluster and objected to what they saw as favoritism and arbitrary actions on his part, such as moving them from theater to theater for no apparent reason.

72. Another source gave the name of the organization as the Colored Operators' Association of Maryland. The first president was John T. Pitts; Charles Robinson was the secretary; William Causby, the vice-president; and George Douglass, treasurer. By 1924, the organization was called The Colored Operators' Protective Association. Their union hall was at Mosher Street and Pennsylvania Avenue. Other early members of the union were Chester Seward, James Mahoney, George Vodery, Joshua Holly, Moxley Willis, Thomas Pitts, Edward Jackson, George Woodlen, Nelson Miller, and Page Herrman.

73. The conditions were: (1) they must not attend union meetings unless invited, (2) they must not participate in the proceedings of meetings, (3) they were not to take positions in any white theater, (4) they were not to accept a position in any theater before first notifying union officials, and (5) they were not to instruct any more African-American projectionists. "Movie Men Form Union," *AA*, August 12, 1921, p. 5.

74. Charles Vodery was a man of many talents. He was a projectionist at the Dunbar. An article in the *Afro-American* of March 21, 1925, claimed he was the "second man to pass the examination for moving picture operators," but the records of the Motion Picture Machine Operators Board of Examiners show that he was not. He got his license in September 1913; George Douglass, Thomas Pitts, Clarence Lee and Leonard Outen all got their licenses in 1910. Vodery was also a pianist, violinist and radio builder.

75. The equipment included two generators, three projectors, two effect and stereopticon projectors, two spotlights, one high intensity spot lamp, three speed indicators, three lenses, 500 sets high intensity carbons, one 15-reel 2000-foot film cabinet, six rheostats, plus other miscellaneous supplies and equipment. Lester B. Isaac, "Then and Now," *Motion Picture Projectionist*, October 1927, p. 26.

76. The changeover worked this way. There were two projectors in each booth. While one was showing one reel, the other was loaded with the next reel. As soon as the dot flashed on the screen, the projectionist knew that 10 feet of film remained on the first reel. One projectionist manned each projector. They each had a foot on the pedal that turned the projector on and off and a hand on the fader control, which adjusted the sound volume. When a second dot appeared on the screen, the operators began a sequence that went something like this. They counted aloud in unison, "one ... two...." On the count of "one" the operator at the projector with the new reel started his machine. On the count of "two" the other operator cut his machine off, and they switched the fader's dial to a new circuit. Usually this went so smoothly that few in the audience noticed anything.

77. IATSE & MPMO feared that these larger reels would "cut in half the work required with a subsequent corresponding decrease in man-power." While it would make the individual projectionist's life a lot easier, it might seem that they were doing less work.

78. The "platter" systems use large flat platters stacked three or four on a holder; the film is prepared on one platter and threaded through the projector; a second platter serves as the take-up reel. An entire show can be contained on a single platter.

79. Douglas Gomery, *Shared Pleasures*, 1992, p. 53.

80. "Ice Plants Boost Summer Attendance," *MPN*, July 11, 1925, p. 180.

Chapter 5

1. "Baltimore's 21,330 Seats Belie Depression Talk," *MPN*, October 25, 1930, p. 54. According to this article, "The automobile is playing a good part in the film business for people watch the advertisements in newspapers and if they see a picture advertised at a neighborhood house they want to see they all pile into the machine and go over to that house to see it."

2. Seven theaters were built outside the city, in Catonsville, Towson, Reisterstown, Essex, Arbutus and Pikesville, while 14 were built outside downtown but still in the city. The latter included the Vilma, Arcade, Northway, Earle and Avon in the northeast, the Senator and Rex in the north, the Gwynn and Ambassador in the northwest, the Westway, Edgewood, and Bridge in the west, the Lord Calvert in the southwest and the Brooklyn in the south.

3. The protest was apparently prompted by fears that promoters had been obtaining permits for theaters on strategic sites throughout the city. The Association failed to send any representatives to the public hearing on the matter and it does not seem to have come up again.

4. "Burlesque's Swan Song Sung, Veteran Show Man Laments," *MS*, January 4, 1928, p. 26.

5. The national average was 12.2 persons per theater seat, so Maryland was not very underseated. Mississippi had 27 persons per seat while Wisconsin had only 1.2 persons per seat. "12 Persons for Each Film Theatre Seat; 15 States Are Underseated," *MPH*, June, 4, 1938, p. 19.

6. D[onald] K[irkley], "Screen. Changes In Operating Policies This Year Among Exhibitors More Marked Than Formerly," *MS*, September 23, 1931, p. 8.

7. "Premiere of Vitaphone," *MS*, January 31, 1927, p. 4.

8. "Vitaphone and 'Don Juan' Are Now at Metropolitan," *Baltimore Daily Post*, January 31, 1927, p. 14.

9. "At the Movies This Week," *MS*, January 10, 1928, p. 9.

10. The previous record holder was the first Vitaphone picture, *Don Juan*. "'The Jazz Singer' Remains at Met for Second Week," *The Jewish Times*, January 13, 1928, p. 36. According to *Motion Picture News* (March 3, 1928, p. 748), the only film run in Baltimore longer than eight weeks was that of *Way Down East* which played at the Lyceum Theater on Charles Street.

11. Quoted in T. M. C. "New Device Is Developed for Talking Movies," *MS*, October 22, 1922, p. Part 6, p. 5.

12. "A Discouraging Prospect," *MS*, December 30, 1928, p. 8.

13. "Doesn't Like Talkies," *MS*, November 4, 1929, p. 8.

14. "Movie Close-Ups," *ES*, February 27, 1929, p. 11.

15. "Dr. Young Is Enthusiastic Over the Baltimore Theater Guild," *ES*, March 25, 1929, p. 19.

16. William N. Jones, "From the Front Row," *AA*, July 27, 1929, p. 9.

17. "Disillusion," *ES*, November 25, 1929, p. 21.

18. "Talking Pictures," *MS*, January 3, 1929, p. 10.

19. "Music at the Movies," *MS*, April 7, 1929, p. 8.

20. Movietone differed from Vitaphone in that the sound track was located on the film rather than on a record.

21. The midnight opening was held in order to circumvent the blue laws prohibiting Sunday movies, which were still in effect.

22. Until there were enough full-length Vitaphone features, the sound films were limited to short vaudeville-type subjects. For example, during the week of May 21, the Vitaphone features at the Regent were (1) Sissle and Blake—Songs of Big Hits, (2) Realization—A Comedy-Drama Sketch, and (3) Roger Wolfe Kahn and His Orchestra. The following week the subjects were (1) Aunt Jemima—The Original Fun Flour Maker, (2) The Lash—One of the Greatest Prison Dramatic Acts, and (3) Waring's Pennsylvanians.

23. Benjamin Cluster v. Moving Picture Operators' Protective Union No. 181, Baltimore City Circuit Court No. 1, October 19, 1923.

24. German-language films were also shown in the Rheinland Hall at the Deutsches Haus.

25. "Building the Sound Theatre," *Exhibitors Herald and Moving Picture World*, Better Theatres Section, September 1, 1928, p. 10.

26. William A. Johnson, "The Theatre Upheaval," *MPN*, July 6, 1929, p. 61.

27. F. W. Strehlau, "Music," *ES*, August 18, 1928, p. 7.

28. See, among many others, "He Insists on Orchestra and Acts," *ES*, October 2, 1928, p. 21, "Supplanting 'Cultured Musicians,'" *ibid.* October 5, 1928, p. 31, and "She Doesn't Like 'Canned Music,'" *ibid.* October 8, 1928, p. 21.

29. "She Might Wear Her Fur Coat and Allow Others to Enjoy the Coolness," *ES*, June 28, 1929, p. 29.

30. *MS*, July 16, 1928, p. 6.

31. "Writer Complains About 'Hot Box' Theaters," *AA*, June 17, 1939, p. [m].

32. Donald Kirkley, "Theaters Vs. Heat," *MS*, September 11, 1941, p. 8.

33. Norman Clark, "3 Theaters Have Their Lights Turned On," *BNP*, August 31, 1949, p. 27.

34. "Says Durkee House Has Choice of Films," *ES*, December 11, 1939, p. 18.

35. This source, a former projectionist who wished to remain anonymous, said that Durkee packed the Motion Picture Theater Owners of Maryland with his own people so that they would vote the way he wanted. This source was a member of Local 181 and did not hide his dislike of the Durkee organization.

36. In Washington the same kind of show was five cents cheaper.

37. "Nickel Candy Sales Do $10,000,000 Business," *MPH*, July 24, 1937, p. 12.

38. Helen Kent, "Extra Profit Potentials and a Service to Theatre Patrons, *Boxoffice*, June 22, 1940, Modern Theatre Section, pp. 48–50. The number of theaters in each city was calculated from lists in the *1940 Film Daily Year Book*.

39. It is not clear how 39 theaters could make use of 800 popcorn machines. Perhaps the number of machines given was for a larger geographic area than the city or perhaps there were multiple machines in some theaters.

40. Both articles were cited in a 1932 pamphlet circulated by the League in 1932.

41. "Unanimous," *ES*, February 24, 1933, p. 21.

42. "Judge Reverses Board's Action on Movie Here," *ES*, January 20, 1931, p. 36.

43. "Judge, As Movie Censor, Overrules State's Board," *ES*, August 28, 1933, p. 26. This was one of the numerous problems for the censor board during the chairmanship of Bernard B. Gough. Among the scenes the board wanted deleted was a scene where a bridegroom was sprucing himself up and another was a baron giving money to the aunt of a young woman in whom he was interested. Gough admitted when he became the chairman that he did not see many movies and that he was "rather narrow."

44. "'Ecstasy' Minus Eighteen Scenes," *MS*, May 26, 1936, p. 10.

45. The ads for the showing at the Europa said, "Suppressed Until Now!! U.S. Customs Has Finally Released Most Amazing Motion Picture Ever Produced. The Film the World Is Talking About."

46. For more on the history of the film *Ecstasy* see: "Now Comes Once Barred 'Ecstasy,' Into Courts to Fight for Title," *MPH*, March 7, 1936, p. 18 and "New Fight Over 'Moral' Aspects of "Ecstasy," *ibid.*, May 16, 1936, p. 40.

47. "Movie Theaters Hit by Daylight Saving," *ES*, June 2, 1922, p. 7.

48. "Movie Attendance Jumps As Daylight Saving Goes," *ES*, August 30, 1922, p. 12.

49. "He Was Converted to Opposition to Daylight Saving," *ES*, May 11, 1926, p. 23. Dr. Judd apparently did not favor daylight saving time.

50. Among those businesses were the Consolidated Gas Electric Light and Power Company, United Railways, numerous banks, and the B & O Railroad.

51. "Daylight Saving and Movies," *ES*, May 15, 1931, p. 33.

52. At first, daylight saving time lasted until the last Sunday in September, but it was extended to the last Sunday in October in 1957. Congress passed the Uniform Time Act in 1966. That law stipulated that a state had to go on daylight saving time unless specifically exempted by the state legislature.

53. Thomas Goldberg, who operated the Harford Theater, said that his valid licenses to operate the theater went along with the building when he leased it to Callan.

54. "Four-Day Town," *ES*, January 23, 1929, p. 21.

55. Second District Councilman, James B. Blake, who was apparently worried about a possible challenge to his seat by John Callan, had introduced the Sunday movie measure in the Council.

56. That spurious argument had been brought up several years earlier and was the subject of a letter to the editor of the *Sun* ("Jews and Sunday Movies," April 7, 1929, p. 8). Major supporters of blue law reform were again characterized as Jews in the savage protest of the so-called "interdenominational ministerial group" which was presented to Mayor Jackson in the spring of 1931. After giving several reasons why the Alliance was opposed to the ordinance, it provided this one. "We are opposed to the ordinance because the majority of those who are active in its interest are citizens who uncompromisingly insist upon the observance of their own Holy Days, no matter how great the sacrifice involved."

57. *Laws of Maryland*, Chapter 287, 1931.

58. Ordinance No. 130 was printed in full in *The Daily Record*, February 27, 1932.

59. Gibbs had also opposed Women's Suffrage in 1920 and was one of the most outspoken critics of the State Censor Board.

60. "Afro Straw Vote This Week," *AA*, April 30, 1932, p. 18.

61. Managers of the Hippodrome, Keith's, Avenue, Valencia, Century, Stanley, Metropolitan, Parkway, Apollo, Rialto, Broadway, Capital, Brodie, Imperial, Royal, Idle Hour, Walbrook, New and Dunbar offered their theaters for the free shows. It is interesting that there was not a single Durkee or Gaertner theater on the list.

62. The liberal Sunday ordinance won in every ward in the city; the foes of the ordinance won in only seven polling places of the 672 in the city.

63. Reprinted in the *ES*, May 5, 1932, p. 25.

64. "Theatres Will Open Doors Here Sunday," *AA*, May 7, 1932, p. 20.

65. Harry Gaertner and his brother Louis operated Ritz Enterprises, which owned the Palace (at Gay and Wolfe streets), Ritz and Vilma in the city and the Strand in Dundalk.

66. St. Mary's County had allowed Sunday movies since around 1908 in apparent violation of state laws.

67. "Second Sight," *ES*, April 13, 1933, p. 23.

68. The Baltimore County law said: "It shall be lawful to ... exhibit motion pictures after two o'clock P.M. on Sunday in said County with or without a charge or admission fee; provided that it shall be unlawful to show any picture having a plot, tone or character which is degrading, indecent or salacious, and which tends to glorify vice and marital infidelity, and to make light of all high ideals." *Laws of Maryland*, 1933, Chapter 534, Section 689A. This law remained part of the Baltimore County Code until it was repealed in 1990. *Laws of Maryland*, 1990, Vol. VI, p. 4060. Other Maryland jurisdictions got Sunday movies during the 1930s. The people of Howard County supported a Sunday movie referendum by a five-to-one margin in 1936. Anne Arundel County got Sunday movies in 1937. In July 1937 Annapolis voters, by almost three to one, approved the repeal of blue laws, which had prohibited movies on Sundays. The Maryland General Assembly passed a bill in 1945 permitting towns and cities to decide on the issue of Sunday movies. It took a long time to change the blue laws throughout the state. As late as the fall of 1948, the Majestic Theater in Mount Savage, Allegany County, was prohibited from showing Sunday movies because of the county blue laws. Cambridge in Dorchester County did not get Sunday movies until 1960.

69. Ira De A. Reid, *Negro Community of Baltimore*, Baltimore: Baltimore Urban League, October 1, 1934.

70. Washington, DC, was somewhat more southern than Baltimore. While there were several small movie houses there that were divided up the middle with whites sitting on one side of the wall and blacks on the other, most of the theaters catered exclusively to either black or white audiences.

71. "Movies Can Exclude Negroes," *MS*, April 12, 1916, p. 5.

72. "'Twas Mr. Kernan's Treat," *AA*, January 2, 1909, p. [4].

73. "Academy Welcomes Race Patronage," *AA*, October 24, 1924, p. 6.

74. "First Balcony at Academy Open to Colored Patrons," *AA*, December 20, 1924, p. 6.

75. "Jim Crow Boomerang Hits Loew Theatre," *AA*, February 4, 1928, p. 9.

76. Interview, Fred Schmuff, Catonsville, Maryland, December 11, 1986.

77. Interview, Sol Goodman, Baltimore, Maryland, June 19, 1996.

78. According to Fred Schmuff, *op.cit.*, Durkee had told Kanter before he built the Gwynn that they owned the property across Liberty Heights and were going to build a theater there at a later date. Despite this warning Kanter applied for the permit to build the Gwynn in July 1933.

79. See, for instance, "Why the Council," *ES*, January 9, 1935, p. 19 and "More Smells," *ibid.*, January 15, 1935, p. 17. The *Sun* in an editorial of January 17, 1935 pointed out that in granting the owners of the Gwynn Theater a building permit, the City Council had violated a number of zoning laws and called for the Council to divest itself of the authority to grant such permits.

80. "A Protest Against a Picture Show Building at Mount Royal and Maryland Avenues," *MS*, May 17, 1910, p. 6.

81. "Protest Against a Moving-Picture Show Close to Branch No. 13 of The Enoch Pratt Library," *MS*, 26 May 1911, p. 6.

82. There was a considerable backlash against the churches both for their nearly universal antipathy towards motion picture theaters anywhere near them and for their stand against Sunday movies. Numerous letters to the editor in the newspapers refer to these protests as "ridiculous" or "embarrassing." A writer in 1928 said that "nothing can break the morale of the church so much as its present narrow-minded stand on the blue laws." Other writers believed that the churches should look at themselves first instead of at their neighbors.

83. Local exhibitors organized the Screen Club, a precursor to the Variety Club, in the fall of 1920. The club was open to movie theater owners, managers, film salesmen, branch managers and others connected to the movie industry. The officers of the new club were Arthur B. Price, president; Frank Durkee, vice-president; Harry Rodman, secretary; and Thomas Goldberg, treasurer; Guy Wonders, Walter Pacy, and Jack Whittle were on the board of directors. The Screen Club did not last very long. "Screen Club Formed," *BN*, October 10, 1920, p. 24.

84. "On the Air," *ES*, September 5, 1928, p. 16.

85. "The 'Talkies' Day," *MS*, September 5, 1928, p. 10.

86. See also *MS*, February 10, 1936, p. 14 and Baltimore *Evening Sun*, February 10, 1936, p. 26.

87. "Coroner Calls Dancer's Death in Lion's Attack an Unavoidable Accident," *ES*, December 14, 1936, p. 36.

88. *MPH*, May 28, 1938, pp. 61, 66.

89. Norman Clark, "Very Busy Week Is This in Theatrical Circles of Baltimore," *BNP*, February 2, 1939, p. 14. The first mention of the new drive-in was in a short article, "Lasky Expands Chain of Open-Air Theaters," in the *Evening Sun* of January 28, 1939, p. 3.

90. In a 1990 interview, Elmer Nolte commented on the Durkee front office's thoughts about drive-ins: "We talked about the North Point Drive-In; they didn't know what we were talking about out here [= in Hamilton]. But [drive-in theaters] were just starting out.... When we opened it down there one of the partners, one of the attorneys that was involved, he said, 'You guys are crazy; the mosquitoes were eating them up the first night.'" Interview, Elmer Nolte, Baltimore, Md., August 24, 1990.

Chapter 6

1. Treasury receipts from amusement admission taxes went from about $10,250,000 in November 1941 to over $16,000,000 in August 1943. Only the weather could keep people away. The well-remembered Palm Sunday Blizzard of 1942 paralyzed the city with two feet of heavy, wet snow. Many theaters, unable to get films because the delivery trucks could not get to Washington to pick them up, closed for the day.

2. Augie Pahl was an East Baltimore saloon owner who also operated two open-air theaters on Monument Street. Pahl died in 1927.

3. Interview, Irwin Cohen, Reisterstown, Md., December 2, 1998.

4. Interview, Sol Goodman, Baltimore, Md., June 19, 1996.

5. Interview, Mrs. Gertrude Epstein, Rossmore, Maryland, November 19, 1990.

6. For more on the Westway case, see "Clearance Victory in Baltimore Is Seen as Bulwark for Defense in Gov't Action," *Boxoffice*, January 13, 1940, p. 5.

7. "Denied 'First-Runs' Complaint of Theater Here Rejected by Supreme Court," *BNP*, January 4, 1954, p. 2. See also, "Distributors Win Vital Test in Supreme Court," *MPH*, January 9, 1954, p. 13.

8. "Baltimore Expecting 'Blackout Practice,'" *Boxoffice*, December 20, 1941, p. 19.

9. Interviews, Charles Reisinger, Baltimore, Maryland, December 18, 1987, and September 30, 1992. Reisinger said that Germans ran the Hindenburg and that plainclothes police appeared in the projection booth one day and told him to stop the show.

10. Approximately 110,000 weekly programs were distributed to patrons in the city.

11. They were Jetsy Parker and Dorothy Schoemer, who called herself a "boogie woogie artist."

12. That amount could have paid for about four destroyers.

13. Although the members of the Motion Picture Owners of Maryland balked at lowering prices for servicemen at first. In a shocking turnaround during the Vietnam War, three Washington area movie theaters, including David Levy's Biograph, told the USO that they would no longer provide free movie tickets to servicemen since it would imply they supported the war. (*Washington Post*, September 28, 1971, p. C1) Apparently no Baltimore theaters followed this shabby example.

14. When a woman did become a manager, it was considered noteworthy enough to rate an article in one of the exhibitors' magazine.

15. "The Stage Possesses Little Glamour for the Girl Usher," *MS*, January 7, 1912, pt. 4, p. 4.

16. "Garden Theatre," *MS*, August 11, 1918, part 3, p. 2.

17. "IATSE Not Worried on Manpower Status," *Boxoffice*, December 26, 1942, p. 28. Walsh saw little chance of women replacing operators in the booths. He said that women were most panicky when it came to fire and easily lost control of themselves. He cited a recent instance where two brothers were breaking in a sister. While in a booth, she dropped a reel which exploded and she was burned to death.

18. "All-Night Movies Requested by Workers," *ES*, April 8, 1943, p. 46.

19. "Yeeeeeeeeeow! War Workers, at the Early Morning Matinee," *MS*, September 16, 1942, p. 28.

20. "For Film Fans," *ES,* July 29, 1943, p. 26.

21. These figures were based on the admission taxes collected by the state and were complicated by several factors, including the fact that servicemen had been admitted to theaters tax-free since 1942. Donald Kirkley, "Baltimore Movie Attendance Shows Decrease of 10 Per Cent," *MS,* September 23, 1943, p. 26. According to an article in *Motion Picture Herald,* U.S. Treasury receipts from amusement taxes reached an all-time high of $16,178,306 in August 1945. The receipts had been increasing since November 1941 when they were slightly less than $10,500,000. ("Admission Tax Receipts Record Box Office in War Year," *MPH,* October 2, 1943, p. 15).

22. An "X" apparently indicated lack of data. "None" indicates that that theater did not play that producer's product.

23. Nationally, ticket prices had been increasing since 1940, when they averaged 32.4 cents including tax. By 1943, they had reached 38 cents, by 1945 they were 43.5 cents and by March 1949 they were 48.8 cents. In May 1949 they had fallen to 47.5 cents.

24. "Victory Day a Hungry One for the Footloose," *ES,* August 16, 1945, p. 32.

25. Sara Wilson, "Escalator, Neon Marquee — Theaters Making Plans for Postwar Renovation," *ES,* January 3, 1945, p. 32.

26. "CPA Limiting Order Comes as Many Ask Building Permits," *MS,* March 28, 1946, p. 30. The theater on Dundalk Avenue was the Carlton, which would not open until 1949; the one on Belair Road was never built.

27. These early popcorn machines consisted of a large hopper mounted on the top of the machine. The hopper was filled with pre-popped corn kept warm by means of a light bulb in the middle. The customer placed a small bag under a chute, inserted money into a slot and popcorn fell into the bag.

28. For more on the history of popcorn, see [Mable Guinan], "The History of Popcorn," *Boxoffice,* May 15, 1978, Modern Theatre Section, pp. 22–26 and June 19, 1978, pp. 22–24 and Smith, *op .cit.*

29. "Cash in the Lobby," *Business Week,* March 15, 1947, p. 22.

30. "Theatre Refreshment Sales Continue to Climb," *Motion Picture Exhibitor — 1966 Theatre Catalog Edition,* April 6, 1966, pp. 58, 60.

31. Eric Johnston, President of the Motion Picture Association, had earlier denied Hughes permission to use advertising that showed Jane Russell lying in a pile of hay with the caption, "How would you like a Tussle with Russell?"

32. The Censor board's Polish Committee, Father Czyz of Holy Rosary Roman Catholic Church and Mrs. Marie Wiltzynski, screened the film and recommended that it be rejected on the grounds that it was communistic propaganda and untrue. Later the entire board, along with two FBI agents, viewed it and supported the rejection. Minutes for May 25, 1949, and June 1, 1949, Maryland State Board of Censors, July 1, 1948–June 30, 1950; Report and Official Opinions of Attorney General 1949, Vol. 34, pp. 100–104.

33. The controversy about *Stromboli* centered more on the private life of Bergman and Rossellini than on the film itself. Bergman had left her husband and run off with Italian director Rossellini. Rose Marie Murphy, the only woman in the Baltimore delegation in the Maryland House of delegates, introduced a measure in the House requesting that theater operators not show it. She said that she just did not think the movie should be shown in the state as it would tend to glorify "a person who in her private life has seriously transgressed the laws of morality and the high duties of family life." Women of that generation still sniffed and looked disapproving when Ingrid Bergman's name was mentioned years after *Stromboli*.

Chapter 7

1. Drive-in construction reached a post-war peak in 1949 when 859 new drive-ins were opened or placed under construction in the U.S. Maryland was still lagging behind most other states in the building of new drive-ins. There were only 10 in the state by the end of 1949.

2. Although there were first-run films being shown in neighborhood theaters as early as 1935, these were not products of the major production companies.

3. The Modern Theatre Section, *Boxoffice,* November 20, 1948, p. 16.

4. The first one seems to have been the Aero, which opened in 1942 in the Aero Shopping Center.

5. The Westview 1, with its subsequent additions, was the lone exception and that was built along a heavily commercialized strip of Route 40 West. Nationwide, the trend was the same. Out of the 285 new theaters reported in 1975, 238 were in shopping centers. "Report 285 New Theatre Constructions in 1975," *Boxoffice,* May 3, 1976, p. 13.

6. Moving pictures were also being shown in the banquet hall of Howard House in Ellicott City during the fall of 1912.

7. "The Boys Given a Treat," Annapolis *Evening Capitol,* December 19, 1901.

8. The theater was presenting the play, *A Flag Is Born,* which was sponsored by the American League for a Free Palestine. Faced with strong opposition from the NAACP and the Citizens Committee for Justice as well as from the League, the management of the theater agreed to this, at least temporary, relaxing of its segregation policy. The Maryland seemed to have an ambivalent attitude toward racial segregation. During a 1930 engagement of the "sepia review" Hot Chocolates, the management of the Maryland had planned to raise the prices of tickets to the first and second balconies, where African Americans had to sit, from 50 cents and $1.00 to $1.00 and $1.50. After a meeting between the theater manager and a representative of the NAACP, the price scale was kept at its original level. The management made another concession at the same time and agreed to set aside an entire section of the first balcony for African Americans rather than have them sit behind white patrons, as was its usual practice. "Local N.A.A.C.P. Wins Theatre Victory," *AA,* January 25, 1930, p. 8.

9. Ruby Dee and Ossie Davis headed the cast.

10. "Theatre Rejects Invited Patrons," *AA,* June 15, 1946, p. 19.

11. "70 Mixed Pickets Protest Policy of Town Theatre," *AA,* January 17, 1948, p. 1.

12. "Theatre Receipts Cut by Picketing," *AA,* January 24, 1948, p. 1.

13. "Balto. Theatre Drops Policy of Segregation," *AA,* May 21, 1949, p. 6.

14. The text of Governor McKeldin's letter and the statement by the Commission are contained in the 1952 *Annual Report of the Commission on Interracial Problems and Relations to the Governor and General Assembly of Maryland.*

15. The theaters were Durkee's Arcade, Boulevard, Senator, and Waverly; Gaertner's Earle and Vilma; Schwaber's Paramount; the Rex, Cameo, Harford, and Northwood.

16. *Annual Report of the Commission on Interracial Problems and Relations to the Governor and General Assembly of Maryland, 1957*, pp. 17–18.

17. For more information on the Northwood demonstrations, see: August Meier, Thomas S. Plaut & Curtis Smothers, "Case Study in Nonviolent Direct Action," *The Crisis*, 71:9 (November 1964), pp. 573–578.

18. For additional details on Goldberg's complaint, see "Washington Tribunal Gets First Plaint," *Boxoffice*, February 15, 1941, p. 9; "Walbrook Case Poses Clearance as Snag," *Boxoffice*, March 29, 1941, pp. 30, 34; and "Blames Baltimore Clearance for Loss," *Boxoffice*, April 19, 1941, p. 34A.

19. "Through the Years," *Showmen's Trade Review*, July 30, 1949, p. 7. For additional information on the consent decree, see *Showmen's Trade Review*, January 11, 1947, p. 15 et seq.; Slide (1986) and Michael Conant, "The Paramount Decrees Reconsidered," in Tino Balio (1985).

20. *1960 Film Daily Yearbook*, p. 105. These figures do not reflect the 18 percent decline in neighborhood attendance and the 25 percent decline for the downtown theaters which were reported for 1944 (see Sara Wilson, "Escalator, Neon Marquee — Theaters Making Plans for Postwar Renovation," *ES*, January 3, 1945, p. 32.) Various sets of figures for grosses and attendance are available, and figures provided by the U.S. Department of Commerce do not always agree with those from the Motion Picture Association of America. Even though they do not agree, they show the same up-and-down trends.

21. "No Movie-Price Cut Seen Here," *ES*, March 26, 1949, p. 18.

22. "Theatre Sales Champions of 1953," *MPH*, March 21, 1953, p. 32.

23. These included the Mayfair and Hampden operated by the Hicks' Circuit and the Horn and Monroe operated by the Hornig family.

24. Cited in the Censor Board's Annual Report for the 1951–52 fiscal year, p. 5.

25. Faced with the overruling of its ban on *The Moon Is Blue*, the board lifted its ban on the Alec Guinness film *The Captain's Paradise*.

26. The case was *Kingsley International Pictures Corp. v. Regents of the Univ. of the State of New York*.

27. "Small Theatre Feels Television Impact, Exhibitor Declares," *Boxoffice*, January 14, 1950, p. 9.

28. Gilbert Kanour, "For Film Fans," *ES*, July 15, 1948, p. 24. There were only about 35,800 television sets in Baltimore homes at this time.

29. Morton G. Thalhimer, "New Influences Affecting Theatre Appraisal," *1952 Theatre Catalog*, pp. 19–23.

30. The *Motion Picture Herald* asked panels composed of members of the exhibition, distribution and production branches of the movie industry to predict what would happen in the industry in 1952. A majority thought that things would get better because of better product, better local advertising and exploitation, more public spending and less effective home TV. The minority thought business would be down because the public lacked money, because of home TV, insufficient good product, competitive amusements, and lack of comfort in theaters. "Panels See First Quarter Gross Up," *MPH*, January 19, 1952, p. 15.

31. "New Theater Will Specialize in Best International Films," *MS*, October 14, 1951, p. 22.

32. Norman Clark, "Two 3-D Pictures Here," *BNP*, April 30, 1953, p. 14.

33. The summary of 3-D that follows is based on the article by Harley W. Lond, "3-D: A Brief History," *Boxoffice*, November 1982, pp. 19–22.

34. A six-reel 3-D film called *The Power of Love*, which used a process involving glasses with red and green celluloid lenses developed by Harry K. Fairall, was shown at the Ambassador Hotel in Los Angeles in September 1922.

35. Neither the *Sun* nor the *Evening Sun's* reviewers mentioned the 3-D short in their reviews of the show at the Century.

36. Four months earlier, the film *The Big Sky* was shown in the RCA process called Synchro Screen. This seems to have been a wide, curved screen process. The Town Theater had one of the first installations in the country for the October 8, 1952 opening of *The Big Sky*. Synchro Screen allowed for the phenomenon of peripheral vision which created a three-dimensional effect. Donald Kirkley, in his October 8, 1952, column, did not think very much of the process, writing only that "the new screen gives a larger image and an illusory third dimension." For more on this process, see "A Greater Theatrical Medium in the Making," *Motion Picture Herald*, January 10, 1953, Better Theaters, pp. 10–12.

37. Donald Kirkley, "Of Stage and Screen. Cinema in the Round," *MS*, January 31, 1953, p. 6.

38. Donald Kirkley, "Of Stage and Screen. But Scenario and Performances Are Strictly 1-D," *MS*, May 22, 1953, p. 12. The author of this book was one of those ducking the flaming arrows that seemed to land in the next seat.

39. The reels were double the size of regular reels and very heavy to lift. For more details on 3-D projection, see: William R. Weaver, "Natural Vision Ready for Public Showing," *Motion Picture Herald*, November 22, 1952, p. 38, "On the House. The Impact of 3-D on Projection," *ibid.*, February 7, 1953, pp. 18–20, and "3-D Projection," *IATSE Official Bulletin*, Spring 1953.

40. One of the earliest uses of a wide screen in a Baltimore movie house was in February 1930 when Keith's installed a larger screen for a showing of the "singing, dancing and color picture" *Show of Shows*. Later in the spring, the Stanley presented a newsreel double-sized on its newly installed larger screen.

41. The Town underwent a $100,000 conversion with the installation of a large deeply-curved screen, three floor-level projection booths, and additional speakers for the stereophonic sound. The decision to use the Town rather than the Stanley was made because the Stanley auditorium was too large.

42. R. H. Gardner, "Of Stage and Screen, Cinerama," *MS*, August 29, 1957, p. 12.

43. Most of the scenting processes used different fragrances dispersed through the air-conditioning system. The Weiss-Rhodia Screen Scent system in 1959 cost $5,000 and utilized an electronic apparatus attached to the projector to trigger each fragrance in synchronization with the appropriate scene on the screen.

44. R. H. Gardner, "Stage Still Fearing 'End of Road' but Movies Have Hopes Widened," *MS*, December 28, 1953, p. 17.

45. According to a source familiar with the ship, the cabin windows were large enough for a person to crawl through.

46. "Missing 7 Years, Man Ruled Dead," *ES*, August 23, 1955, p. 22.

47. Welcher is a variant of welsher, 'one who fails to pay a debt or wager.'

48. Mr. Fruchtman started out in 1929 in the mailroom of Paramount Pictures in New York when he was 14. After spending more than six years at Paramount, where he learned all about the film business, he moved to Washington, D.C., in 1937 where he became the office manager and chief accountant of the local Paramount exchange. In 1940, he and his future wife teamed up to operate the Greenbelt Theater in Prince George's County.

49. Interview, Maurice Rushworth, Pasadena, Md., April 17, 1987.

50. "New Charles Movie House Opens Today," *BNP,* October 2, 1958, p. 16.

51. "The Future Is Bright," *Boxoffice,* January 4, 1960, p. 12.

52. "Show Business. Nato Is a House o' Weenies," *Time,* November 8, 1971, p. 79.

53. Interview with Veazy Craycroft, May 7, 1971. Wyatt and Nolting designed the Capitol Theater (1920) in Baltimore.

54. Letter to the author from Cyril H. Hebrank, A.I.A, dtd. July 20, 1971.

55. Blanke and Zink designed the Rialto Theater in 1918 for Tom Moore. Blanke designed the Rivoli (1921) and Boulevard (1921) theaters in Baltimore. Blanke and Zink also did sketches for St. Paul's Lutheran Church in New York in 1916 and for several buildings in Baltimore.

56. Sparklin was earlier associated with George S. Childs; they designed several theaters in Baltimore including the Bridge (1915), the Regent (1916), and the Rialto (1916).

57. Letter from Albert C. Zink to the author, dtd. August 21, 1971.

58. *Ibid.*

59. Interview with Craycroft, Baltimore, Md., May 7, 1971, and letter from Albert C. Zink, *op.cit.* He may have used this first in a remodeling of the Hippodrome Theater, Baltimore, Md., but this is not yet certain. The original 1914 plans by Thomas Lamb do not indicate a reverse curve.

60. "Baltimorean Designed Tivoli," [Frederick] *Daily News,* December 23, 1926, Special Supplement, p. 5.

61. *Ibid.*

plaining about loud movies. He cites four main points: some films are recorded too loud; the sound systems in theaters are often distorting; many of the sound systems are seriously mistuned and miscalibrated, and producers have been in a kind of contest to make the loudest trailer. Despite all this discussion and agreement that sound is uncomfortably loud, "I have not yet noticed any diminishing of the sound levels. The solution? I use earplugs."

7. Norman Clark, "Whacky Comedy at New," *NA,* August 19, 1964, p. 6B.

8. Credit for the first twin theater in the country is usually given to the twin-auditorium Parkway Theater which was opened in Kansas City in July 1962 by American Multi Cinema.

9. Linda Dunn, "600 At Tower Opening," *MS,* December 20, 1967, p. C24.

10. Norman Clark, "The End of a 'Century'; Movie Palace Goes Dark," *BA,* January 8, 1961, p. 4E.

11. R. H. Gardner, "Show's Over at Stanton Theater," *MS,* April 18, 1965, pp. 16, 14.

12. "Regretful Farewell," *ES* , June 2, 1965, p. A30.

13. R. P. Harriss, "Is the Stanton Worth Keeping?" *NA,* April 18, 1965, p. 6B.

14. "Movie Palace Restoration to By Pass [sic] Baltimore," Baltimore *Daily Record,* September 11, 1979, p. 4.

15. Andrew Sharp, "Death Claims Old Theaters as An Era Comes to an End," *ES,* August 3, 1970, p. C1.

16. Statement by William Pacy to the Maryland General Assembly, September 6, 1972.

17. The admissions tax had had a terrible effect on exhibitors, forcing many smaller theaters to close. After several major efforts in Congress to have the tax reduced or eliminated, President Eisenhower signed legislation boosting the exemption from the 10 percent tax from 50 cents to 90 cents.

18. *Forty-Ninth Annual Report of the Motion Picture Censor Board,* Fiscal Year 1965. Baltimore, p. 4

19. The revised movie censorship code was tested for the first time within a month of its being passed. The censors found the Danish film *A Stranger Knocks* to be objectionable after two cuts they requested were not made. Judge J. Gilbert Prendergast upheld the board's ban. The Maryland Court of Appeals, however, sided with the distributor and producer-director Johan Jacobsen and reversed Judge Prendergast's ruling.

Chapter 8

1. The Perring Plaza Cinema seated 1,184, the Westview seated 1,160, the theater at Harundale Mall seated 1,105, the Hillendale and North Point Plaza theaters seated more than 900.

2. "Theatres Gain 2,333,000 Patrons a Week in 1959," *Boxoffice,* February 1, 1960, p. 7.

3. "Trans-Lux Corp. Annexes Four Baltimore Theatres," *Boxoffice,* August 27, 1962, p. E-1.

4. Gio Gagliardi, "Stereophonic Sound in the Development of New Techniques," *MPH,* April 10, 1954, pp. 16, 34.

5. This was Ken Russell's *Lisztomania.* Robert Schein, "Ten Years of Progress in Motion Picture Sound," *Boxoffice,* December 1985, pp. 118–119.

6. *Boxoffice* discussed the loudness problem in its November 1998 issue, pp. 84–93. John F. Allen in the same issue, "Why Movies Are Not Too Loud," tries to explain why audiences around the world were com-

Chapter 9

1. "$188,270,000 Invested in 540 New Theatres," *Boxoffice,* May 15, 1972, p. 11.

2. The original local ratings were: A — Adults; MY — Mature Young People; FA — Family Audience and NR — Not Rated. In the fall of 1968 a new system was adopted using the abbreviations G — General Audiences, M — Mature Audiences/Adults, R — Restricted (young people not admitted unless accompanied by a parent or guardian), and X — young people not admitted. In 1969 the ratings were again changed, the new system contained four ratings: G — General Audiences, GP — All Ages (Parental Guidance Suggested), R — Restricted (Persons under 16 not admitted unless accompanied by a parent or adult guardian), and X — Persons Under 16 Not Admitted. In 1972 GP was changed to PG . The X-rating was abandoned in the early 1980s and a new rating PG-13, for films which contained material that

might be inappropriate for children 13 and under, was added. The rating system currently (2004) in use has five ratings: G — all ages, PG — all ages (parental guidance suggested), PG-13 — special guidance cautioned, R — restricted (under 17 requires accompanying parent or legal guardian), and NC-17 — no one under 17 admitted.

3. James Jones, "I Remember ... When Movies Showed the Commercials," *MS,* November 25, 1973, Sun Magazine, p. 2.

4. "Entertainment in Baltimore," *ES,* December 10, 1926, p. 29.

5. All the front glass at the Harlem Theater was smashed.

6. Between December 1972 and the end of June 1973, the actual figures were seven new theaters and two new auditoriums added to an existing theater, for a total of 15 new screens.

7. Jeff Valentine, "The Flight of the Flicks. New Film Theaters Burgeoning in Suburbia," *ES,* 17 May 1973, p. E-4.

8. Jacques Kelly, Neighborhood Watch, *NA,* October 1, 1978, p. 1-A, 4-A. In subsequent articles he has written sympathetically and insightfully about Baltimore's movie theaters. Jack Fruchtman claimed that his Hippodrome, Mayfair, and Town were just doing "so-so" by showing often-violent movies directed at black audiences.

9. Editorial, "Goodby, Gayety," *ES,* December 22, 1969, p. A16.

10. The number of local movie theaters showing X-rated films peaked between 1973 and 1976. Currently (2004) the Apex and the Earle are the only theaters in the city that regularly show X-rated product.

11. "Maryland Collects $8.2 million in 1975 Amusement Taxes," *Boxoffice,* September 22, 1975, p. E-7.

12. Mrs. Avara, who died in August 2000 at age 90. was one of the most colorful and controversial members who ever sat on the censor board.

13. Neil Grauer, "Judge Blisters Censors," *NA,* January 11, 1972, p. 2C and George J. Hiltner, "Judge Criticizes Sex Film Approval," *MS,* January 11, 1972, p. C18.

14. For details of the high court's decision see: "Court Toughens Obscenity Stand, School Bias Ban," *MS,* June 22, 1973, p. A1. Between 1957 and 1973, the courts used the following Supreme Court definition of obscene material: "(1) It must deal with sex in a manner appealing to the prurient interest, judged by the average person applying contemporary community standards, and considering its dominant theme as a whole; and (2) it must be patently offensive — so offensive on its face as to affront community standards of decency; and (3) it must be utterly offensive without redeeming social value." Cited in "History of Obscenity Laws in the U.S. Traced From 1815 to Present Period," *Boxoffice,* May 17, 1971, p. 6.

15. See also *Boxoffice,* December 9, 1974, p. E-1. and *Mangum v. Md. St. Bd. of Censors,* 273 Md, 176–194.

16. The Court ruled against the law in a case involving the clerk in an adult bookstore in Baltimore who was convicted and fined for distributing an obscene magazine. The magazine contained stills of Linda Lovelace taken from the film *Deep Throat.* The court held that the Maryland law made unconstitutional distinctions between the different kinds of adult entertainment and said that clerks could not be prosecuted while adult film projectionists were not. The 1974 charges against the North Cinema had been dismissed on a technicality in 1976.

17. George Hanst, "Burch Says Censors Can't Set Standards," *ES,* March 13, 1976, p. 5. A psychologist testified that the film was hard-core pornography and obscene.

18. *Boxoffice,* January 17, 1977, p. E-8.

19. Roy Furchgott and Lottchen Shivers, "Stale Popcorn, Sprung Seats and Scratched-Up Screens," *Baltimore Magazine,* November 1979, pp. 139–145. This article was one of the best that rated local movie theaters; it was intelligently compiled and cleverly written. Of the 15 theaters rated, only three are still open.

20. Mike Giuliano, "Film-watching: A look at the best and worst of the area's silver screens," *NA,* 7 December 1980, p. 1C, 10C.

21. These are just theaters the author knows from personal experience. There are many other fine and horrible theaters the author has never attended.

22. If there were an 11th theater here, it would have to be the wonderful Egyptian megaplex at Arundel Mills. The auditoriums are well planned and comfortable, and the wacky Egyptian murals and statues with the blue-tile Nile River running through the lobby bring some excitement back to movie theaters.

23. Celeste H. Breitenbach, "Cheaper Movie Tickets Might Fill Empty Houses," *MS,* April 27, 1980, The Sun Magazine, p. 21. At the present time, the exhibitor's hands are tied. Distributors demand a minimum admission price per patron for first-run pictures.

24. J. D. Considine, "A guide to cheap movies. All over town, new films at old-time prices," Weekend Section, *NA,* January 2, 1981, Section D, pp. 1–2.

25. Wienholt operated the Beard's Hill Movies 7 in Aberdeen; Cinema 83 near York, Pennsylvania; the Edgewater Twin in Edgewood; the Elkton Movies 4, the Perry Hall Movies 5, Southside Movies 4 in Baltimore; and the Tollgate Movies 7 in Bel Air.

26. Before this type of ticket, tickets came in rolls on which individual tickets were printed and then cut off.

27. A roll of pre-printed perforated tickets was loaded into the ticket-shooter, and the cashier selected a button for the number of tickets purchased. When the cashier stepped on a foot pedal, the ticket(s) emerged from a slot where they were held until torn off by the patron.

28. Robert F. Blaha, "Computerized Movie Theater Ticketing," *Boxoffice,* June 1982, pp. 40–41.

29. Rappaport got his first two theaters around 1915 or 1916 in Philadelphia. He was in and out of the theater business until the Depression hit. At one point Spyros Skouras, later to become president of 20th Century-Fox, suggested that he go down to Baltimore and see about taking over the New Theater. Rappaport came down and, as he was walking around town, he saw a sign on the Hippodrome that it was also available. He decided that he liked the Hippodrome better than the New. Interview, M. Robert Rappaport, Baltimore, Md., April 21, 1994.

30. The Rappaports had a 10-year non-compete clause after they leased their theaters to Trans-Lux. Robert Rappaport had actually gotten back into theaters in 1965, when he acquired a theater in Cleveland.

31. According to a 1979 article, neither the 5-West nor the 7-East were successful as art houses. Earl Arnett, "Is Baltimore a Bad Cinema Town, or Is It Just a Tough Era for Film?" *MS,* February 16, 1979, p. B1.

32. These included four Gaertner theaters — the Strand, Carlton, Vilma, and Earle — the New in Leonardtown and the Park, Plaza, and 235 Drive-In in Lexington Park, Maryland, and four theaters in Lynchburg, Virginia.

33. Another source stated that in 1983, JF had a five-year goal to control between 50 and 75 screens; they did reach this goal. Jeff Seidel, "Movie Chain's Growth Should Spur Competition," *Baltimore Jewish Times*, July 29, 1988, p. 9.

34. Stephen Hunter, "Duplex, triplex, quadriplex, nanoplex — exhibitors see more screens for Baltimore," *MS*, October 14, 1984, pp. 1L, 12L.

35. Many believe that this never actually happened and was an early urban myth, the result of mass hysteria.

36. "Shoots Himself While in Theater," *BA*, October 5, 1920, p. 14.

37. Could the movie have been that bad?

38. I suppose Mrs. Maturio was not facing her husband but, rather, presenting her profile to him.

39. Lauritz Garman was born in Denmark. He worked as a mechanic in Paris and later Cincinnati and London. He became friends with Philadelphia attorney George Flint, and arrived in Baltimore in 1909. Here, he worked for the Crown Cork & Seal Company. In 1914, he and Flint were attending the races at Pimlico, and Flint remarked that Garman should build a theater in Pimlico. Flint offered to finance the venture and along with a local businessman, Morris Wolf, and lawyer, Ben Beck, they opened the Pimlico Theater in March 1914. Garman and his partners went on to control most of the theaters in northwest Baltimore. They took over the Avalon in 1930 and built the New in Reisterstown in 1934, the Pikes in 1938 and the Uptown in 1941. Garman was president of the state exhibitors' organization for a number of years.

40. James L. Whittle, Sr., better known as "Jack," was born in Baltimore in 1892. His 67-year career in the movie business began at the Paradise Theater on North Gay Street in 1906. In 1909 he opened the Celtic Theater on Greenmount Avenue. He later learned how to run a projector and was the projectionist for Augie Pahl in June 1911. He worked as a film salesman for several companies, including Warner Bros. He became a partner in Gwynn Oak Park in 1935 and in 1956 became president of the state branch of the Allied Motion Picture Theater Owners. He retired in 1973 as executive secretary of its successor organization, the National Association of Theater Owners of Maryland.

41. Stephen G. Brenner was born in Canton, Baltimore County, in August 1894. As a child he made his own puppets and gave puppet shows. He also learned to walk the slack wire. When he was in his early teens he was taught to operate a movie projector by Otto P. Steiner at Riverview Park. He ran away with a circus, and worked with wild west shows until he was 17. He developed numerous characters, including Bozo the Clown and Chief Red Moon. He operated the Eagle Theater in Highlandtown and the Elektra Theater in Essex.

42. "John T. M'Caslin, 67, Dies in Jersey," *MS*, February 28, 1944, p. 18.

43. Interview, Fred Schmuff, Catonsville, Md., December 11, 1986.

44. *IATSE Official Bulletin*, Spring 1954.

45. "Fred G. Schmuff. Managed Area Theaters," *MS*, February 24, 1991, p. 6B.

46. Interview, Fred G. Schmuff, Baltimore, Md., December 11, 1986.

47. *Theatre Organ*, June/July 1980. Nuttrell enjoyed hearing organist John Varney at the Metropolitan. Later, after he had learned to play the organ, he played at the Stanley and Valencia. For more on Roland Nuttrell's career, see *Theatre Organ*, November/December 1982, pp. 12–16.

48. Jacques Kelly, "As the Boulevard crumbles, signs of life for old theaters pop up," *ES*, August 21, 1989, pp. B1, B4.

49. Lou Cedrone, "Old Hippodrome and Town Close," *ES*, August 2, 1990, p. D3.

Chapter 10

1. In November 1995, the county's Deputy Zoning Chief ruled against the developer's 16-screen theater at Towson Marketplace but said that they could build a six-screen theater. AMC eventually got a theater in Towson when they acquired the General Cinema theaters in 2002.

2. A 1997 estimate put the cost at between $200,000 and $300,000 per auditorium. Leonard Klady, "Megas Lack Plexuality," *Variety*, March 3–9, 1997, p. 1, 86. In 1996, the estimated cost for a megaplex was about $30 million.

3. Towson developers were still trying in 2001. They proposed a redevelopment plan that included a multiplex theater that would "rival the 24-screen theater at Arundel Mills." Gerald Shields, "New Towson Development Plan Unveiled," *MS*, July 2, 2001, p. B1.

4. The relative sizes of the Maryland theater circuits in 1972 can be judged by the amount of their yearly dues to the National Association of Theater Owners of Maryland. The top ten circuits with their dues were: 1. F. H. Durkee—$5,018. 2. Schwaber Theaters—$2,559. 3. Rome Theaters—$1,950. 4. General Cinema—$1,560. 5. George Brehm—$1,504. 6. R/C Theaters—$1,295. 7. Grant Theaters—$780. 8. Vogel Theaters—$728. 9. Redstone Theaters—$600. 10. Hicks-Baker Theaters—$596. General Cinema was the only out-of-state exhibitor in this group. JF Theaters was not a member at this time.

5. A megaplex may be defined as a movie theater with more than 12 screens and stadium-style high-backed rocking seats. It usually has large concave screens, a digital sound system, large concession areas and, recently, child-care facilities. Megaplexes are typically free-standing.

6. At one time, for some inexplicable reason, the music played in this auditorium during the intermission between shows was Vivaldi's "Four Seasons." It was a welcome change from the usual dismal selections at other theaters.

7. Michelle Schaekel, "New movie house boasts 14 screens, cafe, video room," Bel Air *Aegis*, July 2, 1997, p. C1.

8. It was shocking recently to find that the Regal Theaters, at least the one in Harford County, were not offering Raisinets. Apparently the decision to drop Raisinets was made by the chain's upper management. Whatever could have possessed them?

9. "That Tub of Movie Popcorn Likely Won't Drown You in Coconut Oil," *ES*, April 29, 1994, p. D-1.

10. David Simon, "In mingling principle with politics, City Council loses sight of landmarks," *MS*, December 6, 1987, p. 12C.

11. Editorial, "Hippodrome: Gone Forever," *MS*, August 15, 1990, p. 10A.

12. In September 2002 the Maryland Stadium Authority selected Schamu Machowski Greco as the local architects for the Hippodrome Project.

13. With the demise of the Village and North Point Plaza, if you want to see a theater from the 1960s in nearly vintage condition, you have to look at the Hillendale (1960) or go to Riverdale, Maryland, and look at the Riverdale Plaza Theater (1968). Be quick about visiting the Riverdale Plaza; it's closed and its future looks very bleak.

14. The Columbia Palace 9 would have made a nice choice for the 1980s, but it was demolished after it closed in 2001.

Part II : Baltimore Area Theaters

1. "Baltimore Academy of Music, " *MS*, January 6, 1875, p. 1.

2. Slemmer was the scenic artist at the Holliday Street Theater for more than 43 years and later stage manager at the Palace.

3. At that time, Nixon and Zimmerman controlled 37 theaters across the country, including the Lyceum in Baltimore, the Lafayette Square and Columbia in Washington, and theaters in New York, Philadelphia, Cleveland, Chicago, Denver, Salt Lake City, San Francisco, New Orleans, and Toronto.

4. "The Academy of Music," *BA*, August 30, 1896, p. 2.

5. According to other articles, the painting on the drop curtain was done by the Viennese artist Schweninge Schweninger. "Academy of Music," *MS*, July 16, 1896, p. 8 and "The Academy of Music," *BA*, August 30, 1896, p. 2.

6. "The Academy Reopened," *MS*, September 29, 1896, p. 10.

7. "Grand Opening for Academy," *MS*, September 17, 1911, Section 3, p. 3.

8. Nelson Robins, "Watching 'Em Strut," *DP*, September 21, 1925, p. 9.

9. "Maryland Theater Is Sold; Vaudeville May Come Back," *MS*, April 14, 1942, p. 11.

10. *Boxoffice* magazine of August 26, 1939 reported a theater going up at the new Glynn [sic] Martin settlement. This may have been the Aero. The Aero Acres shopping center was one of the earliest in the Baltimore area. It grew in stages; by July 1942 it had the theater, a bank branch, super market, doctor, dentist, and beauty shop. There were plans for a restaurant, coffee shop, dress shop, haberdashery, barbershop and bowling alley.

11. See especially, letters of W. A. Koontz, April 24, 1912, p. 6, and "Puella," April 27, 1912, p.6.

12. "New Aladdin in Baltimore Is Sold for $10,000 by Mrs. Bamberger, "*MPN*, March 11, 1916, p. 1516.

13. The Kilgen was Opus 4109.

14. "A Novel Plan for a Theatre of 800 Seats," *MPH*, Better Theatres, November 16, 1935, pp. 12–13, 36.

15. "American," *AA*, June 20, 1924, p. 5.

16. "Two Fined in Police Raid on Theatre," *Baltimore News and the Post*, September 4, 1935, p. 4.

17. Earl Arnett, "Life on the Block. Burlesque House Box Office Once Served as Home," *MS*, 16 April 1971, p. B1. Bernard Livingston wrote an enjoyable, thinly disguised semi-autobiographical novel, about a burlesque theater in Baltimore, called *Papa's Burlesque House* (New York: Pyramid Books, 1972). The fictional theater must have been closely modeled after the Clover.

18. Prof. Loose was known as the "singing evangelist." He had been involved in early motion picture exhibition since the late 1890s.

19. It is not clear whether the Spurrier Amusement Company is the same as the Superior Amusement Company, but the names are remarkably similar.

20. The building has been modified many times over its long history. It is built into the granite hillside on the north side of Main Street.

21. Junchen, *op. cit.*, pp. 402, 411, says that the Apollo had a 2/10 Moller organ Opus 3038.

22. However, the earliest newspaper advertisement was on August 2, 1928, when the film *His Tiger Lady* was playing.

23. "The Argonne," *AA*, January 27, 1922, p. 4.

24. The provision to allow a non-fireproof roof seems to have backfired in 1929 when an overheated chimney set the roof on fire.

25. Kernan's first thought was to erect a new building. According to the *American Contractor*, January 17, 1891, Kernan had plans prepared by Washington architect William Bruce Gray for a three-story, 70 × 244 foot theater adjacent to the Academy of Music. The new theater would have cost $75,000, had it been built.

26. One was located in San Francisco, three in Paris, one in Berlin and one in Southampton. "In and About Town. Ice Palace and Summer Roof Garden," *MS*, June 18, 1894, p. 10.

27. "A New Thespian Temple," *BA*, September 29, 1895, p. 19. For additional details, see also, "To Remodel A Theater," *MS*, May 1, 1895, p. 10 and "The Auditorium Rebuilt," *MS*, September 21, 1895, p. 10.

28. "Kernan Houses Ready," *MS*, August 31, 1904, p. 8. According to the *News*, the theater was decorated in Louis XV style, representing "the very latest ideas in the construction of theatres." The stage measurements were 41 feet deep and 64 feet wide, and the seating capacity was 1,800. "Auditorium to Open," *BN*, September 12, 1904, p. 8.

29. The baths occupied a large area below the theater. The entrance was on the south side of the theater through a wide arched doorway and down a flight of marble stairs. The walls of the baths were covered with white tiles with marble finishings. There were 15 private sleeping rooms, 25 dressing rooms, hot rooms, temperate rooms, and steam rooms. all fitted with white marble slabs tiled and enameled in white. Next to the dressing rooms was a large lounging room. There were five large stone-partitioned rooms with marble slabs for the rubbers and masseurs. The hot, cold, needle showers, and ceiling sprinklers were all nickel-plated. In the rear of the baths was a 20 by 40-foot marble and tile pool.

30. During the last week of October, the New was showing the very popular film *The Cock-Eyed World* and had to turn away hundreds of people every day.

31. *MS*, August 21, 1910, p. 4.

32. *BA*, April 10, 1927, p. SS10.

33. Interview, Aaron Seidler, Washington, D.C., October 31, 1991.

34. "A Journey of Exploration to Beautiful Bay Shore," *MS*, May 26, 1907, p. 14.

35. Fr. Kevin A. Mueller, *Bay Shore Park. Fun on the Chesapeake*, p. 8.

36. According to *Exhibitors' Trade Review*, March 1, 1919, p. 1012, William Schnabel, consulting engineer, was preparing plans for a new 1,500-seat theater for Greater Baltimore Theaters on the lot occupied by the Belnord Theater. He must have been working with Sparklin.

37. The theater was named after Bengies Road, and

the corporation was named after nearby Frog Mortar Creek. For more on the Vogel Family and the Bengies Drive-In, see: Randy and Debrean Loy, *Moonlight Magic ... Celebrating 40 Years of Motion Picture Enchantment at Baltimore's Bengies Drive-In Theatre*, Rockville, Md.: Rockville Printing & Graphics.

38. "On the Road: Baltimore," *MPW*, December 25, 1909, p. 924.

39. Letter, Hood and Schultz to Motion Picture Patents Company, July 23, 1910, Defendants' Exhibit No. 58, The United States Government v. The Motion Picture Patents Company. Equity No. 889. District Court. Eastern District of Pennsylvania. pp. 1366–1368 in six-volume transcript.

40. The pipe organ was installed in the Blue Mouse in May 1910, and it may have been the first organ installed in a Baltimore movie house.

41. "Renovated Blue Mouse Theatre Opens," *MPW*, September 14, 1918, p. 1605.

42. Advertisement, *BN*, December 5, 1920, p. 28. This advertisement shows a model of the Boulevard as if the corner drugstore lot had been obtained.

43. The selling price of the theater was a matter of some uncertainty. Contemporary accounts gave widely varying figures from $142,000 to $250,000.

44. The title was finally transferred from the Stanley-Crandell Company to the Grand Company in 1932; the final price was $225,000.

45. "Broadway Theatre an Attractive New House," *MS*, May 21, 1916, part 3, p. 8.

46. Baltimore City, Ordinances and Resolutions, 1926–1927, p. 121.

47. "Round Town in Theatres," *AA*, January 25, 1930, p. 8.

48. Lillian Johnson, "Carey Theatre Spick and Span in New Improvements," *Afro-American*, February 1, 1941, p. [M].

49. The Odd Fellows purchased the lot in the rear of the 1st National Bank of Catonsville in the spring of 1908 for their building.

50. "Rallies for 313th Tonight," *BN*, May 11, 1919, p. 28.

51. *Gardens, Houses and People*, February 1939, p. 17.

52. According to one source, the new theater was going to be called the Cinema Centre ("Cinema Centre to Open Aug. 1," *BNP*, June 22, 1954, p. 10.)

53. "Enter the Century," *BN*, May 1, 1921, p. 20.

54. The main mural measured 36 by 10 feet and the other six were each 15 by 10 feet. They featured a battle of roses on an Arcadian plain between heroic centaurs and wild wood nymphs. Each panel was bordered with Circassian walnut and black marble. "R. McGill Mackall's Fine Murals in the Century Theatre Merit Praise," *MS*, February 20, 1921, part 5, p. 4. Another piece of art played a small role in the history of the Century. In 1924, a local artist, Andrew J. Easter, accepted a commission to paint a picture for the Century Roof. The painting was of a young woman with very little on. The Century's owners refused to pay for it because they said the police would not allow them to exhibit it. The artist sued, and the resulting trial packed the court room with people eager to view the painting. It was described as a nude female figure entitled "Atop the Century." A jury awarded the painter $250.

55. Under Wild, the orchestra consisted of 23 players — six violinists, one viola player, two cellists, two bass players, a flute player, an oboe player, two clarinet players, a bassoon player, two horn players, two cornet players, a trombone player, a drummer, and a piano player.

56. Or Opus 6409 with three manuals, 112 stops and 13 ranks, according to Roland Nuttrell.

57. The Laocoon was supposed to have been donated to the Maryland Institute, but that institution knew nothing about the statue in 2000.

58. Quoted in Loni Ingraham, "Unlikely Stories. Yorkridge Rolls Credits for Its Last Picture Show," *Towson Times*, February 2, 2000, p. 10.

59. "Novel Movie Idea," *BN*, May 9, 1915, p. 15.

60. However, *The Film Index*, August 27, 1910, p. 24, says that Edward L. Anzmann owned and operated the "parlor at 314 North Broadway." He said at the time that he had been in the business for ten months and that he had invested $6,000 in the theater.

61. The vertical sign may have been installed in the fall of 1927. Unfortunately, it had been removed by 1999.

62. According to Judd Walton in his book *Wurlitzer*, the Cluster purchased a Style 100, two-manual three-rank Wurlitzer (Opus 602) on November 23, 1922.

63. The upper theater was scheduled to open during the week of March 18 with C. Nelson Camp & Company's electrical spectacular "Doomsday," but some problems developed and the opening was postponed until April.

64. "Lubin's Theatre Opened,"*MS*, April 2, 1907, p. 12.

65. "Lubin's," *BA*, March 31, 1907, Pt. 2, Sec. 2, p. 2.

66. Sources disagree on the name of the architect. Most sources identify him as Otto Simonson, but the *Star* (October 25, 1910, p. 6) names him as Eustace Simonson of New York.

67. "The Week in Baltimore. Lubin's Theater Reopened," *MPW*, September 23, 1916, p. 2000. The Kimball was a 2/7 organ.

68. Lee McCardell, "Off the Sidewalks of East Baltimore," *MS*, June 30, 1929, Magazine Section, pp. 5–6.

69. By 2002 there was an empty three-story brick building, with a store on the first floor, on the site.

70. "New Columbia Opens Saturday," *MS*, November 13, 1921, p. Part 6, p. 7.

71. Before the Columbia Palace 9 opened, the only movie in Columbia was General Cinema's Columbia Cinema III. The next closest theaters were in Laurel and Catonsville, approximately eight miles to the southeast and northeast respectively.

72. Harry and Herbert Miles opened the first known regular film exchange in the US. in 1903. They also owned nickelodeons and in 1906 were among the first to open one in Manhattan.

73. "Convention Hall," *MS*, January 20, 1903, p. 6.

74. "Theatre to be School," *MS*, May 26, 1907, p. 9.

75. "New Playhouse Opens," *MS*, November 23, 1907, p. 9.

76. "Will Wed Tomorrow in Crescent Theater," *BA*, February 21, 1915, p. 17C.

77. Councilman Muth opposed a bill which would extend the time allowed for the construction of the theater after he learned that the builder, Joseph Myerberg, was one of the builders under investigation for faulty construction of war veterans' homes. "Muth Opposes Theater Plan," *MS*, February 10, 1948, p. 5.

78. According to the *BNP* of February 24, 1949, the mural represented the Three Muses and it was lighted at night.

79. "Crest. Baltimore, Md." *1949–50 Theatre Catalog*, p. 79.

80. For a short history and description of the Hilltop Shopping Center and surrounding area, see Gilbert

Sandler, "Riding the Crest," *Baltimore Jewish Times*, June 25, 1999.

81. The name set in the sidewalk, which was visible in the 1970s, has since disappeared.

82. Brooklyn—Curtis Bay Historical Committee, *A History of Brooklyn-Curtis Bay*, 1976, p. 106.

83. Another source said that the remodeling cost $15,000 ("Erect Row of Handsome Houses," *BN*, April 1, 1909, p. 13).

84. *Ibid.*

85. The average movie tickets cost between 12 and 36 cents; a top-price ticket to a vaudeville show at the Maryland Theater cost $1.00.

86. Apparently the real reason for the film not being shown was that it was refused a seal by the state censor board. Pearl Bowser and Louise Spence in their book *Writing Himself into History* (p. 16), write that, "the Maryland State Board of Motion Picture Censors... demanded twenty-three eliminations [from *Birthright*]." They note that the board was "particularly offended by suggestions of miscegenation, the questioning of white authority, and the depiction of racist attitudes of whites in the everyday interactions between the races."

87. "'Deep Harlem' Promoter First Saw Show at the 'Royal,'" *AA*, January 19, 1929, p. 9.

88. Jackie Mabley stopped the show at the Royal when she played there in "Breezy Rhythm" in January 1937.

89. Quoted in John C. White, "Jazz Greats Played at the Royal," *ES*, February 3, 1971, p. D1.

90. It is very difficult to determine the actual number of seats in the Dunbar at any one time. An ad of February 8, 1924, claimed "the addition of nearly 800 seats" and a 1928 article stated that the theater had 719 seats.

91. "In Spite of Handicap," *AA*, December 15, 1928, pp. 8–10.

92. "Round Town in Theatres, *AA*, January 25, 1930, p. 8.

93. "Earle Theatre to Re-Open Friday of This Week," *Ellicott City Times*, September 10, 1942, p. 1.

94. The Earle has been showing adult movies since at least January 1979, when it announced a re-opening with "two adult movies."

95. In December 1895, Fenneman was negotiating to have one of the buildings of the Atlanta Exposition moved to Baltimore to be used as the theater at Electric Park, but no further reference to this has been found.

96. "Things Theatrical. Suburban Amusement Resort at Electric Park," *MS*, February 6, 1896, p. 7.

97. "Electric Park Opened," *BA*, June 9, 1896, p. 8.

98. "Things Theatrical. Suburban Amusement Resort At Electric Park," *MS*, February 6, 1896, p. 7.

99. "Electric Park," *BA*, May 26, 1907, p. A10. Strictly speaking, the Kinetograph was the camera that took motion pictures which were then shown on a Kinetoscope.

100. In a 1963 article, Robert W. Ward provided a vivid description of the Johnstown Flood: Patrons sat in an auditorium facing a stage where a scale-model of the Johnstown area was set up. A narrator came onstage and began describing the town. In the middle of his description, he would suddenly say, "Oh, my, it looks like a storm's coming up." Then there would be thunder and flashes of lightning. Unperturbed, the narrator would continue describing the town. Soon, he would note that it had begun to rain. Lights played across the model town to make it appear like rain was falling. And suddenly the narrator would shout, "Great God! The dam has burst!" Then, as Ward described it, "Pandemonium broke loose on the stage. The little buildings leaned, then toppled. Bridges fell in heaps. Lights simulated rushing, rising water, beamed across the wreckage. The narrator, screaming over the racket, described the disaster with doom-tinged words." "I Remember When... I piloted that Electric Park Shoot-the-Chute," *MS*, December 8, 1963, *Sun* Magazine, p. 2.

101. Between 1906 and 1910 Fenneman had been managing vaudeville shows at the Suburban.

102. The church building was sold to a real estate dealer in April 1902. His plans called for gutting the building and converting it into an arcade with 28 stores arranged on three new floors. In December 1902, plans had changed, and the church was going to become a theater. The estimated cost of the alterations was $15,000.

103. "Theatres Last Night," *MS*, February 24, 1903, p. 6.

104. Fawcett had a stock company at the Lyceum at the same time, but he agreed to organize a second company at the Oriole.

105. Scarlett's stock company had leased the theater for the 1903–04 season, but in October after the fires, the company was disbanded. A watchman at the theater said that Scarlett had paid him $25 to help him set the fires. Scarlett had just had problems with his leading lady, Miss Mabel Bardine, who refused to let him kiss her in a play. She said, "I am a Southern woman, and for reasons known to me I refuse to allow Mr. Scarlett to kiss me." Scarlett said, "The fact that Miss Bardine would not let me kiss her on the mouth shows that she is headstrong." Scarlett dismissed the headstrong Miss Bardine from his company following the incident.

106. "Theatres Last Night, Blaney's Opens with 'Child Slaves of New York,'" *MS*, September 27, 1904, p. 7.

107. Jacques Kelly, "No Curtain Calls for Blaney's Theater," *ES*, November 3, 1986, p. D1.

108. "Empire Theatre Opens," *MS*, December 26, 1911, p. 12.

109. "Building Boom Just Pauses to Take a Break," *MS*, August 13, 1911, Part 4, p. 5 and "New Empire Ready," *BA*, December 23, 1911, p. 16.

110. "Palace Theatre Opens," *MS*, May 27, 1913, p. 5.

111. "Palace Theater," *BA*, May 25, 1913, p. C21.

112. "Vaudeville at Palace," *BA*, March 19, 1914, p. 16. Watching even a refined burlesque show must have done wonders for the morale of the old soldiers.

113. It is difficult to see how a film like this could be spectacular.

114. "Burlesque's Vigor Here Holds Good," *MS*, February 17, 1929, p. Sect. 2, p. 1.

115. Support for a garage from Ford's and the Hippodrome management may have saved the building. There was a move to tear the theater down and build a parking lot on the site, but manager John A. Little of Ford's said that "a sightly building for housing cars, would be much better than an open-air parking lot which the promoters could establish without any ordinance." "May Put Open Parking Lot on Theater Site," *ES*, October 5, 1937, p. 36.

116. Quoted in "I. Rappaport Opens His New Theatre," *Boxoffice*, January 25, 1947, p. 54.

117. "Palace Theater Sold, Will Be Modern Movie," *BNP*, January 9, 1946, p. 21.

118. Bach was a well-known New York metallurgist and designer. He died in 1957. He was born in Breslau, Germany, but later settled in New York. His metal sculp-

ture is found throughout that city, notably at Rockefeller Center, on the Empire State Building, and the Chase Manhattan Building.

119. These compositions were described in a 1947 article: "The first of these works of art greets one upon entering the lobby. Placed over the door it depicts Drama ... exemplified by the Mask — the actor — in the figure of a woman; and the spectator represented by isolated eyes, forming a half circle around the composition. I have to confess that I always thought this was a modernistic clock. At the right and left of the lobby are two gardens — which Mr. Bach refers to as plant compositions. These each contain one Bach piece. A similar garden, larger in scale is located in the mezzanine lobby and contains a number of Bach compositions. Live plantings of cacti and other plants suitable to the unusual growing conditions are to be found in these indoor gardens." Carl B. Sherred, "Showman Achieves His Lifelong Dream in Baltimore's Beautiful New Town Theatre," *Showmen's Trade Review*, March 1, 1947, p. E17. Rappaport was appalled at the cost of the metal sculpture, but Baylinson insisted that they were needed.

120. The choice of a theater for Cinerama was between the Stanley and the Town. The Stanley Warner Corporation decided that the Town could be more easily remodeled since the back rows of seats were closer to the screen. The Stanley was just too big.

121. Quoted in *MPW*, September 11, 1920, p. 262.

122. There is no record in Junchen (1985) of a Kimball being installed in the Fayette Theater.

123. Call from Jeanie, "Over 50 at 10" with Paul Potter, WITH, December 9, 1992.

124. "Plays Gay Air Averting Panic as Film Blast Terrorizes 300," *BA*, September 16, 1925, p. 1.

125. "Ford's New Opera House — Its Formal Opening," *MS*, October 4, 1871, p. 2.

126. McElfatrick had designed Charles Frohman's Empire Theater at 1428 Broadway, which opened in January 1893.

127. "Before the Footlights," *Sunday Herald*, September 3, 1903, p. 7.

128. Quoted in J. William Joynes, "Thousand and One First Nights," *BA*, February 5, 1961, Section E, p. 1.

129. *Ibid.*

130. Architects Wight and Lockhart asked for the appointment of a receiver in March 1924, claiming that they were owed $300 for designing a new theater for the Fremont Amusement Company.

131. For an interesting account of attending the Garden in the 1950s, see Jim Sizemore's article, "I Remember 'Double Feature' Movies in South Baltimore," *The Sun Magazine*, February 1, 1981, pp. 24–25.

132. The "down-and-out escape" was technically called the Kirker-Bender Patent Spiral Slide Fire-Escape. According to John Kilduff, one night a fight broke out between two patrons at the Jardin de Danse. One hit the other and knocked him back through some curtains and into the mouth of the down-and-out chute. He disappeared, and a few moments later, passers-by on Park Ave. were amazed to see a huge dust ball with arms and legs come hurtling out of a doorway at the back of the theater.

133. The great well-hole unexpectedly provided young hooligans with an ideal site from which to drop paper cups filled with water onto unsuspecting patrons seated below.

134. "Throng at Opening of Garden Theater," *Star*, February 1, 1915 (Extra Edition), p. 8.

135. Evidently the management had not seen many Japanese girls.

136. The Garden seated about 2,700 compared with the Maryland's approximately 1,500.

137. This film was my first experience with 3-D. It scared the pants off me. The first flaming arrow fired in glorious color into the audience seemed to land in the seat next to me and I dove for cover, sure that I could smell the burning cushion.

138. William Ballauf was a popular manager. He had started out a few blocks away from the Gayety as an usher at the Holliday Street Theater under John Albaugh. He moved to the Lyceum when Albaugh opened that theater. He returned to the Holliday Street Theater, where he was treasurer under Kernan & Rife. After that he toured with his own melodrama company. He also managed Fred Irwin's Majestics.

139. Nickel probably obtained a mortgage on the theater which he paid off in the fall of 1924 when title to the theater was conveyed to him. "Hon" Nickel — the "Hon" came from the German name Hans — was born in Germany. His mother came to Baltimore with her youngest son and established a small dairy business in the Canton area. As she was able to save some money, she brought another child over until eventually six of her seven children were here. Nickel was running a small bar in Canton when he bought the Nachman Hotel on East Baltimore Street. That put him in touch with theatrical people. He later purchased the Folly, Gayety and Embassy theaters. Interview with Nickel's daughter, Marian McKew, and granddaughter, Jackie Nickel, Essex, Md., May 5, 1994.

140. Craig Morrison, "Gayety Fire, Balto.," *Marquee*, February 1970, p. 6.

141. Interview, William Lange, Baltimore, Md., February 5, 1981.

142. For a more detailed statement of the management's feelings about Miss McCoy, see "The Gertrude M'Coy," *BA*, October 24, 1915, p. C20.

143. Miss McCoy — her real name was Gertrude Lyons McRae — did not return to live out her days in Baltimore. She returned to her native Georgia after her movie career ended and died in Atlanta in July 1967.

144. F. H. Richardson, the projection editor for *MPW*, was lavish in his praise of the theater and projectionist after a visit in the summer of 1916: "...at the Gertrude McCoy theater I found a progressive operator [F. Clarence Grote], and up-to-date equipment, and a ... spacious well-planned operating room.... The equipment ... consists of a General Electric mercury arc rectifier, two arc controllers, volt and ammeter, two Baird projectors and a motor-driven rewind, with cleaner. Over the roof is a skylight.... The operating room floor is of concrete and the walls are ... plastered. There was a fire proof film case ... metal drawers and cabinet for tools and a water stand containing a five gallon bottle of iced mineral water.... The Gertrude McCoy theater is managed by Frederick Clement Weber, who is a close student of all that pertains to the exhibition of motion pictures. He supplies friend Grote with all things necessary to put the finished result on the screen. The only criticism ... was against the white operating room walls.... I explained ... the advantage to be gained through painting the walls black.... The Gertrude McCoy theater seats 500, projects a 17-foot picture on a Gold fibre screen at 100 feet. The picture lacks a black border, since it fills the entire screen, and this is, of course, not in keeping with the best practice."

145. Goldberg was born around 1884. He was a news-

boy until around 1905, when he opened a small confectionery in Walbrook. In 1913 he decided to build a theater on North Avenue in Walbrook and the following year he opened Goldberg's Theater. In 1917 he was one of the founders of the Exhibitors' League of Maryland. In the same year, he leased the Gordon Theater and bought the Walbrook Theater. In the early 1920s he purchased a part interest in the Harford and operated the Pennington in Curtis Bay and the Strand on Howard Street.

146. "Goldfield Draws Well," *AA*, December 11, 1915, p. 6. The theater was owned at this time by Joseph A. Winkel and J. H. A. Strodel; the projectionist was Charles A. Debrick.

147. There is some confusion about the name. The name on the plans was "Dean," but newspaper advertisements and people who worked there called it the "Jean."

148. "Outdoors Movie to Open Sunday," *MS*, May 12, 1939, p. 5.

149. The Highland Amusement Company was incorporated in May 1913 by Isidore Bucher, William C. F. Wagner, and William Schluderberg.

150. "Grand Theatre Opened," *Baltimore County Sentinel*, November 15, 1913, p. 1.

151. "Handsome Theatre For Highlandtown," *Baltimore County Sentinel*, May 3, 1913, p. 1. The house at 515 was described as one of the oldest in Highlandtown, having been built around 1863.

152. Between 1916 and 1923, the American Photo Player Company purchased a large number of Wicks theater organs and sold them with a nameplate bearing the inscription, "The Robert-Morton. Manufactured by The Robert-Morton Company. Factories. Highland, Ill. Van Nuys, Calif. Division of the American Photo Player Co." (Junchen:695)

153. "New Theater for Amateurs,"*MS*, September 13, 1925, Pt. 2, Section 1, p. 1.

154. There is confusion over who designed the Gwynn. According to *MPH, Better Theaters*, February 13, 1932, p. 53, John J. Zink had prepared plans for a $175,000 theater for F. Price, Jr. The following month, again according to *MPH* (March 12, 1932) p. 53, Frank Price Jr. and J. S. Cook were interested in erecting a one-story, 80 × 150 foot, brick motion picture theater on this site. The architect was named as Edwin H. C. Browne and the theater was going to cost about $175,000. The following year, also according to *MPH* (April 8, 1933) p. 62, Robert Kanter's Gwynn Amusement Company had plans by Kubitz and Koenig for a $20,000, one-story, 46 by 150 foot, brick movie theater at the same location. Finally, the *Daily Record* of September 26, 1933 names the architect as Myers and the engineers as Kubitz and Koenig.

155. However, according to *American Contractor* (September 14, 1912), Laferty was also the architect of the 1912 remodeling.

156. The church had been seriously damaged by a fire before the decision to convert it into a theater was made. Ironically, some very early motion pictures had been shown at the Harlem Park M.E. Church at the beginning of the century.

157. Letter, Charles G. Reigner to Howard W. Bryant, July 31, 1928, Baltimore City Archives, RG 9, S18, 05–51.

158. According to an item in the *News Post* (July 20, 1964), the screen at the Harundale Mall Cinema was second in size only to the one at the Radio City Music Hall in New York.

159. Albers v. Ertel, Baltimore County Circuit Court, June 25, 1913, Maryland State Archives, Baltimore County Judicial Liber WPC No. 248, f. 84 *et seq.*

160. Julius Myerberg was also named as the architect of the Hill.

161. "Install World's First Multi-Channel Transistorized Sound System," The Modern Theatre Section, *Boxoffice*, February 6, 1961, pp. 28–29.

162. Interview, Aaron Seidler, Washington, D.C., October 31, 1991.

163. The Union League Park occupied the block between East McComas and East Donaldson streets and South Charles and Light streets. The entrance was at the corner of McComas and Light.

164. The Eutaw House was built in 1835. It had hosted many well-known guests over the years including Gen. William Henry Harrison, Henry Clay, Daniel Webster, Admiral Farragut, and President Grant.

165. It appears that the first architect selected to draw plans for the theater was Michael McElfatrick. *Engineering News Record*, May 3, 1913 and [*BN*], April 17, 1913. Lamb was named as the architect by September 1913 and all of the plans were signed by Lamb.

166. "New Playhouse Is Nearing Completion," *BN*, August 23, 1914, p. 9.

167. *Ibid.*

168. According to Junchen, I:406, 408, the Hippodrome had at least two Moller organs. Opus 1766 was a two-manual, 17-rank organ purchased in 1914. Later that same year a two-manual, 16-rank organ (Opus 1856) was purchased for $3,100. In 1918, Opus 1856 was enlarged to three manuals and renumbered as Opus 2563.

169. Showings of films like *Birth* were usually portents of disaster for a theater.

170. Norman Clark, "Hipp Closes For Three-Week Period To Don New Garb," *BNP*, June 26, 1941, p. 18. For more on the renovation, see the Baltimore *Home News*, July 2 and July 17, 1941.

171. There were no legitimate theaters in town at the time; Ford's had been demolished in February.

172. Rappaport watched the opening performances of the shows very closely. He had the performers delete all off-color material and dialect jokes. Here is what he had to say when he reopened the Hippodrome in 1931: "People must feel that every week at the Hippodrome will be a pleasant week without inquiring what the bill might be or what star or picture is being presented. The new Hippodrome will be synonymous with the best in entertainment and will be presented at prices which I am sure are within the reach of the most modest purse, and in an atmosphere of cozy luxury such as Baltimore's newest theatre possesses in every nook and corner. The Hippodrome is to be Baltimore's family theatre and at no time will anything be presented on its stage or screen that won't be fit for every member of the family from mother down to the youngest of the kiddies." "Owners Like Baltimore," *BN*, August 28, 1931, p. 21.

173. Data on the performers at the Hippodrome and their salaries are available in manuscript notebooks maintained by the theater's management. These notebooks are in the Hippodrome Collection (MS 34) at the Jewish Museum of Maryland. Some of the salaries for appearances onstage at the Hippodrome that are recorded in these books are: Abbott & Costello (rated as "VG+"): 4-22-1938—$500, 7-26-1945—$9,000; Andrews Sisters (VG+): 7-23-1942—$5,791, 7-7-1949—$12,500; Milton Berle Crazy Show (VG+): 5-27-1948—$6,509; Eddy Duchin & Orchestra (VG): 2-5-1937—$6,500; Spike

Jones Orchestra: 5-3-1945—$8,861.44; Red Skelton (VG+): 12-30-1948—$1,000.

174. Mary Markey, "Restore the Hippodrome," *MS*, November 24, 1991, p. 2N.

175. The plans called for the Hippodrome to become a 2,300-seat theater, big enough to handle the new shows that could not be performed in the Mechanic or Lyric.

176. Hardy Holzman Pfeiffer has a long history of successful theater restorations, including the New Amsterdam, Ohio, and Hawaii theaters.

177. Certainly its name is an inseparable part of a theater. It is the linguistic peg on which years of memories hang and cannot be discarded for a paltry $5 million. Many of us militantly refuse to refer to the magnificent theater on North Howard Street as the Stanton; it will always be the Stanley. One writer to the *Sun* said it well, "...to those of us who remember her in her heyday, the theater will always be 'the Hippodrome.'" (Richard B. Crystal, "Theater is forever 'the Hippodrome,'" *MS*, June 16, 2002).

178. The seating in the balcony didn't fare so well. Many people complained that the seats were too close together and their knees bumped against the backs of the seat row in front of them. Others said that there was something wrong with the angle of the seats. Hopefully this is temporary, and the balcony seating will be modified to make it more comfortable.

179. However, according to a newspaper article, the Hiway was going to open with a Kiddie Show on October 26. "New 'Hiway' to Open with 'Kiddie Show'" *Baltimore County Observer*, October 17, 1946, p. 1.

180. "Local Matters," *MS*, August 4, 1874, p. 1.

181. The scoreboard consisted of a complete reproduction of the game on a large board. Plays were telegraphed by means of a direct wire between the stage of the theater and the baseball grounds and then depicted on the board.

182. "Booth Forgot He Was to Be Killed," *Baltimore Star*, March 8, 1916, p. 15.

183. "He transformed Baltimore theaters with off-screen attractions," *MS*, August 28, 1983, D1, D5.

184. These have been identified as Heywood-Wakefield's TC 706 Airflo "Rocking Chair" Loges.

185. "New Theater Will Specialize in Best 'International Films,'" *MS*, October 14, 1951, p. 22.

186. Much of the material on the original Horn Theater 1909–1920 is from the author's article "Nickelodeon Finances and Operations 1909–1911: The Horn Theater, Baltimore, Maryland," *Marquee*, vol. 13: no. 1 (First Quarter 1981), pp. 21–22.

187. "Flickering Movies of 1913 Recalled," *ES*, April 26, 1940 [m].

188. Also given as 118 Shawan Road.

189. United Artists had signed an agreement in 1995 to put an 11-screen theater in the Hunt Valley Mall, but that project did not develop.

190. Freund had prepared plans for a large theater and stores for the Ideal Theater Company in 1921, but the plans were held up. (*American Builder*, September 10, 1921). In July 1923, architect Beall had plans for a one-story, 140 × 125 foot brick theater to cost $30,000 and he was taking bids on the general contract. (*MPN*, July 7, 1923, p. 120).

191. The Ideal was offered for sale at an auction on May 24, 1960; see *MS*, May 15, 1960, p. 43D.

192. Ella Lott Goodman, "I Remember ... Open-Air Movies 40 Years Ago," *Sun Magazine*, October 27, 1957, p. 2.

193. I am grateful to Bill Hewitt for providing this information.

194. Another source gave the size of the theater as 40 by 90 feet (*ES* November 25, 1910, Real Estate Column).

195. "Dundalk's Second Movie House Set to Open Today," *Community Press*, November 22, 1940, p. 1.

196. [Calvert Silverblatt], "Reel Facts," *The Federationist*, February 25, 1955, p. 3.

197. Interview, Irwin Cohen, Reisterstown, Md., December 2, 1998.

198. "Plans for Germania," *MS*, October 10, 1912, p. 5.

199. "Roslyn Newest Theater Opens Here January 16," *BNP*, December 29, 1941, p. 12.

200. "Reel Facts," *The Federationist*, February 4, 1955, p. 6.

201. *MPW*, February 10, 1917, p. 883.

202. "Overheard in the Wings," *MS*, February 14, 1918, p. 5.

203. "Norman Clark, Nothing in Particular," *BN*, May 12, 1918, p. 18. For more on the Liberty Theaters, see: Alfred Morton Githens, "The Army Libraries and Liberty Theaters," *Architectural Forum*, Vol. 29 (1918): 15–19 and Weldon B. Durham, "The U.S. Army's Liberty Theatres 1917–1919," *Players*, Fall/Winter 1974, pp. 12–17.

204. Githens, *op. cit.*, p. 19.

205. John Carlin was born in Frederick, Maryland, in 1880. He worked in a country store until 1899, when he enlisted in the army. After a tour in the Philippines he returned to civilian life and got a law degree in 1905. He formed a construction company to help rebuild the burned district. He later acquired large tracts in northwest Baltimore where he built moderate-priced homes.

206. For more information, see the write-up under the Circle Theater at Park Circle.

207. This was similar to the arrangement in several early Washington, D.C. movie theaters, although the Washington theaters were divided down the middle by a low wall.

208. Interview with William Lange, Sr., and William Lange, Jr., Baltimore, Md., June 23, 1976.

209. The Guild was founded in Washington by Nathan Machat in the mid–1920s. It showed its first films at the Wardman Park Theater in Northwest Washington in May 1926 and opened the Little Theater there in April 1927.

210. The bowling alleys appear to have been at 519 North Howard Street, two doors south of the theater. They were owned by Wilbert Robinson and John J. McGraw, who were members of the original Baltimore Orioles. Apparently the manager of the bowling alleys, Frank Van Sant, came up with the idea to cut down a set of tenpins. Duckpins was being played in Baltimore as early as July 1900.

211. "Haven for Highbrows," *ES*, December 9, 1927, p. 31.

212. Norman Clark, "Another Film Theatre Opens," *BN*, December 9, 1927, p. 29.

213. Moviegraphs Corporation operated the Fifty-fifth Street Playhouse in New York and several other movie theaters throughout the country.

214. For more on the Fayette Street store, see the ads and articles in the *BA* and *MS* of March 9 and 10, 1908.

215. Architect George Stebbins also prepared plans for this theater.

216. The brick building that housed the Maryland Medical College had earlier been the home of Lester's School for Boys, a dancing school, and the Milton Academy.

217. According to one article, it was going to exceed the Victoria in size and number of seats, but this was apparently merely hype and the Lord Baltimore, as originally built, seated a little more than 1,000. The Victoria seated about 1,400. "Will Soon Build Huge New Theater," *News*, August 2, 1912, p. 15. The largest theater in the metropolitan area outside downtown was the Grand {2}, which seated 1,600 and opened a few days before the Lord Baltimore.

218. Interview, Fred Schmuff, December 11, 1986. It is difficult to believe that architects and builders would forget a projection booth, yet this story persists in many locations. The Knickerbocker Theater in Washington, DC, was another theater where, according to legend, the projection booth was forgotten.

219. According to *MPW*, vol. 8, Jan.–Jun. 1911, p. 185, all of the Lubin theaters in Philadelphia, Baltimore, and Cincinnati were designed by Philadelphia architect Koenig.

220. "New Theatre to Open," *MS*, August 18, 1908, p. 7.

221. "New Theatre Ready, "*MS*, August 25, 1908, p. 21.

222. The area known as Calverton Heights was one of the highest points around the city. Just before the park opened, the Pennsylvania Railroad was allowed to remove a huge poplar tree from park property. It measured 21 feet in circumference at its base and was 196 feet high. It was considered a natural lightning rod and had been struck many times. Even after the tree was taken down, the area was subject to severe lightning. Two months after its removal, a savage storm hit Baltimore and lightning demolished the double roller coaster that was being constructed at the park.

223. "Luna Park Opens," *MS*, May 29, 1910, p. 9.

224. I am grateful to Earl Pruce, formerly of the *Baltimore News-American*, for digging into the Paragon Picture Parlor puzzle and sharing his findings with me.

225. The Wednesday Club was a prosperous amateur music and dramatic club dating from about 1875. The drop curtain for the club's stage was painted by Mr. W. C. Schaeffer of Ford's Theater.

226. Albaugh was one of the great theater men in the late 19th century. He was born in Baltimore in 1837. He began his theatrical career as an actor, making his professional debut in *The Fall of Tarquin* at the old Museum at Baltimore and Calvert streets. He acted for almost 30 years and then turned to management. At one time or another he managed theaters in St. Louis, Albany, Washington, Louisville, Montgomery, Alabama, and Baltimore. He married the well-known actress Mary Lomax Mitchell. His son, John, was also a noted actor. John W. Albaugh died at his daughter's home in Jersey City on February 11, 1909.

227. "Opening of the Lyceum," *BA*, September 25, 1887, p. 3.

228. However, in a letter to the editor of the *Sunday Sun Magazine* (December 30, 1956), Ms. Ottilie Sutro wrote that the exterior of the Lyceum was that of the original Wednesday Club building.

229. I am also indebted to Earl Pruce for much of the history of the Lyceum Theater contained in this article.

230. "To Play at Albaugh's," *MS*, September 17, 1905, p. 14.

231. The cost of tickets to *Way Down East* was astronomical: matinees cost between 50 cents and $1.50 while evenings cost between 50 cents and $2.00. The ads said that the high prices were due to the cost and length of the film and "iron-bound contracts."

232. A photograph of the building suggests that it was a wooden structure. An article in the *Baltimore County Sentinel* (April 6, 1912, p. 4) says the theater was to be of concrete and frame construction.

233. There were eight duckpin bowling alleys under the Lyceum. The pins had wide rubber bands around them to keep the noise down.

234. The other members of the trio were the Kernan (later Congress) Hotel and the Auditorium Theater.

235. Kernan placed a box containing a silver plate, copies of the Sunpaper, programs from the various Kernan theaters, and various medals and other objects in the cornerstone.

236. The art gallery contained some 200 pictures. In addition to Thomas M. Henny's "And Every Soul Was Saved," there was an early painting of George Washington by Rembrandt Peale and a collection of animal studies by Dicksee. Kernan claimed that the painting of Washington had been found in the wreckage of Peale's Baltimore Museum after it burned in 1874. Kernan's collection also included such memorabilia as a weekly statement of the stock company at the Holliday Street Theater signed by Joseph Jefferson, a letter from Melba, and programs dating back to 1775. Schanberger was negotiating with the Actors' Society of America in 1914 to give some of the collection to them to hang in their New York clubrooms as a memorial to James Kernan. In May 1939, 56 pieces of the collection, including Henny's painting, were auctioned off. Only three of the eight oil paintings offered for sale attracted bidders; the centerpiece "And Every Soul Was Saved" was offered to the city in lieu of taxes owed. It languished in a basement for a number of years, then, in 1960 it was found by a art dealer in an auction house. A buyer was found and arrangements were made to have it restored. Sadly, before the restoration could take place, the weight of the paint caused the painting to disintegrate.

237. "New Theater Opens Tonight," *BA*, October 19, 1903, p. 12.

238. The Musical Union had demanded a 50-percent pay raise for the Maryland's musicians and Schanberger could only give them a 25-percent raise. On August 26, just before they were to play, six of the 12 women hired failed to show up at the theater. There was speculation that they had been "spirited away." The remaining six did a good job.

239. In 1993, the architect of the Capitol decided it was not classy enough for the nation's capitol and wanted to take it down. Senator Alan Simpson, then the Republican minority whip, whose office was next to the Small Rotunda, said he liked the chandelier. The chandelier was still there in 2002.

240. The original address was 2431 Greenmount Avenue.

241. The Metropolitan Theater Company was incorporated in December 1921. The president of the company was Dr. Frederick W. Schanze, who ran the drugstore and Schanze's Theater cater-cornered across the street from the new theater.

242. Other estimates for the cost of this theater ranged from $125,000 to $500,000.

243. "Newest Cinema Playhouse Here Cost $325,000," *MS*, December 17, 1922, Part 2, Section 3, p. 7.

244. One organ at the Metropolitan was a three-manual Robert-Morton built in 1922 by the Wicks Organ Company. At some point in its history, the organ was moved from the center of the orchestra pit to the side. It was purchased around 1965 by Arthur R. Aldrich. Aldrich's son gave the organ to the Free State

Organ Society. The Society has restored the organ and installed it in the Rice Auditorium at Spring Grove Hospital in Catonsville, where it is played regularly.

245. "New Midway Theatre Has Grand Opening," *Baltimore County Observer*, September 27, 1945, p. 1.

246. This postcard was published on p. 12 of *Anne Arundel County History Notes*, XXX:3 (April 1999).

247. The bowling alley may have been built in what had earlier been the theater.

248. According to one source, Pahl had a third open-air theater at Monument Street and Montford Avenue.

249. Brennen Jensen, "Brickbats," *Baltimore City Paper*, October 24, 2001. The architect complained that he had not had enough money to do everything he wanted, such as add more lighting, improve the sight-lines, use a better grade of carpet and put fabric on the walls. He described the theater as, "a triumph of economy." R. H. Gardner, "New Theater Has Two-Type Stages," *MS*, January 15, 1967, p. 6D. Inexplicably, the regional meeting of the American Institute of Architects gave Johansen an award for the theater in 1968.

250. "Mt. Royal to be Open to Patrons Tuesday," *BN*, September 5, 1915, p. 12.

251. *Boxoffice*, June 6, 1977, p. 16.

252. *Baltimore Magazine*, November 1979, p. 144.

253. The theaters actually opened to the press and special invitees on December 11.

254. Corinne F. Hammett, "Downtown at the Movies," *NA*, December 13, 1985, p. D1.

255. Jacques Kelly, "Harbor Park: An Architectural Snorefest with Nine Movie Screens," *NA*, December 6, 1985, p. 5A.

256. The Concordia Opera House was located on the west side of Eutaw Street just south of Redwood. It burned on June 10, 1891.

257. For a detailed history of the first three decades of the Lyric, see Edwin Litchfield Turnbull, "Baltimore's Music Hall," *ES*, February 16, 1920, p. 8.

258. The mall was designed by D'Agostino Izzo Quirk of Somerville, Mass., and ID8, a division of RTKL Associates of Baltimore.

259. The columns and statues are made of concrete reinforced with glass-fiber and resemble ancient weathered sandstone.

260. Frederick E. Beall was named as the architect in *American Contractor* of May 21, 1921, but he probably just prepared one early set of plans for the theater.

261. *MPW*, October 15, 1921, p. 800.

262. The first ad for the Eden did not appear in the *AA* until February 18, 1950.

263. The New Theatre Company had been incorporated March 26, 1910, for $200,000.

264. According to the *BN*, this mural was "by Eckhardt of Chicago, executed by Oskar Gross." "New Theater Will Be Opened Dec. 12," *BN*, December 3, 1910, p. 2.

265. "New Theatre Ready," *MS*, December 1, 1910, p. 4.

266. "New Theatre Ready," *ES*, December 16, 1910, p. 9.

267. "Banquet on Stage of New Theater," *BN*, December 17, 1910, p.14.

268. Another source, describing what seems to be the same feature, said that "Where the lobby and this arched recess meet will be on each side a specially modeled life-size figure of a fourteenth century halberdier in full costume of the period. These will stand guard at the entrance." "New Theater To Be Erected Soon," *Baltimore Star*, April 23, 1910, p. 5.

269. "New Theater Will Be Opened Dec. 12," *BN*, December 3, 1910, p. 2.

270. "New Theatre Ready," *MS*, December 1, 1910, p. 4.

271. This was probably opus 2240, a three-manual, 14 rank Moller organ.

272. "New Reopens Tomorrow," *MS*, September 4, 1921, p. Part 6, p. 3.

273. Charles Whitehurst organized a repertory company, known as "The Whitehurst Players," featuring Betty Ross Clark and Ben Taggart to act in the plays. The live productions lasted only about a month; movies were back by May 8, 1922.

274. According to Donald Kirkley, Mechanic decided against tearing the theater down and building a new one from the ground up because he feared that bad weather would hold up outside construction. Using the shell of the original theater, the contractors could work in any kind of weather. Donald Kirkley, "Film Notes," *MS*, December 23, 1945, Section A, p. 7.

275. "Baltimore First Run to Be Reconstructed," *Boxoffice*, October 20, 1945, p. 56D.

276. "Face Changes for Camelot," Baltimore *News-American*, November 5, 1967, p. 8H.

277. One source stated that Abe Cohen bought the building at 524–526 Eastern Avenue and then moved the theater up to 416 Eastern Avenue.

278. The orchestral organ was a mechanical orchestra operated by one person. It could imitate a full band or stringed orchestra, reproducing the sounds of an organ, piano, fife and drum corps, bugle, violin and other instruments. "Mechanical Orchestra," *BN*, September 14, 1913, p. 11.

279. Quoted by Elmer Nolte in an August 24, 1990 interview.

280. Broumas Theaters was operated by John Broumas, one of the first exhibitors to see the possibilities in building movie theaters in suburban shopping centers. He and two partners opened a theater in the newly built Wheaton Plaza Shopping Center in 1962. After the success of that theater, Broumas spent the 1960s ringing the city of Washington with a number of large shopping-center theaters. His expansion into the Baltimore suburbs was probably limited by financial difficulties his organization experienced in 1966. For more on Broumas see, Headley (1999), p. 170 et seq.

281. "Poles Have New Theatre, " *ES*, April 25, 1919, p. 21.

282. Matysek was a native of Czechoslovakia. He was born in 1892 and came to Baltimore with his family when he was seven years old. In 1922 he held the title of "The Strongest Man in America." After various weight-lifting feats, including lifting two boys on a bicycle with one hand, he joined the Baltimore City Police Department. Matysek died in 1963.

283. The original seating capacity could have been as low as 79.

284. Much of the information in this article is taken from Charles E. Nolte's reminiscences, "I Remember ... The Palace on South Broadway," published in the *MS* Sun magazine, October 7, 1951, p. 2.

285. "Princess Theater Leased by Negro," *BN*, March 26, 1911, p. 7.

286. See Mrs. Ella Hoffmeister, "I Remember When ... The Talkies Walked Off Stage," *MS*, February 26, 1950, p. 2.

287. "Palace Being Enlarged," *BN*, June 8, 1919, p. 24.

288. According to another source, this theater was to be erected at 1524 East Monument Street.

289. It was so similar to the Homewood, which opened five months earlier, that the *Home News* used the exact same descriptions for both theaters. (*Home News* May 23, 1946, p. 23 and October 3, 1946, p. 19.)

290. Michael C. Engelmeyer is also named as the architect.

291. According to the ad for the December 1922 auction, the theater had 700 seats.

292. "New Film Theatre Open to the Public," *MS*, January 8, 1922, Part 6, p. 5.

293. Thomas W. Lamb has also been credited with the design of the Parkway, but this is probably in error. Henry Webb did hire Lamb to prepare plans for a theater that was never built at Gay and Federal Streets in 1917. It is possible that the basic plans were Lamb's and that Wight was simply the local architect of record, although Wight was given full credit for the theater's design in the newspaper ad for the opening of the Parkway. *American Builder* (October 27, 1917) listed Wight and Lamb as joint architects.

294. Slightly different figures were given in an undated Loew's document, probably from the mid–1930s, in the author's possession: total —1,007 (orchestra — 599, balcony — 396, boxes —12).

295. The original design for the French rococo interior of the Parkway strongly resembles the interior of the West End Cinema. Richard Gray in *Cinemas in Britain* (London, 1996, p. 30) described the West End as "certainly the most opulent of London's pre–First World War cinemas." The similarities in the two auditoriums can be seen by comparing the drawing on page 31 of Gray's book with photographs of the Parkway's auditorium. Note especially the pavilion boxes at either end of the balcony and the treatment of the proscenium arch.

296. "Baltimore's Newest House Modeled on West End Cinema, London," *MPN*, October 30, 1915, p. 153.

297. "Business Plus Beauty," *Motography*, October 7, 1916, p. 803.

298. Lamb's plans were elaborate and called for the addition of a stage elevator, an increase in the seating capacity, and the construction of a row of loge boxes in the balcony.

299. "Parkway's Brilliant Anniversary," *MPW*, November 11, 1916, p. 887.

300. "York Theater Opens Saturday Afternoon," *Sun*, October 8, 1922, p. Part 6, p. 10.

301. "Pell Mell Theatre Opens in Baltimore," *MPN*, February 13, 1915, p. 110.

302. The original seating plan was maintained after a wall had been constructed down the middle of the auditorium so that the seats in the right auditorium faced slightly to the left and those in the left auditorium faced slightly to the right. This was somewhat disturbing to those watching a movie.

303. "Plaza to Open Soon," *BN*, September 11, 1921, p. 15.

304. It is unclear if the February 1921 report that the Central Theater Company had purchased a site on Poplar Grove Street near Harlem Avenue for the erection of a 65 × 153-foot brick, stone, and terra cotta theater refers to this enlarging.

305. "Under New Management," *Afro-American*, August 8, 1914, p. [5].

306. "New Management to Open Queen Theatre," *Afro-American*, March 4, 1916, p. [8].

307. Sources are not in agreement about the architect of this theater; one source gives the architect as George S. Childs and another gives the architect as W. O. Sparklin. They did a lot of work together and it is possible that they designed the Rainbow as a team.

308. "Towson's All Grown Up Now, But It Has No Movie House," *MS*, August 13, 1922, p. 6.

309. Regan was a semi-professional vaudeville performer. In 1915, he appeared onstage at the Grand Theater impersonating Walter C. Kelly. He received more applause than any of the other acts that afternoon. He also imitated Irish and African-American dialects.

310. This organ has been identified as a Moller, but there is no record of a Moller organ being sold to the Regent in Junchen's definitive study on theater organs.

311. William E. Ready, "The Week's Theatrical Review. The Opening of the New Regent," *AA*, February 4, 1921, p. 4.

312. "Hornstein Cancels Dempsey Film," *AA*, February 7, 1925, p. 5.

313. "Theater to Open Here June 30th," *NA*, June 27, 1965, p. 7D.

314. Rhett Waldman, "Building Boom in Movie Theaters," Baltimore *News-American*, June 2, 1985, p. 6E.

315. Stephen Hunter, "Movie Action: It's Not Just on the Screen," *MS*, May 19, 1985, 1L.

316. Brown took the City to court after it denied him a building permit. He lost in the Baltimore City Superior Court and on appeal to the Maryland Court of Appeals. For additional information on the appeal, see *Maryland Reports*, vol. 128. 1915–16, p. 129 et seq.

317. Fox was also president of the Mount Royal Amusement Company, which had opened the Mount Royal Theater a year earlier.

318. "Rialto Theater, Baltimore, Md.," *MPW*, December 2, 1916, p. 1328–29.

319. It was probably a 2/9 Kimbal (Junchen, 1985, Vol. 1:254). In Junchen, *op.cit.*, there is a record for a 2/9 Kimball organ being installed in a "Linden Th." The Baltimore Linden Theater was not built until 1938, but the Rialto was built by the Linden Company.

320. *Baltimore Magazine*, November 1979, p. 144.

321. The name Point Breeze was apparently given to the site in 1876 by the wife of Harry McGowan.

322. Kernan had planned to build a rival park on Back River, but opted instead to lease River View and build a hotel on the Back River site.

323. The Metropolitan Railway seems like a version of Hale's Tours. Hale's Tours was described as "a two-car 'house' with an ornate stucco front and cost $7,000, including the projection equipment. Admission was 10 cents; and each car was more or less filled — about 60 passengers — 20 to 75 times a day." Each show lasted 20 to 25 minutes. Hale's Tours was popular in summer amusement parks between 1905 and 1907. For a detailed study of Hale's Tours, see Raymond Fielding, "Hale's Tours: Ultrarealism in the pre–1910 Motion Picture," *Cinema Journal*, Fall 1970, Vol. X, No. 1, pp. 33–47.

324. "A Thrill Per Minute at the Moving Pictures," *MS*, April 9, 1911, Part 4, p. 7.

325. Nelson Robins, "Watching 'Em Strut," *DP*, July 10, 1924, p. 4.

326. An article in 1921 claimed that the Rivoli seated 2,560 and was the largest motion picture theater in town. "Rivoli Theatre Opened," *MS*, January 5, 1921, p. 7; another article in the Gas and Electric Company's *Baltimore Gas and Electric News* of February 1921 gave the seating capacity as 2,250. According to *MPN* in the fall of 1930, the seating capacity was 1,982.

327. The Church of the Messiah was built shortly after the Baltimore Fire of 1904 to replace an earlier

church that had been destroyed by that fire. The last service at the church was held on April 11, 1920.

328. *MPW*, October 29, 1921, pp. 2323, 2325.

329. For more on the orchestra, see, Edmund G. Hammerbacher, "I Remember ... the Golden Age of the Movies in Baltimore," *MS*, December 7, 1958, *Sunday Sun Magazine*, p. 2.

330. "Schanze's Theater Opens," *MS*, December 22, 1912, p. 10.

331. An article in 1947 stated that the Morgan was the only air-conditioned movie house on Pennsylvania Avenue. "Know Your Theatre: Morgan, Cool and Comfortable, Lists Future Picture Programs," *AA*, April 5, 1947, p. 16.

332. One source said it would be called the Cinema Art Theater, but the ads retained the name Morgan.

333. Much of the information in this account is taken from the excellent study of Schanze's Theater prepared for the Penn-North Project by Margaret Ann Hoyert in January 1982.

334. A. F. Bryan interview; quoted in Ken Krach, "Durkee Enterprises: The Evolution and Survival of a Baltimore Movie Theatre Chain," ms., 1984.

335. According to Nancy Tommaso in her article "Screen Gem" (*Baltimore Magazine*, October 1989, pp. 48–55, 104–105), Kiefaber was able to purchase the Senator, which was considered the cream of the Durkee theaters, because the Durkee and Nolte families "went out of their way to make the deal possible."

336. Chris Kaltenbach, "A Big Battle Over 'Pearl Harbor,'" *MS*, May 11, 2001, p. 5E.

337. There were 19 mural paintings throughout the theater.

338. One description of the Stanley (*MPN*, October 7, 1927, p. 1118) reported that at least nine different kinds of marble were used in the theater. These included Brecha, Pavazanna, and Flora for the pilasters and columns, Botchina and Lavanto for the railings and bases, a York Fossil for the black bases of some columns, as well as Tennessee, White Italian, and Rouge Royal.

339. Depkin left the Stanley within a few years of its opening and by 1930, he was the general manager of the Warner theaters in Wisconsin. He died in Florida in 1969. Depkin was one of the most popular and successful movie theater managers in Baltimore. He had started out as an assistant to J. Howard Bennett at the Little Pickwick, where he did such an impressive job that he rapidly moved up the managerial ladder to the New Pickwick, Parkway, McHenry, Metropolitan and finally the Stanley.

340. According to Junchen (1985, Vol. 1:254) the Kimball was a 3/28 instrument.

341. "New State Theatre To Open Saturday," *BA*, April 10, 1927, p. SS8.

342. Interview, Roy Insley, Baltimore, Md., April 20, 1998.

343. Interview, Fred Schmuff, Baltimore, Md., September 14, 1988. For more on Abbott and Costello, see *Lou's on First*, p. 24–29.

344. "To Open Thursday," *BN*, March 12, 1916, p. 16.

345. Some newspaper accounts reported that the East opened on November 17, 1965, but the first ads did not appear until late December, and these indicated that the theater would open on Christmas Day.

346. Constantini spells the owner's name phonetically; it was actually spelled Boccuti.

347. Between 1916 and 1930 he toured the country with a musical "tab" show called "Bill Leicht's Teddy Bear Girls." Joe Penner was with this show at one time. A "tab" or "tabloid" show was a whole show in itself featuring a chorus, song and dance acts, and comedy acts. Bill Leicht's group was billed as "A Musical Tabloid of Merit. 11 People of High Class Musical Comedies. Mostly Girls. Real Comedians." In 1923, Leicht joined with comedian Arthur Gardner and the group was called "Leicht and Gardner's Teddy Bear Girls." Leicht was the producer and director, and he wrote additional music for the shows. The Teddy Bear Girls played numerous small towns on the Gus Sun Circuit. In Baltimore, they played at the Brodie and Grand (in Highlandtown). Among the members of the group were Natalie Knight, Margie Wright, Baby Louise, Bob and Merle Broadley, Johnny Hughes, Mignon Rankin and Billie Tucker.

348. The winning name was suggested by 15 contestants who divided a prize of $15 among themselves.

349. It has been unbelievably difficult to build a movie theater on Madison Ave. Only one of eight projected movie theaters for Madison Ave. was completed, and that one lasted only five years.

350. According to another source, the theater was going to be 39 feet wide by 75 feet deep; the final measurements were 39 by 175 feet.

351. "New Amusement Enterprise," *MS*, February 19, 1909, p. 8.

352. "Baltimore's Peabody Taken by Parkway Company Chain," *MPW*, September 21, 1918, p. 1723.

353. The Wizard may have been open as early as October 1906. An advertisement in the *BN* of October 20, 1912, proclaimed the Wizard had "Baltimore's Best Pictures Since 1906."

354. I did not know precisely why that would have been so sensational in 1908. It seems that a directoire gown had a low-cut neckline, usually short sleeves, and a skirt that hung straight down like a tube from a waistline just below the bust. It sounds kind of attractive to me.

355. *Motography*, July 1911, p. 98.

356. "Picture Garden Opens with Many Surprises," *BN*, July 9, 1911, p. 13.

357. "Shots from Film Row. Picture Garden Greatly Improved," *MS*, October 3, 1920, Part 6, p. 9.

358. "Film Notes," *MS*, May 31, 1942, Section 1, p. 7.

359. There were also Laffmovies in New York and Boston.

360. Lewis operated two theaters in New York and a foreign film theater in Hartford, Connecticut. He had run the Carnegie Theater in New York for many years and given many foreign films their American debuts.

361. Traub was furious at Gettinger for not answering his letter requesting an explanation by return mail. During the court hearing he made constant protests. Finally Magistrate Levin told him, "Mr. Traub, you are not running this court. I am running this court and you are going to listen." "Uncensored 'Dante's Inferno' Brings Theater Man Trouble," *MS*, December 27, 1951; "Showing of Film Without Censor Seal Charged," *BNP*, December 27, 1951; "Censor Violation Ruled Technical," *ES*, January 4, 1952, p. 22.

362. According to *Boxoffice* (July 17, 1937, p. 23), Moe Kohn opened "the old Hindenburg, on North Howard, under the label of the Fine Arts Theatre." One source says it was located next to the Hi-Hat nightclub operated by Bill Mechanic, the brother of Morris Mechanic. Two other sources say it was located in the building formerly occupied by the night club. The Hi-Hat Club opened in 1930 at 844 North Howard Street. The location of the Art Theater, which was operating in June 1942 at the same time as the Roslyn, was listed as 844 N. Howard Street.

363. Insurance maps made before 1900 show the original Lehmann's Hall at 852–858 North Howard. After the 1913 rebuilding, the hall was located between 848 and 856 North Howard. Maps made after the construction of the Roslyn show a club at 848 and the Roslyn from 850–858. Baltimore City real estate tax assessment books for 1935 through 1943 show Lehmann's Hall at 844 to 856 North Howard, but no number 848. Finally, city directories for 1929 and 1930 show Lehmann's Hall at 852 while the 1937, 1940 and 1942 city directories show the Three Arts Theater at 844 and the hall at 848. It looks as if the two buildings at 844 and 846 North Howard were remodeled into a single building before 1935.

364. "New Theater Opened Here," *ES*, September 26, 1935, p. 26.

365. The films were *The World of Susie Wong*, *Sanctuary*, *Fanny*, and *Splendor in the Grass*. However, there was a fifth film, *The Roman Spring of Mrs. Stone*, which opened on December 25.

366. "Charles Theater Renovated," *ES*, December 31, 1969, p. C6.

367. Levy was one of the group that opened the Biograph Theater, a successful repertory theater, in Washington, DC in 1967. He later left that theater and ran the nearby Key Theater, also as a repertory house, from 1973 to 1997.

368. A typical month (November) in the first year of the new Charles featured such disparate films as Alexander Korda's *Richard III*, Truffaut's *Love on the Run*, Fellini's *Satyricon*, Kubrick's *Lolita*, the Marx Brothers in *Duck Soup* and *Animal Crackers*, Hitchcock's *Rebecca*, the X-rated *Emmanuelle*, and John Waters' *Pink Flamingos*.

369. The box office was robbed just a month before the theater closed.

370. The funding package included a loan from the Mercantile Bank, a $485,000, 20-year loan from the State Department of Housing and Community Development, and a $79,000 grant from the city.

371. The description above is based in part on Edward Gunts, "A Landmark Monument in City Cinema," *MS*, April 18, 1999, p. 8F.

372. "New Theater to Have Improved Projection," *ES*, December 13, 1967, p. B10.

373. Towson *Jeffersonian*, February 25, 1928, [2 supplemental unnumbered pages].

374. For some, inexplicable reason, the readers of the *Baltimore City Paper* named the Towson Commons Theater as the best suburban movie theater for 2003.

375. Quoted in "Film Fan Gossip," *ES*, January 17, 1927, p. 4.

376. *MS*, December 29, 1908, p. 1.

377. Joe Brodie purchased the old organ for $2,100 and moved it to his Brodie Theater in South Baltimore.

378. The total cost of the theater and ground was estimated at $45,000. Much of the money to build the Walbrook Theater came from residents of the Walbrook neighborhood.

379. "The Walbrook Theater, Baltimore, Md.," *MPW*, August 5, 1916, p. 938.

380. The spectacular fire destroyed nearly the entire block bounded by East Baltimore Street, Jones Falls, Front and Plowman streets. The total loss was about $10,000 for the buildings on Baltimore Street with the Kernans investment in the opera house put at $8,000. "Local Matters. The Baltimore Opera House Destroyed," *MS*, October 13, 1874, p. 1.

381. Carroll Dulaney, "Baltimore Day By Day," *BN Post*, July 27, 1945, p. 23.

382. "Jealousy, Says 'Hon,'" *MS*, January 23, 1919, p. 8. The language must have been pretty strong to demoralize soldiers and sailors. In fact a group of soldiers stationed at Fort McHenry wrote in support of the Folly concluding, "Where does this officer get that stuff about injuring our morals when we have seen 'Wee, Wee, Marie?" According to "Hon" Nickel there was nothing wrong with the show the captain complained about, "we didn't even have a 'cooch.'" Nickel said that he was taking in $2,000 to $3,000 a week and would not stand for any "raw stuff" in his theater "to queer it."

383. Schoenlein was born in Baltimore in 1883. He used the name Americus, a blend of American and Augustus, and at age 16 managed to last more than 15 minutes in the ring with Harvey Parker, the welterweight champion of the world. He became the light heavyweight champion wrestler of the world after defeating Charley Olsen in 1910. He died at the age of 74 in July 1958. For more on Americus see, "Americus Caught Off His Guard by Woman Reporter — Recovers," *MS*, March 8, 1914, p. 3, and "400 'East Baltimore Boys' Fete The Nickel-Beer Days, *MS*, April 28, 1950, p. 36. Shad Link also became a professional wrestler.

384. Many people have commented on the preference for plumper women in the theater of the late 19th century. An anonymous writer to the *Evening Sun* of January 20, 1932 (p. 15) described them this way, "The audiences ... liked their women at least 'pleasingly plump' ... They wore tights, much bare flesh being taboo even in the variety houses. They also wore corsets tightly laced so that the girls resembled a bloated spider or gave the general effect of an hour glass. " Billy Watson's "Beef Trust," was a burlesque act that featured voluptuous young women.

385. Norman Clark, "Mr. Arliss Keeps His Word," *BN*, April 2, 1928, p. 9.

386. "Old Folly Theater Ruins to Be Razed," *MS*, June 25, 1932, p. 5.

387. "Picture Theaters Change Ownership," *Baltimore Star*, October 9, 1909, p. 9.

388. Viola Mussetter Dammann, "I Remember Field Flowers and Rudolph Valentino," *MS Magazine*, April 15, 1979, pp. 23–24.

389. Also given as 1140 Winterson Road.

390. Anne Childress, "The Screen. Would You Believe a Waterfall?" *NA*, November, 18, 1968, p. 4B.

391. Dr. Davidov had a pharmacy next to the theater. His house was moved up Aldershot Road to make room for the theater.

392. By 2003 a third ticket counter had been added near the southeastern entrance.

393. A real estate note in June 1909 gave a lower figure of about 650.

394. This building had been the site of Andrew Jackson's Palace Grand Museum in 1895.

395. "Wilson Theater Opens," *BA*, November 23, 1909, p. 11.

396. "Local Notes," *BN*, May 31, 1914, p. 11.

397. Baltimore City Ordinance 98, March 15, 1916.

398. *Boxoffice*, November 1, 1941, p. 42-G.

399. Letter, Louis S. Diggs to the author, November 17, 1999.

400. An ad for the Wizard in 1913 claimed "Baltimore's Best Pictures Since 1906." According to *American Builder* (May 19, 1906) the dwelling at 402 N. Eutaw was going to be remodeled into the Wizard theater in May 1906. The *Sun* of May 11, 1906, stated that the Maryland Electric and Supply Company had leased that building two doors north of Mulberry and would convert it

into an amusement parlor. See also, *Daily Record* for May 12, 1906, which said that it would be called the Wizard Theatre. It is not clear whether a theater was ever opened at 402 N. Eutaw. The only extant photo is of the Wizard at 219 N. Eutaw.

401. This building, described as a four-story, T-shaped structure, was sold to an investment company for about $75,000 in June 1909 and later became the Picture Garden.

402. Manes Fuld had joined Bohannon and Lewy by this time.

403. There were six dressing rooms in the basement of the Wizard.

404. "Big Picture Theatre," *Sun*, April 8, 1909, p. 8.

405. "Great Wizard," *BA*, October 24, 1909, p. C24.

406. Thomas J. Bohannan et al. v. The Consolidated Amusement Co., Baltimore City Circuit Court No. 2, Equity Papers, March 28, 1910, Maryland State Archives, File 8398A.

407. "New Wizard Has Attractive Features," *MPW*, October 4, 1919, p. 129.

408. *MS*, Real Estate Section, February 6, 1912, p. 4 and February 8, 1912, p. 4.

409. The seating capacity was to be increased from 500 to 900 which would have made the Brodie one of the largest movie theaters in town. However, information on the Brodie is contradictory; plans often announced were never implemented.

410. Anne Childress, "The Screen," *NA*, June 25, 1967, p. 7B.

Appendix 3

1. F. C. Koenig, "The Moving Picture Theater," *MPW*, April 8, 1911, p. 762.

2. *Ibid*.

3. [Auction Sales], Trustees Sale of the Equipment of a Moving-Picture Parlor, Nos. 113 and 115 North Howard St. Known as the New Pickwick," *MS*, October 13, 1917, p. 13.

4. Ben Schlanger, "Motion Picture Theatres of Tomorrow," *MPH*, February 14, 1931, Better Theatres Section, pp. 12–13, 56–57.

5. Sydney B. Self, "New Movie Theatres," *Wall Street Journal*, November 6, 1944, p. 1.

6. "Trends," *MPH*, March 22, 1952, p. 8.

7. $122,880,300 Invested in 383 New Theatres," *Boxoffice*, January 20, 1969, p. 11. The trend toward smaller auditoriums began around 1969 and by 1972 nearly 60 percent of the new theaters were mini-auditoriums seating fewer than 400 people.

8. Interview, Paul Roth, Silver Spring, Maryland, December 11, 1992. According to *Newsweek* "Quads, Six-plexes and Up," September 8, 1969, p. 71, Durwood was the originator of the notion of operating several auditoriums around one projection booth. He first used this concept in 1963 when he was offered two side-by-side bays for a theater in a Kansas City shopping center. Roth returned to Montgomery County and opened the Seven Locks Theater that was the first twin theater in the Washington suburbs.

9. "Veteran Exhibitor Sidney Dreier Sees Theatre Design Changes for the Better," Modern Theatre Section, *Boxoffice*, January 19, 1976, p. 8.

10. Several very nice theaters including the Valley Center 9, UA Snowden Square 14, and Hoyt's Hunt Valley 12 are located behind malls with very little signage to guide the unfamiliar patron to their box offices.

11. An interesting article about future movie theaters appeared in the March 2000 issue of *Boxoffice* magazine. Some of the predictions made there include "skyscraper cinemas" with multi-level auditoriums, bigger screens, the phasing out of stadium seating, portable theaters, motorized seats (perhaps similar to the chairs wired to vibrate for the 1950s film *The Tingler*), and the return of crying rooms. One designer saw the development of more impressive lobbies while another believed that theater interiors needed to become more understated and relaxing. Melissa Morrison, "New Cinema Design," *Boxoffice*, March 2000, pp. 25–29.

Appendix 4

1. Johanna Lochman et al v. The Lord Calvert Theater Co., Baltimore City Circuit Court No. 2, 1922, Equity Papers, Maryland State Archives, Series T56, File 13382-A.

2. "Are Real 'Artistes,' Say Girl Cashiers," *BN*, April 8, 1911, p. 12.

3. Helen Paul White, "Diplomats Of Theater Box Offices," *MS*, November 29, 1925, Magazine Section (Part 4), pp. 1, 7, 9.

4. Robert T. Marhenke, "Action, Off-Screen as Well as On, At the Broadway Theater," *MS*, June 26, 1977, Sun Magazine, pp. 26–27.

5. Blackiston had been a city policeman from 1867 to 1890. He later worked as a ticket-taker on the steamer *Columbia* and a conductor on the Druid Hill line before going to the Auditorium as a special policeman. Blackiston was also a champion swimmer and marksman.

6. Helen Paul White, "Weep with the Poor Theater Usher," *MS*, February 28, 1926. Magazine Section (Part 4), p. 3.

7. "The Stage Possesses Little Glamour for the Girl Usher," *MS*, January 7, 1912, p. 4.

8. Quoted in J. William Joynes, "Movie Managers Face Reel-Life Challenge," *NA*, March 18, 1973, p. F1.

9. "Warm Praise for a Local Manager," *BA*, June 2, 1918, p. C12.

10. "The Details of Successful Exhibition, " *MPW*, November 30, 1918, p. 935.

11. Robert T. Marhenke, *op. cit*.

12. "The Operator Is the Man," *The Film Index*, November 12, 1910, p. 10.

13. Interview, Charles Reisinger, Baltimore, Maryland, September 30, 1992.

14. Jack Wolheim, "When We Were Younger," *The Motion Picture Projectionist*, November 1927, p. 22.

15. "Can This Be True?" *MS*, February 17, 1921, p. 6. A second writer two days later agreed.

16. The records of the State Board of Examiners of Moving Picture Operators reveal many film fires at local theaters between 1910 and 1920. Six months after the terrible Rhoads Opera House fire in Boyertown, Pennsylvania, in January 1908, Capt. Lester L. Kingsbury, the chief electrical inspector for Baltimore, put into effect a sweeping series of rules covering electrical equipment in theaters. Every projector had to be equipped with magazines and operated from within a fireproof booth.

17. According to one projectionist, Davidson got careless and the fire started with a film explosion that literally blew him out of the booth. Another said that he was in the hospital for two years.

Bibliography

Books

Allen, Robert C., and Douglas Gomery. *Film History: Theory and Practice*. New York: Alfred A. Knopf, 1985.

Balio, Tino, ed. *The American Film Industry*. Madison: The University of Wisconsin Press, 1976, 1985.

Bowser, Eileen. *The Transformation of Cinema (1907–1915)*. Vol. 2 in the History of the American Cinema. New York: Charles Scribner's Sons, 1991.

Bowser, Pearl, and Louise Spence. *Writing Himself Into History: Oscar Micheaux, His Silent Films and His Audiences*. New Brunswick, NJ: Rutgers University Press, 2000.

Brenner, Stephen G., Esther M. Sovinsky, and Shirley S. Moore. *My Life Story as a Clown*. Middle River, Md: Gene's Studio, 1978.

Cahn, Julius. *Julius Cahn Official Theatrical Guide* (later *The Cahn-Leighton Official Theatrical Guide* and *Julius Cahn-Gus Hill Theatrical Guide*). New York, 1894–1921.

Cook, David A. *Lost Illusions: American Cinema in the Shadow of Watergate and Vietnam 1970–1979*. Berkeley: University of California Press, 2002.

Costello, Chris, with Raymond Strait. *Lou's on First. A Biography*. New York: St. Martin's Press, 1981.

Diggs, Louis. *It All Started on Winters Lane*. Baltimore: Upton Press, 1995.

———. *From the Meadows to the Point*. Baltimore: Louis Diggs, 2003.

Gomery, Douglas. *The Hollywood Studio System*. New York: St. Martin's Press, 1986.

———. *Shared Pleasures*. Madison: The University of Wisconsin Press, 1992.

———. "Motion Picture Exhibition in 1970s America," in David A. Cook, *Lost Illusions: American Cinema in the Shadow of Watergate and Vietnam 1970–1979*. Berkeley: University of California Press, 2002.

Graves, R. A. *Graves' Moving Picture Theater Directory*. St. Louis: National Trade Directory Publishers, 1914.

Hall, Ben M. *The Best Remaining Seats: The Story of the Golden Age of the Movie Palace*. New York: Bramhall House, 1961.

Hall, Clayton Coleman, gen. ed. *Baltimore Its History and Its People*. 3 vols. New York: Lewis Historical Publishing Co., 1912.

Headley, Robert K., Jr. *EXIT: A History of Movies in Baltimore*. University Park, Maryland: privately published, 1974.

———. *Motion Picture Exhibition in Washington, D. C.: An Illustrated History of Parlors, Palaces and Multiplexes in the Metropolitan Area, 1894–1997*. Jefferson, North Carolina: McFarland & Company, 1999.

Jowett, Garth. *Film: The Democratic Art*. Boston: Little, Brown and Company, 1976.

Junchen, David L. *Encyclopedia of the American Theatre Organ*. 2 vols. Pasadena: Showcase Publications, 1985–1989.

Koszarski, Richard. *An Evening's Entertainment (1915–1928)*. Vol. 3 in the History of the American Cinema. New York: Charles Scribner's Sons, 1991.

Lewis, Howard T. *The Motion Picture Industry*. New York: Van Nostrand, 1933.

The Motion Picture Trade Directory Co. *Motion Picture Theatre List*. New York: The Motion Picture Trade Directory Co., Inc., 1914, 1919–20.

Motion Picture Trade Directory. 1928.

Musser, Charles. *The Emergence of Cinema (Beginnings to 1907)*. Vol. 1 in the History of the American Cinema. New York: Charles Scribner's Sons, 1991a.

———. *Before the Nickelodeon*. Berkeley: University of California Press, 1991b.

Nasaw, David. *Going Out: The Rise and Fall of Public Amusement*. New York: Basic Books, 1993.

Naylor, David. *American Picture Palaces: The Architecture of Fantasy*. New York: Van Nostrand Reinhold, 1981.

Prince, Stephen. *A New Pot of Gold*. Vol. 10 in the History of the American Cinema. New York: Charles Scribner's Sons, 1999.

Ramsaye, Terry. *A Million and One Nights: A History of the Motion Picture Through 1925*. New York: Simon and Schuster, 1926, 1964.

R. L. Polk & Company. *Polk's Baltimore (Maryland) City Directories*. 1907–1942.

Sharp, Dennis. *The Picture Palace*. New York: Frederick A. Praeger, 1969.

Sklar, Robert. *Movie-Made America: A Cultural History of American Movies*. New York: Vintage Books, 1975.

Slide, Anthony. *The American Film Industry. A Historical Dictionary*. New York: Greenwood Press, 1986.

United States House Committee on Education. Hearings on the establishment of a Federal Motion Picture Commission. 63rd Congress, second session. Washington: GPO, 1914.

United States v. Motion Picture Patents Co. and others. United States District Court for the Eastern District of Pennsylvania, September Session, 1912.

Waller, Gregory A., ed. *Moviegoing in America*. Oxford: Blackwell, 2002.

Interviews

Floyd Adams (projectionist), Baltimore, Maryland, July 8, 1988

Leon Back (theater executive), Baltimore, Maryland, interview 1971

Mr. & Mrs. Clarence Bryant, Linthicum, Maryland, December 12, 1991

Irwin Cohen (exhibitor), Reisterstown, Maryland, December 2, 1998

David Colburn (manager), Annapolis, Maryland, May 6, 2000.

Robert Cramblitt (projectionist), Baltimore, Maryland, March 23, 1988

William Curtis (projectionist), Baltimore, Maryland, July 27, 1988 and January 20, 1989

Thurman L. Durst (projectionist), Baltimore, Maryland, October 14, 1988

William E. Eyring, Sr. and Ms. Grace Lopresti (E. Eyring & Sons and Ritz Enterprises), Baltimore Maryland, June 7, 1996

Sol Goodman (exhibitor), Baltimore, Maryland, June 19, 1996

Don Gunther (general manager of JF Theaters), Jarrettsville, Maryland, April 21, 1994

J. Russell Hildebrand, Sr. (projectionist and manager), Baltimore, Maryland, February 20, 1973 and September 1, 1976

Roy Insley (usher, stage hand, and commercial artist), Baltimore, Maryland, April 20, 1998

Edward Kimpel (executive of Rome Theaters), Cockeysville, Maryland, February 20, 1990.

William Lange (projectionist), Baltimore, Maryland, February 5, 1981

Meyer "Mike" Leventhal (theater executive and projectionist), various interviews 1969–1976

Joseph Liberto (theater manager), Catonsville, Maryland, April 8, 1997

Charles A, Lipsey, Sr. (salesman), Baltimore County, Maryland, November 2, 1994

Harry Macer (projectionist), Baltimore, Maryland, February 22, 1988

Sydney Marks (projectionist), Woodlawn, Maryland, January 23, 1986

Marian McKew and Jackie Nickel (daughter & granddaughter of theater owner "Hon" Nickel), Essex, Maryland, May 5, 1994

Elmer and August Nolte (executives with Durkee Enterprises and sons of pioneer exhibitor Charles Nolte), Baltimore, August 24, 1990

M. Robert Rappaport (exhibitor), Baltimore, Maryland, April 21, 1994

Philip Redmond (projectionist), Baltimore, Maryland, December 30, 1986

Charles H. Reisinger (projectionist), Baltimore, Maryland, December 18, 1987 and September 30, 1992

John Robinson, Baltimore, Maryland, January 7, 1992

Fabius Rollins (projectionist), Baltimore, Maryland, May 13, 1988

Maurice Rushworth (projectionist), Pasadena, Maryland, December 18, 1985 and April 17, 1986

Fred Schmuff (executive, Durkee Enterprises), Catonsville, Maryland, December 11, 1986, November 2, 1987 and September 14, 1988

Mrs. John Seamon (organist, Lyceum Theater, Sparrows Point), Dundalk, Maryland, May 19, 1993

Aaron Seidler (manager, booker and film buyer), Washington, D.C., October 31, 1991

Carroll Streeks (projectionist), Towson, Maryland, March 18, 1988

Irving Whitehill (projectionist), Baltimore, Maryland, December 18, 1987, February 22, 1988

James L. "Jack" Whittle (projectionist and NATO official), various interviews, 1973–1976

Ben Womer (steelworker and local historian), Dundalk, Maryland, May 19, 1993

Dr. Leon H. Zeller (theater owner), Baltimore, Maryland, interview 1973

Newspapers

[The following newspapers were systematically scanned during the research for this book. The name of the newspaper is followed by the place and years of publication and the location of the collections used in compiling this book. The abbreviations used are given under Archival and Library Sources.]

Afro-American (Ledger), Baltimore 1898–1915 (EPFL, UMCPM).

Anne Arundel County Star, Glen Burnie, 1959–1968 (EPFL, MSA).

Anne Arundel Times and South County Sentinel (Glen Burnie edition), Annapolis, 1970–? (EPFL).

Argus, Catonsville, 1881–1940 (BCPL, EPFL).

Baltimore American, Baltimore, 1883–1964 (EPFL, MSA, UMCPH).
Baltimore Business Journal, Baltimore, 1983–present (UMCPM).
Baltimore County Guide, Baltimore 1948–1950 (EPFL).
Baltimore County Observer, Middle River, 1945–1946 (EPFL).
Baltimore County Sentinel, Baltimore 1896?–1919 (MSA).
Baltimore County Union, the Towson News, Towson, 1909–1912 (BCPL).
Baltimore (Daily) Post, Baltimore, 1922–1934 (EPFL, MSA).
Baltimore Federationist, Baltimore 1924?–? (EPFL)
Baltimore Herald, Baltimore 1873–1906 (UMCPM).
Baltimore Jewish Times, Baltimore, 1919 — present (EPFL, UMCPH).
Baltimore News, Baltimore 1892–1934 (EPFL, LOC, MSA).
Baltimore News and the Baltimore Post, Baltimore 1934–1936 (EPFL).
Baltimore News-Post, Baltimore 1936–1964 (EPFL).
Baltimore Shoppers Guide, Baltimore 1927–1940 (EPFL).
Baltimore World, Baltimore, 1900–1910 (MSA, EPFL).
Capital, Annapolis, 1981–? (Anne Arundel Community College, EPFL, UMCPH).
Catonsville Herald (and Baltimore Countian), Catonsville, 1928–1940 (BCPL, EPFL).
Catonsville Times (and Herald Argus-Baltimore Countian), Catonsville, 1968–present (EPFL, UMCPH).
Community News (and Baltimore Countian), Reisterstown, 1928–1968 (BCPL, MSA).
Community Press and Baltimore Countian, Dundalk 1935–1968 (EPFL, MSA).
Community Times (and Community News — Baltimore Countian), Randallstown, 1968–present (BCPL, EPFL, MSA).
Daily Record, Baltimore, 1888–present (UMCPH).
Dundalk Eagle, Dundalk, 1969–present (EPFL).
Dundalk Times and Community Press — Baltimore Countian, Dundalk 1968–1977? (EPFL).
Ellicott City Times, Ellicott City, 1870?–1958 (EPFL, UMCPH).
Essex Times (& Eastern Beacon), Essex, 1968–1980 (EPFL).
Evening Capital (and Maryland Gazette), Annapolis, 1884–1981 (EPFL, MSA, UMCPH).
Evening Sun, Baltimore, 1910–199? (UMCPM).
Herald Argus and Baltimore Countian, Catonsville, 1940–1968 (BCPL).
Home News, Baltimore, 1938–1954 (EPFL).
Howard County News, Ellicott City, 1974–1983 (EPFL, UMCPH).
Howard County Times, Columbia, 1958–present (EPFL, UMCPH).
Jeffersonian, Towson, 1911–present (BCPL, MSA).
Maryland Gazette (Glen Burnie News), Annapolis, 1874?–1910; 1922?–1948, 1948–1973 (EPFL, MSA).
Middle River Observer, Middle River, 1944–1945 (EPFL).

New Era, Towson, 1913–1921 (BCPL).
News American, Baltimore, 1964–1986 (EPFL).
Northwest Star, Pikesville 1966–1976, 1980–1988 (EPFL).
Owings Mills Times, Towson, 1986–present (EPFL).
Star, Baltimore, 1908–1920 (EPFL, MSA).
Star, (Northwest edition) Baltimore, 1976–1979? (EPFL).
Southern Maryland Times, Annapolis, 1927–1954? (EPFL, MSA).
Sun, Baltimore, 1837–present (UMCPM).
Towson Times, Towson, 1968–present (BCPL).
Union News, Towson, 1912–1959 (BCPL).

Other Periodicals

American Architect, 1876 –1938 (EPFL, UMCP).
American Contractor, 1889 –1930 (LOC).
Architectural Record, 1911 –1917 (EPFL, UMCP).
Billboard, 1905 –1915 (LOC).
Boxoffice, 1935 –1950, 1958 –1988 (LOC).
Engineering News — Record, 1874 –1921 (EPFL, UMCP).
Exhibitor's Herald (— World), 1928 –(LOCMP).
Exhibitor's Times, 1913 (LOC).
Exhibitor's Trade Review, 1916 –1926 (LOC).
Film Daily Yearbook of Motion Pictures, 1918 –1958, (LOC).
Manufacturer's Record, 1882–1958, (EPFL).
Motion Picture Herald, 1929 –1956, (LOCMP, UMCPM).
Motion Picture News, 1908 –1930, (LOCMP).
Motography, 1911 –1918, (LOCMP).
Moving Picture World, 1907 –1927 (LOCMP).
Nickelodeon, 1909 –1911 (LOCMP).
Theatre Catalog, 1940 –1957 (LOC).
Variety, 1905 – present (LOC, UMCPM).
Views and Film Index, 1906 –1911 (LOC, NYPL).

Archival and Library Sources

Anne Arundel County Historical Society, Glen Burnie, Maryland (AACHS).
Baker Library, Harvard University, Cambridge, Mass.
Baltimore City Archives, Baltimore, Maryland.
Baltimore City Life Museum, Baltimore, Maryland (BCLM) [defunct; collections now part of the Maryland Historical Society].
Baltimore County Public Library, Towson and Catonsville, Maryland (BCPL).
Bowie State University, Bowie, Maryland (BSU) [former home of the *Afro-American* Collection].
Dundalk-Patapsco Neck Historical Society, Dundalk, Maryland (DPNHS).
Enoch Pratt Free Library, Baltimore, Maryland (EPFL).
Laurel Historical Society, Laurel, Maryland (LHS).
Library of Congress, Washington, DC (LOC).
  • Motion Picture, Television and Recorded Sound Division (LOCMP).
  • Newspapers and Periodicals Division (LOCNP).

Maryland Historical Society, Baltimore, Maryland (MHS).
Maryland State Archives, Annapolis, Maryland (MSA).
National Archives and Records Administration, Washington, DC (NARA).
New York Public Library, Theater Collection, Lincoln Center, New York, NY (NYPL).
Prince George's County Memorial Library, Hyattsville, Maryland (PGCML).
University of Maryland, Baltimore County, Albin O. Kuhn Library, Special Collections Department, Catonsville, Maryland (UMBC).
University of Maryland, College Park, Maryland (UMCP).
- McKeldin Library — Periodicals (UMCPM).
- Hornbake Library — Maryland Room (UMCPH).

INDEX

Numbers in ***bold italics*** represent photographs.

Abbey Lane Theater 318
Abbott, Emma 192
Abbott and Costello 131, 180, 306, 403, 485
abdication of King Edward VIII 124
Aberdeen, Maryland 479
Abrahams, S. & Sons 405
Abramowitz, Mitchel 323, 392
Abramson, Myer 217
Academy of Music 7, 8, 12, 23, 37, 40, 45, 46, 54, 56, 57, 70, 71, 96, 103, 121, 134, 189–***190***, 191–192, 208, 343, 395, 396, 400, 410, 457, 462
Accidental Tourist 392
Accust Family 285
Adams, Floyd 441
Adams, Maude 190
Adams, Judge Rowland 114
Ades Brothers 361
Adler, Larry 2
admission fixing 146
admission prices 137, 147, 148, 164, 174
admissions 155; tax 164, 475, 476, 478
Adventures of Don Juan 249
advertisements 20, 21
Aero (Acres) Shopping Center 192, 476, 481
Aero Theater 192–193, 476, 481
African-American audiences 8, 64, 120, 143, 144, 145, 169, 284, 324, 479
African-American exhibitors 47
African American Film Museum and Cinema 366
African-American projectionists 99, 101
African-American theaters 28, 79, 108, 119, 120, 121, 129, 136, 152, 193, 198, 202, 212, 213, 221, 225, 227, 230, 251, 252–256, 266, 271, 273, 279, 281, 289, 298, 299, 300, 301, 302, 310, 318, 324, 345, 359, 360, 366, 373, 374, 375, 376, 380, 381, 382, 385, 388, 389, 391, 407, 412, 430, 440, 441
African-American theaters (Annapolis, Maryland) 143
Afro-American 60, 64, 99, 107, 112, 118, 119, 121, 137, 143
after-midnight movies 135
Agner, Mr., 361
Aiala, Giuseppe 213
Aiken, Herbert C. 200, 291, 407, 432, 433
air conditioning 73, 74, 103, 104, 111, 112, 235, 238, 320, 391, 424, 453, 454
Air Force 136
air raids 132
airdomes 126, 193, 198, 251, 291, 295, 301, 315–316, 318, 341, 343, 443, 453; *see also* open-air theaters
Airport Square Industrial Park 435
Aladdin Theater 52, 193, 468
Albaugh, John W. 2, 8, 307, 330, 331, 484, 487
Albaugh Lyceum Theater 331, 484
Albaugh's Theater 22, 43, 45, 54, 70, 331
Albee, E.F. 396
Albers, Walter 247, 256, 301, 408
Albert, Don 235
Alcazar Theater 202
Aldine Theater 370
Aldrich, Arthur R. 487
Alert Theater (Essex, Maryland) 264
Alexander, John M. 358, 408
Alexandria, Virginia 126, 313
Alhambra Theater 199, 251
Alhambra Theatre Corporation 320, 370
Alhambra Theater (Washington, D.C.) 51
Alice in Wonderland 228
Allegany County, Maryland 119, 474
Allen, John D. 189, 333, 334
Allen, John D. & Company 204, 205, 430
Allen, W.A. 418
Allenbaugh, Oliver J. 35, 308
Alliance Française 109
Allied Motion Picture Theater Owners of Maryland 58, 59, 480
Allied States Association 464
Allied States Association of Motion Picture Exhibitors 464
Aloma of the South Seas 364
Alpha Theater (Catonsville, Maryland) 142, 146, 173, 193–194, ***195***, 390
Alum Chine (ship) 37, 465
Amalgamated Clothing Workers of America 71
Amazing Dobermans 171
Ambassador Theater 133, 146, 149, 157, 160, 166, 173, 185, 193–***196***, ***197***–198, 296, 394, 454, 473
Ambassador Theater (Philadelphia, Pennsylvania) 362
AMC *see* American Multi-Cinemas
AMC Columbia 14 Theaters ***198***
American Amusement Company 248
American Cancer Society 123
American Entertainment Company 143
American Federation of Musicians 110
American Ice Company 315, 375, 387
American Institute of Architects 157
American League for a Free Palestine 476
American Multi-Cinemas (AMC) 176, 182, 183, 184, 359, 434, 478, 480
American Mutoscope and Biograph Company 386
American Mutoscope Company 14

497

American Photo Player Company 485
American Society of Composers, Authors and Publishers (ASCAP) 80
American Theater 198, 356
American Theaters Company 84, 85, 86, 87, 122, 218, 220
American Theaters Corporation 426
American Vitagraph 14
America's Sweetheart 98
Americus 431, 491
Ammenhauser Brothers & Raab 193
Amusea Theater 22, 28, 31, 33, 51, 60, 198–199, 388, 463, 466
Amusea Theater (Ellicott City, Maryland) 199–200
The Amusement Company, Inc. 328
Amusement Corporation of America 373
amusement parks 8
amusement tax 114, 137 476
And Every Soul Was Saved (painting) 333, 487
Anderson, Charles M. 265, 367
Anderson, Charles S. 293
Anderson, Clarence E. 274, 329, 357, 386
Anderson, Marian 144
Anderson Picture Parlor 333
Andrae, Heine C. 229, 410
Andrews Sisters 485
Angel Child 33
Animatograph 9, 276
Anna Lucasta 143, 335
Annapolis Junction 410
Annapolis, Maryland 59, 73, 120, 134, 142, 164, 177, 186, 200, 203
Anne Arundel County, Maryland 141, 164, 169, 182, 203, 289, 293, 343, 385, 405, 434, 474
annual movie ball 59
Another Part of the Forest 335
Anthony, Adrian 398
Anthony Theater (Turner's Station, Maryland) 139, 200
antitrust litigation 131, 141, 146, 261, 454
Antz 358
Anzmann, Edward L. 482
Apex Theater 134, 139, 176, 184, 200, 362, 479
Apfel, Oscar 282
Apollo Theater 78, 79, 91, 108, 112, 137, 174, **200**–201, 217, 385
Apollo Theater Company 200
Apollo Theater (New York, New York) 254
arbitration 146
Arbutus, Maryland 142, 308, 412, 473
Arcade Moving Picture Parlor 357
Arcade Theater 112, 172, **201**, 202, 473, 477

Arcadia Theater 29, 202, 333, 353
Arch Social Club 391
Archbishop Curley High School 418
Archer, Joseph 360
Archer's Laundry 360
Arctic Nu-Air system 103, 227, 238, 255
Arenz, Henry 439
Argonne Theater 202–203
Argonne Theater (Bel Air, Maryland) 142
Arlington Amusement Company 400
Arlington, Maryland 7, 30, 463
Arlington Racecourse 262, 263
Arlington Theater 203, 400
Armat, Christopher 462
Armat, J. Hunter 462
Armat, Thomas 8, 142, 462
Armond, Alfred 33, 218
Armstrong, Bess 2
Armstrong, Louis 212, 254
Around the World in 80 Days 155, 349, 416
Arrow Theater 203–204
Arrowstreet Inc. 313, 434
art deco style 104, 453
Art Theater (Glen Burnie, Maryland) 142, **203**, 204
art theaters 141, 151, 152, 158, 176, 177, 309, 319, 362, 391
Artistic Films 362
Artmore Casino 120, 204
Artoscope Entertainment 50
Arundel Amusement Corporation 204
Arundel Ice Cream stores 193, 245
Arundel Mills Mall 110, 343, 344, 456
As You Like It 277
Ash, Paul 470
Ashkenazi, S. 391
Associated Motion Picture Theater Owners 119
Associated Theaters 182
Associated Theatre Company 411
Association of Commerce 135
Astin, John 2
Astor Theater 112, 373
Astoria Theater 204
Atlanta Exposition 483
Atlanta, Georgia 73
Atlantic City, New Jersey 82
Atlantic Confectionery 256, 257
atmospheric theaters 298, 300, 414
atomic bomb 138
attendance 54, 136, 147, 158
audiences 2, 23, 64
Auditorium Theater *see* Howard Auditorium
Aurora Theater 60, 141, 152, 159, 176, 210, **211**, 230, 257
Ausler and Foss 390
automatic ticket-shooter 175
Autry, Gene 122, 306
Avalon Theater 91, 100, 123, 141, 155, 158, 210–*212*, 401, 410, 411, 480
Avalon Theaters Corporation 210
Avara, Mary 169, 170, 171
The Avenue at White Marsh 438
Avenue Mall 297
Avenue Theater 28, 212, 291
Avon Comedy Four 284
Avon Theater 247, 473
Azrael, Louis 335

B & O Railroad 128, 312
B & O Railroad Building 378
B & O Woman's Music Club 235
Baby Louise 490
Bach, Oscar Bruno 269, 272, 483, 484
Bachelor, James 326
Back, Leon **128**, 168, 405, 457
Back, Samuel 47
Back in Circulation 256
Bacote, Odessa 255
Bailey, Pearl 254
Baird projector 101
Baker, Louis H. 265
Baker, Stanley **128**
Baker Church 407
Balaban & Katz 103, 131
Baldwin, George A. 216
Baldwin, Nelson 62, 468
Baldwin & Pennington 189, 441, 442
Baliko, Alexander 214
Ballauf, William 36, 285, 484
Baltimore American 60, 87, 464
Baltimore Amusement Company 256, 350, 370, 409
Baltimore and Annapolis Railway 127
Baltimore and Washington Film Express 127
Baltimore Association of Commerce 116
Baltimore Association of Jewish Women 67
Baltimore Board of Public Safety 43
Baltimore Bullet 295
Baltimore Center for the Performing Arts 185, 306
Baltimore Chamber of Commerce 116
Baltimore City College 58
Baltimore City Community College 342
Baltimore City Council 39, 53, 61, 84, 85, 86, 115, 116, 117, 118, 122, 123, 164, 184, 194, 204, 298, 412, 428, 430, 475
Baltimore City Paper 392, 417
Baltimore City Quartet 311
Baltimore Civic Opera 321
Baltimore Civilian Defense Committee 132
Baltimore Collector of Water Rents and Licenses 66, 463
Baltimore Committee on Civilian Defense 133

Baltimore Contractors 347
Baltimore County 30, 67, 119, 120, 123, 164, 169, 175, 302, 307, 400, 464, 466, 474
Baltimore Federation of Labor 91
Baltimore Film Exchange 127
Baltimore Film Forum 417
Baltimore Film Society 260, 316, 383
Baltimore Fire 18, 48
Baltimore Gas and Electric Company 387, 424
Baltimore Health Commissioner 71, 72, 73
Baltimore Hebrew Theater 374
Baltimore Heritage 306
Baltimore Housing Authority 412
Baltimore Interracial Fellowship 143
Baltimore Investment Corporation 440
Baltimore Joint Committee on Building Regulations 85
Baltimore Light Artillery 17
Baltimore Moving Picture Company 213
Baltimore News 54, 60, 67, 464, 468
Baltimore Opera House 430
Baltimore Orioles 169, 357, 358, 486
Baltimore police 120
Baltimore Police Board 36, 60, 65, 67
Baltimore Police Department 133
Baltimore Street 29, **30**
Baltimore Symphony Orchestra 157
Baltimore Terrapins 407
Baltimore Theater 81, 213
Baltimore Theater Opera Company 374
Baltimore Theaters: *1910–1911* 40; *1922* 87, 88; *1941* 129; *1962* 159; *1985* 181
Baltimore Theatre Company 243, 285
Baltimore Theatre, Inc. 341
Baltimore Traction Company 407
Baltimore Urban League 120
Baltimore Zoning Board 412
Baltimore Zoning Commission 91
Bamberger, William 193
Bamville 360
Bangert, Prof. James 320
Barber, Mary 179
Bardine, Mabel 483
Barker, Julie 79
barkers 57
Barnes, Adam 316
Barnes, Earl 316
Barnes and King 439
baroque style 104
The Barrets of Wimpole Street 335
Barry, C.E. 202
Barry, Johnny 230
Barrymore, John 106
Barrymore, Lionel 92
Bartlett-Hayward Company 134

Barton, Jim 230
baseball 468
Batchelor, Frank R. 291
Bates, Edward T. 375
Bates, Pegleg 254
Battle Circus 236
Battle Cry 399
Bauer, Harry 148, **149**
Baugher, Elizabeth 252
Baum, Robert H. 352
Baxter, Wilbert 298
Bay Ridge 59
Bay Shore 23, 213–214, 463
Baylinson, S. Brian 269
Bayne, Carroll H. 179, 387
Bayview Brewery 410
Beacon Theater 445
Beall, Frederick E. 203, 225, 240, 248, 260, 261, 275, 276, 314, 315, 328, 373, 390, 403, 440, 453, 488
Bear, Moe 398
Beard's Hill Movies 7 (Aberdeen, Maryland) 479
beaux-arts style 104
Beck, Ben **128**, 179, 372, 420, 480
Beckwith, Clara 430
Bederski, Henry 461
Bedford, John H.C. 62, 99, 179, 468
Beerbohm Tree, Sir Herbert 331
behind-the-screen talkers 31, 32, 199, 271, 292, 301, 322, 324, 359, 361
Bekefi-Delaporte Institute of the Dance, Drama, and Music 415
Bel Air Beltway Plaza Shopping Center 214
Bel-Air Drive-In 126
Bel Air 14 Theaters (Bel Air, Maryland) 183
Bel Air, Maryland 142, 175, 177, 186, 394, 379
Belair Market 20
Bell, Elizabeth 317
Bell Theater 214
Belle Starr 382
Belmar Theater 214, 472
Belnord Theater 79, 82, 90, 91, 112, 123, 149, 163, 166, 214, **215**, 380, 472, 481
Beltway Movies 6 214
Beltway Plaza 2 Theater 214
Belvedere 254
Belvedere Picture Garden 400
Belvedere Theater 400
Belzer, Richard 257
Ben Shomrin 374
Bender, Charles 123, 214, 350
Benesch, Abraham 35, 273
Benesch, Jesse 316
Benesch, Louis 35, 273
Benesch's Excelsior Theater 273
Benesch's Theater 273
Bengies Drive-In 126, 215–216, 482
Ben-Hur 271, 278
Benjamin, Sam **35**, 202
Bennett, Mrs. Howard D. 331

Bennett, J. Howard 35, 65, 352, 370, 371, 414, 490
Benny, Jack 335
Benny, Mr. 341
Bentley Springs 70
Bentum, Harry 216
Berge, E. 277
Berger, Martin A. 254, 373
Bergman, Ingrid 140, 476
Berle, Milton 151, 306, 485
Berlin, Maryland 186
Berlo Vending 237
Berman, Allan L. 418
Berman, Isaac 216
Berman, Joseph 320
Berman, Louis 426
Berman, Samuel 467
Berman, Jean and Allan L. Auditorium 418
Berman's Theater 60, 216
Bermuda Triangle 202
Bernhardt, Elmer F. 316
Bernhardt, Sarah 190, 192, 330, 335
Bernheimer Brothers 327, 408
Bernstein, Nathan 80
Bert-Core Associates 405
Bethlehem-Fairfield shipyard 135
Bethlehem Steel 214, 215, 333
beverages 148
Bickel, Henry 293, 294
Biddle Theater 216
Bien, John H. 324
Big Five 145, 146, 147
Big Sky 271, 477
Bijou Dream Theater (Winchester, Virginia) 51, 216
Bijou Theater (Atlantic City, New Jersey) 82
Bijou Theater 13, 16, 17, 57, 216, 248, 361
Billopp, Christopher 461
Binder, J.W. 67
bingo 151
Biograph 9, 12, 13, 14, 15, 18, 19, 143, 190, 192, 209, 276, 386, 463
Biograph films 261, 311, 343, 413
Biograph Theater (Washington, D.C.) 475, 491
The Birds 174
Birth 113, 268, 305
Birth of a Nation 63, 64, 278, 362, 470
Birthright 252
Bishop, John 301
Bisson, J. 405
Black, Van Lear 179
Black and White Review 62
Black Cat Amusement Company 216
Black Cat Theater 52, 216, 408, 467
black exploitation films 169
Black Hand 223
black light *see* ultra violet lighting
Blackiston, Albert C. 457
blackouts 132, 133
Blackstone 266

Blair, J.O. 411
Blake, Eubie 251, 360
Blake, James B. 474
Blake, Dr. John D. 72
Blake, Capt. Warren A. 247
Bland, Frank Paul 390
Blaney, Charles E. 265
Blaney's Theater 265, 266
Blanke, Ewald G. 156, 218, 219, 238, 298, 316, 332, 387, 388, 410, 411, 430, 453, 471
Blanke and Zink 353, 379
Blaustein, Isador L. 376
Blechman, Harry 370
Blechman, Joseph 218, 367, 414
The Block 13, 20, **30**, 36, 69, 241, 292, 462
block-booking 59, 147, 467
Bloodgood, Clara 2, 461
Bloom, Elizabeth 456
Blue, Monte 2
Blue Bell Theater 71, 216–**217**, 273
Blue Bird Theater 383
blue laws 61, 83, 118, 373, 473
Blue Mouse Theater 31, 33, 36, 60, 75, 82, 90, 217–**218**, 360, 394, 464, 465, 482
Blum, Herman A. 133, 316
Blum, Hyman 426
Blum, Philip 274
Bocutti, Oscar 406
Boer War 209
Bohannon, Tom 28, 47, 67, 341, 441, 442
Bohannon and Lewy 42, 409, 413, 441, 443
Bohannon, Lewy and Fuld 31, 442
Bok Ok, Brian 310
Bon Ton Theater 285
Booker T Theater 193
Boone, Harry S. 375
Booth, Edwin 192, 278, 308, 330
Booth, John Wilkes 308
Booth, Junius Brutus 17, 308
Booth's Theater (New York, New York) 276
Borden's Ice Cream 438
Borge, Victor 306
Boston, Massachusetts 72, 113, 345
Boston Music Company 80
The Boston Orchestra 329
Boston Symphony 343
Boulevard Theater 79, 80, 82, 84, 85, 86, 87, 90, 91, 107, 108, 112, 122, 160, 172, 181, 218–**219**, **220**, 221, 238, 296, 316, 396, 430, 453, 477
Bouse, Senator 83
Bowers, James W., Jr. 193
Bowery Blitzkrieg 131
Bowery Boys 122
Bowie, Maryland 313
Bowie Theaters (Bowie, Maryland) 176
Bowsil, Stanley 193
boxing 462
Boxoffice magazine 155

Boyd Theater (Philadelphia, Pennsylvania) 103
Boys from Syracuse 129
Bozo the Clown 480
Bradford, James C. 470
Brady, William A. 11, 14, 45, 207
Braun, Daniel H. 405
Braun and Baum 42
Braxton, Toni 2
Bredelmeyer, Mr. 361
Breezy Rhythm 483
Brehm, George 178, 262, 412, 435, 480
Breighner, Bernard 297
Breil, C.J. 470
Brenner, Steven 50, **149**, 179, 256, 264, 480
Briant, Ethel 79
Brice, Fanny 278, 335
The Bridge 430
Bridge Theater 47, 60, 71, 166, 173, 221, **222**, 261, 454, 468, 473
Brigode, Ace 79
British films 133, 327, 415
British War Relief Society 132
Britt-Nelson fight 19, 192
Britton, R.L. 191
Broadley, Bob 490
Broadley, Merle 490
Broadway Garden Theater 116, 373
Broadway Market 20
Broadway Theater 70, 78, 108, 109, 112, 124, 137, 160, 216, 221, **223**–224, 406, 456, 458
Broadway Theater Company 213, 221
Brockmeyer, R.C. 214
Brodie, Joe 35, 275, 443, 444, 445, 491
Brodie Theater 70, 71, 443
Broening, Mayor William F. 85, 235, 338, 396
Brooklyn 139, 224, 366, 426
Brooklyn Theater 139, **224**–225, 412, 473
Brooks, George W.E. 50
Broumas, John 161, 177, 488
Broumas Theaters 289, 353, 377, 488
Brown, Alexander 43
Brown, Ambrose S. 383
Brown, "Babe" 440
Brown, E.C. 252
Brown, Harry H. 322
Brown, Harry S. 388
Brown, J. Wilson 293
Brown, Joe E. 268
Brown, Prof. 375
Brown, Robert L. 210
Brown, William 50, 240
Brown, William B. 20, 21, 369
Brown, Dr. Wyatt 332
Brown Demont & Company 324
Browne, Edwin H.C. 485
Browning, Robert 118
Brunet, Arthur 442
Brunier Hair Plant 409

Brunker, Charles 266
Bryan, James Wallace 50
Bryant, Howard W. 67, 83, 94, 115
Brylawski, Aaron 461, 469
Brylawski, Fulton 67, 469
Brylawski, Henry H. 461
Brylawski, Julian 461, 469
Bucher, Isidore 485
Buck, Alfred G. 84, 86, 87, 122, 218, 238, 316, 430
Buckman, Samuel 413
Buedel's Tavern 338
Buffalo Bill 278
Buffalo, New York 17, 18, 336
building permits 40
Bull, Robert B. 238
Bunny, John 225
Bunny Theater 225
Burch, Francis 169
Burgess, Walt 174
Burkhardt, Howard 269
burlesque 18, 62, 69, 104, 105, 199, 266, 268, 269, 285, 286, 287, 335, 351, 409, 426, 431, 453
Burn, G. 456
Burns, Nick 350
Burns, Sandy 252
Burns, Tommy 36
Burrell, Clay 375
Burrill, Austin 277
Burriss and Kemp drugstore 218
Burtis Theater (Annapolis, Maryland) 143
Busch, W.A. 398
Bush, W. Stephen 67
Bushman, Francis X. 59, 461
Busy Moon Theater 359
Butcher, David C. Company 398
Butler, Frank 203
Butter-Kist popcorn 57
Butterbeans & Susie 254
Bwana Devil 153
BWI Airport 182
Byrum, Robert L. 374

Cadden, Magistrate 332
Cadwallader, Capt. Louis 268
Cafe Kaluna 410
Cafe Metropole 417
Cahill, Frank 399
Cahill, J.E. 250
Cahill, Margaret C. 378
Cahill, J.E. Amusement Company 407
Call of the Wild 308
Callahan Film Company 266
Callan, John G. 83, 116, 117, 373
Callis, C.H. 375, 411
Callis, D. Millard 373
Callis, G.R. 109, 409
Callis & Callis 243, 254, 255, 257, 315, 353, 356, 390, 409
Calloway, Cab 2, 254, 306, 324, 382
Caltrider's Hall (Reisterstown, Maryland) 142, 225
Calvert Theater Company 256

Index 501

Calverton Carpet Manufacturing Company 430
Calverton Heights 487
Calverton, Maryland 424
Cambridge, Maryland 73, 474
Cambridge 7 420
Camden, New Jersey 126
Camelot 164
Cameo Theater 65, 144, 145, 362, 468, 477
Cameraphone 32, 307, 352
Cameroni 199, 256
Cammack, Shirley 463
Camp, C. Nelson & Company 463, 482
Camp Dix, NJ 72
Camp Holabird 72
Camp Meade 72, 431; *see also* Fort George G. Meade
Camp Meade Mercantile and Amusement Company 410
Campanari, Giuseppe 46
Campus Hills Theater (Churchville, Maryland) 172, 177, 186
Can-Can 301
candy 113, 139, 148, 184, 454
candy attendants 164
candy butcher 57
Candy Cane Land 424
candy machines 139, 435
Canton 30, 410
Canton Academy 461
Canton Amusement Company 203
Cantor, Eddie 305
capacities of theaters (1938) 125
El Capitan 191
Capitol Theater 78, 79, 91, 100, 108, 117, 131, 132, 225, **226**, 434
Capitol Theater (Washington, D.C.) 75
Capitol Theatre Company 225
Caplan, Abel 373
Caplan, Mildred 416
Capri Theater 325
Captain's Paradise 477
carbon arc 102
Carey Theater 103, 119, 225–**227**, 400
Carley, Fred H. 29, 212
Carlin, John J. 324, 486
Carlin's Drive-In 144, 160, 227–**228**, 324
Carlin's Park 227, 238, 324
Carlos, J.M. 379
Carlos and Valeria 396
Carlton Theater 177, 228, **229**, 458, 476
Carmen 403
Carnegie Theater (New York, New York) 490
Caron, Leslie 154
Carpetbaggers 237
Carr, Robert 255
Carrier Engineering Corporation 111, 320
Carrington, Jerome 380

Carroll, Armand 230, 231, 232, 345, 346, 347, 348
Carroll, Wilson J. 84, 85, 86, 87
Carroll Amusement Company 408
Carroll Island Shopping Center 229
Carroll Theater (Westminster, Maryland) 468
Carrollton Hotel 409
Carrollton Theater 52, 216, 229, 287, 467
Carrollwood Twin Theaters (Middle River, Maryland) 229
Carter, Gaylord 464
cartoons 105
Carver, Dr. George Washington 252
Carver Playhouse 252
Carver Theater 152, 252
cashiers 134, 164, 456
Cashmeyer, Elmer 193
Casino (Sparrows Point, Maryland) 229
Casino Theater **444**, 445
Casino Theater (Washington, D.C.) 425
Casinograph 463
Cassandra Crossing 171
Cassell, Charles E. 327
Cassell, Charles E. & Son 374
Castelle, George 396
Castellucci, Signor 329
Castleberg, Joseph 410
Castro, Alex 416
Caton Moving Picture Parlor (Catonsville, Maryland) 229–230
Catonsville High School 230
Catonsville, Maryland 50, 70, 142, 178, 193, 194, 229, 230, 390, 410, 440, 441, 473, 482
Catonsville Presbyterian Church 230
Catonsville Theatre Corporation 390
Causby, William 101, 472
Cecil B. Demented 295
Cedrone, Lou 171
Celtic Amusement Company 230
Celtic Moving Picture Company 230, 480
censorship 54, 65, 66, 67, 68, 69, 96, 98, 113, 114, 149, 150, 164, 165, 383, 468, 469, 478
Center for Science in the Public Interest 184
Center Park Theater (Calverton, Maryland) 424
Center Stage 413
Centograph 9, 192, 462
Central Park Theater (Chicago, Illinois) 103
Central Theater 430
Central Theater (Sparrows Point, Maryland) 230
Central Theater Company 291, 410, 489

Centre Theater 110, 129, 137, 176, 230–**231**, **232**, 347
Centreville, Maryland 250
Century Roof 235, 422
Century Theater 69, 75, 76, 79, 80, 82, 89, 90, 91, 92, 96, 100, 103, 104, 105, 107, 108, 111, 112, 115, 121, 124, 129, 134, 136, 144, 147, 151, 153, 158, 160, 161, 162, 167, 180, 184, 230–**233**, **234**, 235–236, 388, 396, 414, 422, 424, 443, 453, 457, 470, 477, 482
Century Theater Company 96
Chambers, R.E. 296, 297
Chandu, the Magician 299
changeovers 108, 472
Chaplin, Charlie 2, 335, 426, 461
Charcoal Club 415
charitable work of theaters 37
charities 123
Charles Center 161, 162, 278, 418
Charles Productions 418
The Charles Street Follies 295
Charles Street Theatre Company 416
Charles Theater 141, 144, 155, 168, 172, 175, 177, 184, 210, 310, 416–417
Chase, Charlie 2, **95**, 461
Chase, Plimpton B. 331
Chase Organization 14
Chase's Lyceum Theater 330
Chautauqua 142
Cherry, Hugh 306
Chertkof, J.O. 301
Chertkoff, David W. 412
Chesno, Annie 243
Chesno, John 243
Chestertown, Maryland 186
Chicago, Ill. 103, 131
Chicago Law and Order League 471
Chicago World's Fair 17
Chick, Leonard 218, 464
Chief Red Moon 480
Child Welfare League 69
children 66, 98
Children's Hospital 37
Childs, George S. 221, 341, 380, 489
Childs, Mrs. William T. 11
China Hall 202, 461
Chinese films 109
Chisolm & Tall 216
Chocolate Soldier 121
Christhilf, J. Edward 349
Christian Temple Faith Church 245
Christie Electric Corporation 102
Christmas parties 18, 121, 123, 124
Chronophone 32
Chuck E. Cheese 385
Church Hill, Maryland 186
Church Lane Cinema (Cockeysville, Maryland) 236
Church Lane Shopping Center 236

Church of the Immaculate Conception (Towson, Maryland) 362, 377
Church of the Messiah 387, 489
churches 475
Churchville, Maryland 126
Cinderella 14, 209
Cinema Art Theater 490
Cinema Centre Theater 482
Cinema Club 326
Cinema Eastpoint 238
Cinema 83 Theater (York, Pennsylvania) 479
Cinema North 210
Cinema 1–2 (Lutherville, Maryland) 158, 160, 161, 177, 236, **237**
Cinema-X 240
Cinema Theater 141, 144, 152, 324, 325, 391
CinemaScope 152, 153, 160, 454
Cinematograph 10, 11, 12, 13, 14, 48, 209, 276, 329, 361, 386, 465
Cineograph 11, 12, 14, 16
Cineplex Odeon Corp. 183, 342
Cinerama 153, 271, 454, 484
Circle Theater 87, 238
Circle Theater (Annapolis, Maryland) 112
Circle Theater Corporation 238, 471
Circus Theater 238
Citizen Kane 468
Citizens Committee for Justice 476
Citizens' League of Maryland for Better Motion Pictures 97, 113, 118, 461, 472
Citizens Military Training Camp 340
City Hall Plaza 307
City of Richmond (ship) 154
City Passenger Railway Company 247, 416
civil rights legislation 145
Civilian Mobilization Committee 135
Civilian Production Authority 139
Clark, Betty Ross 488
Clark, Elmer 73
Clark, Garnett 408
Clark, J. Spencer 66, 463
Clark, Kenneth 323
Clark, Norman 74, 112, 126, 306, 326, 423, 431
Clark Bros. Royal Burlesquers 13
Clarke, Samuel 471
Claude Neon Signs 377, 454
Clay, Henry 485
Clay Street Theater (Annapolis, Maryland) 120, 143
Clear Channel Entertainment 307
clearances 146, 147, 470
Cleopatra 306
Cleveland, Ohio 113
Clifton Theater 238
Cline, Maggie 432
Cloistered 252
Clothier, George, Jr. 333

Clover Theater 37, 68, 69, 98, 199, 481
Cloward, F. DuShane 13
Clown Theater 238
Club Charles 225
Clum, Woodworth 343
Cluster, Benjamin 29, 34, 70, 98, 108, 109, 238, 240, 274, 323, 390, 432, 472
Cluster, Harry 99, 100, 132, 148, **149**, 250, 366, 458, 468
Cluster, Herman **149**
Cluster, Isaac 34, 240
Cluster, Max 250
Cluster Amusement Company 203
Cluster Family 47, 98
Cluster Theater 29, 90, 98, 106, 108, 109, 139, 238–**239**, 240, 291, 359, 472
Cluster's Union 100, 148
Coale, Donald Vincent 383
Coats, Dorothy 338
Coblentz, Oscar **128**, 193, 194
Cockeysville, Maryland 182, 236, 313
Codd, John 148, **149**
Cohan, George M. 32, 266, 278, 335
Cohen, Aaron 51, 425
Cohen, Abraham 349, 407, 488
Cohen, Harry 154
Cohen, Irwin 128, 174, 257, 349
Cohen, Israel 191
Cohen, Jacob 203
Cohen, Louis 349, 407
Cohen, Maurice 179, 320
Cohen, Moses 252
Cohen, Scott 257
Cohen Family 128
Colburn, David 164
Coleman, Judge William C. 284
Colgate Creek 386
Colgate Theater 139, 240, 362
Collector of Water Rents and Licenses 440
Collier, Rodney 123, **128**, 398
Collison, Roy 279, 468
Colonial Theater 31, 54, 58, 71, 240, 266
Colonial Theater (Annapolis, Maryland) 143
Colonial Theater (Atlantic City, New Jersey) 82
Colonial Theater Company 240
Colonna, Jerry 306
Colonnade Theater 21, 25, 33, 42, **214**, 240–243, 466
Colony Theater 157, 243
color films 40, 465
Colored Motion Picture Projectionists Association 101
Colored Operators' Association of Maryland 472
Colored Operators' Protective Association 472
Colston, Capt. Frederic M. 343
Columbia Amusement Company 285

Columbia burlesque circuit 18, 268, 285
Columbia City 3 Cinema (Columbia, Maryland) 245, 246, 394; *see also* Columbia Theater (Columbia, Maryland)
Columbia Hall 245
Columbia, Maryland 168, 178, 184, 198, 245, 342, 394, 482
Columbia Moving Picture Parlor 245
Columbia Palace 9 Theater (Columbia, Maryland) 177, 182, 245, **246**, 424, 455, 481
Columbia Phonograph Company 8
Columbia Pictures 122, 137, 146, 152, 153, 223, 315
Columbia School of Architecture 156
Columbia-Shamrock yacht race 14
Columbia Theater 31, 79, 91, 137, 137, 158, 243–**244**, 245, 453
Columbia Theater (Columbia, Maryland) 174, 182, 245, 482; *see also* Columbia City 3 Cinema (Columbia, Maryland)
Columbia Theater (Towson, Maryland) 377
Columbia Theater (Washington, D.C.) 481
Combs, Joe 33, 218
The Comedians 161, 418
Comedy Theater 37, 47, 98, 246, 388, 469
Comet Theater 246
Comic Theater 247, 301
Comiograph 15
commercials 166, 167
Commission on Interracial Problems and Relations 144, 145
Commission on Training Camp Activities 323
Community Church (St. Helena, Maryland) 142, 247
Community Company 202
Community Hall (Glen Burnie, Maryland) 289
Community Hall (St. Helena, Maryland) 247
Community Theater 123, 180, 247
Community Theater (Towson, Maryland) 247
competitive bidding 146
computerized ticketing systems 175
concession stands 140
concessions 57, 113, 139, 184, 459, 468
Concordia Opera House 343, 488
Conesta, Maria 46
Coney Island front 452
confectioners 57
Confederate Home 268
Congress Hotel *see* Hotel Kernan
Conkling Hall 301
Connolly, Jack S. 69
Conreid Opera Company 330

Consolidated Amusement Company 217–218, 360, 442
Consolidated Engineering Company 221, 259
Consolidated Radio Artists, Inc. 335
Consolidated Railway 386
Constantine, C. 200, 329
Constantini, Brian 406
Continental Realty Corp. 177, 306
Convention Hall 15, 16, 17, 247–248, 462
Coogan, Jackie 306
Cook, Eugene A. 210, *211*, 361
Cook, Henry E. 291
Cook, J.S. 485
Cook, John B. 257
Cook, S.B. 357
Cook, William 332
Cooper, Astley D.M. 11, 329
Cooper, Ernie 396, 398
Cooper, Gary 278
Cooper, John W. 380
Cooper, L. Wesley 472
Copeland, Edward 302
Copeland, Henry L. 262
Corbett-Fitzsimmons fight 276, 462
Corbett-McGovern fight 16, 431
Corcozza, Jules 426
Cornell, Katherine 335
Corsican Brothers 192
Cortes Amusement Company 379
Cosmofoto Film Company 67
Cosmopolitan Theater 248
Cosmos Theater (Washington, D.C.) 461
Costco 455
Costello, Maurice 59
Coulbourne, William E. 229
Count Basie 213, 253, 254
Countess Leontine 268
Country Store Nights 438
Coye, Gladys 125
Coyle, Wilbur F. 467
Crabtree, Lotta 308
Crandall, Harry 396
Crandall theaters 124, 396
Crane, William H. 331
Crapo, Henry Theodore 465
Crawford, Samuel 345
Creative Alliance 367
Cremen, James C. 225, 318, 400
Crescent Novelty Company 275
Crescent Theater 29, 52, 248, 273, 318, 378
Crest 99 Theater 250
Crest Theater 131, 142, 160, 173, 174, *249*–250, 454
Crimson Tide 257
Crisis 464
Cromelin, Paul 67
Crothers, Governor Austin L. 37
Crown Amusement Company 254
Crown Imperial Theater 250
Crown Theater 71, 250
Crown Theaters 250

Crystal Amusement Company 250, 432
Crystal Maze 250
Crystal Moving Picture Parlor 250–*251*, 432, 458, 468
Crystal Reception Room 206
Culchia, Charles L. 353
Culp, George 350
Cumberland, Maryland 50, 73, 142, 186, 468
Cupero, E.V. 79, 235, 312
Cupid Amusement Company 247
Cupid Theater 29, 246, 271
Curtis, William *102*
Curtis Bay 72, 139, 367, 485
Curtis Bay Ordnance Depot 72
Curtis Theater 251, 375
Cusack, James "Buzz" 417
Cushen, Patrick J. 265
Cushing, T.M. 80, 91, 106; see also T.M.C.
Cushman, Charlotte 278
Czyz, Father 476

D'Agostino Izzo Quirk 488
Daily News 106
Daily Post 60, 79
Dainty Theater 317
Dakota 200
D'Alesandro, Thomas 118, 382
D'Aljaris Collection 13, 361
Dallas, Texas 113
Daly, William H. 47, 324, 360, 374, 409, 465
Daly Amusement Company 409
Daly's airdome 33, 251
Daly's Why Theater 251, 360
Damnation Alley 171
Dana, Viola 59
The Dance of the Ancient Nile 70
Dante's Inferno 415
DAR 69
Dashiell, Winnet 338
Daugherty, Carlos 254
David Copperfield 278
Davidov, Dr. 491
Davidson, Leonard 390, 458
Davis, Bette 98
Davis, Frank E. 298, 299
Davis, Henry 298, 299
Davis, Meyer 80, 470
Davis, Milton C. 202, 266
Davis, Ossie 476
Davis, Rev. 118, 119
Davis, Ruth 390
Davis, Wiley *102*
Dawes, R.J. 199
daylight saving 104, 115, 116, 474
dead night 213
Deal, Louis 94
Dean, Tunis F. 191, 192
Dean Theater 139, 291
DeBell, Christine 228
Debrick, Charles A. 485
Deception 235
Decker, Dorothy 292
Decker, John 212, 401
Dee, Ruby 476

Deep Harlem 253
Deep Throat 170, 210, 479
deepies 152
Deetjan, Louis T. 375
Degges, Stanley 248
DeHaven, Gloria 348
DeHoff, Louis A. 35, 59, 69, 71, 92, 115, 457
Delaware 128, 156
Dell, Elizabeth 317
Dell'Archiprete, E. 329
Del Manto, Vincent 263
Delmarva Telephone Company 43
Deluxe Roosevelt Theater 389
Deluxe Theater 275
Demme, Charles W. 52, 216, 217, 248
Demon Seed 171
Dempsey, Jack 380, 382
Dempsey-Sharkey fight 37
Dempsey-Tunney fight 37
De Munkacsy 204
Dennis, Judge Samuel 114
Denver, John 245
department stores 1
Depkin, Bernard, Jr. 86, 103, 134, 135, 194, 220, 338, 352, 364, 370, 396, 398, 407, 443, 457, 490
Depression 104, 109, 453
desegregation 144, 159
Detroit, Mi. 113, 336
Deutsches Haus 473
Deutschland (submarine) 70
Developers General Corporation 318
Development Design Group 343, 344
A Devil with Women 113
Dewey, Admiral 14
De Wolfe Hopper Comic Opera Company 121
Diamond, Samuel 124
Diamond Bowling Alleys 326
Diane Theater 47, 251–252
Dick, Herman 33, 352
Dickens, Charles 308
Dickerson, Edwin T. 84, 86, 87
Dickerson & Nice 84, 86, 430, 471
Dickinson High School (Wilmington, Delaware) 399
Dickson, W.K.L. 13
Dicus, V. Larkin 289
Die Hard with a Vengeance 257
Dieter, Louis A. Co. 35
Diggs, Josiah 254
Diggs, Louis S. 440
Diggs and Trimble 380
Diller, Bill 289
Dime Museum 7
Dime Savings Bank 218
Diner 249, 404
Dines, Ralph *102*
discount theaters 174, 175
Disney films 369
distribution 160, 166, 466, 479
District Theaters 254, 301
Divine 2

504 INDEX

Divo Twins 425
Dixie Amusement Company 252
Dixie Theater 47, 114, 152, 252
Dixon, Fred 356
Doc Baker's Flashes of 1931 305
Dockstader, Lew 278
Dodson, Charles 366
Doebereiner's Bakery 440
Dolby sound 160
Don Juan 106, 338, 473
Donnell, Jeff 2
Donohue, John 21, 407
Doomsday 463, 482
doormen 164, 457
Dopman, Austin X. 204
Dorchester County, Maryland 474
Dorsey, Jimmy 306
Dorsey, Tommy 284, 306
Douglas, Justice William O. 169
Douglass, George 101, *102*, 179, 289, 375, 388, 472
Douglass Amusement Company 252
Douglass Theater 91, 101, 252
Doukas, Theodore 373
Down-and-out-chute 281; *see also* Kirker-Bender Patent Spiral Slide Fire-Escape
Downey, Morton 284, 399
downtown 77, 91, 141, 161, 177, 418
Downtown Partnership 185, 306
downtown theaters 99, 105, 110, 134, 136, 144, 160, 167, 168, 169, 174, 175, 176, 477
D'Oyley Carte operetta company 190
Drama-Grams 230
Dramagraph 32, 464
Dream Theater 47, 254
Dreamland Theater 254
Dreier, Sidney 455
dressing for a movie 136
Dressler, Marie 208
drive-in theaters 104, 114, 126, 140, 141, 144, 158, 160, 161, 166, 169, 177, 215, 216, 227, 228, 262, 265, 287, 292, 293, 353, 394, 405, 424, 454, 475, 476
Dryden, William 398
DTS 160
Duchin, Eddy 485
duckpins 486, 487
Dudley, Sherman 345
Dudley Amusement Company 343
Dudley Circuit 375
Duel in the Sun 140
Duffy's Tavern 279
Dumb-Bells 117
Dunbar Amusement Company 254
Dunbar Theater 101, 119, 145, 254–*255*, 256, 472
Dunbar Theater (Philadelphia, Pennsylvania) 252
Dundalk Eagle 257
Dundalk, Maryland 119, 139, 142, 228, 240, 318, 404, 428, 432
Dundon, Bernard H. 84, 86, 87

Dunkin' Donuts 352
Dunn, John Carroll 257, 258, 308, 382, 427, 432
Dunnagan Technical Services 289
Dunnock, Mildred 2
Dupont, Pierre S. 43
Durham, Frank P. 216
Durkee, Frank H. 31, 35, 46, 47, 58, 61, 63, 79, *95*, 100, 101, 112, 122, 123, 127, 134, 137, 179, 194, 240, 243, 247, 264, 360, 361, 373, 385, 392, 468, 473, 475
Durkee, Frank H., Jr. *128*
Durkee, Harry 247
Durkee Enterprises 58, 99, 108, 112, 121, 122, 126, 129, 130, 131, 132, 146, 149, 161, 175, 176, 177, 178, 180, 182, 183, 194, 198, 201, 202, 221, 243, 257, 259, 261, 278, 288, 289, 294, 295, 296, 302, 323, 336, 349, 353, 354, 355, 356, 360, 367, 379, 380, 385, 392, 400, 419, 432, 445, 472, 474, 477, 480
Durwood, Stanley 455, 492
Durwood Theaters 455
Dusman, Henry *128*
Dusman, J.F. 103, 193, 254, 255, 279, 373, 382
Dutton, Charles S. 2

Eagle Theater 247, 256, 301, 472, 480
Eagles' Industrial Exposition 16
Eagleston, Policewoman 65
Earle, Edward 59, 287
Earle, Edward C. 29
Earle, Virginia 17
Earle Theater 177, 184, 256, *257*, 473, 477, 479
Earle Theater (Ellicott City, Maryland) 256
Earle Theater (Washington, D.C.) 75, 155
Earle Theater Company 256
East Theater 406
Easter, Hamilton 10, 11, 48, 465
Eastern Avenue Partnership 295, 367
Eastern Bakery 406
Eastern Industrial Clinic 204
Eastern Theater 256–257
Easterner Theater 257
Easter's Park 463
Easter's Theater 28, 257
Easton, Maryland 73, 186, 250
Eastpoint 4 Theater 257
Eastpoint Shopping Center 238, 257
Eastpoint 10 Theaters 173, 183, 257–*258*
Eastport Cinema (Annapolis, Maryland) 172
Eastway Theater 349
Eberson, Drew 382
Eberson, John 179, 231, 235, 364, 414, 422, 423, 453
Echo Theater 258–*259*

Ecstasy 114, 268, 416, 474
Eden Theater 145, 345
Edgemere Theater 139, 259
Edgewater Twin Theater (Edgewood, Maryland) 479
Edgewood, Maryland 479
Edgewood Theater 112, 130, 141, 146, 157, 259–*260*, 261, 454, 473
Edison films 261, 311
Edison, Thomas A. 8, 9, 442, 471
Edison Kinetophone 465
Edison Manufacturing Company 11
Edison Projecting Kinetoscope 101
Edisonia Theater 250
Edison's Kinedrome 16
Edmondson Amusement Company 221, 260, 410
Edmondson Drive-In 262, 435
Edmondson Theater 47, 221, 260–*261*, 468
Edmondson Village Shopping Center 139, 261
Edmondson Village Theater 139, 142, 161, 173, 174, 261–262, 454
Edouarde, Carl 470
Edwards, Gus 323
Egan and Michael 13
Ehmling's Music Hall 23, 643
Eichenkranz Society 301
Einbinder, Joseph 262, 412, 435
Eintracht Hall 461
Eisenhart, F.J.W. 456
Electone sound system 108
Electric Park 7, 8, 9, 11, 13, 14, 15, 16, 19, 22, 23, 48, 49, 262–264, 400, 462, 463
Electric Park and Exhibition Company 262
Electric Park Improvement Company 264
Elektra Theater *264*, 265, 408, 480
Elite Theater 250, 361
Elkridge Drive-In 265, 454
Elkridge, Maryland 265, 412
Elkton, Maryland 73, 479
Elkton Movies 4 (Elkton, Maryland) 479
Ellicott City, Maryland 50, 70, 142, 186, 199, 256, 265, 412, 476
Ellicott Theater Company 265
Ellington, Duke 213, 254
Elliott, Comstock, and Gest 208
Elterman, John 235, 423
Embassy Theater 91, 104, 139, 154, 268, 426, *427*
emergency house 192
Emerick's Orchestra 390
Emmart, Paul 361, 378, 390, 391, 407, 432
Emmart brothers 434
Emmerich, Henrietta 216, 217
Emmerich, William 216, 217, 248
Emmerich and Demme 52, 216
Emmerson's Famous Moving Pictures 462
Emperor's Nightingale 309

Empire burlesque circuit 18, 266, 431
Empire Theater 16, 17, 265–266, 266–271, 462
Empire Theater (New York, New York) 277, 484
Empire Theater Company 105, 268
Engel, Joan 235
Engelmeyer, Michael C. 362, 489
Engineer's Daughter 31
English, John 323
Ennis, Robert 410
Eno Troupe 132
Enoch Pratt Library 185, 295, 416
Ephraim, Frank 243
epidemics 71, 72, 73
Epstein, Gertrude 128
Equitable Bank 392
Equitable Trust Company 230
Erlanger, Abraham 191, 278
Ertel, John A. 247, 256, 301, 408
Ertel, Nicholas 350
Ertel and Albers Company 408
Erwin, Robert E. 331
Erwood Stock Company 15
Essanay films 261, 311
Essers, Hendrick 79
Essex Amusement Company 264
Essex Hall (Essex, Maryland) 271
Essex, Maryland 128, 264, 271, 349, 407, 473, 480
Essex Theater (Essex, Maryland) 271
Etting, Ruth 235
Euchtman-Macht House 185
Eureka Amusement Company 243, 271, 318
Eureka Theater 71, 245, 271, **273**, 468
Europa Theater 105, 114, 152, 252, 326, 474
European films 109, 152
European Jewish Actors' Ensemble 335
European Summer Garden, Museum and Vaudeville Theater 353
Eutaw House Hotel 51, 302, 485
Evander, E. Bernard 204, 209, 296, 297, 412, 435, 436, 454
Evans, William F. 34
Evening Sun 61, 64, 69, 72, 78, 79, 85, 107, 117, 119, 122, 124, 162, 168, 461
Ewell, George 468
Ewing, Rev. Gene 403
Excelsior Theater 273
Excelsior Theater Company 273
Excess Baggage 208
exhaust fans 74
Exhibitor Merit Award 250
exhibitors 34, 58, 59, 62. 63, 68, 69, 89, 98, 99, 100, 106, 108, 122, 127, 128, 129, 139, 151, 153, 161, 168, 175, 182
Exhibitors' League 464
Exhibitors' League of Maryland, Inc. 58, 60, 61, 67, 98, 99, 115, 375, 467, 468, 485
exhibitors' school 63, 468
Exhibitors' Union 100
Exit 3
Eyer, Charles B. 247
Eyring, Edward 139
Eyring, Erhard 332, 424
Eyring, John F. 179, 202, 228, 229, 256, 257, 318, 349, 370, 372, 404, 412, 420, 421, 428, 454
Eyring, Joseph 424
Eyring, William E., Sr. 204
Eyring, E. and Sons 157, 195, 203, 392

Fagan, Jack B. 225
Fairall, Harry K. 477
Fairmount Theater 274, 375
Fairyland Theater 71, 274, 352
Fait, John 370
Fait, William 34, 47, 66, 242, 246, 254, 323, 370, 378
Family Dollar Store 405
Family Theater 27, 29, 37, 70, 274
Famous Ballroom 417
The Famous Ford 327
Famous Players–Lasky 91, 96
Fanny 491
Fantasia 160
Farcier, Howard 468
Farnan, Thomas F. 65, 66
Farragut, Admiral 485
Farrell, Anthony 203
Farson, Prof. John D. 202, 353
Farson's, Prof. Gwynn Oak Orchestra 33, 199, 242, 347, 353
Farwell, Bernard 292
fast food 148
Faulkner, Kenneth G 78, 338, 443
Fawcett, George 265, 331
Fawcett Stock Company 461
Fayette Theater 274–275
FBI 109, 132, 135, 271, 416
Federal League 407
Federal League Park 357–358
Federal Motion Picture Commission 469
Federal Theater 275
Federalsburg, Maryland 73
Federated Charities of Baltimore 71
Federoff, Herman 225
Federoff's Orchestra 443
Feldman, Herman 260
Feldman, Nathan 411
Fells Point Dinner Theater 224
female ushers 134, 326, 352, 457
Fenhagen, Carl 194
Fenneman, August 8, 262, 263
Fenton and Lichtig 301, 435, 436, 455
Fernandis, William 405
Fetchit, Stepin 324
Fidelity Amusement Company 298, 411
Fields, Joseph B. 31, 179, 320, 387, 388, 390
Fields, Lewis 31
Fields, W.C. 15, 335
Field's Millinery 438
Fields Photo Play Theater 390
Figgs, George 295, 358
fight films 37
Fight for Peace 416
Fighting the Fire Bomb 133
fights 178, 179
Figrani, Angelo 338
Film Art Theater 152
Film Booking Office 91
Film Centre 176, 230
film exchanges 47, 52, 73, 127, 128, 482
film rental 89, 90
Film Row (Washington, D.C.) 128
Film Service Association 52
film shortages 134
film studio 3
Filmart Theater 416
Finan, Judge Thomas B. 169
finances 316
Fine Arts Theater 152, 415, 416, 490
Fingles, W.A. Company 398
Finn, Thomas 34
Finnerty, Steve 236
Finster, George 338
fires 17, 18, 43, 426, 458
first Monday germans 322
First National 91, 254, 399
first-run films 160, 167, 476
first-run theaters 75, 76, 90, 96, 100, 104, 105, 112, 119, 121, 129, 139, 141, 176, 470
Fisher, Frank A. 246
Fisher, Lazarus 278
Fisher, Louis 216, 323
Fisher's Prof. String and Brass band 8, 12, 263, 403
Fiske, Minnie Maddern 16, 334
Fitfy-Fifth Street Playhouse (New York, New York) 486
Fittro, Nellie D. 456
Fitzjarrell, H.A. 218
Fitzsimmons, M.J. 213
5-West Theater 141, 144, 152, 161, 168, 365, 379
Flag Amusement Company 199
A Flag Is Born 476
Flag Theater 37, 275, 472
Flagship Cinemas 412
Flaig, Dottie 285
Flaig, Gus 285
Flaks, Benjamin 254
Flaks, Kalem 198, 356
Flaks, Kalman 324
Flaks, Morris 216, 253, 389
Flaks Brothers 281
Flaks Photoplay Theater 216
Flaming Arrow Theater 34, 79, 82, 275–*276*
Flax, Benjamin 119
Flax, J. 362

Flax, Joseph 445
Flax, Nathan 445
Flax Brothers 301
Fletcher, Frederick A. 210, 212
Fleury, Albert 278
Flint, George 370, 372, 420, 480
Flood's Park 463
Flores Theater (Acapulco, Mexico) 43, 465
flu epidemic 54
Foard, J. Reginald 82, 218
Folk, William 386
Follies of the Day 266
Follow Me 252
Folly Theater 71, 430
Fonda, Henry 335
Ford, Charles E. 8, 9, 73, 262, 277, 278, 398, 462
Ford, Gene 235
Ford, John T. 276, 277, 307
Ford, Robert *102*
Ford Family 277
Ford's Theater 7, 8, 9, 11, 14, 22, 23, 54, 63. 64, 71, 73, 112, 143, 144, 162, 176, 184. 208, 263, 269, 276–278, 340, 400, 462, 464, 468, 483
Ford's Theater (Washington, D.C.) 276
foreign language films 109, 140, 141, 151, 177, 240, 362, 406
Forest, Edwin 308
Forest Park Company 362
Forest Park Motion Picture Company 278
Forest Park Theater 278
Forest Theater 112, 146, 278–*279*
Forever Amber 382
Forman, Charles 375
Forrest, A. Lowther 51, 179, 198, 199, 213, 217, 218, 221, 251, 254, 292, 298, 345, 346, 353, 408, 409, 413, 424, 427, 443, 444, 445, 453
Forrest, Helen 235
Forresters' Hall 202
Forsythe, John R. 370, 372, 379, 409
Forsythe Shoes 438
Fort George G. Meade 323, 339, 410
Fort Howard 213
Fort Howard Band 293
Fort McHenry 72
Fort Ti 153, 284
Forty Thousand Horsemen 209
Fotoplayer 82, 352
Four Musical Kings 425
Four-Star Corporation 321
Four Walls 253
Four Years in Germany 71
Fourth Liberty Loan 71
Fourth Regiment Armory 15
Fourth Regiment Military Orchestra 329
Fourth War Loan 133
Fowler, L.H. 332
Fox 91, 122, 137, 254

The Fox 198
Fox, Harry W. 336
Fox, Myer 71, 383
Fox, Raymond J. 271
Fox, William 76, 96
Foxy Grandpa 207
Foy, Eddie 330
Fradkin Family 259
France-Merrick Foundation 307
Francis, Kay 335
Frank, Benjamin 221, 223
Frankenstein Meets the Wolfman 136
Franklin Theater 327
Frazee, Roy C. 219
Frederick, Maryland 50, 51, 66, 142, 186, 468, 486
Frederick Theater 279
Frederick, Virginia 157
Fredericks, George A. 330
Free State Organ Society 487–488
Freedman, Philip 225
Freedman, Ronald 164, 165, 212, 383
Freitag, William 374
Fremont Amusement Company 279, 484
Fremont Theater 279, *280*, 281, 468
French films 109, 133
Fresh Air Society 71
Freuler, J.R. 52
Freund, John, Jr. 214, 216, 240, 274, 314, 315, 316, 320, 323, 349, 350, 407, 453
Freund & Crawford 240
Frick, Frank 343
Frick, W.F. 191
Friedberg, S. 410
Friedlander, Jacob 388, 389
Friedman, Mr. 193
Friese, Albert H. 258, 259
Frisch, Billy 33, 352
Fritz and Snitz 207
Friz, Clyde N. and Nelson 194
Frizzle's confectionery 256
Frog Mortar Corp. 215
Frog Mortar Creek 482
Frohman, Charles 190, 484
Frohman, Daniel 191
Frohsinn Hall 20
Front Street Theater 7, 8, 43, 465
Froos, Sylvia 305
Fruchtman, Jack 155, 161, 167, 176, 179, 209, 250, 341, 348, 365, 389, 417, 418, 478, 479
fuel crisis 70
fuel shortages 134
Fuld, Manes 464, 492
Fuller, George A. Company 281
Fullerton 214
Fulton Theater 60, 112
Fun Quiz 245
A Funny Thing Happened on the Way to the Forum 278

Gabriel, William F. 380
Gaertner, George 379

Gaertner, Harry 119, 274, 474
Gaertner, Louis 122, 179, 318, 474
Gaertner Theaters 99, 119, 228, 240, 256, 360, 379, 380, 385, 404, 428, 472, 474, 477, 479
Gaffney, G. Horton 352
Gailbraith, Warren Hackett 403
Gaither, Police Commissioner 83, 116, 123, 331
Gallagher, Joseph A. 274
Galveston Cyclone 50
Gamble, Edgar 34
Gambrills, Maryland 412
Gans, Arthur 358
Ganter, Carl 308
Garbo, Greta 97
Garden Bowling and Billiard Academy 281
Garden Roof 62, 281, 282, 470
Garden Theater 58, 62, 70, 71, 74, 75, 76, 78, 80, 89, 91, 92, 96, 100, 103, 112, 176, 281–*282*, *283*–284, 335
Garden Theatre Company 284
Gardner, Arthur 490
Gardner, R.H. 162
Garfink, Joseph 212
Garland, Robert 79
Garman, Lauritz *128*, 137, 179, 212, 349, 370, 372, 420, 480
Garmen-Beck theaters 155, 212, 370, 472
Garrett County, Maryland 56
Gaskill-Mundy-Levitt High Class vaudeville 16
Gatch, T.B. & Sons 411
Gaul, Fritz 59
Gaumont 465
Gay, William 416
Gay Masqueraders 14
Gay Street Museum 284–285
Gayety Theater 18, 36, 42, 54, 57, 62, 71, 98, 132, 162, 166, 168, 185, 243, 268, 285–*286*, 426, 431
Gebhardt, Joel 51, 425
Gee, Lottie 360
Gem Museum 286
Gem Theater 286–287
Gemmel, H.V. 408
General Cinema Corp. 96, 149, 159, 161, 174, 176, 183, 184, 238, 245, 300, 358, 359, 369, 392, 418, 420, 445, 480, 482
General Drive-In Corporation 300
General Electric 35
General Film Company 52, 53, 127, 367, 466, 467
General Pulaski Drive-In 126, 144, 169, 287
George, Anita 124
George, Grover 124
George, H. Barry 366
George, William 468
George Brothers 320
Gerard, Barney 266
Gereson, Hyman 409

Index 507

German language films 132, 473
German theater 109
Germania Maennerchor Society 320, 461
Germania Mannerchor Hall 20
Gertrude McCoy Theater 59, 60, 70, **287–288**, 289, 456, 468, 484
Gerwig, Jacob F. 238, 314, 320, 329, 369, 406
Getchey, Ruth 465
Getting Gertie's Garter 331
Gettinger, Walter 415, 490
Getz Taylor 308, 309
Gewandhaus (Leipzig, Germany) 343
GFS Theatre Corporation 250
Gibbons, Cardinal 12
Gibbs, Cornelia 118
Gibbs, Mrs. Rufus M. 472
Gibelli and Company 398
Gibson, Edgar 203
Gibson, Frank 313
Gibson, John 330
Gieske, Walter M. 229, 320, 321, 410
Gifford, James J. 276, 307
Gigi 231
Gilbert and Sullivan 295, 424
Gilded Lily 234
Gilliece, Mary K. 162
Gilmor Amusement Company 289
Gilmor Theater 289
Girl Friends 417
Girl from Maxim's 469
Giuliano, Mike 172
glass bricks 454
Glaum, Louise 92
Glen Burnie Mall Theater (Glen Burnie, Maryland) 161, 172, 289, 351
Glen Burnie, Maryland 104, 126, 142, 158, 159, 161, 172, 173, 174, 176, 177, 203, 204, 289, 293, 300, 342, 351, 384, 455
Glen Burnie Theater (Glen Burnie, Maryland) 289
Glen Burnie Town Center Cinemas (Glen Burnie, Maryland) 289
Glen Burnie Town Center 7 Theater (Glen Burnie, Maryland) 173, 182, 289
Glen Theater (Glen Burnie, Maryland) 203, 204
Glendening, Governor Parris N. 306
Glenn L. Martin Company 192
Glenville, Peter 161, 418
Glick, Maurice 204
Glidden, Edward H. 247, 278, 279, 424, 427
Globe Moving Picture Parlor 357
Globe Theater 199, 246
Glorious Adventure 40
Go and Get It 387
Go-to-Church Day 60
Goeller, James 313
Goeller, Joe 23

Goelz, Adam 376
Gold Rush 192
Goldberg, Max 326
Goldberg, Nathan 323, 390
Goldberg, Thomas D. 47, 59, 63, 71, 122, 146, 260, 290, 291, 298, 367, 404, 405, 428, 430, 440, 467, 474, 475, 484, 485
Goldberg Theater 71, 290–291, 430
Goldberg's Gwynn Park Theater 290–291
Goldbloom, Leroy **150**
Golden Arrow Theater 291
Golden Ring Mall 342
Golden West Cowboys 306
Goldfield Orchestra 34, 251
Goldfield Theater 60, 101, 178, 203, 291
Goldfinger 160
Goldman, Barry 252, 391
Goldman, L. Edward 305
Gomery, Douglas 103
Gomprecht, Jacob 316
Gone with the Wind 236
Good Time Theater 201, 291
Goodman, Benny 306
Goodman, Ella Lott 315
Goodman, Ethyl 256
Goodman, J.R. 34
Goodman, Julius 61, 123, 314, 315, 357
Goodman, Max 256, 265
Goodman, Mayor Philip H. 145
Goodman, Sol 122, 128
Goodwill Stores 320
Goodwin, Nat 192, 308, 331
Goodwin's Hall (Reisterstown, Maryland) 225
Gordon Realty Company 291
Gordon Theater 291, 485
Gorsuch, Charlie 217
Gorsuch, Marshal 30
Gott, Jackson 247
Gottfried organ 297
Gottleib-Knabe Company 343
Goucher College 145
Gough, Bernard B. 98, 474
Govans Corporation 392
Govans Theater 291, 392
Governor Plaza Shopping Center (Glen Burnie, Maryland) 385
Governor Ritchie Drive-In (Glen Burnie, Maryland) 104, 114, 126, 160, 292, **293**, 454
Grable, Betty 306, 340
Grace and St. Peter's Church 341
Grafanola Company of Norfolk 410
Grand 24 Theaters (Dallas, Texas) 183
Grand Hotel and Cafe 380
grand jury 86, 87
Grand Musee and Theatre 7, 13, 360
Grand Oscar Micheaux Cinema II 302
Grand Rapids, Michigan 463
Grand Theater **30**, 33, 51, 53, 58,
71, 112, 113, 172, 184, 185, 186, 292, 293–**294**, 295, 367, 452, 456, 458, 466, 487, 489
Grand Theater Company 367
Grand United Order of Brothers and Sisters of Good Hope 407, 463
Grant, Irving 145
Grant, Jerome 412
Grant, John A. 55
Grant, Joseph 145, 250, 256, 301, 356, 406, 412
Grant, President Ulysses S. 485
Grant theaters 144, 145, 302, 480
Graphic Theater 361
Graubner's West End Park 15
Graul's Orchestra 193
Gray, William Bruce 204, 330, 481
Gray's Theater 295
Great Duero 33
Great Eastern Amusement Company 257
Great Eastern Film Exchange 127
The Great Lester 327
Great Otillie 432
Great Train Robbery 19, 334
Great Wizard Theater 60, 413, 441, 442
Greater Baltimore Cinema 175, 394
Greater Baltimore Committee, Inc. 185, 306
Greater Baltimore Theater Company 193, 214, 400, 481
Greater Baltimore Theaters *see* Greater Baltimore Theater Company
Greater Cupid Theater 247
Greater Wizard Company 442
Greed 468
Greek films 383, 406
Green, William 440
Greenbaum and Evatt 279
Greenbelt, Maryland 155
Greenbelt Theater (Greenbelt, Maryland) 478
Greenberg, Louis 350
Greenberg, Ronnee 168
Greener, George S. 34, 240, 358
Greenmount Amusement Company 295
Greenmount Gardens 295
Greenspring Bowling Alley 295
Greenspring Shopping Center 176, 295
Greenspring 3 Theaters 182, 295
Greenwich Village Inn (New York, New York) 470
Gregory, George T. "Bunny" 34, 62, 386
Grieves Worrall Wright & O'Hatnick 394
Griffin, R. 366
Griffin, Robert J. 50
Griffith, D.W. 63
Griggs, Harry F. 375
Grisman, Sam 253
Gross, Edward 85

Gross, Oskar 345, 488
Der Grosse Tenor 326
grosses 147, 148, 155
Grosso, Elmer 470
Grote, F. Clarence 34, 456
Group 7 Media 310
Gruver, Bob 351
Gruver, J. Henry 204
Guardaboscia, John 266
Guild Theater 295
Guilford Building Company 202
Guilford Theater 295–296
Gunga Din 292
Gunts, Edward 417
Gus Sun Circuit 490
Gutermuth, Mr. 264
Guterson, Mischa 79, 209, 399, 426
Guth's Gold Medal Candies 252
Gwynn Amusement Company 485
Gwynn Oak Park 23, 463, 480
Gwynn Theater 112, 122, 146, 194, **296**, 473, 475, 485
The Gypsy Baron 330
Gyr, Henry 214

H.M. Rowe Company 298
H.M.S. Pinafore 278
Habighurst, Charles 250
Hackerman, Herman S. 357
Hackett, Francis 64
Haefele Company 103
Hagerstown, Maryland 82, 142, 186, 468
Hagert, Conrad F. 387
Hagwood, Charles 236
Hail Mary 417
Hale's Tours 489
Halethorpe, Md. 405
Haley, Bill 284
Hall, Mr. 301
Hallelujah 121
Hallen and Fuller 12
Halling, Mrs. 409
halls 7, 20
Halsey, Stuart & Company 75
Halsted, Egbert 405
Hamilton 123, 202, 247
Hamilton, G.W. 216
Hamilton Amusement Company 362
Hamilton Corporation 247
Hamilton Presbyterian Church 247
Hammett, Corinne F. 342
Hammond, Harvey 179, 236
Hampden 51, 123, 128, 296, 314, 315
Hampden Hall 461
Hampden Theater 71, 122, 137, **296–297**, **315**, 472, 477
Hand, Judge Learned 114
Hane, Audrey 179
happy endings 2
Happy Johnny 275
Happy Johnny's Talent Hunt 307
The Happy Journey 335
Happyland 21, 297

Harbor Park Garage 342
Harbor Park theaters *see* movies at Harbor Park
Harbor West luxury condominium 342
Hardy Holzman Pfeiffer Associates 186, 306–307, 486
Harford Art Theater 298
Harford Avenue Methodist Episcopal Church 50
Harford County, Maryland 480
Harford Theater 112, 117, 131, 158, **298**, 385, 472, 474, 477, 485
Hargrave, Victor C. 220
Harig, Karl G. 246
Harlem Park 319
Harlem Park Community Baptist Church 300
Harlem Park Methodist Episcopal Church 298, 411
Harlem Square 299
Harlem Theater 129, 151, 250, 298–**299**, 300, 411
Harmans, Maryland 343
Harmon, Tom 323
Harper, Charles E. 67
Harrington, Governor Emerson C. 67, 73
Harris, Britton & Dean 191
Harris, Charles 254, 324
Harris, Patrick 191
Harris, Paul 79, 253, 380
Harris and Rullman 291
Harrison, David 200, 212, 216, 217, 251, 291, 333, 340, 366, 373, 375, 376, 377, 407, 411, 412, 426, 440, 454
Harrison, Mrs. Thomas B. 67, 68, 69
Harrison, Gen. William Henry 485
Hartlove, James J. 35, 47, 238, 248, 250, 275
Hartman, Herbert M. 278
Hart's Tavern 430
Hartz, Michael 51, 425
Harundale Mall 300
Harundale Mall Theater (Glen Burnie, Maryland) 158, 159, 161, 172, 174, 300, 351, 445, 485
Hassan "the Turk" 431
Hasslinger, Daisy 300
Hasslinger, Louis 300
Hasslinger's Daisy Theater 300–301
Haswell, Percy 331
Haubert, Anna 456
Havre de Grace, Maryland 59
Hawkins, John W. 301
Hawkins Airdome 301, 453
Hawley, Ormi 59
Hayes, Margaret 2
Hazazer's Hall 62
Hazelhoff, Carl 390
Hazzard, Stephen 227, 228
Head, T.O. 192
hearing-impaired patrons 387
Heath, Edward 349
heating systems 104

Heatter, Gabriel 131
Hebrew Free School Society 248
Hebrew Ladies' Consumptive Association 60
Hecht Company 278
Hedden's Casino 463
Heinz, John H. 35, 286
Helldorfer, Louis 274
Heller, Fred 431
Heller, Dr. George 97
Hello Dixie 253
Hello, Dolly 340
Helm, Joseph 317
Helmers, Gerhard 338
Helwig, Gottfried 409
Hemberger, Prof. Theodore 320
Hemmick, Lloyd H. 316
Henderson, Mr. 127
Henderson, Newton R. 193
Hendler's Creamery 248
Henny, Thomas M. 487
Henon, D.T. 396
Henon, Paul J., Jr. 396
Henry V 327
Henry, Marshal 69
Herbert, Victor 154, 387
Herckey, Agnes 361
Heritage Playhouse Theater 310
Heritage Shadows of the Silver Screen 302, 366
Herman's New Electric Park 463
Herrington, Frederick J. 60
Herrman, Page 472
Heson and Lee 359
Hess, Harry 468
Hesson, Louis 298
Hesson, Mrs. Louis 465
Hewitt, William, Jr. 164, 165, 202, 265, 486
Heywood-Wakefield seats 177, 325, 340, 435
Hicken, Donald 185, 306
Hicks, C. William 132, 209, 327, 328, 335, 412, 438
Hicks, Charles A. 35, 296
Hicks-Baker theaters 297, 419, 480
Hicks, Muse, Tate & Furst 183
Hicks theaters 194, 221, 297, 327, 335, 435, 477
Higgins, Billy 252
High, Wallace 202, 203, 274, 375
High School Confidential 306
Highland Academy 301
Highland Airdome 301
Highland Amusement Company 293
Highland Park 373
Highland Theater 301, 375
Highlandtown 30, 56, 186, 214, 295, 301, 406, 456, 466, 480, 485
Hi-Hat Club 415, 490
Hildebrand, Curtis **128**
Hildebrand, Russell 179
Hildebrandt, T.T. 403
Hilgartner Company 398

The Hill 406
Hill, Gus 268
Hill Theater 139, 142, 301
Hillendale Theater 158, 160, 172, 175, 176, 182, 301–302, 454, 455, 481
Hilltop Diner 249
Hilltop Players 365
Hilltop Shopping Center 249, 250, 482
Hilltop Theater 144
Hilt and Chick 33
Hilton Amusement Company 440
Hilton Theater 131, **290**–291, 430, 440
Hindenburg Theater 109, 132, 133, 415, 416, 475, 490
Hines, Earl 254
Hinners organ 434
Hippodrome Collection 485
Hippodrome Performing Arts Center 186
Hippodrome Theater 43, 52, 54, 58, 61, 62, 71, 74, 75, 76, 79, 80, 82, 91, 96, 100, 104. 105, 106, 110, 111, 113, 116, 124, 125, 129, 131, 132, 134, 136, 137, 138, 144, 159, 168, 174, 176, 178, 181, 185, 269, 271, 302–**303**, **304** 305–107, 426, 470, 478, 479, 483, 485
Hippodrome Theater Company 413
Hirshberg, Isidore W. 254
Hirshberg, Dr. Leonard K. 254
Hitchcock, Alfred 467
Hitchcock, Harry R. 463
Hitchcock, Walter 19, 20, 463
Hitching Post Coffee and Tea Bar 349
Hitler: The Last Ten Days 245
Hiway Theater (Essex, Maryland) 139, 142, 160, 307
Hobelman Motors 275
Hochschild, Kohn, and Company 326, 382
Hoen Building 45, 46
Hoffberger, S. 210
Hoffman, John 293
Hoffman, Solomon 291
Hoffman, W.S. 200
Hoffman and Henon 103, 394, 395, 396, 453
Hoffman House Casino 463
Hoffmeister, J. George 26, 250, 361
Hoffmeister, William 47
Holliday, Billie 2
Holliday Street Theater 7, 8, 13, 17, 23, 29, 32, 36, 54, 266. 268, 307, 481, 484
Hollingshead, Richard M. 126
Holly, Joshua 472
Hollywood Honeys 335
Hollywood Park 17, 23, 463
Hollywood Theater (Arbutus, Maryland) 142, 174, 175, 308, **309**, 461
Holman, Charlie 431

Holmes, Burton 13, 14, 15, 16, 23, 330, 343, 463
Holthouse, William 294, 458
Holtzman's Bakery 250
Homand, Leo H. 84, 146, 200, 411
Home Amusement Company 332
Home Depot 262
home rule 118
Home Theater 123, 308
Homeland Amusement Company 382
Homewood Amusement Company 353
Homewood Theater 139, 141, 151, 176, 177, 308–310, 325, 362, 489
Homicide 257
hoochie-coochie 70
Hood and Schultz 52, 229
Hook, Jacob W. 194
Hooper, Walter C. 199
Hope, Bob 306
Hopkins, Miriam 335
Hopkins, S. Gordon 366
Hopkins' Trans-Oceanic Star Specialty Company 9
Hopper, De Wolfe 45, 46, 191, 335
Hopper, William J. 305
Horitz Passion Play 12
Horn and Horn 148
Horn Theater 47, 60, 70, 79, 90, 91, 310, **311**, **312**, 340, 390, 477
Horne, Lena 382
Hornig, Al 399
Hornig, Frank A. 35, 47, 59, 69, 133, 135, 179, 310, 311, 340, 390, 477
Hornig, Frank, Jr. **128**
Hornig, Paul 310, 311
Hornsby Theater 406
Hornstein, Henry B. 47, 179, 289
Hornstein, Isaac L. 47, 380, 411
Hornstein, Louis 47, 380, 382
Hornstein, Simon C. 47, 380
Hornstein Family 251, 376, 382
Horton, Edward Everett 2
Hospital for Crippled Children 18
Hot Chocolates 476
Hotel Bayou 59
Hotel Kernan 16, 17, 70, 207, 209, **334**, 335
Hotel Men's Association 83
Hotel Sahara 415
Houck, George H. 307
Houdini, Harry 18, 278, 335
House of Wax 152, 153
Howard, G. Kingston 34, 91, 100, 179, 180, 312, 464, 468
Howard Amusement Company 403
Howard and Johnson 180, 312
Howard Auditorium 7, 8, 9, 11, 12, 13, 14, 15, 17, 19, 23, 40, 54, 70, 71, 79, 96, 105, 106, 111, 129, 134, 185, 204–**205**, 206–109, 335, 338, 395, 409, 457
Howard County 474
Howard House (Ellicott City, Maryland) 476

Howard Kelly Hospital 471
Howard Rollins Cinema I 302
Howard Street 209
Howard Theater 98, 168, 172, 173, 352, 415
Howard Theater (Washington, D.C.) 254
Howe, Lyman H. 22, 23, 464
Hoyert, Margaret Ann 490
Hoyt's Theaters 176, 183, 184, 313, 345, 434
Hoyt's West Nursery 14, 186, 345, 434
Hudson Realty Company 412
Hughes, Governor Harry 171
Hughes, Irvin 253
Hughes, Johnny 490
Hughes' Bill 469
Hull, Henry 208
Hull Theater 51, 312
Hullabaloo 351
Hulse, Robert 468
Humbert, W. Arthur 21, 242
Humes and Lewis 425
Hunt, Edgar 79
Hunt, Guy **102**
Hunt Valley Cinema 12, 176, **313**, 492
Hunt Valley Mall 313, 486
Huntington Building Company 314
Huntington Hall 314
Huntington Theater 313–314, 466
Huntington Theater Company 313
Hupfeldt, H.H. 375
Hurlock, Roger 250, 405
Hutchins, Elmer 217, 370
Hutzler Annex 266
Hutzler Brothers 282
Hutzler's Department Store 266
Huxley, Thomas 190
Hyatt, Robert 212
Hyde, Clifford 34

I Am Curious (Yellow) 169
I Married an Angel 236
I, the Jury 271
IATSE 135
IATSE Local 181 34, 99, 100, 101, 148, 149, 180, 246
IATSE Local 181-A 101, 102
IATSE Local 224 62
Ice Palace 204
Icehouse Theater 375
ID8 488
Ideal Airdome 315–316
Ideal Theater 21, 51, 61, 108, 122, 123, 128, **314–315**, 463, 466, 472
Ideal Theater (Martinsburg, West Virginia) 51
Ideal Theatre Company 410, 486
Idle Hour Theater 38, 71, 100, 316, 415
IDS Group 405
Idzi, Edward D. 223
illustrated songs 39, 42, 58
IMAX 454

510 INDEX

Imperial Russian Court Balalaika Orchestra 190
improper subjects 97
Imwold, Charles H. 279, 394
In Chinatown 324
Independence Day 183
Independent Film Company 426
Independent Motion Picture Exhibitors of America 464
Independent Motion Picture Operators and Managers Union 99, 123
Independent Order of Odd Fellows Hall 142, 229, 247, 388
independent projectionists' union 99, 101, 123, 148, 149, 168
infantile paralysis 71
influenza 71, 72, 73, 92
Inner Harbor 184, 250, 342, 412
Inner Harbor multiplex 161, 178
Inside Nazi Germany 132
Insley, Roy 401
Integration 143, 145
Interfraternal Council of Baltimore 143
intermissions 55
International Alliance of Theatrical Stage Employees (IATSE) 34
International Lady 131
International League 357
International Projecting and Producing Company of Chicago 238
Intolerance 278, 468
Investment Company of Maryland 193
Irma la Douce 392
Iron Master 305
Irving, Sir Henry 190, 192, 331
Irving Amusement Company 391
Irving Theater 84, 87, 316
Irvington 87, 193, 316
Irvington Cinema 316
Irvington Theater 137, 146, 160, 316–*317*, 456, 472
Irvington Theater Company 316
Irwin, Fred 285, 484
Irwin, May 432
Irwin & Luescher 331
Irwin Brothers Compny 9
Isaacson, Sam 23, 62, 99, 100, 179, 386, 468
Islands in the Stream 171
Ismed 268
It Came from Outer Space 153, 271
Italian marble 398
It's a Wonderful Life 271
Itzel, Adam, Jr. 330
Iula, Felice 79, 80, 387, 396, 399, 470
Iula, Frank 470
Iula, Robert Paul 79, 219, 396, 399, 470
Iula, Ruffino 470
Ivanhoe Theater 317
Iverson, George D. 61, 62

J & L Theater Corporation 426
J.S.J. Amusement Company 332
Jackobson, Louis 426
Jackson, Edward 472
Jackson, Mayor Howard W. 118, 194, 292
Jackson, Marie 179
Jackson Park Theater (Chicago, Illinois) 131
Jacobs, A. & Sons 398
Jacobs, George W. 203, 291
Jacoby, Frank W. 85
Jaffe, Morris 390
Jardin de Danse 281, 282
Jaws 168
Jazz Singer 106, 108, 239, 289, 338, 382
Jean Theater 291
Jednosc-Polonia 109
Jefferson, Charles 199
Jefferson, John W. 250, 407
Jefferson, Joseph 192, 331
Jeffries, James J. 36
Jeffries–Johnson fight 36, 37
Jeffries–Ruhlin fight 15
Jeffries–Sharkey fight 14, 209, 276, 431
Jenkins, C. Francis 8
Jenkins, Harry E. 413
Jensen, Brennen 340
Jergens, Diane 306
Jermon, John G. 269
Jessel, George 305
Jeter, Thomas L. 407
Jewel Box Review 254
Jewell, Zella 199
Jewell Theater 158, 317
Jewish Educational Alliance 374
Jewish Museum of Maryland 485
Jews 118, 431
Jezierski, Alexander 124
JF Theaters 141, 144, 155, 164, 168, 169, 174, 175, 177, 178, 182, 183, 210, 228, 237, 238, 245, 250, 254, 256, 262, 271, 289, 306, 318, 327, 328, 340, 342, 377, 382, 389, 399, 400, 404, 416, 418, 424, 427, 480
Johansen, John M. 340
Johnny Jones' Valley Inn Orchestra 253
Johnny Klein's Beer Park 20
Johns Hopkins Hospital 403
Johns Hopkins University 145, 161, 418
Johnson, Augie **102**
Johnson, Calvin 376
Johnson, Clinton 212, 375
Johnson, Edward **102**
Johnson, Jack 36, 254, 382
Johnson, James P. 253
Johnson, John Elgin 271
Johnson, Lillian 227
Johnson, Michael 302, 310, 366
Johnson, Moses 203
Johnson, Richard 101
Johnson, Robert **102**
Johnson, Willie **102**

Johnson–Burns fight 464
Johnston, Eric 476
Johnstown Flood 263, 483
Jolson, Al 106, 306, 335
Jones, Charles J. 273
Jones, John R. 375
Jones, M. Louise 278
Jones, Spike 306, 485–486
Jones, Wallace 203
Jones, William N. 107
Jones and Heimiller 250
Jones Brothers 275
Joppatown Theater 174, 177
Jordan, Richard 171
A Journey to Luna 16, 265
Jowett, Garth 64
Judd, Dr. Zechia 116
Judith 369
Jumpers Mall Theaters (Pasadena, Maryland) 175, 176, 177, 182, 318, 455
Jungnickel, H.M. 189
Junior Order of United American Mechanics Bazaar 15
Juniper Tar 92
Justice Department 146

Kahl, Christian 243
Kahl, John 47, 248
Kahn, Harry 245, 405
Kahn, Jerome 411
Kahn, Robert 238
Kalem films 261, 311
Kaliz, Armand 396
Kaminsky, Evelyn 216
Kane, Thomas J. 301, 317
Kane, William 37325
Kane Theater 373
Kanode, Robert E. 193
Kanour, Gilbert 98, 151
Kansas City, Missouri 455, 478
Kanter, Robert 122, 296, 362, 373, 475, 485
Karmata Travelogues 343
Karp Theater 216
Karr, Harry E. 194
Kassel and Bauman 461
Katz, J.A. 408
Kaufman, David 273
Kaufman, S. Harry 305
Kavanaugh, Maxine 2
Kay Bee Amusement Company 440
Kaye, Danny 306
K/B Theaters 183
Keaton, Buster 19
Keen, Nat 35, 250, 252
Keenan, Joseph D. 292
Keene, Laura 308
Keene, Thomas A. 322
Keene and Smith 323
Keep 'Em Flying 131
Keeper of the Light 31
Keiser, F.H. 252
Keith, B.F. 19
Keith-Albee Organization 91, 305, 396
Keith-Albee Theater 284

Keith-Albee vaudeville 76, 284, 335
Keith's Theater 82, 104, 105, 106, 110, 124, 129, 131, 134, 136, 152, 153, 155, 162, 184, 281–*283*, 284, 338, 477
Keith's Theater (Washington, D.C.) 75
Keith's vaudeville 22, 71, 96, 207, 305, 334, 463, 471
Kelly, C. Markland 138
Kelly, Dr. Howard A. 96
Kelly, Jacques 168, 181, 266, 306, 342, 365, 479
Kelly, Rev. Raymond, Jr. 300
Kelly, Walter C. 489
Kelly Clayton & Mojzisek 214, 245, 246, 369, 394, 424, 425, 455
Kennard and Aler 445
Kennedy, Ambrose J. 83
Kennedy Children's Center 289
Kent Lounge (Towson, Maryland) 377
Kenton, Stan 335
Kentucky 230
Kept Husbands 113
Kernan, Eugene 17, 268
Kernan, James L. 7, 9, 12, 13, 16, 18, 19, 36, 121, 179, 204, 205, 206, 207. 208, 248, 285, 307, 331, 333, 334, 336, 386, 394, 431, 463, 481
Kernan brothers 430
Kernan Hospital for Crippled Children 18, 71, 462, 463
Kernan, James L. Company 284
Kernan, Schanberger and Irvin 248
Kernan theaters 14, 208, 462
Kerney, Bell 316
Kessler, Joseph 431
Kettlebahn, Harry 20
Key, Francis Scott 308
Key Theater (Washington, D.C.) 310
Keyser, Dr. R.E. 398
Keystone Theater 318
Kidd, Frank L. 318, 320
Kidd's Amusement Theater 318
kidnapping 178
Kiefaber, Peter W. 462
Kiefaber, Tom 175, 184, 302, 336, 389, 392, 393
Kiernan, Mr. 248
Kiesler, Hedy 114
Kilduff, John 484
Kilgen organs 82, 202, 419
Kilmer, Harry C. 67
Kimball organs 82, 211, 214, 225, 242, 274, 332, 341, 373, 383, 399, 482, 489
Kimpel, Edward, Jr. *128*, 405
Kinemacolor 40
Kinematographe 9, 10, 209
Kineoptikon 11, 209
Kinetograph 19, 22, 207, 263, 463, 483

Kinetoscope 7, 8, 16, 461, 483
Kinetoscope, Projecting 11
King, Lilly 274
King, Dr. Martin Luther 166, 167
King, King, and King 305
King of the Cowboys 259
Kingdom Within 78
Kingsbury, Capt. Lester L. 492
Kingsmore, Mr. 121
Kirker-Bender Patent Spiral Slide Fire-Escape 484; *see also* down-and-out chute
Kirkley, Donald 105, 112, 113, 114, 121, 153, 415, 468, 477, 488
Kirschenhofer, George 374
Kiss Me, Kate 278
kissing scenes 97, 98, 471, 472, 483
Klaw, Marc 191
Klaw & Erlanger 190, 208
Kleiman, Sigmund 316, 445
Klein, Colman 409
Klein, Morris 47, 201, 225
Klein, Paul 258
Klein, Sol *128*
Klein Amusement Company 374
Kleine, George 45
Kleine, George P. 225
Kleine films 261
Klein's Deer Park 463
Klemm, Gustav *see* Q.E.D.
Kline's Shore Line Park 463
Klotz, Walter 82
Knickerbocker Amusement Company 242, 407
Knickerbocker Motion Picture Company 3
Knickerbocker Theater (Washington, D.C.) 487
Knight, "Al" 294
Knight, Natalie 490
Kocourek, Charles 317, 408
Koenig, Franz 25, 240, 242, 328, 352, 371, 452
Kohlberg Kravis Roberts & Company 183, 184
Kohn, Moe 416, 490
Kolb, Henry 350
Kolb, Louis 123, 214
Kolb, William 243, 271
Konstant, George 373
Korean films 310
Koster & Bial's Music Hall 8
Kourkoules, James 333
Kramer, Robert W. 251, 261, 341, 439
Kraushaar, Otto 145
Kreis, George T. 34
Kreis, John L. 262
Kremen, Alexander 274, 275
Kremer, Jesse 238
Krucoff, Barney 388
Ku Klux Klan 93
Kubitz, D.E. 248
Kubitz & Koenig 296, 485
Kuhn, Major General Joseph E. 323
Kunkel, John F. 229
Kurnel-the-Great 439

Labor Lyceum 461
Lachman, Ed 151
Lachman & Murphy 252
LaCoda, Francis 361
Lacy, Ernest 12
Ladies' Broadway Symphony Orchestra 79, 360
Lady Chatterley's Lover 151
Ladykillers 365
Lafayette Amusement Company 248
Lafayette Players 252
Lafayette Square Theater (Buffalo, New York) 17, 18
Lafayette Square Theater (Washington, D.C.) 17, 481
Lafayette Theater 52, 119, 318, *319*, 378
Laferty, J. Edward 281, 282, 296, 297, 318, 373, 428, 429, 453
Laffmovie 415
La Fontaine Rouge 428
La Gallienne, Eva 335
Lake, E.A. 305
Lamarr, Hedy 114
LaMarr and Boyce 305
Lamb, Thomas W. 51, 156, 179, 194, 281, 283, 302, 303, 335, 363, 364, 409, 478, 489
Land Design/Research, Inc. 342
Lane, Preston 118
Lane of Lights 92
Lane Theater 318
Lange, William, Sr. 179, 286
Langtry, Lily 192, 278
Langville, John T. 275
Lankford, John A. 407, 463
Lansinger, Robert 399
Laocoon statue 236, 482
Lapin Dramagraph 35
Larkin, Nellie 120
Larkins, Magistrate 56
Lash, Lee 206
Lasky, Morris 202, 250
Latin Palace 224
Latrobe Theater 320, 466
Lauder, Harry 45
Laughter Over Broadway 335
Laurel, Maryland 482
Law & Burrell 398
Lawrence, Jack 389, 416
Lawrence of Arabia 209
Lazy H Ranch Boys 307
Leach, Robert F. 86, 87
Leader Theater 31, 51, 109, 320, 359, 410
Leave Her to Heaven 348
Lee, Canada 335
Lee, "Doc" Clarence 101, 472
Lee, Gypsy Rose 285
Lee, H.H. 212
Lee, Robert 216
Lee, Robert R. 200, 440
Lee, Virginia 92
Lee, Walter 338
Lee, William H. 424, 426, 427
Lee and Causby 257
Left Bank Jazz Society 365

Lehmann, Edward G. 320
Lehmann Hall 7, 133, 179, 320–*321*, 322, 415, 416, 461, 491
Leicht, Adam 406
Leicht, Bill 406, 490
Leipzig, Germany 343
Leitz, Edward J. 424
Lemaire & Dawson 305
Lemon Theater 199
Lenox Theater 47, **376**
Leonardtown, Maryland 479
Le-Roi Theater (Towson, Maryland) 377
Leser, C.C. Fulton 400, 453
Lester's School for Boys 486
A Letter to Mother 391
Levan, Flosie 329
Levee, Ray 350
Leventhal, Meyer "Mike" 50, 58, **128**, 179, 275, 431, 465, 468
Levi, Louis 198, 199
Levine, Irvin 68, 316, 317, 370
Levine, Jacob "Jack" 68, **128**, 274, 316, 317, 370
Levine, M. 426
Levinson, Barry 2, 249, 404
Levy, David 310, 417, 475
Levy, Jules 204
Levy, Paul 311, 414
Lewis, C.E. 305
Lewis, Frank 73
Lewis, Martin J. 415
Lewy, Harry 28, 35, 47, 223, 341, 441, 442
Lexington Park, Maryland 177
Lexington Theater 33, 47, **322**–323
Lexway Theater 110, 114, 162, 413, 414
Libertini, J.T. 383
Liberty Amusement Company 323
Liberty Cinemas 175
Liberty Court Shopping Center 323
Liberty Defense League of Maryland 61, 83, 117, 373
Liberty Heights Park 324
Liberty Loan drive 92
Liberty 1–2 Theater 323–324
Liberty Plaza Shopping Center 377
Liberty Theater 161, 323–324
Liberty Theater (New York, New York) 63
Lichtman, Abe 253
Lichtman Theaters 254
Life Boat 134
Lifephonetic Combination 143
Lighston, Ruth 145
Light in the Dark 40
Lights of New York 338
Lili 154
limelight 49
Limelight, Inc. 392
Lincoln Highway Theater 71, 324
Lincoln Number Two Theater 198
Lincoln Theater 28, 29, 47, 324, 356, 360, 389, 465
Linden Amusement Company 383

Linden Company 71
Linden Theater 130, 131, 141, 152, 324–325
Link, Shad 431
Link Brothers 320
Linthicum, Maryland 434
Linwood Amusement Company 213, 326
Linwood Theater 70, 112, **325**–326
lion 124, 125
Lipin, J. 169
Lipps' Society Chocolates 316
Lipsey, Charles 57
Lisztomania 478
litigation 130
Little 3 146, 147
Little Cinema 327
Little Egypt 17, 432
Little Egypt 358
Little Italy 412
Little Moving Picture Palace 327
Little Pickwick Theater 47, 68, 352, 370, 490
Little Princess 257
Little Theater 103, 104, 105, 107, 111, 121, 129, 133, 144, 152, 155, 159, 163, 168, 176, 181, 184, 326–327, 399, 408
Little Theater (Washington, D.C.) 326, 327, 486
Little Washington Theater 361
Little X Theater 327
Livingston, Bernard 199, 481
Lloyd, Archie 33, 352, 414
Lloyd Street Synagogue 60
Lockhart, E.A. 254, 255, 279, 316, 317, 345
Loeb Building 20, 34
Loew, E.M. 292
Loew, Marcus 51, 75, 76, 96, 235, 302, 305, 413
Loew's Cineplex Entertainment 183, 184, 238
Loew's Inc. 261
Loew's Theaters 77, 91, 103, 105, 108, 111, 137, 138, 141, 147, 176, 236, 246, 289, 305, 318, 364, 369, 389, 399, 411, 412, 417, 419, 420, 422
Loew's Theatre Management Corporation 177, 181, 183
Lohmeyer, Harry 398
Lombard Theater 327
London, England 46, 362
Loose, Prof. J. Albert 143, 199
Lopez, Vincent 470
Lord Baltimore Theater 34, 51, 53, 58, 112, 124, 177, 292, 327–**328**, 453, 487
Lord Calvert Amusement Company 287
Lord Calvert Theater 90, 287, 328, 353, 473
Lord Calvert Theaters Company 229, 353, 366, 411, 468
Lord of the Rings: The Return of the King 198

Lord's Day Alliance 29, 60, 61, 117, 118
Loritz Brothers 408
Lost Boundaries 382
Lost in Yonkers 310
Louis, Joe 335
Louis-Savold fight 151, 236
Louise (ship) 54
Louisville, Kentucky 73
Love Dope 68
Lowery, John 386
Loyola College 17
Lubin, Sigmund 25, 31, 42, 59, 241, 242, 328, 329, 407, 452, 463, 466
Lubin films 261
Lubin Marvel projector 101
Lubin's Cineograph 15, 328
Lubin's Family Theater **241**
Lubin's Theater 25, 26, 27, 29, **30**, 47, 60, 65, 98, 160, **241**, 328–329, 452
Luetkemeyer, John A., Jr. 177, 185
Lumiere's Wonderland 11, 12, 329
Luna Park 23, 329
Luna Park Amusement Company 329
Luna Park Theater 329–330
La Lune a un Metre 462
Lunsford, Jimmy 213
Lust, Sidney 150
Lutherville, Maryland 158, 161, 236, 237
Lutwyche, Horace 257
Lyceum Song Slide Service 31
Lyceum Theater 7, 8, 14, 15, 17, 18, 22, 64, 81, 96, 208, 330–332, 481, 484
Lyceum Theater (Sparrow's Point, Maryland) **332**–333
Lyceum Theater (Washington, D.C.) 18
Lynchburg, Va. 479
Lyndhurst Corporation 130, 259
Lyon, Ben 2
Lyric Theater 16, 23, 53, 54, 59, 62, 144, 208, 343, 461
Lyric Theater (Annapolis, Maryland) 143

M.S. Levy Memorial School 374
Maas, Henry L. and Son 293, 439
Mabley, Jackie "Moms" 254, 483
Mac, the Crayon Man 327
MacArthur Theater (Washington, D.C.) 157
Machat, Louis 326
Machat, Nathan 486
Machinery Hall 17
Mack, Matthew 446
Mackall, R. McGill 230, 234
MacKenzie, George Norbury III 418, 419
Madison Amusement Company 409
Madison Square Garden (Baltimore) 301
Madison Theater 139, 216, 333

Index   513

Madonna of the Streets 113
Madstone Theaters 412
Magary's store 345
Magic Johnson 184
magnaphone 44
Magnet Theater (Annapolis, Maryland) 143
Maher-Choynski fight 11, 431
Maher-McCoy fight 14
Mahle, Marshal 30
Mahoney, George P. 214
Mahoney, James 472
Mahool, Mayor J. Barry 36, 40, 123, 329
Maid in the Ozarks 143
Maignan 206
Majestic Motion Picture Parlor 353
Majestic Theater 29, 333, 405, 445
Majestic Theater (Boston, Massachusetts) 345
Majestic Theater (Detroit, Michigan) 336
Majestic Theater (Mt. Savage, Maryland) 474
Majestics 285, 484
Major, Cincinnatus 253
Makover, Isidore K. 212
Makowski, Edward 297
Maltese Falcon 131
Malthan, August 194
Man in the Dark 152, 153
Man in the Moon 13
Man on the Tight Rope 252
managers 81, 457, 475
Mandell-Ballow Jewish deli 250
Mandingo 168
Mandler, Emma 301, 456
Manekin, Bernard 362
Manekin Corp. 412
Mann, Henry P. 247
Mansfield, Richard 331
Mansour, George 417
Maragliotti, Vincent 303
March of Dimes 143
March of Time 132, 414
Marchstein, William R. 276
Marciano-Moore fight 403
Marciano-Walcott fight 151
Marek's Outdoor Garden 375
Marhenke, Robert T. **128**, 131, 132, 307, 324, 367, 405, 432, 456, 458
Marilyn 325
Mariner, John 377
Marion, Dave 268
Markey, Mary 306
Marks and Cooke 245
Marks, G.I. 411
Marks, Sidney 387
Marks, Theresa D. 317
Marley Station Mall (Glen Burnie, Maryland) 342
Marlowe, Julia 190, 278
marquees 454
Marr & Colton organ 428
Marshall, Helen MacNier 235
Martien, William & Company 387

Martin Manor 292
Martin, Ray 292
Martinsburg, West Virginia 51
Mary of Magdala 334
Maryland Attorney General 68, 150, 151, 165, 169
Maryland Avenue Methodist Episcopal Church (Annapolis, Maryland) 143
Maryland Baptist Union Association 83
Maryland Casualty Building 389
Maryland Civil Rights Congress 140
Maryland Commission on Interracial Problems and Relations 65
Maryland Compulsory Work Bureau 71
Maryland Congress of Mothers 469
Maryland Council of Defense 135
Maryland Electric and Supply Company 491
Maryland Exhibitors' League 69
Maryland Film Festival 417
Maryland Finance Corporation 84
Maryland General Assembly 61, 83, 118, 151, 163, 169, 171, 185, 474, 478
Maryland Hygiene Society 431
Maryland Industrial Exposition 15
Maryland Institute 17, 156
Maryland Medical College 327, 486
Maryland Motion Picture Theater Owners' Association 123
Maryland Penitentiary 92
Maryland Senate Finance Committee 113
Maryland Society for the Protection of Children 66
Maryland Society to Protect Children from Cruelty and Immorality 66
Maryland Stadium Authority 185, 480
Maryland State Board of Censors 65, 66, 67, 68, 69, 96, 97, 113, 114, 132, 140, 164, 165, 169, 170, 171, 266, 415, 469, 474, 476, 483
Maryland State Board of Examiners of Moving Picture Operators 34, 53, 58, 99, 468, 472, 492
Maryland State Court of Appeals 61, 93, 94, 117, 123, 164, 169, 170, 247, 469, 478
Maryland State Fairgrounds 417, 418
Maryland State Secretary of Licensing and Regulation 171
Maryland Telephone Company 43
Maryland Theater 7, 16, 17, 18, 19, 22, 23, 29, 36, 37, 54, 56, 62, 70, 71, 76, 78, 96, 112, 121, 134, 143, 144, 167, 206, 207, 209, 268,
284, 323, 333–**334**, 335–336, 395, 465
Maryland Theater Corporation 335
Maryland Theater (Oakland, Maryland) 56
Maryland Theaters, Inc. 373
Maryland Theatres Corporation 258
Maryland Theatrical Agency 257
Mascot Theater 336
Mason, Alfred 279, 280, 357
Mason, Lillian 203
Mason, Judge E. Paul 140
Mason and Mason 207
Mastbaum, Stanley 103
Mastbaum Memorial Theater (Philadelphia, Pennsylvania) 103
Matcher, Henry D. 154, 155, 388
Matthews, George 50
Matthews, Margaret 264
Maturio, Pedro 178
Maturio, Susie 178
Matysek, Antone 357, 488
May Company 327
Mayehoff, Eddie 2
Mayfair Theater 110, 129, 134, 139, 144, 155, 163, 174, 181, 185, 209, 399, 477, 479
Mayfair II Theater 168, 327
Mayflower Laundry (Towson, Maryland) 377
Mayrs, Lew 431
McBride, Robert W. 409
McCale, Larry 285
McCardell, Lee 243
McCaslin, John T. 21, 179, 242, 463
McCleary, Tracy 254
McClellan, Harry H. 317
McClelland, Paul E. 204
McClurg, James P. 409
McComas, H.R. 248
McCormick & Company 342
McCormick Memorial Baptist Church 324
McCorney, Carrie 287
McCoy, Gertrude 59, 287, 484
McCurdy, Eugene 35, 243, 245, 250, 271, 318
McDonald, John L. 217, 370, 406
McDonald, Mickey 217
McDonough, Mitzi 333
McElfatrick, Michael 466, 485
McElfatrick, William H. 266
McElfatrick, J.B. & Sons 204, 205, 206, 276, 285
McFadden, Bernarr 190
McFadden, Nathaniel J. 185
McGovern-Dixon fight 14
McGowan, George 386
McGowan, Harry 386, 489
McGrath, John 415, 432
McGraw, Edmund J. 405
McGraw, John J. 486
McGuffin, Tony 265
McGuirk, John J. 396
McHenry Theater 43, 46, 55, 60,

91, 96, 112, 134, 336, *337*, 442, 453
McHenry Theater Company 336
McKeldin, Theodore 144, 348, 476
McKew, Marian 468
McKim estate 343
McLane, Mayor Robert M. 334
McLaughlin, George E. 320
McLaughlin, J. 240
McLaughlin, Leonard 207, 208, 335
McManus, Margaret 221
McRae, Duncan 287
McRae, Gertrude Lyons 484
McTuerny, Mr. 323
Meade, M.L. 200
Mechanic, Morris 96, 104, 105, 124, 138, 141, 147, 153, 155, 162, 176, 230, 236, 278, 284, 340, 347, 348, 365, 398, 400, 488, 490
Mechanics Hall 266
Meddinger, C.E. 370
Medical Arts Building 461
Medical College 51
megaplexes 182, 434, 435, 455, 480
Meighan, Thomas 59
Meixner Brothers 57
Melba, Nellie 192, 343
Melies, George 13
Menchen, Joseph 11
Mencken, H.L. 2, 118, 326
Mercantile Bank 229
The Merchant of Venice 330
Mercur, Etta Cluster 239
Merriweather Post Pavilion 168, 245
Merry Go Round 121
Mersereau, Violet 59
Methodist Trades Bazaar 10
Metro-Goldwyn 399
Metro Photoplays Theater 216
Metropolitan Amusement Company 408
Metropolitan Concert Orchestra 338
Metropolitan Grand Opera Company 235
Metropolitan Hall and Amusement Company 374
Metropolitan Railway 386, 489
Metropolitan Soloist Ensemble 338
Metropolitan Theater 47, 76, 78, 79, 80, 82, 90, 91, 100, 103, 105, 106, 116, 129, 337–338, *339*, 453, 480
Metropolitan Theater (Los Angeles, California) 103
Metropolitan Theater (Washington, D.C.) 75, 106
Metropolitan Theater Company 337
Mettee, Donald 415
Meyer, Arthur 49
Meyer, Benjamin 250
Meyers, Alexander J. 356
Meyers, Henry 59

Meyers, William *128*
MGM 75, 76, 91, 122, 145, 146, 152, 153, 223, 254, 315
Michael Walter T. 271
Micheaux, Oscar 252
Mickey Theater 406
Middle River Essex Community Children's Christmas Party 307
Middle River, Maryland 126, 139, 192, 215
Middleman, Raoul 342
midnight shows 136
Midway, Battle of 414
Midway Theater (Middle River, Maryland) 139, 338
Mikado 352
Mikulski, Barbara 367
Miles, Herbert 439, 482
Miles Brothers 27, 29, 52, 246, 274, 482
Military Theaters 339–340
military units: 1st Company, Maryland Coast Artillery Corps 70; 15th Infantry Regiment 70; 117th Mortar Battery 70; 313th Infantry Regiment 70, 323
Millard, Arthur 178
Miller, Hal A. 139, 200, 240, 301, 307, 308, 361, 362
Miller, Hyman 373
Miller, J. Henry Company 225
Miller, Kenneth Cameron 139, 261, 262
Miller, Louise Miller 327
Miller, Mark 465
Miller, Nathan 101
Miller, Nelson 472
Miller, Richard 380
Miller, William H. 99, 468
Miller Mercantile Corporation 291
Miller's Oyster Bar 214
Millhauser, Moses 35, 264, 408
Million Dollar Triple Enterprise 16, 17, 18, 206, 207, 333, 334, 394
Milstead, Glen 2
Milton, Walter 327
Milton Academy 486
Mini-Flick Theater 172, 177, 340
mini-theaters 166, 455
Minsky's burlesque 269, 335
Minter, Mary Miles 266
Miracle 149
mirror screen 218
Mirrorphonic Deluxe sound system 416
Miss Clodius 324
Miss Edna's Hiway Kiddie Show 307
Miss Maryland 392
Mississippi River floods 84
Mr. Belvedere Goes to College 348
Mitchell, Grant 208
Mitchell, Mary Lomax 487
Mitchell, Miles E. 291
Mitchell's Back River View Park 463
Mitnick, Eddie 179

Mlle. Corinne 361
Mockery 116
Modern Amusement Company 251
moderne style 104, 453
Modjeska, Helena 192, 330
Moehle, Frederick L.W. 156, 243
Moehle, Frederick L.W. & Associates 338
Moller, E.A. 238
Moller Company 82
Moller organs 82, 221, 236, 245, 271, 278, 298, 303, 316, 336, 347, 360, 363, 372, 380, 413, 414, 430, 442, 481, 485, 489
Mon Oncle d'Amerique 418
Monarch Theater 340
Mondawmin Mall 184
Monogram Pictures 122, 315
Monroe Theater 113, 340, 477
Monroe Theater Company 340
Monsoon ventilation 232, 387
Montgomery, M.V.P. 204
Montgomery County, Maryland 117, 492
Montgomery Ward 380, 465
Monumental Open Air Theater 340
Monumental Theater 7, 8, 11, 13, 14, 15, 16, 17, 18, 22, 23, 266, 268, 285, 430–432, 462
Moon Is Blue 150, 319, 365, 477
Mooney, Captain 117
Mooney, Paul R. 79
Moore, C. Robert 123, 180, 247, 275
Moore, Gary 2
Moore, Tom 52
Moorehead, Harry 33, 34, 35, 463
Moral Education Board 469
Moreno, Antonio 59
Morgan, Basil 468
Morgan Hall 391
Morgan State University 144, 145
Morgan Theater 57, 152, 390, 391, 490
Morrell Park 324
Morrell Theater 472, 324
Morris, William 242, 331
Morris Mechanic Theater 163, 176, 340–341, 424
Morrison, Craig 285
Morrison, J. (singer) 352
Morstein, Harry 193, 225, 375
Morstein, Mendes E. 133
Morton, "Jelly Roll" 212, 253
Mosby, Ada 18
Mosby, Col. John 17, 18
Moseley, Quentin 353
Mosely, Charles W. 375, 380
Moser, Judge Herman 150
Moss, B.S. Enterprises 342
Mothers' Club of Baltimore 469
Mothers' Congress 69
Motiograph projector 101
Motion Picture and Television Operators of Maryland 149
Motion Picture Association of America 166, 476

Motion Picture Board of Trade 67
Motion Picture Exhibitors' League of America 34, 60, 53
Motion Picture Exhibitors of America 464
Motion Picture Guild of Washington 326
Motion Picture Operators and Managers Union No. 1 100
Motion Picture Patents Company 52
Motion Picture Projectionists Union, Inc 132
Motion Picture Theater Association of Maryland 104
Motion Picture Theater Operators of Maryland 137
Motion-Picture Theater Owners and Managers of Maryland 119
Motion Picture Theater Owners' Association of Maryland 133, 135
Motion Picture Theatre Owners of America 92, 464
Motion Picture Theatre Owners of Maryland 59, **128**, 133, 137, 144, 148, 473, 475
Mottu & White 301
Mount Airdome 341
Mount Pelee eruption 15
Mount Royal Amusement Company 341, 489
Mount Royal Theater 60, *341*
Mt. Savage, Maryland 474
Mount St. Mary's College 17
Mount Vernon Drive-In 126
Mount Washington Casino 341
Mt. Winans, Maryland 245
move-over house 424
movie pioneers 179
movie situation 1911 39
Movies at Golden Ring Mall 173, 175, 342, 455
Movies at Harbor Park 175, 179, 182, 342
Movies at Marley Station (Glen Burnie, Maryland) 342-343
Movies I-V 172
Movietone 107, 108, 347, 364, 373, 384, 387, 424
Moving Picture Company of America 329
Moving Picture Exhibitors' Association of Baltimore 34
Moving Picture Row 36
Moving Picture Supply Company 102
The Moving Picture Theater 20, 240
Moviographs, Inc. 105, 326
Moxley, J.E. 224, 243, 244, 412, 438, 453
Mozart Airdome 343
Mozart Hall 461
Mrs. Miniver 136
Mules, Charles F. 117
Mules, Florence 316
Mullinix, Holly 470

multiplex theaters 110, 455
multi-screen theaters 166, 177
Murphy, J. Brady 271
Murphy, Judge James W. 170
Murphy, Rose Marie 476
Murray, Pete 33
Murrow, Edward R. 131
Muse, Clarence 2
Museum of Anatomy 7
music 32, 33, 80, 81, 464
Music Defense League 110
Music Hall 7, 8, 1, 13, 14, 15, 343; *see also* Lyric Theater
Music Hall (Easton, Maryland) 250
Music Man 399
Musical Russells 301
Musical Union 487
musicians 80, 89, 98, 110, 111, 306, 335
Musser, Charles 19
Muth, Councilman 482
Mutoscope Parlor 343
Mutual Amusement Company 409
Mutual Film Corporation 127, 469
Mutual Film Exchange 467
Mutual wheel 268
Muvico 110, 182, 343, 344, 345, 455
Muvico Egyptian 24 Theater (Harmans, Maryland) 343-**344**, 345, 456, 479
My Fair Lady 306
My Wild Irish Rose 201
Myerberg, Joseph 482
Myerberg, Julius 249, 485
Myers, A. Murray 296
Myers, William G. 258, 275

Nachman Hotel 431, 484
Nachos 184
Nagosanosky, William 243
Natatorium 204, 395
The Natatorium and Physical Culture Association of Baltimore City 204
Nation, Carrie 15, 431
National Amusement Company 28, 50, 51, 466
National Association for the Advancement of Colored People (NAACP) 64, 143, 382, 412, 468, 476
National Association of the Motion Picture Industry 464
National Association of Theater Owners of Maryland 59, 163, 168, 361, 457, 480
National Athletic and Amusement Company 345
National Endowment for the Arts 336
National Engineering Corporation 224
National Polish Home Association 357
National Recovery Administration 135
National Theater 79, 101, 345

National Theatre Supply Company 103
Natwick, Mildred 2
Naughty Flirt 113
Nedick's 1
Neely, F.T. 278
Neff, Marion A. 34
Neff & Thompson 410
neighborhood theaters 54, 60, 77, 78, 89, 90, 91, 99, 100, 104, 105, 110, 112, 131, 137, 139, 143, 148, 160, 162, 163, 184, 352, 476, 477
neighborhoods 120
Neilson, J. Crawford 189
Nellie, the Beautiful Cloak Model 432
Nemo Theater 406
Nessul, V. 79
Never on Sunday 310
New Aladdin Theater 193
New Albert Hall 212, 213, 253
New Albert Theater 212, 213
New Amsterdam Theater (New York, New York) 45, 345
New Cameo Art Theatre 362
New Casino Company 353
New Center Follies Theater 318
New Central Theater 430
New Crescent Theater 248
New Eagle Theater 256
New Elektra Theater 264
New Essex Theater 264, 349
New Garden Theater 284, 470
New Gem Theater 349-**350**, *351*
New Gilmor Theater 289
New Glen Art Theater (Glen Burnie, Maryland) 351
New Glen Theater (Glen Burnie, Maryland) 351-352
New Goldfield Theater 203
New Haven, Connecticut 113
New Horn Theater 312
New Kane Theater 373
New Lincoln Theater 324
New Lyceum Theater 331
New Market Theater 274, 352
New Nemo Theater 406
New Paris Follies Theater 318
New Patterson Theater 357, 367
New Peabody Theater 413
New Pickwick Theater 33, 71, 74, 75, 82, 90, 352, 370, 371, 453
New Preston Theater 275
New Queen Theater 193, 375
New Theater 38, 54, 59, 60, 70, 71, 74, 75, 78, 79, 80, 89, 91, 92, 96, 100, 103, 104, 105, 108, 109, 124, 129, 134, 137, 138, 139, 144, 153, 155, 168, 172, 174, 176, 181, 284, 345-**346**, 347, *348*, 349, 457, 468, 472, 479
New Theater (Elkton, Maryland) 156
New Theater (Leonardtown, Maryland) 479
New Theater (Reisterstown, Maryland) 142, 349, 480
New Theatre Company 345

New Victor Theater 424
New Victoria (Buffalo, New York) 336
New Wizard Theater 75
New York Morning Telegraph 80
New York, New York 8, 63, 156, 253, 276, 277, 281, 326, 342, 345, 360, 362, 374, 375, 383, 415, 442, 443, 470, 471, 486
New York Vaudeville Club 206
Newbold, David M., Jr. 266
Newing, DeWitt 331
Newman, David 318, 373
News American 168, 172, 400
News-Post 126
newspapers 20, 21, 25, 35, 37, 60, 238, 464
newsreel theater 104, 414, 415, 416, 424
Newsreel Theaters of America 414
newsreels 150
Nice, Harry W. 84, 86, 87, 194
Nichols, Prof. F.H. 287
Nichols Auto Company 341
Nickel, John "Hon" 285, 426, 431, 468, 484, 491
nickelodeons 23, 24, 25, 28, 30, 35, 38, 91, 324, 371, 452, 453, 456, 463
Nicoland Theater 29, 359
Niederhauser & McCluskey 318, 319
A Night at Earl Carroll's 209
A Night in an English Music Hall 426, 461
Nillson, Christine 192
Niquet, Otto 62
Nixon, Samuel F. 208
Nixon & Zimmerman 37, 51, 96, 191, 192, 302, 330, 334, 481
Nixon-Nirdlinger, Fred G. 336, 426
No Name Theater 212
Nocturne 181
Nolan, Harry M. 214
Nolte, Charles E., Sr. 58, 112, 179, 193, 213, 214, 279, 325, 359, 400, 472
Nolte, Elmer *128*, 326, 475
Nolte, Gus 326
Nolte, Henry *149*
Nolte, Nick 171
Nolte, Vernon *128*
Norfolk, Virginia 154, 377, 410, 461
Norris, George 456
North, Robert 31, 264
North Avenue Baptist Church 123
North Avenue Casino 352–353
North Avenue Casino Company 353
North Avenue Ice Skating Rink 7
North Avenue Market 411
North Bend 193, 438
North Cinema 170, 210, 479
North Crescent Theater 248
North East Park 463

North Point Drive-In 126, 353, *354*, 475
North Point Plaza 353
North Point Plaza Theater 158, 160, 161, 173, 175, 177, 182, 353, 404, 481
North Point State Park 214
North Pole Theater 360
Northeast Drive-In Theatre Corporation 227
Northeast Market 20, 274
Northeastern Amusement Company 240, 360
Northern Amusement Company 349, 353, 362, 363
Northern Neck of Virginia 50
Northern Theater 353
Northway Theater 355–*355*, 356, 473
Northwestern Theater 356
Northwood 99 Theater 357
Northwood Partnership 357
Northwood Shopping Center 356
Northwood Theater 144, 145, 160, 174, *356*–357, 454, 455, 477
Northwood Theater Corporation 356
Novek, Bill 266
Novelty Amusement Company 221
Novelty Theater 98
Nowak, Fritz 70
Nowosci Theater 109, 357
nurseries 225
nursery room 373
Nuttrell, Roland 179, 180, 181, 236, 399, 480

Oakland, Maryland 56
Oberammergau Passion Play 15
Oboler, Arch 153
O'Brien, Geraldine 2
O'Brien, Pat 208
O'Brien, William 31
O'Brien, William C. 291
O'Brien, William G. 330
obscenity 479
O'Conor, Governor Herbert R. 132, 230, 292
Odd Fellows' Hall (Catonsville, Maryland) 142, 229, 441
Odend'hal, Emile S. 79, 387
Odenton, Maryland 126, 323, 405, 410
Odeon Theater 7, 8, 18
O'Dunne, Judge Eugene 93, 94, 347, 361
Oella, Maryland 357
Oella Hall 357
Of Human Bondage 305
O'Hare, Gibbons 252
O'Hare, Lawrence 398
Oklahoma 231
Old Bay Line 154
Old Kentucky 284
Oletsky, Morris *128*, 358, 440
Oletsky, Peter 253, 318, 432
Olevich, Joseph 407

Oliver, Abraham 217
Olsen, Charlie 491
Olson, Peter G. 229
Olympia Theater 357
Olympic Theater 430
Olympic Upholstery Company 214
Omaha, Neb. 455
O'Malley, Edward N. 366
O'Meara, John F. 40
On Polish Lands 140
On the Waterfront 278
One of the Family 208
O'Neill, Thomas 117, 442
Onri, Adele Purvis 9, 263
Ontario Theater (Washington, D.C.) 156
open-air theaters 20, 126, 142, 214, 324, 325, 326, 339, 340, 341, 357, 360, 379, 407, 424, 432, 453, 475; *see also* airdomes
Opera House (Annapolis, Maryland) 142
Opera House (Centreville, Maryland) 250
Opera House (Frederick, Maryland) 51
Optigraph 465
Oratorio Society 204, 469
orchestral organ 488
orchestras 55, 79, 108, 110
O'Ren, John 98, 111
organists 110
organs 82, 352, 482
Oriole Cafeteria 413
Oriole Park 291, 357–358
Oriole Theater 265, 357
Oriole Theatre Company 412
Orpheum Show 15
Orpheum Theater 358, 431
Orpheus 358
Osborn, Charles L.P. 29, 360
Osmond Family 245
Ottenheimer, Reuben 316
Ouch! 153
Outen, Leonard 101, 472
Outlaw 140
outside food 166
Overlea Hall 358
Overlea, Maryland 128, 358
Overlea Shopping Center, Inc. 412
Overlea Theater 119, 358
Overlea Theater Company 358
Owen, Howard 341
Owens, William T. 245
Owens, Bernard F. and Associates 412
Owings Mills Cinema 17 358–*359*
Owings Mills, Maryland 123, 177, 182, 358, 359, 424, 425
Owings Mills Town Center 358–*359*
Owsley, T.E. 380
Oxford Development Corporation 342
Ozonator 35

Pabst Park 463
Pacy, C. William 58, 163, 164, 281, 337, 468
Pacy, Walter 35, **95**, 468, 475
Pacy's Garden Theater 281
Page Miss Glory 194
Pahl, August "Augie" 127, 340, 350, 379, 475, 480
Palace Grand Museum 361, 439, 491
Palace Moving Picture Parlor 360
Palace Musee 361
Palace Museum 360–361
Palace Theater 28, 34, 54, 58, 62, 71, 79, 98, 100, 105, 108, 111, 114, 178, **267**, 268, 269, 359–360, 379, 380, 456, 474
Palace Theater (Dallas, Tex.) 103
Palace Theater (Washington, D.C.) 75, 121
Palacescope photo-plays 268
Palestine Red Cross 123
Palm Garden 206
Palm Sunday Blizzard 475
Palmore, Roy B. 84, 85
Palmore & Homand 84, 85, 103, 122, 127, 295
Pan American Quartet 121
Panhandle 353
Paniz, G.H. 367
Pappas, Victor G. 329
Paradise Amusement Company 210, 361
Paradise Theater **26**, 361, 452, 456, 480
Paragon Amusement Company 329
Paragon Baseball Scoreboard 307
Paragon Park 329
Paragon Picture Parlor 329
Paragon Theater 310
Paramount Associates 237
Paramount Consent Decree 145, 146
Paramount Hall (Towson, Maryland) 362
Paramount Pictures 75, 91, 103, 122, 144, 146, 147, 254, 363, 399, 478
Paramount Theater 139, 160, 361, 477
Parisienne Fine Arts Theatre 367
Park Circle 84, 87
Park Circle Theatre Company 412
Park Heights Amusement Company 412
Park Symphony Orchestra 399
Park Theater 373
Park Theater (Lexington Park, Maryland) 479
Parker, Charlie 254, 491
Parker, Jetsy 475
Parkside Theater 362
Parkville 411
Parkway Theater 38, 43, 46, 60, 70, 71, 75, 76, 78, 79, 80, 89, 90, 91, 92, 96, 100, 105, 108, 111, 115, 129, 134, 141, 147, 152, 180, 181, 185, 235, 336, 362–363, **364**, **365**, 366, 399, 413, 442, 453, 456, 457, 458
Parkway Theater (Kansas City, Mo.) 478
Parkway Theater Company 363, 403, 410, 413, 442
Parkwood Hotel 373
Parr & Parr 407
Parrott, James 461
Pasadena, Maryland 394
Passing Parade 235
Passion 387
Passion of Joan of Arc 107
Passion Play 13, 343
Pastime Company 366
Pastime Theater 101, 225, 257, 287, 291, 366
Patapsco Theater 139, 160, 366, 454
Pathe films 311
Patten, R. 305
Patterson Realty Corp. 274
Patterson Theater 73, 112, 157, 175, 178, 182, 185, 260, 357, 366–367, **368**
Patti, Adelina 192, 334
Paul, Peter D. 384
Paulus, George A. 379
Payne, John 348
Payne, John Howard 308
Peabody Theater 73, 89, 134, 413
Pearce, Charles 35, 49, 50, 52, 445
Pearce, Ida 49
Pearce, Marion S. 20, 34, 35, 36, 47, 49, 50, 53, 58, 59, 428, 466
Pearce, Rev. E. Maurice 465, 466
Pearce, Wilbur 49, 465, 467
Pearce and Scheck 19, 21, 22, 28, 31, 36, 42, 48, 49, 50, 51, 52, 53, 57, 58, 102, 127, 175, 176, 179, 199, 240, 241, 292, 302, 305, 310, 314, 315, 320, 327, 328, 408, 409, 410, 413, 425, 426, 445, 463, 465, 466
Pearl Harbor 131, 132, 134
Peart, Blanche 124, 125
Pee Wee King 306
Pell Mell Theater 367
Penn Mutual Life Insurance Company 209, 335
Penn-North Project 490
Penner, Joe 285, 490
Pennington Theater 367, 485
Pennsylvania Board of Censors 469
penny arcade 42, 367, 369
People's Amusement Company of Baltimore City 273
People's Theatre Company 243
Peranio, Vincent 310
Perdue, Dr. Saul 161
perfume 74, 470
Periscope Optics 436
Perotka, Edward F. 192, 426
Perring Plaza Cinema 158, 159, 160, 161, 166, 174, 182, 300, **369**, 445, 455
Perring Plaza Shopping Center 369
Perrott, Judge James A. 169
Perry, Fred 145, 362
Perry, Lawrence 265
Perry, Oberlin 299
Perry Center Theater 318
Perry Hall, Maryland 369
Perry Hall Movies 5 174, 369, 479
Perry Hall Square 369
pests 56
Peterson, B. 352
Petticoat Minstrels 471
Phantom of the Opera 426
Philadelphia Electric Sign Company 398
Philadelphia Film Exchange 127
Philadelphia, Pennsylvania 103, 118, 252, 305, 334, 362, 396, 398, 401, 426, 430, 431, 442, 443, 462, 479
Philadelphia Record 118
Philanthropy Hall 50
Philip J. Scheck Enterprises, Inc. 58, 252, 292, 328
Phillips, Dorothy 2, 257
Phillips, Sam 257
Photo Players Club of Baltimore 31, 66, 456
photoelectric cells 109
piano players 33, 80, 81, 82, 110, 134, 179, 470
Pic Theater 250
Pickering, John N. 318
Pickwick Theater 21, 29, 32, 42, 60, 90, 178, 322, 323, **371**, 468
Picon, Molly 306
Pictorial Amusement Company 370
Pictorial Theater 370
Picture Garden Theater 33, 60, 90, 218, 413, 414
Pierce, Hazel E. 178
Pietsch, Theodore Wells 167, 179, 213, 214, 264, 273, 298, 329, 360, 409, 439, 453
Pikes Theater 155, 370, 454, 480
Pikesville, Maryland 177, 340, 370, 473
Pimlico 372, 420
Pimlico Theater 82, 370, **372**, 480
The Pink Lady 192
Pinky 213
Pioneer Republican Club 373
pitch men 57
Pitts, Alfred H. 271
Pitts, John T. 101, 472
Pitts, Thomas 472
Pitts Amusement Company 380, 408
Pitt's Park 373
Pittsburgh and Allegheny Telephone Company 43
platter projecting system 102, 473
Play-Arts Guild Theater 295
Playboy bunnies 418
Playhouse Theater 141, 144, 151,

518 INDEX

152, 154, 172, 177, 266, 309–310, 325
Plaza-Randallstown Theater 377
Plaza Theater 243, 373
Plaza Theater (Annapolis, Maryland) 161
Plaza Theater (Lexington Park, Maryland) 479
Pleasant Hour Theater 373
Pleasants, J. Hall 191
Pleasantville 358
Pocomoke City, Maryland 186
Point Breeze 8, 386, 462
Poli, Sylvester Z. 208
Poli Players 208
police 30, 65, 70, 469
Police Boys Club 124, 289
Polish Castle 223
Polish National Home 357
Polish theater 109, 357
popcorn 57, 112, 113, 139, 184, 454, 476
Pope Leo XIII 13, 343
Poplar Amusement Company 373
Poplar Theater 254, 373
Popular Theater 373
Porkie House Sportland 391
Porter, Alexander G. 340
Porter, Cole 278
Porter, Edwin S. 19
Porter, Dr. J. Elmer 253
Porter, Jill 265
Porter, Samuel H. 253
Posluszny, Edward 125
post-war theaters 138
Potomac Valley Chapter, American Association of Theatre Organ Enthusiasts 399
Potts, Cliff 171
Potts, E. 407
Power of Love 477
Powers Cameragraph projector 101
pre-cast concrete 454
Precious Gifts 265
Premier Theaters 183, 318, 382
Prendergast, Judge J. Gilbert 478
preservation 185, 186
Presstman, Marie 2, 472
Preston (building inspector) 207, 307
Preston, Edward D. 431
Preston, Mayor James H. 55
Preston Theater 275, **276**
Pretty Ladies 78
Price, Arthur 35, **95**, 210, 217, 218, 275, 320, 370, 475
Price, Frank, Jr. 485
Primrose, George H. 19
Prince George's County, Maryland 37, 119, 478
Princess Came Across 98
Princess Eulalie 9, 263
Princess Pat 323
Princess Theater 43, 47, 248, 373–**374**, 375
Proctor, William 269
The Producers 186, 307

Producers' Distributing Corporation 91
Professor Cockey 327
Professor Oliver 324
Progress Building 375
Progress Garden 375
Progressive Citizens of America 143
projectionists 34, 62, 63, 73, 77, 81, 83, 98, 99, 100, 101, 102, 108, 109, 135, 148, 149, 150, 153, 179, 458, 459, 464, 472
Projectionists' Ball 62
projectionists' union 62, 91, 148
projectors **10**, **27**, 50, 101
Provident Savings bank 249
Pruce, Earl 487
Pryor, Richard 174
Psycho 210
Pugh, Scotty 214
Purcell, Charles 181
Purity 68
Purity Moving Picture Parlor 375
Pythian Castle Hall 301

Q.E.D. (Gustav Klemm) 106, 113, 464
Quality Amusement Company 266
Quartet 391
Queen, Dick 33
Queen Amusement Company 375
Queen Anne's County, Maryland 117
Queen Theater 28, 193, 375
Quo Vadis 37

R/C Theaters 128, 174, 183, 184, 257, 258, 308, 309, 405, 427, 480
R·K Architects 436
Race Suicide 68
Racoosin, Harry C. 388
Radcliffe, Senator 230
radio 124, 151
Radio Amusement Company 375
Radio Amusement Corp. 411
Radio Pictures 105
Radio Theater 375, **377**
Radnor Park 18
Radziszewski, A.C. 411
Raff & Gammon 8, 461, 462
Raffie's Theater 375
Raheeb, Ahsin 343
Rainbow Theater 375, **376**
Raine's Hall 285
Raisinets 148, 184, 480
Raith, Charles 194
Raith, Susan 409
Rambeau, Marjorie 208
Ramsay Street Players 416
Rand, Sally 285
Randall, Henry 343
Randallstown, Maryland 323, 377
Randallstown Plaza Theater 161, 177, 377
Randolph, "Little Bits" 253
Ranft and Krug 405

Rankin, Mignon 490
Rappaport, Isador 123, 138, 143, 179, 230, 269, 304, 305, 306, 485
Rappaport, M. Robert 113, 178, 182, 318, 385, 417, 479
Rappaport Management, Inc. 178, 295
Rappaport Theaters 105, 144, 155, 159, 176, 210, 257, 327
Ratcliffe, Donald B. 257, 417, 445
ratings 166, 478, 479
Rawson and Baisley 361
RCA Photophone 445
RCA synchroscreen 271
Reade, Roma 266
Read's Drugstore 373
Real Estate Holding Company 210, 251, 410
Realart Theater 317
Rec Room Billiards 420
Recher Brothers 420
Recher Theater (Towson, Maryland) 420
Recreation Theater (Towson, Maryland) 142, 377, **378**
Rector, Enoch 462
Red Cross 84, 92
Red Feather Theater 199
Red Fox Amusement Company 193
Red Mill Amusement Compny 378
Red Mill Theater 52, 318, 378
Red Moon Theater 31, 37, 47, 73, 92, 378–379, 471
Red Raven Theater 359
Red Star Theater 379
Red Wing Theater 112, 340, 360, **379**–380
Reddish, Harry 366, 390
Redmond, Philip **149**, 316
Redstone theaters 228, 480
reduced prices 134
Reed, William 468
Regal Theater (Chicago, Illinois) 254
Regal Theaters 176, 182, 183, 184, 313, 480
Regan, "Joe" 380
Regan's Casino Theater 380
Regent Theater 47, 77, 78, 79, 90, 91, 101, 108, 119, 129, 380–**381**, 382, 408, 473
Rehsen, Frank 79
Reichenback, H.L. 21, 297
Reid, John 73
Reinbold, Benny 329
Reinhard, Samuel E. 408
Reisinger, Charles 133, 148, **149**, 416, 475
Reisterstown, Maryland 142, 225, 349, 473, 480
Reisterstown Plaza Five Star Cinema 182, 382
Reisterstown Road Plaza 382
Reisterstown Road Plaza Theater 160, 177, 382

Reisterstown Shopping Center 427
Reliance-Shamrock yacht race 16
Relkin Edward A. 374
Remember Pearl Harbor 200
Renard Theater 28, 29, 47, 212
Reni, Guido 277
Republic Pictures 122, 315, 399
Republic Theater (Annapolis, Maryland) 143
Requardt, Julius 119
The Rescue of the Princess 70
Return of the Pink Panther 168
Revenge at Daybreak 164
reverse curve 156
Rex Amusement Company 336
Rex Theater 141, 164, 177, 243, 382–383, 416, 473, 477
Rheinland Hall 473
Rhinehart, Eva 201
Rhoads Opera House 43, 465, 492
Rialto Theater 70, 71, 91, 112, 117, 123, 383-**384**
Rialto Theater (New York, New York) 360, 383
Rialto Theater (Washington, D.C.) 478
Rialto Theatre Company 383
Ricci, Armando T. 230
Rice Auditorium 488
Richards, Chuck 203
Richardson, F.H. 484
Richardson, John Holt 293
Richmond, Va. 113, 151
Rife, George W. 36, 105, 207, 266, 268, 307
Riggins, W.S. 403
Riley's Stables 214
Ringgold, Muriel 440
riots 167, 299, 373
Riseman, William 245, 300, 369, 445, 455
Ritchie, Adele 282
Ritchie, Governor Albert C. 61, 97, 100, 235, 305
Ritchie Cinemas 1-2-3 (Glen Burnie, Maryland) 172, 182, 384–385, 455
Ritz, William C. 312
Ritz Enterprises 139, 256, 318, 394, 412, 474; *see also* Gaertner Theaters
Ritz Theater 91, 137, 158, **385**, 474
River View Park 8, 13, 14, 15, 17, 23, 213, 386–387, 462, 463, 480
Riverdale, Maryland 481
Riverdale Plaza Theater (Riverdale, Maryland) 481
Riverside Amusement Company 258
Rivoli Curse 154
Rivoli Theater 2, 40, 46, 79, 80, 82, 90, 91, 98, 100, 104, 105, 106, 108, 111, 115, 116, 129, 139, 154, 155, 162, 184, 275, 387-**388**, **389**, 399, 440, 453, 489
Rivoli Theater (New York, New York) 103

RKO Pictures 75, 122, 137, 145, 146, 147, 152, 153, 223, 315
Roach, George J. & Sons 431
Road to Hong Kong 348
roadshowing 146, 468
Robbins, Fred 282, 470
The Robe 153
Robert-Morton organs 82, 223, 294, 338, 380, 432, 485, 487
Roberts, Frank G. 341
Roberts, Franklin 213
Robertson, H. Charles 331
Robie and Mack's World Beaters 16
Robinson, Harry **102**
Robinson, Walter A. 436
Robinson, Wilbert 486
Robinson & Waldorf 405
Robinson-Maxim fight 151
Robinson-Turpin fight 236
Robinson's Elephants 305
Robitscheck, Kurt 335
Roche, M. Paul 383, 392, 416
Rock, William T. "Pop" 52
Rockwell, David 438
Rocky 171
Rodey, Edward A. 142, 199, 256
Rodman, Harry 475
Rogers, Roy 122
Rogers, Will 335
Roland West's Dairy Maids 305
Rolfs, Herman 266
Rollins, Fabius **149**
Rollins, Howard E., Jr. 2, 310
Rollman, Ed 207
Roma 358
Roman Spring of Mrs. Stone 491
Rome, J. Louis 47, 59, 119, 123, 193, 333, 373, 384
Rome Theaters 47, 78, 99, 108, 122, 126, 129, 130, 131, 194, 201, 203, 217, 239, 250, 276, 296, 299, 320, 338, 362, 373, 384, 405, 410, 434, 472, 480
Romola 332
Rooks, Olive 456
Rooney, Pat 461
Rooney, Pat, Jr. 2
Roosevelt Story 143
Roosevelt Theater 101, 166, 388–389
Rose, Billy 278
Rose, Judge John C. 84, 86
Roseman, Edna 33
Rosen, Abraham 198
Rosen, Morton H. **128**, 412, 440
Rosen, S.I. 35
Rosen Candy Company 198
Rosenbauer, Bruno 258
Rosenberg, Anne 216
Rosenbrock, Charles R. 204
Rosenstein Bros. 221
Rosenthal, Louis 383
Roslyn Theater 110, 129, 320, **321**, 322, 416, 491
Ross, Clifford 252
Ross, James J. 29
Rossellini, Roberto 140, 476

Rossiter, Edward J. 275
Roth, H.P. 408
Roth, Paul 455, 492
Roth circuit 183
Rothier, Leon 46
Rothrock, F.H. 225
Rotunda Cinematheque 390
Rotunda Mall 389
Rotunda Theater 177, 182, 184, 389–390, 417
Rouse, James 300
Routson, H. Ted 152, 310
Roxy Theater 274, 275, 416
Roy Theater 250
Royal Amplitone sound system 108
Royal Artillery Band 213, 386
Royal Moving Picture Parlor 390
Royal Roman Band 329
Royal Symphonic Orchestra 253
Royal Theater 47, 57, 70, 78, 79, 119, 129, 252–254, 311, 390, 457, 458
RTKL Associates 420, 488
Rubenstein, R.L. 225, 291
Ruby Theater 225, 273
Rudolph, C.D. Hardware Store 247
The Runner Stumbles 265
Ruppert's Park 37
Rush and Deruff 408
Rushworth, Maurice 179, 472
Russell, Jane 140, 476
Russell, Stanislaus 225, 227, 265, 326, 328, 388, 405, 409, 411
Russell, Wilson Raymond 379
Russell and Causby 257
Ruth, George Herman "Babe" 50
Ryland, Edward 468

Sachs, Benjamin 376
St. Ambrose's Catholic Church 405
St. Dominic's Drum and Bugle Corps 243
St. Helena, Maryland 142, 247, 375
St. John's Church (Hamilton) 180
St. Mark's Lutheran Church 16, 265
St. Mary's County, Maryland 474
St. Mary's Industrial School 20, 50, 71, 264, 466
St. Mary's Star of the Sea Church 443
St. Michael and All Angels Church 332
St. Patrick's Boys' Band 292
St. Paul's Lutheran Church (New York, New York) 478
St. Paul's Parish 370
St. Wenceslas Bohemian Catholic Church 374
salaries 80, 110
saloons 41
Salvation Army 275
Sanctuary 491
Sandow 15, 190
Sands of Iwo Jima 122
Sappho 266

Sauber, Henry 362
Saunders Drive It Yourself Company 413
Saunner, William 307
Savage, J.R.Y. 230
Savoy Theater 266
Savoygraph 266
Saxton, William K. 111, 123, 136, 138
scandals 84, 91
Scar of Shame 253
Scarlett, Leonard 265, 483
Schacker, George 366
Schaeffer, W.C. 487
Schaffer, Louis 431
Schamu Machowski Greco 307, 480
Schanberger, Frederick C. 9, 18, 121, 134, 192, 208, 268, 284, 331, 334, 335, 462
Schanberger, Frederick C., Jr. 462
Schanberger, J. Lawrence 124, 284, 462
Schanberger and Irvin 263
Schanberger Organization 56, 96, 105
Schanze, Dr. Frederick W. 47, 390, 391, 487
Schanze, Josephine 338
Schanze's Theater 47, 56, 178, 390–***391***, 392, 468
Schapiro, J. Mark 177, 185
Schaum, H.C. 34
Scheck, C. Edna 58
Scheck, John 58
Scheck, Philip J. 20, 47, 49, 50, 53, 58, 411, 428, 466
Scheck, Robert M. 58, 468
Scheck, Ruth 465
Schecter, Louis 382
Schenning, Henry 293
Schenthal, Sylvan 285
Scherr, Oscar M. 289
Schirmer, G. 80
Schlanger, Ben 453
Schleisner, Benjamin 407
Schlenger, Gretchen L. 465
Schleunes, Erwin H., Jr. 409
Schlichter, Louis 47, 221, 273, 410
Schlossberg, Irving 117
Schluderberg, William 293, 485
Schmidt, Charles 266
Schmidt, George 296, 297, 400, 401, 453
Schmidt and Cook 408
Schmoke, Mayor Kurt L. 417
Schmuff, Fred 46, 112, 121, 163, 180, 401, 403, 475
Schnabel, William 481
Schneider, Frederick F. 132
Schneider, George 70
Schneider's American Cinematograph 12
Schoemer, Dorothy 475
Schoenlein, Augustus "Gus" 431, 491
Scholl, Frank M. 178
Schorr's Yiddish Theater 431

Schuck, Edward 274
Schulte United 1
Schwaber, David 430
Schwaber, E.D. 471
Schwaber, Joseph 375
Schwaber, Milton 137, 176, 177, 200, 309, 310
Schwaber Theaters 126, 139, 141, 144, 151, 152, 158, 161, 175, 176, 200, 210, 236, 240, 287, 308, 315, 324, 325, 338, 340, 357, 361, 365, 375, 424, 477, 480
Schwalbe, Harry 52, 221
Schwartz, Emanuel 426
Schwartz, Frank 31, 464
Schwartz, Nicholas 307
Schwartz, Samuel 216
Schweninger, Schweninge 481
Scott, Harry P. 43
scrap drives 134
Screen Club 475
Scribner, Sam A. 15
SDDS 160
Seabord Film Corporation 84
Seaman, David 73
Seamon, Mitzi 81
Sears Roebuck 465
Security Mall Theaters 174, 392, 461
Security Square 8 Theaters 186, 392
Security Square Mall 392
Seduced and Abandoned 237
Seduction 331
Sefton, Charles A. (wagon and truck factory) 345
segregation 120, 121, 335, 476
Seibel, Carl W. 424
Seidenman, Sidney 363, 414
Seidler, Aaron ***128***, 212, 250, 302
Seiler, Roy 211
Seitz, "Doc" 350
Selckmann, E. 373
A Self-Made Failure 316
Selig films 261, 311
Sellmayer, Ludwig 294
Selwyn and Company 208
Senator Theater 157, 160, 172, 173, 184, 185, 336, 389, 392–***393***, 394, 417, 454, 473, 477
Sennett, Mack 2
Sereclicz, Wasil 178
Sergeant York 321
7-East Theater 152, 210, 479
Seven Locks Theater (Rockville, Maryland) 492
Seventh War Loan 134
Sevier, Dorothy 132
Seward, Chester 101, 472
Shadyside Beer Park 20
Shadyside Park 463
Shane 284
Shapiro, M. Sigmund 253
Shapiro Patrauskas Gelber 358, 359
Sharp, Andrew 163
Sharp, Asa C. 97
Shaw, Artie 284

Shaw Stables 408
Shayne and King 425
Shecter family 417
The Sheik 69
Shellman, Jacques M. 50, 55, 56, 463
Sheridan, Rev. Philip H. 362, 377
Sherman, Edward 305, 401, 403
Sherman Antitrust Act 130
Sherry's 398
Sherwood, E.A. 398
Sherwood, Watson E. 34, 50, 58
Shimanauskas, Rafael 251, 375
Shipley, H.C. 345
Shipley estate 329
Shoebridge, Sam 350
Shoemaker, Peggy 307
shootings 178
Shoppers' Special 174
shopping centers 141, 142, 158, 168, 454, 455
Shore, Dinah 306
Shore Drive-In (Pasadena, Maryland) 177, 394
Shoubin, Samuel 250, 391
Show of Shows 477
shows 78
Shriner lot 413
Shubert, Lee 192, 266
Shubert, Lou 350
Shubert, Sam S. 192
Shubert-Fiske-Belasco Organization 331
Shubert Organization 96, 192, 207, 208, 235, 284, 331, 335, 347
Shuman, Charles 326
Sideman Moving Picture Parlor 357
Sidney Perrin's High Flyers 78
Siegal, Samuel 374
Sielke, Leo 219
Siewell, Porter 119, 418, 419
Silver, H.H. 358
Silver, Harry ***128***
Silvers, Phil 285
Sima, Frank 334
Simmons, Cress 253
Simms, Jules 338
Simonson, B. Eustace 407, 482
Simonson, Otto G. 193, 194, 213, 214, 260, 261, 266, 267, 337, 339, 360, 386, 407, 408, 413, 453, 482
Simonson & Pietsch 386
Simpson, Senator Alan 487
Simpson, C.W. 466
Simra, Frank 191
Singer, F.O. 407
Singer-Pentz Construction Company 303
singers 33
single-screen theaters 158, 160, 166
Sins of the Children 111
Sissle and Blake 360, 382
Sizemore, Jim 484
Skelly, James J. 13
Skelton, Red 285, 306, 486

Skidmore, Owings & Merrill 192
Skillman, George 31
Skinner, Otis 190
Skinner organ 82
Skouras, Spyros 479
Skrentney, H.J. 390
slashers 178
slaughterhouses 294
Slaves 306
Slemmer, Milton C. 191, 192
Smallwood, Miss B.P. 378
Smart Brothers 174
Smell-o-Vision 154
Smisel, Philip 316
Smith, Andrew 57
Smith, Bessie 324
Smith, Edwin, Jr. 295
Smith, George 266
Smith, Hilda 465
Smith, Ida 465
Smith, Governor John W. 334
Smith, Joseph 386
Smith, Mamie 254
Smith, Pete 153
Smith, Russell 189, 191
Smith, William S. 322
Smith, Willie "The Lion" 253
Smith, Wilson Porter 298, 299
Smith & May 367, 410
smoking 42, 43, 73, 133
Smoky City Quartet 253
Smyrna Theater (Smyrna, Delaware) 156
Snavely, Ed 230
Snow, Raymond 156
Snowden Square 14 Theaters (Columbia, Maryland) 245, 246, 394, 492
Snowden Square Shopping Center 394
Snuff 170
Social Settlement School Board 469
Society of Friends of Baltimore 469
Society of Social Hygiene 469
Sodaro, Judge Anselm 164
Soistman, Joseph 338
Sokolove, A. 221
Sokolove, Harold 338
Sokolove, Julius 79, 338
Solax Theater 216
Solomon's Theater 394
Solter, Judge George A. 93
Soltz, Samuel 352
Solz, Art 366
Some Wild Oats 266, 268
Somers and Spielman 311
Song of Songs 114
Song of the South 382
Sons of the American Revolution 469
Sony Corp. 183
Soper, Judge Morris A. 61, 85, 86
Soule, Mary 443
Soul's Harbor Full Gospel Church 403
sound 108, 110
sound effects 64, 464

sound levels 160, 467, 478
sound movies 43, 45, 46, 104, 107
Sound of Music 349
sound-on-disk system 108, 109
sound-on-film system 109
sound systems 32, 106, 108, 109, 399
Sousa, Frank 361
Sousa, John Philip 191
South African War 14
Southern Amusement Company 336
Southern Electric Company 48
The Southern Parkway 336
Southside Movies Four 394, 379
Spachner, Leopold 248
Spanish-American War 12, 13, 431
Spanos, Michael 406
Sparklin, William O. 156, 214, 215, 221, 341, 489
Sparklin and Childs 376, 380, 381, 383, 384, 403, 409
Sparrows Point, Maryland 72, 81, 229, 230, 332, 333, 366, 411
Specht, Paul Orchestra 401
Speckman, Fred 297, 357
Spedden, J.C. 275, 327, 328, 408, 443, 444, 453
Spellbring, B.A. 62, 468
Sperry and Hutchinson 413
Spies, Professor 202
Spindler, Mr. 405
spitting 73
Spitzbarth, Paul 338
Splendor in the Grass 491
Spring Grove State Hospital 50, 488
Sprouse, Leon 382
Spurrier, W.G. 286
Spurrier Amusement Company 199, 481
Squire Theater (Reisterstown, Maryland) 349
Stack, John K. 230, 289, 360
stadium seating 455
Stafford Hotel 2
stagehands 98
Stair & Havlin 266
Standard Amusement Company 123
Standiford, John 417
Stanley and Livingston 392
Stanley Company 96, 221, 396, 410
Stanley-Crandall Company 103, 105, 192, 392, 399
Stanley Theater 79, 82, 91, 96, 103, 104, 105, 107, 108, 111, 112, 123, 124, 129, 131, 134, 136, 139, 144, 151, 152, 153, 155, 158, 162, 163, 167, 173, 176, 181, 184, 340, 388, 394, **395**, 396, **397**, 398–400, 410, 435, 453, 456, 477, 480, 484
Stanley Theater (Philadelphia, Pennsylvania) 103
Stanley-Warner Corp. 398, 400
Stanton Theater (Washington, D.C.) 362

Stanton Theater *see* Stanley Theater
Star Spangled Banner 55, 308
Star Theater 101, 254, 375, 400, 440
Star Theater (Annapolis, Maryland) 120, 143
Star Wars 467
Starr, Blaze 285
State Amusement Company 291
State Board of Parole 92
The State Fair Girls 327
State Theater 46, 58, 77, 91, 104, 112, 113, 124, 132, 151, 158, 163, 180, 380, 400–**402**, 403, 453, 457, 457
State Theatre Company 201, 217
Staylor, Sylvester C. 246
Stebbins, George 486
Steele, John 284
Steen, Andrew G. 34, 216, 408
Stehl, J.H. 385
Steinacker, Joseph Henry 193, 194, 349
Steiner, Emma R. 343
Steiner, Otto P. 480
Steinwald, Mr. 425
Stenger, Gus 58, 359
Stenz, George F. 305
stereophonic sound 160
Stereoscopik 153
Stern, Myer H. 411
Steuart, Dr. James A. 204
Stevens, Andrew P. 252
Stewart, Anita 59
Stewart, Arthur 62
Stewart, James 271
Stewart Central Stables 281
Stiefel, Nathan 253
Stierhoff, Walter 117
Stires, Harrison L. 122, 428
Stitt, Milan 265
Stockton, Carey 357
Stockton Theater 403
Stoddard, John L. 13
Stoddard's Palm Garden 463
Stolen Bride 396
Stone, William F. 67
Storck, Edward J. 202
storefront theaters 452
Strand Ballroom 253
Strand Theater 61, 68, 75, 90, 119, 134, 403–404, 442, 485
Strand Theater (Dundalk, Maryland) 142, 160, 177, **404**–405, 428, 474, 479
Strand Theater (New York, NY) 360, 362, 470
A Stranger Knocks 478
Streamlined Divertisements 235
Street Angel 108
Streett, William R. 416
Strehlau, Frederick W. 110
Strodel, J.H.A. 485
Strom, William 409
Stromboli 140, 476
Stuart, Samuel 21, 240, 243
Stubbs, Building Inspector 43

522   INDEX

Stuehler, Tom 428
Stumpf, William E. 100, 201, 291
Stunz, William P. 45
Suburban Amusement and Development Company 372
Suburban Hotel and Gardens 23, 405, 463, 483
Suburban Theater 405
suburban theaters 168
suburbs 126, 161, 453
Sugar Cane 253
Sullavan, Margaret 335
summer slump 59, 103
summer theater season 23
Sumner, George R. 336
Sun 60, 62, 63, 65, 66, 67, 83, 106, 117, 120, 124, 136, 144, 153, 160, 162, 464
Sunburst Theater 405
Sunday Amusement League of Baltimore 83
Sunday movies 29, 30, 53, 59, 60, 61, 62. 68, 82, 83, 104, 110, 116, 117, 118, 119, 120, 123, 473, 474, 475
Sunrise 468
Sunset Boulevard 358
Sunset Theater 248
Super 170 Drive-In (Odenton, Maryland) 126, 405
Superba Theater 90, 405
Superior Amusement Company 199, 481
Sutro, Ottilie 487
Sutton Theater 324, 325
Swaab Film Exchange 442
Swann, Don, Jr. 362, 365
Swanson, Gloria 335
Sweeton, Joe 20
Symington, W. Stuart 51, 302
Symphonie Pastorale 415
Synchro Screen 477
Synchronized Scenario Music Company 80
Synchroscope 32

T.M.C. 153
Taggart, Ben 488
Takoma Theater 405–406
Takoma Theater (Washington, D.C.) 157
Talbot, Laura 199
talking in theaters 56
talking moving pictures 42
Talmadge, Norma 59
Tanguay, Eva 335
Tank piano 35
Tankersley, Roland *149*
Taras Bulba 160
Target 455
Tartuffe 326
Tarzan the Ape Man 399
Tasker, O.J. 464
Taskiana quartet 253
Tatterman Marionettes 295
Taylor, E.B. 235
Taylor, H.W. 257
Taylor, Isaac 256, 265

Taylor, Rose 256, 265
Technicolor 108
Teddy Bear Girls 490
Teddy Bear Parlor 406–407
Tegges, Mamie 456
Tel Aviv Hall 391
television 124, 151, 209, 212, 284, 403, 477
10-cent stores 1
Ten Commandments 278, 348
Terrace Theater (Essex, Maryland) 407
Terrapin Park Open-Air Theater 407
Texan Theater (Houston, Texas) 103
TH-3 Military Theaters 339
Thalhimer, Morton G. 151
Thalia Hall 461
Thalia Theater 431
Thaw-White murder case 285
theater architecture 452–456
theater closings 114, 115
theater district 7
theater names 30
theater openings 114, 115
theater personnel 456–459
theater pooling 147
theater ratings 172, 173, 174
Theatorium 413
Theatre Catalog 156, 309, 356
Theatre Committee for Civilian Defense 133
Theatre Managers' Association of Baltimore 98
Theatrephone 32
Theby, Rosemary 59
Theft of the Secret Service Code 65
Third Dimensional Murder 153
Third Liberty Loan 70
Thirty-One Theater 413–416
This Is Cinerama 153, 271
Thomas, Dr. J. Hanson 191
Thomas, John Charles 192
Thomas, Dr. Joseph H. 200
Thomas, Lowell 131, 153
Thompson, A.H.G. 34
Thompson, Isaiah N. "Ike" 78, 79, 380
Thompson, Mrs. Isaiah 388
Thompson, Otis P. 407
Three Arts Theater 114, 152, 415–416, 491
Three Bouffons 9, 263
Three Coins in the Fountain 394
3-D films 152, 153, 284, 382, 477, 484
The Three Keatons 19
Three Little Pigs 105
Three Sisters Don 9, 263
Three Stooges 306
Three Who Love 305
Through Turbulent Waters 287
Thurston 266
ticket prices 7, 37, 38, 63, 64, 77, 78, 112, 137, 151, 164, 174, 175, 470, 476, 483, 487
ticket-takers 457

tickets 175, 479
Tiffany lamps 317
Tilley, Vesta 18
Tilton, Edward L. 323
Times Theater 110, 129, 136, 141, 155, 416–417
Timonium Cinemas 174, 175, 176, 182, 417, 455
Timonium Drive-In 144, 418, 445–446, 454
Timonium, Maryland 417, 418
Timonium Shopping Center 417
Tinley, Henry J. 274
Titanic (ship) 66, 351
Tivoli Theater (Frederick, Virginia) 157
Tobascoscope 14
Tobias, Earle 426
Tobin, Thomas J. 282
Todd-AO 231
Tolchester, Maryland 54
Tolkins, A.M. 327
Tollgate Movies (Bel Air, Maryland) 177, 394, 379
Tolly, Margaret 361
Tolson, Edward *102*
Tompkins, Mr. *102*
Tompkins, Paul 399
Tonophone sound-on-disk 316
Tormey, Francis E. 60, 210, 211, 287, 310, 312, 408
Tower Showcase Theater 349
Tower Theater 155, 160, 161, 167, 168, 177, 418
Town Theater 110, 129, 137, 143, 144, 153, 159, 172, 173, 174, 176, 181, 185, 186, 269–270, *271*, *272*, 477, 479, 484
Towne, Arthur 362
Townsend, Lt. Gov. Kathleen Kennedy 417
Towson Art Cinemas (Towson, Maryland) 419
Towson Commons Theaters 175, 420
Towson Ice Company 411
Towson Marketplace 480
Towson, Maryland 50, 142, 182, 193, 247, 362, 377, 378, 411, 418, 419, 420, 473, 480
Towson Theater 119, 142, 160, 378, 418–419, *420*
Tracey, Arthur 284
Tracy, Spencer 208
transistorized sound 302
Trans-Lux Corporation 138, 159, 176, 210, 306, 327, 382, 479
Traub, Sydney R. 140, 150, 415, 490
Traveler Theater 318, 420
traveling shows 49
Traymore Amusement Garden 204
Traymore Casino 204
Triangle Film Corporation 3, 316
Trimble, Henry S. 254
Trinity United Methodist Church (Washington, D.C.) 336

Index   523

A Trip to the Moon 462
Triple Million Dollar Enterprise *see* Million Dollar Triple Enterprise
triplexes 455
Truman, President Harry S 137, 138
Tucker, Billie 490
Tunick, Louis 224, 225, 308, 358, 366, 373, 426
Turkish baths 207
Turner, Patrick 336
Turner's Station, Maryland 139, 200, 247
Turpin, Charles *102*
Tuttle, Professor 202
Twele, Louise 383
20th Century-Fox 131, 145, 146, 147, 152, 261, 315
Twilight Amusement Company 243
Twilight Theater 243
twin theaters 158, 161, 177, 478
Twister 183
Two for the Seesaw 198
235 Drive-In Theater (Lexington Park, Maryland) 479
Twombley, Rev. Clifford 69
Tydings, Senator 230
Type A Theaters 323
Tyr, R.E. 214
Tyrone, Pennsylvania 439

Uhlig, R. 456
Ulman, Judge Joseph 113, 114
Ulman, Louis 198
Ulrich, Claire 92, 93, 94, 95, 471
Ulrich, Robert C. 257
ultra violet lighting 209, 420, 454
Uncle Jack's Kiddie Club 306
Uncle Tom's Cabin 17
Uncle Vanya 310
Undying Flame 336
Union League Baseball Park 302, 485
United Amusement Company 263
United Artists 91, 137, 146, 160, 175, 176, 178, 183, 184, 223, 235, 246, 342, 392, 399, 405, 436, 486
United Booking Office 268
United Broadcasting Company 212
United Circuit 375
United Project Company 247
United Railways and Electric Company 15, 43, 48, 213, 386
U.S. Capitol 336
U.S. Marine Band 189
U.S. Supreme Court 67, 131, 146 147, 149, 150, 151, 164, 165, 169, 479
United Theater Company 264
United Theaters 47
United Western Front 225
Universal Film Company 127
Universal-International 152
Universal Pictures 91, 137, 146

University of Maryland 185, 271, 306; Medical School 202
Untouchables 178
Up in Mabel's Room 153
Upshaw Movie Censorship Bill 469
Uptown Amusement Company 420
Uptown Theater 155, 157, 160, 391, 411, 420-*421*, *422*, 454, 480
urban renewal 161
Urbanski, W. 357
usherettes 423
ushers 89, 134, 164, 178, 180, 457, 470
USO 475

V-Day 137
V-J Day 138
Valencia 423
Valencia Theater 79, 91, 100, 103, 104, 105, 108, 111, 123, 147, 160, 162, 176, 232, 235, 236, 326, 399, 422-*423*, 424, 453, 457, 480
Valentine, Jeff 168
Valentini, Vincent A. 298
Valentino, Rudolph 69, 324
Valiant, J.G. Company 282
Valley Centre Mall (Owings Mills, Maryland) 424
Valley Centre 9 Theaters (Owings Mills, Maryland) 424, *425*, 455, 492
Valley Drive-In 161, 169, 177, 424
Valmis Brothers 256
Value Cinema, Inc. 323
Vampire Day 281
Van Den Berg English Grand Opera Company 248
Vanishing Prairie 230
Van Sant, Frank 486
Variety Club 123, 124, 475
Varney, John 211, 480
vaudeville 19, 38, 62, 70, 78, 104, 105, 111, 124, 179, 268, 269, 282, 284, 294, 305, 306, 320, 324, 331, 334, 335, 336, 347, 357, 399, 400, 401, 405, 408, 409, 411, 413, 425, 426, 439, 440, 442, 453, 463, 466
Vaughn, Bridget 409
Vegetable Matinee 71
vending machines 113
ventilation 73, 74, 232, 452, 453, 462
Veriscope 13, 307
Versailles Palace 363
vertical signs 226, 260, 367, 368, 433, 482
Victor Theater 390, 424
Victoria Company 51, 466
Victoria Theater 29, 38, 42, 51, 53, 54, 60, 62, 71, 73, 74, 75, 90, 96, 305, 424-426, *427*, 457, 467, 487
Victory Shows 134
Victory Theater 139, 426

Victory Theater Company 192
Vietnam War 475
Village at Waugh Chapel 412
Village Theater 156, 161, 172, 174, 175, 182, 427-428, 481
Vilma Theater 137, 404, *428*, 473, 474, 477, 479
Vincenti, G.R. 332
Vindex Shirt factory 20
Viola, Mr. 238
Virginia 128, 156, 177
Virginia Avenue 3
Virginia Theater 357
Vitagraph 14, 15, 16, 18, 22, 52, 59, 209, 261, 311, 386, 464
Vitaphone 106, 108, 109, 110, 239, 347, 364, 373, 382, 384, 387, 424, 469, 473
Vitascope 8, 9, 263
Vito, Nicholas 274, 352
Vivaphone 465
Vodery, Charles 101, 254
Vodery, George 472
Vogel, D. Edward 215
Vogel, Hank 215
Vogel, Jack K. 215, 229, 262
Vogel Circuit 192, 215, 480
Vogel Family 482
Vogelstein, Al 338
Vogelstein, Harry 338
Vogue Theater 415
Vokes, Rosina 8
Volkmer, Harry E. 248
Vollbracht, John C. 258
Voltamp Electric Manufacturing Company 464
Von Cello 305

Wad, Emanual 396
Wagner, Philip 301
Wagner, William C.F. 485
Wagonheim, Howard 158, 177, 309, 340
Walbrook 122, 405, 485, 491
Walbrook Amusement Company 428, 440
Walbrook Theater 70, 73, 80, 91, 122, 131, 146, 260, 298, 405, 428-*429*, 430, 440, 472, 485, 491
Walderman, Joseph *128*, 259, 281, 412
Walker, Billy 440
Walker, Charlotte 266
Wallace, Harry E. 398
Waller, Fats 253
Walls, Don 163
Wal-Mart 455
Walnut Spring 463
Walraven, J. Hesser 38
Walsh, Richard F. 135
Walters, William T. 191
Wankoff, William 266
War as It Really Is 70, 343
War Bond Day 133
War Memorial Plaza 308
War Production Board 134
war tax 78, 470

War Time 116
war workers 135, 136
Ward, Fanny 284
Ward, James J., III 420
Ward, Robert W. 483
Ward, Samuel B. 238
Wardman Park Hotel (Washington, D.C.) 398
Wardman Park Theater (Washington, D.C.) 486
Warfield, David 432
Warfield, J. 311
Wargraph 431
Waring, Fred 2, 80, 396, 470
Warner, Charles 268
Warner Bros. 2, 52, 75, 76, 77, 91, 96, 105, 106, 122, 137, 141, 145, 146, 147, 152, 153, 254, 315, 338, 399
Warren, Charles 382
Washington, D.C. 8, 12, 17, 37, 51, 52, 54, 75, 102, 106, 121, 124, 128, 150, 155, 156, 161, 183, 253, 276, 301, 310, 326, 327, 336, 362, 373, 375, 398, 417, 425, 461, 464, 469, 474, 478, 481, 486, 487, 491
Washington Hall Theater 17, 430
Washington Territory 128
Washington Theater 84, 430
Washington Theater Company 430, 471
Waskey, C.C. 316
Wasky, Eva J. 378
WASL Radio 292
Waters, Ethel 324, 382
Waters, John 2, 295, 417
Waters, P.L. 21
Watersedge Shopping Center 432
Watersedge Theater 142, 174, 432
Watersedge Theater Company 432
Watts, Ernest 440
Waverly Amusement Company 432
Waverly Summer Garden 432
Waverly Theater 98, 107, 166, 432, *433*, 477
Waverly Theater Company 291
Way Down East 331, 347, 473
Wayne, John 122
WBMD Radio 307
WCAO Radio 181
WCBM Radio 274
Weaver, Frederick 305
Webb, Chick 254
Webb, George R. 32, 43, 44, 45, 46, 331, 364
Webb, Henry W. 43, 46, 336, 362, 363, 409, 410, 442, 458, 489
Webb, Spike 316
Webb, William G. 43
Webb Talking and Singing Picture Company 44
Webb Talking Pictures Company 46
Webber's Band 301
Webb's Electrical Talking and Singing Pictures 46

Weber, Frederick C. 59, 287, 456, 468
Weber, Joseph N. 110
Weber & Fields 14, 432
Weber's Park 463
Webster, Daniel 485
Wednesday Club 487
Wednesday Club Building 330
Weems, Nick 199, 352
Weidman, John C. 34, 37
Weinberg, Herman G. 326
Weinberg, M. 292
Weinberg, Sam 262
Weinholt, Dr. Herman O. 258
Weiss-Rhodia Screen Scent system 477
Wellby, Dick 230
Weniz, Isidore 35, 103
We're Moving On 349
West, Mae 268
West Baltimore General Hospital 83
West Baltimore Theater 445
West Branch YMCA 19, 52, 445
West End Amusement Company 432
West End Park 329
West End Theater 38, 71, 90, 225, 390, 432, 434, 468
West End Theater (London, England) 362, 489
West North Avenue Garage 291
West Virginia 128, 177
Westergaard, Mrs. Clyde 179, 275
Western Electric Company 386
Western Electric sound system 108
Westminster Cathedral Hall (London, England) 46
Westminster, Maryland 186, 468
Westport 1, 435, 436
Westport Theater 139, **435**, **436**, 454
Westview Cinema 262, 435–436, **437**, 455, 467
Westview Mall 438
Westview Mall 9 Theaters 436–437
Westview Theater 158, 160, 178, 182, 476
Westway Theater 112, 130, 146, 193, 373, 438, 473
WFBR Radio 230, 231
Wheat, Jackson D. 256
Wheaton Plaza Shopping Center 488
Wheeler, William 21
White, Gonzella 253
White, Helen Paul 456
White, Lucius R., Jr. 204, 266, 267, 269
White, Olive 457
White, Theophilus 194
White Cargo 331
White Dog Theater 199
White Marsh Mall 438
White Marsh, Maryland 182, 287, 438

White Marsh 16 Theater 173, 369, **438**–439
Whitehill, Irving **150**
Whitehurst, Camelia 471
Whitehurst, Charles E. 31, 47, 66, 70, 89, 92, 93, 94, 95, 96, 135, 176, 232, 235, 345, 347, 378, 457, 471
Whitehurst, Dr. J. Herbert 93, 94, 235, 471
Whitehurst, Dr. Jesse Harrison 92
Whitehurst, M. Morris 93
Whitehurst, Milton 471
Whitehurst, Wilbur **95**
Whitehurst Organization 61, 75, 76, 91, 93, 99, 124, 175, 176, 231, 281, 284, 336, 364, 413
Whitehurst Players 488
Whitehurst's Baby Broadway 92
Whiteman, Paul 80, 284, 470
Whitter, Crofton S. 34
Whittle, Jack **95**, **128**, 179, 217, 218, 230, 291, 313, 361 375, 400, 475, 480
Who Done It? 309
Wicks theater organs 485, 487
wide screens 477
Wieland, William J. 301
Wienholt, Robert 175, 214, 369, 404
Wight, Oliver B. 201, 202, 240, 247, 254, 255, 279, 295, 316, 317, 328, 336, 337, 345, 346, 352, 362, 364, 384, 409, 410, 411, 413, 414, 442, 443, 453
Wignall and Reinagle 307
Wilcox, Frank 331
Wild One 278
Wild, George 79, 80, 179, 235, 423, 470, 482
Wiley, Edward J. 84, 85, 86, 87, 316
Wilkinson, C.T. 254
Wilkinson, Lloyd 469
Will Rogers Memorial Hospital 124
Willard's Hall (Washington, D.C.) 12
Williams, Charles 373
Williams, Earle 59
Williams, Montel 2
Willis, Moxley 101, 472
Willpaine, Warren M. 235
Wills, Nat 45, 46
Wilmington, Delaware 43, 44, 399
Wilson, Alphonsia R. 50
Wilson, George 439
Wilson, J. Finley 299
Wilson, Jerusa C. 171
Wilson Amusement Company 105, 439
Wilson Theater **30**, 60, 70, 71, 75, 90, 154, 361, 387, 388, **439**–440
Wilson's Restaurant 391
Wiltzynski, Marie 476
Winchester, Virginia 51
Windsor, Walter 279, 325
Windsor Hotel Fire 13, 462

Windsor Theater 131, 430, 440
Winer, J. 406
Winkel, Joseph A. 485
Winona Theater 440
Winters Theater 440–441
Wischhusen, John 406
Within the Law 252
Wizard Theater 28, 31, 33, 38, 42, 67, 90, 92, 134, 413, 441–**444**, 445, 452, 463, 468, 491, 492
Wizard Theater Company 442
WMAR-TV 307
Wolf, Bess 456
Wolf, Chauncey 420
Wolf, Morris H. 372, 480
Wolff, Prof. Fred 341
Wolgast-Moran fight 465
women 92, 134, 135
Women's Army Auxiliary Corps 135
Women's Christian Temperance Union 469
Women's Suffrage 474
Wonders, Guy L. 2, 35, 67. 70, 154, 155,388, 440, 475
Wood, Joe Agency 413
Woodbay Construction Company 342
Woodlen, George 376, 472
Woods, Al 208
Woolley, Claude 32
Workforce Development Corporation 290
World Fare Cinemas 177, 340, 357
World of Susie Wong 491
World Theater 152, 174, 415

World War I 55, 70, 72, 73, 80, 92, 97, 134, 156
World War II 126, 127, 131, 135, 139, 145, 339
Wright, Charles E. 266
Wright, Frank Lloyd 185
Wright, Margie 490
Wright, Rupert W. 410
WSID Radio 307
Wurlitzer-Hope Jones organs 426
Wurlitzer organs 82, 236, 238, 364, 401, 422, 482
Wurlitzer Stringed Orchestra 360
Wyatt and Nolting 156, 225, 226, 320
Wynants, Kate 372

X-rated movies 168, 169, 184, 200, 202, 210, 228, 256, 317, 325, 351, 356, 383, 424, 479
xenon bulb 102

Yarnith, Tobias 71
Yates, Charles 200
Yearly, William N. 408
Yewell, Blanche 13
Yiddish films 109, 216, 391, 431
Yiddish theater 248, 269, 335, 426, 431
Y.M.C.A. 51
YMCA Theater 445, 467
York, Pennsylvania 479
York Road Cinema 159, 160, 161, 174, 420, **445**–446
York Road Plaza Shopping Center 445
York Theater 366

Yorkridge Realty Co. 237
Yorkridge Shopping Center 161, 177, 236
Yorkridge Theaters 182, 237
Yorley, Lillian 322
Young, Clara Kimball 59
Young, Ernie 235
Young, Erwin A. 133
Young Men's Ritchie League 117
Young People's Association 469
Young-O'Brien, A.H. 416
Yueh Yang Lou Chinese Restaurant 223

Zaza 363
Zeit Motor Car Company 278
Zeller, Dr. Leon 179, 250, 274, 275, 321, 417
Zeller circuit 416
Zerker Brothers 359
Ziegfeld Follies 190
Zimlin, Morris 236, 237, 318
Zimmerman, Herbert 258
Zimmerman, Maurice 258
Zinematographe 11
Zink, John J. 155, 156, 157, 179, 193, 194, 195, 196, 221, 222, 231, 233, 243, 259, 260, 266, 267, 269, 298, 302, 324, 326, 351, 355, 367, 368, 390, 392, 393, 430, 432, 433, 453, 454, 485
Zink & Sparklin 410
Zion Lutheran Church 408
Zukor, Adolph 45
Zulu 300

www.ingramcontent.com/pod-product-compliance
Lightning Source LLC
Chambersburg PA
CBHW080802020526
44114CB00046B/2699